The Value of a Missal

"*Hand Missals which are drawn up according to the requirements of the modern liturgical renewal and which contain not only the Ordinary of the Mass but a version of all the liturgical texts approved by the competent authority are still necessary for more perfect understanding of the total mystery of salvation celebrated during the liturgical year, for drawing meditation and fervor from the inexhaustible riches of the liturgical texts, and for facilitating actual participation.*

"*This demands not only that the Word of God be proclaimed within the gathered community and attentively listened to by it, but also that the holy people respond and celebrate the Sacred (Mysteries) by singing or reciting the parts of the Ordinary and Proper [of the Mass], hymns and Psalms.*

"*[Missals are] especially necessary for . . . those who participate in daily Mass, or who desire to live and pray every day in the spirit of the liturgy.*"

Postconciliar Commission for the Implementation
of the Constitution on the Sacred Liturgy

0899429319

9 780899 429311

90000

This Missal belongs to

. . . .

New Saint Joseph
WEEKDAY MISSAL
Complete Edition

Vol. I — Advent to Pentecost

This new Missal has been especially designed to help you participate at Mass . . . in the fullest and most active way possible.

HOW EASY IT IS TO USE THIS MISSAL

● Refer to the Calendars (pp. [20]-[30] and [32]-[37], or use the St. Joseph Missal Guide (No. 920-G).

● This arrow (↓) means *continue to read.* This arrow (→) indicates a *reference* back to the Order of Mass ("Ordinary") or to another part of the "Proper."

● **Boldface** type always indicates the **people's parts** that are to be recited aloud.

The People of God together with Christ worship the heavenly Father.

New . . . St. Joseph

WEEKDAY MISSAL

COMPLETE EDITION

Vol. I — Advent to Pentecost

**All the Proper Mass Texts
for every Weekday and Feast Day
in a Continuous and Easy-to-Use Arrangement
With Short Helpful Notes and Explanations
and a Treasury of Popular Prayers**

**ALL READINGS FOR LITURGICAL YEARS I and II
IN THE "NEW AMERICAN BIBLE" TEXT
FROM THE REVISED WEEKDAY LECTIONARY**

**With the People's Parts
Printed in Boldface Type**

Dedicated to St. Joseph
Patron of the Universal Church

CATHOLIC BOOK PUBLISHING CO.
New Jersey

Published with the approval of the Committee on the Liturgy, United States Conference of Catholic Bishops. Published with ecclesiastical permission.

The St. Joseph Missals have been diligently prepared with the invaluable assistance of a special Board of Editors, including specialists in Liturgy and Sacred Scripture, Catechetics, Sacred Music and Art.

In this Weekday Missal the Scriptural commentaries were prepared by a staff under the direction of Most Reverend James Sullivan.

(T-920)

© 2002 by *Catholic Book Publishing Co., N.J.*
Printed in Korea

PREFACE

Content

This new **St. Joseph Weekday Missal** is a necessary companion to the **St. Joseph Sunday Missal.** It contains the Mass texts for all weekdays of the year. In doing so, it combines the Antiphons and Prayers found in the new **Sacramentary** together with the Readings and Intervenient Chants contained in the **Lectionary for Mass.** The faithful are thus given access to the biblical and liturgical riches that make up the treasury of the Church.

So great is the amount of this treasury that a complete Weekday Missal is not possible in one manageable volume. The present volume contains the texts for the weekday Masses from Pentecost to Advent. It also includes the most commonly used texts for Masses and Prayers for Various Needs and Occasions and Votive Masses (such as those for First Fridays and Saturdays).

Simplified Arrangement

All the texts in this Missal are clearly printed in large type, in an attractive and legible arrangement. All references are immediately visible and one always knows what comes next, and whose part it is. Succinct rubrics inform the reader of the options available and running heads identify the Masses on each page.

Participation Format

A simple, easy-to-understand method of instant identification of the parts of the Mass ensures that everyone will do all of, but only, those parts of the Mass that pertain to his or her office. **Boldface** type is used for all people's parts. All the people's texts are arranged for congregational recitation.

[5]

Order (Ordinary) of the Mass

The complete text of the Order of Mass with all its options is printed in the center of the book and clearly marked for easy use. Each part is numbered to facilitate finding one's place quickly when turning from the Proper to the Ordinary. All the options are given and conveniently arranged.

General Introduction

An extensive General Introduction provides a complete view of the liturgical year, the different liturgical days, the various classifications of celebrations and their makeup, the readings and chants, the color of vestments, and an important note on the type of participation to be attained.

Seasonal Introductions and Mass Themes

Every season of the liturgical year is prefixed by a useful Introduction providing necessary background for the better understanding of the liturgy and the easier use of the Missal. Each weekday Mass is prefaced by a short note focusing on one of the themes of the day's texts and inculcating some particular Christian attitude that may be found in them.

Concise Scriptural Commentaries

A completely original, especially written, and very helpful series of commentaries gives the setting for the Scripture Readings and the lessons to be drawn from them, leading to a more fruitful hearing on the part of the people when they are proclaimed.

Calendars for Quick Reference

Two sets of Calendars are provided to help the reader find the Mass as quickly as possible. One is the General Calendar of feasts that may occur month by month. The second is the Calendar of Sundays and Feasts that gives the precise date for every Sunday and hence week of the year. There is also a more general Table of Principal Celebrations of the Liturgical Year that provides the dates for the two cycles of Scripture Readings until 2025.

Tables of Choices of Masses and Texts

Two handy tables give a bird's-eye view of the choices of Masses and texts available on any given day.

Aids to Prayer and Study

A popular section of private prayers and devotions offers a fine starting point for a better prayer life. An invaluable Index section facilitates a deeper study of the Liturgy by listing all the Masses, Saints, Readings and Intervenient Chants, and Prefaces.

In the Spirit of Vatican II

We trust that this Missal with its many outstanding features will enable all those who attend weekday Mass, in keeping with the desire of the Church, to "be led to that full, conscious, and active participation in liturgical celebrations which is demanded by the very nature of the liturgy" (Vatican II, **On the Sacred Liturgy,** no. 14).

CONTENTS

Proper of Saints

Commons—Antiphons and Prayers

Commons—Readings and Chants

Appendices

Treasury of Prayers

Indices

GENERAL INTRODUCTION

THE LITURGICAL YEAR

The Church celebrates the memory of Christ's saving work on appointed days in the course of the year. Every week the Church celebrates the memorial of the resurrection on Sunday, which is called the Lord's Day. This is also celebrated, together with the passion of Jesus, on the great feast of Easter once a year. Throughout the year the entire mystery of Christ is unfolded, and the birthdays (days of death) of the saints are commemorated.

By means of devotional exercises, instruction, prayer, and works of penance and mercy, the Church, according to traditional practices, completes the formation of the faithful during the various seasons of the liturgical year.

1. The Liturgical Day in General

Each day is made holy through liturgical celebrations of God's people, especially the eucharistic sacrifice and the divine office.

The liturgical day runs from midnight to midnight, but the observance of Sunday and of solemnities begins with the evening of the preceding day.

2. Sunday

The Church celebrates the paschal mystery on the first day of the week, known as the Lord's Day or Sunday. This follows a tradition handed down from the Apostles, which took its origin from the day of Christ's resurrection. Thus Sunday should be considered the original feast day.

Because of its special importance, the celebration of Sunday is replaced only by solemnities or by feasts of the Lord. The Sundays of Advent, Lent, and the Easter Season, however, take precedence over all solemnities and feasts of the Lord. Solemnities that occur on these Sundays are observed on the following Monday.

[11]

3. Solemnities, Feasts, and Memorials

In the course of the year, as the Church celebrates the mystery of Christ, Mary the Mother of God is especially honored, and the martyrs and other saints are proposed as examples for the faithful.

The celebration of the days of saints who have universal significance is required throughout the entire Church. The days of other saints are listed in the calendar as optional or are left to the veneration of particular churches, countries, or religious communities.

The different types of celebrations are distinguished from each other by their importance and are accordingly called solemnities, feasts, and memorials.

a) Solemnities are the days of greatest importance and begin with Evening Prayer I of the preceding day. Several solemnities have their own vigil Mass, to be used when Mass is celebrated in the evening of the preceding day.

The celebration of Easter and Christmas continues for eight days. Each octave is governed by its own rules.

b) Feasts are celebrated within the limits of a natural day and accordingly do not have Evening Prayer I. Exceptions are feasts of the Lord that fall on Sundays in Ordinary Time and in the Christmas Season and that replace the Sunday office.

c) Memorials are either obligatory or optional. Their observance is combined with the celebration of the occurring Weekday according to norms given in the body of the Missal and seen at a glance in the Table of Choices of Masses and Texts, pp. [18]-[19].

Obligatory Memorials that occur on Lenten Weekdays may be celebrated only as Optional Memorials.

Should more than one Optional Memorial fall on the same day, only one is celebrated; the others are omitted.

d) On Saturdays in Ordinary Time when there is no Obligatory Memorial, an Optional Memorial of the Blessed Virgin Mary may be observed.

4. Weekdays

The days following Sunday are called Weekdays. They are celebrated in various ways according to the importance each one has:

a) Ash Wednesday and the days of Holy Week, from Monday to Thursday inclusive, are preferred to all other celebrations.

b) The Weekdays of Advent from December 17 to December 24 inclusive and all the Weekdays of Lent take precedence over Obligatory Memorials.

c) All other Weekdays yield to Solemnities and Feasts and are combined with Memorials.

d) Each Weekday has its own special liturgical texts—at least, insofar as the Readings and Intervenient Chants are concerned.

e) The Weekdays of the major seasons have their own Antiphons and Prayers. The Weekdays of Ordinary Time make use of the Antiphons and Prayers of the preceding Sunday or any of the thirty-four Sundays or those of Masses for Various Needs and Occasions as well as Votive Masses or even Masses for the Dead, as noted in the Table of Choices of Masses and Texts, pp. [18]-[19].

5. Liturgical Seasons

a) The **Advent Season** begins with Evening Prayer I of the Sunday that falls on or closest to November 30 and ends before Evening Prayer I of Christmas.

b) The **Christmas Season** runs from Evening Prayer I of Christmas until Sunday after Epiphany, or after January 6, inclusive.

c) **Lent** lasts from Ash Wednesday to the Mass of the Lord's Supper exclusive.

d) The **Easter Triduum** begins with the evening Mass of the Lord's Supper, reaches its high point in the Easter vigil, and closes with Evening Prayer on Easter Sunday.

e) The **Easter Season** comprises the fifty days from Easter Sunday to Pentecost that are celebrated as one feast day, sometimes called "the great Sunday."

f) **Ordinary Time** comprises the thirty-three or thirty-four weeks in the course of the year that celebrate no particular aspect of the mystery of Christ. Instead, especially on the last Sundays, the mystery of Christ in all its fullness is celebrated. This period is known as Ordinary Time.

Ordinary Time begins on Monday after the Sunday following January 6 and continues until Tuesday before Ash Wednesday inclusive. (See p. 1.) It begins again on Monday after Pentecost and ends before Evening Prayer I of the First Sunday of Advent.

6. Readings and Intervenient Chants

a) On the Weekdays of Advent, Christmas, Lent, and Easter there is a one-year cycle of Readings. These do not change from year to year.

b) On the Weekdays of Ordinary Time, however, there is a two-year cycle for the First Readings and Responsorial Psalms. Those designated "Year I" are read on odd numbered years and those designated "Year II" are read on even numbered years.

c) This Missal has been arranged as follows: The Masses with invariable Readings (for example, those of Advent) are arranged in the traditional order of Antiphons, Prayers, and Readings.

The Masses with variable Readings (for example, the Weekdays in Ordinary Time or the Masses of the Commons) are arranged in two separate sections. One section contains the Antiphons and Prayers (Entrance Antiphon, Opening Prayer, Prayer over the Gifts, Communion Antiphon, and Prayer after Communion), and the other section contains Readings and Intervenient Chants. (Year I and Year II are also found in different sections: see pp. 70 and 767.)

COLOR OF VESTMENTS

Colors in vestments give an effective expression to the celebration of the mysteries of the faith and, in the course of the year, a sense of progress in the Christian life.

1. White is used in Masses of the Easter and Christmas Seasons; on Feasts and Commemorations of the Lord, other than of his Passion; on Feasts and Memorials of Mary, the angels, saints who were not martyrs.

2. Red is used on Passion Sunday (Palm Sunday) and Good Friday, Pentecost, celebrations of the Passion, birthday feasts of the Apostles and evangelists, and feasts of martyrs.

3. Green is used in the offices and Masses of Ordinary Time.

4. Violet is used in Lent and Advent. It may also be used in offices and Masses for the dead.

5. Black may be used in Masses for the dead.

6. Rose may be used on *Gaudete* Sunday (Third Sunday of Advent) and *Laetare* Sunday (Fourth Sunday of Lent).

7. On more solemn days it is permitted to use more precious vestments even if not of the color of the day.

8. Votive Masses of the Lord, the Blessed Virgin Mary, and the saints may be said either with the color proper to the Mass, or with the color proper to the day or Season.

9. Masses for various needs may be said in the color proper either to the day or to the Season.

10. Ritual Masses are said in the color indicated in rubrics of the rite.

11. Adaptations to needs and culture of various regions may be proposed to the Holy See by Episcopal Conferences.

PARTICIPATION AT MASS

1. External and Internal Participation

a) The basic norm is that each one present at Mass has the right and duty to participate externally in the celebration—each one, however, doing wholly but solely what pertains to him or her by reason of the order to which he or she belongs or of the role assigned him or her.

b) In preparing liturgical celebrations, all concerned—whether of clergy or of laity and whether directly interested in ritual or musical or pastoral aspects—should be consulted and should cooperate harmoniously under the leadership of the rector of the church.

c) In order that external participation may produce its full effects, something more is required than mere observance of laws governing valid and licit celebration. Participation should be **internal** also. This consists in right dispositions of faith and charity, cooperation with divine grace and effects.

d) Both internal and external participation is perfected by **spiritual,** and especially (when the law of Church permits) **sacramental,** Communion.

2. Participation of the Faithful

a) Every Mass is an action not only of Christ but of the Church. This is true even if none of the faithful is present; nor is the efficacy or value of the Mass as an action of the Church thereby nullified or essentially impaired. Yet by their presence and association with the celebrant and by the sacramental or at least spiritual Communion the faithful participate in the mystical communion of the Church with Christ in the Paschal Mystery. For it is the Church that is here and now acting in them.

b) Participation of the faithful is not a ministry but an office. This prerogative is theirs, not as individuals but insofar as they unite to form one assembly or congregation. For it is as a community that they are the sacramental sign of the Church. Hence, it is through incorporation into the community, just as it is through incorporation into the Church, that individuals are associated with Christ in the Easter Mystery of his dying and rising in glory.

c) It is of the highest importance, that, whether few or many, the faithful participate in the Mass as one body, united in faith and charity and avoiding every appearance of singularity or division. It is as a group that the Word of God is addressed to them and the Body of the Lord is offered to them and that they are invited to pray, to sing, to perform certain actions and take certain positions. It is, therefore, as a group that they should respond. This common participation, lest it degenerate into mere outward conformity for the sake of good order, should be motivated by a deep religious sense of their relation to one another and to God in Christ and of their office to be a sign of the mystery of the Church.

d) Special importance attaches to acclamations and responses of the faithful. These are not merely external signs of common celebration but effect and foster communion with the celebrant as a sacramental sign of Christ. This degree of active participation is the requisite minimum, in whatever form Mass is celebrated.

e) Next in importance are: the Penitential Rite; Profession of Faith; responses in the Prayer of the Faithful; the Lord's Prayer.

f) Other parts pertaining to the faithful—either alone, or together with celebrant or choir or chanter—are either rites in themselves or accompaniments of rites. To the **former** belong: the **Gloria;** Responsorial Psalm; **Sanctus;** anamnetic acclamation; hymn or silent prayer after Communion. To the **latter** belong: various processional chants (Entrance and Communion Antiphons); chant during preparations for a Gospel; **the Lamb of God** during the rite of the breaking of the bread.

HANDY TABLE OF CHOICES OF MASSES

MASS NOT OF DAY ON ↓	Funeral Requiem	Requiem of Notification of a Death and on First Anniversary	"Daily" or Ordinary Requiem (1)	Nuptial Mass	For Grave Cause (2) with leave of Local Ordinary in Public Mass	For Just Cause (3) in judgment of Celebrant or Rector of church in Public Mass	Saint in Calendar or Martyrology of day	Votive, Public or Private
Easter Triduum — Sundays of Advent, Lent, Easter — Solemnities	No (4)	No	No	No (5)	No	No	No	No
Ash Wed. — Mon. Tues., Wed. of Holy Week	Yes	No	No	Yes	No	No	No	No
Mon. to Sat. of Octave of Easter	Yes	No	No	No (5)	No	No	No	No
Sundays in Seasons of Christmas and "of the year"	Yes	No	No	No (6)	Yes	No	No	No
Ferias of Advent from Dec. 17 and octave of Christmas	Yes	No	No	Yes	Yes	Yes	No (7)	No
Ferias of Lent (exc. Ash Wed. and Holy Week)	Yes	Yes	No	Yes	Yes	Yes	No (7)	No
Ferias of Seasons of Advent to Dec. 16, of Christmas from Jan. 2, and of Easter	Yes	—	No	Yes	Yes	Yes	Yes (8)	No
Feasts	Yes	No	No	Yes	Yes	No	No	No
Obligatory Memorial	Yes	Yes	No	Yes	Yes	Yes	No	Yes
Optional Mass	Yes	Yes	Yes	Yes	Yes	Yes	Yes	Yes
Ferias in Ordinary Time	Yes	Yes	Yes	Yes	Yes	Yes	Yes	Yes

(1) Mass must be applied for deceased — (2) Reference is to Masses for special intentions, including votive Masses, if common good is involved in a serious way — (3) Reference is to same Masses as in (2), if common good is involved in a real, though not necessarily serious way — (4) Funeral Requiem is permitted on a Solemnity, that is not a Holy-day in place — (5) Mass of Day is said instead, with marriage rite included. One of Readings of nuptial Mass can be used in place of corresponding Reading in Mass of Day, exc. in Easter Triduum, on Solemnity if a Holyday in place, and on Solemnities of Christmas, Epiphany, Ascension, Pentecost, and Body and Blood of Christ — (6) Not forbidden, if Mass is not a parish Mass — (7) If Saint is in general calendar, Opening Prayer in honor of the Saint may be said instead of Opening Prayer of Mass of the Day — (8) Applies only to Saint in general or proper calendar.

Composed by: William T. Barry, C.SS.R.

HANDY TABLE OF CHOICES OF TEXTS

CHOICE OF TEXTS for → in ↓	ENTRANCE SONG	OPENING PRAYER	READING AND INTERVENIENT CHANTS	OFFERTORY SONG	PRAYER OVER THE GIFTS	COMMUNION SONG	PRAYER AFTER COMMUNION
Mass of Sunday	If sung: proper, as in Roman or Simple Graduals; or song approved by Bishops' Conference. — If not sung: antiphon in Missal (1)	Proper	Proper, as in Lectionary (2)	If sung: proper, as in Roman or Simple Graduals; or song approved by Bishops' Conference. — If not sung: it is omitted	Proper	If sung: proper, as in Roman or Simple Graduals; or song approved by Bishops' Conference. — If not sung: antiphon in Missal	Proper
Mass of Feria in Advent, Christmas, Lent, Easter, Seasons.	Same as above	Same as above (3)	Same as above (2)	Same as above	Same as above	Same as above	Same as above
Mass of Solemnity or Feast	Same as above. If no proper in Missal or Gradual: from Common	If no proper: from Common	If no proper: from Common (2)	If no proper in Graduals: from Common	Same as above. If no proper: from Common	Same as above. If no proper in Missal or Graduals: from Common.	Same as above. If no proper: from Common
Mass of Memorial	Same as above	Same as above	Same as above (2)	Same as above	If no proper, from Common or current Feria	Same as above	If no proper: from Common or current Feria
Mass of Feria in Ordinary Time	As for Mass of preceding Sunday or of any Sunday in Ordinary Time	As for Mass of any Sunday in Ordinary Time or any Mass for Various Occasions or Various Prayers	Proper, as in Lectionary (2)	As for Mass of preceding Sunday or of any Sunday in Ordinary Time	Same as for Opening Prayer	As for Mass of preceding Sunday or of any Sunday in Ordinary Time	As for Mass of preceding Sunday or of any Sunday in Ordinary Time or any Mass for Various Occasions or Various Prayers
Mass of Dead	If sung: as in Roman or Simple Gradual; or an approved song. — If not sung: antiphon in Missal (1)	Any appropriate prayer for dead in Missal	Any appropriate Readings for the dead in Lectionary (2)	If sung: as in Roman or Simple Graduals; or an approved song. If not sung: it is omitted	Any appropriate prayer for dead in Missal	If sung: as in Roman or Simple Graduals; or an approved song. — If not sung: antiphon in Missal	Any appropriate prayer for dead in Missal

(1) If current Missal is used, only antiphon is read — (2) If Responsorial Psalm after 1st Reading is recited, psalm assigned to Reading in Lectionary is used. If it is sung, it is permitted to use any of the following: psalm assigned to Reading in Lectionary; any psalm & response from common texts given in Lectionary for the season or class to which in the case of a Solemnity, Feast, or Memorial) a Saint belongs. Gradual for the Mass given in Roman Gradual: the responsorial or alleluietic psalm for the Mass given in Simple Gradual. If Alleluia or other chant before Gospel is not sung, it may be omitted — (3) If Memorial in General Calendar occurs on Feria from Dec. 17 to 24 or on Feria within octave of Christmas or (exc. Ash Wed. & Holy Week) on Feria of Lent, Opening Prayer of Memorial may be used in Ferial Mass, instead of Opening Prayer proper to Mass.

Composed by: William T. Barry, C.SS.R.

GENERAL CALENDAR

JANUARY

1.	Octave of Christmas	
	SOLEMNITY OF MARY, MOTHER	
	OF GOD	Solemnity
2.	Sts. Basil the Great and Gregory	
	Nazianzen, Bishops and Doctors	Memorial
3.		
4.	St. Elizabeth Ann Seton, Religious	Memorial
5.	St. John Neumann, Bishop	Memorial
6.	EPIPHANY	Solemnity
	Bl. André Bessette, Religious*	
7.	*St. Raymond of Peñafort, Priest*	
8.		
9.		
10.		
11.		
12.		
13.	*St. Hilary, Bishop and Doctor*	
14.		
15.		
16.		
17.	St. Anthony, Abbot	Memorial
18.		
19.		
20.	*St. Fabian, Pope and Martyr*	
	St. Sebastian, Martyr	
21.	St. Agnes, Virgin and Martyr	Memorial
22.	*St. Vincent, Deacon and Martyr*	
23.		
24.	St. Francis de Sales, Bishop and Doctor	Memorial
25.	THE CONVERSION OF ST. PAUL, APOSTLE	Feast
26.	Sts. Timothy and Titus, Bishops	Memorial
27.	*St. Angela Merici, Virgin*	
28.	St. Thomas Aquinas, Priest and Doctor	Memorial
29.		
30.		
31.	St. John Bosco, Priest	Memorial

Sunday after January 6: BAPTISM OF THE LORD — Feast

*When no rank is given, it is an Optional Memorial.

FEBRUARY

1.
2. THE PRESENTATION OF THE LORD   Feast
3. *St. Blase, Bishop and Martyr*
   St. Ansgar, Bishop
4.
5. St. Agatha, Virgin and Martyr   Memorial
6. St. Paul Miki and His Companions,
       Martyrs   Memorial
7.
8. *St. Jerome Emiliani, Priest*
9.
10. St. Scholastica, Virgin   Memorial
11. *Our Lady of Lourdes*
12.
13.
14. Sts. Cyril and Methodius, Bishops   Memorial
15.
10.
17. *Seven Founders of the Order of Servites, Religious*
18.
19.
20.
21. *St. Peter Damian, Bishop and Doctor*
22. THE CHAIR OF ST. PETER, APOSTLE   Feast
23. St. Polycarp, Bishop and Martyr   Memorial
24.
25.
26.
27.
28.

MARCH

1.
2.
3. *St. Katharine Drexel, Virgin*
4. *St. Casimir*
5.
6.
7. Sts. Perpetua and Felicity, Martyrs   Memorial
8. *St. John of God, Religious*
9. *St. Frances of Rome, Religious*

10.
11.
12.
13.
14.
15.
16.
17.   *St. Patrick, Bishop*
18.   *St. Cyril of Jerusalem, Bishop and Doctor*
19.   ST. JOSEPH, HUSBAND OF MARY   Solemnity
20.
21.
22.
23.   *St. Toribio de Mogrovejo, Bishop*
24.
25.   THE ANNUNCIATION OF THE LORD   Solemnity
26.
27.
28.
29.
30.
31.

APRIL

1.
2.   *St. Francis of Paola, Hermit*
3.
4.   *St. Isidore, Bishop and Doctor*
5.   *St. Vincent Ferrer, Priest*
6.
7.   St. John Baptist de la Salle, Priest   Memorial
8.
9.
10.
11.   *St. Stanislaus, Bishop and Martyr*
12.
13.   *St. Martin I, Pope and Martyr*
14.
15.
16.
17.
18.
19.

20.
21. St. *Anselm, Bishop and Doctor*
22.
23. St. *George, Martyr*
    St. *Adalbert, Bishop and Martyr*
24. St. *Fidelis of Sigmaringen, Priest and Martyr*
25. ST. MARK, EVANGELIST   Feast
26.
27.
28. St. *Peter Chanel, Priest and Martyr*
    St. *Louis Mary de Montfort, Priest*
29. St. Catherine of Siena, Virgin and Doctor   Memorial
30. St. *Pius V, Pope, Religious*

MAY

1. St. *Joseph the Worker*
2. St. Athanasius, Bishop and Doctor   Memorial
3. STS. PHILIP AND JAMES, APOSTLES   Feast
4.
5.
6.
7.
8.
9.
10. Bl. *Damien Joseph de Veuster of Moloka'i, Priest*
11.
12. Sts. *Nereus and Achilleus, Martyrs*
    St. *Pancras, Martyr*
13.
14. ST. MATTHIAS, APOSTLE   Feast
15. St. *Isidore*
16.
17.
18. St. *John I, Pope and Martyr*
19.
20. St. *Bernardine of Siena, Priest*
21.
22.
23.
24.
25. St. *Bede the Venerable, Priest and Doctor*
    St. *Gregory VII, Pope*
    St. *Mary Magdalene de'Pazzi, Virgin*

26.	St. Philip Neri, Priest	Memorial
27.	*St. Augustine of Canterbury, Bishop*	
28.		
29.		
30.		
31.	VISITATION OF THE BLESSED VIRGIN MARY	Feast

First Sunday after Pentecost: HOLY TRINITY   Sol.
Thursday after Holy Trinity: BODY AND
    BLOOD OF CHRIST*   Solemnity
Friday following the Second Sunday after Pentecost:
    SACRED HEART   Solemnity
Saturday following Second Sunday after Pentecost:
    Immaculate Heart of Mary   Memorial

JUNE

1.	St. Justin, Martyr	Memorial
2.	*Sts. Marcellinus and Peter, Martyrs*	
3.	St. Charles Lwanga and Companions, Martyrs	Memorial
4.		
5.	St. Boniface, Bishop and Martyr	Memorial
6.	*St. Norbert, Bishop*	
7.		
8.		
9.	*St. Ephrem, Deacon and Doctor*	
10.		
11.	St. Barnabas, Apostle	Memorial
12.		
13.	St. Anthony of Padua, Priest and Doctor	Memorial
14.		
15.		
16.		
17.		
18.		
19.	*St. Romuald, Abbot*	
20.		
21.	St. Aloysius Gonzaga, Religious	Memorial
22.	*St. Paulinus of Nola, Bishop*	
	St. John Fisher, Bishop and Martyr, and	
	* St. Thomas More, Martyr*	
23.		

* *In the U.S., it is celebrated on the 2nd Sunday after Pentecost.*

24. THE NATIVITY OF ST. JOHN THE BAPTIST   Sol.
25.
26.
27. *St. Cyril of Alexandria, Bishop and Doctor*
28. St. Irenaeus, Bishop and Martyr   Memorial
29. STS. PETER AND PAUL, APOSTLES   Solemnity
30. *The First Holy Martyrs of the Holy Roman Church*

JULY

1. *Bl. Junipero Serra, Priest*
2.
3. ST. THOMAS, APOSTLE   Feast
4. *St. Elizabeth of Portugal*
   Independence Day
5. *St. Anthony Mary Zaccaria, Priest*
6. *St. Maria Goretti, Virgin and Martyr*
7.
8.
9.
10.
11. St. Benedict, Abbot   Memorial
12.
13. *St. Henry*
14. Bl. Kateri Tekakwitha   Memorial
15. St. Bonaventure, Bishop and Doctor   Memorial
16. *Our Lady of Mount Carmel*
17.
18. *St. Camillus de Lellis, Priest*
19.
20.
21. *St. Lawrence of Brindisi, Priest and Doctor*
22. St. Mary Magdalene   Memorial
23. *St. Bridget of Sweden, Religious*
24.
25. ST. JAMES, APOSTLE   Feast
26. Sts. Joachim and Ann, Parents of the
   Blessed Virgin Mary   Memorial
27.
28.
29. St. Martha   Memorial
30. *St. Peter Chrysologus, Bishop and Doctor*
31. St. Ignatius of Loyola, Priest   Memorial

AUGUST

1.	St. Alphonsus Liguori, Bishop and Doctor	Memorial
2.	*St. Eusebius of Vercelli, Bishop*	
	St. Peter Julian Eymard, Priest	
3.		
4.	St. John Mary Vianney, Priest	Memorial
5.	*Dedication of the Basilica of St. Mary Major in Rome*	
6.	THE TRANSFIGURATION OF THE LORD	Feast
7.	*St. Sixtus II, Pope and Martyr, and His Companions, Martyrs*	
	St. Cajetan, Priest	
8.	St. Dominic, Priest	Memorial
9.		
10.	ST. LAWRENCE, DEACON AND MARTYR	Feast
11.	St. Clare, Virgin	Memorial
12.		
13.	*St. Pontian, Pope and Martyr, and St. Hippolytus, Priest and Martyr*	
14.	St. Maximilian Mary Kolbe, Priest and Martyr	Memorial
15.	THE ASSUMPTION OF THE B.V. MARY	Solemnity
16.	*St. Stephen of Hungary*	
17.		
18.	*St. Jane Frances de Chantal, Religious*	
19.	*St. John Eudes, Priest*	
20.	St. Bernard, Abbot and Doctor	Memorial
21.	St. Pius X, Pope	Memorial
22.	The Queenship of the Blessed Virgin Mary	Memorial
23.	*St. Rose of Lima, Virgin*	
24.	ST. BARTHOLOMEW, APOSTLE	Feast
25.	*St. Louis of France*	
	St. Joseph Calasanz, Priest	
26.		
27.	St. Monica	Memorial
28.	St. Augustine, Bishop and Doctor	Memorial
29.	The Martyrdom of St. John the Baptist	Memorial
30.		
31.		

SEPTEMBER

First Monday in September: LABOR DAY

1.
2.
3. St. Gregory the Great, Pope and Doctor   Memorial
4.
5.
6.
7.
8. THE NATIVITY OF THE BLESSED VIRGIN MARY   Feast
9. St. Peter Claver, Priest and Religious   Memorial
10.
11.
12.
13. St. John Chrysostom, Bishop and Doctor   Memorial
14. THE EXALTATION OF THE HOLY CROSS   Feast
15. Our Lady of Sorrows   Memorial
16. St. Cornelius, Pope and Martyr, and
     St. Cyprian, Bishop and Martyr   Memorial
17. *St. Robert Bellarmine, Bishop and Doctor*
18.
19. *St. Januarius, Bishop and Martyr*
20. St. Andrew Kim Taegŏn, Priest and Martyr,
     and St. Paul Chŏng Hasang, Catechist
     and Martyr, and Their Companions   Memorial
21. ST. MATTHEW, APOSTLE AND EVANGELIST   Feast
22.
23.
24.
25.
26. *Sts. Cosmas and Damian, Martyrs*
27. St. Vincent de Paul, Priest   Memorial
28. *St. Lawrence Ruiz, Martyr, and His*
     Companions, Martyrs
     St. Wenceslaus, Martyr
29. STS. MICHAEL, GABRIEL, AND RAPHAEL,
     ARCHANGELS   Feast
30. St. Jerome, Priest and Doctor   Memorial

OCTOBER

1.	St. Thérèse of the Child Jesus, Virgin and Doctor	Memorial
2.	The Guardian Angels	Memorial
3.		
4.	St. Francis of Assisi, Religious	Memorial
5.		
6.	*St. Bruno, Priest*	
	Bl. Marie-Rose Durocher, Virgin	
7.	Our Lady of the Rosary	Memorial
8.		
9.	*St. Denis, Bishop and Martyr, and His Companions, Martyrs*	
	St. John Leonardi, Priest	
10.		
11.		
12.		
13.		
14.	*St. Callistus I, Pope and Martyr*	
15.	St. Teresa of Jesus, Virgin and Doctor	Memorial
16.	*St. Hedwig, Religious*	
	St. Margaret Mary Alacoque, Virgin	
17.	St. Ignatius of Antioch, Bishop and Martyr	Memorial
18.	ST. LUKE, EVANGELIST	Feast
19.	Sts. John de Brébeuf and Isaac Jogues, Priests and Martyrs, and Their Companions, Martyrs	Memorial
20.	*St. Paul of the Cross, Priest*	
21.		
22.		
23.	*St. John of Capistrano, Priest*	
24.	*St. Anthony Mary Claret, Bishop*	
25.		
26.		
27.		
28.	STS. SIMON AND JUDE, APOSTLES	Feast
29.		
30.		
31.		

NOVEMBER

1. ALL SAINTS   Solemnity
2. ALL SOULS
3. *St. Martin de Porres, Religious*
4. St. Charles Borromeo, Bishop   Memorial
5.
6.
7.
8.
9. THE DEDICATION OF THE LATERAN BASILICA
      IN ROME   Feast
10. St. Leo the Great, Pope and Doctor   Memorial
11. St. Martin of Tours, Bishop   Memorial
12. St. Josaphat, Bishop and Martyr   Memorial
13. St. Frances Xavier Cabrini, Virgin   Memorial
14.
15. *St. Albert the Great, Bishop and Doctor*
16. *St. Margaret of Scotland*
     St. Gertrude, Virgin
17. St. Elizabeth of Hungary, Religious   Memorial
18. *Dedication of the Basilica of Sts. Peter*
     and Paul, Apostles
     St. Rose Philippine Duchesne, Virgin
19.
20.
21. The Presentation of the B.V. Mary   Memorial
22. St. Cecilia, Virgin and Martyr   Memorial
23. *St. Clement I, Pope and Martyr*
     St. Columban, Abbot
     Bl. Miguel Agustín Pro, Priest and Martyr
24. *St. Andrew Dung-Lac, Priest and Martyr*
     and His Companions, Martyrs
25.
26.
27.
28.
29.
30. ST. ANDREW, APOSTLE   Feast
Fourth Thursday *Thanksgiving Day*
Last Sunday in Ordinary Time:
      CHRIST THE KING   Solemnity

DECEMBER

1.
2.
3. St. Francis Xavier, Priest   Memorial
4. *St. John of Damascus, Priest and Doctor*
5.
6. *St. Nicholas, Bishop*
7. St. Ambrose, Bishop and Doctor   Memorial
8. THE IMMACULATE CONCEPTION
   OF THE BLESSED VIRGIN MARY   Solemnity
9. *Bl. Juan Diego, Hermit*
10.
11. *St. Damasus I, Pope*
12. OUR LADY OF GUADALUPE   Feast
13. St. Lucy, Virgin and Martyr   Memorial
14. St. John of the Cross, Priest and Doctor   Memorial
15.
16.
17.
18.
19.
20.
21. *St. Peter Canisius, Priest and Doctor*
22.
23. *St. John of Kanty, Priest*
24.
25. CHRISTMAS   Solemnity
26. ST. STEPHEN, FIRST MARTYR   Feast
27. ST. JOHN, APOSTLE AND EVANGELIST   Feast
28. THE HOLY INNOCENTS, MARTYRS   Feast
29. *St. Thomas Becket, Bishop and Martyr*
30.
31. *St. Sylvester I, Pope*
Sunday within the octave of Christmas or
if there is no Sunday within the octave,
December 30: HOLY FAMILY   Feast

PRINCIPAL CELEBRATIONS OF LITURGICAL YEAR

Year	Lectionary Weekday Cycle	Ash Wed.	Easter	Ascension	Pentecost	Body And Blood	First Sun. of Advent
1999	I	17 Feb.	4 Apr.	13 May	23 May	6 June	28 Nov.
2000	II	8 Mar.	23 Apr.	1 June	11 June	25 June	3 Dec.
2001	I	28 Feb.	15 Apr.	24 May	3 June	17 June	29 Nov.
2002	II	13 Feb.	31 Mar.	9 May	19 May	2 June	1 Dec.
2003	I	5 Mar.	20 Apr.	29 May	8 June	22 June	30 Nov.
2004	II	25 Feb.	11 Apr.	20 May	30 May	13 June	28 Nov.
2005	I	9 Feb.	27 Mar.	5 May	15 May	29 May	27 Nov.
2006	II	1 Mar.	16 Apr.	25 May	4 June	18 June	3 Dec.
2007	I	21 Feb.	8 Apr.	17 May	27 May	10 June	2 Dec.
2008	II	6 Feb.	23 Mar.	1 May	11 May	25 May	30 Nov.
2009	I	25 Feb	12 Apr.	21 May	31 May	14 June	29 Nov.
2010	II	17 Feb.	4 Apr.	13 May	23 May	6 June	28 Nov.
2011	I	9 Mar.	24 Apr.	2 June	12 June	26 June	27 Nov.
2012	II	22 Feb.	8 Apr.	17 May	27 May	10 June	2 Dec.
2013	I	13 Feb.	31 Mar.	9 May	19 May	2 June	1 Dec.
2014	II	5 Mar.	20 Apr.	29 May	8 June	26 June	30 Nov.
2015	I	18 Feb.	5 Apr.	14 May	24 May	7 June	29 Nov
2016	II	10 Feb..	27 Mar.	5 May	15 May	29 May	27 Nov.
2017	I	1 Mar.	16 Apr.	25 May	4 June	18 June	3 Dec.
2018	II	14 Feb.	1 Apr.	10 May	20 May	3 June	2 Dec.
2019	I	6 Mar.	21 Apr.	30 May	9 June	23 June	1 Dec.
2020	II	26 Feb.	12 Apr.	21 May	31 May	14 June	29 Nov.
2021	I	17 Feb.	4 Apr.	13 May	23 May	6 June	28 Nov.
2022	II	2 Mar.	17 Apr.	26 May	5 June	19 June	27 Nov.
2023	I	22 Feb.	9 Apr.	18 May	28 May	11 June	3 Dec.
2024	II	14 Feb.	31 Mar.	9 May	19 May	2 June	1 Dec.
2025	I	5 Mar.	20 Apr.	29 May	8 June	22 June	30 Nov.

YEAR A

Sunday or Feast	2001	2004	2007	2010	2013	2016
1st Sun. Advent	2 Dec.	28 Nov.	2 Dec.	28 Nov.	1 Dec.	27 Nov.
Immac. Concep.	8 Dec.	8 Dec.	8 Dec.	8 Dec.	—	8 Dec.
2nd Sun. Advent	9 Dec.	5 Dec.	9 Dec.	5 Dec.	8 Dec.	4 Dec.
3rd Sun. Advent	16 Dec.	12 Dec.	16 Dec.	12 Dec.	15 Dec.	11 Dec.
4th Sun. Advent	23 Dec.	19 Dec.	23 Dec.	19 Dec.	22 Dec.	18 Dec.
Christmas	25 Dec.	25 Dec.	25 Dec.	25 Dec.	25 Dec.	25 Dec.
Holy Family	30 Dec.	26 Dec.	30 Dec.	26 Dec.	29 Dec.	—

Sunday or Feast	2002	2005	2008	2011	2014	2017
Mary, Mother of God	1 Jan.	1 Jan.	1 Jan.	1 Jan.	1 Jan.	1 Jan.
Epiphany of Lord	6 Jan.	2 Jan.	6 Jan.	2 Jan.	5 Jan.	8 Jan.
Baptism of Lord	13 Jan.	9 Jan.	13 Jan.	9 Jan.	12 Jan.	—
2nd Ord. Sun.	20 Jan.	16 Jan.	20 Jan.	16 Jan.	19 Jan.	15 Jan.
3rd Ord. Sun.	27 Jan.	23 Jan.	27 Jan.	23 Jan.	26 Jan.	22 Jan.
4th Ord. Sun.	3 Feb.	30 Jan.	3 Feb.	30 Jan.	2 Feb.	29 Jan.
5th Ord. Sun.	10 Feb.	6 Feb.	—	6 Feb.	9 Feb.	5 Feb.
6th Ord. Sun.	—	—	—	13 Feb.	16 Feb.	12 Feb.
7th Ord. Sun.	—	—	—	20 Feb.	23 Feb.	19 Feb.
8th Ord. Sun.	—	—	—	27 Feb.	2 Mar.	26 Feb.
9th Ord. Sun.	—	—	—	6 Mar.	—	—
1st Sun. of Lent	17 Feb.	13 Feb.	10 Feb.	13 Mar.	9 Mar.	5 Mar.
2nd Sun. of Lent	24 Feb.	20 Feb.	17 Feb.	20 Mar.	16 Mar.	12 Mar.
3rd Sun. of Lent	3 Mar.	27 Feb.	24 Feb.	27 Mar.	23 Mar.	19 Mar.
4th Sun. of Lent	10 Mar.	6 Mar.	2 Mar.	3 Apr.	30 Mar.	26 Mar.
5th Sun. of Lent	17 Mar.	13 Mar.	9 Mar.	10 Apr.	6 Apr.	2 Apr.
Palm Sun.	24 Mar.	20 Mar.	16 Mar.	17 Apr.	13 Apr.	9 Apr.
Holy Thurs.	28 Mar.	24 Mar.	20 Mar.	21 Apr.	17 Apr.	13 Apr.
Holy Thurs.	28 Mar.	24 Mar.	20 Mar.	21 Apr.	17 Apr.	13 Apr.
Good Friday	29 Mar.	25 Mar.	21 Mar.	22 Apr.	18 Apr.	14 Apr.
Easter Vigil	30 Mar.	26 Mar.	22 Mar.	23 Apr.	19 Apr.	15 Apr.
Easter Sunday	31 Mar.	27 Mar.	23 Mar.	24 Apr.	20 Apr.	16 Apr.
2nd Sun. Easter	7 Apr.	3 Apr.	30 Mar.	1 May	27 Apr.	23 Apr.
3rd Sun. Easter	14 Apr.	10 Apr.	6 Apr.	8 May	4 May	30 Apr.
4th Sun. Easter	21 Apr.	17 Apr.	13 Apr.	15 May	11 May	7 May
5th Sun. Easter	28 Apr.	24 Apr.	20 Apr.	22 May	18 May	14 May

YEAR A

Sunday or Feast	2002	2005	2008	2011	2014	2017
6th Sun. Easter	5 May	1 May	27 Apr.	29 May	25 May	21 May
Ascension	9 May	5 May	1 May	2 June	29 May	25 May
7th Sun. Easter	12 May	8 May	4 May	5 June	1 June	28 May
Pentecost Sun.	19 May	15 May	11 May	12 June	8 June	4 June
Trinity Sun.	26 May	22 May	18 May	19 June	15 June	11 June
Body and Blood	2 June	29 May	25 May	26 June	22 June	18 June
9th Ord. Sun.	—	—	1 June	—	—	—
10th Ord. Sun.	9 June	5 June	8 June	—	—	—
11th Ord. Sun.	16 June	12 June	15 June	—	—	—
12th Ord. Sun.	23 June	19 June	22 June	—	—	25 June
13th Ord. Sun.	30 June	26 June	29 June	—	29 June	2 July
14th Ord. Sun.	7 July	3 July	6 July	3 July	6 July	9 July
15th Ord. Sun.	14 July	10 July	13 July	10 July	13 July	16 July
16th Ord. Sun.	21 July	17 July	20 July	17 July	20 July	23 July
17th Ord. Sun.	28 July	24 July	27 July	24 July	27 July	30 July
18th Ord. Sun.	4 Aug.	31 July	3 Aug.	31 July	3 Aug.	6 Aug.
19th Ord. Sun.	11 Aug.	7 Aug.	10 Aug.	7 Aug.	10 Aug.	13 Aug.
Assumption	15 Aug	15 Aug.	15 Aug.	15 Aug.	15 Aug.	15 Aug.
20th Ord. Sun.	18 Aug.	14 Aug.	17 Aug.	14 Aug.	17 Aug.	20 Aug.
21st Ord. Sun.	25 Aug.	21 Aug.	24 Aug.	21 Aug.	24 Aug.	27 Aug.
22nd Ord. Sun.	1 Sept	28 Aug.	31 Aug.	28 Aug.	31 Aug.	3 Sept.
23rd Ord. Sun.	8 Sept.	4 Sept.	7 Sept.	4 Sept.	7 Sept.	10 Sept.
24th Ord. Sun.	15 Sept.	11 Sept.	14 Sept.	11 Sept.	14 Sept.	17 Sept.
25th Ord. Sun.	22 Sept.	18 Sept.	21 Sept.	18 Sept.	21 Sept.	24 Sept.
26th Ord. Sun.	29 Sept.	25 Sept.	28 Sept.	25 Sept.	28 Sept.	1 Oct.
27th Ord. Sun.	6 Oct.	2 Oct.	5 Oct.	2 Oct.	5 Oct.	8 Oct.
28th Ord. Sun.	13 Oct.	9 Oct.	12 Oct.	9 Oct.	12 Oct.	15 Oct.
29th Ord. Sun.	20 Oct.	16 Oct.	19 Oct.	16 Oct.	19 Oct.	22 Oct.
30th Ord. Sun.	27 Oct.	23 Oct.	26 Oct.	23 Oct.	26 Oct.	29 Oct.
All Saints	1 Nov.	1 Nov.	1 Nov.	1 Nov.	1 Nov.	1 Nov.
31st Ord. Sun.	3 Nov.	30 Oct.	2 Nov.	30 Oct.	2 Nov.	5 Nov.
32nd Ord. Sun.	10 Nov.	6 Nov.	9 Nov.	6 Nov.	9 Nov.	12 Nov.
33rd Ord. Sun.	17 Nov.	13 Nov.	16 Nov.	13 Nov.	16 Nov.	19 Nov.
34th Ord. Sun.	24 Nov.	20 Nov.	23 Nov.	20 Nov.	23 Nov.	26 Nov.

YEAR B

Sunday or Feast	2002	2005	2008	2011	2014	2017
1st Sun. Advent	1 Dec.	27 Nov.	30 Nov.	27 Nov.	30 Nov.	3 Dec.
Immac. Concep.	—	8 Dec.	8 Dec.	8 Dec.	8 Dec.	8 Dec.
2nd Sun. Advent	8 Dec.	4 Dec.	7 Dec.	4 Dec.	7 Dec.	10 Dec.
3rd Sun. Advent	15 Dec.	11 Dec.	14 Dec.	11 Dec.	14 Dec.	17 Dec.
4th Sun. Advent	22 Dec.	18 Dec.	21 Dec.	18 Dec.	21 Dec.	24 Dec.
Birth of the Lord	25 Dec.	25 Dec.	25 Dec.	25 Dec.	25 Dec.	25 Dec.
Holy Family	29 Dec.	—	28 Dec.	—	28 Dec.	31 Dec.
Sunday or Feast	**2003**	**2006**	**2009**	**2012**	**2015**	**2018**
Mary, Mother of God	1 Jan.	1 Jan.	1 Jan.	1 Jan.	1 Jan.	1 Jan.
Epiphany of Lord	5 Jan.	8 Jan.	4 Jan.	8 Jan.	4 Jan.	7 Jan.
Baptism of Lord	12 Jan.	—	11 Jan.	—	11 Jan.	—
2nd Ord. Sun.	19 Jan.	15 Jan.	18 Jan.	15 Jan.	18 Jan.	14 Jan.
3rd Ord. Sun.	26 Jan.	22 Jan.	25 Jan.	22 Jan.	25 Jan.	21 Jan.
4th Ord. Sun.	2 Feb.	29 Jan.	1 Feb.	29 Jan.	1 Feb.	28 Jan.
5th Ord. Sun.	9 Feb.	5 Feb.	8 Feb.	5 Feb.	8 Feb.	4 Feb.
6th Ord. Sun.	16 Feb.	12 Feb.	15 Feb.	12 Feb.	15 Feb.	11 Feb.
7th Ord. Sun.	23 Feb.	19 Feb.	22 Feb.	19 Feb.	—	—
8th Ord. Sun.	2 Mar.	26 Feb.	—	—	—	—
9th Ord. Sun.	—	—	—	—	—	—
1st Sun. of Lent	9 Mar.	5 Mar.	1 Mar.	26 Feb.	22 Feb.	18 Feb.
2nd Sun. of Lent	16 Mar.	12 Mar.	8 Mar.	4 Mar.	1 Mar.	25 Feb.
3rd Sun. of Lent	23 Mar.	19 Mar.	15 Mar.	11 Mar.	8 Mar.	4 Mar.
4th Sun. of Lent	30 Mar.	26 Mar.	22 Mar.	18 Mar.	15 Mar.	11 Mar.
5th Sun. of Lent	6 Apr.	2 Apr.	29 Mar.	25 Mar.	22 Mar.	18 Mar.
Palm Sun.	13 Apr.	9 Apr.	5 Apr.	1 Apr.	29 Mar.	25 Mar.
Holy Thurs.	17 Apr.	13 Apr.	9 Apr.	5 Apr.	2 Apr.	29 Mar.
Holy Thurs.	17 Apr.	13 Apr.	9 Apr.	5 Apr.	2 Apr.	29 Mar.
Good Friday	18 Apr.	14 Apr.	10 Apr.	6 Apr.	3 Apr.	30 Mar.
Easter Vigil	19 Apr.	15 Apr.	11 Apr.	7 Apr.	4 Apr.	31 Mar.
Easter Sunday	20 Apr.	16 Apr.	12 Apr.	8 Apr.	5 Apr.	1 Apr.
2nd Sun. Easter	27 Apr.	23 Apr.	19 Apr.	15 Apr.	12 Apr.	8 Apr.
3rd Sun. Easter	4 May	30 Apr.	26 Apr.	22 Apr.	19 Apr.	15 Apr.
4th Sun. Easter	11 May	7 May	3 May	29 Apr.	26 Apr.	22 Apr.
5th Sun. Easter	18 May	14 May	10 May	6 May	3 May	29 Apr.

YEAR B

Sunday or Feast	2003	2006	2009	2012	2015	2018
6th Sun. Easter	25 May	21 May	17 May	13 May	10 May	6 May
Ascension	29 May	25 May	21 May	17 May	14 May	10 May
7th Sun. Easter	1 June	28 May	24 May	20 May	17 May	13 May
Pentecost Sun.	8 June	4 June	31 May	27 May	24 May	20 May
Trinity Sun.	15 June	11 June	7 June	3 June	31 May	27 May
Body and Blood	22 June	18 June	14 June	10 June	7 June	3 June
9th Ord. Sun.	—	—	—	—	—	—
10th Ord. Sun.	—	—	—	—	—	10 June
11th Ord. Sun.	—	—	—	17 June	14 June	17 June
12th Ord. Sun.	—	25 June	21 June	24 June	21 June	24 June
13th Ord. Sun.	29 June	2 July	28 June	1 July	28 June	1 July
14th Ord. Sun.	6 July	9 July	5 July	8 July	5 July	8 July
15th Ord. Sun.	13 July	16 July	12 July	15 July	12 July	15 July
16th Ord. Sun.	20 July	23 July	19 July	22 July	19 July	22 July
17th Ord. Sun.	27 July	30 July	26 July	29 July	26 July	29 July
18th Ord. Sun.	3 Aug.	6 Aug.	2 Aug.	5 Aug.	2 Aug.	5 Aug.
19th Ord. Sun.	10 Aug.	13 Aug.	9 Aug.	12 Aug.	9 Aug.	12 Aug.
Assumption	15 Aug.	15 Aug.	15 Aug.	15 Aug.	15 Aug.	15 Aug.
20th Ord. Sun.	17 Aug.	20 Aug.	16 Aug.	19 Aug.	16 Aug.	19 Aug.
21st Ord. Sun.	24 Aug.	27 Aug.	23 Aug.	26 Aug.	23 Aug.	26 Aug
22nd Ord. Sun.	31 Aug	3 Sept.	30 Aug.	2 Sept.	30 Aug.	2 Sept.
23rd Ord. Sun.	7 Sept.	10 Sept.	6 Sept.	9 Sept.	6 Sept.	9 Sept.
24th Ord. Sun.	14 Sept.	17 Sept.	13 Sept.	16 Sept.	13 Sept.	16 Sept.
25th Ord. Sun.	21 Sept.	24 Sept.	20 Sept.	23 Sept.	20 Sept.	23 Sept.
26th Ord. Sun.	28 Sept.	1 Oct.	27 Sept.	30 Sept.	27 Sept.	30 Sept.
27th Ord. Sun.	5 Oct.	8 Oct.	4 Oct.	7 Oct.	4 Oct.	7 Oct.
28th Ord. Sun.	12 Oct.	15 Oct.	11 Oct.	14 Oct.	11 Oct.	14 Oct.
29th Ord. Sun.	19 Oct.	22 Oct.	18 Oct.	21 Oct.	18 Oct.	21 Oct.
30th Ord. Sun.	26 Oct.	29 Oct.	25 Oct.	28 Oct.	25 Oct.	28 Oct.
All Saints	1 Nov.	1 Nov.	1 Nov.	1 Nov.	1 Nov.	1 Nov.
31st Ord. Sun.	2 Nov.	5 Nov.	—	4 Nov.	—	4 Nov.
32nd Ord. Sun.	9 Nov.	12 Nov.	8 Nov.	11 Nov.	8 Nov.	11 Nov.
33rd Ord. Sun.	16 Nov.	19 Nov.	15 Nov.	18 Nov.	15 Nov.	18 Nov.
34th Ord. Sun.	23 Nov.	26 Nov.	22 Nov.	25 Nov.	22 Nov.	25 Nov.

YEAR C

Sunday or Feast	2003	2006	2009	2012	2015	2018
1st Sun. Advent	30 Nov.	3 Dec.	29 Nov.	2 Dec.	29 Nov.	2 Dec.
Immac. Concep.	8 Dec.	8 Dec.	8 Dec.	8 Dec.	8 Dec.	8 Dec.
2nd Sun. Advent	7 Dec.	10 Dec.	6 Dec.	9 Dec.	6 Dec.	9 Dec.
3rd Sun. Advent	14 Dec.	17 Dec.	13 Dec.	16 Dec.	13 Dec.	16 Dec.
4th Sun. Advent	21 Dec.	24 Dec.	20 Dec.	23 Dec.	20 Dec.	23 Dec.
Birth of the Lord	25 Dec.	25 Dec.	25 Dec.	25 Dec.	25 Dec.	25 Dec.
Holy Family	28 Dec.	31 Dec.	27 Dec.	30 Dec.	27 Dec.	30 Dec.

Sunday or Feast	2004	2007	2010	2013	2016	2019
Mary, Mother of God	1 Jan.	1 Jan.	1 Jan.	1 Jan.	1 Jan.	1 Jan.
Epiphany of Lord	4 Jan.	7 Jan.	3 Jan.	6 Jan.	3 Jan.	6 Jan.
Baptism of Lord	11 Jan	—	10 Jan.	13 Jan.	10 Jan.	13 Jan.
2nd Ord. Sun.	18 Jan.	14 Jan.	17 Jan.	20 Jan..	17 Jan.	20 Jan.
3rd Ord. Sun.	25 Jan.	21 Jan.	24 Jan.	27 Jan	24 Jan.	27 Jan.
4th Ord. Sun.	1 Feb.	28 Jan.	31 Jan.	3 Feb.	31 Jan.	3 Feb.
5th Ord. Sun.	8 Feb.	4 Feb.	7 Feb.	10 Feb.	7 Feb.	10 Feb.
6th Ord. Sun.	15 Feb.	11 Feb.	14 Feb.	—	—	17 Feb.
7th Ord. Sun.	22 Feb.	18 Feb.	—	—	—	24 Feb.
8th Ord. Sun.	—	—	—	—	—	3 Mar.
9th Ord. Sun.	—	—	—	—	—	—
1st Sun. of Lent	29 Feb.	25 Feb.	21 Feb.	17 Feb.	14 Feb.	10 Mar.
2nd Sun. of Lent	7 Mar.	4 Mar.	28 Feb.	24 Feb.	21 Feb.	17 Mar.
3rd Sun. of Lent	14 Mar.	11 Mar.	7 Mar.	3 Mar.	28 Feb.	24 Mar.
4th Sun. of Lent	21 Mar.	18 Mar.	14 Mar.	10 Mar.	6 Mar.	31 Mar.
5th Sun. of Lent	28 Mar.	25 Mar.	21 Mar.	17 Mar.	13 Mar.	7 Apr.
Palm Sun.	4 Apr.	1 Apr.	28 Mar.	24 Mar.	20 Mar.	14 Apr.
Holy Thurs.	8 Apr.	5 Apr.	1Apr.	28 Mar.	24 Mar.	18 Apr.
Holy Thurs.	8 Apr.	5 Apr.	1 Apr.	28 Mar.	24 Mar.	18 Apr.
Good Friday	9 Apr.	6 Apr.	2 Apr.	29 Mar.	25 Mar.	19 Apr.
Easter Vigil	10 Apr.	7 Apr.	3 Apr.	30 Mar.	26 Mar.	20 Apr.
Easter Sunday	11 Apr.	8 Apr.	4 Apr.	31 Mar.	27 Mar.	21 Apr.
2nd Sun. Easter	18 Apr.	15 Apr.	11 Apr.	7 Apr.	3 Apr.	28 Apr.
3rd Sun. Easter	25 Apr.	22 Apr.	18 Apr.	14 Apr.	10 Apr.	5 May
4th Sun. Easter	2 May	29 Apr.	25 Apr.	21 Apr.	17 Apr.	12 May
5th Sun. Easter	9 May	6 May	2 May	28 Apr.	24 Apr.	19 May

YEAR C

Sunday or Feast	2004	2007	2010	2013	2016	2019
6th Sun. Easter	16 May	13 May	9 May	5 May	1 May	26 May
Ascension	20 May	17 May	13 May	9 May	5 May	30 May
7th Sun. Easter	23 May	20 May	16 May	12 May	8 May	2 June
Pentecost Sun.	30 May	27 May	23 May	19 May	15 May	9 June
Trinity Sun.	6 June	3 June	30 May	26 May	22 May	16 June
Body and Blood	13 June	10 June	6 June	2 June	29 May	23 June
9th Ord. Sun.	—	—	—	—	—	—
10th Ord Sun.	—	—	—	9 June	5 June	—
11th Ord. Sun.	—	17 June	13 June	16 June	12 June	—
12th Ord. Sun.	20 June	24 June	20 June	23 June	19 June	—
13th Ord. Sun.	27 June	1 July	27 June	30 June	26 June	30 June
14th Ord. Sun.	4 July	8 July	4 July	7 July	3 July	7 July
15th Ord. Sun.	11 July	15 July	11 July	14 July	10 July	14 July
16th Ord. Sun.	18 July	22 July	18 July	21 July	17 July	21 July
17th Ord. Sun.	25 July	29 July	25 July	28 July	24 July	28 July
18th Ord. Sun.	1 Aug.	5 Aug.	1 Aug.	4 Aug.	31 July	4 Aug.
19th Ord. Sun.	8 Aug.	12 Aug.	8 Aug.	11 Aug.	7 Aug.	11 Aug.
Assumption	15 Aug.	15 Aug.	15 Aug.	15 Aug.	15 Aug.	15 Aug.
20th Ord. Sun.	—	19 Aug.	—	18 Aug.	14 Aug.	18 Aug.
21st Ord. Sun.	22 Aug.	26 Aug.	22 Aug.	25 Aug.	21 Aug.	25 Aug.
22nd Ord. Sun.	29 Aug.	2 Sept.	29 Aug.	1 Sept.	28 Aug.	1 Sept.
23rd Ord. Sun.	5 Sept.	9 Sept.	5 Sept.	8 Sept.	4 Sept.	8 Sept.
24th Ord. Sun.	12 Sept.	16 Sept.	12 Sept.	15 Sept.	11 Sept.	15 Sept.
25th Ord. Sun.	19 Sept.	23 Sept.	19 Sept.	22 Sept.	18 Sept.	22 Sept.
26th Ord. Sun.	26 Sept.	30 Sept.	26 Sept.	29 Sept.	25 Sept.	29 Sept.
27th Ord. Sun.	3 Oct.	7 Oct.	3 Oct.	6 Oct.	2 Oct.	6 Oct.
28th Ord. Sun.	10 Oct.	14 Oct.	10 Oct.	13 Oct.	9 Oct.	13 Oct.
29th Ord. Sun.	17 Oct.	21 Oct.	17 Oct.	20 Oct.	16 Oct.	20 Oct.
30th Ord. Sun.	24 Oct.	28 Oct.	24 Oct.	27 Oct.	23 Oct.	27 Oct.
All Saints	1 Nov.	1 Nov.	1 Nov.	1 Nov.	1 Nov.	1 Nov.
31st Ord. Sun.	31 Oct.	4 Nov.	31 Oct.	3 Nov.	30 Oct.	3 Nov.
32nd Ord. Sun.	7 Nov.	11 Nov.	7 Nov.	10 Nov.	6 Nov.	10 Nov.
33rd Ord. Sun.	14 Nov.	18 Nov.	14 Nov.	17 Nov.	13 Nov.	17 Nov.
34th Ord. Sun.	21 Nov.	25 Nov.	21 Nov.	24 Nov.	20 Nov.	24 Nov.

CHRISTMAS

EASTER

ORDINARY TIME

ADVENT

LENT

PROPER OF SEASONS
ADVENT SEASON

Creation, including ourselves, is submitted to a master-plan, which is in a process of being realized by the Creator. All creation groans and travails in pain till it will be delivered from its slavery to corruption into the freedom of the glory of the sons of God (see Rm 8:21-22).

But when, after millions of years, human beings, created in innocence, finally appeared on the scene—one of the highlights of this divinely-intended evolution—they chose not to cooperate with the process of mysterious growth into the image of the Creator (Gn 1:27). Their state of incompleteness became a sinful deficiency.

And since all have sinned (Rm 3:23), this "sin of the world" brought about the impotence of human beings to realize the divinely-intended freedom into which they are to grow. Hence, Redemption by Jesus, who took away the sin of the world (Jn 1:29), became a necessity. Only in Christ has the earthly person the power to become the heavenly person, as intended by God (1 Cor 15:45-49).

Advent is the time of more than usual eager longing, awaiting our revelation as children of God (Rm 8:19). It is the waiting for Christ's coming in grace on Christmas ever more to us (see Jn 14:23) and for his final coming, when God's plan will be fully realized in all who have put on Christ by faith and baptism (Gal 3:27).

God gives us this plan in the words of the prophets. And the Church gives us their words in Advent. To the great precursors of Isaiah and John the Baptist, she now adds Baruch, Jeremiah, Zephaniah, and Micah. And then comes Jesus, whom St. Paul describes (2 Cor 1:21) as the "Yes" or "Amen"—the fulfillment—of all the promises God has made.

From the day of the Annunciation onward, Mary, more than anyone else in the world, had the privilege of knowing that in all truth God is the One who comes into the world. It is by meditating on his mystery that we begin to understand that One who is called "the Son of the Most High" has linked our lot with his own by becoming man and that he will return to inaugurate his eternal kingdom by saving us.

The Book of Isaiah is one of those in which this Messianic hope is most strongly expressed. It contains the oracles of the great 8th-century-B.C. prophet himself as well as those of two disciples known as Second Isaiah and Third Isaiah. The readings from this Book represent more than half of the First Readings for Advent. The others are taken from various Books and usually have a relation to the Gospel of the day, and some give important Messianic pronouncements. These texts provide a rich tableau of the hope that Christ has come to fulfill and transform.

The Infancy Gospels utilized during Advent and Christmas comprise a prologue to the Gospel that actually begins with the baptism of John (cf. Acts 1:21ff). The evangelists of the infancy (Matthew and Luke) did not intend so much to give biographical detail as to show how Jesus fulfilled God's promises and accomplished human salvation. For Matthew, this meant underlining the signs of Jesus' fulfillment of Scripture: Jesus is the One expected by Israel, the One promised to Abraham and David, a new Moses. For Luke, this meant showing Jesus as the universal Savior, the One who reveals the Father's mercy to sinners and saves them by giving them the Spirit.

During Advent, our constant prayer should be: "Come, Lord Jesus!" (Rv 22:20). We should "reject godless ways and worldly desires, and live temperately, justly, and devoutly in this age as we await our blessed hope, the appearing of the glory of the great God and our Savior Jesus Christ" (Ti 2:12-13).

MONDAY OF THE FIRST WEEK OF ADVENT

"Come, Lord Jesus." This welcome greeting reminds us that Jesus is to come again. His final coming will take place on the last day in the gathering together of the peoples from the east and the west. It will be the time of fulfillment when Jesus will bring peace. We await his glorious coming.

ENTRANCE ANT. See Jer 31:10; Is 35:4

Nations, hear the message of the Lord, and make it known to the ends of the earth: Our Savior is coming. Have no more fear. → No. 2, p. 614

OPENING PRAYER

Lord our God,
help us to prepare
for the coming of Christ your Son.
May he find us waiting,
eager in joyful prayer.
We ask this . . . for ever and ever. ℟. **Amen.** ↓

FIRST READING Is 2:1-5

In year A, when this reading is used on the First Sunday of Advent, the reading below (Is 4:2-6) replaces it.

In his vision Isaiah sees that the Lord's house will be established over all. All peoples shall come and be instructed by God. They will then live in peace and brotherhood.

A reading from the Book of the Prophet Isaiah

THIS is what Isaiah, son of Amoz, saw concerning Judah and Jerusalem.

In days to come,
The mountain of the LORD's house
    shall be established as the highest mountain
    and raised above the hills.
All nations shall stream toward it;
    many peoples shall come and say:
"Come, let us climb the LORD's mountain,
    to the house of the God of Jacob,

3

That he may instruct us in his ways,
    and we may walk in his paths."
For from Zion shall go forth instruction,
    and the word of the LORD from Jerusalem.
He shall judge between the nations,
    and impose terms on many peoples.
They shall beat their swords into plowshares
    and their spears into pruning hooks;
One nation shall not raise the sword against another,
    nor shall they train for war again.

O house of Jacob, come,
    let us walk in the light of the LORD!
The word of the Lord. ℟. **Thanks to be God.** ↓

OR

FIRST READING (for Year A)   Is 4:2-6

The Messiah will come forth in Israel and bring salvation to those who remained steadfast. Joy and happiness will be theirs, for the Lord will protect them.

A reading from the Book of the Prophet Isaiah

ON that day,
    The branch of the LORD will be luster and glory,
    and the fruit of the earth will be honor and splendor
    for the survivors of Israel.
He who remains in Zion
    and he who is left in Jerusalem
Will be called holy:
    every one marked down for life in Jerusalem.
When the LORD washes away
    the filth of the daughters of Zion,
And purges Jerusalem's blood from her midst
    with a blast of searing judgment,
Then will the LORD create,
    over the whole site of Mount Zion
    and over her place of assembly,
A smoking cloud by day
    and a light of flaming fire by night.

For over all, the LORD's glory will be shelter and protection:
  shade from the parching heat of day,
  refuge and cover from storm and rain.
The word of the Lord. ℟. **Thanks be to God.** ↓

RESPONSORIAL PSALM   Ps 122:1-2, 3-4b, 4cd-5, 6-7, 8-9

℟. **Let us go rejoicing to the house of the Lord.**

I rejoiced because they said to me,
  "We will go up to the house of the LORD."
And now we have set foot
  within your gates, O Jerusalem.—℟.

Jerusalem, built as a city
  with compact unity.
To it the tribes go up,
  the tribes of the LORD.—℟.

According to the decree for Israel,
  to give thanks to the name of the LORD.
In it are set up judgment seats,
  seats for the house of David.—℟.

Pray for the peace of Jerusalem!
  May those who love you prosper!
May peace be within your walls,
  prosperity in your buildings.—℟.

Because of my relatives and friends
  I will say, "Peace be within you!"
Because of the house of the LORD, our God,
  I will pray for your good.—℟. ↓

ALLELUIA   See Ps 80:4

℟. **Alleluia, alleluia.**
Come and save us, LORD our God;
let your face shine upon us, that we may be saved.
℟. **Alleluia, alleluia.** ↓

*In place of the Alleluia given for each Weekday Mass, anoth-
er may be selected from pp. 1279-1289.*

GOSPEL   Mt 8:5-11

Jesus heals the centurion's son. Jesus notes the faith of the centurion and at the same time shows that the Kingdom of God is destined to extend to all human beings.

℣. The Lord be with you. ℟. **And also with you.**
✛ A reading from the holy Gospel according to Matthew.
℟. **Glory to you, Lord.**

W HEN Jesus entered Capernaum, a centurion approached him and appealed to him, saying, "Lord, my servant is lying at home paralyzed, suffering dreadfully." He said to him, "I will come and cure him." The centurion said in reply, "Lord, I am not worthy to have you enter under my roof; only say the word and my servant will be healed. For I too am a man subject to authority, with soldiers subject to me. And I say to one, 'Go,' and he goes; and to another, 'Come here,' and he comes; and to my slave, 'Do this,' and he does it." When Jesus heard this, he was amazed and said to those following him, "Amen, I say to you, in no one in Israel have I found such faith. I say to you, many will come from the east and the west, and will recline with Abraham, Isaac, and Jacob at the banquet in the Kingdom of heaven."—The Gospel of the Lord.
℟. **Praise to you, Lord Jesus Christ.**   → No. 15, p. 623

PRAYER OVER THE GIFTS

Father,
from all you give us
we present this bread and wine.
As we serve you now,
accept our offering
and sustain us with your promise of eternal life.
Grant this through Christ our Lord.
℟. **Amen.**   → No. 21, p. 626 (Pref. P 1)

COMMUNION ANT.   See Ps 106:4-5; Is 38:3

Come to us, Lord, and bring us peace. We will rejoice in your presence and serve you with all our heart. ↓

PRAYER AFTER COMMUNION

Father,
may our communion
teach us to love heaven.
May its promise and hope
guide our way on earth.
We ask this through Christ our Lord.
℟. **Amen.**   → No. 32, p. 660

TUESDAY OF THE FIRST WEEK OF ADVENT

Jesus is the promised Messiah who fills the needs that all people have.
We look to him so that our faith will grow and we may understand the
workings of God among his people.

ENTRANCE ANT.   See Zec 14:5, 7

**See, the Lord is coming and with him all his saints. Then
there will be endless day.**   → No. 2, p. 614

OPENING PRAYER

God of mercy and consolation,
help us in our weakness and free us from sin.
Hear our prayers
that we may rejoice at the coming of your Son,
who lives and reigns with you and the Holy Spirit,
one God, for ever and ever. ℟. **Amen.** ↓

FIRST READING   Is 11:1-10

Isaiah describes the power and virtue of the promised king in whom God's
covenant with David will be realized. The Spirit of the Lord will make this
king a man whose virtue, wisdom, and understanding will go beyond all
human dimensions. The Spirit of the Lord will rest on him.

A reading from the Book of the Prophet Isaiah

ON that day,
A shoot shall sprout from the stump of Jesse,
    and from his roots a bud shall blossom.
The Spirit of the LORD shall rest upon him:
    a Spirit of wisdom and of understanding,

A Spirit of counsel and of strength,
    a Spirit of knowledge and of fear of the LORD,
    and his delight shall be the fear of the LORD.
Not by appearance shall he judge,
    nor by hearsay shall he decide,
But he shall judge the poor with justice,
    and decide aright for the land's afflicted.
He shall strike the ruthless with the rod of his mouth,
    and with the breath of his lips he shall slay the wicked.
Justice shall be the band around his waist,
    and faithfulness a belt upon his hips.

Then the wolf shall be a guest of the lamb,
    and the leopard shall lie down with the kid;
The calf and the young lion shall browse together,
    with a little child to guide them.
The cow and the bear shall be neighbors,
    together their young shall rest;
    the lion shall eat hay like the ox.
The baby shall play by the cobra's den,
    and the child lay his hand on the adder's lair.
There shall be no harm or ruin on all my holy mountain;
    for the earth shall be filled with knowledge of the
      LORD,
    as water covers the sea.

    On that day,
The root of Jesse,
    set up as a signal for the nations,
The Gentiles shall seek out,
    for his dwelling shall be glorious.
The word of the Lord. ℟. **Thanks be to God.** ↓

RESPONSORIAL PSALM

Ps 72:1-2, 7-8, 12-13, 17

℟. (see 7) **Justice shall flourish in his time, and fullness
of peace for ever.**

O God, with your judgment endow the king,
    and with your justice, the king's son;

He shall govern your people with justice
　and your afflicted ones with judgment.—℟.

Justice shall flower in his days,
　and profound peace, till the moon be no more.
May he rule from sea to sea,
　and from the River to the ends of the earth.—℟.

He shall rescue the poor when he cries out,
　and the afflicted when he has no one to help him.
He shall have pity for the lowly and the poor;
　the lives of the poor he shall save.—℟.

May his name be blessed forever;
　as long as the sun his name shall remain.
In him shall all the tribes of the earth be blessed;
　all the nations shall proclaim his happiness.—℟. ↓

ALLELUIA

℟. **Alleluia, alleluia.**
Behold, our Lord shall come with power,
he will enlighten the eyes of his servants.
℟. **Alleluia, alleluia.** ↓

GOSPEL　　　　　　　　　　　　　　　　　Lk 10:21-24

From Jesus' prayer of thanksgiving, it is clear that the Father reveals the
mystery of salvation to the little ones, the persons of faith. It is only by
oneness of faith with Jesus, by looking at the Father through his eyes, that
human beings can come to know the unknown God.

℣. The Lord be with you. ℟. **And also with you.**
✟ A reading from the holy Gospel according to Luke.
℟. **Glory to you, Lord.**

JESUS rejoiced in the Holy Spirit and said, "I give you
praise, Father, Lord of heaven and earth, for although
you have hidden these things from the wise and the
learned you have revealed them to the childlike. Yes,
Father, such has been your gracious will. All things have
been handed over to me by my Father. No one knows
who the Son is except the Father, and who the Father is

except the Son and anyone to whom the Son wishes to reveal him."

Turning to the disciples in private he said, "Blessed are the eyes that see what you see. For I say to you, many prophets and kings desired to see what you see, but did not see it, and to hear what you hear, but did not hear it."—The Gospel of the Lord. ℟. **Praise to you, Lord Jesus Christ.**   → No. 15, p. 623

PRAYER OVER THE GIFTS

Lord,
we are nothing without you.
As you sustain us with your mercy,
receive our prayers and offerings.
We ask this through Christ our Lord.
℟. **Amen.**   → No. 21, p. 626 (Pref. P 1)

COMMUNION ANT.   2 Tm 4:8

The Lord is just; he will award the crown of justice to all who have longed for his coming. ↓

PRAYER AFTER COMMUNION

Father,
you give us food from heaven.
By our sharing in this mystery,
teach us to judge wisely the things of earth
and to love the things of heaven.
Grant this through Christ our Lord.
℟. **Amen.**   → No. 32, p. 660

WEDNESDAY OF THE FIRST WEEK OF ADVENT

Our thoughts today plunge us into the next life. We are reminded of the final judgment. As Jesus feeds the hungry in the desert, we come to hope in the banquet of the Lord where we shall be in God's Kingdom. In every Eucharist we are already beginning to eat with the Lord and his heavenly court the feast of rich food and choice wine that in the time of Jesus Christ awaited us "on this mountain."

ENTRANCE ANT.   See Hb 2:3; 1 Cor 4:5

The Lord is coming and will not delay; he will bring every hidden thing to light and reveal himself to every nation.   → No. 2, p. 614

OPENING PRAYER

Lord our God,
grant that we may be ready
to receive Christ when he comes in glory
and to share in the banquet of heaven,
where he lives and reigns with you and the Holy Spirit,
one God, for ever and ever. ℟. **Amen.** ↓

FIRST READING   Is 25:6-10a

Isaiah shows that on the great and final day toward which everything is moving, the Lord and his heavenly court on Mount Zion will feast unendingly with his people who are now seen to come from all over the earth. The rich food and the choice wine which God provides for all his people suggest perfect satisfaction. They show a loving God.

A reading from the Book of the Prophet Isaiah

O N this mountain the LORD of hosts
will provide for all peoples
A feast of rich food and choice wines,
    juicy, rich food and pure, choice wines.
On this mountain he will destroy
    the veil that veils all peoples,
The web that is woven over all nations;
    he will destroy death forever.
The Lord GOD will wipe away
    the tears from all faces;
The reproach of his people he will remove
    from the whole earth; for the LORD has spoken.

    On that day it will be said:
"Behold our God, to whom we looked to save us!
    This is the LORD for whom we looked;
    let us rejoice and be glad that he has saved us!"

For the hand of the LORD will rest on this mountain.
The word of the Lord. ℟. **Thanks be to God.** ↓

RESPONSORIAL PSALM   Ps 23:1-3a, 3b-4, 5, 6

℟. (6cd) **I shall live in the house of the Lord all the
    days of my life.**

The LORD is my shepherd; I shall not want.
    In verdant pastures he gives me repose;
Beside restful waters he leads me;
    he refreshes my soul.—℟.

He guides me in right paths
    for his name's sake.
Even though I walk in the dark valley
    I fear no evil; for you are at my side
With your rod and your staff
    that give me courage. —℟.

You spread the table before me
    in the sight of my foes;
You anoint my head with oil;
    my cup overflows.—℟.

Only goodness and kindness follow me
    all the days of my life;
And I shall dwell in the house of the LORD
    for years to come.—℟. ↓

ALLELUIA

℟. **Alleluia, alleluia.**
Behold, the Lord comes to save his people;
blessed are those prepared to meet him.
℟. **Alleluia, alleluia.** ↓

GOSPEL   Mt 15:29-37

In his ministry, Jesus cures the sick, the blind, and the crippled. Here he
goes beyond the borders of Israel to indicate his meal includes also the
Gentiles. On a hilltop, he provides an abundant heavenly banquet for
them. Not only people of Israel, but pagans, see the wonders of God's sal-

vation and the end of human miseries; they adore a new God—the God of Israel.

℣. The Lord be with you. ℟. **And also with you.**

✢ A reading from the holy Gospel according to Matthew.
℟. **Glory to you, Lord.**

A T that time: Jesus walked by the Sea of Galilee, went up on the mountain, and sat down there. Great crowds came to him, having with them the lame, the blind, the deformed, the mute, and many others. They placed them at his feet, and he cured them. The crowds were amazed when they saw the mute speaking, the deformed made whole, the lame walking, and the blind able to see, and they glorified the God of Israel.

Jesus summoned his disciples and said, "My heart is moved with pity for the crowd, for they have been with me now for three days and have nothing to eat. I do not want to send them away hungry, for fear they may collapse on the way." The disciples said to him, "Where could we ever get enough bread in this deserted place to satisfy such a crowd?" Jesus said to them, "How many loaves do you have?" "Seven," they replied, "and a few fish." He ordered the crowd to sit down on the ground. Then he took the seven loaves and the fish, gave thanks, broke the loaves, and gave them to the disciples, who in turn gave them to the crowds. They all ate and were satisfied. They picked up the fragments left over—seven baskets full.—The Gospel of the Lord. ℟ **Praise to you, Lord Jesus Christ.**   ➙ No. 15, p. 623

PRAYER OVER THE GIFTS

Lord,
may the gift we offer in faith and love
be a continual sacrifice in your honor
and truly become our eucharist and our salvation.
Grant this through Christ our Lord.
℟. **Amen.**   ➙ No. 21, p. 626 (Pref. P 1)

COMMUNION ANT.   Is 40:10; see 34:5

The Lord our God comes in strength and will fill his servants with joy. ↓

PRAYER AFTER COMMUNION

God of mercy,
may this eucharist bring us your divine help,
free us from our sins,
and prepare us for the birthday of our Savior,
who is Lord for ever and ever.
℟. **Amen.**

→ No. 32, p. 660

THURSDAY OF THE FIRST WEEK OF ADVENT

In Advent we live in the hope of a reformed and reestablished world. All are called. The Lord gives hope to his people. Jesus shows his care and concern for people. He looks after both their bodily and their spiritual needs. God takes care of those who come to him.

ENTRANCE ANT.   See Ps 119:151-152

Lord, you are near, and all your commandments are just; long have I known that you decreed them for ever.

→ No. 2, p. 614

OPENING PRAYER

Father,
we need your help.
Free us from sin and bring us to life.
Support us by your power.
Grant this . . . for ever and ever. ℟. **Amen.** ↓

FIRST READING   Is 26:1-6

Isaiah seems to be using a psalm that celebrates liturgically the entrance into the Holy City of God's remnant, a nation newly formed out of the survivors of world devastation. They are God's poor. Isaiah saw the root of Israel's sinfulness in its failure to trust the Lord. The nation did not keep faith and did not live in the covenanted way that God had given them. Isaiah sees the reborn Israel as a nation that is just because it is one that trusts in the Lord forever and keeps faith with him because he is their eternal Rock.

A reading from the Book of the Prophet Isaiah

O N that day they will sing this song in the land of
Judah:
"A strong city have we;
he sets up walls and ramparts to protect us.
Open up the gates
to let in a nation that is just,
one that keeps faith.
A nation of firm purpose you keep in peace;
in peace, for its trust in you."

Trust in the LORD forever!
For the LORD is an eternal Rock.
He humbles those in high places,
and the lofty city he brings down;
He tumbles it to the ground,
levels it with the dust.
It is trampled underfoot by the needy,
by the footsteps of the poor.
The word of the Lord. ℟. **Thanks be to God.** ↓

RESPONSORIAL PSALM   Ps 118:1 and 8-9, 19-21, 25-27a

℟. (26a) **Blessed is he who comes in the name of the Lord.**

℟. Or: **Alleluia.**

Give thanks to the LORD, for he is good,
for his mercy endures forever.
It is better to take refuge in the LORD
than to trust in man.
It is better to take refuge in the LORD
than to trust in princes.—℟.

Open to me the gates of justice;
I will enter them and give thanks to the LORD.
This gate is the LORD's;
the just shall enter it.
I will give thanks to you, for you have answered me
and have been my savior.—℟.

O LORD, grant salvation!
   O LORD, grant prosperity!
Blessed is he who comes in the name of the LORD;
   we bless you from the house of the LORD.
      The LORD is God, and he has given us light.—R̷. ↓

ALLELUIA
Is 55:6

R̷. **Alleluia, alleluia.**
Seek the LORD while he may be found,
call him while he is near.
R̷. **Alleluia, alleluia.** ↓

GOSPEL
Mt 7:21, 24-27

All are called to this Kingdom but not all will be admitted. Only the just will be allowed inside the gates, i.e., those who keep faith, those who are humble, those who accept the Messiah with their whole heart and soul.

V̷. The Lord be with you. R̷. **And also with you.**
✝ A reading from the holy Gospel according to Matthew.
R̷. **Glory to you, Lord.**

JESUS said to his disciples: "Not everyone who says to me, 'Lord, Lord,' will enter the Kingdom of heaven, but only the one who does the will of my Father in heaven.

"Everyone who listens to these words of mine and acts on them will be like a wise man who built his house on rock. The rain fell, the floods came, and the winds blew and buffeted the house. But it did not collapse; it had been set solidly on rock. And everyone who listens to these words of mine but does not act on them will be like a fool who built his house on sand. The rain fell, the floods came, and the winds blew and buffeted the house. And it collapsed and was completely ruined."—The Gospel of the Lord. R̷. **Praise to you, Lord Jesus Christ.**
→ No. 15, p. 623

PRAYER OVER THE GIFTS
Father,
from all you give us

we present this bread and wine.
As we serve you now,
accept our offering
and sustain us with your promise of eternal life.
Grant this through Christ our Lord.
℟. **Amen.** ➜ No. 21, p. 626 (Pref P 1)

COMMUNION ANT. Ti 2:12-13

Let our lives be honest and holy in this present age, as we wait for the happiness to come when our great God reveals himself in glory. ↓

PRAYER AFTER COMMUNION

Father,
may our communion
teach us to love heaven.
May its promise and hope
guide our way on earth.
We ask this through Christ our Lord.
℟. **Amen.** ➜ No. 32, p. 660

FRIDAY OF THE FIRST WEEK OF ADVENT

Jesus is our light and our salvation. He came into the world to show us a way of life. It is through our faith and belief in him and our hope and trust in him that we come to know him and love him all the more.

ENTRANCE ANT.

The Lord is coming from heaven in splendor to visit his people, and bring them peace and eternal life.

➜ No. 2, p. 614

OPENING PRAYER

Jesus, our Lord,
save us from our sins.
Come, protect us from all dangers
and lead us to salvation,
for you live and reign with the Father and the Holy Spirit,
one God, for ever and ever. ℟. **Amen.** ↓

FIRST READING   Is 29:17-24

Isaiah sees the Messiah as a guiding light. From gloom and darkness, the blind shall see. Evildoers will be cut off from him. The children of Jacob shall give praise and honor to the Lord and reverence his name.

A reading from the Book of the Prophet Isaiah

THUS says the Lord GOD:
But a very little while,
    and Lebanon shall be changed into an orchard,
    and the orchard be regarded as a forest!
On that day the deaf shall hear
    the words of a book;
And out of gloom and darkness,
    the eyes of the blind shall see.
The lowly will ever find joy in the LORD,
    and the poor rejoice in the Holy One of Israel.
For the tyrant will be no more
    and the arrogant will have gone;
All who are alert to do evil will be cut off,
    those whose mere word condemns a man,
Who ensnare his defender at the gate,
    and leave the just man with an empty claim.
Therefore thus says the LORD,
    the God of the house of Jacob,
    who redeemed Abraham:
Now Jacob shall have nothing to be ashamed of,
    nor shall his face grow pale.
When his children see
    the work of my hands in his midst,
They shall keep my name holy;
    they shall reverence the Holy One of Jacob,
    and be in awe of the God of Israel.
Those who err in spirit shall acquire understanding,
    and those who find fault shall receive instruction.
The word of the Lord. ℟. **Thanks be to God. ↓**

RESPONSORIAL PSALM   Ps 27:1, 4, 13-14

℟. (1a) **The Lord is my light and my salvation.**

℟. Or: **Alleluia.**

The LORD is my light and my salvation;
    whom should I fear?
The LORD is my life's refuge;
    of whom should I be afraid?—℟.

One thing I ask of the LORD;
    this I seek:
To dwell in the house of the LORD
    all the days of my life,
That I may gaze on the loveliness of the LORD
    and contemplate his temple.—℟.

I believe that I shall see the bounty of the LORD
    in the land of the living.
Wait for the LORD with courage;
    be stouthearted, and wait for the LORD.—℟. ↓

ALLELUIA

℟. **Alleluia, alleluia.**
Behold, our Lord shall come with power,
he will enlighten the eyes of his servants.
℟. **Alleluia, alleluia.** ↓

GOSPEL   Mt 9:27-31

Jesus cures two blind men. To receive light, they had faith in Christ and faith in God's infinite power and unlimited love for human beings. This is a child's faith. It was a condition required by Christ before he would work a miracle. Only this miracle-faith can receive the mystery of light.

℣. The Lord be with you. ℟. **And also with you.**
✠ A reading from the holy Gospel according to Matthew.
℟. **Glory to you, Lord.**

A S Jesus passed by, two blind men followed him, crying out, "Son of David, have pity on us!" When he entered the house, the blind men approached him and Jesus said to them, "Do you believe that I can do this?"

"Yes, Lord," they said to him. Then he touched their eyes and said, "Let it be done for you according to your faith." And their eyes were opened. Jesus warned them sternly, "See that no one knows about this." But they went out and spread word of him through all that land.—The Gospel of the Lord. ℞. **Praise to you, Lord Jesus Christ.**

➡ No. 15, p. 623

PRAYER OVER THE GIFTS

Lord,
we are nothing without you.
As you sustain us with your mercy,
receive our prayers and offerings.
We ask this through Christ our Lord.
℞. **Amen.**   ➡ No. 21, p. 626 (Pref. P 1)

COMMUNION ANT.   Phil 3:20-21

We are waiting for our Savior, the Lord Jesus Christ; he will transfigure our lowly bodies into copies of his own glorious body. ↓

PRAYER AFTER COMMUNION

Father,
you give us food from heaven.
Teach us to live by your wisdom
and to love the things of heaven
by our sharing in this mystery.
Grant this through Christ our Lord.
℞. **Amen.**   ➡ No. 32, p. 660

SATURDAY OF THE FIRST WEEK OF ADVENT

In the days of Isaiah the people did not want a shepherd. Their faith was weak and they were blinded. Today we are living in the time of Jesus. He tells us the harvest is good. Why is it that it rarely takes root in our lives?

ENTRANCE ANT.   Ps 80:4, 2

Come, Lord, from your cherubim throne; let us see your face, and we shall be saved.   ➡ No. 2, p. 614

OPENING PRAYER

God our Father,
you loved the world so much
you gave your only Son to free us
from the ancient power of sin and death.
Help us who wait for his coming,
and lead us to true liberty.
We ask this . . . for ever and ever. ℟. **Amen.** ↓

FIRST READING   Is 30:19-21, 23-26

Isaiah (30:18-19) tells the people: "The LORD is waiting to show you favor, and he rises to pity you. . . . He will be gracious to you when you cry out, as soon as he hears he will answer you." Only their rejection of his word, his shepherding, and their trust and reliance on what is crooked and devious block the manifestation of his favor.

A reading from the Book of the Prophet Isaiah

THUS says the Lord GOD,
  the Holy One of Israel:
O people of Zion, who dwell in Jerusalem,
    no more will you weep;
He will be gracious to you when you cry out,
    as soon as he hears he will answer you.
The Lord will give you the bread you need
    and the water for which you thirst.
No longer will your Teacher hide himself,
    but with your own eyes you shall see your Teacher,
While from behind, a voice shall sound in your ears:
    "This is the way; walk in it,"
    when you would turn to the right or to the left.

He will give rain for the seed
    that you sow in the ground,
And the wheat that the soil produces
    will be rich and abundant.
On that day your flock will be given pasture
    and the lamb will graze in spacious meadows;

The oxen and the asses that till the ground
 will eat silage tossed to them
 with shovel and pitchfork.
Upon every high mountain and lofty hill
 there will be streams of running water.
On the day of the great slaughter,
 when the towers fall,
The light of the moon will be like that of the sun
 and the light of the sun will be seven times greater
 like the light of seven days.
On the day the LORD binds up the wounds of his people,
 he will heal the bruises left by his blows.
The word of the Lord. ℟. **Thanks be to God.** ↓

RESPONSORIAL PSALM   Ps 147:1-2, 3-4, 5-6

℟. (see Is 30:18d) **Blessed are all who wait for the Lord.**

Praise the LORD, for he is good;
 sing praise to our God, for he is gracious;
 it is fitting to praise him.
The LORD rebuilds Jerusalem;
 the dispersed of Israel he gathers.—℟.

He heals the brokenhearted
 and binds up their wounds.
He tells the number of the stars;
 he calls each by name.—℟.

Great is our LORD and mighty in power:
 to his wisdom there is no limit.
The LORD sustains the lowly;
 the wicked he casts to the ground.—℟. ↓

ALLELUIA   Is 33:22

℟. **Alleluia, alleluia.**
The Lord is our Judge, our Lawgiver, our King;
he it is who will save us.
℟. **Alleluia, alleluia.** ↓

GOSPEL Mt 9:35—10:1, 5a, 6-8

The first half of our Gospel reading (9:35-38) is a summary of the situation that Jesus encountered during the early days of his mission in Galilee. He cured "every disease and illness."His heart is moved to pity by much of what he sees, and he tells his disciples: "The harvest is abundant but the laborers are few." Jesus communicates his power to the Apostles and sends them out to do the same work that he is doing. They are to announce the Good News that the Kingdom is fast approaching.

℣. The Lord be with you. ℟. **And also with you.**

✚ A reading from the holy Gospel according to Matthew.
℟. **Glory to you, Lord.**

JESUS went around to all the towns and villages teaching in their synagogues, proclaiming the Gospel of the Kingdom, and curing every disease and illness. At the sight of the crowds, his heart was moved with pity for them because they were troubled and abandoned, like sheep without a shepherd. Then he said to his disciples, "The harvest is abundant but the laborers are few; so ask the master of the harvest to send out laborers for his harvest."

Then he summoned his twelve disciples and gave them authority over unclean spirits to drive them out and to cure every disease and every illness.

Jesus sent out these twelve after instructing them thus, "Go to the lost sheep of the house of Israel. As you go, make this proclamation:'The Kingdom of heaven is at hand.'Cure the sick, raise the dead, cleanse lepers, drive out demons.Without cost you have received; without cost you are to give."—The Gospel of the Lord. ℟. **Praise to you, Lord Jesus Christ.** → No. 15, p. 623

PRAYER OVER THE GIFTS

Lord,
may the gift we offer in faith and love
be a continual sacrifice in your honor
and truly become our eucharist and our salvation.

Grant this through Christ our Lord.
℟. **Amen.**   → No. 21, p. 626 (Pref. P 1)

COMMUNION ANT.   Rv 22:12

I am coming quickly, says the Lord, and will repay each man according to his deeds. ↓

PRAYER AFTER COMMUNION

God of mercy,
may this eucharist bring us your divine help,
free us from our sins,
and prepare us for the birthday of our Savior,
who is Lord for ever and ever.
℟. **Amen.**   → No. 32, p. 660

MONDAY OF THE SECOND WEEK OF ADVENT

The Messiah will bring about peace and prosperity for which the Israelites have prayed. Jesus responds to prayer, to faith, as he cures the sick man. The sign of God's love is shown for his people. Our response should be one of praise and thanks.

ENTRANCE ANT.   See Jer 31:10; Is 35:4

Nations, hear the message of the Lord, and make it known to the ends of the earth: Our Savior is coming. Have no more fear.   → No. 2, p. 614

OPENING PRAYER

Lord,
free us from our sins and make us whole.
Hear our prayer,
and prepare us to celebrate the incarnation of your Son,
who lives and reigns with you and the Holy Spirit,
one God, for ever and ever. ℟. **Amen.** ↓

FIRST READING   Is 35:1-10

Isaiah describes the extraordinary age of prosperity and peace. Yahweh will deliver the people from the bitterness of bondage as in the great Exodus. The Exodus and the Exile restoration are types of the New Exodus through the Life, Death, and Resurrection of Jesus, the new Moses. The blind will see; the ears of the deaf will be opened; the lame will leap like a stag; the dumb will speak.

A reading from the Book of the Prophet Isaiah

THE desert and the parched land will exult;
the steppe will rejoice and bloom.
They will bloom with abundant flowers,
and rejoice with joyful song.
The glory of Lebanon will be given to them,
the splendor of Carmel and Sharon;
They will see the glory of the LORD,
the splendor of our God.
Strengthen the hands that are feeble,
make firm the knees that are weak,
Say to those whose hearts are frightened:
Be strong, fear not!
Here is your God,
he comes with vindication;
With divine recompense
he comes to save you.
Then will the eyes of the blind be opened,
the ears of the deaf be cleared;
Then will the lame leap like a stag,
then the tongue of the mute will sing.

Streams will burst forth in the desert,
and rivers in the steppe.
The burning sands will become pools,
and the thirsty ground, springs of water;
The abode where jackals lurk
will be a marsh for the reed and papyrus.
A highway will be there,
called the holy way;
No one unclean may pass over it,
nor fools go astray on it.
No lion will be there,
nor beast of prey go up to be met upon it.

It is for those with a journey to make,
and on it the redeemed will walk.
Those whom the LORD has ransomed will return
and enter Zion singing,
crowned with everlasting joy;
They will meet with joy and gladness,
sorrow and mourning will flee.

The word of the Lord. ℟. **Thanks be to God.** ↓

RESPONSORIAL PSALM   Ps 85:9ab and 10, 11-12, 13-14

℟. (Is 35:4f) **Our God will come to save us!**

I will hear what God proclaims;
the LORD—for he proclaims peace to his people.
Near indeed is his salvation to those who fear him,
glory dwelling in our land.—℟.

Kindness and truth shall meet;
justice and peace shall kiss.
Truth shall spring out of the earth,
and justice shall look down from heaven.—℟.

The LORD himself will give his benefits;
our land shall yield its increase.
Justice shall walk before him,
and salvation, along the way of his steps.—℟. ↓

ALLELUIA

℟. **Alleluia, alleluia.**
Behold the king will come, the Lord of the earth,
and he himself will lift the yoke of our captivity.
℟. **Alleluia, alleluia.** ↓

GOSPEL   Lk 5:17-26

Jesus demonstrates the power of God over evil—moral and physical. The lame man, now able to carry the mat, begins to glorify God. The healing comes after faith; the response is one of praise and thanks to God.

℣. The Lord be with you. ℟. **And also with you.**
✛ A reading from the holy Gospel according to Luke.
℟. **Glory to you, Lord.**

O NE day as Jesus was teaching, Pharisees and teachers of the law, who had come from every village of Galilee and Judea and Jerusalem, were sitting there, and the power of the Lord was with him for healing. And some men brought on a stretcher a man who was paralyzed; they were trying to bring him in and set him in his presence. But not finding a way to bring him in because of the crowd, they went up on the roof and lowered him on the stretcher through the tiles into the middle in front of Jesus. When Jesus saw their faith, he said, "As for you, your sins are forgiven."

Then the scribes and Pharisees began to ask themselves, "Who is this who speaks blasphemies? Who but God alone can forgive sins?" Jesus knew their thoughts and said to them in reply, "What are you thinking in your hearts? Which is easier, to say, 'Your sins are forgiven,' or to say, 'Rise and walk'? But that you may know that the Son of Man has authority on earth to forgive sins"—he said to the one who was paralyzed, "I say to you, rise, pick up your stretcher, and go home."

He stood up immediately before them, picked up what he had been lying on, and went home, glorifying God. Then astonishment seized them all and they glorified God, and, struck with awe, they said, "We have seen incredible things today."—The Gospel of the Lord. ℟.
Praise to you, Lord Jesus Christ.   → No. 15, p. 623

PRAYER OVER THE GIFTS

Father,
from all you give us
we present this bread and wine.
As we serve you now,
accept our offering
and sustain us with your promise of eternal life.
Grant this through Christ our Lord.
℟. **Amen.**   → No. 21, p. 626 (Pref. P 1)

COMMUNION ANT.   See Ps 106:4-5; Is 38:3

Come to us, Lord, and bring us peace. We will rejoice in your presence and serve you with all our heart. ↓

PRAYER AFTER COMMUNION

Father,
may our communion
teach us to love heaven.
May its promise and hope
guide our way on earth.
We ask this through Christ our Lord.
℟. **Amen.**   ➔ No. 32, p. 660

TUESDAY OF THE SECOND WEEK OF ADVENT

God cares for his people. He looks after them as a just, merciful and loving God. As he formerly looked after the people of Israel by day and by night, he will send his Son into the world to begin a new age to look after his people now, even a single one who may stray.

ENTRANCE ANT   See Zec 14:5, 7

See, the Lord is coming and with him all his saints. Then there will be endless day.   ➔ No. 2, p. 614

OPENING PRAYER

Almighty God,
help us to look forward
to the glory of the birth of Christ our savior:
his coming is proclaimed joyfully
to the ends of the earth
for he lives and reigns with you and the Holy Spirit,
one God, for ever and ever.
℟. **Amen.** ↓

FIRST READING   Is 40:1-11

Isaiah's central message is an announcement of the imminence of salvation for exiled Israel. The punishment proceeds from Yahweh just as he is also the source of comfort. The prophet reveals God as a Shepherd-King, attracting and ever caring for his people.

A reading from the Book of the Prophet Isaiah

COMFORT, give comfort to my people,
    says your God.
Speak tenderly to Jerusalem, and proclaim to her
    that her service is at an end,
        her guilt is expiated;
Indeed, she has received from the hand of the LORD
    double for all her sins.

A voice cries out:
In the desert prepare the way of the LORD!
    Make straight in the wasteland a highway for our
        God!
Every valley shall be filled in,
    every mountain and hill shall be made low;
The rugged land shall be made a plain,
    the rough country, a broad valley.
Then the glory of the LORD shall be revealed,
    and all people shall see it together;
        for the mouth of the LORD has spoken.

A voice says, "Cry out!"
    I answer, "What shall I cry out?"
"All flesh is grass,
    and all their glory like the flower of the field.
The grass withers, the flower wilts,
    when the breath of the LORD blows upon it.
        So then, the people is the grass.
Though the grass withers and the flower wilts,
    the word of our God stands forever."

Go up onto a high mountain,
    Zion, herald of glad tidings;
Cry out at the top of your voice,
    Jerusalem, herald of good news!
Fear not to cry out
    and say to the cities of Judah:
        Here is your God!

Here comes with power
  the Lord GOD,
  who rules by his strong arm;
Here is his reward with him,
  his recompense before him.
Like a shepherd he feeds his flock;
  in his arms he gathers the lambs,
Carrying them in his bosom,
  and leading the ewes with care.
The word of the Lord. ℟. **Thanks be to God.** ↓

RESPONSORIAL PSALM   Ps 96:1-2, 3 and 10ac, 11-12, 13

℟. (see Is 40:10ab) **The Lord our God comes with power.**

Sing to the LORD a new song;
  sing to the LORD, all you lands.
Sing to the LORD; bless his name;
  announce his salvation, day after day.—℟.

Tell his glory among the nations;
  among all peoples, his wondrous deeds.
Say among the nations: The LORD is king;
  he governs the peoples with equity.—℟.

Let the heavens be glad and the earth rejoice;
  let the sea and what fills it resound;
  let the plains be joyful and all that is in them!
Then let all the trees of the forest rejoice.—℟.

They shall exult before the LORD, for he comes;
  for he comes to rule the earth.
He shall rule the world with justice
  and the peoples with his constancy.—℟. ↓

ALLELUIA

℟. **Alleluia, alleluia.**
The day of the Lord is near:
Behold, he comes to save us.
℟. **Alleluia, alleluia.** ↓

GOSPEL   Mt 18:12-14

The love of God for the individual is clear. Christ is not teaching that one person equals ninety-nine, but that even one stray or lost one must be sought out. The shepherds of the Church are called to live the same loving, relentless pursuit of the lowly and sinful. Coaxing, forgiving, looking after the sheep, today's shepherd guides the sheep back to the Father.

℣. The Lord be with you. ℟. **And also with you.**
✠ A reading from the holy Gospel according to Matthew.
℟. **Glory to you, Lord.**

JESUS said to his disciples: "What is your opinion? If a man has a hundred sheep and one of them goes astray, will he not leave the ninety-nine in the hills and go in search of the stray? And if he finds it, amen, I say to you, he rejoices more over it than over the ninety-nine that did not stray. In just the same way, it is not the will of your heavenly Father that one of these little ones be lost."
The Gospel of the Lord. ℟. **Praise to you, Lord Jesus Christ.**   → No. 15, p. 623

PRAYER OVER THE GIFTS

Lord,
we are nothing without you.
As you sustain us with your mercy,
receive our prayers and offerings.
We ask this through Christ our Lord.
℟. **Amen.**   → No. 21, p. 626 (Pref. P 1)

COMMUNION ANT.   2 Tm 4:8

The Lord is just; he will award the crown of justice to all who have longed for his coming. ↓

PRAYER AFTER COMMUNION

Father,
you give us food from heaven.
By our sharing in this mystery,
teach us to judge wisely the things of earth
and to love the things of heaven.

Grant this through Christ our Lord.
R̸. **Amen.**   → No. 32, p. 660

WEDNESDAY OF THE
SECOND WEEK OF ADVENT

The secret of people turning to God is twofold: to see creation in all its splendor and realize that these things are but toys in the hands of God, their Maker, and to experience the weakness and dependence of human beings. These two realities will leave people no other choice than to throw themselves at the mercy of God and his providence. Come, Lord Jesus!

ENTRANCE ANT.   See Hb 2:3; 1 Cor 4:5

The Lord is coming and will not delay; he will bring every hidden thing to light and reveal himself to every nation.   → No. 2, p. 614

OPENING PRAYER

All-powerful Father,
we await the healing power of Christ your Son.
Let us not be discouraged by our weaknesses
as we prepare for his coming.
Keep us steadfast in your love.
We ask this . . . for ever and ever. R̸. **Amen.** ↓

FIRST READING   Is 40:25-31

Isaiah has pleaded with the people to live in a way of holiness rather than in a life of wickedness. He calls the people to live a life worthy of the covenant that God has established with his people. Isaiah frequently calls God by the name "Holy One."

A reading from the Book of the Prophet Isaiah

TO whom can you liken me as an equal?
says the Holy One.
Lift up your eyes on high
    and see who has created these things:
He leads out their army and numbers them,
    calling them all by name.

By his great might and the strength of his power
    not one of them is missing!
Why, O Jacob, do you say,
    and declare, O Israel,
"My way is hidden from the LORD,
    and my right is disregarded by my God"?

Do you not know
    or have you not heard?
The LORD is the eternal God,
    creator of the ends of the earth.
He does not faint nor grow weary,
    and his knowledge is beyond scrutiny.
He gives strength to the fainting;
    for the weak he makes vigor abound.
Though young men faint and grow weary,
    and youths stagger and fall,
They that hope in the LORD will renew their strength,
    they will soar as with eagles' wings;
They will run and not grow weary,
    walk and not grow faint.
The word of the Lord ℟. **Thanks be to God.** ↓

RESPONSORIAL PSALM   Ps 103:1-2, 3-4, 8 and 10

℟. (1) **O bless the Lord, my soul!**
Bless the LORD, O my soul;
    and all my being, bless his holy name.
Bless the LORD, O my soul,
    and forget not all his benefits.—℟.

He pardons all your iniquities,
    he heals all your ills.
He redeems your life from destruction,
    he crowns you with kindness and compassion.—℟.

Merciful and gracious is the LORD,
    slow to anger and abounding in kindness.
Not according to our sins does he deal with us,
    nor does he requite us according to our crimes.—℟. ↓

ALLELUIA

℟. **Alleluia, alleluia.**
Behold, the Lord comes to save his people;
blessed are those prepared to meet him.
℟. **Alleluia, alleluia.** ↓

GOSPEL   Mt 11:28-30

Matthew's Gospel is very sensitive to the poor of spirit. He has preserved
this tender invitation of the Good Shepherd to the weary and burdened
sheep. Jesus can identify with the lowly and the poor to whom he has
come to bring the Good News of salvation.

℣. The Lord be with you. ℟. **And also with you.**
✙ A reading from the holy Gospel according to Matthew.
℟. **Glory to you, Lord.**

JESUS said to the crowds: "Come to me, all you who
labor and are burdened, and I will give you rest. Take
my yoke upon you and learn from me, for I am meek and
humble of heart; and you will find rest for yourselves. For
my yoke is easy, and my burden light."—The Gospel of
the Lord. ℟. **Praise to you, Lord Jesus Christ.**

→ No. 15, p. 623

PRAYER OVER THE GIFTS

Lord,
may the gift we offer in faith and love
be a continual sacrifice in your honor
and truly become our eucharist and our salvation.
Grant this through Christ our Lord.
℟. **Amen.**   → No. 21, p. 626 (Pref. P 1)

COMMUNION ANT.   Is 40:10; see 34:5

**The Lord our God comes in strength and will fill his ser-
vants with joy.** ↓

PRAYER AFTER COMMUNION

God of mercy,
may this eucharist bring us your divine help,

free us from our sins,
and prepare us for the birthday of our Savior,
who is Lord for ever and ever.
℟. **Amen.**

➥ No. 32, p. 660

THURSDAY OF THE SECOND WEEK OF ADVENT

God can become close to his people. The Covenant (promise) is an intimate relationship between creature and Creator. We are blessed to hear the Good News and respond to Christ's word that the Kingdom of God may take root in us.

ENTRANCE ANT.

See Ps 119:151-152

Lord, you are near, and all your commandments are just; long have I known that you decreed them for ever.

➥ No. 2, p. 614

OPENING PRAYER

Almighty Father,
give us the joy of your love
to prepare the way for Christ our Lord.
Help us to serve you and one another.
We ask this . . . for ever and ever. ℟. **Amen.** ↓

FIRST READING

Is 41:13-20

In the Exodus, God offered his love as a saving God and let the Hebrews be his people. Isaiah stresses the complete transcendence of God when he says: "I, the LORD, will answer them," and "The Holy One of Israel has created it." The blessings of the Messianic Kingdom are physical and material.

A reading from the Book of the Prophet Isaiah

I AM the LORD, your God,
who grasp your right hand;
It is I who say to you, "Fear not,
I will help you."
Fear not, O worm Jacob,
O maggot Israel;
I will help you, says the LORD;
your redeemer is the Holy One of Israel.

I will make of you a threshing sledge,
   sharp, new, and double-edged,
To thresh the mountains and crush them,
   to make the hills like chaff.
When you winnow them, the wind shall carry them
      off
   and the storm shall scatter them.
But you shall rejoice in the LORD,
   and glory in the Holy One of Israel.

The afflicted and the needy seek water in vain,
   their tongues are parched with thirst.
I, the LORD, will answer them;
   I, the God of Israel, will not forsake them.
I will open up rivers on the bare heights,
   and fountains in the broad valleys;
I will turn the desert into a marshland,
   and the dry ground into springs of water.
I will plant in the desert the cedar,
   acacia, myrtle, and olive;
I will set in the wasteland the cypress,
   together with the plane tree and the pine,
That all may see and know,
   observe and understand,
That the hand of the LORD has done this,
   the Holy One of Israel has created it.
The word of the Lord. ℟. **Thanks be to God.** ↓

RESPONSORIAL PSALM   Ps 145:1 and 9, 10-11, 12-13ab

℟. (8) **The Lord is gracious and merciful; slow to anger,
   and of great kindness.**

I will extol you, O my God and King,
   and I will bless your name forever and ever.
The LORD is good to all
   and compassionate toward all his works.—℟.

Let all your works give you thanks, O LORD,
   and let your faithful ones bless you.

Let them discourse of the glory of your Kingdom
and speak of your might.—℟.

Let them make known to men your might
and the glorious splendor of your Kingdom.
Your Kingdom is a Kingdom for all ages,
and your dominion endures through all generations.—℟. ↓

ALLELUIA   Is 45:8

℟. **Alleluia, alleluia.**
Let the clouds rain down the Just One,
and the earth bring forth a Savior.
℟. **Alleluia, alleluia.** ↓

GOSPEL   Mt 11:11-15

The role of John the Baptist in the history of human salvation is stressed:
History has not known a man born of woman who was greater. He stands
ahead of the great prophets like Moses, Elijah, Isaiah, and Amos, and
points to the beginning of a new age.

℣. The Lord be with you. ℟. **And also with you.**
✝ A reading from the holy Gospel according to Matthew.
℟. **Glory to you, Lord.**

JESUS said to the crowds: "Amen, I say to you, among
those born of women there has been none greater
than John the Baptist; yet the least in the Kingdom of
heaven is greater than he. From the days of John the
Baptist until now, the Kingdom of heaven suffers violence, and the violent are taking it by force. All the
prophets and the law prophesied up to the time of John.
And if you are willing to accept it, he is Elijah, the one
who is to come. Whoever has ears ought to hear."—The
Gospel of the Lord. ℟. **Praise to you, Lord Jesus
Christ.**   → No. 15, p. 623

PRAYER OVER THE GIFTS

Father,
from all you give us

we present this bread and wine.
As we serve you now,
accept our offering
and sustain us with your promise of eternal life.
Grant this through Christ our Lord.
℞. **Amen.**   → No. 21, p. 626 (Pref. P 1)

COMMUNION ANT   Ti 2:12-13

**Let our lives be honest and holy in this present age, as
we wait for the happiness to come when our great God
reveals himself in glory.** ↓

PRAYER AFTER COMMUNION

Father,
may our communion
teach us to love heaven.
May its promise and hope
guide our way on earth.
We ask this through Christ our Lord.
℞. **Amen.**   → No. 32, p. 660

FRIDAY OF THE SECOND WEEK OF ADVENT

In applying the imagery of the Messianic Kingdom that Isaiah uses, a
poor, sickly, or lonely person without a family could well be close to God
and abundantly wealthy in a spiritual sense, and someone wealthy, in
good health, and with a large family might be very far from the Kingdom
of God. Jesus taught by example, and how much we can learn from him!
"Learn from me," he says on one occasion, "for I am meek and humble of
heart" (Mt 11:29).

ENTRANCE ANT.

**The Lord is coming from heaven in splendor to visit his
people, and bring them peace and eternal life.**

→ No. 2, p. 614

OPENING PRAYER

All-powerful God,
help us to look forward in hope
to the coming of our Savior.

May we live as he has taught,
ready to welcome him with burning love and faith.
We ask this . . . for ever and ever. ℟. **Amen.** ↓

FIRST READING   Is 48:17-19

Isaiah offers a majestic summary of God's Messianic promises. He, the
Holy One, will be our teacher, and to him who will listen, prosperity and
descendants will come.

A reading from the Book of the Prophet Isaiah

THUS says the LORD, your redeemer,
the Holy One of Israel:
I, the LORD, your God,
    teach you what is for your good,
    and lead you on the way you should go.
If you would hearken to my commandments,
    your prosperity would be like a river,
    and your vindication like the waves of the sea;
Your descendants would be like the sand,
    and those born of your stock like its grains,
Their name never cut off
    or blotted out from my presence.
The word of the Lord. ℟. **Thanks be to God.** ↓

RESPONSORIAL PSALM   Ps 1:1-2, 3, 4 and 6

℟. (see Jn 8:12) **Those who follow you, Lord, will have the
    light of life.**

Blessed the man who follows not
    the counsel of the wicked
Nor walks in the way of sinners,
    nor sits in the company of the insolent,
But delights in the law of the LORD
    and meditates on his law day and night.—℟.

He is like a tree
    planted near running water,
That yields its fruit in due season,
    and whose leaves never fade.
Whatever he does, prospers.—℟.

Not so the wicked, not so;
　　they are like chaff which the wind drives away.
For the LORD watches over the way of the just,
　　but the way of the wicked vanishes.—℟. ↓

ALLELUIA

℟. **Alleluia, alleluia.**
The Lord will come; go out to meet him!
He is the prince of peace.
℟. **Alleluia, alleluia.** ↓

GOSPEL　　　　　　　　　　　　　　　　　　Mt 11:16-19

Jesus' message is not accepted by everyone (neither was the message of
John the Baptist). Whatever message would involve change within the
people's own hearts and religious beliefs is rejected immediately; so they
reject John for his austerity, and they reject Jesus because he is not austere enough.

℣. The Lord be with you. ℟. **And also with you.**
✠ A reading from the holy Gospel according to Matthew.
℟. **Glory to you, Lord.**

JESUS said to the crowds: "To what shall I compare this
generation? It is like children who sit in marketplaces
and call to one another,
　　'We played the flute for you, but you did not dance,
　　we sang a dirge but you did not mourn.'
For John came neither eating nor drinking, and they said,
'He is possessed by a demon.' The Son of Man came
eating and drinking and they said, 'Look, he is a glutton
and a drunkard, a friend of tax collectors and sinners.' But
wisdom is vindicated by her works."—The Gospel of the
Lord. ℟. **Praise to you, Lord Jesus Christ.**→ No. 15, p. 623

PRAYER OVER THE GIFTS

Lord,
we are nothing without you.
As you sustain us with your mercy,
receive our prayers and offerings.

We ask this through Christ our Lord.

℟. **Amen.**   → No. 21, p. 626 (Pref. P 1)

COMMUNION ANT.   Phil 3:20-21

We are waiting for our Savior, the Lord Jesus Christ; he will transfigure our lowly bodies into copies of his own glorious body. ↓

PRAYER AFTER COMMUNION

Father,
you give us food from heaven.
Teach us to live by your wisdom
and to love the things of heaven
by our sharing in this mystery.
Grant this through Christ our Lord.

℟. **Amen.**   → No. 32, p. 660

SATURDAY OF THE SECOND WEEK OF ADVENT

We do not know the time or the day of the Parousia. It was thought, according to Malachi, that the "great and terrible day" would be inaugurated by the return of Elijah. This anticipates the Second Coming of Christ, but "of that day or hour, no one knows" (Mk 13:32). Let us be ready no matter what the hour.

ENTRANCE ANT.   Ps 80:4, 2

Come, Lord, from your cherubim throne; let us see your face, and we shall be saved.   → No. 2, p. 614

OPENING PRAYER

Lord,
let your glory dawn to take away our darkness.
May we be revealed as the children of light
at the coming of your Son,
who lives and reigns with you and the Holy Spirit,
one God, for ever and ever.

℟. **Amen.** ↓

FIRST READING   Sir 48:1-4, 9-11

Sirach recounts the heroes of the Jewish faith, he recalls the fiery prophet Elijah who was taken up to heaven in a chariot. It is this prophet that the Jews were expecting to come to usher in the Messianic age, the Day of Yahweh.

A reading from the Book of Sirach

IN those days,
like a fire there appeared the prophet Elijah
    whose words were as a flaming furnace.
Their staff of bread he shattered,
    in his zeal he reduced them to straits;
By the LORD's word he shut up the heavens
    and three times brought down fire.
How awesome are you, Elijah, in your wondrous
        deeds!
    Whose glory is equal to yours?
You were taken aloft in a whirlwind of fire,
    in a chariot with fiery horses.
You were destined, it is written, in time to come
    to put an end to wrath before the day of the LORD,
To turn back the hearts of fathers toward their sons,
    and to re-establish the tribes of Jacob.
Blessed is he who shall have seen you
    and who falls asleep in your friendship.
The word of the Lord. ℟. **Thanks be to God.** ↓

RESPONSORIAL PSALM   Ps 80:2ac and 3b, 15-16, 18-19

℟. (4) **Lord, make us turn to you; let us see your face and
    we shall be saved.**

O shepherd of Israel, hearken,
From your throne upon the cherubim, shine forth.
Rouse your power.—℟.

Once again, O LORD of hosts,
    look down from heaven, and see;
Take care of this vine,
    and protect what your right hand has planted,
    the son of man whom you yourself made strong.—℟.

May your help be with the man of your right hand,
  with the son of man whom you yourself made strong.
Then we will no more withdraw from you;
  give us new life, and we will call upon your name.—
    ℟. ↓

ALLELUIA   Lk 3:4, 6

℟. **Alleluia, alleluia.**
Prepare the way of the Lord, make straight his paths:
All flesh shall see the salvation of God.
℟. **Alleluia, alleluia.** ↓

GOSPEL   Mt 17:9a, 10-13

The disciples of Jesus were aware of the tradition about Elijah. Jesus also
mentioned that the time of decision will consume him just as it did John the
Baptist. The roles of Messiah and Suffering Servant are brought together.

℣. The Lord be with you. ℟. **And also with you.**
✝ A reading from the holy Gospel according to Matthew.
℟. **Glory to you, Lord.**

AS they were coming down from the mountain, the
disciples asked Jesus, "Why do the scribes say that
Elijah must come first?" He said in reply, "Elijah will
indeed come and restore all things; but I tell you that
Elijah has already come, and they did not recognize him
but did to him whatever they pleased. So also will the
Son of Man suffer at their hands." Then the disciples
understood that he was speaking to them of John the
Baptist.—The Gospel of the Lord. ℟. **Praise to you, Lord
Jesus Christ.**   → No. 15, p. 623

PRAYER OVER THE GIFTS

Lord,
may the gift we offer in faith and love
be a continual sacrifice in your honor
and truly become our eucharist and our salvation.
Grant this through Christ our Lord.
℟. **Amen.**   → No. 21, p. 626 (Pref. P 1)

COMMUNION ANT.
Rv 22:12

I am coming quickly, says the Lord, and will repay each man according to his deeds. ↓

PRAYER AFTER COMMUNION

God of mercy,
may this eucharist bring us your divine help,
free us from our sins,
and prepare us for the birthday of our Savior,
who is Lord for ever and ever.
℟. **Amen.**
→ No. 32, p. 660

MONDAY OF THE THIRD WEEK OF ADVENT

For the Masses from December 17 to 24, see pp. 61-89.

All authority in heaven and on earth comes from God. He shares it with us since we are his children, made to his image and likeness. Everyone who exercises this authority, however, must be accountable to God.

ENTRANCE ANT.
See Jer 31:10; Is 35:4

Nations, hear the message of the Lord, and make it known to the ends of the earth: Our Savior is coming. Have no more fear.
→ No. 2, p. 614

OPENING PRAYER

Lord,
hear our voices raised in prayer.
Let the light of the coming of your Son
free us from the darkness of sin.
We ask this . . . for ever and ever. ℟. **Amen.** ↓

FIRST READING
Nm 24:2-7, 15-17a

Balaam foretells what Israel shall do to Moab in the days to come. The stars of Jacob shall prevail and the tribes of Israel shall rise up. Balaam's oracle is wholly and emphatically a blessing on Israel.

A reading from the Book of Numbers

WHEN Balaam raised his eyes and saw Israel encamped, tribe by tribe, the spirit of God came upon him, and he gave voice to his oracle:

The utterance of Balaam, son of Beor,
> the utterance of a man whose eye is true,
The utterance of one who hears what God says,
> and knows what the Most High knows,
Of one who sees what the Almighty sees,
> enraptured, and with eyes unveiled:
How goodly are your tents, O Jacob;
> your encampments, O Israel!
They are like gardens beside a stream,
> like the cedars planted by the LORD.
His wells shall yield free-flowing waters,
> he shall have the sea within reach;
His king shall rise higher,
> and his royalty shall be exalted.

Then Balaam gave voice to his oracle:

The utterance of Balaam, son of Beor,
> the utterance of the man whose eye is true,
The utterance of one who hears what God says,
> and knows what the Most High knows,
Of one who sees what the Almighty sees,
> enraptured, and with eyes unveiled.
I see him, though not now;
> I behold him, though not near:
A star shall advance from Jacob,
> and a staff shall rise from Israel.

The word of the Lord. ℟. **Thanks be to God.** ↓

RESPONSORIAL PSALM Ps 25:4-5ab, 6 and 7bc, 8-9

℟. (4) **Teach me your ways, O Lord.**

Your ways, O LORD, make known to me;
> teach me your paths,

Guide me in your truth and teach me,
  for you are God my savior.—℟.

Remember that your compassion, O LORD,
  and your kindness are from of old.
In your kindness remember me,
  because of your goodness, O LORD.—℟.

Good and upright is the LORD;
  thus he shows sinners the way.
He guides the humble to justice,
  he teaches the humble his way.—℟. ↓

ALLELUIA   Ps 85:8

℟. **Alleluia, alleluia.**
Show us, LORD, your love,
and grant us your salvation.
℟. **Alleluia, alleluia.** ↓

GOSPEL   Mt 21:23-27

The answer of Jesus to the chief priests is a counter question about the
commission of John the Baptist. Jesus' refusal to answer the question
about his own commission is a tacit rejection of the authority of his ques-
tioners.

℣. The Lord be with you. ℟. **And also with you.**
✛ A reading from the holy Gospel according to Matthew.
℟. **Glory to you, Lord.**

WHEN Jesus had come into the temple area, the chief
priests and the elders of the people approached
him as he was teaching and said, "By what authority are
you doing these things? And who gave you this authority?" Jesus said to them in reply, "I shall ask you one question, and if you answer it for me, then I shall tell you by
what authority I do these things. Where was John's baptism from? Was it of heavenly or of human origin?"
They discussed this among themselves and said, "If we
say 'Of heavenly origin,' he will say to us, 'Then why did
you not believe him?' But if we say, 'Of human origin,' we
fear the crowd, for they all regard John as a prophet." So

they said to Jesus in reply, "We do not know." He himself said to them, "Neither shall I tell you by what authority I do these things."—The Gospel of the Lord. ℟. **Praise to you, Lord Jesus Christ.**   ➜ No. 15, p. 623

PRAYER OVER THE GIFTS

Father,
from all you give us
we present this bread and wine.
As we serve you now,
accept our offering
and sustain us with your promise of eternal life.
Grant this through Christ our Lord.
℟. **Amen.**   ➜ No. 21, p. 626 (Pref. P 1)

COMMUNION ANT.   See Ps 106:4-5; Is 38:3

Come to us, Lord, and bring us peace. We will rejoice in your presence and serve you with all our heart. ↓

PRAYER AFTER COMMUNION

Father,
may our communion
teach us to love heaven.
May its promise and hope
guide our way on earth.
We ask this through Christ our Lord.
℟. **Amen.**   ➜ No. 32, p. 660

TUESDAY OF THE THIRD WEEK OF ADVENT

For the Masses from December 17 to 24, see pp. 61-89.

"The LORD is good to all and compassionate toward all his works" (Ps 145:9). His ways differ from ours since we are more like the proud Pharisees. Jesus helps us become aware of our frailty and weakness. We must have sorrow for our sins.

ENTRANCE ANT.   See Zec 14:5, 7

See, the Lord is coming and with him all his saints. Then there will be endless day.   ➜ No. 2, p. 614

OPENING PRAYER

Father of love,
you made a new creation
through Jesus Christ your Son.
May his coming free us from sin
and renew his life within us,
for he lives and reigns with you and the Holy Spirit,
one God, for ever and ever. ℟. **Amen.** ↓

FIRST READING   Zep 3:1-2, 9-13

The time-honored formula for true piety was to hear the Lord (Jer 7:28)
and to trust in him (Hos 6:5). Jerusalem has done neither. Zephaniah pictures an ideal future age in which the Lord triumphs and salvation is for
all. There shall be no lying or deceit. The virtuous, truthful, sincere remnant shall know peace and prosperity.

A reading from the Book of the Prophet Zephaniah

T HUS says the LORD:
 Woe to the city, rebellious and polluted,
   to the tyrannical city!
She hears no voice,
   accepts no correction;
In the LORD she has not trusted,
   to her God she has not drawn near.

For then I will change and purify
   the lips of the peoples,
That they all may call upon the name of the LORD,
   to serve him with one accord;
From beyond the rivers of Ethiopia
   and as far as the recesses of the North,
   they shall bring me offerings.

On that day
You need not be ashamed
   of all your deeds,
   your rebellious actions against me;
For then will I remove from your midst
   the proud braggarts,

And you shall no longer exalt yourself
   on my holy mountain.
But I will leave as a remnant in your midst
   a people humble and lowly,
Who shall take refuge in the name of the LORD:
   the remnant of Israel.
They shall do no wrong
   and speak no lies;
Nor shall there be found in their mouths
   a deceitful tongue;
They shall pasture and couch their flocks
   with none to disturb them.

The word of the Lord. ℟. **Thanks be to God.** ↓

RESPONSORIAL PSALM   Ps 34:2-3, 6-7, 17-18, 19 and 23

℟. (7a) **The Lord hears the cry of the poor.**

I will bless the LORD at all times;
   his praise shall be ever in my mouth.
Let my soul glory in the LORD;
   the lowly will hear me and be glad.—℟.

Look to him that you may be radiant with joy,
   and your faces may not blush with shame.
When the poor one called out, the LORD heard,
   and from all his distress he saved him.—℟.

The LORD confronts the evildoers,
   to destroy remembrance of them from the earth.
When the just cry out, the LORD hears them,
   and from all their distress he rescues them.—℟.

The LORD is close to the brokenhearted;
   and those who are crushed in spirit he saves.
The LORD redeems the lives of his servants;
   no one incurs guilt who takes refuge in him.—℟. ↓

ALLELUIA

℟. **Alleluia, alleluia.**
Come, O Lord, do not delay;

forgive the sins of your people.
℟. **Alleluia, alleluia.** ↓

GOSPEL   Mt 21:28-32

In this parable, the contrast is clear between verbal rebellion and ultimate obedience as opposed to verbal obedience and failure to act. The
adversaries themselves are compelled to admit that action is the test of
obedience. The parable no doubt reflects the faith of the Gentiles as contrasted with the unbelief of the Jews.

℣. The Lord be with you. ℟. **And also with you.**
✛ A reading from the holy Gospel according to Matthew.
℟. **Glory to you, Lord.**

JESUS said to the chief priests and the elders of the
people: "What is your opinion? A man had two sons.
He came to the first and said, 'Son, go out and work in the
vineyard today.' The son said in reply, 'I will not,' but afterwards he changed his mind and went. The man came to
the other son and gave the same order. He said in reply,
'Yes, sir,' but did not go. Which of the two did his father's
will?" They answered, "The first." Jesus said to them,
"Amen, I say to you, tax collectors and prostitutes are
entering the Kingdom of God before you. When John
came to you in the way of righteousness, you did not
believe him; but tax collectors and prostitutes did. Yet
even when you saw that, you did not later change your
minds and believe him."—The Gospel of the Lord. ℟.
Praise to you, Lord Jesus Christ.   → No. 15, p. 623

PRAYER OVER THE GIFTS

Lord,
we are nothing without you.
As you sustain us with your mercy,
receive our prayers and offerings.
We ask this through Christ our Lord.
℟. **Amen.**   → No. 21, p. 626 (Pref. P 1)

COMMUNION ANT.   2 Tm 4:8

The Lord is just; he will award the crown of justice to all who have longed for his coming. ↓

PRAYER AFTER COMMUNION

Father,
you give us food from heaven.
By our sharing in this mystery
teach us to judge wisely the things of earth
and to love the things of heaven.
We ask this through Christ our Lord.
℞. **Amen.**   → No. 32, p. 660

WEDNESDAY OF THE THIRD WEEK OF ADVENT

For the Masses from December 17 to 24, see pp. 61-89.

In all our trials and temptations, divine Providence mercifully guides us and protects us. God endeavors to lead us and keep us to himself. As John sought to know the true identity of Christ through his own words, let us seek through the Gospels and Holy Scripture to find the words of our Savior as they expressly apply to us.

ENTRANCE ANT.   See Hb 2:3; 1 Cor 4:5

The Lord is coming and will not delay; he will bring every hidden thing to light and reveal himself to every nation.   → No. 2, p. 614

OPENING PRAYER

Father,
may the coming celebration of the birth of your Son
bring us your saving help
and prepare us for eternal life.
Grant this . . . for ever and ever. ℞. **Amen.** ↓

FIRST READING   Is 45:6c-8, 18, 21c-25

The year 587 marked an appalling catastrophe for Israel. Jerusalem and the temple were destroyed by the Babylonians. Yet Israel, in spite of its poor, desperate situation, did endure—a testimony to divine mercy and the indestructibility of the divine plan. Isaiah preaches the inevitable, glorious triumphs of Yahweh and the resurrection of Israel.

A reading from the Book of the Prophet Isaiah

I AM the LORD, there is no other;
I form the light, and create the darkness,
I make well-being and create woe;
    I, the LORD, do all these things.
Let justice descend, O heavens, like dew from above,
    like gentle rain let the skies drop it down.
Let the earth open and salvation bud forth;
    let justice also spring up!
    I, the LORD, have created this.

For thus says the LORD,
The creator of the heavens,
    who is God,
The designer and maker of the earth
    who established it,
Not creating it to be a waste,
    but designing it be lived in:
I am the LORD, and there is no other.

Who announced this from the beginning
    and foretold it from of old?
Was it not I, the LORD,
    besides whom there is no other God?
    There is no just and saving God but me.

Turn to me and be safe,
    all you ends of the earth,
    for I am God; there is no other!
By myself I swear,
    uttering my just decree
    and my unalterable word:
To me every knee shall bend;
    by me every tongue shall swear,
Saying, "Only in the LORD
    are just deeds and power.

Before him in shame shall come
all who vent their anger against him.
In the LORD shall be the vindication and the glory
of all the descendants of Israel."
The word of the Lord. ℟. **Thanks be to God.** ↓

RESPONSORIAL PSALM   Ps 85:9ab and 10, 11-12, 13-14

℟. **Let the clouds rain down the Just One, and the earth
bring forth a savior.**

See Monday of the 2nd Week of Advent, p. 26.

ALLELUIA   See Is 40:9-10

℟. **Alleluia, alleluia.**
Raise your voice and tell the Good News:
Behold, the Lord GOD comes with power.
℟. **Alleluia, alleluia.** ↓

GOSPEL   Lk 7:18b-23

John is told that Jesus is the great Prophet. The two disciples sent by John
to Jesus may represent the two witnesses prescribed by the law for the
establishment of the truth. That the poor have the Gospel preached to
them is the clearest sign that our Lord is the Messiah.

℣. The Lord be with you. ℟. **And also with you.**
✛ A reading from the holy Gospel according to Luke.
℟. **Glory to you, Lord.**

A T that time, John summoned two of his disciples and
sent them to the Lord to ask, "Are you the one who is
to come, or should we look for another?" When the men
came to the Lord, they said, "John the Baptist has sent us
to you to ask, 'Are you the one who is to come, or should
we look for another?' " At that time Jesus cured many of
their diseases, sufferings, and evil spirits; he also granted
sight to many who were blind. And Jesus said to them in
reply, "Go and tell John what you have seen and heard: the
blind regain their sight, the lame walk, lepers are
cleansed, the deaf hear, the dead are raised, the poor have
the good news proclaimed to them. And blessed is the one

who takes no offense at me."—The Gospel of the Lord. ℟.
Praise to you, Lord Jesus Christ. → No. 15, p. 623

PRAYER OVER THE GIFTS

Lord,
may the gifts we offer in faith and love
be a continual sacrifice in your honor
and truly become our eucharist and our salvation.
Grant this through Christ our Lord.
℟. **Amen.** → No. 21, p. 626 (Pref. P 1)

COMMUNION ANT.
Is 40:10; see 34:5

The Lord our God comes in strength and will fill his servants with joy. ↓

PRAYER AFTER COMMUNION

God of mercy,
may this eucharist bring us your divine help,
free us from our sins,
and prepare us for the birthday of our Savior,
who is Lord for ever and ever.
℟. **Amen.** → No. 32, p. 660

THURSDAY OF THE THIRD WEEK OF ADVENT

For the Masses from December 17 to 24, see pp. 61-89.

In either the old law or the new law, who can doubt the love that God deserves from us? The answer is, only those who do not know him—only those who are either ignorant or forgetful of his divine perfection. Our Master frequently reminds us of the precept of charity and of our obligation to know God so that we will be led to love and serve him.

ENTRANCE ANT.
See Ps 119:151-152

Lord, you are near, and all your commandments are just; long have I known that you decreed them for ever.
→ No. 2, p. 614

OPENING PRAYER

Lord,
our sins bring us unhappiness.

Hear our prayer for courage and strength.
May the coming of your Son
bring us the joy of salvation.
We ask this . . . for ever and ever. ℟. **Amen.** ↓

FIRST READING   Is 54:1-10

Isaiah places Israel's tragedy in proper perspective as he exhausts the
resources of his language to emphasize the permanence of the new dispensation. The new covenant relationship will be unbreakable. The steadfast love is the inner bond of the covenant of peace, which is also the
everlasting covenant not to be removed.

A reading from the Book of the Prophet Isaiah

R AISE a glad cry, you barren one who did not bear,
  break forth in jubilant song, you who were not in
      labor,
For more numerous are the children of the deserted
      wife
    than the children of her who has a husband,
    says the LORD.
Enlarge the space for your tent,
    spread out your tent cloths unsparingly;
    lengthen your ropes and make firm your stakes.
For you shall spread abroad to the right and to the left;
    your descendants shall dispossess the nations
    and shall people the desolate cities.

Fear not, you shall not be put to shame;
    you need not blush, for you shall not be disgraced.
The shame of your youth you shall forget,
    the reproach of your widowhood no longer remem-
      ber.
For he who has become your husband is your Maker;
    his name is the LORD of hosts;
Your redeemer is the Holy One of Israel,
    called God of all the earth.

The LORD calls you back,
    like a wife forsaken and grieved in spirit,

A wife married in youth and then cast off,
  says your God.
For a brief moment I abandoned you,
  but with great tenderness I will take you back.
In an outburst of wrath, for a moment
  I hid my face from you;
But with enduring love I take pity on you,
  says the LORD, your redeemer.

This is for me like the days of Noah,
  when I swore that the waters of Noah
  should never again deluge the earth;
So I have sworn not to be angry with you,
  or to rebuke you.
Though the mountains leave their place
  and the hills be shaken,
My love shall never leave you
  nor my covenant of peace be shaken,
  says the LORD, who has mercy on you.

The word of the Lord R̸. **Thanks be to God. ↓**

RESPONSORIAL PSALM Ps 30:2 and 4, 5-6, 11-12a and 13b

R̸. (2a) **I will praise you, Lord, for you have rescued me.**

I will extol you, O LORD, for you drew me clear
  and did not let my enemies rejoice over me.
O LORD, you brought me up from the nether world;
  you preserved me from among those going down into
    the pit.—R̸.

Sing praise to the LORD, you his faithful ones,
  and give thanks to his holy name.
For his anger lasts but a moment;
  a lifetime, his good will.
At nightfall, weeping enters in,
  but with the dawn, rejoicing.—R̸.

"Hear, O LORD, and have pity on me;
  O LORD, be my helper."
You changed my mourning into dancing;
  O LORD, my God, forever will I give you thanks.—R̸. ↓

ALLELUIA   Lk 3:4, 6

℟. **Alleluia, alleluia.**
Prepare the way of the Lord, make straight his paths:
All flesh shall see the salvation of God.
℟. **Alleluia, alleluia.** ↓

GOSPEL   Lk 7:24-30

John was a great prophet—and more than a prophet. But a new and final
epoch began with Jesus. Jesus proved he was the Messiah by his miracles. In their baptism, sinners expressed their faith that God would
redeem them and, through the Messiah, reunite them to himself.

℣. The Lord be with you. ℟. **And also with you.**
✤ A reading from the holy Gospel according to Luke.
℟. **Glory to you, Lord.**

WHEN the messengers of John the Baptist had left,
Jesus began to speak to the crowds about John.
"What did you go out to the desert to see—a reed swayed
by the wind? Then what did you go out to see? Someone
dressed in fine garments? Those who dress luxuriously
and live sumptuously are found in royal palaces. Then
what did you go out to see? A prophet? Yes, I tell you, and
more than a prophet. This is the one about whom Scripture says:
   Behold, I am sending my messenger ahead of you,
   he will prepare your way before you.
I tell you, among those born of women, no one is greater
than John; yet the least in the Kingdom of God is greater
than he." (All the people who listened, including the tax
collectors, who were baptized with the baptism of John,
acknowledged the righteousness of God; but the
Pharisees and scholars of the law, who were not baptized
by him, rejected the plan of God for themselves.)—The
Gospel of the Lord. ℟. **Praise to you, Lord Jesus Christ.**
➜ No. 15, p. 623

PRAYER OVER THE GIFTS

Father,
from all you give us

we present this bread and wine.
As we serve you now,
accept our offering
and sustain us with your promise of eternal life.
Grant this through Christ our Lord.

R̸. **Amen.** → No. 21, p. 626 (Pref. P 1)

COMMUNION ANT. Ti 2:12-13

**Let our lives be honest and holy in this present age, as
we wait for the happiness to come when our great God
reveals himself in glory. ↓**

PRAYER AFTER COMMUNION

Father,
may our communion
teach us to love heaven.
May its promise and hope
guide our way on earth.
We ask this through Christ our Lord.

R̸. **Amen.** → No. 32, p. 660

FRIDAY OF THE THIRD WEEK OF ADVENT

For the Masses from December 17 to 24, see pp. 61-89.

John the Baptist was to prepare the way for Jesus. It is the work of every
man to serve God. The Christ-bearer of today must be the lamp on the
mountainside—directing, guiding, and leading to Jesus.

ENTRANCE ANT.

**The Lord is coming from heaven in splendor to visit his
people, and bring them peace and eternal life.**

→ No. 2, p. 614

OPENING PRAYER

All-powerful Father,
guide us with your love
as we await the coming of your Son.
Keep us faithful
that we may be helped through life

and brought to salvation.
We ask this . . . for ever and ever. ℟. **Amen.** ↓

FIRST READING   Is 56:1-3a, 6-8

Isaiah proclaims that those who do what is just will be happy. They are to love the Lord and the Lord will bring them into his house of prayer—a house for all people.

A reading from the Book of the Prophet Isaiah

THUS says the LORD:
  Observe what is right, do what is just;
    for my salvation is about to come,
    my justice, about to be revealed.
Blessed is the man who does this,
    the son of man who holds to it;
Who keeps the sabbath free from profanation,
    and his hand from any evildoing.
Let not the foreigner say,
    when he would join himself to the LORD,
    "The LORD will surely exclude me from his people."

The foreigners who join themselves to the LORD,
    ministering to him,
Loving the name of the LORD,
    and becoming his servants—
All who keep the sabbath free from profanation
    and hold to my covenant,
Them I will bring to my holy mountain
    and make joyful in my house of prayer;
Their burnt offerings and sacrifices
    will be acceptable on my altar,
For my house shall be called
    a house of prayer for all peoples.
Thus says the Lord GOD,
    who gathers the dispersed of Israel:
Others will I gather to him
    besides those already gathered.
The word of the Lord. ℟. **Thanks be to God.** ↓

RESPONSORIAL PSALM　　　　Ps 67:2-3, 5, 7-8

℟. (4) **O God, let all the nations praise you!**

May God have pity on us and bless us;
　　may he let his face shine upon us.
So may your way be known upon earth;
　　among all nations, your salvation.—℟.

May the nations be glad and exult
　　because you rule the peoples in equity;
　　the nations on the earth you guide.—℟.

The earth has yielded its fruits;
　　God, our God, has blessed us.
May God bless us,
　　and may all the ends of the earth fear him!—℟. ↓

ALLELUIA

℟. **Alleluia, alleluia.**
Come, Lord, bring us your peace
that we may rejoice before you with a perfect heart.
℟. **Alleluia, alleluia.** ↓

GOSPEL　　　　Jn 5:33-36

Although John the Baptist pointed out the way to Jesus by his prayer, fasting, and preaching, still the testimony of Jesus is far greater. The very works that Jesus performs speak for themselves. Only God can perform a miracle.

℣. The Lord be with you. ℟. **And also with you.**
✤ A reading from the holy Gospel according to John.
℟. **Glory to you, Lord.**

JESUS said to the Jews: "You sent emissaries to John,
and he testified to the truth. I do not accept testimony
from a human being, but I say this so that you may be
saved. John was a burning and shining lamp, and for a
while you were content to rejoice in his light. But I have
testimony greater than John's. The works that the Father
gave me to accomplish, these works that I perform testify on my behalf that the Father has sent me."—The
Gospel of the Lord. ℟. **Praise to you, Lord Jesus Christ.**
→ No. 15, p. 623

PRAYER OVER THE GIFTS

Lord,
we are nothing without you.
As you sustain us with your mercy,
receive our prayers and offerings.
We ask this through Christ our Lord.
R̸. **Amen.** → No. 21, p. 626 (Pref. P 1)

COMMUNION ANT. Phil 3:20-21

We are waiting for our Savior, the Lord Jesus Christ; he will transfigure our lowly bodies into copies of his own glorious body. ↓

PRAYER AFTER COMMUNION

Father,
you give us food from heaven.
Teach us to live by your wisdom
and to love the things of heaven
by our sharing in this mystery.
Grant this through Christ our Lord.
R̸. **Amen.** → No. 32, p. 660

WEEKDAYS OF ADVENT

from December 17 to December 24

The following Masses are used on the days assigned with the exception of Sunday.

DECEMBER 17

All of us are proud of our ancestry. God promised to send a Redeemer into the world. Today we profess our belief in Jesus that he is the Anointed One, the Son of God born of Mary, the Savior of the World.

ENTRANCE ANT. See Is 49:13

You heavens, sing for joy, and earth exult! Our Lord is coming; he will take pity on those in distress.

→ No 2, p. 614

OPENING PRAYER

Father,
creator and redeemer of mankind,
you decreed, and your Word became man,
born of the Virgin Mary.
May we come to share the divinity of Christ
who humbled himself to share our human nature,
for he lives and reigns with you and the Holy Spirit,
one God, for ever and ever. ℟. **Amen.** ↓

FIRST READING Gn 49:2, 8-10

The sons of Jacob are assured that the strength and the scepter will not pass from Judah. They are to be the holders of authority and preserve the teaching until it can be presented to the one deserving of obedience.

A reading from the Book of Genesis

JACOB called his sons and said to them:
"Assemble and listen, sons of Jacob,
    listen to Israel, your father.

"You, Judah, shall your brothers praise
    —your hand on the neck of your enemies;
    the sons of your father shall bow down to you.
Judah, like a lion's whelp,
    you have grown up on prey, my son.
He crouches like a lion recumbent,
    the king of beasts—who would dare rouse him?
The scepter shall never depart from Judah,
    or the mace from between his legs,
While tribute is brought to him,
    and he receives the people's homage."
The word of the Lord. ℟. **Thanks to be God.** ↓

RESPONSORIAL PSALM Ps 72:1-2, 3-4ab, 7-8, 17

℟. (see 7) **Justice shall flourish in his time, and fullness of
    peace for ever.**

O God, with your judgment endow the king,
    and with your justice, the king's son;

He shall govern your people with justice
 and your afflicted ones with judgment.—℟.

The mountains shall yield peace for the people,
 and the hills justice.
He shall defend the afflicted among the people,
 save the children of the poor.—℟.

Justice shall flower in his days,
 and profound peace, till the moon be no more.
May he rule from sea to sea,
 and from the River to the ends of the earth.—℟.

May his name be blessed forever;
 as long as the sun his name shall remain.
In him shall all the tribes of the earth be blessed;
 all the nations shall proclaim his happiness.—℟. ↓

ALLELUIA

℟. **Alleluia, alleluia.**
O Wisdom of our God Most High,
guiding creation with power and love:
come to teach us the path of knowledge!
℟. **Alleluia, alleluia.** ↓

GOSPEL

Mt 1:1-17

The purpose of the genealogy is to show that Jesus is the Messiah, the end of the history of salvation that was begun with the promise to Abraham. The genealogy of Jesus is of particular significance in support of his claim to be the Messiah, the Son of David. The Savior's Davidic descent was part of the primitive kerygma.

℣. The Lord be with you. ℟. **And also with you.**
✛ A reading from the beginning of the holy Gospel according to Matthew. ℟. **Glory to you, Lord.**

THE book of the genealogy of Jesus Christ, the son of David, the son of Abraham.
 Abraham became the father of Isaac, Isaac the father of Jacob, Jacob the father of Judah and his brothers. Judah became the father of Perez and Zerah, whose

mother was Tamar. Perez became the father of Hezron, Hezron the father of Ram, Ram the father of Amminadab. Amminadab became the father of Nahshon, Nahshon the father of Salmon, Salmon the father of Boaz, whose mother was Rahab. Boaz became the father of Obed, whose mother was Ruth. Obed became the father of Jesse, Jesse the father of David the king.

David became the father of Solomon, whose mother had been the wife of Uriah. Solomon became the father of Rehoboam, Rehoboam the father of Abijah, Abijah the father of Asaph. Asaph became the father of Jehoshaphat, Jehoshaphat the father of Joram, Joram the father of Uzziah. Uzziah became the father of Jotham, Jotham the father of Ahaz, Ahaz the father of Hezekiah. Hezekiah became the father of Manasseh, Manasseh the father of Amos, Amos the father of Josiah. Josiah became the father of Jechoniah and his brothers at the time of the Babylonian exile.

After the Babylonian exile, Jechoniah became the father of Shealtiel, Shealtiel the father of Zerubbabel, Zerubbabel the father of Abiud. Abiud became the father of Eliakim, Eliakim the father of Azor, Azor the father of Zadok. Zadok became the father of Achim, Achim the father of Eliud, Eliud the father of Eleazar. Eleazar became the father of Matthan, Matthan the father of Jacob, Jacob the father of Joseph, the husband of Mary. Of her was born Jesus who is called the Christ.

Thus the total number of generations from Abraham to David is fourteen generations; from David to the Babylonian exile, fourteen generations; from the Babylonian exile to the Christ, fourteen generations.— The Gospel of the Lord. ℟. **Praise to you, Lord Jesus Christ.**　　　　　　　→ No. 15, p. 623

PRAYER OVER THE GIFTS

Lord,
bless these gifts of your Church

and by this eucharist
renew us with the bread from heaven.
We ask this in the name of Jesus the Lord.
℟. **Amen.** ➔ No. 21, p. 626 (Pref. P 2)

COMMUNION ANT. See Hg 2:8

The Desired of all nations is coming, and the house of the Lord will be filled with his glory. ↓

PRAYER AFTER COMMUNION

God our Father,
as you nourish us with the food of life,
give us also your Spirit,
so that we may be radiant with his light
at the coming of Christ your Son,
who is Lord for ever and ever.
℟. **Amen.** ➔ No. 32, p. 660

_____

DECEMBER 18

Isaiah gave a name to the future king—Immanuel, God is with us. Knowing the full course of revelation and history, we know that Jesus alone has fulfilled the words and the hopes of the prophets. God has come to live among his people.

ENTRANCE ANT.

Christ our King is coming, the Lamb whom John proclaimed. ➔ No. 2, p. 614

OPENING PRAYER

All-powerful God,
renew us by the coming feast of your Son
and free us from our slavery to sin.
Grant this . . . for ever and ever.
℟. **Amen.** ↓

FIRST READING Jer 23:5-8

The Messianism here proposed is the fulfillment of sacred kingship as the means chosen by God to realize the blessings of his covenant—the peace and justice of his people in the promised land. Jeremiah predicts the restoration of David's dynasty.

A reading from the Book of the Prophet Jeremiah

BEHOLD, the days are coming, says the LORD,
  when I will raise up a righteous shoot to David;
As king he shall reign and govern wisely,
  he shall do what is just and right in the land.
In his days Judah shall be saved,
  Israel shall dwell in security.
This is the name they give him:
  "The LORD our justice."

Therefore, the days will come, says the LORD, when they shall no longer say, "As the LORD lives, who brought the children of Israel out of the land of Egypt"; but rather, "As the LORD lives, who brought the descendants of the house of Israel up from the land of the north"—and from all the lands to which I banished them; they shall again live on their own land.—The word of the Lord. ℟. **Thanks be to God.** ↓

RESPONSORIAL PSALM   Ps 72:1-2, 12-13, 18-19

℟. (see 7) **Justice shall flourish in his time, and fullness of
  peace for ever.**

O God, with your judgment endow the king,
  and with your justice, the king's son;
He shall govern your people with justice
  and your afflicted ones with judgment.—℟.

For he shall rescue the poor when he cries out,
  and the afflicted when he has no one to help him.
He shall have pity for the lowly and the poor;
  the lives of the poor he shall save.—℟.

Blessed be the LORD, the God of Israel,
  who alone does wondrous deeds.
And blessed forever be his glorious name;
  may the whole earth be filled with his glory.—℟. ↓

ALLELUIA

℟. **Alleluia, alleluia.**
O Leader of the House of Israel,
giver of the Law to Moses on Sinai:
come to rescue us with your mighty power!
℟. **Alleluia, alleluia.** ↓

GOSPEL Mt 1.18-24

Matthew's account of the birth of Christ makes Joseph the central figure. He received the divine revelation through an angel in his dream. Jesus' birth initiated the Messianic age of salvation that the Old Testament anticipated, and Jesus realized the presence of God among his people in an entirely new way.

℣. The Lord be with you. ℟. **And also with you.**
✠ A reading from the holy Gospel according to Matthew.
℟. **Glory to you, Lord.**

THIS is how the birth of Jesus Christ came about. When his mother Mary was betrothed to Joseph, but before they lived together, she was found with child through the Holy Spirit. Joseph her husband, since he was a righteous man, yet unwilling to expose her to shame, decided to divorce her quietly. Such was his intention when, behold, the angel of the Lord appeared to him in a dream and said, "Joseph, son of David, do not be afraid to take Mary your wife into your home. For it is through the Holy Spirit that this child has been conceived in her. She will bear a son and you are to name him Jesus, because he will save his people from their sins." All this took place to fulfill what the Lord had said through the prophet:

Behold, the virgin shall be with child and bear a son,
and they shall name him Emmanuel,

which means "God is with us." When Joseph awoke, he did as the angel of the Lord had commanded him and took his wife into his home. He had no relations with her until she bore a son, and he named him Jesus.—The

Gospel of the Lord. ℟. **Praise to you, Lord Jesus Christ.**

➛ No. 15, p. 623

PRAYER OVER THE GIFTS

Lord,
may this sacrifice
bring us into the eternal life of your Son,
who died to save us from death,
for he is Lord for ever and ever.
℟. **Amen.**

➛ No. 21, p. 626 (Pref. P 2)

COMMUNION ANT. Mt 1:23

His name will be called Emmanuel, which means God is with us. ↓

PRAYER AFTER COMMUNION

Lord,
we receive mercy in your Church.
Prepare us to celebrate with fitting honor
the coming feast of our redemption.
We ask this in the name of Jesus the Lord.
℟. **Amen.**

➛ No. 32, p. 660

DECEMBER 19

John the Baptist's mission was to prepare a people worthy to receive the Lord. He went forth into the desert preaching repentance for sin and a conversion of heart. To concentrate only on the joy and celebration of the coming feast, and to ignore the spiritual preparation, is to miss half of the message that the Church is setting before us through the mouth of John during these weeks.

ENTRANCE ANT. See Heb 10:37

He who is to come will not delay; and then there will be no fear in our lands, because he is our Savior.

➛ No. 2, p. 614

OPENING PRAYER

Father,
you show the world the splendor of your glory

in the coming of Christ, born of the Virgin.
Give to us true faith and love
to celebrate the mystery of God made man.
We ask this . . . for ever and ever.
℞. **Amen.** ↓

FIRST READING Jgs 13:2-7, 24-25a

A nazirite was a person who was consecrated to God, at least for a specific time, in a very special way. The uncut hair, as the story of Samson later reveals, was a sign of strength resulting from this special consecration. The consecration with Samson, however, as with Samuel, was to be a perpetual consecration in order to accomplish a special service for God.

A reading from the Book of Judges

THERE was a certain man from Zorah, of the clan of the Danites, whose name was Manoah. His wife was barren and had borne no children. An angel of the LORD appeared to the woman and said to her, "Though you are barren and have had no children, yet you will conceive and bear a son. Now, then, be careful to take no wine or strong drink and to eat nothing unclean. As for the son you will conceive and bear, no razor shall touch his head, for this boy is to be consecrated to God from the womb. It is he who will begin the deliverance of Israel from the power of the Philistines."

The woman went and told her husband, "A man of God came to me; he had the appearance of an angel of God, terrible indeed. I did not ask him where he came from, nor did he tell me his name. But he said to me, 'You will be with child and will bear a son. So take neither wine nor strong drink, and eat nothing unclean. For the boy shall be consecrated to God from the womb, until the day of his death.' "

The woman bore a son and named him Samson. The boy grew up and the LORD blessed him; the Spirit of the LORD stirred him.—The word of the Lord. ℞. **Thanks be to God.** ↓

RESPONSORIAL PSALM   Ps 71:3-4a, 5-6ab, 16-17

℟. (see 8) **My mouth shall be filled with your praise, and I will sing your glory!**

Be my rock of refuge,
  a stronghold to give me safety,
  for you are my rock and my fortress.
O my God, rescue me from the hand of the wicked.—℟.

For you are my hope, O LORD;
  my trust, O God, from my youth.
On you I depend from birth;
  from my mother's womb you are my strength.—℟.

I will treat of the mighty works of the LORD;
  O God, I will tell of your singular justice.
O God, you have taught me from my youth,
  and till the present I proclaim your wondrous
    deeds.—℟. ↓

ALLELUIA

℟. **Alleluia, alleluia.**
O Root of Jesse's stem,
sign of God's love for all his people:
come to save us without delay!
℟. **Alleluia, alleluia.** ↓

GOSPEL   Lk 1:5-25

The story of the conception of John the Baptist is inseparably linked with the narratives from the Old Testament, in particular the births of Samuel and Samson. "He will be filled with the Holy Spirit even from his mother's womb."

℣. The Lord be with you. ℟. **And also with you.**
✠ A reading from the holy Gospel according to Luke.
℟. **Glory to you, Lord.**

IN the days of Herod, King of Judea, there was a priest named Zechariah of the priestly division of Abijah; his wife was from the daughters of Aaron, and her name was Elizabeth. Both were righteous in the eyes of God, observing all the commandments and ordinances of the Lord blamelessly. But they had no child, because Elizabeth was barren and both were advanced in years.

Once when he was serving as priest in his division's turn before God, according to the practice of the priestly service, he was chosen by lot to enter the sanctuary of the Lord to burn incense. Then, when the whole assembly of the people was praying outside at the hour of the incense offering, the angel of the Lord appeared to him, standing at the right of the altar of incense. Zechariah was troubled by what he saw, and fear came upon him.

But the angel said to him, "Do not be afraid, Zechariah, because your prayer has been heard. Your wife Elizabeth will bear you a son, and you shall name him John. And you will have joy and gladness, and many will rejoice at his birth, for he will be great in the sight of the Lord. He will drink neither wine nor strong drink. He will be filled with the Holy Spirit even from his mother's womb, and he will turn many of the children of Israel to the Lord their God. He will go before him in the spirit and power of Elijah to turn the hearts of fathers toward children and the disobedient to the understanding of the righteous, to prepare a people fit for the Lord." Then Zechariah said to the angel, "How shall I know this? For I am an old man, and my wife is advanced in years." And the angel said to him in reply, "I am Gabriel, who stand before God. I was sent to speak to you and to announce to you this good news. But now you will be speechless and unable to talk until the day these things take place, because you did not believe my words, which will be fulfilled at their proper time."

Meanwhile the people were waiting for Zechariah and were amazed that he stayed so long in the sanctuary. But when he came out, he was unable to speak to them, and they realized that he had seen a vision in the sanctuary. He was gesturing to them but remained mute. Then, when his days of ministry were completed, he went home. After this time his wife Elizabeth conceived, and she went into seclusion for five months, saying, "So has the Lord done for me at a time when he has seen fit to take away my disgrace before others."—The Gospel of the Lord. ℟. **Praise to you, Lord Jesus Christ.**

➜ No. 15, p. 623

PRAYER OVER THE GIFTS

Lord of mercy,
receive the gifts we bring to your altar.
Let your power take away our weakness
and make our offerings holy.
We ask this in the name of Jesus the Lord.
℟. **Amen.**　　　　　➜ No. 21, p. 626 (Pref. P 2)

COMMUNION ANT.　　　　　　　　　Lk 1:78-79

The dawn from on high shall break upon us, to guide our feet on the road to peace. ↓

PRAYER AFTER COMMUNION

Father,
we give you thanks for the bread of life.
Open our hearts in welcome
to prepare for the coming of our Savior,
who is Lord for ever and ever.
℟. **Amen.**　　　　　　　　　➜ No. 32, p. 660

DECEMBER 20

Mary was the object of God's grace and favor. The words of Luke support perfectly the doctrine of the Immaculate Conception—that from the first moment of her existence, she was preserved free from all sin and filled with grace, not because of any merit of her own, but to fit her for her role to be the mother of the Incarnate Word.

ENTRANCE ANT　　　　　　　See Is 11:1; 40:5; Lk 3:6

A shoot will spring from Jesse' stock, and all mankind will see the saving power of God.　　➜ No. 2, p. 614

OPENING PRAYER

God of love and mercy,
help us to follow the example of Mary,
always ready to do your will.
At the message of an angel
she welcomed your eternal Son
and, filled with the light of your Spirit,
she became the temple of your Word,
who lives and reigns with you and the Holy Spirit,
one God, for ever and ever.
℟. **Amen.** ↓

FIRST READING Is 7:10-14

The time, one of turmoil, is approximately 735 B.C. and Ahaz is reigning king of Judah in Jerusalem. Ahaz is weak and worldly, yet he is the legitimate heir to the throne. And so it is to him that God makes his offer. The solemnity of the sign and the use of the word "Emmanuel" show that Isaiah is speaking of more than just a continuation of the royal line.

A reading from the Book of the Prophet Isaiah

T HE LORD spoke to Ahaz: Ask for a sign from the LORD, your God; let it be deep as the nether world, or high as the sky! But Ahaz answered, "I will not ask! I will not tempt the LORD!" Then Isaiah said: Listen, O house of David! Is it not enough for you to weary men, must you also weary my God? Therefore the Lord himself will give you this sign: the virgin shall conceive and bear a son, and shall name him Emmanuel.—The word of the Lord.
℟. **Thanks be to God.** ↓

RESPONSORIAL PSALM Ps 24:1-2, 3-4ab, 5-6

℟. (see 7c and 10b) **Let the Lord enter; he is the king of glory.**

The LORD's are the earth and its fullness;
    the world and those who dwell in it.
For he founded it upon the seas
    and established it upon the rivers.—℟.

Who can ascend the mountain of the LORD?
   or who may stand in his holy place?
He whose hands are sinless, whose heart is clean,
   who desires not what is vain.—R̷̲.

He shall receive a blessing from the LORD,
   a reward from God his savior.
Such is the race that seeks for him,
   that seeks the face of the God of Jacob.—R̷̲. ↓

ALLELUIA

R̷̲. **Alleluia, alleluia.**
O Key of David,
opening the gates of God's eternal Kingdom:
come and free the prisoners of darkness!
R̷̲. **Alleluia, alleluia.** ↓

GOSPEL   Lk 1:26-38

Luke's Gospel now moves from the conception of the Baptist to the Incarnation of the Word of God. In response to the angel, Mary says: "I am the handmaid of the Lord. May it be done to me according to your word." Mary becomes the mother of Jesus.

V̷̲. The Lord be with you. R̷̲. **And also with you.**
✠ A reading from the holy Gospel according to Luke.
R̷̲. **Glory to you, Lord.**

IN the sixth month, the angel Gabriel was sent from God to a town of Galilee called Nazareth, to a virgin betrothed to a man named Joseph, of the house of David, and the virgin's name was Mary. And coming to her, he said, "Hail, full of grace! The Lord is with you." But she was greatly troubled at what was said and pondered what sort of greeting this might be. Then the angel said to her, "Do not be afraid, Mary, for you have found favor with God. Behold, you will conceive in your womb and bear a son, and you shall name him Jesus. He will be great and will be called Son of the Most High, and the Lord God will give him the throne of David his father, and he will rule over the house of Jacob forever, and of his Kingdom there will be no end."

But Mary said to the angel, "How can this be, since I have no relations with a man?" And the angel said to her in reply, "The Holy Spirit will come upon you, and the power of the Most High will overshadow you. Therefore the child to be born will be called holy, the Son of God. And behold, Elizabeth, your relative, has also conceived a son in her old age, and this is the sixth month for her who was called barren; for nothing will be impossible for God."

Mary said, "Behold, I am the handmaid of the Lord. May it be done to me according to your word." Then the angel departed from her.—The Gospel of the Lord. ℟. **Praise to you, Lord Jesus Christ.** → No. 15, p. 623

PRAYER OVER THE GIFTS

Lord,
accept this sacrificial gift.
May the eucharist we share
bring us to the eternal life
we seek in faith and hope.
Grant this through Christ our Lord.
℟. **Amen.** → No. 21, p. 626 (Pref. P 2)

COMMUNION ANT. Lk 1:31

The angel said to Mary: you shall conceive and bear a son, and you shall call him Jesus. ↓

PRAYER AFTER COMMUNION

Lord,
watch over the people you nourish with this eucharist.
Lead them to rejoice in true peace.
We ask this in the name of Jesus the Lord.
℟. **Amen.** → No. 32, p. 660

DECEMBER 21

In the very first chapter of the Gospel we see New Testament spirituality coming into play—that the Christian life is a life of service to others. "Whoever wishes to be great among you shall be your servant" (Mt 20:26). Love of God and love of neighbor cannot be separated, and, as the Apostles warn us, love of neighbor without service is empty and meaningless.

ENTRANCE ANT.
See Is 7:14; 8:10

Soon the Lord God will come, and you will call him Emmanuel, for God is with us. ➜ No. 2, p. 614

OPENING PRAYER

Lord,
hear the prayers of your people.
May we who celebrate the birth of your Son as man
rejoice in the gift of eternal life when he comes in glory,
for he lives and reigns with you and the Holy Spirit,
one God, for ever and ever. ℟. **Amen.** ↓

One of the following Readings may be chosen.

FIRST READING
Sg 2:8-14

The Song of Songs is interpreted in religious terms as a description of the love between God and his people and reflects the mood of lovers in particular situations, whether together or separated. In the beauty of the springtime, the bride awaits her lover as he swiftly speeds to her side.

A reading from the Song of Songs

HARK! my lover—here he comes
    springing across the mountains,
    leaping across the hills.
My lover is like a gazelle
    or a young stag.
Here he stands behind our wall,
    gazing through the windows,
    peering through the lattices.

My lover speaks; he says to me,
"Arise, my beloved, my dove, my beautiful one,
and come!

"For see, the winter is past,
the rains are over and gone.
The flowers appear on the earth,
the time of pruning the vines has come,
and the song of the dove is heard in our land.
The fig tree puts forth its figs,
and the vines, in bloom, give forth fragrance.
Arise, my beloved, my beautiful one,
and come!

"O my dove in the clefts of the rock,
in the secret recesses of the cliff,
Let me see you,
let me hear your voice,
For your voice is sweet,
and you are lovely."
The word of the Lord. ℟. **Thanks be to God.** ↓

OR

FIRST READING   Zep 3:14-18a

The survivors of Israel, only a remnant without possessions, are invited to rejoice because their salvation is at hand. The Lord himself will stand at the head of Israel's army, and with such leadership the nation need fear no enemy.

A reading from the Book of the Prophet Zephaniah

SHOUT for joy, O daughter Zion!
Sing joyfully, O Israel!
Be glad and exult with all your heart,
O daughter Jerusalem!
The LORD has removed the judgment against you,
he has turned away your enemies;
The King of Israel, the LORD, is in your midst,
you have no further misfortune to fear.

On that day, it shall be said to Jerusalem:
Fear not, O Zion, be not discouraged!
The LORD, your God, is in your midst,
a mighty savior;
He will rejoice over you with gladness,
and renew you in his love,
He will sing joyfully because of you,
as one sings at festivals.
The word of the Lord. ℟. **Thanks be to God.** ↓

RESPONSORIAL PSALM   Ps 33:2-3, 11-12, 20-21
℟. (1a; 3a) **Exult, you just, in the Lord! Sing to him a new
song.**

Give thanks to the LORD on the harp;
with the ten-stringed lyre chant his praises.
Sing to him a new song;
pluck the strings skillfully, with shouts of gladness.—℟.

But the plan of the LORD stands forever;
the design of his heart, through all generations.
Blessed the nation whose God is the LORD,
the people he has chosen for his own inheritance.—℟.

Our soul waits for the LORD,
who is our help and our shield,
For in him our hearts rejoice;
in his holy name we trust.—℟. ↓

ALLELUIA
℟. **Alleluia, alleluia.**
O Emmanuel, our King and Giver of Law:
come to save us, Lord our God!
℟. **Alleluia, alleluia.** ↓

GOSPEL   Lk 1:39-45

Mary visits her kinswoman to offer assistance and seek advice. The theme
of joy so connected with Messianic abundance and fulfillment is continued in the words of Elizabeth. Mary proceeds with haste—the greater to
the lesser, Mary to Elizabeth, Christ to John.

℣. The Lord be with you. ℟. **And also with you.**

✣ A reading from the holy Gospel according to Luke.

℟. **Glory to you, Lord.**

MARY set out in those days and traveled to the hill country in haste to a town of Judah, where she entered the house of Zechariah and greeted Elizabeth. When Elizabeth heard Mary's greeting, the infant leaped in her womb, and Elizabeth, filled with the Holy Spirit, cried out in a loud voice and said, "Most blessed are you among women, and blessed is the fruit of your womb. And how does this happen to me, that the mother of my Lord should come to me? For at the moment the sound of your greeting reached my ears, the infant in my womb leaped for joy. Blessed are you who believed that what was spoken to you by the Lord would be fulfilled."—The Gospel of the Lord. ℟. **Praise to you, Lord Jesus Christ.**

→ No. 15, p. 623

PRAYER OVER THE GIFTS

Lord of love,
receive these gifts which you have given to your Church.
Let them become for us
the means of our salvation.
We ask this through Christ our Lord.

℟. **Amen.** → No. 21, p. 626 (Pref. P 2)

COMMUNION ANT. Lk 1:45

Blessed are you for your firm believing, that the promises of the Lord would be fulfilled. ↓

PRAYER AFTER COMMUNION

Lord,
help us to serve you
that we may be brought to salvation.
May this eucharist be our constant protection.
Grant this in the name of Jesus the Lord.

℟. **Amen.** → No. 32, p. 660

DECEMBER 22

"The Almighty has done great things for me" (Gospel). The words of our Blessed Lady speak for all human beings. God has selected her to be the mother of his Son and, in turn, he has given to us a Savior, a Redeemer—Christ, the Lord.

ENTRANCE ANT. Ps 24:7

Gates, lift up your heads! Stand erect, ancient doors, and let in the King of glory. → No. 2, p. 614

OPENING PRAYER

God our Father,
you sent your Son
to free mankind from the power of death.
May we who celebrate the coming of Christ as man
share more fully in his divine life,
for he lives and reigns with you and the Holy Spirit,
one God, for ever and ever.
℟. **Amen.** ↓

FIRST READING 1 Sm 1:24-28

Samuel is a symbol of a child dedicated from the womb to a special service of God. Hannah fulfills her vow—that the child would be consecrated to Gods service in the temple all the days of his life.

A reading from the first Book of Samuel

IN those days, Hannah brought Samuel with her, along with a three-year-old bull, an ephah of flour, and a skin of wine, and presented him at the temple of the LORD in Shiloh. After the boy's father had sacrificed the young bull, Hannah, his mother, approached Eli and said: "Pardon, my lord! As you live, my lord, I am the woman who stood near you here, praying to the LORD. I prayed for this child, and the LORD granted my request. Now I, in turn, give him to the LORD; as long as he lives, he shall be dedicated to the LORD." She left Samuel there.—The word of the Lord. ℟. **Thanks be to God.** ↓

RESPONSORIAL PSALM   1 Sm 2:1, 4-5, 6-7, 8abcd

See Common of the Blessed Virgin Mary, p. 1119, *no.* 1.

ALLELUIA

℟. **Alleluia, alleluia.**
O King of all nations and keystone of the Church:
come and save man, whom you formed from the dust!
℟. **Alleluia, alleluia.** ↓

GOSPEL   Lk 1:46-56

In the Magnificat, all of the Old Testament allusions to the Messiah are
brought together in a hymn of thanksgiving with deep emotion and strong
conviction. The fruits of faith and dependence on a merciful God are
extolled. There is a prophetic or eschatological ring to Mary's words. God
appears as the mighty one, caring for the needy.

℣. The Lord be with you. ℟. **And also with you.**
✠ A reading from the holy Gospel according to Luke.
℟. **Glory to you, Lord.**

MARY said:
    "My soul proclaims the greatness of the Lord;
    my spirit rejoices in God my savior.
    For he has looked upon his lowly servant.
From this day all generations will call me blessed:
    the Almighty has done great things for me,
    and holy is his Name.
    He has mercy on those who fear him
    in every generation.
He has shown the strength of his arm,
    and has scattered the proud in their conceit.
He has cast down the mighty from their thrones
    and has lifted up the lowly.
He has filled the hungry with good things,
    and the rich he has sent away empty.
He has come to the help of his servant Israel
    for he remembered his promise of mercy,
    the promise he made to our fathers,
    to Abraham and his children for ever."

Mary remained with Elizabeth about three months and then returned to her home.—The Gospel of the Lord.
℟. **Praise to you, Lord Jesus Christ.** → No. 15, p. 623

PRAYER OVER THE GIFTS

Lord God,
with confidence in your love
we come with gifts to worship at your altar.
By the mystery of this eucharist
purify us and renew your life within us.
We ask this through Christ our Lord.
℟. **Amen.** → No. 21, p. 626 (Pref. P 2)

COMMUNION ANT
Lk 1:46, 49

My soul proclaims the greatness of the Lord, for the Almighty has done great things for me. ↓

PRAYER AFTER COMMUNION

Lord,
strengthen us by the sacrament we have received.
Help us to go out to meet our Savior
and to merit eternal life
with lives that witness to our faith.
We ask this in the name of Jesus the Lord.
℟. **Amen.** → No. 32, p. 660

DECEMBER 23

God wondrously intervenes among his people. The stage is now set for that moment when God will bend down from heaven and offer us his salvation in the person of his own Son, Jesus.

ENTRANCE ANT.
See Is 9:6; Ps 71:17

A little child is born for us, and he shall be called the mighty God; every race on earth shall be blessed in him. → No. 2, p. 614

OPENING PRAYER

Father,
we contemplate the birth of your Son.
He was born of the Virgin Mary
and came to live among us.
May we receive forgiveness and mercy
through our Lord Jesus Christ, your Son,
who lives and reigns with you and the Holy Spirit,
one God, for ever and ever. ℞. **Amen.** ↓

FIRST READING Mal 3:1-4, 23-24

The fulfillment of the divine promise is announced in prophecy. Malachi
sees that one of the first tasks of the Messiah on the great day of the Lord
is to purify the sons of Levi and to restore once more to his people a sacrifice worthy of the Lord.

A reading from the Book of the Prophet Malachi

THUS says the Lord GOD:
Lo, I am sending my messenger
to prepare the way before me;
And suddenly there will come to the temple
the LORD whom you seek,
And the messenger of the covenant whom you desire.
Yes, he is coming, says the LORD of hosts.
But who will endure the day of his coming?
And who can stand when he appears?
For he is like the refiner's fire,
or like the fuller's lye.
He will sit refining and purifying silver,
and he will purify the sons of Levi,
Refining them like gold or like silver
that they may offer due sacrifice to the LORD.
Then the sacrifice of Judah and Jerusalem
will please the LORD,
as in the days of old, as in years gone by.

Lo, I will send you
Elijah, the prophet,

Before the day of the LORD comes,
  the great and terrible day,
To turn the hearts of the fathers to their children,
  and the hearts of the children to their fathers,
Lest I come and strike
the land with doom.
The word of the Lord. ℟. **Thanks be to God.** ↓

RESPONSORIAL PSALM   Ps 25:4-5ab, 8-9, 10 and 14

℟. (see Lk 21:28) **Lift up your heads and see; your redemption is near at hand.**

Your ways, O LORD, make known to me;
  teach me your paths,
Guide me in your truth and teach me,
  for you are God my savior.—℟.

Good and upright is the LORD;
  thus he shows sinners the way.
He guides the humble to justice,
  he teaches the humble his way.—℟.

All the paths of the LORD are kindness and constancy
  toward those who keep his covenant and his decrees.
The friendship of the LORD is with those who fear him,
  and his covenant, for their instruction.—℟. ↓

ALLELUIA

℟. **Alleluia, alleluia.**
O King of all nations and keystone of the Church:
come and save man, whom you formed from the dust!
℟. **Alleluia, alleluia.** ↓

GOSPEL   Lk 1:57-66

The birth of John the Baptist is described. The name John, given him by the angel, signifies "Yahweh has shown favor," a name that symbolized the role of John in the redemptive plans of God.

℣. The Lord be with you. ℟. **And also with you.**
✛ A reading from the holy Gospel according to Luke.
℟. **Glory to you, Lord.**

WHEN the time arrived for Elizabeth to have her child she gave birth to a son. Her neighbors and relatives heard that the Lord had shown his great mercy toward her, and they rejoiced with her. When they came on the eighth day to circumcise the child, they were going to call him Zechariah after his father, but his mother said in reply, "No. He will be called John." But they answered her, "There is no one among your relatives who has this name." So they made signs, asking his father what he wished him to be called. He asked for a tablet and wrote, "John is his name," and all were amazed. Immediately his mouth was opened, his tongue freed, and he spoke blessing God. Then fear came upon all their neighbors, and all these matters were discussed throughout the hill country of Judea. All who heard these things took them to heart, saying, "What, then, will this child be?" For surely the hand of the Lord was with him.—The Gospel of the Lord.

℟. **Praise to you, Lord Jesus Christ.**   ➔ No. 15, p. 623

PRAYER OVER THE GIFTS

Lord,
you have given us this memorial
as the perfect form of worship.
Restore us to your peace
and prepare us to celebrate the coming of our Savior,
for he is Lord for ever and ever.

℟. **Amen.**   ➔ No. 21, p. 626 (Pref. P 2)

COMMUNION ANT   Rv 3:20

I stand at the door and knock, says the Lord. If anyone hears my voice and opens the door, I will come in and sit down to supper with him and he with me. ↓

PRAYER AFTER COMMUNION

Lord,
as you nourish us with the bread of life,
give peace to our spirits

and prepare us to welcome your Son with ardent faith.
We ask this through Christ our Lord.
℟. **Amen.**   ➜ No. 32, p. 660

DECEMBER 24

MASS IN THE MORNING

In preparing for the birth of Jesus, God asks of us the same openness as Mary had. He is ready to come into our lives and fill us with himself if we put no obstacle in his way and if we are willing to adopt Mary's attitude: "I am the handmaid of the Lord."

ENTRANCE ANT.   See Gal 4:4

The appointed time has come; God has sent his Son into the world.   ➜ No. 2, p. 614

OPENING PRAYER

Come, Lord Jesus,
do not delay;
give new courage to your people who trust in your love.
By your coming, raise us to the joy of your kingdom,
where you live and reign with the Father and the Holy
    Spirit.
one God, for ever and ever. ℟. **Amen.** ↓

FIRST READING   2 Sm 7:1-5, 8b-12, 14a, 16

David decides to build a temple. God reminds him that he has been successful and has become rich and famous, not because of his own power and strength, but through the fatherly care that God has shown toward him. God promises to reward David by making him even more successful and famous in the future. David's dynasty will last forever.

A reading from the second Book of Samuel

WHEN King David was settled in his palace, and the
    LORD had given him rest from his enemies on every
side, he said to Nathan the prophet, "Here I am living in
a house of cedar, while the ark of God dwells in a tent!"
Nathan answered the king, "Go, do whatever you have in

mind, for the LORD is with you." But that night the LORD spoke to Nathan and said: "Go, tell my servant David, 'Thus says the LORD: Should you build me a house to dwell in?

" 'It was I who took you from the pasture and from the care of the flock to be commander of my people Israel. I have been with you wherever you went, and I have destroyed all your enemies before you. And I will make you famous like the great ones of the earth. I will fix a place for my people Israel; I will plant them so that they may dwell in their place without further disturbance. Neither shall the wicked continue to afflict them as they did of old, since the time I first appointed judges over my people Israel. I will give you rest from all your enemies. The LORD also reveals to you that he will establish a house for you. And when your time comes and you rest with your ancestors, I will raise up your heir after you, sprung from your loins, and I will make his Kingdom firm. I will be a father to him, and he shall be a son to me. Your house and your Kingdom shall endure forever before me; your throne shall stand firm forever.' "—The word of the Lord. ℟. **Thanks be to God.** ↓

RESPONSORIAL PSALM   Ps 89:2-3, 4-5, 27 and 29

℟. (2) **For ever I will sing the goodness of the Lord.**

The favors of the LORD I will sing forever;
>through all generations my mouth shall proclaim
>>your faithfulness.

For you have said, "My kindness is established forever";
>in heaven you have confirmed your faithfulness.—℟.

"I have made a covenant with my chosen one,
>I have sworn to David my servant:

Forever will I confirm your posterity
>and establish your throne for all generations."—℟.

"He shall say of me, 'You are my father,
>my God, the rock, my savior.'

Forever I will maintain my kindness toward him,
   and my covenant with him stands firm."—℟. ↓

ALLELUIA

℟. **Alleluia, alleluia.**
O Radiant Dawn,
splendor of eternal light, sun of justice:
come and shine on those who dwell in darkness and in
   the shadow of death.
℟. **Alleluia, alleluia.** ↓

GOSPEL   Lk 1:67-79

A solemn hymn of praise is attributed to Zechariah. This is the recognition of the Prophet of the Most High. The father praises his own son and sees the son as a step closer to the fuller revelation of God.

℣. The Lord be with you. ℟. **And also with you.**
✦ A reading from the holy Gospel according to Luke.
℟. **Glory to you, Lord.**

ZECHARIAH his father, filled with the Holy Spirit,
prophesied, saying:
"Blessed be the Lord, the God of Israel;
   for he has come to his people and set them free.
He has raised up for us a mighty Savior,
   born of the house of his servant David.
Through his prophets he promised of old
   that he would save us from our enemies,
   from the hands of all who hate us.
He promised to show mercy to our fathers
   and to remember his holy covenant.
This was the oath he swore to our father Abraham:
   to set us free from the hand of our enemies,
   free to worship him without fear,
   holy and righteous in his sight
      all the days of our life.
You, my child, shall be called the prophet of the Most
      High,
   for you will go before the Lord to prepare his way,

to give his people knowledge of salvation
by the forgiveness of their sins.
In the tender compassion of our God
the dawn from on high shall break upon us,
to shine on those who dwell in darkness and the shadow of death,
and to guide our feet into the way of peace."
The Gospel of the Lord. ℟. **Praise to you, Lord Jesus Christ.**   ➙ No. 15, p. 623

PRAYER OVER THE GIFTS

Father,
accept the gifts we offer.
By our sharing in this eucharist
free us from sin
and help us to look forward in faith
to the glorious coming of your Son,
who is Lord for ever and ever.
℟. **Amen.**   ➙ No. 21, p. 626 (Pref. P 2)

COMMUNION ANT.   Lk 1:68

Blessed be the Lord God of Israel, for he has visited and redeemed his people. ↓

PRAYER AFTER COMMUNION

Lord,
your gift of the eucharist has renewed our lives.
May we who look forward to the feast of Christ's birth
rejoice for ever in the wonder of his love,
for he is Lord for ever and ever.
℟. **Amen.**   ➙ No. 32, p. 660

CHRISTMAS SEASON

The feasts of the liturgical year place before our minds the sign of some hidden sacred reality that must be applied to all of us. During the Christmas season this hidden sacred reality is the light, the life, and the joy beaming from Christ, the "Sun of Justice," upon mankind in the darkness of ignorance and sin (Mal 4:2).

This mystery of our salvation is to be honored not as something that happened 2,000 years ago, but as something present, for while the act itself (Christ's birth and manifestation) is past, its effects are very present. The hidden reality in this mystery is ultimately Christ and his saving action. He is present in the mystery of Christmas-Epiphany, constantly interceding for us and communicating himself in holy symbols.

We should meditate on and celebrate the Christmas mystery as happening now to us and embrace its mystical effects with an open heart. After the time of waiting (Advent), we enjoy a fuller realization of Christ's presence in us. In the Word made flesh, we see that God is no stranger to the human condition; in the infant born in a stable to simple working people, we come to understand that God who is infinitely great is also one of us.

The Readings of this season provide the salient features of this infant. He is the Servant of Yahweh and the Prince of Peace, whom Isaiah foretold. He is the Light and the Logos, which is greater than human reason and perfects it (John). In him we encounter the Ultimate Transcendent Reality: he reveals the Father (Heb 1) who is gracious to human beings (Titus). This Father comforts and consoles us (Is 52) and promises to unite us his adopted children in Jerusalem, symbols of the Church and brotherly love (Gal 4; Is 68).

Christmas celebrates the Father's gift to us: the revelation of his loving presence. This knowledge has been given to us through Israel and the prophets and supremely through Christ his Son. It must continue to be made manifest through Christ-in-us; "from his fullness we have all received" (John).

Dec. 25—CHRISTMAS

See Vol. I (Sunday Missal), p. 134.

Dec. 26 — ST. STEPHEN, First Martyr

2nd DAY IN THE OCTAVE OF CHRISTMAS

Feast

St. Stephen received the commission from the Apostles to gather food for the poor. The judges accused him before the Sanhedrin, being amazed at his wonderful miracles. St. Stephen, the Church tells us, was the first to give up his life for the Savior. He died praying for those who stoned him.

ENTRANCE ANT.

The gates of heaven opened for Stephen, the first of the martyrs; in heaven, he wears the crown of victory.

→No. 2, p. 614

OPENING PRAYER

Lord,
today we celebrate the entrance of St. Stephen
into eternal glory.
He died praying for those who killed him.
Help us to imitate his goodness
and to love our enemies.
We ask this . . . for ever and ever. ℟. **Amen.** ↓

FIRST READING

Acts 6:8-10; 7:54-59

St. Stephen is "filled with grace and power" through his union with Christ and the presence of the Holy Spirit. The members of the "Synagogue of Freedmen" are closed to God's action and rebel against the prophetic word spoken to them. They try to put Stephen's words out of their minds by stopping up their ears. They attack God's spokesperson and put him to death.

A reading from the Acts of the Apostles

STEPHEN, filled with grace and power, was working great wonders and signs among the people. Certain members of the so-called Synagogue of Freedmen, Cyrenians, and Alexandrians, and people from Cilicia and Asia, came forward and debated with Stephen, but they could not withstand the wisdom and the spirit with which he spoke.

When they heard this, they were infuriated, and they ground their teeth at him. But he, filled with the Holy Spirit, looked up intently to heaven and saw the glory of God and Jesus standing at the right hand of God, and he said, "Behold, I see the heavens opened and the Son of Man standing at the right hand of God." But they cried out in a loud voice, covered their ears, and rushed upon him together. They threw him out of the city, and began to stone him. The witnesses laid down their cloaks at the feet of a young man named Saul. As they were stoning Stephen, he called out "Lord Jesus, receive my spirit."— The word of the Lord. ℟. **Thanks be to God.** ↓

RESPONSORIAL PSALM Ps 31:3cd-4, 6 and 8ab, 16bc and 17

℟. (6) **Into your hands, O Lord, I commend my spirit.**

Be my rock of refuge,
    a stronghold to give me safety.
You are my rock and my fortress;
    for your name's sake you will lead and guide me.—℟.

Into your hands I commend my spirit;
    you will redeem me, O LORD, O faithful God.
I will rejoice and be glad because of your mercy.—℟.

Rescue me from the clutches of my enemies and my per-
    secutors.
Let your face shine upon your servant;
    save me in your kindness.—℟. ↓

ALLELUIA   Ps 118:26a, 27a

℟. **Alleluia, alleluia.**
Blessed is he who comes in the name of the LORD:
the LORD is God and has given us light.
℟. **Alleluia, alleluia.** ↓

GOSPEL   Mt 10:17-22

Christ tells his followers they will experience rejection because of him as
did Stephen. He tells them to be confident and courageous, to live at
peace with him so they can live at peace with themselves, and to conform
to his Gospel and live without fear.

℣. The Lord be with you. ℟. **And also with you.**
✢ A reading from the holy Gospel according to Matthew.
℟. **Glory to you, Lord.**

JESUS said to his disciples: "Beware of men, for they
will hand you over to courts and scourge you in their
synagogues, and you will be led before governors and
kings for my sake as a witness before them and the
pagans. When they hand you over, do not worry about
how you are to speak or what you are to say. You will be
given at that moment what you are to say. For it will not
be you who speak but the Spirit of your Father speaking
through you. Brother will hand over brother to death,
and the father his child; children will rise up against parents and have them put to death. You will be hated by all
because of my name, but whoever endures to the end will
be saved."—The Gospel of the Lord. ℟. **Praise to you,
Lord Jesus Christ.**   → No. 15, p. 623

PRAYER OVER THE GIFTS

Father,
be pleased with the gifts we bring in your honor
as we celebrate the feast of St. Stephen.
Grant this through Christ our Lord.
℟. **Amen.**   → No. 21, p. 626 (Pref. P 3-5)

COMMUNION ANT.　　　　　　　　　　　　　Acts 7:58

As they stoned him, Stephen prayed aloud: Lord Jesus, receive my spirit. ↓

PRAYER AFTER COMMUNION

Lord,
we thank you for the many signs of your love for us.
Save us by the birth of your Son
and give us joy in honoring St. Stephen the martyr.
We ask this through Christ our Lord.
℟. **Amen.**　　　　　　　　　　　　　　　→ No. 32, p. 660

Dec. 27 — ST. JOHN, Apostle and Evangelist

3rd DAY IN THE OCTAVE OF CHRISTMAS

Feast

St. John is the Apostle whom Jesus loved. It was he who reclined on the bosom of the Savior at the Last Supper. He is the author of the sublime Gospel that so emphatically proclaims the Divinity of Christ. To him also our Lord, hanging on the cross, entrusted his beloved Mother. He died about the year 100.

ENTRANCE ANT.　　　　　　　　　　　　　Sir 15:5

The Lord opened his mouth in the assembly, and filled him with the spirit of wisdom and understanding, and clothed him in a robe of glory.

OR

At the last supper, John reclined close to the Lord. Blessed apostle, to you were revealed the heavenly secrets! Your life-giving words have spread over all the earth!　　　　　　　　　　　　　→ No. 2, p. 614

OPENING PRAYER

God our Father,
you have revealed the mysteries of your Word
through St. John the apostle.
By prayer and reflection
may we come to understand the wisdom he taught.
Grant this . . . for ever and ever. ℟. **Amen.** ↓

FIRST READING 1 Jn 1:1-4

John emphasizes that eternal life has been made known in the historical Jesus and that the Church as an apostolic company actually handled, saw, and heard the divine Logos who is the creative Mediator of life.

A reading from the beginning of the first Letter of Saint John

BELOVED:
What was from the beginning,
what we have heard,
what we have seen with our eyes,
what we looked upon
and touched with our hands
concerns the Word of life—
for the life was made visible;
we have seen it and testify to it
and proclaim to you the eternal life
that was with the Father and was made visible to us—
what we have seen and heard
we proclaim now to you,
so that you too may have fellowship with us;
for our fellowship is with the Father
and with his Son, Jesus Christ.
We are writing this so that our joy may be complete.
The word of the Lord. ℟. **Thanks be to God.** ↓

RESPONSORIAL PSALM Ps 97:1-2, 5-6, 11-12

℟. (12) **Rejoice in the Lord, you just!**

The LORD is king; let the earth rejoice;
 let the many isles be glad.
Clouds and darkness are around him,
 justice and judgment are the foundation of his
  throne.—℟.

The mountains melt like wax before the LORD,
 before the LORD of all the earth.
The heavens proclaim his justice,
 and all peoples see his glory.—℟.

Light dawns for the just,
and gladness, for the upright of heart.
Be glad in the LORD, you just,
and give thanks to his holy name.—℟. ↓

ALLELUIA   See *Te Deum*

℟. **Alleluia, alleluia.**
We praise you, O God,
we acclaim you as Lord;
the glorious company of Apostles praise you.
℟. **Alleluia, alleluia.** ↓

GOSPEL   Jn 20:1a and 2-8
John skillfully combines the tradition of the empty tomb with that of
Resurrection appearances. Mary Magdalene reports to Peter and the
"beloved disciple" that the stone has been removed, and the two disciples hurry to the tomb.

℣. The Lord be with you. ℟. **And also with you.**
✟ A reading from the holy Gospel according to John.
℟. **Glory to you, Lord.**

ON the first day of the week, Mary Magdalene ran
and went to Simon Peter and to the other disciple
whom Jesus loved, and told them, "They have taken the
Lord from the tomb, and we do not know where they
put him." So Peter and the other disciple went out and
came to the tomb. They both ran, but the other disciple
ran faster than Peter and arrived at the tomb first; he
bent down and saw the burial cloths there, but did not
go in. When Simon Peter arrived after him, he went
into the tomb and saw the burial cloths there, and the
cloth that had covered his head, not with the burial
cloths but rolled up in a separate place. Then the other
disciple also went in, the one who had arrived at the
tomb first, and he saw and believed.—The Gospel of
the Lord. ℟. **Praise to you, Lord Jesus Christ.**

→ No. 15, p. 623

PRAYER OVER THE GIFTS

Lord,
bless these gifts we present to you.
With St. John may we share
in the hidden wisdom of your eternal Word
which you reveal at this eucharistic table.
We ask this in the name of Jesus the Lord.
℟. **Amen.**   → No. 21, p. 626 (Pref. P 3-5)

COMMUNION ANT.   Jn 1:14-16

The Word of God became man, and lived among us. Of his riches we have all received. ↓

PRAYER AFTER COMMUNION

Almighty Father,
St. John proclaimed that your Word became flesh for our
    salvation.
Through this eucharist may your Son always live in us,
for he is Lord for ever and ever.
℟. **Amen.**   → No. 32, p. 660

Dec. 28 — THE HOLY INNOCENTS, Martyrs

4th DAY IN THE OCTAVE OF CHRISTMAS

Feast

In the slaughter of the Innocents by Herod, the Infant Savior has infant
martyrs. Thus children are held up to our admiration from the very first—
in their death, as in their lives, a pattern to older Christians. All those who
kill innocent children are like Herod and are to be condemned. Even more
corrupt are those who scandalize the innocent and lead them into sin.
Jesus pronounces a terrible punishment upon such people.

ENTRANCE ANT.

**These innocent children were slain for Christ. They fol-
low the spotless Lamb, and proclaim for ever: Glory to
you, Lord.**   → No. 2, p. 614

OPENING PRAYER

Father,
the Holy Innocents offered you praise
by the death they suffered for Christ.
May our lives bear witness
to the faith we profess with our lips.
We ask this . . . for ever and ever. ℟. **Amen.** ↓

FIRST READING   1 Jn 1:5—2:2

John refutes the heretical claims to have fellowship with God and to have no need for redemption from sin. "God is light" means that God is knowable, although invisible, for he reveals himself as Love; and also that he is holy and morally perfect, for the darkness of sin does not exist at all in his being. Every sin must be confessed in the awareness that God knows all and that he is just. John writes to keep "his little ones" from sin.

A reading from the first Letter of Saint John

BELOVED: This is the message that we have heard from Jesus Christ and proclaim to you: God is light, and in him there is no darkness at all. If we say, "We have fellowship with him," while we continue to walk in darkness, we lie and do not act in truth. But if we walk in the light as he is in the light, then we have fellowship with one another, and the Blood of his Son Jesus cleanses us from all sin. If we say, "We are without sin," we deceive ourselves, and the truth is not in us. If we acknowledge our sins, he is faithful and just and will forgive our sins and cleanse us from every wrongdoing. If we say, "We have not sinned," we make him a liar, and his word is not in us.

My children, I am writing this to you so that you may not commit sin. But if anyone does sin, we have an Advocate with the Father, Jesus Christ the righteous one. He is expiation for our sins, and not for our sins only but for those of the whole world.—The word of the Lord. ℟. **Thanks be to God.** ↓

RESPONSORIAL PSALM   Ps 124:2-3, 4-5, 7cd-8

℟. (7) **Our soul has been rescued like a bird from the fowler's snare.**

Had not the LORD been with us—
When men rose up against us,
    then would they have swallowed us alive,
When their fury was inflamed against us.—℟.

Then would the waters have overwhelmed us;
The torrent would have swept over us;
    over us then would have swept the raging waters.—℟.

Broken was the snare,
    and we were freed.
Our help is in the name of the LORD,
    who made heaven and earth.—℟. ↓

ALLELUIA   See *Te Deum*

℟. **Alleluia, alleluia.**
We praise you, O God,
we acclaim you as Lord;
the glorious white-robed army of martyrs praise you.
℟. **Alleluia, alleluia.** ↓

GOSPEL   Mt 2:13-18

The cruelty of Herod has become proverbial, even in Rome. He tries to destroy the child Jesus because he fails to see that the birth of this king was the dawning of hope for salvation. The quotation from Hosea, "Out of Egypt I have called my son," is based on the Hebrew text in which Jesus is presented as reenacting in his own life the career of Israel, for he is the new Israel.

℣. The Lord be with you. ℟. **And also with you.**
✠ A reading from the holy Gospel according to Matthew.
℟. **Glory to you, Lord.**

WHEN the magi had departed, behold, the angel of the Lord appeared to Joseph in a dream and said,

"Rise, take the child and his mother, flee to Egypt, and stay there until I tell you. Herod is going to search for the child to destroy him." Joseph rose and took the child and his mother by night and departed for Egypt. He stayed there until the death of Herod, that what the Lord had said through the prophet might be fulfilled, *Out of Egypt I called my son.*

When Herod realized that he had been deceived by the magi, he became furious. He ordered the massacre of all the boys in Bethlehem and its vicinity two years old and under, in accordance with the time he had ascertained·from the magi. Then was fulfilled what had been said through Jeremiah the prophet:

A voice was heard in Ramah,
    sobbing and loud lamentation;
Rachel weeping for her children,
    and she would not be consoled,
    since they were no more.

The Gospel of the Lord. R̸. **Praise to you, Lord Jesus Christ.** → No. 15, p. 660

PRAYER OVER THE GIFTS

Lord,
you give us your life even before we understand.
Receive the offerings we bring in love,
and free us from sin.
We ask this in the name of Jesus the Lord.
R̸. **Amen.** → No. 21, p. 626 (Pref. P 3-5)

COMMUNION ANT. Rv 14:4

These have been ransomed for God and the Lamb as the first-fruits of mankind; they follow the Lamb wherever he goes. ↓

PRAYER AFTER COMMUNION

Lord,
by a wordless profession of faith in your Son,

the innocents were crowned with life at his birth.
May all people who receive your holy gifts today
come to share in the fullness of salvation.
We ask this through Christ our Lord.
℟. **Amen.**   → No. 32, p. 660

Dec. 29—5th DAY IN THE OCTAVE OF CHRISTMAS

The Mass today stresses the necessity to observe the will of God in obedience and humility. Christ's example of his respect for the law in the shedding of his precious blood in the rite of circumcision had nothing to do with sin. But to atone for that of human beings, he willingly sacrificed himself. He obeyed the command of the old law to the very letter.

ENTRANCE ANT.   Jn 3:16

God loved the world so much, he gave his only Son, that all who believe in him might not perish, but might have eternal life.   → No. 2, p. 614

OPENING PRAYER

All-powerful and unseen God,
the coming of your light into our world
has made the darkness vanish.
Teach us to proclaim the birth of your Son Jesus Christ,
who lives and reigns with you and the Holy Spirit,
one God, for ever and ever. ℟. **Amen.** ↓

FIRST READING   1 Jn 2:3-11

John urges his friends to realize that the one sure way to prove fellowship with God is to do the will of God. In keeping the Commandments, the supreme example that comes to mind is the Lord's precept of love, a commandment that is both old and yet of the new Christian revelation.

A reading from the first Letter of Saint John

BELOVED: The way we may be sure that we know
Jesus is to keep his commandments. Whoever says, "I
know him," but does not keep his commandments is a

liar, and the truth is not in him. But whoever keeps his word, the love of God is truly perfected in him. This is the way we may know that we are in union with him: whoever claims to abide in him ought to walk just as he walked.

Beloved, I am writing no new commandment to you but an old commandment that you had from the beginning. The old commandment is the word that you have heard. And yet I do write a new commandment to you, which holds true in him and among you, for the darkness is passing away, and the true light is already shining. Whoever says he is in the light, yet hates his brother, is still in the darkness. Whoever loves his brother remains in the light, and there is nothing in him to cause a fall. Whoever hates his brother is in darkness; he walks in darkness and does not know where he is going because the darkness has blinded his eyes.—The word of the Lord. ℟. **Thanks be to God.** ↓

RESPONSORIAL PSALM   Ps 96:1-2a, 2b-3, 5b-6

℟. (11a) **Let the heavens be glad and the earth rejoice!**

Sing to the LORD a new song;
  sing to the LORD, all you lands.
Sing to the LORD; bless his name.—℟.

Announce his salvation, day after day.
Tell his glory among the nations;
  among all peoples, his wondrous deeds.—℟.

The LORD made the heavens.
Splendor and majesty go before him;
  praise and grandeur are in his sanctuary.—℟. ↓

ALLELUIA   Lk 2:32

℟. **Alleluia, alleluia.**
A light of revelation to the Gentiles
and glory for your people Israel.
℟. **Alleluia, alleluia.** ↓

GOSPEL   Lk 2:22-35

Mary is seen to be united with Jesus, and possibly with Joseph, in the temple ceremony. Mary's uncleanness is not moral, but only ceremonial, but just as Jesus followed the full Mosaic law and completely immersed himself in humanity, thereby to transform it, so Mary is presented as one with all womankind in giving birth to her child. Her purification, like Jesus' act of redemption, belongs to every one of Israel.

See p. 944 (Long Form), ending at the asterisk (*).

PRAYER OVER THE GIFTS

Lord,
receive our gifts in this wonderful exchange:
from all you have given us
we bring you these gifts,
and in return, you give us yourself.
We ask this through Christ our Lord.
℟. **Amen.**   ➜ No. 21, p. 626 (Pref. P 3-5)

When Eucharistic Prayer I is used, the special Christmas form of In union with the whole Church *is said.*

COMMUNION ANT.   Lk 1:78

Through the tender compassion of our God, the dawn from on high shall break upon us. ↓

PRAYER AFTER COMMUNION

Father of love and mercy,
grant that our lives may always be founded
on the power of this holy mystery.
We ask this in the name of Jesus the Lord.
℟. **Amen.**   ➜ No. 32, p. 660

Dec. 30—6th DAY IN THE OCTAVE OF CHRISTMAS

When there is no Sunday within the octave of Christmas, the feast of the Holy Family is celebrated today. (See Vol. I: Sunday Missal, p. 158.)

We should turn our thoughts today not to the hidden life of Jesus in general, but to the special period of it that formed his boyhood. Our Lord became truly man and went through the different stages of human life, from infancy to the fullness of manhood. He did not come into this world formed in that fullness all at once, as Adam came forth from his Creator's hand, but he came "born of a woman" (Gal 4:4).

ENTRANCE ANT. Wis 18:14-15

When peaceful silence lay over all, and night had run half of her swift course, your all-powerful word, O Lord, leaped down from heaven, from the royal throne.

→ No. 2, p. 614

OPENING PRAYER

All-powerful God,
may the human birth of your Son
free us from our former slavery to sin
and bring us new life.
We ask this . . . for ever and ever. ℟. **Amen.** ↓

FIRST READING 1 Jn 2:12-17

Observance of the law of Christ effectively removes the Christian from the influence of that world from which Christ prayed that his disciples might be free. John continues to address all his Christian readers as "children," whom, however, he now distinguishes as "fathers" and "young men" to emphasize that his appeal extends to the entire Christian community.

A reading from the first Letter of Saint John

I AM writing to you, children, because your sins have been forgiven for his name's sake.

I am writing to you, fathers, because you know him who is from the beginning.

I am writing to you, young men, because you have conquered the Evil One.

I write to you, children, because you know the Father.

I write to you, fathers, because you know him who is from the beginning.

I write to you, young men, because you are strong and the word of God remains in you, and you have conquered the Evil One.

Do not love the world or the things of the world. If anyone loves the world, the love of the Father is not in him. For all that is in the world, sensual lust, enticement for the eyes, and a pretentious life, is not from the Father but is from the world. Yet the world and its enticement are passing away. But whoever does the will of God remains forever.—The word of the Lord. ℟. **Thanks be to God.** ↓

RESPONSORIAL PSALM   Ps 96:7-8a, 8b-9, 10

℟. (11a) **Let the heavens be glad and the earth rejoice!**

Give to the LORD, you families of nations,
    give to the LORD glory and praise;
    give to the LORD the glory due his name!—℟.

Bring gifts, and enter his courts;
    worship the LORD in holy attire.
Tremble before him, all the earth.—℟.

Say among the nations: The LORD is king.
He has made the world firm, not to be moved;
    he governs the peoples with equity.—℟.

ALLELUIA

℟. **Alleluia, alleluia.**
A holy day has dawned upon us.
Come, you nations, and adore the Lord.
Today a great light has come upon the earth.
℟. **Alleluia, alleluia.** ↓

GOSPEL   Lk 2:36-40

It is in the temple, the same place where Anna had for so many years poured out her heart to God, that God pours out his heart to her. Luke points out the necessity of our Lord's hidden life at Nazareth, that he might grow strong in the full experience of a human nature and thus be able to bring the spirit of God into immediate contact with every human area.

℣. The Lord be with you. ℟. **And also with you.**
✝ A reading from the holy Gospel according to Luke.
℟. **Glory to you, Lord.**

THERE was a prophetess, Anna, the daughter of Phanuel, of the tribe of Asher. She was advanced in years, having lived seven years with her husband after her marriage, and then as a widow until she was eighty-four. She never left the temple, but worshiped night and day with fasting and prayer. And coming forward at that very time, she gave thanks to God and spoke about the child to all who were awaiting the redemption of Jerusalem.

When they had fulfilled all the prescriptions of the law of the Lord, they returned to Galilee, to their own town of Nazareth. The child grew and became strong, filled with wisdom; and the favor of God was upon him.—The Gospel of the Lord. ℟. **Praise be to you, Lord Jesus Christ.**

➙ No. 15, p. 623

PRAYER OVER THE GIFTS

Father,
in your mercy accept our gifts.
By sharing in this eucharist
may we come to live more fully the love we profess.
Grant this through Christ our Lord.
℟. **Amen.**

➙ No. 21, p. 626 (Pref. P 3-5)

COMMUNION ANT. Jn 1:16

From his riches we have all received, grace for grace. ↓

PRAYER AFTER COMMUNION

God our Father,
in this eucharist you touch our lives.
Keep your love alive in our hearts
that we may become worthy of you.
We ask this through Christ our Lord.
℟. **Amen.**

➙ No. 32, p. 660

Dec. 31 — 7th DAY IN THE OCTAVE OF CHRISTMAS

"False Christs and false prophets" come to seduce us in the guise of interesting literature and entertainment. These things have nothing in common with the teachings of Jesus. Jesus is the Way, the Truth, and the Life.

ENTRANCE ANT.
Is 9:6

A child is born for us, a son is given to us; dominion is laid on his shoulders, and he shall be called Wonderful-Counselor. → No. 2, p. 614

OPENING PRAYER

Ever-living God,
in the birth of your Son
our religion has its origin and its perfect fulfillment.
Help us to share in the life of Christ
for he is the salvation of mankind,
who lives and reigns with you and the Holy Spirit,
one God, for ever and ever. ℟. **Amen.** ↓

FIRST READING
1 Jn 2:18-21

By "antichrist," John alludes to any and all of the false teachers who afflict the Church in this "last hour." The false teachers who have separated themselves from the Church never truly shared in the Church's life of God. John speaks of this as a self-evident fact to which Christian experience must testify.

A reading from the first Letter of Saint John

CHILDREN, it is the last hour; and just as you heard that the antichrist was coming, so now many antichrists have appeared. Thus we know this is the last hour. They went out from us, but they were not really of our number; if they had been, they would have remained with us. Their desertion shows that none of them was of our number. But you have the anointing that comes from the Holy One, and you all have knowledge. I write to you not because you do not know the truth but because you

do, and because every lie is alien to the truth.—The word
of the Lord. ℟. **Thanks be to God.** ↓

RESPONSORIAL PSALM　　　　　　Ps 96:1-2, 11-12, 13

℟. (11a) **Let the heavens be glad and the earth rejoice!**

Sing to the LORD a new song;
　　sing to the LORD, all you lands.
Sing to the LORD; bless his name;
　　announce his salvation, day after day.—℟.

Let the heavens be glad and the earth rejoice;
　　let the sea and what fills it resound;
　　let the plains be joyful and all that is in them!
Then shall all the trees of the forest exult before the
　　　LORD.—℟.

The LORD comes,
　　he comes to rule the earth.
He shall rule the world with justice
　　and the peoples with his constancy.—℟. ↓

ALLELUIA　　　　　　　　　　　Jn 1:14a, 12a

℟. **Alleluia, alleluia.**
The Word of God became flesh and dwelt among us.
To those who accepted him
he gave power to become the children of God.
℟. **Alleluia, alleluia.** ↓

GOSPEL　　　　　　　　　　　　Jn 1:1-18

In the Old Testament, the Word of God is God's manifestation—the revelation of himself, whether in creation, in deeds of power and of grace, or in prophecy. All these trains of thought are taken up by John who shows that Christ, the Incarnate Word, is the ultimate and complete revelation of God.

℣. The Lord be with you. ℟. **And also with you.**
✠ A reading from the beginning of the holy Gospel
according to John. ℟. **Glory to you, Lord.**

IN the beginning was the Word,
　and the Word was with God,
　　and the Word was God.

He was in the beginning with God.
All things came to be through him,
    and without him nothing came to be.
What came to be through him was life,
    and this life was the light of the human race;
    the light shines in the darkness,
    and the darkness has not overcome it.

A man named John was sent from God. He came for testimony, to testify to the light, so that all might believe through him. He was not the light, but came to testify to the light. The true light, which enlightens everyone, was coming into the world.

He was in the world,
    and the world came to be through him,
    but the world did not know him.
He came to what was his own,
    but his own people did not accept him.

But to those who did accept him he gave power to become children of God, to those who believe in his name, who were born not by natural generation nor by human choice nor by a man's decision but of God.

And the Word became flesh
    and made his dwelling among us,
    and we saw his glory,
    the glory as of the Father's only-begotten Son,
    full of grace and truth.

John testified to him and cried out, saying, "This was he of whom I said, 'The one who is coming after me ranks ahead of me because he existed before me.'" From his fullness we have all received, grace in place of grace, because while the law was given through Moses, grace and truth came through Jesus Christ. No one has ever seen God. The only-begotten Son, God, who is at the Father's side, has revealed him.—The Gospel of the Lord.

℟. **Praise to you, Lord Jesus Christ.** ➜ No. 15, p. 623

PRAYER OVER THE GIFTS

Father of peace,
accept our devotion and sincerity,
and by our sharing in this mystery
draw us closer to each other and to you.
We ask this in the name of Jesus the Lord.
℟. **Amen.**   → No. 21, p. 626 (Pref. P 3-5)

*When Eucharistic Prayer I is used, the special Christmas form
of* In union with the whole Church *is said.*

COMMUNION ANT.   1 Jn 4:9

**God's love for us was revealed when he sent his only Son
into the world, so that we could have life through him.** ↓

PRAYER AFTER COMMUNION

Lord,
may this sacrament be our strength.
Teach us to value all the good you give us
and help us to strive for eternal life.
Grant this through Christ our Lord.
℟. **Amen.**   → No. 32, p. 660

ANTIPHONS AND PRAYERS FOR WEEKDAYS
FROM JANUARY 2 TO EPIPHANY

MONDAY BEFORE EPIPHANY

(After Epiphany, see p. 131.)

The days between the Solemnity of Mary the Mother of God and the Epiphany are devoted to proclaiming the Good News of the identity and work of the One who was born at Bethlehem. He is the Word made flesh, and we have known his glory. Christmas is a joyous time for us because the Son of Mary is the Son of God, the Messiah.

ENTRANCE ANT.

A holy day has dawned upon us. Come, you nations, and adore the Lord. Today a great light has come upon the earth.
→ No. 2, p. 614

OPENING PRAYER

Lord,
keep us true in the faith,
proclaiming that Christ your Son,
who is one with you in eternal glory,
became man and was born of a virgin mother.
Free us from all evil
and lead us to the joy of eternal life.
We ask this . . . for ever and ever. ℟. **Amen.** ↓

READINGS AND INTERVENIENT CHANTS

The *Weekday* Readings and Intervenient Chants corresponding to the day of the month, pp. 118-131.

PRAYER OVER THE GIFTS

Lord,
receive our gifts in this wonderful exchange:
from all you have given us
we bring you these gifts,
and in return, you give you yourself.
We ask this through Christ our Lord.
℟. **Amen.**
→ No. 21, p. 626 (P 3-5)

COMMUNION ANT.   Jn 1:14

We have seen his glory, the glory of the Father's only Son, full of grace and truth. ↓

PRAYER AFTER COMMUNION

Father of love and mercy,
grant that our gifts may always be founded
on the power of this holy mystery.
We ask this in the name of Jesus the Lord.
℟. **Amen.**   → No. 32, p. 660

TUESDAY BEFORE EPIPHANY

(After Epiphany, see p. 134.)

The joy of Christmas must also provide room for penance for our sins. Jesus showed his love by coming to live among us and to offer himself for us, even while we were sinners. The spirit of holiness is given to those who welcome the One whom the Father has given.

ENTRANCE ANT.   Ps 118:26-27

Blessed is he who comes in the name of the Lord; the Lord God shines upon us.   → No. 2, p. 614

OPENING PRAYER

God our Father,
when your Son was born of the Virgin Mary
he became like us in all things but sin.
May we who have been reborn in him
be free from our sinful ways.
We ask this . . . for ever and ever. ℟. **Amen.** ↓

READINGS AND INTERVENIENT CHANTS

The *Weekday* Readings and Intervenient Chants corresponding to the day of the month, pp. 118-131.

PRAYER OVER THE GIFTS

Father,
in your mercy accept our gifts.
By sharing in this eucharist
may we come to live more fully the love we profess.

Grant this through Christ our Lord.
℟. **Amen.**   ➡ No. 21, p. 626 (Pref. P 3-5)

COMMUNION ANT.   Eph 2:4; Rom 8:3

God loved us so much that he sent his own Son in the likeness of sinful flesh. ↓

PRAYER AFTER COMMUNION

God our Father,
in this eucharist you touch our lives.
Keep your love alive in our hearts
that we may become worthy of you.
We ask this through Christ our Lord.
℟. **Amen.**   ➡ No. 32, p. 660

WEDNESDAY BEFORE EPIPHANY

(After Epiphany, see p. 137.)

In the newly revised Missal, God's message in the Readings becomes our thought in the Prayers. We renew our choice to be loyal to God, rather than to follow evil. Jesus is our light and the source of all our good. We ask for the grace to follow him.

ENTRANCE ANT.   Is 9:6

The people who walked in darkness have seen a great light; on those who lived in the shadow of death, light has shone.   ➡ No. 2, p. 614

OPENING PRAYER

All-powerful Father,
you sent your Son Jesus Christ
to bring the new light of salvation to the world.
May he enlighten us with his radiance,
who lives and reigns with you and the Holy Spirit,
one God, for ever and ever. ℟. **Amen.** ↓

READINGS AND INTERVENIENT CHANTS

The *Weekday* Readings and Intervenient Chants corresponding to the day of the month, pp. 118-131.

PRAYER OVER THE GIFTS

Father of peace,
accept our devotion and sincerity,
and by our sharing in this mystery
draw us closer to each other and to you.
We ask this in the name of Jesus the Lord.
℟. **Amen.**   → No. 21, p. 626 (Pref. P 3-5)

COMMUNION ANT.   1 Jn 1:2

**The eternal life which was with the Father has been
revealed to us.** ↓

PRAYER AFTER COMMUNION

Lord,
may this sacrament be our strength.
Teach us to value all the good you give us
and help us to strive for eternal life.
Grant this through Christ our Lord.
℟. **Amen.**   → No. 32, p. 660

THURSDAY BEFORE EPIPHANY

(After Epiphany, see p. 140.)

By the birth of Jesus, heaven came to earth, healing came to sin, and love
broke through the darkness of loneliness and separation. Our Eucharist
today is our gift of thanksgiving for God's gifts by which everything in life
gains a new joy.

ENTRANCE ANT.   See Jn 1:1

**In the beginning, before all ages, the Word was God; that
Word was born a man to save the world.** → No. 2, p. 614

OPENING PRAYER

Father,
you make known the salvation of mankind
at the birth of your Son.
Make us strong in faith
and bring us to the glory you promise.
We ask this . . . for ever and ever. ℟. **Amen.** ↓

READINGS AND INTERVENIENT CHANTS

The *Weekday* Readings and Intervenient Chants corresponding to the day of the month, pp. 118-131.

PRAYER OVER THE GIFTS

Lord,
receive our gifts in this wonderful exchange:
from all you have given us
we bring you these gifts,
and in return, you give us yourself.
We ask this through Christ our Lord.

℞. **Amen.** → No. 21, p. 626 (Pref. P 3-5)

COMMUNION ANT.

Jn 3:16

God loved the world so much, he gave his only Son, that all who believe in him might not perish, but might have eternal life. ↓

PRAYER AFTER COMMUNION

Father of love and mercy,
grant that our lives may always be founded
on the power of this holy mystery.
We ask this in the name of Jesus the Lord.

℞. **Amen.** → No. 32, p. 660

_____

FRIDAY BEFORE EPIPHANY

(After Epiphany, see p. 143.)

Jesus, the child of Bethlehem, the Messiah, the Suffering Servant, the Risen Lord, pours out upon us the gifts of life, especially through the sacraments. Today's Readings and Prayers help us to be aware of how much the Son of God is with us and in us.

ENTRANCE ANT.

Ps 112:4

The Lord is a light in darkness to the upright; he is gracious, merciful, and just. → No. 2, p. 614

OPENING PRAYER

Lord,
fill our hearts with your light.

May we always acknowledge Christ as our Savior
and be more faithful to his gospel,
for he lives and reigns with you and the Holy Spirit,
one God, for ever and ever.
℞. **Amen.**

READINGS AND INTERVENIENT CHANTS

The *Weekday* Readings and Intervenient Chants corresponding to the day of the month, pp. 118-131.

PRAYER OVER THE GIFTS

Father,
in your mercy accept our gifts.
By sharing in this eucharist
may we come to live more fully the love we profess.
Grant this through Christ our Lord.
℞. **Amen.**   ➜ No. 21, p. 626 (Pref. P 3-5)

COMMUNION ANT.   1 Jn 4:9

**God's love for us was revealed when he sent his only Son
into the world, so that we could have life through him.** ↓

PRAYER AFTER COMMUNION

God our Father,
in this eucharist you touch our lives.
Keep your love alive in our hearts
that we may become worthy of you.
We ask this through Christ our Lord.
℞. **Amen.**   ➜ No. 32, p. 660

SATURDAY BEFORE EPIPHANY

(After Epiphany, see p. 146.)

The Son of God came so that we might become the sons and daughters of
God. The great danger to this present and future life is sin. As Jesus
changed the water into wine at Cana, so he can change our minds and
hearts by his grace. This is our prayer today.

ENTRANCE SONG

Gal 4:4-5

God sent his own Son, born of a woman, so that we could be adopted as his sons. → No. 2, p. 614

OPENING PRAYER

All-powerful and ever-living God,
you give us a new vision of your glory
in the coming of Christ your Son.
He was born of the Virgin Mary
and came to share our life.
May we come to share his eternal life
in the glory of your kingdom,
where he lives and reigns with you and the Holy Spirit,
one God, for ever and ever. ℞. **Amen.** ↓

READINGS AND INTERVENIENT CHANTS

The *Weekday* Readings and Intervenient Chants corresponding to the day of the month, pp. 118-131.

PRAYER OVER THE GIFTS

Father of peace,
accept our devotion and sincerity,
and by our sharing in this mystery
draw us closer to each other and to you.
We ask this in the name of Jesus the Lord.
℞. **Amen.** → No. 21, p. 626 (Pref. P 3-5)

COMMUNION ANT.

Jn 1:16

From his riches we have all received, grace for grace. ↓

PRAYER AFTER COMMUNION

Lord,
may this sacrament be our strength.
Teach us to value all the good you give us
and help us to strive for eternal life.
We ask this in the name of Jesus the Lord.
℞. **Amen.** → No. 32, p. 660

READINGS AND INTERVENIENT CHANTS
FOR WEEKDAYS FROM JANUARY 2
TO EPIPHANY

JANUARY 2

FIRST READING   1 Jn 2:22-28

"Christ" here has its full sense as the preferred New Testament designation of our Lord whose words and deeds have proclaimed him the divine Savior of mankind. It is only through the Son that the Father has completely revealed himself.

A reading from the first Letter of Saint John

BELOVED: Who is the liar? Whoever denies that Jesus is the Christ. Whoever denies the Father and the Son, this is the antichrist. Anyone who denies the Son does not have the Father, but whoever confesses the Son has the Father as well.

Let what you heard from the beginning remain in you. If what you heard from the beginning remains in you, then you will remain in the Son and in the Father. And this is the promise that he made us: eternal life. I write you these things about those who would deceive you. As for you, the anointing that you received from him remains in you, so that you do not need anyone to teach you. But his anointing teaches you about everything and is true and not false; just as it taught you, remain in him.

And now, children, remain in him, so that when he appears we may have confidence and not be put to shame by him at his coming.—The word of the Lord. ℟. **Thanks be to God.** ↓

RESPONSORIAL PSALM   Ps 98:1, 2-3ab, 3cd-4

℟. (3cd) **All the ends of the earth have seen the saving power of God.**

See Saturday of the 4th Week of Easter, p. 836.

ALLELUIA Heb 1:1-2

℟. **Alleluia, alleluia.**

In times past, God spoke to our ancestors through the
  prophets:

in these last days, he has spoken to us through his Son.

℟. **Alleluia, alleluia.** ↓

GOSPEL Jn 1:19-28

The question "Who are you?" is asked of John the Baptist. As a prophet,
he answers not by promoting himself but by announcing the presence of
the Messiah whose servant and herald John is.

℣. The Lord be with you. ℟. **And also with you.**

✤ A reading from the holy Gospel according to John.

℟. **Glory to you, Lord.**

THIS is the testimony of John. When the Jews from
 Jerusalem sent priests and Levites to him to ask him,
"Who are you?" he admitted and did not deny it, but
admitted, "I am not the Christ." So they asked him, "What
are you then? Are you Elijah?" And he said, "I am not."
"Are you the Prophet?" He answered, "No." So they said to
him, "Who are you, so we can give an answer to those
who sent us? What do you have to say for yourself?" He
said:

"I am the voice of one crying out in the desert,
  'Make straight the way of the Lord,'

as Isaiah the prophet said." Some Pharisees were also
sent. They asked him, "Why then do you baptize if you are
not the Christ or Elijah or the Prophet?" John answered
them, "I baptize with water; but there is one among you
whom you do not recognize, the one who is coming after
me, whose sandal strap I am not worthy to untie." This
happened in Bethany across the Jordan, where John was
baptizing.—The Gospel of the Lord. ℟. **Praise to you,
Lord Jesus Christ.** → No. 15, p. 623

JANUARY 3

FIRST READING   1 Jn 2:29—3:6

In the truest and most absolute sense, God's gift of love is the gift of his only Son as Savior of the world. It is this gift that makes it possible for us to be called children of God. The Apostle John describes our likeness to God himself: holiness, love, adoption, purity, sinlessness

A reading from the first Letter of Saint John

IF you consider that God is righteous, you also know that everyone who acts in righteousness is begotten by him.

See what love the Father has bestowed on us that we may be called the children of God. Yet so we are. The reason the world does not know us is that it did not know him. Beloved, we are God's children now; what we shall be has not yet been revealed. We do know that when it is revealed we shall be like him, for we shall see him as he is. Everyone who has this hope based on him makes himself pure, as he is pure.

Everyone who commits sin commits lawlessness, for sin is lawlessness. You know that he was revealed to take away sins, and in him there is no sin. No one who remains in him sins; no one who sins has seen him or known him.—The word of the Lord. ℟. **Thanks be to God.** ↓

RESPONSORIAL PSALM   Ps 98:1, 3cd-4, 5-6

℟. (3cd) **All the ends of the earth have seen the saving power of God.**

Sing to the LORD a new song,
    for he has done wondrous deeds;
His right hand has won victory for him,
    his holy arm.—℟.

All the ends of the earth have seen
    the salvation by our God.
Sing joyfully to the LORD, all you lands;
    break into song; sing praise.—℟.

Sing praise to the LORD with the harp,
   with the harp and melodious song.
With trumpets and the sound of the horn
   sing joyfully before the King, the LORD.—℟. ↓

ALLELUIA   Jn 1:14a, 12a

℟. **Alleluia, alleluia.**
The Word of God became flesh and dwelt among us.
To those who accepted him
he gave power to become the children of God.
℟. **Alleluia, alleluia.** ↓

GOSPEL   Jn 1:29-34

John the Baptist brings together the prophecies of the Messiah. Jesus is the lamb offered in sacrifice that accomplishes forgiveness. God's Spirit is upon him, and he gives the Spirit to all who will accept him.

℣. The Lord be with you. ℟. **And also with you.**
✛ A reading from the holy Gospel according to John.
℟. **Glory to you, Lord.**

JOHN the Baptist saw Jesus coming toward him and said, "Behold, the Lamb of God, who takes away the sin of the world. He is the one of whom I said, 'A man is coming after me who ranks ahead of me because he existed before me.' I did not know him, but the reason why I came baptizing with water was that he might be made known to Israel." John testified further, saying, "I saw the Spirit come down like a dove from the sky and remain upon him. I did not know him, but the one who sent me to baptize with water told me, 'On whomever you see the Spirit come down and remain, he is the one who will baptize with the Holy Spirit.' Now I have seen and testified that he is the Son of God."—The Gospel of the Lord. ℟. **Praise to you, Lord Jesus Christ.**   → No. 15, p. 623

JANUARY 4

FIRST READING   1 Jn 3:7-10

God's word presents the choice between two allegiances, either to God or to the devil whose kingdom is already being overcome by Jesus. Virtue and sin are the two opposite characteristics for distinguishing children of God from the children of the devil.

A reading from the first Letter of Saint John

CHILDREN, let no one deceive you. The person who acts in righteousness is righteous, just as he is righteous. Whoever sins belongs to the Devil, because the Devil has sinned from the beginning. Indeed, the Son of God was revealed to destroy the works of the Devil. No one who is begotten by God commits sin, because God's seed remains in him; he cannot sin because he is begotten by God. In this way, the children of God and the children of the Devil are made plain; no one who fails to act in righteousness belongs to God, nor anyone who does not love his brother.—The word of the Lord. ℟. **Thanks be to God.** ↓

RESPONSORIAL PSALM   Ps 98:1, 7-8, 9

℟. (3cd) **All the ends of the earth have seen the saving power of God.**

Sing to the LORD a new song,
    for he has done wondrous deeds;
His right hand has won victory for him,
    his holy arm.—℟.

Let the sea and what fills it resound,
    the world and those who dwell in it;
Let the rivers clap their hands,
    the mountains shout with them for joy before the
        LORD.—℟.

The LORD comes;
    he comes to rule the earth;
He will rule the world with justice
    and the peoples with equity.—℟. ↓

ALLELUIA   Heb 1:1-2

℟. **Alleluia, alleluia.**

In the past God spoke to our ancestors through the
    prophets:

in these last days, he has spoken to us through the Son.
℟. **Alleluia, alleluia.** ↓

GOSPEL

Jn 1:35-42

Jesus receives his first disciples from John the Baptist. Having begun with curiosity, they quickly become convinced that he is the Anointed One of God. The giving of a new name to Peter signifies the taking on of a new way of life.

℣. The Lord be with you. ℟. **And also with you.**
✛ A reading from the holy Gospel according to John.
℟. **Glory to you, Lord.**

JOHN was standing with two of his disciples, and as he watched Jesus walk by, he said, "Behold, the Lamb of God." The two disciples heard what he said and followed Jesus. Jesus turned and saw them following him and said to them, "What are you looking for?" They said to him, "Rabbi" (which translated means Teacher), "where are you staying?" He said to them, "Come, and you will see." So they went and saw where he was staying, and they stayed with him that day. It was about four in the afternoon. Andrew, the brother of Simon Peter, was one of the two who heard John and followed Jesus. He first found his own brother Simon and told him, "We have found the Messiah," which is translated Christ. Then he brought him to Jesus. Jesus looked at him and said, "You are Simon the son of John; you will be called Cephas," which is translated Peter.—The Gospel of the Lord. ℟. **Praise to you, Lord Jesus Christ.**

→ No. 15, p. 623

JANUARY 5

FIRST READING

1 Jn 3:11-21

Charity is the way to life because hatred and selfishness mean slavery to ourselves and to the goods of the world. God's own way is love because he gives life and care to all. To love is to live in God.

A reading from the first Letter of Saint John

BELOVED: This is the message you have heard from the beginning: we should love one another, unlike

Cain who belonged to the Evil One and slaughtered his brother. Why did he slaughter him? Because his own works were evil, and those of his brother righteous. Do not be amazed, then, brothers and sisters, if the world hates you. We know that we have passed from death to life because we love our brothers. Whoever does not love remains in death. Everyone who hates his brother is a murderer, and you know that no murderer has eternal life remaining in him. The way we came to know love was that he laid down his life for us; so we ought to lay down our lives for our brothers. If someone who has worldly means sees a brother in need and refuses him compassion, how can the love of God remain in him? Children, let us love not in word or speech but in deed and truth.

Now this is how we shall know that we belong to the truth and reassure our hearts before him in whatever our hearts condemn, for God is greater than our hearts and knows everything. Beloved, if our hearts do not condemn us, we have confidence in God.—The word of the Lord. ℟. **Thanks be to God.** ↓

RESPONSORIAL PSALM   Ps 100:1b-2, 3, 4, 5

℟. (2a) **Let all the earth cry out to God with joy.**

Sing joyfully to the LORD, all you lands;
    serve the LORD with gladness;
    come before him with joyful song.—℟.

Know that the LORD is God;
    he made us, his we are;
    his people, the flock he tends.—℟.

Enter his gates with thanksgiving,
    his courts with praise;
Give thanks to him; bless his name.—℟.

The LORD is good:
    the LORD, whose kindness endures forever,
    and his faithfulness, to all generations.—℟. ↓

ALLELUIA

℟. **Alleluia, alleluia.**
A holy day has dawned upon us.
Come, you nations, and adore the Lord.
Today a great light has come upon the earth.
℟. **Alleluia, alleluia.** ↓

GOSPEL Jn 1:43-51

Seemingly, Jesus knows of the thoughts and actions of Nathanael without being present, and Nathanael responds to his call: "Follow me." The opening of the sky is foretold in Jacob's vision in Genesis. Jesus is the ladder, or link, between heaven and earth.

℣. The Lord be with you. ℟. **And also with you.**
✟ A reading from the holy Gospel according to John.
℟. **Glory to you, Lord.**

JESUS decided to go to Galilee, and he found Philip. And Jesus said to him, "Follow me." Now Philip was from Bethsaida, the town of Andrew and Peter. Philip found Nathanael and told him, "We have found the one about whom Moses wrote in the law, and also the prophets, Jesus, son of Joseph, from Nazareth." But Nathanael said to him, "Can anything good come from Nazareth?" Philip said to him, "Come and see." Jesus saw Nathanael coming toward him and said of him, "Here is a true child of Israel. There is no duplicity in him." Nathanael said to him, "How do you know me?" Jesus answered and said to him, "Before Philip called you, I saw you under the fig tree." Nathanael answered him, "Rabbi, you are the Son of God; you are the King of Israel." Jesus answered and said to him, "Do you believe because I told you that I saw you under the fig tree? You will see greater things than this." And he said to him, "Amen, amen, I say to you, you will see the sky opened and the angels of God ascending and descending on the Son of Man."—The Gospel of the Lord. ℟. **Praise to you, Lord Jesus Christ.**

→ No. 15, p. 623

JANUARY 6

FIRST READING   1 Jn 5:5-13

The risen Christ, who is not seen by us, is known to be present and active through the visible elements of the sacraments. The water of Baptism, the presence of the Spirit through Confirmation, and our sharing in the blood of Christ in the Eucharist are signs that God is giving us eternal life.

A reading from the first Letter of Saint John

BELOVED: Who indeed is the victor over the world but the one who believes that Jesus is the Son of God?

This is the one who came through water and Blood, Jesus Christ, not by water alone, but by water and Blood. The Spirit is the one who testifies, and the Spirit is truth. So there are three that testify, the Spirit, the water, and the Blood, and the three are of one accord. If we accept human testimony, the testimony of God is surely greater. Now the testimony of God is this, that he has testified on behalf of his Son. Whoever believes in the Son of God has this testimony within himself. Whoever does not believe God has made him a liar by not believing the testimony God has given about his Son. And this is the testimony: God gave us eternal life, and this life is in his Son. Whoever possesses the Son has life; whoever does not possess the Son of God does not have life.

I write these things to you so that you may know that you have eternal life, you who believe in the name of the Son of God.—The word of the Lord. ℟. **Thanks be to God.** ↓

RESPONSORIAL PSALM   Ps 147:12-13, 14-15, 19-20

℟. (12a) **Praise the Lord, Jerusalem.**

℟. Or: **Alleluia.**

Glorify the LORD, O Jerusalem;
   praise your God, O Zion.
For he has strengthened the bars of your gates;
   he has blessed your children within you.—℟.

He has granted peace in your borders;
  with the best of wheat he fills you.
He sends forth his command to the earth;
  swiftly runs his word!—℟.

He has proclaimed his word to Jacob,
  his statutes and his ordinances to Israel.
He has not done thus for any other nation;
    his ordinances he has not made known to them.
      Alleluia.—℟. ↓

ALLELUIA   See Mk 9:6

℟. **Alleluia, alleluia.**
The heavens were opened and the voice of the Father
    thundered:
This is my beloved Son. Listen to him.
℟. **Alleluia, alleluia.** ↓

GOSPEL   Mk 1:7-11

It is only when he baptizes Jesus that the Baptist recognizes him as the
Messiah. This recognition by John is the result of a divine intimation. The
Spirit descends upon our Lord from heaven like a dove and rests upon
him, and this promised heavenly sign reveals him. It is only then, and not
before, that John is conscious of the wondrous truth.

℣. The Lord be with you. ℟. **And also with you.**
✢ A reading from the holy Gospel according to Mark.
℟. **Glory to you, Lord.**

THIS is what John the Baptist proclaimed:"One might-
ier than I is coming after me. I am not worthy to stoop
and loosen the thongs of his sandals. I have baptized you
with water; he will baptize you with the Holy Spirit."

It happened in those days that Jesus came from
Nazareth of Galilee and was baptized in the Jordan by
John. On coming up out of the water he saw the heavens
being torn open and the Spirit, like a dove, descending
upon him. And a voice came from the heavens,"You are
my beloved Son; with you I am well pleased."—The

Gospel of the Lord. ℟. **Praise to you, Lord Jesus Christ.**
➔ No. 15, p. 623

OR   Lk 3:23-38 or 3:23, 31-34, 36, 38

Luke gives a genealogy that is meant not as an historical document but as the assertion of a legal status. Jesus is linked to Joseph, even though it was known that the link was not one of blood; the reason for doing so is that at that time only men and not women had rights. The genealogy then moves back to David without following the line of kings. From that point it continues again, not only as far as Abraham, but—and this is the chief novelty of the passage—as far as Adam, who comes from the hand of God. Luke's intention is to stress the point that Jesus belongs not only to the chosen people but to the entire human race, which he has come to save.

[If the "Short Form" is used, omit indented text in brackets.]

℣. The Lord be with you. ℟. **And also with you.**
✣ A reading from the holy Gospel according to Luke.
℟. **Glory to you, Lord.**

WHEN Jesus began his ministry he was about thirty years of age. He was the son, as was thought, of Joseph, the son of Heli,
[the son of Matthat, the son of Levi, the son of Melchi, the son of Jannai, the son of Joseph, the son of Mattathias, the son of Amos, the son of Nahum, the son of Esli, the son of Naggai, the son of Maath, the son of Mattathias, the son of Semein, the son of Josech, the son of Joda, the son of Joanan, the son of Rhesa, the son of Zerubbabel, the son of Shealtiel, the son of Neri, the son of Melchi, the son of Addi, the son of Cosam, the son of Elmadam, the son of Er, the son of Joshua, the son of Eliezer, the son of Jorim, the son of Matthat, the son of Levi, the son of Simeon, the son of Judah, the son of Joseph, the son of Jonam, the son of Eliakim,]
the son of Melea, the son of Menna, the son of Mattatha, the son of Nathan, the son of David, the son of Jesse, the son of Obed, the son of Boaz, the son of Sala, the son of Nahshon, the son of Amminadab, the son of Admin, the son of Arni, the son of Hezron, the son of Perez, the son

of Judah, the son of Jacob, the son of Isaac, the son of Abraham, the son of Terah, the son of Nahor,
[the son of Serug, the son of Reu, the son of Peleg, the son of Eber, the son of Shelah,]
the son of Cainan, the son of Arphaxad, the son of Shem, the son of Noah, the son of Lamech,
[the son of Methuselah, the son of Enoch, the son of Jared, the son of Mahalaleel, the son of Cainan,]
the son of Enos, the son of Seth, the son of Adam, the son of God.—The Gospel of the Lord. ℟. **Praise to you, Lord Jesus Christ.**   ➙ No. 15, p. 623

JANUARY 7

FIRST READING   1 Jn 5:14-21

God answers all proper prayers made in faith and with willingness for his will to be done. If our brothers and sisters in the Faith commit sins, we pray for them In fraternal love. Fidelity to God's will is the necessary condition of the efficacy of prayer.

A reading from the first Letter of Saint John

B ELOVED: We have this confidence in God, that if we ask anything according to his will, he hears us. And if we know that he hears us in regard to whatever we ask, we know that what we have asked him for is ours. If anyone sees his brother sinning, if the sin is not deadly, he should pray to God and he will give him life. This is only for those whose sin is not deadly. There is such a thing as deadly sin, about which I do not say that you should pray. All wrongdoing is sin, but there is sin that is not deadly.

We know that no one begotten by God sins; but the one begotten by God he protects, and the Evil One cannot touch him. We know that we belong to God, and the whole world is under the power of the Evil One. We also know that the Son of God has come and has given us discernment to know the one who is true. And we are in the one who is true, in his Son Jesus Christ. He is the true God and eternal life. Children, be on your guard against idols.—The word of the Lord. ℟. **Thanks be to God.** ↓

RESPONSORIAL PSALM   Ps 149:1-2, 3-4, 5 and 6a and 9b

℟. (see 4a) **The Lord takes delight in his people.**

℟. Or: **Alleluia.**

Sing to the LORD a new song
of praise in the assembly of the faithful.
Let Israel be glad in their maker,
let the children of Zion rejoice in their king.—℟.

Let them praise his name in the festive dance,
let them sing praise to him with timbrel and harp.
For the LORD loves his people,
and he adorns the lowly with victory.—℟.

Let the faithful exult in glory;
let them sing for joy upon their couches;
Let the high praises of God be in their throats.
This is the glory of all his faithful. Alleluia.—℟. ↓

ALLELUIA   Lk 7:16

℟. **Alleluia, alleluia.**
A great prophet has arisen in our midst
and God has visited his people.
℟. **Alleluia, alleluia.** ↓

GOSPEL   Jn 2:1-11

Jesus' first miracle, performed at the wedding party, shows his blessing
upon married love and upon people having a good time together. It is a
fitting occasion for his presence and for the act of almighty power that
follows, for he is the bridegroom who has come into the world to take his
spouse, the Church.

℣. The Lord be with you. ℟. **And also with you.**
✤ A reading from the holy Gospel according to John.
℟. **Glory to you, Lord.**

THERE was a wedding at Cana in Galilee, and the
mother of Jesus was there. Jesus and his disciples
were also invited to the wedding. When the wine ran
short, the mother of Jesus said to him, "They have no

wine." And Jesus said to her, "Woman, how does your concern affect me? My hour has not yet come." His mother said to the servers, "Do whatever he tells you." Now there were six stone water jars there for Jewish ceremonial washings, each holding twenty to thirty gallons. Jesus told them, "Fill the jars with water." So they filled them to the brim. Then he told them, "Draw some out now and take it to the headwaiter." So they took it. And when the headwaiter tasted the water that had become wine, without knowing where it came from (although the servers who had drawn the water knew), the headwaiter called the bridegroom and said to him, "Everyone serves good wine first, and then when people have drunk freely, an inferior one; but you have kept the good wine until now." Jesus did this as the beginning of his signs at Cana in Galilee and so revealed his glory, and his disciples began to believe in him.—The Gospel of the Lord. ℟. **Praise to you, Lord Jesus Christ.**   → No. 15, p. 623

MONDAY AFTER EPIPHANY (OR JAN. 7)

God is willing and eager to give to us and to the world the gifts of the Spirit that are necessary for faith, unity, and holiness. As long as our minds and desires are in agreement with the Father's, he will hear us and keep us true to himself. Divine healing comes from such loyalty.

ENTRANCE ANT.

A holy day has dawned upon us. Come, you nations, and adore the Lord. Today a great light has come upon the earth.   → No. 2, p. 614

OPENING PRAYER

Lord,
let the light of your glory shine within us,
and lead us through the darkness of this world
to the radiant joy of our eternal home.
We ask this . . . for ever and ever. ℟. **Amen.** ↓

FIRST READING   1 Jn 3:22—4:6

A mysterious communion of life unites us with the Father and with one another. This is the work of the Spirit who enables us to hear, recognize, and accept the voice of Jesus and thus to remain in God.

A reading from the first Letter of Saint John

Beloved: We receive from him whatever we ask, because we keep his commandments and do what pleases him. And his commandment is this: we should believe in the name of his Son, Jesus Christ, and love one another just as he commanded us. Those who keep his commandments remain in him, and he in them, and the way we know that he remains in us is from the Spirit whom he gave us.

Beloved, do not trust every spirit but test the spirits to see whether they belong to God, because many false prophets have gone out into the world. This is how you can know the Spirit of God: every spirit that acknowledges Jesus Christ come in the flesh belongs to God, and every spirit that does not acknowledge Jesus does not belong to God. This is the spirit of the antichrist who, as you heard, is to come, but in fact is already in the world. You belong to God, children, and you have conquered them, for the one who is in you is greater than the one who is in the world. They belong to the world; accordingly, their teaching belongs to the world, and the world listens to them. We belong to God, and anyone who knows God listens to us, while anyone who does not belong to God refuses to hear us. This is how we know the spirit of truth and the spirit of deceit.—The word of the Lord. ℟. **Thanks be to God.** ↓

RESPONSORIAL PSALM   Ps 2:7bc-8, 10-12a

℟. (8ab) **I will give you all the nations for an inheritance.**

The Lord said to me, "You are my Son;
    this day I have begotten you.

Ask of me and I will give you
    the nations for an inheritance
    and the ends of the earth for your possession."—℟.

And now, O kings, give heed;
    take warning, you rulers of the earth.
Serve the LORD with fear, and rejoice before him;
    with trembling rejoice.—℟. ↓

ALLELUIA   See Mt 4:23
℟. **Alleluia, alleluia.**
Jesus proclaimed the Gospel of the Kingdom
and cured every disease among the people.
℟. **Alleluia, alleluia.** ↓

GOSPEL   Mt 4:12-17, 23-25
Jesus returns to Galilee, his own country, to proclaim the Reign. His message is the Good News that the Kingdom of heaven is at hand. His proclamation is accompanied by healing which causes his fame to spread,
attracting followers from Jewish areas and from the lands beyond.

℣. The Lord be with you. ℟. **And also with you.**
✤ A reading from the holy Gospel according to Matthew.
℟. **Glory to you, Lord.**

WHEN Jesus heard that John had been arrested, he
    withdrew to Galilee. He left Nazareth and went to
live in Capernaum by the sea, in the region of Zebulun
and Naphtali, that what had been said through Isaiah the
prophet might be fulfilled:
    Land of Zebulun and land of Naphtali,
        the way to the sea, beyond the Jordan,
        Galilee of the Gentiles,
    the people who sit in darkness
        have seen a great light,
    on those dwelling in a land overshadowed by death
        light has arisen.
From that time on, Jesus began to preach and say,
"Repent, for the Kingdom of heaven is at hand."

He went around all of Galilee, teaching in their synagogues, proclaiming the Gospel of the Kingdom, and curing every disease and illness among the people. His fame spread to all of Syria, and they brought to him all who were sick with various diseases and racked with pain, those who were possessed, lunatics, and paralytics, and he cured them. And great crowds from Galilee, the Decapolis, Jerusalem, and Judea, and from beyond the Jordan followed him.—The Gospel of the Lord. ℟. **Praise to you, Lord Jesus Christ.**   ➜ No. 15, p. 623

PRAYER OVER THE GIFTS

Lord,
receive our gifts in this wonderful exchange:
from all you have given us
we bring you these gifts,
and in return, you give us yourself.
We ask this through Christ our Lord.
℟. **Amen.**   ➜ No. 21, p. 626 (Pref. P 6)

COMMUNION ANT.   Jn 1:14

We have seen his glory, the glory of the Father's only Son, full of grace and truth. ↓

PRAYER AFTER COMMUNION

Father of love and mercy,
grant that our lives may always be founded
on the power of this holy mystery.
We ask this in the name of Jesus the Lord.
℟. **Amen.**   ➜ No. 32, p. 660

TUESDAY AFTER EPIPHANY (OR JAN. 8)

Today we pray that we may become like God. This is a daring request, but it is precisely the life to which we are invited. As we share in this Eucharist, we receive Jesus who remains present within us in order to mold us more and more into images of himself, with our cooperation.

ENTRANCE ANT. Ps 118:26-27

**Blessed is he who comes in the name of the Lord; the
Lord God shines upon us.** → No. 2, p. 614

OPENING PRAYER

Father,
your Son became like us
when he revealed himself in our nature:
help us to become more like him,
who lives and reigns with you and the Holy Spirit,
one God, for ever and ever. ℟. **Amen.** ↓

FIRST READING 1 Jn 4:7-10

God's love expresses so clearly the personality and character of God that
John can say, "God is love." The motive of love is the origin of love in God;
those who love thereby prove that they have their own origin in the same
God with whom they have fellowship. They are born of God.

A reading from the first Letter of Saint John

BELOVED, let us love one another, because love is of
God; everyone who loves is begotten by God and
knows God. Whoever is without love does not know God,
for God is love. In this way the love of God was revealed
to us: God sent his only-begotten Son into the world so
that we might have life through him. In this is love: not
that we have loved God, but that he loved us and sent his
Son as expiation for our sins.—The word of the Lord. ℟.
Thanks be to God. ↓

RESPONSORIAL PSALM Ps 72:1-2, 3-4, 7-8

℟. (see 11) **Lord, every nation on earth will adore you.**

O God, with your judgment endow the king,
    and with your justice, the king's son;
He shall govern your people with justice
    and your afflicted ones with judgment.—℟.

The mountains shall yield peace for the people,
    and the hills justice.

He shall defend the afflicted among the people,
　　save the children of the poor.—℟.

Justice shall flower in his days,
　　and profound peace, till the moon be no more.
May he rule from sea to sea,
　　and from the River to the ends of the earth.—℟. ↓

ALLELUIA　　　　　　　　　　　　　　　　Lk 4:18

℟. **Alleluia, alleluia.**
The Lord has sent me to bring glad tidings to the poor
and to proclaim liberty to captives.
℟. **Alleluia, alleluia.** ↓

GOSPEL　　　　　　　　　　　　　　　　Mk 6:34-44

Jesus' love leads him to provide for all of the needs of those who come to
him. The multiplication of the bread and fish foreshadows the greater
gift, the giving of himself in the sacred meal of the Eucharist.

℣. The Lord be with you. ℟. **And also with you.**
✠ A reading from the holy Gospel according to Mark.
℟. **Glory to you, Lord.**

WHEN Jesus saw the vast crowd, his heart was
moved with pity for them, for they were like sheep
without a shepherd; and he began to teach them many
things. By now it was already late and his disciples
approached him and said, "This is a deserted place and it
is already very late. Dismiss them so that they can go to
the surrounding farms and villages and buy themselves
something to eat." He said to them in reply, "Give them
some food yourselves." But they said to him, "Are we to
buy two hundred days' wages worth of food and give it to
them to eat?" He asked them, "How many loaves do you
have? Go and see." And when they had found out they
said, "Five loaves and two fish." So he gave orders to have
them sit down in groups on the green grass. The people
took their places in rows by hundreds and by fifties.
Then, taking the five loaves and the two fish and looking
up to heaven, he said the blessing, broke the loaves, and

gave them to his disciples to set before the people; he also divided the two fish among them all. They all ate and were satisfied. And they picked up twelve wicker baskets full of fragments and what was left of the fish. Those who ate of the loaves were five thousand men.—The Gospel of the Lord. ℟. **Praise to you, Lord Jesus Christ.**

→ No. 15, p. 623

PRAYER OVER THE GIFTS

Father,
in your mercy accept our gifts.
By sharing in this eucharist
may we come to live more fully the love we profess.
Grant this through Christ our Lord.
℟. **Amen.**   → No. 21, p. 626 (Pref. P 6)

COMMUNION ANT.   Eph 2:4; Rom 8:3

God loved us so much that he sent his own Son in the likeness of sinful flesh. ↓

PRAYER AFTER COMMUNION

God our Father,
in this eucharist you touch our lives.
Keep your love alive in our hearts
that we may become worthy of you.
We ask this through Christ our Lord.
℟. **Amen.**   → No. 32, p. 660

WEDNESDAY AFTER EPIPHANY (OR JAN. 9)

Today's liturgy provides motives for confidence in Jesus as true God and as the Savior. The authors of the Scriptures preserved the knowledge of the life, words, and miracles of Jesus so that we might be drawn to share in their faith. The zeal and apostolic love of the first Christians reaches down to us.

ENTRANCE ANT.   Is 9:2

The people who walked in darkness have seen a great light; on those who lived in the shadow of death, light has shone.   → No. 2, p. 614

OPENING PRAYER

God, light of all nations,
give us the joy of lasting peace,
and fill us with your radiance
as you filled the hearts of our fathers.
We ask this . . . for ever and ever. ℟. **Amen.** ↓

FIRST READING   1 Jn 4:11-18

John assumes the reality of God, the Invisible, and all that the prophetic
faith of the Old Testament has taught about his nature and will. John's
primary desire is to urge Christians to treat one another as God treats
them—to love one another without self-interest, to have faith in God's
fatherly love, and to look forward to the "end of the world" with eagerness
rather than with fear.

A reading from the first Letter of Saint John

BELOVED, if God so loved us, we also must love one
another. No one has ever seen God. Yet, if we love one
another, God remains in us, and his love is brought to
perfection in us.

This is how we know that we remain in him and he in
us, that he has given us of his Spirit. Moreover, we have
seen and testify that the Father sent his Son as savior of
the world. Whoever acknowledges that Jesus is the Son
of God, God remains in him and he in God. We have come
to know and to believe in the love God has for us.

God is love, and whoever remains in love remains in
God and God in him. In this is love brought to perfection
among us, that we have confidence on the day of judgment because as he is, so are we in this world. There is no
fear in love, but perfect love drives out fear because fear
has to do with punishment, and so one who fears is not
yet perfect in love.—The word of the Lord. ℟. **Thanks be
to God.** ↓

RESPONSORIAL PSALM   Ps 72:1-2, 10, 12-13

℟. (see 11) **Lord, every nation on earth will adore you.**

O God, with your judgment endow the king,
    and with your justice, the king's son;
He shall govern your people with justice
    and your afflicted ones with judgment.—℟.

The kings of Tarshish and the Isles shall offer gifts;
    the kings of Arabia and Seba shall bring tribute.—℟.

For he shall rescue the poor when he cries out,
    and the afflicted when he has no one to help him.
He shall have pity for the lowly and the poor;
    the lives of the poor he shall save.—℟. ↓

ALLELUIA   See 1 Tm 3:16
℟. **Alleluia, alleluia.**
Glory to you, O Christ, proclaimed to the Gentiles.
Glory to you, O Christ, believed in throughout the world.
℟. **Alleluia, alleluia.** ↓

GOSPEL   Mk 6:45-52
By feeding the large crowd through a miracle, Jesus showed that the great
signs of God's presence in the world had resumed. In the events on the
lake, he shows that he has power and control over all of creation, even
over the physical characteristics of water. The Apostles are thus prepared
for the growth of their faith and understanding.

℣. The Lord be with you. ℟. **And also with you.**
✤ A reading from the holy Gospel according to Mark.
℟. **Glory to you, Lord.**

A FTER the five thousand had eaten and were satisfied, Jesus made his disciples get into the boat and
precede him to the other side toward Bethsaida, while he
dismissed the crowd. And when he had taken leave of
them, he went off to the mountain to pray. When it was
evening, the boat was far out on the sea and he was alone
on shore. Then he saw that they were tossed about while
rowing, for the wind was against them. About the fourth
watch of the night, he came toward them walking on the
sea. He meant to pass by them. But when they saw him

walking on the sea, they thought it was a ghost and cried out. They had all seen him and were terrified. But at once he spoke with them, "Take courage, it is I, do not be afraid!" He got into the boat with them and the wind died down. They were completely astounded. They had not understood the incident of the loaves. On the contrary, their hearts were hardened.—The Gospel of the Lord. ℟.
Praise to you, Lord Jesus Christ. → No. 15, p. 623

PRAYER OVER THE GIFTS

Father of peace,
accept our devotion and sincerity,
and by our sharing in this mystery
draw us closer to each other and to you.
We ask this in the name of Jesus the Lord.
℟. **Amen.** → No. 21, p. 626 (Pref. P 6)

COMMUNION ANT. 1 Jn 1:2

The eternal life which was with the Father has been revealed to us. ↓

PRAYER AFTER COMMUNION

Lord,
may this sacrament be our strength.
Teach us to value all the good you give us
and help us to strive for eternal life.
Grant this through Christ our Lord.
℟. **Amen.** → No. 32, p. 660

THURSDAY AFTER EPIPHANY (OR JAN. 10)

Today our Epiphany proclamation of faith continues. We wish to show Jesus to one another and to everyone in the world. His teachings and his Spirit truly bring glad tidings to the poor, a new life of liberty, and a new spiritual vision.

ENTRANCE ANT. See Jn 1:1

In the beginning, before all ages, the Word was God: that Word was born a man to save the world. → No. 2, p. 614

OPENING PRAYER

God our Father,
through Christ your Son
the hope of eternal life dawned on our world.
Give to us the light of faith
that we may always acknowledge him as our Redeemer
and come to the glory of his kingdom,
where he lives and reigns with you and the Holy Spirit,
one God, for ever and ever. ℟. **Amen.** ↓

FIRST READING   1 Jn 4:19—5:4

John warns against self-deception in love. No one can pretend to love God
who does not love other human beings. Christ's command is new in its
extension to all people without distinction. Christ's love is not only the
model but also the motive and cause of Christian charity.

A reading from the first Letter of Saint John

BELOVED, we love God because he first loved us. If
anyone says, "I love God," but hates his brother, he is
a liar; for whoever does not love a brother whom he has
seen cannot love God whom he has not seen. This is the
commandment we have from him: Whoever loves God
must also love his brother.

Everyone who believes that Jesus is the Christ is
begotten by God, and everyone who loves the Father loves
also the one begotten by him. In this way we know that we
love the children of God when we love God and obey his
commandments. For the love of God is this, that we keep
his commandments. And his commandments are not burdensome, for whoever is begotten by God conquers the
world. And the victory that conquers the world is our
faith.—The word of the Lord. ℟. **Thanks be to God.** ↓

RESPONSORIAL PSALM   Ps 72:1-2, 14 and 15bc, 17

℟. (see 11) **Lord, every nation on earth will adore you.**

O God, with your judgment endow the king,
    and with your justice, the king's son;

He shall govern your people with justice
 and your afflicted ones with judgment.—℟.

From fraud and violence he shall redeem them,
 and precious shall their blood be in his sight.
May they be prayed for continually;
 day by day shall they bless him.—℟.

May his name be blessed forever;
 as long as the sun his name shall remain.
In him shall all the tribes of the earth be blessed;
 all the nations shall proclaim his happiness.—℟. ↓

ALLELUIA   Lk 4:18

℟. **Alleluia, alleluia.**
The Lord has sent me to bring glad tidings to the poor
and to proclaim liberty to captives.
℟. **Alleluia, alleluia.** ↓

GOSPEL   Lk 4:14-22

Luke shows our Lord in Galilee as a great prophet, possessing the power of
the Spirit. The inhabitants of the city in which the first twenty-nine years of
his life had been spent listen to his message, and they can learn from it that
the time of salvation has begun and that the Savior is present.

℣. The Lord be with you. ℟. **And also with you.**
✛ A reading from the holy Gospel according to Luke.
℟. **Glory to you, Lord.**

JESUS returned to Galilee in the power of the Spirit,
 and news of him spread throughout the whole region.
He taught in their synagogues and was praised by all.

 He came to Nazareth, where he had grown up, and
went according to his custom into the synagogue on the
sabbath day. He stood up to read and was handed a scroll
of the prophet Isaiah. He unrolled the scroll and found
the passage where it was written:
 The Spirit of the Lord is upon me,
  because he has anointed me
   to bring glad tidings to the poor.

He has sent me to proclaim liberty to captives
and recovery of sight to the blind,
to let the oppressed go free,
and to proclaim a year acceptable to the Lord.

Rolling up the scroll, he handed it back to the attendant and sat down, and the eyes of all in the synagogue looked intently at him. He said to them, "Today this Scripture passage is fulfilled in your hearing." And all spoke highly of him and were amazed at the gracious words that came from his mouth.—The Gospel of the Lord. ℟. **Praise to you, Lord Jesus Christ.**   ➜ No. 15, p. 623

PRAYER OVER THE GIFTS

Lord,
receive our gifts in this wonderful exchange:
from all you have given us
we bring you these gifts,
and in return, you give us yourself.
We ask this through Christ our Lord.
℟. **Amen.**   ➜ No. 21, p. 626 (Pref P 6)

COMMUNION ANT.   Jn 3:16

God loved the world so much, he gave his only Son, that all who believe in him might not perish, but might have eternal life. ↓

PRAYER AFTER COMMUNION

Father of love and mercy,
grant that our lives may always be founded
on the power of this holy mystery.
We ask this in the name of Jesus the Lord.
℟. **Amen.**   ➜ No. 32, p. 660

FRIDAY AFTER EPIPHANY (OR JAN. 11)

The Epiphany marks the journey of the wise men who were led by the star. Jesus himself is our star who draws us to himself as the light that shines out in the darkness. As he healed the leper, so he takes us to himself to heal us of leprosy of the spirit.

ENTRANCE ANT.   Ps 112:4

The Lord is a light in darkness to the upright; he is gracious, merciful, and just.   → No. 2, p. 614

OPENING PRAYER

All-powerful Father,
you have made known the birth of the Savior
by the light of a star.
May he continue to guide us with his light,
for he lives and reigns with you and the Holy Spirit,
one God, for ever and ever. ℟. **Amen.** ↓

FIRST READING   1 Jn 5:5-13

The light of faith is nourished by the water of Baptism, the indwelling of the Spirit, the Body and Blood of the Eucharist, and the testimony of the Father through signs and miracles. Eternal life is in the Son, to be enjoyed only by those who possess him.

A reading from the first Letter of Saint John

BELOVED: Who indeed is the victor over the world but the one who believes that Jesus is the Son of God?

This is the one who came through water and Blood, Jesus Christ, not by water alone, but by water and Blood. The Spirit is the one who testifies, and the Spirit is truth. So there are three who testify, the Spirit, the water, and the Blood, and the three are of one accord. If we accept human testimony, the testimony of God is surely greater. Now the testimony of God is this, that he has testified on behalf of his Son. Whoever believes in the Son of God has this testimony within himself. Whoever does not believe God has made him a liar by not believing the testimony God has given about his Son. And this is the testimony: God gave us eternal life, and this life is in his Son. Whoever possesses the Son has life; whoever does not possess the Son of God does not have life.

I write these things to you so that you may know that you have eternal life, you who believe in the name of the Son of God.—The word of the Lord. ℟. **Thanks be to God.** ↓

RESPONSORIAL PSALM   Ps 147:12-13, 14-15, 19-20

See January 6, p. 126.

ALLELUIA   See Mt 4:23

℟. **Alleluia, alleluia.**
Jesus proclaimed the Gospel of the Kingdom
and cured every disease among the people.
℟. **Alleluia, alleluia.** ↓

GOSPEL   Lk 5:12-16

The misfortune of a leper was not only his disease but his enforced isola-
tion from family, friends, and the entire community. By reporting to the
priest after returning to health, the former leper could be reunited with his
family and reenter the community. Similarly, Jesus removes the leprosy of
our sin and pride, and unites us with his family, the Church.

℣. The Lord be with you. ℟. **And also with you.**
✛ A reading from the holy Gospel according to Luke.
℟. **Glory to you, Lord.**

IT happened that there was a man full of leprosy in one
of the towns where Jesus was; and when he saw Jesus,
he fell prostrate, pleaded with him, and said, "Lord, if you
wish, you can make me clean." Jesus stretched out his
hand, touched him, and said, "I do will it. Be made clean."
And the leprosy left him immediately. Then he ordered
him not to tell anyone, but "Go, show yourself to the priest
and offer for your cleansing what Moses prescribed; that
will be proof for them." The report about him spread all
the more, and great crowds assembled to listen to him
and to be cured of their ailments, but he would withdraw
to deserted places to pray.—The Gospel of the Lord. ℟.
Praise to you, Lord Jesus Christ.   → No. 15, p. 623

PRAYER OVER THE GIFTS

Father,
in your mercy accept our gifts.
By sharing in this eucharist
may we come to live more fully the love we profess.

Grant this through Christ our Lord.
℞. **Amen.** → No. 21, p. 626 (Pref. P 6)

COMMUNION ANT. 1 Jn 4:9

God's love for us was revealed when he sent his only Son into the world, so that we could have life through him. ↓

PRAYER AFTER COMMUNION

God our Father,
in this eucharist you touch our lives.
Keep your love alive in our hearts
that we may become worthy of you.
We ask this through Christ our Lord.
℞. **Amen.** → No. 32, p. 660

SATURDAY AFTER EPIPHANY (OR JAN. 12)

The word of God and the coming of Jesus make clear to us that this life and this world are not all there is. There is a life that is so different that it is called a "new creation." The celebration of Christmas and Epiphany is genuine if it has the effect of changing us into new persons according to the pattern of Christ.

ENTRANCE ANT. Gal 4:4-5

God sent his own Son, born of a woman, so that we could be adopted as his sons. → No. 2, p. 614

OPENING PRAYER

God our Father,
through your Son you made us a new creation.
He shared our nature and became one of us;
with his help, may we become more like him,
who lives and reigns with you and the Holy Spirit,
one God, for ever and ever. ℞. **Amen.** ↓

FIRST READING 1 Jn 5:14-21

The Scriptures do not divide body and soul, world and spirit as sharply as we have learned to do from philosophy. The "world" is human life that is ignorant of God and hostile to God's will and values. Those who are in Christ are in the "spirit" and are delivered from the "world" that is fading away.

A reading from the first Letter of Saint John

BELOVED: We have this confidence in him that if we ask anything according to his will, he hears us. And if we know that he hears us in regard to whatever we ask, we know that what we have asked him for is ours. If anyone sees his brother sinning, if the sin is not deadly, he should pray to God and he will give him life. This is only for those whose sin is not deadly. There is such a thing as deadly sin, about which I do not say that you should pray. All wrongdoing is sin, but there is sin that is not deadly.

We know that anyone begotten by God does not sin; but the one begotten by God he protects, and the Evil One cannot touch him. We know that we belong to God, and the whole world is under the power of the Evil One. We also know that the Son of God has come and has given us discernment to know the one who is true. And we are in the one who is true, in his Son Jesus Christ. He is the true God and eternal life. Children, be on your guard against idols.—The word of the Lord. ℟. **Thanks be to God.** ↓

RESPONSORIAL PSALM   Ps 149:1-2, 3-4, 5-6a and 9b
See January 7, p. 130.

ALLELUIA   Mt 4:16
℟. **Alleluia, alleluia.**
The people who sit in darkness have seen a great light, on those dwelling in a land overshadowed by death light has arisen.
℟. **Alleluia, alleluia.** ↓

GOSPEL   Jn 3:22-30
The law of Moses commanded many washings and sprinklings as expressions of life, purification, and renewal. John the Baptist adopted this meaningful custom, and Jesus perfected it in baptism—the sacrament of forgiveness, holiness, life, and rebirth. Baptism is a gift from on high by which Christ increases within us.

℣. The Lord be with you. ℟. **And also with you.**
✤ A reading from the holy Gospel according to John.
℟. **Glory to you, Lord.**

JESUS and his disciples went into the region of Judea, where he spent some time with them baptizing. John was also baptizing in Aenon near Salim, because there was an abundance of water there, and people came to be baptized, for John had not yet been imprisoned. Now a dispute arose between the disciples of John and a Jew about ceremonial washings. So they came to John and said to him, "Rabbi, the one who was with you across the Jordan, to whom you testified, here he is baptizing and everyone is coming to him." John answered and said, "No one can receive anything except what has been given from heaven. You yourselves can testify that I said that I am not the Christ, but that I was sent before him. The one who has the bride is the bridegroom; the best man, who stands and listens for him, rejoices greatly at the bridegroom's voice. So this joy of mine has been made complete. He must increase; I must decrease."—The Gospel of the Lord. ℟.
Praise to you, Lord Jesus Christ.   → No. 15, p. 623

PRAYER OVER THE GIFTS

Father of peace,
accept our devotion and sincerity,
and by our sharing in this mystery
draw us closer to each other and to you.
We ask this in the name of Jesus the Lord.
℟. **Amen.**   → No. 21, p. 626 (Pref. P 6)

COMMUNION ANT.   Jn 1:16

From his riches we have all received, grace for grace. ↓

PRAYER AFTER COMMUNION

Lord,
may this sacrament be our strength.
Teach us to value all the good you give us
and help us to strive for eternal life.
Grant this through Christ our Lord.
℟. **Amen.**   → No. 32, p. 660

ORDINARY TIME

The Sundays and Weekdays of the major seasons of the year are distinguished by their relationship to the Solemnities of Christmas (Advent, Christmas) and Easter (Lent, Easter). On the other hand, Ordinary Time refers to all the other Sundays and Weekdays under the all-embracing heading of celebrations of the "Day of the Lord." These weeks number thirty-three or thirty-four according to the particular character of each year and are assigned to two parts of the liturgical year.

The first part begins with the Sunday after Epiphany (although this First Sunday is perpetually impeded by the Feast of the Baptism of the Lord) and continues until Ash Wednesday. Since the date of Easter varies each year, this part may include as few as four and as many as nine weeks.

The second part of Ordinary Time begins with the day after Pentecost and runs to the Saturday before the first Sunday of Advent. If the number of ordinary weeks is thirty-four, the week after Pentecost is the one that follows immediately the last week celebrated before Lent. The Masses of Pentecost, Trinity Sunday and (in countries where the Body and Blood of Christ is not observed as a holyday of obligation and is therefore celebrated on the following Sunday) the Body and Blood of Christ replace the Sunday Masses in these weeks. If the number of ordinary weeks is thirty-three, the first week that would otherwise follow Pentecost is omitted.

Some of the unique features of these weeks are:

The Gloria and the Profession of Faith are sung or said on Sundays; they are omitted on weekdays.

On Sundays one of the Prefaces for Sundays in Ordinary Time is sung or said; on Weekdays, a Weekday Preface.

Two Antiphons are given for Communion, the first from the Psalms, the second for the most part from the

Gospel. Either one may be selected, but preference should be given to the Antiphon that may happen to come from the Gospel of the Mass.

The most important characteristic of this Ordinary Time is that, in accord with the pastoral needs of the people, any of the thirty-four Sunday Masses may be celebrated on any weekday, regardless of the particular week in which it falls. This does not refer to the Readings and Intervenient Chants which form the "Lectionary texts" and should be taken from the weekday Lectionary for this period, but to the Processional Chants (Entrance and Communion Antiphons) and Presidential Prayers (Opening Prayer, Prayer over the Gifts, and Prayer after Communion), which form the "Sacramentary texts."

Because of this fact, for this period of the year only, Lectionary texts will not be integrated into the Sacramentary texts in this Missal. The Sacramentary texts will be given first and the Lectionary texts will be given in another section. (Solely for the sake of convenience, cross-references according to weeks will be included.)

ANTIPHONS AND PRAYERS
FOR ORDINARY TIME
1st WEEK

Our heavenly Father knows all things. He has made us for himself. In him we live and move and are. Let us pray that all we do will be pleasing to him.

ENTRANCE ANT.

I saw a man sitting on a high throne, being worshiped by a great number of angels who were singing together: This is he whose kingdom will last for ever.

→ No. 2, p. 614

OPENING PRAYER

Father of love,
hear our prayers.
Help us to know your will
and to do it with courage and faith.
Grant this . . . for ever and ever. ℟. **Amen.** ↓

READINGS AND INTERVENIENT CHANTS

The *Weekday* Readings and Intervenient Chants for each day of the 1st Week in Ordinary Time are found on pp. 204-220.

PRAYER OVER THE GIFTS

Lord,
accept our offering.
Make us grow in holiness
and grant what we ask you in faith.
We ask this in the name of Jesus the Lord.
℟. **Amen.**   → No. 21, p. 626 (Pref. P 37-42)

COMMUNION ANT.   Ps 36:10

Lord, you are the source of life, and in the light of your glory we find happiness. ↓

OR   Jn 10:10

I came that men may have life, and have it to the full, says the Lord. ↓

PRAYER AFTER COMMUNION

All-powerful God,
you renew us with your sacraments.
Help us to thank you by lives of faithful service.
We ask this through Christ our Lord.
℟. **Amen.**   → No. 32, p. 660

2nd WEEK

God has made heaven and earth. He made the stars in the heavens and the seasons of the year. He has ordered them all well. Today we pray that his peace and order may abound in the lives of all men.

ENTRANCE ANT.   Ps 66:4

May all the earth give you worship and praise, and break into song to your name, O God, Most High.
                                                    → No. 2, p. 614

OPENING PRAYER

Father of heaven and earth,
hear our prayers,
and show us the way to peace in the world.
Grant this ... for ever and ever. ℟. **Amen.** ↓

ALTERNATIVE OPENING PRAYER

Almighty and ever-present Father,
your watchful care reaches from end to end
and orders all things in such power
that even the tensions and the tragedies of sin
cannot frustrate your loving plans.
Help us to embrace your will,
give us the strength to follow your call,
so that your truth may live in our hearts
and reflect peace to those who believe in your love.
We ask this in the name of Jesus the Lord.
℟. **Amen.** ↓

READINGS AND INTERVENIENT CHANTS

The *Weekday* Readings and Intervenient Chants for each day of the 2nd Week in Ordinary Time are found on pp. 226-250.

PRAYER OVER THE GIFTS

Father,
may we celebrate the eucharist
with reverence and love,
for when we proclaim the death of the Lord
you continue the work of his redemption,
who is Lord for ever and ever.
℞. **Amen.**   ➝ No. 21, p. 626 (Pref. P 37-42)

COMMUNION ANT.   Ps 23:5

The Lord has prepared a feast for me: given wine in plenty for me to drink. ↓

OR   1 Jn 4:16

We know and believe in God's love for us. ↓

PRAYER AFTER COMMUNION

Lord,
you have nourished us with bread from heaven.
Fill us with your Spirit,
and make us one in peace and love.
We ask this through Christ our Lord.
℞. **Amen.**   ➝ No. 32, p. 660

3rd WEEK

St. Paul reminds us that what we do, whether we eat, work, or sleep, all must be done for God. Out of love Jesus came into the world. In return he asks our love.

ENTRANCE ANT.   Ps 96:1, 6

Sing a new song to the Lord! Sing to the Lord, all the earth. Truth and beauty surround him, he lives in holiness and glory.   ➝ No. 2, p. 614

OPENING PRAYER

All-powerful and ever-living God,
direct your love that is within us,
that our efforts in the name of your Son
may bring mankind to unity and peace.
We ask this . . . for ever and ever.
℟. **Amen.** ↓

ALTERNATIVE OPENING PRAYER

Almighty Father,
the love you offer
always exceeds the furthest expression of our human
    longing,
for you are greater than the human heart.
Direct each thought, each effort of our life
so that the limits of our faults and weaknesses
may not obscure the vision of your glory
or keep us from the peace you have promised.
We ask this through Christ our Lord.
℟. **Amen.** ↓

READINGS AND INTERVENIENT CHANTS

The *Weekday* Readings and Intervenient Chants for each
day of the 3rd Week in Ordinary Time are found on 250-273.

PRAYER OVER THE GIFTS

Lord,
receive our gifts.
Let our offerings make us holy
and bring us salvation.
Grant this through Christ our Lord.
℟. **Amen.**   → No. 21, p. 626 (Pref. P 37-42)

COMMUNION ANT.   Ps 34:6

**Look up at the Lord with gladness and smile; your face
will never be ashamed.** ↓

OR Jn 8:12

I am the light of the world, says the Lord; the man who follows me will have the light of life. ↓

PRAYER AFTER COMMUNION

God, all-powerful Father,
may the new life you give us increase our love
and keep us in the joy of your kingdom.
We ask this in the name of Jesus the Lord.
℟. **Amen.** → No. 32, p. 660

4th WEEK

When Jesus came into the world, he left his place in heaven knowing that he was to suffer and die for all human beings. Greater love than this no one has: to lay down one's life for a friend. Let us pray that we may love one another without reserve.

ENTRANCE ANT. Ps 106:47

Save us, Lord our God, and gather us together from the nations, that we may proclaim your holy name and glory in your praise. → No. 2, p. 614

OPENING PRAYER

Lord our God,
help us to love you with all our hearts
and to love all men as you love them.
Grant this . . . for ever and ever.
℟. **Amen.** ↓

ALTERNATIVE OPENING PRAYER

Father in heaven,
from the days of Abraham and Moses
until this gathering of your Church in prayer,
you have formed a people in the image of your Son.
Bless this people with the gift of your kingdom.
May we serve you with our every desire
and show love for one another

even as you have loved us.
Grant this through Christ our Lord. ℟. **Amen.** ↓

READINGS AND INTERVENIENT CHANTS

The *Weekday* Readings and Intervenient Chants for each
day of the 4th Week in Ordinary Time are found on pp. 273-
297.

PRAYER OVER THE GIFTS

Lord,
be pleased with the gifts we bring to your altar,
and make them the sacrament of our salvation.
We ask this through Christ our Lord.
℟. **Amen.**   ➜ No. 21, p. 626 (Pref. P 37-42)

COMMUNION ANT.   Ps 31:17-18

**Let your face shine on your servant, and save me by
your love. Lord, keep me from shame, for I have called
to you. ↓**

OR   Mt 5:3-4

**Happy are the poor in spirit; the kingdom of heaven is
theirs! Happy are the lowly; they shall inherit the land. ↓**

PRAYER AFTER COMMUNION

Lord,
you invigorate us with this help to our salvation.
By this eucharist give the true faith continued growth
throughout the world.
We ask this in the name of Jesus the Lord.
℟. **Amen.**   ➜ No. 32, p. 660

5th WEEK

In Old Testament days God led his people out of bondage. He guided them
with a pillar of fire at night and a cloud during the day. He fed them with
manna in the desert. May God continue to watch over and care for his people of today.

ENTRANCE ANT.   Ps 95:6-7

Come, let us worship the Lord. Let us bow down in the presence of our maker, for he is the Lord our God.

→ No. 2, p. 614

OPENING PRAYER

Father,
watch over your family
and keep us safe in your care,
for all our hope is in you.
Grant this . . . for ever and ever. ℟. **Amen.** ↓

ALTERNATIVE OPENING PRAYER

In faith and love we ask you, Father,
to watch over your family gathered here.
In your mercy and loving kindness
no thought of ours is left unguarded,
no tear unheeded, no joy unnoticed.
Through the prayer of Jesus
may the blessings promised to the poor in spirit
lead us to the treasures of your heavenly kingdom.
We ask this in the name of Jesus the Lord.
℟. **Amen.** ↓

READINGS AND INTERVENIENT CHANTS

The *Weekday* Readings and Intervenient Chants for each day of the 5th Week in Ordinary Time are found on pp. 301-324.

PRAYER OVER THE GIFTS

Lord our God,
may the bread and wine
you give us for our nourishment on earth
become the sacrament of our eternal life.
We ask this through Christ our Lord.
℟. **Amen.**   → No. 21, p. 626 (Pref. P 37-42)

COMMUNION ANT.　　　　　　　　　　　Ps 107:8-9

Give praise to the Lord for his kindness, for his wonderful deeds toward men. He has filled the hungry with good things, he has satisfied the thirsty. ↓

OR　　　　　　　　　　　　　　　　Mt 5:5-6

Happy are the sorrowing; they shall be consoled. Happy those who hunger and thirst for what is right; they shall be satisfied. ↓

PRAYER AFTER COMMUNION

God our Father,
you give us a share in the one bread and the one cup
and make us one in Christ.
Help us to bring your salvation and joy
to all the world.
We ask this through Christ our Lord.
℞. **Amen.** → No. 32, p. 660

6th WEEK

God made a covenant with the Israelites that he would be their God and they would be his people. We pray today that he will look after us and keep us safe from all harm.

ENTRANCE ANT.　　　　　　　　　　　Ps 31:3-4

Lord, be my rock of safety, the stronghold that saves me. For the honor of your name, lead me and guide me.
→ No. 2, p. 614

OPENING PRAYER

God our Father,
you have promised to remain for ever
with those who do what is just and right.
Help us to live in your presence.
We ask this . . . for ever and ever. ℞. **Amen.** ↓

ALTERNATIVE OPENING PRAYER

Father in heaven,
the loving plan of your wisdom took flesh in Jesus Christ,

and changed mankind's history
by his command of perfect love.
May our fulfillment of his command reflect your wisdom
and bring your salvation to the ends of the earth.
We ask this through Christ our Lord.
℟. **Amen.** ↓

READINGS AND INTERVENIENT CHANTS

The *Weekday* Readings and Intervenient Chants for each
day of the 6th Week in Ordinary Time are found on pp. 324-
347.

PRAYER OVER THE GIFTS

Lord,
we make this offering in obedience to your word.
May it cleanse and renew us,
and lead us to our eternal reward.
We ask this in the name of Jesus the Lord.
℟. **Amen.** → No. 21, p. 626 (Pref. P 37-42)

COMMUNION ANT. Ps 78:29-30

**They ate and were filled; the Lord gave them what they
wanted: they were not deprived of their desire.** ↓

OR Jn 3:16

**God loved the world so much, he gave his only Son, that
all who believe in him might not perish, but might have
eternal life.** ↓

PRAYER AFTER COMMUNION

Lord,
you give us food from heaven.
May we always hunger
for the bread of life.
Grant this through Christ our Lord.
℟. **Amen.** → No. 32, p. 660

7th WEEK

Solomon was renowned for his wisdom. Jesus confounded the scribes and Pharisees who tried to trick him. "Give to Caesar what is Caesar's and to God what is God's." May we abide by the revealed word of God and live always according to his commandments.

ENTRANCE ANT.

Ps 13:6

Lord, your mercy is my hope, my heart rejoices in your saving power. I will sing to the Lord for his goodness to me. → No. 2, p. 614

OPENING PRAYER

Father,
keep before us the wisdom and love
you have revealed in your Son.
Help us to be like him
in word and deed,
for he lives and reigns with you and the Holy Spirit,
one God, for ever and ever. ℟. **Amen.** ↓

ALTERNATIVE OPENING PRAYER

Almighty God,
Father of our Lord Jesus Christ,
faith in your word is the way to wisdom,
and to ponder your divine plan is to grow in the truth.
Open our eyes to your deeds,
our ears to the sound of your call,
so that our every act may increase our sharing
in the life you have offered us.
Grant this through Christ our Lord. ℟. **Amen.** ↓

READINGS AND INTERVENIENT CHANTS

The *Weekday* Readings and Intervenient Chants for each day of the 7th Week in Ordinary Time are found on pp. 347-369.

PRAYER OVER THE GIFTS

Lord,
as we make this offering,

may our worship in Spirit and truth
bring us salvation.
We ask this in the name of Jesus the Lord.
℟. **Amen.** → No. 21, p. 626 (Pref. P 37-42)

COMMUNION ANT. Ps 9:2-3

I will tell all your marvelous works. I will rejoice and be glad in you, and sing to your name, Most High. ↓

OR Jn 11:27

Lord, I believe that you are the Christ, the Son of God, who was to come into this world. ↓

PRAYER AFTER COMMUNION

Almighty God,
help us to live the example of love
we celebrate in this eucharist,
that we may come to its fulfillment in your presence.
We ask this through Christ our Lord.
℟. **Amen.** → No. 32, p. 660

8th WEEK

Everything lives in the ever present "now" in the mind of God. We are born only to live for a time wherein we are to serve God. We pray that we may live lives pleasing to God, that we may live in joy and peace.

ENTRANCE ANT. Ps 18:19-20

The Lord has been my strength; he has led me into freedom. He saved me because he loves me. → No. 2, p. 614

OPENING PRAYER

Lord,
guide the course of world events
and give your Church the joy and peace
of serving you in freedom.
We ask this . . . for ever and ever. ℟. **Amen.** ↓

ALTERNATIVE OPENING PRAYER

Father in heaven,
form in us the likeness of your Son
and deepen his life within us.
Send us as witnesses of gospel joy
into a world of fragile peace and broken promises.
Touch the hearts of all men with your love
that they in turn may love one another.
We ask this through Christ our Lord.
℟. **Amen.** ↓

READINGS AND INTERVENIENT CHANTS

The *Weekday* Readings and Intervenient Chants for each
day of the 8th Week in Ordinary Time are found on pp. 369-
391.

PRAYER OVER THE GIFTS

God our Creator,
may this bread and wine we offer
as a sign of our love and worship
lead us to salvation.
Grant this through Christ our Lord.
℟. **Amen.**   ➙ No. 21, p. 626 (Pref. P 37-42)

COMMUNION ANT.   Ps 13:6

**I will sing to the Lord for his goodness to me, I will sing
the name of the Lord, Most High.** ↓

OR   Mt 28:20

**I, the Lord, am with you always, until the end of the
world.** ↓

PRAYER AFTER COMMUNION

God of salvation,
may this sacrament which strengthens us here on earth
bring us to eternal life.
We ask this in the name of Jesus the Lord.
℟. **Amen.**   ➙ No. 32, p. 660

9th WEEK

How much we take for granted as we live in a world of advanced progress! It is easy to become immersed in the affairs around us and they may easily ensnare us. May God who cares for us shield us from all dangers as he provides for our needs.

ENTRANCE ANT.
Ps 25:16, 18

O look at me and be merciful, for I am wretched and alone. See my hardship and my poverty, and pardon all my sins.
→ No. 2, p. 614

OPENING PRAYER

Father,
your love never fails.
Hear our call.
Keep us from danger
and provide for all our needs.
Grant this ... for ever and ever. ℟. **Amen.** ↓

ALTERNATIVE OPENING PRAYER

God our Father,
teach us to cherish the gifts that surround us.
Increase our faith in you
and bring our trust to its promised fulfillment
in the joy of your kingdom.
Grant this through Christ our Lord. ℟. **Amen.** ↓

READINGS AND INTERVENIENT CHANTS

The *Weekday* Readings and Intervenient Chants for each day of the 9th Week in Ordinary Time are found on pp. 391-417.

PRAYER OVER THE GIFTS

Lord,
as we gather to offer our gifts
confident in your love
make us holy by sharing your life with us
and by this eucharist forgive our sins.
We ask this through Christ our Lord.
℟. **Amen.**
→ No. 21, p. 626 (Pref. P 37-42)

COMMUNION ANT.   Ps 17:6

I call upon you, God, for you will answer me; bend your ear and hear my prayer. ↓

OR   Mk 11:23-24

I tell you solemnly, whatever you ask for in prayer, believe that you have received it, and it will be yours, says the Lord. ↓

PRAYER AFTER COMMUNION

Lord,
as you give us the body and blood of your Son,
guide us with your Spirit
that we may honor you
not only with our lips,
but also with the lives we lead,
and so enter your kingdom.
We ask this in the name of Jesus the Lord.
℟. **Amen.**   → No. 32, p. 660

10th WEEK

The life of the Holy Spirit dwells in those chosen by Jesus to carry on his work on earth. The openness of Christ to us through his Spirit is one of love and eternal presence. We are all called upon to be the means by which Christ may reach out to all mankind.

ENTRANCE ANT.   Ps 27:1-2

The Lord is my light and my salvation. Who shall frighten me? The Lord is the defender of my life. Who shall make me tremble?   → No. 2, p. 614

OPENING PRAYER

God of wisdom and love,
source of all good,
send your Spirit to teach us your truth
and guide our actions
in your way of peace.
We ask this . . . for ever and ever. ℟. **Amen.** ↓

ALTERNATIVE OPENING PRAYER

Father in heaven,
words cannot measure the boundaries of love
for those born to new life in Christ Jesus.
Raise us beyond the limits this world imposes,
so that we may be free to love as Christ teaches
and find our joy in your glory.
We ask this through Christ our Lord. ℟. **Amen.** ↓

READINGS AND INTERVENIENT CHANTS

The *Weekday* Readings and Intervenient Chants for the
1st to 9th Weeks in Ordinary Time are found on pp. 204-417.

PRAYER OVER THE GIFTS

Lord, look with love on our service.
Accept the gifts we bring
and help us grow in Christian love.
Grant this through Christ our Lord.
℟. **Amen.**   → No. 21, p. 626 (Pref. P 37-42)

COMMUNION ANT.   Ps 18:3

**I can rely on the Lord; I can always turn to him for shel-
ter. It was he who gave me my freedom. My God, you are
always there to help me!** ↓

OR   1 Jn 4:16

**God is love, and he who lives in love, lives in God, and
God in him.** ↓

PRAYER AFTER COMMUNION

Lord,
may your healing love
turn us from sin
and keep us on the way that leads to you.
We ask this in the name of Jesus the Lord.
℟. **Amen.**   → No. 32, p. 660

11th WEEK

As Christians, we should remember that God's love as exemplified in Christ's dying for all of mankind should bring us to a stronger and more confident abandonment of ourselves in return to God and others. May this Eucharistic liturgy strengthen our confidence in ourselves as receivers and givers of God's love.

ENTRANCE ANT.
Ps 27:7, 9

Lord, hear my voice when I call to you. You are my help; do not cast me off, do not desert me, my Savior God.

→ No. 2, p. 614

OPENING PRAYER

Almighty God,
our hope and our strength,
without you we falter.
Help us to follow Christ
and to live according to your will.
We ask this . . . for ever and ever. ℟. **Amen.** ↓

ALTERNATIVE OPENING PRAYER

God our Father,
we rejoice in the faith that draws us together,
aware that selfishness can drive us apart.
Let your encouragement be our constant strength.
Keep us one in the love that has sealed our lives,
help us to live as one family
the gospel we profess.
We ask this through Christ our Lord. ℟. **Amen.** ↓

READINGS AND INTERVENIENT CHANTS

The *Weekday* Readings and Intervenient Chants for the 1st to 9th Weeks in Ordinary Time are found on pp. 204-417.

PRAYER OVER THE GIFTS

Lord God,
in this bread and wine
you give us food for body and spirit.
May the eucharist renew our strength

and bring us health of mind and body.
We ask this in the name of Jesus the Lord.
℟. **Amen.**   ➜ No. 21, p. 626 (Pref. P 37-42)

COMMUNION ANT.   Ps 27:4

One thing I seek: to dwell in the house of the Lord all the days of my life. ↓

OR   Jn 17:11

Father, keep in your name those you have given me, that they may be one as we are one, says the Lord. ↓

PRAYER AFTER COMMUNION

Lord,
may this eucharist
accomplish in your Church
the unity and peace it signifies.
Grant this through Christ our Lord.
℟. **Amen.**   ➜ No. 32, p. 660

12th WEEK

Jesus Christ is the Good Shepherd who protects us, his sheep. The sheep of his fold come first, and he will do all in his power to save them from harm. Christ our Shepherd laid down his life for us. How he has proved his love for us!

ENTRANCE ANT.   Ps 28:8-9

God is the strength of his people. In him, we his chosen live in safety. Save us, Lord, who share in your life, and give us your blessings; be our shepherd for ever.
                                             ➜ No. 2, p. 614

OPENING PRAYER

Father,
guide and protector of your people,
grant us an unfailing respect for your name,
and keep us always in your love.
Grant this . . . for ever and ever. ℟. **Amen.** ↓

ALTERNATIVE OPENING PRAYER

God of the universe,
we worship you as Lord.
God, ever close to us,
we rejoice to call you Father.
From this world's uncertainty we look to your covenant.
Keep us one in your peace, secure in your love.
We ask this through Christ our Lord. ℟. **Amen.** ↓

READINGS AND INTERVENIENT CHANTS

The *Weekday* Readings and Intervenient Chants for the
1st to 9th Weeks in Ordinary Time are found on pp. 204-417.

PRAYER OVER THE GIFTS

Lord,
receive our offering
and may this sacrifice of praise
purify us in mind and heart
and make us always eager to serve you.
We ask this in the name of Jesus the Lord.
℟. **Amen.**   → No. 21, p. 626 (Pref. P 37-42)

COMMUNION ANT.   Ps 145:15

**The eyes of all look to you, O Lord, and you give them
food in due season.** ↓

OR   Jn 10:11, 15

**I am the Good Shepherd; I give my life for my sheep,
says the Lord.** ↓

PRAYER AFTER COMMUNION

Lord,
you give us the body and blood of your Son
to renew your life within us.
In your mercy, assure our redemption
and bring us to the eternal life
we celebrate in this eucharist.
We ask this through Christ our Lord. ℟. **Amen.**
                                          → No. 32, p. 660

13th WEEK

Jesus Christ, the Light of the World, gives us hope. He lights the way and guides us in the truth. Each day, his light comes to us to help us overcome the darkness. As children of light and followers of Christ, may we support each other and rely on the authority and power of Jesus to live a life of faith.

ENTRANCE ANT. Ps 47:2

All nations, clap your hands. Shout with a voice of joy to God. → No. 2, p. 614

OPENING PRAYER

Father,
you call your children
to walk in the light of Christ.
Free us from darkness
and keep us in the radiance of your truth.
We ask this . . . for ever and ever. ℟. **Amen.** ↓

ALTERNATIVE OPENING PRAYER

Father in heaven,
the light of Jesus
has scattered the darkness of hatred and sin.
Called to that light
we ask for your guidance.
Form our lives in your truth, our hearts in your love
We ask this through Christ our Lord. ℟. **Amen.** ↓

READINGS AND INTERVENIENT CHANTS

The *Weekday* Readings and Intervenient Chants for the 1st to 9th Weeks in Ordinary Time are found on pp. 204-417.

PRAYER OVER THE GIFTS

Lord God,
through your sacraments
you give us the power of your grace.
May this eucharist
help us to serve you faithfully.
We ask this in the name of Jesus the Lord.
℟. **Amen.** → No. 21, p. 626 (Pref. P 37-42)

COMMUNION ANT. Ps 103:1

O, bless the Lord, my soul, and all that is within me, bless his holy name. ↓

OR Jn 17:20-21

Father, I pray for them: may they be one in us, so that the world may believe it was you who sent me. ↓

PRAYER AFTER COMMUNION

Lord,
may this sacrifice and communion
give us a share in your life
and help us bring your love to the world.
Grant this through Christ our Lord.
℟. **Amen.** → No. 32, p. 660

14th WEEK

Each day we are witness to God's dominion over all things. He is the Master of the universe, the Ruler over life and death. All laws of nature are subject to him. We cannot merely recognize that God is all-powerful but must acknowledge that truth in a practical way by conducting our lives in obedience to his Divine Will.

ENTRANCE ANT. Ps 48:10-11

Within your temple, we ponder your loving kindness, O God. As your name, so also your praise reaches to the ends of the earth; your right hand is filled with justice. → No. 2, p. 614

OPENING PRAYER

Father,
through the obedience of Jesus,
your servant and your Son,
you raised a fallen world.
Free us from sin
and bring us the joy that lasts for ever.
We ask this . . . for ever and ever. ℟. **Amen.** ↓

ALTERNATIVE OPENING PRAYER

Father,
in the rising of your Son
death gives birth to new life.
The sufferings he endured restored hope to a fallen world.
Let sin never ensnare us
with empty promises of passing joy.
Make us one with you always,
so that our joy may be holy,
and our love may give life.
We ask this through Christ our Lord. ℟. **Amen.** ↓

READINGS AND INTERVENIENT CHANTS

The *Weekday* Readings and Intervenient Chants for the
1st to 9th Weeks in Ordinary Time are found on pp. 204-417.

PRAYER OVER THE GIFTS

Lord,
let this offering to the glory of your name
purify us and bring us closer to eternal life.
We ask this in the name of Jesus the Lord.
℟. **Amen.**   → No. 21, p. 626 (Pref. P 37-42)

COMMUNION ANT.   Ps 34:9

**Taste and see the goodness of the Lord; blessed is he
who hopes in God.** ↓

OR   Mt 11:28

**Come to me, all you that labor and are burdened, and I
will give you rest, says the Lord.** ↓

PRAYER AFTER COMMUNION

Lord,
may we never fail to praise you
for the fullness of life and salvation
you give us in this eucharist.
We ask this through Christ our Lord.
℟. **Amen.** _____ → No. 32, p. 660

15th WEEK

Jesus showed us that our God is a personal Father who knows the sound of our voice and who always hears the prayers of those who call on him. Jesus himself often prayed to his Father, remembering all of God's goodness and giving him praise. Let us join Jesus in praising the Father and thanking him for all that he has given us.

ENTRANCE ANT.   Ps 17:15

In my justice I shall see your face, O Lord; when your glory appears, my joy will be full.   → No. 2, p. 614

OPENING PRAYER

God our Father,
your light of truth
guides us to the way of Christ.
May all who follow him
reject what is contrary to the gospel.
We ask this . . . for ever and ever. ℟. **Amen.** ↓

ALTERNATIVE OPENING PRAYER

Father,
let the light of your truth
guide us to your kingdom
through a world filled with lights contrary to your own.
Christian is the name and the gospel we glory in.
May your love make us what you have called us to be.
We ask this through Christ our Lord. ℟. **Amen.** ↓

READINGS AND INTERVENIENT CHANTS

The *Weekday* Readings and Intervenient Chants for the 1st to 9th Weeks in Ordinary Time are found on pp. 204-417.

PRAYER OVER THE GIFTS

Lord,
accept the gifts of your Church.
May this eucharist
help us grow in holiness and faith.
We ask this in the name of Jesus the Lord.
℟. **Amen.**   → No. 21, p. 626 (Pref. P 37-42)

COMMUNION ANT. Ps 84:4-5

The sparrow even finds a home, the swallow finds a nest wherein to place her young, near to your altars, Lord of hosts, my King, my God! How happy they who dwell in your house! For ever they are praising you. ↓

OR Jn 6:57

Whoever eats my flesh and drinks my blood will live in me and I in him, says the Lord. ↓

PRAYER AFTER COMMUNION

Lord,
by our sharing in the mystery of this eucharist,
let your saving love grow within us.
Grant this through Christ our Lord
℟. **Amen.** → No. 32, p. 660

16th WEEK

In his goodness and mercy, God has given to men the power to forgive our sins and thereby restore us to friendship with him. He has given to men the power to change bread and wine into his own Body and Blood so that we may have the spiritual strength to meet the problems and trials of life. May we thus serve God in faith, hope, and love!

ENTRANCE ANT. Ps 54:6, 8

God himself is my help. The Lord upholds my life. I will offer you a willing sacrifice; I will praise your name, O Lord, for its goodness. → No. 2, p. 614

OPENING PRAYER

Lord,
be merciful to your people.
Fill us with your gifts
and make us always eager to serve you
in faith, hope, and love.
Grant this . . . for ever and ever. ℟. **Amen.** ↓

ALTERNATIVE OPENING PRAYER

Father,
let the gift of your life
continue to grow in us,
drawing us from death to faith, hope, and love.
Keep us alive in Christ Jesus.
Keep us watchful in prayers,
and true to his teaching
till your glory is revealed in us.
Grant this through Christ our Lord. ℟. **Amen.** ↓

READINGS AND INTERVENIENT CHANTS

The *Weekday* Readings and Intervenient Chants for the
1st to 9th Weeks in Ordinary Time are found on pp. 204-417.

PRAYER OVER THE GIFTS

Lord,
bring us closer to salvation
through these gifts which we bring in your honor.
Accept the perfect sacrifice you have given us,
bless it as you blessed the gifts of Abel.
We ask this through Christ our Lord.
℟. **Amen.**   ➙ No. 21, p. 626 (Pref. P 37-42)

COMMUNION ANT.   Ps 111:4-5

**The Lord keeps in our minds the wonderful things he
has done. He is compassion and love; he always provides
for his faithful.** ↓

OR   Rv 3:20

**I stand at the door and knock, says the Lord. If anyone
hears my voice and opens the door, I will come in and sit
down to supper with him, and he with me.** ↓

PRAYER AFTER COMMUNION

Merciful Father,
may these mysteries
give us new purpose

and bring us to a new life in you.
We ask this in the name of Jesus the Lord.
℟. **Amen.** → No. 32, p. 660

17th WEEK

If we have faith in God, we can be assured that he will provide us with all that we need. God's call is extended to all people, and we have only to accept the invitation to share in his bountiful gifts.

ENTRANCE ANT. Ps 68:6-7, 36

God is in his holy dwelling; he will give a home to the lonely, he gives power and strength to his people.

→ No. 2, p. 614

OPENING PRAYER

God our Father and protector,
without you nothing is holy,
nothing has value.
Guide us to everlasting life
by helping us to use wisely
the blessings you have given to the world.
We ask this . . . for ever and ever. ℟. **Amen.** ↓

ALTERNATIVE OPENING PRAYER

God our Father,
open our eyes to see your hand at work
in the splendor of creation,
in the beauty of human life.
Touched by your hand our world is holy.
Help us to cherish the gifts that surround us,
to share your blessings with our brothers and sisters,
and to experience the joy of life in your presence.
We ask this through Christ our Lord. ℟. **Amen.** ↓

READINGS AND INTERVENIENT CHANTS

The *Weekday* Readings and Intervenient Chants for the 1st to 9th Weeks in Ordinary Time are found on pp. 204-417.

PRAYER OVER THE GIFTS

Lord,
receive these offerings
chosen from your many gifts.
May these mysteries make us holy
and lead us to eternal joy.
Grant this through Christ our Lord.
℟. **Amen.** → No. 21, p. 626 (Pref. P 37-42)

COMMUNION ANT. Ps 103:2

O, bless the Lord, my soul, and remember all his kindness. ↓

OR Mt 5:7-8

**Happy are those who show mercy; mercy shall be theirs.
Happy are the pure of heart, for they shall see God.** ↓

PRAYER AFTER COMMUNION

Lord,
we receive the sacrament
which celebrates the memory
of the death and resurrection of Christ your Son.
May this gift bring us closer to our eternal salvation.
We ask this through Christ our Lord.
℟. **Amen.** → No. 32, p. 660

18th WEEK

The soul requires spiritual food. Jesus offers us himself as the Bread of
Life that will fill our spiritual appetite so that we will never hunger again.
All things of this world are as nothing to us in the presence of our Lord
and Savior whom we receive in the Eucharist.

ENTRANCE ANT. Ps 70:2, 6

**God, come to my help. Lord, quickly give me assistance.
You are the one who helps me and sets me free: Lord, do
not be long in coming.** → No. 2, p. 614

OPENING PRAYER

Father of everlasting goodness,
our origin and guide,
be close to us
and hear the prayers of all who praise you.
Forgive our sins and restore us to life.
Keep us safe in your love.
Grant this . . . for ever and ever. ℟. **Amen.** ↓

ALTERNATIVE OPENING PRAYER

God our Father,
gifts without measure flow from your goodness
to bring us your peace.
Our life is your gift.
Guide our life's journey,
for only your love makes us whole.
Keep us strong in your love.
We ask this through Christ our Lord. ℟. **Amen.** ↓

READINGS AND INTERVENIENT CHANTS

The *Weekday* Readings and Intervenient Chants for the
1st to 9th Weeks in Ordinary Time are found on pp. 204-417.

PRAYER OVER THE GIFTS

Merciful Lord,
make holy these gifts,
and let our spiritual sacrifice
make us an everlasting gift to you.
We ask this in the name of Jesus the Lord.
℟. **Amen.**   → No. 21, p. 626 (Pref. P 37-42)

COMMUNION ANT.   Wis 16:20

**You gave us bread from heaven, Lord: a sweet-tasting
bread that was very good to eat.** ↓

OR   Jn 6:35

**The Lord says: I am the bread of life. A man who comes
to me will not go away hungry, and no one who believes
in me will thirst.** ↓

PRAYER AFTER COMMUNION

Lord,
you give us the strength of new life
by the gift of the eucharist.
Protect us with your love
and prepare us for eternal redemption.
We ask this through Christ our Lord.
℞. **Amen.**

→ No. 32, p. 660

19th WEEK

We have been chosen to be the people of God and to hear the Good News of salvation. We have been reborn in the waters of baptism and we have received the gift of the Holy Spirit, our guide and our protector. We have nothing to fear.

ENTRANCE ANT.

Ps 74:20, 19, 22, 23

Lord, be true to your covenant, forget not the life of your poor ones for ever. Rise up, O God, and defend your cause; do not ignore the shouts of your enemies.

→ No. 2, p. 614

OPENING PRAYER

Almighty and ever-living God,
your Spirit made us your children,
confident to call you Father.
Increase your Spirit within us
and bring us to our promised inheritance.
Grant this . . . for ever and ever. ℞. **Amen.**

ALTERNATIVE OPENING PRAYER

Father,
we come, reborn in the Spirit,
to celebrate our sonship in the Lord Jesus Christ.
Touch our hearts,
help them grow toward the life you have promised.
Touch our lives,
make them signs of your love for all men.
Grant this through Christ our Lord. ℞. **Amen.** ↓

READINGS AND INTERVENIENT CHANTS

The *Weekday* Readings and Intervenient Chants for the 1st to 9th Weeks in Ordinary Time are found on pp. 204-417.

PRAYER OVER THE GIFTS

God of power,
giver of the gifts we bring,
accept the offering of your Church
and make it the sacrament of our salvation.
We ask this through Christ our Lord.
℟. **Amen.**　　　　　→ No. 21, p. 626 (Pref. P 37-42)

COMMUNION ANT.　　　　　　　　　　Ps 147:12-14

Praise the Lord, Jerusalem; he feeds you with the finest wheat. ↓

OR　　　　　　　　　　　　　　　　　Jn 6:52

The bread I shall give is my flesh for the life of the world, says the Lord. ↓

PRAYER AFTER COMMUNION

Lord,
may the eucharist you give us
bring us to salvation
and keep us faithful to the light of your truth.
We ask this in the name of Jesus the Lord.
℟. **Amen.**　　　　　　　　　　　→ No. 32, p. 660

20th WEEK

The Lord's call is universal, meant for all mankind. We are all brothers and sisters in Christ. Each of us must support one another through our concern, and in this way we witness Jesus and his message.

ENTRANCE ANT.　　　　　　　　　　Ps 84:10-11

God, our protector, keep us in mind; always give strength to your people. For if we can be with you even one day, it is better than a thousand without you. → No. 2, p. 614

OPENING PRAYER

God our Father,
may we love you in all things and above all things
and reach the joy you have prepared for us
beyond all our imagining.
We ask this . . . for ever and ever. ℟. **Amen.** ↓

ALTERNATIVE OPENING PRAYER

Almighty God, ever-loving Father,
your care extends beyond the boundaries of race and
   nation
to the hearts of all who live.
May the walls, which prejudice raises between us,
crumble beneath the shadow of your outstretched arm.
We ask this through Christ our Lord. ℟. **Amen.** ↓

READINGS AND INTERVENIENT CHANTS

The *Weekday* Readings and Intervenient Chants for the
1st to 9th Weeks in Ordinary Time are found on pp. 204-417.

PRAYER OVER THE GIFTS

Lord,
accept our sacrifice
as a holy exchange of gifts.
By offering what you have given us
may we receive the gift of yourself.
We ask this in the name of Jesus the Lord.
℟. **Amen.**   → No. 21, p. 626 (Pref. P 37-42)

COMMUNION ANT.   Ps 130:7

**With the Lord there is mercy, and fullness of redemp-
tion.** ↓

OR   Jn 6:51-52

**I am the living bread from heaven, says the Lord; if any-
one eats this bread he will live for ever.** ↓

PRAYER AFTER COMMUNION

God of mercy,
by this sacrament you make us one with Christ.
By becoming more like him on earth,
may we come to share his glory in heaven,
where he lives and reigns for ever and ever.
℞. **Amen.** → No. 32, p. 660

21st WEEK

Jesus alone can lead us to his Father, but we owe him service in order for
him to give us this life. We find this life in loving one another, the same
way Christ loved his Church. He was willing to give up his life to save his
Church.

ENTRANCE ANT. Ps 86:1-3

**Listen, Lord, and answer me. Save your servant who
trusts in you. I call to you all day long; have mercy on me,
O Lord.** → No. 2, p. 614

OPENING PRAYER

Father,
help us to seek the values
that will bring us lasting joy in this changing world.
In our desire for what you promise
make us one in mind and heart.
Grant this ... for ever and ever. ℞. **Amen.** ↓

ALTERNATIVE OPENING PRAYER

Lord our God,
all truth is from you,
and you alone bring oneness of heart.
Give your people the joy
of hearing your word in every sound
and of longing for your presence more than for life itself.
May all the attractions of a changing world
serve only to bring us
the peace of your kingdom which this world does not give.
Grant this through Christ our Lord. ℞. **Amen.** ↓

READINGS AND INTERVENIENT CHANTS

The *Weekday* Readings and Intervenient Chants for the 1st to 9th Weeks in Ordinary Time are found on pp. 204-417.

PRAYER OVER THE GIFTS

Merciful God,
the perfect sacrifice of Jesus Christ
made us your people.
In your love,
grant peace and unity to your Church.
We ask this through Christ our Lord.
℟. **Amen.**   → No. 21, p. 626 (Pref. P 37-42)

COMMUNION ANT.   Ps 104:13-15

Lord, the earth is filled with your gift from heaven; man grows bread from earth, and wine to cheer his heart. ↓

OR   Jn 6:55

The Lord says: The man who eats my flesh and drinks my blood will live for ever; I shall raise him to life on the last day. ↓

PRAYER AFTER COMMUNION

Lord,
may this eucharist increase within us
the healing power of your love.
May it guide and direct our efforts
to please you in all things.
We ask this in the name of Jesus the Lord.
℟. **Amen.**   → No. 32, p. 660

22nd WEEK

Christ calls all persons to him, for all are sinners who need him. He calls us to come to him with repentance and he will not reject us. It is precisely because of our weakness that Christ holds out his hand of mercy and forgiveness to us.

ENTRANCE ANT. Ps 86:3, 5

I call to you all day long, have mercy on me, O Lord. You are good and forgiving, full of love for all who call to you.
➜ No. 2, p. 614

OPENING PRAYER

Almighty God,
every good thing comes from you.
Fill our hearts with love for you,
increase our faith,
and by your constant care
protect the good you have given us.
We ask this . . . for ever and ever. ℞. **Amen.** ↓

ALTERNATIVE OPENING PRAYER

Lord God of power and might,
nothing is good which is against your will,
and all is of value which comes from your hand.
Place in our hearts a desire to please you
and fill our minds with insight into love,
so that every thought may grow in wisdom
and all our efforts may be filled with your peace.
We ask this through Christ our Lord. ℞. **Amen.** ↓

READINGS AND INTERVENIENT CHANTS

The *Weekday* Readings and Intervenient Chants for the
1st to 9th Weeks in Ordinary Time are found on pp. 204-417.

PRAYER OVER THE GIFTS

Lord,
may this holy offering
bring us your blessing
and accomplish within us
its promise of salvation.
Grant this through Christ our Lord.
℞. **Amen.** ➜ No. 21, p. 626 (Pref. P 37-42)

COMMUNION ANT. Ps 31:20

O Lord, how great is the depth of the kindness which you have shown to those who love you. ↓

OR Mt 5:9-10

Happy are the peacemakers; they shall be called sons of God. Happy are they who suffer persecution for justice' sake; the kingdom of heaven is theirs. ↓

PRAYER AFTER COMMUNION

Lord,
you renew us at your table with the bread of life.
May this food strengthen us in love
and help us to serve you in each other.
We ask this in the name of Jesus the Lord.
℟. **Amen.** → No. 32, p. 660

23rd WEEK

In every age and in every place, God makes his presence known to us. We have come to know God through his Son, Jesus. It is our task to share our knowledge of Christ with others.

ENTRANCE ANT. Ps 119:137, 124

Lord, you are just, and the judgments you make are right. Show mercy when you judge me, your servant.
→ No. 2, p. 614

OPENING PRAYER

God our Father,
you redeem us
and make us your children in Christ.
Look upon us,
give us true freedom
and bring us to the inheritance you promised.
Grant this . . . for ever and ever. ℟. **Amen.**

ALTERNATIVE OPENING PRAYER

Lord our God,
in you justice and mercy meet.

With unparalleled love you have saved us from death
and drawn us into the circle of your life.
Open our eyes to the wonders this life sets before us,
that we may serve you free from fear
and address you as God our Father.
We ask this in the name of Jesus the Lord. ℟. **Amen.** ↓

READINGS AND INTERVENIENT CHANTS

The *Weekday* Readings and Intervenient Chants for the
1st to 9th Weeks in Ordinary Time are found on pp. 204-417.

PRAYER OVER THE GIFTS

God of peace and love,
may our offering bring you true worship
and make us one with you.
Grant this through Christ our Lord.
℟. **Amen.**   → No. 21, p. 626 (Pref. P 37-42)

COMMUNION ANT.   Ps 42:2-3

**Like a deer that longs for running streams, my soul longs
for you, my God. My soul is thirsting for the living God.** ↓

OR   Jn 8:12

**I am the light of the world, says the Lord; the man who
follows me will have the light of life.** ↓

PRAYER AFTER COMMUNION

Lord,
your word and your sacrament
give us food and life.
May this gift of your Son
lead us to share his life for ever.
We ask this through Christ our Lord.
℟. **Amen.**

→ No. 32, p. 660

24th WEEK

All of us are called to serve our heavenly Father in some unique way. We must not bury or hide the talents he has given us; we must use those talents by giving good example to others and living at peace.

ENTRANCE ANT.

See Sir 36:18

Give peace, Lord, to those who wait for you and your prophets will proclaim you as you deserve. Hear the prayers of your servant and of your people Israel. ↓

OPENING PRAYER

Almighty God,
our creator and guide,
may we serve you with all our heart
and know your forgiveness in our lives.
We ask this . . . for ever and ever. ℟. **Amen.** ↓

ALTERNATIVE OPENING PRAYER

Father in heaven, Creator of all,
look down upon your people in their moments of need,
for you alone are the source of our peace.
Bring us to the dignity which distinguishes the poor in
    spirit
and show us how great is the call to serve,
that we may share in the peace of Christ
who offered his life in the service of all.
We ask this through Christ our Lord. ℟. **Amen.** ↓

READINGS AND INTERVENIENT CHANTS

The *Weekday* Readings and Intervenient Chants for the 1st to 9th Weeks in Ordinary Time are found on pp. 204-417.

PRAYER OVER THE GIFTS

Lord,
hear the prayers of your people
and receive our gifts.
May the worship of each one here
bring salvation to all.

Grant this through Christ our Lord.
℟. **Amen.** ➜ No. 21, p. 626 (Pref. P 37-42)

COMMUNION ANT. Ps 36:8

O God, how much we value your mercy! All mankind can gather under your protection. ↓

OR See 1 Cor 10:16

The cup that we bless is a communion with the blood of Christ; and the bread that we break is a communion with the body of the Lord. ↓

PRAYER AFTER COMMUNION

Lord,
may the eucharist you have given us
influence our thoughts and actions.
May your Spirit guide and direct us in your way.
We ask this in the name of Jesus the Lord.
℟. **Amen.** ➜ No. 32, p. 660

25th WEEK

Love is a movement of the mind and heart. It is one of humanity's greatest and most powerful emotions. The world has many definitions for the word and places various interpretations upon it. The Gospels tell us love is patient, kind, and never fails.

ENTRANCE ANT.

I am the Savior of all people, says the Lord. Whatever their troubles, I will answer their cry, and I will always be their Lord. ➜ No. 2, p. 614

OPENING PRAYER

Father, guide us, as you guide creation
according to your law of love.
May we love one another
and come to perfection
in the eternal life prepared for us.
Grant this . . . for ever and ever. ℟. **Amen.** ↓

ALTERNATIVE OPENING PRAYER

Father in heaven,
the perfection of justice is found in your love
and all mankind is in need of your law.
Help us to find this love in each other
that justice may be attained
through obedience to your law.
We ask this through Christ our Lord. ℟. **Amen.** ↓

READINGS AND INTERVENIENT CHANTS

The *Weekday* Readings and Intervenient Chants for the
1st to 9th Weeks in Ordinary Time are found on pp. 204-417.

PRAYER OVER THE GIFTS

Lord,
may these gifts which we now offer
to show our belief and our love
be pleasing to you.
May they become for us
the eucharist of Jesus Christ your Son,
who is Lord for ever and ever.
℟. **Amen.** → No. 21, p. 626 (Pref. P 37-42)

COMMUNION ANT. Ps 119:4-5

**You have laid down your precepts to be faithfully kept.
May my footsteps be firm in keeping your commands.** ↓

OR Jn 10:14

**I am the Good Shepherd, says the Lord; I know my
sheep, and mine know me.** ↓

PRAYER AFTER COMMUNION

Lord, help us with your kindness.
Make us strong through the eucharist.
May we put into action
the saving mystery we celebrate.
We ask this in the name of Jesus the Lord.
℟. **Amen.** → No. 32, p. 660

26th WEEK

When we are disobedient to the commandments given by God, we bring sorrow to others, to God, and, in the end, to ourselves. The people of God who shall live forever are those who do his will. Through obedience to God's word, we are enabled to enter into a close personal relationship with our Divine Savior.

ENTRANCE ANT. Dn 3:31, 29, 30, 43, 42

O Lord, you had just cause to judge men as you did: because we sinned against you and disobeyed your will. But now show us your greatness of heart, and treat us with your unbounded kindness. → No. 2, p. 614

OPENING PRAYER

Father,
you show your almighty power
in your mercy and forgiveness.
Continue to fill us with your gifts of love.
Help us to hurry toward the eternal life you promise
and come to share in the joys of your kingdom.
Grant this . . . for ever and ever. ℟. **Amen.** ↓

ALTERNATIVE OPENING PRAYER

Father of our Lord Jesus Christ,
in your unbounded mercy
you have revealed the beauty of your power
through your constant forgiveness of our sins.
May the power of this love be in our hearts
to bring your pardon and your kingdom to all we meet.
We ask this through Christ our Lord. ℟. **Amen.** ↓

READINGS AND INTERVENIENT CHANTS

The *Weekday* Readings and Intervenient Chants for the 1st to 9th Weeks in Ordinary Time are found on pp. 204-417.

PRAYER OVER THE GIFTS

God of mercy,
accept our offering
and make it a source of blessing for us.

We ask this in the name of Jesus the Lord.

℟. **Amen.** → No. 21, p. 626 (Pref. P 37-42)

COMMUNION ANT. Ps 119:49-50

O Lord, remember the words you spoke to me, your servant, which made me live in hope and consoled me when I was downcast. ↓

OR 1 Jn 3:16

This is how we know what love is: Christ gave up his life for us; and we too must give up our lives for our brothers. ↓

PRAYER AFTER COMMUNION

Lord,
may this eucharist
in which we proclaim the death of Christ
bring us salvation
and make us one with him in glory,
for he is Lord for ever and ever.

℟. **Amen.** → No. 32, p. 660

27th WEEK

A just God is present. If we wish to find him, we must seek him. We must not be misled by a world where the just suffer and the unjust prosper. God has given us his Son to remain with us and to show us the way to the Father.

ENTRANCE ANT. Est 13:9, 10-11

O Lord, you have given everything its place in the world, and no one can make it otherwise. For it is your creation, the heavens and the earth and the stars: you are the Lord of all. ↓

OPENING PRAYER

Father,
your love for us
surpasses all our hopes and desires.
Forgive our failings,

keep us in your peace
and lead us in the way of salvation.
We ask this . . . for ever and ever. ℟. **Amen.** ↓

ALTERNATIVE OPENING PRAYER

Almighty and eternal God,
Father of the world to come,
your goodness is beyond what our spirit can touch
and your strength is more than the mind can bear.
Lead us to seek beyond our reach
and give us the courage to stand before your truth.
We ask this through Christ our Lord. ℟. **Amen.** ↓

READINGS AND INTERVENIENT CHANTS

The *Weekday* Readings and Intervenient Chants for the
1st to 9th Weeks in Ordinary Time are found on pp. 204-417.

PRAYER OVER THE GIFTS

Father,
receive these gifts
which our Lord Jesus Christ
has asked us to offer in his memory.
May our obedient service
bring us to the fullness of your redemption.
We ask this in the name of Jesus the Lord.
℟. **Amen.**   → No. 21, p. 626 (Pref. P 37-42)

COMMUNION ANT.   Lam 3:25

**The Lord is good to those who hope in him, to those who
are searching for his love.** ↓

OR   See 1 Cor 10:17

**Because there is one bread, we, though many, are one
body, for we all share in the one loaf and in the one
cup.** ↓

PRAYER AFTER COMMUNION

Almighty God,
let the eucharist we share

fill us with your life.
May the love of Christ
which we celebrate here
touch our lives and lead us to you.
We ask this in the name of Jesus the Lord.
℟. **Amen.** ———————————————— → No. 32, p. 660

28th WEEK

Jesus warns us against being overly concerned about the riches of the world, which can blind us to the spiritual wealth of the Father. In our need to overcome spiritual poverty, we must pray for a healthy detachment from material riches and a realization of the true riches of God.

ENTRANCE ANT.   Ps 130:3-4

If you, O Lord, laid bare our guilt, who could endure it?
But you are forgiving, God of Israel.   → No. 2, p. 614

OPENING PRAYER

Lord,
our help and guide,
make your love the foundation of our lives.
May our love for you express itself
in our eagerness to do good for others.
Grant this . . . for ever and ever. ℟. **Amen.** ↓

ALTERNATIVE OPENING PRAYER

Father in heaven,
the hand of your loving kindness
powerfully yet gently guides all the moments of our day.
Go before us in our pilgrimage of life,
anticipate our needs and prevent our falling.
Send your Spirit to unite us in faith,
that sharing in your service,
we may rejoice in your presence.
We ask this through Christ our Lord. ℟. **Amen.** ↓

READINGS AND INTERVENIENT CHANTS

The *Weekday* Readings and Intervenient Chants for the
1st to 9th Weeks in Ordinary Time are found on pp. 204-417.

PRAYER OVER THE GIFTS

Lord,
accept the prayers and gifts
we offer in faith and love.
May this eucharist bring us to your glory.
We ask this in the name of Jesus the Lord.
℟. **Amen.** → No. 21, p. 626 (Pref. P 37-42)

COMMUNION ANT.
Ps 34:11

**The rich suffer want and go hungry, but nothing shall be
lacking to those who fear the Lord.** ↓

OR
1 Jn 3:2

**When the Lord is revealed we shall be like him, for we
shall see him as he is.** ↓

PRAYER AFTER COMMUNION

Almighty Father,
may the body and blood of your Son
give us a share in his life,
for he is Lord for ever and ever.
℟. **Amen.** → No. 32, p. 660

29th WEEK

Carelessness and indifference may dim our vision; indeed, we may be
spiritually blind. Let us pray that we may see Jesus Christ as the true spiritual guide of our lives and that we may see the light of truth in what God
has revealed.

ENTRANCE ANT.
Ps 17:6, 8

**I call upon you, God, for you will answer me; bend your
ear and hear my prayer. Guard me as the pupil of your
eye; hide me in the shade of your wings.** → No. 2, p. 614

OPENING PRAYER

Almighty and ever-living God,
our source of power and inspiration,
give us strength and joy

in serving you as followers of Christ,
who lives and reigns with you and the Holy Spirit,
one God, for ever and ever. ℟. **Amen.** ↓

ALTERNATIVE OPENING PRAYER

Lord our God, Father of all,
you guard us under the shadow of your wings
and search into the depths of our hearts.
Remove the blindness that cannot know you
and relieve the fear that would hide us from your sight.
We ask this through Christ our Lord. ℟. **Amen.** ↓

READINGS AND INTERVENIENT CHANTS

The *Weekday* Readings and Intervenient Chants for the
1st to 9th Weeks in Ordinary Time are found on pp. 204-417.

PRAYER OVER THE GIFTS

Lord God,
may the gifts we offer
bring us your love and forgiveness
and give us freedom to serve you with our lives.
We ask this in the name of Jesus the Lord.
℟. **Amen.**   ➔ No. 21, p. 626 (Pref. P 37-42)

COMMUNION ANT.   Ps 33:18-19

**See how the eyes of the Lord are on those who fear him,
on those who hope in his love, that he may rescue them
from death and feed them in time of famine.** ↓

OR   Mk 10:45

**The Son of Man came to give his life as a ransom for
many.** ↓

PRAYER AFTER COMMUNION

Lord,
may this eucharist help us to remain faithful.
May it teach us the way to eternal life.
Grant this through Christ our Lord.
℟. **Amen.** _____ ➔ No. 32, p. 660

30th WEEK

The reign of God does not begin at the moment of our death. Rather it begins in each of us at our baptism and continues to grow and flourish throughout our entire life. Let us celebrate and rejoice in the great riches we have as God's people through Christ.

ENTRANCE ANT.   Ps 105:3-4

Let hearts rejoice who search for the Lord. Seek the Lord and his strength, seek always the face of the Lord.

→ No. 2, p. 614

OPENING PRAYER

Almighty and ever-living God,
strengthen our faith, hope, and love.
May we do with loving hearts
what you ask of us
and come to share the life you promise.
We ask this . . . for ever and ever. R̸. **Amen.** ↓

ALTERNATIVE OPENING PRAYER

Praised be you, God and Father of our Lord Jesus Christ.
There is no power for good
which does not come from your covenant,
and no promise to hope in,
that your love has not offered.
Strengthen our faith to accept your covenant
and give us the love to carry out your command.
We ask this through Christ our Lord. R̸. **Amen.** ↓

READINGS AND INTERVENIENT CHANTS

The *Weekday* Readings and Intervenient Chants for the 1st to 9th Weeks in Ordinary Time are found on pp. 204-417.

PRAYER OVER THE GIFTS

Lord God of power and might,
receive the gifts we offer
and let our service give you glory.
Grant this through Christ our Lord.
R̸. **Amen.**   → No. 21, p. 626 (Pref. P 37-42)

COMMUNION ANT.   Ps 20:6

We will rejoice at the victory of God and make our boast in his great name. ↓

OR   Eph 5:2

Christ loved us and gave himself up for us as a fragrant offering to God. ↓

PRAYER AFTER COMMUNION

Lord,
bring to perfection within us
the communion we share in this sacrament.
May our celebration have an effect in our lives.
We ask this in the name of Jesus the Lord
℟. **Amen.**   → No. 32, p. 660

31st WEEK

The Church is the sacrament of Christ's presence in the world. The people of God constitute the Church, and to the extent that we follow Christ's teachings and have an effect on the world, Christ will be present in the world. Let us thank the Lord for his continued presence and love.

ENTRANCE ANT.   Ps 38:22-23

Do not abandon me, Lord. My God, do not go away from me! Hurry to help me, Lord, my Savior.   → No. 2, p. 614

OPENING PRAYER

God of power and mercy,
only with your help
can we offer you fitting service and praise.
May we live the faith we profess
and trust your promise of eternal life.
Grant this . . . for ever and ever. ℟. **Amen.** ↓

ALTERNATIVE OPENING PRAYER

Father in heaven, God of power and Lord of mercy,
from whose fullness we have received,
direct our steps in our everyday efforts.
May the changing moods of the human heart

and the limits which our failings impose on hope
never blind us to you, source of every good.
Faith gives us the promise of peace
and makes known the demands of love.
Remove the selfishness that blurs the vision of faith.
Grant this through Christ our Lord. ℟. **Amen.** ↓

READINGS AND INTERVENIENT CHANTS

The *Weekday* Readings and Intervenient Chants for the
1st to 9th Weeks in Ordinary Time are found on pp. 204-417.

PRAYER OVER THE GIFTS

God of mercy,
may we offer a pure sacrifice
for the forgiveness of our sins.
We ask this through Christ our Lord.
℟. **Amen.**   → No. 21, p. 626 (Pref. P 37-42)

COMMUNION ANT.   Ps 16:11

**Lord, you will show me the path of life and fill me with
joy in your presence.** ↓

OR   Jn 6:58

**As the living Father sent me, and I live because of the
Father, so he who eats my flesh and drinks my blood will
live because of me.** ↓

PRAYER AFTER COMMUNION

Lord,
you give us new hope in this eucharist.
May the power of your love
continue its saving work among us
and bring us to the joy you promise.
We ask this in the name of Jesus the Lord.
℟. **Amen.**   → No. 32, p. 660

32nd WEEK

Jesus inspired the people of his day because his authority was from a
source beyond this world, and the people were in awe as the Spirit worked

in him. So, too, for us. We should be in awe as we look about us at all God's creation, at all that has been given to us.

ENTRANCE ANT. Ps 88:3

Let my prayer come before you, Lord; listen, and answer me. → No. 2, p. 614

OPENING PRAYER

God of power and mercy,
protect us from all harm.
Give us freedom of spirit
and health in mind and body
to do your work on earth.
We ask this . . . for ever and ever. ℟. **Amen.** ↓

ALTERNATIVE OPENING PRAYER

Almighty Father,
strong is your justice and great is your mercy.
Protect us in the burdens and challenges of life.
Shield our minds from the distortion of pride
and enfold our desire with the beauty of truth.
Help us to become more aware of your loving design
so that we may more willingly give our lives in service to all.
We ask this through Christ our Lord. ℟. **Amen.** ↓

READINGS AND INTERVENIENT CHANTS

The *Weekday* Readings and Intervenient Chants for the 1st to 9th Weeks in Ordinary Time are found on pp 204-417.

PRAYER OVER THE GIFTS

God of mercy,
in this eucharist we proclaim the death of the Lord.
Accept the gifts we present
and help us follow him with love,
for he is Lord for ever and ever.
℟. **Amen.** → No. 21, p. 626 (Pref. P 37-42)

COMMUNION ANT. Ps 23:1-2

The Lord is my shepherd; there is nothing I shall want. In green pastures he gives me rest, he leads me beside the waters of peace. ↓

OR Lk 24:35

The disciples recognized the Lord Jesus in the breaking of bread. ↓

PRAYER AFTER COMMUNION

Lord,
we thank you for the nourishment you give us
through your holy gift.
Pour out your Spirit upon us
and in the strength of this food from heaven
keep us single-minded in your service.
We ask this in the name of Jesus the Lord.
℞. **Amen.** _____ → No. 32, p. 660

33rd WEEK

Faith is our instrument of peace, and if it is sincere and good, we do not need miracles to keep it alive. We know that God is with us always, in times of trouble as well as in times of joy. Look about you and believe!

ENTRANCE ANT. Jer 29:11, 12, 14

The Lord says: my plans for you are peace and not disaster; when you call to me, I will listen to you, and I will bring you back to the place from which I exiled you.

→ No. 2, p. 614

OPENING PRAYER

Father of all that is good,
keep us faithful in serving you
for to serve you is our lasting joy.
We ask this . . . for ever and ever. ℞. **Amen.** ↓

ALTERNATIVE OPENING PRAYER

Father in heaven,
ever-living source of all that is good,
from the beginning of time you promised man salvation

through the future coming of your Son, our Lord Jesus
   Christ.
Help us to drink of his truth
and expand our hearts with the joy of his promises,
so that we may serve you in faith and in love
and know for ever the joy of your presence.
We ask this through Christ our Lord. ℟. **Amen.** ↓

READINGS AND INTERVENIENT CHANTS

The *Weekday* Readings and Intervenient Chants for the
1st to 9th Weeks In Ordinary Time are found on pp. 204-417.

PRAYER OVER THE GIFTS

Lord God,
may the gifts we offer
increase our love for you
and bring us to eternal life.
We ask this in the name of Jesus the Lord.
℟. **Amen.**   → No. 21, p. 626 (Pref. P 37-42)

COMMUNION ANT   Ps 72:28

**It is good for me to be with the Lord and to put my hope
in him.** ↓

OR   Mk 11:23, 24

**I tell you solemnly, whatever you ask for in prayer,
believe that you have received it, and it will be yours,
says the Lord.** ↓

PRAYER AFTER COMMUNION

Father,
may we grow in love
by the eucharist we have celebrated
in memory of the Lord Jesus,
who is Lord for ever and ever.
℟. **Amen.**   _____   → No. 32, p. 660

34th WEEK

The Lord speaks of peace to his people. This gives us a note of serenity and
confidence in the midst of our troubles on earth. We are carried along by this
word of the Lord and by the fact that he is with us till the end of the world.

ENTRANCE ANT.
Ps 85:9

The Lord speaks of peace to his holy people, to those who turn to him with all their heart. → No. 2, p. 614

OPENING PRAYER

Lord,
increase our eagerness to do your will
and help us to know the saving power of your love.
Grant this . . . for ever and ever. ℟. **Amen.** ↓

READINGS AND INTERVENIENT CHANTS

The *Weekday* Readings and Intervenient Chants for the 1st to 9th Weeks in Ordinary Time are found on pp. 204-417.

PRAYER OVER THE GIFTS

God of love,
may the sacrifice we offer
in obedience to your command
renew our resolution to be faithful to your word.
We ask this through Christ our Lord.
℟. **Amen.** → No. 21, p. 626 (Pref. P 37-42)

COMMUNION ANT.
Ps 117:1-2

All you nations, praise the Lord, for steadfast is his kindly mercy to us. ↓

OR
Mt 28:20

I, the Lord, am with you always, until the end of the world. ↓

PRAYER AFTER COMMUNION

Almighty God,
in this eucharist
you give us the joy of sharing your life.
Keep us in your presence.
Let us never be separated from you.
We ask this in the name of Jesus the Lord.
℟. **Amen.** → No. 32, p. 660

READINGS AND INTERVENIENT CHANTS FOR ORDINARY TIME

INTRODUCTION FOR 1st TO 4th WEEK

The Letter to the Hebrews—*Written to a community of Christians afflicted with trials and in danger of lapsing into Judaizing practices, this Letter describes most eloquently the eminent superiority of the new dispensation over the old. Inaugurated by the Son of God himself, this new dispensation was God's final revelation to humanity. It completed the message of the Prophets, and brought to perfection all that was of permanent value in the Mosaic covenant. The incarnate Son of God was its High Priest, and his glorious sacrifice was truly efficacious before God in the forgiveness of sin. As suffering and humiliation had an important place in his victory, his followers are exhorted to forego worldly advantage, to bear their trials patiently, and to persevere heroically in the faith.*

The Books of Samuel—*This single work comprises the history of about a century, describing the close of the age of the Judges and the beginnings of monarchy in Israel. By a series of episodes centered around the persons of Samuel, Saul, and David, the writer shows us the conditions and the problems of God's Kingdom on earth. The most important spiritual values imparted are to be found in the work's relation to the Messianic kingdom of Christ. Though David's earthly kingdom crumbled after his death, his greater achievement survived: the foundation of a spiritual Kingdom that would never pass. The people of Israel, freed from their enemies, symbolize the Christian people delivered from spiritual foes.*

The Books of Kings—*In conjunction with the Books of Samuel, these two books, which are originally one work, extend the consecutive history of Israel from the birth of Samuel to the destruction of Jerusalem in 587*

B.C. The purpose of this latter work is to show that the happiness of the Chosen People was intimately associated with the observance of God's law. Hence, the author bitterly denounces the sins of the kings and people. The cardinal sin of the Kingdom of Israel was idolatry, while that of the Kingdom of Judah was the worship of either Yahweh on high places or false deities. The unified worship at the central sanctuary is stressed.

The Gospel of Mark—*Written at Rome about 70 A.D. by Mark, a companion of St. Paul and later a coworker of St. Peter, this Gospel is short, vivid, concrete, and gives the impression of immediate contact with Jesus. It makes use of a familiar style that is occasionally awkward but always direct, and might almost be called photographic in its handling of details. Mark desires to establish a close bond between the Passion of Jesus and his Lordship, showing that the Son of Man had to endure the Cross before attaining his glory and that his destiny is that of the Suffering Servant prophesied by Isaiah (ch. 53). It is also his design to teach us that if we want to encounter the living Christ, we must follow his Way. We will deserve the name of his disciple only if we accept the same destiny as the Master.*

MONDAY OF THE FIRST WEEK IN ORDINARY TIME

─────── YEAR I ───────

FIRST READING   Heb 1:1-6

Jesus is the Son of God. Jesus took upon himself our human nature so that as both God and man he could offer himself as a redemption. Hebrews stresses the uniqueness of Jesus' role, even far superior to that of the angels.

A reading from the beginning of the Letter to the Hebrews

BROTHERS and sisters: In times past, God spoke in partial and various ways to our ancestors through the prophets; in these last days, he spoke to us through the Son, whom he made heir of all things and through whom he created the universe,

who is the refulgence of his glory,
the very imprint of his being,
and who sustains all things by his mighty word.
When he had accomplished purification from sins,
he took his seat at the right hand of the Majesty
on high,
as far superior to the angels
as the name he has inherited is more excellent
than theirs.

For to which of the angels did God ever say:

You are my Son; this day I have begotten you?

Or again:

I will be a father to him, and he shall be a Son to
me?

And again, when he leads the first born into the world, he says:

Let all the angels of God worship him.

The word of the Lord. ℟. **Thanks be to God.** ↓

RESPONSORIAL PSALM   Ps 97:1 and 2b, 6 and 7c, 9

℟. (see 7c) **Let all his angels worship him.**

The LORD is king; let the earth rejoice;
  let the many isles be glad.
    Justice and judgment are the foundation of his
      throne.—℟.

The heavens proclaim his justice,
  and all peoples see his glory.
Let all his angels worship him.—℟.

Because you, O LORD, are the Most High over all the
  earth,
    exalted far above all gods.—℟. ↓

——————— **YEAR II** ———————

FIRST READING   1 Sm 1:1-8

Samuel's identity is established in terms of people and places. The custom of an annual visit to the sanctuary may be taken as a favorable comment on the piety of Elkanah and his family. The climax of the pilgrimage comes with the sacrificial meal, the mood of which is one of gaiety and joy in God.

A reading from the beginning of the first Book of
Samuel

THERE was a certain man from Ramathaim, Elkanah by name, a Zuphite from the hill country of Ephraim. He was the son of Jeroham, son of Elihu, son of Tohu, son of Zuph, an Ephraimite. He had two wives, one named Hannah, the other Peninnah; Peninnah had children, but Hannah was childless. This man regularly went on pilgrimage from his city to worship the LORD of hosts and to sacrifice to him at Shiloh, where the two sons of Eli, Hophni and Phinehas, were ministering as priests of the LORD. When the day came for Elkanah to offer sacrifice, he used to give a portion each to his wife Peninnah and to all her sons and daughters, but a double portion to Hannah because he loved her, though the LORD had made her barren. Her rival, to upset her, turned it into a constant reproach to her that the LORD had left her barren. This went on year after year; each time they made their pilgrimage to the sanctuary of the LORD, Peninnah would approach her, and Hannah would weep and refuse to eat. Her husband Elkanah used to ask her: "Hannah, why do you weep, and why do you refuse to eat? Why do you grieve? Am I not more to you than ten sons?"—The word of the Lord. ℟. **Thanks be to God.** ↓

RESPONSORIAL PSALM   Ps 116:12-13, 14-17, 18-19

℟. (17a) **To you, Lord, I will offer a sacrifice of praise.**

℟. Or: **Alleluia.**

How shall I make a return to the LORD
　　for all the good he has done for me?
The cup of salvation I will take up,
　　and I will call upon the name of the LORD.—℟.

My vows to the LORD I will pay
　　in the presence of all his people.
Precious in the eyes of the LORD
　　is the death of his faithful ones.
O LORD, I am your servant;
　　I am your servant, the son of your handmaid;
　　you have loosed my bonds.—℟.

My vows to the LORD I will pay
　　in the presence of all his people,
In the courts of the house of the LORD,
　　in your midst, O Jerusalem.—℟. ↓

――――― **YEAR I AND II** ―――――

ALLELUIA   Mk 1:15

℟. **Alleluia, alleluia.**
The Kingdom of God is at hand;
repent and believe in the Gospel.
℟. **Alleluia, alleluia.** ↓

GOSPEL   Mk 1:14-20

Mark fixes the arrest of John as the decisive moment for the beginning of the ministry of our Lord. The way had been prepared by John. Christ himself called his message the "good news" (Is 61:1). Christ bids his disciples to leave everything and follow him.

℣. The Lord be with you. ℟. **And also with you.**
℣. A reading from the holy Gospel according to Mark.
℟. **Glory to you, Lord.**

A FTER John had been arrested, Jesus came to Galilee proclaiming the Gospel of God: "This is the time of fulfillment. The Kingdom of God is at hand. Repent, and believe in the Gospel."

As he passed by the Sea of Galilee, he saw Simon and his brother Andrew casting their nets into the sea; they were fishermen. Jesus said to them, "Come after me, and I will make you fishers of men." Then they left their nets and followed him. He walked along a little farther and saw James, the son of Zebedee, and his brother John. They too were in a boat mending their nets. Then he called them. So they left their father Zebedee in the boat along with the hired men and followed him.—The Gospel of the Lord. ℟. **Praise to you, Lord Jesus Christ.**

→ No. 15, p. 623

TUESDAY OF THE FIRST WEEK
IN ORDINARY TIME

——— **YEAR I** ———

FIRST READING   Heb 2:5-12

The world has been made subject to the glorified Son as the climax of an ascending movement that began in the humiliation of Christ's earthly life, suffering, and death. Here the sacred writer regards all things as already subject to Christ in virtue of his exaltation. The designation of our Lord as leader announces the journey of the people of God to the place of rest, the heavenly sanctuary, in the footsteps of our Lord, their forerunner.

A reading from the Letter to the Hebrews

IT was not to angels that God subjected the world to come, of which we are speaking. Instead, someone has testified somewhere:
> *What is man that you are mindful of him,*
>> *or the son of man that you care for him?*
> *You made him for a little while lower than the angels;*
>> *you crowned him with glory and honor,*
>>> *subjecting all things under his feet.*

In "subjecting" all things to him, he left nothing not "subject to him." Yet at present we do not see "all things subject to him," but we do see Jesus "crowned with glory and honor" because he suffered death, he who "for a little while" was made "lower than the angels," that by the grace of God he might taste death for everyone.

For it was fitting that he, for whom and through whom all things exist, in bringing many children to glory, should make the leader to their salvation perfect through suffering. He who consecrates and those who are being consecrated all have one origin. Therefore, he is not ashamed to call them "brothers" saying:
> *I will proclaim your name to my brethren,*
> *in the midst of the assembly I will praise you.*

The word of the Lord. ℟. **Thanks be to God.** ↓

RESPONSORIAL PSALM   Ps 8:2b and 5, 6-7, 8-9

℟. (see 7) **You have given your Son rule over the works of your hands.**

O LORD, our Lord,
> how glorious is your name over all the earth!
What is man that you should be mindful of him,
> or the son of man that you should care for him?—℟.

You have made him little less than the angels,
> and crowned him with glory and honor.
You have given him rule over the works of your hands,
> putting all things under his feet.—℟.

All sheep and oxen,
    yes, and the beasts of the field,
The birds of the air, the fishes of the sea,
    and whatever swims the paths of the seas.—℟. ↓

———— **YEAR II** ————

FIRST READING   1 Sm 1:9-20

Only the birth of a son will console Hannah. She has vowed that if she has a son, she will dedicate him to Yahweh. Her prayers are answered. Hannah names her son Samuel. The name is entirely fitting for one who bears a special mission from God.

A reading from the first Book of Samuel

HANNAH rose after a meal at Shiloh, and presented herself before the LORD; at the time, Eli the priest was sitting on a chair near the doorpost of the LORD's temple. In her bitterness she prayed to the LORD, weeping copiously, and she made a vow, promising: "O LORD of hosts, if you look with pity on the misery of your handmaid, if you remember me and do not forget me, if you give your handmaid a male child, I will give him to the LORD for as long as he lives; neither wine nor liquor shall he drink, and no razor shall ever touch his head." As she remained long at prayer before the LORD, Eli watched her mouth, for Hannah was praying silently; though her lips were moving, her voice could not be heard. Eli, thinking her drunk, said to her, "How long will you make a drunken show of yourself? Sober up from your wine!" "It isn't that, my lord," Hannah answered. "I am an unhappy woman. I have had neither wine nor liquor; I was only pouring out my troubles to the LORD. Do not think your handmaid a ne'er-do-well; my prayer has been prompted by my deep sorrow and misery." Eli said, "Go in peace, and may the God of Israel grant you what you have asked of him." She replied, "Think kindly of your maidservant," and left. She went to her quarters, ate and drank with her husband, and no longer appeared downcast. Early the next morning they worshiped before the LORD, and then returned to their home in Ramah.

When Elkanah had relations with his wife Hannah, the LORD remembered her. She conceived, and at the end of her term bore a son whom she called Samuel, since she had asked the LORD for him.—The word of the Lord.
℟. **Thanks be to God.** ↓

RESPONSORIAL PSALM   1 Sm 2:1, 4-5, 6-7, 8abcd

℟. (see 1) **My heart exults in the Lord, my Savior.**

"My heart exults in the LORD,
    my horn is exalted in my God.
I have swallowed up my enemies;
    I rejoice in my victory."—℟.

"The bows of the mighty are broken,
    while the tottering gird on strength.
The well-fed hire themselves out for bread,
    while the hungry batten on spoil.
The barren wife bears seven sons,
    while the mother of many languishes."—℟.

"The LORD puts to death and gives life;
    he casts down to the nether world;
    he raises up again.
The LORD makes poor and makes rich;
    he humbles, he also exalts."—℟.

"He raises the needy from the dust;
    from the dung heap he lifts up the poor,
To seat them with nobles
    and make a glorious throne their heritage."—℟. ↓

———— **YEAR I AND II** ————

ALLELUIA   See 1 Thes 2:13

℟. **Alleluia, alleluia.**
Receive the word of God, not as the word of men,
but as it truly is, the word of God.
℟. **Alleluia, alleluia.** ↓

GOSPEL   Mk 1:21-28

The teaching and healing by our Lord in Capernaum illustrate his authority in word and act. Christ's teaching is connected with his miraculous power, and it causes amazement. His mighty words are immediately followed by a cluster of miracles, signs even more wondrous than the discourse to which they bore witness.

℣. The Lord be with you. ℟. **And also with you.**
℣. A reading from the holy Gospel according to Mark.
℟. **Glory to you, Lord.**

JESUS came to Capernaum with his followers, and on the sabbath he entered the synagogue and taught. The people were astonished at his teaching, for he taught them as one having authority and not as the scribes. In their synagogue was a man with an unclean spirit; he cried out, "What have you to do with us, Jesus of Nazareth? Have you come to destroy us? I know who you are—the Holy One of God!" Jesus rebuked him and said, "Quiet! Come out of him!" The unclean spirit convulsed him and with a loud cry came out of him. All were amazed and asked one another, "What is this? A new teaching with authority. He commands even the unclean spirits and they obey him." His fame spread everywhere throughout the whole region of Galilee.— The Gospel of the Lord. ℟. **Praise to you, Lord Jesus Christ.**   ➞ No. 15, p. 623

WEDNESDAY OF THE FIRST WEEK
IN ORDINARY TIME

——— **YEAR I** ———

FIRST READING   Heb 2:14-18

In the biblical sense, "Flesh" means human nature considered in its weakness and frailty, and as such it is contrasted with "spirit" and God. Because of the connection between sin and death, the power of death was broken when Christ removed sin. Because of Jesus, the nature of death was changed.

A reading from the Letter to the Hebrews

SINCE the children share in blood and Flesh, Jesus likewise shared in them, that through death he might destroy the one who has the power of death, that is, the Devil, and free those who through fear of death had been subject to slavery all their life. Surely he did not help angels but rather the descendants of Abraham; therefore, he had to become like his brothers and sisters in every way, that he might be a merciful and faithful high priest before God to expiate the sins of the people. Because he himself was tested through what he suffered, he is able to help those who are being tested.—The word of the Lord. ℟. **Thanks be to God.** ↓

RESPONSORIAL PSALM   Ps 105:1-2, 3-4, 6-7, 8-9

℟. (8a) **The Lord remembers his covenant for ever.**

℟. Or: **Alleluia.**

Give thanks to the LORD, invoke his name;
  make known among the nations his deeds.
Sing to him, sing his praise,
  proclaim all his wondrous deeds.—℟.

Glory in his holy name;
  rejoice, O hearts that seek the LORD!
Look to the LORD in his strength;
  seek to serve him constantly.—℟.

You descendants of Abraham, his servants,
  sons of Jacob, his chosen ones!
He, the LORD, is our God;
  throughout the earth his judgments prevail.—℟.

He remembers forever his covenant
  which he made binding for a thousand generations—
Which he entered into with Abraham
  and by his oath to Isaac.—℟. ↓

——— **YEAR II** ———

FIRST READING   1 Sm 3:1-10, 19-20

In Israel the revelation of the Word of God was rare or precious, but the mention of it enhances the significance of the revelation to the young Samuel. He is recognized as a prophet throughout Israel and is represented here as the ruler of all Israel.

A reading from the first Book of Samuel

DURING the time young Samuel was minister to the LORD under Eli, a revelation of the LORD was uncommon and vision infrequent. One day Eli was asleep in his usual place. His eyes had lately grown so weak that he could not see. The lamp of God was not yet extinguished, and Samuel was sleeping in the temple of the LORD where the ark of God was. The LORD called to Samuel, who answered, "Here I am."

Samuel ran to Eli and said, "Here I am. You called me." "I did not call you," Eli said. "Go back to sleep." So he went back to sleep. Again the LORD called Samuel, who rose and went to Eli. "Here I am," he said. "You called me." But Eli answered, "I did not call you, my son. Go back to sleep." At that time Samuel was not familiar with the LORD, because the LORD had not revealed anything to him as yet. The LORD called Samuel again, for the third time. Getting up and going to Eli, he said, "Here I am. You called me." Then Eli understood that the LORD was calling the youth. So Eli said to Samuel, "Go to sleep, and if you are called, reply, 'Speak, LORD, for your servant is listening.'" When Samuel went to sleep in his place, the LORD came and revealed his presence, calling out as before, "Samuel, Samuel!" Samuel answered, "Speak, for your servant is listening."

Samuel grew up, and the LORD was with him, not permitting any word of his to be without effect. Thus all Israel from Dan to Beersheba came to know that Samuel was an accredited prophet of the LORD. —The word of the Lord. ℟. **Thanks be to God.** ↓

RESPONSORIAL PSALM   Ps 40:2 and 5, 7-8a, 8b-9, 10

℟. (8a and 9a) **Here am I, Lord; I come to do your will.**

I have waited, waited for the LORD,
    and he stooped toward me and heard my cry.
Blessed the man who makes the LORD his trust;
    who turns not to idolatry
    or to those who stray after falsehood.—℟.

Sacrifice or oblation you wished not,
    but ears open to obedience you gave me.
Burnt offerings or sin-offerings you sought not;
    then said I, "Behold I come."—℟.

"In the written scroll it is prescribed for me.
To do your will, O my God, is my delight,
    and your law is within my heart!"—℟.

I announced your justice in the vast assembly;
    I did not restrain my lips, as you, O LORD, know.—℟. ↓

———————— **YEAR I AND II** ————————

ALLELUIA   Jn 10:27

℟. **Alleluia, alleluia.**
My sheep hear my voice, says the Lord.
I know them, and they follow me.
℟. **Alleluia, alleluia.** ↓

GOSPEL   Mk 1:29-39

Jesus cures Simon's mother-in-law. When the sun has set, the crowds
bring their sick to the Great Physician to be healed. Jesus enjoins silence
because he does not seek the reputation of a wonder-worker. His own concept of Messiah is vastly different from that of his contemporaries.

℣. The Lord be with you. ℟. **And also with you.**
℣. A reading from the holy Gospel according to Mark.
℟. **Glory to you, Lord.**

O N leaving the synagogue Jesus entered the house of
    Simon and Andrew with James and John. Simon's
mother-in-law lay sick with a fever. They immediately

told him about her. He approached, grasped her hand, and helped her up. Then the fever left her and she waited on them.

When it was evening, after sunset, they brought to him all who were ill or possessed by demons. The whole town was gathered at the door. He cured many who were sick with various diseases, and he drove out many demons, not permitting them to speak because they knew him.

Rising very early before dawn, he left and went off to a deserted place, where he prayed. Simon and those who were with him pursued him and on finding him said, "Everyone is looking for you." He told them, "Let us go on to the nearby villages that I may preach there also. For this purpose have I come." So he went into their synagogues, preaching and driving out demons throughout the whole of Galilee.—The Gospel of the Lord. ℟. **Praise to you, Lord Jesus Christ.**   ➤ No. 15, p. 623

THURSDAY OF THE FIRST WEEK IN ORDINARY TIME

—————— YEAR I ——————

FIRST READING   Heb 3:7-14

God speaks to his people who should always be open to the voice of the Holy Spirit. The followers of Jesus are to support and encourage one another since all are partners in Christ.

A reading from the Letter to the Hebrews

THE Holy Spirit says:
Oh, that today you would hear his voice,
  "Harden not your hearts as at the rebellion
    in the day of testing in the desert,
  where your ancestors tested and tried me
    and saw my works for forty years.

> *Because of this I was provoked with that generation*
>   *and I said, 'They have always been of erring heart,*
>   *and they do not know my ways.'*
> *As I swore in my wrath,*
>   *'They shall not enter into my rest.'"*

Take care, brothers and sisters, that none of you may have an evil and unfaithful heart, so as to forsake the living God. Encourage yourselves daily while it is still "today," so that none of you may grow hardened by the deceit of sin. We have become partners of Christ if only we hold the beginning of the reality 他m until the end.— The word of the Lord. ℟. **Thanks be to God.** ↓

RESPONSORIAL PSALM   Ps 95:6-7c, 8-9, 10-11

℟. (8) **If today you hear his voice, harden not your hearts.**

Come, let us bow down in worship;
    let us kneel before the LORD who made us.
For he is our God,
    and we are the people he shepherds, the flock he
    guides.—℟.

Oh, that today you would hear his voice:
    "Harden not your hearts as at Meribah,
    as in the day of Massah in the desert,
Where your fathers tempted me;
    they tested me though they had seen my works."—℟.

Forty years I was wearied of that generation;
    I said: "This people's heart goes astray,
    they do not know my ways."
Therefore I swore in my anger:
    "They shall never enter my rest."—℟. ↓

YEAR II

FIRST READING   1 Sm 4:1-11

The Israelites are utterly defeated, the Ark is captured, and Eli's two sons are killed. The Elders had felt that the presence of the Ark among the troops would boost their morale. It was not commonly carried to the front lines of battle.

A reading form the first Book of Samuel

THE Philistines gathered for an attack on Israel. Israel went out to engage them in battle and camped at Ebenezer, while the Philistines camped at Aphek. The Philistines then drew up in battle formation against Israel. After a fierce struggle Israel was defeated by the Philistines, who slew about four thousand men on the battlefield. When the troops retired to the camp, the elders of Israel said, "Why has the LORD permitted us to be defeated today by the Philistines? Let us fetch the ark of the LORD from Shiloh that it may go into battle among us and save us from the grasp of our enemies."

So the people sent to Shiloh and brought from there the ark of the LORD of hosts, who is enthroned upon the cherubim. The two sons of Eli, Hophni and Phinehas, were with the ark of God. When the ark of the LORD arrived in the camp, all Israel shouted so loudly that the earth resounded. The Philistines, hearing the noise of shouting, asked, "What can this loud shouting in the camp of the Hebrews mean?" On learning that the ark of the LORD had come into the camp, the Philistines were frightened. They said, "Gods have come to their camp." They said also, "Woe to us! This has never happened before. Woe to us! Who can deliver us from the power of these mighty gods? These are the gods that struck the Egyptians with various plagues and with pestilence. Take courage and be manly, Philistines; otherwise you will become slaves to the Hebrews, as they were your slaves. So fight manfully!" The Philistines fought and Israel was defeated; every man fled to his own tent. It was a disastrous defeat, in which Israel lost thirty thousand foot soldiers. The ark of God was captured, and Eli's two sons, Hophni and Phinehas, were among the dead.—The word of the Lord. ℟. **Thanks be to God.** ↓

RESPONSORIAL PSALM   Ps 44:10-11, 14-15, 24-25

℟. (27b) **Redeem us, Lord, because of your mercy.**

Yet now you have cast us off and put us in disgrace,
    and you go not forth with our armies.
You have let us be driven back by our foes;
    those who hated us plundered us at will.—℟.

You made us the reproach of our neighbors,
    the mockery and the scorn of those around us.
You made us a byword among the nations,
    a laughingstock among the peoples.—℟.

Why do you hide your face,
    forgetting our woe and our oppression?
For our souls are bowed down to the dust,
    our bodies are pressed to the earth.—℟. ↓

——— **YEAR I AND II** ———

ALLELUIA   See Mt 4:23

℟. **Alleluia, alleluia.**
Jesus preached the Gospel of the Kingdom
and cured every disease among the people.
℟. **Alleluia, alleluia.** ↓

GOSPEL   Mk 1:40-45

The miracle of the leper's cure illustrates our Lord's power to save those
who had been excluded from Israel by the Mosaic law. Christ puts forth
his hand and touches the leper. The speech of the leper implies a prayer.
It is a touching profession of perfect faith and a humble "Thy will be
done."

℣. The Lord be with you. ℟. **And also with you.**
℣. A reading from the holy Gospel according to Mark.
℟. **Glory to you, Lord.**

A LEPER came to him and kneeling down begged him
and said, "If you wish, you can make me clean."
Moved with pity, he stretched out his hand, touched the
leper, and said to him, "I do will it. Be made clean." The

leprosy left him immediately, and he was made clean. Then, warning him sternly, he dismissed him at once. Then he said to him, "See that you tell no one anything, but go, show yourself to the priest and offer for your cleansing what Moses prescribed; that will be proof for them." The man went away and began to publicize the whole matter. He spread the report abroad so that it was impossible for Jesus to enter a town openly. He remained outside in deserted places, and people kept coming to him from everywhere.—The Gospel of the Lord. ℟.
Praise to you, Lord Jesus Christ.   → No. 15, p. 623

FRIDAY OF THE FIRST WEEK IN ORDINARY TIME

———— YEAR I ————

FIRST READING   Heb 4:1-5, 11

Hebrews uses New Testament terminology to describe entering heaven. Those who are faithful will enter God's abode, described as a place of rest, rather than as the heavenly sanctuary or the lasting city. There is no thought of hurrying into the rest, but rather of persevering in the effort needed to achieve it.

A reading from the Letter to the Hebrews

LET us be on our guard while the promise of entering into his rest remains, that none of you seem to have failed. For in fact we have received the Good News just as our ancestors did. But the word that they heard did not profit them, for they were not united in faith with those who listened. For we who believed enter into that rest, just as he has said:

As I swore in my wrath,
"They shall not enter into my rest,"

and yet his works were accomplished at the foundation of the world. For he has spoken somewhere about the seventh day in this manner, *And God rested on the seventh day from all his works;* and again, in the previously mentioned place, *They shall not enter into my rest.*

Therefore, let us strive to enter into that rest, so that no one may fall after the same example of disobedience.—The word of the Lord. ℟. **Thanks be to God.** ↓

RESPONSORIAL PSALM   Ps 78:3 and 4bc, 6c-7, 8

℟. (see 7b) **Do not forget the works of the Lord!**

What we have heard and know,
   and what our fathers have declared to us,
   we will declare to the generation to come:
The glorious deeds of the LORD and his strength.—℟.

That they too may rise and declare to their sons
   that they should put their hope in God,
And not forget the deeds of God
   but keep his commands.—℟.

And not be like their fathers,
   a generation wayward and rebellious,
A generation that kept not its heart steadfast
   nor its spirit faithful toward God.—℟. ↓

——————— YEAR II ———————

FIRST READING   1 Sm 8:4-7, 10-22a

Samuel's sons, not of the same caliber as their father, request a king (which amounts to rejecting Yahweh himself). Yahweh grants permission for the appointment of a king in response to the people's request. An unfavorable attitude to kingship is described.

A reading from the first Book of Samuel

ALL the elders of Israel came in a body to Samuel at Ramah and said to him, "Now that you are old, and your sons do not follow your example, appoint a king over us, as other nations have, to judge us."

Samuel was displeased when they asked for a king to judge them. He prayed to the LORD, however, who said in answer: "Grant the people's every request. It is not you they reject, they are rejecting me as their king."

Samuel delivered the message of the LORD in full to those who were asking him for a king. He told them:"The rights of the king who will rule you will be as follows: He will take your sons and assign them to his chariots and horses, and they will run before his chariot. He will also appoint from among them his commanders of groups of a thousand and of a hundred soldiers. He will set them to do his plowing and his harvesting, and to make his implements of war and the equipment of his chariots. He will use your daughters as ointment makers, as cooks, and as bakers. He will take the best of your fields, vineyards, and olive groves, and give them to his officials. He will tithe your crops and your vineyards, and give the revenue to his eunuchs and his slaves. He will take your male and female servants, as well as your best oxen and your asses, and use them to do his work. He will tithe your flocks and you yourselves will become his slaves. When this takes place, you will complain against the king whom you have chosen, but on that day the LORD will not answer you."

The people, however, refused to listen to Samuel's warning and said,"Not so! There must be a king over us. We too must be like other nations, with a king to rule us and to lead us in warfare and fight our battles." When Samuel had listened to all the people had to say, he repeated it to the LORD, who then said to him,"Grant their request and appoint a king to rule them."—The word of the Lord. ℟. **Thanks be to God.** ↓

RESPONSORIAL PSALM   Ps 89:16-17, 18-19

℟. (2) **For ever I will sing the goodness of the Lord.**

Blessed the people who know the joyful shout;
    in the light of your countenance, O LORD, they walk.
At your name they rejoice all the day,
    and through your justice they are exalted.—℟.

For you are the splendor of their strength,
    and by your favor our horn is exalted.

For to the LORD belongs our shield,
and to the Holy One of Israel, our King.—R̹. ↓

——————— **YEAR I AND II** ———————

ALLELUIA   Lk 7:16

R̹. **Alleluia, alleluia.**
A great prophet has arisen in our midst
and God has visited his people.
R̹. **Alleluia, alleluia.** ↓

GOSPEL   Mk 2:1-12

Disease does, in a most convincing manner, set forth the nature of sin.
Disorders of the body aptly represent the disorders of the soul. An almost
insurmountable barrier is overcome because of the earnest desire to bring
the man sick with palsy to Jesus. Jesus says, "Your sins are forgiven you."

V̹. The Lord be with you. R̹. **And also with you.**
V̹. A reading from the holy Gospel according to Mark.
R̹. **Glory to you, Lord.**

WHEN Jesus returned to Capernaum after some days,
it became known that he was at home. Many gathered together so that there was no longer room for them,
not even around the door, and he preached the word to
them. They came bringing to him a paralytic carried by
four men. Unable to get near Jesus because of the crowd,
they opened up the roof above him. After they had broken
through, they let down the mat on which the paralytic was
lying. When Jesus saw their faith, he said to him, "Child,
your sins are forgiven." Now some of the scribes were sitting there asking themselves, "Why does this man speak
that way? He is blaspheming. Who but God alone can forgive sins?" Jesus immediately knew in his mind what they
were thinking to themselves, so he said, "Why are you
thinking such things in your hearts? Which is easier, to
say to the paralytic, 'Your sins are forgiven,' or to say, 'Rise,
pick up your mat and walk'? But that you may know that
the Son of Man has authority to forgive sins on earth"—

he said to the paralytic, "I say to you, rise, pick up your mat, and go home." He rose, picked up his mat at once, and went away in the sight of everyone. They were all astounded and glorified God, saying, "We have never seen anything like this."—The Gospel of the Lord. ℟. **Praise to you, Lord Jesus Christ.**   → No. 15, p. 623

SATURDAY OF THE FIRST WEEK IN ORDINARY TIME

—— YEAR I ——

FIRST READING   Heb 4:12-16

The Letter continues the warning to persevere, for the Word of God judges, and judges rightly. Nothing is unknown to the Word. In its light, those of the present generation will be judged worthy or unfit to enter God's rest. The saving Word of God speaks to human beings, inviting them to belief.

A reading from the Letter to the Hebrews

THE word of God is living and effective, sharper than any two-edged sword, penetrating even between soul and spirit, joints and marrow, and able to discern reflections and thoughts of the heart. No creature is concealed from him, but everything is naked and exposed to the eyes of him to whom we must render an account.

Since we have a great high priest who has passed through the heavens, Jesus, the Son of God, let us hold fast to our confession. For we do not have a high priest who is unable to sympathize with our weaknesses, but one who has similarly been tested in every way, yet without sin. So let us confidently approach the throne of grace to receive mercy and to find grace for timely help.—The word of the Lord. ℟. **Thanks be to God.** ↓

RESPONSORIAL PSALM   Ps 19:8, 9, 10, 15

℟. (see Jn 6:63c) **Your words, Lord, are Spirit and life.**

The law of the LORD is perfect,
    refreshing the soul;

The decree of the LORD is trustworthy,
  giving wisdom to the simple.—℟.

The precepts of the LORD are right,
  rejoicing the heart;
The command of the LORD is clear,
  enlightening the eye.—℟.

The fear of the LORD is pure,
  enduring forever;
The ordinances of the LORD are true,
  all of them just.—℟.

Let the words of my mouth and the thought of my heart
  find favor before you,
  O LORD, my rock and my redeemer.—℟. ↓

——————— **YEAR II** ———————

FIRST READING   1 Sm 9:1-4, 17-19; 10:1

Saul, sent by his father to look for lost asses, is introduced by his servant to Samuel. Samuel entertains Saul. Samuel anoints Saul with oil as a token of consecration to the kingship. Saul is guaranteed signs by which he will know the authority of what has transpired.

A reading from the first Book of Samuel

THERE was a stalwart man from Benjamin named Kish, who was the son of Abiel, son of Zeror, son of Becorath, son of Aphiah, a Benjaminite. He had a son named Saul, who was a handsome young man. There was no other child of Israel more handsome than Saul; he stood head and shoulders above the people.

Now the asses of Saul's father, Kish, had wandered off. Kish said to his son Saul, "Take one of the servants with you and go out and hunt for the asses." Accordingly they went through the hill country of Ephraim, and through the land of Shalishah. Not finding them there, they continued through the land of Shaalim without success. They also went through the land of Benjamin, but they failed to find the animals.

When Samuel caught sight of Saul, the LORD assured him, "This is the man of whom I told you; he is to govern my people."

Saul met Samuel in the gateway and said, "Please tell me where the seer lives." Samuel answered Saul: "I am the seer. Go up ahead of me to the high place and eat with me today. In the morning, before dismissing you, I will tell you whatever you wish."

Then, from a flask he had with him, Samuel poured oil on Saul's head; he also kissed him, saying: "The LORD anoints you commander over his heritage. You are to govern the LORD's people Israel, and to save them from the grasp of their enemies roundabout.

"This will be the sign for you that the LORD has anointed you commander over his heritage."—The word of the Lord. ℟. **Thanks be to God.** ↓

RESPONSORIAL PSALM   Ps 21:2-3, 4-5, 6-7

℟. (2a) **Lord, in your strength the king is glad.**

O LORD, in your strength the king is glad;
  in your victory how greatly he rejoices!
You have granted him his heart's desire;
  you refused not the wish of his lips.—℟.

For you welcomed him with goodly blessings,
  you placed on his head a crown of pure gold.
He asked life of you: you gave him
  length of days forever and ever.—℟.

Great is his glory in your victory;
  majesty and splendor you conferred upon him.
For you made him a blessing forever;
  you gladdened him with the joy of your face.—℟. ↓

———— **YEAR I AND II** ————

ALLELUIA   Lk 4:18

℟. **Alleluia, alleluia.**
The Lord sent me to bring glad tidings to the poor

and to proclaim liberty to captives.
℞. **Alleluia, alleluia.** ↓

GOSPEL   Mk 2:13-17

Jesus lived with his people. He associated with tax collectors and sinners
to the extent of eating with them. The scribes and Pharisees were quick to
criticize Christ. Our Lord gives them a triumphant answer. The healthy do
not need a physician, whereas the sick, or the sinners, do.

℣. The Lord be with you. ℞. **And also with you.**
℣. A reading from the holy Gospel according to Mark.
℞. **Glory to you, Lord.**

JESUS went out along the sea. All the crowd came to
him and he taught them. As he passed by, he saw Levi,
son of Alphaeus, sitting at the customs post. Jesus said to
him, "Follow me." And he got up and followed Jesus.
While he was at table in his house, many tax collectors
and sinners sat with Jesus and his disciples; for there
were many who followed him. Some scribes who were
Pharisees saw that Jesus was eating with sinners and tax
collectors and said to his disciples, "Why does he eat with
tax collectors and sinners?" Jesus heard this and said to
them, "Those who are well do not need a physician, but
the sick do. I did not come to call the righteous but sinners."—The Gospel of the Lord. ℞. **Praise to you, Lord
Jesus Christ.**   → No. 15, p. 623

MONDAY OF THE SECOND WEEK
IN ORDINARY TIME

——— YEAR I ———

FIRST READING   Heb 5:1-10

Christ, "the anointed," was appointed to his heavenly office in the way the
priests of Israel were appointed. He "inherited" this office from God who
begot him as his Son. Priests are the dispensers of the holy mysteries (1
Cor 4:1). The priest is expected to exercise his office faithfully and act
according to the will of Christ whose steward he is.

A reading from the Letter to the Hebrews

BROTHERS and sisters: Every high priest is taken from among men and made their representative before God, to offer gifts and sacrifices for sins. He is able to deal patiently with the ignorant and erring, for he himself is beset by weakness and so, for this reason, must make sin offerings for himself as well as for the people. No one takes this honor upon himself but only when called by God, just as Aaron was. In the same way, it was not Christ who glorified himself in becoming high priest, but rather the one who said to him:

You are my Son:
this day I have begotten you;
just as he says in another place,
You are a priest forever
according to the order of Melchizedek.

In the days when he was in the Flesh, he offered prayers and supplications with loud cries and tears to the one who was able to save him from death, and he was heard because of his reverence. Son though he was, he learned obedience from what he suffered; and when he was made perfect, he became the source of eternal salvation for all who obey him.—The word of the Lord. ℟. **Thanks be to God.** ↓

RESPONSORIAL PSALM Ps 110:1, 2, 3, 4

℟. (4b) **You are a priest for ever, in the line of Melchizedek.**

The LORD said to my Lord:"Sit at my right hand
   till I make your enemies your footstool."—℟.

The scepter of your power the LORD will stretch forth
      from Zion:
   "Rule in the midst of your enemies."—℟.

"Yours is princely power in the day of your birth, in holy
      splendor;
   before the daystar, like the dew, I have begotten
   you."—℟.

The LORD has sworn, and he will not repent:
"You are a priest forever, according to the order of Melchizedek."—R̊. ↓

———— **YEAR II** ————

FIRST READING   1 Sm 15:16-23

Samuel declares that sacrifice without full obedience is of no value and that Saul's disobedience is a rejection of God's Word. Saul explains his action in withholding the best cattle for sacrifice. What was expected of Saul was his active obedience to God. The man who works for God must be dependable—and Saul was not.

A reading from the first Book of Samuel

SAMUEL said to Saul: "Stop! Let me tell you what the LORD said to me last night." Saul replied, "Speak!" Samuel then said: "Though little in your own esteem, are you not leader of the tribes of Israel? The LORD anointed you king of Israel and sent you on a mission, saying, 'Go and put the sinful Amalekites under a ban of destruction. Fight against them until you have exterminated them.' Why then have you disobeyed the LORD? You have pounced on the spoil, thus displeasing the LORD." Saul answered Samuel: "I did indeed obey the LORD and fulfill the mission on which the LORD sent me. I have brought back Agag, and I have destroyed Amalek under the ban. But from the spoil the men took sheep and oxen, the best of what had been banned, to sacrifice to the LORD their God in Gilgal." But Samuel said:

"Does the Lord so delight in burnt offerings and sacrifices
as in obedience to the command of the LORD?
Obedience is better than sacrifice,
and submission than the fat of rams.
For a sin like divination is rebellion,
and presumption is the crime of idolatry.
Because you have rejected the command of the LORD,
he, too, has rejected you as ruler."

The word of the Lord. R̊. **Thanks be to God.** ↓

RESPONSORIAL PSALM   Ps 50:8-9, 16bc-17, 21 and 23
See Tuesday of the 2nd Week of Lent, p. 459.

——————— **YEAR I AND II** ———————

ALLELUIA   Heb 4:12
℟. **Alleluia, alleluia.**
The word of God is living and effective,
able to discern reflections and thoughts of the heart.
℟. **Alleluia, alleluia.** ↓

GOSPEL   Mk 2:18-22
Because the "Bridegroom" is still with them, the significance of the parable about fasting according to the old law indicates that Christ realized his disciples were not yet ready for the new law—Christ's law. Our Lord stresses the incompatibility of the new economy with the old Mosaic law.

℣. The Lord be with you. ℟. **And also with you.**
℣. A reading from the holy Gospel according to Mark.
℟. **Glory to you, Lord.**

T HE disciples of John and of the Pharisees were accustomed to fast. People came to Jesus and objected, "Why do the disciples of John and the disciples of the Pharisees fast, but your disciples do not fast?" Jesus answered them, "Can the wedding guests fast while the bridegroom is with them? As long as they have the bridegroom with them they cannot fast. But the days will come when the bridegroom is taken away from them, and then they will fast on that day. No one sews a piece of unshrunken cloth on an old cloak. If he does, its fullness pulls away, the new from the old, and the tear gets worse. Likewise, no one pours new wine into old wineskins. Otherwise, the wine will burst the skins, and both the wine and the skins are ruined. Rather, new wine is poured into fresh wineskins."—The Gospel of the Lord.
℟. **Praise to you, Lord Jesus Christ.**   ➜ No. 15, p. 623

TUESDAY OF THE SECOND WEEK
IN ORDINARY TIME

———— YEAR I ————

FIRST READING   Heb 6:10-20

Zealous perseverance should mark all Christian work, founded in hope. Christian hope lies in what our Lord carried out in the eternal order of his sacrifice. He has not only entered the heavenly sanctuary but also entered as the "forerunner" of his brothers and sisters.

A reading from the Letter to the Hebrews

BROTHERS and sisters: God is not unjust so as to overlook your work and the love you have demonstrated for his name by having served and continuing to serve the holy ones. We earnestly desire each of you to demonstrate the same eagerness for the fulfillment of hope until the end, so that you may not become sluggish, but imitators of those who, through faith and patience, are inheriting the promises.

When God made the promise to Abraham, since he had no one greater by whom to swear, *he swore by himself,* and said, *I will indeed bless you and multiply you.* And so, after patient waiting, Abraham obtained the promise. Now, men swear by someone greater than themselves; for them an oath serves as a guarantee and puts an end to all argument. So when God wanted to give the heirs of his promise an even clearer demonstration of the immutability of his purpose, he intervened with an oath, so that by two immutable things, in which it was impossible for God to lie, we who have taken refuge might be strongly encouraged to hold fast to the hope that lies before us. This we have as an anchor of the soul, sure and firm, which reaches into the interior behind the veil, where Jesus has entered on our behalf as forerunner, becoming high priest forever according to the order of Melchizedek.—The word of the Lord. ℟. **Thanks be to God.** ↓

RESPONSORIAL PSALM   Ps 111:1-2, 4-5, 9 and 10c

℟. (5) **The Lord will remember his covenant for ever.**

℟. Or: **Alleluia.**

I will give thanks to the LORD with all my heart
   in the company and assembly of the just.
Great are the works of the LORD,
   exquisite in all their delights.—℟.

He has won renown for his wondrous deeds;
   gracious and merciful is the LORD.
He has given food to those who fear him;
   he will forever be mindful of his covenant.—℟.

He has sent deliverance to his people;
   he has ratified his covenant forever;
   holy and awesome is his name.
   His praise endures forever.—℟. ↓

——— **YEAR II** ———

FIRST READING   1 Sm 16:1-13

The anointing of David is told with a certain suspense—the fear of Saul,
the local color, the meeting with the Elders. Bethlehem came to occupy a
special place in salvation history. The name "David" is unique in the Old
Testament. Possession by the Spirit was not just a mark of God's favor but
was virtually limited to leaders of the people—kings and prophets.

A reading from the first Book of Samuel

THE LORD said to Samuel: "How long will you grieve
for Saul, whom I have rejected as king of Israel? Fill
your horn with oil, and be on your way. I am sending you
to Jesse of Bethlehem, for I have chosen my king from
among his sons." But Samuel replied: "How can I go? Saul
will hear of it and kill me." To this the LORD answered:
"Take a heifer along and say, 'I have come to sacrifice to
the LORD.' Invite Jesse to the sacrifice, and I myself will
tell you what to do; you are to anoint for me the one I
point out to you."

Samuel did as the Lord had commanded him. When he entered Bethlehem, the elders of the city came trembling to meet him and inquired, "Is your visit peaceful, O seer?" He replied: "Yes! I have come to sacrifice to the Lord. So cleanse yourselves and join me today for the banquet." He also had Jesse and his sons cleanse themselves and invited them to the sacrifice. As they came, he looked at Eliab and thought, "Surely the Lord's anointed is here before him." But the Lord said to Samuel: "Do not judge from his appearance or from his lofty stature, because I have rejected him. Not as man sees does God see, because he sees the appearance but the Lord looks into the heart." Then Jesse called Abinadab and presented him before Samuel, who said, "The Lord has not chosen him." Next Jesse presented Shammah, but Samuel said, "The Lord has not chosen this one either." In the same way Jesse presented seven sons before Samuel, but Samuel said to Jesse, "The Lord has not chosen any one of these." Then Samuel asked Jesse, "Are these all the sons you have?" Jesse replied, "There is still the youngest, who is tending the sheep." Samuel said to Jesse, "Send for him; we will not begin the sacrificial banquet until he arrives here." Jesse sent and had the young man brought to them. He was ruddy, a youth handsome to behold and making a splendid appearance. The Lord said, "There— anoint him, for this is he!" Then Samuel, with the horn of oil in hand, anointed him in the midst of his brothers; and from that day on, the Spirit of the Lord rushed upon David. When Samuel took his leave, he went to Ramah.— The word of the Lord. ℟. **Thanks be to God.** ↓

RESPONSORIAL PSALM   Ps 89:20, 21-22, 27-28

℟. (21a) **I have found David, my servant.**

Once you spoke in a vision,
    and to your faithful ones you said:

"On a champion I have placed a crown;
  over the people I have set a youth."—℟.

"I have found David, my servant;
  with my holy oil I have anointed him,
That my hand may be always with him,
  and that my arm may make him strong."—℟.

"He shall say of me, 'You are my father,
  my God, the Rock, my savior.'
And I will make him the first-born,
  highest of the kings of the earth."—℟. ↓

——— **YEAR I AND II** ———

ALLELUIA   See Eph 1:17-18
℟. **Alleluia, alleluia.**
May the Father of our Lord Jesus Christ
enlighten the eyes of our hearts,
that we may know what is the hope
that belongs to our call.
℟. **Alleluia, alleluia.** ↓

GOSPEL   Mk 2:23-28
Jesus answers the Pharisees' charge in rabbinic fashion with a counter-question. The Pharisees really do not accuse the disciples of theft, but of profaning the sabbath. However, the law, mercifully, allowed their present act. They were hungry.

℣. The Lord be with you. ℟. **And also with you.**
℣. A reading from the holy Gospel according to Mark.
℟. **Glory to you, Lord.**

A S Jesus was passing through a field of grain on the sabbath, his disciples began to make a path while picking the heads of grain. At this the Pharisees said to him, "Look, why are they doing what is unlawful on the sabbath?" He said to them, "Have you never read what David did when he was in need and he and his companions were hungry? How he went into the house of God when Abiathar was high priest and ate the bread of offering that only the priests could lawfully eat, and shared it with his companions?" Then he said to them, "The sabbath was made for man, not man for the sabbath. That is why the Son of Man is lord even of the sabbath."—The Gospel of the Lord. ℟. **Praise to you, Lord Jesus Christ.**

→ No. 15, p. 623

WEDNESDAY OF THE SECOND WEEK IN ORDINARY TIME

——— YEAR I ———

FIRST READING   Heb 7:1-3, 15-17

It is strange that here Melchizedek is compared to Jesus, rather than the reverse. Jesus received his exaltation after his death on the cross. A priest is a channel of exchange between God and human beings. Christ is the point of exchange through which pass people's submission to his Father and his Father's life to people.

A reading from the Letter to the Hebrews

MELCHIZEDEK, *king of Salem and priest of God Most High, met Abraham as he returned from his defeat of the kings and blessed him.* And Abraham apportioned to him a tenth of everything. His name first means righteous king, and he was also "king of Salem," that is, king of peace. Without father, mother, or ancestry, without beginning of days or end of life, thus made to resemble the Son of God, he remains a priest forever.

It is even more obvious if another priest is raised up after the likeness of Melchizedek, who has become so, not by a law expressed in a commandment concerning physical descent but by the power of a life that cannot be destroyed. For it is testified:

You are a priest forever according to the order of Melchizedek.

The word of the Lord. ℟. **Thanks be to God.** ↓

RESPONSORIAL PSALM   Ps 110:1, 2, 3, 4

℟. (4b) **You are a priest for ever, in the line of Melchizedek.**

The LORD said to my Lord: "Sit at my right hand
   till I make your enemies your footstool."—℟.

The scepter of your power the LORD will stretch forth
      from Zion:
   "Rule in the midst of your enemies."—℟.

"Yours is princely power in the day of your birth, in holy
      splendor;
   before the daystar, like the dew, I have begotten
   you."—℟.

The LORD has sworn, and he will not repent:
   "You are a priest forever, according to the order of
      Melchizedek."—℟. ↓

——————— **YEAR II** ———————

FIRST READING   1 Sm 17:32-33, 37, 40-51

Unable to wear Saul's armor, David goes out with only his sling. David
affirms his loyalty to Yahweh, strikes Goliath down with his sling, and
then dispatches him with the Philistine's own sword. The Philistines take
this as a sign of the Israelites' superiority and flee.

A reading from the first Book of Samuel

DAVID spoke to Saul: "Let your majesty not lose
   courage. I am at your service to go and fight this
Philistine." But Saul answered David, "You cannot go up
against this Philistine and fight with him, for you are only
a youth, while he has been a warrior from his youth."

David continued: "The LORD, who delivered me from
the claws of the lion and the bear, will also keep me safe
from the clutches of this Philistine." Saul answered
David, "Go! the LORD will be with you."

Then, staff in hand, David selected five smooth stones
from the wadi and put them in the pocket of his shep-

herd's bag. With his sling also ready to hand, he approached the Philistine.

With his shield bearer marching before him, the Philistine also advanced closer and closer to David. When he had sized David up, and seen that he was youthful, and ruddy, and handsome in appearance, the Philistine held David in contempt. The Philistine said to David, "Am I a dog that you come against me with a staff?" Then the Philistine cursed David by his gods and said to him, "Come here to me, and I will leave your flesh for the birds of the air and the beasts of the field." David answered him: "You come against me with sword and spear and scimitar, but I come against you in the name of the LORD of hosts, the God of the armies of Israel that you have insulted. Today the LORD shall deliver you into my hand; I will strike you down and cut off your head. This very day I will leave your corpse and the corpses of the Philistine army for the birds of the air and the beasts of the field; thus the whole land shall learn that Israel has a God. All this multitude, too, shall learn that it is not by sword or spear that the LORD saves. For the battle is the LORD's and he shall deliver you into our hands."

The Philistine then moved to meet David at close quarters, while David ran quickly toward the battle line in the direction of the Philistine. David put his hand into the bag and took out a stone, hurled it with the sling, and struck the Philistine on the forehead. The stone embedded itself in his brow, and he fell prostrate on the ground. Thus David overcame the Philistine with sling and stone; he struck the Philistine mortally, and did it without a sword. Then David ran and stood over him; with the Philistine's own sword which he drew from its sheath he dispatched him and cut off his head.—The word of the Lord. ℟. **Thanks be to God.** ↓

RESPONSORIAL PSALM   Ps 144:1b, 2, 9-10

℟. (1) **Blessed be the Lord, my Rock!**

Blessed be the LORD, my rock,
>   who trains my hands for battle, my fingers for
>   war.—R̸.

My refuge and my fortress,
>   my stronghold, my deliverer,
My shield, in whom I trust,
>   who subdues my people under me.—R̸.

O God, I will sing a new song to you;
>   with a ten-stringed lyre I will chant your praise,
You who give victory to kings,
>   and deliver David, your servant, from the evil
>   sword.—R̸. ↓

——————— **YEAR I AND II** ———————

ALLELUIA   See Mt 4:23

R̸. **Alleluia, alleluia.**
Jesus preached the Gospel of the Kingdom
and cured every disease among the people.
R̸. **Alleluia, alleluia.** ↓

GOSPEL   Mk 3:1-6

It is the sabbath and the scribes and Pharisees test Jesus. They know now
he always has compassion on those in need. Still they want to find
grounds for accusing him under the law. Christ knows their murderous
thoughts, but in his compassion, he heals the man. The Pharisees hold
their peace.

V̸. The Lord be with you. R̸. **And also with you.**
V̸. A reading from the holy Gospel according to Mark.
R̸. **Glory to you, Lord.**

JESUS entered the synagogue. There was a man there
who had a withered hand. They watched Jesus closely
to see if he would cure him on the sabbath so that they
might accuse him. He said to the man with the withered
hand, "Come up here before us." Then he said to the
Pharisees, "Is it lawful to do good on the sabbath rather
than to do evil, to save life rather than to destroy it?" But

they remained silent. Looking around at them with anger and grieved at their hardness of heart, Jesus said to the man, "Stretch out your hand." He stretched it out and his hand was restored. The Pharisees went out and immediately took counsel with the Herodians against him to put him to death.—The Gospel of the Lord. ℞. **Praise to you, Lord Jesus Christ.**

→ No 15, p. 623

THURSDAY OF THE SECOND WEEK IN ORDINARY TIME

—— YEAR I ——

FIRST READING   Heb 7:25—8:6

The constant intercession that Jesus makes is a sequel of his completed sacrifice. Christ continues his mediating work on the basis of his unique work of atonement. In contrast to the earthly tabernacle set up by Moses, the heavenly tabernacle was set up by the Lord, and Christ is the ministering priest.

A reading from the Letter to the Hebrews

JESUS is always able to save those who approach God through him, since he lives forever to make intercession for them.

It was fitting that we should have such a high priest: holy, innocent, undefiled, separated from sinners, higher than the heavens. He has no need, as did the high priests, to offer sacrifice day after day, first for his own sins and then for those of the people; he did that once for all when he offered himself. For the law appoints men subject to weakness to be high priests, but the word of the oath, which was taken after the law, appoints a son, who has been made perfect forever.

The main point of what has been said is this: we have such a high priest, who has taken his seat at the right hand of the throne of the Majesty in heaven, a minister of the sanctuary and of the true tabernacle that the Lord, not man, set up. Now every high priest is appointed to offer gifts and sacrifices; thus the necessity for this one also to have something to offer. If then he were on earth, he would not be a priest, since there are those who offer gifts according to the law. They worship in a copy and shadow of the heavenly sanctuary, as Moses was warned when he was about to erect the tabernacle. For God says, "See that you make everything according to the pattern shown you on the mountain." Now he has obtained so much more excellent a ministry as he is mediator of a better covenant, enacted on better promises.—The word of the Lord. ℟. **Thanks be to God.** ↓

RESPONSORIAL PSALM   Ps 40:7-8a, 8b-9, 10, 17

℟. (8a and 9a) **Here am I, Lord; I come to do your will.**

Sacrifice or oblation you wished not,
    but ears open to obedience you gave me.
Burnt offerings or sin-offerings you sought not;
    then said I, "Behold I come."—℟.

"In the written scroll it is prescribed for me,
To do your will, O my God, is my delight,
    and your law is within my heart!"—℟.

I announced your justice in the vast assembly;
    I did not restrain my lips, as you, O Lord, know.—℟.

May all who seek you
    exult and be glad in you,
And may those who love your salvation
    say ever, "The Lord be glorified."—℟. ↓

—————— **YEAR II** ——————

FIRST READING   1 Sm 18:6-9; 19:1-7

The women chant in David's honor. David becomes Saul's successful general. Saul, in his envy, tries to persuade his men, Jonathan among them, to put David to death. Jonathan eloquently pleads David's case, and he is reinstated.

A reading from the first Book of Samuel

WHEN David and Saul approached (on David's return after slaying the Philistine), women came out from each of the cities of Israel to meet King Saul, singing and dancing, with tambourines, joyful songs, and sistrums. The women played and sang:

"Saul has slain his thousands,
and David his ten thousands."

Saul was very angry and resentful of the song, for he thought: "They give David ten thousands, but only thousands to me. All that remains for him is the kingship." And from that day on, Saul was jealous of David.

Saul discussed his intention of killing David with his son Jonathan and with all his servants. But Saul's son Jonathan, who was very fond of David, told him: "My father Saul is trying to kill you. Therefore, please be on your guard tomorrow morning; get out of sight and remain in hiding. I, however, will go out and stand beside my father in the countryside where you are, and will speak to him about you. If I learn anything, I will let you know."

Jonathan then spoke well of David to his father Saul, saying to him: "Let not your majesty sin against his servant David, for he has committed no offense against you, but has helped you very much by his deeds. When he took his life in his hands and slew the Philistine, and the LORD brought about a great victory for all Israel through him, you were glad to see it. Why, then, should you become guilty of shedding innocent blood by killing David without cause?" Saul heeded Jonathan's plea and swore, "As the LORD lives, he shall not be killed." So Jonathan summoned David and repeated the whole conversation to him. Jonathan then brought David to Saul, and David served him as before.—The word of the Lord.
℟. **Thanks be to God.** ↓

RESPONSORIAL PSALM   Ps 56:2-3, 9-10a, 10b-11, 12-13

℞. (5b) **In God I trust; I shall not fear.**

Have mercy on me, O God, for men trample upon me;
  all the day they press their attack against me.
My adversaries trample upon me all the day;
  yes, many fight against me.—℞.

My wanderings you have counted;
  my tears are stored in your flask;
  are they not recorded in your book?
Then do my enemies turn back,
  when I call upon you.—℞.

Now I know that God is with me.
  In God, in whose promise I glory,
  in God I trust without fear;
  what can flesh do against me?—℞.

I am bound, O God, by vows to you;
  your thank offerings I will fulfill.
For you have rescued me from death,
  my feet, too, from stumbling;
  that I may walk before God in the light of the liv-
    ing.—℞. ↓

——————— **YEAR I AND II** ———————

ALLELUIA   See 2 Tm 1:10

℞. **Alleluia, alleluia.**
Our Savior Jesus Christ has destroyed death
and brought life to light through the Gospel.
℞. **Alleluia, alleluia.** ↓

GOSPEL   Mk 3:7-12

This brief narrative shows the interest in the ministry of Jesus. People come from far and near as the rumors of his healings spread. Jesus enjoins silence upon the unclean spirits whose testimony might involve misconceptions about his mission.

℣. The Lord be with you. ℞. **And also with you.**
℣. A reading from the holy Gospel according to Mark.
℞. **Glory to you, Lord.**

JESUS withdrew toward the sea with his disciples. A large number of people followed from Galilee and from Judea. Hearing what he was doing, a large number of people came to him also from Jerusalem, from Idumea, from beyond the Jordan, and from the neighborhood of Tyre and Sidon. He told his disciples to have a boat ready for him because of the crowd, so that they would not crush him. He had cured many and, as a result, those who had diseases were pressing upon him to touch him. And whenever unclean spirits saw him they would fall down before him and shout, "You are the Son of God." He warned them sternly not to make him known.—The Gospel of the Lord. ℟. **Praise to you, Lord Jesus Christ.**

→ No. 15, p. 623

FRIDAY OF THE SECOND WEEK IN ORDINARY TIME

─────── YEAR I ───────

FIRST READING   Heb 8:6-13

Jesus' priesthood is an element of the new and better Covenant of which he is mediator. The promise in the Old Covenant that God will be their God and they will be his people is also the promise in the New Covenant, but this relationship does not constitute the newness of the Covenant.

A reading from the Letter to the Hebrews

BROTHERS and sisters: Now our high priest has obtained so much more excellent a ministry as he is mediator of a better covenant, enacted on better promises.

For if that first covenant had been faultless, no place would have been sought for a second one. But he finds fault with them and says:

Behold, the days are coming, says the Lord,
    when I will conclude a new covenant
        with the house of Israel and the house of Judah.
It will not be like the covenant I made with their
        fathers
    the day I took them by the hand

to lead them forth from the land of Egypt;
    for they did not stand by my covenant
    and I ignored them, says the Lord.
But this is the covenant I will establish with the
       house of Israel
    after those days, says the Lord:
I will put my laws in their minds
    and I will write them upon their hearts.
I will be their God,
    and they shall be my people.
And they shall not teach, each one his fellow citizen
       and kin, saying,
    "Know the Lord,"
    for all shall know me, from least to greatest.
For I will forgive their evildoing
    and remember their sins no more.

When he speaks of a "new" covenant, he declares the first one obsolete. And what has become obsolete and has grown old is close to disappearing.—The word of the Lord. ℟. **Thanks be to God.** ↓

RESPONSORIAL PSALM   Ps 85:8 and 10, 11-12, 13-14

℟. (11a) **Kindness and truth shall meet.**

Show us, O LORD, your mercy,
    and grant us your salvation.
Near indeed is his salvation to those who fear him,
    glory dwelling in our land.—℟.

Kindness and truth shall meet;
    justice and peace shall kiss.
Truth shall spring out of the earth,
    and justice shall look down from heaven.—℟.

The LORD himself will give his benefits;
    our land shall yield its increase.
Justice shall walk before him,
    and salvation, along the way of his steps.—℟. ↓

——————— **YEAR II** ———————

FIRST READING 1 Sm 24:3-21

Saul retires within a cave and unwittingly puts himself within David's reach. David refuses to do any injury to the person of the Lord's anointed. Saul acknowledges David's loyalty to his king and gives David his blessing.

A reading from the first Book of Samuel

SAUL took three thousand picked men from all Israel and went in search of David and his men in the direction of the wild goat crags. When he came to the sheepfolds along the way, he found a cave, which he entered to relieve himself. David and his men were occupying the inmost recesses of the cave.

David's servants said to him, "This is the day of which the LORD said to you, 'I will deliver your enemy into your grasp; do with him as you see fit.'" So David moved up and stealthily cut off an end of Saul's mantle. Afterward, however, David regretted that he had cut off an end of Saul's mantle. He said to his men, "The LORD forbid that I should do such a thing to my master, the LORD's anointed, as to lay a hand on him, for he is the LORD's anointed." With these words David restrained his men and would not permit them to attack Saul. Saul then left the cave and went on his way. David also stepped out of the cave, calling to Saul, "My lord the king!" When Saul looked back, David bowed to the ground in homage and asked Saul: "Why do you listen to those who say, 'David is trying to harm you'? You see for yourself today that the Lord just now delivered you into my grasp in the cave. I had some thought of killing you, but I took pity on you instead. I decided, 'I will not raise a hand against my lord, for he is the LORD's anointed and a father to me.' Look here at this end of your mantle which I hold. Since I cut off an end of your mantle and did not kill you, see and be convinced that I plan no harm and no rebellion. I have done you no wrong, though you are hunting me down to take my life. The LORD will judge between me and you, and the LORD will exact justice from you in my case. I shall not touch you. The old proverb says, 'From the wicked comes forth wickedness.' So I will take no action against you. Against whom are you on campaign, O king of Israel? Whom are you pursuing? A dead dog, or a single flea! The LORD will be the judge; he will decide between me and you. May he see this, and take my part, and grant me justice beyond your reach!"

When David finished saying these things to Saul, Saul answered, "Is that your voice, my son David?" And Saul wept aloud. Saul then said to David: "You are in the right rather than I; you have treated me generously, while I have done you harm. Great is the generosity you showed me today, when the LORD delivered me into your grasp and you did not kill me. For if a man meets his enemy, does he send him away unharmed? May the LORD reward you generously for what you have done this day. And now, I know that you shall surely be king and that sovereignty over Israel shall come into your possession."—The word of the Lord. ℟. **Thanks be to God.** ↓

RESPONSORIAL PSALM   Ps 57:2, 3-4, 6 and 11

℟. (2a) **Have mercy on me, God, have mercy.**

Have mercy on me, O God; have mercy on me,
    for in you I take refuge.
In the shadow of your wings I take refuge,
    till harm pass by.—℟.

I call to God the Most High,
    to God, my benefactor.
May he send from heaven and save me;
    may he make those a reproach who trample upon me;
    may God send his mercy and his faithfulness.—℟.

Be exalted above the heavens, O God;
    above all the earth be your glory!
For your mercy towers to the heavens,
    and your faithfulness to the skies.—℟. ↓

──────── **YEAR I AND II** ────────

ALLELUIA   2 Cor 5:19

℟. **Alleluia, alleluia.**
God was reconciling the world to himself in Christ,
and entrusting to us the message of reconciliation.
℟. **Alleluia, alleluia.** ↓

GOSPEL   Mk 3:13-19

Jesus withdraws to select the Twelve. (The number symbolizes the twelve
tribes of Israel.) Jesus appoints them for the double purpose that is still
the essential function of the Church—fellowship with himself and the
proclamation of the Gospel. Simon is named first in the list.

℣. The Lord be with you. ℟. **And also with you.**
℣. A reading from the holy Gospel according to Mark.
℟. **Glory to you, Lord.**

JESUS went up the mountain and summoned those
whom he wanted and they came to him. He appointed
Twelve, whom he also named Apostles, that they might
be with him and he might send them forth to preach and
to have authority to drive out demons: He appointed the
Twelve: Simon, whom he named Peter; James, son of
Zebedee, and John the brother of James, whom he
named Boanerges, that is, sons of thunder; Andrew,
Philip, Bartholomew, Matthew, Thomas, James the son of
Alphaeus; Thaddeus, Simon the Cananean, and Judas
Iscariot who betrayed him.—The Gospel of the Lord. ℟.
Praise to you, Lord Jesus Christ.   → No. 15, p. 623

─────────────────────

SATURDAY OF THE SECOND WEEK
IN ORDINARY TIME

──────── **YEAR I** ────────

FIRST READING   Heb 9:2-3, 11-14

The sacred writer indicates that the perfect tabernacle is the heavenly
region, the heavenly counterpart of the earthly outer tabernacle through
which our Lord passed into the highest heaven, the abode of God, the
counterpart of the inner tabernacle—the Holy of Holies.

A reading from the Letter to the Hebrews

A TABERNACLE was constructed, the outer one, in which were the lampstand, the table, and the bread of offering; this is called the Holy Place. Behind the second veil was the tabernacle called the Holy of Holies.

But when Christ came as high priest of the good things that have come to be, passing through the greater and more perfect tabernacle not made by hands, that is, not belonging to this creation, he entered once for all into the sanctuary, not with the blood of goats and calves but with his own Blood, thus obtaining eternal redemption. For if the blood of goats and bulls and the sprinkling of a heifer's ashes can sanctify those who are defiled so that their flesh is cleansed, how much more will the Blood of Christ, who through the eternal spirit offered himself unblemished to God, cleanse our consciences from dead works to worship the living God.—The word of the Lord. ℟. **Thanks be to God.** ↓

RESPONSORIAL PSALM   Ps 47:2-3, 6-7, 8-9

℟. (6) **God mounts his throne to shouts of joy; a blare of trumpets for the Lord.**

All you peoples, clap your hands,
    shout to God with cries of gladness,
For the LORD, the Most High, the awesome,
    is the great king over all the earth.—℟.

God mounts his throne amid shouts of joy;
    the LORD, amid trumpet blasts.
Sing praise to God, sing praise;
    sing praise to our king, sing praise.—℟.

For king of all the earth is God:
    sing hymns of praise.
God reigns over the nations,
    God sits upon his holy throne.—℟. ↓

———— **YEAR II** ————

FIRST READING   2 Sm 1:1-4, 11-12, 19, 23-27

The news of the deaths of Saul and Jonathan reaches David at Ziklag. David shows the usual signs of mourning. He composes an elegy in honor of Saul and Jonathan. David extols the bravery and courage of Saul and Jonathan and idealizes their union of spirit.

A reading from the second Book of Samuel

DAVID returned from his defeat of the Amalekites and spent two days in Ziklag. On the third day a man came from Saul's camp, with his clothes torn and dirt on his head. Going to David, he fell to the ground in homage. David asked him, "Where do you come from?" He replied, "I have escaped from the camp of the children of Israel." "Tell me what happened," David bade him. He answered that many of the soldiers had fled the battle and that many of them had fallen and were dead, among them Saul and his son Jonathan.

David seized his garments and rent them, and all the men who were with him did likewise. They mourned and wept and fasted until evening for Saul and his son Jonathan, and for the soldiers of the LORD of the clans of Israel, because they had fallen by the sword.

"Alas! the glory of Israel, Saul,
    slain upon your heights;
    how can the warriors have fallen!

"Saul and Jonathan, beloved and cherished,
    separated neither in life nor in death,
    swifter than eagles, stronger than lions!
Women of Israel, weep over Saul,
    who clothed you in scarlet and in finery,
    who decked your attire with ornaments of gold.

"How can the warriors have fallen—
    in the thick of the battle,
    slain upon your heights!

"I grieve for you, Jonathan my brother!
   most dear have you been to me;
   more precious have I held love for you than love
      for women."

"How can the warriors have fallen,
   the weapons of war have perished!"
The word of the Lord. ℟. **Thanks be to God.** ↓

RESPONSORIAL PSALM   Ps 80:2-3, 5-7

℟. (4b) **Let us see your face, Lord, and we shall be saved.**

O shepherd of Israel, hearken,
   O guide of the flock of Joseph!
From your throne upon the cherubim, shine forth
   before Ephraim, Benjamin and Manasseh.
Rouse your power,
   and come to save us.—℟.

O LORD of hosts, how long will you burn with anger
   while your people pray?
You have fed them with the bread of tears
   and given them tears to drink in ample measure.
You have left us to be fought over by our neighbors,
   and our enemies mock us.—℟. ↓

——————— **YEAR I AND II** ———————

ALLELUIA   See Acts 16:14b

℟. **Alleluia, alleluia.**
Open our hearts, O Lord,
to listen to the words of your Son.
℟. **Alleluia, alleluia.** ↓

GOSPEL   Mk 3:20-21

This statement seems to point out a course of conduct so unexpected and
extraordinary that people failed to understand. Even those who knew
Christ intimately did not realize his compassion and love for the crowd.

℣. The Lord be with you. ℟. **And also with you.**

℣. A reading from the holy Gospel according to Mark.

℟. **Glory to you, Lord.**

JESUS came with his disciples into the house. Again the crowd gathered, making it impossible for them even to eat. When his relatives heard of this they set out to seize him, for they said, "He is out of his mind."—The Gospel of the Lord. ℟. **Praise to you, Lord Jesus Christ.**

→ No. 15, p. 623

MONDAY OF THE THIRD WEEK IN ORDINARY TIME

──────── **YEAR I** ────────

FIRST READING   Heb 9:15, 24-28

Christ as Mediator offered himself one time in the shedding of his Blood. Human beings are to die but once and then they are judged. Through his death Jesus was offered to atone for sin. He will come a second time to judge mankind.

A reading from the Letter to the Hebrews

CHRIST is mediator of a new covenant: since a death has taken place for deliverance from transgressions under the first covenant, those who are called may receive the promised eternal inheritance.

For Christ did not enter into a sanctuary made by hands, a copy of the true one, but heaven itself, that he might now appear before God on our behalf. Not that he might offer himself repeatedly, as the high priest enters each year into the sanctuary with blood that is not his own; if that were so, he would have had to suffer repeatedly from the foundation of the world. But now once for all he has appeared at the end of the ages to take away sin by his sacrifice. Just as it is appointed that human beings die once, and after this the judgment, so also Christ, offered once to take away the sins of many, will appear a second time, not to take away sin but to bring salvation to those who eagerly await him.—The word of the Lord. ℟. **Thanks be to God.** ↓

RESPONSORIAL PSALM   Ps 98:1, 2-3ab, 3cd-4, 5-6

℟. (1a) **Sing to the Lord a new song, for he has done marvelous deeds.**

Sing to the LORD a new song,
    for he has done wondrous deeds;
His right hand has won victory for him,
    his holy arm.—℟.

The LORD has made his salvation known:
    in the sight of the nations he has revealed his justice.
He has remembered his kindness and his faithfulness
    toward the house of Israel.—℟.

All the ends of the earth have seen
    the salvation by our God.
Sing joyfully to the LORD, all you lands;
    break into song; sing praise.—℟.

Sing praise to the LORD with the harp,
    with the harp and melodious song.
With trumpets and the sound of the horn
    sing joyfully before the King, the LORD.—℟. ↓

——————— **YEAR II** ———————

FIRST READING   2 Sm 5:1-7, 10

David becomes king over all Israel, and his accession is ratified by a solemn covenant. He is anointed by the Elders of Israel. David and his men set out to capture Jerusalem. He grows in God's favor.

A reading from the second Book of Samuel

ALL the tribes of Israel came to David in Hebron and said:"Here we are, your bone and your flesh. In days past, when Saul was our king, it was you who led the children of Israel out and brought them back. And the LORD said to you, 'You shall shepherd my people Israel and shall be commander of Israel.'" When all the elders of Israel came to David in Hebron, King David made an agreement with them there before the LORD, and they anointed him king of Israel. David was thirty years old when he became king, and he reigned for forty years: seven years and six months in Hebron over Judah, and thirty-three years in Jerusalem over all Israel and Judah.

Then the king and his men set out for Jerusalem against the Jebusites who inhabited the region. David was told, "You cannot enter here: the blind and the lame will drive you away!" which was their way of saying, "David cannot enter here." But David did take the stronghold of Zion, which is the City of David.

David grew steadily more powerful, for the LORD of hosts was with him.—The word of the Lord. ℟. **Thanks be to God.** ↓

RESPONSORIAL PSALM   Ps 89:20, 21-22, 25-26

℟. (25a) **My faithfulness and my mercy shall be with him.**

Once you spoke in a vision,
    and to your faithful ones you said:
"On a champion I have placed a crown;
    over the people I have set a youth."—℟.

"I have found David, my servant;
    with my holy oil I have anointed him,
That my hand may be always with him,
    and that my arm may make him strong."—℟.

"My faithfulness and my mercy shall be with him,
    and through my name shall his horn be exalted.
I will set his hand upon the sea,
    his right hand upon the rivers."—℟. ↓

—————— **YEAR I AND II** ——————

ALLELUIA   See 2 Tm 1:10

℟. **Alleluia, alleluia.**
Our Savior Jesus Christ has destroyed death

and brought life to light through the Gospel.

℟. **Alleluia, alleluia.** ↓

GOSPEL   Mk 3:22-30

Jesus teaches that a house that is divided falls apart, and with his almighty power he expels Satan by a firm command. Jesus promises that every sin will be forgiven except that which blasphemes against the Holy Spirit.

℣. The Lord be with you. ℟. **And also with you.**

℣. A reading from the holy Gospel according to Mark.

℟. **Glory to you, Lord.**

THE scribes who had come from Jerusalem said of Jesus, "He is possessed by Beelzebul," and "By the prince of demons he drives out demons."

Summoning them, he began to speak to them in parables, "How can Satan drive out Satan? If a kingdom is divided against itself, that kingdom cannot stand. And if a house is divided against itself, that house will not be able to stand. And if Satan has risen up against himself and is divided, he cannot stand; that is the end of him. But no one can enter a strong man's house to plunder his property unless he first ties up the strong man. Then he can plunder his house. Amen, I say to you, all sins and all blasphemies that people utter will be forgiven them. But whoever blasphemes against the Holy Spirit will never have forgiveness, but is guilty of an everlasting sin." For they had said, "He has an unclean spirit."—The Gospel of the Lord. ℟. **Praise to you, Lord Jesus Christ.**

→ No. 15, p. 623

TUESDAY OF THE THIRD WEEK
IN ORDINARY TIME

——— **YEAR I** ———

FIRST READING   Heb 10:1-10

The sacrifices of the Old Covenant only foreshadowed that of Christ. The one sacrifice of Christ Jesus is the source of remission of past sins (Heb 9:15).

Because of its perfection, no further sacrifice is necessary or possible. The offering of Christ's body means the same as the shedding of his blood.

A reading from the Letter to the Hebrews

BROTHERS and sisters: Since the law has only a shadow of the good things to come, and not the very image of them, it can never make perfect those who come to worship by the same sacrifices that they offer continually each year. Otherwise, would not the sacrifices have ceased to be offered, since the worshipers, once cleansed, would no longer have had any consciousness of sins? But in those sacrifices there is only a yearly remembrance of sins, for it is impossible that the blood of bulls and goats take away sins. For this reason, when he came into the world, he said:

Sacrifice and offering you did not desire,
but a body you prepared for me;
in burnt offerings and sin offerings you took no delight.
Then I said, As is written of me in the scroll,
Behold, I come to do your will, O God.

First he says, *Sacrifices and offerings, burnt offerings and sin offerings, you neither desired nor delighted in.* These are offered according to the law. Then he says, *Behold, I come to do your will.* He takes away the first to establish the second. By this "will," we have been consecrated through the offering of the Body of Jesus Christ once for all.—The word of the Lord. ℟. **Thanks be to God.** ↓

RESPONSORIAL PSALM   Ps 40:2 and 4ab, 7-8a, 10, 11

℟. (8a and 9a) **Here am I, Lord; I come to do your will.**

I have waited, waited for the LORD,
    and he stooped toward me.
And he put a new song into my mouth,
    a hymn to our God.—℟.

Sacrifice or oblation you wished not,
    but ears open to obedience you gave me.

Burnt offerings or sin-offerings you sought not;
> then said I, "Behold I come."—℟.

I announced your justice in the vast assembly;
> I did not restrain my lips, as you, O LORD, know.—℟.

Your justice I kept not hid within my heart;
> your faithfulness and your salvation I have spoken of;
I have made no secret of your kindness and your truth
> in the vast assembly.—℟. ↓

——— **YEAR II** ———

FIRST READING   2 Sm 6:12-15b, 17-19

The reception of the ark of the Lord into the City of David is the occasion for exultant celebration. David offers sacrifice and blesses the people. All the people of Israel join in the festivities and share in the delightful repast.

A reading from the second Book of Samuel

DAVID went to bring up the ark of God from the house of Obed-edom into the City of David amid festivities. As soon as the bearers of the ark of the LORD had advanced six steps, he sacrificed an ox and a fatling. Then David, girt with a linen apron, came dancing before the LORD with abandon, as he and all the house of Israel were bringing up the ark of the LORD with shouts of joy and to the sound of the horn. The ark of the LORD was brought in and set in its place within the tent David had pitched for it. Then David offered burnt offerings and peace offerings before the LORD. When he finished making these offerings, he blessed the people in the name of the LORD of hosts. He then distributed among all the people, to each man and each woman in the entire multitude of Israel, a loaf of bread, a cut of roast meat, and a raisin cake. With this, all the people left for their homes.—The word of the Lord. ℟. **Thanks be to God.** ↓

RESPONSORIAL PSALM Ps 24:7, 8, 9, 10
See February 2, p. 942.

————— **YEAR I AND II** —————

ALLELUIA See Mt 11:25

℞. **Alleluia, alleluia.**
Blessed are you, Father, Lord of heaven and earth;
you have revealed to little ones the mysteries of the
Kingdom.
℞. **Alleluia, alleluia.** ↓

GOSPEL Mk 3:31-35

The reign of God makes demands on the personal commitment of a disciple that must transcend at times all natural family bonds. All are brothers and sisters in Christ who made this heavenly kinship possible by giving himself on the cross for our salvation.

℣. The Lord be with you. ℞. **And also with you.**
℣. A reading from the holy Gospel according to Mark.
℞. **Glory to you, Lord.**

THE mother of Jesus and his brothers arrived at the house. Standing outside, they sent word to Jesus and called him. A crowd seated around him told him, "Your mother and your brothers and your sisters are outside asking for you." But he said to them in reply, "Who are my mother and my brothers?" And looking around at those seated in the circle he said, "Here are my mother and my brothers. For whoever does the will of God is my brother and sister and mother."—The Gospel of the Lord. ℞.
Praise to you, Lord Jesus Christ. → No. 15, p. 623

WEDNESDAY OF THE THIRD WEEK IN ORDINARY TIME

—————— YEAR I ——————

FIRST READING　　　　　　　　　　　　　Heb 10:11-18

There is an infinite contrast between the sacrifices of the Old Law for sin and the sublime sacrifice of Jesus. His sacrifice continues in heaven. Once God forgives sins, they are forgiven.

A reading from the Letter to the Hebrews

EVERY priest stands daily at his ministry, offering frequently those same sacrifices that can never take away sins. But this one offered one sacrifice for sins, and took his seat forever at the right hand of God; now he waits until his enemies are made his footstool. For by one offering he has made perfect forever those who are being consecrated. The Holy Spirit also testifies to us, for after saying:

This is the covenant I will establish with them
after those days, says the Lord:
"I will put my laws in their hearts,
and I will write them upon their minds,"

he also says:

Their sins and their evildoing
I will remember no more.

Where there is forgiveness of these, there is no longer offering for sin.—The word of the Lord. ℟. **Thanks be to God.** ↓

RESPONSORIAL PSALM　　　　　　　　Ps 110:1, 2, 3, 4

℟. (4b) **You are a priest for ever, in the line of Melchizedek.**

The LORD said to my Lord: "Sit at my right hand
　　till I make your enemies your footstool."—℟.

The scepter of your power the LORD will stretch forth
　　from Zion:
　　"Rule in the midst of your enemies."—℟.

"Yours is princely power in the day of your birth, in holy
    splendor;
  before the daystar, like the dew, I have begotten
    you."—℟.

The LORD has sworn, and he will not repent:
  "You are a priest forever, according to the order of
    Melchizedek."—℟. ↓

——————— **YEAR II** ———————

FIRST READING   2 Sm 7:4-17

In a night vision, Nathan receives word that David should not build a tem-
ple but is to be given a promise that his house will continue and enjoy
God's favor for all time. The promise to David is a personal one, but Israel,
God's people, will enjoy peace and security.

A reading from the second Book of Samuel

THAT night the LORD spoke to Nathan and said: "Go,
    tell my servant David, 'Thus says the LORD: Should
you build me a house to dwell in? I have not dwelt in a
house from the day on which I led the children of Israel
out of Egypt to the present, but I have been going about
in a tent under cloth. In all my wanderings everywhere
among the children of Israel, did I ever utter a word to
any one of the judges whom I charged to tend my people
Israel, to ask: Why have you not built me a house of
cedar?'

  "Now then, speak thus to my servant David, 'The
LORD of hosts has this to say: It was I who took you from
the pasture and from the care of the flock to be commander of my people Israel. I have been with you wherever you went, and I have destroyed all your enemies
before you. And I will make you famous like the great
ones of the earth. I will fix a place for my people Israel; I
will plant them so that they may dwell in their place without further disturbance. Neither shall the wicked continue to afflict them as they did of old, since the time I first
appointed judges over my people Israel. I will give you

rest from all your enemies. The LORD also reveals to you
that he will establish a house for you. And when your
time comes and you rest with your ancestors, I will raise
up your heir after you, sprung from your loins, and I will
make his Kingdom firm. It is he who shall build a house
for my name. And I will make his royal throne firm forever. I will be a father to him, and he shall be a son to me.
And if he does wrong, I will correct him with the rod of
men and with human chastisements; but I will not withdraw my favor from him as I withdrew it from your pre-
decessor Saul, whom I removed from my presence. Your
house and your kingdom shall endure forever before me;
your throne shall stand firm forever' "

Nathan reported all these words and this entire vision
to David.—The word of the Lord. ℟. **Thanks be to God.** ↓

RESPONSORIAL PSALM   Ps 89:4-5, 27-28, 29-30

℟. (29a) **For ever I will maintain my love for my servant.**

"I have made a covenant with my chosen one;
    I have sworn to David my servant:
I will make your dynasty stand forever
    and establish your throne through all ages."—℟.

"He shall cry to me, 'You are my father,
    my God, the Rock that brings me victory!'
I myself make him firstborn,
    Most High over the kings of the earth."—℟.

"Forever I will maintain my love for him;
    my covenant with him stands firm.
I will establish his dynasty forever,
    his throne as the days of the heavens."—℟. ↓

——————— **YEAR I AND II** ———————

ALLELUIA

℟. **Alleluia, alleluia.**
The seed is the word of God, Christ is the sower;
all who come to him will live for ever.
℟. **Alleluia, alleluia.** ↓

GOSPEL   Mk 4:1-20

Jesus chooses images familiar to his hearers in order to enable them to keep his teaching in daily remembrance. The seed is the Word of God. The sower is Christ, who came forth from the Father.

℣. The Lord be with you. ℟. **And also with you.**
℣. A reading from the holy Gospel according to Mark.
℟. **Glory to you, Lord.**

ON another occasion, Jesus began to teach by the sea. A very large crowd gathered around him so that he got into a boat on the sea and sat down. And the whole crowd was beside the sea on land. And he taught them at length in parables, and in the course of his instruction he said to them, "Hear this! A sower went out to sow. And as he sowed, some seed fell on the path, and the birds came and ate it up. Other seed fell on rocky ground where it had little soil. It sprang up at once because the soil was not deep. And when the sun rose, it was scorched and it withered for lack of roots. Some seed fell among thorns, and the thorns grew up and choked it and it produced no grain. And some seed fell on rich soil and produced fruit. It came up and grew and yielded thirty, sixty, and a hundredfold." He added, "Whoever has ears to hear ought to hear."

And when he was alone, those present along with the Twelve questioned him about the parables. He answered them, "The mystery of the Kingdom of God has been granted to you. But to those outside everything comes in parables, so that

they may look and see but not perceive,
and hear and listen but not understand,
in order that they may not be converted and be forgiven."

Jesus said to them, "Do you not understand this parable? Then how will you understand any of the parables? The sower sows the word. These are the ones on the path where the word is sown. As soon as they hear, Satan comes at once and takes away the word sown in them. And these are the ones sown on rocky ground who, when they hear the word, receive it at once with joy. But they have no roots; they last only for a time. Then when tribulation or persecution comes because of the word, they quickly fall away. Those sown among thorns are another sort. They are the people who hear the word, but worldly anxiety, the lure of riches, and the craving for other things intrude and choke the word, and it bears no fruit. But those sown on rich soil are the ones who hear the word and accept it and bear fruit thirty and sixty and a hundredfold."—The Gospel of the Lord. ℟. **Praise to you, Lord Jesus Christ.** ➡ No. 15, p. 623

THURSDAY OF THE THIRD WEEK IN ORDINARY TIME

———— YEAR I ————

FIRST READING   Heb 10:19-25

The sprinkling designates the purifying power of the sacrifice of Christ that gives salvation. Hope begins at baptism. The assembly is the gathering together of the community for the celebration of the Eucharist. Here Christians should encourage and support one another.

A reading from the Letter to the Hebrews

BROTHERS and sisters: Since through the Blood of Jesus we have confidence of entrance into the sanctuary by the new and living way he opened for us through the veil, that is, his flesh, and since we have "a great priest over the house of God," let us approach with a sincere heart and in absolute trust, with our hearts sprinkled clean from an evil conscience and our bodies washed in pure water. Let us hold unwaveringly to our confession that gives us hope, for he who made the promise is trustworthy. We must consider how to rouse one another to love and good works. We should not stay away from our assembly, as is the custom of some, but encourage one another, and this all the more as you see the day drawing near.—The word of the Lord. ℟. **Thanks be to God.** ↓

RESPONSORIAL PSALM   Ps 24:1-2, 3-4ab, 5-6

℟. (see 6) **Lord, this is the people that longs to see your face.**

The LORD's are the earth and its fullness;
    the world and those who dwell in it.
For he founded it upon the seas
    and established it upon the rivers.—℟.

Who can ascend the mountain of the LORD?
    or who may stand in his holy place?
He whose hands are sinless, whose heart is clean,
    who desires not what is vain.—℟.

He shall receive a blessing from the LORD,
    a reward from God his savior.
Such is the race that seeks for him,
    that seeks the face of the God of Jacob.—℟. ↓

——————— **YEAR II** ———————

FIRST READING   2 Sm 7:18-19, 24-29

David offers a prayer of gratitude to God for the promise and for the initial acts of favor shown to the nation in the Exodus and the settlement. David's conception of the great name achieved by Yahweh plays a vital part in subsequent thought.

A reading from the second Book of Samuel

After Nathan had spoken to King David, the king went in and sat before the LORD and said,"Who am I, Lord GOD, and who are the members of my house, that you have brought me to this point? Yet even this you see as too little, Lord GOD; you have also spoken of the house of your servant for a long time to come: this too you have shown to man, Lord GOD!

"You have established for yourself your people Israel as yours forever, and you, LORD, have become their God.

And now, LORD God, confirm for all time the prophecy you have made concerning your servant and his house, and do as you have promised. Your name will be forever great, when men say, 'The LORD of hosts is God of Israel,' and the house of your servant David stands firm before you. It is you, LORD of hosts, God of Israel, who said in a revelation to your servant, 'I will build a house for you.' Therefore your servant now finds the courage to make this prayer to you. And now, Lord GOD, you are God and your words are truth; you have made this generous promise to your servant. Do, then, bless the house of your servant that it may be before you forever; for you, Lord GOD, have promised, and by your blessing the house of your servant shall be blessed forever."—The word of the Lord. ℟. **Thanks be to God.** ↓

RESPONSORIAL PSALM   Ps 132:1-2, 3-5, 11, 12, 13-14

℟. (Lk 1:32b) **The Lord God will give him the throne of David, his father.**

LORD, remember David
    and all his anxious care;
How he swore an oath to the LORD,
    vowed to the Mighty One of Jacob.—℟.

"I will not enter the house where I live,
    nor lie on the couch where I sleep;
I will give my eyes no sleep,
    my eyelids no rest,
Till I find a home for the LORD,
    a dwelling for the Mighty One of Jacob."—℟.

The LORD swore an oath to David
    a firm promise from which he will not withdraw:
"Your own offspring
    I will set upon your throne."—℟.

"If your sons keep my covenant,
    and the decrees which I shall teach them,

Their sons, too, forever
    shall sit upon your throne."—R̶̸.

For the LORD has chosen Zion,
    he prefers her for his dwelling:
"Zion is my resting place forever;
    in her I will dwell, for I prefer her."—R̶̸. ↓

——————— **YEAR I AND II** ———————

ALLELUIA   Ps 119:105

R̶̸. **Alleluia, alleluia.**
A lamp to my feet is your word,
a light to my path.
R̶̸. **Alleluia, alleluia.** ↓

GOSPEL   Mk 4:21-25

Jesus teaches that his doctrine should not be under a bushel. It is for all human beings. To the Apostles, Christ expounded all mysteries that thereafter they might dispense Light to others also. Jesus warns the Apostles to listen: as you give so shall you receive.

℣. The Lord be with you. R̶̸. **And also with you.**
℣. A reading from the holy Gospel according to Mark.
R̶̸. **Glory to you, Lord.**

JESUS said to his disciples, "Is a lamp brought in to be placed under a bushel basket or under a bed, and not to be placed on a lampstand? For there is nothing hidden except to be made visible; nothing is secret except to come to light. Anyone who has ears to hear ought to hear." He also told them, "Take care what you hear. The measure with which you measure will be measured out to you, and still more will be given to you. To the one who has, more will be given; from the one who has not, even what he has will be taken away."—The Gospel of the Lord. R̶̸. **Praise to you, Lord Jesus Christ.**

→ No. 15, p. 623

FRIDAY OF THE THIRD WEEK
IN ORDINARY TIME

——— YEAR I ———

FIRST READING   Heb 10:32-39

St. Paul recalls persecutions such as those of the Jerusalem church, which involved even the death of some (Acts 8:1). The just must continue to live by faith, awaiting the return of Christ. If they lose faith and fall away, they will displease God.

A reading from the Letter to the Hebrews

REMEMBER the days past when, after you had been enlightened, you endured a great contest of suffering. At times you were publicly exposed to abuse and affliction; at other times you associated yourselves with those so treated. You even joined in the sufferings of those in prison and joyfully accepted the confiscation of your property, knowing that you had a better and lasting possession. Therefore, do not throw away your confidence; it will have great recompense. You need endurance to do the will of God and receive what he has promised.

> *For, after just a brief moment,*
>   *he who is to come shall come;*
>   *he shall not delay.*
> *But my just one shall live by faith,*
>   *and if he draws back I take no pleasure in him.*

We are not among those who draw back and perish, but among those who have faith and will possess life.—The word of the Lord. ℟. **Thanks be to God.** ↓

RESPONSORIAL PSALM   Ps 37:3-4, 5-6, 23-24, 39-40

℟. (39a) **The salvation of the just comes from the Lord.**

Trust in the LORD and do good,
    that you may dwell in the land and be fed in security.
Take delight in the LORD,
    and he will grant you your heart's requests.—℟.

Commit to the LORD your way;
　　trust in him, and he will act.
He will make justice dawn for you like the light;
　　bright as the noonday shall be your vindication.—℟.

By the LORD are the steps of a man made firm,
　　and he approves his way.
Though he fall, he does not lie prostrate,
　　for the hand of the LORD sustains him.—℟.

The salvation of the just is from the LORD;
　　he is their refuge in time of distress.
And the LORD helps them and delivers them;
　　he delivers them from the wicked and saves them,
　　because they take refuge in him.—℟. ↓

———— **YEAR II** ————

FIRST READING　　　　2 Sm 11:1-4a, 5-10a, 13-17

The Ammonite campaign continues but David remains in Jerusalem. He satisfies his lust for Bathsheba, Uriah's wife. To cover his own guilt David arranges for Uriah, who maintains his correct bearing throughout, to meet his death in battle.

A reading from the second Book of Samuel

AT the turn of the year, when kings go out on campaign, David sent out Joab along with his officers and the army of Israel, and they ravaged the Ammonites and besieged Rabbah. David, however, remained in Jerusalem. One evening David rose from his siesta and strolled about on the roof of the palace. From the roof he saw a woman bathing, who was very beautiful. David had inquiries made about the woman and was told, "She is Bathsheba, daughter of Eliam, and wife of Joab's armor bearer Uriah the Hittite." Then David sent messengers and took her. When she came to him, he had relations with her. She then returned to her house. But the woman had conceived, and sent the information to David, "I am with child."

David therefore sent a message to Joab, "Send me Uriah the Hittite." So Joab sent Uriah to David. When he came, David questioned him about Joab, the soldiers, and how the war was going, and Uriah answered that all was well. David then said to Uriah, "Go down to your house and bathe your feet." Uriah left the palace, and a portion was sent out after him from the king's table. But Uriah slept at the entrance of the royal palace with the other officers of his lord, and did not go down to his own house. David was told that Uriah had not gone home. On the day following, David summoned him, and he ate and drank with David, who made him drunk. But in the evening Uriah went out to sleep on his bed among his lord's servants, and did not go down to his home. The next morning David wrote a letter to Joab which he sent by Uriah. In it he directed: "Place Uriah up front, where the fighting is fierce. Then pull back and leave him to be struck down dead." So while Joab was besieging the city, he assigned Uriah to a place where he knew the defenders were strong. When the men of the city made a sortie against Joab, some officers of David's army fell, and among them Uriah the Hittite died.—The word of the Lord. ℟. **Thanks be to God.** ↓

RESPONSORIAL PSALM   Ps 51:3-4, 5-6a, 6bcd-7, 10-11

℟. (see 3a) **Be merciful, O Lord, for we have sinned.**

Have mercy on me, O God, in your goodness;
>   in the greatness of your compassion wipe out my
>   offense.
Thoroughly wash me from my guilt
>   and of my sin cleanse me.—℟.

For I acknowledge my offense,
>   and my sin is before me always:
"Against you only have I sinned,
>   and done what is evil in your sight."—℟.

I have done such evil in your sight
>   that you are just in your sentence,
>   blameless when you condemn.

True, I was born guilty,
   a sinner, even as my mother conceived me.—℟.

Let me hear the sounds of joy and gladness;
   the bones you have crushed shall rejoice.
Turn away your face from my sins,
   and blot out all my guilt.—℟. ↓

────── **YEAR I AND II** ──────

ALLELUIA   See Mt 11:25

℟. **Alleluia, alleluia.**
Blessed are you, Father, Lord of heaven and earth;
you have revealed to little ones the mysteries of the
   Kingdom.
℟. **Alleluia, alleluia.** ↓

GOSPEL   Mk 4:26-34

This is the parable of growing seed. Though the Gospel appears to spread
by human means, it is God who nourishes it. As a seed springs up and
grows, mysteriously, so it is with the growth of Christ's Kingdom on earth.

℣. The Lord be with you. ℟. **And also with you.**
℣. A reading from the holy Gospel according to Mark.
℟. **Glory to you, Lord.**

JESUS said to the crowds: "This is how it is with the
   Kingdom of God; it is as if a man were to scatter seed
on the land and would sleep and rise night and day and
the seed would sprout and grow, he knows not how. Of its
own accord the land yields fruit, first the blade, then the
ear, then the full grain in the ear. And when the grain is
ripe, he wields the sickle at once, for the harvest has
come."

   He said, "To what shall we compare the Kingdom of
God, or what parable can we use for it? It is like a mus-
tard seed that, when it is sown in the ground, is the smallest of all the seeds on the earth. But once it is sown, it
springs up and becomes the largest of plants and puts
forth large branches, so that the birds of the sky can

dwell in its shade." With many such parables he spoke the word to them as they were able to understand it. Without parables he did not speak to them, but to his own disciples he explained everything in private.—The Gospel of the Lord. ℟. **Praise to you, Lord Jesus Christ.**

→ No. 15, p. 623

SATURDAY OF THE THIRD WEEK
IN ORDINARY TIME

——— **YEAR I** ———

FIRST READING Heb 11:1-2, 8-19

Faith is the firm assurance of what is hoped for that is not seen. Christian living is marked by assurance that the good things promised by God will be fully possessed in the future. Jesus' saving death and his heavenly priesthood are indeed facts and not illusions.

A reading from the Letter to the Hebrews

BROTHERS and sisters: Faith is the realization of what is hoped for and evidence of things not seen. Because of it the ancients were well attested.

By faith Abraham obeyed when he was called to go out to a place that he was to receive as an inheritance; he went out, not knowing where he was to go. By faith he sojourned in the promised land as in a foreign country, dwelling in tents with Isaac and Jacob, heirs of the same promise; for he was looking forward to the city with foundations, whose architect and maker is God. By faith he received power to generate, even though he was past the normal age—and Sarah herself was sterile—for he thought that the one who had made the promise was trustworthy. So it was that there came forth from one man, himself as good as dead, descendants as numerous as the stars in the sky and as countless as the sands on the seashore.

All these died in faith. They did not receive what had been promised but saw it and greeted it from afar and acknowledged themselves to be strangers and aliens on earth, for those who speak thus show that they are seeking a homeland. If they had been thinking of the land from which they had come, they would have had opportunity to return. But now they desire a better homeland, a heavenly one. Therefore, God is not ashamed to be called their God, for he has prepared a city for them.

By faith Abraham, when put to the test, offered up Isaac, and he who had received the promises was ready to offer his only son, of whom it was said, *Through Isaac descendants shall bear your name.* He reasoned that God was able to raise even from the dead, and he received Isaac back as a symbol.—The word of the Lord. ℟. **Thanks be to God.** ↓

RESPONSORIAL PSALM   Lk 1:69-70, 71-72, 73-75

℟. (see 68) **Blessed be the Lord the God of Israel; he has come to his people.**

He has raised up for us a mighty savior,
    born of the house of his servant David.—℟.

Through his holy prophets he promised of old
    that he would save us from our sins
    from the hands of all who hate us.
He promised to show mercy to our fathers
    and to remember his holy covenant.—℟.

This was the oath he swore to our father Abraham:
    to set us free from the bonds of our enemies,
    free to worship him without fear,
    holy and righteous in his sight
    all the days of our life.—℟. ↓

———— **YEAR II** ————

FIRST READING   2 Sm 12:1-7a, 10-17

This simple parable of the ewe lamb draws David into an untenable position. It elicits from David the expected judgment of himself. Nathan points out to David that he stands self-condemned because of the wife of Uriah and that what he has done is unworthy of a prince who owes so much to Yahweh.

A reading from the second Book of Samuel

THE LORD sent Nathan to David, and when he came to him, Nathan said: "Judge this case for me! In a certain town there were two men, one rich, the other poor. The rich man had flocks and herds in great numbers. But the poor man had nothing at all except one little ewe lamb that he had bought. He nourished her, and she grew up with him and his children. She shared the little food he had and drank from his cup and slept in his bosom. She was like a daughter to him. Now, the rich man received a visitor, but he would not take from his own flocks and herds to prepare a meal for the wayfarer who had come to him. Instead he took the poor man's ewe lamb and made a meal of it for his visitor." David grew very angry with that man and said to him: "As the LORD lives, the man who has done this merits death! He shall restore the ewe lamb fourfold because he has done this and has had no pity."

Then Nathan said to David: "You are the man! Thus says the LORD God of Israel: 'The sword shall never depart from your house, because you have despised me and have taken the wife of Uriah to be your wife.' Thus says the LORD: 'I will bring evil upon you out of your own house. I will take your wives while you live to see it, and will give them to your neighbor. He shall lie with your wives in broad daylight. You have done this deed in secret, but I will bring it about in the presence of all Israel, and with the sun looking down.'"

Then David said to Nathan, "I have sinned against the LORD." Nathan answered David: "The LORD on his part has forgiven your sin: you shall not die. But since you have utterly spurned the LORD by this deed, the child born to you must surely die." Then Nathan returned to his house.

The LORD struck the child that the wife of Uriah had borne to David, and it became desperately ill. David besought God for the child. He kept a fast, retiring for the night to lie on the ground clothed in sackcloth. The elders of his house stood beside him urging him to rise from the ground; but he would not, nor would he take food with them.—The word of the Lord. ℟. **Thanks be to God.** ↓

RESPONSORIAL PSALM   Ps 51:12-13, 14-15, 16-17

℟. (12a) **Create a clean heart in me, O God.**

A clean heart create for me, O God,
    and a steadfast spirit renew within me.
Cast me not out from your presence,
    and your Holy Spirit take not from me.—℟.

Give me back the joy of your salvation,
    and a willing spirit sustain in me.
I will teach transgressors your ways,
    and sinners shall return to you.—℟.

Free me from blood guilt, O God, my saving God;
    then my tongue shall revel in your justice.
O Lord, open my lips,
    and my mouth shall proclaim your praise.—℟. ↓

——— **YEAR I AND II** ———

ALLELUIA   Jn 3:16

℟. **Alleluia, alleluia.**
God so loved the world that he gave his only-begotten Son,
so that everyone who believes in him might have eternal life.
℟. **Alleluia, alleluia.** ↓

GOSPEL   Mk 4:35-41

The emphasis on the storm and the need of faith is a lesson in discipleship. Christ calms a violent storm. The doubt and fear of the Apostles that he could save them shows that our Lord is trying their faith and awaiting their prayers.

℣. The Lord be with you. ℟. **And also with you.**
℣. A reading from the holy Gospel according to Mark.
℟. **Glory to you, Lord.**

ON that day, as evening drew on, Jesus said to his disciples: "Let us cross to the other side." Leaving the crowd, they took Jesus with them in the boat just as he was. And other boats were with him. A violent squall came up and waves were breaking over the boat, so that it was already filling up. Jesus was in the stern, asleep on a cushion. They woke him and said to him, "Teacher, do you not care that we are perishing?" He woke up, rebuked the wind, and said to the sea, "Quiet! Be still!" The wind ceased and there was great calm. Then he asked them, "Why are you terrified? Do you not yet have faith?" They were filled with great awe and said to one another, "Who then is this whom even wind and sea obey?"—The Gospel of the Lord. ℟. **Praise to you, Lord Jesus Christ.**

→ No. 15, p. 623

MONDAY OF THE FOURTH WEEK
IN ORDINARY TIME

——— YEAR I ———

FIRST READING   Heb 11:32-40

The sacred author passes summarily through some heroes of the Old Testament. The sufferings mentioned are principally those endured by the faithful Israelites during the persecution of the Maccabean revolt. The fulfillment the Old Testament saints awaited did not take place until the saving work of Christ was completed.

A reading from the Letter to the Hebrews

BROTHERS and sisters: What more shall I say? I have not time to tell of Gideon, Barak, Samson, Jephthah, of David and Samuel and the prophets, who by faith conquered kingdoms, did what was righteous, obtained the promises; they closed the mouths of lions, put out raging fires, escaped the devouring sword; out of weakness they were made powerful, became strong in battle, and turned back foreign invaders. Women received back their dead through resurrection. Some were tortured and would not accept deliverance, in order to obtain a better resurrection. Others endured mockery, scourging, even chains and imprisonment. They were stoned, sawed in two, put to death at sword's point; they went about in skins of sheep or goats, needy, afflicted, tormented. The world was not worthy of them. They wandered about in deserts and on mountains, in caves and in crevices in the earth.

Yet all these, though approved because of their faith, did not receive what had been promised. God had foreseen something better for us, so that without us they should not be made perfect.—The word of the Lord. ℟. **Thanks be to God.** ↓

RESPONSORIAL PSALM Ps 31:20, 21, 22, 23, 24

℟. (25) **Let your hearts take comfort, all who hope in the Lord.**

How great is the goodness, O LORD,
    which you have in store for those who fear you,
And which, toward those who take refuge in you,
    you show in the sight of the children of men.—℟.

You hide them in the shelter of your presence
    from the plottings of men;
You screen them within your abode
    from the strife of tongues.—℟.

Blessed be the LORD whose wondrous mercy
    he has shown me in a fortified city.—℟.

Once I said in my anguish,
    "I am cut off from your sight";
Yet you heard the sound of my pleading
    when I cried out to you.—℟.

Love the LORD, all you his faithful ones!
   The LORD keeps those who are constant,
      but more than requites those who act proudly.—℟. ↓

——————— **YEAR II** ———————

FIRST READING   2 Sm 15:13-14, 30; 16:5-13

David, alarmed at the news of the rebellion, leaves Jerusalem with his troops. The ensuing events in David's flight are described succinctly; David is the hunted one, and he is in dismay upon hearing of Absalom's defection.

A reading from the second Book of Samuel

A N informant came to David with the report, "The children of Israel have transferred their loyalty to Absalom." At this, David said to all his servants who were with him in Jerusalem: "Up! Let us take flight, or none of us will escape from Absalom. Leave quickly, lest he hurry and overtake us, then visit disaster upon us and put the city to the sword."

As David went up the Mount of Olives, he wept without ceasing. His head was covered, and he was walking barefoot. All those who were with him also had their heads covered and were weeping as they went.

As David was approaching Bahurim, a man named Shimei, the son of Gera of the same clan as Saul's family, was coming out of the place, cursing as he came. He threw stones at David and at all the king's officers, even though all the soldiers, including the royal guard, were on David's right and on his left. Shimei was saying as he cursed: "Away, away, you murderous and wicked man! The LORD has requited you for all the bloodshed in the family of Saul, in whose stead you became king, and the LORD has given over the kingdom to your son Absalom. And now you suffer ruin because you are a murderer." Abishai, son of Zeruiah, said to the king: "Why should this dead dog curse my lord the king? Let me go over, please, and lop off his head." But the king replied: "What business is it of mine or of yours, sons of Zeruiah, that he curses? Suppose the LORD has told him to curse David; who then will dare to say, 'Why are you doing this?' " Then the king said to Abishai and to all his servants: "If my own son, who came forth from my loins, is seeking my life, how much more might this Benjaminite do so? Let him alone and let him curse, for the LORD has told him to. Perhaps the LORD will look upon my affliction and make it up to me with benefits for the curses he is uttering this day." David and his men continued on the road, while Shimei kept abreast of them on the hillside, all the while cursing and throwing stones and dirt as he went.— The word of the Lord. ℟. **Thanks be to God.** ↓

RESPONSORIAL PSALM   Ps 3:2-3, 4-5, 6-7

℟. (8a) **Lord, rise up and save me.**

O LORD, how many are my adversaries!
    Many rise up against me!
Many are saying of me,
    "There is no salvation for him in God."—℟.

But you, O LORD, are my shield;
    my glory, you lift up my head!
When I call out to the LORD,
    he answers me from his holy mountain.—℟.

When I lie down in sleep,
    I wake again, for the LORD sustains me.
I fear not the myriads of people
    arrayed against me on every side.—℟. ↓

——————— **YEAR I AND II** ———————

ALLELUIA   Lk 7:16

℟. **Alleluia, alleluia.**
A great prophet has arisen in our midst
and God has visited his people.
℟. **Alleluia, alleluia.** ↓

GOSPEL   Mk 5:1-20

Mark dwells graphically on the impossibility of subduing the maniac. The miracle contains many hints as to the nature of demoniacal possession. At the direction of Christ, the healed demoniac returns to his family to tell them of the compassion and mercy of God.

℣. The Lord be with you. ℟. **And also with you.**
℣. A reading from the holy Gospel according to Mark.
℟. **Glory to you, Lord.**

JESUS and his disciples came to the other side of the sea, to the territory of the Gerasenes. When he got out of the boat, at once a man from the tombs who had an unclean spirit met him. The man had been dwelling among the tombs, and no one could restrain him any longer, even with a chain. In fact, he had frequently been bound with shackles and chains, but the chains had been pulled apart by him and the shackles smashed, and no one was strong enough to subdue him. Night and day among the tombs and on the hillsides he was always crying out and bruising himself with stones. Catching sight of Jesus from a distance, he ran up and prostrated himself before him, crying out in a loud voice, "What have you to do with me, Jesus, Son of the Most High God? I adjure you by God, do not torment me!" (He had been saying to him, "Unclean spirit, come out of the man!") He asked him, "What is your name?" He replied, "Legion is my name. There are many of us." And he pleaded earnestly with him not to drive them away from that territory.

Now a large herd of swine was feeding there on the hillside. And they pleaded with him, "Send us into the swine. Let us enter them." And he let them, and the unclean spirits came out and entered the swine. The herd of about two thousand rushed down a steep bank into the sea, where they were drowned. The swineherds ran away and reported the incident in the town and throughout the countryside. And people came out to see what had happened. As they approached Jesus, they caught sight of the man who had been possessed by Legion, sitting there clothed and in his right mind. And they were seized with fear. Those who witnessed the incident explained to them what had happened to the possessed man and to the swine. Then they began to beg him to leave their district. As he was getting into the boat, the man who had been possessed pleaded to remain with him. But Jesus would not permit him but told him instead, "Go home to your family and announce to them all that the Lord in his pity has done for you." Then the man went off and began to proclaim in the Decapolis what Jesus had done for him; and all were amazed.—The Gospel of the Lord. ℟. **Praise to you, Lord Jesus Christ.**   → No. 15, p. 623

TUESDAY OF THE FOURTH WEEK IN ORDINARY TIME

—————— YEAR I ——————

FIRST READING   Heb 12:1-4

All through life there are temptations, wants, and desires that distract from Jesus. The sacred author reminds us to keep in the race with our eyes focused on Jesus in whom we have faith. He did not give up the fight even when faced with death.

A reading from the Letter to the Hebrews

BROTHERS and sisters: Since we are surrounded by so great a cloud of witnesses, let us rid ourselves of every burden and sin that clings to us and persevere in running the race that lies before us while keeping our eyes fixed on Jesus, the leader and perfecter of faith. For the sake of the joy that lay before him Jesus endured the cross, despising its shame, and has taken his seat at the right of the throne of God. Consider how he endured such opposition from sinners, in order that you may not grow weary and lose heart. In your struggle against sin you have not yet resisted to the point of shedding blood. —The word of the Lord. ℟. **Thanks be to God.** ↓

RESPONSORIAL PSALM   Ps 22:26b-27, 28 and 30, 31-32

℟. (see 27b) **They will praise you, Lord, who long for you.**

I will fulfill my vows before those who fear him.
The lowly shall eat their fill;
　　they who seek the LORD shall praise him:
　　"May your hearts be ever merry!"—℟.

All the ends of the earth
　　shall remember and turn to the LORD;
All the families of the nations
　　shall bow down before him.
To him alone shall bow down
　　all who sleep in the earth;
Before him shall bend
　　all who go down into the dust.—℟.

And to him my soul shall live;
　　my descendants shall serve him.
Let the coming generation be told of the LORD
　　that they may proclaim to a people yet to be born
　　the justice he has shown.—℟. ↓

——— **YEAR II** ———

FIRST READING   2 Sm 18:9-10, 14b, 24-25a, 30—19.3

Absalom is caught in a tree, and Joab thrusts three pikes in him. When the news of Absalom's death reaches David, he grieves together with the whole army.

A reading from the second Book of Samuel

ABSALOM unexpectedly came up against David's servants. He was mounted on a mule, and, as the mule passed under the branches of a large terebinth, his hair caught fast in the tree. He hung between heaven and earth while the mule he had been riding ran off. Someone saw this and reported to Joab that he had seen Absalom hanging from a terebinth. And taking three pikes in hand, he thrust for the heart of Absalom, still hanging from the tree alive.

Now David was sitting between the two gates, and a lookout went up to the roof of the gate above the city wall, where he looked about and saw a man running all alone. The lookout shouted to inform the king, who said, "If he is alone, he has good news to report." The king said, "Step aside and remain in attendance here." So he stepped aside and remained there. When the Cushite messenger came in, he said, "Let my lord the king receive the good news that this day the LORD has taken your part, freeing you from the grasp of all who rebelled against you." But the king asked the Cushite, "Is young Absalom safe?" The Cushite replied, "May the enemies of my lord the king and all who rebel against you with evil intent be as that young man!"

The king was shaken, and went up to the room over the city gate to weep. He said as he wept, "My son Absalom! My son, my son Absalom! If only I had died instead of you, Absalom, my son, my son!"

Joab was told that the king was weeping and mourning for Absalom; and that day's victory was turned into mourning for the whole army when they heard that the king was grieving for his son.—The word of the Lord. ℟. **Thanks be to God.** ↓

RESPONSORIAL PSALM   Ps 86:1-2, 3-4, 5-6

℟. (1a) **Listen, Lord, and answer me.**

See Saturday after Ash Wednesday, p. 434.

——————— **YEAR I AND II** ———————

ALLELUIA   Mt 8:17

℟. **Alleluia, alleluia.**
Christ took away our infirmities
and bore our diseases.
℟. **Alleluia, alleluia.** ↓

GOSPEL
Mk 5:21-43

Jesus performs two miracles that are the result of deep faith—the curing of the woman who was sick for years and the raising of Jairus's daughter from death to life. Jesus shows how he responds to those who come to him: "Ask and you shall receive."

℣. The Lord be with you. ℟. **And also with you.**
℣. A reading from the holy Gospel according to Mark.
℟. **Glory to you, Lord.**

WHEN Jesus had crossed again in the boat to the other side, a large crowd gathered around him, and he stayed close to the sea. One of the synagogue officials, named Jairus, came forward. Seeing him he fell at his feet and pleaded earnestly with him, saying, "My daughter is at the point of death. Please, come lay your hands on her that she may get well and live." He went off with him and a large crowd followed him.

There was a woman afflicted with hemorrhages for twelve years. She had suffered greatly at the hands of many doctors and had spent all that she had. Yet she was not helped but only grew worse. She had heard about Jesus and came up behind him in the crowd and touched his cloak. She said, "If I but touch his clothes, I shall be cured." Immediately her flow of blood dried up. She felt in her body that she was healed of her affliction. Jesus, aware at once that power had gone out from him, turned around in the crowd and asked, "Who has touched my clothes?" But his disciples said to him, "You see how the crowd is pressing upon you, and yet you ask, Who touched me?" And he looked around to see who had done it. The woman, realizing what had happened to her, approached in fear and trembling. She fell down before Jesus and told him the whole truth. He said to her, "Daughter, your faith has saved you. Go in peace and be cured of your affliction."

While he was still speaking, people from the synagogue official's house arrived and said, "Your daughter has died; why trouble the teacher any longer?" Disregarding the message that was reported, Jesus said to the synagogue official, "Do not be afraid; just have faith." He did not allow anyone to accompany him inside except Peter, James, and John, the brother of James. When they arrived at the house of the synagogue official, he caught sight of a commotion, people weeping and wailing loudly. So he went in and said to them, "Why this commotion and weeping? The child is not dead but asleep." And they ridiculed him. Then he put them all out. He took along the child's father and mother and those who were with him and entered the room where the child was. He took the child by the hand and said to her, *"Talitha koum,"* which means, "Little girl, I say to you, arise!" The girl, a child of twelve, arose immediately and walked around. At that they were utterly astounded. He gave strict orders that no one should know this and said that she should be given something to eat.—The Gospel of the Lord. ℞. **Praise to you, Lord Jesus Christ.** → No. 15, p. 623

WEDNESDAY OF THE FOURTH WEEK IN ORDINARY TIME

—— **YEAR I** ——

FIRST READING   Heb 12:4-7, 11-15

It is evident that the local church addressed in the Letter shrinks from the thought of persecutions and suffering. However, the Christian should be aware that God trains his people in the hard school of suffering. Trials and suffering are proof of his Fatherly concern and certainly not a sign of his anger.

A reading from the Letter to the Hebrews

BROTHERS and sisters: In your struggle against sin you have not yet resisted to the point of shedding blood. You have also forgotten the exhortation addressed to you as children:

> *My son, do not disdain the discipline of the Lord*
> *or lose heart when reproved by him;*
> *for whom the Lord loves, he disciplines;*
> *he scourges every son he acknowledges.*

Endure your trials as "discipline"; God treats you as his sons. For what "son" is there whom his father does not discipline? At the time, all discipline seems a cause not for joy but for pain, yet later it brings the peaceful fruit of righteousness to those who are trained by it.

So strengthen your drooping hands and your weak knees. Make straight paths for your feet, that what is lame may not be dislocated but healed.

Strive for peace with everyone, and for that holiness without which no one will see the Lord. See to it that no one be deprived of the grace of God, that no bitter root spring up and cause trouble, through which many may become defiled.—The word of the Lord. ℟. **Thanks be to God.** ↓

RESPONSORIAL PSALM   Ps 103:1-2, 13-14, 17-18a

℟. (see 17) **The Lord's kindness is everlasting to those who fear him.**

Bless the LORD, O my soul;
    and all my being, bless his holy name.
Bless the LORD, O my soul,
    and forget not all his benefits.—℟.

As a father has compassion on his children,
    so the LORD has compassion on those who fear him,
For he knows how we are formed;
    he remembers that we are dust.—℟.

But the kindness of the LORD is from eternity
    to eternity toward those who fear him,
And his justice toward children's children
    among those who keep his covenant.—℟. ↓

———— **YEAR II** ————

FIRST READING   2 Sm 24:2, 9-17

David orders a census of the Israelites, but he later repents for testing the Lord. Three choices are given David, and he chooses pestilence for the punishment. God again spares his people.

A reading from the second Book of Samuel

KING David said to Joab and the leaders of the army who were with him, "Tour all the tribes in Israel from Dan to Beer-sheba and register the people, that I may know their number." Joab then reported to the king the number of people registered: in Israel, eight hundred thousand men fit for military service; in Judah, five hundred thousand.

Afterward, however, David regretted having numbered the people, and said to the LORD: "I have sinned grievously in what I have done. But now, LORD, forgive the guilt of your servant, for I have been very foolish." When David rose in the morning, the LORD had spoken to the prophet Gad, David's seer, saying: "Go and say to David, 'This is what the LORD says: I offer you three alternatives; choose one of them, and I will inflict it on you.'" Gad then went to David to inform him. He asked: "Do you want a three years' famine to come upon your land, or to flee from your enemy three months while he pursues you, or to have a three days' pestilence in your land? Now consider and decide what I must reply to him who sent me." David answered Gad: "I am in very serious difficulty. Let us fall by the hand of God, for he is most merciful; but let me not fall by the hand of man." Thus David chose the pestilence. Now it was the time of the wheat harvest when the plague broke out among the people. The LORD then sent a pestilence over Israel from morning until the time appointed, and seventy thousand of the people from Dan to Beer-sheba died. But when the angel stretched forth his hand toward Jerusalem to destroy it, the LORD regretted the calamity and said to the angel causing the destruction among the people, "Enough now! Stay your hand." The angel of the LORD was then standing at the threshing floor of Araunah the Jebusite. When David saw the angel who was striking the people, he said to the LORD: "It is I who have sinned; it is I, the shepherd, who have done wrong. But these are sheep; what have they done? Punish me and my kindred."—The word of the Lord. ℟. **Thanks be to God.** ↓

RESPONSORIAL PSALM   Ps 32:1-2, 5, 6, 7

℟. (see 5c) **Lord, forgive the wrong I have done.**

Blessed is he whose fault is taken away,
    whose sin is covered.
Blessed the man to whom the LORD imputes not guilt,
    in whose spirit there is no guile.—℟.

Then I acknowledged my sin to you,
    my guilt I covered not.
I said, "I confess my faults to the LORD,"
    and you took away the guilt of my sin.—℟.

For this shall every faithful man pray to you
    in time of stress.
Though deep waters overflow,
    they shall not reach him.—℟.

You are my shelter; from distress you will preserve me;
    with glad cries of freedom you will ring me
        round.—℟. ↓

———— **YEAR I AND II** ————

ALLELUIA   Jn 10:27

℟. **Alleluia, alleluia.**
My sheep hear my voice, says the Lord;
I know them, and they follow me.
℟. **Alleluia, alleluia.** ↓

GOSPEL   Mk 6:1-6

Jesus is rejected by his fellow countrymen. It was a Jewish custom to refer to a man as the son of his father. Thus, "son of Mary" may be intended as an insult. Our Lord's miraculous power is rendered ineffective by the disbelief of his countrymen.

℣. The Lord be with you. ℟. **And also with you.**
℣. A reading from the holy Gospel according to Mark.
℟. **Glory to you, Lord.**

JESUS departed from there and came to his native place, accompanied by his disciples. When the sabbath came he began to teach in the synagogue, and many who heard him were astonished. They said, "Where did this man get all this? What kind of wisdom has been given him? What mighty deeds are wrought by his hands! Is he not the carpenter, the son of Mary, and the brother of James and Joseph and Judas and Simon? And are not his sisters here with us?" And they took offense at him. Jesus said to them, "A prophet is not without honor except in his native place and among his own kin and in his own house." So he was not able to perform any mighty deed there, apart from curing a few sick people by laying his hands on them. He was amazed at their lack of faith.— The Gospel of the Lord. ℟. **Praise to you, Lord Jesus Christ.**   → No. 15, p. 623

THURSDAY OF THE FOURTH WEEK
IN ORDINARY TIME

———— YEAR I ————

FIRST READING   Heb 12:18-19, 21-24

The sacred author begins a contrast between the assembly of Israel gathered for the making of the Old Covenant and the giving of the law, and the assembly of those who have entered into the New Covenant.

A reading from the Letter to the Hebrews

BROTHERS and sisters: You have not approached that which could be touched and a blazing fire and gloomy darkness and storm and a trumpet blast and a voice speaking words such that those who heard begged that no message be further addressed to them. Indeed, so fearful was the spectacle that Moses said, "I am terrified and trembling." No, you have approached Mount Zion and the city of the living God, the heavenly Jerusalem, and countless angels in festal gathering, and the assembly of the firstborn enrolled in heaven, and God the judge of all, and the spirits of the just made perfect, and Jesus, the mediator of a new covenant, and the sprinkled Blood that speaks more eloquently than that of Abel.—The word of the Lord. ℟. **Thanks be to God.** ↓

RESPONSORIAL PSALM   Ps 48:2-3ab, 3cd-4, 9, 10-11

℟. (see 10) **O God, we ponder your mercy within your temple.**

Great is the LORD and wholly to be praised
  in the city of our God.
His holy mountain, fairest of heights,
  is the joy of all the earth.—℟.

Mount Zion, "the recesses of the North,"
  the city of the great King.
God is with her castles;
  renowned is he as a stronghold.—℟.

As we had heard, so have we seen
  in the city of the LORD of hosts,
In the city of our God;
  God makes it firm forever.—℟.

O God, we ponder your mercy
  within your temple.
As your name, O God, so also your praise
  reaches to the ends of the earth.
Of justice your right hand is full.—℟. ↓

─────── **YEAR II** ───────

FIRST READING   1 Kgs 2:1-4, 10-12

Just before dying, David instructs Solomon to be courageous and follow the decrees in the law of Moses. David dies and is buried in the City of David. Thereupon, Solomon is seated on the throne of his father.

A reading from the first Book of Kings

WHEN the time of David's death drew near, he gave these instructions to his son Solomon: "I am going the way of all flesh. Take courage and be a man. Keep the mandate of the LORD, your God, following his ways and observing his statutes, commands, ordinances, and decrees as they are written in the law of Moses, that you may succeed in whatever you do, wherever you turn, and the LORD may fulfill the promise he made on my behalf when he said, 'If your sons so conduct themselves that they remain faithful to me with their whole heart and with their whole soul, you shall always have someone of your line on the throne of Israel.' "

David rested with his ancestors and was buried in the City of David. The length of David's reign over Israel was forty years: he reigned seven years in Hebron and thirty-three years in Jerusalem.

Solomon was seated on the throne of his father David, with his sovereignty firmly established.—The word of the Lord. ℟. **Thanks be to God.** ↓

RESPONSORIAL PSALM   1 Chr 29:10, 11ab, 11d-12a, 12bcd

℟. (12b) **Lord, you are exalted over all.**

"Blessed may you be, O LORD,
    God of Israel our father,
    from eternity to eternity."—℟.

"Yours, O LORD, are grandeur and power,
    majesty, splendor, and glory."—℟.

"LORD, you are exalted over all.
   Yours, O LORD, is the sovereignty;
   you are exalted as head over all.
Riches and honor are from you."—R̶.

"In your hand are power and might;
   it is yours to give grandeur and strength to all."—R̶. ↓

——————— **YEAR I AND II** ———————

ALLELUIA   Mk 1:15

R̶. **Alleluia, alleluia.**
The Kingdom of God is at hand;
repent and believe in the Gospel.
R̶. **Alleluia, alleluia.** ↓

GOSPEL   Mk 6:7-13

St. Mark is the only evangelist who mentions that Christ began to send his
disciples forth in pairs. Two were considered better than one, for if one
fell, the companion could lift up his fellow. They work many cures.

℣. The Lord be with you. R̶. **And also with you.**
℣. A reading from the holy Gospel according to Mark.
R̶. **Glory to you, Lord.**

JESUS summoned the Twelve and began to send them
out two by two and gave them authority over unclean
spirits. He instructed them to take nothing for the journey but a walking stick—no food, no sack, no money in
their belts. They were, however, to wear sandals but not a
second tunic. He said to them, "Wherever you enter a
house, stay there until you leave from there. Whatever
place does not welcome you or listen to you, leave there
and shake the dust off your feet in testimony against
them." So they went off and preached repentance. The
Twelve drove out many demons, and they anointed with
oil many who were sick and cured them.—The Gospel of
the Lord. R̶. **Praise to you, Lord Jesus Christ.**

➜ No. 15, p. 623

FRIDAY OF THE FOURTH WEEK
IN ORDINARY TIME

———— YEAR I ————

FIRST READING   Heb 13:1-8

The sacred author speaks of love and appeals for hospitality. Ministry to
the basic needs of one's neighbor is mentioned to show that persons are
judged on their behavior toward their neighbor. Much stress is laid upon
acts of mercy because they are within the reach of all.

A reading from the Letter to the Hebrews

LET brotherly love continue. Do not neglect hospitality, for through it some have unknowingly entertained
angels. Be mindful of prisoners as if sharing their imprisonment, and of the ill-treated as of yourselves, for you
also are in the body. Let marriage be honored among all
and the marriage bed be kept undefiled, for God will
judge the immoral and adulterers. Let your life be free
from love of money but be content with what you have,
for he has said, *I will never forsake you or abandon you.*
Thus we may say with confidence:
　　The Lord is my helper,
　　and I will not be afraid.
　　What can anyone do to me?
Remember your leaders who spoke the word of God to
you. Consider the outcome of their way of life and imitate
their faith. Jesus Christ is the same yesterday, today, and
forever.—The word of the Lord. ℟. **Thanks be to God.** ↓

RESPONSORIAL PSALM   Ps 27:1, 3, 5, 8b-9abc

℟. (1a) **The Lord is my light and my salvation.**

The LORD is my light and my salvation;
　　whom should I fear?
The LORD is my life's refuge;
　　of whom should I be afraid?—℟.

Though an army encamp against me,
  my heart will not fear;
Though war be waged upon me,
  even then will I trust.—℟.

For he will hide me in his abode
  in the day of trouble;
He will conceal me in the shelter of his tent,
  he will set me high upon a rock.—℟.

Your presence, O LORD, I seek.
Hide not your face from me;
  do not in anger repel your servant.
You are my helper: cast me not off.—℟. ↓

——————— **YEAR II** ———————

FIRST READING   Sir 47:2-11

The Lord had given strength to David to slay the giant. The women sang his praises. He destroyed the Philistines and ordered celebrations. The Lord also forgave him his sins.

A reading from the Book of Sirach

L IKE the choice fat of the sacred offerings,
  so was David in Israel.
He made sport of lions as though they were kids,
  and of bears, like lambs of the flock.
As a youth he slew the giant
  and wiped out the people's disgrace,
When his hand let fly the slingstone
  that crushed the pride of Goliath.
Since he called upon the Most High God,
  who gave strength to his right arm
To defeat the skilled warrior
  and raise up the might of his people,
Therefore the women sang his praises,
  and ascribed to him tens of thousands
  and praised him when they blessed the Lord.
When he assumed the royal crown, he battled
  and subdued the enemy on every side.

He destroyed the hostile Philistines
> and shattered their power till our own day.

With his every deed he offered thanks
> to God Most High, in words of praise.

With his whole being he loved his Maker
> and daily had his praises sung.

He set singers before the altar and by their voices
> he made sweet melodies.

He added beauty to the feasts
> and solemnized the seasons of each year

So that when the Holy Name was praised,
> before daybreak the sanctuary would resound.

The LORD forgave him his sins
> and exalted his strength forever;

He conferred on him the rights of royalty
> and established his throne in Israel.

The word of the Lord. ℟. **Thanks be to God.** ↓

RESPONSORIAL PSALM   Ps 18:31, 47 and 50, 51

℟. (see 47b) **Blessed be God my salvation!**

God's way is unerring,
> the promise of the LORD is fire-tried;
> he is a shield to all who take refuge in him.—℟.

The LORD live! And blessed be my Rock!
> Extolled be God my savior.

Therefore will I proclaim you, O LORD, among the nations,
> and I will sing praise to your name.—℟.

You who gave great victories to your king
> and showed kindness to your anointed,
> to David and his posterity forever.—℟. ↓

——————— **YEAR I AND II** ———————

ALLELUIA   See Lk 8:15

℟. **Alleluia, alleluia.**

Blessed are they who have kept the word with a gener-
> ous heart,

and yield a harvest through perseverance.

℟. **Alleluia, alleluia.** ↓

GOSPEL   Mk 6:14-29

The Gospel assigns John's rebuke of Herod's adultery as the reason for his death. When John denounces the adulterous connection of his royal hearer and demands that he put away the guilty woman as the only condition of salvation, John is shut up in prison and ultimately loses his life.

℣. The Lord be with you. ℟. **And also with you.**

℣. A reading from the holy Gospel according to Mark.

℟. **Glory to you, Lord.**

KING Herod heard about Jesus, for his fame had become widespread, and people were saying, "John the Baptist has been raised from the dead; that is why mighty powers are at work in him." Others were saying, "He is Elijah"; still others, "He is a prophet like any of the prophets." But when Herod learned of it, he said, "It is John whom I beheaded. He has been raised up."

Herod was the one who had John arrested and bound in prison on account of Herodias, the wife of his brother Philip, whom he had married. John had said to Herod, "It is not lawful for you to have your brother's wife." Herodias harbored a grudge against him and wanted to kill him but was unable to do so. Herod feared John, knowing him to be a righteous and holy man, and kept him in custody. When he heard him speak he was very much perplexed, yet he liked to listen to him. Herodias had an opportunity one day when Herod, on his birthday, gave a banquet for his courtiers, his military officers, and the leading men of Galilee. His own daughter came in and performed a dance that delighted Herod and his guests. The king said to the girl, "Ask of me whatever you wish and I will grant it to you." He even swore many things to her, "I will grant you whatever you ask of me, even to half of my kingdom." She went out and said to her mother, "What shall I ask for?" Her mother replied, "The head of John the Baptist." The girl hurried back to the king's presence and made her request, "I want you to give me at once on a platter the head of John the Baptist." The king was deeply distressed, but because of his oaths and the guests he did not wish to break his word to her. So he promptly dispatched an executioner with orders to bring back his head. He went off and beheaded him in the prison. He brought in the head on a platter and gave it to the girl. The girl in turn gave it to her mother. When his disciples heard about it, they came and took his body and laid it in a tomb.—The Gospel of the Lord. ℟. **Praise to you, Lord Jesus Christ.**   ➔ No. 15, p. 623

SATURDAY OF THE FOURTH WEEK IN ORDINARY TIME

———— YEAR I ————

FIRST READING   Heb 13:15-17, 20-21

The sacred author exhorts the Christians to praise God constantly through Jesus. They are bound to pray for their pastors, their missionaries, and their teachers. These required petitions and intercessions are as old as the Church itself. The writer prays that his people will receive from God all that is good.

A reading from the Letter to the Hebrews

BROTHERS and sisters: Through Jesus, let us continually offer God a sacrifice of praise, that is, the fruit of lips that confess his name. Do not neglect to do good and to share what you have; God is pleased by sacrifices of that kind.

Obey your leaders and defer to them, for they keep watch over you and will have to give an account, that they may fulfill their task with joy and not with sorrow, for that would be of no advantage to you.

May the God of peace, who brought up from the dead the great shepherd of the sheep by the Blood of the eternal covenant, Jesus our Lord, furnish you with all that is good, that you may do his will. May he carry out in you what is pleasing to him through Jesus Christ, to whom be glory forever and ever. Amen.—The word of the Lord. ℟. **Thanks be to God.** ↓

RESPONSORIAL PSALM   Ps 23:1-3a, 3b-4, 5, 6

℟. (1) **The Lord is my shepherd; there is nothing I shall want.**

The LORD is my shepherd; I shall not want.
    In verdant pastures he gives me repose.
Beside restful waters he leads me;
    he refreshes my soul.—℟.

He guides me in right paths
    for his name's sake.
Even though I walk in the dark valley
    I fear no evil; for you are at my side
With your rod and your staff
    that give me courage.—℟.

You spread the table before me
    in the sight of my foes;
You anoint my head with oil;
    my cup overflows.—℟.

Only goodness and kindness follow me
    all the days of my life;
And I shall dwell in the house of the LORD
    for years to come.—℟. ↓

——————— **YEAR II** ———————

FIRST READING   1 Kgs 3:4-13

The Lord appears to Solomon in a dream telling him to ask any favor. Solomon prays for wisdom to know right from wrong. The Lord promises this and in addition great riches because Solomon has not asked for any selfish gain.

A reading from the first Book of Kings

SOLOMON went to Gibeon to sacrifice there, that was the most renowned high place. Upon

Solomon offered a thousand burnt offerings. In Gibeon the LORD appeared to Solomon in a dream at night. God said, "Ask something of me and I will give it to you." Solomon answered: "You have shown great favor to your servant, my father David, because he behaved faithfully toward you, with justice and an upright heart; and you have continued this great favor toward him, even today, seating a son of his on his throne. O LORD, my God, you have made me, your servant, king to succeed my father David; but I am a mere youth, not knowing at all how to act. I serve you in the midst of the people whom you have chosen, a people so vast that it cannot be numbered or counted. Give your servant, therefore, an understanding heart to judge your people and to distinguish right from wrong. For who is able to govern this vast people of yours?"

The LORD was pleased that Solomon made this request. So God said to him: "Because you have asked for this—not for a long life for yourself, nor for riches, nor for the life of your enemies, but for understanding so that you may know what is right—I do as you requested. I give you a heart so wise and understanding that there has never been anyone like you up to now, and after you there will come no one to equal you. In addition, I give you what you have not asked for, such riches and glory that among kings there is not your like."—The word of the Lord. ℟. **Thanks be to God.** ↓

RESPONSORIAL PSALM   Ps 119:9, 10, 11, 12, 13, 14
See Common of Doctors, p. 1180, no. 3.

———————— **YEAR I AND II** ————————

ALLELUIA   Jn 10:27
℟. **Alleluia, alleluia.**
My sheep hear my voice, says the Lord;

I know them, and they follow me.
℟. **Alleluia, alleluia.** ↓

GOSPEL   Mk 6:30-34

Jesus takes his Apostles aside to converse with them and he teaches them
many things concerning the Kingdom of God. His teaching is connected
with his miraculous powers, and it causes amazement. Our Lord's pity
moves him to assuage the spiritual hunger of the shepherdless people by
bringing God's revelation to them.

℣. The Lord be with you. ℟. **And also with you.**
℣. A reading from the holy Gospel according to Mark.
℟. **Glory to you, Lord.**

T HE Apostles gathered together with Jesus and reported all they had done and taught. He said to them,
"Come away by yourselves to a deserted place and rest a
while." People were coming and going in great numbers,
and they had no opportunity even to eat. So they went off
in the boat by themselves to a deserted place. People saw
them leaving and many came to know about it. They hastened there on foot from all the towns and arrived at the
place before them.

When Jesus disembarked and saw the vast crowd, his
heart was moved with pity for them, for they were like
sheep without a shepherd; and he began to teach them
many things.—The Gospel of the Lord. ℟. **Praise to you,
Lord Jesus Christ.**   ➜ No. 15, p. 623

INTRODUCTION FOR 5th TO 9th WEEK

The Book of Genesis—*The first five Books of the Bible (Genesis, Exodus, Leviticus, Numbers, and Deuteronomy) form what is called the Pentateuch. Though attributed en masse to Moses, they are really the result of a progressive fusion of traditions of diverse origins and times. Their principal theme is God's Covenant with Israel, a contract of the living God with the people he had chosen and whose life he sustained through his fidelity.*

Genesis is the Book of beginnings, the beginnings of the People of God and those of the world. The first eleven chapters paint in broad strokes the history of the world, from its beginning to Abraham, and form the setting for the history of salvation. They give two different pictures of creation, followed by the traditions about the life of the first human beings and the beginning of civilization, the flood, the repeopling of the earth and the dispersion of mankind, manifesting at the same time God's merciful love and humanity's sin.

Their basic purpose, however, is to interpret mankind's present condition and reveal every person's situation before God. Above all, they constitute a profession of faith in the absolute sovereignty of God, the origin and end of all reality, faith in the love and patience of God who has created human beings that they might become his partners and who constantly reestablishes relations with them in spite of the latter's repeated infidelities and incredulity.

The remaining chapters deal with the pre-history of the chosen people through the great patriarchs Abraham, Isaac, and Jacob and his twelve sons. They illustrate the fact that the God of the chosen people is not a far-off deity conceived by some philosopher. He is the God who has manifested himself to Abraham, Isaac, and Jacob, the God who made a Covenant with them and made promises to them, among which is the promise of the Messiah.

The Letter of James—*This Letter is really a sermon set down about 62 A.D. by James, leader of the Jerusalem community and one of the relatives of Jesus. Its purpose was to counter the tendency toward an abstract, non-fruitful practice of Christianity threatening the particular churches known as "the twelve tribes of Israel." The author writes in the spirit of Old Testament wisdom literature and of the moral teaching of Tobit. He presupposes knowledge of the Gospel on the part of his readers and concentrates on reminding them of how Christians ought to live. He also provides a beautiful reproduction of the moral teachings of our Lord's Sermon on the Mount.*

The Book of Sirach—*This Book was written between 200 and 175 B.C. by a sage who lived in Jerusalem and was thoroughly imbued with love for the law, the priesthood, the temple, and divine worship. As a wise and experienced observer of life, he sets forth the true nature of wisdom and indicates the religious and social duties that must be performed in all the vicissitudes of life. It culminates in the personification of wisdom (ch. 24) that laid the groundwork for the revelation of the second person of the Trinity who is the personalized wisdom or word of God.*

The First Letter of Peter—*This Letter was most likely written by St. Peter about 64 A.D. and sets forth the nature of the Christian life begun in baptism as an experience of regeneration. By their acceptance of Christianity the Christian communities of Asia Minor had become separated from their pagan compatriots, who were abusing and persecuting them. The Apostle instructs his readers that Christianity is the true religion in spite of their trials and sufferings, and exhorts them to lead good Christian lives.*

The Book of Tobit—*Written in the second century B.C., this charming book uses the literary form of religious novel (as do Jonah and Judith) for the purpose of instruction and edification. It contains numerous maxims like those found in the Wisdom Books as well as the customary Sapiential themes: fidelity to the law, the intercessory function of angels, piety toward parents, the purity of marriage, reverence for the dead, and the value of almsgiving, prayer, and fasting.*

The Second Letter of Peter—*Probably written by an unknown author about 100-125 A.D., this Letter has a twofold purpose: to undergird faith in the second coming of Christ and to warn against false teachers. In addition to foretelling the imminent doom of the false teachers, the author recalls the apostolic witness as the basis of the Church's proclamation, points to the Messianic prophecies of the Old Testament that have been confirmed by Christ's coming, and attributes the delay of the second coming to God's patience and forbearance.*

The First Letter to Timothy—*The two Letters to Timothy and the one to Titus are called the Pastoral Letters because they are addressed directly, not to any church as a group, but to its head or pastor for his guidance in the rule of the church. This first Letter was written between Paul's liberation from the first imprisonment (63 A.D.) and his death (67 A.D.) and has a twofold purpose: to provide guidance in the problems of church administration and to oppose false teaching of a speculative and moralistic type.*

The Second Letter to Timothy—*This Letter was written in 66 or 67 A.D. while St. Paul was a prisoner in Rome for the second and last time. It is a moving pastoral from a veteran missionary to a younger colleague urging endurance as the main quality of a preacher of the Gospel.*

MONDAY OF THE FIFTH WEEK
IN ORDINARY TIME

———————— YEAR I ————————

FIRST READING   Gn 1:1-19

Genesis presents a brief survey of the religious condition of mankind from the beginning to the time of Abraham. The one God is the sole author of all that exists (1:1), and his created activity is unopposed (1:2). His omnipotence is reflected in the total efficacy of his word, which achieves its effects in the absolute correspondence of the created object to the creating will (1:3ff). Human beings surpass all other created beings by reason of their special relationship to God. The whole visible world came into being as the result of God's divine activity.

A reading from the beginning of the Book of Genesis

IN the beginning, when God created the heavens and the earth, the earth was a formless wasteland, and darkness covered the abyss, while a mighty wind swept over the waters.

Then God said, "Let there be light," and there was light. God saw how good the light was. God then separated the light from the darkness. God called the light "day," and the darkness he called "night." Thus evening came, and morning followed—the first day.

Then God said, "Let there be a dome in the middle of the waters, to separate one body of water from the other." And so it happened: God made the dome, and it separated the water above the dome from the water below it. God called the dome "the sky." Evening came, and morning followed—the second day.

Then God said, "Let the water under the sky be gathered into a single basin, so that the dry land may appear." And so it happened: the water under the sky was gathered into its basin, and the dry land appeared. God called the dry land "the earth," and the basin of the water he called "the sea." God saw how good it was. Then God said, "Let the earth bring forth vegetation: every kind of plant that bears seed and every kind of fruit tree on earth that bears fruit with its seed in it."And so it happened: the earth brought forth every kind of plant that bears seed and every kind of fruit tree on earth that bears fruit with its seed in it. God saw how good it was. Evening came, and morning followed—the third day.

Then God said:"Let there be lights in the dome of the sky, to separate day from night. Let them mark the fixed times, the days and the years, and serve as luminaries in the dome of the sky, to shed light upon the earth."And so it happened: God made the two great lights, the greater one to govern the day, and the lesser one to govern the night; and he made the stars. God set them in the dome of the sky, to shed light upon the earth, to govern the day and the night, and to separate the light from the darkness. God saw how good it was. Evening came, and morning followed—the fourth day.—The word of the Lord. ℟. **Thanks be to God.** ↓

RESPONSORIAL PSALM

Ps 104:1-2a, 5-6, 10 and 12, 24 and 35c

℟. (31b) **May the Lord be glad in his works.**

Bless the LORD, O my soul!
    O LORD, my God, you are great indeed!
You are clothed with majesty and glory,
    robed in light as with a cloak.—℟.

You fixed the earth upon its foundation,
    not to be moved forever;
With the ocean, as with a garment, you covered it;
    above the mountains the waters stood.—℟.

You send forth springs into the watercourses
    that wind among the mountains.
Beside them the birds of heaven dwell;
    from among the branches they send forth their
        song.—℟.

How manifold are your works, O LORD!
    In wisdom you have wrought them all—

the earth is full of your creatures;
Bless the LORD, O my soul! Alleluia.—R/. ↓

——————— **YEAR II** ———————

FIRST READING   1 Kgs 8:1-7, 9-13

The Elders and King Solomon go to Jerusalem to offer sacrifice. The priests take up the Ark of the Covenant. The Lord comes to dwell in a dark cloud and the Lord's glory fills the temple.

A reading from the first Book of Kings

THE elders of Israel and all the leaders of the tribes, the princes in the ancestral houses of the children of Israel, came to King Solomon in Jerusalem, to bring up the ark of the LORD's covenant from the City of David, which is Zion. All the people of Israel assembled before King Solomon during the festival in the month of Ethanim (the seventh month). When all the elders of Israel had arrived, the priests took up the ark; they carried the ark of the LORD and the meeting tent with all the sacred vessels that were in the tent. (The priests and Levites carried them.)

King Solomon and the entire community of Israel present for the occasion sacrificed before the ark sheep and oxen too many to number or count. The priests brought the ark of the covenant of the LORD to its place beneath the wings of the cherubim in the sanctuary, the holy of holies of the temple. The cherubim had their wings spread out over the place of the ark, sheltering the ark and its poles from above. There was nothing in the ark but the two stone tablets which Moses had put there at Horeb, when the LORD made a covenant with the children of Israel at their departure from the land of Egypt.

When the priests left the holy place, the cloud filled the temple of the LORD so that the priests could no longer minister because of the cloud, since the LORD's glory had filled the temple of the LORD. Then Solomon said, "The

LORD intends to dwell in the dark cloud; I have truly built you a princely house, a dwelling where you may abide forever."—The word of the Lord. ℟. **Thanks be to God.** ↓

RESPONSORIAL PSALM

Ps 132:6-7, 8-10

℟. (8a) **Lord, go up to the place of your rest!**

Behold, we heard of it in Ephrathah;
    we found it in the fields of Jaar.
Let us enter into his dwelling,
    let us worship at his footstool.—℟.

Advance, O LORD, to your resting place,
    you and the ark of your majesty.
May your priests be clothed with justice;
    let your faithful ones shout merrily for joy.
For the sake of David your servant,
    reject not the plea of your anointed.—℟. ↓

——————— **YEAR I AND II** ———————

ALLELUIA

See Mt 4:23

℟. **Alleluia, alleluia.**
Jesus preached the Gospel of the Kingdom
and cured every disease among the people.
℟. **Alleluia, alleluia.** ↓

GOSPEL

Mk 6:53-56

Many acts of mercy follow immediately after our Lord's going among the people. Faith is an essential of salvation. Wherever Jesus goes, those who are in need come to him.

℣. The Lord be with you. ℟. **And also with you.**
℣. A reading from the holy Gospel according to Mark.
℟. **Glory to you, Lord.**

AFTER making the crossing to the other side of the sea, Jesus and his disciples came to land at Gennesaret and tied up there. As they were leaving the boat, people immediately recognized him. They scurried about the surrounding country and began to bring in the sick on mats to wherever they heard he was. Whatever villages or towns or countryside he entered, they laid the sick in the marketplaces and begged him that they might touch only the tassel on his cloak; and as many as touched it were healed.—The Gospel of the Lord. ℟. **Praise to you, Lord Jesus Christ.**   ➜ No. 15, p. 623

TUESDAY OF THE FIFTH WEEK
IN ORDINARY TIME
——— YEAR I ———

FIRST READING   Gn 1:20—2:4a

Animals are made superior to plants inasmuch as they are living beings and able to transmit life. Their procreative power is the result of a divine blessing. They are creatures of the one God and therefore good, but human beings alone are made in the image and likeness of God.

A reading from the Book of Genesis

G OD said, "Let the water teem with an abundance of living creatures, and on the earth let birds fly beneath the dome of the sky." And so it happened: God created the great sea monsters and all kinds of swimming creatures with which the water teems, and all kinds of winged birds. God saw how good it was, and God blessed them, saying, "Be fertile, multiply, and fill the water of the seas; and let the birds multiply on the earth." Evening came, and morning followed—the fifth day.

Then God said, "Let the earth bring forth all kinds of living creatures: cattle, creeping things, and wild animals of all kinds." And so it happened: God made all kinds of wild animals, all kinds of cattle, and all kinds of creeping things of the earth. God saw how good it was. Then God said: "Let us make man in our image, after our likeness. Let them have dominion over the fish of the sea, the birds of the air, and the cattle, and over all the wild animals and all the creatures that crawl on the ground."

God created man in his image;
in the divine image he created him;
male and female he created them.
God blessed them, saying: "Be fertile and multiply; fill the earth and subdue it. Have dominion over the fish of the sea, the birds of the air, and all the living things that move on the earth." God also said: "See, I give you every seed-bearing plant all over the earth and every tree that has seed-bearing fruit on it to be your food; and to all the animals of the land, all the birds of the air, and all the living creatures that crawl on the ground, I give all the green plants for food." And so it happened. God looked at everything he had made, and he found it very good. Evening came, and morning followed—the sixth day.

Thus the heavens and the earth and all their array were completed. Since on the seventh day God was finished with the work he had been doing, he rested on the seventh day from all the work he had undertaken. So God blessed the seventh day and made it holy, because on it he rested from all the work he had done in creation.

Such is the story of the heavens and the earth at their creation.—The word of the Lord. ℟. **Thanks be to God.** ↓

RESPONSORIAL PSALM   Ps 8:4-5, 6-7, 8-9

℟. (2ab) **O Lord, our God, how wonderful your name in all the earth!**

When I behold your heavens, the work of your fingers,
the moon and the stars which you set in place—
What is man that you should be mindful of him,
or the son of man that you should care for him?—℟.

You have made him little less than the angels,
and crowned him with glory and honor.
You have given him rule over the works of your hands,
putting all things under his feet.—℟.

All sheep and oxen,
yes, and the beasts of the field,

The birds of the air, the fishes of the sea,
  and whatever swims the paths of the seas.—℟. ↓

——————— **YEAR II** ———————

FIRST READING   1 Kgs 8:22-23, 27-30

Solomon prays for the people in the temple. He acknowledges the august power of the Lord who has chosen to dwell with his people on earth. Solomon asks that God listen to his people.

A reading from the first Book of Kings

SOLOMON stood before the altar of the LORD in the presence of the whole community of Israel, and stretching forth his hands toward heaven, he said, "LORD, God of Israel, there is no God like you in heaven above or on earth below; you keep your covenant of mercy with your servants who are faithful to you with their whole heart.

"Can it indeed be that God dwells on earth? If the heavens and the highest heavens cannot contain you, how much less this temple which I have built! Look kindly on the prayer and petition of your servant, O LORD, my God, and listen to the cry of supplication which I, your servant, utter before you this day. May your eyes watch night and day over this temple, the place where you have decreed you shall be honored; may you heed the prayer which I, your servant, offer in this place. Listen to the petitions of your servant and of your people Israel which they offer in this place. Listen from your heavenly dwelling and grant pardon."—The word of the Lord. ℟. **Thanks be to God.** ↓

RESPONSORIAL PSALM   Ps 84:3, 4, 5 and 10, 11

℟. (2) **How lovely is your dwelling place, Lord, mighty God!**

See Common of Dedication of a Church, p. 1103, no. 3.

—————— **YEAR I AND II** ——————

ALLELUIA   Ps 119:36, 29b

℟. **Alleluia, alleluia.**
Incline my heart, O God, to your decrees;
and favor me with your law.
℟. **Alleluia, alleluia.** ↓

GOSPEL   Mk 7:1-13

This Gospel contains two pronouncements that show our Lord's opposition
to the code of unwritten law so scrupulously observed by the Pharisees.
Christ is the Messiah whose mission extends beyond Judaism and that
contradicts the legalism and particularism of the Pharisaic leaders.

℣. The Lord be with you. ℟. **And also with you.**
℣. A reading from the holy Gospel according to Mark.
℟. **Glory to you, Lord.**

WHEN the Pharisees with some scribes who had
come from Jerusalem gathered around Jesus, they
observed that some of his disciples ate their meals with
unclean, that is, unwashed, hands. (For the Pharisees
and, in fact, all Jews, do not eat without carefully washing their hands, keeping the tradition of the elders. And
on coming from the marketplace they do not eat without
purifying themselves. And there are many other things
that they have traditionally observed, the purification of
cups and jugs and kettles and beds.) So the Pharisees
and scribes questioned him, "Why do your disciples not
follow the tradition of the elders but instead eat a meal
with unclean hands?" He responded, "Well did Isaiah
prophesy about you hypocrites, as it is written:

This people honors me with their lips,
but their hearts are far from me;
In vain do they worship me,
teaching as doctrines human precepts.

You disregard God's commandment but cling to human
tradition." He went on to say, "How well you have set
aside the commandment of God in order to uphold your

tradition! For Moses said, *Honor your father and your mother,* and *Whoever curses father or mother shall die.* Yet you say, 'If someone says to father or mother, "Any support you might have had from me is *qorban*" ' (meaning, dedicated to God), you allow him to do nothing more for his father or mother. You nullify the word of God in favor of your tradition that you have handed on. And you do many such things."—The Gospel of the Lord. ℟. **Praise to you, Lord Jesus Christ.**   ➜ No. 15, p. 623

WEDNESDAY OF THE FIFTH WEEK IN ORDINARY TIME

─────── **YEAR I** ───────

FIRST READING   Gn 2:4b-9, 15-17

The earth is destined for the use of human beings. They have a special kind of life distinguishing them from all earthly beings, a life that comes from God. Adam and Eve's enjoyment of the garden is a gift from God. God gives them a test; their happiness depends upon their remaining subject to God. In this concept lies the whole meaning of the garden.

A reading from the Book of Genesis

AT the time when the LORD God made the earth and the heavens—while as yet there was no field shrub on earth and no grass of the field had sprouted, for the LORD God had sent no rain upon the earth and there was no man to till the soil, but a stream was welling up out of the earth and was watering all the surface of the ground—the LORD God formed man out of the clay of the ground and blew into his nostrils the breath of life, and so man became a living being.

Then the LORD God planted a garden in Eden, in the east, and he placed there the man whom he had formed. Out of the ground the LORD God made various trees grow that were delightful to look at and good for food, with the tree of life in the middle of the garden and the tree of the knowledge of good and evil.

The LORD God then took the man and settled him in the garden of Eden, to cultivate and care for it. The LORD God gave man this order: "You are free to eat from any of the trees of the garden except the tree of knowledge of good and evil. From that tree you shall not eat; the moment you eat from it you are surely doomed to die."—The word of the Lord. ℟. **Thanks be to God.** ↓

RESPONSORIAL PSALM   Ps 104:1-2a, 27-28, 29bc-30

℟. (1a) **O bless the Lord, my soul!**

Bless the LORD, O my soul!
    O LORD, my God, you are great indeed!
You are clothed with majesty and glory,
    robed in light as with a cloak.—℟.

All creatures look to you
    to give them food in due time.
When you give it to them, they gather it;
    when you open your hand, they are filled with good
        things.—℟.

If you take away their breath, they perish
    and return to their dust.
When you send forth your spirit, they are created,
    and you renew the face of the earth.—℟. ↓

———— **YEAR II** ————

FIRST READING   1 Kgs 10:1-10

The Queen of Sheba comes to Jerusalem to see if all she has heard about Solomon's wisdom, wealth, servants, and his rule is true. She is amazed to find that all the reports were true far beyond her expectations.

A reading from the first Book of Kings

THE queen of Sheba, having heard of Solomon's fame, came to test him with subtle questions. She arrived in Jerusalem with a very numerous retinue, and with camels bearing spices, a large amount of gold, and precious stones. She came to Solomon and questioned him on every subject in which she was interested. King Solomon explained everything she asked about, and there remained nothing hidden from him that he could not explain to her.

When the queen of Sheba witnessed Solomon's great wisdom, the palace he had built, the food at his table, the seating of his ministers, the attendance and garb of his waiters, his banquet service, and the burnt offerings he offered in the temple of the Lord, she was breathless. "The report I heard in my country about your deeds and your wisdom is true," she told the king. "Though I did not believe the report until I came and saw with my own eyes, I have discovered that they were not telling me the half. Your wisdom and prosperity surpass the report I heard. Blessed are your men, blessed these servants of yours, who stand before you always and listen to your wisdom. Blessed be the Lord, your God, whom it has pleased to place you on the throne of Israel. In his enduring love for Israel, the Lord has made you king to carry out judgment and justice." Then she gave the king one hundred and twenty gold talents, a very large quantity of spices, and precious stones. Never again did anyone bring such an abundance of spices as the queen of Sheba gave to King Solomon.—The word of the Lord. ℟. **Thanks be to God.** ↓

RESPONSORIAL PSALM   Ps 37:5-6, 30-31, 39-40

℟. (30a) **The mouth of the just murmurs wisdom.**

Commit to the LORD your way;
   trust in him, and he will act.
He will make justice dawn for you like the light;
   bright as the noonday shall be your vindication.—℟.

The mouth of the just man tells of wisdom
   and his tongue utters what is right.
The law of his God is in his heart,
   and his steps do not falter.—℟.

The salvation of the just is from the LORD;
>   he is their refuge in time of distress.
And the LORD helps them and delivers them;
>   he delivers them from the wicked and saves them,
>   because they take refuge in him.—R̸. ↓

———— **YEAR I AND II** ————

ALLELUIA   See Jn 17:17b, 17a

R̸. **Alleluia, alleluia.**
Your word, O Lord, is truth:
consecrate us in the truth.
R̸. **Alleluia, alleluia.** ↓

GOSPEL   Mk 7:14-23

Jesus teaches that thoughts and words proceeding from our inmost self
are those things that defile us. All sin proceeds out of the heart, but people are prone to blame external causes for temptation and so to excuse
themselves. Wicked designs come from within.

V̸. The Lord be with you. R̸. **And also with you.**
V̸. A reading from the holy Gospel according to Mark.
R̸. **Glory to you, Lord.**

JESUS summoned the crowd again and said to them,
"Hear me, all of you, and understand. Nothing that
enters one from outside can defile that person; but the
things that come out from within are what defile."

When he got home away from the crowd his disciples
questioned him about the parable. He said to them, "Are
even you likewise without understanding? Do you not
realize that everything that goes into a person from outside cannot defile, since it enters not the heart but the
stomach and passes out into the latrine?" (Thus he
declared all foods clean.) "But what comes out of the man,
that is what defiles him. From within the man, from his
heart, come evil thoughts, unchastity, theft, murder, adultery, greed, malice, deceit, licentiousness, envy, blasphemy, arrogance, folly. All these evils come from within and

they defile."—The Gospel of the Lord. ℟. **Praise to you, Lord Jesus Christ.**   → No. 15, p. 623

THURSDAY OF THE FIFTH WEEK IN ORDINARY TIME

——— **YEAR I** ———

FIRST READING   Gn 2:18-25

Woman complements man. Man's deep sleep suggests the mystery of creation. The unity of marriage and its monogamous nature are God-ordered. Man and woman are creatures of God, redeemed by Christ; both are children of God and are called to the same supernatural destiny.

A reading from the Book of Genesis

THE LORD God said: "It is not good for the man to be alone. I will make a suitable partner for him." So the LORD God formed out of the ground various wild animals and various birds of the air, and he brought them to the man to see what he would call them; whatever the man called each of them would be its name. The man gave names to all the cattle, all the birds of the air, and all the wild animals; but none proved to be the suitable partner for the man.

So the LORD God cast a deep sleep on the man, and while he was asleep, he took out one of his ribs and closed up its place with flesh. The LORD God then built up into a woman the rib that he had taken from the man. When he brought her to the man, the man said:

"This one, at last, is bone of my bones
      and flesh of my flesh;
this one shall be called 'woman,'
      for out of 'her man' this one has been taken."

That is why a man leaves his father and mother and clings to his wife, and the two of them become one flesh. The man and his wife were both naked, yet they felt no shame.—The word of the Lord. ℟. **Thanks be to God.** ↓

RESPONSORIAL PSALM   Ps 128:1-2, 3, 4-5

℟. (see 1a) **Blessed are those who fear the Lord.**

Blessed are you who fear the LORD,
    who walk in his ways!
For you shall eat the fruit of your handiwork;
    blessed shall you be, and favored.—℟.

Your wife shall be like a fruitful vine
    in the recesses of your home;
Your children like olive plants
    around your table.—℟.

Behold, thus is the man blessed
    who fears the LORD.
The LORD bless you from Zion:
    may you see the prosperity of Jerusalem
    all the days of your life.—℟. ↓

──────── **YEAR II** ────────

FIRST READING   1 Kgs 11:4-13

Solomon falls into worshiping false gods, unlike his father David. The Lord
is angry with him and vows to deprive Solomon's son of all but one tribe
of the kingdom, which will be preserved only because of David.

A reading from the first Book of Kings

WHEN Solomon was old his wives had turned his
    heart to strange gods, and his heart was not entire-
ly with the LORD, his God, as the heart of his father David
had been. By adoring Astarte, the goddess of the
Sidonians, and Milcom, the idol of the Ammonites,
Solomon did evil in the sight of the LORD; he did not follow him unreservedly as his father David had done.
Solomon then built a high place to Chemosh, the idol of
Moab, and to Molech, the idol of the Ammonites, on the
hill opposite Jerusalem. He did the same for all his foreign wives who burned incense and sacrificed to their
gods. The LORD, therefore, became angry with Solomon,
because his heart was turned away from the LORD, the
God of Israel, who had appeared to him twice (for though

the LORD had forbidden him this very act of following strange gods, Solomon had not obeyed him).

So the LORD said to Solomon: "Since this is what you want, and you have not kept my covenant and my statutes which I enjoined on you, I will deprive you of the kingdom and give it to your servant. I will not do this during your lifetime, however, for the sake of your father David; it is your son whom I will deprive. Nor will I take away the whole kingdom. I will leave your son one tribe for the sake of my servant David and of Jerusalem, which I have chosen."—The word of the Lord. ℟. **Thanks be to God.** ↓

RESPONSORIAL PSALM   Ps 106:3-4, 35-36, 37 and 40

℟. (4a) **Remember us, O Lord, as you favor your people.**

Blessed are they who observe what is right,
      who do always what is just.
Remember us, O LORD, as you favor your people;
      visit us with your saving help.—℟.

But they mingled with the nations
      and learned their works.
They served their idols,
      which became a snare for them.—℟.

They sacrificed their sons
      and their daughters to demons.
And the LORD grew angry with his people,
      and abhorred his inheritance.—℟. ↓

——————— **YEAR I AND II** ———————

ALLELUIA   Jas 1:21bc

℟. **Alleluia, alleluia.**
Humbly welcome the word that has been planted in you
and is able to save your souls.
℟. **Alleluia, alleluia.** ↓

GOSPEL   Mk 7:24-30

Jesus goes to the region of Tyre and Sidon in the coastal province of Phoenicia, Gentile territory. This shows Jesus to be the Savior of the

Gentiles as well as of the Jews. A woman asks that a demon be expelled from her daughter.

℣. The Lord be with you. ℟. **And also with you.**
℣. A reading from the holy Gospel according to Mark.
℟. **Glory to you, Lord.**

JESUS went to the district of Tyre. He entered a house and wanted no one to know about it, but he could not escape notice. Soon a woman whose daughter had an unclean spirit heard about him. She came and fell at his feet. The woman was a Greek, a Syrophoenician by birth, and she begged him to drive the demon out of her daughter. He said to her, "Let the children be fed first. For it is not right to take the food of the children and throw it to the dogs." She replied and said to him, "Lord, even the dogs under the table eat the children's scraps." Then he said to her, "For saying this, you may go. The demon has gone out of your daughter." When the woman went home, she found the child lying in bed and the demon gone.—The Gospel of the Lord. ℟. **Praise to you, Lord Jesus Christ.**

→ No. 15, p. 623

FRIDAY OF THE FIFTH WEEK IN ORDINARY TIME

──────── YEAR I ────────

FIRST READING   Gn 3:1-8

Sin begins with some distortion of the truth. The serpent first denies the punishment, offering likeness to God as the result of eating of the tree. The whole of the human family was caught up in Adam's refusal to obey God's command, and by one man's sin, death came into the world for all.

A reading from the Book of Genesis

NOW the serpent was the most cunning of all the animals that the LORD God had made. The serpent asked the woman, "Did God really tell you not to eat from any of the trees in the garden?" The woman answered the serpent: "We may eat of the fruit of the trees in the garden; it is only about the fruit of the tree in the middle of the garden that God said, 'You shall not eat it or even touch it, lest you die.'"But the serpent said to the woman: "You certainly will not die! No, God knows well that the moment you eat of it your eyes will be opened and you will be like gods who know what is good and what is evil."The woman saw that the tree was good for food, pleasing to the eyes, and desirable for gaining wisdom. So she took some of its fruit and ate it; and she also gave some to her husband, who was with her, and he ate it. Then the eyes of both of them were opened, and they realized that they were naked; so they sewed fig leaves together and made loincloths for themselves.

When they heard the sound of the LORD God moving about in the garden at the breezy time of the day, the man and his wife hid themselves from the LORD God among the trees of the garden.—The word of the Lord. R. **Thanks be to God.** ↓

RESPONSORIAL PSALM   Ps 32:1-2, 5, 6, 7

R. (1a) **Blessed are those whose sins are forgiven.**

Blessed is he whose fault is taken away,
    whose sin is covered.
Blessed the man to whom the LORD imputes not guilt,
    in whose spirit there is no guile.—R.

Then I acknowledged my sin to you,
    my guilt I covered not.
I said, "I confess my faults to the LORD,"
    and you took away the guilt of my sin.—R.

For this shall every faithful man pray to you
    in time of stress.
Though deep waters overflow,
    they shall not reach him.—R.

You are my shelter; from distress you will preserve me;
    with glad cries of freedom you will ring me
    round.—R. ↓

———— **YEAR II** ————

FIRST READING 1 Kgs 11:29-32; 12:19

Jeroboam leaves Jerusalem. By cutting up his cloak, Ahijah demonstrates how the kingdom will be divided and only one tribe will remain with the son of Solomon. The ten pieces represent the ten northern tribes of Israel (cf. 2 Sm 19:43).

A reading from the first Book of Kings

JEROBOAM left Jerusalem, and the prophet Ahijah the Shilonite met him on the road. The two were alone in the area, and the prophet was wearing a new cloak. Ahijah took off his new cloak, tore it into twelve pieces, and said to Jeroboam:

"Take ten pieces for yourself; the LORD, the God of Israel, says: 'I will tear away the kingdom from Solomon's grasp and will give you ten of the tribes. One tribe shall remain to him for the sake of David my servant, and of Jerusalem, the city I have chosen out of all the tribes of Israel.' "

Israel went into rebellion against David's house to this day.—The word of the Lord. ℟. **Thanks be to God.** ↓

RESPONSORIAL PSALM Ps 81:10-11ab, 12-13, 14-15

℟. (11a and 9a) **I am the Lord, your God: hear my voice.**

"There shall be no strange god among you
    nor shall you worship any alien god.
I, the LORD, am your God
    who led you forth from the land of Egypt."—℟.

"My people heard not my voice,
    and Israel obeyed me not;
So I gave them up to the hardness of their hearts;
    they walked according to their own counsels."—℟.

"If only my people would hear me,
    and Israel walk in my ways,
Quickly would I humble their enemies;
    against their foes I would turn my hand."—℟. ↓

———— **YEAR I AND II** ————

ALLELUIA See Acts 16:14b

℟. **Alleluia, alleluia.**
Open our hearts, O Lord,
to listen to the words of your Son.
℟. **Alleluia, alleluia.** ↓

GOSPEL Mk 7:31-37

Friends bring a sick man to Christ for healing. Christ cures the man and charges the multitude to say nothing of the miracle, but so much the more do they publish it. The people are amazed at Jesus' powers.

℣. The Lord be with you. ℟. **And also with you.**
℣. A reading from the holy Gospel according to Mark.
℟. **Glory to you, Lord.**

JESUS left the district of Tyre and went by way of Sidon to the Sea of Galilee, into the district of the Decapolis. And people brought to him a deaf man who had a speech impediment and begged him to lay his hand on him. He took him off by himself away from the crowd. He put his finger into the man's ears and, spitting, touched his tongue; then he looked up to heaven and groaned, and said to him, *"Ephphatha!"* (that is, "Be opened!") And immediately the man's ears were opened, his speech impediment was removed, and he spoke plainly. He ordered them not to tell anyone. But the more he ordered them not to, the more they proclaimed it. They were exceedingly astonished and they said, "He has done all things well. He makes the deaf hear and the mute speak."—The Gospel of the Lord. ℟. **Praise to you, Lord Jesus Christ.** → No. 15, p. 623

SATURDAY OF THE FIFTH WEEK
IN ORDINARY TIME

———— YEAR I ————

FIRST READING Gn 3:9-24

In the Garden, Adam and Eve enjoyed an intimacy with God that was disrupted by disobedience. As head of the family, Adam is questioned first. His response is the result of sin. The relationship between the power of evil and humanity is one of enmity that will continue throughout all generations.

A reading from the Book of Genesis

THE LORD God called to Adam and asked him, "Where are you?" He answered, "I heard you in the garden; but I was afraid, because I was naked, so I hid myself." Then he asked, "Who told you that you were naked? You have eaten, then, from the tree of which I had forbidden you to eat!" The man replied, "The woman whom you put here with me—she gave me fruit from the tree, and so I ate it." The LORD God then asked the woman, "Why did you do such a thing?" The woman answered, "The serpent tricked me into it, so I ate it."

Then the LORD God said to the serpent:

"Because you have done this, you shall be banned
    from all the animals
    and from all the wild creatures;
On your belly shall you crawl,
    and dirt shall you eat
    all the days of your life.
I will put enmity between you and the woman,
    and between your offspring and hers;
He will strike at your head,
    while you strike at his heel."

To the woman he said:

"I will intensify the pangs of your childbearing;
    in pain shall you bring forth children.
Yet your urge shall be for your husband,
    and he shall be your master."

To the man he said:"Because you listened to your wife and ate from the tree of which I had forbidden you to eat,

"Cursed be the ground because of you!
In toil shall you eat its yield
all the days of your life.
Thorns and thistles shall it bring forth to you,
as you eat of the plants of the field.
By the sweat of your face
shall you get bread to eat,
Until you return to the ground,
from which you were taken;
For you are dirt,
and to dirt you shall return."

The man called his wife Eve, because she became the mother of all the living.

For the man and his wife the LORD God made leather garments, with which he clothed them. Then the LORD God said: "See! The man has become like one of us, knowing what is good and what is evil! Therefore, he must not be allowed to put out his hand to take fruit from the tree of life also, and thus eat of it and live forever." The LORD God therefore banished him from the garden of Eden, to till the ground from which he had been taken. When he expelled the man, he settled him east of the garden of Eden; and he stationed the cherubim and the fiery revolving sword, to guard the way to the tree of life.—The word of the Lord. ℟. **Thanks be to God.** ↓

RESPONSORIAL PSALM   Ps 90:2, 3-4abc, 5-6, 12-13

℟. (1) **In every age, O Lord, you have been our refuge.**

Before the mountains were begotten
and the earth and the world were brought forth,
from everlasting to everlasting you are God.—℟.

You turn man back to dust,
saying, "Return, O children of men."

For a thousand years in your sight
    are as yesterday, now that it is past,
      or as a watch of the night.—R̷.

You make an end of them in their sleep;
    the next morning they are like the changing grass,
Which at dawn springs up anew,
    but by evening wilts and fades.—R̷.

Teach us to number our days aright,
    that we may gain wisdom of heart.
Return, O LORD! How long?
    Have pity on your servants!—R̷. ↓

——————— **YEAR II** ———————

FIRST READING   1 Kgs 12:26-32; 13:33-34

Jeroboam, in an effort to keep control over the people, builds altars to false gods and establishes feasts in their honor. He will be punished for this sin of leading the people into idolatry.

A reading from the first Book of Kings

JEROBOAM thought to himself: "The kingdom will return to David's house. If now this people go up to offer sacrifices in the temple of the LORD in Jerusalem, the hearts of this people will return to their master, Rehoboam, king of Judah, and they will kill me." After taking counsel, the king made two calves of gold and said to the people: "You have been going up to Jerusalem long enough. Here is your God, O Israel, who brought you up from the land of Egypt." And he put one in Bethel, the other in Dan. This led to sin, because the people frequented those calves in Bethel and in Dan. He also built temples on the high places and made priests from among the people who were not Levites. Jeroboam established a feast in the eighth month on the fifteenth day of the month to duplicate in Bethel the pilgrimage feast of Judah, with sacrifices to the calves he had made; and he stationed in Bethel priests of the high places he had built.

Jeroboam did not give up his evil ways after this, but again made priests for the high places from among the

common people. Whoever desired it was consecrated and
became a priest of the high places. This was a sin on the
part of the house of Jeroboam for which it was to be cut
off and destroyed from the earth.—The word of the Lord.
℟. **Thanks be to God.** ↓

RESPONSORIAL PSALM   Ps 106:6-7ab, 19-20, 21-22

℟. (4a) **Remember us, O Lord, as you favor your people.**

We have sinned, we and our fathers;
 we have committed crimes; we have done wrong.
Our fathers in Egypt
 considered not your wonders.—℟.

They made a calf in Horeb
 and adored a molten image;
They exchanged their glory
 for the image of a grass-eating bullock.—℟.

They forgot the God who had saved them,
 who had done great deeds in Egypt,
Wondrous deeds in the land of Ham,
 terrible things at the Red Sea.—℟. ↓

——————— **YEAR I AND II** ———————

ALLELUIA   Mt 4:4b

℟. **Alleluia, alleluia.**
One does not live on bread alone,
but on every word that comes forth from the mouth of
 God.
℟. **Alleluia, alleluia.** ↓

GOSPEL   Mk 8:1-10

Jesus continually cares for those who follow him. In this miracle of the
multiplying of the seven loaves and two fish, the disciples—not our
Lord—distribute the food to the multitude. All eat until they are filled.

℣. The Lord be with you. ℟. **And also with you.**
℣. A reading from the holy Gospel according to Mark.
℟. **Glory to you, Lord.**

IN those days when there again was a great crowd without anything to eat, Jesus summoned the disciples and said, "My heart is moved with pity for the crowd, because they have been with me now for three days and have nothing to eat. If I send them away hungry to their homes, they will collapse on the way, and some of them have come a great distance." His disciples answered him, "Where can anyone get enough bread to satisfy them here in this deserted place?" Still he asked them, "How many loaves do you have?" They replied, "Seven." He ordered the crowd to sit down on the ground. Then, taking the seven loaves he gave thanks, broke them, and gave them to his disciples to distribute, and they distributed them to the crowd. They also had a few fish. He said the blessing over them and ordered them distributed also. They ate and were satisfied. They picked up the fragments left over—seven baskets. There were about four thousand people.

He dismissed the crowd and got into the boat with his disciples and came to the region of Dalmanutha.—The Gospel of the Lord. ℟. **Praise to you, Lord Jesus Christ.**

→ No. 15, p. 623

MONDAY OF THE SIXTH WEEK IN ORDINARY TIME

——— YEAR I ———

FIRST READING   Gn 4:1-15, 25

The semi-nomadic life of Abel is contrasted to the sedentary life of Cain before the crime and the strictly nomadic life of Cain after killing his brother. The crime of murder confirms the fallen state of human beings. God, although merciful, shows how sin will be justly punished.

A reading from the Book of Genesis

THE man had relations with his wife Eve, and she conceived and bore Cain, saying, "I have produced a man with the help of the LORD." Next she bore his brother Abel. Abel became a keeper of flocks, and Cain a tiller of the soil. In the course of time Cain brought an offering to the LORD from the fruit of the soil, while Abel, for his part, brought one of the best firstlings of his flock. The LORD looked with favor on Abel and his offering, but on Cain and his offering he did not. Cain greatly resented this and was crestfallen. So the LORD said to Cain: "Why are you so resentful and crestfallen? If you do well, you can hold up your head; but if not, sin is a demon lurking at the door: his urge is toward you, yet you can be his master."

Cain said to his brother Abel, "Let us go out in the field." When they were in the field, Cain attacked his brother Abel and killed him. Then the LORD asked Cain, "Where is your brother Abel?" He answered, "I do not know. Am I my brother's keeper?" The LORD then said: "What have you done! Listen: your brother's blood cries out to me from the soil! Therefore you shall be banned from the soil that opened its mouth to receive your brother's blood from your hand. If you till the soil, it shall no longer give you its produce. You shall become a restless wanderer on the earth." Cain said to the LORD: "My punishment is too great to bear. Since you have now banished me from the soil, and I must avoid your presence and become a restless wanderer on the earth, anyone may kill me at sight." "Not so!" the LORD said to him "If anyone kills Cain, Cain shall be avenged sevenfold." So the LORD put a mark on Cain, lest anyone should kill him at sight.

Adam again had relations with his wife, and she gave birth to a son whom she called Seth. "God has granted me more offspring in place of Abel," she said, "because Cain slew him."—The word of the Lord. ℟. **Thanks be to God.** ↓

RESPONSORIAL PSALM   Ps 50:1 and 8, 16bc-17, 20-21

℟. (14a) **Offer to God a sacrifice of praise.**

God the LORD has spoken and summoned the earth,
    from the rising of the sun to its setting.

"Not for your sacrifices do I rebuke you,
     for your burnt offerings are before me always."—℟.

"Why do you recite my statutes,
     and profess my covenant with your mouth
Though you hate discipline
     and cast my words behind you?"—℟.

"You sit speaking against your brother;
     against your mother's son you spread rumors.
When you do these things, shall I be deaf to it?
     Or do you think that I am like yourself?
     I will correct you by drawing them up before your
     eyes."—℟. ↓

——————— **YEAR II** ———————

FIRST READING   Jas 1:1-11

Trials are to be regarded as pure joy (cf. Mt 5:10ff; Jn 10:11). Spiritual maturity and full preparedness for the coming of Christ is achieved by sustaining trials, cultivating endurance, and attaining perfection. All this requires true wisdom, which God readily grants to believing petitioners but withholds from those who doubt. From the religious point of view, the lot of the poor and the lowly is of greater value than that of the rich.

A reading from the beginning of the Letter of
Saint James

JAMES, a servant of God and of the Lord Jesus Christ,
to the twelve tribes in the dispersion, greetings.

Consider it all joy, my brothers and sisters, when you encounter various trials, for you know that the testing of your faith produces perseverance. And let perseverance be perfect, so that you may be perfect and complete, lacking in nothing. But if any of you lacks wisdom, he should ask God who gives to all generously and ungrudgingly, and he will be given it. But he should ask in faith, not doubting, for the one who doubts is like a wave of the sea that is driven and tossed about by the wind. For that person must not suppose that he will receive anything from the Lord, since he is a man of two minds, unstable in all his ways.

The brother in lowly circumstances should take pride in high standing, and the rich one in his lowliness, for he will pass away "like the flower of the field." For the sun comes up with its scorching heat and dries up the grass, its flower droops, and the beauty of its appearance vanishes. So will the rich person fade away in the midst of his pursuits.—The word of the Lord. ℟. **Thanks be to God.** ↓

RESPONSORIAL PSALM   Ps 119:67, 68, 71, 72, 75, 76

℟. (77a) **Be kind to me, Lord, and I shall live.**

Before I was afflicted I went astray,
    but now I hold to your promise.—℟.

You are good and bountiful;
    teach me your statutes.—℟.

It is good for me that I have been afflicted,
    that I may learn your statutes.—℟.

The law of your mouth is to me more precious
    than thousands of gold and silver pieces.—℟.

I know, O LORD, that your ordinances are just,
    and in your faithfulness you have afflicted me.—℟.

Let your kindness comfort me
    according to your promise to your servants.—℟. ↓

——————— **YEAR I AND II** ———————

ALLELUIA   Jn 14:6

℟. **Alleluia, alleluia.**
I am the way and the truth and the life, says the Lord;
no one comes to the Father except through me.
℟. **Alleluia, alleluia.** ↓

GOSPEL   Mk 8:11-13

Boldly, the Pharisees seek a sign from Christ that will substantiate his claims. From their point of view, the request may have been justified. Our Lord's answer is more than a refusal. God will give no sign.

℣. The Lord be with you. ℟. **And also with you.**

℣. A reading from the holy Gospel according to Mark.

℟. **Glory to you, Lord.**

THE Pharisees came forward and began to argue with Jesus, seeking from him a sign from heaven to test him. He sighed from the depth of his spirit and said, "Why does this generation seek a sign? Amen, I say to you, no sign will be given to this generation." Then he left them, got into the boat again, and went off to the other shore.— The Gospel of the Lord. ℟. **Praise to you, Lord Jesus Christ.**

→ No. 15, p. 623

TUESDAY OF THE SIXTH WEEK IN ORDINARY TIME

——— **YEAR I** ———

FIRST READING   Gn 6:5-8; 7:1-5, 10

This passage provides the theological connection between human sin and the natural catastrophe of the flood. The account begins immediately with God's command to Noah to enter the ark. Noah is found "just" in God's sight. Noah's obedience is stressed; he does as directed.

A reading from the Book of Genesis

WHEN the LORD saw how great was man's wickedness on earth, and how no desire that his heart conceived was ever anything but evil, he regretted that he had made man on the earth, and his heart was grieved.

So the LORD said: "I will wipe out from the earth the men whom I have created, and not only the men, but also the beasts and the creeping things and the birds of the air, for I am sorry that I made them." But Noah found favor with the LORD.

Then the LORD said to Noah: "Go into the ark, you and all your household, for you alone in this age have I found to be truly just. Of every clean animal, take with you seven pairs, a male and its mate; and of the unclean animals, one pair, a male and its mate; likewise, of every clean bird of the air, seven pairs, a male and a female, and of all the unclean birds, one pair, a male and a female. Thus you will keep their issue alive over all the earth. Seven days from now I will bring rain down on the earth for forty days and forty nights, and so I will wipe out from the surface of the earth every moving creature that I have made." Noah did just as the LORD had commanded him.

As soon as the seven days were over, the waters of the flood came upon the earth.—The word of the Lord. ℟. **Thanks be to God.** ↓

RESPONSORIAL PSALM Ps 29:1a and 2, 3ac-4, 3b and 9c-10

℟. (11b) **The Lord will bless his people with peace.**

Give to the LORD, you sons of God,
    give to the LORD glory and praise,
Give to the LORD the glory due his name;
    adore the LORD in holy attire.—℟.

The voice of the LORD is over the waters,
    the LORD, over vast waters.
The voice of the LORD is mighty;
    the voice of the LORD is majestic.—℟.

The God of glory thunders,
    and in his temple all say, "Glory!"
The LORD is enthroned above the flood;
    the LORD is enthroned as king forever.—℟. ↓

——— **YEAR II** ———

FIRST READING   Jas 1:12-18

No one tempted may try to evade responsibility by throwing the blame on God. God cannot be the source of temptation. Each one is led astray by personal desires. Sin, becoming mature, gives birth to death. By contrast, the things that come down from God are all good.

A reading from the Letter of Saint James

BLESSED is he who perseveres in temptation, for when he has been proven he will receive the crown of life that he promised to those who love him. No one experiencing temptation should say, "I am being tempted by God"; for God is not subject to temptation to evil, and he himself tempts no one. Rather, each person is tempted when lured and enticed by his desire. Then desire conceives and brings forth sin, and when sin reaches maturity it gives birth to death.

Do not be deceived, my beloved brothers and sisters: all good giving and every perfect gift is from above, coming down from the Father of lights, with whom there is no alteration or shadow caused by change. He willed to give us birth by the word of truth that we may be a kind of firstfruits of his creatures.—The word of the Lord. ℟. **Thanks be to God.** ↓

RESPONSORIAL PSALM   Ps 94:12-13a, 14-15, 18-19

℟. (12a) **Blessed the man you instruct, O Lord.**

Blessed the man whom you instruct, O LORD,
    whom by your law you teach,
Giving him rest from evil days.—℟.

For the LORD will not cast off his people,
    nor abandon his inheritance;
But judgment shall again be with justice,
    and all the upright of heart shall follow it.—℟.

When I say, "My foot is slipping,"
    your mercy, O LORD, sustains me;
When cares abound within me,
    your comfort gladdens my soul.—℟. ↓

——————— **YEAR I AND II** ———————

ALLELUIA   Jn 14:23

℟. **Alleluia, alleluia.**
Whoever loves me will keep my word, says the Lord;
and my Father will love him
and we will come to him.
℟. **Alleluia, alleluia.** ↓

GOSPEL   Mk 8:14-21

The disciples fail to make provision for their own personal needs. Their
usual food was bread. Our Lord warns his followers to beware of the
"leaven" of the Pharisees and the "leaven" of Herod—hypocrisy. Christ's
displeasure is for the disciples' distrust of his providence and power that
could have supplied bread.

℣. The Lord be with you. ℟. **And also with you.**
℣. A reading from the holy Gospel according to Mark.
℟. **Glory to you, Lord.**

THE disciples had forgotten to bring bread, and they
had only one loaf with them in the boat. Jesus
enjoined them, "Watch out, guard against the leaven of
the Pharisees and the leaven of Herod." They concluded
among themselves that it was because they had no
bread. When he became aware of this he said to them,
"Why do you conclude that it is because you have no
bread? Do you not yet understand or comprehend? Are
your hearts hardened? Do you have eyes and not see,
ears and not hear? And do you not remember, when I
broke the five loaves for the five thousand, how many
wicker baskets full of fragments you picked up?" They
answered him, "Twelve." "When I broke the seven loaves
for the four thousand, how many full baskets of fragments did you pick up?" They answered him, "Seven."
He said to them, "Do you still not understand?"—The
Gospel of the Lord. ℟. **Praise to you, Lord Jesus Christ.**

→ No. 15, p. 623

WEDNESDAY OF THE SIXTH WEEK
IN ORDINARY TIME

──────── YEAR I ────────

FIRST READING   Gn 8:6-13, 20-22

Note the suspense of the story. The earth is still covered with water when Noah sends the dove out. It comes back with an olive leaf. In another seven days, the dove is released again and it does not return. The flood story ends with an emphasis upon the restoration of Humanity's life with God.

A reading from the Book of Genesis

AT the end of forty days Noah opened the hatch he had made in the ark, and he sent out a raven, to see if the waters had lessened on the earth. It flew back and forth until the waters dried off from the earth. Then he sent out a dove, to see if the waters had lessened on the earth. But the dove could find no place to alight and perch, and it returned to him in the ark, for there was water all over the earth. Putting out his hand, he caught the dove and drew it back to him inside the ark. He waited seven days more and again sent the dove out from the ark. In the evening the dove came back to him, and there in its bill was a plucked-off olive leaf! So Noah knew that the waters had lessened on the earth. He waited still another seven days and then released the dove once more; and this time it did not come back.

In the six hundred and first year of Noah's life, in the first month, on the first day of the month, the water began to dry up on the earth. Noah then removed the covering of the ark and saw that the surface of the ground was drying up.

Noah built an altar to the LORD, and choosing from every clean animal and every clean bird, he offered burnt offerings on the altar. When the LORD smelled the sweet odor, he said to himself: "Never again will I doom the earth because of man since the desires of man's heart are evil from the start; nor will I ever again strike down all living beings, as I have done.

As long as the earth lasts,
　　seedtime and harvest,
　　cold and heat,
Summer and winter,
　　and day and night
　　shall not cease."

The word of the Lord. ℟. **Thanks be to God.** ↓

RESPONSORIAL PSALM   Ps 116:12-13, 14-15, 18-19

℟. (17a) **To you, Lord, I will offer a sacrifice of praise.**

℟. Or: **Alleluia.**

How shall I make a return to the Lord
　　for all the good he has done for me?
The cup of salvation I will take up,
　　and I will call upon the name of the Lord.—℟.

My vows to the Lord I will pay
　　in the presence of all his people.
Precious in the eyes of the Lord
　　is the death of his faithful ones.—℟.

My vows to the Lord I will pay
　　in the presence of all his people,
In the courts of the house of the Lord,
　　in your midst, O Jerusalem. —℟. ↓

————— **YEAR II** —————

FIRST READING   Jas 1:19-27

Christians must be prompt to hear the Word of God and put it into practice
in their lives. Happiness can result only from conformity of life to this ideal
law of true freedom. Human beings cannot be devout without putting a rein
on their tongues. Neither can they have true worship if they do not look after
orphans and widows, that is, the defenseless and oppressed.

A reading from the Letter of Saint James

KNOW this, my dear brothers and sisters: everyone
should be quick to hear, slow to speak, slow to anger

for anger does not accomplish the righteousness of God. Therefore, put away all filth and evil excess and humbly welcome the word that has been planted in you and is able to save your souls.

Be doers of the word and not hearers only, deluding yourselves. For if anyone is a hearer of the word and not a doer, he is like a man who looks at his own face in a mirror. He sees himself, then goes off and promptly forgets what he looked like. But the one who peers into the perfect law of freedom and perseveres, and is not a hearer who forgets but a doer who acts; such a one shall be blessed in what he does.

If anyone thinks he is religious and does not bridle his tongue but deceives his heart, his religion is vain. Religion that is pure and undefiled before God and the Father is this: to care for orphans and widows in their affliction and to keep oneself unstained by the world.— The word of the Lord. ℟. **Thanks be to God.** ↓

RESPONSORIAL PSALM　　　　　Ps 15:2-3a, 3bc-4ab, 5

℟. (1b) **Who shall live on your holy mountain, O Lord?**

He who walks blamelessly and does justice;
　　who thinks the truth in his heart
　　and slanders not with his tongue.—℟.

Who harms not his fellow man,
　　nor takes up a reproach against his neighbor;
By whom the reprobate is despised,
　　while he honors those who fear the LORD.—℟.

Who lends not his money at usury
　　and accepts no bribe against the innocent.
He who does these things
　　shall never be disturbed.—℟. ↓

———— **YEAR I AND II** ————

ALLELUIA See Eph 1:17-18

℟. **Alleluia, alleluia.**
May the Father of our Lord Jesus Christ
enlighten the eyes of our hearts,
that we may know what is the hope
that belongs to his call.
℟. **Alleluia, alleluia.** ↓

GOSPEL Mk 8:22-26

Jesus cures the blind man, using signs and symbols. It is perhaps implied here that he who came, as foretold, "to open the eyes of the blind" (Is 42:7) will thus sometimes take by the hand those who sit in darkness and guide them into his marvelous light. God spoke through his prophet long before: "I will lead the blind . . . by paths unknown" (Is 42:16).

℣. The Lord be with you. ℟. **And also with you.**
℣. A reading from the holy Gospel according to Mark.
℟. **Glory to you, Lord.**

WHEN Jesus and his disciples arrived at Bethsaida, people brought to him a blind man and begged Jesus to touch him. He took the blind man by the hand and led him outside the village. Putting spittle on his eyes he laid his hands on the man and asked, "Do you see anything?" Looking up the man replied, "I see people looking like trees and walking." Then he laid hands on the man's eyes a second time and he saw clearly; his sight was restored and he could see everything distinctly. Then he sent him home and said, "Do not even go into the village."—The Gospel of the Lord. ℟. **Praise to you, Lord Jesus Christ.** → No. 15, p. 623

THURSDAY OF THE SIXTH WEEK
IN ORDINARY TIME

———— YEAR I ————

FIRST READING   Gn 9:1-13

The first epoch in the division of world history ended with the flood. The second, marked by the covenant of Noah, supposes a theological disorder caused by sin and introduces as normal those adverse conditions of life that everyone encounters. The kingship is exercised, not in peace but through fear.

A reading from the Book of Genesis

GOD blessed Noah and his sons and said to them: "Be fertile and multiply and fill the earth. Dread fear of you shall come upon all the animals of the earth and all the birds of the air, upon all the creatures that move about on the ground and all the fishes of the sea; into your power they are delivered. Every creature that is alive shall be yours to eat; I give them all to you as I did the green plants. Only flesh with its lifeblood still in it you shall not eat. For your own lifeblood, too, I will demand an accounting: from every animal I will demand it, and from one man in regard to his fellow man I will demand an accounting for human life.

If anyone sheds the blood of man,
  by man shall his blood be shed;
For in the image of God
  has man been made.
Be fertile, then, and multiply; abound on earth and subdue it."

God said to Noah and to his sons with him: "See, I am now establishing my covenant with you and your descendants after you and with every living creature that was with you: all the birds, and the various tame and wild animals that were with you and came out of the ark. I will establish my covenant with you, that never again shall all bodily creatures be destroyed by the waters of a flood;

there shall not be another flood to devastate the earth." God added: "This is the sign that I am giving for all ages to come, of the covenant between me and you and every living creature with you: I set my bow in the clouds to serve as a sign of the covenant between me and the earth."—The word of the Lord. ℞. **Thanks be to God.** ↓

RESPONSORIAL PSALM   Ps 102:16-18, 19-21, 29 and 22-23

℞. (20b) **From heaven the Lord looks down on the earth.**

The nations shall revere your name, O LORD,
    and all the kings of the earth your glory,
When the LORD has rebuilt Zion
    and appeared in his glory;
When he has regarded the prayer of the destitute,
    and not despised their prayer.—℞.

Let this be written for the generation to come,
    and let his future creatures praise the LORD:
"The LORD looked down from his holy height,
    from heaven he beheld the earth,
To hear the groaning of the prisoners,
    to release those doomed to die."—℞.

The children of your servants shall abide,
    and their posterity shall continue in your presence,
That the name of the LORD may be declared in Zion,
    and his praise, in Jerusalem,
When the peoples gather together,
    and the kingdoms, to serve the LORD.—℞. ↓

————— **YEAR II** —————

FIRST READING   Jas 2:1-9

In the Christian community, there must be no discrimination against the poor or favoritism toward the rich based on a mistaken exaltation of status or wealth (cf Mt 23:6). Rather, divine favor consists in God's promises, his election, and his rewards elicited by people's faith and response to his love. The impious rich who oppress the poor dishonor the name of Christ.

A reading from the Letter of Saint James

MY brothers and sisters, show no partiality as you adhere to the faith in our glorious Lord Jesus Christ. For if a man with gold rings and fine clothes comes into your assembly, and a poor person with shabby clothes also comes in, and you pay attention to the one wearing the fine clothes and say, "Sit here, please," while you say to the poor one, "Stand there," or "Sit at my feet," have you not made distinctions among yourselves and become judges with evil designs?

Listen, my beloved brothers and sisters. Did not God choose those who are poor in the world to be rich in faith and heirs of the Kingdom that he promised to those who love him? But you dishonored the poor. Are not the rich oppressing you? And do they themselves not haul you off to court? Is it not they who blaspheme the noble name that was invoked over you? However, if you fulfill the royal law according to the Scripture, *You shall love your neighbor as yourself,* you are doing well. But if you show partiality, you commit sin, and are convicted by the law as transgressors.—The word of the Lord. ℟. **Thanks be to God.** ↓

RESPONSORIAL PSALM   Ps 34:2-3, 4-5, 6-7

℟. (7a) **The Lord hears the cry of the poor.**

I will bless the LORD at all times;
    his praise shall be ever in my mouth.
Let my soul glory in the LORD;
    the lowly will hear me and be glad.—℟.

Glorify the LORD with me,
    let us together extol his name.
I sought the LORD, and he answered me
    and delivered me from all my fears.—℟.

Look to him that you may be radiant with joy,
    and your faces may not blush with shame.

When the poor one called out, the LORD heard,
    and from all his distress he saved him.—℟. ↓

─────── **YEAR I AND II** ───────

ALLELUIA   See Jn 6:63c, 68c

℟. **Alleluia, alleluia.**
Your words, Lord, are Spirit and life;
you have the words of everlasting life.
℟. **Alleluia, alleluia.** ↓

GOSPEL   Mk 8:27-33

This passage climaxes our Lord's self-revelation to the disciples as the Messiah. It also introduces the theme of the Suffering Messiah. Peter is the first man to acknowledge openly that our Lord is the expected Deliverer. Christ then prepares the minds of the Apostles for his cross and passion.

℣. The Lord be with you. ℟. **And also with you.**
℣. A reading from the holy Gospel according to Mark.
℟. **Glory to you, Lord.**

JESUS and his disciples set out for the villages of Caesarea Philippi. Along the way he asked his disciples, "Who do people say that I am?" They said in reply, "John the Baptist, others Elijah, still others one of the prophets." And he asked them, "But who do you say that I am?" Peter said to him in reply, "You are the Christ." Then he warned them not to tell anyone about him.

He began to teach them that the Son of Man must suffer greatly and be rejected by the elders, the chief priests, and the scribes, and be killed, and rise after three days. He spoke this openly. Then Peter took him aside and began to rebuke him. At this he turned around and, looking at his disciples, rebuked Peter and said, "Get behind me, Satan. You are thinking not as God does, but as human beings do."—The Gospel of the Lord. ℟. **Praise to you, Lord Jesus Christ.**   → No. 15, p. 623

FRIDAY OF THE SIXTH WEEK
IN ORDINARY TIME

—— YEAR I ——

FIRST READING   Gn 11:1-9

An ancient story, the building of the tower of Babel, is used to give the theological reason for the division of mankind. The sin of the first man resulted in the alienation of human beings from God (Gn 3:22-24) and from their neighbors (Gn 5:1-16). From sin now results the alienation of all human society from God, and human beings from one another.

A reading from the Book of Genesis

THE whole world spoke the same language, using the same words. While the people were migrating in the east, they came upon a valley in the land of Shinar and settled there. They said to one another, "Come, let us mold bricks and harden them with fire." They used bricks for stone, and bitumen for mortar. Then they said, "Come, let us build ourselves a city and a tower with its top in the sky, and so make a name for ourselves; otherwise we shall be scattered all over the earth."

The LORD came down to see the city and the tower that they had built. Then the LORD said: "If now, while they are one people, all speaking the same language, they have started to do this, nothing will later stop them from doing whatever they presume to do. Let us then go down and there confuse their language, so that one will not understand what another says." Thus the LORD scattered them from there all over the earth, and they stopped building the city. That is why it was called Babel, because there the LORD confused the speech of all the world. It was from that place that he scattered them all over the earth.—The word of the Lord. ℟. **Thanks be to God.** ↓

RESPONSORIAL PSALM   Ps 33:10-11, 12-13, 14-15

℟. (12) **Blessed the people the Lord has chosen to be his own.**

The LORD brings to nought the plans of nations;
  he foils the designs of peoples.
But the plan of the LORD stands forever;
  the design of his heart, through all generations.—R⫽.

Blessed the nation whose God is the LORD,
  the people he has chosen for his own inheritance.
From heaven the LORD looks down;
  he sees all mankind.—R⫽.

From his fixed throne he beholds
  all who dwell on the earth,
He who fashioned the heart of each,
  he who knows all their works.—R⫽. ↓

———— **YEAR II** ————

FIRST READING   Jas 2:14-24, 26

Neither faith nor good works can merit salvation without the other. A living faith works through love, as opposed to a dead faith that lacks good works. James does not mean that genuine faith is insufficient for justification, but simply that faith without good works is not genuine. Thus there is no basic disagreement between James and Paul, for whom "faith [works] through love" (Gal 5:6).

A reading from the Letter of Saint James

WHAT good is it, my brothers and sisters, if someone says he has faith but does not have works? Can that faith save him? If a brother or sister has nothing to wear and has no food for the day, and one of you says to them, "Go in peace, keep warm, and eat well," but you do not give them the necessities of the body, what good is it? So also faith of itself, if it does not have works, is dead.

Indeed someone might say, "You have faith and I have works." Demonstrate your faith to me without works, and I will demonstrate my faith to you from my works. You believe that God is one. You do well. Even the demons believe that and tremble. Do you want proof, you ignoramus, that faith without works is useless? Was not

Abraham our father justified by works when he offered his son Isaac upon the altar? You see that faith was active along with his works, and faith was completed by the works. Thus the Scripture was fulfilled that says, *Abraham believed God, and it was credited to him as righteousness, and he was called the friend of God.* See how a person is justified by works and not by faith alone. For just as a body without a spirit is dead, so also faith without works is dead.—The word of the Lord. ℟. **Thanks be to God.** ↓

RESPONSORIAL PSALM   Ps 112:1-2, 3-4, 5-6

℟. (see 1b) **Blessed the man who greatly delights in the Lord's commands.**

Blessed the man who fears the LORD,
    who greatly delights in his commands.
His posterity shall be mighty upon the earth;
    the upright generation shall be blessed.—℟.

Wealth and riches shall be in his house;
    his generosity shall endure forever.
Light shines through the darkness for the upright;
    he is gracious and merciful and just.—℟.

Well for the man who is gracious and lends,
    who conducts his affairs with justice;
He shall never be moved;
    the just man shall be in everlasting remembrance.—℟. ↓

——— **YEAR I AND II** ———

ALLELUIA   Jn 15:15b

℟. **Alleluia, alleluia.**
I call you my friends, says the Lord,
for I have made known to you all that the Father has told
    me.
℟. **Alleluia, alleluia.** ↓

GOSPEL Mk 8:34—9:1

Christ's cross is a symbol of the redemptive suffering that all his followers must bear: "Whoever does not carry his own cross and come after me [that is, does not repent and dedicate himself wholly to God] cannot be my disciple" (Lk 14:27). The pleasures of the world cannot be exchanged for heaven.

℣. The Lord be with you. ℟. **And also with you.**
℣. A reading from the holy Gospel according to Mark.
℟. **Glory to you, Lord.**

JESUS summoned the crowd with his disciples and said to them, "Whoever wishes to come after me must deny himself, take up his cross, and follow me. For whoever wishes to save his life will lose it, but whoever loses his life for my sake and that of the Gospel will save it. What profit is there for one to gain the whole world and forfeit his life? What could one give in exchange for his life? Whoever is ashamed of me and of my words in this faithless and sinful generation, the Son of Man will be ashamed of when he comes in his Father's glory with the holy angels."

He also said to them, "Amen, I say to you, there are some standing here who will not taste death until they see that the Kingdom of God has come in power."—The Gospel of the Lord. ℟. **Praise to you, Lord Jesus Christ.**

→ No. 15, p. 623

SATURDAY OF THE SIXTH WEEK IN ORDINARY TIME

———— YEAR I ————

FIRST READING Heb 11:1-7

The Old Testament does not say why Abel's sacrifice was better than Cain's, but this Letter takes for granted that it was his faith. Without faith, it is impossible to please God. Faith is God's spirit working within us, "the realization of what is hoped for and evidence of things not seen" (Heb 11:1).

A reading from the Letter to the Hebrews

BROTHERS and sisters: Faith is the realization of what is hoped for and evidence of things not seen. Because of it the ancients were well attested. By faith we understand that the universe was ordered by the word of God, so that what is visible came into being through the invisible. By faith Abel offered to God a sacrifice greater than Cain's. Through this, he was attested to be righteous, God bearing witness to his gifts, and through this, though dead, he still speaks. By faith Enoch was taken up so that he should not see death, and *he was found no more because God had taken him.* Before he was taken up, he was attested to have pleased God. But without faith it is impossible to please him, for anyone who approaches God must believe that he exists and that he rewards those who seek him. By faith Noah, warned about what was not yet seen, with reverence built an ark for the salvation of his household. Through this, he condemned the world and inherited the righteousness that comes through faith.—The word of the Lord. ℟. **Thanks be to God.** ↓

RESPONSORIAL PSALM   Ps 145:2-3, 4-5, 10-11

℟. (see 1) **I will praise your name for ever, Lord.**

Every day will I bless you,
    and I will praise your name forever and ever.
Great is the LORD and highly to be praised;
    his greatness is unsearchable.—℟.

Generation after generation praises your works
    and proclaims your might.
They speak of the splendor of your glorious majesty
    and tell of your wondrous works.—℟.

Let all your works give you thanks, O LORD,
    and let your faithful ones bless you.
Let them discourse of the glory of your Kingdom
    and speak of your might.—℟. ↓

———— **YEAR II** ————

FIRST READING   Jas 3:1-10

The use and abuse of the role of teaching are related to the good or bad use of the tongue, the instrument through which teaching was chiefly conveyed. The bit and the rudder are figures of the tongue's control, just as the spark and destroying flames portray the evils of unbridled speech. The tongue should be used to bless and praise God, not to curse one's neighbor.

A reading from the Letter of Saint James

NOT many of you should become teachers, my brothers and sisters, for you realize that we will be judged more strictly, for we all fall short in many respects. If anyone does not fall short in speech, he is a perfect man, able to bridle the whole body also. If we put bits into the mouths of horses to make them obey us, we also guide their whole bodies. It is the same with ships: even though they are so large and driven by fierce winds, they are steered by a very small rudder wherever the pilot's inclination wishes. In the same way the tongue is a small member and yet has great pretensions.

Consider how small a fire can set a huge forest ablaze. The tongue is also a fire. It exists among our members as a world of malice, defiling the whole body and setting the entire course of our lives on fire, itself set on fire by Gehenna. For every kind of beast and bird, of reptile and sea creature, can be tamed and has been tamed by the human species, but no man can tame the tongue. It is a restless evil, full of deadly poison. With it we bless the Lord and Father, and with it we curse men who are made in the likeness of God. From the same mouth come blessing and cursing. My brothers and sisters, this need not be so.—The word of the Lord. ℟. **Thanks be to God.** ↓

RESPONSORIAL PSALM   Ps 12:2-3, 4-5, 7-8

℟. (8a) **You will protect us, Lord.**

Help, O LORD! for no one now is dutiful;
   faithfulness has vanished from among the children of
      men.
Everyone speaks falsehood to his neighbor;
   with smooth lips they speak, and double heart.—℞.

May the LORD destroy all smooth lips,
   every boastful tongue,
Those who say, "We are heroes with our tongues;
   our lips are our own; who is lord over us?"—℞.

The promises of the LORD are sure,
   like tried silver, freed from dross, sevenfold refined.
You, O LORD, will keep us
   and preserve us always from this generation.—℞. ↓

——— **YEAR I AND II** ———

ALLELUIA   See Mk 9:6

℞. **Alleluia, alleluia.**
The heavens were opened and the voice of the Father
   thundered:
This is my beloved Son. Listen to him.
℞. **Alleluia, alleluia.** ↓

GOSPEL   Mk 9:2-13

The original event of the transfiguration is obscure. Yet this story Is based
on some factual occurrence in which the disciples fleetingly recognize the
truth of the revelation at Caesarea Philippi. Although Jesus' Messiahship
involves suffering, he is truly the glorious Son of Man.

℣. The Lord be with you. ℞. **And also with you.**
℣. A reading from the holy Gospel according to Mark.
℞. **Glory to you, Lord.**

JESUS took Peter, James, and John and led them up a
high mountain apart by themselves. And he was trans-
figured before them, and his clothes became dazzling
white, such as no fuller on earth could bleach them. Then
Elijah appeared to them along with Moses, and they

were conversing with Jesus. Then Peter said to Jesus in reply, "Rabbi, it is good that we are here! Let us make three tents: one for you, one for Moses, and one for Elijah." He hardly knew what to say, they were so terrified. Then a cloud came, casting a shadow over them; then from the cloud came a voice, "This is my beloved Son. Listen to him." Suddenly, looking around, the disciples no longer saw anyone but Jesus alone with them.

As they were coming down from the mountain, he charged them not to relate what they had seen to anyone, except when the Son of Man had risen from the dead. So they kept the matter to themselves, questioning what rising from the dead meant. Then they asked him, "Why do the scribes say that Elijah must come first?" He told them, "Elijah will indeed come first and restore all things, yet how is it written regarding the Son of Man that he must suffer greatly and be treated with contempt? But I tell you that Elijah has come and they did to him whatever they pleased, as it is written of him."—The Gospel of the Lord. ℟. **Praise to you, Lord Jesus Christ.**   → No. 15, p. 623

MONDAY OF THE SEVENTH WEEK
IN ORDINARY TIME

—— **YEAR I** ——

FIRST READING   Sir 1:1-10

All wisdom that comes from God always was and always will be. Wisdom belongs to the Lord, and he has placed his wisdom in the works of creation, upon all his works and upon all his friends.

A reading from the beginning of the Book of Sirach

ALL wisdom comes from the LORD
and with him it remains forever, and is before all
    time.
The sand of the seashore, the drops of rain,
    the days of eternity: who can number these?

Heaven's height, earth's breadth,
　the depths of the abyss: who can explore these?
Before all things else wisdom was created;
　and prudent understanding, from eternity.
The word of God on high is the fountain of wisdom
　and her ways are everlasting.
To whom has wisdom's root been revealed?
　Who knows her subtleties?
To whom has the discipline of wisdom been revealed?
　And who has understood the multiplicity of her ways?
There is but one, wise and truly awe-inspiring,
　seated upon his throne:
There is but one, Most High
　all-powerful creator-king and truly awe-inspiring one,
　seated upon his throne and he is the God of dominion.
It is the Lord; he created her through the Holy Spirit,
　has seen her and taken note of her.
He has poured her forth upon all his works,
　upon every living thing according to his bounty;
　he has lavished her upon his friends.
The word of the Lord. ℟. **Thanks be to God.** ↓

RESPONSORIAL PSALM Ps 93:1ab, 1cd-2, 5

℟. (1a) **The Lord is king; he is robed in majesty.**

The Lord is king, in splendor robed;
　robed is the Lord and girt about with strength.—℟.

And he has made the world firm,
　not to be moved.
Your throne stands firm from of old;
　from everlasting you are, O Lord.—℟.

Your decrees are worthy of trust indeed:
　holiness befits your house,
　O Lord, for length of days.—℟. ↓

——— **YEAR II** ———

FIRST READING   Jas 3:13-18

Wisdom shines forth in humility. Jealousy and ambition are cunning. This leads to vile behavior. Wisdom from God, however, is innocent. It leads to a harvest of justice.

A reading from the Letter of Saint James

BELOVED: Who among you is wise and understanding? Let him show his works by a good life in the humility that comes from wisdom. But if you have bitter jealousy and selfish ambition in your hearts, do not boast and be false to the truth. Wisdom of this kind does not come down from above but is earthly, unspiritual, demonic. For where jealousy and selfish ambition exist, there is disorder and every foul practice. But the wisdom from above is first of all pure, then peaceable, gentle, compliant, full of mercy and good fruits, without inconstancy or insincerity. And the fruit of righteousness is sown in peace for those who cultivate peace.—The word of the Lord. ℟. **Thanks be to God.** ↓

RESPONSORIAL PSALM   Ps 19:8, 9, 10, 15

℟. (9a) **The precepts of the Lord give joy to the heart.**

The law of the LORD is perfect,
    refreshing the soul;
The decree of the LORD is trustworthy,
    giving wisdom to the simple.—℟.

The precepts of the LORD are right,
    rejoicing the heart;
The command of the LORD is clear,
    enlightening the eye.—℟.

The fear of the LORD is pure,
    enduring forever;
The ordinances of the LORD are true,
    all of them just.—℟.

Let the words of my mouth and the thought of my heart
   find favor before you,
   O Lord, my rock and my redeemer.—Ř̲. ↓

─────── **YEAR I AND II** ───────

ALLELUIA   See 2 Tm 1:10

Ř̲. **Alleluia, alleluia.**
Our Savior Jesus Christ has destroyed death
and brought life to light through the Gospel.
Ř̲. **Alleluia, alleluia.** ↓

GOSPEL   Mk 9:14-29

A father asks Jesus to expel an evil spirit from his son. The begging father
prays for trust and faith in God. Because of faith Jesus orders the demon
out. Jesus teaches how important prayer is before acting.

V̲̌. The Lord be with you. Ř̲. **And also with you.**
V̲̌. A reading from the holy Gospel according to Mark.
Ř̲. **Glory to you, Lord.**

A S Jesus came down from the mountain with Peter,
   James, John and approached the other disciples,
they saw a large crowd around them and scribes arguing
with them. Immediately on seeing him, the whole crowd
was utterly amazed. They ran up to him and greeted him.
He asked them, "What are you arguing about with them?"
Someone from the crowd answered him, "Teacher, I have
brought to you my son possessed by a mute spirit.
Wherever it seizes him, it throws him down; he foams at
the mouth, grinds his teeth, and becomes rigid. I asked
your disciples to drive it out, but they were unable to do
so." He said to them in reply, "O faithless generation, how
long will I be with you? How long will I endure you?
Bring him to me." They brought the boy to him. And
when he saw him, the spirit immediately threw the boy
into convulsions. As he fell to the ground, he began to roll
around and foam at the mouth. Then he questioned his
father, "How long has this been happening to him?" He
replied, "Since childhood. It has often thrown him into

fire and into water to kill him. But if you can do anything, have compassion on us and help us." Jesus said to him, " 'If you can!' Everything is possible to one who has faith." Then the boy's father cried out, "I do believe, help my unbelief!" Jesus, on seeing a crowd rapidly gathering, rebuked the unclean spirit and said to it, "Mute and deaf spirit, I command you: come out of him and never enter him again!" Shouting and throwing the boy into convulsions, it came out. He became like a corpse, which caused many to say, "He is dead!" But Jesus took him by the hand, raised him, and he stood up. When he entered the house, his disciples asked him in private, "Why could we not drive the spirit out?" He said to them, "This kind can only come out through prayer."—The Gospel of the Lord.
℟. **Praise to you, Lord Jesus Christ.**   ➜ No. 15, p. 623

TUESDAY OF THE SEVENTH WEEK
IN ORDINARY TIME

——— **YEAR I** ———

FIRST READING   Sir 2:1-11

Sirach warns of trials that will come for one who accepts his teaching. Patience and trust in God are the means of emerging victoriously. Adversity is a test for the just.

A reading from the Book of Sirach

MY son, when you come to serve the LORD,
   stand in justice and fear,
   prepare yourself for trials.
Be sincere of heart and steadfast,
   incline your ear and receive the word of understanding,
   undisturbed in time of adversity.
Wait on God, with patience, cling to him, forsake him not;
   thus will you be wise in all your ways.
Accept whatever befalls you,
   when sorrowful, be steadfast,
   and in crushing misfortune be patient;

For in fire gold and silver are tested,
    and worthy people in the crucible of humiliation.
Trust God and God will help you;
    trust in him, and he will direct your way;
    keep his fear and grow old therein.

You who fear the LORD, wait for his mercy,
    turn not away lest you fall.
You who fear the LORD, trust him,
    and your reward will not be lost.
You who fear the LORD, hope for good things,
    for lasting joy and mercy.
You who fear the LORD, love him,
    and your hearts will be enlightened.
Study the generations long past and understand;
    has anyone hoped in the LORD and been disappointed?
Has anyone persevered in his commandments and been
        forsaken?
    has anyone called upon him and been rebuffed?
Compassionate and merciful is the LORD;
    he forgives sins, he saves in time of trouble
    and he is a protector to all who seek him in truth.
The word of the Lord. ℟. **Thanks be to God.** ↓

RESPONSORIAL PSALM   Ps 37:3-4, 18-19, 27-28, 39-40

℟. (see 5) **Commit your life to the Lord, and he will help
    you.**

Trust in the LORD and do good,
    that you may dwell in the land and be fed in security.
Take delight in the LORD,
    and he will grant you your heart's requests.—℟.

The LORD watches over the lives of the wholehearted;
    their inheritance lasts forever.
They are not put to shame in an evil time;
    in days of famine they have plenty.—℟.

Turn from evil and do good,
    that you may abide forever;

For the LORD loves what is right,
and forsakes not his faithful ones.—R′.

The salvation of the just is from the LORD;
he is their refuge in time of distress.
And the LORD helps them and delivers them;
he delivers them from the wicked and saves them,
because they take refuge in him.—R′. ↓

———— **YEAR II** ————

FIRST READING   Jas 4:1-10

Ambition leads to conflicts and disputes, to envy, murder, squandering. These are marks of the world that are contradictory to humility. The Christian should submit to God and resist the devil. He should be humble.

A reading from the Letter of Saint James

BELOVED: Where do the wars and where do the conflicts among you come from? Is it not from your passions that make war within your members? You covet but do not possess. You kill and envy but you cannot obtain; you fight and wage war. You do not possess because you do not ask. You ask but do not receive, because you ask wrongly, to spend it on your passions. Adulterers! Do you not know that to be a lover of the world means enmity with God? Therefore, whoever wants to be a lover of the world makes himself an enemy of God. Or do you suppose that the Scripture speaks without meaning when it says, *The spirit that he has made to dwell in us tends toward jealousy*? But he bestows a greater grace; therefore, it says:

God resists the proud,
but gives grace to the humble.

So submit yourselves to God. Resist the Devil, and he will flee from you. Draw near to God, and he will draw near to you. Cleanse your hands, you sinners, and purify your hearts, you of two minds. Begin to lament, to mourn, to weep. Let your laughter be turned into mourning and your joy into dejection. Humble yourselves before the Lord and he will exalt you.—The word of the Lord. ℟. **Thanks be to God.** ↓

RESPONSORIAL PSALM   Ps 55:7-8, 9-10a, 10b-11a, 23

℟. (23a) **Throw your cares on the Lord, and he will support you.**

And I say,"Had I but wings like a dove,
    I would fly away and be at rest.
Far away I would flee;
    I would lodge in the wilderness."—℟.

"I would wait for him who saves me
    from the violent storm and the tempest."
Engulf them, O Lord; divide their counsels.—℟.

In the city I see violence and strife,
    day and night they prowl about upon its walls.—℟.

Cast your care upon the LORD,
    and he will support you;
    never will he permit the just man to be disturbed.—℟. ↓

——— **YEAR I AND II** ———

ALLELUIA   Gal 6:14

℟. **Alleluia, alleluia.**
May I never boast except in the Cross of our Lord Jesus
    Christ,
through which the world has been crucified to me and I
    to the world.
℟. **Alleluia, alleluia.** ↓

GOSPEL   Mk 9:30-37

Christ tries to give the disciples some preview of what lies before him. The disciples are to reverse the customary practice whereby those in authority rule by force. Their new norm of conduct—to be the servant of all—is made possible by Jesus' own example of his mission of service.

℣. The Lord be with you. ℟. **And also with you.**
℣. A reading from the holy Gospel according to Mark.
℟. **Glory to you, Lord.**

JESUS and his disciples left from there and began a journey through Galilee, but he did not wish anyone to know about it. He was teaching his disciples and telling them, "The Son of Man is to be handed over to men and they will kill him, and three days after his death the Son of Man will rise." But they did not understand the saying, and they were afraid to question him.

They came to Capernaum and, once inside the house, he began to ask them, "What were you arguing about on the way?" But they remained silent. For they had been discussing among themselves on the way who was the greatest. Then he sat down, called the Twelve, and said to them, "If anyone wishes to be first, he shall be the last of all and the servant of all." Taking a child, he placed it in their midst, and putting his arms around it, he said to them, "Whoever receives one child such as this in my name, receives me; and whoever receives me, receives not me but the One who sent me."—The Gospel of the Lord. ℟.
Praise to you, Lord Jesus Christ.   ➜ No. 15, p. 623

WEDNESDAY OF THE SEVENTH WEEK IN ORDINARY TIME

———— **YEAR I** ————

FIRST READING   Sir 4:11-19

True wisdom, which is found only in God and comes from him alone, brings God's blessings down on all who serve her. She puts human beings to the test until their hearts are fully with her. Then she bestows glory and happiness on them.

A reading from the Book of Sirach

WISDOM breathes life into her children
    and admonishes those who seek her.
He who loves her loves life;
    those who seek her will be embraced by the LORD.

He who holds her fast inherits glory;
>   wherever he dwells, the LORD bestows blessings.
Those who serve her serve the Holy One;
>   those who love her the LORD loves.
He who obeys her judges nations;
>   he who hearkens to her dwells in her inmost chambers.
If one trusts her, he will possess her;
>   his descendants too will inherit her.
She walks with him as a stranger
>   and at first she puts him to the test;
Fear and dread she brings upon him
>   and tries him with her discipline
>   until she try him by her laws and trust his soul.
Then she comes back to bring him happiness
>   and reveal her secrets to them
>   and she will heap upon him
>   treasures of knowledge and an understanding of justice.
But if he fails her, she will abandon him
>   and deliver him into the hands of despoilers.
The word of the Lord. ℟. **Thanks be to God.** ↓

RESPONSORIAL PSALM Ps 119:165, 168, 171, 172, 174, 175

℟. (165a) **O Lord, great peace have they who love your law.**

Those who love your law have great peace,
>   and for them there is no stumbling block.—℟.

I keep your precepts and your decrees,
>   for all my ways are before you.—℟.

My lips pour forth your praise,
>   because you teach me your statutes.—℟.

May my tongue sing of your promise,
>   for all your commands are just.—℟.

I long for your salvation, O LORD,
>   and your law is my delight.—℟.

Let my soul live to praise you,
　　and may your ordinances help me.—℟. ↓

——————— **YEAR II** ———————

FIRST READING　　　　　　　　　　　　　Jas 4:13-17

Tomorrow is unknown. Life is like a vapor, appearing now and soon vanishing. Only the will of God merits a reward. Not to do the right thing means that a person sins.

A reading from the Letter of Saint James

B ELOVED: Come now, you who say, "Today or tomorrow we shall go into such and such a town, spend a year there doing business, and make a profit"—you have no idea what your life will be like tomorrow. You are a puff of smoke that appears briefly and then disappears. Instead you should say, "If the Lord wills it, we shall live to do this or that." But now you are boasting in your arrogance. All such boasting is evil. So for one who knows the right thing to do and does not do it, it is a sin.—The word of the Lord. ℟. **Thanks be to God.** ↓

RESPONSORIAL PSALM　　　　Ps 49:2-3, 6-7, 8-10, 11

℟. (Mt 5:3) **Blessed are the poor in spirit; the Kingdom of heaven is theirs!**

Hear this, all you peoples;
　　hearken, all who dwell in the world,
Of lowly birth or high degree,
　　rich and poor alike.—℟.

Why should I fear in evil days
　　when my wicked ensnarers ring me round?
They trust in their wealth;
　　the abundance of their riches is their boast.—℟.

Yet in no way can a man redeem himself,
　　or pay his own ransom to God;
Too high is the price to redeem one's life; he would never
　　　have enough
　　to remain alive always and not see destruction.—℟.

For he can see that wise men die,
    and likewise the senseless and the stupid pass away,
    leaving to others their wealth.—℟. ↓

——————— **YEAR I AND II** ———————

ALLELUIA   Jn 14:6

℟. **Alleluia, alleluia.**
I am the way and the truth and the life, says the Lord;
no one comes to the Father except through me.
℟. **Alleluia, alleluia.** ↓

GOSPEL   Mk 9:38-40

Jesus warns against jealousy and intolerance toward good works such as exorcism, performed in his name by those whose faith is imperfect. The saying "Whoever is not against us is for us" is a broad principle of the divine tolerance.

℣. The Lord be with you. ℟. **And also with you.**
℣. A reading from the holy Gospel according to Mark.
℟. **Glory to you, Lord.**

JOHN said to Jesus, "Teacher, we saw someone driving out demons in your name, and we tried to prevent him because he does not follow us." Jesus replied, "Do not prevent him. There is no one who performs a mighty deed in my name who can at the same time speak ill of me. For whoever is not against us is for us."—The Gospel of the Lord. ℟. **Praise to you, Lord Jesus Christ.**

→ No. 15, p. 623

THURSDAY OF THE SEVENTH WEEK IN ORDINARY TIME

——————— **YEAR I** ———————

FIRST READING   Sir 5:1-8

Whoever has the misfortune to fall away from the Lord should never delay returning to him. The Lord is, indeed, long-suffering and forgiving, but he will not wait forever before sending his anger on the unrepentant sinner.

A reading from the Book of Sirach

RELY not on your wealth;
say not: "I have the power."
Rely not on your strength
in following the desires of your heart.
Say not: "Who can prevail against me?"
or, "Who will subdue me for my deeds?"
for God will surely exact the punishment.
Say not: "I have sinned, yet what has befallen me?"
for the Most High bides his time.
Of forgiveness be not overconfident,
adding sin upon sin.
Say not: "Great is his mercy;
my many sins he will forgive."
For mercy and anger alike are with him;
upon the wicked alights his wrath.
Delay not your conversion to the LORD,
put it not off from day to day.
For suddenly his wrath flames forth;
at the time of vengeance you will be destroyed.
Rely not upon deceitful wrath,
for it will be no help on the day of wrath.
The word of the Lord. ℟. **Thanks be to God.** ↓

RESPONSORIAL PSALM   Ps 1:1-2, 3, 4 and 6

℟. (Ps 40:5a) **Blessed are they who hope in the Lord.**

Blessed the man who follows not
the counsel of the wicked
Nor walks in the way of sinners,
nor sits in the company of the insolent,
But delights in the law of the LORD
and meditates on his law day and night.—℟.

He is like a tree
planted near running water,
That yields its fruit in due season,
and whose leaves never fade.
Whatever he does, prospers.—℟.

Not so the wicked, not so;
  they are like chaff which the wind drives away.
For the LORD watches over the way of the just,
  but the way of the wicked vanishes.—℟. ↓

——————— **YEAR II** ———————

FIRST READING   Jas 5:1-6

Wealth and riches forebode miseries. Only what is stored up for the last day counts. Those who sin in order to gain luxuries isolate themselves from the Lord.

A reading from the Letter of Saint James

COME now, you rich, weep and wail over your impending miseries. Your wealth has rotted away, your clothes have become moth-eaten, your gold and silver have corroded, and that corrosion will be a testimony against you; it will devour your flesh like a fire. You have stored up treasure for the last days. Behold, the wages you withheld from the workers who harvested your fields are crying aloud; and the cries of the harvesters have reached the ears of the Lord of hosts. You have lived on earth in luxury and pleasure; you have fattened your hearts for the day of slaughter. You have condemned; you have murdered the righteous one; he offers you no resistance.—The word of the Lord. ℟. **Thanks be to God.** ↓

RESPONSORIAL PSALM
                          Ps 49:14-15ab, 15cd-16, 17-18, 19-20

℟. (Mt 5:3) **Blessed are the poor in spirit; the Kingdom of heaven is theirs!**

This is the way of those whose trust is folly,
  the end of those contented with their lot:
Like sheep they are herded into the nether world;
  death is their shepherd and the upright rule over them.—℟.

Quickly their form is consumed;
  the nether world is their palace.

But God will redeem me
   from the power of the nether world by receiving
      me.—℟.

Fear not when a man grows rich,
   when the wealth of his house becomes great,
For when he dies, he shall take none of it;
   his wealth shall not follow him down.—℟.

Though in his lifetime he counted himself blessed,
   "They will praise you for doing well for yourself,"
He shall join the circle of his forebears
   who shall never more see light.—℟. ↓

———— **YEAR I AND II** ————

ALLELUIA   See 1 Thes 2:13

℟. **Alleluia, alleluia.**
Receive the word of God, not as the word of men,
but as it truly is, the word of God.
℟. **Alleluia, alleluia.** ↓

GOSPEL   Mk 9:41-50

Christians must avoid giving scandal to others and be prepared to sacrifice anything that is a scandal. They will then escape the torments of hell,
symbolized by the fire and worms that existed in the Valley of Gehenna (a
dumping ground near Jerusalem). To have the salt of the Christian life
means to be at peace with one another.

℣. The Lord be with you. ℟. **And also with you.**
℣. A reading from the holy Gospel according to Mark.
℟. **Glory to you, Lord.**

JESUS said to his disciples: "Anyone who gives you a
cup of water to drink because you belong to Christ,
amen, I say to you, will surely not lose his reward.

   "Whoever causes one of these little ones who believe
in me to sin, it would be better for him if a great millstone
were put around his neck and he were thrown into the
sea. If your hand causes you to sin, cut it off. It is better for
you to enter into life maimed than with two hands to go
into Gehenna, into the unquenchable fire. And if your foot

causes you to sin, cut if off. It is better for you to enter into life crippled than with two feet to be thrown into Gehenna. And if your eye causes you to sin, pluck it out. Better for you to enter into the Kingdom of God with one eye than with two eyes to be thrown into Gehenna, where *their worm does not die, and the fire is not quenched.*

"Everyone will be salted with fire. Salt is good, but if salt becomes insipid, with what will you restore its flavor? Keep salt in yourselves and you will have peace with one another."—The Gospel of the Lord. ℟. **Praise to you, Lord Jesus Christ.**　　　　　　　　→ No. 15, p. 623

FRIDAY OF THE SEVENTH WEEK IN ORDINARY TIME

——— YEAR I ———

FIRST READING　　　　　　　　　　　　　　Sir 6:5-17

True friends are beyond comparison and should be diligently sought by all. They do not desert us in times of trial or turn against us as false friends do. They are a sturdy shelter, and they stand by us; they fear God just as we do.

A reading from the Book of Sirach

A KIND mouth multiplies friends and appeases enemies,
　　and gracious lips prompt friendly greetings.
Let your acquaintances be many,
　　but one in a thousand your confidant.
When you gain a friend, first test him,
　　and be not too ready to trust him.
For one sort is a friend when it suits him,
　　but he will not be with you in time of distress.
Another is a friend who becomes an enemy,
　　and tells of the quarrel to your shame.
Another is a friend, a boon companion,
　　who will not be with you when sorrow comes.
When things go well, he is your other self,
　　and lords it over your servants;

But if you are brought low, he turns against you
    and avoids meeting you.
Keep away from your enemies;
    be on your guard with your friends.
A faithful friend is a sturdy shelter;
    he who finds one finds a treasure.
A faithful friend is beyond price,
    no sum can balance his worth.
A faithful friend is a life-saving remedy,
    such as he who fears God finds;
For he who fears God behaves accordingly,
    and his friend will be like himself.
The word of the Lord. ℟. **Thanks be to God.** ↓

RESPONSORIAL PSALM   Ps 119:12, 16, 18, 27, 34, 35

℟. (35a) **Guide me, Lord, in the way of your commands.**

Blessed are you, O LORD;
    teach me your statutes.—℟.

In your statutes I will delight;
    I will not forget your words.—℟.

Open my eyes, that I may consider
    the wonders of your law.—℟.

Make me understand the way of your precepts,
    and I will meditate on your wondrous deeds.   ℟.

Give me discernment, that I may observe your law
    and keep it with all my heart.—℟.

Lead me in the path of your commands,
    for in it I delight.—℟. ↓

——— **YEAR II** ———

FIRST READING   Jas 5:9-12

A Christian does not grumble. The judge stands and waits. The prophets
are past models of suffering; they have endured hardship patiently.
Speech should be open and honest.

A reading from the Letter of Saint James

DO not complain, brothers and sisters, about one another, that you may not be judged. Behold, the Judge is standing before the gates. Take as an example of hardship and patience, brothers and sisters, the prophets who spoke in the name of the Lord. Indeed we call blessed those who have persevered. You have heard of the perseverance of Job, and you have seen the purpose of the Lord, because *the Lord is compassionate and merciful.*

But above all, my brothers and sisters, do not swear, either by heaven or by earth or with any other oath, but let your "Yes" mean "Yes" and your "No" mean "No," that you may not incur condemnation.—The word of the Lord. ℟. **Thanks be to God.** ↓

RESPONSORIAL PSALM   Ps 103:1-2, 3-4, 8-9, 11-12

℟. (8a) **The Lord is kind and merciful.**

Bless the LORD, O my soul;
    and all my being, bless his holy name.
Bless the LORD, O my soul,
    and forget not all his benefits.—℟.

He pardons all your iniquities,
    he heals all your ills.
He redeems your life from destruction,
    he crowns you with kindness and compassion.

Merciful and gracious is the LORD,
    slow to anger and abounding in kindness.
He will not always chide,
    nor does he keep his wrath forever.—℟.

For as the heavens are high above the earth,
    so surpassing is his kindness toward those who fear
      him.
As far as the east is from the west,
    so far has he put our transgressions from us.—℟. ↓

——— **YEAR I AND II** ———

ALLELUIA   See Jn 17:17b, 17a

℟. **Alleluia, alleluia.**
Your word, O Lord, is truth;
consecrate us in the truth.
℟. **Alleluia, alleluia.** ↓

GOSPEL   Mk 10:1-12

In answer to a test-question Jesus declares that divorce is not part of
God's original plan for man and woman in marriage. They are no longer
two but one flesh. Therefore, neither one can divorce the other.

℣. The Lord be with you. ℟. **And also with you.**
℣. A reading from the holy Gospel according to Mark.
℟. **Glory to you, Lord.**

JESUS came into the district of Judea and across the
Jordan. Again crowds gathered around him and, as
was his custom, he again taught them. The Pharisees
approached him and asked, "Is it lawful for a husband to
divorce his wife?" They were testing him. He said to
them in reply, "What did Moses command you?" They
replied, "Moses permitted a husband to write a bill of
divorce and dismiss her." But Jesus told them, "Because of
the hardness of your hearts he wrote you this commandment. But from the beginning of creation, *God made
them male and female. For this reason a man shall leave
his father and mother and be joined to his wife, and the
two shall become one flesh.* So they are no longer two
but one flesh. Therefore what God has joined together, no
human being must separate." In the house the disciples
again questioned Jesus about this. He said to them,
"Whoever divorces his wife and marries another commits adultery against her; and if she divorces her husband and marries another, she commits adultery."—The
Gospel of the Lord. ℟. **Praise to you, Lord Jesus Christ.**

➔ No. 15, p. 623

SATURDAY OF THE SEVENTH WEEK
IN ORDINARY TIME

——————— YEAR I ———————

FIRST READING   Sir 17:1-15

The Lord created men and women in his own image and likeness. He made them masters of creation and bestowed marvelous blessings and gifts upon them. He made a covenant with them and exhorted them to do good and avoid evil. He continues to watch over them, and all their actions are clear to him.

A reading from the Book of Sirach

GOD from the earth created man,
    and in his own image he made him.
He makes man return to earth again,
    and endows him with a strength of his own.
Limited days of life he gives him,
    with power over all things else on earth.
He puts the fear of him in all flesh,
    and gives him rule over beasts and birds.
He created for them counsel, and a tongue and eyes and
        ears,
    and an inventive heart,
    and filled them with the discipline of understanding.
He created in them knowledge of the spirit;
With wisdom he fills their heart;
    good and evil he shows them.
He put the fear of himself upon their hearts,
    and showed them his mighty works,
That they might glory in the wonder of his deeds
    and praise his holy name.
He has set before them knowledge,
    a law of life as their inheritance;
An everlasting covenant he has made with them,
    his justice and his judgments he has revealed to them.
His majestic glory their eyes beheld,
    his glorious voice their ears heard.

He says to them, "Avoid all evil";
  each of them he gives precepts about his fellow men.
Their ways are ever known to him,
  they cannot be hidden from his eyes.
Over every nation he places a ruler,
  but God's own portion is Israel.
All their actions are clear as the sun to him,
  his eyes are ever upon their ways.
The word of the Lord. ℟. **Thanks be to God.** ↓

RESPONSORIAL PSALM   Ps 103:13-14, 15-16, 17-18

℟. (see 17) **The Lord's kindness is everlasting to those
  who fear him.**

As a father has compassion on his children,
  so the LORD has compassion on those who fear him,
For he knows how we are formed;
  he remembers that we are dust.—℟.

Man's days are like those of grass;
  like a flower of the field he blooms;
The wind sweeps over him and he is gone,
  and his place knows him no more.—℟.

But the kindness of the LORD is from eternity
  to eternity toward those who fear him,
And his justice toward children's children
  among those who keep his covenant.—℟. ↓

———— **YEAR II** ————

FIRST READING   Jas 5:13-20

The Lord will answer the prayers of the just. Those who are sick should call
in God's ministers to pray for them. If they are sincere, their sins will be
forgiven. To help those in sin will merit a handsome reward.

A reading from the Letter of Saint James

BELOVED: Is anyone among you suffering? He should
  pray. Is anyone in good spirits? He should sing a
song of praise. Is anyone among you sick? He should
summon the presbyters of the Church, and they should

pray over him and anoint him with oil in the name of the Lord. The prayer of faith will save the sick person, and the Lord will raise him up. If he has committed any sins, he will be forgiven.

Therefore, confess your sins to one another and pray for one another, that you may be healed. The fervent prayer of a righteous person is very powerful. Elijah was a man like us; yet he prayed earnestly that it might not rain, and for three years and six months it did not rain upon the land. Then Elijah prayed again, and the sky gave rain and the earth produced its fruit.

My brothers and sisters, if anyone among you should stray from the truth and someone bring him back, he should know that whoever brings back a sinner from the error of his way will save his soul from death and will cover a multitude of sins.—The word of the Lord. ℟. **Thanks be to God.** ↓

RESPONSORIAL PSALM   Ps 141:1-2, 3 and 8

℟. (2a) **Let my prayer come like incense before you.**

O LORD, to you I call; hasten to me;
    hearken to my voice when I call upon you.
Let my prayer come like incense before you;
    the lifting up of my hands, like the evening sacrifice.—℟.

O LORD, set a watch before my mouth,
    a guard at the door of my lips.
For toward you, O God, my LORD, my eyes are turned;
    in you I take refuge; strip me not of life.—℟. ↓

─────── **YEAR I AND II** ───────

ALLELUIA   See Mt 11:25

℟. **Alleluia, alleluia.**
Blessed are you, Father, Lord of heaven and earth;
you have revealed to little ones the mysteries of the
    Kingdom.
℟. **Alleluia, alleluia.** ↓

GOSPEL   Mk 10:13-16

See Common of Holy Men and Women, p. 1233, no. 16.

MONDAY OF THE EIGHTH WEEK
IN ORDINARY TIME

———— **YEAR I** ————

FIRST READING   Sir 17:20-24

The mercy of the Lord is great and God forgives all who return to him. His mercy far surpasses that of human beings. They must hate sin and offer living praise to God while they have the opportunity to do so on earth.

A reading from the Book of Sirach

TO the penitent God provides a way back,
he encourages those who are losing hope
   and has chosen for them the lot of truth.
Return to him and give up sin,
   pray to the LORD and make your offenses few.
Turn again to the Most High and away from your sin,
   hate intensely what he loathes,
   and know the justice and judgments of God,
Stand firm in the way set before you,
   in prayer to the Most High God.

Who in the nether world can glorify the Most High
   in place of the living who offer their praise?
Dwell no longer in the error of the ungodly,
   but offer your praise before death.
No more can the dead give praise
   than those who have never lived;
You who are alive and well
   shall praise and glorify God in his mercies.
How great the mercy of the LORD,
   his forgiveness of those who return to him!
The word of the Lord. ℟. **Thanks be to God.** ↓

RESPONSORIAL PSALM   Ps 32:1-2, 5, 6, 7

℟. (11a) **Let the just exult and rejoice in the Lord.**

Blessed is he whose fault is taken away,
    whose sin is covered.
Blessed the man to whom the LORD imputes not guilt,
    in whose spirit there is no guile.—℟.

Then I acknowledged my sin to you,
    my guilt I covered not.
I said, "I confess my faults to the LORD,"
    and you took away the guilt of my sin.—℟.

For this shall every faithful man pray to you
    in time of stress.
Though deep waters overflow,
    they shall not reach him.—℟.

You are my shelter; from distress you will preserve me;
    with glad cries of freedom you will ring me
    round.—℟. ↓

——— **YEAR II** ———

FIRST READING   1 Pt 1:3-9

Through his resurrection Jesus has given to human beings a new hope, a
new birth. This is cause for rejoicing. It is by faith that we believe in him
to achieve salvation.

A reading from the first Letter of Saint Peter

BLESSED be the God and Father of our Lord Jesus
Christ, who in his great mercy gave us a new birth to
a living hope through the resurrection of Jesus Christ
from the dead, to an inheritance that is imperishable,
undefiled, and unfading, kept in heaven for you who by
the power of God are safeguarded through faith, to a salvation that is ready to be revealed in the final time. In this
you rejoice, although now for a little while you may have
to suffer through various trials, so that the genuineness

of your faith, more precious than gold that is perishable
even though tested by fire, may prove to be for praise,
glory, and honor at the revelation of Jesus Christ.
Although you have not seen him you love him; even
though you do not see him now yet you believe in him,
you rejoice with an indescribable and glorious joy, as you
attain the goal of faith, the salvation of your souls.—The
word of the Lord. ℟. **Thanks be to God.** ↓

RESPONSORIAL PSALM   Ps 111:1-2, 5-6, 9 and 10c

℟. (5) **The Lord will remember his covenant for ever**.

℟. Or: **Alleluia.**

I will give thanks to the LORD with all my heart
   in the company and assembly of the just.
Great are the works of the LORD,
   exquisite in all their delights.—℟.

He has given food to those who fear him;
   he will forever be mindful of his covenant.
He has made known to his people the power of his works,
   giving them the inheritance of the nations.—℟.

He has sent deliverance to his people,
   he has ratified his covenant forever;
holy and awesome is his name.
   His praise endures forever.—℟. ↓

———— **YEAR I AND II** ————

ALLELUIA   2 Cor 8:9

℟. **Alleluia, alleluia.**
Jesus Christ became poor although he was rich,
so that by his poverty you might become rich.
℟. **Alleluia, alleluia.** ↓

GOSPEL   Mk 10:17-27

Jesus' contemporaries consider wealth a sign of divine favor. When he
denies this and shows that wealth can obstruct the spiritual perception
of his message, the disciples conclude that virtually no one can be saved.

Jesus replies that the rich as well as the poor are dependent on God for their salvation.

℣. The Lord be with you. ℟. **And also with you.**

℣. A reading from the holy Gospel according to Mark.

℟. **Glory to you, Lord.**

AS Jesus was setting out on a journey, a man ran up, knelt down before him, and asked him, "Good teacher, what must I do to inherit eternal life?" Jesus answered him, "Why do you call me good? No one is good but God alone. You know the commandments: *You shall not kill; you shall not commit adultery; you shall not steal; you shall not bear false witness; you shall not defraud; honor your father and your mother.*" He replied and said to him, "Teacher, all of these I have observed from my youth." Jesus, looking at him, loved him and said to him, "You are lacking in one thing. Go, sell what you have, and give to the poor and you will have treasure in heaven; then come, follow me." At that statement, his face fell, and he went away sad, for he had many possessions.

Jesus looked around and said to his disciples, "How hard it is for those who have wealth to enter the Kingdom of God!" The disciples were amazed at his words. So Jesus again said to them in reply, "Children, how hard it is to enter the Kingdom of God! It is easier for a camel to pass through the eye of a needle than for one who is rich to enter the Kingdom of God." They were exceedingly astonished and said among themselves, "Then who can be saved?" Jesus looked at them and said, "For men it is impossible, but not for God. All things are possible for God."—The Gospel of the Lord. ℟. **Praise to you, Lord Jesus Christ.**

➨ No. 15, p. 623

TUESDAY OF THE EIGHTH WEEK
IN ORDINARY TIME

———— **YEAR I** ————

FIRST READING   Sir 35:1-12

God is a God of justice, who knows no favorites. He always repays human beings for their good works, and he does so to the seventh degree, that is, to the perfect degree. Hence, we should observe God's commandments and present a perfect sacrifice to God.

A reading from the Book of Sirach

TO keep the law is a great oblation,
  and he who observes the commandments sacrifices
     a peace offering.
In works of charity one offers fine flour,
  and when he gives alms he presents his sacrifice of
     praise.
To refrain from evil pleases the LORD,
  and to avoid injustice is an atonement.
Appear not before the LORD empty-handed,
  for all that you offer is in fulfillment of the precepts.
The just one's offering enriches the altar
  and rises as a sweet odor before the Most High.
The just one's sacrifice is most pleasing,
  nor will it ever be forgotten.
In a generous spirit pay homage to the LORD,
  be not sparing of freewill gifts.
With each contribution show a cheerful countenance,
  and pay your tithes in a spirit of joy.
Give to the Most High as he has given to you,
  generously, according to your means.

For the LORD is one who always repays,
  and he will give back to you sevenfold.
But offer no bribes, these he does not accept!
  Trust not in sacrifice of the fruits of extortion.
For he is a God of justice,
  who knows no favorites.
The word of the Lord. ℟. **Thanks be to God.** ↓

RESPONSORIAL PSALM Ps 50:5-6, 7-8, 14 and 23

℟. (23b) **To the upright I will show the saving power of God.**

"Gather my faithful ones before me,
    those who have made a covenant with me by sacri-
        fice."
And the heavens proclaim his justice;
    for God himself is the judge.—℟.

"Hear, my people, and I will speak;
    Israel, I will testify against you;
    God, your God, am I.
Not for your sacrifices do I rebuke you,
    for your burnt offerings are before me always.—℟.

"Offer to God praise as your sacrifice
    and fulfill your vows to the Most High.
He that offers praise as a sacrifice glorifies me;
    and to him that goes the right way I will show the sal-
        vation of God."—℟. ↓

——————— **YEAR II** ———————

FIRST READING 1 Pt 1:10-16

The prophets were witnesses to the future coming of Christ. They directed
their lives to foreshadowing Jesus. Peter directs Christians to live soberly, hoping in the fulfillment of the Gospel. Scripture says, "Be holy, for I
am holy" (1 Pt 1:16).

A reading from the first Letter of Saint Peter

BELOVED: Concerning the salvation of your souls the
    prophets who prophesied about the grace that was to
be yours searched and investigated it investigating the
time and circumstances that the Spirit of Christ within
them indicated when it testified in advance to the sufferings destined for Christ and the glories to follow them. It
was revealed to them that they were serving not themselves but you with regard to the things that have now
been announced to you by those who preached the Good

News to you through the Holy Spirit sent from heaven, things into which angels longed to look.

Therefore, gird up the loins of your mind, live soberly, and set your hopes completely on the grace to be brought to you at the revelation of Jesus Christ. Like obedient children, do not act in compliance with the desires of your former ignorance but, as he who called you is holy, be holy yourselves in every aspect of your conduct, for it is written, *Be holy because I am holy.*—The word of the Lord. ℟. **Thanks be to God.** ↓

RESPONSORIAL PSALM
Ps 98:1, 2-3ab, 3cd-4

℟. (2a) **The Lord has made known his salvation.**

See Saturday of the 4th Week of Easter, p. 836.

———— **YEAR I AND II** ————

ALLELUIA
See Mt 11:25

℟. **Alleluia, alleluia.**
Blessed are you, Father, Lord of heaven and earth;
you have revealed to little ones the mysteries of the
    Kingdom.
℟. **Alleluia, alleluia.** ↓

GOSPEL
Mk 10:28-31

Peter expresses the concern of all who follow Christ faithfully and closely in this life in spite of every difficulty. Jesus promises that voluntary renunciation of self, home, property, and relatives for his sake will be rewarded by God in this life and the next.

℣. The Lord be with you. ℟. **And also with you.**
℣. A reading from the holy Gospel according to Mark.
℟. **Glory to you, Lord.**

PETER began to say to Jesus, "We have given up everything and followed you." Jesus said, "Amen, I say to you, there is no one who has given up house or brothers or sisters or mother or father or children or lands for my sake and for the sake of the Gospel who will not receive a hundred times more now in this present age: houses and brothers and sisters and mothers and children and lands, with persecutions, and eternal life in the age to come. But many that are first will be last, and the last will be first."—The Gospel of the Lord. ℟. **Praise to you, Lord Jesus Christ.**   → No. 15, p. 623

WEDNESDAY OF THE EIGHTH WEEK IN ORDINARY TIME

———— **YEAR I** ————

FIRST READING   Sir 36:1, 4-5a, 10-17

In the name of the people Sirach asks God to give new signs and work new wonders on their behalf. Thus the nations will know, as the People of God do, that there is no other God. They ask him to hear the prayers of his servants and so show that he is the eternal God.

A reading from the Book of Sirach

COME to our aid, O God of the universe,
    look upon us, show us the light of your mercies,
    and put all the nations in dread of you!
Thus they will know, as we know,
    that there is no God but you, O Lord.

Give new signs and work new wonders.

Gather all the tribes of Jacob,
    that they may inherit the land as of old,
Show mercy to the people called by your name;
    Israel, whom you named your firstborn.
Take pity on your holy city,
    Jerusalem, your dwelling place.
Fill Zion with your majesty,
    your temple with your glory.

Give evidence of your deeds of old;
    fulfill the prophecies spoken in your name,

Reward those who have hoped in you,
   and let your prophets be proved true.
Hear the prayer of your servants,
   for you are ever gracious to your people;
   and lead us in the way of justice.
Thus it will be known to the very ends of the earth
   that you are the eternal God.
The word of the Lord. ℟. **Thanks be to God.** ↓

RESPONSORIAL PSALM   Ps 79:8, 9, 11 and 13

℟. (Sir 36:1b) **Show us, O Lord, the light of your kindness.**

Remember not against us the iniquities of the past;
   may your compassion quickly come to us,
   for we are brought very low.—℟.

Help us, O God our savior,
   because of the glory of your name;
Deliver us and pardon our sins
   for your name's sake.—℟.

Let the prisoners' sighing come before you;
   with your great power free those doomed to death.
Then we, your people and the sheep of your pasture,
   will give thanks to you forever;
      through all generations we will declare your
      praise.—℟. ↓

——————— **YEAR II** ———————

FIRST READING   1 Pt 1:18-25

The faithful have been delivered not by gold or silver but by the blood of
Jesus Christ. Through him they are believers. By obedience to him, they
become purified. In this way human beings learn to love one another.

A reading from the first Letter of Saint Peter

B ELOVED: Realize that you were ransomed from your
   futile conduct, handed on by your ancestors, not with
perishable things like silver or gold but with the precious

Blood of Christ as of a spotless unblemished Lamb. He was known before the foundation of the world but revealed in the final time for you, who through him believe in God who raised him from the dead and gave him glory, so that your faith and hope are in God.

Since you have purified yourselves by obedience to the truth for sincere brotherly love, love one another intensely from a pure heart. You have been born anew, not from perishable but from imperishable seed, through the living and abiding word of God, for:

"All flesh is like grass,
    and all its glory like the flower of the field;
the grass withers,
    and the flower wilts;
but the word of the Lord remains forever."

This is the word that has been proclaimed to you.—The word of the Lord. ℟. **Thanks be to God.** ↓

RESPONSORIAL PSALM   Ps 147:12-13, 14-15, 19-20

℟. (12a) **Praise the Lord, Jerusalem.**

℟. Or: **Alleluia.**

Glorify the LORD, O Jerusalem;
    praise your God, O Zion.
For he has strengthened the bars of your gates;
    he has blessed your children within you.—℟.

He has granted peace in your borders;
    with the best of wheat he fills you.
He sends forth his command to the earth;
    swiftly runs his word!—℟.

He has proclaimed his word to Jacob,
    his statutes and his ordinances to Israel.
He has not done thus for any other nation;
    his ordinances he has not made known to them.
        Alleluia.—℟. ↓

———— YEAR I AND II ————

ALLELUIA Mk 10:45

℟. **Alleluia, alleluia.**
The Son of Man came to serve,
and to give his life as a ransom for many.
℟. **Alleluia, alleluia.** ↓

GOSPEL Mk 10:32-45

Jesus predicts his passion once again and then emphasizes that whatever authority the disciples (and, of course, their successors) exercise is to be viewed, like the authority of Jesus, in terms of service to others rather than as a sign of personal eminence.

℣. The Lord be with you. ℟. **And also with you.**
℣. A reading from the holy Gospel according to Mark.
℟. **Glory to you, Lord.**

THE disciples were on the way, going up to Jerusalem, and Jesus went ahead of them. They were amazed, and those who followed were afraid. Taking the Twelve aside again, he began to tell them what was going to happen to him. "Behold, we are going up to Jerusalem, and the Son of Man will be handed over to the chief priests and the scribes, and they will condemn him to death and hand him over to the Gentiles who will mock him, spit upon him, scourge him, and put him to death, but after three days he will rise."

Then James and John, the sons of Zebedee, came to Jesus and said to him, "Teacher, we want you to do for us whatever we ask of you." He replied, "What do you wish me to do for you?" They answered him, "Grant that in your glory we may sit one at your right and the other at your left." Jesus said to them, "You do not know what you are asking. Can you drink the chalice that I drink or be baptized with the baptism with which I am baptized?" They said to him, "We can." Jesus said to them, "The chalice that I drink, you will drink, and with the baptism with which I am baptized, you will be baptized; but to sit at my right or at my left is not mine to give but is for those for whom it has been prepared." When the ten heard this, they became indignant at James and John. Jesus summoned them and said to them, "You know that those who are recognized as rulers over the Gentiles lord it over them, and their great ones make their authority over them felt. But it shall not be so among you. Rather, whoever wishes to be great among you will be your servant; whoever wishes to be first among you will be the slave of all. For the Son of Man did not come to be served but to serve and to give his life as a ransom for many."—The Gospel of the Lord. ℟. **Praise to you, Lord Jesus Christ.**

→ No. 15, p. 623

THURSDAY OF THE EIGHTH WEEK IN ORDINARY TIME

——— **YEAR I** ———

FIRST READING Sir 42:15-25

God is great and his glory fills all his works. His wisdom is almighty and he is from all eternity one and the same. His works are beautiful, and his creatures are all good, differing from one another, and filled with splendor.

A reading from the Book of Sirach

NOW will I recall God's works;
    what I have seen, I will describe.
At God's word were his works brought into being;
    they do his will as he has ordained for them.
As the rising sun is clear to all,
    so the glory of the LORD fills all his works;
Yet even God's holy ones must fail
    in recounting the wonders of the LORD,
Though God has given these, his hosts, the strength
    to stand firm before his glory.

He plumbs the depths and penetrates the heart;
  their innermost being he understands.
The Most High possesses all knowledge,
  and sees from of old the things that are to come:
He makes known the past and the future,
  and reveals the deepest secrets.
No understanding does he lack;
  no single thing escapes him.
Perennial is his almighty wisdom;
  he is from all eternity one and the same,
With nothing added, nothing taken away;
  no need of a counselor for him!
How beautiful are all his works!
  even to the spark and fleeting vision!
The universe lives and abides forever;
  to meet each need, each creature is preserved.
All of them differ, one from another,
  yet none of them has he made in vain,
For each in turn, as it comes, is good;
  can one ever see enough of their splendor?
The word of the Lord. ℟. **Thanks be to God.** ↓

RESPONSORIAL PSALM   Ps 33:2-3, 4-5, 6-7, 8-9

℟. (6a) **By the word of the Lord the heavens were made.**

Give thanks to the LORD on the harp;
  with the ten-stringed lyre chant his praises.
Sing to him a new song;
    pluck the strings skillfully, with shouts of gladness.—℟.

For upright is the word of the LORD,
  and all his works are trustworthy.
He loves justice and right;
  of the kindness of the LORD the earth is full.—℟.

By the word of the LORD the heavens were made;
  by the breath of his mouth all their host.
He gathers the waters of the sea as in a flask;
  in cellars he confines the deep.—℟.

Let all the earth fear the L<small>ORD</small>;
　let all who dwell in the world revere him.
For he spoke, and it was made;
　he commanded, and it stood forth.—R̶). ↓

─────── **YEAR II** ───────

FIRST READING　　　　　　　　　1 Pt 2:2-5, 9-12

Come to Jesus. He is the cornerstone and we are living stones. The faithful are a chosen people, a consecrated race. God delivers them to a marvelous light. They are not to be disturbed by slanderous criticism. By good works they give glory to God.

A reading from the first Letter of Saint Peter

B<small>ELOVED</small>: Like newborn infants, long for pure spiritual milk so that through it you may grow into salvation, for you have tasted that the Lord is good. Come to him, a living stone, rejected by human beings but chosen and precious in the sight of God, and, like living stones, let yourselves be built into a spiritual house to be a holy priesthood to offer spiritual sacrifices acceptable to God through Jesus Christ.

You are *a chosen race, a royal priesthood, a holy nation, a people of his own, so that you may announce the praises* of him who called you out of darkness into his wonderful light.

Once you were *no people*
　　but now you are God's people;
you had not received mercy
　　but now you have received mercy.

Beloved, I urge you as aliens and sojourners to keep away from worldly desires that wage war against the soul. Maintain good conduct among the Gentiles, so that if they speak of you as evildoers, they may observe your good works and glorify God on the day of visitation.—The word of the Lord. R̶). **Thanks be to God.** ↓

RESPONSORIAL PSALM   Ps 100:2, 3, 4, 5

℟. (2c) **Come with joy into the presence of the Lord.**

Sing joyfully to the LORD, all you lands;
>   serve the LORD with gladness;
>   come before him with joyful song.—℟.

Know that the LORD is God;
>   he made us, his we are;
>   his people, the flock he tends.—℟.

Enter his gates with thanksgiving,
>   his courts with praise;
Give thanks to him;
>   bless his name.—℟.

The LORD is good:
>   his kindness endures forever,
>   and his faithfulness, to all generations.—℟. ↓

——————— **YEAR I AND II** ———————

ALLELUIA   Jn 8:12

℟. **Alleluia, alleluia.**
I am the light of the world, says the Lord;
whoever follows me will have the light of life.
℟. **Alleluia, alleluia.** ↓

GOSPEL   Mk 10:46-52

The blind man, unaffected by what he heard of Jesus' lowly condition,
addresses him with the Messianic title, "Son of David." He asks to be
cured and his faith is rewarded.

℣. The Lord be with you. ℟. **And also with you.**
℣. A reading from the holy Gospel according to Mark.
℟. **Glory to you, Lord.**

AS Jesus was leaving Jericho with his disciples and a
sizable crowd, Bartimaeus, a blind man, the son of
Timaeus, sat by the roadside begging. On hearing that it
was Jesus of Nazareth, he began to cry out and say,
"Jesus, son of David, have pity on me." And many

rebuked him, telling him to be silent. But he kept calling out all the more, "Son of David, have pity on me." Jesus stopped and said, "Call him." So they called the blind man, saying to him, "Take courage; get up, Jesus is calling you." He threw aside his cloak, sprang up, and came to Jesus. Jesus said to him in reply, "What do you want me to do for you?" The blind man replied to him, "Master, I want to see." Jesus told him, "Go your way; your faith has saved you." Immediately he received his sight and followed him on the way.—The Gospel of the Lord. ℟. **Praise to you, Lord Jesus Christ.** → No. 15, p. 623

FRIDAY OF THE EIGHTH WEEK IN ORDINARY TIME

──── **YEAR I** ────

FIRST READING   Sir 44:1, 9-13

The memory of good deeds and virtue is never blotted out, just as the merciful deeds of ancestors insured that their name would live on for generations. The glory of those who are faithful to God's Covenant will endure forever.

A reading from the Book of Sirach

NOW will I praise those godly men,
  our ancestors, each in his own time.
But of others there is no memory,
  for when they ceased, they ceased.
And they are as though they had not lived,
  they and their children after them.
Yet these also were godly men
  whose virtues have not been forgotten;
Their wealth remains in their families,
  their heritage with their descendants;
Through God's covenant with them their family endures,
  their posterity, for their sake.
And for all time their progeny will endure,
  their glory will never be blotted out.
The word of the Lord. ℟. **Thanks be to God.** ↓

RESPONSORIAL PSALM   Ps 149:1b-2, 3-4, 5-6a and 9b

℟. (see 4a) **The Lord takes delight in his people.**

℟. Or: **Alleluia.**

Sing to the LORD a new song
of praise in the assembly of the faithful.
Let Israel be glad in their maker,
let the children of Zion rejoice in their king.—℟.

Let them praise his name in the festive dance,
let them sing praise to him with timbrel and harp.
For the LORD loves his people,
and he adorns the lowly with victory.—℟.

Let the faithful exult in glory;
let them sing for joy upon their couches;
Let the high praises of God be in their throats.
This is the glory of all his faithful. Alleluia.—℟. ↓

——— **YEAR II** ———

FIRST READING   1 Pt 4:7-13

Love must be constant. It covers up for many sins. Followers of Christ
should not complain. They are to deliver the Gospel message and serve
one another. This gives glory to God.

A reading from the first Letter of Saint Peter

BELOVED: The end of all things is at hand. Therefore
be serious and sober-minded so that you will be able
to pray. Above all, let your love for one another be
intense, because love covers a multitude of sins. Be hospitable to one another without complaining. As each one
has received a gift, use it to serve one another as good
stewards of God's varied grace. Whoever preaches, let it
be with the words of God; whoever serves, let it be with
the strength that God supplies, so that in all things God
may be glorified through Jesus Christ, to whom belong
glory and dominion forever and ever. Amen.

Beloved, do not be surprised that a trial by fire is occurring among you, as if something strange were happening to you. But rejoice to the extent that you share in the sufferings of Christ, so that when his glory is revealed you may also rejoice exultantly.—The word of the Lord. R̖. **Thanks be to God.** ↓

RESPONSORIAL PSALM   Ps 96:10, 11-12, 13

R̖. (13b) **The Lord comes to judge the earth.**

Say among the nations: The LORD is king.
He has made the world firm, not to be moved;
   he governs the peoples with equity.—R̖.

Let the heavens be glad and the earth rejoice;
   let the sea and what fills it resound;
   let the plains be joyful and all that is in them!
Then shall all the trees of the forest exult.—R̖.

Before the LORD, for he comes;
   for he comes to rule the earth.
He shall rule the world with justice
   and the peoples with his constancy.—R̖. ↓

——————— **YEAR I AND II** ———————

ALLELUIA   See Jn 15:16

R̖. **Alleluia, alleluia.**
I chose you from the world,
to go and bear fruit that will last, says the Lord.
R̖. **Alleluia, alleluia.** ↓

GOSPEL   Mk 11:11-26

Jesus curses a barren fig tree symbolizing his judgment on barren Israel for failing to receive his teaching. Later he drives the money changers from the temple. Jesus insists that his house is a house of prayer. Whoever is ready to believe will receive whatever he asks for in prayer. We must always forgive others and put our trust completely in God.

V̖. The Lord be with you. R̖. **And also with you.**
V̖. A reading from the holy Gospel according to Mark.
R̖. **Glory to you, Lord.**

JESUS entered Jerusalem and went into the temple area. He looked around at everything and, since it was already late, went out to Bethany with the Twelve.

The next day as they were leaving Bethany he was hungry. Seeing from a distance a fig tree in leaf, he went over to see if he could find anything on it. When he reached it he found nothing but leaves; it was not the time for figs. And he said to it in reply, "May no one ever eat of your fruit again!" And his disciples heard it.

They came to Jerusalem, and on entering the temple area he began to drive out those selling and buying there. He overturned the tables of the money changers and the seats of those who were selling doves. He did not permit anyone to carry anything through the temple area. Then he taught them saying, "Is it not written:

My house shall be called a house of prayer for all
    peoples?
    But you have made it a den of thieves."

The chief priests and the scribes came to hear of it and were seeking a way to put him to death, yet they feared him because the whole crowd was astonished at his teaching. When evening came, they went out of the city.

Early in the morning, as they were walking along, they saw the fig tree withered to its roots. Peter remembered and said to him, "Rabbi, look! The fig tree that you cursed has withered." Jesus said to them in reply, "Have faith in God. Amen, I say to you, whoever says to this mountain, 'Be lifted up and thrown into the sea,' and does not doubt in his heart but believes that what he says will happen, it shall be done for him. Therefore I tell you, all that you ask for in prayer, believe that you will receive it and it shall be yours. When you stand to pray, forgive anyone against whom you have a grievance, so that your heavenly Father may in turn forgive you your transgressions."—The Gospel of the Lord. ℟. **Praise to you, Lord Jesus Christ.**   ➔ No. 15, p. 623

SATURDAY OF THE EIGHTH WEEK
IN ORDINARY TIME

———— YEAR I ————

FIRST READING   Sir 51:12cd-20

True wisdom is a gift of God. Among other things she enables human
beings to do good and avoid evil. They should ask God for her and thank
him on receiving her, for she holds the key to eternal life.

A reading from the Book of Sirach

I THANK the LORD and I praise him;
I bless the name of the LORD.
When I was young and innocent,
    I sought wisdom openly in my prayer;
I prayed for her before the temple,
    and I will seek her until the end,
    and she flourished as a grape soon ripe.
My heart delighted in her,
My feet kept to the level path
    because from earliest youth I was familiar with her.
In the short time I paid heed,
    I met with great instruction.
Since in this way I have profited,
    I will give my teacher grateful praise.
I became resolutely devoted to her—
    the good I persistently strove for.
My soul was tormented in seeking her,
My hand opened her gate
    and I came to know her secrets.
I directed my soul to her,
    and in cleanness I attained to her.
The word of the Lord. ℟. **Thanks be to God.** ↓

RESPONSORIAL PSALM   Ps 19:8, 9, 10, 11

℟. (9ab) **The precepts of the Lord give joy to the heart.**

The law of the LORD is perfect,
    refreshing the soul.

The decree of the LORD is trustworthy,
   giving wisdom to the simple.—℟.

The precepts of the LORD are right,
   rejoicing the heart.
The command of the LORD is clear,
   enlightening the eye.—℟.

The fear of the LORD is pure,
   enduring forever;
The ordinances of the LORD are true,
   all of them just.

They are more precious than gold,
   than a heap of purest gold;
Sweeter also than syrup
   or honey from the comb.—℟. ↓

——————— **YEAR II** ———————

FIRST READING   Jude 17, 20b-25

Remember the teaching of the Apostles. Persevere in the love of God.
Correct those who are confused. God can protect all of his people. Glory
be to him forever.

A reading from the Letter of Saint Jude

BELOVED, remember the words spoken beforehand
by the Apostles of our Lord Jesus Christ. Build yourselves up in your most holy faith; pray in the Holy Spirit.
Keep yourselves in the love of God and wait for the
mercy of our Lord Jesus Christ that leads to eternal life.
On those who waver, have mercy; save others by snatch-
ing them out of the fire; on others have mercy with fear,
abhorring even the outer garment stained by the flesh.

    To the one who is able to keep you from stumbling
and to present you unblemished and exultant, in the
presence of his glory, to the only God, our savior, through
Jesus Christ our Lord be glory, majesty, power, and
authority from ages past, now, and for ages to come.
Amen.—The word of the Lord. ℟. **Thanks be to God.** ↓

RESPONSORIAL PSALM   Ps 63:2, 3-4, 5-6

℟. (2b) **My soul is thirsting for you, O Lord my God.**

O God, you are my God whom I seek;
    for you my flesh pines and my soul thirsts
    like the earth, parched, lifeless and without water.—℟.

Thus have I gazed toward you in the sanctuary
    to see your power and your glory,
For your kindness is a greater good than life;
    my lips shall glorify you.—℟.

Thus will I bless you while I live;
    lifting up my hands, I will call upon your name.
As with the riches of a banquet shall my soul be satisfied,
        and with exultant lips my mouth shall praise
        you.—℟. ↓

──────── **YEAR I AND II** ────────

ALLELUIA   See Col 3:16a, 17c

℟. **Alleluia, alleluia.**
Let the word of Christ dwell in you richly;
giving thanks to God the Father through him.
℟. **Alleluia, alleluia.** ↓

GOSPEL   Mk 11:27-33

Jesus shows by his verbal jousting with his opponents that he needs no "references." His authority imposes itself from within on all those whose heart is free of intrigue and self-service. But his message, like that of the Baptist and the prophets, is opposed by the leaders who are jealous of their position.

℣. The Lord be with you. ℟. **And also with you.**
℣. A reading from the holy Gospel according to Mark.
℟. **Glory to you, Lord.**

JESUS and his disciples returned once more to Jerusalem. As he was walking in the temple area, the chief priests, the scribes, and the elders approached him and said to him, "By what authority are you doing these things? Or who gave you this authority to do them?" Jesus said to them, "I shall ask you one question. Answer me, and I will tell you by what authority I do these things. Was John's baptism of heavenly or of human origin? Answer me." They discussed this among themselves and said, "If we say, 'Of heavenly origin,' he will say, 'Then why did you not believe him?' But shall we say, 'Of human origin'?"—they feared the crowd, for they all thought John really was a prophet. So they said to Jesus in reply, "We do not know." Then Jesus said to them, "Neither shall I tell you by what authority I do these things."—The Gospel of the Lord. ℟. **Praise to you, Lord Jesus Christ.**

→ No. 15, p. 623

MONDAY OF THE NINTH WEEK IN ORDINARY TIME

———— **YEAR I** ————

FIRST READING   Tb 1:3; 2:1a-8

The story of Tobit takes place during the exile in Babylon. Tobit and his family remain faithful to God in unfriendly surroundings and are outstanding for their love of neighbor. Tobit shows his loyalty and trust regardless of criticism.

A reading from the Book of Tobit

I, TOBIT, have walked all the days of my life on the paths of truth and righteousness. I performed many charitable works for my kinsmen and my people who had been deported with me to Nineveh, in Assyria.

On our festival of Pentecost, the feast of Weeks, a fine dinner was prepared for me, and I reclined to eat. The table was set for me, and when many different dishes were placed before me, I said to my son Tobiah: "My son, go out and try to find a poor man from among our kinsmen exiled here in Nineveh. If he is a sincere worshiper of God, bring him back with you, so that he can share this meal with me. Indeed, son, I shall wait for you to come back."

Tobiah went out to look for some poor kinsman of ours. When he returned he exclaimed, "Father!" I said to him, "What is it, son?" He answered, "Father, one of our people has been murdered! His body lies in the market place where he was just strangled!" I sprang to my feet, leaving the dinner untouched; and I carried the dead man from the street and put him in one of the rooms, so that I might bury him after sunset. Returning to my own quarters, I washed myself and ate my food in sorrow. I was reminded of the oracle pronounced by the prophet Amos against Bethel:

"All your festivals shall be turned into mourning,
    and all your songs into lamentation."
And I wept. Then at sunset I went out, dug a grave, and buried him.

The neighbors mocked me, saying to one another: "He is still not afraid! Once before he was hunted down for execution because of this very thing; yet now that he has scarcely escaped, here he is again burying the dead!"— The word of the Lord. ℞. **Thanks be to God.** ↓

RESPONSORIAL PSALM   Ps 112:1b-2, 3b-4, 5-6

℞. (1b) **Blessed the man who fears the Lord.**

℞. Or: **Alleluia.**

Blessed the man who fears the LORD,
    who greatly delights in his commands.
His posterity shall be mighty upon the earth;
    the upright generation shall be blessed.—℞.

His generosity shall endure forever.
Light shines through the darkness for the upright;
    he is gracious and merciful and just.—℞.

Well for the man who is gracious and lends,
    who conducts his affairs with justice;

He shall never be moved;
>   the just man shall be in everlasting remem-
>   brance.—℟. ↓

——————— **YEAR II** ———————

FIRST READING   2 Pt 1:2-7

God has given his people the means and grace for a holy life. In this way they share in his divine nature. This is reason enough to live a life of self-control leading to piety and care for one another.

A reading from the second Letter of Saint Peter

BELOVED: May grace and peace be yours in abundance through knowledge of God and of Jesus our Lord.

His divine power has bestowed on us everything that makes for life and devotion, through the knowledge of him who called us by his own glory and power. Through these, he has bestowed on us the precious and very great promises, so that through them you may come to share in the divine nature, after escaping from the corruption that is in the world because of evil desire. For this very reason, make every effort to supplement your faith with virtue, virtue with knowledge, knowledge with self-control, self-control with endurance, endurance with devotion, devotion with mutual affection, mutual affection with love.— The word of the Lord. ℟. **Thanks be to God.** ↓

RESPONSORIAL PSALM   Ps 91:1-2, 14-15b, 15c-16

℟. (see 2b) **In you, my God, I place my trust.**

You who dwell in the shelter of the Most High,
>   who abide in the shadow of the Almighty,
Say to the Lord, "My refuge and my fortress,
>   my God, in whom I trust."—℟.

Because he clings to me, I will deliver him;
>   I will set him on high because he acknowledges my
>   name.

He shall call upon me, and I will answer him;
  I will be with him in distress.—℟.

I will deliver him and glorify him;
  with length of days I will gratify him
  and will show him my salvation.—℟. ↓

——————— **YEAR I AND II** ———————

ALLELUIA   See Rev 1:5ab

℟. **Alleluia, alleluia.**
Jesus Christ, you are the faithful witness,
the firstborn of the dead;
you have loved us and freed us from our sins by your
  Blood.
℟. **Alleluia, alleluia.** ↓

GOSPEL   Mk 12:1-12

In the parable, the servants who are killed represent the prophets, and the son who is slain represents Jesus himself. However, his death will become his victory. He will rise again as Lord, the keystone of the Church, as foretold.

℣. The Lord be with you. ℟. **And also with you.**
℣. A reading from the holy Gospel according to Mark.
℟. **Glory to you, Lord.**

JESUS began to speak to the chief priests, the scribes, and the elders in parables. "A man planted a vineyard, put a hedge around it, dug a wine press, and built a tower. Then he leased it to tenant farmers and left on a journey. At the proper time he sent a servant to the tenants to obtain from them some of the produce of the vineyard. But they seized him, beat him, and sent him away empty-handed. Again he sent them another servant. And that one they beat over the head and treated shamefully. He sent yet another whom they killed. So, too, many others; some they beat, others they killed. He had one other to send, a beloved son. He sent him to them last of all, thinking, 'They will respect my son.' But those tenants said to one another, 'This is the heir. Come, let us kill him, and the inheritance will be ours.' So they seized him and killed him, and threw him out of the vineyard. What then will the owner of the vineyard do? He will come, put the tenants to death, and give the vineyard to others. Have you not read this Scripture passage:

The stone that the builders rejected
has become the cornerstone;
by the Lord has this been done,
and it is wonderful in our eyes?"

They were seeking to arrest him, but they feared the crowd, for they realized that he had addressed the parable to them. So they left him and went away.—The Gospel of the Lord. ℟. **Praise to you, Lord Jesus Christ.**

➜ No. 15, p. 623

TUESDAY OF THE NINTH WEEK IN ORDINARY TIME

——— **YEAR I** ———

FIRST READING Tb 2:9-14

In spite of exile, blindness, and his own misjudgments, Tobit still hopes in God. God's watchful care will bring a solution to Tobit's problems. He has trust in God.

A reading from the Book of Tobit

ON the night of Pentecost, after I had buried the dead, I, Tobit, went into my courtyard to sleep next to the courtyard wall. My face was uncovered because of the heat. I did not know there were birds perched on the wall above me, till their warm droppings settled in my eyes, causing cataracts. I went to see some doctors for a cure but the more they anointed my eyes with various salves, the worse the cataracts became, until I could see no more. For four years I was deprived of eyesight, and all my kinsmen were grieved at my condition. Ahiqar, however, took care of me for two years, until he left for Elymais.

At that time, my wife Anna worked for hire at weaving cloth, the kind of work women do. When she sent back the goods to their owners, they would pay her. Late in winter on the seventh of Dystrus, she finished the cloth and sent it back to the owners. They paid her the full salary and also gave her a young goat for the table. On entering my house the goat began to bleat.

I called to my wife and said: "Where did this goat come from? Perhaps it was stolen! Give it back to its owners; we have no right to eat stolen food!" She said to me, "It was given to me as a bonus over and above my wages." Yet I would not believe her, and told her to give it back to its owners. I became very angry with her over this. So she retorted: "Where are your charitable deeds now? Where are your virtuous acts? See! Your true character is finally showing itself!"—The word of the Lord. ℟. **Thanks be to God.** ↓

RESPONSORIAL PSALM Ps 112:1-2, 7-8, 9

℟. (see 7c) **The heart of the just one is firm, trusting in the Lord.**

℟. Or: **Alleluia.**

Blessed the man who fears the LORD,
   who greatly delights in his commands.
His posterity shall be mighty upon the earth;
   the upright generation shall be blessed.—℟.

An evil report he shall not fear;
   his heart is firm, trusting in the LORD.
His heart is steadfast; he shall not fear
   till he looks down upon his foes.—℟.

Lavishly he gives to the poor;
   his generosity shall endure forever;
   his horn shall be exalted in glory.—℟. ↓

——————— **YEAR II** ———————

FIRST READING 2 Pt 3:12-15a, 17-18

Anxiously the faithful await the coming of Jesus—a new heaven and a new earth. During this waiting the followers of Christ should be found without stain or sin. They should be on guard against false teaching.

A reading from the second Letter of Saint Peter

BELOVED: Wait for and hasten the coming of the day of God, because of which the heavens will be dissolved in flames and the elements melted by fire. But according to his promise we await new heavens and a new earth in which righteousness dwells.

Therefore, beloved, since you await these things, be eager to be found without spot or blemish before him, at peace. And consider the patience of our Lord as salvation.

Therefore, beloved, since you are forewarned, be on your guard not to be led into the error of the unprincipled and to fall from your own stability. But grow in grace and in the knowledge of our Lord and savior Jesus Christ. To him be glory now and to the day of eternity. Amen.—The word of the Lord. ℟. **Thanks be to God.** ↓

RESPONSORIAL PSALM   Ps 90:2, 3-4, 10, 14 and 16

℟. (1) **In every age, O Lord, you have been our refuge.**

Before the mountains were begotten
> and the earth and the world were brought forth,
> from everlasting to everlasting you are God.—℟.

You turn man back to dust,
> saying, "Return, O children of men."
For a thousand years in your sight
> are as yesterday, now that it is past,
> or as a watch of the night.—℟.

Seventy is the sum of our years,
> or eighty, if we are strong,
And most of them are fruitless toil,
> for they pass quickly and we drift away.—℟.

Fill us at daybreak with your kindness,
> that we may shout for joy and gladness all our days.
Let your work be seen by your servants
> and your glory by their children.—℟. ↓

——— **YEAR I AND II** ———

ALLELUIA See Eph 1:17-18

℟. **Alleluia, alleluia.**
May the Father of our Lord Jesus Christ
enlighten the eyes of our hearts,
that we may know what is the hope
that belongs to his call.
℟. **Alleluia, alleluia.** ↓

GOSPEL Mk 12:13-17

Jesus answers a trick question with an important principle. Secularism would exclude God from this world; some religionists would forget the world in favor of God. Jesus uses the coin of tribute to teach loyalty to God and country.

℣. The Lord be with you. ℟. **And also with you.**
℣. A reading from the holy Gospel according to Mark.
℟. **Glory to you, Lord.**

SOME Pharisees and Herodians were sent to Jesus to ensnare him in his speech. They came and said to him, "Teacher, we know that you are a truthful man and that you are not concerned with anyone's opinion. You do not regard a person's status but teach the way of God in accordance with the truth. Is it lawful to pay the census tax to Caesar or not? Should we pay or should we not pay?" Knowing their hypocrisy he said to them, "Why are you testing me? Bring me a denarius to look at." They brought one to him and he said to them, "Whose image and inscription is this?" They replied to him, "Caesar's." So Jesus said to them, "Repay to Caesar what belongs to Caesar and to God what belongs to God." They were utterly amazed at him.—The Gospel of the Lord. ℟.
Praise to you, Lord Jesus Christ. → No. 15, p. 623

WEDNESDAY OF THE NINTH WEEK
IN ORDINARY TIME

———— **YEAR I** ————

FIRST READING   Tb 3:1-11a, 16-17a

Tobit prays to God and summarizes God's blessings and the sins of his people. The author uses the trials and problems of Tobit and Sarah to show that God loves his people and will help them by his power, even when all seems lost.

A reading from the Book of Tobit

GRIEF-STRICKEN in spirit, I, Tobit, groaned and wept aloud. Then with sobs I began to pray:
"You are righteous, O Lord,
    and all your deeds are just;
All your ways are mercy and truth;
    you are the judge of the world.
And now, O Lord, may you be mindful of me,
    and look with favor upon me.
Punish me not for my sins,
    nor for my inadvertent offenses,
    nor for those of my ancestors.

"We sinned against you,
    and disobeyed your commandments.
So you handed us over to plundering, exile, and death,
    till you made us the talk and reproach of all the nations
    among whom you had dispersed us.

"Yes, your judgments are many and true
    in dealing with me as my sins
    and those of my ancestors deserve.
For we have not kept your commandments,
    nor have we trodden the paths of truth before you.

"So now, deal with me as you please,
>and command my life breath to be taken from me,
>that I may go from the face of the earth into dust.
It is better for me to die than to live,
>because I have heard insulting calumnies,
>and I am overwhelmed with grief.

"Lord, command me to be delivered from such
>anguish;
>let me go to the everlasting abode;
>Lord, refuse me not.
For it is better for me to die
>than to endure so much misery in life,
>and to hear these insults!"

On the same day, at Ecbatana in Media, it so happened that Raguel's daughter Sarah also had to listen to abuse, from one of her father's maids. For she had been married to seven husbands, but the wicked demon Asmodeus killed them off before they could have intercourse with her, as it is prescribed for wives. So the maid said to her: "You are the one who strangles your husbands! Look at you! You have already been married seven times, but you have had no joy with any one of your husbands. Why do you beat us? Is it on account of your seven husbands, because they are dead? May we never see a son or daughter of yours!"

The girl was deeply saddened that day, and she went into an upper chamber of her house, where she planned to hang herself.

But she reconsidered, saying to herself: "No! People would level this insult against my father: 'You had only one beloved daughter, but she hanged herself because of ill fortune!' And thus would I cause my father in his old age to go down to the nether world laden with sorrow. It is far better for me not to hang myself, but to beg the Lord to have me die, so that I need no longer live to hear such insults."

At that time, then, she spread out her hands, and facing the window, poured out her prayer:

"Blessed are you, O Lord, merciful God,
and blessed is your holy and honorable name.
Blessed are you in all your works for ever!"

At that very time, the prayer of these two suppliants was heard in the glorious presence of Almighty God. So Raphael was sent to heal them both: to remove the cataracts from Tobit's eyes, so that he might again see God's sunlight; and to marry Raguel's daughter Sarah to Tobit's son Tobiah, and then drive the wicked demon Asmodeus from her.—The word of the Lord. ℟. **Thanks be to God.** ↓

RESPONSORIAL PSALM   Ps 25:2-3, 4-5ab, 6 and 7bc, 8-9

℟. (1) **To you, O Lord, I lift my soul.**

In you I trust; let me not be put to shame,
     let not my enemies exult over me.
No one who waits for you shall be put to shame;
     those shall be put to shame who heedlessly break
       faith.—℟.

Your ways, O LORD, make known to me;
     teach me your paths,
Guide me in your truth and teach me,
     for you are God my savior.—℟.

Remember that your compassion, O LORD,
     and your kindness are from of old.
In your kindness remember me,
     because of your goodness, O LORD.—℟.

Good and upright is the LORD;
     thus he shows sinners the way.
He guides the humble to justice,
     he teaches the humble his way.—℟. ↓

—————— **YEAR II** ——————

FIRST READING   2 Tm 1:1-3, 6-12

Paul reminds Timothy to stir up the graces given him in Holy Orders. The Spirit of God makes people strong. God has called his people to a holy life through the power of the Gospel.

A reading from the beginning of the second Letter
of Saint Paul to Timothy

PAUL, an Apostle of Christ Jesus by the will of God for the promise of life in Christ Jesus, to Timothy, my dear child: grace, mercy, and peace from God the Father and Christ Jesus our Lord.

I am grateful to God, whom I worship with a clear conscience as my ancestors did, as I remember you constantly in my prayers, night and day.

For this reason, I remind you to stir into flame the gift of God that you have through the imposition of my hands. For God did not give us a spirit of cowardice but rather of power and love and self-control. So do not be ashamed of your testimony to our Lord, nor of me, a prisoner for his sake; but bear your share of hardship for the Gospel with the strength that comes from God.

He saved us and called us to a holy life, not according to our works but according to his own design and the grace bestowed on us in Christ Jesus before time began, but now made manifest through the appearance of our savior Christ Jesus, who destroyed death and brought life and immortality to light through the Gospel, for which I was appointed preacher and Apostle and teacher. On this account I am suffering these things; but I am not ashamed, for I know him in whom I have believed and am confident that he is able to guard what has been entrusted to me until that day.—The word of the Lord. ℟.
Thanks be to God. ↓

RESPONSORIAL PSALM   Ps 123:1b-2ab, 2cdef

℟. (1b) **To you, O Lord, I lift up my eyes.**

To you I lift up my eyes
    who are enthroned in heaven.
Behold, as the eyes of servants
    are on the hands of their masters.—℟.

As the eyes of a maid
    are on the hands of her mistress,
So are our eyes on the LORD, our God,
    till he have pity on us.—℟. ↓

——————— **YEAR I AND II** ———————

ALLELUIA   Jn 11:25a, 26

℟. **Alleluia, alleluia.**
I am the resurrection and the life, says the Lord;
whoever believes in me will never die.
℟. **Alleluia, alleluia.** ↓

GOSPEL   Mk 12:18-27

St. Mark relates another trick question used to challenge Jesus. Jesus proclaims that the ancestors of the Jews are still alive and are with God. Marriage teaches love and prepares for the fullness of love in heaven. God is the God of the living, not the dead.

℣. The Lord be with you. ℟. **And also with you.**
℣. A reading from the holy Gospel according to Mark.
℟. **Glory to you, Lord.**

SOME Sadducees, who say there is no resurrection, came to Jesus and put this question to him, saying, "Teacher, Moses wrote for us, *'If someone's brother dies, leaving a wife but no child, his brother must take the wife and raise up descendants for his brother.'* Now there were seven brothers. The first married a woman and died, leaving no descendants. So the second brother married her and died, leaving no descendants, and the third likewise. And the seven left no descendants. Last of all the woman also died. At the resurrection when they arise whose wife will she be? For all seven had been married to her." Jesus said to them, "Are you not misled because you do not know the Scriptures or the power of God? When they rise from the dead, they neither marry nor are given in marriage, but they are like the angels in heaven. As for the dead being raised, have you not read in the Book of Moses, in the passage about the bush, how God told him, *I am the God of Abraham, the God of Isaac, and the God of Jacob*? He is not God of the dead but of the living. You are greatly misled."—The Gospel of the Lord. ℟. **Praise to you, Lord Jesus Christ.**   ➜ No. 15, p. 623

THURSDAY OF THE NINTH WEEK IN ORDINARY TIME

─────── **YEAR I** ───────

FIRST READING   Tb 6:10-11; 7:1bcde, 9-17; 8:4-9a

The old saying holds that marriages are made in heaven. The young Tobiah and Sarah recognize that God is giving them to each other. They thank God and ask for his grace to live together to a happy old age.

A reading from the Book of Tobit

WHEN the angel Raphael and Tobiah had entered Media and were getting close to Ecbatana, Raphael said to the boy, "Tobiah, my brother!" He replied: "Here I am!" He said: "Tonight we must stay with Raguel, who is a relative of yours. He has a daughter named Sarah."

So he brought him to the house of Raguel, whom they found seated by his courtyard gate. They greeted him first. He said to them, "Greetings to you too, brothers! Good health to you, and welcome!" And he brought them into his home.

Raguel slaughtered a ram from the flock and gave them a cordial reception. When they had bathed and reclined to eat, Tobiah said to Raphael, "Brother Azariah, ask Raguel to let me marry my kinswoman Sarah." Raguel overheard the words; so he said to the boy: "Eat

and drink and be merry tonight, for no man is more enti-
tled to marry my daughter Sarah than you, brother.
Besides, not even I have the right to give her to anyone
but you, because you are my closest relative. But I will
explain the situation to you very frankly. I have given her
in marriage to seven men, all of whom were kinsmen of
ours, and all died on the very night they approached her.
But now, son, eat and drink. I am sure the Lord will look
after you both." Tobiah answered, "I will eat or drink
nothing until you set aside what belongs to me."

Raguel said to him: "I will do it. She is yours according to the decree of the Book of Moses. Your marriage to
her has been decided in heaven! Take your kinswoman;
from now on you are her love, and she is your beloved.
She is yours today and ever after. And tonight, son, may
the Lord of heaven prosper you both. May he grant you
mercy and peace." Then Raguel called his daughter
Sarah, and she came to him. He took her by the hand
and gave her to Tobiah with the words: "Take her
according to the law. According to the decree written in
the Book of Moses she is your wife. Take her and bring
her back safely to your father. And may the God of
heaven grant both of you peace and prosperity." Raguel
then called Sarah's mother and told her to bring a
scroll, so that he might draw up a marriage contract
stating that he gave Sarah to Tobiah as his wife according to the decree of the Mosaic law. Her mother brought
the scroll, and Raguel drew up the contract, to which
they affixed their seals.

Afterward they began to eat and drink. Later Raguel
called his wife Edna and said, "My love, prepare the other
bedroom and bring the girl there." She went and made
the bed in the room, as she was told, and brought the girl
there. After she had cried over her, she wiped away the
tears and said: "Be brave, my daughter. May the Lord
grant you joy in place of your grief. Courage, my daughter." Then she left.

When the girl's parents left the bedroom and closed the door behind them, Tobiah arose from bed and said to his wife, "My love, get up. Let us pray and beg our Lord to have mercy on us and to grant us deliverance." She got up, and they started to pray and beg that deliverance might be theirs. And they began to say:

"Blessed are you, O God of our fathers,
praised be your name forever and ever.
Let the heavens and all your creation
praise you forever.
You made Adam and you gave him his wife Eve
to be his help and support;
and from these two the human race descended.
You said, 'It is not good for the man to be alone;
let us make him a partner like himself.'
Now, Lord, you know that I take this wife of mine
not because of lust,
but for a noble purpose.
Call down your mercy on me and on her,
and allow us to live together to a happy old age."

They said together, "Amen, amen," and went to bed for the night.—The word of the Lord. ℟. **Thanks be to God.** ↓

RESPONSORIAL PSALM   Ps 128:1-2, 3, 4-5

℟. (see 1a) **Blessed are those who fear the Lord.**

Blessed are you who fear the LORD,
who walk in his ways!
For you shall eat the fruit of your handiwork;
blessed shall you be, and favored.—℟.

Your wife shall be like a fruitful vine
in the recesses of your home;
Your children like olive plants
around your table.—℟.

Behold, thus is the man blessed
who fears the LORD.

The Lord bless you from Zion:
>   may you see the prosperity of Jerusalem
>   all the days of your life.—℞. ↓

——————— **YEAR II** ———————

FIRST READING   2 Tm 2:8-15

Paul preaches about Jesus Christ who is risen. In preaching Paul has suffered much. but the word of God cannot be silenced. He directs Timothy to keep reminding the people that if they deny Jesus, he will deny them. They must try to be worthy of God's approval.

A reading from the second Letter of Saint Paul
to Timothy

BELOVED: Remember Jesus Christ, raised from the dead, a descendant of David: such is my Gospel, for which I am suffering, even to the point of chains, like a criminal. But the word of God is not chained. Therefore, I bear with everything for the sake of those who are chosen, so that they too may obtain the salvation that is in Christ Jesus, together with eternal glory. This saying is trustworthy:
>   If we have died with him
>   we shall also live with him;
>   if we persevere
>   we shall also reign with him.
>   But if we deny him
>   he will deny us.
>   If we are unfaithful
>   he remains faithful,
>   for he cannot deny himself.

Remind people of these things and charge them before God to stop disputing about words. This serves no useful purpose since it harms those who listen. Be eager to present yourself as acceptable to God, a workman who causes no disgrace, imparting the word of truth without deviation.—The word of the Lord. ℞. **Thanks be to God.** ↓

RESPONSORIAL PSALM   Ps 25:4-5ab, 8-9, 10 and 14

℟. (4) **Teach me your ways, O Lord.**

Your ways, O LORD, make known to me;
    teach me your paths,
Guide me in your truth and teach me,
    for you are God my savior.—℟.

Good and upright is the LORD;
    thus he shows sinners the way.
He guides the humble to justice,
    he teaches the humble his way.—℟.

All the paths of the LORD are kindness and constancy
    toward those who keep his covenant and his decrees.
The friendship of the LORD is with those who fear him,
    and his covenant, for their instruction.—℟. ↓

———— **YEAR I AND II** ————

ALLELUIA   See 2 Tm 1:10

℟. **Alleluia, alleluia.**
Our Savior Jesus Christ has destroyed death
and brought life to light through the Gospel.
℟. **Alleluia, alleluia.** ↓

GOSPEL   Mk 12:28-34

Jesus takes the two great commandments from the Old Testament, and he
makes them the spirit that must give life to every law. In this way, the law
teaches how human beings may truly love one another. This double law
brings life and the Kingdom.

℣. The Lord be with you. ℟. **And also with you.**
℣. A reading from the holy Gospel according to Mark.
℟. **Glory to you, Lord.**

ONE of the scribes came to Jesus and asked him,
"Which is the first of all the commandments?" Jesus
replied, "The first is this: *Hear, O Israel! The Lord our God
is Lord alone! You shall love the Lord your God with all
your heart, with all your soul, with all your mind, and*

with all your strength. The second is this: *You shall love your neighbor as yourself.* There is no other commandment greater than these." The scribe said to him, "Well said, teacher. You are right in saying, *He is One and there is no other than he.* And *to love him with all your heart, with all your understanding, with all your strength, and to love your neighbor as yourself* is worth more than all burnt offerings and sacrifices." And when Jesus saw that he answered with understanding, he said to him, "You are not far from the Kingdom of God." And no one dared to ask him any more questions.—The Gospel of the Lord. ℟.
Praise to you, Lord Jesus Christ. → No. 15, p. 623

FRIDAY OF THE NINTH WEEK IN ORDINARY TIME

─────── **YEAR I** ───────

FIRST READING Tb 11:5-17

The trust of Anna is shown as she awaits her son's return. The story uses the medical ideas of its time, and the aged Tobit praises God in thanksgiving for his sight.

A reading from the Book of Tobit

A NNA sat watching the road by which her son was to come. When she saw him coming, she exclaimed to his father, "Tobit, your son is coming, and the man who traveled with him!"

Raphael said to Tobiah before he reached his father: "I am certain that his eyes will be opened. Smear the fish gall on them. This medicine will make the cataracts shrink and peel off from his eyes; then your father will again be able to see the light of day."

Then Anna ran up to her son, threw her arms around him, and said to him, "Now that I have seen you again, son, I am ready to die!" And she sobbed aloud.

Tobit got up and stumbled out through the courtyard gate. Tobiah went up to him with the fish gall in his hand,

and holding him firmly, blew into his eyes. "Courage, father," he said. Next he smeared the medicine on his eyes, and it made them smart. Then, beginning at the corners of Tobit's eyes, Tobiah used both hands to peel off the cataracts.

When Tobit saw his son, he threw his arms around him and wept. He exclaimed, "I can see you, son, the light of my eyes!" Then he said:

"Blessed be God,
>   and praised be his great name,
>   and blessed be all his holy angels.
May his holy name be praised
>   throughout all the ages,
Because it was he who scourged me,
>   and it is he who has had mercy on me.
Behold, I now see my son Tobiah!"

Then Tobit went back in, rejoicing and praising God with full voice for everything that had happened. Tobiah told his father that the Lord God had granted him a successful journey; that he had brought back the money; and that he had married Raguel's daughter Sarah, who would arrive shortly, for she was approaching the gate of Nineveh.

Tobit and Anna rejoiced and went out to the gate of Nineveh to meet their daughter-in-law. When the people of Nineveh saw Tobit walking along briskly, with no one leading him by the hand, they were amazed. Before them all Tobit proclaimed how God had mercifully restored sight to his eyes. When Tobit reached Sarah, the wife of his son Tobiah, he greeted her: "Welcome, my daughter! Blessed be your God for bringing you to us, daughter! Blessed is your father, and blessed is my son Tobiah, and blessed are you, daughter! Welcome to your home with blessing and joy. Come in, daughter!" That day there was joy for all the Jews who lived in Nineveh.— The word of the Lord. ℟. **Thanks be to God.** ↓

RESPONSORIAL PSALM   Ps 146:1b-2, 6c-7, 8-9a, 9bc-10

℟. (1b) **Praise the Lord, my soul!**

℟. Or: **Alleluia.**

Praise the LORD, O my soul;
    I will praise the LORD all my life;
    I will sing praise to my God while I live.—℟.

The LORD keeps faith forever,
    secures justice for the oppressed,
    gives food to the hungry.
The LORD sets captives free.—℟.

The LORD gives sight to the blind.
The LORD raises up those who are bowed down;
    the LORD loves the just.
The LORD protects strangers.—℟.

The fatherless and the widow he sustains,
    but the way of the wicked he thwarts
The LORD shall reign forever,
    your God, O Zion, through all generations! Alleluia.—℟. ↓

——————— **YEAR II** ———————

FIRST READING   2 Tm 3:10-17

Paul recalls for Timothy his persecutions because of teaching the Gospel message. Anyone who lives wholly for Jesus will be persecuted. The Scriptures are a source of wisdom. They are inspired by God, training us for holiness.

A reading from the second Letter of Saint Paul to Timothy

YOU have followed my teaching, way of life, purpose, faith, patience, love, endurance, persecutions, and sufferings, such as happened to me in Antioch, Iconium, and Lystra, persecutions that I endured. Yet from all these things the Lord delivered me. In fact, all who want to live religiously in Christ Jesus will be persecuted. But wicked people and charlatans will go from bad to worse, deceivers and deceived. But you, remain faithful to what you have learned and believed, because you know from whom you learned it, and that from infancy you have known the sacred Scriptures, which are capable of giving you wisdom for salvation through faith in Christ Jesus. All Scripture is inspired by God and is useful for teaching, for refutation, for correction, and for training in righteousness, so that one who belongs to God may be competent, equipped for every good work.—The word of the Lord. ℟. **Thanks be to God.** ↓

RESPONSORIAL PSALM Ps 119:157, 160, 161, 165, 166, 168

℟. (165a) **O Lord, great peace have they who love your law.**

Though my persecutors and my foes are many,
　　I turn not away from your decrees.—℟.

Permanence is your word's chief trait;
　　each of your just ordinances is everlasting.—℟.

Princes persecute me without cause
　　but my heart stands in awe of your word.

Those who love your law have great peace,
　　and for them there is no stumbling block.—℟.

I wait for your salvation, O LORD,
　　and your commands I fulfill.—℟.

I keep your precepts and your decrees,
　　for all my ways are before you.—℟. ↓

——————— **YEAR I AND II** ———————

ALLELUIA Jn 14:23

℟. **Alleluia, alleluia.**
Whoever loves me will keep my word,
and my Father will love him
and we will come to him.
℟. **Alleluia, alleluia.** ↓

GOSPEL Mk 12:35-37

After being challenged by his enemies, Jesus poses a hard question of his own. Jesus is both the Son of God and the Son of Man. He is Lord and the Savior of his human brothers and sisters, in the one person.

℣. The Lord be with you. ℟. **And also with you.**

℣. A reading from the holy Gospel according to Mark.

℟. **Glory to you, Lord.**

AS Jesus was teaching in the temple area he said, "How do the scribes claim that the Christ is the son of David? David himself, inspired by the Holy Spirit, said:

The Lord said to my lord,

'Sit at my right hand

until I place your enemies under your feet.'

David himself calls him 'lord'; so how is he his son?" The great crowd heard this with delight.—The Gospel of the Lord. ℟. **Praise to you, Lord Jesus Christ.**

→ No. 15, p. 623

SATURDAY OF THE NINTH WEEK IN ORDINARY TIME

——— **YEAR I** ———

FIRST READING Tb 12:1, 5-15, 20

Tobit and his family discover that they have been aided by an angel of God. Raphael recommends thanksgiving and almsgiving as pleasing to God. God shows his care and concern for those who love him.

A reading from the Book of Tobit

TOBIT called his son Tobiah and said to him, "Son, see to it that you give what is due to the man who made the journey with you; give him a bonus too." So he called Raphael and said, "Take as your wages half of all that you have brought back, and go in peace."

Raphael called the two men aside privately and said to them: "Thank God! Give him the praise and the glory. Before all the living, acknowledge the many good things he has done for you, by blessing and extolling his name in song. Honor and proclaim God's deeds, and do not be slack in praising him. A king's secret it is prudent to keep, but the works of God are to be declared and made known. Praise them with due honor. Do good, and evil will not find its way to you. Prayer and fasting are good, but better than either is almsgiving accompanied by righteousness. A little with righteousness is better than abundance with wickedness. It is better to give alms than to store up gold; for almsgiving saves one from death and expiates every sin. Those who regularly give alms shall enjoy a full life; but those habitually guilty of sin are their own worst enemies.

"I will now tell you the whole truth; I will conceal nothing at all from you. I have already said to you, 'A king's secret it is prudent to keep, but the works of God are to be made known with due honor.' I can now tell you that when you, Tobit, and Sarah prayed, it was I who presented and read the record of your prayer before the Glory of the Lord; and I did the same thing when you used to bury the dead. When you did not hesitate to get up and leave your dinner in order to go and bury the dead, I was sent to put you to the test. At the same time, however, God commissioned me to heal you and your daughter-in-law Sarah. I am Raphael, one of the seven angels who enter and serve before the Glory of the Lord."

"So now get up from the ground and praise God. Behold, I am about to ascend to him who sent me; write down all these things that have happened to you."—The word of the Lord. ℟. **Thanks be to God.** ↓

RESPONSORIAL PSALM   Tb 13:2, 6efgh, 7, 8

℟. (1b) **Blessed be God, who lives for ever.**

He scourges and then has mercy;
   he casts down to the depths of the nether world,
   and he brings up from the great abyss.
No one can escape his hand.—℟.

So now consider what he has done for you,
　　and praise him with full voice.
Bless the Lord of righteousness,
　　and exalt the King of ages.—℟.

In the land of my exile I praise him
　　and show his power and majesty to a sinful na-
　　　tion.—℟.

Bless the Lord, all you his chosen ones,
　　and may all of you praise his majesty.
Celebrate days of gladness, and give him praise.—℟. ↓

———— **YEAR II** ————

FIRST READING　　　　　　　　　　　　　　2 Tm 4:1-8

Paul exhorts Timothy to preach the Good News at all times—correcting, reproving, appealing. But the time is coming when people will ignore sound doctrine. Paul admits he has fought a good fight and he awaits his crown in heaven.

A reading from the second Letter of Saint Paul
to Timothy

BELOVED: I charge you in the presence of God and of Christ Jesus, who will judge the living and the dead, and by his appearing and his kingly power: proclaim the word; be persistent whether it is convenient or inconvenient; convince, reprimand, encourage through all patience and teaching. For the time will come when people will not tolerate sound doctrine but, following their own desires and insatiable curiosity, will accumulate teachers and will stop listening to the truth and will be diverted to myths. But you, be self-possessed in all circumstances; put up with hardship; perform the work of an evangelist; fulfill your ministry.

For I am already being poured out like a libation, and the time of my departure is at hand. I have competed well; I have finished the race; I have kept the faith. From now on the crown of righteousness awaits me, which the

Lord, the just judge, will award to me on that day, and not only to me, but to all who have longed for his appearance.—The word of the Lord. ℟. **Thanks be to God.** ↓

RESPONSORIAL PSALM　　　　Ps 71:8-9, 14-15ab, 16-17, 22

℟. (see 15ab) **I will sing of your salvation.**

My mouth shall be filled with your praise,
　　with your glory day by day.
Cast me not off in my old age;
　　as my strength fails, forsake me not.—℟.

But I will always hope
　　and praise you ever more and more.
My mouth shall declare your justice,
　　day by day your salvation.—℟.

I will treat of the mighty works of the Lord;
　　O God, I will tell of your singular justice.
O God, you have taught me from my youth,
　　and till the present I proclaim your wondrous
　　　　deeds.—℟.

So will I give you thanks with music on the lyre,
　　for your faithfulness, O my God!
I will sing your praises with the harp,
　　O Holy One of Israel!—℟. ↓

——————— **YEAR I AND II** ———————

ALLELUIA　　　　　　　　　　　　　Mt 5:3

℟. **Alleluia, alleluia.**
Blessed are the poor in spirit;
for theirs is the Kingdom of heaven.
℟. **Alleluia, alleluia.** ↓

GOSPEL　　　　　　　　　　　　　　Mk 12:38-44

Jesus teaches that outward show is vain. He uses the widow's mite by way of example. It is not the amount that is given that has value, but what matters in the sight of God is the spirit in which the gift is given. And so, the poor widow gave "more" than the rich gave.

℣. The Lord be with you. ℟. **And also with you.**

℣. A reading from the holy Gospel according to Mark.

℟. **Glory to you, Lord.**

IN the course of his teaching Jesus said, "Beware of the scribes, who like to go around in long robes and accept greetings in the marketplaces, seats of honor in synagogues, and places of honor at banquets. They devour the houses of widows and, as a pretext, recite lengthy prayers. They will receive a very severe condemnation."

He sat down opposite the treasury and observed how the crowd put money into the treasury. Many rich people put in large sums. A poor widow also came and put in two small coins worth a few cents. Calling his disciples to himself, he said to them, "Amen, I say to you, this poor widow put in more than all the other contributors to the treasury. For they have all contributed from their surplus wealth, but she, from her poverty, has contributed all she had, her whole livelihood."—The Gospel of the Lord. ℟.

Praise to you, Lord Jesus Christ. ➙ No. 15, p. 623

LENTEN SEASON

The word "Lent" is an ancient word for spring. The season of Lent is a time in our personal lives for new life to appear, and for old frozen attitudes to disappear. It is a time to clear the ground, to clear away rubbish. A time for sowing, so that one day, the Day of the Lord, there will be a harvest.

Lent is six weeks. It is not too long to prepare for the Easter event, the Paschal Mystery, that changed history and human life. Jesus went through this time of reflection that the forty days of Lent present to us. He made new choices. He thought about his direction in life, his awareness of the Father, his use of time, power, and personal gifts.

Jesus came into the world to share his life with us. We say we are "in him." We could examine the priorities in our lives with his mission in mind. His mission is to bring each person to human dignity, and all persons to be brothers and sisters, leading them to the Father. He sought to do the will of his Father. "My Father is at work until now, so I am at work" (Jn 5:17), he said. What does that mean, for us?

Lent is a time of instruction. Faith comes by hearing, which certainly includes reading, and study, and good conversation. And today it would include the communication that comes from good film and art. Faith needs to grow, to ask questions, and to reflect on the answers. To grow in faith calls for an alert and attentive person, one who listens. The person of faith listens to others, and to self, to one's speech and one's conscience—and at the same time also listens to the world.

In the early Christian centuries Lent was and (in parishes that prepare adults to enter the Church) still is a time of preparation for baptism on Easter Eve. If we are already baptized, then it is a time to think what that Covenant should mean to us. Covenant is promise.

Promise of what? Perhaps we promised nothing; it was all done for us. But should we look into that Covenant and decide to renew it for ourselves? The Church provides a baptismal renewal at Easter. A serious spiritual effort in Lent will keep that renewal from becoming an empty gesture.

Lent is a time of listening. The Word of God is given to us in abundance. Look at the texts of the Lenten Sundays (and all the weekdays), the rich parables, the choice of Gospels, the great themes of faith, conversion, and turning back to a God who is already waiting and loving us. We are asked to do more than listen in this Lenten season. We are asked to make the Word of God a judgment upon our lives. Lent is a time for special penance and personal evaluation. We are reminded of the words of Christ that unless we do penance we shall all likewise perish: "Take up [your] cross and follow me" (Mt 16:24).

The Gospel during Lent is chosen each day in accord with the major Lenten themes and preparation for baptism: penance, prayer, effort to live a good Christian life, and acceptance of the mystery of salvation through the cross. Up until the end of the third week the texts are chosen from the Synoptic Gospels and follow one another without any real order. However, beginning with the fourth week, the Gospel of St. John is read in order. On the last day a text of Matthew's Gospel is read—the one concerning the betrayal by Judas.

The First Reading is taken every day from the Old Testament. It is chosen to accord with the theme of the Gospel or a Lenten theme. On the last three days the Songs of the Suffering Servant are read from the Book of Isaiah in order to prepare for the reading of the fourth Song on Good Friday, the Song that represents the spiritual summit of the Old Testament.

ASH WEDNESDAY

In today's Mass, ashes from palm branches or the branches of other trees, which were blessed in the preceding year, are blessed and imposed. In the Introductory Rites, the Penitential Rite is omitted since the giving of ashes takes its place. The ashes are blessed and given to the people after the Homily.

(The blessing and giving of ashes may also take place outside Mass. In this case, the Liturgy of the Word may be celebrated, using the Entrance Song, Opening Prayer and the readings with their chants as at Mass. The Homily and the blessing and giving of ashes follow. The rite concludes with the General Intercessions.)

Ashes remind us of ancient forms of penance and also that the human glamor of this life will soon come to an end when God calls us to himself for judgment.

ENTRANCE ANT. See Wis 11:24, 25, 27

Lord, you are merciful to all, and hate nothing you have created. You overlook the sins of men to bring them to repentance. You are the Lord our God.

→ No. 2, p. 614 (Omit Penitential Prayers and Gloria)

OPENING PRAYER

Let us pray
　　[for the grace to keep Lent faithfully]

Lord,
protect us in our struggle against evil.
As we begin the discipline of Lent,
make this season holy by our self-denial.
Grant this . . . for ever and ever. R̕. **Amen.** ↓

ALTERNATIVE OPENING PRAYER

Let us pray
　　[in quiet remembrance of our need for redemption]

Father in heaven,
the light of your truth bestows sight
to the darkness of sinful eyes.
May this season of repentance
bring us the blessing of your forgiveness

and the gift of your light.
Grant this through Christ our Lord. ℟. **Amen.** ↓

FIRST READING Jl 2:12-18

Joel warns that the Day of Yahweh is near. He recalls the actual situation caused by the locust plague and pleads, in Yahweh's name, for heartfelt repentance. The priests are invited to join in the general penitence after they have proclaimed a national day of fasting and prayer. The Lord's response implies he will send them food and renew the gift of prophecy and wisdom.

A reading from the Book of the Prophet Joel

EVEN now, says the LORD,
return to me with your whole heart,
with fasting, and weeping, and mourning;
Rend your hearts, not your garments,
and return to the LORD, your God.
For gracious and merciful is he,
slow to anger, rich in kindness,
and relenting in punishment.
Perhaps he will again relent
and leave behind him a blessing,
Offerings and libations
for the LORD, your God.

Blow the trumpet in Zion!
proclaim a fast,
call an assembly;
Gather the people,
notify the congregation;
Assemble the elders,
gather the children
and the infants at the breast;
Let the bridegroom quit his room
and the bride her chamber.
Between the porch and the altar
let the priests, the ministers of the LORD, weep,
And say, "Spare, O LORD, your people,
and make not your heritage a reproach,
with the nations ruling over them!

Why should they say among the peoples,
    'Where is their God?'"
    Then the LORD was stirred to concern for his land and took pity on his people.—The word of the Lord. ℟.
Thanks be to God. ↓

RESPONSORIAL PSALM Ps 51:3-4, 5-6ab, 12-13, 14 and 17

℟. (see 3a) **Be merciful, O Lord, for we have sinned.**

Have mercy on me, O God, in your goodness;
    in the greatness of your compassion wipe out my
       offense.
Thoroughly wash me from my guilt
    and of my sin cleanse me.—℟.

For I acknowledge my offense,
    and my sin is before me always:
"Against you only have I sinned,
    and done what is evil in your sight."—℟.

A clean heart create for me, O God,
    and a steadfast spirit renew within me.
Cast me not out from your presence,
    and your Holy Spirit take not from me.—℟.

Give me back the joy of your salvation,
    and a willing spirit sustain in me.
O Lord, open my lips,
    and my mouth shall proclaim your praise.—℟. ↓

SECOND READING   2 Cor 5:20—6:2

Paul describes an apostle's work. He is God's instrument. In one sense, reconciliation is obtained with the acceptance of the first justifying grace, but in another, it is not achieved until one enters into definitive possession of the eternal reward.

A reading from the second Letter of Saint Paul
to the Corinthians

BROTHERS and sisters: We are ambassadors for
Christ, as if God were appealing through us. We

implore you on behalf of Christ, be reconciled to God. For our sake he made him to be sin who did not know sin, so that we might become the righteousness of God in him. Working together, then, we appeal to you not to receive the grace of God in vain. For he says:

In an acceptable time I heard you,
and on the day of salvation I helped you.

Behold, now is a very acceptable time; behold, now is the day of salvation.—The word of the Lord. ℟. **Thanks be to God.** ↓

VERSE BEFORE THE GOSPEL
See Ps 95:8

℟. **Glory and praise to you, Lord Jesus Christ!***
If today you hear his voice,
harden not your hearts.
℟. **Glory and praise to you, Lord Jesus Christ** ↓

GOSPEL
Mt 6:1-6, 16-18

Righteousness is illustrated by three basic acts of Jewish piety: almsgiving, prayer, and fasting. Works of piety should not be done for vain display. Prayer and fasting should be carried out joyfully without display. God will then give the reward.

℣. The Lord be with you. ℟. **And also with you.**
℣. A reading from the holy Gospel according to Matthew.
℟. **Glory to you, Lord.**

JESUS said to his disciples: "Take care not to perform righteous deeds in order that people may see them; otherwise, you will have no recompense from your heavenly Father. When you give alms, do not blow a trumpet before you, as the hypocrites do in the synagogues and in the streets to win the praise of others. Amen, I say to you, they have received their reward. But when you give alms, do not let your left hand know what your right is doing, so that your almsgiving may be secret. And your Father who sees in secret will repay you.

* See p. 620 for other Gospel Acclamations.

"When you pray, do not be like the hypocrites, who love to stand and pray in the synagogues and on street corners so that others may see them. Amen, I say to you, they have received their reward. But when you pray, go to your inner room, close the door, and pray to your Father in secret. And your Father who sees in secret will repay you.

"When you fast, do not look gloomy like the hypocrites. They neglect their appearance, so that they may appear to others to be fasting. Amen, I say to you, they have received their reward. But when you fast, anoint your head and wash your face, so that you may not appear to be fasting, except to your Father who is hidden. And your Father who sees what is hidden will repay you."—The Gospel of the Lord. ℞. **Praise to you, Lord Jesus Christ.** ↓

BLESSING AND GIVING OF ASHES

After the homily the priest joins his hands and says:
Dear friends in Christ, let us ask our Father to bless these ashes which we will use as the mark of our repentance. ↓
Pause for silent prayer.

Lord,
bless the sinner who asks for your forgiveness
and bless ✝ all those who receive these ashes.
May they keep this lenten season
in preparation for the joy of Easter.
We ask this through Christ our Lord. ℞. **Amen.** ↓

OR:

Lord,
bless these ashes ✝
by which we show that we are dust.
Pardon our sins
and keep us faithful to the discipline of Lent,
for you do not want sinners to die
but to live with the risen Christ,
who reigns with you for ever and ever. ℞. **Amen.** ↓

He sprinkles the ashes with holy water in silence.

The priest then places ashes on those who come forward, saying to each:

Turn away from sin and be faithful to the gospel. (Mk 1:15)

OR:

Remember, man, you are dust
and to dust you will return. (See Gn 3:19)

Meanwhile some of the following antiphons or other appropriate songs are sung.

ANTIPHON 1 See Jl 2:13

Come back to the Lord with all your heart; leave the past in ashes, and turn to God with tears and fasting, for he is slow to anger and ready to forgive.

ANTIPHON 2 See Jl 2:17; Est 13:17

Let the priests and ministers of the Lord lament before his altar, and say: Spare us, Lord; spare your people! Do not let us die for we are crying out to you.

ANTIPHON 3 Ps 51:3

Lord, take away our wickedness.

These may be repeated after each verse of Psalm 51, Have mercy on me, O God.

RESPONSORY See Bar 3:5

Direct our hearts to better things, O Lord; heal our sin and ignorance. Lord, do not face us suddenly with death, but give us time to repent.

℟. **Turn to us with mercy, Lord; we have sinned against you.**

℣. **Help us, God our savior, rescue us for the honor of your name.** (Ps 79:9)

℟. **Turn to us with mercy, Lord; we have sinned against you.**

*After the giving of ashes the priest washes his hands; the rite
concludes with the General Intercessions or Prayer of the
Faithful. The Profession of Faith is not said.*

PRAYER OVER THE GIFTS

Lord,
help us to resist temptation
by our lenten works of charity and penance.
By this sacrifice
may we be prepared to celebrate
the death and resurrection of Christ our Savior
and be cleansed from sin and renewed in spirit.
We ask this through Christ our Lord.
℟. **Amen.**   ➜ No. 21, p. 626 (Pref. P 11)

COMMUNION ANT   Ps 1:2-3

**The man who mediates day and night on the law of the
Lord will yield fruit in due season.** ↓

PRAYER AFTER COMMUNION

Lord,
through this communion
may our lenten penance give you glory
and bring us your protection.
We ask this in the name of Jesus the Lord.
℟. **Amen.**   ➜ No. 32, p. 660

THURSDAY AFTER ASH WEDNESDAY

Just as the Israelites had to make a choice between good and evil in the
life they were to live, we must also make a choice between what is good
and pleasing to God, and what is evil and of the devil. We should therefore gird ourselves with justice, truth, and good works. The shield of faith,
which teaches us how richly God rewards virtue, gives us confidence in
God and the hope of heaven.

ENTRANCE ANT.   See Ps 55:17-20, 23

**When I cry to the Lord, he hears my voice and saves me
from the foes who threaten me. Unload your burden
onto the Lord, and he will support you.**   ➜ No. 2, p. 614

OPENING PRAYER

Lord,
may everything we do
begin with your inspiration,
continue with your help,
and reach perfection under your guidance.
We ask this . . . for ever and ever. ℟. **Amen.** ↓

FIRST READING Dt 30:15-20

The liturgy of covenant renewal confronts the community with committing itself to a binding decision. The life in question is fullness of life in the Promised Land. The calling of witnesses was an essential feature of ancient covenants. The Israelites were to choose such a life

A reading from the Book of Deuteronomy

MOSES said to the people: "Today I have set before you life and prosperity, death and doom. If you obey the commandments of the LORD, your God, which I enjoin on you today, loving him, and walking in his ways, and keeping his commandments, statutes and decrees, you will live and grow numerous, and the LORD, your God, will bless you in the land you are entering to occupy. If, however, you turn away your hearts and will not listen, but are led astray and adore and serve other gods, I tell you now that you will certainly perish; you will not have a long life on the land that you are crossing the Jordan to enter and occupy. I call heaven and earth today to witness against you: I have set before you life and death, the blessing and the curse. Choose life, then, that you and your descendants may live, by loving the LORD, your God, heeding his voice, and holding fast to him. For that will mean life for you, a long life for you to live on the land that the LORD swore he would give to your fathers Abraham, Isaac and Jacob."—The word of the Lord. ℟. **Thanks be to God.** ↓

RESPONSORIAL PSALM Ps 1:1-2, 3, 4 and 6

℟. (Ps 40:5a) **Blessed are they who hope in the Lord.**

Blessed the man who follows not
  the counsel of the wicked
Nor walks in the way of sinners,
  nor sits in the company of the insolent,
But delights in the law of the LORD
  and meditates on his law day and night.—℟.

He is like a tree
  planted near running water,
That yields its fruit in due season,
  and whose leaves never fade.
  Whatever he does, prospers.—℟.

Not so the wicked, not so;
  they are like chaff which the wind drives away.
For the LORD watches over the way of the just,
  but the way of the wicked vanishes.—℟. ↓

VERSE BEFORE THE GOSPEL Mt 4:17

℟. **Glory and praise to you, Lord Jesus Christ!***
Repent, says the Lord,
the Kingdom of heaven is at hand.
℟. **Glory and praise to you, Lord Jesus Christ!** ↓

GOSPEL Lk 9:22-25

Jesus foretells his passion and death. He warns that disciples too must
be prepared to suffer and die in true apostleship in imitation of his suffering. True disciples take up their cross daily.

℣. The Lord be with you. ℟. **And also with you.**
℣. A reading from the holy Gospel according to Luke.
℟. **Glory to you, Lord.**

JESUS said to his disciples: "The Son of Man must suffer greatly and be rejected by the elders, the chief
priests, and the scribes, and be killed and on the third day
be raised."

* See p. 620 for other Gospel Acclamations.

Then he said to all, "If anyone wishes to come after me, he must deny himself and take up his cross daily and follow me. For whoever wishes to save his life will lose it, but whoever loses his life for my sake will save it. What profit is there for one to gain the whole world yet lose or forfeit himself?"—The Gospel of the Lord. ℟. **Praise to you, Lord Jesus Christ.** ➔ No. 15, p. 623

PRAYER OVER THE GIFTS

Lord,
accept these gifts.
May they bring us your mercy
and give you honor and praise.
We ask this in the name of Jesus the Lord.
℟. **Amen.** ➔ No. 21, p. 626 (Pref. P 8-11)

COMMUNION ANT.
Ps 51:12

Create a clean heart in me, O God; give me a new and steadfast spirit. ↓

PRAYER AFTER COMMUNION

Merciful Father,
may the gifts and blessings we receive
bring us pardon and salvation.
Grant this through Christ our Lord.
℟. **Amen.** ➔ No. 32, p. 660

FRIDAY AFTER ASH WEDNESDAY

It is a good and holy practice to humble ourselves by abstaining from other than mere food for the body. The eye should abstain from all vain and curious sights, the ears from listening to idle talk, the tongue from detraction and frivolous words. True sorrow for past sins can best be expressed through acts of love and charity toward others.

ENTRANCE ANT.
Ps 30:11

The Lord heard me and took pity on me. He came to my help. ➔ No. 2, p. 614

OPENING PRAYER

Lord,
with your loving care
guide the penance we have begun.
Help us to persevere with love and sincerity.
Grant this . . . for ever and ever. ℟. **Amen.** ↓

FIRST READING

Is 58:1-9a

Fasting should unite rich and poor. Only the wealthy can fast; they alone have something of which to deprive themselves. In fasting, they share the lot of the poor who are always hungry. To fast and neglect the poor is a form of conceit.

A reading from the Book of the Prophet Isaiah

THUS says the Lord GOD:
Cry out full-throated and unsparingly,
lift up your voice like a trumpet blast;
Tell my people their wickedness,
and the house of Jacob their sins.
They seek me day after day,
and desire to know my ways,
Like a nation that has done what is just
and not abandoned the law of their God;
They ask me to declare what is due them,
pleased to gain access to God.
"Why do we fast, and you do not see it?
afflict ourselves, and you take no note of it?"

Lo, on your fast day you carry out your own pursuits,
and drive all your laborers.
Yes, your fast ends in quarreling and fighting,
striking with wicked claw.
Would that today you might fast
so as to make your voice heard on high!
Is this the manner of fasting I wish,
of keeping a day of penance:
That a man bow his head like a reed
and lie in sackcloth and ashes?

Do you call this a fast,
>   a day acceptable to the LORD?
This, rather, is the fasting that I wish:
>   releasing those bound unjustly,
>   untying the thongs of the yoke;
Setting free the oppressed,
>   breaking every yoke;
Sharing your bread with the hungry,
>   sheltering the oppressed and the homeless;
Clothing the naked when you see them,
>   and not turning your back on your own.
Then your light shall break forth like the dawn,
>   and your wound shall quickly be healed;
Your vindication shall go before you,
>   and the glory of the LORD shall be your rear guard.
Then you shall call, and the LORD will answer,
>   you shall cry for help, and he will say: Here I am!

The word of the Lord. ℟. **Thanks be to God.** ↓

RESPONSORIAL PSALM   Ps 51:3-4, 5-6ab, 18-19

℟. (19b) **A heart contrite and humbled, O God, you will
not spurn.**

Have mercy on me, O God, in your goodness;
>   in the greatness of your compassion wipe out my
>   offense.
Thoroughly wash me from my guilt
>   and of my sin cleanse me.—℟.

For I acknowledge my offense,
>   and my sin is before me always:
"Against you only have I sinned,
>   and done what is evil in your sight."—℟.

For you are not pleased with sacrifices;
>   should I offer a burnt offering, you would not accept
>   it.
My sacrifice, O God, is a contrite spirit;
>   a heart contrite and humbled, O God, you will not
>   spurn.—℟. ↓

VERSE BEFORE THE GOSPEL See Am 5:14

℟. **Glory and praise to you, Lord Jesus Christ!***
Seek good and not evil so that you may live,
and the Lord will be with you.
℟. **Glory and praise to you, Lord Jesus Christ!** ↓

GOSPEL Mt 9:14-15

In the Old Testament, fasting appears as a token of mourning or of repentance. A fast meant abstinence from food for the entire day. Jesus answers the question of not fasting by saying that his sojourn with his disciples is considered a time of joy when fasting is out of place.

℣. The Lord be with you. ℟. **And also with you.**
℣. A reading from the holy Gospel according to Matthew.
℟. **Glory to you, Lord.**

THE disciples of John approached Jesus and said, "Why do we and the Pharisees fast much, but your disciples do not fast?" Jesus answered them, "Can the wedding guests mourn as long as the bridegroom is with them? The days will come when the bridegroom is taken away from them, and then they will fast."—The Gospel of the Lord. ℟. **Praise to you, Lord Jesus Christ.**

→ No. 15, p. 623

PRAYER OVER THE GIFTS

Lord,
through this lenten eucharist
may we grow in your love and service
and become an acceptable offering to you.
We ask this through Christ our Lord.
℟. **Amen.** → No. 21, p. 626 (Pref. P 8-11)

COMMUNION ANT.

Teach us your ways, O Lord, and lead us in your paths. ↓

---

* *See p. 620 for other Gospel Acclamations.*

PRAYER AFTER COMMUNION

Lord,
may our sharing in this mystery
free us from our sins
and make us worthy of your healing.
We ask this in the name of Jesus the Lord.
℟. **Amen.**

→ No. 32, p. 660

SATURDAY AFTER ASH WEDNESDAY

To serve God lovingly and to be content with few things always brings rich rewards, if not in this life, at least in the next. Christ promised the Kingdom of Heaven to the poor in spirit, that is, not only to the humble but also to the poor who imitate Christ in all patience and resignation.

ENTRANCE ANT. Ps 69:17

Answer us, Lord, with your loving kindness, turn to us in your great mercy. → No. 2, p. 614

OPENING PRAYER

Father,
look upon our weakness
and reach out to help us with your loving power.
We ask this . . . for ever and ever. ℟. **Amen.** ↓

FIRST READING Is 58:9b-14

The prophet's thoughts expand to include the eschatological day. When lowliness unites all people, then God will fill the need of the whole world with his glorious presence. Fasting makes the wealthy poor, and the poor will impart their spirit of humble waiting upon God to the wealthy.

A reading from the Book of the Prophet Isaiah

THUS says the LORD:
If you remove from your midst oppression,
    false accusation and malicious speech;
If you bestow your bread on the hungry
    and satisfy the afflicted;
Then light shall rise for you in the darkness,
    and the gloom shall become for you like midday;

Then the LORD will guide you always
 and give you plenty even on the parched land.
He will renew your strength,
 and you shall be like a watered garden,
 like a spring whose water never fails.
The ancient ruins shall be rebuilt for your sake,
 and the foundations from ages past you shall raise up;
"Repairer of the breach," they shall call you,
 "Restorer of ruined homesteads."

If you hold back your foot on the sabbath
 from following your own pursuits on my holy day;
If you call the sabbath a delight,
 and the LORD's holy day honorable;
If you honor it by not following your ways,
 seeking your own interests, or speaking with malice—
Then you shall delight in the LORD,
 and I will make you ride on the heights of the earth;
I will nourish you with the heritage of Jacob, your father,
 for the mouth of the Lord has spoken.
The word of the Lord. ℟. **Thanks be to God.** ↓

RESPONSORIAL PSALM   Ps 86:1-2, 3-4, 5-6

℟. (11ab) **Teach me your way, O Lord, that I may walk in
 your truth.**

Incline your ear, O LORD; answer me,
 for I am afflicted and poor.
Keep my life, for I am devoted to you;
 save your servant who trusts in you.
 You are my God.—℟.

Have mercy on me, O Lord,
 for to you I call all the day.
Gladden the soul of your servant,
 for to you, O Lord, I lift up my soul.—℟.

For you, O LORD, are good and forgiving,
 abounding in kindness to all who call upon you.

Hearken, O LORD, to my prayer
and attend to the sound of my pleading.—℟. ↓

VERSE BEFORE THE GOSPEL Ez 33:11

℟. **Glory and praise to you, Lord Jesus Christ!***
I take no pleasure in the death of the wicked man, says
the Lord,
but rather in his conversion, that he may live.
℟. **Glory and praise to you, Lord Jesus Christ!** ↓

GOSPEL Lk 5:27-32

Jesus invites Levi (Matthew) to leave his tax post and follow him. The Pharisees and scribes could not understand why Jesus would eat with the unclean. Our Lord refers ironically to the self-righteous. Jesus invites sinners who repent to become his guests at the heavenly banquet.

℣. The Lord be with you. ℟. **And also with you.**
℣. A reading from the holy Gospel according to Luke.
℟. **Glory to you, Lord.**

JESUS saw a tax collector named Levi sitting at the customs post. He said to him, "Follow me." And leaving everything behind, he got up and followed him. Then Levi gave a great banquet for him in his house, and a large crowd of tax collectors and others were at table with them. The Pharisees and their scribes complained to his disciples, saying, "Why do you eat and drink with tax collectors and sinners?" Jesus said to them in reply, "Those who are healthy do not need a physician, but the sick do. I have not come to call the righteous to repentance but sinners."—The Gospel of the Lord. ℟. **Praise to you, Lord Jesus Christ.** → No. 15, p. 623

PRAYER OVER THE GIFTS

Lord,
receive our sacrifice of praise and reconciliation.

---

* *See p. 620 for other Gospel Acclamations.*

Let it free us from sin
and enable us to give you loving service.
We ask this in the name of Jesus the Lord.
℟. **Amen.**   ➜ No. 21, p. 626 (Pref. P 8-11)

COMMUNION ANT.   Mt 9:13

It is mercy that I want, and not sacrifice, says the Lord; I did not come to call the virtuous, but sinners. ↓

PRAYER AFTER COMMUNION

Lord,
we are nourished by the bread of life you give us.
May this mystery we now celebrate
help us to reach eternal life with you.
Grant this through Christ our Lord.
℟. **Amen.**   ➜ No. 32, p. 660

MONDAY OF THE FIRST WEEK OF LENT

The same precept that binds us to love God also binds us to love our neighbor. We are bound to love our neighbor in thought, word, and deed from the motive of divine charity. This is a superior love and a higher order of charity, and it is grounded on faith and the love of God. Let us strive to purify ourselves of all our sins and, with the proper motive, perform good works with true charity and love toward God's "little ones."

ENTRANCE ANT.   Ps 123:2-3

As the eyes of servants are on the hands of their master, so our eyes are fixed on the Lord our God, pleading for his mercy. Have mercy on us, Lord, have mercy.

➜ No. 2, p. 614

OPENING PRAYER

God our savior,
bring us back to you
and fill our minds with your wisdom.
May we be enriched by our observance of Lent.
Grant this . . . for ever and ever. ℟. **Amen.** ↓

FIRST READING Lv 19:1-2, 11-18

The general theme of Leviticus is, "Be holy, because I, the LORD, your God, am holy." One directive comes out in a positive way in this passage: "You shall love your neighbor as yourself. . . ." People must not cheat or lie. There must be strict, impartial justice, no gossip, and no plotting against the life of a fellow-citizen.

A reading from the Book of Leviticus

THE LORD said to Moses, "Speak to the whole assembly of the children of Israel and tell them: Be holy, for I, the LORD, your God, am holy.

"You shall not steal. You shall not lie or speak falsely to one another. You shall not swear falsely by my name, thus profaning the name of your God. I am the LORD.

"You shall not defraud or rob your neighbor. You shall not withhold overnight the wages of your day laborer. You shall not curse the deaf, or put a stumbling block in front of the blind, but you shall fear your God. I am the LORD.

"You shall not act dishonestly in rendering judgment. Show neither partiality to the weak nor deference to the mighty, but judge your fellow men justly. You shall not go about spreading slander among your kin; nor shall you stand by idly when your neighbor's life is at stake. I am the LORD.

"You shall not bear hatred for your brother in your heart. Though you may have to reprove him, do not incur sin because of him. Take no revenge and cherish no grudge against your fellow countrymen. You shall love your neighbor as yourself. I am the LORD."—The word of the Lord. ℟. **Thanks be to God.** ↓

RESPONSORIAL PSALM Ps 19:8, 9, 10, 15

℟. (Jn 6:63b) **Your words, Lord, are Spirit and life.**

The law of the LORD is perfect,
refreshing the soul.

The decree of the LORD is trustworthy,
  giving wisdom to the simple.—R̸.

The precepts of the LORD are right,
  rejoicing the heart.
The command of the LORD is clear,
  enlightening the eye.—R̸.

The fear of the LORD is pure,
  enduring forever;
The ordinances of the LORD are true,
  all of them just.—R̸.

Let the words of my mouth and the thought of my heart
  find favor before you,
  O LORD, my rock and my redeemer.—R̸.

VERSE BEFORE THE GOSPEL   2 Cor 6:2b

R̸. **Glory to you, Lord Jesus Christ, Wisdom of God the
  Father!***
Behold, now is a very acceptable time;
behold, now is the day of salvation.
R̸. **Glory to you, Lord Jesus Christ, Wisdom of God the
  Father!** ↓

GOSPEL   Mt 25:31-46

The final judgment by God will depend on how each person has lived. The
accent falls on Jesus' repeated phrase: Truly I say to you, as you did it— or
did it not—to one of the least of these my brothers and sisters, you did
it—or did it not—to me.

*See Common of Holy Men and Women, p. 1231, no. 13 (Long
Form).*

PRAYER OVER THE GIFTS

Lord,
may this offering of our love
be acceptable to you.
Let it transform our lives
and bring us your mercy.

---

* *See p. 620 for other Gospel Acclamations.*

We ask this through Christ our Lord.
℟. **Amen.**   → No. 21, p. 626 (Pref. P 8-11)

COMMUNION ANT.   Mt 25:40, 34

I tell you, anything you did for the least of my brothers, you did for me, says the Lord. Come, you whom my Father has blessed; inherit the kingdom prepared for you since the foundation of the world. ↓

PRAYER AFTER COMMUNION

Lord,
through this sacrament
may we rejoice in your healing power
and experience your saving love in mind and body.
We ask this in the name of Jesus the Lord.
℟. **Amen.**   → No. 32, p. 660

TUESDAY OF THE FIRST WEEK OF LENT

Lent is for special graces; marvelous things happen during this sacred time. We ourselves do not lay down the conditions for our salvation. God does that. When we pray, we should mean what we say and keep our mind on what we are doing. Glorify God, adore him, praise him—then ask!

ENTRANCE ANT.   Ps 90:1-2

In every age, O Lord, you have been our refuge. From all eternity, you are God.   → No. 2, p. 614

OPENING PRAYER

Father,
look on us, your children.
Through the discipline of Lent
help us to grow in our desire for you.
We ask this . . . for ever and ever. ℟. **Amen.** ↓

FIRST READING   Is 55:10-11

Isaiah directs his hearers to come to the Lord, especially when in need. It is necessary to seek the Lord while he may be found. God alone lays down the conditions for salvation.

A reading from the Book of the Prophet Isaiah

THUS says the LORD:
Just as from the heavens
    the rain and snow come down
And do not return there
    till they have watered the earth,
    making it fertile and fruitful,
Giving seed to the one who sows
    and bread to the one who eats,
So shall my word be
    that goes forth from my mouth;
It shall not return to me void,
    but shall do my will,
    achieving the end for which I sent it.
The word of the Lord. ℟. **Thanks be to God.** ↓

RESPONSORIAL PSALM   Ps 34:4-5, 6-7, 16-17, 18-19

℟. (18b) **From all their distress God rescues the just.**

Glorify the LORD with me,
    let us together extol his name.
I sought the LORD, and he answered me
    and delivered me from all my fears.—℟.

Look to him that you may be radiant with joy,
    and your faces may not blush with shame.
When the poor one called out, the LORD heard,
    and from all his distress he saved him.—℟.

The LORD has eyes for the just,
    and ears for their cry.
The LORD confronts the evildoers,
    to destroy remembrance of them from the earth.—℟.

When the just cry out, the LORD hears them,
    and from all their distress he rescues them.
The LORD is close to the brokenhearted;
    and those who are crushed in spirit he saves.—℟. ↓

VERSE BEFORE THE GOSPEL Mt 4:4b

℟. **Glory to you, Lord Jesus Christ, Wisdom of God the Father!***

One does not live on bread alone,
but on every word that comes forth from the mouth of God.

℟. **Glory to you, Lord Jesus Christ, Wisdom of God the Father!** ↓

GOSPEL Mt 6:7-15

Jesus gives advice about prayer. He notes that sincerity and attention are required. Then he gives an example of how to pray. God forgives those who forgive others' faults.

℣. The Lord be with you. ℟. **And also with you.**

℣. A reading from the holy Gospel according to Matthew.
℟. **Glory to you, Lord.**

JESUS said to his disciples: "In praying, do not babble like the pagans, who think that they will be heard because of their many words. Do not be like them. Your Father knows what you need before you ask him.

"This is how you are to pray:

Our Father who art in heaven,
hallowed be thy name,
thy Kingdom come,
thy will be done,
on earth as it is in heaven.
Give us this day our daily bread;
and forgive us our trespasses,
as we forgive those who trespass against us;
and lead us not into temptation,
but deliver us from evil.

"If you forgive men their transgressions, your heavenly Father will forgive you. But if you do not forgive men, neither will your Father forgive your transgres-

* *See p. 620 for other Gospel Acclamations.*

sions."—The Gospel of the Lord. ℟. **Praise to you, Lord Jesus Christ.**   → No. 15, p. 623

PRAYER OVER THE GIFTS

Father of creation,
from all you have given us
we bring you this bread and wine.
May it become for us the food of eternal life.
We ask this in the name of Jesus the Lord.
℟. **Amen.**   → No. 21, 626 (Pref. P 8-11)

COMMUNION ANT   Ps 4:2

My God of justice, you answer my cry; you come to my help when I am in trouble. Take pity on me, Lord, and hear my prayer. ↓

PRAYER AFTER COMMUNION

Lord,
may we who receive this sacrament
restrain our earthly desires
and grow in love for the things of heaven.
Grant this through Christ our Lord.
℟. **Amen.**   → No. 32, p. 660

WEDNESDAY OF THE FIRST WEEK OF LENT

Many of those now separated from God will again one day hear the voice of God as did the people of Nineveh. This should help us reflect on the tremendous love God has for his people. Let us consider Jesus' great love for us, and we shall be led to offer him our love in return. Our Divine Master shows his love by his sufferings for us.

ENTRANCE ANT.   Ps 25:6, 3, 22

Remember your mercies, Lord, your tenderness from ages past. Do not let our enemies triumph over us; O God, deliver Israel from all her distress. → No. 2, p. 614

OPENING PRAYER

Lord,
look upon us and hear our prayer.

By the good works you inspire,
help us to discipline our bodies
and to be renewed in spirit.
Grant this . . . for ever and ever. ℟. **Amen.** ↓

FIRST READING   Jon 3:1-10

Jonah was running away from his job of preaching penance to the people
of Nineveh who were offending God by their wickedness. But God directs
Jonah to encourage the people to repent. They listen and begin a fast. God
is moved by their actions and spares them.

A reading from the Book of the Prophet Jonah

The word of the LORD came to Jonah a second time:
"Set out for the great city of Nineveh, and announce
to it the message that I will tell you." So Jonah made
ready and went to Nineveh, according to the LORD's bidding. Now Nineveh was an enormously large city; it took
three days to go through it. Jonah began his journey
through the city, and had gone but a single day's walk
announcing, "Forty days more and Nineveh shall be
destroyed," when the people of Nineveh believed God;
they proclaimed a fast and all of them, great and small,
put on sackcloth.

When the news reached the king of Nineveh, he rose
from his throne, laid aside his robe, covered himself with
sackcloth, and sat in the ashes. Then he had this proclaimed throughout Nineveh, by decree of the king and
his nobles: "Neither man nor beast, neither cattle nor
sheep, shall taste anything; they shall not eat, nor shall
they drink water. Man and beast shall be covered with
sackcloth and call loudly to God; every man shall turn
from his evil way and from the violence he has in hand.
Who knows, God may relent and forgive, and withhold
his blazing wrath, so that we shall not perish." When
God saw by their actions how they turned from their evil
way, he repented of the evil that he had threatened to do
to them; he did not carry it out.—The word of the Lord.
℟. **Thanks be to God.** ↓

RESPONSORIAL PSALM   Ps 51:3-4, 12-13, 18-19

℞. (19b) **A heart contrite and humbled, O God, you will not spurn.**

Have mercy on me, O God, in your goodness;
    in the greatness of your compassion wipe out my offense.
Thoroughly wash me from my guilt
    and of my sin cleanse me.—℞.

A clean heart create for me, O God,
    and a steadfast spirit renew within me.
Cast me not out from your presence,
    and your Holy Spirit take not from me.—℞.

For you are not pleased with sacrifices;
    should I offer a burnt offering, you would not accept it.
My sacrifice, O God, is a contrite spirit;
    a heart contrite and humbled, O God, you will not spurn.—℞. ↓

VERSE BEFORE THE GOSPEL   Jl 2:12-13

℞. **Glory to you, Lord Jesus Christ, Wisdom of God the Father!***
Even now, says the LORD,
return to me with your whole heart
for I am gracious and merciful.
℞. **Glory to you, Lord Jesus Christ, Wisdom of God the Father!** ↓

GOSPEL   Lk 11:29-32

The Son of. Man is a sign far greater than that of Jonah, but the scribes and Pharisees are not converted. Jesus speaks as the one sent. He is not only the prophet but also the Redeemer. Jesus praises the people of Nineveh, but the present generation will be judged by their response.

---

* *See p. 620 for other Gospel Acclamations.*

℣. The Lord be with you. ℟. **And also with you.**
℣. A reading from the holy Gospel according to Luke.
℟. **Glory to you, Lord.**

WHILE still more people gathered in the crowd, Jesus said to them, "This generation is an evil generation; it seeks a sign, but no sign will be given it, except the sign of Jonah. Just as Jonah became a sign to the Ninevites, so will the Son of Man be to this generation. At the judgment the queen of the south will rise with the men of this generation and she will condemn them, because she came from the ends of the earth to hear the wisdom of Solomon, and there is something greater than Solomon here. At the judgment the men of Nineveh will arise with this generation and condemn it, because at the preaching of Jonah they repented, and there is something greater than Jonah here."—The Gospel of the Lord. ℟. **Praise to you, Lord Jesus Christ.**   → No. 15, p. 623

PRAYER OVER THE GIFTS

Lord,
from all you have given us,
we bring you these gifts in your honor.
Make them the sacrament of our salvation.
We ask this through Christ our Lord.
℟. **Amen.**   → No. 21, p. 626 (Pref. P 8-11)

COMMUNION ANT.   Ps 5:12

Lord, give joy to all who trust in you; be their defender and make them happy for ever. ↓

PRAYER AFTER COMMUNION

Father,
you have never failed to give us the food of life.
May this eucharist renew our strength
and bring us to salvation.
Grant this through Christ our Lord.
℟. **Amen.**   → No. 32, p. 660

THURSDAY OF THE FIRST WEEK OF LENT

God promises the necessities of life and at the same time expects us to perform our daily duties in order to obtain them. Let us avoid all undue anxiety and inordinate care about the things of this life. "Your heavenly Father knows that you need them all. But seek first the Kingdom [of God] and his righteousness, and all these things will be given you besides" (Mt 6:32-33).

ENTRANCE ANT.   Ps 5:2-3

Let my words reach your ears, Lord; listen to my groaning, and hear the cry of my prayer, O my King, my God.

→ No. 2, p. 614

OPENING PRAYER

Father,
without you we can do nothing.
By your Spirit help us to know what is right
and to be eager in doing your will.
We ask this . . . for ever and ever. ℟. **Amen.** ↓

FIRST READING   Est C:12, 14-16, 23-25

Esther became queen of Persia, and King Ahasuerus fixed a date for the extermination of all Jews. Esther intervenes, asking help from the Lord, and the Jews are victorious. Esther's prayer and penance earned God's care. This Book shows how God protected his people.

A reading from the Book of Esther

Queen Esther, seized with mortal anguish, had recourse to the LORD. She lay prostrate upon the ground, together with her handmaids, from morning until evening, and said: "God of Abraham, God of Isaac, and God of Jacob, blessed are you. Help me, who am alone and have no help but you, for I am taking my life in my hand. As a child I used to hear from the books of my forefathers that you, O LORD, always free those who are pleasing to you. Now help me, who am alone and have no one but you, O LORD, my God.

"And now, come to help me, an orphan. Put in my mouth persuasive words in the presence of the lion and turn his heart to hatred for our enemy, so that he and those who are in league with him may perish. Save us from the hand of our enemies; turn our mourning into gladness and our sorrows into wholeness."—The word of the Lord. ℟. **Thanks be to God.** ↓

RESPONSORIAL PSALM Ps 138:1-2ab, 2cde-3, 7c-8

℟. (3a) **Lord, on the day I called for help, you answered me.**

I will give thanks to you, O LORD, with all my heart,
    for you have heard the words of my mouth;
    in the presence of the angels I will sing your praise;
I will worship at your holy temple,
    and give thanks to your name.—℟.

Because of your kindness and your truth,
    you have made great above all things
    your name and your promise.
When I called, you answered me;
    you built up strength within me.—℟.

Your right hand saves me.
The LORD will complete what he has done for me;
    your kindness, O LORD, endures forever;
    forsake not the work of your hands.—℟. ↓

VERSE BEFORE THE GOSPEL Ps 51:12a, 14a

℟. **Glory to you, Lord Jesus Christ, Wisdom of God the Father!***
A clean heart create for me, God;
give me back the joy of your salvation.
℟. **Glory to you, Lord Jesus Christ, Wisdom of God the Father!** ↓

GOSPEL Mt 7:7-12

Jesus advised how important it is to keep clear the notion of God's power and goodness, especially in prayer. The faith necessary for prayer is really a firm hope that springs from belief in Jesus. God will answer those who call upon him.

---

* *See p. 620 for other Gospel Acclamations.*

℣. The Lord be with you. ℟. **And also with you.**
℣. A reading from the holy Gospel according to Matthew.
℟. **Glory to you, Lord.**

JESUS said to his disciples: "Ask and it will be given to you; seek and you will find; knock and the door will be opened to you. For everyone who asks, receives; and the one who seeks, finds; and to the one who knocks, the door will be opened. Which one of you would hand his son a stone when he asked for a loaf of bread, or a snake when he asked for a fish? If you then, who are wicked, know how to give good gifts to your children, how much more will your heavenly Father give good things to those who ask him.

"Do to others whatever you would have them do to you. This is the law and the prophets."—The Gospel of the Lord. ℟. **Praise to you, Lord Jesus Christ.** ➜ No. 15, p. 623

PRAYER OVER THE GIFTS

Lord,
be close to your people,
accept our prayers and offerings,
and let us turn to you with all our hearts.
We ask this in the name of Jesus the Lord.
℟. **Amen.** ➜ No. 21, p. 626 (Pref. P 8-11)

COMMUNION ANT. Mt 7:8

Everyone who asks will receive; whoever seeks shall find, and to him who knocks it shall be opened. ↓

PRAYER AFTER COMMUNION

Lord our God,
renew us by these mysteries.
May they heal us now
and bring us eternal salvation.
Grant this through Christ our Lord.
℟. **Amen.** ➜ No. 32, p. 660

FRIDAY OF THE FIRST WEEK OF LENT

The second commandment is like the first in that it is concerned with love—the love of our neighbor as ourself. We must love our neighbor in thought, word, and deed—in thought, by never judging anything evil of others; in word, by carefully abstaining from any calumny or detraction; in deed, by being charitable in our actions. "Let us love not in word or speech but in deed and truth," says St. John (1 Jn 3:18).

ENTRANCE ANT. Ps 25:17-18

Lord, deliver me from my distress. See my hardship and my poverty, and pardon all my sins. → No. 2, p. 614

OPENING PRAYER

Lord,
may our observance of Lent
help to renew us and prepare us
to celebrate the death and resurrection of Christ,
who lives and reigns with you and the Holy Spirit,
one God, for ever and ever. ℟. **Amen.** ↓

FIRST READING Ez 18:21-28

Ezekiel was the prophet during the Babylonian exile. Ezekiel preaches the same message that Jeremiah did: Repent and all will be well. He brings out personal accountability. A person lives only by keeping God's law joyfully.

A reading from the Book of the Prophet Ezekiel

THUS says the Lord GOD: If the wicked man turns away from all the sins he committed, if he keeps all my statutes and does what is right and just, he shall surely live, he shall not die. None of the crimes he committed shall be remembered against him; he shall live because of the virtue he has practiced. Do I indeed derive any pleasure from the death of the wicked? says the Lord GOD. Do I not rather rejoice when he turns from his evil way that he may live?

And if the virtuous man turns from the path of virtue to do evil, the same kind of abominable things that the wicked man does, can he do this and still live? None of his virtuous deeds shall be remembered, because he has broken faith and committed sin; because of this, he shall die. You say, "The LORD's way is not fair!" Hear now, house of Israel: Is it my way that is unfair, or rather, are not your ways unfair? When someone virtuous turns away from virtue to commit iniquity, and dies, it is because of the iniquity he committed that he must die. But if the wicked, turning from the wickedness he has committed, does what is right and just, he shall preserve his life; since he has turned away from all the sins that he committed, he shall surely live, he shall not die.—The word of the Lord. ℟. **Thanks be to God.** ↓

RESPONSORIAL PSALM   Ps 130:1-2, 3-4, 5-7a, 7bc-8

℟. (3) **If you, O Lord, mark iniquities, who can stand?**

Out of the depths I cry to you, O LORD;
    LORD, hear my voice!
Let your ears be attentive
    to my voice in supplication.—℟.

If you, O LORD, mark iniquities,
    LORD, who can stand?
But with you is forgiveness,
    that you may be revered.—℟.

I trust in the LORD;
    my soul trusts in his word.
My soul waits for the LORD
    more than sentinels wait for the dawn.
    Let Israel wait for the LORD.—℟.

For with the LORD is kindness
    and with him is plenteous redemption;
And he will redeem Israel
    from all their iniquities.—℟. ↓

VERSE BEFORE THE GOSPEL   Ez 18:31

℟. **Glory to you, Lord Jesus Christ, Wisdom of God the Father!***

---

* *See p. 620 for other Gospel Acclamations.*

Cast away from you all the crimes you have committed,
   says the Lord,
and make for yourselves a new heart and a new spirit.

℟. **Glory to you, Lord Jesus Christ, Wisdom of God the Father!** ↓

GOSPEL   Mt 5:20-26

Christ talks about occasions of sin—do not get angry and you will not be a murderer. It is not easy to understand the gradations of guilt that our Lord mentions in this passage. We are under God's judgment when we cherish hatred and anger. We should seek forgiveness of others if we wrong them.

℣. The Lord be with you. ℟. **And also with you.**
℣. A reading from the holy Gospel according to Matthew.
℟. **Glory to you, Lord.**

JESUS said to his disciples: "I tell you, unless your righteousness surpasses that of the scribes and Pharisees, you will not enter into the Kingdom of heaven.

"You have heard that it was said to your ancestors, *You shall not kill; and whoever kills will be liable to judgment.* But I say to you, whoever is angry with his brother will be liable to judgment, and whoever says to his brother, *Raqa,* will be answerable to the Sanhedrin, and whoever says, 'You fool,' will be liable to fiery Gehenna. Therefore, if you bring your gift to the altar, and there recall that your brother has anything against you, leave your gift there at the altar, go first and be reconciled with your brother, and then come and offer your gift. Settle with your opponent quickly while on the way to court. Otherwise your opponent will hand you over to the judge, and the judge will hand you over to the guard, and you will be thrown into prison. Amen, I say to you, you will not be released until you have paid the last penny."— The Gospel of the Lord. ℟. **Praise to you, Lord Jesus Christ.**   → No. 15, p. 623

PRAYER OVER THE GIFTS

Lord of mercy,
in your love accept these gifts.
May they bring us your saving power.
We ask this in the name of Jesus the Lord.
℞. **Amen.**   → No. 21, p. 626 (Pref. P 8-11)

COMMUNION ANT   Ez 33:11

**By my life, I do not wish the sinner to die, says the Lord,
but to turn to me and live.** ↓

PRAYER AFTER COMMUNION

Lord,
may the sacrament you give us
free us from our sinful ways and bring us new life.
May this eucharist lead us to salvation.
Grant this through Christ our Lord.
℞. **Amen.**   → No. 32, p. 660

SATURDAY OF THE FIRST WEEK OF LENT

St. Bernard tells us that perfection is a sincere purpose to go forward and
increase in virtue, that is to say, in loving God and our neighbor. Prayer is
a necessary means of perfection. The test of repentant sinners is how
courageously they can cut out the roots of evil habits and how wholeheartedly they are able to forgive their neighbor. The touch of the Divine
Hand is never absent.

ENTRANCE ANT.   Ps 19:8

**The law of the Lord is perfect, reviving the soul; his com-
mandments are the wisdom of the simple.**

                              → No. 2, p. 614

OPENING PRAYER

Eternal Father,
turn our hearts to you.
By seeking your kingdom
and loving one another,
may we become a people who worship you

in spirit and truth.

Grant this . . . for ever and ever. ℟. **Amen.** ↓

FIRST READING Dt 26:16-19

The Book of Deuteronomy literally means the Book of the Second Law, which is concerned with the Ten Commandments. The Jewish people are told by God to observe these laws with all their heart and soul. It is in this pact that God makes the Jewish people a people chosen to be his own.

A reading from the Book of Deuteronomy

Moses spoke to the people, saying: "This day the LORD, your God, commands you to observe these statutes and decrees. Be careful, then, to observe them with all your heart and with all your soul. Today you are making this agreement with the LORD: he is to be your God and you are to walk in his ways and observe his statutes, commandments and decrees, and to hearken to his voice. And today the LORD is making this agreement with you: you are to be a people peculiarly his own, as he promised you; and provided you keep all his commandments, he will then raise you high in praise and renown and glory above all other nations he has made, and you will be a people sacred to the LORD, your God, as he promised."— The word of the Lord. ℟. **Thanks be to God.** ↓

RESPONSORIAL PSALM Ps 119:1-2, 4-5, 7-8

℟. (1b) **Blessed are they who follow the law of the Lord!**

Blessed are they whose way is blameless,
  who walk in the law of the LORD.
Blessed are they who observe his decrees,
  who seek him with all their heart.—℟.

You have commanded that your precepts
  be diligently kept.
Oh, that I might be firm in the ways
  of keeping your statutes!—℟.

I will give you thanks with an upright heart,
  when I have learned your just ordinances.

I will keep your statutes;
do not utterly forsake me.—℟. ↓

VERSE BEFORE THE GOSPEL   2 Cor 6:2b

℟. **Glory to you, Lord Jesus Christ, Wisdom of God the Father!***
Behold, now is a very acceptable time;
behold, now is the day of salvation.
℟. **Glory to you, Lord Jesus Christ, Wisdom of God the Father!** ↓

GOSPEL   Mt 5:43-48

The law of Christian love is not hard to practice when no harm has been done, but to love an enemy is difficult. Jesus' command is to love our enemies and pray for our persecutors. In this way, we become perfect.

℣. The Lord be with you. ℟. **And also with you.**
℣. A reading from the holy Gospel according to Matthew.
℟. **Glory to you, Lord.**

JESUS said to his disciples: "You have heard that it was said, *You shall love your neighbor and hate your enemy.* But I say to you, love your enemies, and pray for those who persecute you, that you may be children of your heavenly Father, for he makes his sun rise on the bad and the good, and causes rain to fall on the just and the unjust. For if you love those who love you, what recompense will you have? Do not the tax collectors do the same? And if you greet your brothers and sisters only, what is unusual about that? Do not the pagans do the same? So be perfect, just as your heavenly Father is perfect."—The Gospel of the Lord. ℟. **Praise to you, Lord Jesus Christ.**

→ No. 15, p. 623

PRAYER OVER THE GIFTS
Lord,
may we be renewed by this eucharist.

* *See p. 620 for other Gospel Acclamations.*

May we become more like Christ your Son,
who is Lord for ever and ever.
℞. **Amen.** ➜ No. 21, p. 626 (Pref. P 8-11)

COMMUNION ANT. Mt 5:48

Be perfect, as your heavenly Father is perfect, says the Lord. ↓

PRAYER AFTER COMMUNION

Lord,
may the word we share
be our guide to peace in your kingdom.
May the food we receive
assure us of your constant love.
We ask this in the name of Jesus the Lord.
℞. **Amen.** ➜ No. 32, p. 660

MONDAY OF THE SECOND WEEK OF LENT

The Mass today teaches us not to look around for someone to accuse and to blame. We should recognize our own personal sinfulness and not be too ready to give ourselves absolution. How often do we pray: "Forgive us our trespasses as we forgive those who trespass against us"?

ENTRANCE ANT. Ps 26:11-12

Redeem me, Lord, and have mercy on me; my foot is set on the right path, I worship you in the great assembly.
➜ No. 2, p. 614

OPENING PRAYER

God our Father,
teach us to find new life through penance.
Keep us from sin,
and help us live by your commandment of love.
We ask this . . . for ever and ever. ℞. **Amen.** ↓

FIRST READING Dn 9:4b-10

Daniel makes a sort of national act of contrition. Punishments on a people must be suffered right here when there is a question of corporate blame for defying God's law, or credit for keeping it.

A reading from the Book of the Prophet Daniel

"LORD, great and awesome God, you who keep your merciful covenant toward those who love you and observe your commandments! We have sinned, been wicked and done evil; we have rebelled and departed from your commandments and your laws. We have not obeyed your servants the prophets, who spoke in your name to our kings, our princes, our fathers, and all the people of the land. Justice, O Lord, is on your side; we are shamefaced even to this day: we, the men of Judah, the residents of Jerusalem, and all Israel, near and far, in all the countries to which you have scattered them because of their treachery toward you. O LORD, we are shamefaced, like our kings, our princes, and our fathers, for having sinned against you. But yours, O Lord, our God, are compassion and forgiveness! Yet we rebelled against you and paid no heed to your command, O LORD, our God, to live by the law you gave us through your servants the prophets."—The word of the Lord. ℞. **Thanks be to God.** ↓

RESPONSORIAL PSALM Ps 79:8, 9, 11 and 13

℞. (see Ps 103:10a) **Lord, do not deal with us according to our sins.**

See Wednesday of the 8th Week—Year II, p. 377.

VERSE BEFORE THE GOSPEL Jn 6:63c, 68c

℞. **Glory to you, Word of God, Lord Jesus Christ!***
Your words, Lord, are Spirit and life;
you have the words of everlasting life.
℞. **Glory to you, Word of God, Lord Jesus Christ!** ↓

---

* See p. 620 *for other Gospel Acclamations.*

GOSPEL

Lk 6:36-38

Jesus teaches that his disciples should be compassionate, should not judge others, should not condemn. Pardon, forgiveness, generosity are marks of a Christian. Measure for measure is the reward.

℣. The Lord be with you. ℟. **And also with you.**
℣. A reading from the holy Gospel according to Luke.
℟. **Glory to you, Lord.**

JESUS said to his disciples: "Be merciful, just as your Father is merciful.

"Stop judging and you will not be judged. Stop condemning and you will not be condemned. Forgive and you will be forgiven. Give and gifts will be given to you; a good measure, packed together, shaken down, and overflowing, will be poured into your lap. For the measure with which you measure will in return be measured out to you."—The Gospel of the Lord. ℟. **Praise to you, Lord Jesus Christ.** → No. 15, p. 623

PRAYER OVER THE GIFTS

Father of mercy,
hear our prayer.
May the grace of this mystery
prevent us from becoming absorbed in material things.
Grant this through Christ our Lord.
℟. **Amen.** → No. 21, p. 626 (Pref. P 8-11)

COMMUNION ANT.

Lk 6:36

Be merciful as your Father is merciful, says the Lord. ↓

PRAYER AFTER COMMUNION

Lord,
may this communion bring us pardon
and lead us to the joy of heaven.
We ask this in the name of Jesus the Lord.
℟. **Amen.** → No. 32, p. 660

TUESDAY OF THE SECOND WEEK OF LENT

No advance in virtue is possible until we know our faults, and know them as God knows them. A full knowledge of past sinfulness ought to be reached by mere memory. But that faculty gives us only facts and figures. It takes no reckoning of guilt, which enters the Christian's mind through a supernatural influence. One of our rudimentary graces is appreciation of sin.

ENTRANCE ANT. Ps 13:4-5

Give light to my eyes, Lord, lest I sleep in death, and my enemy say: I have overcome him. ➙ No. 2, p. 614

OPENING PRAYER

Lord,
watch over your Church,
and guide it with your unfailing love.
Protect us from what could harm us
and lead us to what will save us.
Help us always,
for without you we are bound to fail.
Grant this . . . for ever and ever. ℞. **Amen.** ↓

FIRST READING Is 1:10, 16-20

The prophets spoke out and most of them met a sudden death. "Your hands are full of blood," Isaiah warns, and he tells the people to wash themselves clean. In repentance sins are washed clean as snow. The obstinate will suffer by the sword.

A reading from the Book of the Prophet Isaiah

HEAR the word of the LORD,
princes of Sodom!
Listen to the instruction of our God,
people of Gomorrah!

Wash yourselves clean!
Put away your misdeeds from before my eyes;
cease doing evil; learn to do good.
Make justice your aim: redress the wronged,
hear the orphan's plea, defend the widow.

Come now, let us set things right,
says the LORD:

Though your sins be like scarlet,
  they may become white as snow;
Though they be crimson red,
  they may become white as wool.
If you are willing, and obey,
  you shall eat the good things of the land;
But if you refuse and resist,
  the sword shall consume you:
    for the mouth of the LORD has spoken!
The word of the Lord. ℟. **Thanks be to God.** ↓

RESPONSORIAL PSALM   Ps 50:8-9, 16bc-17, 21 and 23

℟. (23b) **To the upright I will show the saving power of God.**

"Not for your sacrifices do I rebuke you,
  for your burnt offerings are before me always.
I take from your house no bullock,
  no goats out of your fold."—℟.

"Why do you recite my statutes,
  and profess my covenant with your mouth,
Though you hate discipline
  and cast my words behind you?"—℟.

"When you do these things, shall I be deaf to it?
  Or do you think that I am like yourself?
  I will correct you by drawing them up before your
    eyes.
He that offers praise as a sacrifice glorifies me;
  and to him that goes the right way I will show the sal-
    vation of God."—℟. ↓

VERSE BEFORE THE GOSPEL   Ez 18:31

℟. **Glory to you, Word of God, Lord Jesus Christ!***
Cast away from you all the crimes you have committed,
  says the Lord,
and make for yourselves a new heart and a new spirit.
℟. **Glory to you, Word of God, Lord Jesus Christ!** ↓

---

* *See p. 620 for other Gospel Acclamations.*

GOSPEL

Mt 23:1-12

Christ complains about the rigor of scribal interpretation and the vanity and hypocrisy of the scribes and Pharisees. The Pharisees do not practice what they preach. Jesus teaches by his humble example.

℣. The Lord be with you. ℟. **And also with you.**

℣. A reading from the holy Gospel according to Matthew. ℟. **Glory to you, Lord.**

JESUS spoke to the crowds and to his disciples, saying, "The scribes and the Pharisees have taken their seat on the chair of Moses. Therefore, do and observe all things whatsoever they tell you, but do not follow their example. For they preach but they do not practice. They tie up heavy burdens hard to carry and lay them on people's shoulders, but they will not lift a finger to move them. All their works are performed to be seen. They widen their phylacteries and lengthen their tassels. They love places of honor at banquets, seats of honor in synagogues, greetings in marketplaces, and the salutation 'Rabbi.' As for you, do not be called 'Rabbi.' You have but one teacher, and you are all brothers. Call no one on earth your father; you have but one Father in heaven. Do not be called 'Master'; you have but one master, the Christ. The greatest among you must be your servant. Whoever exalts himself will be humbled; but whoever humbles himself will be exalted."—The Gospel of the Lord. ℟. **Praise to you, Lord Jesus Christ.**   ➔ No. 15, p. 623

PRAYER OVER THE GIFTS

Lord,
bring us closer to you by this celebration.
May it cleanse us from our faults
and lead us to the gifts of heaven.
We ask this through Christ our Lord.
℟. **Amen.**   ➔ No. 21, p. 626 (Pref. P 8-11)

COMMUNION ANT.

Ps 9:2-3

I will tell all your marvelous works. I will rejoice and be glad in you, and sing to your name, Most High. ↓

PRAYER AFTER COMMUNION

Lord,
may the food we receive
bring us your constant assistance
that we may live better lives.
We ask this in the name of Jesus the Lord.
R̝. **Amen.**   → No. 32, p. 660

WEDNESDAY OF THE SECOND WEEK OF LENT

We should be honest enough to behave before others according to God's knowledge of human beings. How would our thoughts, words, and deeds stand examination before Christ? Let us follow the Master's maxim: "If any man desires to be first, he shall be the last of all and the minister of all" (Mk 9:35).

ENTRANCE ANT.   Ps 38:22-23

Do not abandon me, Lord. My God, do not go away from me! Hurry to help me, Lord, my Savior.   → No. 2, p. 614

OPENING PRAYER

Father,
teach us to live good lives,
encourage us with your support
and bring us to eternal life.
We ask this . . . for ever and ever. R̝. **Amen.** ↓

FIRST READING   Jer 18:18-20

Although his enemies plot to destroy Jeremiah, he prays for them: "Remember that I stood before you to speak in their behalf, to turn away your wrath from them." However, God's forgiveness has to be earned by a change of heart, by repentance.

A reading from the Book of the Prophet Jeremiah

THE people of Judah and the citizens of Jerusalem said, "Come, let us contrive a plot against Jeremiah. It will not mean the loss of instruction from the priests, nor of counsel from the wise, nor of messages from the prophets. And so, let us destroy him by his own tongue; let us carefully note his every word."

Heed me, O LORD,
    and listen to what my adversaries say.
Must good be repaid with evil
    that they should dig a pit to take my life?
Remember that I stood before you
    to speak in their behalf,
    to turn away your wrath from them.

The word of the Lord. ℟. **Thanks be to God.** ↓

RESPONSORIAL PSALM   Ps 31:5-6, 14, 15-16

℟. (17b) **Save me, O Lord, in your kindness.**

You will free me from the snare they set for me,
    for you are my refuge.
Into your hands I commend my spirit;
    you will redeem me, O LORD, O faithful God.—℟.

I hear the whispers of the crowd, that frighten me from
      every side,
    as they consult together against me, plotting to take
    my life.—℟.

But my trust is in you, O LORD;
    I say, "You are my God."
In your hands is my destiny; rescue me
    from the clutches of my enemies and my persecu-
    tors.—℟. ↓

VERSE BEFORE THE GOSPEL   Jn 8:12

℟. **Glory to you, Word of God, Lord Jesus Christ!***
I am the light of the world, says the Lord;
whoever follows me will have the light of life.
℟. **Glory to you, Word of God, Lord Jesus Christ!** ↓

GOSPEL   Mt 20:17-28

The last journey to Jerusalem and the mentioning of the cross are here used for the first time. The ransom of all human beings will be paid by

---

* *See p. 620 for other Gospel Acclamations.*

Christ by his own life. Jesus replies to the mother of Zebedee's sons by promising they will drink his cup to the full but his Father alone will award the places of honor in the next life. Anyone who aspires to greatness must be willing to serve.

℣. The Lord be with you. ℟. **And also with you.**

℣. A reading from the holy Gospel according to Matthew. ℟. **Glory to you, Lord.**

AS Jesus was going up to Jerusalem, he took the Twelve disciples aside by themselves, and said to them on the way, "Behold, we are going up to Jerusalem, and the Son of Man will be handed over to the chief priests and the scribes, and they will condemn him to death, and hand him over to the Gentiles to be mocked and scourged and crucified, and he will be raised on the third day."

Then the mother of the sons of Zebedee approached Jesus with her sons and did him homage, wishing to ask him for something. He said to her, "What do you wish?" She answered him, "Command that these two sons of mine sit, one at your right and the other at your left, in your kingdom." Jesus said in reply, "You do not know what you are asking. Can you drink the chalice that I am going to drink?" They said to him, "We can." He replied, "My chalice you will indeed drink, but to sit at my right and at my left, this is not mine to give but is for those for whom it has been prepared by my Father." When the ten heard this, they became indignant at the two brothers. But Jesus summoned them and said, "You know that the rulers of the Gentiles lord it over them, and the great ones make their authority over them felt. But it shall not be so among you. Rather, whoever wishes to be great among you shall be your servant; whoever wishes to be first among you shall be your slave. Just so, the Son of Man did not come to be served but to serve and to give his life as a ransom for many."—The Gospel of the Lord. ℟. **Praise to you, Lord Jesus Christ.** ➜ No. 15, p. 623

PRAYER OVER THE GIFTS

Lord,
accept this sacrifice,
and through this holy exchange of gifts
free us from the sins that enslave us.
We ask this in the name of Jesus the Lord.
℞. **Amen.** ➙ No. 21, p. 626 (Pref. P 8-11)

COMMUNION ANT. Mt 20:28

The Son of Man did not come to be served, but to serve, and to give his life as a ransom for many. ↓

PRAYER AFTER COMMUNION

Lord our God,
may the eucharist you give us
as a pledge of unending life
help us to salvation.
Grant this through Christ our Lord.
℞. **Amen.** ➙ No. 32, p. 660

THURSDAY OF THE SECOND WEEK OF LENT

To be detached from all material comforts for Jesus' sake is to be poor in spirit. We can be truly poor in spirit, not only by helping but also by deeply sympathizing with those who are poor. Poverty is closely related to holy wisdom. Jesus said of himself: "Foxes have dens and birds of the sky have nests, but the Son of Man has nowhere to rest his head" (Mt 8:20).

ENTRANCE ANT Ps 139:23-24

Test me, O God, and know my thoughts; see whether I step in the wrong path, and guide me along the everlasting way. ➙ No. 2, p. 614

OPENING PRAYER

God of love,
bring us back to you.
Send your Spirit to make us strong in faith
and active in good works.
Grant this . . . for ever and ever. ℞. **Amen.** ↓

FIRST READING Jer 17:5-10

Jeremiah paints a beautiful picture of fidelity in his prophecy. Just as a person cannot depend upon other human beings in some of the crises of life, so others cannot depend upon that person either unless he or she has an authentic and direct relation to God.

A reading from the Book of the Prophet Jeremiah

THUS says the LORD:
Cursed is the man who trusts in human beings,
   who seeks his strength in flesh,
   whose heart turns away from the LORD.
He is like a barren bush in the desert
   that enjoys no change of season,
But stands in a lava waste,
   a salt and empty earth.
Blessed is the man who trusts in the LORD,
   whose hope is the LORD.
He is like a tree planted beside the waters
   that stretches out its roots to the stream:
It fears not the heat when it comes,
   its leaves stay green;
In the year of drought it shows no distress,
   but still bears fruit.
More tortuous than all else is the human heart,
   beyond remedy; who can understand it?
I, the LORD, alone probe the mind
   and test the heart,
To reward everyone according to his ways,
   according to the merit of his deeds.
The word of the Lord. ℟. **Thanks be to God.** ↓

RESPONSORIAL PSALM Ps 1:1-2, 3, 4-6

℟. (Ps 40:5a) **Blessed are they who hope in the Lord.**

Blessed the man who follows not
   the counsel of the wicked
Nor walks in the way of sinners,
   nor sits in the company of the insolent,

But delights in the law of the LORD
    and meditates on his law day and night.—℟.

He is like a tree
    planted near running water,
That yields its fruit in due season,
    and whose leaves never fade.
      Whatever he does, prospers.—℟.

Not so, the wicked, not so;
    they are like chaff which the wind drives away.
For the LORD watches over the way of the just,
    but the way of the wicked vanishes.—℟. ↓

VERSE BEFORE THE GOSPEL   See Lk 8:15
℟. **Glory to you, Word of God, Lord Jesus Christ!***
Blessed are they who have kept the word with a gener-
    ous heart
and yield a harvest through perseverance.
℟. **Glory to you, Word of God, Lord Jesus Christ!** ↓

GOSPEL   Lk 16:19-31

In this story of the rich man and Lazarus, our Lord addresses the Pharisees who are fond of money. Those who make bad use of earthly riches will be punished with everlasting torments, while those who follow Christ's example and lead poor but virtuous lives will be eternally rewarded.

℣. The Lord be with you. ℟. **And also with you.**
℣. A reading from the holy Gospel according to Luke.
℟. **Glory to you, Lord.**

JESUS said to the Pharisees: "There was a rich man who dressed in purple garments and fine linen and dined sumptuously each day. And lying at his door was a poor man named Lazarus, covered with sores, who would gladly have eaten his fill of the scraps that fell from the rich man's table. Dogs even used to come and

---

* See p. 620 for other Gospel Acclamations.

lick his sores. When the poor man died, he was carried away by angels to the bosom of Abraham. The rich man also died and was buried, and from the netherworld, where he was in torment, he raised his eyes and saw Abraham far off and Lazarus at his side. And he cried out, 'Father Abraham, have pity on me. Send Lazarus to dip the tip of his finger in water and cool my tongue, for I am suffering torment in these flames.' Abraham replied, 'My child, remember that you received what was good during your lifetime while Lazarus likewise received what was bad; but now he is comforted here, whereas you are tormented. Moreover, between us and you a great chasm is established to prevent anyone from crossing who might wish to go from our side to yours or from your side to ours.' He said, 'Then I beg you, father, send him to my father's house, for I have five brothers, so that he may warn them, lest they too come to this place of torment.' But Abraham replied, 'They have Moses and the prophets. Let them listen to them.' He said, 'Oh no, father Abraham, but if someone from the dead goes to them, they will repent.' Then Abraham said, 'If they will not listen to Moses and the prophets, neither will they be persuaded if someone should rise from the dead.'"—The Gospel of the Lord. ℟. **Praise to you, Lord Jesus Christ.**

→ No. 15, p. 623

PRAYER OVER THE GIFTS

Lord,
may this sacrifice bless our lenten observance.
May it lead us to sincere repentance.
We ask this through Christ our Lord.
℟. **Amen.**

→ No. 21, p. 626 (Pref. P 8-11)

COMMUNION ANT. Ps 119:1

Happy are those of blameless life, who follow the law of the Lord. ↓

PRAYER AFTER COMMUNION

Lord,
may the sacrifice we have offered strengthen our faith
and be seen in our love for one another.
We ask this in the name of Jesus the Lord.
R). **Amen.**   ➜ No. 32, p. 660

FRIDAY OF THE SECOND WEEK OF LENT

Envy is either a kind of sadness because of another's prosperity or joy at
his misfortunes. Such was the envy of Saul toward David, and of the
Pharisees toward Christ. Envy is one of the most detestable of vices
because it is so frequently found among us, and nothing else so destroys
individual happiness as well as the welfare of whole nations.

ENTRANCE ANT.   Ps 31:2, 5

To you, Lord, I look for protection, never let me be disgraced. You are my refuge; save me from the trap they have laid for me.   ➜ No. 2, p. 614

OPENING PRAYER

Merciful Father,
may our acts of penance bring us your forgiveness,
open our hearts to your love,
and prepare us for the coming feast of the resurrection.
We ask this . . . for ever and ever. R). **Amen.** ↓

FIRST READING   Gn 37:3-4, 12-13a, 17-28a

This reading reveals that God consistently brings good out of evil, success
out of failure, triumph out of defeat. Joseph is a type of the redeeming
Messiah. Jesus is loved by his Father, but rejected by his brothers, as
Joseph was.

A reading from the Book of Genesis

ISRAEL loved Joseph best of all his sons, for he was the
child of his old age; and he had made him a long tunic.

When his brothers saw that their father loved him best of all his sons, they hated him so much that they would not even greet him.

One day, when his brothers had gone to pasture their father's flocks at Shechem, Israel said to Joseph, "Your brothers, you know, are tending our flocks at Shechem. Get ready; I will send you to them."

So Joseph went after his brothers and caught up with them in Dothan. They noticed him from a distance, and before he came up to them, they plotted to kill him. They said to one another: "Here comes that master dreamer! Come on, let us kill him and throw him into one of the cisterns here; we could say that a wild beast devoured him. We shall then see what comes of his dreams."

When Reuben heard this, he tried to save him from their hands, saying, "We must not take his life. Instead of shedding blood," he continued, "just throw him into that cistern there in the desert; but do not kill him outright." His purpose was to rescue him from their hands and return him to his father. So when Joseph came up to them, they stripped him of the long tunic he had on; then they took him and threw him into the cistern, which was empty and dry.

They then sat down to their meal. Looking up, they saw a caravan of Ishmaelites coming from Gilead, their camels laden with gum, balm and resin to be taken down to Egypt. Judah said to his brothers: "What is to be gained by killing our brother and concealing his blood? Rather, let us sell him to these Ishmaelites, instead of doing away with him ourselves. After all, he is our brother, our own flesh." His brothers agreed. They sold Joseph to the Ishmaelites for twenty pieces of silver. —The word of the Lord. ℟. **Thanks be to God.** ↓

RESPONSORIAL PSALM   Ps 105:16-17, 18-19, 20-21

℟. (5a) **Remember the marvels the Lord has done.**

When the LORD called down a famine on the land
and ruined the crop that sustained them,
He sent a man before them,
Joseph, sold as a slave.—R̠.

They had weighed him down with fetters,
and he was bound with chains,
Till his prediction came to pass
and the word of the LORD proved him true.—R̠.

The king sent and released him,
the ruler of the peoples set him free.
He made him lord of his house
and ruler of all his possessions.—R̠. ↓

VERSE BEFORE THE GOSPEL   Jn 3:16

R̠. **Glory to you, Word of God, Lord Jesus Christ!***
God so loved the world that he gave his only-begotten
Son;
so that everyone who believes in him might have eternal
life.
R̠. **Glory to you, Word of God, Lord Jesus Christ!** ↓

GOSPEL   Mt 21:33-43, 45-46

The theme of Joseph is carried into the Gospel. It represents the same
principle: what is rejected by human beings may become vital for salvation. The chosen people who reject Christ are really turning him over to the
whole world.

V̠. The Lord be with you. R̠. **And also with you.**
V̠. A reading from the holy Gospel according to Matthew.
R̠. **Glory to you, Lord.**

JESUS said to the chief priests and the elders of the
people: "Hear another parable. There was a landowner
who planted a vineyard, put a hedge around it, dug a
wine press in it, and built a tower. Then he leased it to tenants and went on a journey. When vintage time drew

---

* *See p. 620 for other Gospel Acclamations.*

near, he sent his servants to the tenants to obtain his produce. But the tenants seized the servants and one they beat, another they killed, and a third they stoned. Again he sent other servants, more numerous than the first ones, but they treated them in the same way. Finally, he sent his son to them, thinking, 'They will respect my son.' But when the tenants saw the son, they said to one another, 'This is the heir. Come, let us kill him and acquire his inheritance.' They seized him, threw him out of the vineyard, and killed him. What will the owner of the vineyard do to those tenants when he comes?" They answered him, "He will put those wretched men to a wretched death and lease his vineyard to other tenants who will give him the produce at the proper times." Jesus said to them, "Did you never read in the Scriptures:

> *The stone that the builders rejected*
> *has become the cornerstone;*
> *by the Lord has this been done,*
> *and it is wonderful in our eyes*?

Therefore, I say to you, the Kingdom of God will be taken away from you and given to a people that will produce its fruit." When the chief priests and the Pharisees heard his parables, they knew that he was speaking about them. And although they were attempting to arrest him, they feared the crowds, for they regarded him as a prophet.— The Gospel of the Lord. ℟. **Praise to you, Lord Jesus Christ.**   → No. 15, p. 623

PRAYER OVER THE GIFTS

God of mercy,
prepare us to celebrate these mysteries.
Help us to live the love they proclaim.
We ask this in the name of Jesus the Lord.
℟. **Amen.**   → No. 21, p. 626 (Pref. P 8-11)

COMMUNION ANT.   1 Jn 4:10

God loved us and sent his Son to take away our sins. ↓

PRAYER AFTER COMMUNION

Lord,
may this communion so change our lives
that we may seek more faithfully
the salvation it promises.
Grant this through Christ our Lord.
℟. **Amen.**   → No. 32, p. 660

SATURDAY OF THE SECOND WEEK OF LENT

The two passages from the Bible for today's Mass are closely related. They are trustworthy testimony to the willingness of God the Father to receive everyone at all times with the most compassionate love. His love embraces even the greatest of sinners who truly repents. His mercy is unlimited for the contrite. How we must love God in his goodness!

ENTRANCE ANT   Ps 145:8-9

The Lord is loving and merciful, to anger slow, and full of love; the Lord is kind to all, and compassionate to all his creatures.   → No. 2, p. 614

OPENING PRAYER

God our Father,
by your gifts to us on earth
we already share in your life.
In all we do,
guide us to the light of your kingdom.
Grant this . . . for ever and ever. ℟. **Amen.** ↓

FIRST READING   Mi 7:14-15, 18-20

Micah denounced Israel's sins, particularly its social crimes, and he wrote about a new Israel. the latter idea may have a hidden reference to the future redemption of humanity by Christ and the founding of the Kingdom of God. Micah is presenting God in his readiness to forgive the contrite.

A reading from the Book of the Prophet Micah

SHEPHERD your people with your staff,
the flock of your inheritance,

That dwells apart in a woodland,
  in the midst of Carmel.
Let them feed in Bashan and Gilead,
  as in the days of old;
As in the days when you came from the land of Egypt,
  show us wonderful signs.

Who is there like you, the God who removes guilt
  and pardons sin for the remnant of his inheritance;
Who does not persist in anger forever,
  but delights rather in clemency,
And will again have compassion on us,
  treading underfoot our guilt?
You will cast into the depths of the sea all our sins;
You will show faithfulness to Jacob,
  and grace to Abraham,
As you have sworn to our fathers
  from days of old.
The word of the Lord. ℞. **Thanks be to God.** ↓

RESPONSORIAL PSALM   Ps 103:1-2, 3-4, 9-10, 11-12

℞. (8a) **The Lord is kind and merciful.**

Bless the LORD, O my soul;
  and all my being, bless his holy name.
Bless the LORD, O my soul,
  and forget not all his benefits.—℞.

He pardons all your iniquities,
  he heals all your ills.
He redeems your life from destruction,
  he crowns you with kindness and compassion.—℞.

He will not always chide,
  nor does he keep his wrath forever.
Not according to our sins does he deal with us,
  nor does he requite us according to our crimes.—℞.

For as the heavens are high above the earth,
  so surpassing is his kindness toward those who fear
    him.

As far as the east is from the west,
   so far has he put our transgressions from us.—℟. ↓

VERSE BEFORE THE GOSPEL   Lk 15:18

℟. **Glory to you, Word of God, Lord Jesus Christ!***
I will get up and go to my father and shall say to him,
Father, I have sinned against heaven and against you.
℟. **Glory to you, Word of God, Lord Jesus Christ!** ↓

GOSPEL   Lk 15:1-3, 11-32

The story of the Prodigal Son is the ideal story of contrition. He resents the
boredom of family life and discipline and so asserts his rights, but he
soon finds out that his total freedom is bringing him nothing but misery.
The father receives his son back and forgives him.

℣. The Lord be with you. ℟. **And also with you.**
℣. A reading from the holy Gospel according to Luke.
℟. **Glory to you, Lord.**

TAX collectors and sinners were all drawing near to
listen to Jesus, but the Pharisees and scribes began to
complain, saying, "This man welcomes sinners and eats
with them." So to them Jesus addressed this parable. "A
man had two sons, and the younger son said to his father,
'Father, give me the share of your estate that should come
to me.' So the father divided the property between them.
After a few days, the younger son collected all his
belongings and set off to a distant country where he
squandered his inheritance on a life of dissipation. When
he had freely spent everything, a severe famine struck
that country, and he found himself in dire need. So he
hired himself out to one of the local citizens who sent
him to his farm to tend the swine. And he longed to eat
his fill of the pods on which the swine fed, but nobody
gave him any. Coming to his senses he thought, 'How
many of my father's hired workers have more than
enough food to eat, but here am I, dying from hunger. I
shall get up and go to my father and I shall say to him,

---

* *See p. 620 for other Gospel Acclamations.*

"Father, I have sinned against heaven and against you. I no longer deserve to be called your son; treat me as you would treat one of your hired workers." ' So he got up and went back to his father. While he was still a long way off, his father caught sight of him, and was filled with compassion. He ran to his son, embraced him and kissed him. His son said to him, 'Father, I have sinned against heaven and against you; I no longer deserve to be called your son.' But his father ordered his servants, 'Quickly, bring the finest robe and put it on him; put a ring on his finger and sandals on his feet. Take the fattened calf and slaughter it. Then let us celebrate with a feast, because this son of mine was dead, and has come to life again; he was lost, and has been found.' Then the celebration began. Now the older son had been out in the field and, on his way back, as he neared the house, he heard the sound of music and dancing. He called one of the servants and asked what this might mean. The servant said to him, 'Your brother has returned and your father has slaughtered the fattened calf because he has him back safe and sound.' He became angry, and when he refused to enter the house, his father came out and pleaded with him. He said to his father in reply, 'Look, all these years I served you and not once did I disobey your orders; yet you never gave me even a young goat to feast on with my friends. But when your son returns who swallowed up your property with prostitutes, for him you slaughter the fattened calf.' He said to him, 'My son, you are here with me always; everything I have is yours. But now we must celebrate and rejoice, because your brother was dead and has come to life again; he was lost and has been found.' "—The Gospel of the Lord. ℞. **Praise to you, Lord Jesus Christ.**   → No. 15, p. 623

PRAYER OVER THE GIFTS

Lord,
may the grace of these sacraments

help us to reject all harmful things
and lead us to your spiritual gifts.
We ask this through Christ our Lord.
℟. **Amen.** → No. 21, p. 626 (Pref. P 8-11)

COMMUNION ANT. Lk 15:32

**My son, you should rejoice, because your brother was
dead and has come back to life; he was lost and is
found.** ↓

PRAYER AFTER COMMUNION

Lord,
give us the spirit of love
and lead us to share in your life.
We ask this in the name of Jesus the Lord.
℟. **Amen.** → No. 32, p. 660

_____

OPTIONAL READINGS AND INTERVENIENT
CHANTS FOR THE THIRD WEEK OF LENT

*These Readings and Intervenient Chants may be used on any
day of this week, especially when the Gospel of the Samaritan
woman is not read on the 3rd Sunday of Lent.*

FIRST READING Ex 17:1-7

The journey through the desert presents numerous difficulties for the
Israelites. They have been specially cared for by God, but now they are
without water. Impatient with Moses, they begin to complain. When Moses
asks God for help, water miraculously comes from out of a rock.

A reading from the Book of Exodus

FROM the desert of Sin the whole congregation of the
children of Israel journeyed by stages, as the LORD
directed, and encamped at Rephidim.

There was no water for the people to drink. They
quarreled, therefore, with Moses and said, "Give us water
to drink." Moses replied, "Why do you quarrel with me?
Why do you put the LORD to a test?" Then, in their thirst
for water, the people grumbled against Moses, saying,
"Why did you ever make us leave Egypt? Was it just to

have us die here of thirst with our children and our live-stock?" So Moses cried out to the LORD, "What shall I do with this people? A little more and they will stone me!" The LORD answered Moses, "Go over there in front of the people, along with some of the elders of Israel, holding in your hand, as you go, the staff with which you struck the river. I will be standing there in front of you on the rock in Horeb. Strike the rock, and the water will flow from it for the people to drink." This Moses did, in the presence of the elders of Israel. The place was called Massah and Meribah, because the children of Israel quarreled there and tested the LORD, saying, "Is the Lord in our midst or not?"—The word of the Lord. ℟. **Thanks be to God.** ↓

RESPONSORIAL PSALM　　　　Ps 95:1-2, 6-7ab, 7c-9
See Thursday of the 3rd Week of Lent, p. 491.

VERSE BEFORE THE GOSPEL　　　　See Jn 4:42, 15

℟. **Glory to you, Lord Jesus Christ, Son of the living God!***
Lord, you are truly the Savior of the world;
give me living water, that I may never thirst again.
℟. **Glory to you, Lord Jesus Christ, Son of the living God!** ↓

GOSPEL　　　　Jn 4:5-42

Just as God gave water to the Israelites in the desert, Jesus offers the Samaritan woman at the well life-giving water that will provide eternal life. He also shows her that he knows her past. She recognizes Jesus as a prophet, and Jesus admits that he is the Messiah.

℣. The Lord be with you. ℟. **And also with you.**
℣. A reading from the holy Gospel according to John.
℟. **Glory to you, Lord.**

AT that time, Jesus came to a town of Samaria called Sychar, near the plot of land that Jacob had given to his son Joseph. Jacob's well was there. Jesus, tired from his journey, sat down there at the well. It was about noon.

———
* See p. 620 for other Gospel Acclamations.

A woman of Samaria came to draw water. Jesus said to her, "Give me a drink." His disciples had gone into the town to buy food. The Samaritan woman said to him, "How can you, a Jew, ask me, a Samaritan woman, for a drink?"—For Jews use nothing in common with Samaritans.—Jesus answered and said to her, "If you knew the gift of God and who is saying to you, 'Give me a drink,' you would have asked him and he would have given you living water." The woman said to him, "Sir, you do not even have a bucket and the cistern is deep; where then can you get this living water? Are you greater than our father Jacob, who gave us this cistern and drank from it himself with his children and his flocks?" Jesus answered and said to her, "Everyone who drinks this water will be thirsty again; but whoever drinks the water I shall give will never thirst; the water I shall give will become in him a spring of water welling up to eternal life." The woman said to him, "Sir, give me this water, so that I may not be thirsty or have to keep coming here to draw water."

Jesus said to her, "Go call your husband and come back." The woman answered and said to him, "I do not have a husband." Jesus answered her, "You are right in saying, 'I do not have a husband.' For you have had five husbands, and the one you have now is not your husband. What you have said is true." The woman said to him, "Sir, I can see that you are a prophet. Our ancestors worshiped on this mountain; but you people say that the place to worship is in Jerusalem." Jesus said to her, "Believe me, woman, the hour is coming when you will worship the Father neither on this mountain nor in Jerusalem. You people worship what you do not understand; we worship what we understand, because salvation is from the Jews. But the hour is coming, and is now here, when true worshipers will worship the Father in Spirit and truth; and indeed the Father seeks such people to worship him. God is Spirit, and those who worship him must worship in Spirit and truth." The woman said to him, "I know that the Christ is coming, the one called the Anointed; when he comes, he will tell us everything." Jesus said to her, "I am he, the one speaking with you."

At that moment his disciples returned, and were amazed that he was talking with a woman, but still no one said, "What are you looking for?" or "Why are you talking with her?" The woman left her water jar and went into the town and said to the people, "Come see a man who told me everything I have done. Could he possibly be the Christ?" They went out of the town and came to him. Meanwhile, the disciples urged him, "Rabbi, eat." But he said to them, "I have food to eat of which you do not know." So the disciples said to one another, "Could someone have brought him something to eat?" Jesus said to them, "My food is to do the will of the one who sent me and to finish his work. Do you not say, 'In four months the harvest will be here'? I tell you, look up and see the fields ripe for the harvest. The reaper is already receiving payment and gathering crops for eternal life, so that the sower and reaper can rejoice together. For here the saying is verified that 'One sows and another reaps.' I sent you to reap what you have not worked for; others have done the work, and you are sharing the fruits of their work."

Many of the Samaritans of that town began to believe in him because of the word of the woman who testified, "He told me everything I have done." When the Samaritans came to him, they invited him to stay with them; and he stayed there two days. Many more began to believe in him because of his word, and they said to the woman, "We no longer believe because of your word; for we have heard for ourselves, and we know that this is truly the savior of the world."—The Gospel of the Lord. ℟. **Praise to you, Lord Jesus Christ.** ➔ No. 15, p. 623

MONDAY OF THE THIRD WEEK OF LENT

The Gentiles may not be as worthy as the Jews, but God in his mercy has chosen us for his own. The Nazarenes despised our Savior because of his humble birth, but when they learned of his miracles, they asked that he would also heal their sick. But he refused their request because they were without faith. If we desire not to be abandoned by God, as were the Nazarenes, we must have a lively faith. This is a gift of God for which we should daily pray.

ENTRANCE ANT.   Ps 84:3

My soul is longing and pining for the courts of the Lord; my heart and my flesh sing for joy to the living God.

→ No. 2, p. 614

OPENING PRAYER

God of mercy,
free your Church from sin
and protect it from evil.
Guide us, for we cannot be saved without you.
We ask this . . . for ever and ever. ℟. **Amen.** ↓

FIRST READING   2 Kgs 5:1-15ab

The story of the cure of Naaman represents an important point in the process of the forgiveness of sin. The cure of leprosy is a good comparison. When Naaman is cured after doing what he is told, he cannot help exclaiming: "Now I know that there is no God in all the earth, except in Israel!"

A reading from the second Book of Kings

Naaman, the army commander of the king of Aram, was highly esteemed and respected by his master, for through him the Lord had brought victory to Aram. But valiant as he was, the man was a leper. Now the Arameans had captured in a raid on the land of Israel a little girl, who became the servant of Naaman's wife. "If only my master would present himself to the prophet in Samaria," she said to her mistress, "he would cure him of his leprosy." Naaman went and told his lord just what the slave girl from the land of Israel had said. "Go," said the king of Aram. "I will send along a letter to the king of

Israel." So Naaman set out, taking along ten silver talents, six thousand gold pieces, and ten festal garments. To the king of Israel he brought the letter, which read: "With this letter I am sending my servant Naaman to you, that you may cure him of his leprosy."

When he read the letter, the king of Israel tore his garments and exclaimed: "Am I a god with power over life and death, that this man should send someone to me to be cured of leprosy? Take note! You can see he is only looking for a quarrel with me!" When Elisha, the man of God, heard that the king of Israel had torn his garments, he sent word to the king: "Why have you torn your garments? Let him come to me and find out that there is a prophet in Israel."

Naaman came with his horses and chariots and stopped at the door of Elisha's house. The prophet sent him the message: "Go and wash seven times in the Jordan, and your flesh will heal, and you will be clean." But Naaman went away angry, saying, "I thought that he would surely come out and stand there to invoke the LORD his God, and would move his hand over the spot, and thus cure the leprosy. Are not the rivers of Damascus, the Abana and the Pharpar, better than all the waters of Israel? Could I not wash in them and be cleansed?" With this, he turned about in anger and left.

But his servants came up and reasoned with him. "My father," they said, "if the prophet had told you to do something extraordinary, would you not have done it? All the more now, since he said to you, 'Wash and be clean,' should you do as he said." So Naaman went down and plunged into the Jordan seven times at the word of the man of God. His flesh became again like the flesh of a little child, and he was clean.

He returned with his whole retinue to the man of God. On his arrival he stood before him and said, "Now I know that there is no God in all the earth, except in Israel."— The word of the Lord. ℟. **Thanks be to God.** ↓

RESPONSORIAL PSALM	Pss 42:2, 3; 43:3, 4

℟. (see Ps 42:3) **Athirst is my soul for the living God.**
When shall I go and behold the face of God?

As the hind longs for the running waters,
  so my soul longs for you, O God.—℟.

Athirst is my soul for God, the living God.
  When shall I go and behold the face of God?—℟.

Send forth your light and your fidelity;
  they shall lead me on
And bring me to your holy mountain,
  to your dwelling-place.—℟.

Then will I go in to the altar of God,
  the God of my gladness and joy;
Then will I give you thanks upon the harp,
  O God, my God!—℟. ↓

VERSE BEFORE THE GOSPEL	See Ps 130:5, 7

℟. **Glory to you, Lord Jesus Christ, Son of the living God!***
I hope in the Lord, I trust in his word;
with him there is kindness and plenteous redemption.
℟. **Glory to you, Lord Jesus Christ, Son of the living**
God! ↓

GOSPEL	Lk 4:24-30

Our Lord reminds his hearers of the cure of the non-Jew Naaman. Part of
his message was that he was not accepted by his own people and that,
therefore, the wonders of his Kingdom would be shared by so-called out-
siders. A prophet is not without honor except in his native town.

℣. The Lord be with you. ℟. **And also with you.**
℣. A reading from the holy Gospel according to Luke.
℟. **Glory to you, Lord.**

JESUS said to the people in the synagogue at Nazareth:
  "Amen, I say to you, no prophet is accepted in his own

---

* *See p. 620 for other Gospel Acclamations.*

native place. Indeed, I tell you, there were many widows in Israel in the days of Elijah when the sky was closed for three and a half years and a severe famine spread over the entire land. It was to none of these that Elijah was sent, but only to a widow in Zarephath in the land of Sidon. Again, there were many lepers in Israel during the time of Elisha the prophet; yet not one of them was cleansed, but only Naaman the Syrian." When the people in the synagogue heard this, they were all filled with fury. They rose up, drove him out of the town, and led him to the brow of the hill on which their town had been built, to hurl him down headlong. But he passed through the midst of them and went away.—The Gospel of the Lord.
℟. **Praise to you, Lord Jesus Christ.**   ➔ No. 15, p. 623

PRAYER OVER THE GIFTS

Father,
bless these gifts
that they may become the sacrament of our salvation.
We ask this in the name of Jesus the Lord.
℟. **Amen.**   ➔ No. 21, p. 626 (Pref. P 8-11)

COMMUNION ANT.   Ps 117:1-2

All you nations, praise the Lord, for steadfast is his kindly mercy to us. ↓

PRAYER AFTER COMMUNION

Lord,
forgive the sins of those
who receive your sacrament,
and bring us together in unity and peace.
Grant this through Christ our Lord.
℟. **Amen.**   ➔ No. 32, p. 660

TUESDAY OF THE THIRD WEEK OF LENT

We cannot expect forgiveness unless we forgive others. The first and most important disposition necessary for obtaining pardon in the sacrament of Penance is a sincere sorrow for having offended God, which includes a firm resolution of sinning no more and a willing intention of satisfying God's justice.

ENTRANCE ANT.   Ps 17:6, 8

I call upon you, God, for you will answer me; bend your ear and hear my prayer. Guard me as the pupil of your eye; hide me in the shade of your wings. → No 2, p. 614

OPENING PRAYER

Lord,
you call us to your service
and continue your saving work among us.
May your love never abandon us.
We ask this . . . for ever and ever. ℟. **Amen.** ↓

FIRST READING   Dn 3:25, 34-43

Contrition for sin is a great act of worship. It takes deep faith, true humility, and complete obedience. The prayer of Azariah, whose Babylonian name was Abednego, is a national, public act of repentance. He prays to God with a contrite heart.

A reading from the Book of the Prophet Daniel

AZARIAH stood up in the fire and prayed aloud:

"For your name's sake, O Lord, do not deliver us up
     for ever,
   or make void your covenant.
Do not take away your mercy from us,
   for the sake of Abraham, your beloved,
   Isaac your servant, and Israel your holy one,
To whom you promised to multiply their offspring
   like the stars of heaven,
   or the sand on the shore of the sea.
For we are reduced, O Lord, beyond any other nation,
   brought low everywhere in the world this day
   because of our sins.
We have in our day no prince, prophet, or leader,
   no burnt offering, sacrifice, oblation, or incense,
   no place to offer first fruits, to find favor with you.

But with contrite heart and humble spirit
  let us be received;
As though it were burnt offerings of rams and bullocks,
  or thousands of fat lambs,
So let our sacrifice be in your presence today
  as we follow you unreservedly;
  for those who trust in you cannot be put to shame.
And now we follow you with our whole heart,
  we fear you and we pray to you.
Do not let us be put to shame,
  but deal with us in your kindness and great mercy.
Deliver us by your wonders,
  and bring glory to your name, O Lord."
The word of the Lord. ℟. **Thanks be to God.** ↓

RESPONSORIAL PSALM   Ps 25:4-5ab, 6 and 7bc, 8-9

℟. (6a) **Remember your mercies, O Lord.**

Your ways, O LORD, make known to me;
  teach me your paths,
Guide me in your truth and teach me,
  for you are God my savior.—℟.

Remember that your compassion, O LORD,
  and your kindness are from of old.
In your kindness remember me,
  because of your goodness, O LORD.

Good and upright is the LORD;
  thus he shows sinners the way.
He guides the humble to justice,
  he teaches the humble his way.—℟. ↓

VERSE BEFORE THE GOSPEL   Jl 2:12-13

℟. **Glory to you, Lord Jesus Christ, Son of the living
  God!***
Even now, says the LORD,
return to me with your whole heart;

---

* *See p. 620 for other Gospel Acclamations.*

for I am gracious and merciful.

℟. **Glory to you, Lord Jesus Christ, Son of the living God!** ↓

GOSPEL   Mt 18:21-35

Jesus teaches that forgiving others is a requirement for being forgiven. He presents an exaggerated difference of debt in the story. It is not the statistic he is emphasizing, but the need of forgiving others.

℣. The Lord be with you. ℟. **And also with you.**
℣. A reading from the holy Gospel according to Matthew.
℟. **Glory to you, Lord.**

PETER approached Jesus and asked him, "Lord, if my brother sins against me, how often must I forgive him? As many as seven times?" Jesus answered, "I say to you, not seven times but seventy-seven times. That is why the Kingdom of heaven may be likened to a king who decided to settle accounts with his servants. When he began the accounting, a debtor was brought before him who owed him a huge amount. Since he had no way of paying it back, his master ordered him to be sold, along with his wife, his children, and all his property, in payment of the debt. At that, the servant fell down, did him homage, and said, 'Be patient with me, and I will pay you back in full.' Moved with compassion the master of that servant let him go and forgave him the loan. When that servant had left, he found one of his fellow servants who owed him a much smaller amount. He seized him and started to choke him, demanding, 'Pay back what you owe.' Falling to his knees, his fellow servant begged him, 'Be patient with me, and I will pay you back.' But he refused. Instead, he had him put in prison until he paid back the debt. Now when his fellow servants saw what had happened, they were deeply disturbed, and went to their master and reported the whole affair. His master summoned him and said to him, 'You wicked servant! I forgave you your entire debt because you begged me to. Should you not have had pity on your fellow servant, as

I had pity on you?' Then in anger his master handed him over to the torturers until he should pay back the whole debt. So will my heavenly Father do to you, unless each of you forgives your brother from your heart."—The Gospel of the Lord. ℟. **Praise to you, Lord Jesus Christ.**

→ No. 15, p. 623

PRAYER OVER THE GIFTS

Lord,
may the saving sacrifice we offer
bring us your forgiveness,
so that freed from sin, we may always please you.
Grant this through Christ our Lord.
℟. **Amen.**   → No. 21, p. 626 (Pref. P 8-11)

COMMUNION ANT.   Ps 15:1-2

Lord, who may stay in your dwelling place? Who shall live on your holy mountain? He who walks without blame and does what is right. ↓

PRAYER AFTER COMMUNION

Lord,
may our sharing in this holy mystery
bring us your protection, forgiveness and life.
We ask this in the name of Jesus the Lord.
℟. **Amen.**   → No. 32, p. 660

WEDNESDAY OF THE THIRD WEEK OF LENT

The great obedience that shows our love of God is fidelity to conscience— to conscience enlightened by Christ's teaching in the Holy Church. To this is joined patient submission to God in our daily lives. This is especially applicable in this time of renewal. Let us be aware that the teachings of the Second Vatican Council were inspired by the Holy Spirit.

ENTRANCE ANT.   Ps 119:133

Lord, direct my steps as you have promised, and let no evil hold me in its power.   → No. 2, p. 614

OPENING PRAYER

Lord,
during this lenten season
nourish us with your word of life
and make us one in love and prayer.
Grant this . . . for ever and ever. ℟. **Amen.** ↓

FIRST READING   Dt 4:1, 5-9

This beautiful prayer of Moses shows the relationship of human beings to God. It would serve as an ideal base for love of country and homeland. He admonishes that God's people should remember God's teachings and pass them on to their children.

A reading from the Book of Deuteronomy

MOSES spoke to the people and said: "Now, Israel, hear the statutes and decrees which I am teaching you to observe, that you may live, and may enter in and take possession of the land which the LORD, the God of your fathers, is giving you. Therefore, I teach you the statutes and decrees as the LORD, my God, has commanded me, that you may observe them in the land you are entering to occupy. Observe them carefully, for thus will you give evidence of your wisdom and intelligence to the nations, who will hear of all these statutes and say, 'This great nation is truly a wise and intelligent people.' For what great nation is there that has gods so close to it as the LORD, our God, is to us whenever we call upon him? Or what great nation has statutes and decrees that are as just as this whole law which I am setting before you today?

"However, take care and be earnestly on your guard not to forget the things which your own eyes have seen, nor let them slip from your memory as long as you live, but teach them to your children and to your children's children."—The word of the Lord. ℟. **Thanks be to God.** ↓

RESPONSORIAL PSALM   Ps 147:12-13, 15-16, 19-20

℟. (12a) **Praise the Lord, Jerusalem.**

Glorify the LORD, O Jerusalem;
    praise your God, O Zion.
For he has strengthened the bars of your gates;
    he has blessed your children within you.—℟.

He sends forth his command to the earth;
    swiftly runs his word!
He spreads snow like wool;
    frost he strews like ashes.—℟.

He has proclaimed his word to Jacob,
    his statutes and his ordinances to Israel.
He has not done thus for any other nation;
    his ordinances he has not made known to them.—℟. ↓

VERSE BEFORE THE GOSPEL   Jn 6:63c, 68c

℟. **Glory to you, Lord Jesus Christ, Son of the living God!*
Your words, Lord, are Spirit and life;
you have the words of everlasting life.
℟. **Glory to you, Lord Jesus Christ, Son of the living
    God!** ↓

GOSPEL   Mt 5:17-19

Jesus carries out the precept of obeying God's law. He did not come to
change God's law but to carry it out to its fullest extent. Whoever keeps
God's law will be great in his Kingdom.

℣. The Lord be with you. ℟. **And also with you.**
℣. A reading from the holy Gospel according to Matthew.
℟. **Glory to you, Lord.**

JESUS said to his disciples: "Do not think that I have
come to abolish the law or the prophets. I have come
not to abolish but to fulfill. Amen, I say to you, until heav-
en and earth pass away, not the smallest letter or the
smallest part of a letter will pass from the law, until all
things have taken place. Therefore, whoever breaks one
of the least of these commandments and teaches others

* *See p.* 620 *for other Gospel Acclamations.*

to do so will be called least in the Kingdom of heaven. But whoever obeys and teaches these commandments will be called greatest in the Kingdom of heaven."—The Gospel of the Lord. ℟. **Praise to you, Lord Jesus Christ.**
→ No. 15, p. 623

PRAYER OVER THE GIFTS

Lord,
receive our prayers and offerings.
In time of danger,
protect all who celebrate this sacrament.
We ask this in the name of Jesus the Lord.
℟. **Amen.**   → No. 21, p. 626 (Pref. P 8-11)

COMMUNION ANT.   Ps 16:11

Lord, you will show me the path of life and fill me with joy in your presence. ↓

PRAYER AFTER COMMUNION

Lord,
may this eucharist forgive our sins,
make us holy,
and prepare us for the eternal life you promise.
We ask this through Christ our Lord.
℟. **Amen.**   → No. 32, p. 660

THURSDAY OF THE THIRD WEEK OF LENT

Those who expect to reap a harvest of divine benefit other than through faith in Christ will find their hopes and their labor in vain. It is only by serving God alone that we are with and in God. Those who are against God can bring only destruction and damnation upon themselves.

ENTRANCE ANT.

I am the Savior of all people, says the Lord. Whatever their troubles, I will answer their cry, and I will always be their Lord.   → No. 2, p. 614

OPENING PRAYER

Father,
help us to be ready to celebrate the great paschal mystery.
Make our love grow each day
as we approach the feast of our salvation.
We ask this . . . for ever and ever. ℞. **Amen.** ↓

FIRST READING Jer 7:23-28

Jeremiah speaks of what God commands his people. Nations are made up of individuals, but when the majority of individuals break away from God, the nation becomes godless even though a few righteous and holy people are scattered here and there. Because of deaf ears, the word of God is not among them.

A reading from the Book of the Prophet Jeremiah

THUS says the LORD: This is what I commanded my people: Listen to my voice; then I will be your God and you shall be my people. Walk in all the ways that I command you, so that you may prosper.

But they obeyed not, nor did they pay heed. They walked in the hardness of their evil hearts and turned their backs, not their faces, to me. From the day that your fathers left the land of Egypt even to this day, I have sent you untiringly all my servants the prophets. Yet they have not obeyed me nor paid heed; they have stiffened their necks and done worse than their fathers. When you speak all these words to them, they will not listen to you either; when you call to them, they will not answer you. Say to them: This is the nation that does not listen to the voice of the LORD, its God, or take correction. Faithfulness has disappeared; the word itself is banished from their speech.— The word of the Lord. ℞. **Thanks be to God.** ↓

RESPONSORIAL PSALM Ps 95:1-2, 6-7, 8-9

℞. (8) **If today you hear his voice, harden not your hearts.**

Come, let us sing joyfully to the LORD;
let us acclaim the Rock of our salvation.

Let us come into his presence with thanksgiving;
> let us joyfully sing psalms to him.—℟.

Come, let us bow down in worship;
> let us kneel before the LORD who made us.

For he is our God,
> and we are the people he shepherds, the flock he
> guides.—℟.

Oh, that today you would hear his voice:
> "Harden not your hearts as at Meribah,
> as in the day of Massah in the desert,

Where your fathers tempted me;
> they tested me though they had seen my works."—℟. ↓

VERSE BEFORE THE GOSPEL   Jl 2:12-13

℟. **Glory to you, Lord Jesus Christ, Son of the living God!***
Even now, says the LORD,
return to me with your whole heart,
for I am gracious and merciful.
℟. **Glory to you, Lord Jesus Christ, Son of the living
God!** ↓

GOSPEL   Lk 11:14-23

*Jesus expels a devil. This text is an appropriate conclusion to the whole
argument between our Lord and his enemies: "Whoever is not with me is
against me, and whoever does not gather with me scatters." There is no
such thing as a neutral position in the kingdom of God.*

℣. The Lord be with you. ℟. **And also with you.**
℣. A reading from the holy Gospel according to Luke.
℟. **Glory to you, Lord.**

JESUS was driving out a demon that was mute, and
when the demon had gone out, the mute man spoke
and the crowds were amazed. Some of them said, "By the
power of Beelzebul, the prince of demons, he drives out
demons." Others, to test him, asked him for a sign from

---

* *See p. 620 for other Gospel Acclamations.*

heaven. But he knew their thoughts and said to them, "Every kingdom divided against itself will be laid waste and house will fall against house. And if Satan is divided against himself, how will his kingdom stand? For you say that it is by Beelzebul that I drive out demons. If I, then, drive out demons by Beelzebul, by whom do your own people drive them out? Therefore they will be your judges. But if it is by the finger of God that I drive out demons, then the Kingdom of God has come upon you. When a strong man fully armed guards his palace, his possessions are safe. But when one stronger than he attacks and overcomes him, he takes away the armor on which he relied and distributes the spoils. Whoever is not with me is against me, and whoever does not gather with me scatters."—The Gospel of the Lord. ℟. **Praise to you, Lord Jesus Christ.**   → No. 15, p. 623

PRAYER OVER THE GIFTS

Lord,
take away our sinfulness and be pleased with our offerings.
Help us to pursue the true gifts you promise
and not become lost in false joys.
Grant this through Christ our Lord.
℟. **Amen.**   → No. 21, p. 626 (Pref. P 8-11)

COMMUNION ANT.   Ps 119:4-5

You have laid down your precepts to be faithfully kept. May my footsteps be firm in keeping your commands. ↓

PRAYER AFTER COMMUNION

Lord,
may your sacrament of life
bring us the gift of salvation
and make our lives pleasing to you.
We ask this in the name of Jesus the Lord.
℟. **Amen.**   → No. 32, p. 660

FRIDAY OF THE THIRD WEEK OF LENT

The love of God is summed up in "the whole law and the prophets." This love of God is the greatest and the First Commandment. The Second is very like it and is next in importance in the eyes of the Lord. Love for others is true Christian charity. Christ says plainly; "I say to you, love your enemies, and pray for those who persecute you" (Mt 5:44).

ENTRANCE ANT.   Ps 86:8, 10

Lord, there is no god to compare with you; you are great and do wonderful things, you are the only God.

→ No. 2, p. 614

OPENING PRAYER

Merciful Father,
fill our hearts with your love
and keep us faithful to the gospel of Christ.
Give us the grace to rise above our human weakness.
Grant this . . . forever and ever. ℟. **Amen.** ↓

FIRST READING   Hos 14:2-10

How many times the Jews turned from God! Through the prayer of the Prophet Hosea who lived about 750 B.C., God again shows his forgiveness and promises them a flourishing future. They shall bear much fruit.

A reading from the Book of the Prophet Hosea

THUS says the LORD:
Return, O Israel, to the LORD, your God;
 you have collapsed through your guilt.
Take with you words,
 and return to the LORD;
Say to him, "Forgive all iniquity,
 and receive what is good, that we may render
 as offerings the bullocks from our stalls.
Assyria will not save us,
 nor shall we have horses to mount;
We shall say no more, 'Our god,'
 to the work of our hands;
 for in you the orphan finds compassion."

I will heal their defection, says the LORD,
   I will love them freely;
   for my wrath is turned away from them.
I will be like the dew for Israel:
   he shall blossom like the lily;
He shall strike root like the Lebanon cedar,
   and put forth his shoots.
His splendor shall be like the olive tree
   and his fragrance like the Lebanon cedar.
Again they shall dwell in his shade
   and raise grain;
They shall blossom like the vine,
   and his fame shall be like the wine of Lebanon.

Ephraim! What more has he to do with idols?
   I have humbled him, but I will prosper him.
"I am like a verdant cypress tree"—
   Because of me you bear fruit!

Let him who is wise understand these things;
   let him who is prudent know them.
Straight are the paths of the LORD,
   in them the just walk,
   but sinners stumble in them.
The word of the Lord. ℟. **Thanks be to God.** ↓

RESPONSORIAL PSALM

Ps 81:6c-8a, 8bc-9, 10-11ab, 14 and 17

℟. (see 11 and 9a) **I am the Lord your God: hear my voice.**
An unfamiliar speech I hear:
   "I relieved his shoulder of the burden;
   his hands were freed from the basket.
In distress you called, and I rescued you."—℟.

"Unseen, I answered you in thunder;
   I tested you at the waters of Meribah.
Hear, my people, and I will admonish you;
   O Israel, will you not hear me?"—℟.

"There shall be no strange god among you
   nor shall you worship any alien god.

I, the Lord, am your God
　who led you forth from the land of Egypt."—℟.

"If only my people would hear me,
　and Israel walk in my ways,
I would feed them with the best of wheat,
　and with honey from the rock I would fill them."—℟. ↓

VERSE BEFORE THE GOSPEL　　　　　　　Mt 4:17

℟. **Glory to you, Lord Jesus Christ, Son of the living God!***
Repent, says the Lord;
the Kingdom of heaven is at hand.
℟. **Glory to you, Lord Jesus Christ, Son of the living
God!** ↓

GOSPEL　　　　　　　　　　　　　　Mk 12:28-34

In answering the question concerning the most important commandment,
Jesus replies that the greatest commandment is to place the adoration of
God above all else and the love of neighbor next.

℣. The Lord be with you. ℟. **And also with you.**
℣. A reading from the holy Gospel according to Mark.
℟. **Glory to you, Lord.**

ONE of the scribes came to Jesus and asked him,
　"Which is the first of all the commandments?" Jesus
replied, "The first is this: *Hear, O Israel! The Lord our God
is Lord alone! You shall love the Lord your God with all
your heart, with all your soul, with all your mind, and
with all your strength.* The second is this: *You shall love
your neighbor as yourself.* There is no other commandment greater than these." The scribe said to him, "Well
said, teacher. You are right in saying, *He is One and there
is no other than he.* And *to love him with all your heart,
with all your understanding, with all your strength, and
to love your neighbor as yourself* is worth more than all
burnt offerings and sacrifices." And when Jesus saw that
he answered with understanding, he said to him, "You are

---

* *See p. 620 for other Gospel Acclamations.*

not far from the Kingdom of God." And no one dared to ask him any more questions.—The Gospel of the Lord. ℟. **Praise to you, Lord Jesus Christ.**   ➔ No. 15, p. 623

PRAYER OVER THE GIFTS

Lord,
bless the gifts we have prepared.
Make them acceptable to you
and a lasting source of salvation.
We ask this in the name of Jesus the Lord.
℟. **Amen.**   ➔ No. 21, p. 626 (Pref. P 8-11)

COMMUNION ANT.   See Mk 12:33

To love God with all your heart, and your neighbor as yourself, is a greater thing than all the temple sacrifices. ↓

PRAYER AFTER COMMUNION

Lord,
fill us with the power of your love.
As we share in this eucharist,
may we come to know fully the redemption we have received.
We ask this through Christ our Lord.
℟. **Amen.**   ➔ No. 32, p. 660

SATURDAY OF THE THIRD WEEK OF LENT

The Lord says, "It is love that I desire, not sacrifice, and knowledge of God rather than holocausts." This demand of our love by God applies even today when we celebrate the one and only Sacrifice of the New Covenant offered by Jesus Christ through the Mass. Even the Mass means nothing unless we turn to God with love!

ENTRANCE ANT.   Ps 103:2-3

Bless the Lord, my soul, and remember all his kindnesses, for he pardons all my faults.   ➔ No. 2, p. 614

OPENING PRAYER

Lord,
make this lenten observance
of the suffering, death and resurrection of Christ
bring us to the full joy of Easter.
We ask this . . . for ever and ever. ℟. **Amen.** ↓

FIRST READING   Hos 6:1-6

Hosea was a prophet who sometimes is called the prophet of divine love.
He uses the imagery of a father's love for his son and the husband's love
for his wife in describing God's love for his people. They are wayward people, but God pursues them, asking for their love in return.

A reading from the Book of the Prophet Hosea

"COME, let us return to the LORD,
   it is he who has rent, but he will heal us;
      he has struck us, but he will bind our wounds.
He will revive us after two days;
      on the third day he will raise us up,
   to live in his presence.
Let us know, let us strive to know the LORD;
      as certain as the dawn is his coming,
      and his judgment shines forth like the light of day!
He will come to us like the rain,
      like spring rain that waters the earth."

What can I do with you, Ephraim?
What can I do with you, Judah?
Your piety is like a morning cloud,
      like the dew that early passes away.
For this reason I smote them through the prophets,
      I slew them by the words of my mouth;
For it is love that I desire, not sacrifice,
      and knowledge of God rather than burnt offerings.
The word of the Lord. ℟. **Thanks be to God.** ↓

RESPONSORIAL PSALM   Ps 51:3-4, 18-19, 20-21ab
℟. (see Hos 6:6) **It is mercy I desire, and not sacrifice.**

Have mercy on me, O God, in your goodness;
> in the greatness of your compassion wipe out my
> offense.

Thoroughly wash me from my guilt
> and of my sin cleanse me.—℟.

For you are not pleased with sacrifices;
> should I offer a burnt offering, you would not accept
> it.

My sacrifice, O God, is a contrite spirit;
> a heart contrite and humbled, O God, you will not
> spurn.—℟.

Be bountiful, O Lord, to Zion in your kindness
> by rebuilding the walls of Jerusalem;

Then shall you be pleased with due sacrifices,
> burnt offerings and holocausts.—℟. ↓

VERSE BEFORE THE GOSPEL   Ps 95:8

℟. **Glory to you, Lord Jesus Christ, Son of the living God!***
If today you hear his voice,
harden not your hearts.
℟. **Glory to you, Lord Jesus Christ, Son of the living
God!** ↓

GOSPEL   Lk 18:9-14

Jesus teaches by contrast. The Pharisee believes that his external religious practices justify him before God. He assumes he is good, while the
other, a publican, begs for mercy and receives mercy. The proud shall
become humble.

℣. The Lord be with you. ℟. **And also with you.**
℣. A reading from the holy Gospel according to Luke.
℟. **Glory to you, Lord.**

JESUS addressed this parable to those who were convinced of their own righteousness and despised everyone else. "Two people went up to the temple area to pray;

---

* *See p.* 620 *for other Gospel Acclamations.*

one was a Pharisee and the other was a tax collector. The Pharisee took up his position and spoke this prayer to himself, 'O God, I thank you that I am not like the rest of humanity—greedy, dishonest, adulterous—or even like this tax collector. I fast twice a week, and I pay tithes on my whole income.' But the tax collector stood off at a distance and would not even raise his eyes to heaven but beat his breast and prayed, 'O God, be merciful to me a sinner.' I tell you, the latter went home justified, not the former; for everyone who exalts himself will be humbled, and the one who humbles himself will be exalted."—The Gospel of the Lord. ℟. **Praise to you, Lord Jesus Christ.**

➜ No. 15, p. 623

PRAYER OVER THE GIFTS

Lord,
by your grace you enable us
to come to these mysteries with renewed lives.
May this eucharist give you worthy praise.
Grant this through Christ our Lord.
℟. **Amen.**

➜ No. 21, p. 626 (Pref. P 8-11)

COMMUNION ANT.   Lk 18:13

He stood at a distance and beat his breast, saying: O God, be merciful to me, a sinner. ↓

PRAYER AFTER COMMUNION

God of mercy,
may the holy gifts we receive
help us to worship you in truth,
and to receive your sacraments with faith.
We ask this in the name of Jesus the Lord.
℟. **Amen.**

➜ No. 32, p. 660

OPTIONAL READINGS AND INTERVENIENT CHANTS FOR THE FOURTH WEEK OF LENT

These Readings and Intervenient Chants may be used on any day of this week, especially when the Gospel of the man born blind is not read on the Fourth Sunday of Lent.

FIRST READING   Mi 7:7-9

Micah says that God will be his Savior. Even though he is living in darkness, God will hear him when he prays to him. He has sinned and will be punished, but God will show him his justice.

A reading from the Book of the Prophet Micah

I will look to the LORD,
 I will put my trust in God my savior;
  my God will hear me!

Rejoice not over me, O my enemy!
  though I have fallen, I will arise;
  though I sit in darkness, the LORD is my light.
The wrath of the LORD I will endure
  because I have sinned against him,
Until he takes up my cause,
  and establishes my right.
He will bring me forth to the light;
  I will see his justice.
The word of the Lord. ℟. **Thanks be to God.** ↓

RESPONSORIAL PSALM   Ps 27:1, 7-8a, 8b 9abc, 13-14

℟. (1a) **The Lord is my light and my salvation.**

The LORD is my light and my salvation;
  whom should I fear?
The LORD is my life's refuge;
  of whom should I be afraid?—℟.

Hear, O LORD, the sound of my call;
  have pity on me and answer me.
Of you my heart speaks; you my glance seeks.—℟.

Your presence, O LORD, I seek!
Hide not your face from me;

do not in anger repel your servant.
You are my helper; cast me not off.—℟.

I believe that I shall see the bounty of the LORD
in the land of the living.
Wait for the LORD with courage;
be stouthearted, and wait for the LORD!—℟. ↓

VERSE BEFORE THE GOSPEL   Jn 8:12

℟. **Praise and honor to you, Lord Jesus Christ!***
I am the light of the world, says the Lord;
whoever follows me will have the light of life.
℟. **Praise and honor to you, Lord Jesus Christ!** ↓

GOSPEL   Jn 9:1-41

The man who is cured from his blindness was chosen by God to show forth the divine power of Jesus. The man believes in Jesus and obeys him. There follows a full court investigation, but the man is faithful in professing his anxious belief in the Son of Man regardless of criticism or reprisal.

℣. The Lord be with you. ℟. **And also with you.**
℣. A reading from the holy Gospel according to John.
℟. **Glory to you, Lord.**

AS Jesus passed by he saw a man blind from birth. His disciples asked him, "Rabbi, who sinned, this man or his parents, that he was born blind?" Jesus answered, "Neither he nor his parents sinned; it is so that the works of God might be made visible through him. We have to do the works of the one who sent me while it is day. Night is coming when no one can work. While I am in the world, I am the light of the world." When he had said this, he spat on the ground and made clay with the saliva, and smeared the clay on his eyes, and said to him, "Go, wash in the Pool of Siloam"—which means Sent—. So he went and washed, and came back able to see.

His neighbors and those who had seen him earlier as a beggar said, "Isn't this the one who used to sit and beg?"

---

* *See p. 620 for other Gospel Acclamations.*

Some said, "It is," but others said, "No, he just looks like him." He said, "I am." So they said to him, "How were your eyes opened?" He replied, "The man called Jesus made clay and anointed my eyes and told me, 'Go to Siloam and wash.' So I went there and washed and was able to see." And they said to him, "Where is he?" He said, "I don't know."

They brought the one who was once blind to the Pharisees. Now Jesus had made clay and opened his eyes on a sabbath. So then the Pharisees also asked him how he was able to see. He said to them, "He put clay on my eyes, and I washed, and now I can see." So some of the Pharisees said, "This man is not from God, because he does not keep the sabbath." But others said, "How can a sinful man do such signs?" And there was a division among them. So they said to the blind man again, "What do you have to say about him, since he opened your eyes?" He said, "He is a prophet."

Now the Jews did not believe that he had been blind and gained his sight until they summoned the parents of the one who had gained his sight. They asked them, "Is this your son, who you say was born blind? How does he now see?" His parents answered and said, "We know that this is our son and that he was born blind. We do not know how he sees now, nor do we know who opened his eyes. Ask him, he is of age; he can speak for himself." His parents said this because they were afraid of the Jews, for the Jews had already agreed that if anyone acknowledged him as the Christ, he would be expelled from the synagogue. For this reason his parents said, "He is of age; question him."

So a second time they called the man who had been blind and said to him, "Give God the praise! We know that this man is a sinner." He replied, "If he is a sinner, I do not know. One thing I do know is that I was blind and now I see." So they said to him, "What did he do to you? How did he open your eyes?" He answered them, "I told you already and you did not listen. Why do you want to hear it again? Do you want to become his disciples, too?" They ridiculed him and said, "You are that man's disciple; we are disciples of Moses! We know that God spoke to Moses, but we do not know where this one is from." The man answered and said to them, "This is what is so amazing, that you do not know where he is from, yet he opened my eyes. We know that God does not listen to sinners, but if one is devout and does his will, he listens to him. It is unheard of that anyone ever opened the eyes of a person born blind. If this man were not from God, he would not be able to do anything." They answered and said to him, "You were born totally in sin, and are you trying to teach us?" Then they threw him out.

When Jesus heard that they had thrown him out, he found him and said, "Do you believe in the Son of Man?" He answered and said, "Who is he, sir, that I may believe in him?" Jesus said to him, "You have seen him, and the one speaking with you is he." He said, "I do believe, Lord," and he worshiped him. Then Jesus said, "I came into this world for judgment, so that those who do not see might see, and those who do see might become blind."

Some of the Pharisees who were with him heard this and said to him, "Surely we are not also blind, are we?" Jesus said to them, "If you were blind, you would have no sin; but now you are saying, 'We see,' so your sin remains."—The Gospel of the Lord. ℟. **Praise to you, Lord Jesus Christ.**

➝ No. 15, p. 623

MONDAY OF THE FOURTH WEEK OF LENT

Today we have placed before us the thoughts of our eternal happiness in heaven, which we are to enjoy after the labors of this short life are ended. We may think of ourselves as mere pilgrims passing through for a time because it is the only way to our true home in heaven. Christ told his disciples that their journey through this vale of tears to his Kingdom would last only a little while, and when they arrived, their sorrow would be turned to joy.

ENTRANCE ANT.   Ps 31:7-8

Lord, I put my trust in you; I shall be glad and rejoice in your mercy, because you have seen my affliction.

→ No. 2, p. 614

OPENING PRAYER

Father, creator,
you give the world new life by your sacraments.
May we, your Church, grow in your life
and continue to receive your help on earth.
Grant this . . . for ever and ever. ℟. **Amen.** ↓

FIRST READING   Is 65:17-21

In an optimistic passage, Isaiah talks of renewal. This is God's response to our interior renewal. Isaiah describes a Jerusalem of joy and happiness.

A reading from the Book of the Prophet Isaiah

THUS says the LORD:
Lo, I am about to create new heavens
    and a new earth;
The things of the past shall not be remembered
    or come to mind.
Instead, there shall always be rejoicing and happiness
    in what I create;
For I create Jerusalem to be a joy
    and its people to be a delight;
I will rejoice in Jerusalem
    and exult in my people.
No longer shall the sound of weeping be heard there,
    or the sound of crying;
No longer shall there be in it
    an infant who lives but a few days,
        or an old man who does not round out his full life
        time;
He dies a mere youth who reaches but a hundred
    years,
        and he who fails of a hundred shall be thought
        accursed.

They shall live in the houses they build,
     and eat the fruit of the vineyards they plant.
The word of the Lord. ℟. **Thanks be to God.** ↓

RESPONSORIAL PSALM Ps 30:2 and 4, 5-6, 11-12a and 13b
See Thursday of the 3rd Week of Advent, p. 56.

VERSE BEFORE THE GOSPEL   Am 5:14

℟. **Praise and honor to you, Lord Jesus Christ!***
Seek good and not evil so that you may live,
and the LORD will be with you.
℟. **Praise and honor to you, Lord Jesus Christ!** ↓

GOSPEL   Jn 4:43-54

Jesus performed few miracles in Galilee. There was little faith there and
he was not accepted by his own. Presumably, the "royal official" is not a
native. He has only to believe the word of Jesus, and he does so.

℣. The Lord be with you. ℟. **And also with you.**
℣. A reading from the holy Gospel according to John.
℟. **Glory to you, Lord.**

AT that time Jesus left [Samaria] for Galilee. For Jesus
himself testified that a prophet has no honor in his
native place. When he came into Galilee, the Galileans
welcomed him, since they had seen all he had done in
Jerusalem at the feast; for they themselves had gone to
the feast.

    Then he returned to Cana in Galilee, where he had
made the water wine. Now there was a royal official
whose son was ill in Capernaum. When he heard that
Jesus had arrived in Galilee from Judea, he went to him
and asked him to come down and heal his son, who was
near death. Jesus said to him, "Unless you people see
signs and wonders, you will not believe." The royal official said to him, "Sir, come down before my child dies."
Jesus said to him, "You may go; your son will live." The

---

* See p. 620 *for other Gospel Acclamations.*

man believed what Jesus said to him and left. While the man was on his way back, his slaves met him and told him that his boy would live. He asked them when he began to recover. They told him, "The fever left him yesterday, about one in the afternoon." The father realized that just at that time Jesus had said to him, "Your son will live," and he and his whole household came to believe. Now this was the second sign Jesus did when he came to Galilee from Judea.—The Gospel of the Lord. ℟. **Praise to you, Lord Jesus Christ.**   ➜ No. 15, p. 623

PRAYER OVER THE GIFTS

Lord,
through the gifts we present
may we receive the grace
to cast off the old ways of life
and to redirect our course toward the life of heaven.
We ask this in the name of Jesus the Lord.
℟. **Amen.**   ➜ No. 21, p. 626 (Pref. P 8-11)

COMMUNION ANT.   Ez 36:27

I shall put my spirit within you, says the Lord; you will obey my laws and keep my decrees. ↓

PRAYER AFTER COMMUNION

Lord,
may your gifts bring us life and holiness
and lead us to the happiness of eternal life.
We ask this through Christ our Lord.
℟. **Amen.**   ➜ No. 32, p. 660

TUESDAY OF THE FOURTH WEEK OF LENT

Christ restores us to eternal life with God. This life comes through the Church and the sacraments. Baptism gives us supernatural life. The confessional brings the medicine to keep us alive. The Blessed Eucharist gives us strength. Left to ourselves, we have but a short cycle of life from birth to death. But through Christ and his Church we have the promise of life forever.

ENTRANCE ANT.   See Is 55:1

**Come to the waters, all who thirst; though you have no
money, come and drink with joy.**   → No. 2, p. 614

OPENING PRAYER

Father,
may our lenten observance
prepare us to embrace the paschal mystery
and to proclaim your salvation with joyful praise.
We ask this . . . for ever and ever. ℟. **Amen.** ↓

FIRST READING   Ez 47:1-9, 12

Ezekiel uses the motif of the River of God with its life-giving waters, but
in his own way he develops the concept of a temple-centered land. From
beneath the threshold of the east gate of the Sanctuary, he sees a stream
of water issue forth to the east, from the holy mount to the lifeless waters
of the sea. Its waters become fresh and healthy.

A reading from the Book of Prophet Ezekiel

THE angel brought me, Ezekiel, back to the entrance of
the temple of the LORD, and I saw water flowing out
from beneath the threshold of the temple toward the east,
for the façade of the temple was toward the east; the
water flowed down from the right side of the temple,
south of the altar. He led me outside by the north gate,
and around to the outer gate facing the east, where I saw
water trickling from the right side. Then when he had
walked off to the east with a measuring cord in his hand,
he measured off a thousand cubits and had me wade
through the water, which was ankle-deep. He measured
off another thousand and once more had me wade
through the water, which was now knee-deep. Again he
measured off a thousand and had me wade; the water
was up to my waist. Once more he measured off a thousand, but there was now a river through which I could
not wade; for the water had risen so high it had become
a river that could not be crossed except by swimming. He
asked me, "Have you seen this, son of man?" Then he

brought me to the bank of the river, where he had me sit. Along the bank of the river I saw very many trees on both sides. He said to me, "This water flows into the eastern district down upon the Arabah, and empties into the sea, the salt waters, which it makes fresh. Wherever the river flows, every sort of living creature that can multiply shall live, and there shall be abundant fish, for wherever this water comes the sea shall be made fresh. Along both banks of the river, fruit trees of every kind shall grow; their leaves shall not fade, nor their fruit fail. Every month they shall bear fresh fruit, for they shall be watered by the flow from the sanctuary. Their fruit shall serve for food, and their leaves for medicine."—The word of the Lord. ℟. **Thanks be to God.** ↓

RESPONSORIAL PSALM   Ps 46:2-3, 5-6, 8-9

℟. (8) **The Lord of hosts is with us; our stronghold is the God of Jacob.**

God is our refuge and our strength,
    an ever-present help in distress.
Therefore we fear not, though the earth be shaken
    and mountains plunge into the depths of the sea.—℟.

There is a stream whose runlets gladden the city of God,
    the holy dwelling of the Most High.
God is in its midst; it shall not be disturbed;
    God will help it at the break of dawn.—℟.

The LORD of hosts is with us;
    our stronghold is the God of Jacob.
Come! behold the deeds of the LORD,
    the astounding things he has wrought on earth.—℟. ↓

VERSE BEFORE THE GOSPEL   Ps 51:12a, 14a

℟. **Praise and honor to you, Lord Jesus Christ!***
A clean heart create for me, O God;

---

* *See p.* 620 *for other Gospel Acclamations.*

give me back the joy of your salvation.
℞. **Praise and honor to you, Lord Jesus Christ!** ↓

GOSPEL Jn 5:1-16

Water is featured again. The angel stirs the pool and all who enter are made well and strong. The poor man who keeps trying to get in has his faith rewarded when our Lord comes along. At last he is cured.

℣. The Lord be with you. ℞. **And also with you.**
℣. A reading from the holy Gospel according to John.
℞. **Glory to you, Lord.**

THERE was a feast of the Jews, and Jesus went up to Jerusalem. Now there is in Jerusalem at the Sheep Gate a pool called in Hebrew Bethesda, with five porticoes. In these lay a large number of ill, blind, lame, and crippled. One man was there who had been ill for thirty-eight years. When Jesus saw him lying there and knew that he had been ill for a long time, he said to him, "Do you want to be well?" The sick man answered him, "Sir, I have no one to put me into the pool when the water is stirred up; while I am on my way, someone else gets down there before me." Jesus said to him, "Rise, take up your mat, and walk." Immediately the man became well, took up his mat, and walked.

Now that day was a sabbath. So the Jews said to the man who was cured, "It is the sabbath, and it is not lawful for you to carry your mat." He answered them, "The man who made me well told me, 'Take up your mat and walk.'" They asked him, "Who is the man who told you, 'Take it up and walk'?" The man who was healed did not know who it was, for Jesus had slipped away, since there was a crowd there. After this Jesus found him in the temple area and said to him, "Look, you are well; do not sin any more, so that nothing worse may happen to you." The man went and told the Jews that Jesus was the one who had made him well. Therefore, the Jews began to persecute Jesus because he did this on a sabbath.—The Gospel of the Lord. ℟. **Praise to you, Lord Jesus Christ.**   → No. 15, p. 623

PRAYER OVER THE GIFTS

Lord,
may your gifts of bread and wine
which nourish us here on earth
become the food of our eternal life.
Grant this through Christ our Lord.
℟. **Amen.**   → No. 21, p. 626 (Pref. P 8-11)

COMMUNION ANT.   Ps 23:1-2

The Lord is my shepherd; there is nothing I shall want. In green pastures he gives me rest, he leads me beside the waters of peace. ↓

PRAYER AFTER COMMUNION

Lord,
may your holy sacraments cleanse and renew us;
may they bring us your help
and lead us to salvation.
We ask this in the name of Jesus the Lord.
℟. **Amen.**   → No. 32, p. 660

WEDNESDAY OF THE FOURTH WEEK OF LENT

Jesus is identified as the Suffering Servant of Isaiah. As Messiah and Prophet and Son of God, he fulfilled the role completely. In these days of Lent, we begin to discern more and more the significance of Christ's sufferings. Millions of people have suffered since time began, but the sufferings of the Son of God for us take on a special redemptive value. In those sufferings, Jesus was carrying out the special mission of uniting man with God.

ENTRANCE ANT.   Ps 69:14

I pray to you, O God, for the time of your favor. Lord, in your great love, answer me.   → No. 2, p. 614

OPENING PRAYER

Lord,
you reward virtue
and forgive the repentant sinner.
Grant us your forgiveness
as we come before you confessing our guilt.
We ask this . . . for ever and ever. ℟. **Amen.** ↓

FIRST READING   Is 49:8-15

Isaiah proclaims the wondrous reversal of Israel's fortunes. Salvation comes through God's pleasure. God is a shepherd leading his sheep along a new exodus. The Lord comforts his people but Zion exclaims, "The Lord has forsaken me. . . ."

A reading from the Book of the Prophet Isaiah

THUS says the LORD:
    In a time of favor I answer you,
        on the day of salvation I help you;
        and I have kept you and given you as a covenant to
            the people,
To restore the land
        and allot the desolate heritages,
Saying to the prisoners: Come out!
To those in darkness: Show yourselves!
Along the ways they shall find pasture,
        on every bare height shall their pastures be.
They shall not hunger or thirst,
        nor shall the scorching wind or the sun strike them;
For he who pities them leads them
        and guides them beside springs of water.
I will cut a road through all my mountains,
        and make my highways level.
See, some shall come from afar,
        others from the north and the west,
        and some from the land of Syene.
Sing out, O heavens, and rejoice, O earth,
        break forth into song, you mountains.

For the LORD comforts his people
> and shows mercy to his afflicted.

But Zion said, "The LORD has forsaken me;
> my Lord has forgotten me."
Can a mother forget her infant,
> be without tenderness for the child of her womb?
Even should she forget,
> I will never forget you.
The word of the Lord. ℞. **Thanks be to God.** ↓

RESPONSORIAL PSALM   Ps 145:8-9, 13cd-14, 17-18

℞. (8a) **The Lord is gracious and merciful.**

The LORD is gracious and merciful,
> slow to anger and of great kindness.
The LORD is good to all
> and compassionate toward all his works.—℞.

The LORD is faithful in all his words
> and holy in all his works.
The LORD lifts up all who are falling
> and raises up all who are bowed down.—℞.

The LORD is just in all his ways
> and holy in all his works.
The LORD is near to all who call upon him,
> to all who call upon him in truth.—℞. ↓

VERSE BEFORE THE GOSPEL   Jn 11:25a, 26

℞. **Praise and honor to you, Lord Jesus Christ!***
I am the resurrection and the life, says the Lord;
whoever believes in me will never die.
℞. **Praise and honor to you, Lord Jesus Christ!** ↓

GOSPEL   Jn 5:17-30

The Servant of Yahweh is Christ. God made his beloved Son the source of
life for all human beings. This is the specific meaning of "redeeming."

---

* See p. 620 *for other Gospel Acclamations.*

Jesus openly says that he has been appointed the supreme judge of life and death.

℣. The Lord be with you. ℟. **And also with you.**

℣. A reading from the holy Gospel according to John.

℟. **Glory to you, Lord.**

JESUS answered the Jews: "My Father is at work until now, so I am at work." For this reason they tried all the more to kill him, because he not only broke the sabbath but he also called God his own father, making himself equal to God.

Jesus answered and said to them, "Amen, amen, I say to you, the Son cannot do anything on his own, but only what he sees the Father doing; for what he does, the Son will do also. For the Father loves the Son and shows him everything that he himself does, and he will show him greater works than these, so that you may be amazed. For just as the Father raises the dead and gives life, so also does the Son give life to whomever he wishes. Nor does the Father judge anyone, but he has given all judgment to the Son, so that all may honor the Son just as they honor the Father. Whoever does not honor the Son does not honor the Father who sent him. Amen, amen, I say to you, whoever hears my word and believes in the one who sent me has eternal life and will not come to condemnation, but has passed from death to life. Amen, amen, I say to you, the hour is coming and is now here when the dead will hear the voice of the Son of God, and those who hear will live. For just as the Father has life in himself, so also he gave to the Son the possession of life in himself. And he gave him power to exercise judgment, because he is the Son of Man. Do not be amazed at this, because the hour is coming in which all who are in the tombs will hear his voice and will come out, those who have done good deeds to the resurrection of life, but those who have done wicked deeds to the resurrection of condemnation.

"I cannot do anything on my own; I judge as I hear, and my judgment is just, because I do not seek my own will but the will of the one who sent me."—The Gospel of the Lord. ℟. **Praise to you, Lord Jesus Christ.**

➙ No. 15, p. 623

PRAYER OVER THE GIFTS

Lord God,
may the power of this sacrifice wash away our sins,
renew our lives and bring us to salvation.
We ask this in the name of Jesus the Lord.
℟. **Amen.**   ➙ No. 21, p. 626 (Pref. P 8-11)

COMMUNION ANT.   Jn 3:17

God sent his Son into the world, not to condemn it, but so that the world might be saved through him. ↓

PRAYER AFTER COMMUNION

Lord,
may we never misuse your healing gifts,
but always find in them a source of life and salvation.
Grant this through Christ our Lord.
℟. **Amen.**   ➙ No. 32, p. 660

THURSDAY OF THE FOURTH WEEK OF LENT

How often we refuse to bear witness to Christ and do not hear the words of God. Sin darkens the understanding, blunts the spiritual faculties, and deprives us of true faith. Christ suffered and died that we might be ransomed. We can help ourselves by learning more and more of the depth of God's love for us by devout meditation on Christ's sacred Passion.

ENTRANCE ANT.   Ps 105:3-4

Let hearts rejoice who search for the Lord. Seek the Lord and his strength, seek always the face of the Lord.

➙ No. 2, p. 614

OPENING PRAYER

Merciful Father,
may the penance of our lenten observance

make us your obedient people.
May the love within us be seen in what we do
and lead us to the joy of Easter.
Grant this . . . for ever and ever. ℞. **Amen.** ↓

FIRST READING   Ex 32:7-14

While Moses is speaking to God, the Jewish people mold a golden calf. God is angry but Moses implores God to forgive them. Moses recalls the promise God had made to Abraham, Isaac and Jacob. So God relents.

A reading from the Book of Exodus

THE LORD said to Moses, "Go down at once to your people whom you brought out of the land of Egypt, for they have become depraved. They have soon turned aside from the way I pointed out to them, making for themselves a molten calf and worshiping it, sacrificing to it and crying out, 'This is your God, O Israel, who brought you out of the land of Egypt!' " The LORD said to Moses, "I see how stiff-necked this people is. Let me alone, then, that my wrath may blaze up against them to consume them. Then I will make of you a great nation."

But Moses implored the LORD, his God, saying, "Why, O LORD, should your wrath blaze up against your own people, whom you brought out of the land of Egypt with such great power and with so strong a hand? Why should the Egyptians say, 'With evil intent he brought them out, that he might kill them in the mountains and exterminate them from the face of the earth'? Let your blazing wrath die down; relent in punishing your people. Remember your servants Abraham, Isaac and Israel, and how you swore to them by your own self, saying, 'I will make your descendants as numerous as the stars in the sky; and all this land that I promised, I will give your descendants as their perpetual heritage.' " So the LORD relented in the punishment he had threatened to inflict on his people.— The word of the Lord. ℞. **Thanks be to God.** ↓

RESPONSORIAL PSALM   Ps 106:19-20, 21-22, 23

℟. (4a) **Remember us, O Lord, as you favor your people.**

Our fathers made a calf in Horeb
   and adored a molten image;
They exchanged their glory
   for the image of a grass-eating bullock. — ℟.

They forgot the God who had saved them,
   who had done great deeds in Egypt,
Wondrous deeds in the land of Ham,
   terrible things at the Red Sea.—℟.

Then he spoke of exterminating them,
   but Moses, his chosen one,
Withstood him in the breach
   to turn back his destructive wrath.—℟. ↓

VERSE BEFORE THE GOSPEL   Jn 3:16

℟. **Praise and honor to you, Lord Jesus Christ!***
God so loved the world that he gave his only-begotten
   Son,
so that everyone who believes in him might have eternal
   life.
℟. **Praise and honor to you, Lord Jesus Christ!** ↓

GOSPEL   Jn 5:31-47

Jesus says that John was his lamp. More than this, Jesus' divine works just speak for themselves. Even the Scriptures foretold the works of the Messiah. He has come in his Father's name.

℣. The Lord be with you. ℟. **And also with you.**
℣. A reading from the holy Gospel according to John.
℟. **Glory to you, Lord.**

JESUS said to the Jews: "If I testify on my own behalf, my testimony is not true. But there is another who testifies on my behalf, and I know that the testimony he gives on my behalf is true. You sent emissaries to John,

---

* *See p.* 620 *for other Gospel Acclamations.*

and he testified to the truth. I do not accept human testimony, but I say this so that you may be saved. He was a burning and shining lamp, and for a while you were content to rejoice in his light. But I have testimony greater than John's. The works that the Father gave me to accomplish, these works that I perform testify on my behalf that the Father has sent me. Moreover, the Father who sent me has testified on my behalf. But you have never heard his voice nor seen his form, and you do not have his word remaining in you, because you do not believe in the one whom he has sent. You search the Scriptures, because you think you have eternal life through them; even they testify on my behalf. But you do not want to come to me to have life.

"I do not accept human praise; moreover, I know that you do not have the love of God in you. I came in the name of my Father, but you do not accept me; yet if another comes in his own name, you will accept him. How can you believe, when you accept praise from one another and do not seek the praise that comes from the only God? Do not think that I will accuse you before the Father: the one who will accuse you is Moses, in whom you have placed your hope. For if you had believed Moses, you would have believed me, because he wrote about me. But if you do not believe his writings, how will you believe my words?"—The Gospel of the Lord. ℟.
Praise to you, Lord Jesus Christ.   ➙ No. 15, p. 623

PRAYER OVER THE GIFTS

All-powerful God,
look upon our weakness.
May the sacrifice we offer
bring us purity and strength.
We ask this in the name of Jesus the Lord.
℟. **Amen.**   ➙ No. 21, p. 626 (Pref. P 8-11)

COMMUNION ANT. Jer 31:33

I will put my law within them, I will write it on their hearts; then I shall be their God, and they will be my people. ↓

PRAYER AFTER COMMUNION

Lord,
may the sacraments we receive
cleanse us of sin and free us from guilt,
for our sins bring us sorrow
but your promise of salvation brings us joy.
We ask this through Christ our Lord.
℟. **Amen.** → No. 32, p. 660

FRIDAY OF THE FOURTH WEEK OF LENT

The Passion that we are approaching in the Sacred Liturgy will give us a supreme opportunity to concentrate our thoughts on that awful occasion brought about by the plots of wicked people. In the face of all that is human, remember the presence of that which is Divine. Let us be filled with cheerful certainty that in the Church, the time of sorrow will pass away and days of triumph and victory will return again.

ENTRANCE ANT. Ps 54:3-4

Save me, O God, by your power, and grant me justice! God, hear my prayer; listen to my plea. → No. 2, p. 614

OPENING PRAYER

Father, our source of life,
you know our weakness.
May we reach out with joy to grasp your hand
and walk more readily in your ways.
We ask this . . . for ever and ever. ℟. **Amen.** ↓

FIRST READING Wis 2:1a, 12-22

The Book of Wisdom was written very close to the time of Christ—perhaps only 50 years before him. It represents the whole history of people's dealings with their neighbors. Wickedness blinded those who were mistaken and who doubted. They did not learn the counsels of God. Let people uphold goodness and virtue and the observance of the Law.

A reading from the Book of Wisdom

THE wicked said among themselves,
thinking not aright:
"Let us beset the just one, because he is obnoxious to us;
    he sets himself against our doings,
Reproaches us for transgressions of the law
    and charges us with violations of our training.
He professes to have knowledge of God
    and styles himself a child of the LORD.
To us he is the censure of our thoughts;
    merely to see him is a hardship for us,
Because his life is not like that of others,
    and different are his ways.
He judges us debased;
    he holds aloof from our paths as from things
    impure.
He calls blest the destiny of the just
    and boasts that God is his Father.
Let us see whether his words be true;
    let us find out what will happen to him.
For if the just one be the son of God, he will defend him
    and deliver him from the hand of his foes.
With revilement and torture let us put him to the test
    that we may have proof of his gentleness
    and try his patience.
Let us condemn him to a shameful death;
    for according to his own words, God will take care
    of him."
These were their thoughts, but they erred;
    for their wickedness blinded them,
And they knew not the hidden counsels of God;
    neither did they count on a recompense of holiness
    nor discern the innocent souls' reward.
The word of the Lord. ℟. **Thanks be to God.** ↓

RESPONSORIAL PSALM   Ps 34:17-18, 19-20, 21 and 23

℟. (19a) **The Lord is close to the brokenhearted.**

The LORD confronts the evildoers,
    to destroy remembrance of them from the earth.
When the just cry out, the LORD hears them,
    and from all their distress he rescues them.—℟.

The LORD is close to the brokenhearted;
    and those who are crushed in spirit he saves.
Many are the troubles of the just man,
    but out of them all the LORD delivers him.—℟.

He watches over all his bones;
    not one of them shall be broken.
The LORD redeems the lives of his servants;
    no one incurs guilt who takes refuge in him.—℟. ↓

VERSE BEFORE THE GOSPEL   Mt 4:4b

℟. **Praise and honor to you, Lord Jesus Christ!***
One does not live on bread alone,
but on every word that comes forth from the mouth of
    God.
℟. **Praise and honor to you, Lord Jesus Christ!** ↓

GOSPEL   Jn 7:1-2, 10, 25-30

Those in Galilee begin to realize that Jesus is doomed. Voices are heard in
all directions asking, "Is he not the one they are trying to kill?" But Jesus
faces them unafraid, and when he speaks in the temple, he sets their
malicious wills against him irrevocably.

℣. The Lord be with you. ℟. **And also with you.**
℣. A reading from the holy Gospel according to John.
℟. **Glory to you, Lord.**

JESUS moved about within Galilee; he did not wish to
travel in Judea, because the Jews were trying to kill
him. But the Jewish feast of Tabernacles was near.

---

* See p. 620 *for other Gospel Acclamations.*

But when his brothers had gone up to the feast, he himself also went up, not openly but as it were in secret.

Some of the inhabitants of Jerusalem said, "Is he not the one they are trying to kill? And look, he is speaking openly and they say nothing to him. Could the authorities have realized that he is the Christ? But we know where he is from. When the Christ comes, no one will know where he is from." So Jesus cried out in the temple area as he was teaching and said, "You know me and also know where I am from. Yet I did not come on my own, but the one who sent me, whom you do not know, is true. I know him, because I am from him, and he sent me." So they tried to arrest him, but no one laid a hand upon him, because his hour had not yet come.—The Gospel of the Lord. ℟. **Praise to you, Lord Jesus Christ.**

➙ No. 15, p. 623

PRAYER OVER THE GIFTS

All-powerful God,
may the healing power of this sacrifice
free us from sin
and help us to approach you with pure hearts.
Grant this through Christ our Lord.
℟. **Amen.**   ➙ No. 21, p. 626 (Pref. P 8-11)

COMMUNION ANT.   Eph 1:7

In Christ, through the shedding of his blood, we have redemption and forgiveness of our sins by the abundance of his grace. ↓

PRAYER AFTER COMMUNION

Lord,
in this eucharist we pass from death to life.
Keep us from our old and sinful ways
and help us to continue in the new life.
We ask this in the name of Jesus the Lord.
℟. **Amen.**   ➙ No. 32, p. 660

SATURDAY OF THE FOURTH WEEK OF LENT

Jesus knows what we are thinking. He knows what we believe and what we hesitate to believe and what we do not want to believe. But once we accept him, we believe everything he tells us. A just God probes our hearts.

ENTRANCE ANT Ps 18:5-7

The snares of death overtook me, the ropes of hell tightened around me; in my distress I called upon the Lord, and he heard my voice. → No. 2, p. 614

OPENING PRAYER

Lord,
guide us in your gentle mercy,
for left to ourselves
we cannot do your will.
Grant this . . . for ever and ever. ℟. **Amen.** ↓

FIRST READING Jer 11:18-20

This part of Jeremiah's prophecy gives a picture of his readiness to suffer. As the prophet expresses his loving spirit, he would seem to be unsuspecting. The vision is of patient resignation. His enemies decide they must obliterate him.

A reading from the Book of the Prophet Jeremiah

I KNEW their plot because the LORD informed me; at that time you, O LORD, showed me their doings.

Yet I, like a trusting lamb led to slaughter, had not realized that they were hatching plots against me: "Let us destroy the tree in its vigor; let us cut him off from the land of the living, so that his name will be spoken no more."

But, you, O LORD of hosts, O just Judge,
 searcher of mind and heart,
Let me witness the vengeance you take on them,
 for to you I have entrusted my cause!
The word of the Lord. ℟. **Thanks be to God.** ↓

RESPONSORIAL PSALM   Ps 7:2-3, 9bc-10, 11-12

℟. (2a) **O Lord, my God, in you I take refuge.**

O LORD, my God, in you I take refuge;
 save me from all my pursuers and rescue me,
Lest I become like the lion's prey,
 to be torn to pieces, with no one to rescue me.—℟.

Do me justice, O LORD, because I am just,
 and because of the innocence that is mine.
Let the malice of the wicked come to an end,
 but sustain the just,
  O searcher of heart and soul, O just God.—℟.

A shield before me is God,
 who saves the upright of heart;
A just judge is God,
 a God who punishes day by day.—℟. ↓

VERSE BEFORE THE GOSPEL   See Lk 8:15

℟. **Praise and honor to you, Lord Jesus Christ!***
Blessed are they who have kept the word with a generous heart
and yield a harvest through perseverance.
℟. **Praise and honor to you, Lord Jesus Christ!** ↓

GOSPEL   Jn 7:40-53

The scribes and Pharisees are discussing Christ. The last sentence in this excerpt from St. John's Gospel says everything: They all went home! No consensus is reached. The major accusation against Jesus is that he came from Galilee, and evidently Nazareth was the worst place to come from in Galilee.

℣. The Lord be with you. ℟. **And also with you.**
℣. A reading from the holy Gospel according to John.
℟. **Glory to you, Lord.**

SOME in the crowd who heard these words of Jesus
said, "This is truly the Prophet." Others said, "This is
the Christ." But others said, "The Christ will not come

---

* *See p. 620 for other Gospel Acclamations.*

from Galilee, will he? Does not Scripture say that the Christ will be of David's family and come from Bethlehem, the village where David lived?" So a division occurred in the crowd because of him. Some of them even wanted to arrest him, but no one laid hands on him.

So the guards went to the chief priests and Pharisees, who asked them, "Why did you not bring him?" The guards answered, "Never before has anyone spoken like this man." So the Pharisees answered them, "Have you also been deceived? Have any of the authorities or the Pharisees believed in him? But this crowd, which does not know the law, is accursed." Nicodemus, one of their members who had come to him earlier, said to them, "Does our law condemn a man before it first hears him and finds out what he is doing?" They answered and said to him, "You are not from Galilee also, are you? Look and see that no prophet arises from Galilee."

Then each went to his own house.—The Gospel of the Lord. ℟. **Praise to you, Lord Jesus Christ.** ➔ No. 15, p. 623

PRAYER OVER THE GIFTS

Father,
accept our gifts
and make our hearts obedient to your will.
We ask this in the name of Jesus the Lord.
℟. **Amen.**   ➔ No. 21, p. 626 (Pref. P 8-11)

COMMUNION ANT.   1 Pt 1:19

We have been ransomed with the precious blood of Christ, as with the blood of a lamb without blemish or spot. ↓

PRAYER AFTER COMMUNION

Lord,
may the power of your holy gifts free us from sin
and help us to please you in our daily lives.
We ask this through Christ our Lord.
℟. **Amen.**   ➔ No. 32, p. 660

The practice of covering crosses and images in the church may be observed if the episcopal conference decides. The crosses are to be covered until the end of the celebration of the Lord's Passion on Good Friday. Images are to remain covered until the beginning of the Easter vigil.

OPTIONAL READINGS AND INTERVENIENT CHANTS FOR THE FIFTH WEEK OF LENT

These Readings and Intervenient Chants may be used on any day of this week when the Gospel of Lazarus is not read on the Fifth Sunday of Lent.

FIRST READING   2 Kgs 4:18b-21, 32-37

The son of the Shunammite woman becomes ill working in the field. He is carried home and dies in his mother's arms. Through the prayer of Elisha, the man of God, the boy's life is restored. How grateful is his mother!

A reading from the second Book of Kings

THE day came when the child of the Shunammite woman was old enough to go out to his father among the reapers. "My head hurts!" he complained to his father. "Carry him to his mother," the father said to a servant. The servant picked him up and carried him to his mother; he stayed with her until noon, when he died in her lap. The mother took him upstairs and laid him on the bed of the man of God. Closing the door on him, she went out.

When Elisha reached the house, he found the boy lying dead. He went in, closed the door on them both, and prayed to the LORD. Then he lay upon the child on the bed, placing his mouth upon the child's mouth, his eyes upon the eyes, and his hands upon the hands. As Elisha stretched himself over the child, the body became warm. He arose, paced up and down the room, and then once more lay down upon the boy, who now sneezed seven times and opened his eyes. Elisha summoned Gehazi and said, "Call the Shunammite." She came at his call, and Elisha said to her, "Take your son." She came in and fell at his feet in gratitude; then she took her son and left the room.—The word of the Lord. ℟. **Thanks be to God.** ↓

RESPONSORIAL PSALM   Ps 17:1, 6-7, 8b and 15

℟. (15b) **Lord, when your glory appears, my joy will be full.**

Hear, O LORD, a just suit;
    attend to my outcry;
    hearken to my prayer from lips without deceit.—℟.

I call upon you, for you will answer me, O God;
    incline your ear to me; hear my word.
Show your wondrous mercies,
    O savior of those who flee
    from their foes to refuge at your right hand.—℟.

Hide me in the shadow of your wings.
But I in justice shall behold your face;
    on waking, I shall be content in your presence.—℟. ↓

VERSE BEFORE THE GOSPEL   Jn 11:25a, 26

℟. **Praise to you, Lord Jesus Christ, King of endless glory!***
I am the resurrection and the life, says the Lord;
whoever believes in me will never die.

℟. **Praise to you, Lord Jesus Christ, King of endless glory!** ↓

GOSPEL   Jn 11:1-45

Jesus was a close friend of Mary, Martha, and Lazarus. When Lazarus becomes ill, his sisters send for Jesus. When Jesus arrives, he finds that Lazarus has been dead for four days. Jesus comforts Mary and Martha and brings Lazarus back to life.

℣. The Lord be with you. ℟. **And also with you.**
℣. A reading from the holy Gospel according to John.
℟. **Glory to you, Lord.**

---

* *See p. 620 for other Gospel Acclamations.*

THERE was a man who was ill, Lazarus from Bethany, the village of Mary and her sister Martha. Mary was the one who had anointed the Lord with perfumed oil and dried his feet with her hair; it was her brother Lazarus who was ill. So the sisters sent word to Jesus saying, "Master, the one you love is ill." When Jesus heard this he said, "This illness is not to end in death, but is for the glory of God, that the Son of God may be glorified through it." Now Jesus loved Martha and her sister and Lazarus. So when he heard that he was ill, he remained for two days in the place where he was. Then after this he said to his disciples, "Let us go back to Judea." The disciples said to him, "Rabbi, the Jews were just trying to stone you, and you want to go back there?" Jesus answered, "Are there not twelve hours in a day? If one walks during the day, he does not stumble, because he sees the light of this world. But if one walks at night, he stumbles, because the light is not in him." He said this, and then told them, "Our friend Lazarus is asleep, but I am going to awaken him." So the disciples said to him, "Master, if he is asleep, he will be saved." But Jesus was talking about his death, while they thought that he meant ordinary sleep. So then Jesus said to them clearly, "Lazarus has died. And I am glad for you that I was not there, that you may believe. Let us go to him." So Thomas, called Didymus, said to his fellow disciples, "Let us also go to die with him."

When Jesus arrived, he found that Lazarus had already been in the tomb for four days. Now Bethany was near Jerusalem, only about two miles away. And many of the Jews had come to Martha and Mary to comfort them about their brother. When Martha heard that Jesus was coming, she went to meet him; but Mary sat at home. Martha said to Jesus, "Lord, if you had been here, my brother would not have died. But even now I know that whatever you ask of God, God will give you." Jesus said to her, "Your brother will rise." Martha said to him, "I know he will rise, in the resurrection on the last day." Jesus told her, "I am the resurrection and the life; whoever believes in me, even if he dies, will live, and everyone who lives and believes in me will never die. Do you believe this?" She said to him, "Yes, Lord. I have come to believe that you are the Christ, the Son of God, the one who is coming into the world."

When she had said this, she went and called her sister Mary secretly, saying, "The teacher is here and is asking for you." As soon as she heard this, she rose quickly and went to him. For Jesus had not yet come into the village, but was still where Martha had met him. So when the Jews who were with her in the house comforting her saw Mary get up quickly and go out, they followed her, presuming that she was going to the tomb to weep there. When Mary came to where Jesus was and saw him, she fell at his feet and said to him, "Lord, if you had been here, my brother would not have died." When Jesus saw her weeping and the Jews who had come with her weeping, he became perturbed and deeply troubled, and said, "Where have you laid him?" They said to him, "Sir, come and see." And Jesus wept. So the Jews said, "See how he loved him." But some of them said, "Could not the one who opened the eyes of the blind man have done something so that this man would not have died?"

So Jesus, perturbed again, came to the tomb. It was a cave, and a stone lay across it. Jesus said, "Take away the stone." Martha, the dead man's sister, said to him, "Lord, by now there will be a stench; he has been dead for four days." Jesus said to her, "Did I not tell you that if you believe you will see the glory of God?" So they took away the stone. And Jesus raised his eyes and said, "Father, I thank you for hearing me. I know that you always hear me; but because of the crowd here I have said this, that they may believe that you sent me." And when he had said this, he cried out in a loud voice, "Lazarus, come out!" The dead man came out, tied hand and foot with burial bands, and his face was wrapped in a cloth. So Jesus said to them, "Untie him and let him go."

Now many of the Jews who had come to Mary and seen what he had done began to believe in him.—The Gospel of the Lord. ℟. **Praise to you, Lord Jesus Christ.**

→ No. 15, p. 623

MONDAY OF THE FIFTH WEEK OF LENT

Jesus is the light of the world. In him we find perfect justice as he search-es into the hearts of human beings. We live in an imperfect world and our human weakness often makes us prone to error. God alone is all-just. He is triumphant in eternal vindication, which is proved in the Resurrection. Jesus was judged by evil-minded people.

ENTRANCE ANT.   Ps 56:2

God, take pity on me! My enemies are crushing me; all day long they wage war on me.   → No. 2, p. 614

OPENING PRAYER

Father of love, source of all blessings,
help us to pass from our old life of sin
to the new life of grace.
Prepare us for the glory of your kingdom.
We ask this . . . for ever and ever. ℟. **Amen.** ↓

FIRST READING   Dn 13:1-9, 15-17, 19-30, 33-62 or 13:41c-62

[If the "Short Form" is used, omit indented text in brackets.]

The last two chapters of the Book of Daniel develop stories about Daniel. In the shorter form of the story about Susanna, the author comes quickly to the point that in God there is perfect justice and vindication, whereas the judgment of humans is always in danger of being erroneous.

A reading from the Book of the Prophet Daniel

[IN Babylon there lived a man named Joakim, who married a very beautiful and God-fearing woman,

Susanna, the daughter of Hilkiah; her pious parents had trained their daughter according to the law of Moses. Joakim was very rich; he had a garden near his house, and the Jews had recourse to him often because he was the most respected of them all.

That year, two elders of the people were appointed judges, of whom the Lord said, "Wickedness has come out of Babylon: from the elders who were to govern the people as judges." These men, to whom all brought their cases, frequented the house of Joakim. When the people left at noon, Susanna used to enter her husband's garden for a walk. When the old men saw her enter every day for her walk, they began to lust for her. They suppressed their consciences; they would not allow their eyes to look to heaven, and did not keep in mind just judgments.

One day, while they were waiting for the right moment, she entered the garden as usual, with two maids only. She decided to bathe, for the weather was warm. Nobody else was there except the two elders, who had hidden themselves and were watching her. "Bring me oil and soap," she said to the maids, "and shut the garden doors while I bathe."

As soon as the maids had left, the two old men got up and hurried to her. "Look," they said, "the garden doors are shut, and no one can see us; give in to our desire, and lie with us. If you refuse, we will testify against you that you dismissed your maids because a young man was here with you."

"I am completely trapped," Susanna groaned. "If I yield, it will be my death; if I refuse, I cannot escape your power. Yet it is better for me to fall into your power without guilt than to sin before the Lord." Then Susanna shrieked, and the old men also shouted at her, as one of them ran to open the garden doors.

When the people in the house heard the cries from the garden, they rushed in by the side gate to see what had happened to her. At the accusations by the old men, the servants felt very much ashamed, for never had any such thing been said about Susanna.

When the people came to her husband Joakim the next day, the two wicked elders also came, fully determined to put Susanna to death. Before all the people they ordered: "Send for Susanna, the daughter of Hilkiah, the wife of Joakim." When she was sent for, she came with her parents, children and all her relatives. All her relatives and the onlookers were weeping.

In the midst of the people the two elders rose up and laid their hands on her head. Through tears she looked up to heaven, for she trusted in the Lord wholeheartedly. The elders made this accusation: "As we were walking in the garden alone, this woman entered with two girls and shut the doors of the garden, dismissing the girls. A young man, who was hidden there, came and lay with her. When we, in a corner of the garden, saw this crime, we ran toward them. We saw them lying together, but the man we could not hold, because he was stronger than we; he opened the doors and ran off. Then we seized her and asked who the young man was, but she refused to tell us. We testify to this."

The assembly believed them, since they were elders and judges of the people, and they condemned her to death.]

*[Short Form only:*The assembly condemned Susanna to death.]

But Susanna cried aloud: "O eternal God, you know what is hidden and are aware of all things before they come to be: you know that they have testified falsely against me. Here I am about to die, though I have done none of the things with which these wicked men have charged me."

The Lord heard her prayer. As she was being led to execution, God stirred up the holy spirit of a young boy named Daniel, and he cried aloud: "I will have no part in the death of this woman." All the people turned and asked him, "What is this you are saying?" He stood in their midst and continued, "Are you such fools, O children of Israel! To condemn a woman of Israel without examination and without clear evidence? Return to court, for they have testified falsely against her."

Then all the people returned in haste. To Daniel the elders said, "Come, sit with us and inform us, since God has given you the prestige of old age." But he replied, "Separate these two far from each other that I may examine them."

After they were separated one from the other, he called one of them and said: "How you have grown evil with age! Now have your past sins come to term: passing unjust sentences, condemning the innocent, and freeing the guilty, although the Lord says, 'The innocent and the just you shall not put to death.' Now, then, if you were a witness, tell me under what tree you saw them together." "Under a mastic tree," he answered. Daniel replied, "Your fine lie has cost you your head, for the angel of God shall receive the sentence from him and split you in two." Putting him to one side, he ordered the other one to be brought. Daniel said to him, "Offspring of Canaan, not of Judah, beauty has seduced you, lust has subverted your conscience. This is how you acted with the daughters of Israel, and in their fear they yielded to you; but a daughter of Judah did not tolerate your wickedness. Now, then, tell me under what tree you surprised them together." "Under an oak," he said. Daniel replied, "Your fine lie has cost you also your head, for the angel of God waits with a sword to cut you in two so as to make an end of you both."

The whole assembly cried aloud, blessing God who saves those who hope in him. They rose up against the two elders, for by their own words Daniel had convicted them of perjury. According to the law of Moses, they inflicted on them the penalty they had plotted to impose on their neighbor: they put them to death. Thus was innocent blood spared that day.—The word of the Lord. ℟. **Thanks be to God.** ↓

RESPONSORIAL PSALM   Ps 23:1-3a, 3b-4, 5, 6

℟. (4ab) **Even though I walk in the dark valley I fear no evil; for you are at my side.**

See Saturday of the 4th Week in Ordinary Time, p. 295.

VERSE BEFORE THE GOSPEL   Ez 33:11

℟. **Praise to you, Lord Jesus Christ, King of endless glory!***

I take no pleasure in the death of the wicked man, says the Lord,

but rather in his conversion, that he may live.

℟. **Praise to you, Lord Jesus Christ, King of endless glory!** ↓

GOSPEL   Jn 8:1-11

The Pharisees bring a woman accused of adultery to Jesus. They ask him to judge the case in the light of their law. Without speaking, Jesus writes in the sand. Let him who has no sin cast the first stone. One by one, they leave and Jesus also forgives her.

℣. The Lord be with you. ℟. **And also with you.**

℣. A reading from the holy Gospel according to John.

℟. **Glory to you, Lord.**

JESUS went to the Mount of Olives. But early in the morning he arrived again in the temple area, and all the people started coming to him, and he sat down and taught them. Then the scribes and the Pharisees brought a woman who had been caught in adultery and made her stand in the middle. They said to him, "Teacher, this

---

* *See p. 620 for other Gospel Acclamations.*

woman was caught in the very act of committing adultery. Now in the law, Moses commanded us to stone such women. So what do you say?" They said this to test him, so that they could have some charge to bring against him. Jesus bent down and began to write on the ground with his finger. But when they continued asking him, he straightened up and said to them, "Let the one among you who is without sin be the first to throw a stone at her." Again he bent down and wrote on the ground. And in response, they went away one by one, beginning with the elders. So he was left alone with the woman before him. Then Jesus straightened up and said to her, "Woman, where are they? Has no one condemned you?" She replied, "No one, sir." Then Jesus said, "Neither do I condemn you. Go, and from now on do not sin any more."—The Gospel of the Lord. ℞. **Praise to you, Lord Jesus Christ.**

➔ No. 15, p. 623

OR

In Year C, when the above Gospel is read on the preceding Sunday, the following text is used.

GOSPEL   Jn 8:12-20

This incident is connected with routing the accusers of the woman taken in adultery. Jesus says the worst thing he could have said to the Pharisees, the intellectuals of the time. "I," he says, "am the light of the world." This would mean "not you." And, of course, they react.

℣. The Lord be with you. ℞. **And also with you.**
℣. A reading from the holy Gospel according to John.
℞. **Glory to you, Lord.**

JESUS spoke to them again, saying, "I am the light of the world. Whoever follows me will not walk in darkness, but will have the light of life." So the Pharisees said to him, "You testify on your own behalf, so your testimony cannot be verified." Jesus answered and said to them, "Even if I do testify on my own behalf, my testimony can be verified, because I know where I came from and where I am going. But you do not know where I come from or where I am going. You judge by appearances, but I do not judge anyone. And even if I should judge, my judgment is valid, because I am not alone, but it is I and the Father who sent me. Even in your law it is written that the testimony of two men can be verified. I testify on my behalf and so does the Father who sent me." So they said to him, "Where is your father?" Jesus answered, "You know neither me nor my Father. If you knew me, you would know my Father also." He spoke these words while teaching in the treasury in the temple area. But no one arrested him, because his hour had not yet come.—The Gospel of the Lord. ℟. **Praise to you, Lord Jesus Christ.**

→ No. 15, p. 623

PRAYER OVER THE GIFTS

Lord,
as we come with joy
to celebrate the mystery of the eucharist,
may we offer you hearts
purified by bodily penance.
Grant this through Christ our Lord.
℟. **Amen.**   → No. 21, p. 626 (Pref. P 17)

COMMUNION ANT.

When the Gospel of the adulteress is read (Year C):

Jn 8:10-11

Has no one condemned you? The woman answered: No one, Lord. Neither do I condemn you: go and do not sin again. ↓

When other Gospels are read:

Jn 8:12

I am the light of the world, says the Lord; the man who follows me will have the light of life. ↓

PRAYER AFTER COMMUNION

Father,
through the grace of your sacraments

may we follow Christ more faithfully
and come to the joy of your kingdom,
where he is Lord for ever and ever.
℟. **Amen.**   ➜ No. 32 p. 660

TUESDAY OF THE FIFTH WEEK OF LENT

In our humanity, the great obedience is fidelity to conscience—to conscience enlightened by Christ's teachings in the Church. It must be a prompt conformity to all lawful authority, beginning with our parents in early days. This practice smoothes differences, blends with kindness, and pleases God exceedingly.

ENTRANCE ANT.   Ps 27:14

Put your hope in the Lord. Take courage and be strong.
    ➜ No. 2, p. 614

OPENING PRAYER

Lord,
help us to do your will
that your Church may grow
and become more faithful in your service.
Grant this . . . for ever and ever. ℟. **Amen.** ↓

FIRST READING   Nm 21:4-9

Again the Israelites rebel against God and are punished. There is a deep symbolism in the mounting of the bronze serpent who saved those Israelites, victims of deadly stings in the desert. But first there is retribution for complaining against God.

A reading from the Book of Numbers

FROM Mount Hor the children of Israel set out on the Red Sea road, to bypass the land of Edom. But with their patience worn out by the journey, the people complained against God and Moses, "Why have you brought us up from Egypt to die in this desert, where there is no food or water? We are disgusted with this wretched food!"

In punishment the Lord sent among the people saraph serpents, which bit the people so that many of them died. Then the people came to Moses and said, "We have sinned in complaining against the Lord and you. Pray the Lord to take the serpents away from us." So Moses prayed for the people, and the Lord said to Moses, "Make a saraph and mount it on a pole, and whoever looks at it after being bitten will live." Moses accordingly made a bronze serpent and mounted it on a pole, and whenever anyone who had been bitten by a serpent looked at the bronze serpent, he lived.—The word of the Lord. ℟. **Thanks be to God.** ↓

RESPONSORIAL PSALM   Ps 102:2-3, 16-18, 19-21

℟. (2) **O Lord, hear my prayer, and let my cry come to you.**

O Lord, hear my prayer,
    and let my cry come to you.
Hide not your face from me
    in the day of my distress.
Incline your ear to me;
    in the day when I call, answer me speedily.—℟.

The nations shall revere your name, O Lord,
    and all the kings of the earth your glory,
When the Lord has rebuilt Zion
    and appeared in his glory;
When he has regarded the prayer of the destitute,
    and not despised their prayer.—℟.

Let this be written for the generation to come,
    and let his future creatures praise the Lord:
"The Lord looked down from his holy height,
    from heaven he beheld the earth,
To hear the groaning of the prisoners,
    to release those doomed to die."—℟. ↓

VERSE BEFORE THE GOSPEL

℟. **Praise to you, Lord Jesus Christ, king of endless glory!***
The seed is the word of God, Christ is the sower;
all who come to him will live for ever.

℟. **Praise to you, Lord Jesus Christ, king of endless glory!** ↓

GOSPEL   Jn 8:21-30

Jesus' words are clear only for those who are disposed to believe. His words may be wasted on the Pharisees to whom he is speaking, but there are others listening who may be saved. In this passage Jesus speaks as one who is sent with authority.

℣. The Lord be with you. ℟. **And also with you.**
℣. A reading from the holy Gospel according to John.
℟. **Glory to you, Lord.**

JESUS said to the Pharisees: "I am going away and you will look for me, but you will die in your sin. Where I am going you cannot come." So the Jews said, "He is not going to kill himself, is he, because he said, 'Where I am going you cannot come'?" He said to them, "You belong to what is below, I belong to what is above. You belong to this world, but I do not belong to this world. That is why I told you that you will die in your sins. For if you do not believe that I AM, you will die in your sins." So they said to him, "Who are you?" Jesus said to them, "What I told you from the beginning. I have much to say about you in condemnation. But the one who sent me is true, and what I heard from him I tell the world." They did not realize that he was speaking to them of the Father. So Jesus said to them, "When you lift up the Son of Man, then you will realize that I AM, and that I do nothing on my own, but I say only what the Father taught me. The one who sent me is with me. He has not left me alone, because I always do what is pleasing to him." Because he spoke this way

---

* *See p. 620 for other Gospel Acclamations.*

many came to believe in him.—The Gospel of the Lord.
℟. **Praise to you, Lord Jesus Christ.** → No. 15, p. 623

PRAYER OVER THE GIFTS

Merciful Lord,
we offer this gift of reconciliation
so that you will forgive our sins
and guide our wayward hearts.
We ask this through Christ our Lord.
℟. **Amen.** → No. 21, p. 626 (Pref. P 17)

COMMUNION ANT. Jn 12:32

When I am lifted up from the earth, I will draw all men to myself, says the Lord. ↓

PRAYER AFTER COMMUNION

All-powerful God,
may the holy mysteries we share in this eucharist
make us worthy to attain the gift of heaven.
We ask this in the name of Jesus the Lord.
℟. **Amen.** → No. 32, p. 660

WEDNESDAY OF THE FIFTH WEEK OF LENT

We are slaves to sin, slaves to envy and hatred of our neighbors, bound to human weakness from which, without true repentance and faith in the grace of God, we can never know spiritual freedom. We must realize that we have been called to live in freedom, but not to give free rein to freedom of the flesh. Love for our neighbors ensures this freedom for us.

ENTRANCE ANT. Ps 18:48-49

Lord, you rescue me from raging enemies, you lift me up above my attackers, you deliver me from violent men.
→ No. 2, p. 614

OPENING PRAYER

Father of mercy,
hear the prayers of your repentant children
who call on you in love.

Enlighten our minds and sanctify our hearts.
We ask this . . . for ever and ever. ℟. **Amen.** ↓

FIRST READING   Dn 3:14-20, 91-92, 95

Nebuchadnezzar builds a golden statue and commands everyone to worship it. The three youths do not obey, and being denounced to the king by certain Chaldeans, they are thrown into a furnace of extreme heat. Nevertheless, they are not consumed, but walk unharmed in the midst of the fire. With them is a fourth, whose aspect is like a "Son of God."

A reading from the Book of the Prophet Daniel

KING Nebuchadnezzar said: "Is it true, Shadrach, Meshach, and Abednego, that you will not serve my god, or worship the golden statue that I set up? Be ready now to fall down and worship the statue I had made, whenever you hear the sound of the trumpet, flute, lyre, harp, psaltery, bagpipe, and all the other musical instruments; otherwise, you shall be instantly cast into the white-hot furnace; and who is the God who can deliver you out of my hands?" Shadrach, Meshach, and Abednego answered King Nebuchadnezzar, "There is no need for us to defend ourselves before you in this matter. If our God, whom we serve, can save us from the white-hot furnace and from your hands, O king, may he save us! But even if he will not, know, O king, that we will not serve your god or worship the golden statue that you set up."

King Nebuchadnezzar's face became livid with utter rage against Shadrach, Meshach, and Abednego. He ordered the furnace to be heated seven times more than usual and had some of the strongest men in his army bind Shadrach, Meshach, and Abednego and cast them into the white-hot furnace.

Nebuchadnezzar rose in haste and asked his nobles, "Did we not cast three men bound into the fire?" "Assuredly, O king," they answered. "But," he replied, "I see four men unfettered and unhurt, walking in the fire, and the fourth looks like a son of God." Nebuchadnezzar exclaimed, "Blessed be the God of Shadrach, Meshach,

and Abednego, who sent his angel to deliver the servants who trusted in him; they disobeyed the royal command and yielded their bodies rather than serve or worship any god except their own God."—The word of the Lord. ℟.
Thanks be to God. ↓

RESPONSORIAL PSALM Dn 3:52, 53, 54, 55, 56

℟. (52b) **Glory and praise for ever!**

"Blessed are you, O LORD, the God of our fathers,
  praiseworthy and exalted above all forever;
And blessed is your holy and glorious name,
  praiseworthy and exalted above all for all ages."—℟.

"Blessed are you in the temple of your holy glory,
  praiseworthy and exalted above all forever.—℟.

"Blessed are you on the throne of your kingdom,
  praiseworthy and exalted above all forever."—℟.

"Blessed are you who look into the depths
  from your throne upon the cherubim;
  praiseworthy and exalted above all forever."—℟.

"Blessed are you in the firmament of heaven,
  praiseworthy and glorious forever."—℟. ↓

VERSE BEFORE THE GOSPEL See Lk 8:15

℟. **Praise to you, Lord Jesus Christ, King of endless glory!***
Blessed are they who have kept the word with a generous heart
and yield a harvest through perseverance.

℟. **Praise to you, Lord Jesus Christ, King of endless glory!** ↓

GOSPEL Jn 8:31-42

The Jews who were listening to Jesus' words were definitely hoping to become a world power through some indomitable leader. Christ was dispelling such notions by insisting that his mission was to redeem human beings from themselves, that is, from sin—a slavery to self.

---

* *See p. 620 for other Gospel Acclamations.*

℣. The Lord be with you. ℟. **And also with you.**
℣. A reading from the holy Gospel according to John.
℟. **Glory to you, Lord.**

JESUS said to those Jews who believed in him, "If you remain in my word, you will truly be my disciples, and you will know the truth, and the truth will set you free." They answered him, "We are descendants of Abraham and have never been enslaved to anyone. How can you say, 'You will become free'?" Jesus answered them, "Amen, amen, I say to you, everyone who commits sin is a slave of sin. A slave does not remain in a household forever, but a son always remains. So if the Son frees you, then you will truly be free. I know that you are descendants of Abraham. But you are trying to kill me, because my word has no room among you. I tell you what I have seen in the Father's presence; then do what you have heard from the Father."

They answered and said to him, "Our father is Abraham." Jesus said to them, "If you were Abraham's children, you would be doing the works of Abraham. But now you are trying to kill me, a man who has told you the truth that I heard from God; Abraham did not do this. You are doing the works of your father!" So they said to him, "We were not born of fornication. We have one Father, God." Jesus said to them, "If God were your Father, you would love me, for I came from God and am here; I did not come on my own, but he sent me."—The Gospel of the Lord. ℟. **Praise to you, Lord Jesus Christ.** ➧ No. 15, p. 623

PRAYER OVER THE GIFTS

Lord,
you have given us these gifts to honor your name.
Bless them,
and let them become a source of health and strength.
We ask this through Christ our Lord.
℟. **Amen.**　　　　　　　　　　➧ No. 21, p. 626 (Pref. P 17)

COMMUNION ANT. Col. 1:13-15

God has transferred us into the kingdom of the Son he loves; in him we are redeemed, and find forgiveness of our sins. ↓

PRAYER AFTER COMMUNION

Lord,
may the mysteries we receive heal us,
remove sin from our hearts,
and make us grow strong
under your constant protection.
Grant this through Christ our Lord.
℞. **Amen.**

→ No. 32, p. 660

THURSDAY OF THE FIFTH WEEK OF LENT

Almighty God is eager to forgive us. With his gift of his only Son to be our salvation, he waits for us to come to him, and it will be the same until the Second Coming. We should waste no time in putting our house in order and be ready for that great summons!

ENTRANCE ANT. Heb 9:15

Christ is the mediator of a new covenant so that, since he has died, those who are called may receive the eternal inheritance promised to them. → No. 2, p. 614

OPENING PRAYER

Lord,
come to us:
free us from the stain of our sins.
Help us to remain faithful to a holy way of life,
and guide us to the inheritance you have promised.
Grant this . . . for ever and ever. ℞. **Amen.** ↓

FIRST READING Gn 17:3-9

Abram, "the father," becomes Abraham, indicating "father of a multitude." The new item here is the extension of the Covenant to succeeding generations, and the promise of the land is here stated solemnly. Abraham and his descendants are to keep the covenant.

A reading from the Book of Genesis

WHEN Abram prostrated himself, God spoke to him: "My covenant with you is this: you are to become the father of a host of nations. No longer shall you be called Abram; your name shall be Abraham, for I am making you the father of a host of nations. I will render you exceedingly fertile; I will make nations of you; kings shall stem from you. I will maintain my covenant with you and your descendants after you throughout the ages as an everlasting pact, to be your God and the God of your descendants after you. I will give to you and to your descendants after you the land in which you are now staying, the whole land of Canaan, as a permanent possession; and I will be their God."

God also said to Abraham: "On your part, you and your descendants after you must keep my covenant throughout the ages."—The word of the Lord. ℟. **Thanks be to God.** ↓

RESPONSORIAL PSALM   Ps 105:4-5, 6-7, 8-9

℟. (8a) **The Lord remembers his covenant for ever.**

Look to the LORD in his strength;
    seek to serve him constantly.
Recall the wondrous deeds that he has wrought,
    his portents, and the judgments he has uttered.—℟.

You descendants of Abraham, his servants,
    sons of Jacob, his chosen ones!
He, the LORD, is our God;
    throughout the earth his judgments prevail.—℟.

He remembers forever his covenant
    which he made binding for a thousand generations—
Which he entered into with Abraham
    and by his oath to Isaac.—℟. ↓

VERSE BEFORE THE GOSPEL Ps 95:8

℟. **Praise to you, Lord Jesus Christ, King of endless glory!***
If today you hear his voice,
harden not your hearts.
℟. **Praise to you, Lord Jesus Christ, King of endless glory!** ↓

GOSPEL Jn 8:51-59

Still superficial in their judgment, the Jews protest the possibility of Christ giving eternal life. Jesus answers that it is the testimony of the Father that is involved—the testimony that they refuse to receive. Abraham himself knew that the promises made to him pointed to a blessedness to come.

℣. The Lord be with you. ℟. **And also with you.**
℣. A reading from the holy Gospel according to John.
℟. **Glory to you, Lord.**

JESUS said to the Jews: "Amen, amen, I say to you, whoever keeps my word will never see death." So the Jews said to him, "Now we are sure that you are possessed. Abraham died, as did the prophets, yet you say, 'Whoever keeps my word will never taste death.' Are you greater than our father Abraham, who died? Or the prophets, who died? Who do you make yourself out to be?" Jesus answered, "If I glorify myself, my glory is worth nothing; but it is my Father who glorifies me, of whom you say, 'He is our God.' You do not know him, but I know him. And if I should say that I do not know him, I would be like you a liar. But I do know him and I keep his word. Abraham your father rejoiced to see my day; he saw it and was glad." So the Jews said to him, "You are not yet fifty years old and you have seen Abraham?" Jesus said to them, "Amen, amen, I say to you, before Abraham came to be, I AM." So they picked up stones to throw at him; but Jesus hid and went out of the

---

* *See p. 620 for other Gospel Acclamations.*

temple area.—The Gospel of the Lord. ℟. **Praise to you, Lord Jesus Christ.** → No. 15, p. 623

PRAYER OVER THE GIFTS

Merciful Lord,
accept the sacrifice we offer you
that it may help us grow in holiness
and advance the salvation of the world.
We ask this in the name of Jesus the Lord.
℟. **Amen.** → No. 21, p. 626 (Pref. P 17)

COMMUNION ANT.
Rom 8:32

God did not spare his own Son, but gave him up for us all: with Christ he will surely give us all things. ↓

PRAYER AFTER COMMUNION

Lord of mercy,
let the sacrament which renews us
bring us to eternal life.
We ask this through Christ our Lord.
℟. **Amen.** → No. 32, p. 660

FRIDAY OF THE FIFTH WEEK OF LENT

Faith alone is not sufficient for salvation. "Just as a body without a spirit is dead, so also faith without works is dead," says St. James (2:26), and, again, "You believe that God is one. You do well. Even the demons believe that and shudder" (2:19). We should believe as if our salvation depended on God alone and work as if it depended only on us. God will listen to those who come to him.

ENTRANCE ANT.
Ps 31:10, 16, 18

Have mercy on me, Lord, for I am in distress; rescue me from the hands of my enemies. Lord, keep me from shame, for I have called to you. → No. 2, p. 614

OPENING PRAYER

Lord,
grant us your forgiveness,

and set us free from our enslavement to sin.
We ask this . . . for ever and ever. ℟. **Amen.** ↓

FIRST READING
Jer 20:10-13

Jeremiah knows that God is with him. This confidence has its foundation in Yahweh's promise that the prophet often recalls. In the midst of strong contradictions, he keeps his faith in God's loyalty.

A reading from the Book of the Prophet Jeremiah

I HEAR the whisperings of many:
  "Terror on every side!
    Denounce! let us denounce him!"
All those who were my friends
    are on the watch for any misstep of mine.
"Perhaps he will be trapped; then we can prevail,
    and take our vengeance on him."
But the LORD is with me, like a mighty champion:
    my persecutors will stumble, they will not triumph.
In their failure they will be put to utter shame,
    to lasting, unforgettable confusion.
O LORD of hosts, you who test the just,
    who probe mind and heart,
Let me witness the vengeance you take on them,
    for to you I have entrusted my cause.
Sing to the LORD,
    praise the LORD,
For he has rescued the life of the poor
    from the power of the wicked!
The word of the Lord. ℟. **Thanks be to God.** ↓

RESPONSORIAL PSALM
Ps 18:2-3a, 3bc-4, 5-6, 7

℟. (see 7) **In my distress I called upon the Lord, and he heard my voice.**

I love you, O LORD, my strength,
    O LORD, my rock, my fortress, my deliverer.—℟.
My God, my rock of refuge,
    my shield, the horn of my salvation, my stronghold!

Praised be the LORD, I exclaim,
  and I am safe from my enemies.—℞.

The breakers of death surged round about me,
  the destroying floods overwhelmed me;
The cords of the nether world enmeshed me,
  the snares of death overtook me.—℞.

In my distress I called upon the LORD
  and cried out to my God;
From his temple he heard my voice,
  and my cry to him reached his ears.—℞. ↓

VERSE BEFORE THE GOSPEL   Jn 6:63c, 68c

℞. **Praise to you, Lord Jesus Christ, King of endless
  glory!***
Your words, Lord, are Spirit and life;
you have the words of everlasting life.
℞. **Praise to you, Lord Jesus Christ, King of endless
  glory!** ↓

GOSPEL   Jn 10:31-42

The sinful men who wanted to stone our Lord when they had accused him
of blasphemy heard what Jesus spoke when he said he was of one sub-
stance with the Father. He is known for who he is because he does the
work of the Father. The people recall what John taught about Jesus.

℣. The Lord be with you. ℞. **And also with you.**
℣. A reading from the holy Gospel according to John.
℞. **Glory to you, Lord.**

T HE Jews picked up rocks to stone Jesus. Jesus
  answered them, "I have shown you many good works
from my Father. For which of these are you trying to
stone me?" The Jews answered him, "We are not stoning
you for a good work but for blasphemy. You, a man, are
making yourself God." Jesus answered them, "Is it not
written in your law, 'I said, "You are gods" '? If it calls

* See p. 620 for other Gospel Acclamations.

them gods to whom the word of God came, and Scripture cannot be set aside, can you say that the one whom the Father has consecrated and sent into the world blasphemes because I said, 'I am the Son of God'? If I do not perform my Father's works, do not believe me; but if I perform them, even if you do not believe me, believe the works, so that you may realize and understand that the Father is in me and I am in the Father." Then they tried again to arrest him; but he escaped from their power.

He went back across the Jordan to the place where John first baptized, and there he remained. Many came to him and said, "John performed no sign, but everything John said about this man was true." And many there began to believe in him.—The Gospel of the Lord. ℟. **Praise to you, Lord Jesus Christ.**   ➙ No. 15, p. 623

PRAYER OVER THE GIFTS

God of mercy,
may the gifts we present at your altar
help us to achieve eternal salvation.
Grant this through Christ our Lord.
℟. **Amen.**   ➙ No. 21, p. 626 (Pref. P 17)

COMMUNION ANT.   1 Pt 2:24

Jesus carried our sins in his own body on the cross so that we could die to sin and live in holiness; by his wounds we have been healed. ↓

PRAYER AFTER COMMUNION

Lord,
may we always receive the protection of this sacrifice.
May it keep us safe from all harm.
We ask this in the name of Jesus the Lord.
℟. **Amen.**   ➙ No. 32, p. 660

SATURDAY OF THE FIFTH WEEK OF LENT

Jesus offered his life for all of us. This is the example of ultimate love. By thinking of this we can gradually transform and motivate ourselves to become more understanding of one another. We too, like Christ, can give of ourselves in prayer, thought, word, and action.

ENTRANCE ANT.   Ps 22:20, 7

Lord, do not stay away; come quickly to help me! I am a worm and no man: men scorn me, people despise me.

→ No. 2, p. 614

OPENING PRAYER

God our Father,
you always work to save us,
and now we rejoice in the great love
you give to your chosen people.
Protect all who are about to become your children,
and continue to bless those who are already baptized.
Grant this . . . for ever and ever. ℟. **Amen.** ↓

FIRST READING   Ez 37:21-28

The union of all tribes is a frequent element in Messianic prophecy. God is to unite the nation in a new Covenant in which there are five essential elements: Yahweh, its God; Israel, his people; life, "on the land where their fathers lived"; "my sanctuary among them," as a sign of the presence of the Lord and law; David, as the one shepherd over them.

A reading from the Book of the Prophet Ezekiel

THUS says the Lord GOD: I will take the children of Israel from among the nations to which they have come, and gather them from all sides to bring them back to their land. I will make them one nation upon the land, in the mountains of Israel, and there shall be one prince for them all. Never again shall they be two nations, and never again shall they be divided into two kingdoms.

No longer shall they defile themselves with their idols, their abominations, and all their transgressions. I will deliver them from all their sins of apostasy, and cleanse them so that they may be my people and I may be their God. My servant David shall be prince over them, and there shall be one shepherd for them all; they shall live by my statutes and carefully observe my decrees. They shall live on the land that I gave to my servant Jacob, the land where their fathers lived; they shall live on it forever, they, and their children, and their children's children, with my servant David their prince forever. I will make with them a covenant of peace; it shall be an everlasting covenant with them, and I will multiply them, and put my sanctuary among them forever. My dwelling shall be with them; I will be their God, and they shall be my people. Thus the nations shall know that it is I, the LORD, who make Israel holy, when my sanctuary shall be set up among them forever.—The word of the Lord. ℟. **Thanks be to God.** ↓

RESPONSORIAL PSALM   Jer 31:10, 11-12abcd, 13

℟. (see 10d) **The Lord will guard us, as a shepherd
    guards his flock.**

Hear the word of the LORD, O nations,
    proclaim it on distant isles, and say:
He who scattered Israel, now gathers them together,
    he guards them as a shepherd his flock.—℟.

The LORD shall ransom Jacob,
    he shall redeem him from the hand of his conqueror.
Shouting, they shall mount the heights of Zion,
    they shall come streaming to the LORD's blessings:
The grain, the wine, and the oil,
    the sheep and the oxen.—℟.

Then the virgins shall make merry and dance,
    and young men and old as well.
I will turn their mourning into joy,
    I will console and gladden them after their sorrows.—℟. ↓

VERSE BEFORE THE GOSPEL Ez 18:31

℟. **Praise to you, Lord Jesus Christ, King of endless glory!***

Cast away from you all the crimes you have committed,
  says the Lord,
and make for yourselves a new heart and a new spirit.

℟. **Praise to you, Lord Jesus Christ, King of endless glory!** ↓

GOSPEL Jn 11:45-56

With each day the hatred of Jesus' enemies increases, and the more astounding the deeds Jesus performs, the more determined they are to put him to death. Caiaphas prophesies: "It is better that one man should die instead of the people, so that the whole nation may not perish."

℣. The Lord be with you. ℟. **And also with you.**
℣. A reading from the holy Gospel according to John.
℟. **Glory to you, Lord.**

MANY of the Jews who had come to Mary and seen what Jesus had done began to believe in him. But some of them went to the Pharisees and told them what Jesus had done. So the chief priests and the Pharisees convened the Sanhedrin and said, "What are we going to do? This man is performing many signs. If we leave him alone, all will believe in him, and the Romans will come and take away both our land and our nation." But one of them, Caiaphas, who was high priest that year, said to them, "You know nothing, nor do you consider that it is better for you that one man should die instead of the people, so that the whole nation may not perish." He did not say this on his own, but since he was high priest for that year, he prophesied that Jesus was going to die for the nation, and not only for the nation, but also to gather into one the dispersed children of God. So from that day on they planned to kill him.

---

* *See p. 620 for other Gospel Acclamations.*

So Jesus no longer walked about in public among the Jews, but he left for the region near the desert, to a town called Ephraim, and there he remained with his disciples.

Now the Passover of the Jews was near, and many went up from the country to Jerusalem before Passover to purify themselves. They looked for Jesus and said to one another as they were in the temple area, "What do you think? That he will not come to the feast?"—The Gospel of the Lord. ℞. **Praise to you, Lord Jesus Christ.**

➜ No. 15, p. 623

PRAYER OVER THE GIFTS

Ever-living God,
in baptism, the sacrament of our faith,
you restore us to life.
Accept the prayers and gifts of your people:
forgive our sins and fulfill our hopes and desires.
We ask this in the name of Jesus the Lord.
℞. **Amen.**   ➜ No. 21, p. 626 (Pref. P 17)

COMMUNION ANT.   Jn 11:52

Christ was sacrificed so that he could gather together the scattered children of God. ↓

PRAYER AFTER COMMUNION

Father of mercy and power,
we thank you for nourishing us
with the body and blood of Christ
and for calling us to share in his divine life,
for he is Lord for ever and ever.
℞. **Amen.**   ➜ No. 32, p. 660

MONDAY OF HOLY WEEK

We are in the final week of the New Creation. Jesus makes it clear that all of us have varied tasks and responsibilities in the Kingdom of God. In working out our salvation we must be careful to attend to them and uproot our failings and sins that turn us away from God.

ENTRANCE ANT. Ps 35:1-2; 140:8

Defend me, Lord, from all my foes: take up your arms and come swiftly to my aid for you have the power to save me. → No. 2, p. 614

OPENING PRAYER

All-powerful God,
by the suffering and death of your Son,
strengthen and protect us in our weakness.
We ask this . . . for ever and ever. ℟. **Amen.** ↓

FIRST READING Is 42:1-7

The Suffering Servant represents the finest qualities of Israel and her great leaders. In this song he is a "chosen one" like Moses, David, and all Israel. As the Servant, he fulfills the role of Davidic king and prophet.

A reading from the Book of the Prophet Isaiah

HERE is my servant whom I uphold,
my chosen one with whom I am pleased,
Upon whom I have put my Spirit;
he shall bring forth justice to the nations,
Not crying out, not shouting,
not making his voice heard in the street.
A bruised reed he shall not break,
and a smoldering wick he shall not quench,
Until he establishes justice on the earth;
the coastlands will wait for his teaching.

Thus says God, the LORD,
who created the heavens and stretched them out,
who spreads out the earth with its crops,
Who gives breath to its people
and spirit to those who walk on it:
I, the LORD, have called you for the victory of justice,
I have grasped you by the hand;
I formed you, and set you
as a covenant of the people,
a light for the nations,

To open the eyes of the blind,
>> to bring out prisoners from confinement,
>>> and from the dungeon, those who live in darkness.
The word of the Lord. ℟. **Thanks be to God. ↓**

RESPONSORIAL PSALM
Ps 27:1, 2, 3, 13-14

℟. (1a) **The Lord is my light and my salvation.**

The Lord is my light and my salvation;
>> whom should I fear?
The Lord is my life's refuge;
>> of whom should I be afraid?—℟.

When evildoers come at me
>> to devour my flesh,
My foes and my enemies
>> themselves stumble and fall.—℟.

Though an army encamp against me,
>> my heart will not fear;
Though war be waged upon me,
>> even then will I trust.—℟.

I believe that I shall see the bounty of the Lord
>> in the land of the living.
Wait for the Lord with courage;
>> be stouthearted, and wait for the Lord.—℟. ↓

VERSE BEFORE THE GOSPEL

℟. **Marvelous and great are your works, O Lord!***
Hail to you, our King;
you alone are compassionate with our faults.
℟. **Marvelous and great are your works, O Lord! ↓**

GOSPEL
Jn 12:1-11

John describes the supper at Bethany on the sabbath before the Passover. Martha waits upon Jesus as he reclines at the table. Mary anoints the feet of Jesus with ointment and wipes his feet with her hair. Judas objects to the use of the expensive ointment, making religion a cloak for his covetousness.

* *See p. 620 for other Gospel Acclamations.*

℣. The Lord be with you. ℟. **And also with you.**

℣. A reading from the holy Gospel according to John.

℟. **Glory to you, Lord.**

SIX days before Passover Jesus came to Bethany, where Lazarus was, whom Jesus had raised from the dead. They gave a dinner for him there, and Martha served, while Lazarus was one of those reclining at table with him. Mary took a liter of costly perfumed oil made from genuine aromatic nard and anointed the feet of Jesus and dried them with her hair; the house was filled with the fragrance of the oil. Then Judas the Iscariot, one of his disciples, and the one who would betray him, said, "Why was this oil not sold for three hundred days' wages and given to the poor?" He said this not because he cared about the poor but because he was a thief and held the money bag and used to steal the contributions. So Jesus said, "Leave her alone. Let her keep this for the day of my burial. You always have the poor with you, but you do not always have me."

The large crowd of the Jews found out that he was there and came, not only because of him, but also to see Lazarus, whom he had raised from the dead. And the chief priests plotted to kill Lazarus too, because many of the Jews were turning away and believing in Jesus because of him—The Gospel of the Lord. ℟. **Praise to you, Lord Jesus Christ.** → No. 15, p. 623

PRAYER OVER THE GIFTS

Lord,
look with mercy on our offerings.
May the sacrifice of Christ, your Son,
bring us to eternal life,
for he is Lord for ever and ever.

℟. **Amen.** → No. 21, p. 626 (Pref. P 18)

COMMUNION ANT. Ps 102:3

When I am in trouble, Lord, do not hide your face from me; hear me when I call, and answer me quickly. ↓

PRAYER AFTER COMMUNION

God of mercy,
be close to your people.
Watch over us who receive this sacrament of salvation,
and keep us in your love.
We ask this in the name of Jesus the Lord.
℟. **Amen.**   ➜ No. 32, p. 660

TUESDAY OF HOLY WEEK

In times of trial and discouragement, we might conceivably lose sight of the fact that God has in store for us things never dreamed of in the mind of humans. In spite of our weakness and errors, he has extended his mission to the "ends of the earth." We should seek our reward with God because we trust him to reveal the fruit of our efforts.

ENTRANCE ANT.   Ps 27:12

False witnesses have stood up against me, and my enemies threaten violence; Lord, do not surrender me into their power!   ➜ No. 2, p. 614

OPENING PRAYER

Father,
may we receive your forgiveness and mercy
as we celebrate the passion and death of the Lord,
who lives and reigns with you and the Holy Spirit,
one God, for ever and ever. ℟. **Amen.** ↓

FIRST READING   Is 49:1-6

The second Servant Song presents the Servant as another Jeremiah: he is called from his mother's womb (Jer 1:5); he has a vocation to the Gentiles (Jer 1:10); he brings a message of both doom and happiness (Jer 16:19-21).

A reading from the Book of the Prophet Isaiah

HEAR me, O islands,
listen, O distant peoples.
The LORD called me from birth,
from my mother's womb he gave me my name.

He made of me a sharp-edged sword
  and concealed me in the shadow of his arm.
He made me a polished arrow,
  in his quiver he hid me.
You are my servant, he said to me,
  Israel, through whom I show my glory.

Though I thought I had toiled in vain,
  and for nothing, uselessly, spent my strength,
Yet my reward is with the LORD,
  my recompense is with my God.
For now the LORD has spoken
  who formed me as his servant from the womb,
That Jacob may be brought back to him
  and Israel gathered to him;
And I am made glorious in the sight of the LORD,
  and my God is now my strength!
It is too little, he says, for you to be my servant,
  to raise up the tribes of Jacob,
  and restore the survivors of Israel;
I will make you a light to the nations,
  that my salvation may reach to the ends of the
  earth.

The word of the Lord. ℟. **Thanks be to God.** ↓

RESPONSORIAL PSALM Ps 71:1-2, 3-4a, 5ab-6ab, 15 and 17

℟. (see 15ab) **I will sing of your salvation.**

In you, O LORD, I take refuge;
  let me never be put to shame.
In your justice rescue me, and deliver me;
  incline your ear to me, and save me.—℟.

Be my rock of refuge,
  a stronghold to give me safety,
  for you are my rock and my fortress.
O my God, rescue me from the hand of the wicked.—℟.

For you are my hope, O Lord;
  my trust, O God, from my youth.

On you I depend from birth;
> from my mother's womb you are my strength.—℟.

My mouth shall declare your justice,
> day by day your salvation.
O God, you have taught me from my youth,
> and till the present I proclaim your wondrous
> deeds.—℟. ↓

VERSE BEFORE THE GOSPEL

℟. **Marvelous and great are your works, O Lord!***
Hail to you, our King, obedient to the Father;
you were led to your crucifixion like a gentle lamb to the
> slaughter.
℟. **Marvelous and great are your works, O Lord!** ↓

GOSPEL   Jn 13:21-33, 36-38

Our Lord's statement that one of the Twelve will betray him strikes fear in
the hearts of each of them. Peter understands nothing of the mystery of
the cross and suspects that Christ doubts his courage or his zeal. Jesus
tells Peter that Peter will deny even knowing him—three times before the
cock crows.

℣. The Lord be with you. ℟. **And also with you.**
℣. A reading from the holy Gospel according to John.
℟. **Glory to you, Lord.**

R ECLINING at table with his disciples, Jesus was
deeply troubled and testified, "Amen, amen, I say to
you, one of you will betray me." The disciples looked at
one another, at a loss as to whom he meant. One of his
disciples, the one whom Jesus loved, was reclining at
Jesus' side. So Simon Peter nodded to him to find out
whom he meant. He leaned back against Jesus' chest and
said to him, "Master, who is it?" Jesus answered, "It is the
one to whom I hand the morsel after I have dipped it." So
he dipped the morsel and took it and handed it to Judas,
son of Simon the Iscariot. After Judas took the morsel,

---

* *See p. 620 for other Gospel Acclamations.*

Satan entered him. So Jesus said to him, "What you are going to do, do quickly." Now none of those reclining at table realized why he said this to him. Some thought that since Judas kept the money bag, Jesus had told him, "Buy what we need for the feast," or to give something to the poor. So Judas took the morsel and left at once. And it was night.

When he had left, Jesus said, "Now is the Son of Man glorified, and God is glorified in him. If God is glorified in him, God will also glorify him in himself, and he will glorify him at once. My children, I will be with you only a little while longer. You will look for me, and as I told the Jews, 'Where I go you cannot come,' so now I say it to you."

Simon Peter said to him, "Master, where are you going?" Jesus answered him, "Where I am going, you cannot follow me now, though you will follow later." Peter said to him, "Master, why can I not follow you now? I will lay down my life for you." Jesus answered, "Will you lay down your life for me? Amen, amen, I say to you, the cock will not crow before you deny me three times."— The Gospel of the Lord. ℟. **Praise to you, Lord Jesus Christ.**   ➙ No. 15, p. 623

PRAYER OVER THE GIFTS

Lord,
look with mercy on our offerings.
May we who share the holy gifts
receive the life they promise.
We ask this in the name of Jesus the Lord.
℟. **Amen.**   ➙ No. 21, p. 626 (Pref. P 18)

COMMUNION ANT.   Rom 8:32

God did not spare his own Son, but gave him up for us all. ↓

PRAYER AFTER COMMUNION

God of mercy,
may the sacrament of salvation
which now renews our strength
bring us a share in your life for ever.
Grant this through Christ our Lord.
℞. **Amen.**   ➔ No. 32, p. 660

WEDNESDAY OF HOLY WEEK

It should always be remembered that those who suffer persecution in the defense of the truth, the faith, and Christian virtues and who cling firmly to God and permit nothing to turn them from their duties as Christians will, like the saints, receive the heavenly crown. God will be our Redeemer and our helper. All who live in Christ, our Lord, shall suffer persecution (2 Tm 3:12).

ENTRANCE ANT.   Phil 2:10, 8, 11

At the name of Jesus every knee must bend, in heaven, on earth, and under the earth: Christ became obedient for us even to death, dying on the cross. Therefore, to the glory of God the Father, Jesus is Lord.   ➔ No. 2, p. 614

OPENING PRAYER

Father,
in your plan of salvation
your Son Jesus Christ accepted the cross
and freed us from the power of the enemy.
May we come to share the glory of his resurrection,
for he lives and reigns with you and the Holy Spirit,
one God, for ever and ever. ℞. **Amen.** ↓

FIRST READING   Is 50:4-9a

Isaiah speaks with a spirit of resignation. The Suffering Servant opens with the statement that God's Word is the source of salvation. The servant must first be a disciple, prayerfully receiving God's words, before he can presume to teach others.

A reading from the Book of the Prophet Isaiah

THE Lord GOD has given me
a well-trained tongue,
That I might know how to speak to the weary
a word that will rouse them.
Morning after morning
he opens my ear that I may hear;
And I have not rebelled,
have not turned back.
I gave my back to those who beat me,
my cheeks to those who plucked my beard;
My face I did not shield
from buffets and spitting

The Lord GOD is my help,
therefore I am not disgraced;
I have set my face like flint,
knowing that I shall not be put to shame.
He is near who upholds my right;
if anyone wishes to oppose me,
let us appear together.
Who disputes my right?
Let him confront me.
See, the Lord GOD is my help;
who will prove me wrong?
The word of the Lord. ℟. **Thanks be to God.** ↓

RESPONSORIAL PSALM   Ps 69:8-10, 21-22, 31 and 33-34

℟. (14c) **Lord, in your great love, answer me.**

For your sake I bear insult,
and shame covers my face.
I have become an outcast to my brothers,
a stranger to my mother's sons,
because zeal for your house consumes me,
and the insults of those who blaspheme you fall upon
me.—℟.

Insult has broken my heart, and I am weak,
　　I looked for sympathy, but there was none;
　　for consolers, not one could I find.
Rather they put gall in my food,
　　and in my thirst they gave me vinegar to drink.—℟.

I will praise the name of God in song,
　　and I will glorify him with thanksgiving:
"See, you lowly ones, and be glad;
　　you who seek God, may your hearts revive!
For the LORD hears the poor,
　　and his own who are in bonds he spurns not."—℟. ↓

VERSE BEFORE THE GOSPEL

℟. **Marvelous and great are your works, O Lord!***
Hail to you, our King,
you alone are compassionate with our errors.
℟. **Marvelous and great are your works, O Lord!** ↓

OR

℟. **Marvelous and great are your works, O Lord!***
Hail to you, our King, obedient to the Father;
you were led to your crucifixion like a gentle lamb to the
　　slaughter.
℟. **Marvelous and great are your works, O Lord!** ↓

GOSPEL   Mt 26:14-25

"One of the Twelve" is to betray Jesus. The enormity of the deed is under-
lined by the fact that it was done for money, for thirty pieces of silver.
Jesus predicts that Judas is the betrayer.

℣. The Lord be with you. ℟. **And also with you.**
℣. A reading from the holy Gospel according to Matthew.
℟. **Glory to you, Lord.**

ONE of the Twelve, who was called Judas Iscariot,
　　went to the chief priests and said, "What are you
willing to give me if I hand him over to you?" They paid

---

* *See p.* 620 *for other Gospel Acclamations.*

him thirty pieces of silver, and from that time on he looked for an opportunity to hand him over.

On the first day of the Feast of Unleavened Bread, the disciples approached Jesus and said, "Where do you want us to prepare for you to eat the Passover?" He said, "Go into the city to a certain man and tell him, 'The teacher says, "My appointed time draws near; in your house I shall celebrate the Passover with my disciples." ' " The disciples then did as Jesus had ordered, and prepared the Passover.

When it was evening, he reclined at table with the Twelve. And while they were eating, he said, "Amen, I say to you, one of you will betray me." Deeply distressed at this, they began to say to him one after another, "Surely it is not I, Lord?" He said in reply, "He who has dipped his hand into the dish with me is the one who will betray me. The Son of Man indeed goes, as it is written of him, but woe to that man by whom the Son of Man is betrayed. It would be better for that man if he had never been born." Then Judas, his betrayer, said in reply, "Surely it is not I, Rabbi?" He answered, "You have said so."—The Gospel of the Lord. ℟. **Praise to you, Lord Jesus Christ.**

➜ No. 15, p. 623

PRAYER OVER THE GIFTS

Lord,
accept the gifts we present
as we celebrate this mystery
of the suffering and death of your Son.
May we share in the eternal life he won for us,
for he is Lord for ever and ever.
℟. **Amen.**   ➜ No. 21, p. 626 (Pref. P 18)

COMMUNION ANT.   Mt 20:28

The Son of Man did not come to be served, but to serve, and to give his life as a ransom for many. ↓

PRAYER AFTER COMMUNION

All-powerful God,
the eucharist proclaims the death of your Son.
Increase our faith in its saving power
and strengthen our hope in the life it promises.
We ask this in the name of Jesus the Lord.
℟. **Amen.** → No. 32, p. 660

HOLY THURSDAY

CHRISM MASS

This Mass, which the bishop concelebrates with his presbyterium and at which the oils are blessed, shows the communion of the priests with their bishops. It is thus desirable that, if possible, all the priests take part in it, together with parish representatives, and receive communion under both kinds. To show the unity of the presbyterium, the priests who concelebrate with the bishop should come from different parts of the diocese. This day also is dedicated to the renewal of priestly ministry.

ENTRANCE ANT. Rv 1:6

Jesus Christ has made us a kingdom of priests to serve his God and Father: glory and kingship be his for ever and ever. Amen. → No. 2, p. 614

The Gloria *is sung or said.*

OPENING PRAYER

Father,
by the power of the Holy Spirit
you anointed your only Son Messiah and Lord of creation;
you have given us a share in his consecration
to priestly service in your Church.
Help us to be faithful witnesses in the world
to the salvation Christ won for all mankind.
We ask this through our Lord Jesus Christ, your Son,
who lives and reigns with you and the Holy Spirit
one God, for ever and ever. ℟. **Amen.** ↓

FIRST READING Is 61:1-3ab, 6a, 8b-9

Isaiah the prophet, anointed by God to bring the Good News to the poor, proclaims a message filled with hope. It is one that replaces mourning with gladness. Their descendants will be renowned among all nations. God has blessed them.

A reading from the Book of the Prophet Isaiah

THE Spirit of the Lord GOD is upon me,
  because the LORD has anointed me;
He has sent me to bring glad tidings to the poor,
    to heal the brokenhearted,
To proclaim liberty to the captives
    and release to the prisoners,
To announce a year of favor from the LORD
    and a day of vindication by our God,
    to comfort all who mourn;
To place on those who mourn in Zion
    a diadem instead of ashes,
To give them oil of gladness in place of mourning,
    a glorious mantle instead of a listless spirit.
You yourselves shall be named priests of the LORD,
    ministers of our God you shall be called.
I will give them their recompense faithfully,
    a lasting covenant I will make with them.
Their descendants shall be renowned among the
      nations,
    and their offspring among the peoples;
All who see them shall acknowledge them
    as a race the LORD has blessed.
The word of the Lord. ℟. **Thanks be to God.** ↓

RESPONSORIAL PSALM Ps 89:21-22, 25 and 27 (℟. 2)

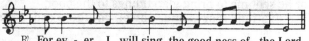

℟. **For ev - er I will sing the good-ness of the Lord.**

"I have found David, my servant;
  with my holy oil I have anointed him,

That my hand may always be with him;
　　and that my arm may make him strong."—℟.

"My faithfulness and my mercy shall be with him;
　　and through my name shall his horn be exalted.
He shall say of me, 'You are my father,
　　my God, the Rock, my savior!' "—℟. ↓

SECOND READING　　　　　　　　　　Rv 1:5-8

God says, "I am the beginning and the end, the one who is and who was and who is to come, the almighty!" All shall see God as he comes amid the clouds.

A reading from the Book of Revelation

JESUS Christ is the faithful witness, the firstborn of the dead and ruler of the kings of the earth. To him who loves us and has freed us from our sins by his blood, who has made us into a kingdom, priests for his God and Father, to him be glory and power forever and ever! Amen.

　　Behold, he is coming amid the clouds,
　　　　and every eye will see him,
　　　　even those who pierced him.
　　All the peoples of the earth will lament him.
　　　　Yes. Amen.
"I am the Alpha and the Omega," says the Lord God, "the one who is and who was and who is to come, the almighty."—The word of the Lord. ℟. **Thanks be to God.** ↓

VERSE BEFORE THE GOSPEL　　　Is 61:1 (cited in Lk 4:18)

℟. **Salvation, glory, and power to the Lord Jesus Christ!*
The Spirit of the Lord is upon me
for he sent me to bring glad tidings to the poor.
℟. **Salvation, glory, and power to the Lord Jesus Christ!** ↓

---

* *See p. 620 for other Gospel Acclamations.*

GOSPEL
Lk 4:16-21

Jesus reads in the synagogue at Nazareth the words of Isaiah quoted in the First Reading. Jesus is the Anointed One. He tells the people that today Isaiah's prophecy is fulfilled in their hearing.

℣. The Lord be with you. ℟. **And also with you.**

℣. A reading from the holy Gospel according to Matthew.

℟. **Glory to you, Lord.**

J ESUS came to Nazareth, where he had grown up, and went according to his custom into the synagogue on the sabbath day. He stood up to read and was handed a scroll of the prophet Isaiah. He unrolled the scroll and found the passage where it was written:

The Spirit of the Lord is upon me;
because he has anointed me
to bring glad tidings to the poor.
He has sent me to proclaim liberty to captives
and recovery of sight to the blind,
to let the oppressed go free,
and to proclaim a year acceptable to the Lord.

Rolling up the scroll, he handed it back to the attendant and sat down, and the eyes of all in the synagogue looked intently at him. He said to them, "Today this Scripture passage is fulfilled in your hearing."—The Gospel of the Lord. ℟. **Praise to you, Lord Jesus Christ.** ➜ No. 14, p. 18

In his Homily the bishop should urge the priests to be faithful in fulfilling their office in the Church and should invite them to renew publicly their priestly promises.

Renewal of Commitment to Priestly Service

After the Homily the bishop speaks to the priests in these or similar words:

My brothers,
today we celebrate the memory of the first eucharist
at which our Lord Jesus Christ
shared with his apostles and with us
his call to the priestly service of his Church.

Now, in the presence of your bishop and God's holy
people,

are you ready to renew your own dedication to Christ
as priests of his new covenant?

Priests: I am.

Bishop: At your ordination
you accepted the responsibilities of the priesthood
out of love for the Lord Jesus and his Church.
Are you resolved to unite yourselves more closely to
   Christ
and to try to become more like him
by joyfully sacrificing your own pleasure and ambition
to bring his peace and love to your brothers and sisters?

Priests: I am.

Bishop: Are you resolved
to be faithful ministers of the mysteries of God,
to celebrate the eucharist and the other liturgical services
with sincere devotion?
Are you resolved to imitate Jesus Christ,
the head and shepherd of the Church,
by teaching the Christian faith
without thinking of your own profit,
solely for the well-being of the people
you were sent to serve?

Priests: I am.

Then the bishop addresses the people:

My brothers and sisters,
pray for your priests.
Ask the Lord to bless them with the fullness of his love,
to help them be faithful ministers of Christ the High
   Priest,
so that they will be able to lead you to him,
the fountain of your salvation.

People: Lord Jesus Christ, hear us and answer our prayer.

Bishop: Pray also for me
that despite my own unworthiness

I may faithfully fulfill the office of apostle
which Jesus Christ has entrusted to me.
Pray that I may become more like
our High Priest and Good Shepherd
the teacher and servant of all,
and so be a genuine sign
of Christ's loving presence among you.

People: Lord Jesus Christ, hear us and answer our prayer.

Bishop: May the Lord in his love
keep you close to him always,
and may he bring all of us,
his priests and people,
to eternal life.

All: Amen.

The Profession of Faith and General Intercessions are omitted.

→ No. 17, p. 624

PRAYER OVER THE GIFTS

Lord God,
may the power of this sacrifice
cleanse the old weakness of our human nature.
Give us a newness of life
and bring us to salvation.
Grant this through Christ our Lord. ℟. **Amen.** ↓

PREFACE (P 20)

℣. The Lord be with you. ℟. **And also with you.**
℣. Lift up your hearts. ℟. **We lift them up to the Lord.**
℣. Let us give thanks to the Lord our God. ℟. **It is right to give him thanks and praise.**

Father, all-powerful and ever-living God,
we do well always and everywhere to give you thanks.
By your Holy Spirit
you anointed your only Son
High Priest of the new and eternal covenant.

With wisdom and love you have planned
that this one priesthood should continue in the Church.
Christ gives the dignity of a royal priesthood
to the people he has made his own.
From these, with a brother's love,
he chooses men to share his sacred ministry
by the laying on of hands.
He appoints them to renew in his name
the sacrifice of our redemption
as they set before your family his paschal meal.
He calls them to lead your holy people in love,
nourish them by your word,
and strengthen them through the sacraments.
Father, they are to give their lives in your service
and for the salvation of your people
as they strive to grow in the likeness of Christ
and honor you by their courageous witness of faith and
　　love.
We praise you, Lord, with all the angels and saints
in their song of joy:　　　　　　　　　　→ No. 23, p. 627

COMMUNION ANT.　　　　　　　　　　　　　　Ps 89:2

**For ever I will sing the goodness of the Lord; I will pro-
claim your faithfulness to all generations.** ↓

PRAYER AFTER COMMUNION

Lord God almighty,
you have given us fresh strength
in these sacramental gifts.
Renew in us the image of Christ's goodness.
We ask this in the name of Jesus the Lord.
℟. **Amen.**　　　　　　　　　　　　　　　→ No. 32, p. 660

Optional Solemn Blessings, p. 692, and Prayers over the
People, p. 699.

"Do this in remembrance of me."

EASTER TRIDUUM

HOLY THURSDAY

EVENING MASS OF THE LORD'S SUPPER

The Evening Mass of the Lord's Supper commemorates the institution of the Holy Eucharist and the sacrament of Holy Orders. It was at this Mass that Jesus changed bread and wine into his Body and Blood. He then directed his disciples to carry out this same ritual: "Do this in remembrance of me."

Introductory Rites and Liturgy of the Word

ENTRANCE ANT.   See Gal 6:14

We should glory in the cross of our Lord Jesus Christ, for he is our salvation, our life and our resurrection; through him we are saved and made free. → No. 2, p. 614

During the singing of the Gloria, the church bells are rung and then remain silent until the Easter Vigil, unless the conference of bishops or the Ordinary decrees otherwise.

OPENING PRAYER

God our Father,
we are gathered here to share in the supper
which your only Son left to his Church to reveal his love.

He gave it to us when he was about to die
and commanded us to celebrate it as the new and eternal
   sacrifice.
We pray that in this eucharist
we may find the fullness of love and life.
Grant this through our Lord Jesus Christ, your Son,
who lives and reigns with you and the Holy Spirit,
one God, for ever and ever. ℟. **Amen.** ↓

FIRST READING   Ex 12:1-8, 11-14

For the protection of the Jewish people, strict religious and dietary
instructions are given to Moses by God. The law of the Passover meal
requires that the doorposts and lintels of each house be marked with the
blood of the sacrificial animal so that the Lord can "go through Egypt,
striking down every firstborn of the land, both man and beast."

A reading from the Book of Exodus

THE LORD said to Moses and Aaron in the land of
Egypt,"This month shall stand at the head of your calendar; you shall reckon it the first month of the year. Tell
the whole community of Israel: On the tenth of this
month every one of your families must procure for itself
a lamb, one apiece for each household. If a family is too
small for a whole lamb, it shall join the nearest household in procuring one and shall share in the lamb in proportion to the number of persons who partake of it. The
lamb must be a year-old male and without blemish. You
may take it from either the sheep or the goats. You shall
keep it until the fourteenth day of this month, and then,
with the whole assembly of Israel present, it shall be
slaughtered during the evening twilight. They shall take
some of its blood and apply it to the two doorposts and
the lintel of every house in which they partake of the
lamb. That same night they shall eat its roasted flesh with
unleavened bread and bitter herbs.

    "This is how you are to eat it: with your loins girt, san-
dals on your feet and your staff in hand, you shall eat like
those who are in flight. It is the Passover of the LORD. For

on this same night I will go through Egypt, striking down every firstborn of the land, both man and beast, and executing judgment on all the gods of Egypt—I, the LORD! But the blood will mark the houses where you are. Seeing the blood, I will pass over you; thus, when I strike the land of Egypt, no destructive blow will come upon you.

"This day shall be a memorial feast for you, which all your generations shall celebrate with pilgrimage to the LORD, as a perpetual institution."—The word of the Lord. ℟. **Thanks be to God.** ↓

RESPONSORIAL PSALM

Ps 116:12-13, 15-16bc, 17-18 (℟. cf. 1 Cor 10:16)

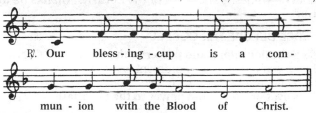

℟. Our bless-ing -cup is a com-mun-ion with the Blood of Christ.

How shall I make a return to the LORD
　　for all the good he has done for me?
The cup of salvation I will take up,
　　and I will call upon the name of the LORD.—℟.

Precious in the eyes of the LORD
　　is the death of his faithful ones.
I am your servant, the son of your handmaid;
　　you have loosed my bonds.—℟.

To you will I offer sacrifice of thanksgiving,
　　and I will call upon the name of the LORD.
My vows to the LORD I will pay
　　in the presence of all his people.—℟. ↓

SECOND READING

1 Cor 11:23-26

Paul recounts the events of the Last Supper which were handed down to him. The changing of bread and wine into the Body and Blood of the Lord proclaimed again his death. It was to be a sacrificial meal.

A reading from the first Letter of Saint Paul
to the Corinthians

BROTHERS and sisters: I received from the Lord what
I also handed on to you, that the Lord Jesus, on the
night he was handed over, took bread, and, after he had
given thanks, broke it and said, "This is my body that is
for you. Do this in remembrance of me." In the same way
also the cup, after supper, saying, "This cup is the new
covenant in my blood. Do this, as often as you drink it, in
remembrance of me." For as often as you eat this bread
and drink the cup, you proclaim the death of the Lord
until he comes.—The word of the Lord. ℟. **Thanks be to
God.** ↓

VERSE BEFORE THE GOSPEL   Jn 13:34

℟. **Salvation, glory, and power to the Lord Jesus Christ!***
I give you a new commandment, says the Lord:
love one another as I have loved you.
℟. **Salvation, glory, and power to the Lord Jesus Christ!** ↓

GOSPEL   Jn 13:1-15

Jesus washes the feet of his disciples to prove to them his sincere love
and great humility which they should imitate. He teaches them that,
although free from sin and not unworthy to receive his most holy body and
blood, they should be purified of all evil inclinations.

℣. The Lord be with you. ℟. **And also with you.**
✠ A reading from the holy Gospel according to John.
℟. **Glory to you, Lord.**

BEFORE the feast of Passover, Jesus knew that his
hour had come to pass from this world to the Father.
He loved his own in the world and he loved them to the
end. The devil had already induced Judas, son of Simon
the Iscariot, to hand him over. So, during supper, fully
aware that the Father had put everything into his power

---

* *See p.* 620 *for other Gospel Acclamations.*

and that he had come from God and was returning to God, he rose from supper and took off his outer garments. He took a towel and tied it around his waist. Then he poured water into a basin and began to wash the disciples' feet and dry them with the towel around his waist. He came to Simon Peter, who said to him, "Master, are you going to wash my feet?" Jesus answered and said to him, "What I am doing, you do not understand now, but you will understand later." Peter said to him, "You will never wash my feet." Jesus answered him, "Unless I wash you, you will have no inheritance with me." Simon Peter said to him, "Master, then not only my feet, but my hands and head as well." Jesus said to him, "Whoever has bathed has no need except to have his feet washed, for he is clean all over; so you are clean, but not all." For he knew who would betray him; for this reason, he said, "Not all of you are clean."

So when he had washed their feet and put his garments back on and reclined at table again, he said to them, "Do you realize what I have done for you? You call me 'teacher' and 'master,' and rightly so, for indeed I am. If I, therefore, the master and teacher, have washed your feet, you ought to wash one another's feet. I have given you a model to follow, so that as I have done for you, you should also do."—The Gospel of the Lord. ℟. **Praise to you, Lord Jesus Christ.**   → No. 14, p. 622

The homily should explain the principal mysteries which are commemorated in this Mass: the institution of the eucharist, the institution of the priesthood, and Christ's commandment of brotherly love.

Washing of Feet

Depending on pastoral circumstances, the washing of feet follows the homily.

The men who have been chosen are led by the ministers to chairs prepared in a suitable place. Then the priest (removing his chasuble if necessary) goes to each man. With the help of the ministers, he pours water over each one's feet and dries them.

Meanwhile some of the following antiphons or other appropriate songs are sung.

ANTIPHON 1   See Jn 13:4, 5,15

The Lord Jesus,
when he had eaten with his disciples,
poured water into a basin
and began to wash their feet, saying:
This example I leave you.

ANTIPHON 2   Jn 13:6, 7, 8

Lord, do you wash my feet?
Jesus said to him:
If I do not wash your feet,
you can have no part with me.

℣. So he came to Simon Peter,
who said to him:
Lord, do you wash my feet?

℣. Now you do not know what I am doing,
but later you will understand.
Lord, do you wash my feet?

ANTIPHON 3   See Jn 13:14

If I, your Lord and Teacher, have washed your feet, then
surely you must wash one another's feet.

ANTIPHON 4   Jn 13:35

If there is this love among you,
all will know that you are my disciples.

℣. Jesus said to his disciples:
If there is this love among you,
all will know that you are my disciples.

ANTIPHON 5   Jn 13:34

I give you a new commandment:
love one another as I have loved you, says the Lord.

ANTIPHON 6 1 Cor 13:13

Faith, hope, and love,
let these endure among you;
and the greatest of these is love.

The general intercessions follow the washing of feet, or, if this does not take place, they follow the homily. The profession of faith is not said in this Mass.

The Liturgy of the Eucharist

At the beginning of the liturgy of the eucharist, there may be a procession of the faithful with gifts for the poor. During the procession the following may be sung, or another appropriate song.

Ant. ℣. **Where charity and love are found, there is God.**
℣. **The love of Christ has gathered us together into one.**
℣. **Let us rejoice and be glad in him.**
℣. **Let us fear and love the living God,**
℣. **and love each other from the depths of our heart.**
Ant. **Where charity and love are found, there is God.**
℣. **Therefore when we are together,**
℣. **let us take heed not to be divided in mind.**
℣. **Let there be an end to bitterness and quarrels, an end to strife,**
℣. **and in our midst be Christ our God.**
Ant. **Where charity and love are found, there is God.**
℣. **And, in company with the blessed, may we see**
℣. **your face in glory, Christ our God,**
℣. **pure and unbounded joy**
℣. **for ever and ever.**
Ant. **Where charity and love are found, there is God.**

➜ No. 17, p. 624

PRAYER OVER THE GIFTS

Lord,
make us worthy to celebrate these mysteries.
Each time we offer this memorial sacrifice
the work of our redemption is accomplished.

We ask this in the name of Jesus the Lord.

℞. **Amen.**   → No. 21, p. 626 (Pref. P 47)

When Eucharistic Prayer I is used, the special Holy Thursday forms of In union with the whole Church, Father, accept this offering, *and* The day before he suffered *are said:*

In union with the whole Church
we celebrate that day
when Jesus Christ, our Lord,
was betrayed for us.
We honor Mary,
the ever-virgin mother of Jesus Christ our Lord and God.
We honor Joseph, her husband,
the apostles and martyrs
Peter and Paul, Andrew,
(James, John, Thomas,
James, Philip,
Bartholomew, Matthew, Simon and Jude;
we honor Linus, Cletus, Clement, Sixtus,
Cornelius, Cyprian, Lawrence, Chrysogonus,
John and Paul, Cosmas and Damian)
and all the saints.
May their merits and prayers
gain us your constant help and protection.
(Through Christ our Lord. Amen.)

Father, accept this offering
from your whole family
in memory of the day when Jesus Christ, our Lord,
gave the mysteries of his body and blood
for his disciples to celebrate.
Grant us your peace in this life,
save us from final damnation,
and count us among those you have chosen.
(Through Christ our Lord. Amen.)

Bless and approve our offering;
make it acceptable to you,

an offering in spirit and in truth.
Let it become for us
the body and blood of Jesus Christ,
your only Son, our Lord.

The day before he suffered
to save us and all men,
that is, today,
he took bread in his sacred hands
and looking up to heaven,
to you, his almighty Father,
he gave you thanks and praise.
He broke the bread,
gave it to his disciples, and said:

Take this, all of you, and eat it:
this is my body which will be given up for you.

The rest follows the Roman canon, pp. 630-632.

COMMUNION ANT.   1 Cor 11:24-25

This body will be given for you. This is the cup of the new covenant in my blood; whenever you receive them, do so in remembrance of me. ↓

After the distribution of communion, the ciborium with hosts for Good Friday is left on the altar.

A period of silence may be observed after communion, or a psalm or song of praise may be sung.

PRAYER AFTER COMMUNION

Almighty God,
we receive new life
from the supper your Son gave us in this world.
May we find full contentment
in the meal we hope to share
in your eternal kingdom.
We ask this through Christ our Lord. ℟. **Amen.**

The Mass concludes with this prayer.

Transfer of the Holy Eucharist

*After the prayer the priest stands before the altar and puts
incense in the thurible. Kneeling, he incenses the Blessed
Sacrament three times. Then he receives the humeral veil,
takes the ciborium, and covers it with the ends of the veil.*

*The Blessed Sacrament is carried through the church in pro-
cession, led by a cross-bearer and accompanied by candles
and incense, to the place of reposition prepared in a chapel
suitably decorated for the occasion. During the procession the
hymn* Pange, lingua *(exclusive of the last two stanzas) or
some other eucharistic song is sung.*

PANGE LINGUA

Sing my tongue, the Savior's
 glory,
Of his flesh the mystery sing;
Of his blood all price exceed-
 ing,
Shed by our immortal king,
Destined for the world's
 redemption,
From a noble womb to
 spring.

Of a pure and spotless Virgin
Born for us on earth below,
He, as man with man con-
 versing,
Stayed the seeds of truth to
 sow;
Then he closed in solemn
 order
Wondrously his life of woe.

On the night of that Last
 Supper,
Seated with his chosen band,
He, the paschal victim eating,
First fulfills the law's com-
 mand;
Then as food to all his
 brethren
Gives himself with his own
 hand.

Word made Flesh, the bread
 of nature,
By his word to flesh he turns,
Wine into his blood he
 changes:
What though sense no
 change discerns,
Only be the heart in earnest,
Faith her lesson quickly
 learns.

*When the procession reaches the place of reposition, the priest
sets the ciborium down. Then he puts incense in the thurible
and, kneeling, incenses the Blessed Sacrament, while*
Tantum ergo Sacramentum *is sung. The tabernacle of reposition is then closed.*

Down in adoration falling,
Lo! the sacred host we hail,
Lo! o'er ancient forms departing
Newer rites of grace prevail;
Faith for all defects supplying,
Where the feeble senses fail.

To the everlasting Father,
And the Son who reigns on high
With the Holy Spirit proceeding
Forth from each eternally,
Be salvation, honor, blessing,
Might and endless majesty.
Amen.

After a period of silent adoration, the priest and ministers genuflect and return to the sacristy.

Then the altar is stripped and, if possible, the crosses are removed from the church. It is desirable to cover any crosses which remain in the church.

The faithful should be encouraged to continue adoration before the Blessed Sacrament for a suitable period of time during the night.

"And bowing his head, [Jesus] handed over the spirit."

GOOD FRIDAY

CELEBRATION OF THE LORD'S PASSION

The liturgy of Good Friday recalls graphically the passion and death of Jesus. The reading of the passion describes the suffering and death of Jesus. Today we show great reverence for the crucifix, the sign of our redemption.

According to the Church's ancient tradition, the sacraments, except for Penance and the Anointing of the Sick, are not cel-

ebrated today or tomorrow. The celebration of the Lord's passion takes place in the afternoon, about three o'clock, unless pastoral reasons suggest a later hour.

The priest and deacon, wearing red Mass vestments, go to the altar. There they make a reverence and prostrate themselves, or they may kneel. All pray silently for a while. Then the priest goes to the chair with the ministers. He faces the people and, with hands joined, sings or says one of the following prayers.

PRAYER

Lord,
by shedding his blood for us,
your Son, Jesus Christ,
established the paschal mystery.
In your goodness, make us holy
and watch over us always.
We ask this through Christ our Lord. ℟. **Amen.** ↓

OR

Lord,
by the suffering of Christ your Son
you have saved us all from the death
we inherited from sinful Adam.
By the law of nature
we have borne the likeness of his manhood.
May the sanctifying power of grace
help us to put on the likeness of our Lord in heaven,
who lives and reigns for ever and ever. ℟. **Amen.** ↓

PART ONE: LITURGY OF THE WORD

FIRST READING   Is 52:13—53:12

The suffering Servant shall be raised up and exalted. The Servant remains one with all people in sorrow and yet distinct from each of them in innocence of life and total service to God. The doctrine of expiatory suffering finds supreme expression in these words.

A reading from the Book of the Prophet Isaiah

SEE, my servant shall prosper,
he shall be raised high and greatly exalted.

Even as many were amazed at him—
> so marred was his look beyond human semblance
> and his appearance beyond that of the sons of
> > man—
so shall he startle many nations,
> because of him kings shall stand speechless;
for those who have not been told shall see,
> those who have not heard shall ponder it.

Who would believe what we have heard?
> To whom has the arm of the Lord been revealed?
He grew up like a sapling before him,
> like a shoot from the parched earth;
there was in him no stately bearing to make us look
> > at him,
> nor appearance that would attract us to him.
He was spurned and avoided by people,
> a man of suffering, accustomed to infirmity,
one of those from whom people hide their faces,
> spurned, and we held him in no esteem.

Yet it was our infirmities that he bore,
> our sufferings that he endured,
while we thought of him as stricken,
> as one smitten by God and afflicted.
But he was pierced for our offenses,
> crushed for our sins;
upon him was the chastisement that makes us whole,
> by his stripes we were healed.
We had all gone astray like sheep,
> each following his own way;
but the LORD laid upon him
> the guilt of us all.

Though he was harshly treated, he submitted
> and opened not his mouth;
like a lamb led to the slaughter
> or a sheep before the shearers,
> he was silent and opened not his mouth.

Oppressed and condemned, he was taken away,
    and who would have thought any more of his des-
        tiny?
When he was cut off from the land of the living,
    and smitten for the sin of his people,
a grave was assigned him among the wicked
    and a burial place with evildoers,
though he had done no wrong
    nor spoken any falsehood.
But the Lord was pleased
    to crush him in infirmity.

If he gives his life as an offering for sin,
    he shall see his descendants in a long life,
    and the will of the Lord shall be accomplished
        through him.
Because of his affliction
    he shall see the light in fullness of days;
through his suffering, my servant shall justify many,
    and their guilt he shall bear.
Therefore I will give him his portion among the great,
    and he shall divide the spoils with the mighty,
because he surrendered himself to death
    and was counted among the wicked;
and he shall take away the sins of many,
    and win pardon for their offenses.

The word of the Lord. ℟. **Thanks be to God.** ↓

RESPONSORIAL PSALM

        Ps 31:2, 6, 12-13, 15-16, 17, 25 (℟. Lk 23:46)

℟. **Fa - ther, in - to your hands I com - mend my spir - it.**

In you, O Lord, I take refuge;
    let me never be put to shame.
In your justice rescue me.
Into your hands I commend my spirit;
    you will redeem me, O Lord, O faithful God.

℞. **Father, into your hands I commend my spirit.**

For all my foes I am an object of reproach,
a laughingstock to my neighbors, and a dread to my
friends;
they who see me abroad flee from me.
I am forgotten like the unremembered dead;
I am like a dish that is broken.

℞. **Father, into your hands I commend my spirit.**

But my trust is in you, O LORD;
I say, "You are my God."
In your hands is my destiny; rescue me
from the clutches of my enemies and my persecutors.

℞. **Father, into your hands I commend my spirit.**

Let your face shine upon your servant;
save me in your kindness.
Take courage and be stouthearted,
all you who hope in the LORD.

℞. **Father, into your hands I commend my spirit.** ↓

SECOND READING   Heb 4:14-16; 5:7-9

The theme of the compassionate high priest appears again in this passage. In him the Christian can approach God confidently and without fear. Christ learned obedience from his sufferings whereby he became the source of eternal life for all.

A reading from the Letter to the Hebrews

BROTHERS and sisters: Since we have a great high priest who has passed through the heavens, Jesus, the Son of God, let us hold fast to our confession. For we do not have a high priest who is unable to sympathize with our weaknesses, but one who has similarly been tested in every way, yet without sin. So let us confidently approach the throne of grace to receive mercy and to find grace for timely help.

In the days when Christ was in the flesh, he offered prayers and supplications with loud cries and tears to the one who was able to save him from death, and he was heard because of his reverence. Son though he was, he learned obedience from what he suffered; and when he was made perfect, he became the source of eternal salvation for all who obey him.—The word of the Lord. ℟. **Thanks be to God.** ↓

VERSE BEFORE THE GOSPEL   Phil 2:8-9

℟. **Salvation, glory, and power to the Lord Jesus Christ!***
Christ became obedient to the point of death,
even death on a cross.
Because of this, God greatly exalted him
and bestowed on him the name which is above every
    other name.
℟. **Salvation, glory, and power to the Lord Jesus Christ!** ↓

GOSPEL   Jn 18:1—19:42

The Passion may be read by lay readers, with the part of Christ, if possible, read by a priest. The Narrator is noted by N, the words of Jesus by a ✠ and the words of others by V (Voice) and C (Crowd). The part of the Crowd (C) printed in boldface type may be recited by the people.

We participate in the passion narrative in several ways: by reading it and reflecting on it during the week ahead; by listening with faith as it is proclaimed; by respectful posture during the narrative; by reverent silence after the passage about Christ's death.

The message of the liturgy in proclaiming the passion narratives in full is to enable the assembly to see vividly the love of Christ for each person, despite their sins, a love that even death could not vanquish. The crimes during the Passion of Christ cannot be attributed indiscriminately to all Jews of that time, nor to Jews today. The Jewish people should not be referred to as though rejected or cursed, as if this view followed from Scripture. The Church ever keeps in mind that Jesus, his mother Mary, and the Apostles were Jewish. As the

---

* *See p. 620 for other Gospel Acclamations.*

*Church has always held, Christ freely suffered his passion
and death because of the sins of all, that all might be saved.*

The beginning scene is Christ's agony in the garden. Our Lord knows what
is to happen. The Scriptures recount the betrayal, the trial, the condemn-
nation, and the crucifixion of Jesus.

N. **T**HE Passion of our Lord Jesus Christ according
to John

N. **J**ESUS went out with his disciples across the
Kidron valley to where there was a garden, into
which he and his disciples entered. Judas his betrayer
also knew the place, because Jesus had often met there
with his disciples. So Judas got a band of soldiers and
guards from the chief priests and the Pharisees and went
there with lanterns, torches, and weapons. Jesus, knowing everything that was going to happen to him, went
out and said to them, ✝ *"Whom are you looking for?"* **N.**
They answered him, **C. "Jesus the Nazorean."** **N.** He said
to them, ✝ *"I AM."* **N.** Judas his betrayer was also with
them. When he said to them, "I AM," they turned away
and fell to the ground. So he again asked them, ✝
"Whom are you looking for?" **N.** They said, **C. "Jesus the
Nazorean."** **N.** Jesus answered, ✝ *"I told you that I AM.
So if you are looking for me, let these men go."* **N.** This
was to fulfill what he had said, "I have not lost any of
those you gave me." Then Simon Peter, who had a sword,
drew it, struck the high priest's slave, and cut off his
right ear. The slave's name was Malchus. Jesus said to
Peter, ✝ *"Put your sword into its scabbard. Shall I not
drink the cup that the Father gave me?"*

N. So the band of soldiers, the tribune, and the Jewish
guards seized Jesus, bound him, and brought him to
Annas first. He was the father–in–law of Caiaphas, who
was high priest that year. It was Caiaphas who had
counseled the Jews that it was better that one man
should die rather than the people.

N. S IMON Peter and another disciple followed Jesus. Now the other disciple was known to the high priest, and he entered the courtyard of the high priest with Jesus. But Peter stood at the gate outside. So the other disciple, the acquaintance of the high priest, went out and spoke to the gatekeeper and brought Peter in. Then the maid who was the gatekeeper said to Peter, **C. "You are not one of this man's disciples, are you?" N.** He said, **V.** "I am not." **N.** Now the slaves and the guards were standing around a charcoal fire that they had made, because it was cold, and were warming themselves. Peter was also standing there keeping warm.

N. T HE high priest questioned Jesus about his disciples and about his doctrine. Jesus answered him, ✠ *"I have spoken publicly to the world. I have always taught in a synagogue or in the temple area where all the Jews gather, and in secret I have said nothing. Why ask me? Ask those who heard me what I said to them. They know what I said." N.* When he had said this, one of the temple guards standing there struck Jesus and said, **V.** "Is this the way you answer the high priest?" **N.** Jesus answered him, ✠ *"If I have spoken wrongly, testify to the wrong; but if I have spoken rightly, why do you strike me?" N.* Then Annas sent him bound to Caiaphas the high priest.

N. N OW Simon Peter was standing there keeping warm. And they said to him, **C. "You are not one of his disciples, are you?" N.** He denied it and said, **V.** "I am not." **N.** One of the slaves of the high priest, a relative of the one whose ear Peter had cut off, said, **C. "Didn't I see you in the garden with him?" N.** Again Peter denied it. And immediately the cock crowed.

N. T HEN they brought Jesus from Caiaphas to the praetorium. It was morning. And they themselves did not enter the praetorium, in order not to be defiled so that they could eat the Passover. So Pilate came out to them and said, **V.** "What charge do you bring against this man?" **N.** They answered and said to him, **C. "If he were not a criminal, we would not have handed him over to you."** **N.** At this, Pilate said to them, **V.** "Take him yourselves, and judge him according to your law." **N.** The Jews answered him, **C. "We do not have the right to execute anyone,"** **N.** in order that the word of Jesus might be fulfilled that he said indicating the kind of death he would die. So Pilate went back into the praetorium and summoned Jesus and said to him, **V.** "Are you the King of the Jews?" **N.** Jesus answered, ✠ *"Do you say this on your own or have others told you about me?"* **N.** Pilate answered, **V.** "I am not a Jew, am I? Your own nation and the chief priests handed you over to me. What have you done?" **N.** Jesus answered, ✠ *"My kingdom does not belong to this world. If my kingdom did belong to this world, my attendants would be fighting to keep me from being handed over to the Jews. But as it is, my kingdom is not here."* **N.** So Pilate said to him, **V.** "Then you are a king?" **N.** Jesus answered, ✠ *"You say I am a king. For this I was born and for this I came into the world, to testify to the truth. Everyone who belongs to the truth listens to my voice."* **N.** Pilate said to him, **V.** "What is truth?"

N. W HEN he had said this, he again went out to the Jews and said to them, **V.** "I find no guilt in him. But you have a custom that I release one prisoner to you at Passover. Do you want me to release to you the King of the Jews?" **N.** They cried out again, **C.**

"Not this one but Barabbas!" N. Now Barabbas was a revolutionary.

N. THEN Pilate took Jesus and had him scourged. And the soldiers wove a crown out of thorns and placed it on his head, and clothed him in a purple cloak, and they came to him and said, **C. "Hail, King of the Jews!" N.** And they struck him repeatedly. Once more Pilate went out and said to them, **V.** "Look, I am bringing him out to you, so that you may know that I find no guilt in him." **N.** So Jesus came out, wearing the crown of thorns and the purple cloak. And Pilate said to them, **V.** "Behold, the man!" **N.** When the chief priests and the guards saw him they cried out, **C. "Crucify him, crucify him!" N.** Pilate said to them, **V.** "Take him yourselves and crucify him. I find no guilt in him." **N.** The Jews answered, **C. "We have a law, and according to that law he ought to die, because he made himself the Son of God." N.** Now when Pilate heard this statement, he became even more afraid, and went back into the praetorium and said to Jesus, **V.** "Where are you from?" **N.** Jesus did not answer him. So Pilate said to him, **V.** "Do you not speak to me? Do you not know that I have power to release you and I have power to crucify you?" **N.** Jesus answered him, ✠ *"You would have no power over me if it had not been given to you from above. For this reason the one who handed me over to you has the greater sin."* **N.** Consequently, Pilate tried to release him; but the Jews cried out, **C. "If you release him, you are not a Friend of Caesar. Everyone who makes himself a king opposes Caesar."**

N. WHEN Pilate heard these words he brought Jesus out and seated him on the judge's bench in the place called Stone Pavement, in Hebrew,

Gabbatha. It was preparation day for Passover, and it was about noon. And he said to the Jews, **V.** "Behold, your king!" **N.** They cried out, **C.** "Take him away, take him away! Crucify him!" **C.** Pilate said to them, **V.** "Shall I crucify your king?" **N.** The chief priests answered, **C.** "We have no king but Caesar." **N.** Then he handed him over to them to be crucified.

N. SO they took Jesus, and, carrying the cross himself, he went out to what is called the Place of the Skull, in Hebrew, Golgotha. There they crucified him, and with him two others, one on either side, with Jesus in the middle. Pilate also had an inscription written and put on the cross. It read, "Jesus the Nazorean, the King of the Jews." Now many of the Jews read this inscription, because the place where Jesus was crucified was near the city; and it was written in Hebrew, Latin, and Greek. So the chief priests of the Jews said to Pilate, **C.** "Do not write 'The King of the Jews,' but that he said, 'I am the King of the Jews.'" **N.** Pilate answered, **V.** "What I have written, I have written."

N. WHEN the soldiers had crucified Jesus, they took his clothes and divided them into four shares, a share for each soldier. They also took his tunic, but the tunic was seamless, woven in one piece from the top down. So they said to one another, **C.** "Let's not tear it, but cast lots for it to see whose it will be," **N.** in order that the passage of Scripture might be fulfilled that says:

> *They divided my garments among them,*
> *and for my vesture they cast lots.*

This is what the soldiers did. Standing by the cross of Jesus were his mother and his mother's sister, Mary the wife of Clopas, and Mary of Magdala. When Jesus saw his mother and the disciple there whom he loved he said to his mother, ✝ *"Woman, behold, your son."* **N.** Then he said to the disciple, ✝ *"Behold, your mother."* **N.** And from that hour the disciple took her into his home.

After this, aware that everything was now finished, in order that the Scripture might be fulfilled, Jesus said, ✝ *"I thirst."* **N.** There was a vessel filled with common wine. So they put a sponge soaked in wine on a sprig of hyssop and put it up to his mouth. When Jesus had taken the wine, he said, ✝ *"It is finished."* **N.** And bowing his head, he handed over the spirit.

Here all kneel and pause for a short time.

N. **N**OW since it was preparation day, in order that the bodies might not remain on the cross on the sabbath, for the sabbath day of that week was a solemn one, the Jews asked Pilate that their legs be broken and that they be taken down. So the soldiers came and broke the legs of the first and then of the other one who was crucified with Jesus. But when they came to Jesus and saw that he was already dead, they did not break his legs, but one soldier thrust his lance into his side, and immediately blood and water flowed out. An eyewitness has testified, and his testimony is true; he knows that he is speaking the truth, so that you also may come to believe. For this happened so that the Scripture passage might be fulfilled:

Not a bone of it will be broken.

And again another passage says:

They will look upon him whom they have pierced.

N. **A**FTER this, Joseph of Arimathea, secretly a disciple of Jesus for fear of the Jews, asked Pilate if he could remove the body of Jesus. And Pilate permitted it. So he came and took his body. Nicodemus, the one who had first come to him at night, also came bringing a mixture of myrrh and aloes weighing about one hundred pounds. They took the body of Jesus and bound it with burial cloths along with the spices, according to the Jewish burial custom. Now in the place where he had been crucified there was a garden, and in the garden a new tomb, in which no one had yet been buried. So they laid Jesus there because of the Jewish preparation day; for the tomb was close by.— The Gospel of the Lord. ℟. **Praise to you, Lord Jesus Christ.** ➜ No. 14, p. 622

GENERAL INTERCESSIONS

The general intercessions conclude the liturgy of the word. The deacon, standing at the ambo, sings or says the introduction in which each intention is stated. All kneel and pray silently for some period of time, and then the priest, with hands outstretched, standing either at the chair or at the altar, sings or says the prayer. The people may either kneel or stand throughout the entire period of the general intercessions.

I. For the Church

Let us pray, dear friends,
for the holy Church of God throughout the world,
that God the almighty Father
guide it and gather it together
so that we may worship him
in peace and tranquility.

Silent prayer. Then the priest sings or says:

Almighty and eternal God,
you have shown your glory to all nations
in Christ, your Son.
Guide the work of your Church.
Help it to persevere in faith,
proclaim your name,

and bring your salvation to people everywhere.
We ask this through Christ our Lord. ℟. **Amen.** ↓

II. For the Pope

Let us pray
for our Holy Father, Pope N.,
that God who chose him to be bishop
may give him health and strength
to guide and govern God's holy people.

Silent prayer. Then the priest sings or says:

Almighty and eternal God,
you guide all things by your word,
you govern all Christian people.
In your love protect the Pope you have chosen for us.
Under his leadership deepen our faith
and make us better Christians.
We ask this through Christ our Lord. ℟. **Amen.** ↓

III. For the clergy and laity of the Church

Let us pray
for N., our bishop,
for all bishops, priests and deacons,
for all who have a special ministry in the Church
and for all God's people.

Silent prayer. Then the priest sings or says:

Almighty and eternal God,
your Spirit guides the Church
and makes it holy.
Listen to our prayers
and help each of us
in his own vocation
to do your work more faithfully.
We ask this through Christ our Lord. ℟. **Amen.** ↓

IV. For those preparing for baptism

Let us pray
for those [among us] preparing for baptism,

that God in his mercy
make them responsive to his love,
forgive their sins through the waters of new birth,
and give them life in Jesus Christ our Lord.

Silent prayer. Then the priest sings or says:

Almighty and eternal God,
you continually bless your Church with new members.
Increase the faith and understanding
of those [among us] preparing for baptism.
Give them a new birth in these living waters
and make them members of your chosen family.
We ask this through Christ our Lord. ℟. **Amen.** ↓

V. For the unity of Christians

Let us pray
for all our brothers and sisters
who share our faith in Jesus Christ,
that God may gather and keep together in one Church
all those who seek the truth with sincerity.

Silent prayer. Then the priest sings or says:

Almighty and eternal God,
you keep together those you have united.
Look kindly on all who follow Jesus your Son.
We are all consecrated to you by our common baptism.
Make us one in the fullness of faith,
and keep us one in the fellowship of love.
We ask this through Christ our Lord. ℟. **Amen.** ↓

VI. For the Jewish people

Let us pray
for the Jewish people,
the first to hear the word of God,
that they may continue to grow in the love of his name
and in faithfulness to his covenant.

Silent prayer. Then the priest sings or says:

Almighty and eternal God,
long ago you gave your promise to Abraham and his pos-
    terity.
Listen to your Church as we pray
that the people you first made your own
may arrive at the fullness of redemption.
We ask this through Christ our Lord. ℟. **Amen.** ↓

VII. For those who do not believe in Christ

Let us pray
for those who do not believe in Christ,
that the light of the Holy Spirit
may show them the way to salvation.
Silent prayer. Then the priest sings or says:

Almighty and eternal God,
enable those who do not acknowledge Christ
to find the truth
as they walk before you in sincerity of heart.
Help us to grow in love for one another,
to grasp more fully the mystery of your godhead,
and to become more perfect witnesses of your love
in the sight of men.
We ask this through Christ our Lord. ℟. **Amen.** ↓

VIII. For those who do not believe in God

Let us pray
for those who do not believe in God,
that they may find him
by sincerely following all that is right.
Silent prayer. Then the priest sings or says:

Almighty and eternal God,
you created mankind
so that all might long to find you
and have peace when you are found.
Grant that, in spite of the hurtful things
that stand in their way,
they may all recognize in the lives of Christians

the tokens of your love and mercy,
and gladly acknowledge you
as the one true God and Father of us all.
We ask this through Christ our Lord. ℟. **Amen.** ↓

IX. For all in public office

Let us pray
for those who serve us in public office,
that God may guide their minds and hearts,
so that all men may live in true peace and freedom.
Silent prayer. Then the priest sings or says:

Almighty and eternal God,
you know the longings of men's hearts
and you protect their rights.
In your goodness
watch over those in authority,
so that people everywhere may enjoy
religious freedom, security, and peace.
We ask this through Christ our Lord. ℟. **Amen.** ↓

X. For those in special need

Let us pray, dear friends,
that God the almighty Father
may heal the sick,
comfort the dying,
give safety to travelers,
free those unjustly deprived of liberty,
and rid the world of falsehood,
hunger, and disease.
Silent prayer. Then the priest sings or says:

Almighty, ever-living God,
you give strength to the weary
and new courage to those who have lost heart.
Hear the prayers of all who call on you in any trouble
that they may have the joy of receiving your help in their
    need.
We ask this through Christ our Lord. ℟. **Amen.** ↓

PART TWO: VENERATION OF THE CROSS

After the general intercessions, the veneration of the cross takes place. Pastoral demands will determine which of the two forms is more effective and should be chosen.

First Form of Showing the Cross

The veiled cross is carried to the altar, accompanied by two ministers with lighted candles. Standing at the altar, the priest takes the cross, uncovers the upper part of it, then elevates it and begins the invitation This is the wood of the cross. *He is assisted in the singing by the deacon or, if convenient, by the choir. All respond:* Come, let us worship. *At the end of the singing all kneel and venerate the cross briefly in silence; the priest remains standing and holds the cross high.*

Then the priest uncovers the right arm of the cross, lifts it up, and again begins the invitation This is the wood of the cross, *and the rite is repeated as before.*

Finally he uncovers the entire cross, lifts it up, and begins the invitation This is the wood of the cross *a third time, and the rite is repeated as before.*

Accompanied by two ministers with lighted candles, the priest then carries the cross to the entrance of the sanctuary or to another suitable place. There he lays the cross down or hands it to the ministers to hold. Candles are placed on either side of the cross, and the veneration follows as below.

Second Form of Showing the Cross

The priest or deacon, accompanied by the ministers or by another suitable minister, goes to the church door. There he takes the (uncovered) cross, and the ministers take lighted candles. They go in procession through the church to the sanctuary. Near the entrance of the church, in the middle of the church, and at the entrance to the sanctuary, the one carrying the cross stops, lifts it up and sings the invitation This is the wood of the cross. *All respond:* Come, let us worship. *After each response all kneel and venerate the cross briefly in silence as above.*

Then the cross and candles are placed at the entrance to the sanctuary.

INVITATION

℣. This is the wood of the cross, on which hung the Savior of the world.

℟. **Come, let us worship.**

Veneration of the Cross

*The priest, clergy, and faithful approach to venerate the cross
in a kind of procession. They make a simple genuflection or
perform some other appropriate sign of reverence according to
local custom, for example, kissing the cross.*

During the veneration the antiphon We worship you, Lord,
*the reproaches or other suitable songs are sung. All who have
venerated the cross return to their places and sit.*

*Only one cross should be used for the veneration. If the number
of people makes it impossible for everyone to venerate the cross
individually, the priest may take the cross, after some of the
faithful have venerated it, and stand in the center in front of the
altar. In a few words he invites the people to venerate the cross
and then holds it up briefly for them to worship in silence.*

*In the United States, if pastoral reasons suggest that there be
individual veneration even though the number of people is
very large, a second or third cross may be used.*

*After the veneration, the cross is carried to its place at the
altar, and the lighted candles are placed around the altar or
near the cross.*

Songs at the Veneration of the Cross

*Individual parts are indicated by no. 1 (first choir) and no. 2
(second choir); parts sung by both choirs together are indicated by nos. 1 and 2.*

ANTIPHON

1 and 2: Antiphon
**We worship you, Lord,
we venerate your cross,
we praise your resurrection.
Through the cross you brought joy to the world.**

1: Psalm 67:2
**May God be gracious and bless us;
and let his face shed its light upon us.**

1 and 2: Antiphon
**We worship you, Lord,
we venerate your cross,
we praise your resurrection.
Through the cross you brought joy to the world.**

I

REPROACHES

1 and 2: **My people, what have I done to you?
how have I offended you? Answer me!**

1: **I led you out of Egypt, from slavery to freedom,
but you led your Savior to the cross.**

2. **My people, what have I done to you?
How have I offended you? Answer me!**

1: **Holy is God!**

2: **Holy and strong!**

1: **Holy immortal One,
have mercy on us!**

1 and 2: **For forty years I led you safely through the
desert.
I fed you with manna from heaven,
and brought you to a land of plenty;
but you led your Savior to the cross.**

1: **Holy is God!**

2: **Holy and strong!**

1: **Holy immortal One,
have mercy on us!**

1 and 2: **What more could I have done for you?
I planted you as my fairest vine,
but you yielded only bitterness:
when I was thirsty you gave me vinegar to drink,
and you pierced your Savior with a lance.**

1: **Holy is God!**

2: **Holy and strong!**

1: **Holy immortal One,
have mercy on us!**

II

1: **For your sake I scourged your captors and their firstborn sons,
but you brought your scourges down on me.**

2: **My people, what have I done to you?
How have I offended you? Answer me!**

1: **I led you from slavery to freedom
and drowned your captors in the sea,
but you handed me over to your high priests.**

2: **My people, what have I done to you?
How have I offended you? Answer me!**

1: **I opened the sea before you,
but you opened my side with a spear.**

2: **My people, what have I done to you?
How have I offended you? Answer me!**

1: **I led you on your way in a pillar of cloud,
but you led me to Pilate's court.**

2: **My people, what have I done to you?
How have I offended you? Answer me!**

1: **I bore you up with manna in the desert,
but you struck me down and scourged me.**

2: **My people, what have I done to you?
How have I offended you? Answer me!**

1: **I gave you saving water from the rock,
but you gave me gall and vinegar to drink.**

2: **My people, what have I done to you?
How have I offended you? Answer me!**

1: **For you I struck down the kings of Canaan,
but you struck my head with a reed.**

2: **My people, what have I done to you?
How have I offended you? Answer me!**

1: **I gave you a royal scepter,
but you gave me a crown of thorns.**

2: **My people, what have I done to you?
How have I offended you? Answer me!**

1: I raised you to the height of majesty,
   but you have raised me high on a cross.

2: My people, what have I done to you?
   How have I offended you? Answer me!

HYMN: PANGE LINGUA

Sing, my tongue, the Savior's glory;
  tell his triumph far and wide;
Tell aloud the famous story
  of his body crucified;
How upon the cross a victim,
  vanquishing in death, he died.

Eating of the tree forbidden,
  man had sunk in Satan's snare,
When our pitying Creator did
  this second tree prepare;
Destined, many ages later,
  that first evil to repair.

Such the order God appointed
  when for sin he would atone;
To the serpent thus opposing
  schemes yet deeper than his own;
Thence the remedy procuring,
  when the fatal wound had come.

So when now at length the fullness
  of the sacred time drew nigh,

Then the Son, the world's Creator,
  left his Father's throne on high;
From a virgin's womb appearing,
  clothed in our mortality.

All within a lowly manger,
  lo, a tender babe he lies!
See his gentle Virgin Mother
  lull to sleep his infant cries!
While the limbs of God incarnate
  round with swathing bands she ties.

Thus did Christ to perfect manhood
  in our mortal flesh attain:
Then of his free choice he goeth
  to a death of bitter pain;
And as a lamb, upon the altar
  of the cross, for us is slain.

Lo, with gall his thirst he quenches!
  See the thorns upon his brow!
Nails his tender flesh are rending!

See, his side is opened now!
Whence, to cleanse the whole creation,
streams of blood and water flow.

Lofty tree, bend down thy branches,
to embrace thy sacred load;
Oh, relax the native tension of that all too rigid wood;
Gently, gently bear the members
of thy dying King and God.

Tree, which solely wast found worthy

the world's great Victim to sustain.
Harbor from the raging tempest!
Ark, that saved the world again!
Tree, with sacred blood anointed
of the Lamb for sinners slain.

Blessing, honor everlasting, to the immortal Deity;
To the Father, Son, and Spirit, equal praises ever be;
Glory through the earth and heaven
to Trinity in Unity. Amen.

PART THREE: HOLY COMMUNION

The altar is covered with a cloth and the corporal and book are placed on it. Then the deacon or, if there is no deacon, the priest brings the ciborium with the Blessed Sacrament from the place of reposition to the altar without any procession, while all stand in silence.

The priest comes from his chair, genuflects, and goes up to the altar. With hands joined, he says aloud:

Let us pray with confidence to the Father
in the words our Savior gave us:

He extends his hands and continues, with all present:

Our Father . . .

With hands extended, the priest continues alone:

Deliver us, Lord, from every evil,
and grant us peace in our day.
In your mercy keep us free from sin
and protect us from all anxiety

as we wait in joyful hope
for the coming of our Savior, Jesus Christ.

The people end the prayer with the acclamation:

**For the kingdom, the power, and the glory are yours,
now and for ever.**

Then the priest says quietly:

Lord Jesus Christ, with faith in your love and mercy I eat
    your body and drink your blood.
Let it not bring me condemnation, but health in mind and
    body.

Taking the host, the priest says aloud:

This is the Lamb of God
who takes away the sins of the world.
Happy are those who are called to his supper.

He adds, once only, with the people:

**Lord, I am not worthy to receive you,
but only say the word and I shall be healed.**

Facing the altar, he reverently consumes the body of Christ.

Then communion is distributed to the faithful. Any appropriate song may be sung during communion.

When the communion has been completed, a suitable minister may take the ciborium to a place prepared outside the church or, if circumstances require, may place it in the tabernacle.

A period of silence may now be observed. The priest then says the following prayer:

Let us pray.
Almighty and eternal God,
you have restored us to life
by the triumphant death and resurrection of Christ.
Continue this healing work within us.
May we who participate in this mystery
never cease to serve you.
We ask this through Christ our Lord. ℟. **Amen.** ↓

For the dismissal the priest faces the people, extends his hands toward them, and says the following prayer:

PRAYER OVER THE PEOPLE

Lord,
send down your abundant blessing
upon your people who have devoutly recalled the death
 of your Son
in the sure hope of the resurrection.
Grant them pardon; bring them comfort.
May their faith grow stronger
and their eternal salvation be assured.
We ask this through Christ our Lord. ℟. **Amen.** ↓

All depart in silence. The altar is stripped at a convenient time.

HOLY SATURDAY

On Holy Saturday the Church waits at the Lord's tomb, meditating on his suffering and death. The altar is left bare, and the sacrifice of the Mass is not celebrated. Only after the solemn vigil during the night, held in anticipation of the resurrection, does the Easter celebration begin, with a spirit of joy that overflows into the following period of fifty days.

608

COMMUNION PRAYERS

PRAYERS BEFORE HOLY COMMUNION

Act of Faith

Lord Jesus Christ, I firmly believe that you are present in this Blessed Sacrament as true God and true Man, with your Body and Blood, Soul and Divinity. My Redeemer and my Judge, I adore your Divine Majesty together with the angels and saints. I believe, O Lord; increase my faith.

Act of Hope

Good Jesus, in you alone I place all my hope. You are my salvation and my strength, the Source of all good. Through your mercy, through your Passion and Death, I hope to obtain the pardon of my sins, the grace of final perseverance and a happy eternity.

Act of Love

Jesus, my God, I love you with my whole heart and above all things, because you are the one supreme Good and an infinitely perfect Being. You have given your life for me, a poor sinner, and in your mercy you have even offered yourself as food for my soul. My God, I love you. Inflame my heart so that I may love you more.

Act of Contrition

O my Savior, I am truly sorry for having offended you because you are infinitely good and sin displeases you. I detest all the sins of my life and I desire to atone for them. Through the merits of your Precious Blood, wash from my soul all stain of sin, so that, cleansed in body and soul, I may worthily approach the Most Holy Sacrament of the Altar.

PRAYERS AFTER HOLY COMMUNION

Act of Faith

Jesus, I firmly believe that you are present within me as God and Man, to enrich my soul with graces and to fill my heart with the happiness of the blessed. I believe that you are Christ, the Son of the living God!

Act of Adoration

With deepest humility, I adore you, my Lord and God; you have made my soul your dwelling place. I adore you as my Creator from whose hands I came and with whom I am to be happy forever.

Act of Love

Dear Jesus, I love you with my whole heart, my whole soul, and with all my strength. May the love of your own Sacred Heart fill my soul and purify it so that I may die to the world for love of you, as you died on the Cross for love of me. My God, you are all mine; grant that I may be all yours in time and in eternity.

Act of Thanksgiving

From the depths of my heart I thank you, dear Lord, for your infinite kindness in coming to me. How good you are to me! With your most holy Mother and all the angels, I praise your mercy and generosity toward me, a poor sinner. I thank you for nourishing my soul with your Sacred Body and Precious Blood. I will try to show my gratitude to you in the Sacrament of your love, by obedience to your holy commandments, by fidelity to my duties, by kindness to my neighbor and by an earnest endeavor to become more like you in my daily conduct.

Act of Offering

Jesus, you have given yourself to me; now let me give myself to you. I give you my body, that it may be chaste and pure. I give you my souls, that it may be free from sin. I give you my heart, that it may always love you. I give you every thought, word, and deed of my life, and I offer all for your honor and glory.

Prayer to Christ the King

O Christ Jesus, I acknowledge you King of the universe. All that has been created has been made for you. Exercise upon me all your rights. I renew my baptismal promises, renouncing Satan and all his works and pomps. I promise to live a good Christian life and to do all in my power to procure the triumph of the rights of God and your Church.

Divine Heart of Jesus, I offer you my poor actions in order to obtain that all hearts may acknowledge your sacred Royalty, and that thus the reign of your peace may be established throughout the universe. Amen.

Indulgenced prayer before a Crucifix

Look down upon me, good and gentle Jesus, while before your face I humbly kneel, and with a burning soul pray and beseech you to fix deep in my heart lively sentiments of faith, hope, and charity, true contrition for my sins, and a firm purpose of amendment, while I contemplate with great love and tender pity your five wounds, pondering over them within me, calling to mind the words that David, your prophet, said of you, my good Jesus: "They have pierced my hands and my feet; they have numbered all my bones" (Ps 22:17-18).

A *plenary indulgence* is granted on each Friday of Lent and Passiontide to the faithful, who after Communion piously recite the above prayer before an image of Christ crucified; on other days of the year the indulgence is *partial*. (No. 22).

Prayer to Mary

O Jesus living in Mary, come and live in your servants, in the spirit of your holiness, in the fulness of your power, in the perfection of your ways, in the truth of your mysteries. Reign in us over all adverse power by your Holy Spirit, and for the glory of the Father. Amen.

Mary, I come to you with childlike confidence and earnestly beg you to take me under your powerful protection. Grant me a place in your loving motherly Heart. I place my immortal soul into your hands and give you my own poor heart.

Anima Christi

Partial indulgence (No. 10)

Soul of Christ, sanctify me.
Body of Christ, save me.
Blood of Christ, inebriate me.
Water from the side of Christ, wash me.
Passion of Christ, strengthen me.
O good Jesus, hear me.
Within your wounds hide me.
Separated from you let me never be.
From the malignant enemy, defend me.
At the hour of death, call me.
And close to you bid me.
That with your saints I may be
Praising you, for all eternity. Amen.

PLAN OF THE MASS

INTRODUCTORY RITES
1. Entrance Antiphon **(Proper)**
2. Greeting
3. Blessing and Sprinkling Holy Water
4. Penitential Rite
5. Kyrie
6. Gloria
7. Opening Prayer **(Proper)**

LITURGY OF THE WORD
8. First Reading **(Proper)**
9. Responsorial Psalm **(Proper)**
10. Second Reading **(Proper)**
11. Alleluia **(Proper)**
12. Gospel **(Proper)**
13. Homily
14. Profession of Faith **(Creed)**
15. General Intercessions

(Preparation of the Gifts)
16. Offertory Song
17. Preparation of the Bread
18. Preparation of the Wine
19. Invitation to Prayer
20. Prayer over the Gifts **(Proper)**

(Eucharistic Prayer)
LITURGY OF THE EUCHARIST
21. Introductory Dialogue
22. Preface
23. Sanctus
   Eucharistic Prayer
   1, 2, 3, 4
   Children 1, 2, 3
   Reconciliation 1, 2

(Communion Rite)
24. Lord's Prayer
25. Sign of Peace
26. Breaking of the Bread
27. Prayers before Communion
28. Reception of Communion
29. Communion Antiphon **(Proper)**
30. Silence after Communion
31. Prayer after Communion **(Proper)**

CONCLUDING RITE
32. Greeting
33. Blessing
34. Dismissal

THE ORDER OF MASS

Options are indicated by A, B, C, D in the margin.

INTRODUCTORY RITES

Acts of prayer and penitence prepare us to meet Christ as he comes in Word and Sacrament. We gather as a worshiping community to celebrate our unity with him and with one another in faith.

1 ENTRANCE ANTIPHON   `STAND`

If it is not sung, it is recited by all or some of the people.

Joined together as Christ's people, we open the celebration by raising our voices in praise of God who is present among us. This song should deepen our unity as it introduces the Mass we celebrate today.

→ `Turn to Today's Mass`

2 GREETING (3 forms)

When the priest comes to the altar, he makes the customary reverence with the ministers and kisses the altar. Then, with the ministers, he goes to his seat. After the entrance song, all make the sign of the cross:

Priest: In the name of the Father, ✠ and of the Son, and of the Holy Spirit.

PEOPLE: **Amen.**

The priest welcomes us in the name of the Lord. We show our union with God, our neighbor, and the priest by a united response to his greeting.

A ─────────────────────────────────

Priest: The grace of our Lord Jesus Christ and the love of God and the fellowship of the Holy Spirit be with you all.

PEOPLE: And also with you.

B ──────────────── OR ────────────────

Priest: The grace and peace of God our Father and the Lord Jesus Christ be with you.

PEOPLE: Blessed be God, the Father of our Lord Jesus Christ.

or:

And also with you.

C ──────────────── OR ────────────────

Priest: The Lord be with you.

PEOPLE: And also with you.

[Bishop: Peace be with you.

People: **And also with you.**]

3 RITE OF BLESSING and SPRINKLING HOLY WATER

The rite of blessing and sprinkling holy water may be celebrated in all churches and chapels at all Sunday Masses celebrated on Sunday or Saturday evening. See pp. 662-664.

4 PENITENTIAL RITE (3 forms)

(Omitted when the rite of blessing and sprinkling holy water has taken place or some part of the liturgy of the hours has preceded.)

Before we hear God's word, we acknowledge our sins humbly, ask for mercy, and accept his pardon.

Invitation to repent:

After the introduction to the day's Mass, the priest invites the people to recall their sins and to repent of them in silence:

A As we prepare to celebrate the mystery of Christ's love,
let us acknowledge our failures
and ask the Lord for pardon and strength.

B Coming together as God's family,
with confidence let us ask the Father's forgiveness,
for he is full of gentleness and compassion.

C My brothers and sisters,
to prepare ourselves to celebrate the sacred mysteries,
let us call to mind our sins.

Then, after a brief silence, one of the following forms is used.

A

Priest and **People**:
**I confess to almighty God,
and to you, my brothers and sisters,
that I have sinned through my own fault**

They strike their breast:

**in my thoughts and in my words,
in what I have done,**

and in what I have failed to do;
and I ask blessed Mary, ever virgin,
all the angels and saints,
and you, my brothers and sisters,
to pray for me to the Lord our God.

B ———————— OR ————————

Priest: Lord, we have sinned against you:
Lord, have mercy.

PEOPLE: Lord, have mercy.

Priest: Lord, show us your mercy and love.

PEOPLE: And grant us your salvation.

C ———————— OR ————————

Priest or other minister:

You were sent to heal the contrite:
Lord, have mercy.

PEOPLE: Lord have mercy.

Priest or other minister:

You came to call sinners:
Christ, have mercy.

PEOPLE: Christ, have mercy.

Priest or other minister:

You plead for us at the right hand of the
Father:
Lord, have mercy.

PEOPLE: Lord, have mercy.

(Other invocations may be used as on pp. 665-667.)

Absolution:

At the end of any of the forms of the penitential rite:

Priest: May almighty God have mercy on us,
forgive us our sins,
and bring us to everlasting life.

PEOPLE: Amen.

5 KYRIE

Unless included in the penitential rite, the Kyrie is sung or said by all, with alternating parts for the choir or cantor and for the people:

℣. Lord have mercy.

℟. **Lord, have mercy.**

℣. Christ, have mercy.

℟. **Christ, have mercy.**

℣. Lord, have mercy.

℟. **Lord, have mercy.**

6 GLORIA

As the Church assembled in the Spirit we praise and pray to the Father and the Lamb.

When the Gloria is sung or said, the priest or the cantors or everyone together may begin it. It is omitted on most Weekdays but said on Solemnities and Feasts.

Glory to God in the highest,
and peace to his people on earth.

Lord God, heavenly King,
almighty God and Father,
we worship you, we give you thanks,
we praise you for your glory.

Lord Jesus Christ, only Son of the Father,
Lord God, Lamb of God,
you take away the sin of the world:
   have mercy on us;
you are seated at the right hand of the Father:
   receive our prayer.

For you alone are the Holy One,
you alone are the Lord,
you alone are the Most High,
   Jesus Christ,
   with the Holy Spirit,
   in the glory of God the Father. Amen.

7 OPENING PRAYER

The priest invites us to pray silently for a moment and then, in our name, expresses the theme of the day's celebration and petitions God the Father through the mediation of Christ in the Holy Spirit.

Priest: Let us pray.

→ **Turn to Today's Mass**

Priest and people pray silently for a while. Then the priest says the opening prayer and concludes:

Priest: For ever and ever.*

PEOPLE: Amen.

*The complete conclusion is:

We ask this (Grant this) through our Lord Jesus Christ,
   your Son,
who lives and reigns with you and the Holy Spirit,
one God, for ever and ever.

LITURGY OF THE WORD

The proclamation of God's Word is always centered on Christ, present through his Word. Old Testament writings prepare for him; New Testament books speak of him directly. All of scripture calls us to believe once more and to follow. After the reading we reflect on God's words and respond to them.

As in Today's Mass **SIT**

8 FIRST READING

At the end of the reading: Reader: The word of the Lord.

PEOPLE: Thanks be to God.

9 RESPONSORIAL PSALM

The people repeat the response sung by the cantor the first time and then after each verse.

10 SECOND READING

At the end of the reading: Reader: The word of the Lord.

PEOPLE: Thanks be to God.

11 ALLELUIA (Gospel Acclamation) **STAND**

Jesus will speak to us in the Gospel. We rise now out of respect and prepare for his message with the alleluia.

The people repeat the alleluia after cantor's alleluia and then after the verse. During Lent one of the following invocations is used as a response instead of the alleluia:

(1) Glory and praise to you, Lord Jesus Christ!
(2) Glory to you, Lord Jesus Christ, Wisdom of God the Father!
(3) Glory to you, Word of God, Lord Jesus Christ!
(4) Glory to you, Lord Jesus Christ, Son of the Living God!

(5) **Praise and honor to you, Lord Jesus Christ!**
(6) **Praise to you, Lord Jesus Christ, King of endless glory!**
(7) **Marvelous and great are your works, O Lord!**
(8) **Salvation, glory, and power to the Lord Jesus Christ!**

12 GOSPEL

Before proclaiming the Gospel, the deacon asks the priest:
Father, give me your blessing. *The priest says:*

The Lord be in your heart and on your lips
that you may worthily proclaim his gospel.
In the name of the Father, and of the Son, ✤ and of
the Holy Spirit. *The deacon answers:* Amen.

If there is no deacon, the priest says inaudibly:

Almighty God, cleanse my heart and my lips that I
may worthily proclaim your gospel.

Deacon (or Priest):
        The Lord be with you.
PEOPLE: And also with you.

Deacon (or Priest):

✤ A reading from the holy Gospel according to N.
PEOPLE: Glory to you, Lord.

At the end:

Deacon (or priest):
        The Gospel of the Lord.
PEOPLE: Praise to you, Lord Jesus Christ.

Then the deacon (or priest) kisses the book, saying inaudibly: May the words of the Gospel wipe away our sins.

13 HOMILY   `SIT`

God's word is spoken again in the homily. The Holy Spirit speaking through the lips of the preacher explains and applies today's biblical readings to the needs of this particular congregation. He calls us to respond to Christ through the life we lead.

14 PROFESSION OF FAITH (CREED) STAND

As a people we express our acceptance of God's message in the scriptures and homily. We summarize our faith by proclaiming a creed handed down from the early Church.

All say the profession of faith on Sundays and Solemnities.

THE NICENE CREED

We believe in one God,
  the Father, the Almighty,
  maker of heaven and earth,
  of all that is seen and unseen.
We believe in one Lord, Jesus Christ,
  the only Son of God,
  eternally begotten of the Father,
  God from God, Light from Light,
  true God from true God,
  begotten, not made, one in Being with the Father.
  Through him all things were made.
For us men and for our salvation
    he came down from heaven:
by the power of the Holy Spirit
    he was born of the Virgin Mary, } *bow*
      and became man.
For our sake he was crucified under Pontius Pilate;
    he suffered, died, and was buried.
  On the third day he rose again
    in fulfillment of the Scriptures;
  he ascended into heaven
    and is seated at the right hand of the Father.
He will come again in glory to judge the living and
      the dead,
    and his kingdom will have no end.
We believe in the Holy Spirit, the Lord, the giver of life,
  who proceeds from the Father and the Son.
  With the Father and the Son he is worshiped and
      glorified.
  He has spoken through the Prophets.
We believe in one holy catholic and apostolic Church.

We acknowledge one baptism for the forgiveness of
    sins.
We look for the resurrection of the dead,
    and the life of the world to come. Amen.

OR ——————— APOSTLES' CREED ———————

In celebrations of Masses with children, the Apostles'
Creed may be said after the homily.

I believe in God, the Father almighty,
    creator of heaven and earth.

I believe in Jesus Christ, his only Son, our Lord.
    He was conceived by the power of the Holy Spirit
        and born of the Virgin Mary.
    He suffered under Pontius Pilate,
        was crucified, died, and was buried.
    He descended to the dead.
    On the third day he rose again.
    He ascended into heaven,
        and is seated at the right hand of the Father.
    He will come again to judge the living and the dead.

I believe in the Holy Spirit,
    the holy catholic Church,
    the communion of saints,
    the forgiveness of sins,
    the resurrection of the body,
    and the life everlasting. Amen.

15 GENERAL INTERCESSIONS   (Prayer of the Faithful)

As a priestly people we unite with one another to pray for
today's needs in the Church and the world.

After the priest gives the introduction the deacon or other
minister sings or says the invocations.

PEOPLE: Lord, hear our prayer.
(or other response, according to local custom)
At the end the priest says the concluding prayer:

PEOPLE: Amen.

LITURGY OF THE EUCHARIST

Made ready by reflection on God's Word, we enter now into the eucharistic sacrifice itself, the Supper of the Lord. We celebrate the memorial which the Lord instituted at his Last Supper. We are God's new people, the redeemed brothers and sisters of Christ, gathered by him around his table. We are here to bless God and to receive the gift of Jesus' body and blood so that our faith and life may be transformed.

PREPARATION OF THE GIFTS

16 OFFERTORY SONG `SIT`

The bread and wine for the Eucharist, with our gifts for the Church and the poor, are gathered and brought to the altar. We prepare our hearts by song or in silence as the Lord's table is being set.

While the people's gifts are brought forward to the priest and are placed on the altar, the offertory song is sung.

17 PREPARATION OF THE BREAD

Before placing the bread on the altar, the priest says inaudibly:

Blessed are you, Lord, God of all creation.
Through your goodness we have this bread to offer,
which earth has given and human hands have made.
It will become for us the bread of life.

If there is no singing, the priest may say this prayer aloud, and the people may respond:

PEOPLE: Blessed be God for ever.

18 PREPARATION OF THE WINE

When he pours wine and a little water into the chalice, the deacon (or the priest) says inaudibly:

624

By the mystery of this water and wine
may we come to share in the divinity of Christ,
who humbled himself to share in our humanity.

Before placing the chalice on the altar, he says:

Blessed are you, Lord, God of all creation.
Through your goodness we have this wine to offer,
fruit of the vine and work of human hands.
It will become our spiritual drink.

*If there is no singing, the priest may say this prayer
aloud, and the people may respond:*

PEOPLE: Blessed be God for ever.

The priest says inaudibly:

Lord God, we ask you to receive us
and be pleased with the sacrifice we offer you
with humble and contrite hearts.

Then he washes his hands, saying:

Lord, wash away my iniquity;
cleanse me from my sin.

19 INVITATION TO PRAYER   `STAND`

Priest: Pray, brethren, that our sacrifice may be
acceptable to God, the almighty Father.

PEOPLE:

**May the Lord accept the sacrifice at your hands
for the praise and glory of his name,
for our good, and the good of all his Church.**

20 PRAYER OVER THE GIFTS

*The priest, speaking in our name, asks the Father to bless
and accept these gifts.*

→ `Turn to Today's Mass`

At the end, **PEOPLE: Amen.**

EUCHARISTIC PRAYER

We begin the eucharistic service of praise and thanksgiving, the center of the entire celebration, the central prayer of worship. We lift our hearts to God, and offer praise and thanks as the priest addresses this prayer to the Father through Jesus Christ. Together we join Christ in his sacrifice, celebrating his memorial in the holy meal and acknowledging with him the wonderful works of God in our lives.

21 INTRODUCTORY DIALOGUE

Priest: The Lord be with you.

PEOPLE: And also with you.

Priest: Lift up your hearts.

PEOPLE: We lift them up to the Lord.

Priest: Let us give thanks to the Lord our God.

PEOPLE: It is right to give him thanks and praise.

22 PREFACE

As indicated in the individual Masses of this Missal, the priest may say one of the following Prefaces (listed in numerical order). (The Prefaces whose numbers are missing are found together with the Proper texts of the Masses to which they belong or are found in the Sunday Missal since they are used only on Sundays.)

626

---

23 ACCLAMATION

Priest and **People**:

Holy, holy, holy Lord, God of power and might, heaven and earth are full of your glory.

   Hosanna in the highest.

Blessed is he who comes in the name of the Lord.

   Hosanna in the highest.   `KNEEL`

Then the priest continues with one of the following Eucharistic Prayers.

The Roman Canon

(This Eucharistic Prayer is especially suitable for Sundays and Masses with proper "Communicantes" and "Hanc Igitur.")

[The words within brackets may be omitted.]

[Praise to the Father]

We come to you, Father,
with praise and thanksgiving,
through Jesus Christ your Son.
Through him we ask you to accept and bless
these gifts we offer you in sacrifice.

[Intercessions: For the Church]

We offer them for your holy catholic Church,
watch over it, Lord, and guide it;
grant it peace and unity throughout the world.
We offer them for N. our Pope,
for N. our bishop,
and for all who hold and teach the catholic faith
that comes to us from the apostles.
Remember, Lord, your people,
especially those for whom we now pray, N. and N.

Remember all of us gathered here before you.
You know how firmly we believe in you
and dedicate ourselves to you.
We offer you this sacrifice of praise
for ourselves and those who are dear to us.
We pray to you, our living and true God,
for our well-being and redemption.

[In Communion with the Saints]

1

In union with the whole Church*
we honor Mary,
the ever-virgin mother of Jesus Christ our Lord and
     God.
We honor Joseph, her husband,
the apostles and martyrs
Peter and Paul, Andrew,
[James, John, Thomas,
James, Philip,
Bartholomew, Matthew, Simon and Jude;
we honor Linus, Cletus, Clement, Sixtus,
Cornelius, Cyprian, Lawrence, Chrysogonus,
John and Paul, Cosmas and Damian]
and all the saints.
May their merits and prayers
gain us your constant help and protection.
[Through Christ our Lord. Amen.]

Father, accept this offering*
from your whole family.
Grant us your peace in this life,
save us from final damnation,
and count us among those you have chosen.
[Through Christ our Lord. Amen.]

Bless and approve our offering;.
make it acceptable to you,
an offering in spirit and in truth.
Let it become for us
the body and blood of Jesus Christ,
your only Son, our Lord.
[Through Christ our Lord. Amen.]

See p. 690 for special Communicantes and Hanc Igitur.

[The Lord's Supper]

1 The day before he suffered
he took bread in his sacred hands
and looking up to heaven,
to you, his almighty Father,
he gave you thanks and praise.
He broke the bread,
gave it to his disciples, and said:

Take this, all of you, and eat it:
this is my body which will be given up for you.

When supper was ended,
he took the cup.
Again he gave you thanks and praise,
gave the cup to his disciples, and said:

Take this, all of you, and drink from it:
this is the cup of my blood,
the blood of the new and everlasting covenant.
It will be shed for you and for all
so that sins may be forgiven.
Do this in memory of me.

[Memorial Acclamation]

Priest: Let us proclaim the mystery of faith.
PEOPLE:

A Christ has died,
Christ is risen,
Christ will come again.

B Dying you destroyed our death,
rising you restored our life.
Lord Jesus, come in glory.

1

C When we eat this bread and drink this cup,
we proclaim your death, Lord Jesus,
until you come in glory

D Lord, by your cross and resurrection
you have set us free.
You are the Savior of the world.

[The Memorial Prayer]

Father, we celebrate the memory of Christ, your
Son.
We, your people and your ministers,
recall his passion,
his resurrection from the dead,
and his ascension into glory;
and from the many gifts you have given us
we offer to you, God of glory and majesty,
this holy and perfect sacrifice:
the bread of life
and the cup of eternal salvation.
Look with favor on these offerings
and accept them as once you accepted
the gifts of your servant Abel,
the sacrifice of Abraham, our father in faith,
and the bread and wine offered by your priest
Melchisedech.
Almighty God,
we pray that your angel may take this sacrifice
to your altar in heaven.
Then, as we receive from this altar
the sacred body and blood of your Son,
let us be filled with every grace and blessing.
[Through Christ our Lord. Amen.]

1

[For the Dead]

Remember, Lord, those who have died
and have gone before us marked with the sign of
　　　faith,
especially those for whom we now pray, N. and N.
May these, and all who sleep in Christ,
find in your presence
light, happiness, and peace.
[Through Christ our Lord. Amen.]

For ourselves, too, we ask
some share in the fellowship of your apostles and
　　　martyrs,
with John the Baptist, Stephen, Matthias, Barnabas,
[Ignatius, Alexander, Marcellinus, Peter,
Felicity, Perpetua, Agatha, Lucy,
Agnes, Cecilia, Anastasia]
and all the saints.
Though we are sinners,
we trust in your mercy and love.
Do not consider what we truly deserve,
but grant us your forgiveness.
Through Christ our Lord.

Through him you give us all these gifts.
You fill them with life and goodness,
you bless them and make them holy.

[Concluding Doxology]

Through him,
with him,
in him,
in the unity of the Holy Spirit,
all glory and honor is yours,
almighty Father,
for ever and ever.

All reply: **Amen.** *Continue with the Mass, as on p. 656.*

(This Eucharistic Prayer is particularly suitable on Weekdays or for special circumstances)

STAND

℣. The Lord be with you.
℟. **And also with you.**
℣. Lift up your hearts.
℟. **We lift them up to the Lord.**
℣. Let us give thanks to the Lord our God.
℟. **It is right to give him thanks and praise.**

PREFACE   *[Praise to the Lord]*

Father, it is our duty and our salvation,
always and everywhere
to give you thanks
through your beloved Son, Jesus Christ.

He is the Word through whom you made the universe,
the Savior you sent to redeem us.

By the power of the Holy Spirit
he took flesh and was born of the Virgin Mary.

For our sake he opened his arms on the cross;
he put an end to death
and revealed the resurrection.

In this he fulfilled your will
and won for you a holy people.

And so we join the angels and the saints
in proclaiming your glory
as we sing (say):

2

SANCTUS

[First Acclamation of the People]

**Holy, holy, holy Lord, God of power and might,
heaven and earth are full of your glory.**
　　Hosanna in the highest.
Blessed is he who comes in the name of the Lord.
　　Hosanna in the highest.

KNEEL

[Invocation of the Holy Spirit]

Lord, you are holy indeed,
the fountain of all holiness.

Let your Spirit come upon these gifts to make
　　them holy,
so that they may become for us
the body and blood of our Lord, Jesus Christ.

[The Lord's Supper]

Before he was given up to death,
a death he freely accepted,
he took bread and gave you thanks.
He broke the bread,
gave it to his disciples, and said:

Take this, all of you, and eat it:
this is my body which will be given up for you.

When supper was ended, he took the cup.
Again he gave you thanks and praise,
gave the cup to his disciples, and said:

Take this, all of you, and drink from it:
this is the cup of my blood,
the blood of the new and everlasting covenant.
It will be shed for you and for all
so that sins may be forgiven.
Do this in memory of me.

2

[Memorial Acclamation]

Priest: Let us proclaim the mystery of faith.

PEOPLE:

A Christ has died,
   Christ is risen,
   Christ will come again.

B Dying you destroyed our death,
   rising you restored our life.
   Lord Jesus, come in glory.

C When we eat this bread and drink this cup,
   we proclaim your death, Lord Jesus,
   until you come in glory.

D Lord, by your cross and resurrection
   you have set us free.
   You are the Savior of the world.

[The Memorial Prayer]

In memory of his death and resurrection,
we offer you, Father, this life-giving bread,
this saving cup.
We thank you for counting us worthy
to stand in your presence and serve you.

[Invocation of the Holy Spirit]

May all of us who share in the body and blood of
      Christ
be brought together in unity by the Holy Spirit.

[Intercessions: For the Church]

2 Lord, remember your Church throughout the
world;
make us grow in love,
together with N. our Pope,
N. our bishop, and all the clergy.*

[For the Dead]

Remember our brothers and sisters
who have gone to their rest
in the hope of rising again;
bring them and all the departed
into the light of your presence.

[In Communion with the Saints]

Have mercy on us all;
make us worthy to share eternal life
with Mary, the virgin Mother of God,
with the apostles, and with all the saints
who have done your will throughout the ages.
May we praise you in union with them,
and give you glory
through your Son, Jesus Christ.

[Concluding Doxology]

Through him,
with him,
in him,
in the unity of the Holy Spirit,
all glory and honor is yours,
almighty Father,
for ever and ever.

All reply: **Amen.** *Continue with the Mass, as on p. 656.*

---

* *In Masses for the Dead the following may be added:*

Remember N., whom you have called from this life.
In baptism he (she) died with Christ:
may he (she) also share his resurrection.

(This Eucharistic Prayer may be used with any Preface and preferably on Sundays and feast days)

KNEEL

[Praise to the Father]

Father, you are holy indeed,
and all creation rightly gives you praise.
All life, all holiness comes from you
through your Son, Jesus Christ our Lord,
by the working of the Holy Spirit.

From age to age you gather a people to yourself,
so that from east to west
a perfect offering may be made
to the glory of your name.

[Invocation of the Holy Spirit]

And so, Father, we bring you these gifts.
We ask you to make them holy by the power of
    your Spirit,
that they may become the body and blood
of your Son, our Lord Jesus Christ,
at whose command we celebrate this eucharist.

[The Lord's Supper]

On the night he was betrayed,
he took bread and gave you thanks and praise.
He broke the bread, gave it to his disciples, and
    said:

Take this, all of you, and eat it:
this is my body which will be given up for you.

3 When supper was ended, he took the cup.
Again he gave you thanks and praise,
gave the cup to his disciples, and said:

Take this, all of you, and drink from it:
this is the cup of my blood,
the blood of the new and everlasting covenant.
It will be shed for you and for all
so that sins may be forgiven.
Do this in memory of me.

[Memorial Acclamation]

Priest: Let us proclaim the mystery of faith.

PEOPLE:

A **Christ has died,**
Christ is risen,
Christ will come again.

B **Dying you destroyed our death,**
rising you restored our life.
Lord Jesus, come in glory.

C **When we eat this bread and drink this cup,**
we proclaim your death, Lord Jesus,
until you come in glory.

D **Lord, by your cross and resurrection**
you have set us free.
You are the Savior of the world.

[The Memorial Prayer]

Father, calling to mind the death your Son endured
    for our salvation,
his glorious resurrection and ascension into heaven,
and ready to greet him when he comes again,
we offer you in thanksgiving this holy and living
    sacrifice.

Look with favor on your Church's offering,
and see the Victim whose death has reconciled us
    to yourself.

3

[Invocation of the Holy Spirit]

Grant that we, who are nourished by his body
    and blood,
may be filled with his Holy Spirit,
and become one body, one spirit in Christ.

[Intercessions: In Communion with the Saints]

May he make us an everlasting gift to you
and enable us to share in the inheritance of your
    saints,
with Mary, the virgin Mother of God;
with the apostles, the martyrs,
(Saint *N.—the saint of the day or the patron saint*) and
    all your saints,
on whose constant intercession we rely for help.

[For the Church]

Lord, may this sacrifice,
which has made our peace with you,
advance the peace and salvation of all the world.
Strengthen in faith and love your pilgrim Church
    on earth;
your servant, Pope *N.,* our bishop *N.,*
and all the bishops,
with the clergy and the entire people your Son
    has gained for you.
Father, hear the prayers of the family you have
    gathered here before you.
In mercy and love unite all your children
wherever they may be.*

*See p. 640 for special prayer for Mass for the Dead.

[For the Dead]

3 Welcome into your kingdom our departed brothers and sisters,
and all who have left this world in your friendship.
We hope to enjoy for ever the vision of your glory,
through Christ our Lord, from whom all good things come.

[Concluding Doxology]

Through him,
with him,
in him,
in the unity of the Holy Spirit,
all glory and honor is yours,
almighty Father,
for ever and ever.
All reply: **Amen.**

Continue with the Mass, as on p. 656.

---

*In Masses for the Dead the following is said:

Remember N.
In baptism he (she) died with Christ:
may he (she) also share his resurrection,
when Christ will raise our mortal bodies
and make them like his own in glory.

Welcome into your kingdom our departed brothers and sisters,
and all who have left this world in your friendship.
There we hope to share in your glory
when every tear will be wiped away.
On that day we shall see you, our God, as you are.
We shall become like you
and praise you for ever through Christ our Lord,
from whom all good things come.
Through him, etc., *as above.*

℣. The Lord be with you.   STAND
℟. **And also with you.**
℣. Lift up your hearts.
℟. **We lift them up to the Lord.**
℣. Let us give thanks to the Lord our God.
℟. **It is right to give him thanks and praise.**

PREFACE   *[Praise to the Father]*

Father in heaven,
it is right that we should give you thanks and
    glory:
you are the one God, living and true.
Through all eternity you live in unapproachable
    light.
Source of life and goodness, you have created all
    things,
to fill your creatures with every blessing
and lead all men to the joyful vision of your light.
Countless hosts of angels stand before you to do
    your will;
they look upon your splendor
and praise you, night and day.
United with them,
and in the name of every creature under heaven,
we too praise your glory as we sing (say):

SANCTUS   *[First Acclamation of the People]*

**Holy, holy, holy Lord, God of power and might,
heaven and earth are full of your glory.**
    Hosanna in the highest.
Blessed is he who comes in the name of the Lord.
    Hosanna in the highest.

4 Father, we acknowledge your greatness:
all your actions show your wisdom and love.
You formed man in your own likeness
and set him over the whole world
to serve you, his creator,
and to rule over all creatures.
Even when he disobeyed you and lost your
      friendship
you did not abandon him to the power of death,
but helped all men to seek and find you.
Again and again you offered a covenant to man,
and through the prophets taught him to hope for
      salvation.
Father, you so loved the world
that in the fullness of time you sent your only Son
      to be our Savior.
He was conceived through the power of the Holy
      Spirit,
and born of the Virgin Mary,
a man like us in all things but sin.
To the poor he proclaimed the good news of sal-
      vation,
to prisoners, freedom,
and to those in sorrow, joy.
In fulfillment of your will
he gave himself up to death;
but by rising from the dead,
he destroyed death and restored life.
And that we might live no longer for ourselves
      but for him,
he sent the Holy Spirit from you, Father,
as his first gift to those who believe,

to complete his work on earth
and bring us the fullness of grace.

4

[Invocation of the Holy Spirit]

Father, may this Holy Spirit sanctify these offerings.
Let them become the body ✚ and blood of Jesus
Christ our Lord
as we celebrate the great mystery
which he left us as an everlasting covenant.

[The Lord's Supper]

He always loved those who were his own in the
world.
When the time came for him to be glorified by
you, his heavenly Father,
he showed the depth of his love.
While they were at supper,
he took bread, said the blessing, broke the bread,
and gave it to his disciples, saying:

Take this, all of you, and eat it:
this is my body which will be given up for you.

In the same way, he took the cup, filled with wine.
He gave you thanks, and giving the cup to his disciples, said:

Take this, all of you, and drink from it:
this is the cup of my blood,
the blood of the new and everlasting covenant.
It will be shed for you and for all
so that sins may be forgiven.
Do this in memory of me.

[Memorial Acclamation]

Priest: Let us proclaim the mystery of faith.

PEOPLE:

4

A Christ has died,
Christ is risen,
Christ will come again.

B Dying you destroyed our death,
rising you restored our life.
Lord Jesus, come in glory.

C When we eat this bread and drink this cup,
we proclaim your death, Lord Jesus,
until you come in glory.

D Lord, by your cross and resurrection
you have set us free.
You are the Savior of the world.

[The Memorial Prayer]

Father, we now celebrate this memorial of our
redemption.
We recall Christ's death, his descent among the
dead,
his resurrection, and his ascension to your right
hand;
and, looking forward to his coming in glory,
we offer you his body and blood,
the acceptable sacrifice
which brings salvation to the whole world.

Lord, look upon this sacrifice which you have
given to your Church;
and by your Holy Spirit, gather all who share this
one bread and one cup
into the one body of Christ, a living sacrifice of
praise.

4

[Intercessions: For the Church]

Lord, remember those for whom we offer this sacrifice,
especially N. our Pope,
N. our bishop, and bishops and clergy everywhere.
Remember those who take part in this offering,
those here present and all your people,
and all who seek you with a sincere heart.

[For the Dead]

Remember those who have died in the peace of Christ
and all the dead whose faith is known to you alone.

[In Communion with the Saints]

Father, in your mercy grant also to us, your children,
to enter into our heavenly inheritance
in the company of the Virgin Mary, the Mother of God,
and your apostles and saints.
Then, in your kingdom, freed from the corruption of sin and death,
we shall sing your glory with every creature through Christ our Lord,
through whom you give us everything that is good.

[Concluding Doxology]

Through him,
with him,
in him,
in the unity of the Holy Spirit,
all glory and honor is yours,
almighty Father,
for ever and ever.

All reply: **Amen.** *Continue with the Mass, as on p. 656.*

R 1 EUCHARISTIC PRAYER FOR MASSES OF RECONCILIATION I

STAND

℣. The Lord be with you.

℟. **And also with you.**

℣. Lift up your hearts.

℟. **We lift them up to the Lord.**

℣. Let us give thanks to the Lord our God.

℟. **It is right to give him thanks and praise.**

Father, all-powerful and ever-living God,
we do well always and everywhere to give you
    thanks and praise.
You never cease to call us
to a new and more abundant life.

God of love and mercy,
you are always ready to forgive;
we are sinners,
and you invite us
to trust in your mercy.

Time and time again
we broke your covenant,
but you did not abandon us.
Instead, through your Son, Jesus our Lord,
you bound yourself even more closely to the
    human family
by a bond that can never be broken.

Now is the time
for your people to turn back to you
and to be renewed in Christ your Son,
a time of grace and reconciliation.

R 1

You invite us
to serve the family of mankind
by opening our hearts
to the fullness of your Holy Spirit.

In wonder and gratitude,
we join our voices with the choirs of heaven
to proclaim the power of your love
and to sing of our salvation in Christ:

All say:

**Holy, holy, holy Lord, God of power and might,
heaven and earth are full of your glory.**
> **Hosanna in the highest.**
Blessed is he who comes in the name of the Lord.
> **Hosanna in the highest.**

KNEEL

Father,
from the beginning of time
you have always done what is good for man
so that we may be holy as you are holy.

Look with kindness on your people
gathered here before you:
send forth the power of your Spirit
so that these gifts may become for us
the body ✠ and blood of your beloved Son, Jesus
> the Christ,
in whom we have become your sons and daugh-
> ters.

R 1

When we were lost
and could not find the way to you,
you loved us more than ever:
Jesus, your Son, innocent and without sin,
gave himself into our hands
and was nailed to a cross.
Yet before he stretched out his arms between
    heaven and earth
in the everlasting sign of your covenant,
he desired to celebrate the Paschal feast
in the company of his disciples.

While they were at supper,
he took bread and gave you thanks and praise.
He broke the bread, gave it to his disciples, and
    said:

Take this, all of you, and eat it:
this is my body which will be given up for you.

At the end of the meal,
knowing that he was to reconcile all things in
    himself
by the blood of his cross,
he took the cup, filled with wine.
Again he gave you thanks,
handed the cup to his friends, and said:

Take this, all of you, and drink from it:
this is the cup of my blood,
the blood of the new and everlasting covenant.
It will be shed for you and for all
so that sins may be forgiven.
Do this in memory of me.

Priest: Let us proclaim the mystery of faith.

PEOPLE:

A **Christ has died,**
    Christ is risen,
    Christ will come again.

B **Dying you destroyed our death,**
    rising you restored our life.
    Lord Jesus, come in glory.

C **When we eat this bread and drink this cup,**
    we proclaim your death, Lord Jesus,
    until you come in glory.

D **Lord, by your cross and resurrection**
    you have set us free.
    You are the Savior of the world.

We do this in memory of Jesus Christ,
our Passover and our lasting peace.
We celebrate his death and resurrection
and look for the coming of that day
when he will return to give us the fullness of joy.
Therefore we offer you, God ever faithful and true,
the sacrifice which restores man to your friendship.

Father,
look with love
on those you have called
to share in the one sacrifice of Christ.
By the power of your Holy Spirit
make them one body,
healed of all division.

R 1 Keep us all
in communion of mind and heart
with *N.*, our pope, and *N.*, our bishop.
Help us to work together
for the coming of your kingdom,
until at last we stand in your presence
to share the life of the saints,
in the company of the Virgin Mary and the
   apostles,
and of our departed brothers and sisters
whom we commend to your mercy.

Then, freed from every shadow of death,
we shall take our place in the new creation
and give you thanks
with Christ, our risen Lord.

Through him,
with him,
in him,
in the unity of the Holy Spirit,
all glory and honor is yours,
almighty Father,
for ever and ever.

The people respond: **Amen.**

Continue with the Mass, as on p. 656.

EUCHARISTIC PRAYER FOR
MASSES OF RECONCILIATION II

STAND

℣. The Lord be with you.
℟. **And also with you.**
℣. Lift up your hearts.
℟. **We lift them up to the Lord.**
℣. Let us give thanks to the Lord our God.
℟. **It is right to give him thanks and praise.**

Father, all-powerful and ever-living God,
we praise and thank you through Jesus Christ our
      Lord
for your presence and action in the world.

In the midst of conflict and division,
we know it is you
who turn our minds to thoughts of peace.
Your Spirit changes our hearts:
enemies begin to speak to one another,
those who were estranged join hands in friend-
      ship,
and nations seek the way of peace together.

Your Spirit is at work
when understanding puts an end to strife,
when hatred is quenched by mercy,
and vengeance gives way to forgiveness.

For this we should never cease
to thank and praise you.
We join with all the choirs of heaven
as they sing for ever to your glory:

**R
2**

All say:
**Holy, holy, holy Lord, God of power and might,
heaven and earth are full of your glory.**
  Hosanna in the highest.
Blessed is he who comes in the name of the Lord.
  Hosanna in the highest.

God of power and might,   **KNEEL**
we praise you through your Son, Jesus Christ,
who comes in your name.
He is the Word that brings salvation.
He is the hand you stretch out to sinners.
He is the way that leads to your peace.

God our Father,
we had wandered far from you,
but through your Son you have brought us back.
You gave him up to death
so that we might turn again to you
and find our way to one another.

Therefore we celebrate the reconciliation
Christ has gained for us.

We ask you to sanctify these gifts
by the power of your Spirit,
as we now fulfill your Son's ✛ command.

While he was at supper
on the night before he died for us,
he took bread in his hands,
and gave you thanks and praise.

R 2

He broke the bread,
gave it to his disciples, and said:

Take this, all of you, and eat it:
this is my body which will be given up for you.

At the end of the meal he took the cup.
Again he praised you for your goodness,
gave the cup to his disciples, and said:

Take this, all of you, and drink from it:
this is the cup of my blood,
the blood of the new and everlasting covenant.
It will be shed for you and for all
so that sins may be forgiven.
Do this in memory of me.

Priest: Let us proclaim the mystery of faith.

PEOPLE:

A Christ has died,
    Christ is risen,
    Christ will come again.

B Dying you destroyed our death,
    rising you restored our life.
    Lord Jesus, come in glory.

C When we eat this bread and drink this cup,
    we proclaim your death, Lord Jesus,
    until you come in glory.

D Lord, by your cross and resurrection
    you have set us free.
    You are the Savior of the world.

R 2 Lord our God,
your Son has entrusted to us
this pledge of his love.
We celebrate the memory of his death and resurrec-
     tion
and bring you the gift you have given us,
the sacrifice of reconciliation.
Therefore, we ask you, Father,
to accept us, together with your Son.

Fill us with his Spirit
through our sharing in this meal.
May he take away all that divides us.

May this Spirit keep us always in communion
with N., our pope, N., our bishop,
with all the bishops and all your people.
Father, make your Church throughout the world
a sign of unity and an instrument of your peace.

You have gathered us here
around the table of your Son,
in fellowship with the Virgin Mary, Mother of God,
     and all the saints.

In that new world where the fullness of your peace
     will be revealed,
gather people of every race, language, and way of
     life
to share in the one eternal banquet
with Jesus Christ the Lord.

Through him,
with him,
in him,
in the unity of the Holy Spirit,
all glory and honor is yours,
almighty Father,
for ever and ever.

The people respond: **Amen.**

COMMUNION RITE

To prepare for the paschal meal, to welcome the Lord, we pray for forgiveness and exchange a sign of peace. Before eating Christ's body and drinking his blood, we must be one with him and with all our brothers and sisters in the Church.

24 LORD'S PRAYER

Priest: **STAND**

A Let us pray with confidence to the Father
in the words our Savior gave us.

B Jesus taught us to call God our Father,
and so we have the courage to say:

C Let us ask our Father to forgive our sins
and to bring us to forgive those who sin against
us.

D Let us pray for the coming of the kingdom
as Jesus taught us.

Priest and **PEOPLE**:

> **Our Father, who art in heaven,**
> **hallowed be thy name;**
> **thy kingdom come;**
> **thy will be done on earth as it is in heaven.**
> **Give us this day our daily bread;**
> **and forgive us our trespasses**
> **as we forgive those who trespass against us;**
> **and lead us not into temptation,**
> **but deliver us from evil.**

Priest: Deliver us, Lord, from every evil,
and grant us peace in our day.

656

In your mercy keep us free from sin
and protect us from all anxiety
as we wait in joyful hope
for the coming of our Savior, Jesus Christ.

**PEOPLE: For the kingdom, the power and the glory
are yours, now and for ever.**

25 SIGN OF PEACE

The Church is a community of Christians joined by the Spirit in love. It needs to express, deepen, and restore its peaceful unity before eating the one Body of the Lord and drinking from the one cup of salvation. We do this by a sign of peace.

The priest says the prayer for peace:

Lord Jesus Christ, you said to your apostles:
I leave you peace, my peace I give you.
Look not on our sins, but on the faith of your
    Church,
and grant us the peace and unity of your kingdom
where you live for ever and ever.

PEOPLE: Amen.

Priest: The peace of the Lord be with you always.

PEOPLE: And also with you.

Deacon (or priest):
  Let us offer each other the sign of peace.

The people exchange a sign of peace and love, according to local custom.

26 BREAKING OF THE BREAD

Christians are gathered for the "breaking of the bread," another name for the Mass. In communion, though many we are made one body in the one bread, which is Christ.

Then the following is sung or said:

PEOPLE:

**Lamb of God, you take away the sins of the
world:**
have mercy on us.
**Lamb of God, you take away the sins of the
world:**
have mercy on us.
**Lamb of God, you take away the sins of the
world:**
grant us peace.

*The hymn may be repeated until the breaking of the bread
is finished, but the last phrase is always: "Grant us
peace."*

*Meanwhile the priest breaks the host over the paten and
places a small piece in the chalice, saying inaudibly:*

May this mingling of the body and blood of our
    Lord Jesus Christ
bring eternal life to us who receive it.

KNEEL

27 PRAYERS BEFORE COMMUNION

We pray in silence and then voice words of humility and hope
as our final preparation before meeting Christ in the eucharist.

*Before communion, the priest says inaudibly one of the
following prayers:*

Lord Jesus Christ, Son of the living God, by the will
of the Father and the work of the Holy Spirit your
death brought life to the world. By your holy body
and blood free me from all my sins, and from every
evil. Keep me faithful to your teaching, and never
let me be parted from you.

OR

Lord Jesus Christ, with faith in your love and mercy I eat your body and drink your blood. Let it not bring me condemnation, but health in mind and body.

28 RECEPTION OF COMMUNION

The priest genuflects. Holding the host elevated slightly over the paten, the priest says:

Priest: This is the Lamb of God
            who takes away the sins of the world.
            Happy are those who are called to his supper.

Priest and **People** (once only):
**Lord, I am not worthy to receive you,
but only say the word and I shall be healed.**

Before receiving communion, the priest says inaudibly:

May the body of Christ bring me to everlasting life.
May the blood of Christ bring me to everlasting life.
He then gives communion to the people.

Priest: The body of Christ. Communicant: **Amen.**
Priest: The blood of Christ. Communicant: **Amen.**

29 COMMUNION SONG or ANTIPHON

The Communion Psalm or other appropriate Song or Hymn is sung while Communion is given to the faithful. If there is no singing, the Communion Antiphon is said:

➡ **Turn to Today's Mass**

The vessels are cleansed by the priest or deacon or acolyte. Meanwhile he says inaudibly:

Lord, may I receive these gifts in purity of heart.
May they bring me healing and strength, now and
      for ever.

30 PERIOD OF SILENCE or Song of Praise

After communion there may be a period of silence, or a song of praise may be sung.

31 PRAYER AFTER COMMUNION　　`STAND`

The priest prays in our name that we may live the life of faith since we have been strengthened by Christ himself. Our *Amen* makes his prayer our own.

Priest: Let us pray.

Priest and people may pray silently for a while. Then the priest says the prayer after communion.

➡ `Turn to Today's Mass`

At the end, **PEOPLE: Amen.**

CONCLUDING RITE

We have heard God's Word and eaten the body of Christ. Now it is time for us to leave, to do good works, to praise and bless the Lord in our daily lives.

32 GREETING　　`STAND`

After any brief announcements (sit), the blessing and dismissal follow:

Priest:　The Lord be with you.

PEOPLE:　And also with you.

33 BLESSING

A　Simple form

Priest: May almighty God bless you,
the Father, and the Son, ✠ and the Holy Spirit.

PEOPLE: Amen.

On certain days or occasions another more solemn form of blessing or prayer over the people may be used as the rubrics direct.

B Solemn blessing

Texts of all the solemn blessings are given on pp. 692-699.

Deacon: Bow your heads and pray for God's blessing.

The priest always concludes the solemn blessings by adding:

May almighty God bless you,
the Father, and the Son, ✠ and the Holy Spirit.

PEOPLE: Amen.

C Prayer over the people

Texts of all prayers over the people are given on pp. 699-703.

After the prayer over the people, the priest always adds:

May almighty God bless you,
the Father, and the Son, ✠ and the Holy Spirit.

PEOPLE: Amen.

34 DISMISSAL

Deacon (or priest):

A Go in the peace of Christ.

B The Mass is ended, go in peace.

C Go in peace to love and serve the Lord.

PEOPLE: Thanks be to God.

If any liturgical service follows immediately, the rite of dismissal is omitted.

RITE OF BLESSING AND
SPRINKLING HOLY WATER

When this rite is celebrated it takes the place of the penitential rite at the beginning of Mass. The Kyrie is also omitted.

After greeting the people the priest remains standing at his chair. A vessel containing the water to be blessed is placed before him. Facing the people, he invites them to pray, using these or similar words:

Dear friends,
this water will be used
to remind us of our baptism.
Let us ask God to bless it,
and to keep us faithful
to the Spirit he has given us.

After a brief silence, he joins his hands and continues:

A.

God our Father,
your gift of water
brings life and freshness to the earth;
it washes away our sins
and brings us eternal life.

We ask you now
to bless ✠ this water,
and to give us your protection on this day
which you have made your own.
Renew the living spring of your life within us
and protect us in spirit and body,
that we may be free from sin
and come into your presence
to receive your gift of salvation.
We ask this through Christ our Lord. R̲. **Amen.**

B. Or:

Lord God almighty,
creator of all life,
of body and soul,
we ask you to bless ✠ this water:
as we use it in faith
forgive our sins
and save us from all illness
and the power of evil.

Lord,
in your mercy
give us living water,
always springing up as a fountain of salvation:
free us, body and soul, from every danger,
and admit us to your presence
in purity of heart.
Grant this through Christ our Lord. ℟. **Amen.**

C. Or (during the Easter season):

Lord God almighty,
hear the prayers of your people:
we celebrate our creation and redemption.
Hear our prayers and bless ✠ this water
which gives fruitfulness to the fields,
and refreshment and cleansing to man.
You chose water to show your goodness
when you led your people to freedom
through the Red Sea
and satisfied their thirst in the desert
with water from the rock.
Water was the symbol used by the prophets
to foretell your new covenant with man.
You made the water of baptism holy
by Christ's baptism in the Jordan:
by it you give us a new birth
and renew us in holiness.
May this water remind us of our baptism,
and let us share the joy

of all who have been baptized at Easter.
We ask this through Christ our Lord. ℟. **Amen.**

*Where it is customary, salt may be mixed with the holy water.
The priest blesses the salt, saying:*

Almighty God,
we ask you to bless ✤ this salt
as once you blessed the salt scattered over the water
by the prophet Elisha.
Wherever this salt and water are sprinkled,
drive away the power of evil,
and protect us always
by the presence of your Holy Spirit.
Grant this through Christ our Lord. ℟. **Amen.**

Then he pours the salt into the water in silence.

*Taking the sprinkler, the priest sprinkles himself and his
ministers, then the rest of the clergy and people. He may
move through the church for the sprinkling of the people.
Meanwhile, an antiphon or another appropriate song is
sung.*

*When he returns to his place and the song is finished, the
priest faces the people and, with joined hands, says:*

May almighty God cleanse us of our sins,
and through the eucharist we celebrate
make us worthy to sit at his table
in his heavenly kingdom.

The people answer: **Amen.**

When it is prescribed, the Gloria is then sung or said.

PENITENTIAL RITE

ALTERNATIVE FORMS FOR C (p. 617)

ii

Priest or other minister:
Lord Jesus, you came to gather the nations
into the peace of God's kingdom:
Lord, have mercy.

People: **Lord, have mercy.**

Priest or other minister:
You come in word and sacrament to strengthen us in
holiness:
Christ, have mercy.

People: **Christ, have mercy.**

Priest or other minister:
You will come in glory with salvation for your people:
Lord, have mercy.

People: **Lord, have mercy.** (→ p. 617)

iii

Priest or other minister:
Lord Jesus, you are mighty God and Prince of peace:
Lord, have mercy.

People: **Lord, have mercy.**

Priest or other minister:
Lord Jesus, you are Son of God and Son of Mary:
Christ, have mercy.

People: **Christ, have mercy.**

Priest or other minister:
Lord Jesus, you are Word made flesh and splendor of the
Father:
Lord, have mercy.

People: **Lord, have mercy.** (→ p. 617)

665

iv

Priest or other minister:
Lord Jesus, you came to reconcile us
to one another and to the Father:
Lord, have mercy.

People: **Lord, have mercy.**

Priest or other minister:
Lord Jesus, you heal the wounds of sin and division:
Christ, have mercy.

People: **Christ, have mercy.**

Priest or other minister:
Lord Jesus, you intercede for us with your Father:
Lord, have mercy.

People: **Lord, have mercy.** (➜ p. 617)

v

Priest or other minister:
You raise the dead to life in the Spirit:
Lord, have mercy.

People: **Lord, have mercy.**

Priest or other minister:
You bring pardon and peace to the sinner:
Christ, have mercy.

People: **Christ, have mercy.**

Priest or other minister:
You bring light to those in darkness:
Lord, have mercy.

People: **Lord, have mercy.** (➜ p. 617)

vi

Priest or other minister:
Lord Jesus, you raise us to new life:
Lord, have mercy.

People: **Lord, have mercy.**

Priest or other minister:
Lord Jesus, you forgive us our sins:

Christ, have mercy.

People: **Christ, have mercy.**

Priest or other minister:
Lord Jesus, you feed us with your body and blood:
Lord, have mercy.

People: **Lord, have mercy.** (→ p. 617)

vii

Priest or other minister:
Lord Jesus, you have shown us the way to the Father:
Lord, have mercy.

People: **Lord, have mercy.**

Priest or other minister:
Lord Jesus, you have given us the consolation of the truth:
Christ, have mercy.

People: **Christ, have mercy.**

Priest or other minister:
Lord Jesus, you are the Good Shepherd,
leading us into everlasting life:
Lord, have mercy.

People: **Lord, have mercy.** (→ p. 617)

viii

Priest or other minister:
Lord Jesus, you healed the sick:
Lord, have mercy.

People: **Lord, have mercy.**

Priest or other minister:
Lord Jesus, you forgave sinners:
Christ, have mercy.

People: **Christ, have mercy.**

Priest or other minister:
Lord Jesus, you give us yourself to heal us and bring us
    strength:
Lord, have mercy.

People: **Lord, have mercy.** (→ p. 617)

PREFACES

ADVENT I (P 1)

The Two Comings of Christ
(From the First Sunday of Advent to December 16)

Father, all-powerful and ever-living God,
we do well always and everywhere to give you thanks
through Jesus Christ our Lord.

When he humbled himself to come among us as a man,
he fulfilled the plan you formed long ago
and opened for us the way to salvation.

Now we watch for the day,
hoping that the salvation promised us will be ours
when Christ our Lord will come again in his glory.

And so, with all the choirs of angels in heaven
we proclaim your glory
and join in their unending hymn of praise: → No. 23, p. 627

ADVENT II (P 2)

Waiting for the Two Comings of Christ
(From December 17 to December 24)

Father, all-powerful and ever-living God,
we do well always and everywhere to give you thanks
through Jesus Christ our Lord.

His future coming was proclaimed by all the prophets.
The virgin mother bore him in her womb
with love beyond all telling.
John the Baptist was his herald
and made him known when at last he came.

In his love he has filled us with joy
as we prepare to celebrate his birth,
so that when he comes he may find us watching in prayer,
our hearts filled with wonder and praise.

And so, with all the choirs of angels in heaven
we proclaim your glory
and join in their unending hymn of praise: → No. 23, p. 627

CHRISTMAS I (P 3)

Christ the Light
(From Christmas to Saturday before Epiphany)

Father, all-powerful and ever-living God,
we do well always and everywhere to give you thanks
through Jesus Christ our Lord.

In the wonder of the incarnation
your eternal Word has brought to the eyes of faith
a new and radiant vision of your glory.
In him we see our God made visible
and so are caught up in love of the God we cannot see.

And so, with all the choirs of angels in heaven
we proclaim you glory
and join in the unending hymn of praise: → No. 23, p. 627

CHRISTMAS II (P 4)

Christ Restores Unity to All Creation
(From Christmas to Saturday before Epiphany)

Father, all-powerful and ever-living God,
we do well always and everywhere to give you thanks
through Jesus Christ our Lord.

Today you fill our hearts with joy
as we recognize in Christ the revelation of your love.
No eye can see his glory as our God,
yet now he is seen as one like us.

Christ is your Son before all ages,
yet now he is born in time.
He has come to lift up all things to himself,
to restore unity to creation,
and to lead mankind from exile into your heavenly kingdom.

With all the angels of heaven
we sing our joyful hymn of praise: → No. 23, p. 627

CHRISTMAS III (P 5)

*Divine and Human Exchange in the Incarnation of
the Word*
(From Christmas to Saturday before Epiphany)

Father, all-powerful and ever-living God,
we do well always and everywhere to give you thanks

through Jesus Christ our Lord.

Today in him a new light has dawned upon the world:
God has become one with man,
and man has become one again with God.

Your eternal Word has taken upon himself our human weakness,
giving our mortal nature immortal value.
So marvelous is this oneness between God and man
that in Christ man restores to man the gift of everlasting life.

In our joy we sing to your glory
with all the choirs of angels: ➙ No. 23, p. 627

EPIPHANY (P 6)

Christ the Light of the Nations

Father, all-powerful and ever-living God,
we do well always and everywhere to give you thanks.

Today you revealed in Christ your eternal plan of salvation
and showed him as the light of all peoples.
Now that his glory has shone among us
you have renewed humanity in his immortal image.

Now, with angels and archangels,
and the whole company of heaven,
we sing the unending hymn of your praise: ➙ No. 23, p. 627

LENT I (P 8)

The Spiritual Meaning of Lent

Father, all-powerful and ever-living God,
we do well always and everywhere to give you thanks
through Jesus Christ our Lord.

Each year you give us this joyful season
when we prepare to celebrate the paschal mystery
with mind and heart renewed.
You give us a spirit of loving reverence for you, our Father,
and of willing service to our neighbor.

As we recall the great events that gave us new life in Christ,
you bring the image of your Son to perfection within us.

Now, with angels and archangels,
and the whole company of heaven,
we sing the unending hymn of your praise: → No. 23, p. 627

LENT II (P 9)

The Spirit of Penance

Father, all-powerful and ever-living God,
we do well always and everywhere to give you thanks.

This great season of grace is your gift to your family
to renew us in spirit.
You give us strength to purify our hearts,
to control our desires,
and so to serve you in freedom.
You teach us how to live in this passing world
with our heart set on the world that will never end.

Now, with all the saints and angels,
we praise you for ever: → No. 23, p. 627

LENT III (P 10)

The Fruits of Self-denial

Father, all-powerful and ever-living God,
we do well always and everywhere to give you thanks.

You ask us to express our thanks by self-denial.
We are to master our sinfulness and conquer our pride.
We are to show to those in need your goodness to ourselves.

Now, with all the saints and angels,
we praise you for ever: → No. 23, p. 627

LENT IV (P 11)

The Reward of Fasting

Father, all-powerful and ever-living God,
we do well always and everywhere to give you thanks.

Through our observance of Lent
you correct our faults and raise our minds to you,
you help us grow in holiness,
and offer us the reward of everlasting life
through Jesus Christ our Lord.

Through him the angels and all the choirs of heaven
worship in awe before your presence.
May our voices be one with theirs
as they sing with joy the hymn of your glory:

→ No. 23, p. 627

PASSION OF THE LORD I (P 17)

The Power of the Cross

Father, all-powerful and ever-living God,
we do well always and everywhere to give you thanks.

The suffering and death of your Son
brought life to the whole world,
moving our hearts to praise your glory.
The power of the cross reveals your judgment on this world
and the kingship of Christ crucified.

We praise you, Lord,
with all the angels and saints in their song of joy:

→ No. 23, p. 627

PASSION OF THE LORD II (P 18)

The Victory of the Passion

Father, all-powerful and ever-living God,
we do well always and everywhere to give you thanks
through Jesus Christ our Lord.

The days of his life-giving death and glorious resurrection
are approaching.
This is the hour when he triumphed over Satan's pride,
the time when we celebrate the great event of our redemption.

Through Christ
the angels of heaven offer their prayer of adoration
as they rejoice in your presence for ever.
May our voices be one with theirs
in their triumphant hymn of praise: → No. 23, p. 627

EASTER I (P 21)

The Paschal Mystery

(Easter Vigil, Easter Sunday and during the octave)

Father, all-powerful and ever-living God,
we do well always and everywhere to give you thanks
through Jesus Christ our Lord.

We praise you with greater joy than ever
on this Easter night (day) (in this Easter season),
when Christ became our paschal sacrifice.

He is the true Lamb who took away the sins of the world.
By dying he destroyed our death;
by rising he restored our life.

And so, with all the choirs of angels in heaven
we proclaim your glory
and join in their unending hymn of praise: ➜ No. 23, p. 627

EASTER II (P 22)

New Life in Christ

Father, all-powerful and ever-living God,
we do well always and everywhere to give you thanks
through Jesus Christ our Lord.

We praise you with greater joy than ever in this Easter season,
when Christ became our paschal sacrifice.

He has made us children of the light,
rising to new and everlasting life.
He has opened the gates of heaven
to receive his faithful people.

His death is our ransom from death;
his resurrection is our rising to life.

The joy of the resurrection renews the whole world,
while the choirs of heaven sing for ever to your glory:
➜ No. 23, p. 627

EASTER III (P 23)

Christ Lives and Intercedes for Us For Ever

Father, all-powerful and ever-living God,
we do well always and everywhere to give you thanks
through Jesus Christ our Lord.

We praise you with greater joy than ever in this Easter season,
when Christ became our paschal sacrifice.
He is still our priest,
our advocate who always pleads our cause.
Christ is the victim who dies no more,
the Lamb, once slain, who lives for ever.
The joy of the resurrection renews the whole world,
while the choirs of heaven sing for ever to your glory:

→ No. 23, p. 627

EASTER IV (P 24)

The Restoration of the Universe through the Paschal Mystery

Father, all-powerful and ever-living God,
we do well always and everywhere to give you thanks
through Jesus Christ our Lord.
We praise you with greater joy than ever in this Easter season,
when Christ became our paschal sacrifice.
In him a new age has dawned,
the long reign of sin is ended,
a broken world has been renewed,
and man is once again made whole.
The joy of the resurrection renews the whole world,
while the choirs of heaven sing for ever to your glory:

→ No. 23, p. 627

EASTER V (P 25)

Christ Is Priest and Victim

Father, all-powerful and ever-living God,
we do well always and everywhere to give you thanks
through Jesus Christ our Lord.
We praise you with greater joy than ever in this Easter season,
when Christ became our paschal sacrifice.
As he offered his body on the cross,
his perfect sacrifice fulfilled all others.

As he gave himself into your hands for our salvation,
he showed himself to be the priest, the altar, and the lamb of
  sacrifice.

The joy of the resurrection renews the whole world,
while the choirs of heaven sing for ever to your glory:

→ No. 23, p. 627

ASCENSION I (P 26)

The Mystery of the Ascension
(Ascension to the Saturday before Pentecost inclusive)

Father, all-powerful and ever-living God,
we do well always and everywhere to give you thanks.

[Today] the Lord Jesus, the king of glory,
the conqueror of sin and death,
ascended to heaven while the angels sang his praises.

Christ, the mediator between God and man,
judge of the world and Lord of all,
has passed beyond our sight,
not to abandon us but to be our hope.

Christ is the beginning, the head of the Church;
where he has gone, we hope to follow.

The joy of the resurrection and ascension renews the whole
  world,
while the choirs of heaven sing for ever to your glory:

→ No. 23, p. 627

ASCENSION II (P 27)

The Mystery of the Ascension
(Ascension to the Saturday before Pentecost inclusive)

Father, all-powerful and ever-living God,
we do well always and everywhere to give you thanks
through Jesus Christ our Lord.

In his risen body he plainly showed himself to his disciples
and was taken up to heaven in their sight
to claim for us a share in his divine life.

And so, with all the choirs of angels in heaven
we proclaim your glory
and join in their unending hymn of praise: → No. 23, p. 627

WEEKDAYS I (P 37)

All Things Made One in Christ
(For Masses without Proper or Seasonal Preface)

Father, all-powerful and ever-living God,
we do well always and everywhere to give you thanks
through Jesus Christ our Lord.

In him you have renewed all things
and you have given us all a share in his riches.

Though his nature was divine,
he stripped himself of glory
and by shedding his blood on the cross
he brought his peace to the world.

Therefore he was exalted above all creation
and became the source of eternal life
to all who serve him.

And so, with all the choirs of angels in heaven
we proclaim your glory
and join in their unending hymn of praise:

→ No. 23, p. 627

WEEKDAYS II (P 38)

Salvation through Christ
(For Masses without Proper or Seasonal Preface)

Father, all-powerful and ever-living God,
we do well always and everywhere to give you thanks.

In love you created man,
in justice you condemned him,
but in mercy you redeemed him,
through Jesus Christ our Lord.

Through him the angels and all the choirs of heaven
worship in awe before your presence.
May our voices be one with theirs
as they sing with joy
the hymn of your glory:

→ No. 23, p. 627

WEEKDAYS III (P 39)

The Praise of God in Creation and through the Conversion of Man
(For Masses without Proper or Seasonal Preface)

Father, all-powerful and ever-living God,
we do well always and everywhere to give you thanks.

Through your beloved Son
you created our human family.
Through him you restored us to your likeness.

Therefore it is your right
to receive the obedience of all creation,
the praise of the Church on earth,
the thanksgiving of your saints in heaven.

We too rejoice with the angels
as we proclaim your glory for ever: → No. 23, p. 627

WEEKDAYS IV (P 40)

Praise of God Is His Gift
(For Masses without Proper or Seasonal Preface)

Father, all-powerful and ever living God,
we do well always and everywhere to give you thanks.

You have no need of our praise,
yet our desire to thank you is itself your gift.
Our prayer of thanksgiving adds nothing to your greatness,
but makes us grow in your grace,
through Jesus Christ our Lord.

In our joy we sing to your glory
with all the choirs of angels: → No. 23, p. 627

WEEKDAYS V (P 41)

The Mystery of Christ Is Proclaimed
(For Masses without Proper or Seasonal Preface)

Father, all-powerful and ever-living God,
we do well always and everywhere to give you thanks
through Jesus Christ our Lord.

With love we celebrate his death.
With living faith we proclaim his resurrection.

With unwavering hope we await his return in glory.
Now, with the saints and all the angels
we praise you for ever: → No. 23, p. 627

WEEKDAYS VI (P 42)

Salvation in Christ

(For Masses without Proper or Seasonal Preface)

Father, it is our duty and our salvation,
always and everywhere
to give you thanks
through your beloved Son, Jesus Christ.
He is the Word through whom you made the universe,
the Savior you sent to redeem us.
By the power of the Holy Spirit
he took flesh and was born of the Virgin Mary.
For our sake he opened his arms on the cross;
he put an end to death
and revealed the resurrection.
In this he fulfilled your will
and won for you a holy people.
And so we join the angels and the saints
in proclaiming your glory: → No. 23, p. 627

HOLY EUCHARIST I (P 47)

The Sacrifice and Sacrament of Christ

Father, all-powerful and ever-living God,
we do well always and everywhere to give you thanks
through Jesus Christ our Lord.
He is the true and eternal priest
who established this unending sacrifice.
He offered himself as a victim for our deliverance
and taught us to make this offering in his memory.
As we eat his body which he gave for us,
we grow in strength.
As we drink his blood which he poured out for us,
we are washed clean.
Now, with angels and archangels,
and the whole company of heaven,
we sing the unending hymn of your praise: → No. 23, p. 627

HOLY EUCHARIST II (P 48)

The Effects of the Holy Eucharist

Father, all-powerful and ever-living God,
we do well always and everywhere to give you thanks
through Jesus Christ our Lord.

At the last supper, / as he sat at table with his apostles,
he offered himself to you as the spotless lamb,
the acceptable gift that gives you perfect praise.
Christ has given us this memorial of his passion
to bring us its saving power until the end of time.

In this great sacrament you feed your people
and strengthen them in holiness,
so that the family of mankind
may come to walk in the light of one faith,
in one communion of love.
We come then to this wonderful sacrament
to be fed at your table
and grow into the likeness of the risen Christ.

Earth unites with heaven / to sing the new song of creation
as we adore and praise you for ever: → No. 23, p. 627

DEDICATION OF A CHURCH I (P 52)

The Mystery of God's Temple, Which Is the Church
(In the Dedicated Church)

Father, all-powerful and ever-living God,
we do well always and everywhere to give you thanks.

We thank you now for this house of prayer
in which you bless your family
as we come to you on pilgrimage.
Here you reveal your presence / by sacramental signs,
and make us one with you
through the unseen bond of grace.

Here you build your temple of living stones,
and bring the Church to its full stature
as the body of Christ throughout the world,
to reach its perfection at last
in the heavenly city of Jerusalem,
which is the vision of your peace.

In communion with all the angels and saints
we bless and praise your greatness
in the temple of your glory:
→ No. 23, p. 627

DEDICATION OF A CHURCH II (P 53)

*The Mystery of the Church, the Bride of Christ and
the Temple of the Spirit*

(Outside the Dedicated Church)

Father, all-powerful and ever-living God,
we do well always and everywhere to give you thanks.

Your house is a house of prayer,
and your presence makes it a place of blessing.
You give us grace upon grace
to build the temple of your Spirit,
creating its beauty from the holiness of our lives.

Your house of prayer
is also the promise of the Church in heaven.
Here your love is always at work.
preparing the Church on earth / for its heavenly glory
as the sinless bride of Christ,
the joyful mother of a great company of saints.

Now, with the saints and all the angels
we praise you for ever:
→ No. 23, p. 627

HOLY SPIRIT I (P 54)

The Spirit Sent by the Lord upon His Church

(For Votive Masses of the Holy Spirit)

Father, all-powerful and ever-living God,
we do well always and everywhere to give you thanks
through Jesus Christ our Lord.

He ascended above all the heavens,
and from his throne at your right hand
poured into the hearts of your adopted children
the Holy Spirit of your promise.

With steadfast love / we sing your unending praise;
we join with the hosts of heaven
in their triumphant song:
→ No. 23, p. 627

HOLY SPIRIT II (P 55)

The Working of the Spirit in the Church
(For Votive Masses of the Holy Spirit)

Father, all-powerful and ever-living God,
we do well always and everywhere to give you thanks.

You give your gifts of grace
for every time and season
as you guide the Church
in the marvelous ways of your providence.

You give us your Holy Spirit
to help us always by his power,
so that with loving trust
we may turn to you in all our troubles,
and give you thanks in all our joys,
through Jesus Christ our Lord.

In our joy we sing to your glory
with all the choirs of angels: → No. 23, p. 627

BLESSED VIRGIN MARY I (P 56)

Motherhood of Mary

Father, all-powerful and ever-living God,
we do well always and everywhere to give you thanks
(as we celebrate . . . of the Blessed Virgin Mary).
(as we honor the Blessed Virgin Mary).

Through the power of the Holy Spirit,
she became the virgin mother of your only Son,
our Lord Jesus Christ,
who is for ever the light of the world.

Through him the choirs of angels
and all the powers of heaven
praise and worship your glory.
May our voices blend with theirs
as we join in their unending hymn: → No. 23, p. 627

BLESSED VIRGIN MARY II (P 57)

The Church Echoes Mary's Song of Praise

Father, all-powerful and ever-living God,
we do well always and everywhere to give you thanks,
and to praise you for your gifts
as we contemplate your saints in glory.

In celebrating the memory of the Blessed Virgin Mary,
it is our special joy to echo her song of thanksgiving.
What wonders you have worked throughout the world.
All generations have shared the greatness of your love.
When you looked on Mary your lowly servant,
you raised her to be the mother of Jesus Christ, your Son,
    our Lord,
the savior of all mankind.

Through him the angels of heaven
offer their prayer of adoration
as they rejoice in your presence for ever.
May our voices be one with theirs
in their triumphant hymn of praise: ➡ No. 23, p. 627

ANGELS (P 60)
The Glory of God in the Angels

Father, all-powerful and ever-living God,
we do well always and everywhere to give you thanks.

In praising your faithful angels and archangels,
we also praise your glory,
for in honoring them, we honor you, their creator.
Their splendor shows us your greatness,
which surpasses in goodness the whole of creation.

Through Christ our Lord
the great army of angels rejoices in your glory.
In adoration and joy
we make their hymn of praise our own: ➡ No. 23, p. 627

APOSTLES I (P 64)
The Apostles Are Shepherds of God's People
(For Masses of the apostles)

Father, all-powerful and ever-living God,
we do well always and everywhere to give you thanks.

You are the eternal Shepherd
who never leaves his flock untended.
Through the apostles
you watch over us and protect us always.
You made them shepherds of the flock
to share in the work of your Son,
and from their place in heaven they guide us still.

And so, with all the choirs of angels in heaven
we proclaim your glory
and join in their unending hymn of praise: → No. 23, p. 627

APOSTLES II (P 65)

Apostolic Foundation and Witness
(For Masses of the apostles and evangelists)

Father, all-powerful and ever-living God,
we do well always and everywhere to give you thanks.

You founded your Church on the apostles
to stand firm for ever
as the sign on earth of your infinite holiness
and as the living gospel for all men to hear.

With steadfast love
we sing your unending praise:
we join with the hosts of heaven
in their triumphant song: → No. 23, p. 627

MARTYRS (P 66)

The Sign and Example of Martyrdom
(For solemnities and feasts of martyrs)

Father, all powerful and ever-living God,
we do well always and everywhere to give you thanks.

Your holy martyr N. followed the example of Christ,
and gave his (her) life for the glory of your name.
His (her) death reveals your power
shining through our human weakness.
You choose the weak and make them strong
in bearing witness to you,
through Jesus Christ our Lord.

In our unending joy we echo on earth
the song of the angels in heaven
as they praise your glory for ever: → No. 23, p. 627

PASTORS (P 67)

The Presence of Shepherds in the Church
(For solemnities and feasts of pastors)

Father, all-powerful and ever-living God,
we do well always and everywhere to give you thanks.

You give the Church this feast in honor of Saint N.;
you inspire us by his holy life,
instruct us by his preaching,
and give us your protection in answer to his prayers.

We join the angels and the saints
as they sing their unending hymn of praise:→ No. 23, p. 627

VIRGINS AND RELIGIOUS (P 68)
The Sign of a Life Consecrated to God
(For solemnities and feasts of virgins and religious)

Father, all-powerful and ever-living God,
we do well always and everywhere to give you thanks.

Today we honor your saints
who consecrated their lives to Christ
for the sake of the kingdom of heaven.
What love you show us
as you recall mankind to its innocence,
and invite us to taste on earth
the gifts of the world to come!

Now, with the saints and all the angels
we praise you for ever: → No. 23, p. 627

HOLY MEN AND WOMEN I (P 69)
The Glory of the Saints
(For Masses of all saints, patrons, and titulars of churches, and
on the solemnities and feasts of saints which have no Proper Preface)

Father, all-powerful and ever-living God,
we do well always and everywhere to give you thanks.

You are glorified in your saints,
for their glory is the crowning of your gifts.
In their lives on earth
you give us an example.
In our communion with them,
you give us their friendship.
In their prayer for the Church
you give us strength and protection.
This great company of witnesses spurs us on to victory,
to share their prize of everlasting glory,
through Jesus Christ our Lord.

With angels and archangels
and the whole company of saints
we sing our unending hymn of praise: → No. 23, p. 627

HOLY MEN AND WOMEN II (P 70)

The Activity of the Saints
(For Masses of all saints, patrons, and titulars of churches, and
on the solemnities and feasts of saints which have no Proper Preface)

Father, all-powerful and ever-living God,
we do well always and everywhere to give you thanks.

You renew the Church in every age
by raising up men and women outstanding in holiness,
living witnesses of your unchanging love.
They inspire us by their heroic lives,
and help us by their constant prayers
to be the living sign of your saving power.

We praise you, Lord, with all the angels and saints
in their song of joy: → No. 23, p. 627

RELIGIOUS PROFESSION (P 75)

The Religious Life, Serving God by Imitating Christ

Father, all-powerful and ever-living God,
we do well always and everywhere to give you thanks
through Jesus Christ our Lord.

He came, the son of a virgin mother,
named those blessed who were pure of heart,
and taught by his whole life the perfection of chastity.
He chose always to fulfill your holy will,
and became obedient even to dying for us,
offering himself to you as a perfect oblation.

He consecrated more closely to your service
those who leave all things for your sake,
and promised that they would find a heavenly treasure.

And so, we join the angels and saints
as they sing their unending hymn of praise: → No. 23, p. 627

CHRISTIAN UNITY (P 76)

The Unity of Christ's Body, Which Is the Church

Father, all-powerful and ever-living God,
we do well always and everywhere to give you thanks
through Jesus Christ our Lord.

Through Christ you bring us to the knowledge of your truth,
that we may be united by one faith and one baptism
to become his body.
Through Christ you have given the Holy Spirit to all peoples.

How wonderful are the works of the Spirit,
revealed in so many gifts!
Yet how marvelous is the unity
the Spirit creates from their diversity,
as he dwells in the hearts of your children,
filling the whole Church with his presence
and guiding it with his wisdom!

In our joy we sing to your glory
with all the choirs of angels: → No. 23, p. 627

CHRISTIAN DEATH I (P 77)

The Hope of Rising in Christ

Father, all-powerful and ever-living God,
we do well always and everywhere to give you thanks
through Jesus Christ our Lord.

In him, who rose from the dead,
our hope of resurrection dawned.
The sadness of death gives way
to the bright promise of immortality.

Lord, for your faithful people life is changed, not ended.
When the body of our earthly dwelling lies in death
we gain an everlasting dwelling place in heaven.

And so, with all the choirs of angels in heaven
we proclaim your glory
and join in their unending hymn of praise:

→ No. 23, p. 627

CHRISTIAN DEATH II (P 78)

Christ's Death, Our Life

Father, all-powerful and ever-living God,
we do well always and everywhere to give you thanks
through Jesus Christ our Lord.

He chose to die
that he might free all men from dying.
He gave his life
that we might live to you alone for ever.

In our joy we sing to your glory
with all the choirs of angels:　　　　→ No. 23, p. 627

CHRISTIAN DEATH III (P 79)

Christ, Salvation and Life

Father, all-powerful and ever-living God,
we do well always and everywhere to give you thanks
through Jesus Christ our Lord.

In him the world is saved,
man is reborn,
and the dead rise again to life.

Through Christ the angels of heaven
offer their prayer of adoration
as they rejoice in your presence for ever.
May our voices be one with theirs
in their triumphant hymn of praise:　　　→ No. 23, p. 627

CHRISTIAN DEATH IV (P 80)

From Earthly Life to Heaven's Glory

Father, all-powerful and ever-living God,
we do well always and everywhere to give you thanks.

By your power you bring us to birth.
By your providence you rule our lives.
By your command you free us at last from sin
as we return to the dust from which we came.
Through the saving death of your Son
we rise at your word to the glory of the resurrection.

Now we join the angels and the saints
as they sing their unending hymn of praise:→ No. 23, p. 627

CHRISTIAN DEATH V (P 81)

Our Resurrection through Christ's Victory

Father, all-powerful and ever-living God,
we do well always and everywhere to give you thanks
through Jesus Christ our Lord.

Death is the just reward for our sins,
yet, when at last we die,
your loving kindness calls us back to life
in company with Christ,
whose victory is our redemption.

Our hearts are joyful,
for we have seen your salvation,
and now with the angels and saints
we praise you for ever: → No. 23, p. 627

INDEPENDENCE DAY AND OTHER CIVIC OBSERVANCES I (P 82)

Father, / all-powerful and ever-living God,
we do well to sing your praise for ever,
and to give you thanks in all we do
through Jesus Christ our Lord.

He spoke to men a message of peace
and taught us to live as brothers.
His message took form in the vision of our fathers
as they fashioned a nation
where men might live as one.
This message lives on in our midst
as a task for men today
and a promise for tomorrow.

We thank you, Father, for your blessings in the past
and for all that, with your help, we must yet achieve.
And so, with hearts full of love,
we join the angels today and every day of our lives,
to sing your glory in a hymn of endless praise:
→ No. 23, p. 627

INDEPENDENCE DAY AND OTHER CIVIC OBSERVANCES II (P 83)

Father, all-powerful and ever-living God,
we praise your oneness and truth.

We praise you as the God of creation,

and the Father of Jesus, the Savior of mankind,
in whose image we seek to live.
He loved the children of the lands he walked
and enriched them with his witness of justice and truth.
He lived and died that we might be reborn in the Spirit
and filled with love of all men.

And so, with hearts full of love,
we join the angels, today and every day of our lives,
to sing your glory in a hymn of endless praise:

➙ No. 23, p. 627

THANKSGIVING DAY (P 84)

Father, / we do well to join all creation,
in heaven and on earth,
in praising you, our mighty God
through Jesus Christ our Lord.

You made man to your own image
and set him over all creation.
Once you chose a people
and gave them a destiny
and, when you brought them out of bondage to freedom,
they carried with them the promise
that all men would be blessed
and all men could be free.

What the prophets pledged
was fulfilled in Jesus Christ,
your Son and our saving Lord.
It has come to pass in every generation
for all men who have believed that Jesus
by his death and resurrection
gave them a new freedom in his Spirit.

It happened to our fathers,
who came to this land as if out of the desert
into a place of promise and hope.
It happens to us still, in our time,
as you lead all men through your Church
to the blessed vision of peace.

And so, with hearts full of love,
we join the angels, today and every day of our lives,
to sing your glory in a hymn of endless praise:

➙ No. 23, p. 627

PROPER COMMUNICANTES
AND HANC IGITUR

FOR EUCHARISTIC PRAYER I

Communicantes for Christmas

In union with the whole Church
we celebrate that day (night)
when Mary without loss of her virginity
gave the world its savior.
We honor Mary,
the ever-virgin mother of Jesus Christ, our Lord and God,
    etc., **p. 629.**

Communicantes for the Epiphany

In union with the whole Church
we celebrate that day
when your only Son,
sharing your eternal glory,
showed himself in a human body.
We honor Mary, etc., **p. 629.**

Communicantes for Easter

In union with the whole Church
we celebrate that day (night)
when Jesus Christ, our Lord,
rose from the dead in his human body.
We honor Mary, etc., **p. 629.**

Hanc Igitur for Easter

Father, accept this offering
from your whole family
and from those born into the new life
of water and the Holy Spirit,
with all their sins forgiven.
Grant us your peace in this life,
save us from final damnation,
and count us among those you have chosen.
[Through Christ our Lord. Amen.]

➜ *Canon,* **p. 629:** *Bless, etc.*

Communicantes for the Ascension

In union with the whole Church
we celebrate that day
when your Son, our Lord,
took his place with you
and raised our frail human nature to glory.
We honor Mary, etc., **p. 629.**

Communicantes for Pentecost

In union with the whole Church
we celebrate the day of Pentecost
when the Holy Spirit appeared to the apostles
in the form of countless tongues.
We honor Mary, etc., **p, 629.**

SOLEMN BLESSINGS

The following blessings may be used, at the discretion of the priest, at the end of Mass, or after the liturgy of the word, the office, and the celebration of the sacraments.

The deacon, or in his absence the priest himself, gives the invitation: **Bow your heads and pray for God's blessing.** *Another form of invitation may be used. Then the priest extends his hands over the people while he says or sings the blessings. All respond:* **Amen.**

I. Celebrations during the Proper of Seasons

1. ADVENT

You believe that the Son of God once came to us;
you look for him to come again.
May his coming bring you the light of his holiness
and free you with his blessing. ℟. **Amen.**

May God make you steadfast in faith,
joyful in hope, and untiring in love
all the days of your life. ℟. **Amen.**

You rejoice that our Redeemer came to live with us as man.
When he comes again in glory,
may he reward you with endless life. ℟. **Amen.**

May almighty God bless you,
the Father, and the Son, ✤ and the Holy Spirit. ℟. **Amen.**

2. CHRISTMAS

When he came to us as man,
the Son of God scattered the darkness of this world,
and filled this holy night (day) with his glory.
May the God of infinite goodness
scatter the darkness of sin
and brighten your hearts with holiness. ℟. **Amen.**

God sent his angels to shepherds
to herald the great joy of our Savior's birth.
May he fill you with joy
and make you heralds of his gospel. ℟. **Amen.**

When the Word became man,
earth was joined to heaven.

May he give you his peace and good will,
and fellowship with all the heavenly host. ℟. **Amen.**

May almighty God bless you,
the Father, and the Son, ✠ and the Holy Spirit. ℟. **Amen.**

3. BEGINNING OF THE NEW YEAR

Every good gift comes from the Father of light.
May he grant you his grace and every blessing,
and keep you safe throughout the coming year. ℟. **Amen.**

May he grant you unwavering faith,
constant hope, and love that endures to the end. ℟. **Amen.**

May he order your days and work in his peace,
hear your every prayer,
and lead you to everlasting life and joy. ℟. **Amen.**

May almighty God bless you,
the Father, and the Son, ✠ and the Holy Spirit. ℟. **Amen.**

4. EPIPHANY

God has called you out of darkness
into his wonderful light.
May you experience his kindness and blessings,
and be strong in faith, in hope, and in love. ℟. **Amen.**

Because you are followers of Christ,
who appeared on this day as a light shining in darkness,
may he make you a light to all your sisters and brothers.℟.
    Amen.

The wise men followed the star,
and found Christ who is light from light.
May you too find the Lord
when your pilgrimage is ended. ℟. **Amen.**

May almighty God bless you,
the Father, and the Son, ✠ and the Holy Spirit. ℟. **Amen.**

5. PASSION OF THE LORD

The Father of mercies has given us an example of unselfish
    love
in the sufferings of his only Son.
Through your service of God and neighbor
may you receive his countless blessings.℟. **Amen.**

You believe that by his dying
Christ destroyed death for ever.
May he give you everlasting life. ℟. **Amen.**

He humbled himself for our sakes.
May you follow his example
and share in his resurrection. ℟. **Amen.**

May almighty God bless you,
the Father, and the Son, ✚ and the Holy Spirit. ℟. **Amen.**

6. EASTER VIGIL AND EASTER SUNDAY

May almighty God bless you on this solemn feast of Easter,
and may he protect you against all sin. ℟. **Amen.**

Through the resurrection of his Son
God has granted us healing.
May he fulfill his promises,
and bless you with eternal life. ℟. **Amen.**

You have mourned for Christ's sufferings;
now you celebrate the joy of his resurrection.
May you come with joy to the feast which lasts for ever. ℟.
   Amen.

May almighty God bless you,
the Father, and the Son, ✚ and the Holy Spirit. ℟. **Amen.**

7. EASTER SEASON

Through the resurrection of his Son
God has redeemed you and made you his children.
May he bless you with joy. ℟. **Amen.**

The Redeemer has given you lasting freedom.
May you inherit his everlasting life. ℟. **Amen.**

By faith you rose with him in baptism.
May your lives be holy,
so that you will be united with him for ever. ℟. **Amen.**

May almighty God bless you,
the Father, and the Son, ✚ and the Holy Spirit. ℟. **Amen.**

8. ASCENSION

May almighty God bless you on this day
when his only Son ascended into heaven
to prepare a place for you. ℟. **Amen.**

After his resurrection, Christ was seen by his disciples.
When he appears as judge
may you be pleasing for ever in his sight. ℟. **Amen.**.
You believe that Jesus has taken his seat in majesty
at the right hand of the Father.
May you have the joy of experiencing
that he is also with you to the end of time,
according to his promise. ℟. **Amen.**

May almighty God bless you,
the Father, and the Son, ✚ and the Holy Spirit. ℟. **Amen.**

9. HOLY SPIRIT

(This day) the Father of light
has enlightened the minds of the disciples
by the outpouring of the Holy Spirit.
May he bless you
and give you the gifts of the Spirit for ever. ℟. **Amen.**

May that fire which hovered over the disciples
as tongues of flame
burn out all evil from your hearts
and made them glow with pure light. ℟. **Amen.**

God inspired speech in different tongues
to proclaim one faith.
May he strengthen your faith
and fulfill your hope of seeing him face to face. ℟. **Amen.**

May almighty God bless you,
the Father, and the Son, ✚ and the Holy Spirit.℟. **Amen.**

10. ORDINARY TIME I

Blessing of Aaron (Num 6:24-26)

May the Lord bless you and keep you. ℟. **Amen.**

May his face shine upon you,
and be gracious to you. ℟. **Amen.**

May he look upon you with kindness,
and give you his peace. ℟. **Amen.**

May almighty God bless you,
the Father, and the Son, ✚ and the Holy Spirit. ℟. **Amen.**

11. ORDINARY TIME II (Phil 4:7)

May the peace of God
which is beyond all understanding
keep your hearts and minds
in the knowledge and love of God
and of his Son, our Lord Jesus Christ. ℟. **Amen.**

May almighty God bless you,
the Father, and the Son, ✚ and the Holy Spirit. ℟. **Amen.**

12. ORDINARY TIME III

May almighty God bless you in his mercy,
and make you always aware of his saving wisdom. ℟. **Amen.**

May he strengthen your faith with proofs of his love,
so that you will persevere in good works. ℟. **Amen.**

May he direct your steps to himself,
and show you how to walk in charity and peace. ℟. **Amen.**

May almighty God bless you,
the Father, and the Son, ✚ and the Holy Spirit. ℟. **Amen.**

13. ORDINARY TIME IV

May the God of all consolation
bless you in every way
and grant you peace all the days of your life. ℟. **Amen.**

May he free you from all anxiety
and strengthen your hearts in his love. ℟. **Amen.**

May he enrich you with his gifts of faith, hope, and love,
so that what you do in this life
will bring you to the happiness of everlasting life. ℟. **Amen.**

May almighty God bless you,
the Father, and the Son, ✚ and the Holy Spirit. ℟. **Amen.**

14. ORDINARY TIME V

May almighty God keep you from all harm
and bless you with every good gift. ℟. **Amen.**

May he set his Word in your heart
and fill you with lasting joy. ℟. **Amen.**

May you walk in his ways,
always knowing what is right and good,
until you enter your heavenly inheritance. ℟. **Amen.**

May almighty God bless you,
the Father, and the Son, ✚ and the Holy Spirit. ℟. **Amen.**

II. Celebrations of Saints

15. BLESSED VIRGIN MARY

Born of the Blessed Virgin Mary,
the Son of God redeemed mankind.
May he enrich you with his blessings. ℟. **Amen.**

You received the author of life through Mary.
May you always rejoice in her loving care. ℟. **Amen.**

You have come to rejoice at Mary's feast.
May you be filled with the joys of the Spirit
and the gifts of your eternal home. ℟. **Amen.**

May almighty God bless you,
the Father, and the Son, ✚ and the Holy Spirit. ℟. **Amen.**

16. PETER AND PAUL

The Lord has set you firm within his Church,
which he built upon the rock of Peter's faith.
May he bless you with a faith that never falters. ℟. **Amen.**

The Lord has given you knowledge of the faith
through the labors and preaching of St. Paul.
May his example inspire you to lead others to Christ
by the manner of your life. ℟. **Amen.**

May the keys of Peter, and the words of Paul,
their undying witness and their prayers,
lead you to the joy of that eternal home
which Peter gained by his cross, and Paul by the sword.
℟. **Amen.**

May almighty God bless you,
the Father, and the Son, ✚ and the Holy Spirit. ℟. **Amen.**

17. APOSTLES

May God who founded his Church upon the apostles
bless you through the prayers of St. N. (and St. N.). ℟. **Amen.**

May God inspire you to follow the example of the apostles,
and give witness to the truth before all men. ℟. **Amen.**

The teaching of the apostles has strengthened your faith.
May their prayers lead you
to your true and eternal home. ℟. **Amen.**

May almighty God bless you,
the Father, and the Son, ✛ and the Holy Spirit. ℟. **Amen.**

18. ALL SAINTS

God is the glory and joy of all his saints,
whose memory we celebrate today.
May his blessing be with you always. ℟. **Amen.**

May the prayers of the saints deliver you from present evil.
May their example of holy living
turn your thoughts to service of God and neighbor. ℟. **Amen.**

God's holy Church rejoices that her saints
have reached their heavenly goal,
and are in lasting peace.
May you come to share all the joys of our Father's house. ℟.
     Amen.

May almighty God bless you,
the Father, and the Son, ✛ and the Holy Spirit. ℟. **Amen.**

III. Other Blessings

19. DEDICATION OF A CHURCH

The Lord of earth and heaven
has assembled you before him this day
to dedicate this house of prayer
(to recall the dedication of this church).
May he fill you with the blessings of heaven. ℟. **Amen.**

God the Father wills that all his children
scattered throughout the world
become one family in his Son.
May he make you his temple,
the dwelling-place of his Holy Spirit. ℟. **Amen.**

May God free you from every bond of sin,
dwell within you and give you joy.

May you live with him for ever
in the company of all his saints.
May almighty God bless you,
the Father, and the Son, ✤ and the Holy Spirit. ℟. **Amen.**

20. THE DEAD

In his great love,
the God of all consolation gave man the gift of life.
May he bless you with faith
in the resurrection of his Son,
and with the hope of rising to new life. ℟. **Amen.**

To us who are alive
may he grant forgiveness,
and to all who have died
a place of light and peace. ℟. **Amen.**

As you believe that Jesus rose from the dead,
so may you live with him for ever in joy. ℟. **Amen.**

May almighty God bless you,
the Father, and the Son, ✤ and the Holy Spirit. ℟. **Amen.**

PRAYERS OVER THE PEOPLE

*The following prayers may be used, at the discretion of the
priest, at the end of the Mass, or after the liturgy of the word,
the office, and the celebration of the sacraments.*

*The deacon, or in his absence the priest himself, gives the invi-
tation:* **Bow your heads and pray for God's blessing**. *Another
form of invitation may be used. Then the priest extends his
hands over the people while he says or sings the prayer. All
respond:* **Amen.**

After the prayer, the priest always adds:

May Almighty God bless you,
the Father, and the Son, ✤ and the Holy Spirit. ℟. **Amen.**

1. Lord,
    have mercy on your people.
    Grant us in this life the good things
    that lead to the everlasting life you prepare for us.
    We ask this through Christ our Lord.

2. Lord,
grant your people your protection and grace.
Give them health of mind and body,
perfect love for one another,
and make them always faithful to you.
Grant this through Christ our Lord.

3. Lord,
may all Christian people both know and cherish
the heavenly gifts they have received.
We ask this in the name of Jesus the Lord.

4. Lord,
bless your people and make them holy
so that, avoiding evil,
they may find in you the fulfillment of their longing.
We ask this through Christ our Lord.

5. Lord,
bless and strengthen your people.
May they remain faithful to you
and always rejoice in your mercy.
We ask this in the name of Jesus the Lord.

6. Lord,
you care for your people even when they stray.
Grant us a complete change of heart,
so that we may follow you with greater fidelity.
Grant this through Christ our Lord.

7. Lord,
send your light upon your family.
May they continue to enjoy your favor
and devote themselves to doing good.
We ask this through Christ our Lord.

8. Lord,
we rejoice that you are our creator and ruler.
As we call upon your generosity,
renew and keep us in your love.
Grant this through Christ our Lord.

9. Lord,
we pray for your people who believe in you.
May they enjoy the gift of your love,

share it with others
and spread it everywhere.
We ask this in the name of Jesus the Lord.

10. Lord,
bless your people who hope for your mercy.
Grant that they may receive
the things they ask for at your prompting.
Grant this through Christ our Lord.

11. Lord,
bless us with your heavenly gifts,
and in your mercy make us ready to do your will.
We ask this through Christ our Lord.

12. Lord,
protect your people always,
that they may be free from every evil
and serve you with all their hearts.
We ask this through Christ our Lord.

13. Lord,
help your people to seek you with all their hearts
and to deserve what you promise.
Grant this through Christ our Lord.

14. Father,
help your people to rejoice in the mystery of redemption
and to win its reward.
We ask this in the name of Jesus the Lord.

15. Lord,
have pity on your people;
help them each day to avoid what displeases you
and grant that they may serve you with joy.
We ask this through Christ our Lord.

16. Lord,
care for your people and purify them.
Console them in this life
and bring them to the life to come.
We ask this in the name of Jesus the Lord.

17. Father,
look with love upon your people,
the love which our Lord Jesus Christ showed us

when he delivered himself to evil men
and suffered the agony of the cross,
for he is Lord for ever.

18. Lord,
grant that your faithful people
may continually desire to relive the mystery of the
    eucharist
and so be reborn to lead a new life.
We ask this through Christ our Lord.

19. Lord God,
in your great mercy,
enrich your people with your grace
and strengthen them by your blessing
so that they may praise you always.
Grant this through Christ our Lord.

20. May God bless you with every good gift from on high.
May he keep you pure and holy in his sight at all times.
May he bestow the riches of his grace upon you,
bring you the good news of salvation,
and always fill you with love for all men.
We ask this through Christ our Lord.

21. Lord,
make us pure in mind and body,
that we will avoid all evil pleasures
and always delight in you.
We ask this in the name of Jesus the Lord.

22. Lord,
bless your people and fill them with zeal.
Strengthen them by your love to do your will.
We ask this through Christ our Lord.

23. Lord,
come, live in your people
and strengthen them by your grace.
Help them to remain close to you in prayer
and give them a true love for one another.
Grant this through Christ our Lord.

24. Father,
    look kindly on your children who put their trust in you;
    bless them and keep them from all harm,
    strengthen them against the attacks of the devil.
    May they never offend you
    but seek to love you in all they do.
    We ask this through Christ our Lord.

FEASTS OF SAINTS

25. God our Father,
    may all Christian people rejoice in the glory of your
        saints.
    Give us fellowship with them
    and unending joy in your kingdom.
    We ask this in the name of Jesus the Lord.

26. Lord,
    you have given us many friends in heaven.
    Through their prayers we are confident
    that you will watch over us always
    and fill our hearts with your love.
    Grant this through Christ our Lord.

EASTER SEASON

In our analysis of Advent, we mentioned that creation and ourselves in it, as unfinished beings, are in a process of change. The Creator evolves his plan and the first creature in whom this master-plan was fully realized is our risen Lord Jesus Christ. Creation, where it became self-conscious human beings, did not cooperate. They sinned; hence God reestablished all things in Christ Jesus (Eph 1:10).

According to the purpose of God's will, we are predestined to grow into the full realization of that divine plan (Eph 1:5), presupposing the cooperation we have given during Lent. In Christ all will be made to live—but each in his or her own turn, Christ as firstfruits, then they who are Christ's, who have believed, at his coming (1 Cor 15:22-23).

It is through faith and baptism that we now share in Christ's glorious Resurrection, till we fully share in it by partaking in his Ascension into heaven. Therefore both mysteries: Christ's Resurrection and our partaking in it through Baptism, are celebrated in the Easter Liturgy.

And after we had heard the Good News of our salvation and believed in it, we were sealed with the Holy Spirit (Eph 1:13). Our full initiation into God's people is by Confirmation. The feast of Pentecost celebrates the outpouring of this pledge of our inheritance (Eph 1:14).

Again, Easter, Ascension, and Pentecost are not past but present to us. (Note "this day" in the Propers of these feasts.)

We should read about God's plan of salvation in Eph 1:3-14 and consider prayerfully how it is celebrated at Easter, the Ascension, and Pentecost.

There is no Easter victory unless there is a personal victory in which love becomes stronger than hate, moving us to forgive each other and to live together in mutual respect and brotherhood. If we are "Easter people," as St. Augustine called us, we should also be a joyous people. There is no reason for prolonged sadness at life's defeats or the end that *death brings to our visible existence. Easter is a reminder that death has lost its victory and its sting. Sin will always be with us, but the knowledge that this man Jesus seeks out sinners and eats with them, as the Gospel often relates, will lead us to show our gratitude in a good life and a glad heart.*

The Gospels for the first week of Easter reproduce the accounts of the Resurrection as found in the four Gospels. In the ensuing weeks the Gospel of John is read omitting the parts already used for Lent. We can thus meditate on the message of Jesus as seen in the light of Easter.

The First Readings for the entire season are taken from the Acts of the Apostles. In this way the Church sets before us the history of the primitive community with its accent on the joy and fervor of Christians flowing from the knowledge of Christ's Resurrection.

"He is not here, for he has been raised."

EASTER VIGIL

In accord with ancient tradition, this night is one of vigil for the Lord (Ex 12:42). The Gospel of Luke (12:35ff) is a reminder to the faithful to have their lamps burning ready, to be like men awaiting their master's return so that when he arrives he will find them wide awake and will seat them at his table.

The night vigil is arranged in four parts: (a) a brief service of light; (b) the liturgy of the word, when the Church meditates on all the wonderful things God has done for his people from the beginning; (c) the liturgy of baptism, when new members of the Church are reborn as the day of resurrection approaches; and (d) the liturgy of the eucharist, when the whole Church is called to the table which the Lord has prepared for his people through his death and resurrection.

PART ONE

SOLEMN BEGINNING OF THE VIGIL:
THE SERVICE OF LIGHT

Blessing of the Fire and Lighting the Candle

All the lights in the church are put out.

A large fire is prepared in a suitable place outside the church. When the people have assembled, the priest goes there with the ministers, one of whom carries the Easter candle.

If it is not possible to light the fire outside the church, the rite is carried out as below, p. 709.

The priest greets the congregation in the usual manner and briefly instructs them about the vigil in these or similar words:

Dear friends in Christ,
on this most holy night,
when our Lord Jesus Christ passed from death to life,
the Church invites her children throughout the world
to come together in vigil and prayer.
This is the passover of the Lord:
if we honor the memory of his death and resurrection
by hearing his word and celebrating his mysteries,
then we may be confident
that we shall share his victory over death
and live with him for ever in God.

Then the fire is blessed.

Let us pray.
Father,
we share in the light of your glory
through your Son, the light of the world.
Make this new fire ✝ holy, and inflame us with new hope.
Purify our minds by this Easter celebration
and bring us one day to the feast of eternal light.
We ask this through Christ our Lord. ℟. **Amen.** ↓

The Easter candle is lighted from the new fire.

Preparation of the Candle

Depending on the nature of the congregation, it may seem appropriate to stress the dignity and significance of the Easter candle with other symbolic rites. This may be done as follows:

After the blessing of the new fire, an acolyte or one of the ministers brings the Easter candle to the celebrant, who cuts a cross in the wax with a stylus. Then he traces the Greek letter alpha above the cross, the letter omega below, and the numerals of the current year between the arms of the cross. Meanwhile he says:

1. Christ yesterday and today (*as he traces the vertical arm of the cross*),

2. the beginning and the end *(the horizontal arm)*,
3. Alpha *(alpha, above the cross)*,
4. and Omega *(omega, below the cross)*;
5. all time belongs to him *(the first numeral, in the upper left corner of the cross)*,
6. and all the ages *(the second numeral in the upper right corner)*;
7. to him be glory and power *(the third numeral in the lower left corner)*,
8. through every age for ever. Amen *(the last numeral in the lower right corner)*.

```
        A
    2  |  0
    ───┼───
    0  |
        Ω
```

When the cross and other marks have been made, the priest may insert five grains of incense in the candle. He does this in the form of a cross, saying:

1. By his holy	1
2. and glorious wounds	4 2 5
3. may Christ our Lord	3
4. guard us	
5. and keep us. Amen.	

The priest lights the candle from the new fire, saying:

May the light of Christ, rising in glory,
dispel the darkness of our hearts and minds.

Any or all of the preceding rites may be used, depending on local pastoral circumstances. The conferences of bishops may also determine other rites better adapted to the culture of the people.

Where it may be difficult to have a large fire, the blessing of the fire is adapted to the circumstances. When the people have assembled in the church as on other occasions, the priest goes with the ministers (carrying the Easter candle) to the church door. If possible, the people turn to face the priest.

The greeting and brief instruction take place as above, p. 708. Then the fire is blessed and, if desired, the candle is prepared and lighted as above.

Procession

Then the deacon or, if there is no deacon, the priest takes the Easter candle, lifts it high, and sings alone:

Christ our light.

All answer:

Thanks be to God.

The conferences of bishops may determine a richer acclamation.

Then all enter the church, led by the deacon with the Easter candle. If incense is used, the thurifer goes before the deacon.

At the church door the deacon lifts the candle high and sings a second time:

Christ our light.

All answer:

Thanks be to God.

All light their candles from the Easter candle and continue in the procession.

When the deacon arrives before the altar, he faces the people and sings a third time:

Christ our light.

All answer:

Thanks be to God.

Then the lights in the church are put on.

Easter Proclamation (Exsultet)

When he comes to the altar, the priest goes to his chair. The deacon places the Easter candle on a stand in the middle of the sanctuary or near the lectern. If incense is used, the priest puts some in the censer, as at the gospel of Mass. Then the deacon asks the blessing of the priest, who says in a low voice:

The Lord be in your heart and on your lips,
that you may worthily proclaim his Easter praise.
In the name of the Father, and of the Son ✠ and of the
Holy Spirit. ℟. **Amen.** ↓

The book and candle may be incensed. Then the deacon or, if there is no deacon, the priest sings the Easter proclamation at the lectern or pulpit. All stand and hold lighted candles.

If necessary, the Easter proclamation may be sung by one who is not a deacon. In this case the bracketed words are omitted.

[When the short form is used, omit the *italicized* parts.]

Rejoice, heavenly powers! Sing, choirs of angels!
Exult, all creation around God's throne!
Jesus Christ, our King, is risen!
Sound the trumpet of salvation!

Rejoice, O earth, in shining splendor,
radiant in the brightness of your King!
Christ has conquered! Glory fills you!
Darkness vanishes for ever!

Rejoice, O Mother Church! Exult in glory!
The risen Savior shines upon you!
Let this place resound with joy,
echoing the mighty song of all God's people!

*[My dearest friends, standing with me in this holy
     light,
join me in asking God for mercy,
that he may give his unworthy minister
grace to sing his Easter praises.]*

[℣. The Lord be with you. ℟. **And also with you.]**
℣. Lift up your hearts. ℟. **We lift them up to the Lord.**
℣. Let us give thanks to the Lord our God. ℟. **It is right to
give him thanks and praise.**

It is truly right
that with full hearts and minds and voices
we should praise the unseen God, the all-powerful Father,
and his only Son, our Lord Jesus Christ.
For Christ has ransomed us with his blood,
    and paid for us the price of Adam's sin
    to our eternal Father!

This is our passover feast,
   when Christ, the true Lamb, is slain,
   whose blood consecrates the homes of all believers.
This is the night when first you saved our fathers:
   you freed the people of Israel from their slavery
   and led them dry-shod through the sea.
This is the night when the pillar of fire
   destroyed the darkness of sin!
This is the night when Christians everywhere,
   washed clean of sin
   and freed from all defilement,
   are restored to grace and grow together in holiness.
This is the night when Jesus Christ
   broke the chains of death
   and rose triumphant from the grave.
What good would life have been to us,
   had Christ not come as our Redeemer?
Father, how wonderful your care for us!
   How boundless your merciful love!
   To ransom a slave
   you gave away your Son.
O happy fault, O necessary sin of Adam,
   which gained for us so great a Redeemer!
Most blessed of all nights, chosen by God
   to see Christ rising from the dead!
Of this night scripture says:
   "The night will be as clear as day:
   it will become my light, my joy."
The power of this holy night
   dispels all evil, washes guilt away,
   restores lost innocence, brings mourners joy;
   it casts out hatred, brings us peace, and humbles
      earthly pride.
Night truly blessed when heaven is wedded to earth
   and man is reconciled with God!

Therefore, heavenly Father, in the joy of this night,
  receive our evening sacrifice of praise,
  your Church's solemn offering.
Accept this Easter candle,
  a flame divided but undimmed,
  a pillar of fire that glows to the honor of God.

> *Short form only:*
> May it always dispel the darkness of this night!

Let it mingle with the lights of heaven
  and continue bravely burning
  to dispel the darkness of this night!
May the Morning Star which never sets find this flame
    still burning:
  Christ, that Morning Star, who came back from the
    dead,
  and shed his peaceful light on all mankind,
  your Son who lives and reigns for ever and ever.
R̸. **Amen.** ↓

PART TWO

LITURGY OF THE WORD

In this vigil, the mother of all vigils, nine Readings are provided, seven from the Old Testament and two from the New Testament (the Epistle and Gospel).

The number of Readings from the Old Testament may be reduced for pastoral reasons, but it must always be borne in mind that the reading of the word of God is the fundamental element of the Easter Vigil. At least three Readings from the Old Testament should be read, although for more serious reasons the number may be reduced to two. The reading of Exodus 14 (Reading 3), however, is never to be omitted.

After the Easter proclamation, the candles are put aside and all sit down. Before the Readings begin, the priest speaks to the people in these or similar words:

Dear friends in Christ,
we have begun our solemn vigil.
Let us now listen attentively to the word of God,
recalling how he saved his people throughout history
and, in the fullness of time,
sent his own Son to be our Redeemer.
Through this Easter celebration,
may God bring to perfection
the saving work he has begun in us.

The Readings follow. A reader goes to the lectern and pro-claims the First Reading. Then the cantor leads the psalm and the people respond. All rise and the priest sings or says Let us pray. *When all have prayed silently for a while, he sings or says the prayer.*

Instead of the Responsorial Psalm a period of silence may be observed. In this case the pause after Let us pray *is omitted.*

FIRST READING   Gn 1:1—2:2 or 1:1, 26-31a

God created the world and all that is in it. He saw that it was good. This reading from the first Book of the Bible shows that God loved all that he made.

[If the Short Form" is used, omit indented text in brackets.]

A reading from the Book of Genesis

IN the beginning, when God created the heavens and the earth,

[the earth was a formless wasteland, and dark-ness covered the abyss, while a mighty wind swept over the waters.

Then God said, "Let there be light," and there was light. God saw how good the light was. God then sep-arated the light from the darkness. God called the light "day," and the darkness he called "night." Thus evening came, and morning followed—the first day.

Then God said, "Let there be a dome in the middle of the waters, to separate one body of water from the other." And so it happened: God made the dome, and it separated the water above the dome from the water below it. God called the dome "the sky." Evening came, and morning followed—the second day.

Then God said, "Let the water under the sky be gathered into a single basin, so that the dry land may appear." And so it happened: the water under the sky was gathered into its basin, and the dry land appeared. God called the dry land "the earth," and the basin of the water he called "the sea." God saw how good it was. Then God said, "Let the earth bring forth vegetation: every kind of plant that bears seed and every kind of fruit tree on earth that bears fruit with its seed in it." And so it happened: the earth brought forth every kind of plant that bears seed and every kind of fruit tree on earth that bears fruit with its seed in it. God saw how good it was. Evening came, and morning followed—the third day.

Then God said: "Let there be lights in the dome of the sky, to separate day from night. Let them mark the fixed times, the days and the years, and serve as luminaries in the dome of the sky, to shed light upon the earth." And so it happened: God made the two great lights, the greater one to govern the day, and the lesser one to govern the night; and he made the stars. God set them in the dome of the sky, to shed light upon the earth, to govern the day and the night, and to separate the light from the darkness. God saw how good it was. Evening came, and morning followed—the fourth day.

Then God said, "Let the water teem with an abundance of living creatures, and on the earth let birds fly beneath the dome of the sky." And so it happened: God created the great sea monsters and all kinds of swimming creatures with which the water teems, and all kinds of winged birds. God saw how good it was, and God blessed them, saying, "Be fertile, multiply, and fill the water of the seas; and let the birds multiply on the earth." Evening came, and morning followed—the fifth day.

Then God said, "Let the earth bring forth all kinds of living creatures: cattle, creeping things, and wild animals of all kinds." And so it happened: God made all kinds of wild animals, all kinds of cattle, and all kinds of creeping things of the earth. God saw how good it was. Then]

God said: "Let us make man in our image, after our likeness. Let them have dominion over the fish of the sea, the birds of the air, and the cattle, and over all the wild animals and all the creatures that crawl on the ground."

God created man in his image;
in the divine image he created him;
male and female he created them.

God blessed them, saying: "Be fertile and multiply; fill the earth and subdue it. Have dominion over the fish of the sea, the birds of the air, and all the living things that move on the earth." God also said: "See, I give you every seed-bearing plant all over the earth and every tree that has seed-bearing fruit on it to be your food; and to all the animals of the land, all the birds of the air, and all the living creatures that crawl on the ground, I give all the green plants for food." And so it happened. God looked at everything he had made, and he found it very good.

[Evening came, and morning followed—the sixth day.

Thus the heavens and the earth and all their array were completed. Since on the seventh day God was finished with the work he had been doing, he rested on the seventh day from all the work he had undertaken.]

The word of the Lord. ℟. **Thanks be to God.** ↓

RESPONSORIAL PSALM

Ps 104:1-2, 5-6, 10, 12, 13-14, 24, 35 (R̸.:30)

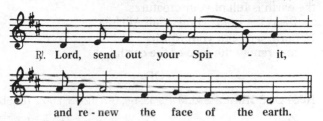

R̸. Lord, send out your Spir - it, and re-new the face of the earth.

Bless the LORD, O my soul!
O LORD, my God, you are great indeed!
You are clothed with majesty and glory,
    robed in light as with a cloak.

R̸. **Lord, send out your Spirit,**
    and renew the face of the earth.

You fixed the earth upon its foundation,
    not to be moved forever;
with the ocean, as with a garment, you covered it;
    above the mountains the waters stood.

R̸. **Lord, send out your Spirit,**
    and renew the face of the earth.

You send forth springs into the watercourses
    that wind among the mountains.
Beside them the birds of heaven dwell;
    from among the branches they send forth their song.

R̸. **Lord, send out your Spirit,**
    and renew the face of the earth.

You water the mountains from your palace;
    the earth is replete with the fruit of your works.
You raise grass for the cattle,
    and vegetation for men's use,
producing bread from the earth.

R̸. **Lord, send out your Spirit,**
    and renew the face of the earth.

How manifold are your works, O LORD!
　　In wisdom you have wrought them all—
the earth is full of your creatures.
　　Bless the LORD, O my soul! Alleluia.

℟. **Lord, send out your Spirit,
　　and renew the face of the earth.**↓

OR

RESPONSORIAL PSALM　Ps 33:4-5, 6-7, 12-13, 20-22 (℟.:5b)

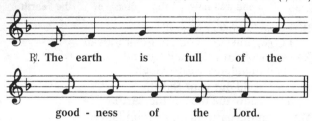

℟. The earth is full of the good-ness of the Lord.

Upright is the word of the LORD,
　　and all his works are trustworthy.
He loves justice and right;
　　of the kindness of the LORD the earth is full.

℟. **The earth is full of the goodness of the Lord.**

By the word of the LORD the heavens were made;
　　by the breath of his mouth all their host.
He gathers the waters of the sea as in a flask;
　　in cellars he confines the deep.

℟. **The earth is full of the goodness of the Lord.**

Blessed the nation whose God is the LORD,
　　the people he has chosen for his own inheritance.
From heaven the LORD looks down;
　　he sees all mankind.

℟. **The earth is full of the goodness of the Lord.**

Our soul waits for the LORD,
　　who is our help and our shield.

May your kindness, O LORD, be upon us
  who have put our hope in you.
℞. **The earth is full of the goodness of the Lord.** ↓

PRAYER

Let us pray.
Almighty and eternal God,
you created all things in wonderful beauty and order.
Help us now to perceive
how still more wonderful is the new creation
by which in the fullness of time
you redeemed your people
through the sacrifice of our passover, Jesus Christ,
who lives and reigns for ever and ever. ℞. **Amen.** ↓

OR

PRAYER (on the creation of man)

Let us pray.
Lord God,
the creation of man was a wonderful work,
his redemption still more wonderful.
May we persevere in right reason
against all that entices to sin
and so attain to everlasting joy.
We ask this through Christ our Lord. ℞. **Amen.** ↓

SECOND READING   Gn 22:1-18 or 22:1-2, 9a, 10-13, 15-18

Abraham is obedient to the will of God. Because God asks him, without
hesitation he prepares to sacrifice his son Isaac. In the new order, God
sends his Son to redeem man by his death on the cross.

[If the "Short Form" is used, omit indented text in brackets.]

A reading from the Book of Genesis

GOD put Abraham to the test. He called to him,
"Abraham!" "Here I am," he replied. Then God said:

"Take your son Isaac, your only one, whom you love, and go to the land of Moriah. There you shall offer him up as a holocaust on a height that I will point out to you."

[Early the next morning Abraham saddled his donkey, took with him his son Isaac, and two of his servants as well, and with the wood that he had cut for the holocaust, set out for the place of which God had told him.

On the third day Abraham got sight of the place from afar. Then he said to his servants: "Both of you stay here with the donkey, while the boy and I go on over yonder. We will worship and then come back to you." Thereupon Abraham took the wood for the holocaust and laid it on his son Isaac's shoulders, while he himself carried the fire and the knife. As the two walked on together, Isaac spoke to his father Abraham. "Father!" Isaac said. "Yes, son," he replied. Isaac continued, "Here are the fire and the wood, but where is the sheep for the holocaust?" "Son," Abraham answered, "God himself will provide the sheep for the holocaust." Then the two continued going forward.]

When they came to the place of which God had told him, Abraham built an altar there and arranged the wood on it.

[Next he tied up his son Isaac, and put him on top of the wood on the altar.]

Then he reached out and took the knife to slaughter his son. But the LORD's messenger called to him from heaven, "Abraham, Abraham!" "Here I am," he answered. "Do not lay your hand on the boy," said the messenger. "Do not do the least thing to him. I know now how devoted you are to God, since you did not withhold from me your own beloved son." As Abraham looked about, he spied a ram caught by its horns in the thicket. So he went and took the ram and offered it up as a holocaust in place of his son.

[Abraham named the site Yahweh-yireh; hence people now say, "On the mountain the LORD will see."]

Again the LORD's messenger called to Abraham from heaven and said: "I swear by myself, declares the LORD, that because you acted as you did in not withholding from me your beloved son, I will bless you abundantly and make your descendants as countless as the stars of the sky and the sands of the seashore; your descendants shall take possession of the gates of their enemies, and in your descendants all the nations of the earth shall find blessing—all this because you obeyed my command."— The word of the Lord. ℟. **Thanks be to God.** ↓

RESPONSORIAL PSALM   Ps 16:5, 8, 9-10, 11 (℟.:1)

℟. You   are   my   in-   her - i -tance,   O   Lord.

O LORD, my allotted portion and my cup,
   you it is who hold fast my lot.
I set the LORD ever before me;
   with him at my right I shall not be disturbed.

℟. **You are my inheritance, O Lord.**

Therefore my heart is glad and my soul rejoices,
   my body, too, abides in confidence;
because you will not abandon my soul to the nether-
      world,
   nor will you suffer your faithful one to undergo cor-
      ruption.

℟. **You are my inheritance, O Lord.**

You will show me the path to life,
   fullness of joys in your presence,
   the delights at your right hand forever.

℟. **You are my inheritance, O Lord.** ↓

PRAYER

Let us pray.
God and Father of all who believe in you,
you promised Abraham that he would become the father
    of all nations,
and through the death and resurrection of Christ
you fulfill that promise:
everywhere throughout the world you increase your cho-
    sen people.
May we respond to your call
by joyfully accepting your invitation to the new life of
    grace.
We ask this through Christ our Lord. ℟. **Amen.** ↓

THIRD READING   Ex 14:15—15:1

Moses leads the Israelites out of Egypt. He opens a path of escape
through the Red Sea. God protects his people. Through the waters of baptism, human beings are freed from sin.

A reading from the Book of Exodus

THE LORD said to Moses, "Why are you crying out to
me? Tell the Israelites to go forward. And you, lift up
your staff and, with hand outstretched over the sea, split
the sea in two, that the Israelites may pass through it on
dry land. But I will make the Egyptians so obstinate that
they will go in after them. Then I will receive glory
through Pharaoh and all his army, his chariots and charioteers. The Egyptians shall know that I am the LORD,
when I receive glory through Pharaoh and his chariots
and charioteers."

The angel of God, who had been leading Israel's camp,
now moved and went around behind them. The column of
cloud also, leaving the front, took up its place behind
them, so that it came between the camp of the Egyptians
and that of Israel. But the cloud now became dark, and
thus the night passed without the rival camps coming any
closer together all night long. Then Moses stretched out

his hand over the sea, and the LORD swept the sea with a strong east wind throughout the night and so turned it into dry land. When the water was thus divided, the Israelites marched into the midst of the sea on dry land, with the water like a wall to their right and to their left.

The Egyptians followed in pursuit; all Pharaoh's horses and chariots and charioteers went after them right into the midst of the sea. In the night watch just before dawn the LORD cast through the column of the fiery cloud upon the Egyptian force a glance that threw it into a panic; and he so clogged their chariot wheels that they could hardly drive. With that the Egyptians sounded the retreat before Israel, because the LORD was fighting for them against the Egyptians.

Then the LORD told Moses, "Stretch out your hand over the sea, that the water may flow back upon the Egyptians, upon their chariots and their charioteers." So Moses stretched out his hand over the sea, and at dawn the sea flowed back to its normal depth. The Egyptians were fleeing head on toward the sea, when the LORD hurled them into its midst. As the water flowed back, it covered the chariots and the charioteers of Pharaoh's whole army which had followed the Israelites into the sea. Not a single one of them escaped. But the Israelites had marched on dry land through the midst of the sea, with the water like a wall to their right and to their left. Thus the LORD saved Israel on that day from the power of the Egyptians. When Israel saw the Egyptians lying dead on the seashore and beheld the great power that the LORD had shown against the Egyptians, they feared the LORD and believed in him and in his servant Moses.

Then Moses and the Israelites sang this song to the LORD:

I will sing to the LORD, for he is gloriously triumphant;
horse and chariot he has cast into the sea.

The word of the Lord. ℞. **Thanks be to God.** ↓

RESPONSORIAL PSALM   Ex 15:1-2, 3-4, 5-6, 17-18 (℟.:1b)

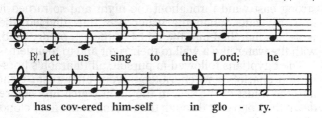

℟. Let us sing to the Lord; he has cov-ered him-self in glo - ry.

I will sing to the LORD, for he is gloriously triumphant;
   horse and chariot he has cast into the sea.
My strength and my courage is the LORD,
   and he has been my savior.
He is my God, I praise him;
   the God of my father, I extol him.

℟. **Let us sing to the Lord;**
   he has covered himself in glory.

The LORD is a warrior,
   LORD is his name!
Pharaoh's chariots and army he hurled into the sea;
   the elite of his officers were submerged into the Red
      Sea.

℟. **Let us sing to the Lord;**
   he has covered himself in glory.

The flood waters covered them,
   they sank into the depths like a stone.
Your right hand, O LORD, magnificent in power,
   your right hand, O LORD, has shattered the enemy.

℟. **Let us sing to the Lord;**
   he has covered himself in glory.

You brought in the people you redeemed
   and planted them on the mountain of your inheri-
      tance—

the place where you made your seat, O LORD,
　the sanctuary, O LORD, which your hands established.
The LORD shall reign forever and ever.

℟. **Let us sing to the Lord;**
　he has covered himself in glory. ↓

PRAYER

Let us pray.
Father,
even today we see the wonders
of the miracles you worked long ago.
You once saved a single nation from slavery,
and now you offer that salvation to all through baptism.
May the peoples of the world become true sons of
　Abraham
and prove worthy of the heritage of Israel.
We ask this through Christ our Lord. ℟. **Amen.** ↓

OR

PRAYER

Let us pray.
Lord God,
in the new covenant
you shed light on the miracles you worked in ancient
　times:
the Red Sea is a symbol of our baptism,
and the nation you freed from slavery
is a sign of your Christian people.
May every nation
share the faith and privilege of Israel
and come to new birth in the Holy Spirit.
We ask this through Christ our Lord. ℟. **Amen.** ↓

FOURTH READING　　　　　　　　　　　　Is 54:5-14

For a time, God hid from his people, but his love for them is everlasting.
He takes pity on them and promises them prosperity.

A reading from the Book of the Prophet Isaiah

THE One who has become your husband is your
    Maker;
  his name is the Lord of hosts;
your redeemer is the Holy One of Israel,
    called God of all the earth.
The LORD calls you back,
    like a wife forsaken and grieved in spirit,
    a wife married in youth and then cast off,
    says your God.
For a brief moment I abandoned you,
    but with great tenderness I will take you back.
In an outburst of wrath, for a moment
    I hid my face from you;
but with enduring love I take pity on you,
    says the LORD, your redeemer.
This is for me like the days of Noah,
    when I swore that the waters of Noah
    should never again deluge the earth;
so I have sworn not to be angry with you,
    or to rebuke you.
Though the mountains leave their place
    and the hills be shaken,
my love shall never leave you
    nor my covenant of peace be shaken,
    says the LORD, who has mercy on you.
O afflicted one, storm-battered and unconsoled,
    I lay your pavements in carnelians,
    and your foundations in sapphires;
I will make your battlements of rubies,
    your gates of carbuncles,
    and all your walls of precious stones.
All your sons shall be taught by the LORD,
    and great shall be the peace of your children.
In justice shall you be established,
    far from the fear of oppression,
    where destruction cannot come near you.
The word of the Lord. ℟. **Thanks be to God.** ↓

RESPONSORIAL PSALM   Ps 30:2, 4, 5-6, 11-12, 13 (℟.:2a)

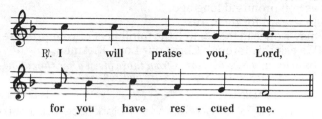

℟. I will praise you, Lord, for you have res - cued me.

I will extol you, O LORD, for you drew me clear
　　and did not let my enemies rejoice over me.
O LORD, you brought me up from the netherworld;
　　you preserved me from among those going down into
　　　　the pit.

℟. **I will praise you, Lord,
　　for you have rescued me.**

Sing praise to the LORD, you his faithful ones,
　　and give thanks to his holy name.
For his anger lasts but a moment;
　　a lifetime, his good will.
At nightfall, weeping enters in,
　　but with the dawn, rejoicing.

℟. **I will praise you, Lord,
　　for you have rescued me.**

Hear, O LORD, and have pity on me;
　　O LORD, be my helper.
You changed my mourning into dancing;
　　O LORD, my God, forever will I give you thanks.

℟. **I will praise you, Lord,
　　for you have rescued me.** ↓

PRAYER

Let us pray.
Almighty and eternal God,

glorify your name by increasing your chosen people
as you promised long ago.
In reward for their trust,
may we see in the Church the fulfillment of your promise.
We ask this through Christ our Lord. ℟. **Amen.** ↓

Prayers may also be chosen from those given after the following Readings, if the Readings are omitted.

FIFTH READING   Is 55:1-11

God is a loving Father and he calls his people back. He promises an everlasting covenant with them. God is merciful, generous, and forgiving.

A reading from the Book of the Prophet Isaiah

THUS says the LORD:
All you who are thirsty,
    come to the water!
You who have no money,
    come, receive grain and eat;
come, without paying and without cost,
    drink wine and milk!
Why spend your money for what is not bread;
    your wages for what fails to satisfy?
Heed me, and you shall eat well,
    you shall delight in rich fare.
Come to me heedfully,
    listen, that you may have life.
I will renew with you the everlasting covenant,
    the benefits assured to David.
As I made him a witness to the peoples,
    a leader and commander of nations,
so shall you summon a nation you knew not,
    and nations that knew you not shall run to you,
because of the LORD, your God,
    the Holy One of Israel, who has glorified you.

Seek the LORD while he may be found,
    call him while he is near.
Let the scoundrel forsake his way,
    and the wicked man his thoughts;

let him turn to the LORD for mercy;
   to our God, who is generous in forgiving.
For my thoughts are not your thoughts,
   nor are your ways my ways, says the LORD.
As high as the heavens are above the earth,
   so high are my ways above your ways,
   and my thoughts above your thoughts.

For just as from the heavens
   the rain and snow come down
and do not return there
   till they have watered the earth,
   making it fertile and fruitful,
giving seed to the one who sows
   and bread to the one who eats,
so shall my word be
   that goes forth from my mouth;
my word shall not return to me void,
   but shall do my will,
   achieving the end for which I sent it.
The word of the Lord. ℞. **Thanks be to God.** ↓

RESPONSORIAL PSALM   Is 12:2-3, 4, 5-6 (℞.:3)

℞. You will draw water joyfully from the springs of salvation.

God indeed is my savior;
   I am confident and unafraid.
My strength and my courage is the LORD,
   and he has been my savior.

With joy you will draw water
  at the fountain of salvation.

℟. **You will draw water joyfully from the springs of salvation.**

Give thanks to the LORD, acclaim his name;
  among the nations make known his deeds,
  proclaim how exalted is his name.

℟. **You will draw water joyfully from the springs of salvation.**

Sing praise to the LORD for his glorious achievement;
  let this be known throughout all the earth.
Shout with exultation, O city of Zion,
  for great in your midst
  is the Holy One of Israel!

℟. **You will draw water joyfully from the springs of salvation.** ↓

PRAYER

Let us pray.
Almighty, ever-living God,
only hope of the world,
by the preaching of the prophets
you proclaimed the mysteries we are celebrating tonight.
Help us to be your faithful people,
for it is by your inspiration alone
that we can grow in goodness.
We ask this through Christ our Lord. ℟. **Amen.** ↓

SIXTH READING   Bar 3:9-15, 32—4:4

Baruch tells the people of Israel to walk in the ways of God. They have to learn prudence, wisdom, understanding. Then they will have peace forever.

A reading from the Book of the Prophet Baruch

HEAR, O Israel, the commandments of life:
listen, and know prudence!

How is it, Israel,
>   that you are in the land of your foes,
>   grown old in a foreign land,
defiled with the dead,
>   accounted with those destined for the netherworld?
You have forsaken the fountain of wisdom!
>   Had you walked in the way of God,
>   you would have dwelt in enduring peace.
Learn where prudence is,
>   where strength, where understanding;
that you may know also
>   where are length of days, and life,
>   where light of the eyes, and peace.
Who has found the place of wisdom,
>   who has entered into her treasuries?

The One who knows all things knows her;
>   he has probed her by his knowledge—
the One who established the earth for all time,
>   and filled it with four-footed beasts;
he who dismisses the light, and it departs,
>   calls it, and it obeys him trembling;
before whom the stars at their posts
>   shine and rejoice;
when he calls them, they answer, "Here we are!"
>   shining with joy for their Maker.
Such is our God;
>   no other is to be compared to him:
he has traced out all the way of understanding,
>   and has given her to Jacob, his servant,
>   to Israel, his beloved son.

Since then she has appeared on earth,
>   and moved among people.
She is the book of the precepts of God,
>   the law that endures forever;
all who cling to her will live,
>   but those will die who forsake her.

Turn, O Jacob, and receive her:
  walk by her light toward splendor.
Give not your glory to another,
  your privileges to an alien race.
Blessed are we, O Israel;
  for what pleases God is known to us!
The word of the Lord. ℟. **Thanks be to God.** ↓

RESPONSORIAL PSALM   Ps 19:8, 9, 10, 11 (℟.:Jn 6:68c)

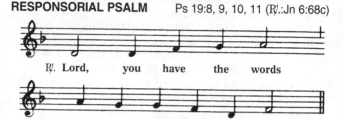

℟. Lord, you have the words of ev-er-last-ing life.

The law of the LORD is perfect,
  refreshing the soul;
the decree of the LORD is trustworthy,
  giving wisdom to the simple.

℟. **Lord, you have the words of everlasting life.**

The precepts of the LORD are right,
  rejoicing the heart;
the command of the LORD is clear,
  enlightening the eye.

℟. **Lord, you have the words of everlasting life.**

The fear of the LORD is pure,
  enduring forever;
the ordinances of the LORD are true,
  all of them just.

℟. **Lord, you have the words of everlasting life.**

They are more precious than gold,
  than a heap of purest gold;

sweeter also than syrup
   or honey from the comb.

℟. **Lord, you have the words of everlasting life.** ↓

PRAYER

Let us pray.
Father,
you increase your Church
by continuing to call all people to salvation.
Listen to our prayers
and always watch over those you cleanse in baptism.
We ask this through Christ our Lord. ℟. **Amen.** ↓

SEVENTH READING   Ez 36:16-17a, 18-28

Ezekiel, as God's prophet, speaks for God who is to keep his name holy
among his people. All shall know the holiness of God. He will cleanse his
people from idol worship and make them his own again. This promise is
again fulfilled in baptism in the restored order of redemption.

A reading from the Book of the Prophet Ezekiel

THE word of the LORD came to me, saying: Son of man,
when the house of Israel lived in their land, they
defiled it by their conduct and deeds. Therefore I poured
out my fury upon them because of the blood that they
poured out on the ground, and because they defiled it
with idols. I scattered them among the nations, dispers-
ing them over foreign lands; according to their conduct
and deeds I judged them. But when they came among the
nations, wherever they came, they served to profane my
holy name, because it was said of them: "These are the
people of the LORD, yet they had to leave their land." So I
have relented because of my holy name which the house
of Israel profaned among the nations where they came.
Therefore say to the house of Israel: Thus says the Lord
GOD: Not for your sakes do I act, house of Israel, but for
the sake of my holy name, which you profaned among
the nations to which you came. I will prove the holiness

of my great name, profaned among the nations, in whose midst you have profaned it. Thus the nations shall know that I am the LORD, says the Lord GOD, when in their sight I prove my holiness through you. For I will take you away from among the nations, gather you from all the foreign lands, and bring you back to your own land. I will sprinkle clean water upon you to cleanse you from all your impurities, and from all your idols I will cleanse you. I will give you a new heart and place a new spirit within you, taking from your bodies your stony hearts and giving you natural hearts. I will put my spirit within you and make you live by my statutes, careful to observe my decrees. You shall live in the land I gave your fathers; you shall be my people, and I will be your God.—The word of the Lord. ℟. **Thanks be to God.** ↓

When baptism is celebrated, Responsorial Psalm 42 is used; when baptism is not celebrated, Is 12 or Ps 51 is used.

RESPONSORIAL PSALM   Ps 42:3, 5; 43:3, 4 (℟.:Ps 42:2)

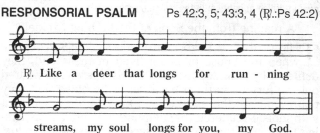

℟. Like a deer that longs for run-ning streams, my soul longs for you, my God.

Athirst is my soul for God, the living God.
     When shall I go and behold the face of God?

℟. **Like a deer that longs for running streams,
     my soul longs for you, my God.**

I went with the throng
     and led them in procession to the house of God,
amid loud cries of joy and thanksgiving,
     with the multitude keeping festival.

℟. **Like a deer that longs for running streams,
my soul longs for you, my God.**

Send forth your light and your fidelity;
    they shall lead me on
and bring me to your holy mountain,
    to your dwelling-place.

℟. **Like a deer that longs for running streams,
my soul longs for you, my God.**

Then will I go into the altar of God,
    the God of my gladness and joy;
then will I give you thanks upon the harp,
    O God, my God!

℟. **Like a deer that longs for running streams,
my soul longs for you, my God.** ↓

OR

*When baptism is not celebrated, the Responsorial Psalm after
the Fifth Reading (Is 12:2-3, 4bcd, 5-6) as above, p. 729, may be
used; or the following:*

RESPONSORIAL PSALM Ps 51:12-13, 14-15, 18-19 (℟.:12a)

℟. Cre - ate a clean heart in me, O God.

A clean heart create for me, O God,
    and a steadfast spirit renew within me.
Cast me not out from your presence,
    and your holy spirit take not from me.

℟. **Create a clean heart in me, O God.**

Give me back the joy of your salvation,
    and a willing spirit sustain in me.
I will teach transgressors your ways,
    and sinners shall return to you.

℟. **Create a clean heart in me, O God.**

For you are not pleased with sacrifices;
   should I offer a holocaust, you would not accept it.
My sacrifice, O God, is a contrite spirit;
   a heart contrite and humbled, O God, you will not
      spurn.

℟. **Create a clean heart in me, O God.** ↓

PRAYER

Let us pray.
God of unchanging power and light,
look with mercy and favor on your entire Church.
Bring lasting salvation to mankind,
so that the world may see
the fallen lifted up,
the old made new,
and all things brought to perfection,
through him who is their origin,
our Lord Jesus Christ,
who lives and reigns for ever and ever. ℟. **Amen.** ↓

OR

PRAYER

Let us pray.
Father,
you teach us in both the Old and the New Testament
to celebrate this passover mystery.
Help us to understand your great love for us.
May the goodness you now show us
confirm our hope in your future mercy.
We ask this through Christ our Lord. ℟. **Amen.** ↓

*After the last Reading from the Old Testament with its respon-
sory and prayer, the altar candles are lighted, and the priest
intones the* Gloria, *which is taken up by all present. The
church bells are rung, according to local custom.*

*At the end of the hymn, the priest sings or says the Opening
Prayer in the usual way.*

OPENING PRAYER

Let us pray.
Lord God,
you have brightened this night
with the radiance of the risen Christ.
Quicken the spirit of sonship in your Church;
renew us in mind and body
to give you whole-hearted service.
Grant this through our Lord Jesus Christ, your Son,
who lives and reigns with you and the Holy Spirit,
one God, for ever and ever. ℟. **Amen.** ↓

Then a reader proclaims the Reading from the Apostle Paul.

EPISTLE   Rom 6:3-11

By Baptism the Christian is not merely identified with the dying Christ,
who has won a victory over sin, but is introduced into the very act by which
Christ died to sin.

A reading from the Letter of Saint Paul to the Romans

BROTHERS and sisters: Are you unaware that we who
were baptized into Christ Jesus were baptized into
his death? We were indeed buried with him through baptism into death, so that, just as Christ was raised from the
dead by the glory of the Father, we too might live in newness of life.

For if we have grown into union with him through a
death like his, we shall also be united with him in the
resurrection. We know that our old self was crucified
with him, so that our sinful body might be done away
with, that we might no longer be in slavery to sin. For a
dead person has been absolved from sin. If, then, we have
died with Christ, we believe that we shall also live with
him. We know that Christ, raised from the dead, dies no
more; death no longer has power over him. As to his
death, he died to sin once for all; as to his life, he lives
for God. Consequently, you too must think of yourselves

as being dead to sin and living for God in Christ Jesus.—
The word of the Lord. ℟. **Thanks be to God.** ↓

After the Epistle all rise, and the priest solemnly intones the
Alleluia, *which is repeated by all present.*

RESPONSORIAL PSALM   Ps 118:1-2, 16-17, 22-23

℟. **Al - le - lu - ia. Al - le - lu - ia.   Al - le - lu - ia.**

Give thanks to the LORD, for he is good,
   for his mercy endures forever.
Let the house of Israel say,
   "His mercy endures forever."

℟. **Alleluia. Alleluia. Alleluia.**

The right hand of the LORD has struck with power;
   the right hand of the LORD is exalted.
I shall not die, but live,
   and declare the works of the LORD.

℟. **Alleluia. Alleluia. Alleluia.**

The stone which the builders rejected
   has become the cornerstone.
By the LORD has this been done;
   it is wonderful in our eyes.

℟. **Alleluia. Alleluia. Alleluia.** ↓

Incense may be used at the Gospel, but candles are not carried.

Years A, B, and C each have their proper Gospel, as given below.

— Year A —

2002, 2005, 2008, 2011, 2014, 2017

GOSPEL   Mt 28:1-10

Jesus has risen; he is not here. The cross has yielded to the empty tomb.
Although Peter is singled out, the Easter message is first announced to
the faithful, devoted women who followed Jesus.

℣. The Lord be with you. ℟. **And also with you.**

✠ A reading from the holy Gospel according to Matthew.

℟. **Glory to you, Lord.**

A FTER the sabbath, as the first day of the week was dawning, Mary Magdalene and the other Mary came to see the tomb. And behold, there was a great earthquake; for an angel of the Lord descended from heaven, approached, rolled back the stone, and sat upon it. His appearance was like lightning and his clothing was white as snow. The guards were shaken with fear of him and became like dead men. Then the angel said to the women in reply, "Do not be afraid! I know that you are seeking Jesus the crucified. He is not here, for he has been raised just as he said. Come and see the place where he lay. Then go quickly and tell his disciples, 'He has been raised from the dead, and he is going before you to Galilee; there you will see him.' Behold, I have told you." Then they went away quickly from the tomb, fearful yet overjoyed, and ran to announce this to his disciples. And behold, Jesus met them on their way and greeted them. They approached, embraced his feet, and did him homage. Then Jesus said to them, "Do not be afraid. Go tell my brothers to go to Galilee, and there they will see me."—The Gospel of the Lord. ℟. **Praise to you, Lord Jesus Christ.** → No. 14, p. 18

The Homily follows the Gospel, and then the Liturgy of Sacraments of Initiation begins, p. 741.

— Year B —

2003, 2006, 2009, 2012, 2015, 2018

GOSPEL Mk 16:1-8

On Easter morning, Mary Magdalene, Mary the mother of James, and Salome go to anoint the body of Jesus. An angel announces to them the amazing news that Jesus of Nazareth is risen as he had said and is on his way to Galilee. . . . Alleluia.

℣. The Lord be with you. ℟. **And also with you.**
✛ A reading from the holy Gospel according to Mark.
℟. **Glory to you, Lord.**

WHEN the sabbath was over, Mary Magdalene, Mary, the mother of James, and Salome brought spices so that they might go and anoint him. Very early when the sun had risen, on the first day of the week, they came to the tomb. They were saying to one another, "Who will roll back the stone for us from the entrance to the tomb?" When they looked up, they saw that the stone had been rolled back; it was very large. On entering the tomb they saw a young man sitting on the right side, clothed in a white robe, and they were utterly amazed. He said to them, "Do not be amazed! You seek Jesus of Nazareth, the crucified. He has been raised; he is not here. Behold the place where they laid him. But go and tell his disciples and Peter, 'He is going before you to Galilee; there you will see him, as he told you.'"—The Gospel of the Lord.
℟. **Praise to you, Lord Jesus Christ.**

The Homily follows the Gospel, and then the Liturgy of Sacraments of Initiation begins, p. 741.

— Year C —

2004, 2007, 2010, 2013, 2016, 2019

GOSPEL   Lk 24:1-12

Christ has died, Christ has risen, Christ will come again! God's mercy brings us forgiveness and salvation

℣. The Lord be with you. ℟. **And also with you.**
✛ A reading from the holy Gospel according to Luke.
℟. **Glory to you, Lord.**

AT daybreak on the first day of the week the women who had come from Galilee with Jesus took the spices they had prepared and went to the tomb. They found the stone rolled away from the tomb; but when they entered, they did not find the body of the Lord Jesus. While they were puzzling over this, behold, two men in dazzling garments appeared to them. They were terrified and bowed their faces to the ground. They said to them, "Why do you seek the living one among the dead? He is not here, but he has been raised. Remember what he said to you while he was still in Galilee, that the Son of Man must be handed over to sinners and be crucified, and rise on the third day." And they remembered his words. Then they returned from the tomb and announced all these things to the eleven and to all the others. The women were Mary Magdalene, Joanna, and Mary the mother of James; the others who accompanied them also told this to the apostles, but their story seemed like nonsense and they did not believe them. But Peter got up and ran to the tomb, bent down, and saw the burial cloths alone; then he went home amazed at what had happened.—The Gospel of the Lord. ℟. **Praise to you, Lord Jesus Christ.**

The Homily follows the Gospel, and then the Liturgy of Sacraments of Initiation begins.

PART THREE

LITURGY OF SACRAMENTS OF INITIATION

The following is taken from the Rite of Christian Initiation of Adults.

Celebration of Baptism

PRESENTATION OF THE CANDIDATES

An assisting deacon or other minister calls the candidates for baptism forward and their godparents present them. The invitation to prayer and the Litany of the Saints follow.

INVITATION TO PRAYER

The celebrant addresses the following or a similar invitation for the assembly to join in prayer for the candidates for baptism.

Dear friends, let us pray to almighty God for our brothers and sisters, N. and N., who are asking for baptism. He has called them and brought them to this moment; may he grant them light and strength to follow Christ with resolute hearts and to profess the faith of the Church. May he give them the new life of the Holy Spirit, whom we are about to call down on this water.

LITANY OF THE SAINTS

The singing of the Litany of the Saints is led by cantors and may include, at the proper place, names of other saints (for example, the titular of the church, the patron saints of the place or of those to be baptized) or petitions suitable to the occasion.

Lord, have mercy.
Lord, have mercy.

Christ, have mercy.
Christ, have mercy.

Lord, have mercy.
Lord, have mercy.

Holy Mary, Mother of God, **pray for us.**

Saint Michael, **pray for us.**

Holy angels of God, **pray for us.**

Saint John the Baptist, **pray for us.**

Saint Joseph, **pray for us.**

Saint Peter and Saint Paul, **pray for us.**

Saint Andrew, **pray for us.**

Saint John, **pray for us.**

Saint Mary Magdalene, **pray for us.**

Saint Stephen, **pray for us.**

Saint Ignatius, **pray for us.**

Saint Lawrence, **pray for us.**

Saint Perpetua and Saint Felicity, **pray for us.**

Saint Agnes, **pray for us.**

Saint Gregory, **pray for us.**

Saint Augustine, **pray for us.**

Saint Athanasius, **pray for us.**

Saint Basil, **pray for us.**

Saint Martin, **pray for us.**

Saint Benedict, **pray for us.**

Saint Francis and Saint Dominic, **pray for us.**

Saint Francis Xavier, **pray for us.**

Saint John Vianney, **pray for us.**

Saint Catherine, **pray for us.**

Saint Teresa, **pray for us.**

All holy men and women, **pray for us.**

Lord, be merciful, **Lord, save your people.**

From all evil, **Lord, save your people.**

From every sin, **Lord, save your people.**

From everlasting death, **Lord, save your people.**

By your coming as man, **Lord, save your people.**

By your death and rising to new life, **Lord, save your people.**

By your gift of the Holy Spirit, **Lord, save your people.**

Be merciful to us sinners, **Lord, hear our prayer.**

Give new life to these chosen ones by the grace of baptism, **Lord, hear our prayer.**

Jesus, Son of the living God, **Lord, hear our prayer.**

Christ, hear us. **Christ, hear us.**

Lord Jesus, hear our prayer. **Lord Jesus, hear our prayer.**

BLESSING OF THE WATER

Facing the font (or vessel) containing the water, the celebrant sings or says the following:

Father,
you give us grace through sacramental signs,
which tell us the wonders of your unseen power.
In baptism we use your gift of water,
which you have made a rich symbol of the grace
you give us in this sacrament.
At the very dawn of creation
your Spirit breathed on the waters,
making them the wellspring of all holiness.
The waters of the great flood
you made a sign of the waters of baptism,
that make an end of sin
and a new beginning of goodness.
Through the waters of the Red Sea
you led Israel out of slavery,

to be an image of God's holy people,
set free from sin by baptism.
In the waters of the Jordan
your Son was baptized by John
and anointed with the Spirit.
Your Son willed that water and blood should flow from
    his side
as he hung upon the cross.
After his resurrection he told his disciples:
"Go out and teach all nations,
baptizing them in the name of the Father and of the Son
    and of the Holy Spirit."
Father,
look now with love upon your Church,
and unseal for it the fountain of baptism.
By the power of the Spirit
give to this water the grace of your Son,
so that in the sacrament of baptism
all those whom you have created in your likeness may be
    cleansed from sin
and rise to a new birth of innocence
by water and the Holy Spirit.

*Here, if this can be done conveniently, the celebrant before
continuing lowers the Easter candle into the water once or
three times, then holds it there until the acclamation at the
end of the blessing.*

We ask you, Father, with your Son
to send the Holy Spirit upon the waters of this font.
May all who are buried with Christ in the death of bap-
    tism
rise also with him to newness of life.
We ask this through Christ our Lord.
All: **Amen.**

*The celebrant then raises it and the people sing the following
or another suitable acclamation:*

> **Springs of water, bless the Lord.**
> **Give him glory and praise for ever.**

PROFESSION OF FAITH

After the blessing of the water, the celebrant continues with the profession of faith, which includes the renunciation of sin and the profession itself.

RENUNCIATION OF SIN

Using one of the following formularies, the celebrant questions all the elect together; or, after being informed of each candidate's name by the godparents, he may use the same formularies to question the candidates individually.

A

Do you reject sin so as to live in the freedom of God's children? **I do.**

Do you reject the glamour of evil, and refuse to be mastered by sin? **I do.**

Do you reject Satan, father of sin and prince of darkness? **I do.**

B

Do you reject Satan, and all his works, and all his empty promises? **I do.**

C

Do you reject Satan? **I do.**

And all his works? **I do.**

And all his empty promises? **I do.**

PROFESSION OF FAITH

Then the celebrant, informed again of each candidate's name by the godparents, questions each candidate individually. Each candidate is baptized immediately after his or her profession of faith.

Celebrant: N., do you believe in God, the Father almighty, creator of heaven and earth?

Candidate: **I do.**

Celebrant: Do you believe in Jesus Christ, his only Son, our Lord,

who was born of the Virgin Mary,
was crucified, died and was buried,
rose from the dead,
and is now seated at the right hand of the Father?
Candidate: **I do.**
Celebrant: Do you believe in the Holy Spirit,
the holy Catholic Church, the communion of saints,
the forgiveness of sins, the resurrection of the body,
and the life everlasting?
Candidate: **I do.**

BAPTISM

The celebrant baptizes each candidate either by immersion or by the pouring of water.

N., I baptize you in the name of the Father, and of the Son, and of the Holy Spirit.

EXPLANATORY RITES

The celebration of baptism continues with the explanatory rites, after which the celebration of confirmation normally follows.

ANOINTING AFTER BAPTISM

If the confirmation of those baptized is separated from their baptism, the celebrant anoints them with chrism immediately after baptism.

The God of power and Father of our Lord Jesus Christ
has freed you from sin
and brought you to new life
through water and the Holy Spirit.

He now anoints you with the chrism of salvation,
so that, united with his people,
you may remain for ever a member of Christ
who is Priest, Prophet, and King.

Newly baptized: **Amen.**

In silence each of the newly baptized is anointed with chrism on the crown of the head.

CLOTHING WITH A BAPTISMAL GARMENT

The garment used in this rite may be white or of a color that conforms to local custom. If circumstances suggest, this rite may be omitted.

N. and N., you have become a new creation
and have clothed yourselves in Christ.
Receive this baptismal garment
and bring it unstained to the judgment seat of our Lord
   Jesus Christ,
so that you may have everlasting life.

Newly baptized: **Amen.**

PRESENTATION OF A LIGHTED CANDLE

The celebrant takes the Easter candle in his hands or touches it, saying:

Godparents, please come forward to give to the newly baptized the light of Christ.

A godparent of each of the newly baptized goes to the celebrant, lights a candle from the Easter candle, then presents it to the newly baptized.

You have been enlightened by Christ.
Walk always as children of the light
and keep the flame of faith alive in your hearts.
When the Lord comes, may you go out to meet him
with all the saints in the heavenly kingdom.

Newly baptized: **Amen.**

Renewal of Baptismal Promises

INVITATION

After the celebration of baptism, the celebrant addresses the community, in order to invite those present to the renewal of their baptismal promises; the candidates for reception into full communion join the rest of the community in this renunciation of sin and profession of faith. All stand and hold lighted candles. The celebrant may use the following or similar words.

Dear friends, through the paschal mystery we have been buried with Christ in baptism, so that we may rise with him to newness of life. Now that we have completed our Lenten observance, let us renew the promises we made in baptism when we rejected Satan and his works, and promised to serve God faithfully in his holy Catholic Church.

RENEWAL OF BAPTISMAL PROMISES

RENUNCIATION OF SIN

A

Celebrant: Do you reject sin so as to live in the freedom of God's children?
All: **I do.**

Celebrant: Do you reject the glamour of evil,
and refuse to be mastered by sin?
All: **I do.**

Celebrant: Do you reject Satan, father of sin and prince of darkness?
All: **I do.**

B

Celebrant: Do you reject Satan?
All: **I do.**
Celebrant: And all his works?
All: **I do.**
Celebrant: And all his empty promises?
All: **I do.**

PROFESSION OF FAITH

Then the celebrant continues:

Celebrant: Do you believe in God, the Father almighty, creator of heaven and earth?
All: **I do.**

Celebrant: Do you believe in Jesus Christ, his only Son, our Lord,

who was born of the Virgin Mary,
was crucified, died and was buried,
rose from the dead,
and is now seated at the right hand of the Father?
All: **I do.**
Celebrant: Do you believe in the Holy Spirit,
the holy Catholic Church, the communion of saints,
the forgiveness of sins, the resurrection of the body,
and the life everlasting?
All: **I do.**

SPRINKLING WITH BAPTISMAL WATER

The celebrant sprinkles all the people with the blessed baptismal water, while all sing the following song or any other that is baptismal in character.

Antiphon

See Ez 47:1-2, 9

I saw water flowing
from the right side of the temple, alleluia.
It brought God's life and his salvation,
and the people sang in joyful praise:
alleluia, alleluia.

The celebrant then concludes with the following prayer.

God, the all-powerful Father of our Lord Jesus Christ, has given us a new birth by water and the Holy Spirit and forgiven all our sins.
May he also keep us faithful to our Lord Jesus Christ for ever and ever.
All: **Amen.**

Celebration of Reception

INVITATION

If baptism has been celebrated at the font, the celebrant, the assisting ministers, and the newly baptized with their godparents proceed to the sanctuary. As they do so the assembly may sing a suitable song.

Then in the following or similar words the celebrant invites the candidates for reception, along with their sponsors, to come into the sanctuary and before the community to make a profession of faith.

N. and N., of your own free will you have asked to be received into the full communion of the Catholic Church. You have made your decision after careful thought under the guidance of the Holy Spirit. I now invite you to come forward with your sponsors and in the presence of this community to profess the Catholic faith. In this faith you will be one with us for the first time at the eucharistic table of the Lord Jesus, the sign of the Church's unity.

PROFESSION BY THE CANDIDATES

When the candidates for reception and their sponsors have taken their places in the sanctuary, the celebrant asks the candidates to make the following profession of faith. The candidates say:

I believe and profess all that the holy Catholic Church believes, teaches, and proclaims to be revealed by God.

ACT OF RECEPTION

Then the candidates with their sponsors go individually to the celebrant, who says to each candidate (laying his right hand on the head of any candidate who is not to receive confirmation):

N., the Lord receives you into the Catholic Church.
His loving kindness has led you here,
so that in the unity of the Holy Spirit
you may have full communion with us
in the faith that you have professed in the presence of his
     family.

Celebration of Confirmation

INVITATION

The newly baptized with their godparents and, if they have not received the sacrament of confirmation, the newly received with their sponsors, stand before the celebrant. He first speaks briefly to the newly baptized and the newly received in these or similar words.

My dear candidates for confirmation, by your baptism you have been born again in Christ and you have become members of Christ and of his priestly people. Now you are to share in the outpouring of the Holy Spirit among us, the Spirit sent by the Lord upon his apostles at Pentecost and given by them and their successors to the baptized.

The promised strength of the Holy Spirit, which you are to receive, will make you more like Christ and help you to be witnesses to his suffering, death, and resurrection. It will strengthen you to be active members of the Church and to build up the Body of Christ in faith and love.

My dear friends, let us pray to God our Father, that he will pour out the Holy Spirit on these candidates for confirmation to strengthen them with his gifts and anoint them to be more like Christ, the Son of God.

All pray briefly in silence.

LAYING ON OF HANDS

The celebrant holds his hands outstretched over the entire group of those to be confirmed and says the following prayer.

All-powerful God, Father of our Lord Jesus Christ,
by water and the Holy Spirit
you freed your sons and daughters from sin
and gave them new life.
Send your Holy Spirit upon them
to be their helper and guide.
Give them the spirit of wisdom and understanding,
the spirit of right judgment and courage,
the spirit of knowledge and reverence.
Fill them with the spirit of wonder and awe in your presence.
We ask this through Christ our Lord.
℟. **Amen.**

ANOINTING WITH CHRISM

Either or both godparents and sponsors place the right hand on the shoulder of the candidate; and a godparent or a sponsor of the candidate gives the candidate's name to the minister of the sacrament. During the conferral of the sacrament an appropriate song may be sung.

The minister of the sacrament dips his right thumb in the chrism and makes the sign of the cross on the forehead of the one to be confirmed as he says:

N., be sealed with the Gift of the Holy Spirit.
Newly confirmed: **Amen.**
Minister: Peace be with you.
Newly confirmed: **And also with you.**

After all have received the sacrament, the newly confirmed as well as the godparents and sponsors are led to their places in the assembly.

[Since the Profession of Faith is not said, the General Intercessions (no. 15, p. 623) begin immediately and for the first time the neophytes take part in them.]

PART FOUR

LITURGY OF THE EUCHARIST

The priest goes to the altar and begins the Liturgy of the Eucharist in the usual way.

It is fitting that the bread and wine be brought forward by the newly baptized.

PRAYER OVER THE GIFTS

Lord,
accept the prayers and offerings of your people.
With your help
may this Easter mystery of our redemption
bring to perfection the saving work you have begun in us.
We ask this through Christ our Lord. ℟. **Amen.** ↓

Preface of Easter I (P 21: on this Easter day), p. 673.

When Eucharistic Prayer I is used, the special Easter forms of In union with the whole Church, *and* Father, accept this offering *are said.*

COMMUNION ANT. 1 Cor 5:7-8

Christ has become our paschal sacrifice; let us feast with the unleavened bread of sincerity and truth, alleluia. ↓

PRAYER AFTER COMMUNION

Lord,
you have nourished us with your Easter sacraments.
Fill us with your Spirit,
and make us one in peace and love.
We ask this through Christ our Lord. ℞. **Amen.**

The deacon (or the priest) sings or says the dismissal as follows:

Go in the peace of Christ, alleluia, alleluia.

OR

The Mass is ended, go in peace, alleluia, alleluia.

OR

Go in peace to love and serve the Lord, alleluia, alleluia.
℞. **Thanks be to God, alleluia, alleluia.**

MONDAY OF THE OCTAVE OF EASTER

Jesus Christ has risen from the dead. He allowed himself to undergo the sufferings of the cross, but then he was raised to life. In Jesus we live and move and have our being. Let us rejoice and be glad for the Lord is risen. Alleluia.

ENTRANCE ANT.   Ex 13:5, 9

The Lord brought you to a land flowing with milk and honey, so that his law would always be given honor among you, alleluia.

OR:

The Lord has risen from the dead, as he foretold. Let there be happiness and rejoicing for he is our King for ever, alleluia.   → No. 2, p. 614

OPENING PRAYER

Father,
you give your Church constant growth
by adding new members to your family.
Help us put into action in our lives
the baptism we have received with faith.
We ask this . . . for ever and ever. ℟. **Amen.** ↓

FIRST READING   Acts 2:14, 22-33

In short summary, St. Peter proposes the name, works, death and resurrection of Jesus. He speaks to the Jews and all in Jerusalem, and he includes the facts about the resurrection.

A reading from the Acts of the Apostles

ON the day of Pentecost, Peter stood up with the Eleven, raised his voice, and proclaimed: "You who are Jews, indeed all of you staying in Jerusalem. Let this be known to you, and listen to my words.

"You who are children of Israel, hear these words. Jesus the Nazorean was a man commended to you by God with mighty deeds, wonders, and signs, which God worked through him in your midst, as you yourselves know. This man, delivered up by the set plan and foreknowledge of God, you killed, using lawless men to crucify him. But God raised him up, releasing him from the throes of death, because it was impossible for him to be held by it. For David says of him:

> *I saw the Lord ever before me,*
>> *with him at my right hand I shall not be disturbed.*
>
> *Therefore my heart has been glad and my tongue has exulted;*
>> *my flesh, too, will dwell in hope,*
>
> *because you will not abandon my soul to the nether world,*
>> *nor will you suffer your holy one to see corruption.*
>
> *You have made known to me the paths of life;*
>> *you will fill me with joy in your presence.*

"My brothers, one can confidently say to you about the patriarch David that he died and was buried, and his tomb is in our midst to this day. But since he was a prophet and knew that God had sworn an oath to him that he would set one of his descendants upon his throne, he foresaw and spoke of the resurrection of the Christ, that neither was he abandoned to the netherworld nor did his flesh see corruption. God raised this Jesus; of this we are all witnesses. Exalted at the right hand of God, he poured forth the promise of the Holy Spirit that he received from the Father, as you both see and hear."—The word of the Lord. ℟. **Thanks be to God.** ↓

RESPONSORIAL PSALM   Ps 16:1-2a and 5, 7-8, 9-10, 11

℟. (1) **Keep me safe, O God; you are my hope.**

℟. Or: **Alleluia.**

Keep me, O God, for in you I take refuge;
    I say to the LORD, "My Lord are you."
O LORD, my allotted portion and my cup,
    you it is who hold fast my lot.—℟.

I bless the LORD who counsels me;
>even in the night my heart exhorts me.

I set the LORD ever before me;
>with him at my right hand I shall not be disturbed.—R̸.

Therefore my heart is glad and my soul rejoices,
>my body, too, abides in confidence;

Because you will not abandon my soul to the nether world,
>nor will you suffer your faithful one to undergo corruption.—R̸.

You will show me the path to life,
>fullness of joys in your presence,
>>the delights at your right hand forever.—R̸. ↓

SEQUENCE (Optional)

Christians, to the Paschal Victim
>**Offer your thankful praises!**
A Lamb the sheep redeems;
>**Christ, who only is sinless,**
>**Reconciles sinners to the Father.**
Death and life have contended in that combat stupendous:
>**The Prince of life, who died, reigns immortal.**
Speak, Mary, declaring
>**What you saw, wayfaring.**
"The tomb of Christ, who is living,
>**The glory of Jesus' resurrection;**
Bright angels attesting,
>**The shroud and napkin resting.**
Yes, Christ my hope is arisen;
>**To Galilee he goes before you."**
Christ indeed from death is risen, our new life obtaining.
>**Have mercy, victor King, ever reigning!**
>**Amen. Alleluia.** ↓

ALLELUIA Ps 118:24

℟. **Alleluia, alleluia.**
This is the day the LORD has made;
let us be glad and rejoice in it.
℟. **Alleluia, alleluia.** ↓

GOSPEL Mt 28:8-15

The apparition of Christ himself completes the Resurrection narrative. The empty tomb has ceased to be a place of mourning and has become a place of exultant joy. Jesus repeats to the women the message the angel has already given for the disciples. Even now the elders and chief priests continue their scheme of plotting against the Jews.

℣. The Lord be with you. ℟. **And also with you.**
✠ A reading from the holy Gospel according to Matthew.
℟. **Glory to you, Lord.**

MARY Magdalene and the other Mary went away quickly from the tomb, fearful yet overjoyed, and ran to announce the news to his disciples. And behold, Jesus met them on their way and greeted them. They approached, embraced his feet, and did him homage. Then Jesus said to them, "Do not be afraid. Go tell my brothers to go to Galilee, and there they will see me."

While they were going, some of the guard went into the city and told the chief priests all that had happened. The chief priests assembled with the elders and took counsel; then they gave a large sum of money to the soldiers, telling them, "You are to say, 'His disciples came by night and stole him while we were asleep.' And if this gets to the ears of the governor, we will satisfy him and keep you out of trouble." The soldiers took the money and did as they were instructed. And this story has circulated among the Jews to the present day.—The Gospel of the Lord. ℟. **Praise to you, Lord Jesus Christ.**

→ No. 15, p. 623

PRAYER OVER THE GIFTS

Father,
you have given us new light by baptism
and the profession of your name.
Accept the gifts of your children
and bring us to eternal joy in your presence.
We ask this in the name of Jesus the Lord.
℟. **Amen.** → No. 21, p. 626 (Pref. P 21)

When Eucharistic Prayer I is used, the special Easter forms of In union with the whole Church *and* Father, accept this offering *are said.*

COMMUNION ANT. Rom 6:9

Christ now raised from the dead will never die again; death no longer has power over him, alleluia. ↓

PRAYER AFTER COMMUNION

Lord,
may the life we receive in these Easter sacraments
continue to grow in our hearts.
As you lead us along the way of eternal salvation,
make us worthy of your many gifts.
Grant this through Christ our Lord.
℟. **Amen.** → No. 32, p. 660

TUESDAY OF THE OCTAVE OF EASTER

If our love of God is perfect and unselfish as was Mary's, shown in her grief and tenderness as she stood at the empty tomb, we can express this kind of love and loyalty by our sincere desire to keep God's commands. Our love will be from the heart that binds us to God and also binds us to our neighbor. For his sake, may we love our neighbor in thought, word, and deed.

ENTRANCE ANT. Sir 15:3-4

If men desire wisdom, she will give them the water of knowledge to drink. They will never waver from the truth; they will stand firm for ever, alleluia.

→ No. 2, p. 614

OPENING PRAYER

Father,
by this Easter mystery you touch our lives
with the healing power of your love.
You have given us the freedom of the sons of God.
May we who now celebrate your gift
find joy in it for ever in heaven.
Grant this . . . for ever and ever. ℟. **Amen.** ↓

FIRST READING   Acts 2:36-41

St. Peter reminds the Jews that Christ has been crucified and they are summoned to penance and to conversion, which will be accomplished by the mystery of baptism in the name of Jesus Christ. Three thousand are baptized that very day.

A reading from the Acts of the Apostles

O N the day of Pentecost, Peter said to the Jewish people, "Let the whole house of Israel know for certain that God has made him both Lord and Christ, this Jesus whom you crucified."

Now when they heard this, they were cut to the heart, and they asked Peter and the other Apostles, "What are we to do, my brothers?" Peter said to them, "Repent and be baptized, every one of you, in the name of Jesus Christ, for the forgiveness of your sins; and you will receive the gift of the Holy Spirit. For the promise is made to you and to your children and to all those far off, whomever the Lord our God will call." He testified with many other arguments, and was exhorting them, "Save yourselves from this corrupt generation." Those who accepted his message were baptized, and about three thousand persons were added that day.—The word of the Lord. ℟. **Thanks be to God.** ↓

RESPONSORIAL PSALM   Ps 33:4-5, 18-19, 20 and 22

℟. (5b) **The earth is full of the goodness of the Lord.**

℟. Or: **Alleluia.**

Upright is the word of the LORD,
  and all his works are trustworthy.
He loves justice and right;
  of the kindness of the LORD the earth is full.—℞.

See, the eyes of the LORD are upon those who fear him,
  upon those who hope for his kindness,
To deliver them from death
  and preserve them in spite of famine.—℞.

Our soul waits for the LORD,
  who is our help and our shield.
May your kindness, O LORD, be upon us
  who have put our hope in you.—℞. ↓

→ Sequence (Optional), p. 756

ALLELUIA   Ps 118:24

℞. **Alleluia, alleluia.**
This is the day the LORD has made;
let us be glad and rejoice in it.
℞. **Alleluia, alleluia.** ↓

GOSPEL   Jn 20:11-18

As Mary Magdalene stands weeping at Jesus' tomb, she believes the Lord has been taken away. But he appears, and at first Mary fails to recognize him. It is sufficient for Jesus to call Mary by name for her to recognize him.

℣. The Lord be with you. ℞. **And also with you.**
✠ A reading from the holy Gospel according to John.
℞. **Glory to you, Lord.**

MARY Magdalene stayed outside the tomb weeping. And as she wept, she bent over into the tomb and saw two angels in white sitting there, one at the head and one at the feet where the Body of Jesus had been. And they said to her, "Woman, why are you weeping?" She said to them, "They have taken my Lord, and I don't know where they laid him." When she had said this, she turned around and saw Jesus there, but did not know it was Jesus. Jesus said to her, "Woman, why are you weeping? Whom are you looking for?" She thought it was the gardener and said to him, "Sir, if you carried him away, tell me where you laid him, and I will take him." Jesus said to her, "Mary!" She turned and said to him in Hebrew, "Rabbouni," which means Teacher. Jesus said to her, "Stop holding on to me, for I have not yet ascended to the Father. But go to my brothers and tell them, 'I am going to my Father and your Father, to my God and your God.' " Mary went and announced to the disciples, "I have seen the Lord," and then reported what he had told her.—The Gospel of the Lord. ℟. **Praise to you, Lord Jesus Christ.**

→ No. 15, p. 623

PRAYER OVER THE GIFTS

Lord,
accept these gifts from your family.
May we hold fast to the life you have given us
and come to the eternal gifts you promise.
We ask this in the name of Jesus the Lord.
℟. **Amen.**

→ No. 21, p. 626 (Pref. P 21)

When Eucharistic Prayer I is used, the special Easter forms of In union with the whole Church *and* Father, accept this offering *are said.*

COMMUNION ANT.

Col. 3:1-2

If you have been raised with Christ, seek the things that are above, where Christ is seated at the right hand of God, alleluia. ↓

PRAYER AFTER COMMUNION

All-powerful Father,
hear our prayers.
Prepare for eternal joy
the people you have renewed in baptism.
We ask this through Christ our Lord.
℟. **Amen.**

→ No. 32, p. 660

WEDNESDAY OF THE OCTAVE OF EASTER

The glorious mystery of the Holy Eucharist is in itself a continuing miracle of the love of God for his children. Christ our Lord expects us to prepare for the worthy reception of it. Through our work and in the company of our brothers and sisters, we shall help to bring to completion the creative and redemptive work of God. Each day through the Eucharist we will then move one step closer to attaining the fullness of Christ.

ENTRANCE ANT.   Mt 25:34

Come, you whom my Father has blessed; inherit the kingdom prepared for you since the foundation of the world, alleluia.   → No. 2, p. 614

OPENING PRAYER

God our Father,
on this solemn feast you give us the joy of recalling
the rising of Christ to new life.
May the joy of our annual celebration
bring us to the joy of eternal life.
We ask this . . . for ever and ever. ℟. **Amen.** ↓

FIRST READING   Acts 3:1-10

Our Lord's healing ministry is continued by his chosen Apostles. It is Peter who speaks and acts for the Twelve. Peter's admission that he has neither silver nor gold shows the depth of his faith and prepares for the name of Jesus as a powerful source of salvation.

A reading from the Acts of the Apostles

PETER and John were going up to the temple area for the three o'clock hour of prayer. And a man crippled from birth was carried and placed at the gate of the temple called "the Beautiful Gate" every day to beg for alms from the people who entered the temple. When he saw Peter and John about to go into the temple, he asked for alms. But Peter looked intently at him, as did John, and said, "Look at us." He paid attention to them, expecting to receive something from them. Peter said, "I have neither silver nor gold, but what I do have I give you: in the name of Jesus Christ the Nazorean, rise and walk."Then Peter took him by the right hand and raised him up, and immediately his feet and ankles grew strong. He leaped up, stood, and walked around, and went into the temple with them, walking and jumping and praising God. When all the people saw him walking and praising God, they recognized him as the one who used to sit begging at the Beautiful Gate of the temple, and they were filled with amazement and astonishment at what had happened to him.—The word of the Lord. ℟. **Thanks be to God.** ↓

RESPONSORIAL PSALM   Ps 105:1-2, 3-4, 6-7, 8-9

℟. (3b) **Rejoice, O hearts that seek the Lord.**

℟. Or: **Alleluia.**

Give thanks to the LORD, invoke his name;
    make known among the nations his deeds.
Sing to him, sing his praise,
    proclaim all his wondrous deeds.—℟.

Glory in his holy name;
    rejoice, O hearts that seek the LORD!
Look to the LORD in his strength;
    seek to serve him constantly.—℟.

You descendants of Abraham, his servants,
    sons of Jacob, his chosen ones!
He, the LORD, is our God;
    throughout the earth his judgments prevail.—℟.

He remembers forever his covenant
    which he made binding for a thousand generations—
Which he entered into with Abraham
    and by his oath to Isaac.—℟. ↓

→ Sequence (Optional) p. 756

ALLELUIA   Ps 118:24

℟. **Alleluia, alleluia.**
This is the day the LORD has made;

let us be glad and rejoice in it.
℟. **Alleluia, alleluia.** ↓

GOSPEL   Lk 24:13-35

While walking on the road to Emmaus, the two disciples are troubled and
do not understand why Jesus is absent. They seem to recognize Jesus in
the stranger but do not believe their senses. After recognition, these men
do not hesitate to believe. Once recognized, Jesus disappears.

℣. The Lord be with you. ℟. **And also with you.**
✠ A reading from the holy Gospel according to Luke.
℟. **Glory to you, Lord.**

THAT very day, the first day of the week, two of Jesus'
disciples were going to a village seven miles from
Jerusalem called Emmaus, and they were conversing
about all the things that had occurred. And it happened
that while they were conversing and debating, Jesus himself drew near and walked with them, but their eyes were
prevented from recognizing him. He asked them, "What
are you discussing as you walk along?" They stopped,
looking downcast. One of them, named Cleopas, said to
him in reply, "Are you the only visitor to Jerusalem who
does not know of the things that have taken place there
in these days?" And he replied to them, "What sort of
things?" They said to him, "The things that happened to
Jesus the Nazarene, who was a prophet mighty in deed
and word before God and all the people, how our chief
priests and rulers both handed him over to a sentence of
death and crucified him. But we were hoping that he
would be the one to redeem Israel; and besides all this, it
is now the third day since this took place. Some women
from our group, however, have astounded us: they were
at the tomb early in the morning and did not find his
Body; they came back and reported that they had indeed
seen a vision of angels who announced that he was alive.
Then some of those with us went to the tomb and found
things just as the women had described, but him they did
not see." And he said to them, "Oh, how foolish you are!

How slow of heart to believe all that the prophets spoke! Was it not necessary that the Christ should suffer these things and enter into his glory?" Then beginning with Moses and all the prophets, he interpreted to them what referred to him in all the Scriptures. As they approached the village to which they were going, he gave the impression that he was going on farther. But they urged him, "Stay with us, for it is nearly evening and the day is almost over." So he went in to stay with them. And it happened that, while he was with them at table, he took bread, said the blessing, broke it, and gave it to them. With that their eyes were opened and they recognized him, but he vanished from their sight. Then they said to each other, "Were not our hearts burning within us while he spoke to us on the way and opened the Scriptures to us?" So they set out at once and returned to Jerusalem where they found gathered together the Eleven and those with them who were saying, "The Lord has truly been raised and has appeared to Simon!" Then the two recounted what had taken place on the way and how he was made known to them in the breaking of the bread.— The Gospel of the Lord. ℟. **Praise to you, Lord Jesus Christ.**   → No. 15, p. 623

PRAYER OVER THE GIFTS

Lord,
accept this sacrifice of our redemption
and accomplish in us salvation of mind and body.
Grant this through Christ our Lord.
℟. **Amen.**   → No. 21, p. 626 (Pref. P 21)

When Eucharistic Prayer I is used, the special Easter forms of In union with the whole Church *and* Father, accept this offering *are said.*

COMMUNION ANT.   Lk 24:35

The disciples recognized the Lord Jesus in the breaking of bread, alleluia. ↓

PRAYER AFTER COMMUNION

Lord,
may this sharing in the sacrament of your Son
free us from our old life of sin
and make us your new creation.
We ask this in the name of Jesus the Lord.
℟. **Amen.**   → No. 32, p. 660

THURSDAY OF THE OCTAVE OF EASTER

May our faith have the strength to make us pleasing to God. We should ever guard and preserve the gift of true faith. We cannot expose it to danger. In a manner of speaking, we are engraved on Jesus' hands and feet and in his heart. We are strengthened by these sacred wounds. Let us strive, therefore, to live so that these wounds may be our consolation.

ENTRANCE ANT.   Wis 10:20-21

Your people praised your great victory, O Lord. Wisdom opened the mouth that was dumb, and made the tongues of babies speak, alleluia.   → No. 2, p. 614

OPENING PRAYER

Father,
you gather the nations to praise your name.
May all who are reborn in baptism
be one in faith and love.
Grant this . . . for ever and ever. ℟. **Amen.** ↓

FIRST READING   Acts 3:11-26

Peter refuses as false any claim that the miracle was wrought because of either John's or his piety. He stresses the power of prayer. Peter tells the people how they killed Jesus but God raised him from the dead.

A reading from the Acts of the Apostles

A S the crippled man who had been cured clung to Peter and John, all the people hurried in amazement toward them in the portico called "Solomon's Portico." When Peter saw this, he addressed the people, "You children of Israel, why are you amazed at this, and why do you look so intently at us as if we had made him walk by our own power or piety? The God of Abraham, the God of Isaac, and the God of Jacob, the God of our fathers, has glorified his servant Jesus whom you handed over and denied in Pilate's presence, when he had decided to release him. You denied the Holy and Righteous One and asked that a murderer be released to you. The author of life you put to death, but God raised him from the dead; of this we are witnesses. And by faith in his name, this man, whom you see and know, his name has made strong, and the faith that comes through it has given him this perfect health, in the presence of all of you. Now I know, brothers and sisters, that you acted out of ignorance, just as your leaders did; but God has thus brought to fulfillment what he had announced beforehand through the mouth of all the prophets, that his Christ would suffer. Repent, therefore, and be converted, that your sins may be wiped away, and that the Lord may grant you times of refreshment and send you the Christ already appointed for you, Jesus, whom heaven must receive until the times of universal restoration of which God spoke through the mouth of his holy prophets from of old. For Moses said:

> *A prophet like me will the Lord, your God, raise up*
> *   for you*
> *   from among your own kin;*
> *to him you shall listen in all that he may say to*
> *   you.*
> *Everyone who does not listen to that prophet*
> *   will be cut off from the people.*

"Moreover, all the prophets who spoke, from Samuel and those afterwards, also announced these days. You are the children of the prophets and of the covenant that God made with your ancestors when he said to Abraham, *In your offspring all the families of the earth shall be blessed.* For you first, God raised up his servant and sent him to bless you by turning each of you from your evil ways."—The word of the Lord. ℟. **Thanks be to God.** ↓

RESPONSORIAL PSALM   Ps 8:2ab and 5, 6-7, 8-9

℟. (2ab) **O Lord, our God, how wonderful your name in all the earth!**

℟. Or: **Alleluia.**

O LORD, our Lord,
    how glorious is your name over all the earth!
What is man that you should be mindful of him,
    or the son of man that you should care for him?—℟.

You have made him little less than the angels,
    and crowned him with glory and honor.
You have given him rule over the works of your hands,
    putting all things under his feet.—℟.

All sheep and oxen,
    yes, and the beasts of the field,
The birds of the air, the fishes of the sea,
    and whatever swims the paths of the seas.—℟. ↓

→ Sequence (Optional), p. 756

ALLELUIA   Ps 118:24

℟. **Alleluia, alleluia.**
This is the day the LORD has made;
let us be glad and rejoice in it.
℟. **Alleluia, alleluia.** ↓

GOSPEL   Lk 24:35-48

Without a sound or a step being heard, "Jesus stood in their midst." Peace, the last word of the prophecy of Zechariah, is the first word which is heard from Jesus lips when he is risen from the dead. He shows them his hands and his feet, and the Apostles are convinced.

℣. The Lord be with you. ℟. **And also with you.**
✝ A reading from the holy Gospel according to Luke.
℟. **Glory to you, Lord.**

The disciples of Jesus recounted what had taken place along the way, and how they had come to recognize him in the breaking of bread.

While they were still speaking about this, he stood in their midst and said to them, "Peace be with you." But they were startled and terrified and thought that they were seeing a ghost. Then he said to them, "Why are you troubled? And why do questions arise in your hearts? Look at my hands and my feet, that it is I myself. Touch me and see, because a ghost does not have flesh and bones as you can see I have." And as he said this, he showed them his hands and his feet. While they were still incredulous for joy and were amazed, he asked them, "Have you anything here to eat?" They gave him a piece of baked fish; he took it and ate it in front of them.

He said to them, "These are my words that I spoke to you while I was still with you, that everything written about me in the law of Moses and in the prophets and psalms must be fulfilled." Then he opened their minds to understand the Scriptures. And he said to them, "Thus it is written that the Christ would suffer and rise from the dead on the third day and that repentance, for the forgiveness of sins, would be preached in his name to all the nations, beginning from Jerusalem. You are witnesses of these things."—The Gospel of the Lord. ℟. **Praise to you, Lord Jesus Christ.** → No. 15, p. 623

PRAYER OVER THE GIFTS

Lord,
accept our gifts
and grant your continuing protection
to all who have received new life in baptism.
We ask this in the name of Jesus the Lord.
℟. **Amen.** → No. 21, p. 626 (Pref. P 21)

When Eucharistic Prayer I is used, the special Easter forms of In union with the whole Church *and* Father, accept this offering *are said.*

COMMUNION ANT. 1 Pt 2:9

You are a people God claims as his own, to praise him who called you out of darkness into his marvelous light, alleluia. ↓

PRAYER AFTER COMMUNION

Lord,
may this celebration of our redemption
help us in this life
and lead us to eternal happiness.
We ask this through Christ our Lord.
℟. **Amen.** ➙ No. 32, p. 660

FRIDAY OF THE OCTAVE OF EASTER

True faith in the name of Jesus and its power to save us is one that firmly believes all that God has revealed, whether written or unwritten. It imposes upon us a life in accordance with that faith. This we do for the love of God who is eternal Truth and cannot be deceived. In a small way, we must suffer "martyrdom" by crucifying the flesh, in the words of St. John Chrysostom, "that you may obtain the martyr's crown."

ENTRANCE ANT. Ps 78:53

The Lord led his people out of slavery. He drowned their enemies in the sea, alleluia. ➙ No. 2, p. 614

OPENING PRAYER

Eternal Father,
you gave us the Easter mystery
as our covenant of reconciliation.
May the new birth we celebrate
show its effects in the way we live.
We ask this . . . for ever and ever. ℟. **Amen.** ↓

FIRST READING Acts 4:1-12

The arrest of Peter and John at the moment when salvation is being announced to Israel begins the tide of opposition. Peter explains that the miracle of curing the lame man was done in the name of Jesus. He reminds the authorities of how they rejected Jesus, the cornerstone. Only in the name of Jesus is salvation possible.

A reading from the Acts of the Apostles

AFTER the crippled man had been cured, while Peter and John were still speaking to the people, the priests, the captain of the temple guard, and the Sadducees confronted them, disturbed that they were teaching the people and proclaiming in Jesus the resurrection of the dead. They laid hands on Peter and John and put them in custody until the next day, since it was already evening. But many of those who heard the word came to believe and the number of men grew to about five thousand.

On the next day, their leaders, elders, and scribes were assembled in Jerusalem, with Annas the high priest, Caiaphas, John, Alexander, and all who were of the high-priestly class. They brought them into their presence and questioned them, "By what power or by what name have you done this?" Then Peter, filled with the Holy Spirit, answered them, "Leaders of the people and elders: If we are being examined today about a good deed done to a cripple, namely, by what means he was saved, then all of you and all the people of Israel should know that it was in the name of Jesus Christ the Nazorean whom you crucified, whom God raised from the dead; in his name this man stands before you healed. He is *the stone rejected by you, the builders, which has become the cornerstone.* There is no salvation through anyone else, nor is there any other name under heaven given to the human race by which we are to be saved."— The word of the Lord. ℟. **Thanks be to God.** ↓

RESPONSORIAL PSALM   Ps 118:1-2 and 4, 22-24, 25-27a

℟. (22) **The stone rejected by the builders has become the cornerstone.**

℟. Or: **Alleluia.**

Give thanks to the LORD, for he is good,
   for his mercy endures forever.

Let the house of Israel say,
  "His mercy endures forever."
Let those who fear the LORD say,
  "His mercy endures forever."—R̲̅.

The stone which the builders rejected
  has become the cornerstone.
By the LORD has this been done;
  it is wonderful in our eyes.
This is the day the LORD has made;
  let us be glad and rejoice in it.—R̲̅.

O LORD, grant salvation!
  O LORD, grant prosperity!
Blessed is he who comes in the name of the LORD;
  we bless you from the house of the LORD.
  The LORD is God, and he has given us light.—R̲̅. ↓

➔ Sequence (Optional), p. 756

ALLELUIA   Ps 118:24

R̲̅. **Alleluia, alleluia.**
This is the day the LORD has made;
let us be glad and rejoice in it.
R̲̅. **Alleluia, alleluia.** ↓

GOSPEL   Jn 21:1-14

Jesus shows himself to his disciples again collectively while they are fishing unsuccessfully. At his word they cast all their nets, and the miracle of fish proves that Jesus is with them. Peter swims to shore to be with Jesus.

V̷. The Lord be with you. R̲̅. **And also with you.**
✦ A reading from the holy Gospel according to John.
R̲̅. **Glory to you, Lord.**

JESUS revealed himself again to his disciples at the Sea of Tiberias. He revealed himself in this way. Together were Simon Peter, Thomas called Didymus, Nathanael from Cana in Galilee, Zebedee's sons, and two others of his disciples. Simon Peter said to them, "I am going fishing." They said to him, "We also will come with you." So they went out and got into the boat, but that night they

caught nothing. When it was already dawn, Jesus was standing on the shore; but the disciples did not realize that it was Jesus. Jesus said to them, "Children, have you caught anything to eat?" They answered him, "No." So he said to them, "Cast the net over the right side of the boat and you will find something." So they cast it, and were not able to pull it in because of the number of fish. So the disciple whom Jesus loved said to Peter, "It is the Lord." When Simon Peter heard that it was the Lord, he tucked in his garment, for he was lightly clad, and jumped into the sea. The other disciples came in the boat, for they were not far from shore, only about a hundred yards, dragging the net with the fish. When they climbed out on shore, they saw a charcoal fire with fish on it and bread. Jesus said to them, "Bring some of the fish you just caught." So Simon Peter went over and dragged the net ashore full of one hundred fifty-three large fish. Even though there were so many, the net was not torn. Jesus said to them, "Come, have breakfast." And none of the disciples dared to ask him, "Who are you?" because they realized it was the Lord. Jesus came over and took the bread and gave it to them, and in like manner the fish. This was now the third time Jesus was revealed to his disciples after being raised from the dead.—The Gospel of the Lord. ℟. **Praise to you, Lord Jesus Christ.**
→ No. 15, p. 623

PRAYER OVER THE GIFTS

Lord,
bring to perfection the spirit of life
we receive from these Easter gifts.
Free us from seeking after the passing things in life
and help us set our hearts on the kingdom of heaven.
Grant this through Christ our Lord.
℟. **Amen.**
→ No. 21, p. 626 (Pref. P 21)

When Eucharistic Prayer I is used, the special Easter forms of In union with the whole Church *and* Father, accept this offering *are said.*

COMMUNION ANT.

See Jn 21:12-13

Jesus said to his disciples: Come and eat. And he took the bread and gave it to them, alleluia. ↓

PRAYER AFTER COMMUNION

Lord,
watch over those you have saved in Christ.
May we who are redeemed by his suffering and death
always rejoice in his resurrection,
for he is Lord for ever and ever.
℟. **Amen.**

→ No. 32, p. 660

SATURDAY OF THE OCTAVE OF EASTER

In applying the doubts of the Apostles to our own frequent doubts, we should have in mind that though the assent of faith is in a sense obscure, it is still most reasonable. When God reveals his truths to us, he provides us with abundant motives for believing and gives us his own authority for them. If we are blessed with the gift of true faith, we can never forget that it is bestowed through the mercy and goodness of God and the merits of Jesus Christ and not because of any merit of our own.

ENTRANCE ANT.

Ps 105:43

The Lord led his people to freedom and they shouted with joy and gladness, alleluia. → No. 2, p. 614

OPENING PRAYER

Father of love,
by the outpouring of your grace
you increase the number of those who believe in you.
Watch over your chosen family.
Give undying life to all
who have been born again in baptism.
Grant this . . . for ever and ever. ℟. **Amen.** ↓

FIRST READING

Acts 4:13-21

The fearlessness of the Apostles astonishes the elders and priests. It was known that they were uneducated men, but their self-assurance is a traditional attribute of the preaching of God's word. No legal fault can be found with the preaching of the Gospel.

A reading from the Acts of the Apostles

OBSERVING the boldness of Peter and John and perceiving them to be uneducated, ordinary men, the leaders, elders, and scribes were amazed, and they recognized them as the companions of Jesus. Then when they saw the man who had been cured standing there with them, they could say nothing in reply. So they ordered them to leave the Sanhedrin, and conferred with one another, saying, "What are we to do with these men? Everyone living in Jerusalem knows that a remarkable sign was done through them, and we cannot deny it. But so that it may not be spread any further among the people, let us give them a stern warning never again to speak to anyone in this name."

So they called them back and ordered them not to speak or teach at all in the name of Jesus. Peter and John, however, said to them in reply, "Whether it is right in the sight of God for us to obey you rather than God, you be the judges. It is impossible for us not to speak about what we have seen and heard." After threatening them further, they released them, finding no way to punish them, on account of the people who were all praising God for what had happened.—The word of the Lord. ℟. **Thanks be to God.** ↓

RESPONSORIAL PSALM Ps 118:1 and 14-15ab, 16-18, 19-21

℟. (21a) **I will give thanks to you, for you have answered me.**

℟. Or: **Alleluia.**

Give thanks to the LORD, for he is good,
    for his mercy endures forever.
My strength and my courage is the LORD,
    and he has been my savior.
The joyful shout of victory
    in the tents of the just.—℟.

"The right hand of the LORD is exalted;
    the right hand of the LORD has struck with power."

I shall not die, but live,
  and declare the works of the LORD.
Though the LORD has indeed chastised me,
  yet he has not delivered me to death.—R̷.

Open to me the gates of justice;
  I will enter them and give thanks to the LORD.
This is the gate of the LORD;
  the just shall enter it.
I will give thanks to you, for you have answered me
  and have been my savior.—R̷. ↓

→ Sequence (Optional), p. 756.

ALLELUIA   Ps 118:24

R̷. **Alleluia, alleluia.**
This is the day the LORD has made;
let us be glad and rejoice in it.
R̷. **Alleluia, alleluia.** ↓

GOSPEL   Mk 16:9-15

Jesus rose from the dead and appeared to Mary Magdalene, but the faithful followers refuse to believe. Jesus rebukes the apostles for disbelieving the evidence of Mary Magdalene and the others. He then tells the apostles to proclaim the Good News to all creation.

℣. The Lord be with you. R̷. **And also with you.**
✛ A reading from the holy Gospel according to Mark.
R̷. **Glory to you, Lord.**

WHEN Jesus had risen, early on the first day of the week, he appeared first to Mary Magdalene, out of whom he had driven seven demons. She went and told his companions who were mourning and weeping. When they heard that he was alive and had been seen by her, they did not believe. After this he appeared in another form to two of them walking along on their way to the country. They returned and told the others; but they did not believe them either.

But later, as the Eleven were at table, he appeared to them and rebuked them for their unbelief and hardness of heart because they had not believed those who saw him after he had been raised. He said to them, "Go into the whole world and proclaim the Gospel to every creature."—The Gospel of the Lord. ℟. **Praise to you, Lord Jesus Christ.**

→ No. 15, p. 623

PRAYER OVER THE GIFTS

Lord,
give us joy by these Easter mysteries.
Let the continuous offering of this sacrifice
by which we are renewed
bring us to eternal happiness.
We ask this in the name of Jesus the Lord.
℟. **Amen.**   → No. 21, p. 626 (Pref. P 21)

When Eucharistic Prayer I is used, the special Easter forms of
In union with the whole Church *and* Father, accept this
offering *are said.*

COMMUNION ANT.   Gal 3:27

All you who have been baptized have been clothed in Christ, alleluia. ↓

PRAYER AFTER COMMUNION

Lord,
look on your people with kindness
and by these Easter mysteries
bring us to the glory of the resurrection.
We ask this in the name of Jesus the Lord.
℟. **Amen.**   → No. 32, p. 660

MONDAY OF THE SECOND WEEK OF EASTER

"Be renewed in the spirit of your minds, and put on the new self" (Eph 4:23-24). To accomplish this we must make a radical and complete change in all our ways. We may have lived what is called a virtuous life, but if we have not had the proper spirit and motive, our actions will not have rendered us pleasing and holy in the sight of God.

ENTRANCE ANT. Rom 6:9

Christ now raised from the dead will never die again; death no longer has power over him, alleluia.

→ No. 2, p. 614

OPENING PRAYER

Almighty and ever-living God,
your Spirit made us your children,
confident to call you Father.
Increase your Spirit of love within us
and bring us to our promised inheritance.
Grant this . . . for ever and ever. ℟. **Amen.** ↓

FIRST READING Acts 4:23-31

When the believers prayed, they were supported by their faith in the omnipotence of God who made heaven and earth. This is one of the original and fundamental truths of revelation from which faith continually derives. They were filled with the Holy Spirit.

A reading from the Acts of the Apostles

AFTER their release Peter and John went back to their own people and reported what the chief priests and elders had told them. And when they heard it, they raised their voices to God with one accord and said, "Sovereign Lord, maker of heaven and earth and the sea and all that is in them, you said by the Holy Spirit through the mouth of our father David, your servant:

*Why did the Gentiles rage
    and the peoples entertain folly?
The kings of the earth took their stand
    and the princes gathered together
    against the Lord and against his anointed.*

"Indeed they gathered in this city against your holy servant Jesus whom you anointed, Herod and Pontius Pilate, together with the Gentiles and the peoples of Israel, to do what your hand and your will had long ago planned to take place. And now, Lord, take note of their threats, and enable your servants to speak your word with all boldness, as you stretch forth your hand to heal, and signs and wonders are done through the name of your holy servant Jesus." As they prayed, the place where they were gathered shook, and they were all filled with the Holy Spirit and continued to speak the word of God with boldness.— The word of the Lord. ℟. **Thanks be to God.** ↓

RESPONSORIAL PSALM Ps 2:1-3, 4-7a, 7b-9

℟. (see 11d) **Blessed are all who take refuge in the Lord.**

℟. Or: **Alleluia.**

Why do the nations rage
    and the peoples utter folly?
The kings of the earth rise up,
    and the princes conspire together
    against the LORD and against his anointed:
"Let us break their fetters
    and cast their bonds from us!"—℟.

He who is throned in heaven laughs;
    the LORD derides them.
Then in anger he speaks to them;
    he terrifies them in his wrath:
"I myself have set up my king
    on Zion, my holy mountain."
I will proclaim the decree of the LORD.—℟.

The LORD said to me, "You are my Son;
    this day I have begotten you.
Ask of me and I will give you
    the nations for an inheritance
    and the ends of the earth for your possession.
You shall rule them with an iron rod;
    you shall shatter them like an earthen dish."—℟. ↓

ALLELUIA Col 3:1

℟. **Alleluia, alleluia.**
If then you were raised with Christ,

seek what is above,
where Christ is seated at the right hand of God.
℟. **Alleluia, alleluia.** ↓

GOSPEL   Jn 3:1-8

In view of the official opposition to Jesus, Nicodemus could only have
come to see him secretly. Nicodemus' profession of faith would be of no
value unless it fixed itself upon our Lord as he really is. The Kingdom of
God can only be experienced through a spiritual rebirth.

℣. The Lord be with you. ℟. **And also with you.**
✣ A reading from the holy Gospel according to John.
℟. **Glory to you, Lord.**

THERE was a Pharisee named Nicodemus, a ruler of
the Jews. He came to Jesus at night and said to him,
"Rabbi, we know that you are a teacher who has come
from God, for no one can do these signs that you are
doing unless God is with him." Jesus answered and said
to him, "Amen, amen, I say to you, unless one is born from
above, he cannot see the Kingdom of God." Nicodemus
said to him, "How can a man once grown old be born
again? Surely he cannot reenter his mother's womb and
be born again, can he?" Jesus answered, "Amen, amen, I
say to you, unless one is born of water and Spirit he cannot enter the Kingdom of God. What is born of flesh is
flesh and what is born of spirit is spirit. Do not be
amazed that I told you, 'You must be born from above.'
The wind blows where it wills, and you can hear the
sound it makes, but you do not know where it comes
from or where it goes; so it is with everyone who is born
of the Spirit."—The Gospel of the Lord. ℟. **Praise to you,
Lord Jesus Christ.**   ➔ No. 15, p. 623

PRAYER OVER THE GIFTS

Lord,
receive these gifts from your Church.
May the great joy you give us
come to perfection in heaven.

Grant this through Christ our Lord.

℟. **Amen.**   → No. 21, p. 626 (Pref. P 22-25)

COMMUNION ANT.   Jn 20:19

Jesus came and stood among his disciples and said to them: Peace be with you, alleluia. ↓

PRAYER AFTER COMMUNION

Lord,
look on your people with kindness
and by these Easter mysteries
bring us to the glory of the resurrection.
We ask this in the name of Jesus the Lord.

℟. **Amen.**   → No. 32, p. 660

TUESDAY OF THE SECOND WEEK OF EASTER

The real proof of our love of God is our hatred of sin and our sincere desire to keep his commandments. If this love strives for perfection, we will love our neighbor, whom we are bound to love in thought, word and deed, from the motive of divine charity. This is a superior love and a higher order of charity that is grounded on faith and the love of God

ENTRANCE ANT.   Rv 19:7, 6

Let us shout out our joy and happiness, and give glory to God, the Lord of all, because he is our King, alleluia.
     → No. 2, p. 614

OPENING PRAYER

All-powerful God,
help us to proclaim the power of the Lord's resurrection.
May we who accept this sign of the love of Christ
come to share the eternal life he reveals,
for he lives and reigns with you and the Holy Spirit,
one God, for ever and ever. ℟. **Amen.** ↓

FIRST READING   Acts 4:32-37

The union in spirit among the disciples was not only a union in faith but also one in brotherly love, and demonstrates that the Christians were truly regenerated and in a state of grace. Barnabas gives his wealth to the Church.

A reading from the Acts of the Apostles

THE community of believers was of one heart and mind, and no one claimed that any of his possessions was his own, but they had everything in common. With great power the Apostles bore witness to the resurrection of the Lord Jesus, and great favor was accorded them all. There was no needy person among them, for those who owned property or houses would sell them, bring the proceeds of the sale, and put them at the feet of the Apostles, and they were distributed to each according to need.

Thus Joseph, also named by the Apostles Barnabas (which is translated "son of encouragement"), a Levite, a Cypriot by birth, sold a piece of property that he owned, then brought the money and put it at the feet of the Apostles.—The word of the Lord. ℞. **Thanks be to God.** ↓

RESPONSORIAL PSALM   Ps 93:1ab, 1cd-2, 5

℞. (1a) **The Lord is king; he is robed in majesty.**

℞. Or: **Alleluia**

The LORD is king, in splendor robed;
    robed is the LORD and girt about with strength.—℞.

And he has made the world firm,
    not to be moved.
Your throne stands firm from of old;
    from everlasting you are, O LORD.—℞.

Your decrees are worthy of trust indeed:
    holiness befits your house,
    O LORD, for length of days.—℞. ↓

ALLELUIA   Jn 3:14-15

℞. **Alleluia, alleluia.**
The Son of Man must be lifted up,
so that everyone who believes in him
may have eternal life.
℞. **Alleluia, alleluia.** ↓

GOSPEL   Jn 3:7b-15

The "heavenly things" of which Christ has spoken cannot be grasped by anyone at will. Nicodemus asks how they can come about, and Jesus alone can answer with authority since he is the only person who has come down from heaven. Those who believe in him will have eternal life.

℣. The Lord be with you. ℞. **And also with you.**
✠ A reading from the holy Gospel according to John.
℞. **Glory to you, Lord.**

JESUS said to Nicodemus: " 'You must be born from above.' The wind blows where it wills, and you can hear the sound it makes, but you do not know where it comes from or where it goes; so it is with everyone who is born of the Spirit." Nicodemus answered and said to him, "How can this happen?" Jesus answered and said to him, "You are the teacher of Israel and you do not understand this? Amen, amen, I say to you, we speak of what we know and we testify to what we have seen, but you people do not accept our testimony. If I tell you about earthly things and you do not believe, how will you believe if I tell you about heavenly things? No one has gone up to heaven except the one who has come down from heaven, the Son of Man. And just as Moses lifted up the serpent in the desert, so must the Son of Man be lifted up, so that everyone who believes in him may have eternal life."—The Gospel of the Lord. ℞. **Praise to you, Lord Jesus Christ.**   → No. 15, p. 623

PRAYER OVER THE GIFTS

Lord,
give us joy by these Easter mysteries.
Let the continuous offering of this sacrifice
by which we are renewed
bring us to eternal happiness.
We ask this in the name of Jesus the Lord.
℞. **Amen.**   → No. 21, p. 626 (Pref. P 22-25)

COMMUNION ANT.   See Lk 24:46, 26

Christ had to suffer and to rise from the dead, and so enter into his glory, alleluia. ↓

PRAYER AFTER COMMUNION

Lord,
may this celebration of our redemption
help us in this life
and lead us to eternal happiness.
We ask this through Christ our Lord.
℟. **Amen.**   → No. 32, p. 660

WEDNESDAY OF THE SECOND WEEK OF EASTER

Even the just suffer tribulations and are surrounded by dangers of every kind. Friends prove false; sickness strikes; death and misfortunes may follow. But if God is with us, the winds of adversity blow in vain. God in his mercy will not permit us to be tried beyond our strength

ENTRANCE ANT.   Ps 18:50; 21:23

I will be a witness to you in the world, O Lord. I will spread the knowledge of your name among my brothers, alleluia.   → No. 2, p. 614

OPENING PRAYER

God of mercy,
you have filled us with the hope of resurrection
by restoring man to his original dignity.
May we who relive this mystery each year
come to share it in perpetual love.
Grant this . . . for ever and ever. ℟. **Amen.** ↓

FIRST READING   Acts 5:17-26

The Apostles are arrested, but they are delivered by the angel who opens the prison doors and brings them forth. The guard and high priests cannot understand the release of the prisoners who are free and teaching the people.

A reading from the Acts of the Apostles

THE high priest rose up and all his companions, that is, the party of the Sadducees, and, filled with jealousy, laid hands upon the Apostles and put them in the public jail. But during the night, the angel of the Lord opened the doors of the prison, led them out, and said, "Go and take your place in the temple area, and tell the people everything about this life." When they heard this, they went to the temple early in the morning and taught. When the high priest and his companions arrived, they convened the Sanhedrin, the full senate of the children of Israel, and sent to the jail to have them brought in. But the court officers who went did not find them in the prison, so they came back and reported, "We found the jail securely locked and the guards stationed outside the doors, but when we opened them, we found no one inside." When the captain of the temple guard and the chief priests heard this report, they were at a loss about them, as to what this would come to. Then someone came in and reported to them, "The men whom you put in prison are in the temple area and are teaching the people." Then the captain and the court officers went and brought them, but without force, because they were afraid of being stoned by the people.— The word of the Lord. ℞. **Thanks be to God.** ↓

RESPONSORIAL PSALM   Ps 34:2-3, 4-5, 6-7, 8-9

℞. (7a) **The Lord hears the cry of the poor.**

℞. Or: **Alleluia**

I will bless the LORD at all times;
   his praise shall be ever in my mouth.
Let my soul glory in the LORD;
   the lowly will hear me and be glad.—℞.

Glorify the LORD with me,
   let us together extol his name.

I sought the LORD, and he answered me
and delivered me from all my fears.—℟.

Look to him that you may be radiant with joy,
and your faces may not blush with shame.
When the poor one called out, the LORD heard,
and from all his distress he saved him.—℟.

The angel of the LORD encamps
around those who fear him, and delivers them.
Taste and see how good the LORD is;
blessed the man who takes refuge in him.—℟. ↓

ALLELUIA   Jn 3:16
℟. **Alleluia, alleluia.**
God so loved the world that he gave his only-begotten
Son,
so that everyone who believes in him might have eternal
life.
℟. **Alleluia, alleluia.** ↓

GOSPEL   Jn 3:16-21
The gift of eternal life made possible in the Redemption is the result of
God's incredible love for the world. Christ has been sent into the world to
bring eternal life. The evildoer is the child of darkness. Christ, the Light,
"acts in truth."

℣. The Lord be with you. ℟. **And also with you.**
✠ A reading from the holy Gospel according to John.
℟. **Glory to you, Lord.**

GOD so loved the world that he gave his only-begotten
Son, so that everyone who believes in him might not
perish but might have eternal life. For God did not send
his Son into the world to condemn the world, but that the
world might be saved through him. Whoever believes in
him will not be condemned, but whoever does not believe
has already been condemned, because he has not
believed in the name of the only-begotten Son of God.
And this is the verdict, that the light came into the world,

but people preferred darkness to light, because their works were evil. For everyone who does wicked things hates the light and does not come toward the light, so that his works might not be exposed. But whoever lives the truth comes to the light, so that his works may be clearly seen as done in God.—The Gospel of the Lord. ℟. **Praise to you, Lord Jesus Christ.**   → No. 15, p. 623

PRAYER OVER THE GIFTS

Lord God,
by this holy exchange of gifts
you share with us your divine life.
Grant that everything we do
may be directed by the knowledge of your truth.
We ask this in the name of Jesus the Lord.
℟. **Amen.**   → No. 21, p. 626 (Pref. P 22-25)

COMMUNION ANT.   See Jn 15:16, 19

The Lord says, I have chosen you from the world to go and bear fruit that will last, alleluia. ↓

PRAYER AFTER COMMUNION

Merciful Father,
may these mysteries give us new purpose
and bring us to a new life in you.
Grant this through Christ our Lord.
℟. **Amen.**   → No. 32, p. 660

THURSDAY OF THE SECOND WEEK OF EASTER

One of the greatest miracles of all time was the marvelous establishment of the Christian religion itself—rapid, universal, and lasting in character. It has been victorious over innumerable persecutions. We are blessed in having been given the faith that guides our eternal salvation. The Divine Word given to us by the successors of Christ and the Apostles still has the same power it had when Christ and the Apostles first preached it, so that our "faith might rest not on human wisdom but on the power of God" (1 Cor 2:5).

ENTRANCE ANT.   See Ps 68:8-9, 20

When you walked at the head of your people, O God, and lived with them on their journey, the earth shook at your presence, and the skies poured forth their rain, alleluia.

→ No. 2, p. 614

OPENING PRAYER

God of mercy,
may the Easter mystery we celebrate
be effective throughout our lives.
Grant this . . . for ever and ever. ℟. **Amen.** ↓

FIRST READING   Acts 5:27-33

The leaders of the people clearly feel powerless in preventing the teaching of Christ by the Apostles. The people are enthusiastic and listen with great attention. The disciples continue to preach the "Good News." It is better to obey God than human beings.

A reading from the Acts of the Apostles

WHEN the court officers had brought the Apostles in and made them stand before the Sanhedrin, the high priest questioned them, "We gave you strict orders, did we not, to stop teaching in that name. Yet you have filled Jerusalem with your teaching and want to bring this man's blood upon us." But Peter and the Apostles said in reply, "We must obey God rather than men. The God of our ancestors raised Jesus, though you had him killed by hanging him on a tree. God exalted him at his right hand as leader and savior to grant Israel repentance and forgiveness of sins. We are witnesses of these things, as is the Holy Spirit whom God has given to those who obey him." When they heard this, they became infuriated and wanted to put them to death.—The word of the Lord. ℟. **Thanks be to God.** ↓

RESPONSORIAL PSALM   Ps 34:2 and 9, 17-18, 19-20

℟. (7a) **The Lord hears the cry of the poor.**

℟. Or: **Alleluia.**

I will bless the LORD at all times;
>his praise shall be ever in my mouth.

Taste and see how good the LORD is;
>blessed the man who takes refuge in him.—℟.

The LORD confronts the evildoers,
>to destroy remembrance of them from the earth.

When the just cry out, the LORD hears them,
>and from all their distress he rescues them.—℟.

The LORD is close to the brokenhearted;
>and those who are crushed in spirit he saves.

Many are the troubles of the just man,
>but out of them all the LORD delivers him.—℟. ↓

ALLELUIA   Jn 20:29

℟. **Alleluia, alleluia.**
You believe in me, Thomas, because you have seen me,
>says the Lord;

blessed are those who have not seen, but still believe!

℟. **Alleluia, alleluia.** ↓

GOSPEL   Jn 3:31-36

Jesus brings eternal life. Whoever receives the testimony of Christ testifies to God's truthfulness, even as God certifies to the truthfulness of Christ. Since Christ is the Messenger of God, the fullness of God's revelation has come only in Christ.

℣. The Lord be with you. ℟. **And also with you.**

✛ A reading from the holy Gospel according to John.

℟. **Glory to you, Lord.**

THE one who comes from above is above all. The one who is of the earth is earthly and speaks of earthly things. But the one who comes from heaven is above all. He testifies to what he has seen and heard, but no one accepts his testimony. Whoever does accept his testimony certifies that God is trustworthy. For the one whom God sent speaks the words of God. He does not ration his gift of the Spirit. The Father loves the Son and has given everything over to him. Whoever believes in the Son has eternal life, but whoever disobeys the Son will not see life, but the wrath of God remains upon him.—The Gospel of the Lord. ℟. **Praise to you, Lord Jesus Christ.**

➜ No. 15, p. 623

PRAYER OVER THE GIFTS

Lord,
accept our prayers and offerings.
Make us worthy of your sacraments of love
by granting us your forgiveness.
We ask this in the name of Jesus the Lord.
℟. **Amen.**   ➜ No. 21, p. 626 (Pref. P 22-25)

COMMUNION ANT.   Mt 28:20

I, the Lord, am with you always, until the end of the world, alleluia. ↓

PRAYER AFTER COMMUNION

Almighty and ever-living Lord,
you restored us to life
by raising Christ from death.
Strengthen us by this Easter sacrament;
may we feel its saving power in our daily life.
We ask this through Christ our Lord.
℟. **Amen.**   ➜ No. 32, p. 660

FRIDAY OF THE SECOND WEEK OF EASTER

Jesus fed about five thousand by the miraculous multiplication of the loaves and fish. This was the foreshadowing of the supreme Banquet of the Most Holy Sacrament—the spiritual food he has given to us for all time for the attainment of our eternal life. Our Savior delights to be with human beings. He invites us to the Divine Banquet to comfort and console us. "Come to me, all you who labor and are burdened, and I will give you rest" (Mt 11:28).

ENTRANCE ANT. Rv 5:9-10

By your blood, O Lord, you have redeemed us from every tribe and tongue, from every nation and people: you have made us into the kingdom of God, alleluia.

➜ No. 2, p. 614

OPENING PRAYER

Father,
in your plan of salvation
your Son Jesus Christ accepted the cross
and freed us from the power of the enemy.
May we come to share the glory of his resurrection,
for he lives and reigns with you and the Holy Spirit,
one God, for ever and ever. ℟. **Amen.** ↓

FIRST READING Acts 5:34-42

Gamaliel cautions the Sanhedrin because he is well aware of their motives in the trial of Jesus. Gamaliel is expedient and prudent, but he also has knowledge of God. The Sanhedrin are eager to "save face" and are willing to punish the Apostles by having them flogged and then released

A reading from the Acts of the Apostles

A PHARISEE in the Sanhedrin named Gamaliel, a teacher of the law, respected by all the people, stood up, ordered the Apostles to be put outside for a short time, and said to the Sanhedrin, "Fellow children of Israel, be careful what you are about to do to these men. Some time ago, Theudas appeared, claiming to be someone important, and about four hundred men joined him, but he was killed, and all those who were loyal to him were disbanded and came to nothing. After him came Judas the Galilean at the time of the census. He also drew people after him, but he too perished and all who were loyal to him were scattered. So now I tell you, have nothing to do with these men, and let them go. For if this endeavor or this activity is of human origin, it will destroy itself. But if it comes from God, you will not be able to destroy them; you may even find yourselves fighting against God." They were persuaded by him. After recalling the Apostles, they had them flogged, ordered them to stop speaking in the name of Jesus, and dismissed them. So they left the presence of the Sanhedrin, rejoicing that they had been found worthy to suffer dishonor for the sake of the name. And all day long, both at the temple and in their homes, they did not stop teaching and proclaiming the Christ, Jesus.—The word of the Lord. ℟. **Thanks be to God.** ↓

RESPONSORIAL PSALM   Ps 27:1, 4, 13-14

℟. (see 4abc) **One thing I seek: to dwell in the house of the Lord.**

℟. Or: **Alleluia.**

The LORD is my light and my salvation;
    whom should I fear?
The LORD is my life's refuge;
    of whom should I be afraid?—℟.

One thing I ask of the LORD;
    this I seek:
To dwell in the house of the LORD
    all the days of my life,
That I may gaze on the loveliness of the LORD
    and contemplate his temple.—℟.

I believe that I shall see the bounty of the LORD
    in the land of the living.
Wait for the LORD with courage;
    be stouthearted, and wait for the LORD.—℟. ↓

ALLELUIA   Mt 4:4b

℟. **Alleluia, alleluia.**
One does not live on bread alone,
but on every word that comes forth from the mouth of
    God.
℟. **Alleluia, alleluia.** ↓

GOSPEL   Jn 6:1-15

John recounts the multiplication of the loaves. The miracle is a Eucharistic symbol. The people correctly see in this miracle an indication that Jesus is the Prophet like Moses, who has come to found the New Israel. Jesus promises his flesh to eat and his blood to drink.

℣. The Lord be with you. ℟. **And also with you.**

✢ A reading from the holy Gospel according to John.

℟. **Glory to you, Lord.**

JESUS went across the Sea of Galilee. A large crowd followed him, because they saw the signs he was performing on the sick. Jesus went up on the mountain, and there he sat down with his disciples. The Jewish feast of Passover was near. When Jesus raised his eyes and saw that a large crowd was coming to him, he said to Philip, "Where can we buy enough food for them to eat?" He said this to test him, because he himself knew what he was going to do. Philip answered him, "Two hundred days' wages worth of food would not be enough for each of them to have a little." One of his disciples, Andrew, the brother of Simon Peter, said to him, "There is a boy here who has five barley loaves and two fish; but what good are these for so many?" Jesus said, "Have the people recline." Now there was a great deal of grass in that place. So the men reclined, about five thousand in number. Then Jesus took the loaves, gave thanks, and distributed them to those who were reclining, and also as much of the fish as they wanted. When they had had their fill, he said to his disciples, "Gather the fragments left over, so that nothing will be wasted." So they collected them, and filled twelve wicker baskets with fragments from the five barley loaves that had been more than they could eat. When the people saw the sign he had done, they said, "This is truly the Prophet, the one who is to come into the world." Since Jesus knew that they were going to come and carry him off to make him king, he withdrew again to the mountain alone.—The Gospel of the Lord. ℟. **Praise to you, Lord Jesus Christ.**

➜ No. 15, p. 623

PRAYER OVER THE GIFTS

Lord,
accept these gifts from your family.
May we hold fast to the life you have given us
and come to the eternal gifts you promise.
We ask this in the name of Jesus the Lord.
℞. **Amen.**   → No. 21, p. 626 (Pref. P 22-25)

COMMUNION ANT.   Rom 4:25

**Christ our Lord was put to death for our sins; and he
rose again to make us worthy of life, alleluia. ↓**

PRAYER AFTER COMMUNION

Lord,
watch over those you have saved in Christ.
May we who are redeemed by his suffering and death
always rejoice in his resurrection,
or he is Lord for ever and ever.
℞. **Amen.**   → No. 32, p. 660

SATURDAY OF THE SECOND WEEK OF EASTER

The Church is a community of persons created in God's image. The human family is a unity—a family of sons and daughters with but one Father. Like the early Christians, we should strive for fraternity so that we become true children of a loving Father. Growth in the love of the Father is accomplished only by the sacrifice of self-love.

ENTRANCE ANT.   1 Pt 2:9

**You are a people God claims as his own, to praise him
who called you out of darkness into his marvelous light,
alleluia.**   → No. 2, p. 614

OPENING PRAYER

God our Father,
look upon us with love.
You redeem us and make us your children in Christ.
Give us true freedom

and bring us to the inheritance you promised.
We ask this . . . for ever and ever. ℟. **Amen.** ↓

FIRST READING Acts 6:1-7

The followers of Jesus are now an international group. The apostles select deacons to carry out the works of religion among the poor and to help instruct the people about the new life.

A reading from the Acts of the Apostles

AS the number of disciples continued to grow, the Hellenists complained against the Hebrews because their widows were being neglected in the daily distribution. So the Twelve called together the community of the disciples and said, "It is not right for us to neglect the word of God to serve at table. Brothers, select from among you seven reputable men, filled with the Spirit and wisdom, whom we shall appoint to this task, whereas we shall devote ourselves to prayer and to the ministry of the word." The proposal was acceptable to the whole community, so they chose Stephen, a man filled with faith and the Holy Spirit, also Philip, Prochorus, Nicanor, Timon, Parmenas, and Nicholas of Antioch, a convert to Judaism. They presented these men to the Apostles who prayed and laid hands on them. The word of God continued to spread, and the number of the disciples in Jerusalem increased greatly; even a large group of priests were becoming obedient to the faith.—The word of the Lord. ℟. **Thanks be to God.** ↓

RESPONSORIAL PSALM Ps 33:1-2, 4-5, 18-19

℟. (22) **Lord, let your mercy be on us, as we place our trust in you.**

℟. Or: **Alleluia.**

Exult, you just, in the LORD;
    praise from the upright is fitting.
Give thanks to the LORD on the harp;
    with the ten-stringed lyre chant his praises.—℟.

Upright is the word of the LORD,
  and all his works are trustworthy.
He loves justice and right;
  of the kindness of the LORD the earth is full.—℟.

See, the eyes of the LORD are upon those who fear him,
  upon those who hope for his kindness,
To deliver them from death
  and preserve them in spite of famine.—℟. ↓

ALLELUIA

℟. **Alleluia, alleluia.**
Christ is risen, who made all things;
he has shown mercy on all people.
℟. **Alleluia, alleluia.** ↓

GOSPEL   Jn 6:16-21

When Jesus walks upon the water and comes to the disciples, they become
frightened. But he assures them there is no need to be afraid.

℣. The Lord be with you. ℟. **And also with you.**
✠ A reading from the holy Gospel according to John.
℟. **Glory to you, Lord.**

W HEN it was evening, the disciples of Jesus went
  down to the sea, embarked in a boat, and went
across the sea to Capernaum. It had already grown dark,
and Jesus had not yet come to them. The sea was stirred
up because a strong wind was blowing. When they had
rowed about three or four miles, they saw Jesus walking
on the sea and coming near the boat, and they began to
be afraid. But he said to them, "It is I. Do not be afraid."
They wanted to take him into the boat, but the boat
immediately arrived at the shore to which they were
heading.—The Gospel of the Lord. ℟. **Praise to you, Lord
Jesus Christ.**   → No. 15, p. 623

PRAYER OVER THE GIFTS

Merciful Lord,
make holy these gifts

and let our spiritual sacrifice
make us an everlasting gift to you.
We ask this in the name of Jesus the Lord.
℟. **Amen.**   → No. 21, p. 626 (Pref. P 22-25)

COMMUNION ANT.   Jn 17:24

**Father, I want the men you have given me to be with me
where I am, so that they may see the glory you have
given me, alleluia. ↓**

PRAYER AFTER COMMUNION

Lord,
may this eucharist,
which we have celebrated in memory of your Son,
help us to grow in love.
We ask this in the name of Jesus the Lord.
℟. **Amen.**   → No. 32, p. 660

MONDAY OF THE THIRD WEEK OF EASTER

The persecution of the early Christians served to spread the rapid growth
of the Church into the far reaches of the then-civilized world. In our day,
we may not expect to suffer martyrdom; still, this is a continual reminder
of the suffering offered by Christ to the Father. Our frustrations and disappointments must be taken up daily by those who would serve with
Christ our Lord.

ENTRANCE ANT.

**The Good Shepherd is risen! He who laid down his life
for his sheep, who died for his flock, he is risen, alleluia.**
                                   → No. 2, p. 614

OPENING PRAYER

God our Father,
your light of truth
guides us to the way of Christ.
May all who follow him
reject what is contrary to the gospel.
We ask this . . . for ever and ever. ℟. **Amen.** ↓

FIRST READING Acts 6:8-15

The deacon St. Stephen is filled with the Holy Spirit through the grace of the risen Christ. He courageously gives witness that Jesus fulfills the promises of the Scriptures. In the Spirit, he faces his trial without fear.

A reading from the Acts of the Apostles

STEPHEN, filled with grace and power, was working great wonders and signs among the people. Certain members of the so-called Synagogue of Freedmen, Cyrenians, and Alexandrians, and people from Cilicia and Asia, came forward and debated with Stephen, but they could not withstand the wisdom and the Spirit with which he spoke. Then they instigated some men to say, "We have heard him speaking blasphemous words against Moses and God." They stirred up the people, the elders, and the scribes, accosted him, seized him, and brought him before the Sanhedrin. They presented false witnesses who testified, "This man never stops saying things against this holy place and the law. For we have heard him claim that this Jesus the Nazorean will destroy this place and change the customs that Moses handed down to us." All those who sat in the Sanhedrin looked intently at him and saw that his face was like the face of an angel.—The word of the Lord. ℟. **Thanks be to God.** ↓

RESPONSORIAL PSALM Ps 119:23-24, 26-27, 29-30

℟. (1ab) **Blessed are they who follow the law of the Lord!**

℟. Or: **Alleluia.**

Though princes meet and talk against me,
    your servant meditates on your statutes.
Yes, your decrees are my delight;
    they are my counselors.—℟.

I declared my ways, and you answered me;
    teach me your statutes.
Make me understand the way of your precepts,
    and I will meditate on your wondrous deeds.—℟.

Remove from me the way of falsehood,
    and favor me with your law.
The way of truth I have chosen;
    I have set your ordinances before me.—℟. ↓

ALLELUIA   Mt 4:4b

℟. **Alleluia, alleluia.**
One does not live on bread alone
but on every word that comes forth from the mouth of
    God.
℟. **Alleluia, alleluia.** ↓

GOSPEL   Jn 6:22-29
The crowd wants to proclaim Jesus their Messiah, but he leaves them and
goes off alone. The people search for him. When found, Jesus tells them of
their concern—that they are looking for signs, wonders, perishable food.

℣. The Lord be with you. ℟. **And also with you.**
✠ A reading from the holy Gospel according to John.
℟. **Glory to you, Lord.**

[A FTER Jesus had fed the five thousand men, his disciples saw him walking on the sea.] The next day,
the crowd that remained across the sea saw that there
had been only one boat there, and that Jesus had not
gone along with his disciples in the boat, but only his disciples had left. Other boats came from Tiberias near the
place where they had eaten the bread when the Lord
gave thanks. When the crowd saw that neither Jesus nor
his disciples were there, they themselves got into boats
and came to Capernaum looking for Jesus. And when
they found him across the sea they said to him, "Rabbi,
when did you get here?" Jesus answered them and said,
"Amen, amen, I say to you, you are looking for me not
because you saw signs but because you ate the loaves
and were filled. Do not work for food that perishes but
for the food that endures for eternal life, which the Son
of Man will give you. For on him the Father, God, has set

his seal." So they said to him, "What can we do to accomplish the works of God?" Jesus answered and said to them, "This is the work of God, that you believe in the one he sent."—The Gospel of the Lord. ℟. **Praise to you, Lord Jesus Christ.** → No. 15, p. 623

PRAYER OVER THE GIFTS

Lord,
accept our prayers and offerings.
Make us worthy of your sacraments of love
by granting us your forgiveness.
We ask this in the name of Jesus the Lord.
℟. **Amen.** → No. 21, p. 626 (Pref. P 22-25)

COMMUNION ANT. Jn 14:27

The Lord says, peace I leave with you, my own peace I give you; not as the world gives, do I give, alleluia. ↓

PRAYER AFTER COMMUNION

Almighty and ever-living Lord,
you restored us to life by raising Christ from death.
Strengthen us by this Easter sacrament.
We ask this through Christ our Lord.
℟. **Amen.** → No. 32, p. 660

TUESDAY OF THE THIRD WEEK OF EASTER

Severe as the accusations were, they did not disturb Stephen because his conscience acquitted him. There is no greater tormentor than a bad conscience and no better defender than a good one, for a good conscience is a continual feast (Prv 15:15). It is the best comforter in all adversity; it goes with us into prison, is with us in distress, in death, and even before the judgment seat of God.

ENTRANCE ANT. Rv 19:5; 12:10

All you who fear God, both the great and the small, give praise to him! For his salvation and strength have come, the power of Christ, alleluia. → No. 2, p. 614

OPENING PRAYER

Father,
you open the kingdom of heaven
to those born again by water and the Spirit.
Increase your gift of love in us.
May all who have been freed from sins in baptism
receive all that you have promised.
We ask this . . . for ever and ever. ℞. **Amen.** ↓

FIRST READING   Acts 7:51—8:1a

Stephen boldly reminds the early Christians of how Jesus suffered and died. Those who listen become angered and begin to stone him. Stephen prays for his persecutors. Saul consents to the execution, but later is to become the great St. Paul.

A reading from the Acts of the Apostles

STEPHEN said to the people, the elders, and the scribes: "You stiff-necked people, uncircumcised in heart and ears, you always oppose the Holy Spirit; you are just like your ancestors. Which of the prophets did your ancestors not persecute? They put to death those who foretold the coming of the righteous one, whose betrayers and murderers you have now become. You received the law as transmitted by angels, but you did not observe it."

When they heard this, they were infuriated, and they ground their teeth at him. But Stephen, filled with the Holy Spirit, looked up intently to heaven and saw the glory of God and Jesus standing at the right hand of God, and Stephen said, "Behold, I see the heavens opened and the Son of Man standing at the right hand of God." But they cried out in a loud voice, covered their ears, and rushed upon him together. They threw him out of the city, and began to stone him. The witnesses laid down their cloaks at the feet of a young man named Saul. As they were stoning Stephen, he called out, "Lord Jesus, receive my spirit." Then he fell to his knees and cried out in a loud voice, "Lord, do not hold this sin against them"; and when he said this, he fell asleep.

Now Saul was consenting to his execution.—The word of the Lord. ℟. **Thanks be to God.** ↓

RESPONSORIAL PSALM

Ps 31:3cd-4, 6 and 7b and 8a, 17 and 21ab

℟. (6a) **Into your hands, O Lord, I commend my spirit.**

℟. Or: **Alleluia.**

Be my rock of refuge,
  a stronghold to give me safety.
You are my rock and my fortress;
  for your name's sake you will lead and guide me.—℟.

Into your hands I commend my spirit;
  you will redeem me, O LORD, O faithful God.
My trust is in the LORD;
  I will rejoice and be glad of your mercy.—℟.

Let your face shine upon your servant;
  save me in your kindness.
You hide them in the shelter of your presence
  from the plottings of men.—℟. ↓

ALLELUIA

Jn 6:35ab

℟. **Alleluia, alleluia.**
I am the bread of life, says the Lord;
whoever comes to me will never hunger.
℟. **Alleluia, alleluia.** ↓

GOSPEL

Jn 6:30-35

Jesus teaches that the manna provided to the Hebrews in the desert during the Exodus was a symbol of the true bread from heaven that he would give. Jesus explains that he is the bread of life. Those who come to him will never hunger or thirst again.

℣. The Lord be with you. ℟. **And also with you.**
✝ A reading from the holy Gospel according to John.
℟. **Glory to you, Lord.**

T HE crowd said to Jesus: "What sign can you do, that we may see and believe in you? What can you do? Our ancestors ate manna in the desert, as it is written:

He gave them bread from heaven to eat."

So Jesus said to them, "Amen, amen, I say to you, it was not Moses who gave the bread from heaven; my Father gives you the true bread from heaven. For the bread of God is that which comes down from heaven and gives life to the world."

So they said to Jesus, "Sir, give us this bread always." Jesus said to them, "I am the bread of life; whoever comes to me will never hunger, and whoever believes in me will never thirst."—The Gospel of the Lord. ℟. **Praise to you, Lord Jesus Christ.**   → No. 15, p. 623

PRAYER OVER THE GIFTS

Lord,
receive these gifts from your Church.
May the great joy you give us
come to perfection in heaven.
Grant this through Christ our Lord.
℟. **Amen.**   → No. 21, p. 626 (Pref. P 22-25)

COMMUNION ANT.   Rom 6:8

Because we have died with Christ, we believe that we shall also come to life with him, alleluia. ↓

PRAYER AFTER COMMUNION

Lord,
look on your people with kindness
and by these Easter mysteries
bring us to the glory of the resurrection.
We ask this in the name of Jesus the Lord.
℟. **Amen.**   → No. 32, p. 660

WEDNESDAY OF THE THIRD WEEK OF EASTER

Regardless of what sins we have committed, nothing is too vicious to be unforgiven if we have true repentance. If we can no longer hear the voice of God calling us to repentance and can no longer ask for mercy and forgiveness, our condition is indeed serious. But we must never despair of God's mercy, for "the Lord is good to all and compassionate toward all his works" (Ps 145:9). When the grace of God touches the sinner's heart, tears of repentance will follow.

ENTRANCE ANT.   Ps 71:8, 23

Fill me with your praise and I will sing your glory; songs of joy will be on my lips, alleluia.   → No. 2, p. 614

OPENING PRAYER

Merciful Lord,
hear the prayers of your people.
May we who have received your gift of faith
share for ever in the new life of Christ.
Grant this . . . for ever and ever. ℞. **Amen.** ↓

FIRST READING   Acts 8:1b-8

The violent death of the deacon Stephen begins a general persecution. The Christian faithful disperse to safer areas and bring the word of God to many more people. God certifies the truth of their words by miracles and signs.

A reading from the Acts of the Apostles

THERE broke out a severe persecution of the Church in Jerusalem, and all were scattered throughout the countryside of Judea and Samaria, except the Apostles. Devout men buried Stephen and made a loud lament over him. Saul, meanwhile, was trying to destroy the Church; entering house after house and dragging out men and women, he handed them over for imprisonment.

Now those who had been scattered went about preaching the word. Thus Philip went down to the city of Samaria and proclaimed the Christ to them. With one accord, the crowds paid attention to what was said by

Philip when they heard it and saw the signs he was doing. For unclean spirits, crying out in a loud voice, came out of many possessed people, and many paralyzed and crippled people were cured. There was great joy in that city.—The word of the Lord. ℟. **Thanks be to God.** ↓

RESPONSORIAL PSALM   Ps 66:1-3a, 4-5, 6-7a

℟. (1) **Let all the earth cry out to God with joy.**

℟. Or: **Alleluia.**

Shout joyfully to God, all the earth,
    sing praise to the glory of his name;
    proclaim his glorious praise.
Say to God, "How tremendous are your deeds!"—℟.

"Let all on earth worship and sing praise to you,
    sing praise to your name!"
Come and see the works of God,
    his tremendous deeds among the children of
        Adam.—℟.

He has changed the sea into dry land;
    through the river they passed on foot;
    therefore let us rejoice in him.
He rules by his might forever.—℟. ↓

ALLELUIA   See Jn 6:40

℟. **Alleluia, alleluia.**
Everyone who believes in the Son has eternal life,
and I shall raise him on the last day, says the Lord.
℟. **Alleluia, alleluia.** ↓

GOSPEL   Jn 6:35-40

St. John continues his presentation of the words of Jesus about the Bread of Life, the Holy Eucharist. Those who eat his Body and drink his Blood will share in the risen life of Christ and will have their spiritual hunger satisfied.

℣. The Lord be with you. ℟. **And also with you.**
✤ A reading from the holy Gospel according to John.
℟. **Glory to you, Lord.**

JESUS said to the crowds, "I am the bread of life; whoever comes to me will never hunger, and whoever believes in me will never thirst. But I told you that although you have seen me, you do not believe. Everything that the Father gives me will come to me, and I will not reject anyone who comes to me, because I came down from heaven not to do my own will but the will of the one who sent me. And this is the will of the one who sent me, that I should not lose anything of what he gave me, but that I should raise it on the last day. For this is the will of my Father, that everyone who sees the Son and believes in him may have eternal life, and I shall raise him on the last day."—The Gospel of the Lord. ℟. **Praise to you, Lord Jesus Christ.** → No. 15, p. 623

PRAYER OVER THE GIFTS

Lord,
restore us by these Easter mysteries.
May the continuing work of our Redeemer
bring us eternal joy.
We ask this through Christ our Lord.
℟. **Amen.** → No. 21, p. 626 (Pref. P 22-25)

COMMUNION ANT.

Christ has risen and shines upon us, whom he has redeemed by his blood, alleluia. ↓

PRAYER AFTER COMMUNION

Lord,
may this celebration of our redemption
help us in this life
and lead us to eternal happiness.
We ask this through Christ our Lord.
℟. **Amen.** → No. 32, p. 660

THURSDAY OF THE THIRD WEEK OF EASTER

We who have the precious treasure of faith have a grave responsibility. It is not enough to be satisfied with mere profit from the message we have received. We must also communicate it to others. Thus we shall assist in the good work of spreading the Gospel of Christ and share in the reward promised by God to those who lead others to grace and virtue.

ENTRANCE ANT. Ex 15:1-2

Let us sing to the Lord, he has covered himself in glory! The Lord is my strength, and I praise him: he is the Savior of my life, alleluia. → No. 2, p. 614

OPENING PRAYER

Father,
in this holy season
we come to know the full depth of your love.
You have freed us from the darkness of error and sin.
Help us to cling to your truths with fidelity.
We ask this . . . for ever and ever. ℟. **Amen.** ↓

FIRST READING Acts 8:26-40

In a mysterious way Philip meets a man anxious to hear the Gospel. The prophecy of the sufferings of the Messiah is applied to Christ. Philip brings the man into the life of the risen Christ by baptizing him, and the man rejoices in God's gift.

A reading from the Acts of the Apostles

THE angel of the Lord spoke to Philip, "Get up and head south on the road that goes down from Jerusalem to Gaza, the desert route." So he got up and set out. Now there was an Ethiopian eunuch, a court official of the Candace, that is, the queen of the Ethiopians, in charge of her entire treasury, who had come to Jerusalem to worship, and was returning home. Seated in his chariot, he was reading the prophet Isaiah. The Spirit said to Philip, "Go and join up with that chariot." Philip ran up and heard him reading Isaiah the prophet and said, "Do you understand what you are reading?" He replied, "How can I, unless someone instructs me?" So he invited Philip to get in and sit with him. This was the Scripture passage he was reading:

> *Like a sheep he was led to the slaughter,*
> > *and as a lamb before its shearer is silent,*
> > > *so he opened not his mouth.*
> *In his humiliation justice was denied him.*
> > *Who will tell of his posterity?*
> > > *For his life is taken from the earth.*

Then the eunuch said to Philip in reply, "I beg you, about whom is the prophet saying this? About himself or about someone else?" Then Philip opened his mouth and, beginning with this Scripture passage, he proclaimed Jesus to him. As they traveled along the road they came to some water, and the eunuch said, "Look, there is water. What is to prevent my being baptized?" Then he ordered the chariot to stop, and Philip and the eunuch both went down into the water, and he baptized him. When they came out of the water, the Spirit of the Lord snatched Philip away, and the eunuch saw him no more, but continued on his way rejoicing. Philip came to Azotus, and went about proclaiming the good news to all the towns until he reached Caesarea.—The word of the Lord. ℟.
Thanks be to God. ↓

RESPONSORIAL PSALM   Ps 66:8-9, 16-17, 20

℟. (1) **Let all the earth cry out to God with joy.**

℟. Or: **Alleluia.**

Bless our God, you peoples,
    loudly sound his praise;
He has given life to our souls,
    and has not let our feet slip.—℟.

Hear now, all you who fear God, while I declare
    what he has done for me.
When I appealed to him in words,
    praise was on the tip of my tongue.—℟.

Blessed be God who refused me not
　　my prayer or his kindness!—℟. ↓

ALLELUIA
Jn 6:51

℟. **Alleluia, alleluia.**
I am the living bread that came down from heaven,
says the Lord;
whoever eats this bread will live forever.
℟. **Alleluia, alleluia.** ↓

GOSPEL
Jn 6:44-51

Jesus teaches that the only way to life is through himself. He reveals the
Father and his will. Through faith and the Eucharist, we will not die, but
we will share in the life of the Father forever.

℣. The Lord be with you. ℟. **And also with you.**
✠ A reading from the holy Gospel according to John.
℟. **Glory to you, Lord.**

JESUS said to the crowds: "No one can come to me
unless the Father who sent me draw him, and I will
raise him on the last day. It is written in the prophets:
　　They shall all be taught by God.
Everyone who listens to my Father and learns from him
comes to me. Not that anyone has seen the Father except
the one who is from God; he has seen the Father. Amen,
amen, I say to you, whoever believes has eternal life. I am
the bread of life. Your ancestors ate the manna in the
desert, but they died; this is the bread that comes down
from heaven so that one may eat it and not die. I am the
living bread that came down from heaven; whoever eats
this bread will live forever; and the bread that I will give
is my Flesh for the life of the world."—The Gospel of the
Lord. ℟. **Praise to you, Lord Jesus Christ.**→ No. 15, p. 623

PRAYER OVER THE GIFTS

Lord God,
by this holy exchange of gifts
you share with us your divine life.

Grant that everything we do
may be directed by the knowledge of your truth.
We ask this in the name of Jesus the Lord.
℟. **Amen.**   ➙ No. 21, p. 626 (Pref. P 22-25)

COMMUNION ANT.   2 Cor 5:15

**Christ died for all, so that living men should not live for
themselves, but for Christ who died and was raised to
life for them, alleluia.** ↓

PRAYER AFTER COMMUNION

Merciful Father,
may these mysteries give us new purpose
and bring us to a new life in you.
Grant this through Christ our Lord.
℟. **Amen.**   ➙ No. 32, p. 660

FRIDAY OF THE THIRD WEEK OF EASTER

St. Paul in his life, as after his death by martyrdom, worked numberless
miracles. He had so deeply impressed the name of Jesus in his heart that it
was almost continually on his lips, "for from the fullness of the heart
the mouth speaks" (Mt 12:34). Would that we loved Jesus as St. Paul
loved him, to be ready to do his will and suffer for him.

ENTRANCE ANT.   Rv 5:12

**The Lamb who was slain is worthy to receive strength
and divinity, wisdom and power and honor, alleluia.**
                                                ➙ No. 2, p. 614

OPENING PRAYER

Father,
by the love of your Spirit,
may we who have experienced
the grace of the Lord's resurrection
rise to the newness of life in joy.
Grant this . . . for ever and ever. ℟. **Amen.** ↓

FIRST READING   Acts 9:1-20

Saul is stricken from his horse on the road to Damascus and has a vision of Jesus as the Lord. Christ himself has been persecuted by Saul's attacks upon the faithful. Saul receives the gift of faith.

A reading from the Acts of the Apostles

SAUL, still breathing murderous threats against the disciples of the Lord, went to the high priest and asked him for letters to the synagogues in Damascus, that, if he should find any men or women who belonged to the Way, he might bring them back to Jerusalem in chains. On his journey, as he was nearing Damascus, a light from the sky suddenly flashed around him. He fell to the ground and heard a voice saying to him, "Saul, Saul, why are you persecuting me?" He said, "Who are you, sir?" The reply came, "I am Jesus, whom you are persecuting. Now get up and go into the city and you will be told what you must do." The men who were traveling with him stood speechless, for they heard the voice but could see no one. Saul got up from the ground, but when he opened his eyes he could see nothing; so they led him by the hand and brought him to Damascus. For three days he was unable to see, and he neither ate nor drank.

There was a disciple in Damascus named Ananias, and the Lord said to him in a vision, "Ananias." He answered, "Here I am, Lord." The Lord said to him, "Get up and go to the street called Straight and ask at the house of Judas for a man from Tarsus named Saul. He is there praying, and in a vision he has seen a man named Ananias come in and lay his hands on him, that he may regain his sight." But Ananias replied, "Lord, I have heard from many sources about this man, what evil things he has done to your holy ones in Jerusalem. And here he has authority from the chief priests to imprison all who call upon your name." But the Lord said to him, "Go, for this man is a chosen instrument of mine to carry my name before Gentiles, kings, and children of Israel, and I will show him what he will have to suffer for my name." So Ananias went and entered the house; laying his hands on him, he said, "Saul, my brother, the Lord has sent me, Jesus who appeared to you on the way by which you came, that you may regain your sight and be filled with the Holy Spirit." Immediately things like scales fell from his eyes and he regained his sight. He got up and was baptized, and when he had eaten, he recovered his strength.

He stayed some days with the disciples in Damascus, and he began at once to proclaim Jesus in the synagogues, that he is the Son of God.—The word of the Lord. ℟. **Thanks be to God.** ↓

RESPONSORIAL PSALM   Ps 117:1bc, 2

℟. (Mk 16:15) **Go out to all the world and tell the Good News.**

℟. Or: **Alleluia.**

Praise the LORD, all you nations;
    glorify him, all you peoples!—℟.

For steadfast is his kindness toward us,
    and the fidelity of the Lord endures forever.—℟. ↓

ALLELUIA   Jn 6:56

℟. **Alleluia, alleluia.**
Whoever eats my Flesh and drinks my Blood,
remains in me and I in him, says the Lord.
℟. **Alleluia, alleluia.** ↓

GOSPEL   Jn 6:52-59

The announcement of his Flesh and Blood as food and drink produces wonderment and objection, but Jesus stresses the real meaning of his words. Whoever eats the Flesh of the Son of Man and drinks his Blood remains in Jesus and will live forever.

℣. The Lord be with you. ℟. **And also with you.**
✣ A reading from the holy Gospel according to John.
℟. **Glory to you, Lord.**

THE Jews quarreled among themselves, saying, "How can this man give us his Flesh to eat?" Jesus said to them, "Amen, amen, I say to you, unless you eat the Flesh of the Son of Man and drink his Blood, you do not have life within you. Whoever eats my Flesh and drinks my Blood has eternal life, and I will raise him on the last day. For my Flesh is true food, and my Blood is true drink. Whoever eats my Flesh and drinks my Blood remains in me and I in him. Just as the living Father sent me and I have life because of the Father, so also the one who feeds on me will have life because of me. This is the bread that came down from heaven. Unlike your ancestors who ate and still died, whoever eats this bread will live forever." These things he said while teaching in the synagogue in Capernaum.—The Gospel of the Lord. ℟. **Praise to you, Lord Jesus Christ.** ➙ No. 15, p. 623

PRAYER OVER THE GIFTS

Merciful Lord,
make holy these gifts
and let our spiritual sacrifice
make us an everlasting gift to you.
We ask this in the name of Jesus the Lord.
℟. **Amen.** ➙ No. 21, p. 626 (Pref. P 22-25)

COMMUNION ANT.

The man who died on the cross has risen from the dead, and has won back our lives from death, alleluia. ↓

PRAYER AFTER COMMUNION

Lord,
may this eucharist,
which we have celebrated in memory of your Son,
help us to grow in love.
We ask this in the name of Jesus the Lord.
℟. **Amen.** ➙ No. 32, p. 660

SATURDAY OF THE THIRD WEEK OF EASTER

Jesus said: "Without me you can do nothing" (Jn 15:5). Our grace must come from God, and it enables us to practice good works. By prayer and a lively faith, we can do anything! We have but to ask with every confidence in God's will and power to help us. This is the reason why all the saints and the spiritual writers insist upon the practice of prayer as an essential means of salvation.

ENTRANCE ANT.   Col 2:12

In baptism we have died with Christ, and we have risen to new life in him, because we believed in the power of God who raised him from the dead, alleluia.

→ No. 2, p. 614

OPENING PRAYER

God our Father,
by the waters of baptism
you give new life to the faithful.
May we not succumb to the influence of evil
but remain true to your gift of life.
We ask this . . . for ever and ever. ℟. **Amen.** ↓

FIRST READING   Acts 9:31-42

During his missionary journeys, St. Peter cures the sick and raises the dead. The signs that Jesus performed are now done by the Apostles, but by prayer to Christ rather than by their own personal power.

A reading from the Acts of the Apostles

THE Church throughout all Judea, Galilee, and Samaria was at peace. She was being built up and walked in the fear of the Lord, and with the consolation of the Holy Spirit she grew in numbers.

As Peter was passing through every region, he went down to the holy ones living in Lydda. There he found a man named Aeneas, who had been confined to bed for eight years, for he was paralyzed. Peter said to him, "Aeneas, Jesus Christ heals you. Get up and make your bed." He got up at once. And all the inhabitants of Lydda and Sharon saw him, and they turned to the Lord.

Now in Joppa there was a disciple named Tabitha (which translated is Dorcas). She was completely occupied with good deeds and almsgiving. Now during those days she fell sick and died, so after washing her, they laid her out in a room upstairs. Since Lydda was near Joppa, the disciples, hearing that Peter was there, sent two men to him with the request, "Please come to us without delay." So Peter got up and went with them. When he arrived, they took him to the room upstairs where all the widows came to him weeping and showing him the tunics and cloaks that Dorcas had made while she was with them. Peter sent them all out and knelt down and prayed. Then he turned to her body and said, "Tabitha, rise up." She opened her eyes, saw Peter, and sat up. He gave her his hand and raised her up, and when he had called the holy ones and the widows, he presented her alive. This became known all over Joppa, and many came to believe in the Lord.—The word of the Lord. ℟. **Thanks be to God.** ↓

RESPONSORIAL PSALM   Ps 116:12-13, 14-15, 16-17

℟. (12) **How shall I make a return to the Lord for all the good he has done for me?**

℟. Or: **Alleluia.**

How shall I make a return to the Lord
  for all the good he has done for me?
The cup of salvation I will take up,
  and I will call upon the name of the Lord.—℟.

My vows to the Lord I will pay
  in the presence of all his people.
Precious in the eyes of the Lord
  is the death of his faithful ones.—℟.

O Lord, I am your servant;
  I am your servant, the son of your handmaid;
  you have loosed my bonds.

To you will I offer sacrifice of thanksgiving,
  and I will call upon the name of the LORD.—℟. ↓

ALLELUIA   See Jn 6:63c, 68c
℟. **Alleluia, alleluia.**
Your words, Lord, are Spirit and life;
you have the words of everlasting life.
℟. **Alleluia, alleluia.** ↓

GOSPEL   Jn 6:60-69
The Bread of Life discourse leads many of Jesus' followers to abandon
him. Jesus explains that his promise is possible because of his coming
passage into the risen life of heaven. Jesus challenges his Apostles to
accept his words because of their faith in him.

℣. The Lord be with you. ℟. **And also with you.**
✤ A reading from the holy Gospel according to John.
℟. **Glory to you, Lord.**

MANY of the disciples of Jesus who were listening
said, "This saying is hard; who can accept it?" Since
Jesus knew that his disciples were murmuring about this,
he said to them, "Does this shock you? What if you were
to see the Son of Man ascending to where he was before?
It is the Spirit that gives life, while the flesh is of no avail.
The words I have spoken to you are Spirit and life. But
there are some of you who do not believe." Jesus knew
from the beginning the ones who would not believe and
the one who would betray him. And he said, "For this reason I have told you that no one can come to me unless it
is granted him by my Father."

  As a result of this, many of his disciples returned to
their former way of life and no longer walked with him.
Jesus then said to the Twelve, "Do you also want to
leave?" Simon Peter answered him, "Master, to whom
shall we go? You have the words of eternal life. We have
come to believe and are convinced that you are the Holy
One of God."—The Gospel of the Lord. ℟. **Praise to you,
Lord Jesus Christ.**   → No. 15, p. 623

PRAYER OVER THE GIFTS

Lord,
accept these gifts from your family.
May we hold fast to the life you have given us
and come to the eternal gifts you promise.
We ask this in the name of Jesus the Lord.
℞. **Amen.**   ➞ No. 21, p. 626 (Pref. P 22-25)

COMMUNION ANT.   Jn 17:20-21

**Father, I pray for them: may they be one in us, so that the
world may believe it was you who sent me, alleluia. ↓**

PRAYER AFTER COMMUNION

Lord,
watch over those you have saved in Christ.
May we who are redeemed by his suffering and death
always rejoice in his resurrection,
for he is Lord for ever and ever.
℞. **Amen.**   ➞ No. 32, p. 660

MONDAY OF THE FOURTH WEEK OF EASTER

More than nineteen centuries have passed since Christ founded the
Church upon the blessed Apostle Peter, and although thousands of heresies have risen, the foundation yet stands unshaken, serene and
unharmed in apostolic dignity. We, like Peter, should assist in spreading
the Gospel of Christ, remembering that "whoever brings back a sinner
from the error of his way will save his soul from death and will cover a
multitude of sins" (Jas 5:20).

ENTRANCE ANT.   Rom 6:9

**Christ now raised from the dead will never die again;
death no longer has power over him, alleluia.**

➞ No. 2, p. 614

OPENING PRAYER

Father,
through the obedience of Jesus,

your servant and your Son,
you raised a fallen world.
Free us from sin
and bring us the joy that lasts for ever.
We ask this . . . for ever and ever. R̸. **Amen.** ↓

FIRST READING　　　　　　　　　　　　　　Acts 11:1-18

By receiving a Roman family into the Church, Peter sets off a major controversy about the obligation of the law of Moses after the coming of Christ. Peter explains the will of Christ, thus opening the Church to the Gentiles, that is, to non-Jews, without imposing the Mosaic law.

A reading from the Acts of the Apostles

THE Apostles and the brothers who were in Judea heard that the Gentiles too had accepted the word of God. So when Peter went up to Jerusalem the circumcised believers confronted him, saying, "You entered the house of uncircumcised people and ate with them." Peter began and explained it to them step by step, saying, "I was at prayer in the city of Joppa when in a trance I had a vision, something resembling a large sheet coming down, lowered from the sky by its four corners, and it came to me. Looking intently into it, I observed and saw the four-legged animals of the earth, the wild beasts, the reptiles, and the birds of the sky. I also heard a voice say to me, 'Get up, Peter. Slaughter and eat.' But I said, 'Certainly not, sir, because nothing profane or unclean has ever entered my mouth.' But a second time a voice from heaven answered, 'What God has made clean, you are not to call profane.' This happened three times, and then everything was drawn up again into the sky. Just then three men appeared at the house where we were, who had been sent to me from Caesarea. The Spirit told me to accompany them without discriminating. These six brothers also went with me, and we entered the man's house. He related to us how he had seen the angel standing in his house, saying, 'Send someone to Joppa and summon Simon, who is called Peter, who will speak words to you by which you and all your household will be saved.' As I began to speak, the Holy Spirit fell upon them as it had upon us at the beginning, and I remembered the word of the Lord, how he had said, 'John baptized with water but you will be baptized with the Holy Spirit.' If then God gave them the same gift he gave to us when we came to believe in the Lord Jesus Christ, who was I to be able to hinder God?" When they heard this, they stopped objecting and glorified God, saying, "God has then granted life-giving repentance to the Gentiles too."—The word of the Lord. ℟. **Thanks be to God.** ↓

RESPONSORIAL PSALM Ps 42:2-3; 43:3, 4

℟. (see 3a) **Athirst is my soul for the living God.**

℟. Or: **Alleluia.**

As the hind longs for the running waters,
    so my soul longs for you, O God.
Athirst is my soul for God, the living God.
    When shall I go and behold the face of God?—℟.

Send forth your light and your fidelity;
    they shall lead me on
And bring me to your holy mountain,
    to your dwelling-place.—℟.

Then will I go in to the altar of God,
    the God of my gladness and joy;
Then will I give you thanks upon the harp,
    O God, my God!—℟. ↓

ALLELUIA Jn 10:14

℟. **Alleluia, alleluia.**
I am the good shepherd, says the Lord;
I know my sheep, and mine know me.
℟. **Alleluia, alleluia.** ↓

GOSPEL   Jn 10:1-10

By using two related comparisons, that of a shepherd leading his flock and that of a sheepfold protecting the sheep, Jesus promises that whoever enters the fold through him will be safe.

℣. The Lord be with you. ℟. **And also with you.**
✛ A reading from the holy Gospel according to John.
℟. **Glory to you, Lord.**

JESUS said: "Amen, amen, I say to you, whoever does not enter a sheepfold through the gate but climbs over elsewhere is a thief and a robber. But whoever enters through the gate is the shepherd of the sheep. The gatekeeper opens it for him, and the sheep hear his voice, as he calls his own sheep by name and leads them out. When he has driven out all his own, he walks ahead of them, and the sheep follow him, because they recognize his voice. But they will not follow a stranger; they will run away from him, because they do not recognize the voice of strangers." Although Jesus used this figure of speech, they did not realize what he was trying to tell them.

So Jesus said again, "Amen, amen, I say to you, I am the gate for the sheep. All who came before me are thieves and robbers, but the sheep did not listen to them. I am the gate. Whoever enters through me will be saved, and will come in and go out and find pasture. A thief comes only to steal and slaughter and destroy; I came so that they might have life and have it more abundantly."— The Gospel of the Lord. ℟. **Praise to you, Lord Jesus Christ.**   → No. 15, p. 623

OR

In year A, when the Gospel above is read on the preceding Sunday, the following text is used.

GOSPEL   Jn 10:11-18

Christ is the Good Shepherd. He loves his sheep and lays down his life for them. The Father loves him because he lays down his life freely. Jesus announces that he has other sheep who will one day be part of the one fold.

℣. The Lord be with you. ℟. **And also with you.**

✤ A reading from the holy Gospel according to John.

℟. **Glory to you, Lord.**

JESUS said: "I am the good shepherd. A good shepherd lays down his life for the sheep. A hired man, who is not a shepherd and whose sheep are not his own, sees a wolf coming and leaves the sheep and runs away, and the wolf catches and scatters them. This is because he works for pay and has no concern for the sheep. I am the good shepherd, and I know mine and mine know me, just as the Father knows me and I know the Father; and I will lay down my life for the sheep. I have other sheep that do not belong to this fold. These also I must lead, and they will hear my voice, and there will be one flock, one shepherd. This is why the Father loves me, because I lay down my life in order to take it up again. No one takes it from me, but I lay it down on my own. I have power to lay it down, and power to take it up again. This command I have received from my Father."—The Gospel of the Lord. ℟. **Praise to you, Lord Jesus Christ.**   → No. 15, p. 623

PRAYER OVER THE GIFTS

Lord,
receive these gifts from your Church.
May the great joy you give us
come to perfection in heaven.
Grant this through Christ our Lord.
℟. **Amen.**   → No. 21, p. 626 (Pref. P 22-25)

COMMUNION ANT.   Jn 20:9

Jesus came and stood among his disciples and said to them: Peace be with you, alleluia. ↓

PRAYER AFTER COMMUNION

Lord,
look on your people with kindness
and by these Easter mysteries

bring us to the glory of the resurrection.
We ask this in the name of Jesus the Lord.
℟. **Amen.**

→ No. 32, p. 660

TUESDAY OF THE FOURTH WEEK OF EASTER

In all places they reached, the disciples established Christian communities. Jesus cast aside Paganism and Judaism and promulgated a new religion and founded this true Church. There is but one flock and one shepherd. The apostolic Church thus founded and continued was watered with the blood of thousands of holy martyrs. We must be ever ready to show our gratitude and to suffer, if required, to foster the faith that is our gift from God.

ENTRANCE ANT.   Rv 19:7, 6

Let us shout out our joy and happiness, and give glory to God, the Lord of all, because he is our King, alleluia.

→ No. 2, p. 614

OPENING PRAYER

Almighty God,
as we celebrate the resurrection,
may we share with each other
the joy the risen Christ has won for us.
We ask this . . . for ever and ever. ℟. **Amen.** ↓

FIRST READING   Acts 11:19-26

The message of Christ reaches Greek areas, especially Cyprus. Barnabas has been commissioned to oversee the development of the Church in Antioch. Barnabas in turn selects Paul to work with him.

A reading from the Acts of the Apostles

THOSE who had been scattered by the persecution that arose because of Stephen went as far as Phoenicia, Cyprus, and Antioch, preaching the word to no one but Jews. There were some Cypriots and Cyrenians among them, however, who came to Antioch and began to speak to the Greeks as well, proclaiming the Lord Jesus. The hand of the Lord was with them and a great number who believed turned to the Lord. The news about them reached the ears of the Church in Jerusalem, and they sent Barnabas to go to Antioch. When he arrived and saw the grace of God, he rejoiced and encouraged them all to remain faithful to the Lord in firmness of heart, for he was a good man, filled with the Holy Spirit and faith. And a large number of people was added to the Lord. Then he went to Tarsus to look for Saul, and when he had found him he brought him to Antioch. For a whole year they met with the Church and taught a large number of people, and it was in Antioch that the disciples were first called Christians.—The word of the Lord. ℟. **Thanks be to God.** ↓

RESPONSORIAL PSALM   Ps 87:1b-3, 4-5, 6-7

℟. (Ps 117:1a) **All you nations, praise the Lord.**

℟. Or: **Alleluia.**

His foundation upon the holy mountains
    the LORD loves:
The gates of Zion,
    more than any dwelling of Jacob.
Glorious things are said of you,
    O city of God!—℟.

I tell of Egypt and Babylon
    among those who know the LORD;
Of Philistia, Tyre, Ethiopia:
    "This man was born there."
And of Zion they shall say:
    "One and all were born in her;
And he who has established her
    is the Most High LORD."—℟.

They shall note, when the peoples are enrolled:
    "This man was born there."
And all shall sing, in their festive dance:
    "My home is within you."—℟. ↓

ALLELUIA
Jn 10:27

℟. **Alleluia, alleluia.**
My sheep hear my voice, says the Lord;
I know them, and they follow me.
℟. **Alleluia, alleluia.** ↓

GOSPEL
Jn 10:22-30

John recorded many statements by Jesus concerning his identity as the
Son of God. In this Gospel passage, Jesus says he and the Father are one,
and he directs our attention to his works—which prove his claim.

℣. The Lord be with you. ℟. **And also with you.**
✛ A reading from the holy Gospel according to John.
℟. **Glory to you, Lord.**

THE feast of the Dedication was taking place in
Jerusalem. It was winter. And Jesus walked about in
the temple area on the Portico of Solomon. So the Jews
gathered around him and said to him, "How long are you
going to keep us in suspense? If you are the Christ, tell us
plainly." Jesus answered them, "I told you and you do not
believe. The works I do in my Father's name testify to me.
But you do not believe, because you are not among my
sheep. My sheep hear my voice; I know them, and they
follow me. I give them eternal life, and they shall never
perish. No one can take them out of my hand. My Father,
who has given them to me, is greater than all, and no one
can take them out of the Father's hand. The Father and I
are one."—The Gospel of the Lord. ℟. **Praise to you, Lord
Jesus Christ.**
→ No. 15, p. 623

PRAYER OVER THE GIFTS

Lord,
give us joy by these Easter mysteries;
let the continuous offering of this sacrifice
by which we are renewed
bring us to eternal happiness.
We ask this in the name of Jesus the Lord.
℟. **Amen.**
→ No. 21, p. 626 (Pref. P 22-25)

COMMUNION ANT.   See Lk 24:46, 26

Christ had to suffer and to rise from the dead, and so enter into his glory, alleluia. ↓

PRAYER AFTER COMMUNION

Lord,
may this celebration of our redemption
help us in this life
and lead us to eternal happiness.
We ask this through Christ our Lord.
℟. **Amen.**   → No. 32, p. 660

WEDNESDAY OF THE FOURTH WEEK OF EASTER

Jesus is the Way by his holy doctrine and example. He is the Truth by the fulfillment of all prophecies, by his mysteries, his promises and warnings. He is the Life because by his death he has obtained for us the life of grace and glory. We have but to listen and obey.

ENTRANCE ANT.   Ps 18: 50; 21:23

I will be a witness to you in the world, O Lord. I will spread the knowledge of your name among my brothers, alleluia.   → No. 2, p. 614

OPENING PRAYER

God our Father,
life of the faithful,
glory of the humble,
happiness of the just,
hear our prayer.
Fill our emptiness
with the blessing of this eucharist,
the foretaste of eternal joy.
We ask this . . . for ever and ever. ℟. **Amen.** ↓

FIRST READING   Acts 12:24—13:5a

As the community of believers spreads in numbers and in area, preachers and ministers are added to the original twelve apostles. Barnabas and Paul are ordained by the will of the Spirit and accepted into the college of the Apostles.

A reading from the Acts of the Apostles

THE word of God continued to spread and grow. After Barnabas and Saul completed their relief mission, they returned to Jerusalem, taking with them John, who is called Mark.

Now there were in the Church at Antioch prophets and teachers: Barnabas, Symeon who was called Niger, Lucius of Cyrene, Manaen who was a close friend of Herod the tetrarch, and Saul. While they were worshiping the Lord and fasting, the Holy Spirit said, "Set apart for me Barnabas and Saul for the work to which I have called them." Then, completing their fasting and prayer, they laid hands on them and sent them off.

So they, sent forth by the Holy Spirit, went down to Seleucia and from there sailed to Cyprus. When they arrived in Salamis, they proclaimed the word of God in the Jewish synagogues.—The word of the Lord. ℟. **Thanks to be God.** ↓

RESPONSORIAL PSALM   Ps 67:2-3, 5, 6 and 8

℟. (4) **O God, let all the nations praise you!**

℟. Or: **Alleluia.**

May God have pity on us and bless us;
    may he let his face shine upon us.
So may your way be known upon earth;
    among all nations, your salvation.—℟.

May the nations be glad and exult
    because you rule the peoples in equity;
    the nations on the earth you guide.—℟.

May the peoples praise you, O God;
    may all the peoples praise you!
May God bless us,
    and may all the ends of the earth fear him!—℟. ↓

ALLELUIA   Jn 8:12
℟. **Alleluia, alleluia.**
I am the light of the world, says the Lord;
whoever follows me will have the light of life.
℟. **Alleluia, alleluia.** ↓

GOSPEL   Jn 12:44-50
Jesus teaches that he is the light of the world. The Jews followed a pillar
of light out of slavery into the promised land. Jesus is the light leading all
human beings to eternal life. Whoever rejects Jesus and does not believe
already has his judge.

℣. The Lord be with you. ℟. **And also with you.**
✚ A reading from the holy Gospel according to John.
℟. **Glory to you, Lord.**

JESUS cried out and said, "Whoever believes in me
believes not only in me but also in the one who sent
me, and whoever sees me sees the one who sent me. I
came into the world as light, so that everyone who
believes in me might not remain in darkness. And if anyone hears my words and does not observe them, I do not
condemn him, for I did not come to condemn the world
but to save the world. Whoever rejects me and does not
accept my words has something to judge him: the word
that I spoke, it will condemn him on the last day, because
I did not speak on my own, but the Father who sent me
commanded me what to say and speak. And I know that
his commandment is eternal life. So what I say, I say as
the Father told me."—The Gospel of the Lord. ℟. **Praise to
you, Lord Jesus Christ.**   ➜ No. 15, p. 623

PRAYER OVER THE GIFTS
Lord God,
by this holy exchange of gifts

you share with us your divine life.
Grant that everything we do
may be directed by the knowledge of your truth.
We ask this in the name of Jesus the Lord.
℟. **Amen.**   ➔ No. 21, p. 626 (Pref. P 22-25)

COMMUNION ANT.   See Jn 15:16, 19

**The Lord says, I have chosen you from the world to go
and bear fruit that will last, alleluia. ↓**

PRAYER AFTER COMMUNION

Merciful Father,
may these mysteries give us new purpose
and bring us to a new life in you.
Grant this through Christ our Lord.
℟. **Amen.**   ➔ No. 32, p. 660

THURSDAY OF THE FOURTH WEEK OF EASTER

Even in the most difficult of circumstances, nothing is impossible for God.
We should ever be aware that God abandons no one, no matter what his
or her sin and weakness, if that person is truly repentant. How anxious
God is to care for all of us. We need but come to him as we do at Mass
today.

ENTRANCE ANT.   See Ps 68:8-9, 20

**When you walked at the head of your people, O God, and
lived with them on their journey, the earth shook at your
presence and the skies poured forth their rain, alleluia.**
                                                ➔ No. 2, p. 614

OPENING PRAYER

Father,
in restoring human nature
you have given us a greater dignity
than we had in the beginning.
Keep us in your love
and continue to sustain those
who have received new life in baptism.
We ask this . . . for ever and ever. ℟. **Amen. ↓**

FIRST READING   Acts 13:13-25

Paul gives a summary of the case for Jesus Christ as the promised Messiah to groups of Jews he meets during his travels. Jesus fulfills the Old Testament. Jewish history has been the preparation for the coming of Christ.

A reading from the Acts of the Apostles

From Paphos, Paul and his companions set sail and arrived at Perga in Pamphylia. But John left them and returned to Jerusalem. They continued on from Perga and reached Antioch in Pisidia. On the sabbath they entered into the synagogue and took their seats. After the reading of the law and the prophets, the synagogue officials sent word to them, "My brothers, if one of you has a word of exhortation for the people, please speak."

So Paul got up, motioned with his hand, and said, "Fellow children of Israel and you others who are God-fearing, listen. The God of this people Israel chose our ancestors and exalted the people during their sojourn in the land of Egypt. With uplifted arm he led them out, and for about forty years he put up with them in the desert. When he had destroyed seven nations in the land of Canaan, he gave them their land as an inheritance at the end of about four hundred and fifty years. After these things he provided judges up to Samuel the prophet. Then they asked for a king. God gave them Saul, son of Kish, a man from the tribe of Benjamin, for forty years. Then he removed him and raised up David as their king; of him he testified, *I have found David, son of Jesse, a man after my own heart; he will carry out my every wish.* From this man's descendants God, according to his promise, has brought to Israel a savior, Jesus. John heralded his coming by proclaiming a baptism of repentance to all the people of Israel; and as John was completing his course, he would say, 'What do you suppose that I am? I am not he. Behold, one is coming after me; I am not worthy to unfasten the sandals of his feet.'"—The word of the Lord. ℟. **Thanks be to God.** ↓

RESPONSORIAL PSALM   Ps 89:2-3, 21-22, 25 and 27

℟. (2) **For ever I will sing the goodness of the Lord.**

℟. Or: **Alleluia.**

The favors of the LORD I will sing forever;
>   through all generations my mouth shall proclaim
>   your faithfulness.
For you have said, "My kindness is established forever";
>   in heaven you have confirmed your faithfulness.—℟.

"I have found David, my servant;
>   with my holy oil I have anointed him,
That my hand may be always with him,
>   and that my arm may make him strong."—℟.

"My faithfulness and my mercy shall be with him,
>   and through my name shall his horn be exalted.
He shall say of me, 'You are my father,
>   my God, the Rock, my savior.' "—℟. ↓

ALLELUIA   See Rv 1:5ab

℟. **Alleluia, alleluia.**
Jesus Christ, you are the faithful witness,
the firstborn of the dead,
you have loved us and freed us from our sins by your
>   Blood.
℟. **Alleluia, alleluia.** ↓

GOSPEL   Jn 13:16-20

The scene is that of the Last Supper. Jesus washed the feet of his
Apostles, thus showing his love and self-sacrifice for them. He expects his
followers to love one another as he has loved all human beings and to
help those who preach his coming.

℣. The Lord be with you. ℟. **And also with you.**

✛ A reading from the holy Gospel according to John.

℟. **Glory to you, Lord.**

WHEN Jesus had washed the disciples' feet, he said to
them: "Amen, amen, I say to you, no slave is greater

than his master nor any messenger greater than the one who sent him. If you understand this, blessed are you if you do it. I am not speaking of all of you. I know those whom I have chosen. But so that the Scripture might be fulfilled, *The one who ate my food has raised his heel against me.* From now on I am telling you before it happens, so that when it happens you may believe that I AM. Amen, amen, I say to you, whoever receives the one I send receives me, and whoever receives me receives the one who sent me."—The Gospel of the Lord. ℟. **Praise to you, Lord Jesus Christ.**   → No. 15, p. 623

PRAYER OVER THE GIFTS

Lord,
accept our prayers and offerings.
Make us worthy of your sacraments of love
by granting us your forgiveness.
We ask this in the name of Jesus the Lord.
℟. **Amen.**   → No. 21, p. 626 (Pref. P 22-25)

COMMUNION ANT.   Mt 28:20

I, the Lord, am with you always, until the end of the world, alleluia. ↓

PRAYER AFTER COMMUNION

Almighty and ever-living Lord,
you restored us to life
by raising Christ from death.
Strengthen us by this Easter sacrament;
may we feel its saving power in our daily life.
We ask this through Christ our Lord.
℟. **Amen.**   → No. 32, p. 660

FRIDAY OF THE FOURTH WEEK OF EASTER

By his Death and Resurrection, Jesus has rendered perfect satisfaction and effected the redemption. But we must not imagine there is no further need for doing penance or for working out our salvation. As the children of Israel, though freed from Pharaoh's bondage, had to fight long and constantly against many enemies in order to gain the Promised Land, so also we, though freed by Christ, must battle against our enemies to the end of our lives to obtain the promised heavenly land.

ENTRANCE ANT.   Rv 5:9-10

By your blood, O Lord, you have redeemed us from every tribe and tongue, from every nation and people: you have made us into the kingdom of God, alleluia.

↦ No. 2, p. 614

OPENING PRAYER

Father of our freedom and salvation,
hear the prayers of those redeemed by your Son's suffering.
Through you may we have life;
with you may we have eternal joy.
We ask this . . . for ever and ever. ℟. **Amen.** ↓

FIRST READING   Acts 13:26-33

Paul tries to convert to Christ the Jews who are settled in the cities of the Roman empire. He goes to their synagogues, and he proclaims that God's plan was fulfilled by the Death and the Resurrection of Jesus Christ, the Savior and the Son of God.

A reading from the Acts of the Apostles

WHEN Paul came to Antioch in Pisidia, he said in the synagogue: "My brothers, children of the family of Abraham, and those others among you who are God-fearing, to us this word of salvation has been sent. The inhabitants of Jerusalem and their leaders failed to recognize him, and by condemning him they fulfilled the oracles of the prophets that are read sabbath after sabbath. For even though they found no grounds for a death sentence, they asked Pilate to have him put to death, and when they had accomplished all that was written about him, they took him down from the tree and placed him in a tomb. But God raised him from the dead, and for many days he appeared to those who had come up with him from Galilee to Jerusalem. These are now his witnesses before the people. We ourselves are proclaiming this good news to you that what God promised our fathers he has brought to fulfillment for us, their children, by raising up Jesus, as it is written in the second psalm, *You are my Son; this day I have begotten you.*"—The word of the Lord. ℟. **Thanks be to God.** ↓

RESPONSORIAL PSALM   Ps 2:6-7, 8-9, 10-11ab

℟. (7bc) **You are my Son; this day I have begotten you.**

℟. Or: **Alleluia.**

"I myself have set up my king
    on Zion, my holy mountain."
I will proclaim the decree of the LORD:
    The LORD said to me, "You are my Son;
    this day I have begotten you."—℟.

"Ask of me and I will give you
    the nations for an inheritance
    and the ends of the earth for your possession.
You shall rule them with an iron rod;
    you shall shatter them like an earthen dish."—℟.

And now, O kings, give heed;
    take warning, you rulers of the earth.
Serve the LORD with fear, and rejoice before him;
    with trembling rejoice.—℟. ↓

ALLELUIA   Jn 14:6

℟. **Alleluia, alleluia.**
I am the way and the truth and the life, says the Lord;
no one comes to the Father except through me.
℟. **Alleluia, alleluia.** ↓

GOSPEL   Jn 14:1-6

Before Easter Sunday, Jesus foretold his Death and Resurrection. He passed over into heaven to prepare a place for his followers, his brothers and sisters. Thus, Jesus is the Way, the Truth, and the Life.

℣. The Lord be with you. ℟. **And also with you.**
✠ A reading from the holy Gospel according to John.
℟. **Glory to you, Lord.**

JESUS said to his disciples: "Do not let your hearts be troubled. You have faith in God; have faith also in me. In my Father's house there are many dwelling places. If there were not, would I have told you that I am going to prepare a place for you? And if I go and prepare a place for you, I will come back again and take you to myself, so that where I am you also may be. Where I am going you know the way." Thomas said to him, "Master, we do not know where you are going; how can we know the way?" Jesus said to him, "I am the way and the truth and the life. No one comes to the Father except through me."—The Gospel of the Lord. ℟. **Praise to you, Lord Jesus Christ.**

→ No. 15, p. 623

PRAYER OVER THE GIFTS

Lord,
accept these gifts from your family.
May we hold fast to the life you have given us
and come to the eternal gifts you promise.
We ask this in the name of Jesus the Lord.
℟. **Amen.**   → No. 21, p. 626 (Pref. P 22-25)

COMMUNION ANT.   Rom 4:25

Christ our Lord was put to death for our sins; and he rose again to make us worthy of life, alleluia. ↓

PRAYER AFTER COMMUNION

Lord,
watch over those you have saved in Christ.
May we who are redeemed by his suffering and death
always rejoice in his resurrection,
for he is Lord for ever and ever.
℟. **Amen.**   → No. 32, p. 660

SATURDAY OF THE FOURTH WEEK OF EASTER

May God grant us a lively and firm faith, one secure in the knowledge that through our Lord Jesus Christ we have all the knowledge that is necessary to make us pleasing to God. Let us often pray with the Apostles, "Lord, increase our faith."

ENTRANCE ANT.   1 Pt 2:9

You are a people God claims as his own, to praise him who called you out of darkness into his marvelous light, alleluia.   → No. 2, p. 614

OPENING PRAYER

Father,
may we whom you renew in baptism
bear witness to our faith by the way we live.
By the suffering, death, and resurrection of your Son
may we come to eternal joy.
We ask this . . . for ever and ever. ℟. **Amen.** ↓

FIRST READING   Acts 13:44-52

Since the teaching of the Apostles is not always well received and Paul is rejected by some of the Jews of Antioch, he turns his work to the Gentiles who welcome the new faith. Rejected by his own people, Paul then continues his journeys.

A reading from the Acts of the Apostles

ON the following sabbath almost the whole city gathered to hear the word of the Lord. When the Jews saw the crowds, they were filled with jealousy and with violent abuse contradicted what Paul said. Both Paul and Barnabas spoke out boldly and said, "It was necessary that the word of God be spoken to you first, but since you reject it and condemn yourselves as unworthy of eternal life, we now turn to the Gentiles. For so the Lord has commanded us, *I have made you a light to the Gentiles, that you may be an instrument of salvation to the ends of the earth.*"

The Gentiles were delighted when they heard this and glorified the word of the Lord. All who were destined for eternal life came to believe, and the word of the Lord continued to spread through the whole region. The Jews, however, incited the women of prominence who were worshipers and the leading men of the city, stirred up a persecution against Paul and Barnabas, and expelled them from their territory. So they shook the dust from their feet in protest against them and went to Iconium. The disciples were filled with joy and the Holy Spirit.—The word of the Lord. ℟. **Thanks be to God.** ↓

RESPONSORIAL PSALM Ps 98:1, 2-3ab, 3cd-4

℟. (3cd) **All the ends of the earth have seen the saving power of God.**

℟. Or: **Alleluia.**

Sing to the LORD a new song,
  for he has done wondrous deeds;
His right hand has won victory for him,
  his holy arm.—℟.

The LORD has made his salvation known:
  in the sight of the nations he has revealed his justice.
He has remembered his kindness and his faithfulness
  toward the house of Israel.—℟.

All the ends of the earth have seen
  the salvation by our God.
Sing joyfully to the LORD, all you lands;
  break into song; sing praise.—℟. ↓

ALLELUIA Jn 8:31b-32

℟. **Alleluia, alleluia.**
If you remain in my word, you will truly be my disciples,
and you will know the truth, says the Lord.
℟. **Alleluia, alleluia.** ↓

GOSPEL   Jn 14:7-14

Jesus teaches the disciples that he and the Father are fully and equally the one God, and yet that Father and Son are distinct from one another. Philip asks to see the Father. Jesus promises that anything asked from the Father in his name will be granted.

℣. The Lord be with you. ℟. **And also with you.**
✢ A reading from the holy Gospel according to John.
℟. **Glory to you, Lord.**

JESUS said to his disciples: "If you know me, then you will also know my Father. From now on you do know him and have seen him." Philip said to Jesus, "Master, show us the Father, and that will be enough for us." Jesus said to him, "Have I been with you for so long a time and you still do not know me, Philip? Whoever has seen me has seen the Father. How can you say, 'Show us the Father'? Do you not believe that I am in the Father and the Father is in me? The words that I speak to you I do not speak on my own. The Father who dwells in me is doing his works. Believe me that I am in the Father and the Father is in me, or else, believe because of the works themselves. Amen, amen, I say to you, whoever believes in me will do the works that I do, and will do greater ones than these, because I am going to the Father. And whatever you ask in my name, I will do, so that the Father may be glorified in the Son. If you ask anything of me in my name, I will do it."—The Gospel of the Lord. ℟. **Praise to you, Lord Jesus Christ.**   → No. 15, p. 623

PRAYER OVER THE GIFTS

Merciful Lord,
make holy these gifts
and let our spiritual sacrifice
make us an everlasting gift to you.
We ask this in the name of Jesus the Lord.
℟. **Amen.**   → No. 21, p. 626 (Pref. P 22-25)

COMMUNION ANT. Jn 17:24

Father, I want the men you have given me to be with me where I am, so that they may see the glory you have given me, alleluia. ↓

PRAYER AFTER COMMUNION

Lord,
may this eucharist,
which we have celebrated in memory of your Son,
help us to grow in love.
We ask this in the name of Jesus the Lord.
℟. **Amen.** → No. 32, p. 660

MONDAY OF THE FIFTH WEEK OF EASTER

All Christians should learn to be obedient to the commandments of God and of the Church. God has united life or death, blessing or rejection, with obedience or disobedience to his commandments, and the Bible shows that obedience pleases God more than sacrifices. If our obedience is meant with all our heart, we show the Father our greatest love and gratitude and eagerness always to be pleasing to him.

ENTRANCE ANT.

The Good Shepherd is risen! He who laid down his life for his sheep, who died for his flock, he is risen, alleluia.
→ No. 2, p. 614

OPENING PRAYER

Father,
help us to seek the values
that will bring us eternal joy in this changing world.
In our desire for what you promise
make us one in mind and heart.
Grant this . . . for ever and ever. ℟. **Amen.** ↓

FIRST READING Acts 14:5-18

Paul cures a crippled man in Lystra, a stronghold of pagan belief. The darkness of paganism shows itself in the reaction. Paul patiently tries to explain the truth.

A reading from the Acts of the Apostles

THERE was an attempt in Iconium by both the Gentiles and the Jews, together with their leaders, to attack and stone Paul and Barnabas. They realized it, and fled to the Lycaonian cities of Lystra and Derbe and to the surrounding countryside, where they continued to proclaim the Good News.

At Lystra there was a crippled man, lame from birth, who had never walked. He listened to Paul speaking, who looked intently at him, saw that he had the faith to be healed, and called out in a loud voice, "Stand up straight on your feet." He jumped up and began to walk about. When the crowds saw what Paul had done, they cried out in Lycaonian, "The gods have come down to us in human form." They called Barnabas "Zeus" and Paul "Hermes," because he was the chief speaker. And the priest of Zeus, whose temple was at the entrance to the city, brought oxen and garlands to the gates, for he together with the people intended to offer sacrifice.

The Apostles Barnabas and Paul tore their garments when they heard this and rushed out into the crowd, shouting, "Men, why are you doing this? We are of the same nature as you, human beings. We proclaim to you good news that you should turn from these idols to the living God, *who made heaven and earth and sea and all that is in them.* In past generations he allowed all Gentiles to go their own ways; yet, in bestowing his goodness, he did not leave himself without witness, for he gave you rains from heaven and fruitful seasons, and filled you with nourishment and gladness for your hearts." Even with these words, they scarcely restrained the crowds from offering sacrifice to them.—The word of the Lord. ℟. **Thanks be to God.** ↓

RESPONSORIAL PSALM   Ps 115:1-2, 3-4, 15-16

℟. (1ab) **Not to us, O Lord, but to your name give the glory.**

℟. Or: **Alleluia.**

Not to us, O LORD, not to us
　　but to your name give glory
　　because of your mercy, because of your truth.
Why should the pagans say,
　　"Where is their God?"—℟.

Our God is in heaven;
　　whatever he wills, he does.
Their idols are silver and gold,
　　the handiwork of men.—℟.

May you be blessed by the LORD,
　　who made heaven and earth.
Heaven is the heaven of the LORD,
　　but the earth he has given to the children of
　　men.—℟. ↓

ALLELUIA　　　　　　　　　　　　　　　　　Jn 14:26

℟. **Alleluia, alleluia.**
The Holy Spirit will teach you everything
and remind you of all I told you.
℟. **Alleluia, alleluia.** ↓

GOSPEL　　　　　　　　　　　　　　　　　　Jn 14:21-26

Jesus teaches that an understanding of God depends upon goodwill and
the gift of faith. He sent the Holy Spirit into the world that human beings
may understand and follow God's word. The Holy Spirit will emphasize the
message Jesus preached.

℣. The Lord be with you. ℟. **And also with you.**
✝ A reading from the holy Gospel according to John.
℟. **Glory to you, Lord.**

JESUS said to his disciples: "Whoever has my commandments and observes them is the one who loves
me. Whoever loves me will be loved by my Father, and I
will love him and reveal myself to him." Judas, not the
Iscariot, said to him, "Master, then what happened that
you will reveal yourself to us and not to the world?" Jesus

answered and said to him, "Whoever loves me will keep my word, and my Father will love him, and we will come to him and make our dwelling with him. Whoever does not love me does not keep my words; yet the word you hear is not mine but that of the Father who sent me.

"I have told you this while I am with you. The Advocate, the Holy Spirit whom the Father will send in my name—he will teach you everything and remind you of all that I told you."—The Gospel of the Lord. ℞. **Praise to you, Lord Jesus Christ.**   → No. 15, p. 623

PRAYER OVER THE GIFTS

Lord,
accept our prayers and offerings.
Make us worthy of your sacraments of love
by granting us your forgiveness.
We ask this in the name of Jesus the Lord.
℞. **Amen.**   → No. 21, p. 626 (Pref. P 22-25)

COMMUNION ANT.   Jn 14:27

The Lord says, peace I leave with you, my own peace I give you; not as the world gives, do I give, alleluia. ↓

PRAYER AFTER COMMUNION

Almighty and ever-living Lord,
you restored us to life
by raising Christ from death.
Strengthen us by this Easter sacrament.
We ask this through Christ our Lord.
℞. **Amen.**   → No. 32, p. 660

TUESDAY OF THE FIFTH WEEK OF EASTER

By faith, true Christian faith, we are imbued with love and gratitude to God. As believers of his word, we are his witnesses. The further we advance in the ways of faith, the deeper becomes that faith. If we but approach the Gospels as the Word of God inspired by the Holy Spirit, we will find in them eternal life.

ENTRANCE ANT.

Rv 19:5; 12:10

All you who fear God, both the great and the small, give praise to him! For his salvation and strength have come, the power of Christ, alleluia. → No. 2, p. 614

OPENING PRAYER

Father,
you restored your people to eternal life
by raising Christ your Son from death.
Make our faith strong and our hope sure.
May we never doubt that you will fulfill
the promises you have made.
Grant this . . . for ever and ever. ℟. **Amen.** ↓

FIRST READING

Acts 14:19-28

Paul and his companion Barnabas complete their first great missionary journey, bringing the faith to many far-distant towns, but also encountering much opposition. They willingly accept the trials, as Christ did, to build the Kingdom.

A reading from the Acts of the Apostles

IN those days, some Jews from Antioch and Iconium arrived and won over the crowds. They stoned Paul and dragged him out of the city, supposing that he was dead. But when the disciples gathered around him, he got up and entered the city. On the following day he left with Barnabas for Derbe.

After they had proclaimed the good news to that city and made a considerable number of disciples, they returned to Lystra and to Iconium and to Antioch. They strengthened the spirits of the disciples and exhorted them to persevere in the faith, saying, "It is necessary for us to undergo many hardships to enter the Kingdom of God." They appointed presbyters for them in each Church and, with prayer and fasting, commended them to the Lord in whom they had put their faith. Then they traveled through Pisidia and reached Pamphylia. After proclaiming the word at Perga they went down to Attalia. From there they sailed to Antioch, where they had been commended to the grace of God for the work they had now accomplished. And when they arrived, they called the Church together and reported what God had done with them and how he had opened the door of faith to the Gentiles. Then they spent no little time with the disciples.—The word of the Lord. ℟. **Thanks be to God.** ↓

RESPONSORIAL PSALM   Ps 145:10-11, 12-13ab, 21

℟. (see 12) **Your friends make known, O Lord, the glorious splendor of your kingdom.**

℟. Or: **Alleluia.**

Let all your works give you thanks, O LORD,
   and let your faithful ones bless you.
Let them discourse of the glory of your kingdom
   and speak of your might.—℟.

Making known to men your might
   and the glorious splendor of your kingdom.
Your kingdom is a kingdom for all ages,
   and your dominion endures through all generations.—℟.

May my mouth speak the praise of the LORD,
   and may all flesh bless his holy name forever and ever.—℟. ↓

ALLELUIA   See Lk 24:46, 26

℟. **Alleluia, alleluia.**
Christ had to suffer and to rise from the dead,
and so enter into his glory.
℟. **Alleluia, alleluia.** ↓

GOSPEL   Jn 14:27-31a

Jesus speaks of peace only a few hours before his sufferings and death. His victory over death meant that peace is possible, but only if his followers take up the cross of self-sacrifice as Jesus himself did.

℣. The Lord be with you. ℟. **And also with you.**
✠ A reading from the holy Gospel according to John.
℟. **Glory to you, Lord.**

JESUS said to his disciples: "Peace I leave with you; my peace I give to you. Not as the world gives do I give it to you. Do not let your hearts be troubled or afraid. You heard me tell you, 'I am going away and I will come back to you.' If you loved me, you would rejoice that I am going to the Father; for the Father is greater than I. And now I have told you this before it happens, so that when it happens you may believe. I will no longer speak much with you, for the ruler of the world is coming. He has no power over me, but the world must know that I love the Father and that I do just as the Father has commanded me."— The Gospel of the Lord. ℟. **Praise to you, Lord Jesus Christ.** ➥ No. 15, p. 623

PRAYER OVER THE GIFTS

Lord,
receive these gifts from your Church.
May the great joy you give us
come to perfection in heaven.
Grant this through Christ our Lord.
℟. **Amen.** ➥ No. 21, p. 626 (Pref. P 22-25)

COMMUNION ANT. Rom 6:8

Because we have died with Christ, we believe that we shall also come to life with him, alleluia. ↓

PRAYER AFTER COMMUNION

Lord,
look on your people with kindness
and by these Easter mysteries
bring us to the glory of the resurrection.
We ask this in the name of Jesus the Lord.
℟. **Amen.** ➥ No. 32, p. 660

WEDNESDAY OF THE FIFTH WEEK OF EASTER

We are incapable of judging the degree of success or failure of the work of anyone in the sight of God. Often the most apparently successful results are the saddest failures, just as the most shining piety, which obtains for a person the respect of neighbors, is not always the most solid or the most perfect in the sight of God. "Unless the Lord build the house, they labor in vain who build it" (Ps 127:1).

ENTRANCE ANT.   Ps 71:8, 23

Fill me with your praise and I will sing your glory; songs of joy will be on my lips, alleluia.   ➙ No. 2, p. 614

OPENING PRAYER

Father of all holiness,
guide our hearts to you.
Keep in the light of your truth
all those you have freed from the darkness of unbelief.
We ask this . . . for ever and ever. ℟. **Amen.** ↓

FIRST READING   Acts 15:1-6

Agitation to impose the Mosaic Law upon Christians was a repeated difficulty faced by the Apostles. Paul holds that the gift of faith given to so many pagans is a sign that the Law of Moses cannot be made an obligation under the New Covenant in Christ.

A reading from the Acts of the Apostles

SOME who had come down from Judea were instructing the brothers, "Unless you are circumcised according to the Mosaic practice, you cannot be saved." Because there arose no little dissension and debate by Paul and Barnabas with them, it was decided that Paul, Barnabas, and some of the others should go up to Jerusalem to the Apostles and presbyters about this question. They were sent on their journey by the Church, and passed through Phoenicia and Samaria telling of the conversion of the Gentiles, and brought great joy to all the brethren. When they arrived in Jerusalem, they were welcomed by the

Church, as well as by the Apostles and the presbyters, and they reported what God had done with them. But some from the party of the Pharisees who had become believers stood up and said, "It is necessary to circumcise them and direct them to observe the Mosaic law."

The Apostles and the presbyters met together to see about this matter.—The word of the Lord. ℟. **Thanks be to God.** ↓

RESPONSORIAL PSALM   Ps 122:1-2, 3-4ab, 4cd-5

℟. (see 1) **Let us go rejoicing to the house of the Lord.**

℟. Or: **Alleluia.**

I rejoiced because they said to me,
    "We will go up to the house of the Lord."
And now we have set foot
    within your gates, O Jerusalem.—℟.

Jerusalem, built as a city
    with compact unity.
To it the tribes go up,
    the tribes of the Lord.—℟.

According to the decree for Israel,
    to give thanks to the name of the Lord.
In it are set up judgment seats,
    seats for the house of David.—℟. ↓

ALLELUIA   Jn 15:4a, 5b

℟. **Alleluia, alleluia.**
Remain in me, as I remain in you, says the Lord;
whoever remains in me will bear much fruit.
℟. **Alleluia, alleluia.** ↓

GOSPEL   Jn 15:1-8

The symbol of the vine and the branches is similar to Paul's image of the Mystical Body. True life and adoptive relationship to the Father depend on union with Christ. Jesus teaches that only the branch that is connected to the vine will bear fruit.

℣. The Lord be with you. ℟. **And also with you.**
✤ A reading from the holy Gospel according to John.
℟. **Glory to you, Lord.**

JESUS said to his disciples:"I am the true vine, and my
Father is the vine grower. He takes away every branch
in me that does not bear fruit, and everyone that does he
prunes so that it bears more fruit.You are already pruned
because of the word that I spoke to you. Remain in me, as
I remain in you. Just as a branch cannot bear fruit on its
own unless it remains on the vine, so neither can you
unless you remain in me. I am the vine, you are the
branches. Whoever remains in me and I in him will bear
much fruit, because without me you can do nothing.
Anyone who does not remain in me will be thrown out
like a branch and wither; people will gather them and
throw them into a fire and they will be burned. If you
remain in me and my words remain in you, ask for whatever you want and it will be done for you. By this is my
Father glorified, that you bear much fruit and become my
disciples."—The Gospel of the Lord. ℟. **Praise to you,
Lord Jesus Christ.**   ➔ No. 15, p. 623

PRAYER OVER THE GIFTS

Lord,
restore us by these Easter mysteries.
May the continuing work of our Redeemer
bring us eternal joy.
We ask this through Christ our Lord.
℟. **Amen.**   ➔ No. 21, p. 626 (Pref. P 22-25)

COMMUNION ANT.

**Christ has risen and shines upon us, whom he has
redeemed by his blood, alleluia.** ↓

PRAYER AFTER COMMUNION

Lord,
may this celebration of our redemption

help us in this life
and lead us to eternal happiness.
We ask this through Christ our Lord.
℟. **Amen.**   ⟶ No. 32, p. 660

THURSDAY OF THE FIFTH WEEK OF EASTER

We should always remember that we are all one under the Good Shepherd.
We cannot bar anyone from our circle of friends. All human beings are our
brothers and sisters, and our belief in the Father is proof that we are
related to every human being. Faith imposes upon us this underlying unity
and is the foundation of lasting peace. Christ our Lord showed charity and
love in the salvation of all human beings.

ENTRANCE ANT.   Ex 15:1-2

**Let us sing to the Lord, he has covered himself in glory!
The Lord is my strength, and I praise him: he is the
Savior of my life, alleluia.**   ⟶ No. 2, p. 614

OPENING PRAYER

Father,
in your love you have brought us
from evil to good and from misery to happiness.
Through your blessings
give the courage of perseverance
to those you have called and justified by faith.
Grant this . . . for ever and ever. ℟. **Amen.** ↓

FIRST READING   Acts 15:7-21

The Apostles, as the divinely appointed guides and teachers of the
Church, decide that the Old Testament regulations were a preparation for
Christ and had passed away. James urges the faithful to be considerate
of the feelings of their Jewish brethren.

A reading from the Acts of the Apostles

AFTER much debate had taken place, Peter got up and
said to the Apostles and the presbyters, "My brothers, you are well aware that from early days God made
his choice among you that through my mouth the

Gentiles would hear the word of the Gospel and believe. And God, who knows the heart, bore witness by granting them the Holy Spirit just as he did us. He made no distinction between us and them, for by faith he purified their hearts. Why, then, are you now putting God to the test by placing on the shoulders of the disciples a yoke that neither our ancestors nor we have been able to bear? On the contrary, we believe that we are saved through the grace of the Lord Jesus, in the same way as they." The whole assembly fell silent, and they listened while Paul and Barnabas described the signs and wonders God had worked among the Gentiles through them.

After they had fallen silent, James responded, "My brothers, listen to me. Symeon has described how God first concerned himself with acquiring from among the Gentiles a people for his name. The words of the prophets agree with this, as is written:

After this I shall return
    and rebuild the fallen hut of David;
from its ruins I shall rebuild it
    and raise it up again,
so that the rest of humanity may seek out the Lord,
    even all the Gentiles on whom my name is
    invoked.
Thus says the Lord who accomplishes these things,
    known from of old.

It is my judgment, therefore, that we ought to stop troubling the Gentiles who turn to God, but tell them by letter to avoid pollution from idols, unlawful marriage, the meat of strangled animals, and blood. For Moses, for generations now, has had those who proclaim him in every town, as he has been read in the synagogues every sabbath."—The word of the Lord. ℟. **Thanks be to God.** ↓

RESPONSORIAL PSALM   Ps 96:1-2a, 2b-3, 10

℟. (3) **Proclaim God's marvelous deeds to all the nations.**

℟. Or: **Alleluia.**

Sing to the LORD a new song;
    sing to the LORD, all you lands.
Sing to the LORD; bless his name.—℟.

Announce his salvation, day after day.
Tell his glory among the nations;
    among all peoples, his wondrous deeds.—℟.

Say among the nations: The LORD is king.
He has made the world firm, not to be moved;
    he governs the peoples with equity.—℟. ↓

ALLELUIA Jn 10:27

℟. **Alleluia, alleluia.**
My sheep hear my voice, says the Lord;
I know them, and they follow me.
℟. **Alleluia, alleluia.** ↓

GOSPEL Jn 15:9-11

Jesus gives the spirit of obedience to the law. The letter kills, but the spirit gives life. The Christian obeys because of his love, and so he shares in the love and in the life of God.

℣. The Lord be with you. ℟. **And also with you.**
✖ A reading from the holy Gospel according to John.
℟. **Glory to you, Lord.**

JESUS said to his disciples: "As the Father loves me, so I also love you. Remain in my love. If you keep my commandments, you will remain in my love, just as I have kept my Father's commandments and remain in his love.

"I have told you this so that my joy might be in you and your joy might be complete."—The Gospel of the Lord. ℟.
Praise to you, Lord Jesus Christ. → No. 15, p. 623

PRAYER OVER THE GIFTS

Lord God,
by this holy exchange of gifts
you share with us your divine life.

Grant that everything we do
may be directed by the knowledge of your truth.
We ask this in the name of Jesus the Lord.
℟. **Amen.** → No. 21, p. 626 (Pref. P 22-25)

COMMUNION ANT. 2 Cor 5:15

Christ died for all, so that living men should not live for themselves, but for Christ who died and was raised to life for them, alleluia. ↓

PRAYER AFTER COMMUNION

Merciful Father,
may these mysteries give us new purpose
and bring us to a new life in you.
Grant this through Christ our Lord.
℟. **Amen.** → No. 32, p. 660

FRIDAY OF THE FIFTH WEEK OF EASTER

It is our duty to bear witness to the divinity of Christ and his teaching by the example of our own Christ-like virtues by which all human beings should recognize us as faithful followers of our Divine Master. The virtue of charity, or love, is then the true test of the Christian. It is a most essential characteristic. If we are without it, we are not of Christ.

ENTRANCE ANT. Rv 5:12

The Lamb who was slain is worthy to receive strength and divinity, wisdom and power and honor, alleluia.
→ No. 2, p. 614

OPENING PRAYER

Lord,
by this Easter mystery
prepare us for eternal life.
May our celebration of Christ's death and resurrection

guide us to salvation.
We ask this . . . for ever and ever. ℟. **Amen.** ↓

FIRST READING Acts 15:22-31

The decision by the Apostles about the Mosaic law clearly shows the authoritative position that they held in the young Church. They state that their decisions are guaranteed by the Holy Spirit. Their letter is read by the faithful teachers of the Gospel to those embracing the faith.

A reading from the Acts of the Apostles

THE Apostles and presbyters, in agreement with the whole Church, decided to choose representatives and to send them to Antioch with Paul and Barnabas. The ones chosen were Judas, who was called Barsabbas, and Silas, leaders among the brothers. This is the letter delivered by them: "The Apostles and the presbyters, your brothers, to the brothers in Antioch, Syria, and Cilicia of Gentile origin: greetings. Since we have heard that some of our number who went out without any mandate from us have upset you with their teachings and disturbed your peace of mind, we have with one accord decided to choose representatives and to send them to you along with our beloved Barnabas and Paul, who have dedicated their lives to the name of our Lord Jesus Christ. So we are sending Judas and Silas who will also convey this same message by word of mouth: 'It is the decision of the Holy Spirit and of us not to place on you any burden beyond these necessities, namely, to abstain from meat sacrificed to idols, from blood, from meats of strangled animals, and from unlawful marriage. If you keep free of these, you will be doing what is right. Farewell.' "

And so they were sent on their journey. Upon their arrival in Antioch they called the assembly together and delivered the letter. When the people read it, they were delighted with the exhortation.—The word of the Lord. ℟. **Thanks be to God.** ↓

RESPONSORIAL PSALM   Ps 57:8-9, 10 and 12

℟. (10a) **I will give you thanks among the peoples, O Lord.**

℟. Or: **Alleluia.**

My heart is steadfast, O God; my heart is steadfast;
  I will sing and chant praise.
Awake, O my soul; awake, lyre and harp!
  I will wake the dawn.—℟.

I will give thanks to you among the peoples, O LORD,
  I will chant your praise among the nations.
For your mercy towers to the heavens,
  and your faithfulness to the skies.
Be exalted above the heavens, O God;
  above all the earth be your glory!—℟. ↓

ALLELUIA   Jn 15:15b

℟. **Alleluia, alleluia.**
I call you my friends, says the Lord,
for I have made known to you all that the Father has told
  me.
℟. **Alleluia, alleluia.** ↓

GOSPEL   Jn 15:12-17

The theme of the law is continued with the announcement of the supreme
law of Christ, the law of love. Jesus gives the perfect example of how people
are to love one another, that is, with complete unselfishness and without
expecting thanks from others.

℣. The Lord be with you. ℟. **And also with you.**

✠ A reading from the holy Gospel according to John.

℟. **Glory to you, Lord.**

JESUS said to his disciples: "This is my commandment:
love one another as I love you. No one has greater love
than this, to lay down one's life for one's friends. You are
my friends if you do what I command you. I no longer call
you slaves, because a slave does not know what his master is doing. I have called you friends, because I have told
you everything I have heard from my Father. It was not
you who chose me, but I who chose you and appointed

you to go and bear fruit that will remain, so that whatever you ask the Father in my name he may give you. This I command you: love one another."—The Gospel of the Lord. ℟. **Praise to you, Lord Jesus Christ.**➙ No. 15, p. 623

PRAYER OVER THE GIFTS

Merciful Lord,
make holy these gifts
and let our spiritual sacrifice
make us an everlasting gift to you.
We ask this in the name of Jesus the Lord.
℟. **Amen.**　　　　　　　➙ No. 21, p. 626 (Pref. P 22-25)

COMMUNION ANT.

The man who died on the cross has risen from the dead, and has won back our lives from death, alleluia. ↓

PRAYER AFTER COMMUNION

Lord,
may this eucharist,
which we have celebrated in memory of your Son,
help us to grow in love.
We ask this in the name of Jesus the Lord.
℟. **Amen.**　　　　　　　　　　　➙ No. 32, p. 660

SATURDAY OF THE FIFTH WEEK OF EASTER

True Christians have no easy task to live and be pleasing to God. The unjust persecute them on all sides, but if they are abused, they must pray for those who abuse them. As Christians we must not be ashamed because the world despises us and opposes our virtuous life. This was the lot of the Apostles, and even of Christ himself. They entered heaven only through suffering trials and many persecutions.

ENTRANCE ANT.　　　　　　　　　　　　　　　　Col 2:12

In baptism we have died with Christ, and we have risen to new life in him, because we believed in the power of God who raised him from the dead, alleluia.

➙ No. 2, p. 614

OPENING PRAYER

Loving Father,
through our rebirth in baptism
you give us your life and promise immortality.
By your unceasing care,
guide our steps toward the life of glory.
Grant this . . . for ever and ever. ℟. **Amen.** ↓

FIRST READING   Acts 16:1-10

After his first journey, Paul goes forth again on a longer and more difficult missionary tour. As he teaches, many plead for the faith. God directs
the work of his chosen missionary.

A reading from the Acts of the Apostles

PAUL reached also Derbe and Lystra where there was
a disciple named Timothy, the son of a Jewish woman
who was a believer, but his father was a Greek. The
brothers in Lystra and Iconium spoke highly of him, and
Paul wanted him to come along with him. On account of
the Jews of that region, Paul had him circumcised, for
they all knew that his father was a Greek. As they traveled from city to city, they handed on to the people for
observance the decisions reached by the Apostles and
presbyters in Jerusalem. Day after day the churches
grew stronger in faith and increased in number.

They traveled through the Phrygian and Galatian territory because they had been prevented by the Holy
Spirit from preaching the message in the province of
Asia. When they came to Mysia, they tried to go on into
Bithynia, but the Spirit of Jesus did not allow them, so
they crossed through Mysia and came down to Troas.
During the night Paul had a vision. A Macedonian stood
before him and implored him with these words, "Come
over to Macedonia and help us." When he had seen the
vision, we sought passage to Macedonia at once, concluding that God had called us to proclaim the Good

News to them.—The word of the Lord. ℟. **Thanks be to God.** ↓

RESPONSORIAL PSALM   Ps 100:1b-2, 3, 5

℟. (2a) **Let all the earth cry out to God with joy.**

℟. Or: **Alleluia.**

Sing joyfully to the LORD, all you lands;
    serve the LORD with gladness;
    come before him with joyful song.—℟.

Know that the LORD is God;
    he made us, his we are;
    his people, the flock he tends.—℟.

The LORD is good:
    his kindness endures forever,
    and his faithfulness, to all generations.—℟. ↓

ALLELUIA   Col 3:1

℟. **Alleluia, alleluia.**
If then you were raised with Christ,
seek what is above,
where Christ is seated at the right hand of God.
℟. **Alleluia, alleluia.** ↓

GOSPEL   Jn 15:18-21

Jesus warns that Christians cannot be fully at home in the world. The "world" means society insofar as it is contrary to the plan of God and ignores God. Followers of Christ are to have different values in life, based on their hope in the coming of Christ.

℣. The Lord be with you. ℟. **And also with you.**
✚ A reading from the holy Gospel according to John.
℟. **Glory to you, Lord.**

JESUS said to his disciples:"If the world hates you, realize that it hated me first. If you belonged to the world, the world would love its own; but because you do not belong to the world, and I have chosen you out of the

world, the world hates you. Remember the word I spoke to you, 'No slave is greater than his master.' If they persecuted me, they will also persecute you. If they kept my word, they will also keep yours. And they will do all these things to you on account of my name, because they do not know the one who sent me."—The Gospel of the Lord. ℟.
Praise to you, Lord Jesus Christ.   → No. 15, p. 623

PRAYER OVER THE GIFTS

Lord,
accept these gifts from your family.
May we hold fast to the life you have given us
and come to the eternal gifts you promise.
We ask this in the name of Jesus the Lord.
℟. **Amen.**   → No. 21, p. 626 (Pref. P 22-25)

COMMUNION ANT.   Jn 17:20-21

Father, I pray for them: may they be one in us, so that the world may believe it was you who sent me, alleluia. ↓

PRAYER AFTER COMMUNION

Lord,
watch over those you have saved in Christ.
May we who are redeemed by his suffering and death
always rejoice in his resurrection,
for he is Lord for ever and ever.
℟. **Amen.**   → No. 32, p. 660

MONDAY OF THE SIXTH WEEK OF EASTER

We are born of God by the saving waters of baptism by which the merits of Christ are applied to our souls. Our faith overcomes the world. By this faith we truly believe that jesus is the Son of God who saved us not merely by the waters of baptism but by his own blood. What a deep debt of gratitude we owe to our Creator!

ENTRANCE ANT. Rom 6:9

Christ now raised from the dead will never die again; death no longer has power over him, alleluia.

→ No. 2, p. 614

OPENING PRAYER

God of mercy,
may our celebration of your Son's resurrection
help us to experience its effect in our lives.
We ask this . . . for ever and ever. ℟. **Amen.** ↓

FIRST READING Acts 16:11-15

The writer of Acts, St. Luke, now says "we," indicating that he accompanied St. Paul. The Kingdom of God is spread not by the Spirit alone, but by men and women who cooperate with the Spirit and who work with one another.

A reading from the Acts of the Apostles

WE set sail from Troas, making a straight run for Samothrace, and on the next day to Neapolis, and from there to Philippi, a leading city in that district of Macedonia and a Roman colony. We spent some time in that city. On the sabbath we went outside the city gate along the river where we thought there would be a place of prayer. We sat and spoke with the women who had gathered there. One of them, a woman named Lydia, a dealer in purple cloth, from the city of Thyatira, a worshiper of God, listened, and the Lord opened her heart to pay attention to what Paul was saying. After she and her household had been baptized, she offered us an invitation, "If you consider me a believer in the Lord, come and stay at my home," and she prevailed on us.—The word of the Lord. ℟. **Thanks be to God.** ↓

RESPONSORIAL PSALM Ps 149:1b-2, 3-4, 5-6a and 9b

℟. (see 4a) **The Lord takes delight in his people.**

℟. Or: **Alleluia.**

Sing to the L<small>ORD</small> a new song
  of praise in the assembly of the faithful.
Let Israel be glad in their maker,
  let the children of Zion rejoice in their king.—R̷.

Let them praise his name in the festive dance,
  let them sing praise to him with timbrel and harp.
For the L<small>ORD</small> loves his people,
  and he adorns the lowly with victory.—R̷.

Let the faithful exult in glory;
  let them sing for joy upon their couches.
Let the high praises of God be in their throats.
  This is the glory of all his faithful. Alleluia.—R̷. ↓

ALLELUIA   Jn 15:26b, 27a
R̷. **Alleluia, alleluia.**
The Spirit of truth will testify to me, says the Lord,
and you also will testify.
R̷. **Alleluia, alleluia.** ↓

GOSPEL   Jn 15:26—16:4
The message of Christ is the means to eternal salvation. Nevertheless, he
entrusts the future of his work to chosen men. Therefore, Christ promises
to give the Spirit, who will preserve his words accurately throughout the
centuries. The Holy Spirit will bear witness to the Good News.

℣. The Lord be with you. R̷. **And also with you.**
✠ A reading from the holy Gospel according to John.
R̷. **Glory to you, Lord.**

J<small>ESUS</small> said to his disciples: "When the Advocate comes
  whom I will send you from the Father, the Spirit of
truth who proceeds from the Father, he will testify to me.
And you also testify, because you have been with me
from the beginning.

  "I have told you this so that you may not fall away.
They will expel you from the synagogues; in fact, the
hour is coming when everyone who kills you will think
he is offering worship to God. They will do this because
they have not known either the Father or me. I have told

you this so that when their hour comes you may remember that I told you."—The Gospel of the Lord. ℟. **Praise to you, Lord Jesus Christ.**   → No. 15, p. 623

PRAYER OVER THE GIFTS

Lord,
receive these gifts from your Church.
May the great joy you give us
come to perfection in heaven.
Grant this through Christ our Lord.
℟. **Amen.**   → No. 21, p. 626 (Pref. P 22-25)

COMMUNION ANT.   Jn 20:19

Jesus came and stood among his disciples and said to them: Peace be with you, alleluia. ↓

PRAYER AFTER COMMUNION

Lord,
look on your people with kindness
and by these Easter mysteries
bring us to the glory of the resurrection.
We ask this in the name of Jesus the Lord.
℟. **Amen.**   → No. 32, p. 660

TUESDAY OF THE SIXTH WEEK OF EASTER

Though the assent of faith is in a sense obscure, it is still most reasonable, for when God reveals his truths to us, he provides us with abundant motives for believing and gives us his own authority for them. Nothing increases the rich flow of his grace and love to us so much as our humble thankfulness for and acknowledgment of his mercy and kindness.

ENTRANCE ANT.   Rv 19:7, 6

Let us shout out our joy and happiness, and give glory to God, the Lord of all, because he is our King, alleluia.
   → No. 2, p. 614

OPENING PRAYER

God our Father,
may we look forward with hope to our resurrection,

for you have made us your sons and daughters,
and restored the joy of our youth.
We ask this . . . for ever and ever. ℟. **Amen.** ↓

FIRST READING   Acts 16:22-34

St. Paul is arrested, flogged, and jailed. Freed by the Lord, his faith and
his firm commitment stimulate faith in his jailer. Today, strong faith and
patient forgiveness will be a sign that we have indeed found God, and will
draw others to him.

A reading from the Acts of the Apostles

THE crowd in Philippi joined in the attack on Paul and
Silas, and the magistrates had them stripped and
ordered them to be beaten with rods. After inflicting
many blows on them, they threw them into prison and
instructed the jailer to guard them securely. When he
received these instructions, he put them in the innermost
cell and secured their feet to a stake.

About midnight, while Paul and Silas were praying
and singing hymns to God as the prisoners listened, there
was suddenly such a severe earthquake that the foundations of the jail shook; all the doors flew open, and the
chains of all were pulled loose. When the jailer woke up
and saw the prison doors wide open, he drew his sword
and was about to kill himself, thinking that the prisoners
had escaped. But Paul shouted out in a loud voice, "Do no
harm to yourself; we are all here." He asked for a light
and rushed in and, trembling with fear, he fell down
before Paul and Silas. Then he brought them out and
said, "Sirs, what must I do to be saved?" And they said,
"Believe in the Lord Jesus and you and your household
will be saved." So they spoke the word of the Lord to him
and to everyone in his house. He took them in at that
hour of the night and bathed their wounds; then he and
all his family were baptized at once. He brought them up
into his house and provided a meal and with his household rejoiced at having come to faith in God.—The word
of the Lord. ℟. **Thanks be to God.** ↓

RESPONSORIAL PSALM   Ps 138:1-2ab, 2cde-3, 7c-8

℟. (7a) **Your right hand saves me, O Lord.**

℟. Or: **Alleluia.**

I will give thanks to you, O LORD, with all my heart,
    for you have heard the words of my mouth;
    in the presence of the angels I will sing your praise;
I will worship at your holy temple,
    and give thanks to your name.—℟.

Because of your kindness and your truth,
    you have made great above all things
    your name and your promise.
When I called, you answered me;
    you built up strength within me.—℟.

Your right hand saves me.
The LORD will complete what he has done for me;
    your kindness, O LORD, endures forever;
    forsake not the work of your hands.—℟. ↓

ALLELUIA   See Jn 16:7, 13

℟. **Alleluia, alleluia.**
I will send to you the Spirit of truth, says the Lord;
he will guide you to all truth.
℟. **Alleluia, alleluia.** ↓

GOSPEL   Jn 16:5-11

Jesus says that he has to go in order for the Holy Spirit to come. Jesus
promises the coming of the Spirit by passing over into the presence of the
Father as the perfect gift.

℣. The Lord be with you. ℟. **And also with you.**
✠ A reading from the holy Gospel according to John.
℟. **Glory to you, Lord.**

JESUS said to his disciples: "Now I am going to the one
who sent me, and not one of you asks me, 'Where are
you going?' But because I told you this, grief has filled
your hearts. But I tell you the truth, it is better for you that

I go. For if I do not go, the Advocate will not come to you. But if I go, I will send him to you. And when he comes he will convict the world in regard to sin and righteousness and condemnation: sin, because they do not believe in me; righteousness, because I am going to the Father and you will no longer see me; condemnation, because the ruler of this world has been condemned."—The Gospel of the Lord. ℟. **Praise to you, Lord Jesus Christ.**

➜ No. 15, p. 623

PRAYER OVER THE GIFTS

Lord,
give us joy by these Easter mysteries;
let the continuous offering of this sacrifice
by which we are renewed
bring us to eternal happiness.
We ask this in the name of Jesus the Lord.
℟. **Amen.** ➜ No. 21, p. 626 (Pref. P 22-25)

COMMUNION ANT. See Lk 24:46, 26

Christ had to suffer and to rise from the dead, and so enter into his glory, alleluia. ↓

PRAYER AFTER COMMUNION

Lord,
may this celebration of our redemption
help us in this life and lead us to eternal happiness.
We ask this through Christ our Lord.
℟. **Amen.** ➜ No. 32, p. 660

WEDNESDAY OF THE SIXTH WEEK OF EASTER

Our greatest source of encouragement, strength, and consolation, as we labor in the Lord's vineyard, is absolute certainty that we are guided in our efforts by the Holy Spirit. He is our divine and infallible guide to God in the teachings and precepts of the Church. This is the sublime promise of our Savior. The Holy Spirit will always guide us in the right direction.

ENTRANCE ANT.   Ps 18:50; 22:23

I will be a witness to you in the world, O Lord. I will spread the knowledge of your name among my brothers, alleluia.   → No. 2, p. 614

OPENING PRAYER

Lord,
as we celebrate your Son's resurrection,
so may we rejoice with all the saints
when he returns in glory,
who lives and reigns with you and the Holy Spirit,
one God, for ever and ever. ℟. **Amen.** ↓

FIRST READING   Acts 17:15, 22—18:1

When he reaches Athens, the center of Greek culture, Paul presents the message of Christ in a way adapted to his hearers' habits of thought. In God all live and move and are. Some are baptized and others ask to hear Paul again.

A reading from the Acts of the Apostles

AFTER Paul's escorts had taken him to Athens, they came away with instructions for Silas and Timothy to join him as soon as possible.

Then Paul stood up at the Areopagus and said:

"You Athenians, I see that in every respect you are very religious. For as I walked around looking carefully at your shrines, I even discovered an altar inscribed, 'To an Unknown God.' What therefore you unknowingly worship, I proclaim to you. The God who made the world and all that is in it, the Lord of heaven and earth, does not dwell in sanctuaries made by human hands, nor is he served by human hands because he needs anything. Rather it is he who gives to everyone life and breath and everything. He made from one the whole human race to dwell on the entire surface of the earth, and he fixed the ordered seasons and the boundaries of their regions, so that people might seek God, even perhaps grope for him and find him, though indeed he is not far from any one of

us. For 'In him we live and move and have our being,' as
even some of your poets have said, 'For we too are his offspring.' Since therefore we are the offspring of God, we
ought not to think that the divinity is like an image fashioned from gold, silver, or stone by human art and imagi-
nation. God has overlooked the times of ignorance, but
now he demands that all people everywhere repent
because he has established a day on which he will 'judge
the world with justice' through a man he has appointed,
and he has provided confirmation for all by raising him
from the dead." When they heard about resurrection of
the dead, some began to scoff, but others said, "We should
like to hear you on this some other time." And so Paul left
them. But some did join him, and became believers.
Among them were Dionysius, a member of the Court of
the Areopagus, a woman named Damaris, and others
with them.

After this he left Athens and went to Corinth.—The
word of the Lord. ℟. **Thanks be to God.** ↓

RESPONSORIAL PSALM   Ps 148:1-2, 11-12, 13, 14

℟. **Heaven and earth are full of your glory.**

℟. Or: **Alleluia.**

Praise the LORD from the heavens;
    praise him in the heights.
Praise him, all you his angels;
    praise him, all you his hosts.—℟.

Let the kings of the earth and all peoples,
    the princes and all the judges of the earth,
Young men too, and maidens,
    old men and boys.—℟.

Praise the name of the LORD,
    for his name alone is exalted;
His majesty is above earth and heaven.—℟.

He has lifted up the horn of his people;
Be this his praise from all his faithful ones,

from the children of Israel, the people close to him.
Alleluia.—℟. ↓

ALLELUIA
Jn 14:16

℟. **Alleluia, alleluia.**
I will ask the Father
and he will give you another Advocate
to be with you always.
℟. **Alleluia, alleluia.** ↓

GOSPEL
Jn 16:12-15

Jesus promises that when the Spirit comes, he will guide people to all
truth. He will teach of things to come.

℣. The Lord be with you. ℟. **And also with you.**
✝ A reading from the holy Gospel according to John.
℟. **Glory to you, Lord.**

JESUS said to his disciples: "I have much more to tell
you, but you cannot bear it now. But when he comes,
the Spirit of truth, he will guide you to all truth. He will
not speak on his own, but he will speak what he hears,
and will declare to you the things that are coming. He
will glorify me, because he will take from what is mine
and declare it to you. Everything that the Father has is
mine; for this reason I told you that he will take from
what is mine and declare it to you."—The Gospel of the
Lord. ℟. **Praise to you, Lord Jesus Christ.**

→ No. 15, p. 623

PRAYER OVER THE GIFTS
Lord God,
by this holy exchange of gifts
you share with us your divine life.
Grant that everything we do
may be directed by the knowledge of your truth.
We ask this in the name of Jesus the Lord.
℟. **Amen.**   → No. 21, p. 626 (Pref. P 22-25)

COMMUNION ANT. See Jn 15:16, 19

The Lord says, I have chosen you from the world to go and bear fruit that will last, alleluia. ↓

PRAYER AFTER COMMUNION

Merciful Father,
may these mysteries give us new purpose
and bring us to a new life in you.
Grant this through Christ our Lord.
℟. **Amen.** → No. 32, p. 660

THURSDAY OF THE SIXTH WEEK OF EASTER

This Mass is celebrated in dioceses where the celebration of the Ascension is transferred to the Seventh Sunday of Easter. (See Sunday Missal, pp. 454, 838, 1208.)

Jesus came into the world to give us an example of how we are to live. In him we live and move and are. Just as the Apostles of the early Church taught about Jesus in both word and act, we, as the Apostles of today born into the faith, should share our belief with others. Let us be conscious today of our every thought, word, and deed that they may reflect the life of Jesus.

ENTRANCE ANT. See Ps 68:8-9, 20

When you walked at the head of your people, O God, and lived with them on their journey, the earth shook at your presence, and the skies poured forth their rain, alleluia.
→ No. 2, p. 614

OPENING PRAYER

Father,
may we always give you thanks
for raising Christ our Lord to glory,
because we are his people
and share the salvation he won,
for he lives and reigns with you and the Holy Spirit,
one God, for ever and ever. ℟. **Amen.** ↓

FIRST READING   Acts 18:1-8

Paul relies upon the help of zealous lay people in making Christ known.
He preaches that Jesus was the Messiah. When he is persecuted by his
compatriots, he turns to the Gentiles.

A reading from the Acts of the Apostles

PAUL left Athens and went to Corinth. There he met a
Jew named Aquila, a native of Pontus, who had
recently come from Italy with his wife Priscilla because
Claudius had ordered all the Jews to leave Rome. He
went to visit them and, because he practiced the same
trade, stayed with them and worked, for they were tent-
makers by trade. Every sabbath, he entered into discus-
sions in the synagogue, attempting to convince both Jews
and Greeks.

When Silas and Timothy came down from Macedonia, Paul began to occupy himself totally with preaching the word, testifying to the Jews that the Christ was
Jesus. When they opposed him and reviled him, he shook
out his garments and said to them, "Your blood be on
your heads! I am clear of responsibility. From now on I
will go to the Gentiles." So he left there and went to a
house belonging to a man named Titus Justus, a worshiper of God; his house was next to a synagogue.
Crispus, the synagogue official, came to believe in the
Lord along with his entire household, and many of the
Corinthians who heard believed and were baptized.—
The word of the Lord. ℟. **Thanks be to God.** ↓

RESPONSORIAL PSALM   Ps 98:1, 2-3ab, 3cd-4

℟. (see 2b) **The Lord has revealed to the nations his sav-
    ing power.**

℟. Or: **Alleluia.**

Sing to the LORD a new song,
    for he has done wondrous deeds;

His right hand has won victory for him,
    his holy arm.—℟.

The LORD has made his salvation known:
    in the sight of the nations he has revealed his justice.
He has remembered his kindness and his faithfulness
    toward the house of Israel.—℟.

All the ends of the earth have seen
    the salvation by our God.
Sing joyfully to the LORD, all you lands;
    break into song; sing praise.—℟. ↓

ALLELUIA   See Jn 14:18

℟. **Alleluia, alleluia.**
I will not leave you orphans, says the Lord;
I will come back to you, and your hearts will rejoice.
℟. **Alleluia, alleluia.** ↓

GOSPEL   Jn 16:16-20

As the Hebrews passed over from Egypt to the Promised Land, so Jesus will pass over from this alienated world to the right hand of the Father. Jesus predicts his leaving this world. The disciples fail to understand and they question him. In the end Jesus promises their sorrow will be turned to joy.

℣. The Lord be with you. ℟. **And also with you.**
✠ A reading from the holy Gospel according to John.
℟. **Glory to you, Lord.**

JESUS said to his disciples: "A little while and you will no longer see me, and again a little while later and you will see me." So some of his disciples said to one another, "What does this mean that he is saying to us, 'A little while and you will not see me, and again a little while and you will see me,' and 'Because I am going to the Father'?" So they said, "What is this 'little while' of which he speaks? We do not know what he means." Jesus knew that they wanted to ask him, so he said to them, "Are you discussing with one another what I said, 'A little while and you will not see me, and again a little while and you will see me'? Amen, amen, I say to you, you will weep and mourn, while the world rejoices; you will grieve, but your grief will become joy."—The Gospel of the Lord. ℟. **Praise to you, Lord Jesus Christ.**

→ No. 15, p. 623

PRAYER OVER THE GIFTS

Lord,
accept our prayers and offerings.
Make us worthy of your sacraments of love
by granting us your forgiveness.
We ask this in the name of Jesus the Lord.
℟. **Amen.**

→ No. 21, p. 626 (Pref. P 22-25)

COMMUNION ANT.   Mt 28:20

I, the Lord, am with you always, until the end or the world, alleluia. ↓

PRAYER AFTER COMMUNION

Almighty and ever-living Lord,
you restored us to life
by raising Christ from death.
Strengthen us by this Easter sacrament;
may we feel its saving power in our daily life.
We ask this through Christ our Lord.
℟. **Amen.**

→No. 32, p. 660

FRIDAY OF THE SIXTH WEEK OF EASTER

Jesus is our mediator, and although we may be depressed with the memory of our many weaknesses and transgressions, we should have confidence that he is always helping us. We must first let him take us under his protecting arm, and then we shall be certain to receive every good gift for which we ask.

ENTRANCE ANT.   See Rv 5:9-10

By your blood, O Lord, you have redeemed us from every tribe and tongue, from every nation and people: you have made us into the kingdom of God, alleluia.

→ No. 2, p. 614

OPENING PRAYER

Father,
you have given us eternal life
through Christ your Son who rose from the dead
and now sits at your right hand.
When he comes again in glory,
may he clothe with immortality
all who have been born again in baptism.
We ask this . . . for ever and ever. ℟. **Amen.** ↓

*In dioceses where the Ascension is celebrated on the Seventh
Sunday of Easter, the following Opening Prayer is said:*

Lord,
hear our prayer
that your gospel may reach all men
and that we who receive salvation through your Word
may be your children in deed as well as in name.
We ask this . . . for ever and ever. ℟. **Amen.** ↓

FIRST READING   Acts 18:9-18

Luke recounts more of the difficulties encountered by Paul. In a vision the
Lord encourages Paul. Paul is brought to trial, but the judge sees it is a
political trial and discontinues the hearing.

A reading from the Acts of the Apostles

ONE night while Paul was in Corinth, the Lord said to
him in a vision, "Do not be afraid. Go on speaking,
and do not be silent, for I am with you. No one will attack
and harm you, for I have many people in this city." He settled there for a year and a half and taught the word of
God among them.

But when Gallio was proconsul of Achaia, the Jews
rose up together against Paul and brought him to the tribunal, saying, "This man is inducing people to worship
God contrary to the law." When Paul was about to reply,
Gallio spoke to the Jews, "If it were a matter of some
crime or malicious fraud, I should with reason hear the

complaint of you Jews; but since it is a question of arguments over doctrine and titles and your own law, see to it yourselves. I do not wish to be a judge of such matters." And he drove them away from the tribunal. They all seized Sosthenes, the synagogue official, and beat him in full view of the tribunal. But none of this was of concern to Gallio.

Paul remained for quite some time, and after saying farewell to the brothers he sailed for Syria, together with Priscilla and Aquila. At Cenchreae he had shaved his head because he had taken a vow.—The word of the Lord. ℟. **Thanks be to God.** ↓

RESPONSORIAL PSALM   Ps 47:2-3, 4-5, 6-7

℟. (8a) **God is king of all the earth.**

℟. Or: **Alleluia.**

All you peoples, clap your hands,
    shout to God with cries of gladness,
For the LORD, the Most High, the awesome,
    is the great king over all the earth.—℟.

He brings people under us;
    nations under our feet.
He chooses for us our inheritance,
    the glory of Jacob, whom he loves.—℟.

God mounts his throne amid shouts of joy;
    the LORD, amid trumpet blasts.
Sing praise to God, sing praise;
    sing praise to our king, sing praise.—℟. ↓

ALLELUIA   See Lk 24:46, 26

℟. **Alleluia, alleluia.**
Christ had to suffer and to rise from the dead,
and so enter into his glory.
℟. **Alleluia, alleluia.** ↓

GOSPEL   Jn 16:20-23

The coming of the Kingdom is described in terms of childbirth. The process requires time and patient endurance, but the result will be a joy that will never be taken away.

℣. The Lord be with you. ℟. **And also with you.**

✠ A reading from the holy Gospel according to John.

℟. **Glory to you, Lord.**

JESUS said to his disciples: "Amen, amen, I say to you, you will weep and mourn, while the world rejoices; you will grieve, but your grief will become joy. When a woman is in labor, she is in anguish because her hour has arrived; but when she has given birth to a child, she no longer remembers the pain because of her joy that a child has been born into the world. So you also are now in anguish. But I will see you again, and your hearts will rejoice, and no one will take your joy away from you. On that day you will not question me about anything. Amen, amen, I say to you, whatever you ask the Father in my name he will give you."—The Gospel of the Lord. ℟.
Praise to you, Lord Jesus Christ.   → No. 15, p. 623

PRAYER OVER THE GIFTS

Lord,
accept these gifts from your family.
May we hold fast to the life you have given us
and come to the eternal gifts you promise.
We ask this in the name of Jesus the Lord.
℟. **Amen.**   → No. 21, p. 626

If the Ascension has been celebrated on Thursday of this week: Preface of Ascension I or II (P 26-27). If the Ascension is celebrated on the Seventh Sunday of Easter: Preface of Easter II-V (P 22-25).

COMMUNION ANT.   Rom 4:25

Christ our Lord was put to death for our sins; and he rose again to make us worthy of life, alleluia. ↓

PRAYER AFTER COMMUNION

Lord,
watch over those you have saved in Christ.
May we who are redeemed by his suffering and death
always rejoice in his resurrection,
for he is Lord for ever and ever.
℟. **Amen.**

➜ No. 32, p. 660

SATURDAY OF THE SIXTH WEEK OF EASTER

Jesus himself has expressly promised that our prayers shall be heard if only we ask them in his name through the Father. It is a mistake to imagine that consideration of or meditation on the eternal truths is a spiritual exercise reserved for those who have specially consecrated their lives to the service of God in the religious state. It is necessary for all the faithful. Let us recall our Lord's promise: "Whatever you ask the Father in my name he will give to you" (Jn 16:23).

ENTRANCE ANT.

1 Pt 2:9

You are a people God claims as his own, to praise him who called you out of darkness into his marvelous light, alleluia.

➜ No. 2, p. 614

OPENING PRAYER

Father,
at your Son's ascension into heaven
you promised to send the Holy Spirit on your apostles.
You filled them with heavenly wisdom:
fill us also with the gift of your Spirit.
Grant this . . . for ever and ever. ℟. **Amen.** ↓

In dioceses where the Ascension is celebrated on the Seventh Sunday of Easter, the following Opening Prayer is said:

Lord,
teach us to know you better
by doing good to others.
Help us to grow in your love

and come to understand the eternal mystery
of Christ's death and resurrection.
We ask this . . . for ever and ever. ℟. **Amen.** ↓

FIRST READING   Acts 18:23-28

The Christian preacher Apollos shows from the Scriptures that Jesus was
the Messiah. He preaches fearlessly. Since he had only heard of John's
baptism, Priscilla and Aquila instruct him in greater depth about Jesus.

A reading from the Acts of the Apostles

A FTER staying in Antioch some time, Paul left and
traveled in orderly sequence through the Galatian
country and Phrygia, bringing strength to all the disciples.

A Jew named Apollos, a native of Alexandria, an elo-
quent speaker, arrived in Ephesus. He was an authority
on the Scriptures. He had been instructed in the Way of
the Lord and, with ardent spirit, spoke and taught accurately about Jesus, although he knew only the baptism of
John. He began to speak boldly in the synagogue; but
when Priscilla and Aquila heard him, they took him aside
and explained to him the Way of God more accurately.
And when he wanted to cross to Achaia, the brothers
encouraged him and wrote to the disciples there to welcome him. After his arrival he gave great assistance to
those who had come to believe through grace. He vigorously refuted the Jews in public, establishing from the
Scriptures that the Christ is Jesus.—The word of the
Lord. ℟. **Thanks be to God.** ↓

RESPONSORIAL PSALM   Ps 47:2-3, 8-9, 10

℟. (8a) **God is king of all the earth.**

℟. Or: **Alleluia.**

All you peoples, clap your hands;
    shout to God with cries of gladness.
For the LORD, the Most High, the awesome,
    is the great king over all the earth.—℟.

For king of all the earth is God;
  sing hymns of praise.
God reigns over the nations,
  God sits upon his holy throne.—℟.

The princes of the peoples are gathered together
  with the people of the God of Abraham.
For God's are the guardians of the earth;
  he is supreme.—℟. ↓

ALLELUIA   Jn 16:28

℟. **Alleluia, alleluia.**
I came from the Father and have come into the world;
now I am leaving the world and going back to the Father.
℟. **Alleluia, alleluia.** ↓

GOSPEL   Jn 16:23b-28

Jesus is not only willing to present prayers to the Father; he strongly urges
his followers to ask "in his name," that is, in accord with what is truly
good according to the wisdom of God.

℣. The Lord be with you. ℟. **And also with you.**
✠ A reading from the holy Gospel according to John.
℟. **Glory to you, Lord.**

JESUS said to his disciples: "Amen, amen, I say to you,
whatever you ask the Father in my name he will give
you. Until now you have not asked anything in my name;
ask and you will receive, so that your joy may be complete.

  "I have told you this in figures of speech. The hour is
coming when I will no longer speak to you in figures but
I will tell you clearly about the Father. On that day you
will ask in my name, and I do not tell you that I will ask
the Father for you. For the Father himself loves you,
because you have loved me and have come to believe that
I came from God. I came from the Father and have come
into the world. Now I am leaving the world and going
back to the Father."—The Gospel of the Lord. ℟. **Praise to
you, Lord Jesus Christ.**   ➜ No. 15, p. 623

PRAYER OVER THE GIFTS

Merciful Lord,
make holy these gifts,
and let our spiritual sacrifice
make us an everlasting gift to you.
We ask this in the name of Jesus the Lord.
℟. **Amen.**   ➜ No. 21, p. 626

If the Ascension has been celebrated on Thursday of this week: Preface of Ascension I or II (P 26-27). If the Ascension is celebrated on the Seventh Sunday of Easter: Preface of Easter II-V (P 22-25).

COMMUNION ANT.   Jn 17:24

Father, I want the men you have given me to be with me where I am, so that they may see the glory you have given me, alleluia. ↓

PRAYER AFTER COMMUNION

Lord,
may this eucharist,
which we have celebrated in memory of your Son,
help us to grow in love.
We ask this in the name of Jesus the Lord.
℟. **Amen.**   ➜ No. 32, p. 660

─────────────────

MONDAY OF THE SEVENTH WEEK OF EASTER

When the Holy Spirit descended upon the Apostles and made the power of God's grace manifest, he came to dwell for all time in the hearts of the faithful. The gift of divine charity was thus infused into their souls. We should examine ourselves and see what results have been produced in us by the many visits of the Holy Spirit that we have been privileged to receive. The gift of the Holy Spirit is the secret of the complete change of heart, true conversion.

ENTRANCE ANT.   Acts 1:8

You will receive power when the Holy Spirit comes upon you. You will be my witnesses to all the world, alleluia.
                                    ➜ No. 2, p. 614

OPENING PRAYER

Lord,
send the power of your Holy Spirit upon us
that we may remain faithful
and do your will in our daily lives.
We ask this . . . for ever and ever. ℟. **Amen.** ↓

FIRST READING Acts 19:1-8

The giving of the Holy Spirit to the twelve men by Paul is called "Little Pentecost." The event is a Scriptural indication of the sacraments of Baptism and Confirmation. Through Christ, the Spirit is available to all. Paul continues to preach Jesus as the Lord, the Risen Savior.

A reading from the Acts of the Apostles

WHILE Apollos was in Corinth, Paul traveled through the interior of the country and down to Ephesus where he found some disciples. He said to them, "Did you receive the Holy Spirit when you became believers?" They answered him, "We have never even heard that there is a Holy Spirit." He said, "How were you baptized?" They replied, "With the baptism of John." Paul then said, "John baptized with a baptism of repentance, telling the people to believe in the one who was to come after him, that is, in Jesus." When they heard this, they were baptized in the name of the Lord Jesus. And when Paul laid his hands on them, the Holy Spirit came upon them, and they spoke in tongues and prophesied. Altogether there were about twelve men.

He entered the synagogue, and for three months debated boldly with persuasive arguments about the Kingdom of God.—The word of the Lord. ℟. **Thanks be to God.** ↓

RESPONSORIAL PSALM Ps 68:2-3ab, 4-5acd, 6-7ab

℟. (33a) **Sing to God, O kingdoms of the earth.**

℟. Or: **Alleluia.**

God arises; his enemies are scattered,
  and those who hate him flee before him.

As smoke is driven away, so are they driven;
   as wax melts before the fire.—R̸.

But the just rejoice and exult before God;
   they are glad and rejoice.
Sing to God, chant praise to his name;
   whose name is the LORD.—R̸.

The father of orphans and the defender of widows
   is God in his holy dwelling.
God gives a home to the forsaken;
   he leads forth prisoners to prosperity.—R̸. ↓

ALLELUIA   Col 3:1
R̸. **Alleluia, alleluia.**
If then you were raised with Christ,
seek what is above,
where Christ is seated at the right hand of God.
R̸. **Alleluia, alleluia.** ↓

GOSPEL   Jn 16:29-33
The disciples finally make a profession of their belief in Jesus. They admit
that he is from God. Jesus then warns them of their future, their sufferings, but he promises that he will overcome the world.

℣. The Lord be with you. R̸. **And also with you.**
✚ A reading from the holy Gospel according to John.
R̸. **Glory to you, Lord.**

THE disciples said to Jesus, "Now you are talking
plainly, and not in any figure of speech. Now we realize that you know everything and that you do not need to
have anyone question you. Because of this we believe
that you came from God." Jesus answered them, "Do you
believe now? Behold, the hour is coming and has arrived
when each of you will be scattered to his own home and
you will leave me alone. But I am not alone, because the
Father is with me. I have told you this so that you might
have peace in me. In the world you will have trouble, but
take courage, I have conquered the world."—The Gospel

of the Lord. ℟. **Praise to you, Lord Jesus Christ.**

→ No. 15, p. 623

PRAYER OVER THE GIFTS

Lord,
may these gifts cleanse us from sin
and make our hearts live with your gift of grace.
Grant this through Christ our Lord.
℟. **Amen.**

→ No. 21, p. 626 (Pref. P 26-27)

COMMUNION ANT.   Jn 14:18; 16:22

**The Lord said: I will not leave you orphans. I will come
back to you, and your hearts will rejoice, alleluia. ↓**

PRAYER AFTER COMMUNION

Merciful Father,
may these mysteries give us new purpose
and bring us to a new life in you.
Grant this through Christ our Lord.
℟. **Amen.**

→No. 32, p. 660

TUESDAY OF THE SEVENTH WEEK OF EASTER

The final proof of our redemption, which was given through the
Incarnation and Passion, was completed when our Savior took his place
as true God and as true man at the right hand of his Eternal Father in the
Kingdom of heaven. Our faith is that which the Apostles and their successors received with their commission to preach and teach and to bear
witness to the truths of the Gospel. Our faith, too, must be ever steadfast,
and it will become strong as we imitate our Divine Master.

ENTRANCE ANT.   Rv 1:17-18

**I am the beginning and the end of all things. I have met
death, but I am alive, and I shall live for eternity, alleluia.**

→ No. 2, p. 614

OPENING PRAYER

God of power and mercy,
send your Holy Spirit
to live in our hearts

and make us temples of his glory.
We ask this . . . for ever and ever. ℟. **Amen.** ↓

FIRST READING   Acts 20:17-27

Luke exposes the inner spirit of the great Apostle Paul. He has abandoned
any thought of a life for himself and has become the servant of the plan
of God. He finds his joy in serving others. He wants to finish the race of
life and attain the crown of victory.

A reading from the Acts of the Apostles

FROM Miletus Paul had the presbyters of the Church at
Ephesus summoned. When they came to him, he
addressed them, "You know how I lived among you the
whole time from the day I first came to the province of
Asia. I served the Lord with all humility and with the
tears and trials that came to me because of the plots of
the Jews, and I did not at all shrink from telling you what
was for your benefit, or from teaching you in public or in
your homes. I earnestly bore witness for both Jews and
Greeks to repentance before God and to faith in our Lord
Jesus. But now, compelled by the Spirit, I am going to
Jerusalem. What will happen to me there I do not know,
except that in one city after another the Holy Spirit has
been warning me that imprisonment and hardships
await me. Yet I consider life of no importance to me, if
only I may finish my course and the ministry that I
received from the Lord Jesus, to bear witness to the
Gospel of God's grace.

"But now I know that none of you to whom I preached
the kingdom during my travels will ever see my face
again. And so I solemnly declare to you this day that I am
not responsible for the blood of any of you, for I did not
shrink from proclaiming to you the entire plan of God."—
The word of the Lord. ℟. **Thanks be to God.** ↓

RESPONSORIAL PSALM   Ps 68:10-11, 20-21

℟. **(33a) Sing to God, O kingdoms of the earth.**

℟. Or: **Alleluia.**

A bountiful rain you showered down, O God, upon your
    inheritance;
  you restored the land when it languished;
Your flock settled in it;
    in your goodness, O God, you provided it for the
    needy.—℟.

Blessed day by day be the Lord,
  who bears our burdens; God, who is our salvation.
God is a saving God for us;
    the LORD, my Lord, controls the passageways of
    death.—℟. ↓

ALLELUIA
Jn 14:16

℟. **Alleluia, alleluia.**
I will ask the Father
and he will give you another Advocate
to be with you always.
℟. **Alleluia, alleluia.** ↓

GOSPEL
Jn 17:1-11a

Jesus speaks of his coming death. The Son of Man will suffer and enter
into his glory at the right hand of the Father. He prays about how the chosen disciples have heard the message of the Father. Jesus prays especially for them since they, too, belong to the Father.

℣. The Lord be with you. ℟. **And also with you.**
✢ A reading from the holy Gospel according to John.
℟. **Glory to you, Lord.**

JESUS raised his eyes to heaven and said, "Father, the
hour has come. Give glory to your son, so that your
son may glorify you, just as you gave him authority over
all people, so that your son may give eternal life to all you
gave him. Now this is eternal life, that they should know
you, the only true God, and the one whom you sent, Jesus
Christ. I glorified you on earth by accomplishing the
work that you gave me to do. Now glorify me, Father,
with you, with the glory that I had with you before the
world began.

"I revealed your name to those whom you gave me out of the world. They belonged to you, and you gave them to me, and they have kept your word. Now they know that everything you gave me is from you, because the words you gave to me I have given to them, and they accepted them and truly understood that I came from you, and they have believed that you sent me. I pray for them. I do not pray for the world but for the ones you have given me, because they are yours, and everything of mine is yours and everything of yours is mine, and I have been glorified in them. And now I will no longer be in the world, but they are in the world, while I am coming to you."—The Gospel of the Lord. ℟. **Praise to you, Lord Jesus Christ.**   → No. 15, p. 623

PRAYER OVER THE GIFTS

Father,
accept the prayers and offerings of your people
and bring us to the glory of heaven,
where Jesus is Lord for ever and ever.
℟. **Amen.**   → No. 21, p. 626 (Pref. P 26-27)

COMMUNION ANT.   Jn 14:26

The Lord says, the Holy Spirit whom the Father will send in my name will teach you all things, and remind you of all I have said to you, alleluia. ↓

PRAYER AFTER COMMUNION

Lord,
may this eucharist,
which we have celebrated in memory of your Son,
help us to grow in love.
We ask this in the name of Jesus the Lord.
℟. **Amen.**   → No. 32, p. 660

WEDNESDAY OF THE SEVENTH WEEK OF EASTER

The apostolic mission of the Church is the same as Christ's mission from the Father. The Church shows us the love of Almighty God for human beings and reminds us how noble, generous, and truly divine is the charity of our Heavenly Father. When God created us, he did so because he was goodness and love itself, and our Lord Jesus Christ was one with him. In humility, let us try to be one with the Father and the Son, to be holy and pleasing to the Creator through our Blessed Savior.

ENTRANCE ANT. Ps 47:2

All nations, clap your hands. Shout with a voice of joy to God, alleluia. → No. 2, p. 614

OPENING PRAYER

God of mercy,
unite your Church in the Holy Spirit
that we may serve you with all our hearts
and work together with unselfish love.
Grant this . . . for ever and ever. ℟. **Amen.** ↓

FIRST READING Acts 20:28-38

Paul entrusts the protection of the true faith and the guidance of the faithful to the appointed ministers of each community. He warns of false teachers. Paul refers to his own example, and before leaving Ephesus he prays with the community.

A reading from the Acts of the Apostles

AT Miletus, Paul spoke to the presbyters of the Church of Ephesus: "Keep watch over yourselves and over the whole flock of which the Holy Spirit has appointed you overseers, in which you tend the Church of God that he acquired with his own Blood. I know that after my departure savage wolves will come among you, and they will not spare the flock. And from your own group, men will come forward perverting the truth to draw the disciples away after them. So be vigilant and remember that for three years, night and day, I unceasingly admonished each of you with tears. And now I commend you to God and to that gracious word of his that can build you up and give you the inheritance among all who are consecrated. I have never wanted anyone's silver or gold or clothing. You know well that these very hands have served my needs and my companions. In every way I have shown you that by hard work of that sort we must help the weak, and keep in mind the words of the Lord Jesus who himself said, 'It is more blessed to give than to receive.'"

When he had finished speaking he knelt down and prayed with them all. They were all weeping loudly as they threw their arms around Paul and kissed him, for they were deeply distressed that he had said that they would never see his face again. Then they escorted him to the ship.—The word of the Lord. ℟. **Thanks be to God.** ↓

RESPONSORIAL PSALM   Ps 68:29-30, 33-35a, 35bc-36ab

℟. (33a) **Sing to God, O kingdoms of the earth.**

℟. Or: **Alleluia.**

Show forth, O God, your power,
    the power, O God, with which you took our part;
For your temple in Jerusalem
    let the kings bring you gifts.—℟.

You kingdoms of the earth, sing to God,
    chant praise to the Lord
who rides on the heights of the ancient heavens.
Behold, his voice resounds, the voice of power:
    "Confess the power of God!"—℟.

Over Israel is his majesty;
    his power is in the skies.
Awesome in his sanctuary is God, the God of Israel;
    he gives power and strength to his people.—℟. ↓

ALLELUIA   See Jn 17:17b, 17a

℟. **Alleluia, alleluia.**
Your word, O Lord, is truth;
consecrate us in the truth.
℟. **Alleluia, alleluia.** ↓

GOSPEL   Jn 17:11b-19

Jesus prays at the Last Supper that all may be one. The mutual bond of the followers of Jesus is that all are the adopted children of the Father, gathered to hear him and to worship him. Jesus asks that these followers be guarded from the evil one.

℣. The Lord be with you. ℟. **And also with you.**
✚ A reading from the holy Gospel according to John.
℟. **Glory to you, Lord.**

LIFTING up his eyes to heaven, Jesus prayed, saying: "Holy Father, keep them in your name that you have given me, so that they may be one just as we are one. When I was with them I protected them in your name that you gave me, and I guarded them, and none of them was lost except the son of destruction, in order that the Scripture might be fulfilled. But now I am coming to you. I speak this in the world so that they may share my joy completely. I gave them your word, and the world hated them, because they do not belong to the world any more than I belong to the world. I do not ask that you take them out of the world but that you keep them from the Evil One. They do not belong to the world any more than I belong to the world. Consecrate them in the truth. Your word is truth. As you sent me into the world, so I sent them into the world. And I consecrate myself for them, so that they also may be consecrated in truth."—The Gospel of the Lord. ℟. **Praise to you, Lord Jesus Christ.**

➜ No. 15, p. 623

PRAYER OVER THE GIFTS

Lord,
accept this offering we make at your command.
May these sacred mysteries by which we worship you
bring your salvation to perfection within us.
We ask this in the name of Jesus the Lord.
℟. **Amen.**   ➜ No. 21, p. 626 (Pref. P 26-27)

COMMUNION ANT. Jn 15:26-27

The Lord says: When the Holy Spirit comes to you, the Spirit whom I shall send, the Spirit of truth who proceeds from the Father, he will bear witness to me, and you also will be my witnesses, alleluia. ↓

PRAYER AFTER COMMUNION

Lord,
may our participation in the eucharist
increase your life in us, cleanse us from sin,
and make us increasingly worthy of this holy sacrament.
We ask this through Christ our Lord.
℟. **Amen.** ➙ No. 32, p. 660

THURSDAY OF THE SEVENTH WEEK OF EASTER

As courage was infused into Paul by God before what was to be the end of his missionary work, the Church endeavors to renew our courage and strength and a trust and confidence in his mercy and power. No matter what our condition may be, we must never despair of God's mercy, for "the Lord is good to all and compassionate toward all his works" (Ps 145:9).

ENTRANCE ANT. Heb 4:16

Let us come to God's presence with confidence, because we will find mercy, and strength when we need it, alleluia. ➙ No. 2, p. 614

OPENING PRAYER

Father,
let your Spirit come upon us with power
to fill us with his gifts.
May he make our hearts pleasing to you,
and ready to do your will.
We ask this . . . for ever and ever. ℟. **Amen.** ↓

FIRST READING Acts 22:30; 23:6-11

After reaching Jerusalem at the end of his third journey, Paul is arrested. Even then, he witnesses to the Resurrection of Jesus and influences many. At night God appears to Paul to give him courage to persevere.

A reading from the Acts of the Apostles

WISHING to determine the truth about why Paul was being accused by the Jews, the commander freed him and ordered the chief priests and the whole Sanhedrin to convene. Then he brought Paul down and made him stand before them.

Paul was aware that some were Sadducees and some Pharisees, so he called out before the Sanhedrin, "My brothers, I am a Pharisee, the son of Pharisees; I am on trial for hope in the resurrection of the dead." When he said this, a dispute broke out between the Pharisees and Sadducees, and the group became divided. For the Sadducees say that there is no resurrection or angels or spirits, while the Pharisees acknowledge all three. A great uproar occurred, and some scribes belonging to the Pharisee party stood up and sharply argued, "We find nothing wrong with this man. Suppose a spirit or an angel has spoken to him?" The dispute was so serious that the commander, afraid that Paul would be torn to pieces by them, ordered his troops to go down and rescue Paul from their midst and take him into the compound. The following night the Lord stood by him and said, "Take courage. For just as you have borne witness to my cause in Jerusalem, so you must also bear witness in Rome."—The word of the Lord. ℟. **Thanks be to God.** ↓

RESPONSORIAL PSALM   Ps 16:1-2a and 5, 7-8, 9-10, 11

℟. (1) **Keep me safe, O God; you are my hope.**

℟. Or: **Alleluia.**

Keep me, O God, for in you I take refuge;
    I say to the LORD, "My Lord are you."
O LORD, my allotted portion and my cup,
    you it is who hold fast my lot.—℟.

I bless the LORD who counsels me;
    even in the night my heart exhorts me.
I set the LORD ever before me;
    with him at my right hand I shall not be disturbed.—℟.

Therefore my heart is glad and my soul rejoices,
  my body, too, abides in confidence;
Because you will not abandon my soul to the nether
    world,
  nor will you suffer your faithful one to undergo cor-
    ruption.—℟.

You will show me the path to life,
  fullness of joys in your presence,
    the delights at your right hand forever.—℟. ↓

ALLELUIA   Jn 17:21
℟. **Alleluia, alleluia.**
May they all be one as you, Father, are in me and I in you,
that the world may believe that you sent me, says the
  Lord.
℟. **Alleluia, alleluia.** ↓

GOSPEL   Jn 17:20-26
Jesus prays for unity so that all will believe in him and in his Gospel. He
prays that all may be one in the Father and him. Jesus reveals the Father
and will continue to carry out his mission.

℣. The Lord be with you. ℟. **And also with you.**
✤ A reading from the holy Gospel according to John.
℟. **Glory to you, Lord.**

LIFTING up his eyes to heaven, Jesus prayed, saying:"I
  pray not only for these, but also for those who will
believe in me through their word, so that they may all be
one, as you, Father, are in me and I in you, that they also
may be in us, that the world may believe that you sent
me. And I have given them the glory you gave me, so that
they may be one, as we are one, I in them and you in me,
that they may be brought to perfection as one, that the
world may know that you sent me, and that you loved
them even as you loved me. Father, they are your gift to
me. I wish that where I am they also may be with me, that
they may see my glory that you gave me, because you
loved me before the foundation of the world. Righteous

Father, the world also does not know you, but I know you, and they know that you sent me. I made known to them your name and I will make it known, that the love with which you loved me may be in them and I in them."—The Gospel of the Lord. ℟. **Praise to you, Lord Jesus Christ.**

→ No. 15, p. 623

PRAYER OVER THE GIFTS

Merciful Lord,
make holy these gifts,
and let our spiritual sacrifice
make us an everlasting gift to you.
We ask this in the name of Jesus the Lord.
℟. **Amen.** → No. 21, p. 626 (Pref. P 26.27)

COMMUNION ANT.
Jn 16:7

This is the word of Jesus: It is best for me to leave you; because if I do not go, the Spirit will not come to you, alleluia. ↓

PRAYER AFTER COMMUNION

Lord,
renew us by the mysteries we have shared.
Help us to know you
and prepare us for the gifts of the Spirit.
We ask this through Christ our Lord.
℟. **Amen.** → No. 32, p. 660

FRIDAY OF THE SEVENTH WEEK OF EASTER

We should refrain from judging others and even examining their motives. Let us leave all judgment in the hands of God. Thus, we shall have prepared the way of the Lord according to his own directions, and by his grace we shall be prepared to meet him by receiving Holy Communion. Jesus Christ is the Lamb of God who takes away the sins of the world.

ENTRANCE ANT.
Rv 1:5-6

Christ loved us and has washed away our sins with his blood, and has made us a kingdom of priests to serve his God and Father, alleluia. → No. 2, p. 614

OPENING PRAYER

Father,
in glorifying Christ and sending us your Spirit,
you open the way to eternal life.
May our sharing in this gift increase our love
and make our faith grow stronger.
Grant this . . . for ever and ever. ℟. **Amen.** ↓

FIRST READING   Acts 25:13b-21

The imprisonment of Paul brings much good. Several high Roman officials
hear of Jesus Christ and of Paul's firm conviction that Jesus is the risen
Lord. Paul will soon announce the Good News in Rome itself.

A reading from the Acts of the Apostles

KING Agrippa and Bernice arrived in Caesarea on a
visit to Festus. Since they spent several days there,
Festus referred Paul's case to the king, saying, "There is a
man here left in custody by Felix. When I was in
Jerusalem the chief priests and the elders of the Jews
brought charges against him and demanded his condemnation. I answered them that it was not Roman practice
to hand over an accused person before he has faced his
accusers and had the opportunity to defend himself
against their charge. So when they came together here, I
made no delay; the next day I took my seat on the tribunal and ordered the man to be brought in. His accusers
stood around him, but did not charge him with any of the
crimes I suspected. Instead they had some issues with
him about their own religion and about a certain Jesus
who had died but who Paul claimed was alive. Since I
was at a loss how to investigate this controversy, I asked
if he were willing to go to Jerusalem and there stand trial
on these charges. And when Paul appealed that he be
held in custody for the Emperor's decision, I ordered him
held until I could send him to Caesar."—The word of the
Lord. ℟. **Thanks be to God.** ↓

RESPONSORIAL PSALM   Ps 103:1-2, 11-12, 19-20ab

℟. (19a) **The Lord has established his throne in heaven.**

℟. Or: **Alleluia.**

Bless the LORD, O my soul;
　　and all my being, bless his holy name.
Bless the LORD, O my soul,
　　and forget not all his benefits.—℟.

For as the heavens are high above the earth,
　　so surpassing is his kindness toward those who fear
　　　him.
As far as the east is from the west,
　　so far has he put our transgressions from us.—℟.

The LORD has established his throne in heaven,
　　and his kingdom rules over all.
Bless the LORD, all you his angels,
　　you mighty in strength, who do his bidding.—℟. ↓

ALLELUIA   Jn 14:26

℟. **Alleluia, alleluia.**
The Holy Spirit will teach you everything
and remind you of all I told you.
℟. **Alleluia, alleluia.** ↓

GOSPEL   Jn 21:15-19

Jesus makes the Apostle Peter the shepherd of his flock on earth after
Peter answers the threefold question of Jesus. Then Jesus foretells how
Peter will die.

℣. The Lord be with you. ℟. **And also with you.**
✛ A reading from the holy Gospel according to John.
℟. **Glory to you, Lord.**

A FTER Jesus had revealed himself to his disciples and
　eaten breakfast with them, he said to Simon Peter,
"Simon, son of John, do you love me more than these?"
Simon Peter answered him, "Yes, Lord, you know that I
love you." Jesus said to him, "Feed my lambs." He then

said to Simon Peter a second time, "Simon, son of John, do you love me?" Simon Peter answered him, "Yes, Lord, you know that I love you." He said to him, "Tend my sheep." He said to him the third time, "Simon, son of John, do you love me?" Peter was distressed that he had said to him a third time, "Do you love me?" and he said to him, "Lord, you know everything; you know that I love you." Jesus said to him, "Feed my sheep. Amen, amen, I say to you, when you were younger, you used to dress yourself and go where you wanted; but when you grow old, you will stretch out your hands, and someone else will dress you and lead you where you do not want to go." He said this signifying by what kind of death he would glorify God. And when he had said this, he said to him, "Follow me."—The Gospel of the Lord. ℟. **Praise to you, Lord Jesus Christ.** → No. 15, p. 623

PRAYER OVER THE GIFTS

Father of love and mercy,
we place our offering before you.
Send your Holy Spirit to cleanse our lives
so that our gifts may be acceptable.
We ask this through Christ our Lord.
℟. **Amen.** → No. 21, p. 626 (Pref. P 26-27)

COMMUNION ANT. Jn 16:13

When the Spirit of truth comes, says the Lord, he will lead you to the whole truth, alleluia. ↓

PRAYER AFTER COMMUNION

God our Father,
the eucharist is our bread of life
and the sacrament of our forgiveness.
May our sharing in this mystery
bring us to eternal life,
where Jesus is Lord for ever and ever.
℟. **Amen.** → No. 32, p. 660

SATURDAY OF THE SEVENTH WEEK OF EASTER

MASS IN THE MORNING

We should be aware that the chosen people of Israel, favored though they were by God's most special care, are but a figure of us, enriched as we have been by God's choicest favors. We should try to realize that we are often called to repentance, but we have been careless in accepting such tender invitations. Let us purify the "holy temple" by casting out all affection for sin and its occasions.

ENTRANCE ANT.   Acts 1:14

The disciples were constantly at prayer together, with Mary the mother of Jesus, the other women, and the brothers of Jesus, alleluia.   ➙ No. 2, p. 614

OPENING PRAYER

Almighty Father,
let the love we have celebrated in this Easter season
be put into practice in our daily lives.
We ask this . . . for ever and ever. ℟. **Amen.** ↓

FIRST READING   Acts 28:16-20, 30-31

This passage concludes the Acts of the Apostles. The faith has been planted according to the directions of Jesus to teach all human beings. Paul is held in custody but welcomes any visitors. He proclaims the Kingdom of God and teaches about Jesus.

A reading from the Acts of the Apostles

WHEN he entered Rome, Paul was allowed to live by himself, with the soldier who was guarding him.

Three days later he called together the leaders of the Jews. When they had gathered he said to them, "My brothers, although I had done nothing against our people or our ancestral customs, I was handed over to the Romans as a prisoner from Jerusalem. After trying my case the Romans wanted to release me, because they found nothing against me deserving the death penalty. But when the Jews objected, I was obliged to appeal to Caesar, even though I had no accusation to make against my own nation. This is the reason, then, I have requested to see you and to speak with you, for it is on account of the hope of Israel that I wear these chains."

He remained for two full years in his lodgings. He received all who came to him, and with complete assurance and without hindrance he proclaimed the Kingdom of God and taught about the Lord Jesus Christ.—The word of the Lord. ℟. **Thanks to be God.** ↓

RESPONSORIAL PSALM   Ps 11:4, 5 and 7

℟. (see 7b) **The just will gaze on your face, O Lord.**

℟. Or: **Alleluia.**

The LORD is in his holy temple;
    the LORD's throne is in heaven.
His eyes behold,
    his searching glance is on mankind.—℟.

The LORD searches the just and the wicked;
    the lover of violence he hates.
For the LORD is just, he loves just deeds;
    the upright shall see his face.—℟. ↓

ALLELUIA   Jn 16:7, 13

℟. **Alleluia, alleluia.**
I will send to you the Spirit of truth, says the Lord;
he will guide you to all truth.
℟. **Alleluia, alleluia.** ↓

GOSPEL   Jn 21:20-25

John speaks of himself as the disciple whom Jesus loved and as the witness to the events of Christ's life. Peter asks about John but Jesus reminds him of his mission. John ends his account by admitting much more could have been written about Jesus.

℣. The Lord be with you. ℟. **And also with you.**

✢ A reading from the holy Gospel according to John.

℟. **Glory to you, Lord.**

PETER turned and saw the disciple following whom Jesus loved, the one who had also reclined upon his chest during the supper and had said, "Master, who is the one who will betray you?" When Peter saw him, he said to Jesus, "Lord, what about him?" Jesus said to him, "What if I want him to remain until I come? What concern is it of yours? You follow me." So the word spread among the brothers that that disciple would not die. But Jesus had not told him that he would not die, just "What if I want him to remain until I come? What concern is it of yours?"

It is this disciple who testifies to these things and has written them, and we know that his testimony is true. There are also many other things that Jesus did, but if these were to be described individually, I do not think the whole world would contain the books that would be written.—The Gospel of the Lord. ℟. **Praise to you, Lord Jesus Christ.**   → No. 15, p. 623

PRAYER OVER THE GIFTS

Lord,
may the coming of the Holy Spirit
prepare us to receive these holy sacraments,
for he is our forgiveness.
We ask this in the name of Jesus the Lord.
℟. **Amen.**   → No. 21, p. 626 (Pref. P 26-27)

COMMUNION ANT.   Jn 16:14

The Lord says: The Holy Spirit will give glory to me, because he takes my words from me and will hand them to you, alleluia. ↓

PRAYER AFTER COMMUNION

Father of mercy,
hear our prayers

that we may leave our former selves behind
and serve you with holy and renewed hearts.
Grant this through Christ our Lord.
℟. **Amen.**

→ No. 32, p. 660

PROPER OF SAINTS

"In celebrating the annual cycle of Christ's mysteries, holy Church honors with special love the Blessed Mary, Mother of God, who is joined by an inseparable bond to the saving work of her Son. In her the Church holds up and admires the most excellent fruit of the redemption, and joyfully contemplates, as in a faultless model, that which she herself wholly desires and hopes to be.

"The Church has also included in the annual cycle days devoted to the memory of the martyrs and the other saints. Raised up to perfection by the manifold grace of God, and already in possession of eternal salvation, they sing God's perfect praise in heaven and offer prayers for us. By celebrating the passage of these saints from earth to heaven the Church proclaims the paschal mystery as achieved in the saints who have suffered and been glorified with Christ; she proposes them to the faithful as examples who draw all to the Father through Christ, and through their merits she pleads for God's favors" (Vatican II, Constitution on the Sacred Liturgy, nos. 103-104).

Solemnities and Feasts

A proper Mass is provided in its entirety for each Solemnity and Feast. There is no substitute for the Processional Chants, Presidential Prayers, and SPECIAL Readings and Intervenient Chants given for these days.

Obligatory Memorials

1) Processional Chants and Presidential Prayers

a) Proper texts, given on some days, should always be used.

b) When there is a reference to a particular common, appropriate texts should be chosen according to the principles at the beginning of the Commons. The page reference in each case indicates only the beginning of the common to which reference is made.

c) If the reference is to more than one common, one or the other may be used, according to pastoral need. It is always permissible to interchange texts from several Masses within the same common.

For example, if a saint is both a martyr and a bishop, either the Common of Martyrs or the Common of Pastors (for bishops) may be used.

d) In addition to the commons that express a special characteristic holiness (e.g., of martyrs, virgins, or pastors), the texts from the Common of Holy Men and Women, referring to holiness in general, may always be used.

For example, in the case of a saint who is both a virgin and a martyr, texts from the Common of Holy Men and Women in general may be used, in addition to texts from the Common of Martyrs or the Common of Virgins.

e) The Prayer over the Gifts and Prayer after Communion, unless there are proper prayers, may be taken either from the common or from the current liturgical season.

2) Readings and Intervenient Chants

a) The WEEKDAY Readings and Intervenient Chants are to be preferred.

b) However, sometimes SPECIAL Readings are assigned, that is, readings that mention the saint or mystery being celebrated; these are to be said in place of the Weekday Readings. (Whenever this is the case, a clear indication is given in this Missal.)

c) In all other cases the readings found in the Proper of Saints are used only if special reasons (particularly of a pastoral nature) exist. Sometimes, these readings will be APPROPRIATE, that is, they will shed light on some outstanding trait of the saint's spiritual life. Others will be simply references to the GENERAL Readings in the Commons so as to facilitate a selection. However, they are only suggestions; in place of these APPROPRIATE *Readings or suggested* GENERAL *Readings, any other Reading from the common indicated may be said.*

d) *Whenever there are compelling reasons for doing so, readings can always be chosen from the Common of Holy Men and Women.*

Optional Memorials

The category of Optional Memorials is like that of Obligatory Memorials as far as choice of texts is concerned but it allows many more options of Masses to be chosen. In place of the Mass of the Optional Memorial, the priest has the option to choose the Mass of the Weekday, or of one of the saints commemorated or mentioned in the martyrology on that day, or a Mass for Various Needs and Occasions, or a Votive Mass.

Masses of the saints from the martyrology can be taken from the Mass of a saint in the Missal who is in a similar category, e.g., a martyr, priest, etc.

— NOVEMBER —

Nov 30 — ST. ANDREW, Apostle

Feast

St. Andrew, the brother of St. Peter, was a native of the town of Bethsaida in Galilee. A fisherman by profession and a disciple of St. John the Baptist, he and his brother, St. Peter, joined Jesus as members of the Apostolic College. After the dispersion of the Apostles, St. Andrew preached in Greece and several other countries. He suffered martyrdom in Patras, Greece, and, according to common opinion, by crucifixion on a cross made in the form of the letter X.

ENTRANCE ANT.   See Mt 4:18-19

By the Sea of Galilee the Lord saw two brothers, Peter and Andrew. He called them: Come and follow me, and I will make you fishers of men.   → No. 2, p. 614

OPENING PRAYER

Lord,
in your kindness hear our petitions.
You called Andrew the apostle
to preach the gospel and guide your Church in faith.
May he always be our friend in your presence
to help us with his prayers.
We ask this . . . for ever and ever. ℟. **Amen.** ↓

FIRST READING   Rom 10:9-18

An inner faith is demanded that will guide the whole person, but it is also an assent to an expression of that faith. The person seeking justification and salvation is called on to acknowledge Christ as the risen Lord.

A reading from the Letter of Saint Paul to the Romans

Brothers and sisters: If you confess with your mouth that Jesus is Lord and believe in your heart that God raised him from the dead, you will be saved. For one believes with the heart and so is justified, and one confesses with the mouth and so is saved. The Scripture says, *No one who believes in him will be put to shame.* There is no distinction between Jew and Greek; the same Lord is Lord of all, enriching all who call upon him. *For everyone who calls on the name of the Lord will be saved.*

But how can they call on him in whom they have not believed? And how can they believe in him of whom they have not heard? And how can they hear without someone to preach? And how can people preach unless they are sent? As it is written, *How beautiful are the feet of those who bring the good news!* But not everyone has heeded the good news; for Isaiah says, *Lord, who has believed what was heard from us?* Thus faith comes from what is heard, and what is heard comes through the word of Christ. But I ask, did they not hear? Certainly they did; for

> Their voice has gone forth to all the earth,
> and their words to the ends of the world.

The word of the Lord. ℟. **Thanks be to God.** ↓

RESPONSORIAL PSALM   Ps 19:8, 9, 10, 11

℟. (10) **The judgments of the Lord are true, and all of them are just.**

℟. Or: (Jn 6:63) **Your words, Lord, are Spirit and life.**

The law of the LORD is perfect,
    refreshing the soul;
The decree of the Lord is trustworthy,
    giving wisdom to the simple.—℟.

The precepts of the LORD are right,
    rejoicing the heart;
The command of the LORD is clear,
    enlightening the eye.—℟.

The fear of the LORD is pure,
    enduring forever;
The ordinances of the LORD are true,
    all of them just.—℟.

They are more precious than gold,
    than a heap of purest gold;

Sweeter also than syrup
   or honey from the comb.—℟. ↓

ALLELUIA   Mt 4:19

℟. **Alleluia, alleluia.**
Come after me, says the Lord,
and I will make you fishers of men.
℟. **Alleluia, alleluia.** ↓

GOSPEL   Mt 4:18-22

Peter, Andrew, James, and John follow our Lord immediately. They drop their
fishing nets, leave their families and become disciples. The promise of Christ
to make them "fishers of men" is an intimation of the apostolic office.

℣. The Lord be with you. ℟. **And also with you**.
✠ A reading from the holy Gospel according to Matthew.
℟. **Glory to you, Lord.**

AS Jesus was walking by the Sea of Galilee, he saw
two brothers, Simon who is called Peter, and his
brother Andrew, casting a net into the sea; they were
fishermen. He said to them, "Come after me, and I will
make you fishers of men." At once they left their nets and
followed him. He walked along from there and saw two
other brothers, James, the son of Zebedee, and his brother John. They were in a boat, with their father Zebedee,
mending their nets. He called them, and immediately
they left their boat and their father and followed him.—
The Gospel of the Lord. ℟. **Praise to you, Lord Jesus
Christ.**   → No. 15, p. 623

PRAYER OVER THE GIFTS

All-powerful God,
may these gifts we bring on the feast of St. Andrew
be pleasing to you
and give life to all who receive them.
We ask this in the name of Jesus the Lord.
℟. **Amen.**   → No. 21, p. 626 (Pref. P 64-65)

COMMUNION ANT. Jn 1:41-42

Andrew told his brother Simon: We have found the Messiah, the Christ; and he brought him to Jesus. ↓

PRAYER AFTER COMMUNION

Lord,
may the sacrament we have received give us courage
to follow the example of Andrew the apostle.
By sharing in Christ's suffering
may we live with him for ever in glory,
for he is Lord for ever and ever.
℟. **Amen.** → No. 32, p. 660

— DECEMBER —

Dec. 3 — ST. FRANCIS XAVIER, Priest

Memorial

St. Francis Xavier was born in Navarre, Spain, 1506. From St. Ignatius Loyola, he heard the words: "What does it profit a man, if he gains the whole world, but suffers the loss of his own soul?" He renounced his worldly life, and became one of the most zealous apostles who have ever preached.

Common of Pastors: for Missionaries, p. 1067.

OPENING PRAYER

God our Father,
by the preaching of Francis Xavier
you brought many nations to yourself.
Give his zeal for the faith to all who believe in you,
that your Church may rejoice in continued growth
throughout the world.
Grant this . . . for ever and ever. ℟. **Amen.**

First Reading (1 Cor 9:16-19, 22-23), p. 1163, no. 4.
Responsorial Psalm (Ps 117), p. 1161, no. 8.
Alleluia (Mt 28:19a, 20b), p. 1168, no.2.
Gospel (Mk 16:15-20), p. 1171, no. 6.

PRAYER OVER THE GIFTS

Lord,
receive the gifts we bring on the feast of Francis Xavier.
As his zeal for the salvation of mankind
led him to the ends of the earth,
may we be effective witnesses to the gospel
and come with our brothers and sisters
to be with you in the joy of your kingdom.
We ask this through Christ our Lord.
℟. **Amen.**   ➜ No. 21, p. 626 (Pref. P 1)

PRAYER AFTER COMMUNION

Lord God,
may this eucharist fill us with the same love
that inspired Francis Xavier
to work for the salvation of all.

Help us to live in a manner more worthy of our Christian
   calling
and so inherit the promise of eternal life.
We ask this in the name of Jesus the Lord.
℟. **Amen.**

→ No. 32, p. 660

Dec. 4 — ST. JOHN OF DAMASCUS, Priest, Religious, and Doctor

Optional Memorial

St. John distinguished himself against the Emperor of
Constantinople for his defense of the veneration of sacred
images. He was famous for his great knowledge and for his
theological method. He died in the 8th century.

*Common of Pastors, p. 1061; or Common of Doctors of the
Church, p. 1072.*

OPENING PRAYER

Lord,
may the prayers of St. John Damascene help us,
and may the true faith he taught so well
always be our light and our strength.
We ask this . . . for ever and ever. ℟. **Amen.**

First Reading (2 Tm 1:13-14; 2:1-3), p. 1167, no. 11.
Responsorial Psalm (Ps 19), p. 1179, no. 1.
Alleluia (Jn 14:23), p. 1224, no. 11.
Gospel (Mt 25:14-30), p. 1231, no. 12 (or Mt 25:14-23).

Dec. 6 — ST. NICHOLAS, Bishop

Optional Memorial

St. Nicholas is distinguished in the Church for his holy austerity and childlike innocence. Chosen as Bishop of Myra in
Lycia, Asia Minor, he distinguished himself for his charity
and liberality. He was particularly solicitous for the care of
the young, and thus is venerated as the patron of children.

Common of Pastors: for Bishops, p. 1059.

OPENING PRAYER

Father,
hear our prayers for mercy,
and by the help of St. Nicholas

keep us safe from all danger,
and guide us on the way of salvation.
Grant this . . . for ever and ever. ℟. **Amen.**

First Reading (Is 6:1-8), p. 1153, no. 4.

RESPONSORIAL PSALM   Ps 40:2 and 4, 7-8a, 8b-9, 10, 11

℟. (8a and 9a) **Here I am, Lord; I come to do your will.**

I have waited, waited for the LORD,
    and he stooped toward me and heard my cry.
And he put a new song into my mouth,
    a hymn to our God.—℟.

Sacrifice or oblation you wished not,
    but ears open to obedience you gave me.
Burnt offerings or sin-offerings you sought not;
    then said I, "Behold I come."—℟.

"In the written scroll it is prescribed for me,
To do your will, O my God, is my delight,
    and your law is within my heart!"—℟.

I announced your justice in the vast assembly;
    I did not restrain my lips, as you, O LORD, know.—℟.

Your justice I kept not hid within my heart;
    your faithfulness and your salvation I have spoken of;
I have made no secret of your kindness and your truth
    in the vast assembly.—℟. ↓

Alleluia (Lk 4:18), p. 1168, no. 4.
Gospel (Lk 10:1-9), p. 1172, no. 8.

Dec. 7—ST. AMBROSE, Bishop and Doctor

Memorial

St. Ambrose was one of the four great Latin Fathers and
Doctors of the Western Church. As Bishop of Milan, he
witnessed the conversion of St. Augustine, whom he baptized in 387. He enriched Latin literature with many works
on Scripture, the priesthood, doctrinal subjects, and hym-
nology. The liturgy of Milan is known as the "Ambrosian
Rite." He died in 397.

*Common of Pastors: for Bishops, p. 1059; or Common of
Doctors of the Church, p. 1072.*

OPENING PRAYER

Lord,
you made St. Ambrose
an outstanding teacher of the Catholic faith
and gave him the courage of an apostle.
Raise up in your Church more leaders after your own
    heart,
to guide us with courage and wisdom.
We ask this . . . for ever and ever. ℟. **Amen.**

First Reading (Eph 3:8-12), p. 1183, no. 4.
Responsorial Psalm (Ps 89), p. 1159, no. 4.
Alleluia (Jn 10:14), p. 1168, no. 5.
Gospel (Jn 10:11-16), p. 1173, no. 10.

PRAYER OVER THE GIFTS

Lord,
as we celebrate these holy rites,
send your Spirit to give us the light of faith
which guided St. Ambrose to make your glory known.
We ask this in the name of Jesus the Lord.
℟. **Amen.**   → No. 21, p. 626 (Pref. P 1)

PRAYER AFTER COMMUNION

Father,
you have renewed us by the power of this sacrament.
Through the teachings of St. Ambrose,
may we follow your way with courage
and prepare ourselves for the feast of eternal life.
Grant this through Christ our Lord.
℟. **Amen.**   → No. 32, p. 660

Dec. 8 — Immaculate Conception

See Vol. I, Sunday Missal, p. 1499.

[In the dioceses of the United States]

Dec. 9 — ST. JUAN DIEGO, Hermit

Juan Diego, to whom our Lady appeared at Tepeyac on December 9, 1531, was a member of the Chichimeca people, one of the more culturally advanced groups living in the Valley of Anahuac, as the area that is now Mexico City was once known. After the apparitions of the Blessed Virgin Mary, Juan Diego lived as a hermit in a small hut near the chapel that was built on Tepeyac. There he cared for the church and the first pilgrims who came to see the miraculous image and pray to the Mother of Jesus. His contemporaries were impressed with his holiness; parents used to bless their children with the wish, "May God make you like Juan Diego." He was canonized by John Paul II in 2002.

Common of Holy Men and Women, p. 1080.

OPENING PRAYER

Lord God,
through blessed Juan Diego
you made known the love of Our Lady of Guadalupe
toward your people.
Grant by his intercession
that we who follow the counsel of Mary, our Mother,
may strive continually to do your will.
We ask this . . . for ever and ever. ℟. **Amen.**

Dec. 11 — ST. DAMASUS I, Pope

Optional Memorial

Born in Spain, St. Damasus governed the Church from 366 to 384. He commanded St. Jerome to translate the New Testament into Latin, combatted the Apollinarist and Macedonian heresies and confirmed the second ecumenical council of Constantinople which had condemned the Arian heresy. He died in 384.

Common of Pastors: for Popes, p. 1057.

OPENING PRAYER

Father,
as St. Damasus loved and honored your martyrs,

so may we continue to celebrate their witness for Christ,
who lives and reigns with you and the Holy Spirit,
one God, for ever and ever. ℟. **Amen.**

First Reading (Acts 20:17-18a, 28-32, 36), p. 1157, no. 2.
Responsorial Psalm (Ps 110), p. 1161, no. 7.
Alleluia (Jn 15:15b), p. 1169, no. 7.
Gospel (Jn 15:9-17), p. 1238, no. 25.

[In the dioceses of the United States]

Dec. 12 — OUR LADY OF GUADALUPE

Feast

The Shrine of Our Lady of Guadalupe, near Mexico City, is
one of the most celebrated places of pilgrimage in North
America. On Dec. 9, 1531, the Blessed Virgin Mary appeared to an Indian convert, Juan Diego, and left with
him a picture of herself impressed upon his cloak.
Devotion to Mary under this title has continually
increased and today she is Patroness of the Americas.

ENTRANCE ANT.
Ru 12:1

**A great sign appeared in the sky, a woman clothed with
the sun, with the moon under her feet, and on her head
a crown of twelve stars.**   → No. 2, p. 614

OPENING PRAYER

God of power and mercy,
you blessed the Americas at Tepeyac
with the presence of the Virgin Mary of Guadalupe.
May her prayers help all men and women
to accept each other as brothers and sisters.
Through your justice present in our hearts
may your peace reign in the world.
We ask this . . . for ever and ever. ℟. **Amen.**

First Reading (Zec 2:14-17), p. 1117, no. 11,
        or (Rv 11:19a; 12:1-6a, 10ab), p. 1117, no. 2.
Responsorial Psalm (Jdt 13), p. 1119, no. 2.
Alleluia ("Blessed . . . our God), p. 1123, no. 5
Gospel (Lk 1:26-38), p. 1126, no. 4,
        or (Lk 1:39-47), p. 1127, no. 5.

PRAYER OVER THE GIFTS

Lord,
accept the gifts we present to you
on this feast of Our Lady of Guadalupe,
and grant that this sacrifice
will strengthen us to fulfill your commandments
as true sons and daughters of the Virgin Mary.
We ask this through Christ our Lord.
℟. **Amen.**　　　　　→ No. 21, p. 626 (Pref. P 56 or P 57)

COMMUNION ANT.　　　　　Lk 1:52

**The Lord has cast down the mighty from their thrones,
and has lifted up the lowly. ↓**

OR　　　　　See Ps 147:20

**God has not acted thus for any other nation; to no other
people has he shown his love so clearly. ↓**

PRAYER AFTER COMMUNION

Lord,
may the Body and Blood of your Son,
which we receive in this sacrament,
reconcile us always in your love.
May we who rejoice in the holy Mother of Guadalupe
live united and at peace in this world
until the day of the Lord dawns in glory.
We ask this through Christ our Lord.
℟. **Amen.**　　　　　→ No. 32, p. 660

Dec. 13 — ST. LUCY, Virgin and Martyr

Memorial

Lucy is the name of an early martyr of Syracuse (Sicily)
honored in the Roman Church from the 6th century
onward. She is invoked for protection against eye ailments.

Common of Martyrs, p. 1047; or Common of Virgins, p. 1075.

OPENING PRAYER

Lord,
give us courage through the prayers of St. Lucy.
As we celebrate her entrance into eternal glory,
we ask to share her happiness in the life to come.
Grant this . . . for ever and ever. ℞. **Amen.**

First Reading (2 Cor 10:17—11:2), p. 1194, no. 2.
Responsorial Psalm (Ps 31), p. 1139, no. 1.
Alleluia ("This is the wise virgin . . ."), p. 1194, no. 2.
Gospel (Mt 25:1-13), p. 1196, no. 2.

Dec. 14 — ST. JOHN OF THE CROSS, Priest and Doctor

Memorial

John Yepez was born at Fontiberas in Old Castile, Spain, in 1524. He took the Carmelite habit in 1563 and gave himself up to the practice of the greatest austerities. Later he collaborated with St. Teresa of Avila in reforming the Carmelite Order. He is known in the Church as one of the greatest contemplatives and teachers of mystical theology. After much physical and mental suffering, he died in peace in 1591.

ENTRANCE ANT.   Gal 6:14

I should boast of nothing but the cross of our Lord Jesus Christ; through him the world is crucified to me, and I to the world.   → No. 2, p. 614

OPENING PRAYER

Father,
you endowed John of the Cross with a spirit of self-denial
and a love of the cross.
By following his example,
may we come to the eternal vision of your glory.
We ask this . . . for ever and ever. ℞. **Amen.**

Readings and Intervenient Chants are taken from the Common of Pastors, p. 1151, or the Common of Doctors of the Church, p. 1176.

First Reading (1 Cor 2:1-10a), p. 1182, no. 2.
Responsorial Psalm (Ps 37), p. 1180, no. 2.

ALLELUIA   Mt 5:3

℟. **Alleluia, alleluia.**
Blessed are the poor in spirit;
the Kingdom of heaven is theirs.
℟. **Alleluia, alleluia.**

Gospel (Lk 14:25-33), p. 1237, no. 23.

PRAYER OVER THE GIFTS

Almighty God,
look upon the gifts we offer
in memory of St. John of the Cross.
May we imitate the love we proclaim
as we celebrate the mystery
of the suffering and death of Christ,
who is Lord for ever and ever.
℟. **Amen.**   → No. 21, p. 626 (Pref. P. 1)

COMMUNION ANT.   Mt 16:24

**If anyone wishes to come after me, he must renounce
himself, take up his cross, and follow me, says the
Lord.** ↓

PRAYER AFTER COMMUNION

God our Father,
you have shown us the mystery of the cross
in the life of St. John.
May this sacrifice make us strong,
keep us faithful to Christ
and help us to work in the Church
for the salvation of all mankind.
We ask this in the name of Jesus the Lord.
℟. **Amen.**   → No. 32, p. 660

Dec. 21 — ST. PETER CANISIUS, Priest and Doctor

Optional Memorial

This eminent Jesuit, who was born in Holland, became the second great Apostle of Germany. He enriched the Church with his standard Catechism and won the title of Doctor of the Church. He died in 1598.

Common of Pastors p. 1061; *or Common of Doctors of the Church, p.* 1072

OPENING PRAYER

Lord,
you gave St. Peter Canisius
wisdom and courage to defend the Catholic faith.
By the help of his prayers
may all who seek the truth rejoice in finding you,
and may all who believe in you
be loyal in professing their faith.
Grant this ... for ever and ever. ℟. **Amen.**

First Reading (2 Tm 4:1-5), p. 1167, no. 12.
Responsorial Psalm (Ps 40), p. 908.
Alleluia (Mt 5:16), p. 1185, no. 1.
Gospel (Mt 5:13-19), p. 1186, no. 1.

Dec. 23 — ST. JOHN OF KANTY, Priest

Optional Memorial

Born at Kanty, Poland, St. John attended the University of Cracow, where he later became a professor. He was famous for his charity and love for the poor. He died in 1473.

Common of Pastors, p. 1061, *or Common of Holy Men and Women: for Those Who Work for the Underprivileged, p.* 1089.

OPENING PRAYER

Almighty Father,
through the example of John of Kanty
may we grow in the wisdom of the saints.
As we show understanding and kindness to others,
may we receive your forgiveness.
We ask this ... for ever and ever. ℟. **Amen.**

First Reading (Jas 2:14-17), p. 1220, no. 13.
Responsorial Psalm (Ps 112), p. 1213, no. 7.
Alleluia (Jn 13:34), p. 1224, no. 10.
Gospel (Lk 6:27-38), p. 1234, no. 18.

Dec. 26, 27, 28

See pp. 91-101.

Dec. 29 — ST. THOMAS BECKET,
Bishop and Martyr

Optional Memorial

Thomas Becket, after having served as chancellor of
Henry II, was made Archbishop of Canterbury. He fought
against the King for the liberty of the Church. He was
slain on December 29, 1171.

Common of Martyrs, p. 1047; *or Common of Pastors: for
Bishops, p.* 1059.

OPENING PRAYER

Almighty God,
you granted the martyr Thomas
the grace to give his life for the cause of justice.
By his prayers
make us willing to renounce for Christ
our life in this world
so that we may find it in heaven.
We ask this . . . for ever and ever. ℟. **Amen.**

First Reading (2 Tm 2:8-13; 3:10-12), p. 1143, no. 5.
Responsorial Psalm (Ps 34), p. 1139, no. 2.
Alleluia (Mt 5:6), p. 1223, no. 2.
Gospel (Mt 16:24-27), p. 1225, no. 6.

Dec. 31 — ST. SYLVESTER I, Pope

Optional Memorial

Little is known of the reign of Pope Sylvester I. He took
an active part in the negotiations in regard to the heresy
of Arius and in the first Ecumenical Council of Nicea in
325. He died in 335.

Common of Pastors: for Popes, p. 1057.

OPENING PRAYER

Lord,
help and sustain your people
by the prayers of Pope Sylvester.
Guide us always in this present life
and bring us to the joy that never ends.
We ask this . . . for ever and ever. ℟. **Amen.**

First Reading (Ez 34:11-16), p. 1156, no. 9.
Responsorial Psalm (Ps 23), p. 1158, no. 2.
Alleluia (Mt 1:17), p. 1168, no. 3.
Gospel (Mt 16:13-19), p. 1169, no. 2.

—JANUARY —

Jan. 2—STS. BASIL THE GREAT AND GREGORY NAZIANZEN, Bishops and Doctors

Memorial

St. Basil, one of the four great Doctors of the East, was born at Cappadocia in Asia Minor. He became a monk and combatted the Arian heresy with great zeal. He wrote the famous Basilian rule of monasticism and framed the Basilian Liturgy. He died in 379.

St. Gregory, called "The Theologian," because of his profound knowledge of Sacred Scripture, was born at Nazianzen in Cappadocia, Asia Minor. He became successively the Bishop of Sosina, Nazianzen, and Patriarch of Constantinople. He died in the latter part of the 4th century after having written many pious works of Scriptural eloquence.

Common of Pastors: for Bishops, p. 1059; or Common of Doctors of the Church, p. 1072.

OPENING PRAYER

God our Father,
you inspired the Church
with the example and teaching of your saints Basil and
    Gregory.
In humility may we come to know your truth
and put it into action with faith and love.
Grant this . . . for ever and ever. ℟. **Amen.**

First Reading (Eph 4:1-7, 11-13), p. 1165, no. 8.
Responsorial Psalm (Ps 23), p. 1158, no. 2.
Alleluia (Mt 23:9b, 10b), p. 1168, no. 1.
Gospel (Mt 23, 8-12), p. 1170, no. 3.

[In the dioceses of the United States]

Jan. 4—ST. ELIZABETH ANN SETON, Religious

Memorial

Upon the death of her husband, by whom she had five children, Elizabeth Seton became a convert and in 1809 established a religious community of teaching sisters. She died in 1821 at the age of 46 and was beatified in 1963. She was canonized in September 1975.

ENTRANCE ANT. See Prv 14:1-2

Praise to the holy woman whose home is built on faithful love and whose pathway leads to God.

OR Ps 23

This is the generation which seeks the face of the God of Jacob. → No. 2, p. 614

OPENING PRAYER

Lord God,
you blessed Elizabeth Seton with gifts of grace
as wife and mother, educator and foundress,
so that she might spend her life in service to your people.
Through her example and prayers
may we learn to express our love for you
in love for others.
We ask this . . . for ever and ever. ℟. **Amen.**

Readings and Intervenient Chants are taken from the Common of Holy Men and Women, p. 1197.

PRAYER OVER THE GIFTS

Lord,
give to us who offer these gifts at your altar
the same spirit of love that filled St. Elizabeth Seton.
By celebrating this sacred eucharist with pure minds and
    loving hearts
may we offer a sacrifice that pleases you,
and bring salvation to us.
Grant this through Christ our Lord.
℟. **Amen.** → No. 21, p. 626

COMMUNION ANT. Jn 6:51

I am the living bread from heaven, says the Lord. Whoever eats this bread will live forever; the bread I shall give is my flesh for the life of the world. ↓

PRAYER AFTER COMMUNION

Lord,
we have shared
in the mystery of your love.
May we be strengthened in faith and love for the
　　eucharist
as we recall the example of St. Elizabeth Seton.
We ask this through Christ our Lord.
℟. **Amen.**

→ No. 32, p. 660

[In the dioceses of the United States]

Jan. 5 — ST. JOHN NEUMANN, Bishop

Memorial

Born in Bohemia in 1811, John Neumann came to the United
States, became a priest, and joined the Redemptorists. In
1852 he was consecrated bishop of Philadelphia and labored
zealously to establish parish schools and erect many
parishes. He died in 1860 and was canonized in 1977.

ENTRANCE ANT.   Ps 16:5-6

**O Lord, my allotted portion and my cup, you it is who
hold fast my lot. For me the measuring lines have fallen
on pleasant sites; fair to me indeed is my inheritance.**

→ No. 2, p. 614

OPENING PRAYER

Almighty God,
you called St. John Neumann
to a life of zeal and compassion
for the guidance of your people in the new world.
By his prayers
help us to build up the community of the Church
through our dedication to the Christian education of
　　youth
and through the witness of our brotherly love.
Grant this . . . for ever and ever. ℟. **Amen.**

*Readings and Intervenient Chants are taken from the
Common of Pastors, p. 1151.*

PRAYER OVER THE GIFTS

Father of mercies,
look upon the gifts
that we present in memory of Christ your Son.
Form us in his likeness
as you formed St. John,
who imitated what he handled
in these holy mysteries.
We ask this in the name of Jesus the Lord.
℞. **Amen.**   → No. 21, p. 626

COMMUNION ANT.   Mt 19:29

**Everyone who has given up home, brothers, or sisters,
father or mother, wife or children or property for my
sake will receive many times as much and inherit everlasting life.** ↓

PRAYER AFTER COMMUNION

Father of our Lord Jesus Christ,
you have united us with our Redeemer
in this memorial of his death and resurrection.
By the power of this sacrament,
help us to live,
one in spirit and in truth,
in the communion of Christ's body.
Grant this through Christ our Lord.
℞. **Amen.**   → No. 32, p. 660

[In the dioceses of the United States]

Jan. 6 — BLESSED ANDRÉ BESSETTE, Religious
Optional Memorial

Born near Quebec in 1845, André entered the Congregation
of the Holy Cross as a Brother. Because of poor health as
a child, André had been unable to attend school regularly
and could not read or write. He was assigned as a door-
keeper at the College of Notre Dame in Montreal and
remained in that capacity for over forty years. He also

performed the tasks of janitor, infirmarian, barber, gardener, and lamplighter.

André also developed a great devotion to St. Joseph and imparted it to others. In time, he was able to have a chapel built to St. Joseph. After his death on January 6, 1937, the shrine grew into the great basilica of St. Joseph's Oratory in Montreal, which is visited by pilgrims from all over the world. He was beatified in 1982 by Pope John Paul II.

Common of Holy Men and Women, p. 1080.

OPENING PRAYER

Lord our God, friend of the lowly,
you gave your servant, Brother André,
a great devotion to Saint Joseph
and a special commitment to the poor and afflicted.
Through his intercession
help us to follow his example of prayer and love
and so come to share with him in your glory.
We ask this . . . for ever and ever. ℟. **Amen.**

Readings and Intervenient Chants are taken from the Common of Holy Men and Women: for Religious, p. 1197.

Jan. 7 — ST. RAYMOND OF PEÑAFORT, Priest

Optional Memorial

Born at Barcelona, Spain, in 1175, St. Raymond labored zealously for the redemption of slaves. By order of Gregory IX he wrote five books of Decretals which are now a valuable part of the Canon Law of the Church. He died in 1275.

Common of Pastors, p. 1061.

OPENING PRAYER

Lord,
you gave St. Raymond the gift of compassion
in his ministry to sinners.
May his prayers free us from the slavery of sin
and help us to love and serve you in liberty.
We ask this . . . for ever and ever. ℟. **Amen.**

First Reading (2 Cor 5:14-20), p. 1165, no. 7.
Responsorial Psalm (Ps 103), p. 1212, no. 6.

Alleluia (Lk 21:36), p. 1224, no. 7.
Gospel (Lk 12:35-40), p. 1236, no. 22.

Jan. 13 — ST. HILARY, Bishop and Doctor

Optional Memorial

St. Hilary, Bishop of Poitiers, one of the greatest religious luminaries of France in the 4th century, strenuously defended the Church against the Arian heresy. He wrote 12 books about the Holy Trinity. He died in 368.

Common of Pastors: for Bishops, p. 1059; or Common of Doctors of the Church, p. 1072.

OPENING PRAYER

All-powerful God,
as St. Hilary defended the divinity of Christ your Son,
give us a deeper understanding of this mystery
and help us to profess it in all truth.
Grant this . . . for ever and ever. ℟. **Amen.** ↓

FIRST READING   1 Jn 2:18-25

John warns that many antichrists have appeared. They show that they are impostors because of what they say and do. They are not of the truth, and they deny that Jesus is the Christ, the Son of God. Jesus alone is the promise of eternal life.

A reading from the first Letter of John

CHILDREN, it is the last hour; and just as you heard that the antichrist was coming, so now many antichrists have appeared. Thus we know this is the last hour. They went out from us, but they were not really of our number; if they had been, they would have remained with us. Their desertion shows that none of them was of our number. But you have the anointing that comes from the Holy One, and you all have knowledge. I write to you not because you do not know the truth but because you do, and because every lie is alien to the truth. Who is the liar? Whoever denies that Jesus is the Christ. Whoever denies the Father and the Son, this is the antichrist.

Anyone who denies the Son does not have the Father, but whoever confesses the Son has the Father as well.

Let what you heard from the beginning remain in you. If what you heard from the beginning remains in you, then you will remain in the Son and in the Father. And this is the promise that he made us: eternal life.—The word of the Lord. ℟. **Thanks be to God.**

Responsorial Psalm (Ps 110), p. 1161, no. 7.
Alleluia (Mt 5:16), p. 1185, no. 1.
Gospel (Mt 5:13-19), p. 1186, no. 1.

Jan. 17 — ST. ANTHONY, Abbot

Memorial

At eighteen years of age, St. Anthony retired to the desert. He is called the Patriarch of Monks, not that before his advent the monastical life was nonexistent, but precisely because he was the first Abbot to form a stable rule for his family of monks dedicated to Divine Service. He died in 356, at 105 years of age.

ENTRANCE ANT.

Ps 92:13-14

The just man will flourish like the palm tree. Planted in the courts of God's house, he will grow like the cedars of Lebanon. ➔ No. 2, p. 614

OPENING PRAYER

Father,
you called St. Anthony
to renounce the world
and serve you in the solitude of the desert.
By his prayers and example,
may we learn to deny ourselves
and to love you above all things.
We ask this . . . for ever and ever. ℟. **Amen.**

Readings and Intervenient Chants are taken from the Common of Holy Men and Women: for Religious, p. 1197.

First Reading (Eph 6:10-13, 18), p. 1217, no. 8.
Responsorial Psalm (Ps 16), p. 1210, no. 3.
Alleluia (Jn 8:31b-32), p. 1224, no. 9

GOSPEL   Mt 19:16-26

Jesus teaches that to attain everlasting life, it is necessary to keep the
commandments. To seek absolute perfection, however, Jesus counsels his
disciples to sell all their possessions, give to the poor, and then follow him.

℣. The Lord be with you. ℟. **And also with you.**
✛ A reading from the holy Gospel according to Matthew.
℟. **Glory to you, Lord.**

SOMEONE approached Jesus and said, "Teacher, what
good must I do to gain eternal life?" Jesus answered
him, "Why do you ask me about the good? There is only
One who is good. If you wish to enter into life, keep the
commandments." He asked him, "Which ones?" And Jesus
replied, *"You shall not kill; you shall not commit adultery; you shall not steal; you shall not bear false witness;
honor your father and your mother; and you shall love
your neighbor as yourself."* The young man said to him,
"All of these I have observed. What do I still lack?" Jesus
said to him, "If you wish to be perfect, go, sell what you
have and give to the poor, and you will have treasure in
heaven. Then come, follow me." When the young man
heard this statement, he went away sad, for he had many
possessions. Then Jesus said to his disciples, "Amen, I say
to you, it will be hard for one who is rich to enter the
Kingdom of heaven. Again I say to you, it is easier for a
camel to pass through the eye of a needle than for one
who is rich to enter the Kingdom of God." When the disciples heard this, they were greatly astonished and said,
"Who then can be saved?" Jesus looked at them and said,
"For men this is impossible, but for God all things are
possible."—The Gospel of the Lord. ℟. **Praise to you,
Lord Jesus Christ.**   → No. 15, p. 623

PRAYER OVER THE GIFTS
Lord,
accept the sacrifice we offer at your altar
in commemoration of St. Anthony.

May no earthly attractions keep us from loving you.
Grant this through Christ our Lord.
℟. **Amen.** → No. 21, p. 626 (Pref. P 37-42)

COMMUNION ANT. Mt 19:21

**If you wish to be perfect, go, sell what you own, give it
all to the poor, then come, follow me.**

PRAYER AFTER COMMUNION

Lord,
you helped St. Anthony conquer the powers of darkness.
May your sacrament strengthen us
in our struggle with evil.
We ask this in the name of Jesus the Lord.
℟. **Amen.** → No. 32, p. 660

Jan. 20—ST. FABIAN, Pope and Martyr

Optional Memorial

St. Fabian, Supreme Pontiff, suffered martyrdom in 250
during the persecution of Decius.

*Common of Martyrs, p. 1047; or Common of Pastors: for Popes,
p. 1057.*

OPENING PRAYER

God our Father, glory of your priests,
may the prayers of your martyr Fabian
help us to share his faith
and offer you loving service.
Grant this . . . for ever and ever. ℟. **Amen.**

First Reading (1 Pt 5:1-4), p. 1168, no. 13.
Responsorial Psalm (Ps 40), p. 1159, no. 3.
Alleluia (Jn 10:14), p. 1168, no. 5.
Gospel (Jn 21:15-17), p. 1174, no. 12.

The Same Day, Jan. 20
ST. SEBASTIAN, Martyr

St. Sebastian, finding life too easy in his native city of Milan, went to Rome where Christians were valiantly suffering for their faith. He became their companion and "he too suffered and was crowned" (St. Ambrose).

Common of Martyrs, p. 1047.

OPENING PRAYER

Lord,
fill us with that spirit of courage
which gave your martyr Sebastian
strength to offer his life in faithful witness.
Help us to learn from him to cherish your law
and to obey you rather than men.
We ask this . . . for ever and ever. R̸. **Amen.**

First Reading (1 Pt 3:14-17), p. 1145, no. 8.
Responsorial Psalm (Ps 34), p. 1139, no. 2.
Alleluia (Jas 1:12), p. 1146, no. 4.
Gospel (Mt 10:28-33), p. 1147, no. 2.

Jan. 21 — ST. AGNES, Virgin and Martyr

Memorial

According to St. Augustine and St. Ambrose, St. Agnes, a noble Roman virgin, was about thirteen years of age when she won the martyr's crown. She was tortured by fire or decapitated in 304. Her name is inscribed in Eucharistic Prayer No. 1, and she is universally venerated as the Patroness of the Children of Mary Sodality.

Common of Martyrs, p. 1047; or Common of Virgins, p. 1075.

OPENING PRAYER

Almighty, eternal God,
you choose what the world considers weak
to put the worldly power to shame.
May we who celebrate the birth of St. Agnes into eternal
    joy
be loyal to the faith she professed.
Grant this . . . for ever and ever. R̸. **Amen.**

First Reading (1 Cor 1:26-31), p. 1215, no. 3.
Responsorial Psalm (Ps 23), p. 1158, no. 2.
Alleluia (Jn 15:9b, 5b), p. 1224, no. 13.
Gospel (Mt 13:44-46), p. 1227, no. 5.

Jan. 22—ST. VINCENT, Deacon and Martyr

Optional Memorial

St. Vincent, born at Huesca in Spain, is one of the great
Deacons of the Church. For his defense of Christianity he
suffered martyrdom about 300.

Common of Martyrs, p. 1047.

OPENING PRAYER

Eternal Father,
you gave St. Vincent
the courage to endure torture and death for the gospel:
fill us with your Spirit
and strengthen us in your love.
We ask this . . . for ever and ever. ℟. **Amen.**

First Reading (2 Cor 4:7-15), p. 1142, no. 3.
Responsorial Psalm (Ps 34), p. 1139, no. 2.
Alleluia (Mt 5:10), p. 1146, no. 1.
Gospel (Mt 10:17-22), p. 1147, no. 1.

Jan. 24 — ST. FRANCIS DE SALES, Bishop and Doctor

Memorial

St. Francis was born near Annecy in Savoy in 1567. After
many victories and conversions which were the fruits of
his apostolic zeal in combatting Calvinism, St. Francis
succeeded to the bishopric of Geneva. With St. Frances de
Chantal he founded the Visitation Order. After writing
several devout treatises for the edification of the faithful,
he died at Lyons, France, in 1622. He was canonized in 1655,
and in 1877, Pius IX placed him among the Doctors of the
Church.

*Common of Pastors: for Bishops, p. 1059; or Common of
Doctors of the Church, p. 1072.*

OPENING PRAYER

Father,
you gave Francis de Sales the spirit of compassion
to befriend all men on the way to salvation.
By his example, lead us to show your gentle love
in the service of our fellow men.
Grant this . . . for ever and ever. ℟. **Amen.**

First Reading (Eph 3:8-12), p. 1183, no. 4.
Responsorial Psalm (Ps 37), p. 1180, no. 2.
Alleluia (Jn 13:34), p. 1224, no. 10.
Gospel (Jn 15:9-17), p. 1238, no. 25.

PRAYER OVER THE GIFTS

Lord,
by this offering
may the divine fire of your Holy Spirit,
which burned in the gentle heart of Francis de Sales,
inspire us with compassion and love.
We ask this through Christ our Lord.
℟. **Amen.**   → No. 21, p. 626

PRAYER AFTER COMMUNION

Merciful Father,
may the sacrament we have received
help us to imitate Francis de Sales in love and service;
bring us to share with him the glory of heaven.
We ask this in the name of Jesus the Lord.
℟. **Amen.**   → No. 32, p. 660

Jan. 25 — THE CONVERSION OF ST. PAUL,
Apostle

Feast

The conversion of Saul while journeying to Damascus is
perhaps the greatest miracle in the history of the
Primitive Church. The doctrine of the Mystical Body of
Christ, which teaches us that all the faithful are members
of the same Body, whose Head Christ is, receives a very
clear meaning in the words of Christ addressed to Saul,

the persecutor of Christians: "Saul, Saul, why are you persecuting me?"

ENTRANCE ANT.   2 Tm 1:12; 4:8

I know whom I have believed. I am sure that he, the just judge, will guard my pledge until the day of judgment.

➜ No. 2, p. 614

OPENING PRAYER

God our Father,
you taught the gospel to all the world
through the preaching of Paul your apostle.
May we who celebrate his conversion to the faith
follow him in bearing witness to your truth.
We ask this . . . for ever and ever. ℟. **Amen.** ↓

FIRST READING   Acts 22:3-16

Before the mission to the Gentiles is officially begun, Luke must incorporate Saul into the early Church. The narrative of Saul's conversion is introduced. It is not merely a conversion story; it is rather the story of his call "to the Gentiles."

A reading from the Acts of the Apostles

PAUL addressed the people in these words: "I am a Jew, born in Tarsus in Cilicia, but brought up in this city. At the feet of Gamaliel I was educated strictly in our ancestral law and was zealous for God, just as all of you are today. I persecuted this Way to death, binding both men and women and delivering them to prison. Even the high priest and the whole council of elders can testify on my behalf. For from them I even received letters to the brothers and set out for Damascus to bring back to Jerusalem in chains for punishment those there as well.

"On that journey as I drew near to Damascus, about noon a great light from the sky suddenly shone around me. I fell to the ground and heard a voice saying to me, 'Saul, Saul, why are you persecuting me?' I replied, 'Who are you, sir?' And he said to me, 'I am Jesus the Nazorean whom you are persecuting.'My companions saw the light but did not hear the voice of the one who spoke to me. I asked, 'What shall I do, sir?' The Lord answered me, 'Get up and go into Damascus, and there you will be told about everything appointed for you to do.' Since I could see nothing because of the brightness of that light, I was led by hand by my companions and entered Damascus.

"A certain Ananias, a devout observer of the law, and highly spoken of by all the Jews who lived there, came to me and stood there and said, 'Saul, my brother, regain your sight.' And at that very moment I regained my sight and saw him. Then he said, 'The God of our ancestors designated you to know his will, to see the Righteous One, and to hear the sound of his voice; for you will be his witness before all to what you have seen and heard. Now, why delay? Get up and have yourself baptized and your sins washed away, calling upon his name.' "—The word of the Lord. ℟. **Thanks be to God.** ↓

OR

FIRST READING   Acts 9:1-22

Saul in his former life persecuted the Church founded by Jesus Christ. The reality of Saul's vision on the road to Damascus is recognized as the operation of grace bestowed upon him by the Lord. Henceforth, Jesus will make of him a servant and take possession of him.

A reading from the Acts of the Apostles

SAUL, still breathing murderous threats against the disciples of the Lord, went to the high priest and asked him for letters to the synagogues in Damascus, that, if he should find any men or women who belonged to the Way, he might bring them back to Jerusalem in chains. On his journey, as he was nearing Damascus, a light from the sky suddenly flashed around him. He fell to the ground and heard a voice saying to him, "Saul, Saul, why are you persecuting me?" He said, "Who are you, sir?" The reply came, "I am Jesus, whom you are persecuting. Now get up and go into the city and you will be told what you must do." The men who were traveling with him stood speechless, for they heard the voice but could see no one. Saul got up from the ground, but when he opened his eyes he could see nothing; so they led him by the hand and brought him to Damascus. For three days he was unable to see, and he neither ate nor drank.

There was a disciple in Damascus named Ananias, and the Lord said to him in a vision, "Ananias." He answered, "Here I am, Lord." The Lord said to him, "Get up and go to the street called Straight and ask at the house of Judas for a man from Tarsus named Saul. He is there praying, and in a vision he has seen a man named Ananias come in and lay his hands on him, that he may regain his sight." But Ananias replied, "Lord, I have heard from many sources about this man, what evil things he has done to your holy ones in Jerusalem. And here he has authority from the chief priests to imprison all who call upon your name." But the Lord said to him, "Go, for this man is a chosen instrument of mine to carry my name before Gentiles, kings, and children of Israel, and I will show him what he will have to suffer for my name." So Ananias went and entered the house; laying his hands on him, he said, "Saul, my brother, the Lord has sent me, Jesus who appeared to you on the way by which you came, that you may regain your sight and be filled with the Holy Spirit." Immediately things like scales fell from his eyes and he regained his sight. He got up and was baptized, and when he had eaten, he recovered his strength.

He stayed some days with the disciples in Damascus, and he began at once to proclaim Jesus in the synagogues, that he is the Son of God. All who heard him were astounded and said, "Is not this the man who in Jerusalem ravaged those who call upon this name, and came here expressly to take them back in chains to the chief priests?" But Saul grew all the stronger and confounded the Jews who lived in Damascus, proving that this is the Christ.—The word of the Lord. ℟. **Thanks be to God.** ↓

RESPONSORIAL PSALM   Ps 117:1bc, 2

℟. (Mk 16:15) **Go out to all the world and tell the Good News.**

℟. Or: **Alleluia, alleluia.**

Praise the LORD, all you nations;
  glorify him, all you peoples!—℟.

For steadfast is his kindness toward us,
  and the fidelity of the LORD endures forever.—℟. ↓

ALLELUIA   See Jn 15:16

℟. **Alleluia, alleluia.**
I chose you from the world,
to go and bear fruit that will last, says the Lord.
℟. **Alleluia, alleluia.** ↓

GOSPEL   Mk 16:15-18

Christ's commission to his disciples is emphatic. Repentance and remission of sins are to be preached among all nations. In spreading this Gospel, they are to be saved from danger.

℣. The Lord be with you. ℟. **And also with you.**
✛ A reading from the holy Gospel according to Mark.
℟. **Glory to you, Lord.**

JESUS appeared to the Eleven and said to them: "Go into the whole world and proclaim the Gospel to every creature. Whoever believes and is baptized will be saved; whoever does not believe will be condemned. These signs will accompany those who believe: in my name they will drive out demons, they will speak new languages. They will pick up serpents with their hands, and if they drink any deadly thing, it will not harm them. They will lay hands on the sick, and they will recover."—The Gospel of the Lord. ℟. **Praise to you, Lord Jesus Christ.**

→ No. 15, p. 623

PRAYER OVER THE GIFTS   [God's Power and Glory]

Lord,
may your Spirit who helped Paul the apostle
to preach your power and glory
fill us with the light of faith
as we celebrate this holy eucharist.
We ask this in the name of Jesus the Lord.
℟. **Amen.**   ➜ No. 21, p. 626 (Pref. P 64-65)

COMMUNION ANT.   Gal 2:20

I live by faith in the Son of God, who loved me and sacrificed himself for me. ↓

PRAYER AFTER COMMUNION

Lord God,
you filled Paul the apostle
with love for all the churches:
may the sacrament we have received
foster in us this love for your people.
Grant this through Christ our Lord.
℟. **Amen.**   ➜ No. 32, p. 660

Jan. 26 — STS. TIMOTHY AND TITUS, Bishops

Memorial

When St. Paul preached at Ephesus, Timothy admired his virtues, renounced all his worldly possessions in order to be his disciple, and accompanied him in the evangelization of many cities. He was consecrated Bishop of Ephesus by St. Paul. He died in the year 97.

St. Titus was the friend and disciple of St. Paul. He was also ordained Bishop of Crete by St. Paul. One of the canonical Letters addressed by St. Paul to Titus forms part of the New Testament. He died at the age of 105. St. John Chrysostom and St. Jerome eulogized him.

Common of Pastors: for Bishops, p. 1059.

OPENING PRAYER

God our Father,
you gave your saints Timothy and Titus
the courage and wisdom of the apostles:
may their prayers help us to live holy lives
and lead us to heaven, our true home.
Grant this . . . for ever and ever. ℟. **Amen.** ↓

The First Reading is proper *in this Memorial, and one of the following is always to be read.*

FIRST READING 2 Tm 1:1-8

Paul sees God's power at work in the souls of all Christians and in his fellow worker, Timothy. Paul reminds Timothy of God's gift of grace, which dwells in him as a result of the imposition of hands. As an office-bearer, Timothy has received. together with this gift of grace the Spirit of strength and love.

A reading from the beginning of the second Letter of
Saint Paul to Timothy

PAUL, an Apostle of Christ Jesus by the will of God for the promise of life in Christ Jesus, to Timothy, my dear child: grace, mercy, and peace from God the Father and Christ Jesus our Lord.

I am grateful to God, whom I worship with a clear conscience as my ancestors did, as I remember you constantly in my prayers, night and day. I yearn to see you again, recalling your tears, so that I may be filled with joy, as I recall your sincere faith that first lived in your grandmother Lois and in your mother Eunice and that I am confident lives also in you.

For this reason, I remind you to stir into flame the gift of God that you have through the imposition of my hands. For God did not give us a spirit of cowardice but rather of power and love and self-control. So do not be ashamed of your testimony to our Lord, nor of me, a prisoner for his sake; but bear your share of hardship for the Gospel with the strength that comes from God.—The word of the Lord. ℟. **Thanks be to God.** ↓

OR

FIRST READING Ti 1:1-5

In the beginning of his Letter to Titus, Paul calls himself an Apostle. Without reservation, he acknowledges his mission to spread the work of God. Paul tells Titus to carry on the work he started, especially to appoint more leaders in the Church.

A reading from the beginning of the Letter of
Saint Paul to Titus

PAUL, a slave of God and Apostle of Jesus Christ for the sake of the faith of God's chosen ones and the recognition of religious truth, in the hope of eternal life that God, who does not lie, promised before time began, who indeed at the proper time revealed his word in the proclamation with which I was entrusted by the command of God our savior, to Titus, my true child in our common faith: grace and peace from God the Father and Christ Jesus our savior.

For this reason I left you in Crete so that you might set right what remains to be done and appoint presbyters in every town, as I directed you.—The word of the Lord. ℟. **Thanks be to God.** ↓

RESPONSORIAL PSALM Ps 96:1-2a, 2b-3, 7-8a, 10

℟. (3) **Proclaim God's marvelous deeds to all the nations.**

Sing to the LORD a new song;
    sing to the LORD, all you lands.
Sing to the LORD; bless his name.—℟.

Announce his salvation, day after day.
Tell his glory among the nations;
    among all peoples, his wondrous deeds.—℟.

Give to the LORD, you families of nations,
    give to the LORD glory and praise;
    give to the LORD the glory due his name!—℟.

Say among the nations: The LORD is king.
He has made the world firm, not to be moved;
   he governs the peoples with equity.—R̶.̶ ↓

ALLELUIA   Lk 4:18

R̶.̶ **Alleluia, alleluia.**
The Lord sent me to bring glad tidings to the poor
and to proclaim liberty to captives.
R̶.̶ **Alleluia, alleluia.** ↓

Gospel (Lk 10:1-9), p. 1172, no. 8.

Jan. 27 — ST. ANGELA MERICI, Virgin

Optional Memorial

St. Angela was born on the shores of Lake Giarda. She founded the Order of the Ursulines, the first teaching Order for women approved by the Church. She died in 1540.

Common of Virgins, p. 1075; *or Common of Holy Men and Women: for Teachers*, p. 1090.

OPENING PRAYER

Lord,
may St. Angela commend us to your mercy;
may her charity and wisdom help us
to be faithful to your teaching
and to follow it in our lives.
We ask this . . . for ever and ever. R̶.̶ **Amen.**

First Reading (1 Pt 4:7b-11), p. 1221, no. 15.
Responsorial Psalm (Ps 148), p. 1192, no. 2.
Alleluia (See Mt 11:25), p. 1223, no. 4.
Gospel (Mk 9:34b-37), p. 1233, no. 15.

Jan. 28—ST. THOMAS AQUINAS, Priest and Doctor

Memorial

Thomas' undisputed mastery in scholastic theology gained for him the title of *Angelic Doctor*. He is one of the greatest glories of the Dominican Order. Pope Leo XIII declared him patron of all Catholic Schools. He left the great monument of his learning, the *Summa Theologica*, unfinished, for, on his way to the Council of Lyons, in 1274. he fell sick and died in the Cistercian monastery of Fossa Nuova, Italy.

Common of Doctors of the Church, p. 1073; or Common of Pastors, p. 1061,

OPENING PRAYER

God our Father,
you made Thomas Aquinas known for his holiness and
    learning.
Help us to grow in wisdom by his teaching,
and in holiness by imitating his faith.
Grant this ... for ever and ever. R̃. **Amen.**

First Reading (Wis 7:7-10, 15-16), p. 1176, no. 2.
Responsorial Psalm (Ps 119), p. 1180, no. 3.
Alleluia (Mt 23:9b, 10b), p. 1185, no. 2.
Gospel (Mt 23:8-12), p. 1188, no. 4.

Jan. 31 — ST. JOHN BOSCO, Priest

Memorial

This admirable "Apostle of Youth" is almost our contemporary. He founded the Salesian Society of St. Francis de Sales, and the Daughters of Mary, Help of Christians. His lifework was consecrated to the care of young boys and girls. He died in 1888 and was canonized by Pope Pius XI in 1934. The motto on the Salesian coat of arms: "Give me only souls and keep the rest," bears witness to Don Bosco's Christian ideal.

Common of Pastors, p. 1061; or Common of Holy Men and Women: for Teachers, p. 1090.

OPENING PRAYER

Lord,
you called John Bosco
to be a teacher and father to the young.
Fill us with love like his:
may we give ourselves completely to your service
and to the salvation of mankind.
We ask this ... for ever and ever. R̃. **Amen.**

First Reading (Phil 4:4-9), p. 1218, no. 10.
Responsorial Psalm (Ps 103), p. 1212, no. 6.
Alleluia (Mt 23:11, 12b), p. 1223, no. 6.
Gospel (Mt 18:1-5), p. 1227, no. 7.

—FEBRUARY—

Feb. 2 — THE PRESENTATION OF THE LORD

Feast

We have evidence going back to the 5th century of the celebration at Jerusalem of the feast of the Presentation of the Lord in the temple. The feast was accepted at Rome in the 7th century under the name Hypapante. Beginning with the 10th century Western liturgical books emphasized the purification of Mary, which henceforth gave its name to the feast. In full accord with the traditions of the Eastern Church, the Code of Rubrics in 1960 established that this must be regarded as a feast of the Lord.

Candles are blessed on this day, a symbolic representation of the words of holy Simeon concerning Christ: "A light of revelation to the Gentiles." A procession of the faithful with lighted candles is held to commemorate the entry of Christ, the Light of the World, into the temple of Jerusalem.

BLESSING OF CANDLES AND PROCESSION

First Form: Procession

The people gather in a chapel or other suitable place outside the church where the Mass will be celebrated. They carry unlighted candles.

While the candles are being lighted, this canticle or another hymn is sung:

The Lord will come with mighty power,
and give light to the eyes of all who serve him, alleluia.

The priest greets the people as usual, and briefly invites the people to take an active part in this celebration. He may use these or similar words:

Forty days ago we celebrated the joyful feast of the birth of our Lord Jesus Christ. Today we recall the holy day on which he was presented in the temple, fulfilling the law of Moses and at the same time going to meet his faithful people. Led by the Spirit, Simeon and Anna came to the temple, recognized Christ as their Lord, and proclaimed him with joy.

United by the Spirit, may we now go to the house of God to welcome Christ the Lord. There we shall recognize him in the breaking of bread until he comes again in glory.

Then the priest joins his hands and blesses the candles:

Let us pray.
God our Father, source of all light,
today you revealed to Simeon
your Light of revelation to the nations.
Bless ✚ these candles and make them holy.
May we who carry them to praise your glory
walk in the path of goodness
and come to the light that shines for ever.
Grant this through Christ our Lord. ℞. **Amen.** ↓

OR

Let us pray.
God our Father, source of eternal light,
fill the hearts of all believers
with the light of faith.
May we who carry these candles in your church
come with joy to the light of glory.
We ask this through Christ our Lord. ℞. **Amen.** ↓

He sprinkles the candles in silence.

The priest then takes the candle prepared for him, and the procession begins with the acclamation:

Let us go in peace to meet the Lord.

During the procession, the following canticle or another hymn is sung:

ANTIPHON

**Christ is the light of the nations
and the glory of Israel his people.**

CANTICLE

Now, Lord, you have kept your word:
let your servant go in peace.

The Antiphon is repeated: "Christ is the light, etc."

With my own eyes I have seen the salvation
which you have prepared in the sight of every people.

The Antiphon is repeated: "Christ is the light, etc."

A light to reveal you to the nations
and the glory of your people Israel.

The Antiphon is repeated: "Christ is the light, etc."

As the procession enters the church, the Entrance Antiphon of the Mass is sung. When the priest reaches the altar, he venerates it, and may incense it. Then he goes to the chair (and replaces the cope with the chasuble). After the Gloria, *he sings or says the Opening Prayer. The Mass continues as usual.*

Second Form: Solemn Entrance

The people, carrying unlighted candles, assemble in the church. The priest, vested in white, is accompanied by his ministers and by a representative group of the faithful. They go to a suitable place (either in front of the door or in the church itself) where most of the congregation can easily take part.

Then the candles are lighted while the antiphon, The Lord will come, *or another hymn is sung.*

After the greeting and introduction, he blesses the candles, as above, and goes in procession to the altar, while all are singing. The Mass is as described above.

THE MASS

ENTRANCE ANT. Ps 48:10-11

Within your temple, we ponder your loving kindness, O god. As your name, so also your praise reaches to the ends of the earth. Your right hand is filled with justice.

→ No. 2, p. 614

OPENING PRAYER

All-powerful Father,
Christ your Son became man for us

and was presented in the temple.
May he free our hearts from sin
and bring us into your presence.
We ask this . . . for ever and ever. ℟. **Amen.** ↓

When this feast occurs apart from Sunday, only one of the first two Readings is read before the Gospel.

FIRST READING   Mal 3:1-4

Malachi presents the eschatological moment in the language of God's great interventions in sacred history. Malachi does not reject the Jerusalem sacrifice altogether, but he awaits its transformation just as he expects the priestly messenger of the Covenant to be perfected and transcended by the Lord.

A reading from the Book of the Prophet Malachi

THUS says the Lord God:
Lo, I am sending my messenger
    to prepare the way before me;
And suddenly there will come to the temple
    the LORD whom you seek,
And the messenger of the covenant whom you desire.
    Yes, he is coming, says the LORD of hosts.
But who will endure the day of his coming?
    And who can stand when he appears?
For he is like the refiner's fire,
    or like the fuller's lye.
He will sit refining and purifying silver,
    and he will purify the sons of Levi,
Refining them like gold or like silver
    that they may offer due sacrifice to the LORD.
Then the sacrifice of Judah and Jerusalem
    will please the LORD,
        as in the days of old, as in years gone by.
The word of the Lord. ℟. **Thanks be to God.** ↓

RESPONSORIAL PSALM   Ps 24:7, 8, 9, 10

℟. (8) **Who is this king of glory? It is the Lord!**

Lift up, O gates, your lintels;
    reach up, you ancient portals,
      that the king of glory may come in!—℟.

Who is this king of glory?
    The LORD, strong and mighty,
      the LORD, mighty in battle.—℟.

Lift up, O gates, your lintels;
    reach up, you ancient portals,
      that the king of glory may come in!—℟.

Who is this king of glory?
    The LORD of hosts; he is the king of glory.—℟. ↓

SECOND READING   Heb 2:14-18

In the biblical sense, "flesh" means human nature considered in its weakness and frailty. It is contrasted with "spirit" and God. Because of the connection between sin and death, Christ overcomes the power of death through his priestly work. In Christ's Death and Resurrection, the nature of death is changed.

A reading from the Letter to the Hebrews

SINCE the children share in blood and flesh, Jesus likewise shared in them, that through death he might destroy the one who has the power of death, that is, the Devil, and free those who through fear of death had been subject to slavery all their life. Surely he did not help angels but rather the descendants of Abraham; therefore, he had to become like his brothers and sisters in every way, that he might be a merciful and faithful high priest before God to expiate the sins of the people. Because he himself was tested through what he suffered, he is able to help those who are being tested.—The word of the Lord.
℟. **Thanks be to God.** ↓

ALLELUIA   Lk 2:32
℟. **Alleluia, alleluia.**
A light of revelation to the Gentiles,
and glory for your people Israel.
℟. **Alleluia, alleluia.** ↓

GOSPEL   Lk 2:22-40 or 2:22-32

Mary and Joseph come with the Christ Child to the temple ceremony to present Jesus according to the prescriptions of the Jewish law. Jesus is formally stamped as a member of God's chosen people through whom world salvation is to be achieved.

[If the "Short Form" is used, omit indented tent in brackets.]

℣. The Lord be with you. ℟. **And also with you.**
✚ A reading from the holy Gospel according to Luke.
℟. **Glory to you, Lord.**

WHEN the days were completed for their purification according to the law of Moses, Mary and Joseph took Jesus up to Jerusalem to present him to the Lord, just as it is written in the law of the Lord, *Every male that opens the womb shall be consecrated to the Lord,* and to offer the sacrifice of *a pair of turtledoves or two young pigeons,* in accordance with the dictate in the law of the Lord.

Now there was a man in Jerusalem whose name was Simeon. This man was righteous and devout, awaiting the consolation of Israel, and the Holy Spirit was upon him. It had been revealed to him by the Holy Spirit that he should not see death before he had seen the Christ of the Lord. He came in the Spirit into the temple; and when the parents brought in the child Jesus to perform the custom of the law in regard to him, he took him into his arms and blessed God, saying:

> "Now, Master, you may let your servant go
> in peace, according to your word,
> for my eyes have seen your salvation,
> which you prepared in the sight of all the peoples:
> a light for revelation to the Gentiles,
> and glory for your people Israel."

[The child's father and mother were amazed at what was said about him; and Simeon blessed them and said to Mary his mother, "Behold, this child is destined for the fall and rise of many in Israel, and to be a sign that will be contradicted—and you yourself a sword will pierce—so that the thoughts of many hearts may be revealed." * There was also a prophetess, Anna, the daughter of Phanuel, of the tribe of Asher. She was advanced in years, having lived seven years with her husband after her marriage, and then as a widow until she was eighty-four. She never left the temple, but worshiped night and day with fasting and prayer. And coming forward at that very time, she gave thanks to God and spoke about the child to all who were awaiting the redemption of Jerusalem.

When they had fulfilled all the prescriptions of the law of the Lord, they returned to Galilee, to their own town of Nazareth. The child grew and became strong, filled with wisdom; and the favor of God was upon him.]

The Gospel of the Lord. ℟. **Praise to you, Lord Jesus Christ** → No. 15, p. 623

PRAYER OVER THE GIFTS

Lord,
accept the gifts your Church offers you with joy,
since in fulfillment of your will
your Son offered himself as a lamb without blemish
for the life of the world.
We ask this through Christ our Lord. ℟. **Amen.** ↓

PREFACE (P 49)

℣. The Lord be with you. ℟. **And also with you.**
℣. Lift up your hearts. ℟. **We lift them up to the Lord.**
℣. Let us give thanks to the Lord our God. ℟. **It is right to give him thanks and praise.**

Father, all-powerful and ever-living God,
we do well always and everywhere to give you thanks
through Jesus Christ our Lord.

---

* When this Gospel is used on Dec. 30, it ends here.

Today your Son,
who shares your eternal splendor,
was presented in the temple,
and revealed by the Spirit
as the glory of Israel
and the light of all peoples.
Our hearts are joyful,
for we have seen your salvation,
and now with the angels and saints
we praise you for ever: ➤ No. 23, p. 627

COMMUNION ANT. Lk 2:30-31

With my own eyes I have seen the salvation which you have prepared in the sight of all the nations. ↓

PRAYER AFTER COMMUNION

Lord,
you fulfilled the hope of Simeon,
who did not die
until he had been privileged to welcome the Messiah.
May this communion perfect your grace in us
and prepare us to meet Christ
when he comes to bring us into everlasting life,
for he is Lord for ever and ever.
℟. **Amen.** ➤ No. 32, p. 660

Optional Solemn Blessings, p. 692, and Prayers over the People, p. 699.

Feb. 3 — ST. BLASE, Bishop and Martyr

Optional Memorial

St. Blase, Bishop of Sebaste, was beheaded after terrible torments, under Licinius in 317. Among his many miracles, there is cited one in which he cured a boy who was choking from a fishbone. Thus, he is venerated as the patron saint against diseases of the throat.

Common of Martyrs, p. 1047; or Common of Pastors: for Bishops, p. 1059.

OPENING PRAYER

Lord,
hear the prayers of your martyr Blase.
Give us the joy of your peace in this life
and help us to gain the happiness that will never end.
Grant this . . . for ever and ever. ℟. **Amen.**

First Reading (Rom 5:1-5), p. 1141, no. 1.
Responsorial Psalm (Ps 117), p. 1161, no. 8.
Alleluia (Mt 28:19a, 20b), p. 1168, no. 2.
Gospel (Mk 16:15-20), p. 1171, no. 6.

The Same Day, Feb. 3
ST. ANSGAR, Bishop

Optional Memorial

St. Ansgar died in Bremen, Germany, on February 3, 865.
Since the holy apostles of Germany, England and the
Slavic countries were added to the liturgical calendar in
the 19th century, it was only right to include the apostle
of Denmark and Switzerland in the latest calendar
reform.

Common of Pastors: for Missionaries, p. 1067, *or for Bishops,
p.* 1059.

OPENING PRAYER

Father, you sent St. Ansgar
to bring the light of Christ to many nations.
May his prayers help us
to walk in the light of your truth.
We ask this . . . for ever and ever. ℟. **Amen.**

First Reading (Is 52:7-10), p. 1153, no. 5.
Responsorial Psalm (Ps 96), p. 1160, no. 5.
Alleluia (Mk 1:17), p. 1168, no. 3.
Gospel (Mk 1:14-20), p. 1171, no. 5.

Feb. 5 — ST. AGATHA, Virgin and Martyr

Memorial

St. Agatha, an illustrious Sicilian virgin, was martyred
at Catania in 251 for refusing the solicitations of a Roman
Senator. Her name appears in the First Eucharistic
Prayer.

Common of Martyrs, p. 1047; or Common of Virgins, p. 1075.

OPENING PRAYER

Lord,
let your forgiveness be won for us
by the pleading of St. Agatha,
who found favor with you by her chastity
and by her courage in suffering death for the gospel.
Grant this . . . for ever and ever. ℟. **Amen.**

First Reading (1 Cor 1:26-31), p. 1215, no. 2.
Responsorial Psalm (Ps 31), p. 1139, no. 1.
Alleluia (1 Pt 4:14), p. 1147, no. 5.
Gospel (Lk 9:23-26), p. 1148, no. 4.

Feb. 6 — ST. PAUL MIKI and HIS COMPANIONS, Martyrs

Memorial

St. Paul Miki and his twenty-five companions were crucified at Nagasaki, Japan, on February 5, 1597. They were
the first martyrs of the Far East to be canonized (1862)
and included priests and laymen, European missionaries
and Japanese Christians.

Common of Martyrs, p. 1041.

OPENING PRAYER

God our Father,
source of strength for all your saints,
you led Paul Miki and his companions
through the suffering of the cross
to the joy of eternal life.
May their prayers give us the courage
to be loyal until death in professing our faith.
We ask this . . . for ever and ever. ℟. **Amen.**

First Reading (Gal 2:19-20), p. 1216, no. 5.
Responsorial Psalm (Ps 126), p. 1140, no. 4.
Alleluia (Mt 28:19a, 20b), p. 1168, no. 2.
Gospel (Mt 28:16-20), p. 1170, no. 4.

Feb. 8 — ST. JEROME EMILIANI, Priest

Optional Memorial

St. Jerome was born in Venice and left everything for the sake of the Lord. He founded a Congregation that was dedicated to orphanages, schools, and the education of children. He died of the plague in 1537.

Common of Holy Men and Women: for Teachers, p. 1090.

OPENING PRAYER

God of mercy'
you chose Jerome Emiliani
to be a father and friend of orphans.
May his prayers keep us faithful
to the Spirit we have received,
who makes us your children.
Grant this . . . for ever and ever. ℟. **Amen.**

First Reading (Tb 12:6-13), p. 1200, no. 8.
Responsorial Psalm (Ps 34), p. 1211, no. 5.
Alleluia (Mt 5:3), p. 1223, no. 1.
Gospel (Mk 10:17-30 or 17-27), p. 1233, no. 17.

Feb. 10 — ST. SCHOLASTICA, Virgin

Memorial

St. Scholastica was the twin sister of St. Benedict. Embracing the rule of her brother, she founded the Order of Benedictine nuns. She died in 542.

Common of Virgins, p. 1075; or Common of Holy Men and Women: for Religious, p. 1086.

OPENING PRAYER

Lord,
as we recall the memory of St. Scholastica,
we ask that by her example
we may serve you with love and obtain perfect joy.
Grant this . . . for ever and ever. ℟. **Amen.**

First Reading (Sg 8:6-7), p. 1190, no. 1.
Responsorial Psalm (Ps 148), p. 1193, no. 2.
Alleluia (Jn 14:23), p. 1194, no. 1.
Gospel (Lk 10:38-42), p. 1196, no. 3.

Feb. 11 — OUR LADY OF LOURDES
Optional Memorial

The first of the eighteen apparitions of the Blessed Virgin Mary to the humble Bernadette took place at Lourdes on February 11, 1858. On March 25, when Bernadette asked the Beautiful Lady her name, she replied: "I am the Immaculate Conception." The devotion of people in all parts of the world to our Lady of Lourdes, together with the countless miracles that have been wrought through her intercession. has caused one of the most marvelous spiritual regenerations in the history of the Church.

Common of the Blessed Virgin Mary, p. 1032.

OPENING PRAYER

God of mercy,
we celebrate the feast of Mary,
the sinless mother of God.
May her prayers help us
to rise above our human weakness.
We ask this . . . for ever and ever. ℟. **Amen.**

FIRST READING   Is 66:10-14c

The power of the Lord is manifest to his servants. They are to rejoice and exult in the fulfillment that he gives them. He will give them wealth and comfort.

A reading from the Book of the Prophet Isaiah

REJOICE with Jerusalem and be glad because of her,
all you who love her;
Exult, exult with her,
    all you who were mourning over her!
Oh, that you may suck fully
    of the milk of her comfort,
That you may nurse with delight
    at her abundant breasts!
    For thus says the LORD:
Lo, I will spread prosperity over her like a river,
    and the wealth of the nations like an overflowing
        torrent.

As nurslings, you shall be carried in her arms,
  and fondled in her lap;
As a mother comforts her child,
  so will I comfort you;
  in Jerusalem you shall find your comfort.

When you see this, your heart shall rejoice,
  and your bodies flourish like the grass;
The LORD's power shall be known to his servants.
The word of the Lord. ℟. **Thanks be to God.**

Responsorial Psalm (Jdt 13), p. 1119, no. 2.
Alleluia (See Lk 1:45), p. 1123, no. 2.
Gospel (Jn 2:1-11), p. 1130, no. 11.

Feb. 14 — STS. CYRIL and METHODIUS, Bishops

Memorial

Born in Thessalonica, these two brothers evangelized
Moravia, Bohemia, and Bulgaria. Consecrated Bishops by
Pope Adrian II, St. Cyril died at Rome in the year 869 and
St. Methodius in the year 885.

*Common of Pastors: for Founders of Churches. p. 1065, or for
Missionaries, p. 1067.*

OPENING PRAYER

Father,
you brought the light of the gospel to the Slavic nations
through St. Cyril and his brother St. Methodius.
Open our hearts to understand your teaching
and help us to become one in faith and praise.
Grant this . . . for ever and ever. ℟. **Amen.**

First Reading (Acts 13:46-49) p. 1156, no. 1.
Responsorial Psalm (Ps 117), p. 1161, no. 8.
Alleluia (Lk 4:18), p. 1168, no. 4.
Gospel (Lk 10:1-9), p. 1172, no. 8.

Feb. 17 — SEVEN FOUNDERS OF THE ORDER OF SERVITES, Religious

Optional Memorial

In 1233 seven members of a Florentine Confraternity founded the Order of Servites of the Blessed Virgin Mary. The Servites led an austere life, meditating constantly on the Passion of our Lord and venerating the Blessed Virgin as Our Lady of Sorrows.

Common of Holy Men and Women: for Religious, p. 1086.

OPENING PRAYER

Lord,
fill us with the love
which inspired the seven holy brothers
to honor the mother of God with special devotion
and to lead your people to you.
We ask this . . . for ever and ever. ℟. **Amen.**

First Reading (Rom 8:26-30), p. 1214, no. 1.
Responsorial Psalm (Ps 34), p. 1211, no. 5.
Alleluia (Mt 5:3), p. 1223, no. 1.
Gospel (Mt 19:27-29), p. 1229, no. 9.

Feb. 21 —ST. PETER DAMIAN, Bishop and Doctor

Optional Memorial

Peter Damian a Benedictine monk, rendered immense services to Gregory VII in his struggle for the rights of the Church. He died in 1072.

Common of Doctors of the Church, p. 1082; or Common of Pastors: for Bishops, p. 1069.

OPENING PRAYER

All-powerful God,
help us to follow the teachings and example of Peter
    Damian.
By making Christ and the service of his Church
the first love of our lives,
may we come to the joys of eternal light,

where he lives and reigns with you and the Holy Spirit, one God, for ever and ever. ℟. **Amen.**

Readings and Intervenient Chants may also be taken from the Common of Holy Men and Women: for Religious, p. 1197.

First Reading (2 Tm 4:1-5), p. 1184, no. 7.
Responsorial Psalm (Ps 16), p. 1210, no. 3.
Alleluia (Jn 15:9b, 5b), p. 1223, no. 1.
Gospel (Jn 15:1-8), p. 1237, no. 24.

Feb. 22 — THE CHAIR OF ST. PETER, Apostle

Feast

The feast of the Chair of St. Peter was originally celebrated on February 22. However in Gaul it came to be celebrated on January 18. Pope Paul IV believed that there were two different feasts; therefore in 1558 he doubled the original feast: on January 18 he placed St. Peter's Pontificate at Rome and on February 22 his Pontificate at Antioch. As of 1961, the duplicate feast of January 18 was abolished and the original feast remains in honor of St. Peter's Pontifical Authority.

ENTRANCE ANT.   Lk 22:32

The Lord said to Simon Peter: I have prayed that your faith may not fail; and you in your turn must strengthen your brothers.   → No. 2, p. 614

OPENING PRAYER

All-powerful Father,
you have built your Church
on the rock of St. Peter's confession of faith.
May nothing divide or weaken
our unity in faith and love.
Grant this . . . for ever and ever. ℟. **Amen.** ↓

FIRST READING   1 Pt 5:1-4

The presbyters are entrusted with an administrative function in the Christian community. The pastoral care of the Church is entrusted to the elders. Christ in his parousia is depicted in the role of shepherd, bringing out the pastoral aspects of his activity and his relationship to others in the Church.

A reading from the first Letter of Saint Peter

BELOVED: I exhort the presbyters among you, as a fellow presbyter and witness to the sufferings of Christ and one who has a share in the glory to be revealed. Tend the flock of God in your midst, overseeing not by constraint but willingly, as God would have it, not for shameful profit but eagerly. Do not lord it over those assigned to you, but be examples to the flock. And when the chief Shepherd is revealed, you will receive the unfading crown of glory.—The word of the Lord. ℟. **Thanks be to God.** ↓

RESPONSORIAL PSALM   Ps 23:1-3a, 4, 5, 6

℟. (1) **The Lord is my shepherd; there is nothing I shall want.**

The LORD is my shepherd; I shall not want.
    In verdant pastures he gives me repose;
Beside restful waters he leads me;
    he refreshes my soul.—℟.

Even though I walk in the dark valley
    I fear no evil; for you are at my side
With your rod and your staff
    that give me courage.—℟.

You spread the table before me
    in the sight of my foes;
You anoint my head with oil;
    my cup overflows.—℟.

Only goodness and kindness follow me
    all the days of my life;
And I shall dwell in the house of the LORD
    for years to come.—℟. ↓

ALLELUIA   Mt 16:18

℟. **Alleluia, alleluia.**
You are Peter, and upon this rock I will build my Church;

the gates of the netherworld shall not prevail against it.
℟. **Alleluia, alleluia.** ↓

GOSPEL
Mt 16:13-19

The question of Jesus concerns his Messianic title, the Son of Man. He directly puts the question to the disciples. It is a challenge. Peter answers for all with a profession that Christ is the Messiah. Simon is given the name by which he is usually known in the New Testament.

℣. The Lord be with you. ℟. **And also with you.**
✚ A reading from the holy Gospel according to Matthew.
℟. **Glory to you, Lord.**

WHEN Jesus went into the region of Caesarea Philippi he asked his disciples, "Who do people say that the Son of Man is?" They replied, "Some say John the Baptist, others Elijah, still others Jeremiah or one of the prophets." He said to them, "But who do you say that I am?" Simon Peter said in reply, "You are the Christ, the Son of the living God." Jesus said to him in reply, "Blessed are you, Simon son of Jonah. For flesh and blood has not revealed this to you, but my heavenly Father. And so I say to you, you are Peter, and upon this rock I will build my Church, and the gates of the netherworld shall not prevail against it. I will give you the keys to the Kingdom of heaven. Whatever you bind on earth shall be bound in heaven; and whatever you loose on earth shall be loosed in heaven."—The Gospel of the Lord. ℟. **Praise to you, Lord Jesus Christ.**
→ No. 15, p. 623

PRAYER OVER THE GIFTS

Lord,
accept the prayers and gifts of your Church.
With St. Peter as our shepherd,
keep us true to the faith he taught
and bring us to your eternal kingdom.
We ask this through Christ our Lord.
℟. **Amen.**   → No. 21, p. 626 (Pref. P 64-65)

COMMUNION ANT. Mt 16:16, 18

Peter said: You are the Christ, the Son of the living God. Jesus answered: You are Peter, the rock on which I will build my Church. ↓

PRAYER AFTER COMMUNION

God our Father,
you have given us the body and blood of Christ
as the food of life.
On this feast of Peter the apostle,
may this communion bring us redemption
and be the sign and source of our unity and peace.
We ask this in the name of Jesus the Lord.
℟. **Amen.**

→ No. 32, p. 660

Feb. 23—ST. POLYCARP, Bishop and Martyr

Memorial

St. Polycarp was a disciple of St. John the Evangelist, who converted him to Christianity. Late in life he was elevated to the Bishopric of Smyrna. When he was carried to the amphitheatre, the pro-consul exhorted him to renounce Jesus Christ, and he responded: "For eighty-six years I have served him and he has never wronged me; how can I renounce the king who has saved me?" He suffered martyrdom about the year 155.

Common of Martyrs, p. 1047; or Common of Pastors: for Bishops, p. 1059.

OPENING PRAYER

God of all creation,
you gave your bishop Polycarp
the privilege of being counted among the saints
who gave their lives in faithful witness to the gospel.
May his prayers give us the courage
to share with him the cup of suffering
and to rise to eternal glory.
We ask this . . . for ever and ever. ℟. **Amen.** ↓

FIRST READING Rv 2:8-11

To the church in Smyrna, John is directed to write that there will be suffering and poverty in spite of riches. The devil will bring about imprisonment and persecution, but for those who are faithful, the crown of life will be received. The victor will not suffer a second death.

A reading from the Book of Revelation

"To the angel of the Church in Smyrna, write this:

" 'The first and the last, who once died but came to life, says this: "I know your tribulation and poverty, but you are rich. I know the slander of those who claim to be Jews and are not, but rather are members of the assembly of Satan. Do not be afraid of anything that you are going to suffer. Indeed, the Devil will throw some of you into prison, that you may be tested, and you will face an ordeal for ten days. Remain faithful until death, and I will give you the crown of life.

" ' "Whoever has ears ought to hear what the Spirit says to the churches. The victor shall not be harmed by the second death." ' "—The word of the Lord. ℟. **Thanks be to God.**

Responsorial Psalm (Ps 31), p. 1139, no. 1.
Alleluia (See *Te Deum*), p. 1147, no. 6.
Gospel (Jn 15:18-21), p. 1149, no. 6.

MARCH

[In the dioceses of the United States]

MAR. 3 — ST. KATHARINE DREXEL, Virgin

Katharine Drexel was born in Philadelphia on November 26, 1858, the daughter of Francis A. Drexel, a prominent banker. Katharine gave her fortune and her life to serve the poor and oppressed, particularly African American and Native American people. She helped finance many missions among them. In 1891, she founded a missionary community, The Sisters of the Blessed Sacrament. The eucharist was the center of and sustenance for her life; she saw it as the source of unity among races. Katharine died on March 3, 1955 and was canonized by Pope John Paul II in 2000.

Common of Virgins, p. 1075.

OPENING PRAYER

Ever-loving God,
you called St. Katharine Drexel
to teach the message of the Gospel
and to bring the life of the Eucharist
to the African American and Native American peoples.
By her prayers and example,
enable us to work for justice
among the poor and the oppressed,
and keep us undivided in love
in the eucharistic community of your Church.
Grant this . . . for ever and ever. ℟. **Amen.**

Readings and Intervenient Chants may be taken from the Common of Virgins, p. 1191, *or Common of Holy Men and Women: for Religious, p.* 1197.

Mar. 4 — ST. CASIMIR

Optional Memorial

St. Casimir was the son of King Casimir IV of Poland and Elizabeth of Austria. Amidst the moral dangers of the court, he was an example of piety and above all preserved his chastity. While on a journey to Lithuania he died at the court of Grodno, March 4, 1484.

Common of Holy Men and Women, p. 1080.

OPENING PRAYER

All-powerful God,
to serve you is to reign:
by the prayers of St. Casimir,
help us to serve you in holiness and justice.
Grant this . . . for ever and ever. ℟. **Amen.**

First Reading (Phil 3:8-14), p. 1218, no. 9.
Responsorial Psalm (Ps 15), p. 1210, no. 2.
Alleluia (Jn 13:34), p. 1224, no. 10.
Gospel (Jn 15:9-17), p. 1238, no. 25.

Mar. 7 — STS. PERPETUA and FELICITY, Martyrs
Memorial

Perpetua, a noble lady of Carthage with a nursing child, and Felicity an expectant mother, were exposed to the ferocity of wild beasts. They were finally beheaded in the year 202 during the persecution of Severus.

Common of Martyrs, p. 1041; or Common of Holy Men and Women, p. 1092.

OPENING PRAYER

Father,
your love gave the saints Perpetua and Felicity
courage to suffer a cruel martyrdom.
By their prayers, help us to grow in love of you.
We ask this . . . for ever and ever. ℟. **Amen.**

First Reading (Rom 8:31b-39), p. 1141, no. 2.
Responsorial Psalm (Ps 124), p. 1140, no. 3.
Alleluia (Mt 5:10), p. 1146, no. 1.
Gospel (Mt 10:34-39), p. 1148, no. 3.

Mar. 8 — ST. JOHN OF GOD, Religious
Optional Memorial

After a stormy youth, St. John listened to the word of God when he was forty years old, and lived thereafter a penitent life. He founded the Order of "Brothers Hospitallers of St. John of God," who devote themselves to the healing of sick bodies and souls. He died in 1550.

Common of Holy Men and Women: for Religious, p. 1086, or for Those Who Work for the Underprivileged, p. 1089.

OPENING PRAYER

Father,
you gave John of God
love and compassion for others.
Grant that by doing good for others
we may be counted among the saints in your kingdom.
We ask this . . . for ever and ever. ℟. **Amen.**

First Reading (1 Jn 3:14-18), p. 1221, no. 16.
Responsorial Psalm (Ps 112), p. 1213, no. 7.
Alleluia (Jn 13:34), p. 1224, no. 10.
Gospel (Mt 25:31-40—Short Form), p. 1231, no. 13.

Mar. 9 — ST. FRANCES OF ROME, Religious

Optional Memorial

At eleven years of age, St. Frances married Lorenzo de Ponziani, with whom she had six children. She was the perfect Christian spouse. She founded the Benedictine Oblate Congregation of Tor di Specchi, and died in 1440.

Common of Holy Men and Women: for Religious, p. 1086.

OPENING PRAYER

Merciful Father,
in Frances of Rome
you have given us a unique example of love in marriage
as well as in religious life.
Keep us faithful in your service,
and help us to see and follow you
in all the aspects of life
We ask this . . . for ever and ever. ℟. **Amen.**

First Reading (Prv 31:10-13, 19-20, 30-31), p. 1202, no. 11.
Responsorial Psalm (Ps 34), p. 1211, no. 5.
Alleluia (Jn 13:34), p. 1224, no. 10.
Gospel (Mt 22:34-40), p. 1229, no. 10.

Mar. 17—ST. PATRICK, Bishop

Optional Memorial

St. Patrick, Apostle and Patron of Ireland, was born in Scotland in 387. Pope St. Celestine commissioned him to evangelize Ireland, and in the thirty-three years of his apostolate, he succeeded in converting the whole country, which, in the Middle Ages, was known as "Island of Saints," resplendent with churches and monasteries. St. Patrick died in the year 464.

Common of Pastors: for Missionaries, p. 1067, *or for Bishops, p.* 1059.

OPENING PRAYER

Let us pray
    [that like St. Patrick the missionary
    we will be fearless witnesses
    to the gospel of Jesus Christ]
God our Father,
you sent St. Patrick
to preach your glory to the people of Ireland.
By the help of his prayers,
may all Christians proclaim your love to all men.
Grant this . . . for ever and ever. ℟. **Amen.**

ALTERNATIVE OPENING PRAYER

Let us pray
    [that, like St. Patrick,
    we may be loyal to our faith in Christ]
Father in heaven,
you sent the great bishop Patrick
to the people of Ireland to share his faith
and to spend his life in loving service.
May our lives bear witness
to the faith we profess,
and our love bring others
to the peace and joy of your gospel.
We ask this through Christ our Lord. ℟. **Amen.**

First Reading (1 Pt 4:7b-11), p. 1221, no. 15.
Responsorial Psalm (Ps 96), p 1160, no. 5.
Alleluia (Mk 1:17), p. 1168, no. 3.
Gospel (Lk 5:1-11), p. 1172, no. 7.

Mar. 18 — ST. CYRIL OF JERUSALEM, Bishop and Doctor

Optional Memorial

When he was a simple priest, St. Cyril instructed the Catechumens during Lent. His instructions which are extant show conclusively that Catholic doctrine was the same then as now. The Arians exiled him three times. He died in 386.

Common of Pastors: for Bishops, p. 1059; *or Common of Doctors of the Church*, p. 1072.

OPENING PRAYER

Father,
through Cyril of Jerusalem
you led your Church to a deeper understanding
of the mysteries of salvation.
Let his prayers help us to know your Son better
and to have eternal life in all its fullness.
We ask this . . . for ever and ever. ℟. **Amen.**

First Reading (1 Jn 5:1-5), p. 1222, no. 18.
Responsorial Psalm (Ps 19), p. 1179, no. 1.
Alleluia (Jn 15:9b, 5b), p. 1224, no. 13.
Gospel (Jn 15:1-8), p. 1237, no. 24.

Mar. 19 — ST. JOSEPH, HUSBAND OF THE BLESSED VIRGIN MARY

Solemnity

From the end of the 10th century St. Joseph has been honored on March 19 in many Western calendars. His feast was accepted at Rome in 1479 and established on the same date; and in 1621 it was inserted into the universal calendar. Since the Solemnity of St. Joseph always falls in Lent, the episcopal conferences have the faculty to transfer it to another day, outside Lent.

ENTRANCE ANT.

Lk 12:42

The Lord has put his faithful servant in charge of his household. → No. 2, p. 614

OPENING PRAYER

Let us pray
   [that the Church will continue
   the saving work of Christ]
Father,
you entrusted our Savior to the care of St. Joseph.
By the help of his prayers
may your Church continue to serve its Lord, Jesus Christ,
who lives and reigns with you and the Holy Spirit,
one God, for ever and ever. ℟. **Amen.** ↓

FIRST READING   2 Sm 7:4-5a, 12-14a, 16

This text probes deeply into the stupendous mystery of the Incarnation.
God is the Father of his eternal Son, Jesus Christ, and Mary is his mother
by the power of the Holy Spirit. But Jesus is also the Son of David. Joseph
was of the Davidic line, and so was Mary.

A reading from the second Book of Samuel

THE LORD spoke to Nathan and said: "Go, tell my servant David, 'When your time comes and you rest with your ancestors, I will raise up your heir after you, sprung from your loins, and I will make his kingdom firm. It is he who shall build a house for my name. And I will make his royal throne firm forever. I will be a father to him, and he shall be a son to me. Your house and your kingdom shall endure forever before me; your throne shall stand firm forever.' "—The word of the Lord. ℟. **Thanks be to God.** ↓

RESPONSORIAL PSALM   Ps 89:2-3, 4-5, 27 and 29

℟. (37) **The son of David will live for ever.**

The promises of the LORD I will sing forever;
   through all generations my mouth shall proclaim
     your faithfulness,
For you have said, "My kindness is established forever";
   in heaven you have confirmed your faithfulness.—℟.

"I have made a covenant with my chosen one,
   I have sworn to David my servant:

Forever will I confirm your posterity
and establish your throne for all generations."—R̶).

"He shall say of me, 'You are my father,
my God, the Rock, my savior.'
Forever I will maintain my kindness toward him,
and my covenant with him stands firm."—R̶). ↓

SECOND READING   Rom 4:13, 16-18, 22

St. Paul brings full pressure to bear on faith as we think over the mystery
of God's coming to earth under the protection of Joseph. Abraham's faith
is held up to us as the ideal. Joseph's faith was like Abraham's, and by
that faith he became the spiritual father of millions.

A reading from the Letter of Saint Paul to the Romans

BROTHERS and sisters: It was not through the law
that the promise was made to Abraham and his
descendants that he would inherit the world, but through
the righteousness that comes from faith. For this reason,
it depends on faith, so that it may be a gift, and the
promise may be guaranteed to all his descendants, not to
those who only adhere to the law but to those who follow
the faith of Abraham, who is the father of all of us, as it
is written, *I have made you father of many nations.* He is
our father in the sight of God, in whom he believed, who
gives life to the dead and calls into being what does not
exist. He believed, hoping against hope, that he would
become *the father of many nations,* according to what
was said, *Thus shall your descendants be.* That is why *it
was credited to him as righteousness.*— The word of the
Lord. R̶). **Thanks be to God.** ↓

VERSE BEFORE THE GOSPEL OR ALLELUIA

R̶). **[Alleluia, alleluia.]***
Blessed are those who dwell in your house, O Lord;

---

* *See p. 620 for Gospel Acclamations during Lent.*

they never cease to praise you.

℟. **[Alleluia, alleluia.]** ↓

GOSPEL Mt 1:16, 18-21, 24a

Joseph's faith was tested from the start. First there was a crisis of integrity, and a great tension arose in his just heart. Mary was with child. Then an angel of the Lord revealed the whole majestic and ineffable truth. Mary had conceived by the Holy Spirit. She was the all-holy tabernacle of our redemption.

℣. The Lord be with you. ℟. **And also with you.**

✝ A reading from the holy Gospel according to Matthew.

℟. **Glory to you, Lord.**

JACOB was the father of Joseph, the husband of Mary. Of her was born Jesus who is called the Christ.

Now this is how the birth of Jesus Christ came about. When his mother Mary was betrothed to Joseph, but before they lived together, she was found with child through the Holy Spirit. Joseph her husband, since he was a righteous man, yet unwilling to expose her to shame, decided to divorce her quietly. Such was his intention when, behold, the angel of the Lord appeared to him in a dream and said, "Joseph, son of David, do not be afraid to take Mary your wife into your home. For it is through the Holy Spirit that this child has been conceived in her. She will bear a son and you are to name him Jesus, because he will save his people from their sins." When Joseph awoke, he did as the angel of the Lord had commanded him and took his wife into his home.—The Gospel of the Lord. ℟. **Praise to you, Lord Jesus Christ.** → No. 14, p. 622

OR

GOSPEL Lk 2:41-51a

Mary and Joseph were religious people and they observed the Passover. During the return journey from Jerusalem, they could not find Jesus. Returning to Jerusalem, they found him in the temple. Jesus returned with his parents to Nazareth and was obedient to them.

℣. The Lord be with you. ℟. **And also with you.**

✤ A reading from the holy Gospel according to Luke.

℟. **Glory to you, Lord.**

EACH year Jesus' parents went to Jerusalem for the feast of Passover, and when he was twelve years old, they went up according to festival custom. After they had completed its days, as they were returning, the boy Jesus remained behind in Jerusalem, but his parents did not know it. Thinking that he was in the caravan, they journeyed for a day and looked for him among their relatives and acquaintances, but not finding him, they returned to Jerusalem to look for him. After three days they found him in the temple, sitting in the midst of the teachers, listening to them and asking them questions, and all who heard him were astounded at his understanding and his answers. When his parents saw him, they were astonished, and his mother said to him, "Son, why have you done this to us? Your father and I have been looking for you with great anxiety." And he said to them, "Why were you looking for me? Did you not know that I must be in my Father's house?" But they did not understand what he said to them. He went down with them and came to Nazareth, and was obedient to them.—The Gospel of the Lord. ℟. **Praise to you, Lord Jesus Christ.**

➜ No. 14, p. 623

PRAYER OVER THE GIFTS

Father,
with unselfish love St. Joseph cared for your Son,
born of the Virgin Mary.
May we also serve you at your altar with pure hearts.
We ask this in the name of Jesus the Lord.
℟. **Amen.** ↓

PREFACE (P 62)

℣. The Lord be with you. ℟. **And also with you.**

℣. Lift up your hearts. ℟. **We lift them up to the Lord.**

℣. Let us give thanks to the Lord our God. ℟. **It is right to give him thanks and praise.**

Father, all-powerful and ever-living God,
we do well always and everywhere to give you thanks
as we honor St. Joseph.
He is that just man,
that wise and loyal servant,
whom you placed at the head of your family.
With a husband's love he cherished Mary,
the virgin Mother of God.
With fatherly care he watched over Jesus Christ your
    Son,
conceived by the power of the Holy Spirit.
Through Christ the choirs of angels
and all the powers of heaven
praise and worship your glory.
May our voices blend with theirs
as we join in their unending hymn: → No. 23, p. 627

COMMUNION ANT.   Mt 25:21

Come, good and faithful servant! Share the joy of your Lord! ↓

PRAYER AFTER COMMUNION

Lord,
today you nourish us at this altar
as we celebrate the feast of St. Joseph.
Protect your Church always,
and in your love watch over the gifts you have given us.
Grant this through Christ our Lord.
℟. **Amen.**   → No. 32, p. 660

Mar. 23 — ST. TORIBIO DE MOGROVEJO, Bishop

Optional Memorial

St. Toribio Alphonsus de Mogrovejo died at Lima, Peru, on March 23, 1606. He was canonized in 1726. He has been inscribed in the general calendar because of his important contribution toward the establishment of ecclesiastical discipline in the Church of Latin America.

Common of Pastors: for Bishops, p. 1059.

OPENING PRAYER

Lord,
through the apostolic work of St. Toribio
and his unwavering love of truth,
you helped your Church to grow.
May your chosen people continue to grow
in faith and holiness.
Grant this. . . for ever and ever. ℟. **Amen.**

First Reading (2 Tm 1:13-14; 2:1-3), p. 1167, no. 11.
Responsorial Psalm (Ps 96), p. 1160, no. 5.
Alleluia (Jn 10:14), p. 1168, no. 5.
Gospel (Mt 9:35-38), p. 1169, no. 1.

Mar. 25 — THE ANNUNCIATION OF THE LORD

Solemnity

The Solemnity of the Annunciation, of Eastern origin, was accepted at Rome in the 7th century under the title "Annunciation of the Lord" as attested by the "Liber Pontificalis." The Eastern Rites as well as the Ambrosian Rite have always regarded it as a feast of the Lord. Hence the name of this Solemnity has now been changed. It is called "The Annunciation of the Lord" to make it more evident that it is above all a feast of the Lord.

ENTRANCE ANT.   Heb 10:5, 7

As Christ came into the world, he said: Behold! I have come to do your will, O God.   → No. 2, p. 614

OPENING PRAYER

Let us pray
    [that Christ, the Word made flesh,
    will make us more like him]
God our Father,
your Word became man and was born of the Virgin Mary.
May we become more like Jesus Christ,

whom we acknowledge as our redeemer, God and man.
We ask this . . . for ever and ever. ℟. **Amen.** ↓

ALTERNATIVE OPENING PRAYER

Let us pray
  [that we may become more like Christ
  who chose to become one of us]
Almighty Father of our Lord Jesus Christ,
you have revealed the beauty of your power
by exalting the lowly virgin of Nazareth
and making her the mother of our Savior.
May the prayers of this woman
bring Jesus to the waiting world
and fill the void of incompletion
with the presence of her child
who lives and reigns with you and the Holy Spirit,
one God, for ever and ever. ℟. **Amen.** ↓

FIRST READING   Is 7:10-14; 8:10

On this feast of the Incarnation of our Lord, we celebrate the moment of
his taking on of our flesh in the womb of his mother by the power of the
Holy Spirit.

A reading from the Book of the Prophet Isaiah

THE LORD spoke to Ahaz, saying: Ask for a sign from
the LORD, your God; let it be deep as the nether world,
or high as the sky! But Ahaz answered, "I will not ask! I
will not tempt the LORD!" Then Isaiah said: Listen, O
house of David! Is it not enough for you to weary people,
must you also weary my God? Therefore the Lord himself
will give you this sign: the virgin shall be with child, and
bear a son, and shall name him Emmanuel, which means
"God is with us!"—The word of the Lord. ℟. **Thanks be to
God.** ↓

RESPONSORIAL PSALM   Ps 40:7-8a, 8b-9, 10, 11

℟. (8a and 9a) **Here I am, Lord; I come to do your will.**

Sacrifice or oblation you wished not,
  but ears open to obedience you gave me.
Holocausts or sin-offerings you sought not;
  then said I, "Behold I come."—℟.

"In the written scroll it is prescribed for me,
To do your will, O my God, is my delight,
  and your law is within my heart!"—℟.

I announced your justice in the vast assembly;
  I did not restrain my lips, as you, O LORD, know.—℟.

Your justice I kept not hid within my heart;
  your faithfulness and your salvation I have spoken of;
I have made no secret of your kindness and your truth
  in the vast assembly.—℟. ↓

SECOND READING   Heb 10:4-10

Christ is shown making a free offering of himself for us. It was an act of his all-holy will to be the Son of Mary and Brother of us all. Mary is God's mother, Jesus is God's Son. We will be made holy by the offering of his body!

A reading from the Letter to the Hebrews

BROTHERS and sisters: It is impossible that the blood of bulls and goats take away sins. For this reason, when Christ came into the world, he said:
  "Sacrifice and offering you did not desire,
    but a body you prepared for me;
  in holocausts and sin offerings you took no delight.
  Then I said, 'As is written of me in the scroll,
  behold, I come to do your will, O God.' "
First he says, "Sacrifices and offerings, holocausts and sin offerings, you neither desired nor delighted in." These are offered according to the law. Then he says, "Behold, I come to do your will." He takes away the first to establish the second. By this "will," we have been consecrated through the offering of the Body of Jesus Christ once for all.—The word of the Lord. ℟. **Thanks be to God.** ↓

VERSE BEFORE THE GOSPEL OR ALLELUIA Jn 1:14ab

℟. **[Alleluia, alleluia.]***
The Word of God became flesh and made his dwelling
    among us;
and we saw his glory.
℟. **[Alleluia, alleluia.]** ↓

GOSPEL Lk 1:26-38

St. Luke tells the story. The most we know about the doctrine of the
Incarnation is contained in these few paragraphs. This is an event that
puts Christ in the middle of all history. And the exquisite Lady who
received the message gave herself to God with her newly conceived Son.

℣. The Lord be with you. ℟. **And also with you.**
✢ A reading from the holy Gospel according to Luke.
℟. **Glory to you, Lord.**

THE angel Gabriel was sent from God to a town of
Galilee called Nazareth, to a virgin betrothed to a
man named Joseph, of the house of David, and the virgin's name was Mary. And coming to her, he said, "Hail,
full of grace! The Lord is with you." But she was greatly
troubled at what was said and pondered what sort of
greeting this might be. Then the angel said to her, "Do not
be afraid, Mary, for you have found favor with God.
Behold, you will conceive in your womb and bear a son,
and you shall name him Jesus. He will be great and will
be called Son of the Most High, and the Lord God will
give him the throne of David his father, and he will rule
over the house of Jacob forever, and of his Kingdom
there will be no end." But Mary said to the angel, "How
can this be, since I have no relations with a man?" And
the angel said to her in reply, "The Holy Spirit will come
upon you, and the power of the Most High will overshadow you. Therefore the child to be born will be called
holy, the Son of God. And behold, Elizabeth, your rela-

---

* *See p. 620 for Gospel Acclamations during Lent.*

tive, has also conceived a son in her old age, and this is the sixth month for her who was called barren; for nothing will be impossible for God." Mary said, "Behold, I am the handmaid of the Lord. May it be done to me according to your word." Then the angel departed from her.— The Gospel of the Lord. ℟. **Praise to you, Lord Jesus Christ.** → No. 14, p. 622

In the Profession of Faith, all genuflect at the words, and became man.

PRAYER OVER THE GIFTS

Almighty Father,
as we recall the beginning of the Church
when your Son became man,
may we celebrate with joy today
this sacrament of your love.
We ask this through Christ our Lord. ℟. **Amen.** ↓

PREFACE (P 44)

℣. The Lord be with you. ℟. **And also with you.**
℣. Lift up your hearts. ℟. **We lift them up to the Lord.**
℣. Let us give thanks to the Lord our God. ℟. **It is right to give him thanks and praise.**

Father, all-powerful and ever-living God,
we do well always and everywhere to give you thanks
through Jesus Christ our Lord.
He came to save mankind by becoming a man himself.
The Virgin Mary, receiving the angel's message in faith,
conceived by the power of the Spirit
and bore your Son in purest love.
In Christ, the eternal truth,
your promise to Israel came true.
In Christ, the hope of all peoples,
man's hope was realized beyond all expectation.
Through Christ the angels of heaven
offer their prayer of adoration
as they rejoice in your presence for ever.

May our voices be one with theirs
in their triumphant hymn of praise.   → No. 23, p. 627

COMMUNION ANT.   Is 7:14

**The Virgin is with child and shall bear a son, and she will
call him Emmanuel.** ↓

PRAYER AFTER COMMUNION

Lord,
may the sacrament we share
strengthen our faith and hope in Jesus, born of a virgin
and truly God and man.
By the power of his resurrection
may we come to eternal joy.
We ask this in the name of Jesus the Lord.
℞. **Amen.**   → No. 32, p. 660

—APRIL—

Apr. 2 — ST. FRANCIS OF PAOLA, Hermit

Optional Memorial

St. Francis founded the Order of Minims, whose name shows that they wished to be regarded as the least in the household of God. He died in 1507.

Common of Holy Men and Women: for Religious, p. 1086.

OPENING PRAYER

Father of the lowly,
you raised St. Francis of Paola
to the glory of your saints.
By his example and prayers,
may we come to the rewards
you have promised the humble.
We ask this . . . for ever and ever. ℟. **Amen.**

First Reading (Phil 3:8-14), p. 1218, no. 9.
Responsorial Psalm (Ps 16), p. 1210, no. 3.
Alleluia (Mt 5:3), p. 1223, no. 1.
Gospel (Lk 12:32-34), p. 1236, no. 21.

Apr. 4 — ST. ISIDORE, Bishop and Doctor

Optional Memorial

St. Isidore, who restored Catholicism in Spain, was admired for his preaching, his miracles, and his work for the liturgy and ecclesiastical discipline. He presided at the Council of Toledo (633) and died in 636.

Common of Pastors: for Bishops, p. 1059; or Common of Doctors of the Church, p. 1072.

OPENING PRAYER

Lord,
hear the prayers we offer in commemoration of St. Isidore.
May your Church learn from his teaching
and benefit from his intercession.
Grant this . . . for ever and ever. ℟. **Amen.**

First Reading (2 Cor 4:1-2, 5-7), p. 1164, no. 6.
Responsorial Psalm (Ps 37), p. 1180, no. 2.
Alleluia (Jn 15:5), p. 1885, no. 4.
Gospel (Lk 6:43-45), p. 1189, no. 6.

Apr. 5 — ST. VINCENT FERRER, Priest

Optional Memorial

St. Vincent Ferrer was born in Valencia, Spain, January 23, 1350. He was educated at the Dominican school in Barcelona, and later entered the Order. He is said to have had the gift of tongues, so amazing was the speed with which he mastered the many varied dialects of Western Europe. He converted thousands of sinners, Jews, and infidels by his preaching. He died in France in 1419.

Common of Pastors: for Missionaries, p. 1067.

OPENING PRAYER

Father,
you called St. Vincent Ferrer
to preach the gospel of the last judgment.
Through his prayers may we come with joy
to meet your Son in the kingdom of heaven,
where he lives and reigns with you and the Holy Spirit,
one God, for ever and ever. ℟. **Amen.**

First Reading (2 Tm 4:1-5), p. 1167, no. 12.

RESPONSORIAL PSALM   Ps 40:2, 4, 7-8, 8-9, 10, 11

℟. (8a and 9a) **Here I am, Lord; I come to do your will.**

I have waited, waited for the LORD,
    and he stooped toward me and heard my cry.
And he put a new song into my mouth,
    a hymn to our God.—℟.

Sacrifice or oblation you wished not,
    but ears open to obedience you gave me.
Burnt offerings or sin-offerings you sought not;
    then said I, "Behold I come."—℟.

"In the written scroll it is prescribed for me,
To do your will, O my God, is my delight,
    and your law is within my heart!"—℟.

I announced your justice in the vast assembly;
    I did not restrain my lips, as you, O LORD, know.—℟.

Your justice I kept not hid within my heart;
    your faithfulness and your salvation I have spoken of;

I have made no secret of your kindness and your truth
    in the vast assembly.—℟.

Alleluia (Lk 21:36), p. 1224, no. 7.
Gospel (Lk 12:35-40), p. 1236, no. 22.

Apr. 7 — ST. JOHN BAPTIST DE LA SALLE, Priest
Memorial

Founder of the Institute of the Brothers of the Christian
Schools, St. John Baptist de la Salle is called the father of
modern pedagogy. In 1678 he was ordained to the priesthood and received his doctorate in theology in 1680. In 1691
he founded his first novitiate of Brothers at Vangirard,
France. He died in Rouen, in 1719 and was canonized on
May 24, 1900.

Common of Pastors, p. 1061; *or Common of Holy Men and
Women: for Teachers*, p. 1090.

OPENING PRAYER

Father,
you chose St. John Baptist de la Salle
to give young people a Christian education.
Give your Church teachers who will devote themselves
to helping your children grow
as Christian men and women.
We ask this . . . for ever and ever. ℟. **Amen.**

First Reading (2 Tm 1:13-14; 2:1-3), p. 1167, no. 11.
Responsorial Psalm (Ps 1), p. 1209, no. 1.
Alleluia (Mt 23:11, 12b), p. 1223, no. 6.
Gospel (Mt 18:1-5), p. 1227, no. 7.

Apr. 11 — ST. STANISLAUS, Bishop and Martyr
Memorial

St. Stanislaus was born in Poland. As Bishop of Cracow he
reproached King Boleslaw II for his dissolute life. Boleslaw
slew him during the Holy Sacrifice of the Mass in 1079.

Common of Martyrs, p. 1052; *or Common of Pastors: for
Bishops* p. 1059.

OPENING PRAYER

Father,
to honor you, St. Stanislaus faced martyrdom with
  courage.
Keep us strong and loyal in our faith until death.
Grant this . . . for ever and ever. ℟. **Amen.**

First Reading (Rv 12:10-12a), p. 1138, no. 3.
Responsorial Psalm (Ps 34), p. 1211, no. 5.
Alleluia (2 Cor 1:3b-4a), p. 1146, no. 3.
Gospel (Jn 17:11b-19), p. 1149, no. 7.

Apr. 13 — ST. MARTIN I, Pope and Martyr

Optional Memorial

St. Martin was continually persecuted by the heretics of
his time. The horrible treatment to which he was subjected hastened his death in 655.

*Common of Martyrs, p. 1052; or Common of Pastors: for Popes,
p. 1057.*

OPENING PRAYER

Merciful God, our Father,
neither hardship, pain, nor the threat of death
could weaken the faith of St. Martin.
Through our faith, give us courage
to endure whatever sufferings the world may inflict upon
  us.
We ask this . . . for ever and ever. ℟. **Amen.**

First Reading (2 Tm 2:8-13; 3:10-12), p. 1143, no. 5.
Responsorial Psalm (Ps 126), p. 1140, no. 4.
Alleluia (See *Te Deum*), p. 1147, no. 6.
Gospel (Jn 15:18-21), p. 1149, no. 6.

Apr. 21 — ST. ANSELM, Bishop and Doctor

Optional Memorial

A Benedictine Monk, St. Anselm governed the Monastery
of Bec and was elevated to the Archbishopric of Canterbury. He died in 1109 and is called the Father of Scholastic
Theology.

Common of Pastors: for Bishops, p. 1059; or Common of Doctors of the Church, p. 1072.

OPENING PRAYER

Father,
you called St. Anselm
to study and teach the sublime truths you have revealed.
Let your gift of faith come to the aid of our understanding
and open our hearts to your truth.
Grant this . . . for ever and ever. ℟. **Amen.**

First Reading (Eph 3:14-19), p. 1217, no. 7.
Responsorial Psalm (Ps 34), p. 1211, no. 5.
Alleluia (Jn 6:63c, 68c), p. 1185, no. 3.
Gospel (Mt 7:21-29), p. 1186, no. 2.

Apr. 23 — ST. GEORGE, Martyr

Optional Memorial

Son of an illustrious family of Cappadocia, St. George was elevated at a young age by Diocletian to one of the highest offices of the Imperial ministry. When the Emperor promulgated an edict against the Christians, St. George professed his faith publicly. He died in 303. He is the Patron Saint of England.

Common of Martyrs, p. 1052.

OPENING PRAYER

Lord,
hear the prayers of those who praise your mighty power.
As St. George was ready to follow Christ in suffering and death,
so may he be ready to help us in our weakness.
We ask this . . . for ever and ever. ℟. **Amen.**

First Reading (Rv 21:5-7), p. 1138, no. 4.
Responsorial Psalm (Ps 126), p. 1140, no. 4.
Alleluia (1 Pt 4:14), p. 1147, no. 5.
Gospel (Lk 9:23-26), p. 1148, no. 4.

The Same Day, Apr. 23
ST. ADALBERT, Bishop and Martyr

Optional Memorial

Born in Bohemia about the year 956, Adalbert became a priest and eventually the second Bishop of Prague in 986. Later, he became a Benedictine at Rome. However, acceding to the people's request, he returned to Prague and undertook to correct the Prussians. He met with fierce resistance and was martyred on April 23, 997.

Common of Martyrs, p. 1052; or Common of Pastors: for Bishops, p.1059.

OPENING PRAYER

God our Father,
you have honored the Church with the victorious witness
    of St. Adalbert,
who died for his faith.
As he imitated the sufferings and death of the Lord,
may we follow in his footsteps and come to eternal joy.

Or: Opening Prayer, p. 1059.

First Reading (2 Cor 6:4-10), p. 1143, no. 4.
Responsorial Psalm (Ps 31), p. 1139, no. 1.
Alleluia (Jn 17:19), p. 1146, no. 2.
Gospel (Jn 10:11-16), p. 1173, no. 10.

Apr. 24 — ST. FIDELIS OF SIGMARINGEN,
Priest and Martyr

Optional Memorial

St. Fidelis was born at Sigmaringen, Germany, in 1577. He was at first "The Advocate of the Poor." He then entered the Order of Friars Minor and preached the Word of God. He was martyred in the Capuchin reform in 1622 and is the Protomartyr of the "Congregation of the Propagation of the Faith."

Common of Martyrs, p. 1052; or Common of Pastors, p. 1061.

OPENING PRAYER

Father,
you filled St. Fidelis with the fire of your love

and gave him the privilege of dying
that the faith might live.
Let his prayers keep us firmly grounded in your love,
and help us to come to know the power of Christ's resurrection.
We ask this . . . for ever and ever. ℟. **Amen.**

First Reading (Col 1:24-29), p. 1166, no. 9.
Responsorial Psalm (Ps 34), p. 1139, no. 2.
Alleluia (Jn 13:34), p. 1224, no. 10.
Gospel (Jn 17:20-26), p. 1239, no. 26.

Apr. 25 — ST. MARK, Evangelist

Feast

St. Mark was a disciple of St. Paul and the author of the
second Gospel under the inspiration of the Holy Spirit. He
begins his account with the Mission of John the Baptist,
"crying in the desert"; thus he is represented with a lion
at his feet, since the lion, one of the symbolic living creatures of Ezekiel's vision, shakes the desert with his roars.
He founded the Church at Alexandria in Egypt and was
martyred there in the latter part of the 1st century.

ENTRANCE ANT. Mk 16:15

**Go out to the whole world, and preach the gospel to all
creation, alleluia.** ➔ No. 2, p. 14

OPENING PRAYER

Father,
you gave St. Mark
the privilege of proclaiming your gospel.
May we profit by his wisdom
and follow Christ more faithfully.
Grant this . . . for ever and ever. ℟. **Amen.** ↓

FIRST READING 1 Pt 5:5b-14

St. Peter tells us that we are to be obedient toward those in authority and
humble toward one another, with complete trust in God's loving care. As
a reward for our faith and trust in God, we will be strengthened and attain
glory in Christ.

A reading from the first Letter of Saint Peter

BELOVED: Clothe yourselves with humility in your dealings with one another, for:
God opposes the proud
but bestows favor on the humble.
So humble yourselves under the mighty hand of God, that he may exalt you in due time. Cast all your worries upon him because he cares for you.

Be sober and vigilant. Your opponent the Devil is prowling around like a roaring lion looking for someone to devour. Resist him, steadfast in faith, knowing that your brothers and sisters throughout the world undergo the same sufferings. The God of all grace who called you to his eternal glory through Christ Jesus will himself restore, confirm, strengthen, and establish you after you have suffered a little. To him be dominion forever. Amen.

I write you this briefly through Silvanus, whom I consider a faithful brother, exhorting you and testifying that this is the true grace of God. Remain firm in it. The chosen one at Babylon sends you greeting, as does Mark, my son. Greet one another with a loving kiss. Peace to all of you who are in Christ.—The word of the Lord. ℟. **Thanks be to God.** → No. 15, p. 623

RESPONSORIAL PSALM Ps 89:2-3, 6-7, 16-17

℟. (2) **For ever I will sing the goodness of the Lord.**

℟. Or: **Alleluia.**

The favors of the LORD I will sing forever;
    through all generations my mouth shall proclaim
        your faithfulness.
For you have said, "My kindness is established forever";
    in heaven you have confirmed your faithfulness.—℟.

The heavens proclaim your wonders, O LORD,
    and your faithfulness, in the assembly of the holy ones.
For who in the skies can rank with the LORD?
    Who is like the LORD among the sons of God?—℟.

Blessed the people who know the joyful shout;
in the light of your countenance, O LORD, they walk.
At your name they rejoice all the day,
and through your justice they are exalted.—℟. ↓

ALLELUIA   1 Cor 1:23a-24b

℟. **Alleluia, alleluia.**
We proclaim Christ crucified;
he is the power of God and the wisdom of God.
℟. **Alleluia, alleluia.** ↓

GOSPEL   Mk 16:15-20

Together with Christ, our human nature has been glorified at God's right hand. To those who have this certitude Jesus entrusts the mission to continue his work of salvation, and he promises them his help.

℣. The Lord be with you. ℟. **And also with you.**
✛ A reading from the holy Gospel according to Mark.
℟. **Glory to you, Lord.**

JESUS appeared to the Eleven and said to them: "Go into the whole world and proclaim the Gospel to every creature. Whoever believes and is baptized will be saved; whoever does not believe will be condemned. These signs will accompany those who believe: in my name they will drive out demons, they will speak new languages. They will pick up serpents with their hands, and if they drink any deadly thing, it will not harm them. They will lay hands on the sick, and they will recover."

Then the Lord Jesus, after he spoke to them, was taken up into heaven and took his seat at the right hand of God. But they went forth and preached everywhere, while the Lord worked with them and confirmed the word through accompanying signs.—The Gospel of the Lord. ℟. **Praise to you, Lord Jesus Christ**.

→ No. 15, p. 623

PRAYER OVER THE GIFTS

Lord,
as we offer the sacrifice of praise
on the feast of St. Mark,
we pray that your Church may always be faithful
to the preaching of the gospel.
We ask this through Christ our Lord.
℞. **Amen.**   → No. 21, p. 626 (Pref. P 65)

COMMUNION ANT.   Mt 28:20

**I, the Lord, am with you always, until the end of the
world, alleluia.** ↓

PRAYER AFTER COMMUNION

All-powerful God,
may the gifts we have received at this altar
make us holy, and strengthen us
in the faith of the gospel preached by St. Mark.
We ask this in the name of Jesus the Lord.
℞. **Amen.**   → No. 32, p. 660

Apr. 28 — ST. PETER CHANEL, Priest and Martyr

Optional Memorial

St. Peter Chanel died a martyr's death on the island of
Futuna in Polynesia April 28, 1841. He was canonized in
1954. It seems quite fitting that the first martyr of
Oceania should be inscribed in the general calendar of the
Church.

Common of Martyrs, p. 1052; or *Common of Pastors: for
Missionaries*, p. 1067.

OPENING PRAYER

Father,
you called St. Peter Chanel to work for your Church
and gave him the crown of martyrdom.
May our celebration of Christ's death and resurrection
make us faithful witnesses to the new life he brings,

for he lives and reigns with you and the Holy Spirit,
one God, for ever and ever. ℟. **Amen.**

First Reading (1 Cor 1:18-25), p. 1162, no. 2.
Responsorial Psalm (Ps 117), p. 1161, no. 8.
Alleluia (Mk 1:17), p. 1168, no. 3.
Gospel (Mk 1:14-20), p. 1171, no. 5.

The Same Day, Apr. 28
ST. LOUIS MARY DE MONTFORT, Priest

Optional Memorial

Louis Mary Grignion was born to a poor family on
January 21, 1673, at Montfort, France. He was ordained in
1700 and shortly thereafter he organized a group of women
into the congregation of the Daughters of Divine Wisdom.
Eventually Louis went to Rome where Pope Clement XI
appointed him missionary apostolic, and he began to
preach in Britanny. He was successful, especially in fur-
thering devotion to the Blessed Virgin through the
Rosary. He also wrote a popular book, *True Devotion to the
Blessed Virgin*. In 1715, Louis organized several priests and
formed the Missionaries of the Company of Mary. He died
in 1716 at Saint-Laurent-sur Sèvre, France, and was canonized in 1947 by Pope Pius XII.

Common of Pastors: for Missionaries, p. 1067.

OPENING PRAYER

God of eternal wisdom,
you made your priest Louis Mary
an outstanding witness and teacher
of total dedication to Christ your Son
through the hands of the blessed Mother,
Grant that we may follow that same spiritual path
and extend your kingdom on earth.
We ask this . . . for ever and ever. ℟. **Amen.**

First Reading (1 Cor 1:18-25), p. 1162, no. 2.
Responsorial Psalm (Ps 40), p. 1159, no. 3.
Alleluia (Lk 4:18), p. 1168, no. 4.
Gospel (Mt 28:16-20), p. 1170, no. 4.

Apr. 29 — ST. CATHERINE OF SIENA, Virgin and Doctor

Memorial

A Dominican tertiary, St. Catherine pacified the civil discords of her country and was largely responsible for the return of Pope Gregory XI from Avignon to Rome. She was imprinted with the sacred Stigmata and died at Rome in 1380 at thirty-three years of age. In 1970 Pope Paul VI proclaimed her a Doctor of the Church.

ENTRANCE ANT.

Here is a wise and faithful virgin who went with lighted lamp to meet her Lord, alleluia. → No. 2, p. 12

OPENING PRAYER

Father,
in meditating on the sufferings of your Son
and in serving your Church,
St. Catherine was filled with the fervor of your love.
By her prayers,
may we share in the mystery of Christ's death
and rejoice in the revelation of his glory,
for he lives and reigns with you and the Holy Spirit,
one God, for ever and ever. ℟. **Amen.** ↓

Readings and Intervenient Chants are taken from the Common of Virgins, p. 1190.

FIRST READING
1 Jn 1:5—2:2

The Blood of Jesus Christ cleanses us of all sin. We are saved through the Blood of Christ who is the perfect offering for our sins.

A reading from the first Letter of Saint John

BELOVED: This is the message that we have heard from Jesus Christ and proclaim to you: God is light, and in him there is no darkness at all. If we say, "We have fellowship with him," while we continue to walk in darkness, we lie and do not act in truth. But if we walk in the light as he is in the light, then we have fellowship with one another, and the Blood of his Son Jesus cleanses us from all sin. If we say, "We are without sin," we deceive ourselves, and the truth is not in us. If we acknowledge our sins, he is faithful and just and will forgive our sins and cleanse us from every wrongdoing. If we say, "We have not sinned," we make him a liar, and his word is not in us.

My children, I am writing this to you so that you may not commit sin. But if anyone does sin, we have an Advocate with the Father, Jesus Christ the righteous one. He is expiation for our sins, and not for our sins only but for those of the whole world.—The word of the Lord. ℟.
Thanks be to God.

Responsorial Psalm (Ps 103), p. 1212, no. 6.
Alleluia (See Mt 11:25), p. 1223, no. 4.
Gospel (Mt 11:25-30), p. 1226, no. 4.

PRAYER OVER THE GIFTS

Lord,
accept this saving sacrifice
we offer on the feast of St. Catherine.
By following her teaching and example,
may we offer more perfect praise to you.
Grant this through Christ our Lord.
℟. **Amen.**   ➔ No. 21, p. 626 (Pref. P 22-25)

COMMUNION ANT.   1 Jn 1:7

If we walk in the light, as God is in light, there is fellowship among us, and the blood of his Son, Jesus Christ, will cleanse us from all sin, alleluia. ↓

PRAYER AFTER COMMUNION

Lord,
may the eucharist,
which nourished St. Catherine in this life,
bring us eternal life.
We ask this in the name of Jesus the Lord.
℟. **Amen.**   ➔ No. 32, p. 660

Apr. 30 — ST. PIUS V, Pope

Optional Memorial

St. Pius V, of the Dominican Order, was a Pope of great sanctity. His pontificate was one of the most glorious of the 16th century. He enforced obedience to the decrees of the Council of Trent, and revised the Missal and the Breviary. He died in 1572.

Common of Pastors: for Popes, p, 1057.

OPENING PRAYER

Father,
you chose St. Pius V as pope of your Church
to protect the faith and give you more fitting worship.
By his prayers,
help us to celebrate your holy mysteries
with a living faith and an effective love.
We ask this . . . for ever and ever. ℟. **Amen.**

First Reading (1 Cor 4:1-5), p. 1163, no. 3.
Responsorial Psalm (Ps 110), p. 1161, no. 7.
Alleluia (Jn 10:14), p. 1168, no. 5.
Gospel (Jn 21:15-17), p. 1174, no. 12.

—MAY—

May 1 — ST. JOSEPH THE WORKER

Optional Memorial

The feast of St. Joseph the Worker was instituted in 1955 by Pius XII, and its celebration was fixed on May 1, which is the day on which human labor is honored in many countries.

ENTRANCE ANT.　　　　　　　　　　　　　　　　Ps 128:1-2

Happy are all who fear the Lord and walk in his ways. You shall enjoy the fruits of your labor, you will prosper and be happy, alleluia.　　　　　→ No. 2, p. 614

OPENING PRAYER

God our Father,
creator and ruler of the universe,
in every age you call man
to develop and use his gifts for the good of others.
With St. Joseph as our example and guide,
help us to do the work you have asked
and come to the rewards you have promised.
We ask this . . . for ever and ever. ℟. **Amen.** ↓

FIRST READING　　　　　　　　　　　　　　　　Gn 1:26—2:3

God has given the world he created into the care of human beings. We are to work with it, subdue it and rule over it. It is our responsibility to develop the essential goodness that God has given to all creation.

A reading from the Book of Genesis

GOD said: "Let us make man in our image, after our likeness. Let them have dominion over the fish of the sea, the birds of the air, and the cattle, and over all the wild animals and all the creatures that crawl on the ground."

　　God created man in his image;
　　　　in the divine image he created him;
　　　　male and female he created them.

God blessed them, saying: "Be fertile and multiply; fill the earth and subdue it. Have dominion over the fish of the sea, the birds of the air, and all the living things that move on the earth." God also said: "See, I give you every seed-bearing plant all over the earth and every tree that has seed-bearing fruit on it to be your food; and to all the animals of the land, all the birds of the air, and all the living creatures that crawl on the ground, I give all the green plants for food." And so it happened. God looked at everything he had made, and he found it very good. Evening came, and morning followed—the sixth day.

Thus the heavens and the earth and all their array were completed. Since on the seventh day God was finished with the work he had been doing, God rested on the seventh day from all the work he had undertaken. So God blessed the seventh day and made it holy, because on it he rested from all the work he had done in creation.—The word of the Lord. ℟. **Thanks be to God.** ↓

OR

FIRST READING Col 3:14-15, 17, 23-24

Everything we do must be done in the name of the Lord Jesus, for all we have and do comes to us through him from the Father. We must give our all in the service of the Lord.

A reading from the Letter of Saint Paul to the Colossians

BROTHERS and sisters: Over all these things put on love, that is, the bond of perfection. And let the peace of Christ control your hearts, the peace into which you were also called in one Body. And be thankful. And whatever you do, in word or in deed, do everything in the name of the Lord Jesus, giving thanks to God the Father through him.

Whatever you do, do from the heart, as for the Lord and not for men, knowing that you will receive from the Lord the due payment of the inheritance; be slaves of the Lord Christ.—The word of the Lord. ℟. **Thanks be to God.** ↓

RESPONSORIAL PSALM　　Ps 90:2, 3-4, 12-13, 14 and 16

℟. (see 17b) **Lord, give success to the work of our hands.**

℟. Or: **Alleluia.**

Before the mountains were begotten
　　and the earth and the world were brought forth,
　　from everlasting to everlasting you are God.—℟.

You turn men back to dust,
　　saying, "Return, O children of men."
For a thousand years in your sight
　　are as yesterday, now that it is past,
　　or as a watch of the night.—℟.

Teach us to number our days aright,
　　that we may gain wisdom of heart.
Return, O LORD! How long?
　　Have pity on your servants!—℟.

Fill us at daybreak with your kindness,
　　that we may shout for joy and gladness all our days.
Let your work be seen by your servants
　　and your glory by their children.—℟. ↓

ALLELUIA　　Ps 68:20

℟. **Alleluia, alleluia.**
Blessed be the Lord day by day,
God, our salvation, who bears our burdens.
℟. **Alleluia, alleluia.** ↓

The Gospel is proper *in this Optional Memorial.*

GOSPEL　　Mt 13:54-58

The people of Nazareth spurned Jesus because they knew he was the son of a simple carpenter. If only they had had the vision to see how noble was the work of Joseph and Jesus, they might not have rejected Jesus out of hand.

℣. The Lord be with you. ℟. **And also with you.**
✠ A reading from the holy Gospel according to Matthew.
℟. **Glory to you, Lord.**

JESUS came to his native place and taught the people in their synagogue. They were astonished and said, "Where did this man get such wisdom and mighty deeds? Is he not the carpenter's son? Is not his mother named Mary and his brothers James, Joseph, Simon, and Judas? Are not his sisters all with us? Where did this man get all this?" And they took offense at him. But Jesus said to them, "A prophet is not without honor except in his native place and in his own house." And he did not work many mighty deeds there because of their lack of faith.—The Gospel of the Lord. ℟. **Praise to you, Lord Jesus Christ.**

→ No. 15, p. 623

PRAYER OVER THE GIFTS

Lord God,
fountain of all mercy,
look upon our gifts on this feast of St. Joseph.
Let our sacrifice
become the protection of all who call on you.
We ask this in the name of Jesus the Lord.
℟. **Amen.** → No. 21, p. 626 (Pref. P 62)

COMMUNION ANT. Col. 3:17

Let everything you do or say be in the name of the Lord with thanksgiving to God, alleluia. ↓

PRAYER AFTER COMMUNION

Lord,
hear the prayers of those you nourish in this eucharist.
Inspired by the example of St. Joseph,
may our lives manifest your love;
may we rejoice for ever in your peace.
Grant this through Christ our Lord.
℟. **Amen.** → No. 32, p. 660

May 2 — ST. ATHANASIUS, Bishop and Doctor

Memorial

St. Athanasius was born at Alexandria late in the 3rd century. Elevated to the Bishopric of Alexandria, he became the champion of the Faith against Arianism. He died in 373, leaving many religious and apologetic writings.

Common of Pastors: for Bishops, p. 1059; or Common of Doctors of the Church, p. 1072.

OPENING PRAYER

Father,
you raised up St. Athanasius
to be an outstanding defender
of the truth of Christ's divinity.
By his teaching and protection
may we grow in your knowledge and love.
Grant this . . . for ever and ever. ℟. **Amen.**

First Reading (1 Jn 5:1-5), p. 1146, no. 10.
Responsorial Psalm (Ps 37), p. 1180, no. 2.

ALLELUIA
Mt 5:10

℟. **Alleluia, alleluia.**
Blessed are they who are persecuted for the sake of righteousness,
for theirs is the Kingdom of heaven.
℟. **Alleluia, alleluia.** ↓

GOSPEL
Mt 10:22-25

The missionaries are told not to risk their lives unnecessarily. Jesus implies, not that he expects the Second Coming and God's final judgment before the termination of his disciples' mission, but rather that the divine plan of Israel's salvation will not be completed before the Second Coming.

℣. The Lord be with you. ℟. **And also with you.**
✛ A reading from the holy Gospel according to Matthew.
℟. **Glory to you, Lord.**

JESUS said to the Twelve: "You will be hated by all because of my name, but whoever endures to the end will be saved. When they persecute you in one town, flee to another. Amen, I say to you, you will not finish the towns of Israel before the Son of Man comes. No disciple is above his teacher, no slave above his master. It is enough for the disciple that he become like the teacher, and the slave that he become like the master. If they have called the master of the house Beelzebub, how much more those of his household!"—The Gospel of the Lord.

℟. **Praise to you, Lord Jesus Christ.** → No. 15, p. 623

PRAYER OVER THE GIFTS

Lord,
look upon the gifts we offer
on the feast of St. Athanasius.
Keep us true to the faith he professed
and let our own witness to your truth
bring us closer to salvation.
We ask this through Christ our Lord.

℟. **Amen.** → No. 21, p. 626 (Pref. P 22-25)

PRAYER AFTER COMMUNION

All-powerful God,
we join St. Athanasius in professing our belief
in the true divinity of Christ your Son.
Through this sacrament
may our faith always give us life and protection.
We ask this through Christ our Lord.

℟. **Amen.** → No. 32, p. 660

May 3 — STS. PHILIP AND JAMES, Apostles

Feast

St. Philip, like Peter and Andrew, was from Bethsaida. He was crucified at Hierapolis in Phrygia where he preached the Gospel. St. James the Less was a cousin of our Lord and a brother of the apostle Jude. He wrote one of the Letters of the New Testament. He was hurled down from the terrace of the temple and clubbed to death.

ENTRANCE ANT.

The Lord chose these holy men for their unfeigned love, and gave them eternal glory, alleluia. → No. 2, p. 614

OPENING PRAYER

God our Father,
every year you give us joy
on the festival of the apostles Philip and James.
By the help of their prayers
may we share in the suffering, death, and resurrection
of your only Son
and come to the eternal vision of your glory.
We ask this . . . for ever and ever. ℟. **Amen.**

FIRST READING   1 Cor 15:1-8

St. Paul summarizes the basic facts of the Good News. Our faith rests upon the eyewitness testimony of the Apostles, who saw Jesus after his Death and Resurrection, as well as upon their successors, our bishops.

A reading from the first Letter of Saint Paul to the
Corinthians

I AM reminding you, brothers and sisters, of the Gospel I preached to you, which you indeed received and in which you also stand. Through it you are also being saved, if you hold fast to the word I preached to you, unless you believed in vain. For I handed on to you as of first importance what I also received: that Christ died for our sins in accordance with the Scriptures; that he was buried; that he was raised on the third day in accordance with the Scriptures; that he appeared to Cephas, then to the Twelve. After that, he appeared to more than five hundred brothers and sisters at once, most of whom are still living, though some have fallen asleep. After that he appeared to James, then to all the Apostles. Last of all, as to one born abnormally, he appeared to me.—The word of the Lord. ℟. **Thanks be to God.** ↓

RESPONSORIAL PSALM   Ps 19:2-3, 4-5

℟. (5) **Their message goes out through all the earth.**

℟. Or: **Alleluia.**

The heavens declare the glory of God;
    and the firmament proclaims his handiwork.

Day pours out the word to day;
   and night to night imparts knowledge.—℟.

Not a word nor a discourse
   whose voice is not heard;
Through all the earth their voice resounds,
   and to the ends of the world, their message.—℟. ↓

ALLELUIA   Jn 14:6b, 9c

℟. **Alleluia, alleluia.**
I am the way, the truth, and the life, says the Lord;
Philip, whoever has seen me has seen the Father.
℟. **Alleluia, alleluia.** ↓

GOSPEL   Jn 14:6-14

The question of Philip, who is honored today, was answered by Christ with a clear statement of his divinity. The Apostles are to share in the saving mission of the Son of God, who will watch over them and will answer their needs.

℣. The Lord be with you. ℟. **And also with you.**
✠ A reading from the holy Gospel according to John.
℟. **Glory to you, Lord.**

JESUS said to Thomas, "I am the way and the truth and the life. No one comes to the Father except through me. If you know me, then you will also know my Father. From now on you do know him and have seen him." Philip said to him, "Master, show us the Father, and that will be enough for us." Jesus said to him, "Have I been with you for so long a time and you still do not know me, Philip? Whoever has seen me has seen the Father. How can you say, 'Show us the Father'? Do you not believe that I am in the Father and the Father is in me? The words that I speak to you I do not speak on my own. The Father who dwells in me is doing his works. Believe me that I am in the Father and the Father is in me, or else, believe because of the works themselves. Amen, amen, I say to you, whoever believes in me will do the works that I do, and will do greater ones than these, because I am going to the Father. And whatever you ask in my name, I will do, so that the

Father may be glorified in the Son. If you ask anything of me in my name, I will do it."—The Gospel of the Lord. ℟.
Praise to you, Lord Jesus Christ.   → No. 15, p. 623

PRAYER OVER THE GIFTS

Lord,
accept our gifts
at this celebration in honor of the apostles Philip and
     James.
Make our religion pure and undefiled.
We ask this through Christ our Lord.
℟. **Amen.**   → No. 21, p. 626 (Pref. P 64-65)

COMMUNION ANT.   Jn 14:8-9

Lord, let us see the Father, and we shall be content. And Jesus said: Philip, he who sees me, sees the Father, alleluia. ↓

PRAYER AFTER COMMUNION

Father,
by the holy gifts we have received
free our minds and hearts from sin.
With the apostles Philip and James
may we see you in your Son
and be found worthy to have eternal life.
We ask this through Christ our Lord.
℟. **Amen.**   → No. 32, p. 660

[In the dioceses of the United States]

May 10 — BLESSED DAMIEN JOSEPH DE VEUSTER OF MOLOKA'I, Priest

Optional Memorial

Born in Belgium in 1840, Damien entered the congregation of the Sacred Hearts and became a missionary priest to the island of Hawaii. In 1873 he began caring for the spiritual and physical needs of those in the leper colony on the island of Moloka'i and remained there till his death from leprosy on April 15, 1889. He was beatified in 1995 by Pope John Paul II, who called him a Servant of Humanity.

Common of Pastors, p. 1067; or Common of Holy Men and Women, p. 1086.

May 12 — STS. NEREUS and ACHILLEUS, Martyrs

Optional Memorial

Nereus and Achilleus were Roman soldiers who embraced the true faith and refused to serve any longer. As a result, they were martyred, probably during the reign of Diocletian. Their tomb is located in the cemetery on the Via Ardeatina, where a basilica was erected in their honor.

Common of Martyrs, p. 1041 *or* 1050.

OPENING PRAYER

Father,
we honor Saints Nereus and Achilleus for their courage
in dying to profess their faith in Christ.
May we experience the help of their prayers
at the throne of your mercy.
Grant this . . . for ever and ever. ℟. **Amen.**

First Reading (Rv 7:9-17), p. 1137, no. 2.
Responsorial Psalm (Ps 124), p. 1140, no. 3.
Alleluia (Mt 5:10), p. 1146, no. 1.
Gospel (Mt 10:17-22), p. 1226, no. 4.

The Same Day, May 12
ST. PANCRAS, Martyr

Optional Memorial

St. Pancras was martyred at the age of fourteen, during the reign of Diocletian about 304. He was buried on the Via Aurelia and Pope Symmachus built a church over his tomb.

Common of Martyrs, p. 1047 *or* 1052.

OPENING PRAYER

God of mercy,
give your Church joy and confidence
through the prayers of St. Pancras.
Keep us faithful to you
and steadfast in your service.
We ask this . . . for ever and ever. ℟. **Amen.**

First Reading (Rv 19:1, 5-9a), p. 1208, no. 3.
Responsorial Psalm (Ps 103), p. 1212, no. 6.

Alleluia (See Mt 11:25), p. 1223, no. 4.
Gospel (Mt 11:25-30), p. 1226, no. 4.

May 14 — ST. MATTHIAS, Apostle

Feast

After the Ascension of our Lord, St. Peter proposed that the disciples draw lots to select an Apostle to take the place of Judas. "The lot fell upon Matthias, and he was counted with the Eleven Apostles." He propagated the Faith in Palestine, and was stoned to death in the year 64.

ENTRANCE ANT. 　　　　　　　　　　　　　　　Jn 15:16

You have not chosen me; I have chosen you. Go and bear fruit that will last, alleluia. 　　　　　　→ No. 2, p. 614

OPENING PRAYER

Father,
you called St. Matthias to share in the mission of the
　　apostles.
By the help of his prayers
may we receive with joy the love you share with us
and be counted among those you have chosen.
We ask this . . . for ever and ever. ℟. **Amen.** ↓

FIRST READING 　　　　　　　　　　　　　Acts 1:15-17, 20-26

Peter discusses the question of Judas and his replacement. Two men of irreputable life are nominated, Joseph Barsabbas and Matthias. Then lots are drawn by the disciples and the choice falls on Matthias, who is added to the Apostles.

A reading from the Acts of the Apostles

PETER stood up in the midst of the brothers and sisters (there was a group of about one hundred and twenty persons in the one place). He said, "My brothers and sisters, the Scripture had to be fulfilled which the Holy Spirit spoke beforehand through the mouth of David, concerning Judas, who was the guide for those who arrested Jesus. Judas was numbered among us and was allotted a share in this ministry. For it is written in the Book of Psalms:

> *Let his encampment become desolate,*
> *and may no one dwell in it.*

and:

> *May another take his office.*

Therefore, it is necessary that one of the men who accompanied us the whole time the Lord Jesus came and went among us, beginning from the baptism of John until the day on which he was taken up from us, become with us a witness to his resurrection." So they proposed two, Joseph called Barsabbas, who was also known as Justus, and Matthias. Then they prayed, "You, Lord, who know the hearts of all, show which one of these two you have chosen to take the place in this apostolic ministry from which Judas turned away to go to his own place." Then they gave lots to them, and the lot fell upon Matthias, and he was counted with the Eleven Apostles.—The word of the Lord. ℟. **Thanks be to God.** ↓

RESPONSORIAL PSALM   Ps 113:1-2, 3-4, 5-6, 7-8

℟. (9) **The Lord will give him a seat with the leaders of his people.**

℟. Or: **Alleluia.**

Praise, you servants of the LORD,
  praise the name of the LORD.
Blessed be the name of the LORD
  both now and forever.—℟.

From the rising to the setting of the sun
  is the name of the LORD to be praised.
High above all nations is the LORD;
  above the heavens is his glory.—℟.

Who is like the LORD, our God, who is enthroned on high
  and looks upon the heavens and the earth below?—℟.

He raises up the lowly from the dust;
    from the dunghill he lifts up the poor
To seat them with princes,
    with the princes of his own people.—℟. ↓

ALLELUIA
See Jn 15:16

℟. **Alleluia, alleluia.**
I chose you from the world,
to go and bear fruit that will last, says the Lord.
℟. **Alleluia, alleluia.** ↓

GOSPEL
Jn 15:9-17

Jesus admonishes the disciples to continue the love he has shown to them. Their keeping of the commandments will be a proof of this. "Love one another. . . . [It was] I who chose you."

℣. The Lord be with you. ℟. **And also with you.**
✠ A reading from the holy Gospel according to John.
℟. **Glory to you, Lord.**

JESUS said to his disciples: "As the Father loves me, so I also love you. Remain in my love. If you keep my commandments, you will remain in my love, just as I have kept my Father's commandments and remain in his love.

"I have told you this so that my joy might be in you and your joy might be complete. This is my commandment: love one another as I love you. No one has greater love than this, to lay down one's life for one's friends. You are my friends if you do what I command you. I no longer call you slaves, because a slave does not know what his master is doing. I have called you friends, because I have told you everything I have heard from my Father. It was not you who chose me, but I who chose you and appointed you to go and bear fruit that will remain, so that whatever you ask the Father in my name he may give you. This I command you: love one another."—The Gospel of the Lord. ℟. **Praise to you, Lord Jesus Christ.**

→ No. 15, p. 623

PRAYER OVER THE GIFTS

Lord,
accept the gifts your Church offers
on the feast of the apostle, Matthias,
and by this eucharist
strengthen your grace within us.
We ask this through Christ our Lord.
℟. **Amen.**   ➜ No. 21, p. 626 (Pref. P 64-65)

COMMUNION ANT.   Jn 15:12

This is my commandment: love one another as I have loved you. ↓

PRAYER AFTER COMMUNION

Lord,
you constantly give life to your people
in this holy eucharist.
By the prayers of the apostle Matthias
prepare us to take our place
among your saints in eternal life.
We ask this through Christ our Lord.
℟. **Amen.**   ➜ No. 32, p. 660

[In the dioceses of the United States]

May 15 — ST. ISIDORE

Optional Memorial

St. Isidore was born at Madrid, Spain, in the latter half of
the 12th century. For the greater part of his life he was
employed as a laborer on a farm outside the city. Many marvelous happenings accompanied his lifelong work in the
fields and continued long after his death. St. Isidore was
canonized in 1622. In 1947 he was proclaimed the patron of
the National Rural Life Conference in the United States.

Common of Holy Men and Women, p. 1080.

OPENING PRAYER

Lord God,
all creation is yours, and you call us to serve you

by caring for the gifts that surround us.
May the example of St. Isidore urge us
to share our food with the hungry
and to work for the salvation of mankind.
We ask this . . . for ever and ever. ℟. **Amen.**

May 18 — ST JOHN I, Pope and Martyr

Optional Memorial

St. John I was Pope under the Arian King Theodoric.
Captured and brought to Ravenna, he died in prison shortly after in 526.

Common of Martyrs, p. 1047 *or* 1052; *or Common of Pastors: for
Popes*, p. 1057.

OPENING PRAYER

God our Father,
rewarder of all who believe,
hear our prayers
as we celebrate the martyrdom of Pope John.
Help us to follow him in loyalty to the faith.
Grant this . . . for ever and ever. ℟. **Amen.**

First Reading (Rv 3:14b, 20-22), p. 1208, no. 2.
Responsorial Psalm (Ps 23), p. 1211, no. 4.
Alleluia (Jn 15:15b), p. 1169, no. 7.
Gospel (Lk 22:24-30), p. 1173, no. 9.

May 20 — ST. BERNARDINE OF SIENA, Priest

Optional Memorial

St. Bernardine, born of noble parentage, left all and
entered the Franciscan Order and became one of its chief
glories. He preached devotion to the Name of Jesus in
every place he went. He died in 1444.

Common of Pastors: for Missionaries, p. 1067.

OPENING PRAYER

Father,
you gave St. Bernardine a special love
for the holy name of Jesus.

By the help of his prayers,
may we always be alive with the spirit of your love.
We ask this . . . for ever and ever. ℟. **Amen.**

FIRST READING   Acts 4:8-12

Peter explains the cure of the cripple. It was a miracle performed in the name of Jesus, whom the people had rejected and crucified. There is no salvation except in Jesus.

A reading from the Acts of the Apostles

PETER, filled with the Holy Spirit, answered them: "Leaders of the people and elders: If we are being examined today about a good deed done to a cripple, namely, by what means he was saved, then all of you and all the people of Israel should know that it was in the name of Jesus Christ the Nazorean whom you crucified, whom God raised from the dead; in his name this man stands before you healed. He is the stone rejected by you, the builders, which has become the cornerstone. There is no salvation through anyone else, nor is there any other name under heaven given to the human race by which we are to be saved."—The word of the Lord. ℟. **Thanks be to God.**

Responsorial Psalm (Ps 40), p. 975.
Alleluia (Jn 8:12), p. 1224, no. 8.
Gospel (Lk 9:57-62), p. 1235, no. 18.

May 25 — ST. BEDE THE VENERABLE, Priest and Doctor

Optional Memorial

St. Bede, who lived in the 8th century, was a member of the Order of St. Benedict. Because of the enormous amount of his writings, full of sound doctrine, he was called "Venerable" while still living. He is rightly termed "The Father of English History." He died in 735.

Common of Doctors of the Church, p. 1072; or Common of Holy Men and Women: for Religious, p. 1086.

OPENING PRAYER

Lord,
you have enlightened your Church
with the learning of St. Bede.
In your love
may your people learn from his wisdom
and benefit from his prayers.
Grant this . . . for ever and ever. ℟. **Amen.**

*Readings and Intervenient Chants may also be taken from the
Common of Pastors, p. 1151.*

First Reading (1 Cor 2:10b-16), p. 1182, no. 3.
Responsorial Psalm (Ps 119), p. 1180, no. 3.
Alleluia (See Jn 6:63c, 68c), p. 1185, no. 3.
Gospel (Mt 7:21-29), p. 1186, no. 2.

The Same Day, May 25
ST. GREGORY VII, Pope, Religious

Optional Memorial

Before ascending to the Papacy, St. Gregory was known as
Hildebrand, a monk of the Benedictine Order. As a monk
and Pope (1073) he fought against the abuses within the
Church. He died in 1085.

Common of Pastors: for Popes, p. 1057.

OPENING PRAYER

Lord,
give your Church
the spirit of courage and love for justice
which distinguished Pope Gregory.
Make us courageous in condemning evil
and free us to pursue justice with love.
We ask this . . . for ever and ever. ℟. **Amen.**

First Reading (Acts 20:17-18a, 28-32, 36), p. 1157, no. 2.
Responsorial Psalm (Ps 110), p. 1161, no. 7.
Alleluia (Mk 1:17), p. 1168, no. 3.
Gospel (Mt 16:13-19), p. 1169, no. 2.

The Same Day, May 25
ST. MARY MAGDALENE DE' PAZZI, Virgin

Optional Memorial

At ten years of age. St. Mary Magdalene consecrated her virginity to God. When she was nineteen, she received the Carmelite habit. Her constant exclamation was: "To suffer and not to die." She died in 1607.

Common of Virgins, p. 1075; or Common of Holy Men and Women: for Religious, p. 1086.

OPENING PRAYER

Father,
you love those who give themselves completely to your
    service,
and you filled St. Mary Magdalene de Pazzi
with heavenly gifts and the fire of your love.
As we honor her today
may we follow her example of purity and charity.
Grant this . . . for ever and ever. R̞. **Amen.**

First Reading (1 Cor 7:25-35), p. 1193, no. 1.
Responsorial Psalm (Ps 148), p. 1192, no. 2.
Alleluia (Jn 8:31b-32), p. 1224, no. 9.
Gospel (Mk 3:31-35), p. 1232, no. 14.

May 26—ST. PHILIP NERI, Priest

Memorial

St. Philip Neri was born in Florence. Ordained a priest, he founded the Congregation of the Priests of the Oratory. He is noted for his zeal in converting sinners by means of the confessional. He died at 80 years of age, in 1595, after having demonstrated many miraculous gifts.

Common of Pastors, p. 1061; or Common of Holy Men and Women: for Religious, p. 1086.

OPENING PRAYER

Father,
you continually raise up your faithful
to the glory of holiness.
In your love
kindle in us the fire of the Holy Spirit

who so filled the heart of Philip Neri.
We ask this . . . for ever and ever. R̹. **Amen.**

First Reading (Phil 4:4-9), p. 1218, no. 10.
Responsorial Psalm (Ps 34), p. 1211, no. 5.
Alleluia (Jn 15:9b, 5b), p. 1224, no. 13.
Gospel (Jn 17:20-26), p. 1239, no. 26.

PRAYER OVER THE GIFTS

Lord,
help us who offer you this sacrifice of praise
to follow the example of St. Philip.
Keep us always cheerful in our work
for the glory of your name and the good of our neighbor.
Grant this through Christ our Lord.
R̹. **Amen.**

→ No. 21, p. 626

PRAYER AFTER COMMUNION

Lord,
strengthen us with the bread of life.
May we always imitate St. Philip
by hungering after this sacrament
in which we find true life.
We ask this in the name of Jesus the Lord.
R̹. **Amen.**

→ No. 32, p. 660

May 27 — ST. AUGUSTINE OF CANTERBURY, Bishop

Optional Memorial

St. Augustine was sent by St. Gregory the Great to
England to convert the people to Christianity. At
Canterbury he erected a monastery, and there established
his Episcopal See. He is said to have baptized thousands of
Englishmen in one day. He died in the year 604.

*Common of Pastors: for Missionaries, p. 1067; or for Bishops,
p. 1059.*

OPENING PRAYER

Father,
by the preaching of St. Augustine of Canterbury,

you led the people of England to the gospel.
May the fruits of his work continue in your Church.
Grant this . . . for ever and ever. ℟. **Amen.**

First Reading (1 Thes 2:2b-8), p. 1166, no. 10.
Responsorial Psalm (Ps 96), p. 1160, no. 5.
Alleluia (Jn 10:14), p. 1168, no. 5.
Gospel (Mt 9:35-38), p. 1169, no. 1.

May 31 — VISITATION

Feast

The feast of the Visitation was instituted in 1389 by Urban VI to obtain the end of the Western schism, and it was inserted in the Roman Calendar on July 2, the date on which it had already been celebrated by the Franciscans since 1263. Its new date (May 31) places this feast between the Solemnity of the Annunciation of the Lord and the Nativity of St. John the Baptist, to conform more closely to the Gospel account.

ENTRANCE ANT.   Ps 66:16

Come, all you who fear God, and hear the great things the Lord has done for me.   ➜ No. 2, p. 614

OPENING PRAYER

Eternal Father,
you inspired the Virgin Mary, mother of your Son,
to visit Elizabeth and assist her in her need.
Keep us open to the working of your Spirit,
and with Mary may we praise you for ever.
We ask this . . . for ever and ever. ℟. **Amen.** ↓

FIRST READING   Zep 3:14-18a

"Shout for joy . . . the Lord is in your midst." The chosen people are told they are understood and forgiven; therefore, they have nothing to fear. Their hearts are to be filled with joy and gladness as he is renewing them in his love.

A reading from the Book of the Prophet Zephaniah

S HOUT for joy, O daughter Zion!
Sing joyfully, O Israel!

Be glad and exult with all your heart,
   O daughter Jerusalem!
The L ORD has removed the judgment against you,
   he has turned away your enemies;
The King of Israel, the L ORD, is in your midst,
   you have no further misfortune to fear.
On that day, it shall be said to Jerusalem:
   Fear not, O Zion, be not discouraged!
The L ORD, your God, is in your midst,
   a mighty savior;
He will rejoice over you with gladness,
   and renew you in his love,
He will sing joyfully because of you,
   as one sings at festivals.
The word of the Lord. ℟. **Thanks be to God.** ↓

OR

FIRST READING   Rom 12:9-16

*"Let love be sincere." Be patient, hospitable, concerned, sympathetic,
brotherly to the lowly. By these ways, you serve the Lord, and you can
rejoice in hope.*

A reading from the Letter of Saint Paul to the Romans

B ROTHERS and sisters: Let love be sincere; hate what
is evil, hold on to what is good; love one another with
mutual affection; anticipate one another in showing
honor. Do not grow slack in zeal, be fervent in spirit,
serve the Lord. Rejoice in hope, endure in affliction,
persevere in prayer. Contribute to the needs of the holy
ones, exercise hospitality. Bless those who persecute
you, bless and do not curse them. Rejoice with those
who rejoice, weep with those who weep. Have the same
regard for one another; do not be haughty but associ-
ate with the lowly; do not be wise in your own estima-
tion.—The word of the Lord. ℟. **Thanks be to God.** ↓

RESPONSORIAL PSALM Is 12:2-3, 4bcd, 5-6

℟. (6) **Among you is the great and Holy One of Israel.**

God indeed is my savior;
   I am confident and unafraid.
My strength and my courage is the LORD,
   and he has been my savior.
With joy you will draw water
   at the fountain of salvation.—℟.

Give thanks to the LORD, acclaim his name;
   among the nations make known his deeds,
   proclaim how exalted is his name.—℟.

Sing praise to the LORD for his glorious achievement;
   let this be known throughout all the earth.
Shout with exultation, O city of Zion,
   for great in your midst
   is the Holy One of Israel!—℟. ↓

ALLELUIA See Lk 1:45

℟. **Alleluia, alleluia.**
Blessed are you, O Virgin Mary, who believed
that what was spoken to you by the Lord would be fulfilled.
℟. **Alleluia, alleluia.** ↓

GOSPEL Lk 1:39-56

Filled with unutterable joy, Mary had to share her feelings with Elizabeth,
who was mentioned by the angel. Joyfully, they revealed their secrets and
found themselves exultantly praising God in all his ways.

℣. The Lord be with you. ℟. **And also with you.**
✚ A reading from the holy Gospel according to Luke.
℟. **Glory to you, Lord.**

MARY set out and traveled to the hill country in haste
to a town of Judah, where she entered the house of
Zechariah and greeted Elizabeth. When Elizabeth heard
Mary's greeting, the infant leaped in her womb, and

Elizabeth, filled with the Holy Spirit, cried out in a loud voice and said, "Most blessed are you among women, and blessed is the fruit of your womb. And how does this happen to me, that the mother of my Lord should come to me? For at the moment the sound of your greeting reached my ears, the infant in my womb leaped for joy. Blessed are you who believed that what was spoken to you by the Lord would be fulfilled."

And Mary said:

"My soul proclaims the greatness of the Lord;
>   my spirit rejoices in God my Savior,
>   for he has looked with favor on his lowly servant.
From this day all generations will call me blessed:
>   the Almighty has done great things for me,
>   and holy is his Name.

He has mercy on those who fear him
>   in every generation.
He has shown the strength of his arm,
>   he has scattered the proud in their conceit.
He has cast down the mighty from their thrones,
>   and has lifted up the lowly.
He has filled the hungry with good things,
>   and the rich he has sent away empty.
He has come to the help of his servant Israel
>   for he has remembered his promise of mercy,
>   the promise he made to our fathers,
>   to Abraham and his children for ever."

Mary remained with her about three months and then returned to her home.—The Gospel of the Lord. ℟. **Praise to you, Lord Jesus Christ.**   → No. 15, p. 623

PRAYER OVER THE GIFTS

Father,
make our sacrifice acceptable and holy
as you accepted the love of Mary,
the mother of your Son, Jesus Christ,

who is Lord for ever and ever.
℟. **Amen.** → No. 21, p. 626 (Pref. P 56-57)

COMMUNION ANT. Lk 1:48-49

**All generations will call me blessed, for the Almighty
has done great things for me. Holy is his name.** ↓

PRAYER AFTER COMMUNION

Lord,
let the Church praise you
for the great things you have done for your people.
May we always recognize with joy
the presence of Christ in the eucharist we celebrate,
as John the Baptist hailed the presence
of our Savior in the womb of Mary.
We ask this through Christ our Lord.
℟. **Amen.** → No. 32, p. 660

Saturday following the Second Sunday
after Pentecost

IMMACULATE HEART OF MARY

Memorial

Our Lady of Fatima is said to have asked for the Consecration of the world to her Immaculate Heart in order to obtain world peace and the conversion of Russia. To it must be added devout prayers, true repentance, and penance for people's sins. In 1942, Pope Pius XII consecrated the world to the Immaculate Heart of Mary. In 1945, the sovereign Pontiff established this new Feast to promote devotion to the Immaculate Heart of Mary and extended it to the Universal Church.

ENTRANCE ANT. Ps 13:6

My heart rejoices in your saving power. I will sing to the Lord for his goodness to me. → No. 2, p. 614

OPENING PRAYER

Father,
you prepared the heart of the Virgin Mary
to be a fitting home for your Holy Spirit.
By her prayers
may we become a more worthy temple of your glory.
Grant this . . . for ever and ever. R̹. **Amen.**

Readings and Intervenient Chants are taken from the Common of the Blessed Virgin Mary, p. 1110.

First Reading (Is 61:9-11), p. 1115, no. 9.
Responsorial Psalm (1 Sm 2), p. 1119, no. 1.

ALLELUIA See Lk 2:19

R̹. **Alleluia, alleluia.**
Blessed is the Virgin Mary who kept the word of God,
and pondered it in her heart.
R̹. **Alleluia, alleluia.** ↓

The Gospel is proper *in this Memorial.*

GOSPEL   Lk 2:41-51

Jesus and his parents go to Jerusalem for the Passover. Upon returning, Jesus is separated from them. Mary and Joseph find him in the temple, teaching. When Mary asks why, Jesus replies that he must be doing his Father's work. Jesus returns with Mary and Joseph to Nazareth.

℣. The Lord be with you. ℟. **And also with you**.
✛ A reading from the holy Gospel according to Luke.
℟. **Glory to you, Lord.**

EACH year Jesus' parents went to Jerusalem for the feast of Passover, and when he was twelve years old, they went up according to festival custom. After they had completed its days, as they were returning, the boy Jesus remained behind in Jerusalem, but his parents did not know it. Thinking that he was in the caravan, they journeyed for a day and looked for him among their relatives and acquaintances, but not finding him, they returned to Jerusalem to look for him. After three days they found him in the temple, sitting in the midst of the teachers, listening to them and asking them questions, and all who heard him were astounded at his understanding and his answers. When his parents saw him, they were astonished, and his mother said to him, "Son, why have you done this to us? Your father and I have been looking for you with great anxiety." And he said to them, "Why were you looking for me? Did you not know that I must be in my Father's house?" But they did not understand what he said to them. He went down with them and came to Nazareth, and was obedient to them; and his mother kept all these things in her heart.—The Gospel of the Lord. ℟. **Praise to you, Lord Jesus Christ.**   ➜ No. 15, p. 623

PRAYER OVER THE GIFTS

Lord,
accept the prayers and gifts we offer
in honor of Mary, the Mother of God.

May they please you
and bring us your help and forgiveness.
We ask this in the name of Jesus the Lord.
℟. **Amen.** → No. 21, p. 626 (P 56-57)

COMMUNION ANT. Lk 2:19

**Mary treasured all these words and pondered them in
her heart.** ↓

PRAYER AFTER COMMUNION

Lord,
you have given us the sacrament of eternal redemption.
May we who honor the mother of your Son
rejoice in the abundance of your blessings
and experience the deepening of your life within us.
We ask this through Christ our Lord. → No. 32, p. 660

— JUNE —

June 1 — ST. JUSTIN, Martyr

Memorial

St. Justin was converted from being a pagan philosopher to Christianity. He then became the most illustrious opponent of pagan philosophers. He addressed two Apologies to the Emperor Antoninus and the Roman Senate. He died in 165.

ENTRANCE ANT. See Ps 119:85, 46

The wicked tempted me with their fables against your law, but I proclaimed your decrees before kings without fear or shame. → No. 2, p. 614

OPENING PRAYER

Father,
through the folly of the cross
you taught St. Justin the sublime wisdom of Jesus
    Christ.
May we too reject falsehood
and remain loyal to the faith.
We ask this . . . for ever and ever. ℟. **Amen.**

Readings and Intervenient Chants are taken from the Common of Martyrs, p. 1132.

First Reading (1 Cor 1:18-25), p. 1162, no. 2.
Responsorial Psalm (Ps 34), p. 1139, no. 2.
Alleluia (Mt 5:16), p. 1185, no. 1.
Gospel (Mt 5:13-19), p. 1186, no. 1.

PRAYER OVER THE GIFTS

Lord,
help us to worship you as we should
when we celebrate these mysteries
which St. Justin vigorously defended.
We ask this in the name of Jesus the Lord.
℟. **Amen.** → No. 21, p. 626

COMMUNION ANT. 1 Cor 2:2

I resolved that while I was with you I would think of nothing but Jesus Christ and him crucified. ↓

PRAYER AFTER COMMUNION

Lord,
hear the prayer of those you renew with spiritual food.
By following the teaching of St. Justin
may we offer constant thanks for the gifts we receive.
Grant this through Christ our Lord.
℟. **Amen.** → No. 32, p. 660

June 2 — STS. MARCELLINUS and PETER, Martyrs

Optional Memorial

The exorcist Peter succeeded in converting his jailer and his family. All were baptized by St. Marcellinus. Both were beheaded in 304.

Common of Martyrs, p. 1041 or 1051.

OPENING PRAYER

Father,
may we benefit from the example
of your martyrs Marcellinus and Peter,
and be supported by their prayers.
Grant this . . . for ever and ever. ℟. **Amen.**

First Reading (2 Cor 6:4-10), p. 1143, no. 4.
Responsorial Psalm (Ps 124), p. 1140, no. 3.
Alleluia (2 Cor 1:3b-4a), p. 1146, no. 3.
Gospel (Jn 17:11b-19), p. 1149, no. 7.

June 3 — STS. CHARLES LWANGA and COMPANIONS, Martyrs

Memorial

St. Charles Lwanga and his companions, martyrs of Uganda, are the first martyrs of black Africa. St. Charles was martyred with twelve companions near Rubaga on

June 3, 1886; the others were killed between May 26, 1886 and January 27, 1887. They were canonized in 1964.

Common of Martyrs, p. 1041 or 1051.

OPENING PRAYER

Father,
you have made the blood of the martyrs
the seed of Christians.
May the witness of St. Charles and his companions
and their loyalty to Christ in the face of torture
inspire countless men and women
to live the Christian faith.
We ask this . . . for ever and ever. ℟. **Amen.**

First Reading (2 Mc 7:1-2, 9-14), p. 1133, no. 3.
Responsorial Psalm (Ps 124), p. 1140, no. 3.
Alleluia (Mt 5:3), p. 1223, no. 1.
Gospel (Mt 5:1-12a), p. 1225, no. 1.

PRAYER OVER THE GIFTS

Lord,
accept the gifts we present at your altar.
As you gave your holy martyrs courage to die rather than
    sin,
help us to give ourselves completely to you.
We ask this in the name of Jesus the Lord.
℟. **Amen.**   ➙ No. 21, p. 626

PRAYER AFTER COMMUNION

Lord,
at this celebration of the triumph of your martyrs,
we have received the sacraments
which helped them endure their sufferings.
In the midst of our own hardships
may this eucharist keep us steadfast in faith and love.
Grant this through Christ our Lord.
℟. **Amen.**   ➙ No. 32, p. 660

June 5 — ST. BONIFACE, Bishop and Martyr

Memorial

Born in England about 680, St. Boniface became a Benedictine monk. He preached in Germany and later was consecrated first Bishop of Germany by Pope Gregory II. He died a martyr, together with thirty companions, in 754.

Common of Martyrs, p. 1047 or 1052; or Common of Pastors: for Missionaries, p. 1067.

OPENING PRAYER

Lord,
your martyr Boniface
spread the faith by his teaching
and witnessed to it with his blood.
By the help of his prayers
keep us loyal to our faith
and give us the courage to profess it in our lives.
Grant this . . . for ever and ever. ℟. **Amen.**

First Reading (Acts 26:19-23), p. 1157, no. 3.
Responsorial Psalm (Ps 117), p. 1161, no. 8.
Alleluia (Jn 10:14), p. 1168, no. 5.
Gospel (Jn 10:11-16), p. 1173, no. 10.

June 6 — ST. NORBERT, Bishop

Optional Memorial

St. Norbert was born at Xanten, Germany, in 1080. After a somewhat worldly and licentious life, he retired to Prémontre and there founded the Premonstratensians under the rule of St. Augustine. He died in 1134 while holding the exalted office of Archbishop of Magdeburg.

Common of Pastors: for Bishops, p, 1059; or Common of Holy Men and Women: for Religious, p. 1086.

OPENING PRAYER

Father,
you made the bishop Norbert

an outstanding minister of your Church,
renowned for his preaching and pastoral zeal.
Always grant to your Church faithful shepherds
to lead your people to eternal salvation.
We ask this . . . for ever and ever. ℟. **Amen.**

First Reading (Ez 34:11-16), p. 1156, no. 9.
Responsorial Psalm (Ps 23), p. 1158, no. 2.
Alleluia (Mt 5:3), p. 1223, no. 1.
Gospel (Lk 14:25-33), p. 1237, no. 23.

June 9 — ST. EPHREM, Deacon and Doctor

Optional Memorial

St. Ephrem, of Nisibis in Mesopotamia, was cast forth
from his home by his father, a pagan priest. He lived as a
hermit but was later ordained a deacon of Edessa and
became renowned as a poet, orator, and holy monk. He
died in 373.

Common of Doctors of the Church, p. 1072.

OPENING PRAYER

Lord,
in your love fill our hearts with the Holy Spirit,
who inspired the deacon Ephrem to sing the praise of
    your mysteries
and gave him strength to serve you alone.
Grant this . . . for ever and ever. ℟. **Amen.**

First Reading (Col 3:12-17), p. 1219, no. 11.
Responsorial Psalm (Ps 37), p 1180, no. 2.
Alleluia (Jn 15:5), p. 1185, no. 4.
Gospel (Lk 6:43-45), p. 1189, no. 6.

June 11 — ST. BARNABAS, Apostle

Memorial

St. Barnabas was the companion of St. Paul in the evangelization of the pagans in Cyprus. After having won over

many souls for Christ, Barnabas died a martyr at Cyprus during Nero's reign with the Gospel of St. Matthew, written by his own hand, on his chest.

ENTRANCE ANT.　　　　　See Acts 11:24

Blessed are you, St. Barnabas: you were a man of faith filled with the Holy Spirit and counted among the apostles.　　　　　→ No. 2, p. 614

OPENING PRAYER

God our Father,
you filled St. Barnabas with faith and the Holy Spirit,
and sent him to convert the nations.
Help us to proclaim the gospel by word and deed.
We ask this . . . for ever and ever. ℟. **Amen.** ↓

The First Reading is proper in this Memorial.

FIRST READING　　　　　Acts 11:21b-26; 13:1-3

Today's saint, Barnabas, is commended as a man full of the Spirit of faith. St. Barnabas introduced St. Paul to the Christian community. Together, they were added to the number of the apostles and were sent to the Gentiles.

A reading from the Acts of the Apostles

IN those days a great number who believed turned to the Lord. The news about them reached the ears of the Church in Jerusalem, and they sent Barnabas to go to Antioch. When he arrived and saw the grace of God, he rejoiced and encouraged them all to remain faithful to the Lord in firmness of heart, for he was a good man, filled with the Holy Spirit and faith. And a large number of people was added to the Lord. Then he went to Tarsus to look for Saul, and when he had found him he brought him to Antioch. For a whole year they met with the Church and taught a large number of people, and it was in Antioch that the disciples were first called Christians.

Now there were in the Church at Antioch prophets and teachers: Barnabas, Symeon who was called Niger,

Lucius of Cyrene, Manaen who was a close friend of Herod the tetrarch, and Saul. While they were worshiping the Lord and fasting, the Holy Spirit said, "Set apart for me Barnabas and Saul for the work to which I have called them." Then, completing their fasting and prayer, they laid hands on them and sent them off.—The word of the Lord. ℟. **Thanks be to God.** ↓

RESPONSORIAL PSALM　　　　Ps 98:1, 2-3ab, 3cd-4, 5-6

℟. (see 2b) **The Lord has revealed to the nations his saving power.**

Sing to the LORD a new song,
　　for he has done wondrous deeds;
His right hand has won victory for him,
　　his holy arm.—℟.

The LORD has made his salvation known:
　　in the sight of the nations he has revealed his justice.
He has remembered his kindness and his faithfulness
　　toward the house of Israel.—℟.

All the ends of the earth have seen
　　the salvation by our God.
Sing joyfully to the LORD, all you lands;
　　break into song; sing praise.—℟.

Sing praise to the LORD with the harp,
　　with the harp and melodious song.
With trumpets and the sound of the horn
　　sing joyfully before the King, the LORD.—℟. ↓

ALLELUIA　　　　　　　　　　　　Mt 28:19a, 20b

℟. **Alleluia, alleluia.**
Go and teach all nations, says the Lord;
I am with you always, until the end of the world.
℟. **Alleluia, alleluia.** ↓

GOSPEL Mt 10:7-13

Jesus empowered his apostles to work wonders and miracles, to prove their teaching about Christ. The greater miracles are men who still leave everything today, in order to preach the Good News. Miracles of grace accompany such dedication.

℣. The Lord be with you. ℟. **And also with you**.

✤ A reading from the holy Gospel according to Matthew.
℟. **Glory to you, Lord.**

JESUS said to the Twelve: "As you go, make this proclamation: 'The Kingdom of heaven is at hand.' Cure the sick, raise the dead, cleanse the lepers, drive out demons. Without cost you have received; without cost you are to give. Do not take gold or silver or copper for your belts; no sack for the journey, or a second tunic, or sandals, or walking stick. The laborer deserves his keep. Whatever town or village you enter, look for a worthy person in it, and stay there until you leave. As you enter a house, wish it peace. If the house is worthy, let your peace come upon it; if not, let your peace return to you."—The Gospel of the Lord. ℟. **Praise to you, Lord Jesus Christ.**

→ No. 15, p. 623

PRAYER OVER THE GIFTS

Lord,
bless these gifts we present to you.
May they kindle in us the flame of love
by which St. Barnabas brought the light of the gospel
to the nations.
Grant this through Christ our Lord.
℟. **Amen.** → No. 21, p. 626 (Pref. P 64-65)

COMMUNION ANT. Jn 15:15

No longer shall I call you servants, for a servant knows not what his master does. Now I shall call you friends, for I have revealed to you all that I have heard from my Father. ↓

PRAYER AFTER COMMUNION   [Pledge of Life]

Lord,

hear the prayers of those who receive the pledge of eternal life

on the feast of St. Barnabas.

May we come to share the salvation

we celebrate in this sacrament.

We ask this in the name of Jesus the Lord.

℟. **Amen.**   → No. 32, p. 660

COMMONS
ANTIPHONS AND PRAYERS

1) The following Mass formularies are used for all Masses of Saints who have no complete formulary in the Proper of Saints. In each case, an appropriate rubric gives the page number of the specific Common or Commons that may be used.

2) In the individual Commons, several Mass formularies, with Antiphons and Prayers, are arranged for convenience.

The priest, however, may interchange Antiphons and Prayers of the same Common choosing according to the circumstances those texts which seem pastorally appropriate.

In addition, for Masses of Memorial, the Prayer over the Gifts and the Prayer after Communion may be taken from the weekdays of the current liturgical season as well as from the Commons.

3) In the Common of Martyrs and in the Common of Holy Men and Women, all the Prayers may be used of men or women with the necessary change of gender.

4) In the individual Commons, texts in the singular may be changed to the plural and vice versa.

5) Certain Masses that are given for specific seasons and circumstances should be used for those seasons and circumstances.

6) During the Easter Season an alleluia should be added at the end of the Entrance and Communion Antiphons.

7) In accord with the rules given in the Introduction to the Proper of Saints, the Readings and Intervenient Chants in the Common of Saints may always be used in any individual celebration in honor of the Saints when there are pastoral reasons for doing so.

COMMON OF THE DEDICATION OF A CHURCH

The Common of the Dedication of a Church comprises three formularies. The first is said on the day of the dedication. The others are used on the anniversary of the dedication: the second in the dedicated church itself, for example, the parish church; and the third outside the dedicated church, for example on the feast of St. John Lateran (Nov. 9) or of the Cathedral of the local diocese.

1. ON THE DAY OF DEDICATION

ENTRANCE ANT.

God in his holy dwelling, God who has gathered us together in his house: he will strengthen and console his people.

OR Ps 123:1

Let us go rejoicing to the house of the Lord. → No. 2, p. 614

OPENING PRAYER

Lord,
fill this place with your presence,
and extend your hand
to all those who call upon you.
May your word here proclaimed
and your sacraments here celebrated
strengthen the hearts of all the faithful.
We ask this . . . for ever and ever. ℟. **Amen.** ↓

READINGS AND INTERVENIENT CHANTS

See pp. 1096-1109.

PRAYER OVER THE GIFTS

Lord,
accept the gifts of a rejoicing Church.
May your people,
who are gathered in this sacred place,
arrive at eternal salvation
through the mysteries in which they share.
Grant this through Christ our Lord. ℟. **Amen.**

PREFACE (P 53-A)

℣. The Lord be with you. ℟. **And also with you.** ℣. Lift up your hearts. ℟. **We lift them up to the Lord.** ℣. Let us give thanks to the Lord our God. ℟. **It is right to give him thanks and praise.**

Father, all-powerful and ever-living God,
we do well always and everywhere to give you thanks.
The whole world is your temple,
shaped to resound with your name.
Yet you also allow us to dedicate to your service
places designed for your worship.
With hearts full of joy
we consecrate to your glory
this work of our hands, this house of prayer.
Here is foreshadowed the mystery of your true temple;
this church is the image on earth of your heavenly city.
For you made the body of your Son
born of the Virgin,
a temple consecrated to your glory,
the dwelling place of your godhead in all its fullness.
You have established the Church as your holy city,
founded on the apostles,
with Jesus Christ its cornerstone.
You continue to build your Church with chosen stones,
enlivened by the Spirit,
and cemented together by love.
In that holy city you will be all in all for endless ages,
and Christ will be its light for ever.
Through Christ we praise you, Lord,
with all the angels and saints in their song of joy:

→ No. 23, p. 627

When Eucharistic Prayer I is used, the special form of Father,
accept this offering *is said:*

Father,
accept this offering
from your whole family,

and from your servants
who with heart and hand
have given and built this church
as an offering to you (in honor of N.).
Grant us your peace in this life,
save us from final damnation,
and count us among those you have chosen.

When Eucharistic Prayer III is used, in the Intercessions after
the words with . . . the entire people your Son has gained
for you, *the following is said:*

Father,
accept the prayers of those who dedicate this church to you.
May it be a place of salvation and sacrament
where your Gospel of peace is proclaimed
and your holy mysteries celebrated.
Guided by your word and secure in your peace
may your chosen people now journeying through life
arrive safely at their eternal home.
There may all your children
now scattered abroad
be settled at last in your city of peace.   (→ p. 639)

COMMUNION ANT.   Mt 21:13; Lk 11:10

My house shall be called a house of prayer, says the Lord:
in it all who ask shall receive, all who seek shall find, and all
who knock shall have the door opened to them (alleluia). ↓

OR   Ps 129:3

May the children of the Church be like olive branches
around the table of the Lord (alleluia). ↓

PRAYER AFTER COMMUNION

Lord,
through these gifts
increase the vision of your truth in our minds.
May we always worship you in your holy temple,
and rejoice in your presence with all your saints.

Grant this through Christ our Lord.

℟. **Amen.** → No. 32, p. 660 (Solemn Blessing, no. 19, p. 698)

2. ANNIVERSARY OF DEDICATION

A. IN THE DEDICATED CHURCH

ENTRANCE ANT   Ps 68:36

Greatly to be feared is God in his sanctuary; he, the God of Israel, gives power and strength to his people. Blessed be God!   → No. 2, p. 614

OPENING PRAYER

Father,
each year we recall the dedication of this church
to your service.
Let our worship always be sincere
and help us to find your saving love in this church.
Grant this . . . for ever and ever. ℟. **Amen.** ↓

READINGS AND INTERVENIENT CHANTS

See pp. 1097-1109.

PRAYER OVER THE GIFTS

Lord,
as we recall the day you filled this church
with your glory and holiness,
may our lives also become an acceptable offering to you.
Grant this in the name of Jesus the Lord
℟. **Amen.**   → No. 21, p. 626 (Pref. P 52)

COMMUNION ANT.   1 Cor 3:16-17

You are the temple of God, and God's Spirit dwells in you. The temple of God is holy; you are that temple. ↓

PRAYER AFTER COMMUNION

Lord,
we know the joy and power of your blessing in our lives.

As we celebrate the dedication of this church,
may we give ourselves once more to your service.
Grant this through Christ our Lord.
℟. **Amen.**   ➜ No. 32, p. 660 (Solemn Blessing no. 19, p. 698)

B. OUTSIDE THE DEDICATED CHURCH

ENTRANCE ANT.   Rv 21:2

I saw the holy city, new Jerusalem, coming down from God out of heaven, like a bride adorned in readiness for her husband.   ➜ No. 2, p. 614

OPENING PRAYER

God our Father,
from living stones, your chosen people,
you built an eternal temple to your glory.
Increase the spiritual gifts you have given to your Church,
so that your faithful people may continue to grow
into the new and eternal Jerusalem.
We ask this . . . for ever and ever. ℟. **Amen.**

OR

Father,
you called your people to be your Church.
As we gather together in your name,
may we love, honor, and follow you
to eternal life in the kingdom you promise.
Grant this . . . for ever and ever. ℟. **Amen.** ↓

READINGS AND INTERVENIENT CHANTS

See pp. 1097-1109.

PRAYER OVER THE GIFTS

Lord,
receive our gifts.
May we who share this sacrament
experience the life and power it promises,
and hear the answer to our prayers.

We ask this in the name of Jesus the Lord.
℟. **Amen.** ➜ No. 21, p. 626 (Pref. P 53)

COMMUNION ANT. 1 Pt 2:5

Like living stones let yourselves be built on Christ as a spiritual house, a holy priesthood. ↓

PRAYER AFTER COMMUNION

Father,
you make your Church on earth
a sign of the new and eternal Jerusalem
By sharing in this sacrament
may we become the temple of your presence
and the home of your glory.
Grant this in the name of Jesus the Lord.
℟. **Amen.** ➜ No. 32, p. 660 (Solemn Blessing no. 19, p. 698)

COMMON OF THE BLESSED
VIRGIN MARY

The Common of the Blessed Virgin Mary comprises six Mass formularies and one Prayer formulary. These are used on feasts of the Virgin Mary during the year as indicated in the Missal. They are also utilized for the Mass of the Blessed Virgin Mary on Saturday in Ordinary Time when there is no feast higher than an optional Memorial.

These Masses are also used for the Saturday celebrations of the Blessed Virgin Mary and for votive Masses of the Blessed Virgin Mary.

1

ENTRANCE ANT. Sedulius

Hail, holy Mother! The child to whom you gave birth is the King of heaven and earth for ever. ➔ No. 2, p. 614

OPENING PRAYER

Lord God,
give to your people the joy
of continual health in mind and body.
With the prayers of the Virgin Mary to help us,
guide us through the sorrows of this life
to eternal happiness in the life to come.
Grant this . . . for ever and ever. ℟. **Amen.** ↓

OR

Lord,
take away the sins of your people.
May the prayers of Mary the mother of your Son help us,
for alone and unaided we cannot hope to please you.
We ask this . . . for ever and ever. ℟. **Amen.** ↓

READINGS AND INTERVENIENT CHANTS

See pp. 1110-1131.

PRAYER OVER THE GIFTS

Father,
the birth of Christ your Son

deepened the virgin mother's love for you,
and increased her holiness.
May the humanity of Christ
give us courage in our weakness;
may it free us from our sins,
and make our offering acceptable.
We ask this through Christ our Lord.
℟. **Amen.**   → No. 21, p. 626 (Pref. P 56-57)

COMMUNION ANT.   See Lk 11:27

Blessed is the womb of the Virgin Mary; she carried the Son of the eternal Father. ↓

PRAYER AFTER COMMUNION

Lord,
we rejoice in your sacraments and ask your mercy
as we honor the memory of the Virgin Mary.
May her faith and love
inspire us to serve you more faithfully
in the work of salvation.
Grant this in the name of Jesus the Lord.
℟. **Amen.**   → No. 32, p. 660

2

ENTRANCE ANT.

Blessed are you, Virgin Mary, who carried the creator of all things in your womb; you gave birth to your maker, and remain for ever a virgin.   → No. 2, p. 614

OPENING PRAYER

God of mercy,
give us strength.
May we who honor the memory of the Mother of God
rise above our sins and failings with the help of her prayers.
Grant this . . . for ever and ever. ℟. **Amen.** ↓

OR

Lord,
may the prayers of the Virgin Mary
bring us protection from danger
and freedom from sin
that we may come to the joy of your peace.
We ask this . . . for ever and ever. R̶̷. **Amen.** ↓

READINGS AND INTERVENIENT CHANTS
See pp. 1110-1131.

PRAYER OVER THE GIFTS

Lord,
we honor the memory of the mother of your Son.
May the sacrifice we share
make of us an everlasting gift to you.
Grant this through Christ our Lord.
R̶̷. **Amen.**   → No. 21, p. 626 (Pref. P 56-57)

COMMUNION ANT.   Lk 1:49

The Almighty has done great things for me. Holy is his name. ↓

PRAYER AFTER COMMUNION

Lord,
you give us the sacraments of eternal redemption.
May we who honor the memory of the mother of your Son
rejoice in the abundance of your grace
and experience your unfailing help.
We ask this through Christ our Lord.
R̶̷. **Amen.**   → No. 32, p. 660

3

ENTRANCE ANT.   See Jdt 13:23, 25

You have been blessed, O Virgin Mary, above all other women on earth by the Lord the most high God; he has so exalted your name that your praises shall never fade from the mouths of men.   → No. 2, p. 614

OPENING PRAYER

Lord,
as we honor the glorious memory of the Virgin Mary,
we ask that by the help of her prayers
we too may come to share the fullness of your grace.
Grant this . . . for ever and ever. ℟. **Amen.** ↓

OR

Lord Jesus Christ,
you chose the Virgin Mary to be your mother,
a worthy home in which to dwell.
By her prayers keep us from danger
and bring us to the joy of heaven,
where you live and reign with the Father and the Holy Spirit,
one God, for ever and ever. ℟. **Amen.** ↓

READINGS AND INTERVENIENT CHANTS

See pp. 1110-1131.

PRAYER OVER THE GIFTS

Lord,
we bring you our sacrifice of praise
at this celebration in honor of Mary, the mother of your Son.
May this holy exchange of gifts
help us on our way to eternal salvation.
We ask this in the name of Jesus the Lord.
℟. **Amen.**   → No. 21, p. 626 (Pref. P 56-57)

COMMUNION ANT.   See Lk 1:48

All generations will call me blessed, because God has looked upon his lowly handmaid. ↓

PRAYER AFTER COMMUNION

Lord,
we eat the bread of heaven.
May we who honor the memory of the Virgin Mary
come one day to your banquet of eternal life.

Grant this through Christ our Lord.
℟. **Amen.**   → No. 32, p. 660

---

4. ADVENT SEASON

ENTRANCE ANT.   Is 45:8

**Let the clouds rain down the Just One, and the earth bring
forth a Savior.**

OR   Lk 1:30-32

**The angel said to Mary: You have won God's favor. You will
conceive and bear a Son, and he will be called Son of the
Most High.**   → No. 2, p. 614

OPENING PRAYER

Father,
in your plan for our salvation
your Word became man,
announced by an angel and born of the Virgin Mary.
May we who believe that she is the Mother of God
receive the help of her prayers.
We ask this . . . for ever and ever. ℟. **Amen.** ↓

READINGS AND INTERVENIENT CHANTS

See pp. 1110-1131.

PRAYER OVER THE GIFTS

Lord,
may the power of your Spirit,
which sanctified Mary the mother of your Son,
make holy the gifts we place upon this altar.
We ask this through Christ our Lord.
℟. **Amen.**   → No. 21, p. 626 (Pref. P 56-57 or P 2)

COMMUNION ANT.   Is 7:14

**The Virgin is with child and shall bear a son, and she will
call him Emmanuel.** ↓

PRAYER AFTER COMMUNION

Lord our God,
may the sacraments we receive
show us your forgiveness and love.
May we who honor the mother of your Son
be saved by his coming among us as man,
for he is Lord for ever and ever.
℟. **Amen.**

→ No. 32, p. 660

5. CHRISTMAS SEASON

ENTRANCE ANT.

**Giving birth to the King whose reign is unending, Mary
knows the joys of motherhood together with a virgin's
honor; none like her before, and there shall be none here-
after.**

OR

**O virgin Mother of God, the universe cannot hold him, and
yet, becoming man, he confined himself in your womb.**

→ No. 2, p. 614

OPENING PRAYER

Father,
you gave the human race eternal salvation
through the motherhood of the Virgin Mary.
May we experience the help of her prayers in our lives,
for through her we received the very source of life,
your Son, our Lord Jesus Christ,
who lives and reigns with you and the Holy Spirit,
one God, for ever and ever. ℟. **Amen.** ↓

READINGS AND INTERVENIENT CHANTS

See pp. 1110-1131.

PRAYER OVER THE GIFTS

Lord,
accept our gifts and prayers

and fill our hearts with the light of your Holy Spirit.
Help us to follow the example of the Virgin Mary:
to seek you in all things
and to do your will with gladness.
We ask this in the name of Jesus the Lord.
R̸. **Amen.**   → No. 21, p. 626 (Pref. P 56-57)

COMMUNION ANT.   Jn 1:14

**The Word of God became man, and lived among us, full of
grace and truth.** ↓

PRAYER AFTER COMMUNION

Lord,
as we celebrate this feast of the Blessed Virgin Mary,
you renew us with the body and blood of Christ your Son.
May this sacrament give us a share in his life,
for he is Lord for ever and ever.
R̸. **Amen.**   → No. 32, p. 660

------

6. EASTER SEASON

ENTRANCE ANT.   See Acts 1:14

**The disciples were constantly at prayer together, with Mary
the mother of Jesus, alleluia.**   → No. 2, p. 614

OPENING PRAYER

God our Father,
you give joy to the world
by your resurrection of your Son, our Lord Jesus Christ.
Through the prayers of his mother, the Virgin Mary,
bring us to the happiness of eternal life.
We ask this . . . for ever and ever. R̸. **Amen.** ↓

OR

God our Father,
you gave the Holy Spirit to your apostles

as they joined in prayer with Mary, the mother of Jesus.
By the help of her prayers
keep us faithful in your service
and let our words and actions be so inspired
as to bring glory to your name.
Grant this . . . for ever and ever. ℟. **Amen.** ↓

READINGS AND INTERVENIENT CHANTS

See pp. 1110-1131.

PRAYER OVER THE GIFTS

Father,
as we celebrate the memory of the Virgin Mary,
we offer you our gifts and prayers.
Sustain us by the love of Christ,
who offered himself as a perfect sacrifice on the cross,
and is Lord for ever and ever.
℟. **Amen.**   → No. 21, p. 626 (Pref. P 56-57)

COMMUNION ANT.

Rejoice, virgin mother, for Christ has arisen from his grave, alleluia. ↓

PRAYER AFTER COMMUNION

Lord,
may this sacrament strengthen the faith in our hearts.
May Mary's Son, Jesus Christ,
whom we proclaim to be God and man,
bring us to eternal life
by the saving power of his resurrection,
for he is Lord for ever and ever.
℟. **Amen.**   → No. 32, p. 660

OTHER PRAYERS FOR MASSES OF THE
BLESSED VIRGIN MARY

OPENING PRAYER

All-powerful God,
we rejoice in the protection of the holy Virgin Mary.
May her prayers help to free us from all evils here on earth
and lead us to eternal joy in heaven.
Grant this . . . for ever and ever. ℟. **Amen.** ↓

READINGS AND INTERVENIENT CHANTS

See pp. 1110-1131.

PRAYER OVER THE GIFTS

Lord,
accept the prayers and gifts we present today
as we honor Mary, the Mother of God.
May they please you
and bring us your forgiveness and help.
We ask this in the name of Jesus the Lord.
℟. **Amen.** → No. 21, p. 626

PRAYER AFTER COMMUNION

Lord,
we are renewed with the sacraments of salvation.
May we who celebrate the memory of the Mother of God
come to realize the eternal redemption you promise.
We ask this . . . for ever and ever. ℟. **Amen.** → No. 32, p. 660

COMMON OF MARTYRS

The Common of Martyrs comprises ten Mass formularies and three Prayer formularies. Since the Martyrs were associated in a very special way with the mystery of Christ's death and resurrection, their worship takes on special significance when it is celebrated during the Easter Season. That is why the formularies are separated into those for Martyrs "outside the Easter Season" and "in the Easter Season."

1. FOR SEVERAL MARTYRS, OUTSIDE THE EASTER SEASON

ENTRANCE ANT.

The saints are happy in heaven because they followed Christ. They rejoice with him for ever because they shed their blood for love of him. → No. 2, p. 614

OPENING PRAYER

Father,
we celebrate the memory of Saints N. and N.
who died for their faithful witnessing to Christ.
Give us the strength to follow their example,
loyal and faithful to the end.
We ask this . . . for ever and ever. ℟. **Amen.** ↓

READINGS AND INTERVENIENT CHANTS

See pp. 1132-1150.

PRAYER OVER THE GIFTS

Father,
receive the gifts we bring
in memory of your holy martyrs.
Keep us strong in our faith
and in our witness to you.
Grant this through Christ our Lord.
℟. **Amen.** → No. 21, p. 626

COMMUNION ANT.   Lk 22:28-30

You are the men who have stood by me faithfully in my trials, and now I confer a kingdom on you, says the Lord. You will eat and drink at my table in my kingdom. ↓

PRAYER AFTER COMMUNION

God our Father,
in your holy martyrs you show us the glory of the cross.
Through this sacrifice, strengthen our resolution
to follow Christ faithfully
and to work in your Church for the salvation of all.
We ask this through Christ our Lord.
℟. **Amen.**   → No. 32, p. 660

2. FOR SEVERAL MARTYRS, OUTSIDE THE EASTER SEASON

ENTRANCE ANT.   Ps 34:20-21

Many are the sufferings of the just, and from them all the Lord has delivered them; the Lord preserves all their bones, not one of them shall be broken.   → No. 2, p. 614

OPENING PRAYER

All-powerful, ever-living God,
turn our weakness into strength.
As you gave your martyrs N. and N.
the courage to suffer death for Christ,
give us the courage to live in faithful witness to you.
Grant this . . . for ever and ever. ℟. **Amen.** ↓

READINGS AND INTERVENIENT CHANTS

See pp. 1132-1150.

PRAYER OVER THE GIFTS

Lord,
accept the gifts we bring
to celebrate the feast of your martyrs.

May this sacrifice free us from sin
and make our service pleasing to you.
We ask this through Christ our Lord.
℟. **Amen.** → No. 21, p. 626

COMMUNION ANT. Jn 15:13

**No one has greater love, says the Lord, than the man who
lays down his life for his friends.** ↓

PRAYER AFTER COMMUNION

Lord,
we eat the bread from heaven
and become one body in Christ.
Never let us be separated from his love
and help us to follow your martyrs N. and N.
by having the courage to overcome all things through
    Christ,
who loved us all,
and lives and reigns with you for ever and ever.
℟. **Amen.** → No. 32, p. 660

3. FOR SEVERAL MARTYRS, OUTSIDE THE EASTER SEASON

ENTRANCE ANT. Ps 37:39

**The salvation of the just comes from the Lord. He is their
strength in time of need.** → No. 2, p. 614

OPENING PRAYER

Lord,
may the victory of your martyrs give us joy.
May their example strengthen our faith,
and their prayers give us renewed courage.
We ask this . . . for ever and ever. ℟. **Amen.** ↓

OR

Lord,
hear the prayers of the martyrs N. and N.

and give us courage to bear witness to your truth.
Grant this . . . for ever and ever. ℟. **Amen.** ↓

READINGS AND INTERVENIENT CHANTS

See pp. 1132-1150.

PRAYER OVER THE GIFTS

Lord,
accept the gifts of your people
as we honor the suffering and death
of your martyrs N. and N.
As the eucharist gave them strength in persecution
may it keep us faithful in every difficulty.
We ask this through Christ our Lord.
℟. **Amen.**   → No. 21, p. 626

COMMUNION ANT.   Mk 8:35

**Whoever loses his life for my sake and the gospel, says the
Lord, will save it.** ↓

PRAYER AFTER COMMUNION

Lord,
keep this eucharist effective within us.
May the gift we receive
on this feast of the martyrs N. and N.
bring us salvation and peace.
Grant this in the name of Jesus the Lord.
℟. **Amen.**   → No. 32, p. 660

---

4. FOR SEVERAL MARTYRS, OUTSIDE THE EASTER SEASON

ENTRANCE ANT.   Ps 34:18

**The Lord will hear the just when they cry out, from all their
afflictions he will deliver them.**   → No. 2, p. 614

OPENING PRAYER

God our Father,
every year you give us the joy

of celebrating this feast of Saints N. and N.
May we who recall their birth to eternal life
imitate their courage in suffering for you.
Grant this . . . for ever and ever. ℟. **Amen.** ↓

OR

God our Father,
your generous gift of love
brought Saints N. and N. to unending glory.
Through the prayers of your martyrs
forgive our sins and free us from every danger.
We ask this . . . for ever and ever. ℟. **Amen.** ↓

READINGS AND INTERVENIENT CHANTS

See pp. 1132-1150.

PRAYER OVER THE GIFTS

Lord,
you gave Saints N. and N. the fulfillment of their faith
in the vision of your glory.
May the gifts we bring to honor their memory
gain us your pardon and peace.
We ask this in the name of Jesus the Lord.
℟. **Amen.**   → No. 21, p. 626

COMMUNION ANT.   2 Cor 4:11

**We are given over to death for Jesus, that the life of Jesus
may be revealed in our dying flesh.** ↓

PRAYER AFTER COMMUNION

Lord,
may this food of heaven
bring us a share in the grace you gave the martyrs N. and N.
From their bitter sufferings may we learn to become strong
and by patient endurance earn the victory of rejoicing in
    your holiness.
Grant this through Christ our Lord.
℟. **Amen.**   → No. 32, p. 660

5. FOR SEVERAL MARTYRS, OUTSIDE THE EASTER SEASON

ENTRANCE ANT.

The holy martyrs shed their blood on earth for Christ; therefore they have received an everlasting reward.

→ No. 2, p. 614

OPENING PRAYER

Lord,
we honor your martyrs N. and N.
who were faithful to Christ
even to the point of shedding their blood for him.
Increase our own faith and free us from our sins,
and help us to follow their example of love.
We ask this . . . for ever and ever. ℟. **Amen.** ↓

READINGS AND INTERVENIENT CHANTS

See pp. 1132-1150.

PRAYER OVER THE GIFTS

Lord,
be pleased with the gifts we bring.
May we who celebrate the mystery of the passion of your
    Son
make this mystery part of our lives
by the inspiration of the martyrs N. and N.
Grant this through Christ our Lord. ℟. **Amen.**

OR

Lord,
may these gifts which we bring you in sacrifice
to celebrate the victory of Saints N. and N.
fill our hearts with your love
and prepare us for the reward you promise
to those who are faithful.
We ask this in the name of Jesus the Lord.
℟. **Amen.**

→ No. 21, p. 626

COMMUNION ANT. See Rom 8:38-39

Neither death nor life nor anything in all creation can come between us and Christ's love for us. ↓

PRAYER AFTER COMMUNION

Lord,
you give us the body and blood of Christ your only Son
on this feast of your martyrs N. and N.
By being faithful to your love
may we live in you,
receive life from you,
and always be true to your inspiration.
We ask this in the name of Jesus the Lord.
℟. **Amen.** → No. 32, p. 660

---

6. FOR ONE MARTYR, OUTSIDE THE EASTER SEASON

ENTRANCE ANT.

This holy man fought to the death for the law of his God, never cowed by the threats of the wicked; his house was built on solid rock. → No. 2, p. 614

OPENING PRAYER

God of power and mercy,
you gave N., your martyr, victory over pain and suffering.
Strengthen us who celebrate this day of his triumph
and help us to be victorious over the evils that threaten us.
Grant this . . for ever and ever. ℟. **Amen.** ↓

READINGS AND INTERVENIENT CHANTS

See pp. 1132-1150.

PRAYER OVER THE GIFTS

Lord,
bless our offerings and make them holy.
May these gifts fill our hearts

with the love which gave St. N. victory
over all his suffering.
We ask this through Christ our Lord. ℟. **Amen.**

OR

Lord,
accept the gifts we offer in memory of the martyr N.
May they be pleasing to you
as was the shedding of his blood for the faith.
Grant this through Christ our Lord. ℟. **Amen.**

→ No. 21, p. 626

COMMUNION ANT.   Mt 16:24

**If anyone wishes to come after me, he must renounce
himself, take up his cross, and follow me, says the Lord.** ↓

PRAYER AFTER COMMUNION

Lord,
may the mysteries we receive
give us the spiritual courage which made your martyr N.
faithful in your service and victorious in his suffering.
Grant this in the name of Jesus the Lord.
℟. **Amen.**   → No. 32, p. 660

---

7. FOR ONE MARTYR, OUTSIDE THE EASTER SEASON

ENTRANCE ANT.

**Here is a true martyr who shed his blood for Christ; his
judges could not shake him by their menaces, and so he
won through to the kingdom of heaven.**   → No. 2, p. 614

OPENING PRAYER

All-powerful, ever-living God,
you gave St. N. the courage to witness to the gospel of
    Christ

even to the point of giving his life for it.
By his prayers help us to endure all suffering for love of
you
and to seek you with all our hearts,
for you alone are the source of life.
Grant this . . . for ever and ever. ℟. **Amen.** ↓

READINGS AND INTERVENIENT CHANTS

See pp. 1132-1150.

PRAYER OVER THE GIFTS

God of love,
pour out your blessing on our gifts
and make our faith strong,
the faith which St. N. professed by shedding his blood.
We ask this through Christ our Lord. ℟. **Amen.**

OR

Lord,
accept these gifts we present in memory of St. N.,
for no temptation could turn him away from you.
We ask this through Christ our Lord. ℟. **Amen.**

→ No. 21, p. 626

COMMUNION ANT.   Jn 15:5

**I am the vine and you are the branches, says the Lord; he
who lives in me, and I in him, will bear much fruit.** ↓

PRAYER AFTER COMMUNION

Lord,
we are renewed by the mystery of the eucharist.
By imitating the fidelity of St. N. and by your patience
may we come to share the eternal life you have promised.
We ask this in the name of Jesus the Lord.
℟. **Amen.**

→ No. 32, p. 660

8. FOR SEVERAL MARTYRS, IN THE EASTER SEASON

ENTRANCE ANT. Mt 25:34

Come, you whom my Father has blessed; inherit the kingdom prepared for you since the foundation of the world, alleluia. → No. 2, p. 614

OPENING PRAYER

Father,
you gave your martyrs N. and N.
the courage to die in witness to Christ and the gospel.
By the power of your Holy Spirit,
give us the humility to believe
and the courage to profess
the faith for which they gave their lives.
We ask this . . . for ever and ever. ℟. **Amen.** ↓

OR

God our all-powerful Father,
you strengthen our faith
and take away our weakness.
Let the prayers and example of your martyrs N. and N. help
us
to share in the passion and resurrection of Christ
and bring us to eternal joy with all your saints.
We ask this . . . for ever and ever. ℟. **Amen.** ↓

READINGS AND INTERVENIENT CHANTS

See pp. 1132-1150.

PRAYER OVER THE GIFTS

Lord,
we celebrate the death of your holy martyrs.
May we offer the sacrifice which gives all martyrdom its
meaning.
Grant this through Christ our Lord.
℟. **Amen.** → No. 21, p. 626

COMMUNION ANT. Rv 2:7

Those who are victorious I will feed from the tree of life, which grows in the paradise of my God, alleluia. ↓

PRAYER AFTER COMMUNION

Lord,
at this holy meal
we celebrate the heavenly victory of your martyrs N. and N.
May this bread of life
give us the courage to conquer evil,
so that we may come to share the fruit of the tree of life in paradise.
We ask this through Christ our Lord.
℟. **Amen.**

→ No. 32, p. 660

9. FOR SEVERAL MARTYRS, IN THE EASTER SEASON

ENTRANCE ANT. Rv 12:11

These are the saints who were victorious in the blood of the Lamb, and in the face of death they did not cling to life; therefore they are reigning with Christ for ever, alleluia.

→ No. 2, p. 614

OPENING PRAYER

Lord,
you gave your martyrs N. and N.
the privilege of shedding their blood
for boldly proclaiming the death and resurrection of your Son.
May this celebration of their victory give them honor among your people.
We ask this . . . for ever and ever. ℟. **Amen.** ↓

READINGS AND INTERVENIENT CHANTS

See pp. 1132–1150.

PRAYER OVER THE GIFTS

Lord,
fill these gifts with the blessing of your Holy Spirit
and fill our hearts with the love
which gave victory to Saints N. and N.
in dying for the faith.
We ask this through Christ our Lord.
℟. **Amen.**   → No. 21, p. 626

COMMUNION ANT.   2 Tm 2:11-12

**If we die with Christ, we shall live with him, and if we are
faithful to the end, we shall reign with him, alleluia.** ↓

PRAYER AFTER COMMUNION

Lord,
we are renewed by the breaking of one bread
in honor of the martyrs N. and N.
Keep us in your love
and help us to live the new life Christ won for us.
Grant this in the name of Jesus the Lord.
℟. **Amen.**   → No. 32, p. 660

---

10. FOR ONE MARTYR, IN THE EASTER SEASON

ENTRANCE ANT.   See 4 Ezr 2:35

Light for ever will shine on your saints, O Lord, alleluia.
→ No. 2, p. 614

OPENING PRAYER

God our Father,
you have honored the Church with the victorious witness of
    St. N.,
who died for his faith.
As he imitated the sufferings and death of the Lord,
may we follow in his footsteps and come to eternal joy.
We ask this . . . for ever and ever. ℟. **Amen.** ↓

READINGS AND INTERVENIENT CHANTS
See pp. 1132-1150.

PRAYER OVER THE GIFTS

Lord,
accept this offering of praise and peace
in memory of your martyr N.
May it bring us your forgiveness
and inspire us to give you thanks now and for ever.
Grant this in the name of Jesus the Lord.
℞. **Amen.**

→ No. 21, p. 626

COMMUNION ANT. Jn 12:24-25

I tell you solemnly: Unless a grain of wheat falls on the ground and dies, it remains a single grain; but if it dies, it yields a rich harvest, alleluia. ↓

PRAYER AFTER COMMUNION

Lord,
we receive your gifts from heaven
at this joyful feast.
May we who proclaim at this holy table
the death and resurrection of your Son
come to share his glory with all your holy martyrs.
Grant this through Christ our Lord.
℞. **Amen.**

→ No. 32, p. 660

OTHER PRAYERS FOR MARTYRS

FOR MISSIONARY MARTYRS

OPENING PRAYER

God of mercy and love,
through the preaching of your martyrs N. and N.
you brought the good news of Christ
to people who had not known him.
May the prayers of Saints N. and N.

make our own faith grow stronger.
We ask this . . . for ever and ever. ℟. **Amen.** ↓

READINGS AND INTERVENIENT CHANTS

See pp. 1132-1150.

PRAYER OVER THE GIFTS

Lord,
at this celebration of the eucharist
we honor the suffering and death of your martyrs N. and N.
In offering this sacrifice
may we proclaim the death of your Son
who gave these martyrs courage not only by his words
but also by the example of his own passion,
for he is Lord for ever and ever.
℟. **Amen.**   → No. 21, p. 626

PRAYER AFTER COMMUNION

Lord,
may we who eat at your holy table
be inspired by the example of Saints N. and N.
May we keep before us the loving sacrifice of your Son,
and come to the unending peace of your kingdom.
We ask this in the name of Jesus the Lord.
℟. **Amen.**   → No. 32, p. 660

FOR A VIRGIN MARTYR

OPENING PRAYER

God our Father,
you give us joy each year
in honoring the memory of St. N.
May her prayers be a source of help for us,
and may her example of courage and chastity be our inspi-
    ration.
Grant this . . . for ever and ever. ℟. **Amen.** ↓

READINGS AND INTERVENIENT CHANTS

See pp. 1132-1150.

PRAYER OVER THE GIFTS

Lord,
receive our gifts
as you accepted the suffering and death of St. N.
in whose honor we celebrate this eucharist.
We ask this through Christ our Lord.
℟. **Amen.**

→ No. 21, p. 626

PRAYER AFTER COMMUNION

Lord God,
you gave St. N. the crown of eternal joy
because she gave her life
rather than renounce the virginity she had promised
in witness to Christ.
With the courage this eucharist brings
help us to rise out of the bondage of our earthly desires
and attain to the glory of your kingdom.
Grant this through Christ our Lord.
℟. **Amen.**

→ No. 32, p. 660

FOR A HOLY WOMAN MARTYR

OPENING PRAYER

Father,
in our weakness your power reaches perfection.
You gave St. N. the strength
to defeat the power of sin and evil.
May we who celebrate her glory share in her triumph.
We ask this . . . for ever and ever. ℟. **Amen.** ↓

READINGS AND INTERVENIENT CHANTS

See pp. 1132-1150

PRAYER OVER THE GIFTS

Lord,
today we offer this sacrifice in joy
as we recall the victory of St. N.

...y we proclaim to others the great things
...ou have done for us
...nd rejoice in the constant help of your martyr's prayers.
Grant this through Christ our Lord.
℟. **Amen.** → No. 21, p. 626

PRAYER AFTER COMMUNION

Lord,
by this sacrament you give us eternal joys
as we recall the memory of St. N.
May we always embrace the gift of life
we celebrate at this eucharist.
We ask this in the name of Jesus the Lord.
℟. **Amen.** → No. 32, p. 660

COMMON OF PASTORS

The Common of Pastors comprises twelve Mass formularies: two for a Pope or Bishop (nos. 1-2); two for a Bishop (nos. 3-4); one for a Pastor (no. 5); two for several Pastors (nos. 6-7); one for a Founder of Churches (no. 8); one for several Founders of Churches (no. 9); and three for a Missionary Pastor (nos. 10-12).

1. FOR POPES OR BISHOPS

ENTRANCE ANT.

The Lord chose him to be his high priest; he opened his treasures and made him rich in all goodness. → No. 2, p. 614

OPENING PRAYER

(for popes)

All-powerful and ever-living God,
you called St. N. to guide your people
by his word and example.
With him we pray to you:
watch over the pastors of your Church
with the people entrusted to their care,
and lead them to salvation.
We ask this . . . for ever and ever. ℟. **Amen.** ↓

OR

(for bishops)
Father,
you gave St. N. to your Church
as an example of a good shepherd.
May his prayers help us on our way to eternal life.
Grant this . . . for ever and ever. ℟. **Amen.** ↓

READINGS AND INTERVENIENT CHANTS

See pp. 1151-1175.

PRAYER OVER THE GIFTS

Lord,
we offer you this sacrifice of praise

1057

in memory of your saints.
May their prayers keep us from evil
now and in the future.
Grant this through Christ our Lord.
℟. **Amen.**   ➡ No. 21, p. 626

COMMUNION ANT.   See Jn 10:11

The good shepherd gives his life for his sheep. ↓

PRAYER AFTER COMMUNION

Lord God,
St. N. loved you
and gave himself completely in the service of your Church.
May the eucharist awaken in us that same love.
We ask this in the name of Jesus the Lord.
℟. **Amen.**   ➡ No. 32, p. 660

2. FOR POPES OR BISHOPS

ENTRANCE ANT.   See Sir 45:30

**The Lord sealed a covenant of peace with him, and made
him a prince, bestowing the priestly dignity upon him for
ever.**   ➡ No. 2, p. 614

OPENING PRAYER

(for popes)

Father,
you made St. N. shepherd of the whole Church
and gave to us the witness of his virtue and teaching.
Today as we honor this outstanding bishop,
we ask that our light may shine before men
and that our love for you may be sincere.
Grant this . . . for ever and ever. ℟. **Amen. ↓**

OR (for bishops)

All-powerful God,
you made St. N. a bishop and leader of the Church
to inspire your people with his teaching and example.
May we give fitting honor to his memory

and always have the assistance of his prayers.
We ask this . . . for ever and ever. R̸. **Amen.** ↓

READINGS AND INTERVENIENT CHANTS

See pp. 1151-1175.

PRAYER OVER THE GIFTS

Lord,
may the sacrifice which wipes away the sins of all the world
bring us your forgiveness.
Help us as we offer it
on this yearly feast in honor of St. N.
Grant this through Christ our Lord.
R̸. **Amen.**
→ No. 21, p. 626

COMMUNION ANT.
Jn 21:17

Lord, you know all things: you know that I love you. ↓

PRAYER AFTER COMMUNION

Lord God,
let the power of the gifts we receive
on this feast of St. N.
take full effect within us.
May this eucharist bring us your help in this life
and lead us to happiness in the unending life to come.
We ask this through Christ our Lord.
R̸. **Amen.**
→ No. 32, p. 660

3. FOR BISHOPS

ENTRANCE ANT.
Ez 34:11, 23-24

**I will look after my sheep, says the Lord, and I will raise up
one shepherd who will pasture them. I, the Lord, will be
their God.**
→ No. 2, p. 614

OPENING PRAYER

All-powerful, ever-living God,
you made St. N. bishop and leader of your people.

May his prayers help to bring us your forgiveness and love.
We ask this . . . for ever and ever. ℟. **Amen.** ↓

READINGS AND INTERVENIENT CHANTS

See pp. 1151-1175.

PRAYER OVER THE GIFTS

Lord,
accept the gifts we bring to your holy altar
on this feast of St. N.
May our offering bring honor to your name
and pardon to your people.
We ask this through Christ our Lord.
℟. **Amen.**   → No. 21, p. 626

COMMUNION ANT.   Jn 15:16

**You have not chosen me; I have chosen you. Go and bear
fruit that will last.** ↓

PRAYER AFTER COMMUNION

Lord,
may we who receive this sacrament
be inspired by the example of St. N.
May we learn to proclaim what he believed
and put his teaching into action.
We ask this in the name of Jesus the Lord.
℟. **Amen.**   → No. 32, p. 660

4. FOR BISHOPS

ENTRANCE ANT.   1 Sm 2:35

**I will raise up for myself a faithful priest; he will do what is
in my heart and in my mind, says the Lord.** → No. 2, p. 614

OPENING PRAYER

Lord God,
you counted St. N. among your holy pastors,
renowned for faith and love which conquered evil in this
    world.
By the help of his prayers

keep us strong in faith and love
and let us come to share his glory.
Grant this . . . for ever and ever. ℟. **Amen.** ↓

READINGS AND INTERVENIENT CHANTS

See pp. 1151-1175.

PRAYER OVER THE GIFTS

Lord,
accept the gifts your people offer you
on this feast of St. N.
May these gifts bring us
your help for which we long.
We ask this through Christ our Lord.
℟. **Amen.**

→ No. 21, p. 626

COMMUNION ANT.

Jn 10:10

I came that men may have life, and have it to the full, says the Lord. ↓

PRAYER AFTER COMMUNION

Lord our God,
you give us the holy body and blood
of your Son.
May the salvation we celebrate
be our undying hope.
Grant this through Christ our Lord.
℟. **Amen.**

→ No. 32, p. 660

5. FOR PASTORS

ENTRANCE ANT.

Lk 4:18

The Spirit of God is upon me; he has anointed me. He sent me to bring good news to the poor, and to heal the broken-hearted.

→ No. 2, p. 614

OPENING PRAYER

God our Father,
in St. (bishop) N. you gave

a light to your faithful people.
You made him a pastor of the Church
to feed your sheep with his word
and to teach them by his example.
Help us by his prayers to keep the faith he taught
and follow the way of life he showed us.
Grant this . . . for ever and ever. ℟. **Amen.** ↓

READINGS AND INTERVENIENT CHANTS

See pp. 1151-1175.

PRAYER OVER THE GIFTS

Father of mercy,
we have these gifts to offer in honor of your saints
who bore witness to your mighty power.
May the power of the eucharist
bring us your salvation.
Grant this through Christ our Lord.
℟. **Amen.**

→ No. 21, p. 626

COMMUNION ANT.   Mt 28:20

I, the Lord, am with you always, until the end of the world. ↓

PRAYER AFTER COMMUNION

Lord,
may the mysteries we receive
prepare us for the eternal joys
St. N. won by his faithful ministry.
We ask this in the name of Jesus the Lord.
℟. **Amen.** ↓

OR

All-powerful God,
by our love and worship
may we who share this holy meal
always follow the example of St. N.
Grant this in the name of Jesus the Lord.
℟. **Amen.**

→ No. 32, p. 660

6. FOR PASTORS

ENTRANCE ANT. Jer 3:15

I will give you shepherds after my own heart, and they shall feed you on knowledge and sound teaching.

OR Dan 3:84, 87

Priests of God, bless the Lord; praise God, all you that are holy and humble of heart. → No. 2, p. 614

OPENING PRAYER

Lord God,
you gave your Saints (bishops) N. and N.
the spirit of truth and love
to shepherd your people.
May we who honor them on this feast
learn from their example
and be helped by their prayers.
We ask this . . . for ever and ever. ℟. **Amen.** ↓

READINGS AND INTERVENIENT CHANTS

See pp. 1151-1175.

PRAYER OVER THE GIFTS

Lord,
accept these gifts from your people.
May the eucharist we offer to your glory
in honor of Saints N. and N.
help us on our way to salvation.
Grant this in the name of Jesus the Lord.
℟. **Amen.** → No. 21, p. 626

COMMUNION ANT. Mt 20:28

The Son of Man did not come to be served, but to serve, and to give his life as a ransom for many. ↓

PRAYER AFTER COMMUNION

Lord,
we receive the bread of heaven

as we honor the memory of your Saints N. and N.
May the eucharist we now celebrate
lead us to eternal joys.
Grant this in the name of Jesus the Lord.
R̸̲. **Amen.**   → No. 32, p. 660

7. FOR PASTORS

ENTRANCE ANT.   Ps 132:9

**Lord, may your priests be clothed in justice, and your holy
ones leap for joy.**   → No. 2, p. 614

OPENING PRAYER

All-powerful God,
hear the prayers of Saints N. and N.
Increase your gifts within us
and give us peace in our days.
We ask this . . . for ever and ever. R̸̲. **Amen.** ↓

READINGS AND INTERVENIENT CHANTS

See pp. 1151-1175.

PRAYER OVER THE GIFTS

Lord,
accept the gifts we bring to your altar
in memory of your Saints N. and N.
As you led them to glory through these mysteries,
grant us also your pardon and love.
We ask this in the name of Jesus the Lord.
R̸̲. **Amen.**   → No. 21, p. 626

COMMUNION ANT.   Mt 24:46-47

**Blessed is the servant whom the Lord finds watching when
he comes; truly I tell you, he will set him over all his possessions.** ↓

OR   Lk 12:42

**The Lord has put his faithful servant in charge of his house-
hold, to give them their share of bread at the proper time.** ↓

PRAYER AFTER COMMUNION

All-powerful God,
by the eucharist we share at your holy table
on this feast of Saints N. and N.
increase our strength of character and love for you.
May we guard from every danger the faith you have given
us
and walk always in the way that leads to salvation.
Grant this in the name of Jesus the Lord.
℟. **Amen.**

→ No. 32, p. 660

8. FOR FOUNDERS OF CHURCHES

ENTRANCE ANT.   Is 59:21; 56:7

**My words that I have put in your mouth, says the Lord, will
never be absent from your lips, and your gifts will be
accepted on my altar.**   → No. 2, p. 614

OPENING PRAYER

God of mercy,
you gave our fathers the light of faith
through the preaching of St. N.
May we who glory in the Christian name
show in our lives the faith we profess.
We ask this . . . for ever and ever. ℟. **Amen.** ↓

OR

Lord,
look upon the family whom your St. (bishop) N. brought to
life
with the word of truth
and nourished with the sacrament of life.
By his ministry you gave us the faith;
by his prayers help us grow in love.
Grant this . . . for ever and ever. ℟. **Amen.** ↓

READINGS AND INTERVENIENT CHANTS

See pp. 1151-1175.

PRAYER OVER THE GIFTS

Lord,
may the gifts your people bring
in memory of St. N.
bring us your gifts from heaven.
We ask this in the name of Jesus the Lord.
℞. **Amen.**   → No. 21, p. 626

COMMUNION ANT.   Mk 10:45

The Son of Man came to give his life as a ransom for many. ↓

PRAYER AFTER COMMUNION

Lord,
may this pledge of our eternal salvation
which we receive on this feast of St. N.
be our help now and always.
Grant this through Christ our Lord.
℞. **Amen.**   → No. 32, p. 660

9. FOR FOUNDERS OF CHURCHES

ENTRANCE ANT.

The Lord chose these holy men for their unfeigned love, and gave them eternal glory. The Church has light by their teaching.   → No. 2, p. 614

OPENING PRAYER

Lord,
look with love on the church of N.
Through the apostolic zeal of Saints N. and N.
you gave us the beginnings of our faith:
through their prayers keep alive our Christian love.
We ask this . . . for ever and ever. ℞. **Amen.** ↓

OR

God,
you called our fathers to the light of the gospel

by the preaching of your bishop N.
By his prayers help us to grow in the love and knowledge
of your Son, our Lord Jesus Christ,
who lives and reigns with you and the Holy Spirit,
one God, for ever and ever. ℟. **Amen.** ↓

READINGS AND INTERVENIENT CHANTS

See pp. 1151-1175.

PRAYER OVER THE GIFTS

Lord,
accept the gifts your people bring
on this feast of Saints N. and N.
Give us purity of heart
and make us pleasing to you.
We ask this through Christ our Lord.
℟. **Amen.**   → No. 21, p. 626

COMMUNION ANT.   Jn 15:15

No longer shall I call you servants, for a servant knows not
what his master does. Now I shall call you friends, for I have
revealed to you all that I have heard from my Father. ↓

PRAYER AFTER COMMUNION

Lord,
as we share in your gifts,
we celebrate this feast of Saints N. and N.
We honor the beginnings of our faith
and proclaim your glory in the saints.
May the salvation we receive from your altar
be our unending joy.
Grant this through Christ our Lord.
℟. **Amen.**   → No. 32, p. 660

10. FOR MISSIONARIES

ENTRANCE ANT.

These are holy men who became God's friends and glorious
heralds of his truth.   → No. 2, p. 614

OPENING PRAYER

Father,
through your St. (bishop) N.
you brought those who had no faith
out of darkness into the light of truth.
By the help of his prayers,
keep us strong in our faith
and firm in the hope of the gospel he preached.
Grant this . . . for ever and ever. ℟. **Amen.** ↓

OR

All-powerful and ever-living God,
you made this day holy
by welcoming St. N. into the the glory of your kingdom.
Keep us true to the faith he professed with untiring zeal,
and help us to bring it to perfection by acting in love.
We ask this . . . for ever and ever. ℟. **Amen.** ↓

READINGS AND INTERVENIENT CHANTS

See pp. 1151-1175.

PRAYER OVER THE GIFTS

All-powerful God,
look upon the gifts we bring on this feast
in honor of St. N.
May we who celebrate the mystery of the death of the Lord
imitate the love we celebrate.
We ask this through Christ our Lord.
℟. **Amen.**   → No. 21, p. 626

COMMUNION ANT.   Ez 34:15

I will feed my sheep, says the Lord, and give them repose. ↓

PRAYER AFTER COMMUNION

Lord,
St. N. worked tirelessly for the faith,
spending his life in its service.
With the power this eucharist gives

make your people strong in the same true faith
and help us to proclaim it everywhere
by all we say and do.
℟. **Amen.**

→ No. 32, p. 660

---

11. FOR MISSIONARIES

ENTRANCE ANT. Is 52:7

**How beautiful on the mountains are the feet of the man
who brings tidings of peace, joy and salvation.**

→ No. 2, p. 614

OPENING PRAYER

Father,
you made your Church grow
through the Christian zeal and apostolic work of
St. N.
By the help of his prayers
give your Church continued growth in holiness and faith.
Grant this . . . for ever and ever. ℟. **Amen.** ↓

READINGS AND INTERVENIENT CHANTS
See pp. 1151-1175.

PRAYER OVER THE GIFTS

Lord,
be pleased with our prayers
and free us from all guilt.
In your love, wash away our sins
that we may celebrate the mysteries which set us free.
Grant this in the name of Jesus the Lord.
℟. **Amen.**

→ No. 21, p. 626

COMMUNION ANT. Mk 16:15; Mt 28:20

**Go out to all the world, and tell the good news: I am with
you always, says the Lord.** ↓

OR   Jn 15:4-5

**Live in me and let me live in you, says the Lord; he who
lives in me, and I in him, will bear much fruit.** ↓

PRAYER AFTER COMMUNION

Lord our God,
by these mysteries help our faith grow to maturity
in the faith the apostles preached and taught,
and the faith which St. N. watched over with such
    care.
We ask this through Christ our Lord.
R̂. **Amen.**   → No. 32, p. 660

---

12. FOR MISSIONARIES

ENTRANCE ANT.   Ps 96:3-4

**Proclaim his glory among the nations, his marvelous deeds
to all the peoples; great is the Lord and worthy of all
praise.**   → No. 2, p. 614

OPENING PRAYER

God of mercy,
you gave us St. N. to proclaim the riches of Christ.
By the help of his prayers
may we grow in knowledge of you,
be eager to do good,
and learn to walk before you
by living the truth of the gospel.
Grant this . . . for ever and ever. R̂. **Amen.** ↓

OR (for martyrs)

All-powerful God,
help us to imitate with steadfast love
the faith of Saints N. and N.

who won the crown of martyrdom
by giving their lives in the service of the gospel.
We ask this . . . for ever and ever. ℞. **Amen.** ↓

READINGS AND INTERVENIENT CHANTS

See pp. 1151-1175.

PRAYER OVER THE GIFTS

Lord,
we who honor the memory of St. N.
ask you to send your blessing on these gifts.
By receiving them may we be freed from all guilt
and share in the food from the heavenly table.
We ask this through Christ our Lord.
℞. **Amen.** ➜ No. 21, p. 626

COMMUNION ANT. See Lk 10:1, 9

**The Lord sent disciples to proclaim to all the towns: the
kingdom of God is very near to you.**

PRAYER AFTER COMMUNION

Lord,
let the holy gifts we receive fill us with life
so that we who rejoice in honoring the memory of St. N.
may also benefit from his example of apostolic zeal.
Grant this through Christ our Lord.
℞. **Amen.** ➜ No. 32, p. 660

COMMON OF DOCTORS OF
THE CHURCH

The Common of Doctors of the Church comprises only two Mass formularies. One of the reasons for this is that the relatively few saints who fit into this category also fall into another—for example, pastors or religious. Thus a combination of the texts of these categories offers ample opportunity for the desired variety.

1

ENTRANCE ANT. Sir 15:5

The Lord opened his mouth in the assembly, and filled him with the spirit of wisdom and understanding, and clothed him in a robe of glory.

OR Ps 37:30-31

The mouth of the just man utters wisdom, and his tongue speaks what is right; the law of his God is in his heart.

→ No. 2, p. 614

OPENING PRAYER

God our Father,
you made your St. (bishop) N. a teacher in your Church.
By the power of the Holy Spirit
establish his teaching in our hearts.
As you give him to us as a patron,
may we have the protection of his prayers.
Grant this . . . for ever and ever. ℟. **Amen.** ↓

READINGS AND INTERVENIENT CHANTS

See pp. 1176-1189.

PRAYER OVER THE GIFTS

Lord,
accept our sacrifice on this feast of St. N.,
and following his example
may we give you our praise
and offer you all we have.

Grant this in the name of Jesus the Lord.

℟. **Amen.** → No. 21, p. 626

COMMUNION ANT. Lk 12:42

The Lord has put his faithful servant in charge of his household, to give them their share of bread at the proper time. ↓

PRAYER AFTER COMMUNION

God our Father,
Christ the living bread renews us.
Let Christ our teacher instruct us
that on this feast of St. N.
we may learn your truth
and practice it in love.
We ask this through Christ our Lord.

℟. **Amen.** → No. 32, p. 660

2

ENTRANCE ANT. Dn 12:3

The learned will shine like the brilliance of the firmament, and those who train many in the ways of justice will sparkle like the stars for all eternity.

OR See Sir 44:15, 14

Let the peoples declare the wisdom of the saints and the Church proclaim their praises; their names shall live for ever. → No. 2, p. 614

OPENING PRAYER

Lord God,
you filled St. N. with heavenly wisdom.
By his (her) help may we remain true to his (her) teaching
and put it into practice.
We ask this . . . for ever and ever. ℟. **Amen.** ↓

READINGS AND INTERVENIENT CHANTS

See pp. 1176-1189.

PRAYER OVER THE GIFTS

Lord,
by this celebration,
may your Spirit fill us with the same light of faith
that shines in the teaching of St. N.
We ask this through Christ our Lord.
℟. **Amen.**

→ No. 21, p. 626

COMMUNION ANT.   1 Cor 1:23-24

We preach a Christ who was crucified; he is the power and the wisdom of God. ↓

PRAYER AFTER COMMUNION

Lord,
you renew us with the food of heaven.
St. N. remain our teacher and example
and keep us thankful for all we have received.
Grant this in the name of Jesus the Lord.
℟. **Amen.**

→ No. 32, p. 660

COMMON OF VIRGINS

The Common of Virgins comprises four Mass formularies, three for one Virgin and the last for several Virgins. The saint who is a Virgin in many cases also fits into another category. One may thus use both categories in choosing the texts for each celebration.

1

ENTRANCE ANT.

Here is a wise and faithful virgin who went with lighted lamp to meet her Lord. ➙ No. 2, p. 614

OPENING PRAYER

God our Savior,
as we celebrate with joy the memory of the virgin N.,
may we learn from her example of faithfulness and love.
We ask this . . . for ever and ever. ℟. **Amen.** ↓

READINGS AND INTERVENIENT CHANTS

See pp. 1190-1195.

PRAYER OVER THE GIFTS

Lord,
we see the wonder of your love
in the life of the virgin N.
and her witness to Christ.
Accept our gifts of praise
and make our offering pleasing to you.
Grant this through Christ our Lord.
℟. **Amen.** ➙ No. 21, p. 626

COMMUNION ANT. Mt 25:5

The bridegroom is here; let us go out to meet Christ the Lord. ↓

PRAYER AFTER COMMUNION

Lord God,
may this eucharist renew our courage and strength.
May we remain close to you, like St. N.,

by accepting in our lives
a share in the suffering of Jesus Christ,
who lives and reigns with you for ever and ever.
℟. **Amen.**   → No. 32, p. 660

2

ENTRANCE ANT.

Let us rejoice and shout for joy, because the Lord of all things has favored this holy and glorious virgin with his love.   → No. 2, p. 614

OPENING PRAYER

Lord God,
you endowed the virgin N. with gifts from heaven.
By imitating her goodness here on earth
may we come to share her joy in eternal life.
We ask this . . . for ever and ever. ℟. **Amen.** ↓

OR (for a virgin foundress)

Lord our God,
may the witness of your faithful bride the virgin N.
awaken the fire of divine love in our hearts.
May it inspire other young women to give their lives
to the service of Christ and his Church.
Grant this . . . for ever and ever. ℟. **Amen.** ↓

READINGS AND INTERVENIENT CHANTS

See pp. 1190-1195.

PRAYER OVER THE GIFTS

Lord,
may the gifts we bring you
help us follow the example of St. N.
Cleanse us from our earthly way of life
and teach us to live the new life of your kingdom.
We ask this through Christ our Lord.
℟. **Amen.**   → No. 21, p. 626

COMMUNION ANT. Mt 25:4, 6

The five sensible virgins took flasks of oil as well as their lamps. At midnight a cry was heard: the bridegroom is here; let us go out to meet Christ the Lord. ↓

PRAYER AFTER COMMUNION

Lord,
may our reception of the body and blood of your Son
keep us from harmful things.
Help us by the example of St. N.
to grow in your love on earth
that we may rejoice for ever in heaven.
We ask this in the name of Jesus the Lord.
℟. **Amen.** → No. 32, p. 660

3

ENTRANCE ANT.

Come, bride of Christ, and receive the crown, which the Lord has prepared for you for ever. → No. 2, p. 614

OPENING PRAYER

Lord,
you have told us that you live for ever
in the hearts of the chaste.
By the prayers of the virgin N.,
help us to live by your grace
and to become a temple of your Spirit.
Grant this . . . for ever and ever. ℟. **Amen.** ↓

OR

Lord,
hear the prayers of those who recall the devoted life of the
virgin N.
Guide us on our way and help us to grow
in love and devotion as long as we live.
We ask this . . . for ever and ever. ℟. **Amen.** ↓

READINGS AND INTERVENIENT CHANTS
See pp. 1190-1195.

PRAYER OVER THE GIFTS

Lord,
receive our worship in memory of N. the virgin.
By this perfect sacrifice
make us grow in unselfish love for you
and for our brothers.
We ask this through Christ our Lord.
℟. **Amen.**   ➜ No. 21, p. 626

COMMUNION ANT.   See Lk 10:42

**The wise virgin chose the better part for herself, and it shall
not be taken away from her.** ↓

PRAYER AFTER COMMUNION

God of mercy,
we rejoice that on this feast of St. N.
you give us the bread of heaven.
May it bring us pardon for our sins,
health of body,
your grace in this life,
and glory in heaven.
Grant this through Christ our Lord.
℟. **Amen.**   ➜ No. 32, p. 660

4

ENTRANCE ANT.   Ps 148:12-14

**Let virgins praise the name of the Lord, for his name alone
is supreme; its majesty outshines both earth and heaven.**
                                                ➜ No. 2, p. 614

OPENING PRAYER

Lord,
increase in us your gifts of mercy and forgiveness.
May we who rejoice at this celebration

in honor of the virgins N. and N.
receive the joy of sharing eternal life with them.
We ask this. . . for ever and ever. ℟. **Amen.** ↓

READINGS AND INTERVENIENT CHANTS

See pp. 1190-1195.

PRAYER OVER THE GIFTS

Lord,
we bring you our gifts and prayers.
We praise your glory on this feast of the virgins N. and N.,
whose witness to Christ was pleasing to you.
Be pleased also with the eucharist we now offer.
Grant this through Christ our Lord.
℟. **Amen.** → No. 21, p. 626

COMMUNION ANT.

Mt 25:10

The bridegroom has come, and the virgins who were ready
have gone in with him to the wedding. ↓

OR

Jn 14:21, 23

Whoever loves me will be loved by my Father. We shall
come to him and make our home with him. ↓

PRAYER AFTER COMMUNION

Lord,
may the mysteries we receive
on this feast of the virgins N. and N.
keep us alert and ready to welcome your Son at his return,
that he may welcome us to the feast of eternal life.
Grant this through Christ our Lord.
℟. **Amen.** → No. 32, p. 660

COMMON OF HOLY MEN AND WOMEN

The Common of Holy Men and Women comprises twelve Mass formularies. The first six refer to the saints in general: the first to one (no. 1) and the others to several (nos. 2-6). The other six refer to some specific state and field of endeavor: religious (nos. 7-8), those who worked for the underprivileged (no. 9), teachers (no. 10), and those who were especially noteworthy for holiness (nos. 11-12).

The following Masses, if indicated for a particular rank of saints, are used for saints of that rank. If no indication is given, the Masses may be used for saints of any rank.

1

ENTRANCE ANT. Ps 145:10-11

May all your works praise you, Lord, and your saints bless you; they will tell of the glory of your kingdom and proclaim your power. → No. 2, p. 614

OPENING PRAYER

Ever-living God,
the signs of your love are manifest
in the honor you give your saints.
May their prayers and their example encourage us
to follow your Son more faithfully.
We ask this . . . for ever and ever. R̸. **Amen.** ↓

READINGS AND INTERVENIENT CHANTS

See pp. 1197-1239.

PRAYER OVER THE GIFTS

Lord,
in your kindness hear our prayers
and the prayers which the saints offer on our behalf.
Watch over us that we may offer fitting service at your altar.
Grant this in the name of Jesus the Lord.
R̸. **Amen.** → No. 21, p. 626

COMMUNION ANT. Ps 68:4

May the just rejoice as they feast in God's presence, and delight in gladness of heart. ↓

OR Lk 12:37

Blessed are those servants whom the Lord finds watching when he comes; truly I tell you, he will seat them at his table and wait on them. ↓

PRAYER AFTER COMMUNION

Father, our comfort and peace,
we have gathered as your family
to praise your name and honor your saints.
Let the sacrament we have received
be the sign and pledge of our salvation.
We ask this through Christ our Lord.
℟. **Amen.** → No. 32, p. 660

2

ENTRANCE ANT. Ps 64:11

The just man will rejoice in the Lord and hope in him, and all the upright of heart will be praised. → No. 2, p. 614

OPENING PRAYER

God our Father,
you alone are holy;
without you nothing is good.
Trusting in the prayers of St. N.
we ask you to help us
to become the holy people you call us to be.
Never let us be found undeserving
of the glory you have prepared for us.
We ask this . . . for ever and ever. ℟. **Amen.** ↓

READINGS AND INTERVENIENT CHANTS
See pp. 1197-1239.

PRAYER OVER THE GIFTS

All-powerful God,
may the gifts we present
bring honor to your saints,
and free us from sin in mind and body.

We ask this in the name of Jesus the Lord.

℟. **Amen.**   → No. 21, p. 626

COMMUNION ANT.   Jn 12:26

He who serves me, follows me, says the Lord; and where I am, my servant will also be. ↓

PRAYER AFTER COMMUNION

Lord,
your sacramental gifts renew us
at this celebration of the birth of your saints to glory.
May the good things you give us
lead us to the joy of your kingdom.
We ask this through Christ our Lord.

℟. **Amen.**   → No. 32, p. 660

3

ENTRANCE ANT.   Ps 21:2-3

Lord, your strength gives joy to the just; they greatly delight in your saving help. You have granted them their heart's desire.   → No. 2, p. 614

OPENING PRAYER

Father,
your saints guide us when in our weakness we tend to stray.
Help us who celebrate the birth of St. N. to glory
grow closer to you by following his (her) example.
We ask this . . . for ever and ever. ℟. **Amen.** ↓

READINGS AND INTERVENIENT CHANTS

See pp. 1197-1239.

PRAYER OVER THE GIFTS

Lord,
let the sacrifice we offer
in memory of St. N.

bring to your people the gifts of unity and peace.
Grant this in the name of Jesus the Lord.
℟. **Amen.** → No. 21, p. 626

COMMUNION ANT. Mt 16:24

If anyone wishes to come after me, he must renounce himself, take up his cross, and follow me, says the Lord. ↓

PRAYER AFTER COMMUNION

Lord,
may the sacraments we receive
on this feast in honor of N.
give us holiness of mind and body
and bring us into your divine life.
We ask this through Christ our Lord.
℟. **Amen.** → No. 32, p. 660

4

ENTRANCE ANT. Mal 2:6

The teaching of truth was in his mouth, and no wrong was found on his lips; he walked with me in peace and justice, and turned many away from wickedness. → No. 2, p. 614

OPENING PRAYER

Merciful Father,
we fail because of our weakness.
Restore us to your love
through the example of your saints.
We ask this . . . for ever and ever. ℟. **Amen.** ↓

READINGS AND INTERVENIENT CHANTS
See pp. 1107-1239.

PRAYER OVER THE GIFTS

Lord,
may this sacrifice we share

on the feast of your St. N.
give you praise
and help us on our way to salvation.
Grant this in the name of Jesus the Lord.
R̸. **Amen.** → No. 21, p. 626

COMMUNION ANT. Mt 5:8-9

**Happy are the pure of heart for they shall see God. Happy
the peacemakers; they shall be called the sons of God.
Happy are they who suffer persecution for justice' sake; the
kingdom of heaven is theirs.** ↓

PRAYER AFTER COMMUNION

Lord,
our hunger is satisfied by your holy gift.
May we who have celebrated this eucharist
experience in our lives the salvation which it brings.
We ask this in the name of Jesus the Lord.
R̸. **Amen.** → No. 32, p. 660

5

ENTRANCE ANT. Ps 92:13-14

**The just man will flourish like the palm tree. Planted in the
courts of God's house, he will grow great like the cedars of
Lebanon.** → No. 2, p. 614

OPENING PRAYER

Lord,
may the prayers of the saints
bring help to your people.
Give to us who celebrate the memory of your saints
a share in their eternal joy.
Grant this . . . for ever and ever. R̸. **Amen.** ↓

READINGS AND INTERVENIENT CHANTS

See pp. 1197-1239.

PRAYER OVER THE GIFTS

Lord,
give to us who offer these gifts at your altar
the same spirit of love that filled St. N.
By celebrating this sacred eucharist with pure minds and
loving hearts
may we offer a sacrifice that pleases you,
and brings salvation to us.
Grant this through Christ our Lord.
℟. **Amen.**

→ No. 21, p. 626

COMMUNION ANT. Mt 11:28

Come to me, all you that labor and are burdened, and I will give you rest, says the Lord. ↓

PRAYER AFTER COMMUNION

Lord,
may the sacrament of holy communion which we receive
bring us health and strengthen us
in the light of your truth.
We ask this in the name of Jesus the Lord.
℟. **Amen.**

→ No. 32, p. 660

6

ENTRANCE ANT. Jer 17:7-8

Blessed is the man who puts his trust in the Lord; he will be like a tree planted by the waters, sinking its roots into the moist earth; he will have nothing to fear in time of drought.

→ No. 2, p. 614

OPENING PRAYER

All-powerful God,
help us who celebrate the memory of St. N.
to imitate his (her) way of life.

May the example of your saints
be our challenge to live holier lives.
Grant this . . . for ever and ever. R̸. **Amen.** ↓

READINGS AND INTERVENIENT CHANTS

See pp. 1197-1239.

PRAYER OVER THE GIFTS

Lord,
we bring our gifts to your holy altar
on this feast of your saints.
In your mercy let this eucharist
give you glory
and bring us to the fullness of your love.
Grant this through Christ our Lord.
R̸. **Amen.**

→ No. 21, p. 626

COMMUNION ANT.   Jn 15:9

**As the Father has loved me, so have I loved you; remain in
my love.** ↓

PRAYER AFTER COMMUNION

Lord our God,
may the divine mysteries we celebrate
in memory of your saint
fill us with eternal peace and salvation.
We ask this in the name of Jesus the Lord.
R̸. **Amen.**

→ No. 32, p. 660

---

7. FOR RELIGIOUS

ENTRANCE ANT.   Ps 16:5-6

**The Lord is my inheritance and my cup; he alone will give
me my reward. The measuring line has marked a lovely
place for me; my inheritance is my great delight.**

→ No. 2, p. 614

OPENING PRAYER

Lord God,
you kept St. N. faithful to Christ's pattern of poverty and
    humility.
May his (her) prayers help us to live in fidelity to our calling
and bring us to the perfection you have shown us in your
    Son,
who lives and reigns with you and the Holy Spirit,
one God, for ever and ever. ℟. **Amen.** ↓

OR (for an abbot)

Lord,
in your abbot N.
you give an example of the gospel lived to perfection.
Help us to follow him
by keeping before us the things of heaven
amid all the changes of this world.
Grant this . . . for ever and ever. ℟. **Amen.** ↓

READINGS AND INTERVENIENT CHANTS

See pp. 1197-1239.

PRAYER OVER THE GIFTS

God of all mercy,
you transformed St. N.
and made him (her) a new creature in your image.
Renew us in the same way
by making our gifts of peace acceptable to you.
We ask this in the name of Jesus the Lord.
℟. **Amen.**   → No. 21, p. 626

COMMUNION ANT.   See Mt 19.27-29

**I solemnly tell you: those who have left everything and fol-
lowed me will be repaid a hundredfold and will gain eternal
life.** ↓

PRAYER AFTER COMMUNION

All-powerful God,
may we who are strengthened by the power of this sacra-
    ment
learn from the example of St. N.
to seek you above all things
and to live in this world as your new creation.
We ask this through Christ our Lord.
℟. **Amen.**   → No. 32, p. 660

---

8. FOR RELIGIOUS

ENTRANCE ANT.   See Ps 24:5-6

**These are the saints who received blessings from the Lord,
a prize from God their Savior. They are the people that long
to see his face.**   → No. 2, p. 614

OPENING PRAYER

God our Father,
you called St. N. to seek your kingdom in this world
by striving to live in perfect charity.
With his (her) prayers to give us courage,
help us to move forward with joyful hearts in the way of
    love.
We ask this . . . for ever and ever. ℟. **Amen.** ↓

READINGS AND INTERVENIENT CHANTS

See pp. 1197-1239.

PRAYER OVER THE GIFTS

Lord,
may the gifts we bring to your altar
in memory of St. N.
be acceptable to you.
Free us from the things that keep us from you
and teach us to seek you as our only good.
We ask this through Christ our Lord.
℟. **Amen.**   → No. 21, p. 626

COMMUNION ANT. Ps 34:9

Taste and see the goodness of the Lord; blessed is he who hopes in God. ↓

PRAYER AFTER COMMUNION

Lord,
by the power of this sacrament and the example of St. N.
guide us always in your love.
May the good work you have begun in us
reach perfection in the day of Christ Jesus
who is Lord for ever and ever.
℟. **Amen.** → No. 32, p. 660

9. FOR THOSE WHO WORK FOR THE UNDERPRIVILEGED

ENTRANCE ANT. Mt 25:34, 36, 40

Come, you whom my Father has blessed, says the Lord: I was ill and you comforted me. I tell you, anything you did for one of my brothers, you did for me. → No. 2, p. 614

OPENING PRAYER

Lord God,
you teach us that the commandments of heaven
are summarized in love of you and love of our neighbor.
By following the example of St. N.
in practicing works of charity
may we be counted among the blessed in your kingdom.
Grant this . . . for ever and ever. ℟. **Amen.** ↓

READINGS AND INTERVENIENT CHANTS
See pp. 1197-1239.

PRAYER OVER THE GIFTS

Lord,
accept the gifts of your people.

May we who celebrate the love of your Son
also follow the example of your saints
and grow in love for you and for one another.
We ask this through Christ our Lord.
℟. **Amen.**   → No. 21, p. 626

COMMUNION ANT.   Jn 15:13

**No one has greater love, says the Lord, than the man who
lays down his life for his friends.** ↓

OR   Jn 13:35

**By the love you have for one another, says the Lord, every-
one will know that you are my disciples.** ↓

PRAYER AFTER COMMUNION

Lord,
may we who are renewed by these mysteries
follow the example of St. N.
who worshiped you with love
and served your people with generosity.
We ask this through Christ our Lord. ℟. **Amen.**

OR

Lord,
we who receive the sacrament of salvation ask your mercy.
Help us to imitate the love of St. N.
and give to us a share in his (her) glory.
Grant this through Christ our Lord. ℟. **Amen.**

→ No. 32, p. 660

---

10. FOR TEACHERS

ENTRANCE ANT.   Mk 10:14

**Let the children come to me, and do not stop them, says the
Lord; to such belongs the kingdom of God.**

OR Mt 5:19

The man that keeps these commandments and teaches them, he is the one who will be called great in the kingdom of heaven, says the Lord.

→ No. 2, p. 614

OPENING PRAYER

Lord God,
you called St. N. to serve you in the Church
by teaching his (her) fellow man the way of salvation.
Inspire us by his (her) example:
help us to follow Christ our teacher
and lead us to our brothers and sisters in heaven.
We ask this . . . for ever and ever. R̷. **Amen.** ↓

READINGS AND INTERVENIENT CHANTS

See pp. 1197-1239.

PRAYER OVER THE GIFTS

Lord,
accept the gifts your people bring
in memory of your saints.
May our sharing in this mystery
help us to live the example of love you give us.
Grant this in the name of Jesus the Lord.
R̷. **Amen.** → No. 21, p. 626

COMMUNION ANT. Mt 18:3

Unless you change, and become like little children, says the Lord, you shall not enter the kingdom of heaven. ↓

OR Jn 8:12

I am the light of the world, says the Lord; the man who follows me will have the light of life. ↓

PRAYER AFTER COMMUNION

All-powerful God,
may this holy meal help us

to follow the example of your saints
by showing in our lives
the light of truth and love for our brothers.
We ask this in the name of Jesus the Lord.
℟. **Amen.**   → No. 32, p. 660

---

11. FOR HOLY WOMEN

ENTRANCE ANT.   See Prv 31:30, 28

Honor the woman who fears the Lord. Her sons will bless her, and her husband praise her.   → No. 2, p. 614

OPENING PRAYER

God our Father,
every year you give us joy on this feast of St. N.
As we honor her memory by this celebration,
may we follow the example of her holy life.
We ask this . . . for ever and ever. ℟. **Amen.** ↓

OR (for several)

All-powerful God,
may the prayers of Saints N. and N. bring us help from heaven
as their lives have already given us
an example of holiness.
We ask this . . . for ever and ever. ℟. **Amen.** ↓

READINGS AND INTERVENIENT CHANTS

See pp. 1197-1239.

PRAYER OVER THE GIFTS

Lord,
may the gifts we present in memory of St. N.
bring us your forgiveness and salvation.
We ask this in the name of Jesus the Lord.
℟. **Amen.**   → No. 21, p. 626

COMMUNION ANT. Mt 13:45-46

The kingdom of heaven is like a merchant in search of fine pearls; on finding one rare pearl he sells everything he has and buys it. ↓

PRAYER AFTER COMMUNION

All-powerful God,
fill us with your light and love
by the sacrament we receive on the feast of St. N.
May we burn with love for your kingdom
and let our light shine before men.
We ask this through Christ our Lord.
℟. **Amen.** → No. 32, p. 660

12. FOR HOLY WOMEN

ENTRANCE ANT. See Prv 14:1-2

Praise to the holy woman whose home is built on faithful love and whose pathway leads to God. → No. 2, p. 614

OPENING PRAYER

Father,
rewarder of the humble,
you blessed St. N. with charity and patience.
May her prayers help us, and her example inspire us
to carry our cross and to love you always.
We ask this . . . for ever and ever. ℟. **Amen.** ↓

OR

Lord,
pour upon us the spirit of wisdom and love
with which you filled your servant St. N.
By serving you as she did,
may we please you with our faith and our actions.
Grant this . . . for ever and ever. ℟. **Amen.** ↓

READINGS AND INTERVENIENT CHANTS

See pp. 1197-1239.

PRAYER OVER THE GIFTS

Lord,
receive the gifts your people bring to you
in honor of your saints.
By the eucharist we celebrate
may we progress toward salvation.
Grant this in the name of Jesus the Lord.
℞. **Amen.**

→ No. 21, p. 626

COMMUNION ANT.   Mt 12:50

**Whoever does the will of my Father in heaven is my broth-
er and sister and mother, says the Lord.** ↓

PRAYER AFTER COMMUNION

Lord,
we receive your gifts
at this celebration in honor of St. N.
May they free us from sin
and strengthen us by your grace.
We ask this in the name of Jesus the Lord.
℞. **Amen.**

→ No. 32, p. 660

OPTIONAL ANTIPHONS FOR SOLEMNITIES AND FEASTS

1

Let us rejoice in the Lord, and keep a festival in honor of the holy (martyr, pastor) N. Let us join with the angels in joyful praise to the Son of God.

2

Let us all rejoice in the Lord as we honor St. N., our protector. On this day this faithful friend of God entered heaven to reign with Christ for ever.

3

Let us rejoice in celebrating the victory of our patron saint. On earth he proclaimed Christ's love for us. Now Christ leads him to a place of honor before his Father in heaven.

4

Let us rejoice in celebrating the feast of the blessed martyr N. He fought for the law of God on earth; now Christ has granted him an everlasting crown of glory.

5

All his saints and all who fear the Lord, sing your praises to our God; for the Lord our almighty God is King of all creation. Let us rejoice and give him glory.

6

We celebrate the day when blessed N. received his reward; with all the saints he is seated at the heavenly banquet in glory.

COMMONS

READINGS AND INTERVENIENT CHANTS

DEDICATION OF A CHURCH

1. ON THE DAY OF DEDICATION

FIRST READING   Neh 8:2-4a, 5-6, 8-10

A reading from the Book of the Prophet Nehemiah

EZRA the priest brought the law before the assembly, which consisted of men, women, and those children old enough to understand. Standing at one end of the open place that was before the Water Gate, he read out of the book from daybreak till midday, in the presence of the men, the women, and those children old enough to understand; and all the people listened attentively to the book of the law. Ezra the scribe stood on a wooden platform that had been made for the occasion. He opened the scroll so that all the people might see it (for he was standing higher up than any of the people); and, as he opened it, all the people rose. Ezra blessed the LORD, the great God, and all the people, their hands raised high, answered, "Amen, amen!" Then they bowed down and prostrated themselves before the LORD, their faces to the ground. Ezra read plainly from the book of the law of God, interpreting it so that all could understand what was read. Then Nehemiah, that is, His Excellency, and Ezra the priest-scribe and the Levites who were instructing the people said to all the people: "Today is holy to the LORD your God. Do not be sad, and do not weep"—for all the people were weeping as they heard the words of the law. He said further: "Go, eat rich foods and drink sweet drinks, and allot portions to those who had nothing prepared; for today is holy to our LORD. Do not be saddened this day, for rejoicing in the LORD must be your strength!"—The word of the Lord.

RESPONSORIAL PSALM   Ps 19:8, 9, 10, 15

℞. (Jn 10:64b) **Your words, Lord, are Spirit and life.**

The law of the LORD is perfect,
    refreshing the soul;
the decree of the LORD is trustworthy,
    giving wisdom to the simple.—℞.

The precepts of the LORD are right,
    rejoicing the heart;
the command of the LORD is clear,
    enlightening the eye.—℞.

The fear of the LORD is pure,
    enduring forever;
the ordinances of the LORD are true,
    all of them just.—℞.

Let the words of my mouth and the thought of my heart
    find favor before you,
O LORD, my rock and my redeemer.—℞. ↓

The Second Reading, Alleluia, and Gospel are taken from pp. 1104-1109.

---

2. ON THE ANNIVERSARY OF DEDICATION

READING I FROM THE OLD TESTAMENT

1   1 Kgs 8:22-23, 27-30

A reading from the first Book of Kings

IN those days: Solomon stood before the altar of the LORD in the presence of the whole community of Israel, and stretching forth his hands toward heaven, he said, "LORD, God of Israel, there is no God like you in heaven above or on earth below; you keep your covenant of mercy with your servants who are faithful to you with their whole heart.

"Can it indeed be that God dwells on earth? If the heavens and the highest heavens cannot contain you, how much less this temple which I have built! Look kindly on the prayer and petition of your servant, O LORD, my God, and listen to the cry of supplication I, your servant, utter before you this day. May your eyes watch night and day over this temple, the place where you have decreed you shall be honored; may you heed the prayer which I, your servant, offer in this place. Listen to the petitions of your servant and of your people Israel which they offer in this place. Listen from your heavenly dwelling and grant pardon."—The word of the Lord.

2   2 Chr 5:6-10, 13—6:2

A reading from the second Book of Chronicles

KING Solomon and the entire community of Israel gathered about him before the ark were sacrificing sheep and oxen so numerous that they could not be counted or numbered. The priests brought the ark of the covenant of the LORD to its place beneath the wings of the cherubim in the sanctuary, the holy of holies of the temple. The cherubim had their wings spread out over the place of the ark, sheltering the ark and its poles from above. The poles were long enough so that their ends could be seen from that part of the holy place nearest the sanctuary; however, they could not be seen beyond. The ark has remained there to this day. There was nothing in it but the two tablets which Moses put there on Horeb, the tablets of the covenant which the LORD made with the children of Israel at their departure from Egypt.

When the trumpeters and singers were heard as a single voice praising and giving thanks to the LORD, and when they raised the sound of the trumpets, cymbals and other musical instruments to "give thanks to the LORD, for he is good, for his mercy endures forever," the building of the LORD's temple was filled with a cloud. The priests could not continue to minister because of the cloud, since the LORD's glory filled the house of God.

Then Solomon said: "The LORD intends to dwell in the dark cloud. I have truly built you a princely house and dwelling, where you may abide forever."—The word of the Lord.

---

3   Is 56:1, 6-7

A reading from the Book of the Prophet Isaiah

THUS says the LORD:
Observe what is right, do what is just;
    for my salvation is about to come,
    my justice, about to be revealed.

The foreigners who join themselves to the LORD,
    ministering to him,
Loving the name of the LORD,
    and becoming his servants—
All who keep the sabbath free from profanation
    and hold to my covenant,
Them I will bring to my holy mountain
    and make joyful in my house of prayer;
Their burnt offerings and sacrifices
    will be acceptable on my altar,
For my house shall be called
    a house of prayer for all peoples.
The word of the Lord.

---

4   Ez 43:1-2, 3c-7a

A reading from the Book of the Prophet Ezekiel

THE angel led me to the gate which faces the east, and there I saw the glory of the God of Israel coming from the east. I heard a sound like the roaring of many waters, and the earth shone with his glory. I fell prone as the glory of the LORD entered the temple by way of the gate which faces the east, but spirit lifted me up and brought me to the inner court. And I saw that the temple was filled with the glory of the LORD. Then I heard someone speaking to me from the temple, while the man stood beside me. The voice said to me: Son of man, this is where my throne shall be, this is where I will set the soles of my feet; here I will dwell among the children of Israel forever.—The word of the Lord.

5️⃣   Ez 47:1-2, 8-9, 12

A reading from the Book of the Prophet Ezekiel

THE angel brought me back to the entrance of the temple, and I saw water flowing out from beneath the threshold of the temple toward the east, for the façade of the temple was toward the east; the water flowed down from the right side of the temple, south of the altar. He led me outside by the north gate, and around to the outer gate facing the east, where I saw water trickling from the right side. He said to me, "This water flows into the eastern district down upon the Arabah, and empties into the sea, the salt waters, which it makes fresh. Wherever the river flows, every sort of living creature that can multiply shall live, and there shall be abundant fish, for wherever this water comes the sea shall be made fresh. Along both banks of the river, fruit trees of every kind shall grow; their leaves shall not fade, nor their fruit fail. Every month they shall bear fresh fruit, for they shall be watered by the flow from the sanctuary. Their fruit shall serve for food, and their leaves for medicine."—The word of the Lord.

READING I FROM THE NEW TESTAMENT DURING THE SEASON OF EASTER

1️⃣   Acts 7:44-50

A reading from the Acts of the Apostles

STEPHEN said to the people, the elders and the scribes: "Our ancestors had the tent of testimony in the desert just as the One who spoke to Moses directed him to make it according to the pattern he had seen. Our ancestors who inherited it brought it with Joshua when they dispossessed the nations that God drove out from before our ancestors, up to the time of David, who found favor in the sight of God and asked that he might find a dwelling place for the house of Jacob. But Solomon built a house for him. Yet the Most High does not dwell in houses made by human hands. As the prophet says:

The heavens are my throne,
*   the earth is my footstool.*
What kind of house can you build for me?
*   says the Lord,*
*   or what is to be my resting place?*
Did not my hand make all these things?"

The word of the Lord.

---

2   Rv 21:1-5a

A reading from the Book of Revelation

I, JOHN, saw a new heaven and a new earth. The former heaven and the former earth had passed away, and the sea was no more. I also saw the holy city, a new Jerusalem, coming down out of heaven from God, prepared as a bride adorned for her husband. I heard a loud voice from the throne saying, "Behold, God's dwelling is with the human race. He will dwell with them and they will be his people and God himself will always be with them as their God. He will wipe every tear from their eyes, and there shall be no more death or mourning, wailing or pain, for the old order has passed away."

The One who sat on the throne said, "Behold, I make all things new."—The word of the Lord.

---

3   Rv 21:9-14

A reading from the Book of Revelation

THE angel spoke to me, saying: "Come here. I will show you the bride, the wife of the Lamb." He took me in spirit to a great, high mountain and showed me the holy city Jerusalem coming down out of heaven from God. It gleamed with the splendor of God. Its radiance was like that of a precious stone, like jasper, clear as crystal. It had a massive, high wall, with twelve gates where twelve angels were stationed and on which names were inscribed, the names of the twelve tribes of the children of Israel. There were three gates facing east, three north, three south, and three west. The wall of the city had twelve courses of stones as its foundation, on which were inscribed the twelve names of the twelve Apostles of the Lamb.—The word of the Lord.

RESPONSORIAL PSALM

1   1 Chr 29:10, 11, 12

℟. (13b) **We praise your glorious name, O mighty God.**

"Blessed may you be, O LORD,
 God of Israel our father,
 from eternity to eternity."—℟.

"Yours, O LORD, are grandeur and power,
 majesty, splendor, and glory.
For all in heaven and on earth is yours."—℟.

"Yours, O LORD, is the sovereignty;
 you are exalted as head over all.
Riches and honor are from you."—℟.

"You have dominion over all.
In your hands are power and might;
 it is yours to give grandeur and strength to all."—℟.

---

2   Ps 46:2-3, 5-6, 8-9

℟. (5) **There is a stream whose runlets gladden the city of God, the holy dwelling of the Most High!**

God is our refuge and our strength,
 an ever-present help in distress.
Therefore we fear not, though the earth be shaken
 and mountains plunge into the depths of the sea.—℟.

There is a stream whose runlets gladden the city of God,
    the holy dwelling of the Most High.
God is in its midst; it shall not be disturbed;
    God will help it at the break of dawn.—℟.

The LORD of hosts is with us;
    our stronghold is the God of Jacob.
Come! behold the deeds of the LORD,
    the astounding things he has wrought on earth.—℟.

---

3   Ps 84:3, 4, 5 and 10, 11

℟. **How lovely is your dwelling-place, Lord, mighty God!**

℟. Or: **Here God lives among his people.**

My soul yearns and pines
    for the courts of the LORD.
My heart and my flesh
    cry out for the living God.—℟.

Even the sparrow finds a home,
    and the swallow a nest
    in which she puts her young—
Your altars, O LORD of hosts,
    my king and my God!—℟.

Blessed they who dwell in your house!
    continually they praise you.
O God, behold our shield,
    and look upon the face of your anointed.—℟.

I had rather one day in your courts
    than a thousand elsewhere;
I had rather lie at the threshold of the house of my God
    than dwell in the tents of the wicked.—℟.

---

4   Ps 95:1-2, 3-5, 6-7

℟. (2) **Let us come before the Lord and praise him.**

Come, let us sing joyfully to the LORD;
    let us acclaim the Rock of our salvation.

Let us come into his presence with thanksgiving;
> let us joyfully sing psalms to him.—R̦.

For the LORD is a great God,
> and a great king above all gods;

In his hands are the depths of the earth,
> and the tops of the mountains are his.

His is the sea, for he has made it,
> and the dry land, which his hands have formed.—R̦.

Come, let us bow down in worship;
> let us kneel before the LORD who made us.

For he is our God,
> and we are the people he shepherds, the flock he guides.—R̦.

---

5   Ps 122:1-2, 3-4ab, 8-9

R̦. (1) **Let us go rejoicing to the house of the Lord!**

I rejoiced because they said to me,
> "We will go up to the house of the LORD."

And now we have set foot
> within your gates, O Jerusalem.—R̦.

Jerusalem, built as a city
> with compact unity.

To it the tribes go up,
> the tribes of the LORD.—R̦.

Because of my relatives and friends
> I will say, "Peace be within you!"

Because of the house of the LORD, our God,
> I will pray for your good.—R̦.

READING II FROM THE NEW TESTAMENT

1   1 Cor 3:9c-11, 16-17

A reading from the first Letter of Saint Paul to the
Corinthians

BROTHERS and sisters: You are God's building.

According to the grace of God given to me, like a wise master builder I laid a foundation, and another is building upon it. But each one must be careful how he builds upon it, for no one can lay a foundation other than the one that is there, namely, Jesus Christ. Do you not know that you are the temple of God, and that the Spirit of God dwells in you? If anyone destroys God's temple, God will destroy that person; for the temple of God, which you are, is holy.—The word of the Lord.

---

2   Eph 2:19-22

A reading from the Letter of Saint Paul to the Ephesians

BROTHERS and sisters: You are no longer strangers and sojourners, but you are fellow citizens with the holy ones and members of the household of God, built upon the foundation of the Apostles and prophets, with Christ Jesus himself as the capstone. Through him the whole structure is held together and grows into a temple sacred in the Lord; in him you also are being built together into a dwelling place of God in the Spirit.—The word of the Lord.

---

3   Heb 12:18-19, 22-24

A reading from the Letter to the Hebrews

BROTHERS and sisters: You have not approached that which could be touched and a blazing fire and gloomy darkness and storm and a trumpet blast and a voice speaking words such that those who heard begged that no message be further addressed to them. No, you have approached Mount Zion and the city of the living God, the heavenly Jerusalem, and countless angels in festal gathering, and the assembly of the firstborn enrolled in heaven, and God the judge of all, and the spirits of the just made perfect, and

Jesus, the mediator of a new covenant, and the sprinkled Blood that speaks more eloquently than that of Abel.—The word of the Lord.

---

4   1 Pt 2:4-9

A reading from the first Letter of Saint Peter

BELOVED: Come to the Lord, a living stone, rejected by human beings but chosen and precious in the sight of God, and, like living stones, let yourselves be built into a spiritual house to be a holy priesthood to offer spiritual sacrifices acceptable to God through Jesus Christ. For it says in Scripture:

Behold, I am laying a stone in Zion,

a cornerstone, chosen and precious,

and whoever believes in it shall not be put to shame.

Therefore, its value is for you who have faith, but for those without faith:

The stone which the builders rejected

has become the cornerstone,

and

A stone which will make people stumble,

and a rock that will make them fall.

They stumble by disobeying the word, as is their destiny. You are *a chosen race, a royal priesthood, a holy nation, a people of his own, so that you may announce the praises* of him who called you out of darkness into his wonderful light.—The word of the Lord.

ALLELUIA VERSE AND
VERSE BEFORE THE GOSPEL

1   2 Chr 7:16

I have chosen and consecrated this house, says the Lord, that my name may be there forever.

2   Is 66:1

The heavens are my throne, the earth is my footstool, says
    the Lord.
What kind of house can you build for me?

3   Ez 37:27

My dwelling shall be with them, says the Lord;
I will be their God and they shall be my people.

4   See Mt 7:8

In my house, says the Lord, everyone who asks will receive;
the one who seeks, finds; and to the one who knocks, the
    door will be opened.

5   Mt 16:18

You are Peter, and upon this rock I will build my Church,
and the gates of the netherworld shall not prevail against it.

GOSPEL

1   Mt 16:13-19

✠ A reading from the holy Gospel according to Matthew

WHEN Jesus went into the region of Caesarea Philippi
he asked his disciples, "Who do people say that the
Son of Man is?" They replied, "Some say John the Baptist,
others Elijah, still others Jeremiah or one of the prophets."
He said to them, "But who do you say that I am?" Simon Peter
said in reply, "You are the Christ, the Son of the living God."
Jesus said to him in reply, "Blessed are you, Simon son of
Jonah. For flesh and blood has not revealed this to you, but
my heavenly Father. And so I say to you, you are Peter, and
upon this rock I will build my Church, and the gates of the
netherworld shall not prevail against it. I will give you the
keys to the Kingdom of heaven. Whatever you bind on earth

hall be bound in heaven; and whatever you loose on earth shall be loosed in heaven."—The Gospel of the Lord.

2

Lk 19:1-10

✝ A reading from the holy Gospel according to Luke

AT that time, Jesus came to Jericho and intended to pass through the town. Now a man there named Zacchaeus, who was a chief tax collector and also a wealthy man, was seeking to see who Jesus was; but he could not see him because of the crowd, for he was short in stature. So he ran ahead and climbed a sycamore tree in order to see Jesus, who was about to pass that way. When he reached the place, Jesus looked up and said, "Zacchaeus, come down quickly, for today I must stay at your house." And he came down quickly and received him with joy. When they saw this, they began to grumble, saying, "He has gone to stay at the house of a sinner." But Zacchaeus stood there and said to the Lord, "Behold, half of my possessions, Lord, I shall give to the poor, and if I have extorted anything from anyone I shall repay it four times over." And Jesus said to him, "Today salvation has come to this house because this man too is a descendant of Abraham. For the Son of Man has come to seek and to save what was lost."—The Gospel of the Lord.

3

Jn 2:13-22

✝ A reading from the holy Gospel according to John

SINCE the Passover of the Jews was near, Jesus went up to Jerusalem. He found in the temple area those who sold oxen, sheep, and doves, as well as the money-changers seated there. He made a whip out of cords and drove them all out of the temple area, with the sheep and oxen, and spilled the coins of the money-changers and overturned their tables, and to those who sold doves he said, "Take these out of here, and stop making my Father's house a marketplace." His disciples recalled the words of Scripture, *Zeal for your house will consume me.* At this the Jews answered and said to him, "What sign can you show us for doing this?" Jesus answered and said to them, "Destroy this temple and in three days I will raise it up." The Jews said, "This temple has been under construction for forty-six years, and you will raise it up in three days?" But he was speaking about the temple of his Body. Therefore, when he was raised from the dead, his disciples remembered that he had said this, and they came to believe the Scripture and the word Jesus had spoken.—The Gospel of the Lord.

---

4   Jn 4:19-24

✠ A reading from the holy Gospel according to John

THE Samaritan woman said to Jesus, "Sir, I can see that you are a prophet. Our ancestors worshiped on this mountain; but you people say that the place to worship is in Jerusalem." Jesus said to her, "Believe me, woman, the hour is coming when you will worship the Father neither on this mountain nor in Jerusalem. You people worship what you do not understand; we worship what we understand, because salvation is from the Jews. But the hour is coming, and is now here, when true worshipers will worship the Father in Spirit and truth; and indeed the Father seeks such people to worship him. God is Spirit, and those who worship him must worship in Spirit and truth."—The Gospel of the Lord.

COMMON OF THE
BLESSED VIRGIN MARY

READING I FROM THE OLD TESTAMENT

1

Gn 3:9-15, 20

A reading from the Book of Genesis

AFTER the man, Adam, had eaten of the tree, the LORD God called to the man and asked him, "Where are you?" He answered, "I heard you in the garden; but I was afraid, because I was naked, so I hid myself." Then he asked, "Who told you that you were naked? You have eaten, then, from the tree of which I had forbidden you to eat!" The man replied, "The woman whom you put here with me—she gave me fruit from the tree, and so I ate it." The LORD God then asked the woman, "Why did you do such a thing?" The woman answered, "The serpent tricked me into it, so I ate it."

Then the LORD God said to the serpent:

"Because you have done this, you shall be banned
from all the animals
and from all the wild creatures;
On your belly shall you crawl,
and dirt shall you eat
all the days of your life.
I will put enmity between you and the woman,
and between your offspring and hers;
He will strike at your head,
while you strike at his heel."

The man called his wife Eve, because she became the mother of all the living.—The word of the Lord.

2

Gn 12:1-7

A reading from the Book of Genesis

THE LORD said to Abram: "Go forth from the land of your kinsfolk and from your father's house to a land that I will show you.

1110

"I will make of you a great nation,
  and I will bless you;
I will make your name great,
  so that you will be a blessing.
I will bless those who bless you
  and curse those who curse you.
All the communities of the earth
  shall find blessing in you."

Abram went as the LORD directed him, and Lot went with him. Abram was seventy-five years old when he left Haran. Abram took his wife Sarai, his brother's son Lot, all the possessions that they had accumulated, and the persons they had acquired in Haran, and they set out for the land of Canaan. When they came to the land of Canaan, Abram passed through the land as far as the sacred place at Shechem, by the terebinth of Moreh. (The Canaanites were then in the land.)

The LORD appeared to Abram and said, "To your descendants I will give this land." So Abram built an altar there to the LORD who had appeared to him.—The word of the Lord.

---

3   2 Sm 7:1-5, 8-11, 16

A reading from the second Book of Samuel

WHEN King David was settled in his palace, and the LORD had given him rest from his enemies on every side, he said to Nathan the prophet, "Here I am living in a house of cedar, while the ark of God dwells in a tent!" Nathan answered the king, "Go, do whatever you have in mind, for the LORD is with you." But that night the LORD spoke to Nathan and said: "Go tell my servant David, 'Thus says the LORD: Should you build me a house to dwell in?'

" 'It was I who took you from the pasture and from the care of the flock to be commander of my people Israel. I have been with you wherever you went, and I have destroyed all your enemies before you. And I will make you famous like

e great ones of the earth. I will fix a place for my people
Israel; I will plant them so that they may dwell in their place
without further disturbance. Neither shall the wicked continue to afflict them as they did of old, since the time I first
appointed judges over my people Israel. I will give you rest
from all your enemies. The LORD also reveals to you that he
will establish a house for you. Your house and your kingdom
shall endure forever before me; your throne shall stand firm
forever.' "—The word of the Lord.

---

4   1 Chr 15:3-4, 15-16; 16:1-2

A reading from the first Book of Chronicles

DAVID assembled all Israel in Jerusalem to bring the ark
of the LORD to the place which he had prepared for it.
David also called together the sons of Aaron and the Levites.
The Levites bore the ark of God on their shoulders with
poles, as Moses had ordained according to the word of the
LORD.

David commanded the chiefs of the Levites to appoint
their brethren as chanters, to play on musical instruments,
harps, lyres, and cymbals to make a loud sound of rejoicing.

They brought in the ark of God and set it within the tent
which David had pitched for it. Then they offered up burnt
offerings and peace offerings to God. When David had finished offering up the burnt offerings and peace offerings, he
blessed the people in the name of the LORD.—The word of
the Lord.

---

5   Prv 8:22-31

A reading from the Book of Proverbs

THE Wisdom of God says:
"The LORD begot me, the firstborn of his ways,
    the forerunner of his prodigies of long ago;
From of old I was poured forth,
    at the first, before the earth.

When there were no depths I was brought forth,
  when there were no fountains or springs of water;
Before the mountains were settled into place,
  before the hills, I was brought forth;
While as yet the earth and fields were not made,
  nor the first clods of the world.

"When he established the heavens I was there,
  when he marked out the vault over the face of the deep;
When he made firm the skies above,
  when he fixed fast the foundations of the earth;
When he set for the sea its limit,
  so that the waters should not transgress his command;
Then was I beside him as his craftsman,
  and I was his delight day by day,
Playing before him all the while,
  playing on the surface of his earth;
  and I found delight in the sons of men."
The word of the Lord.

---

6   Sir 24:1-2, 3-4, 8-12, 18-21

A reading from the Book of Sirach

WISDOM sings her own praises
  and is honored in God,
  before her own people she proclaims her glory;
In the assembly of the Most High she opens her mouth,
  in the presence of his power she declares her worth.

"From the mouth of the Most High I came forth
  the first-born before all creatures.
I made that in the heavens there should arise
  light that never fades
  and mistlike covered the earth.
In the highest heavens did I dwell,
  my throne on a pillar of cloud.

"Then the Creator of all gave me his command,
  and he who formed me chose the spot for my tent,

Saying, 'In Jacob make your dwelling,
   in Israel your inheritance,
   and among my chosen put down your roots.'
Before all ages, in the beginning, he created me,
   and through all ages I shall not cease to be.
In the holy tent I ministered before him,
   and in Zion I fixed my abode.
Thus in the chosen city he has given me rest,
   in Jerusalem is my domain.
I have struck root among the glorious people,
   in the portion of the LORD, his heritage,
   and in the company of the holy ones do I linger.

"Come to me, all you that yearn for me,
   and be filled with my fruits;
You will remember me as sweeter than honey,
   better to have than the honeycomb;
   my memory is unto everlasting generations.
Whoever eats of me will hunger still,
   whoever drinks of me will thirst for more;
Whoever obeys me will not be put to shame,
   whoever serves me will never fail."
The word of the Lord.

7
                                       Is 7:10-14; 8:10

A reading from the Book of the Prophet Isaiah

THE LORD spoke to Ahaz: Ask for a sign from the LORD, your God; let it be deep as the nether world, or high as the sky! But Ahaz answered, "I will not ask! I will not tempt the LORD!" Then Isaiah said: Listen, O house of David! Is it not enough for you to weary people, must you also weary my God? Therefore the Lord himself will give you this sign: the virgin shall conceive, and bear a son, and shall name him Emmanuel which means "God is with us."—The word of the Lord.

---

8   Is 9:1-6

A reading from the Book of the Prophet Isaiah

THE people who walked in darkness
  have seen a great light;
Upon those who dwelt in the land of gloom
  a light has shone.
You have brought them abundant joy
  and great rejoicing,
As they rejoice before you as at the harvest,
  as people make merry when dividing spoils.
For the yoke that burdened them,
  the pole on their shoulder,
And the rod of their taskmaster
  you have smashed, as on the day of Midian.
For every boot that tramped in battle,
  every cloak rolled in blood,
  will be burned as fuel for flames.

For a child is born to us, a son is given us;
  upon his shoulder dominion rests.
They name him Wonder-Counselor, God-Hero,
  Father-Forever, Prince of Peace.
His dominion is vast
  and forever peaceful,
From David's throne, and over his kingdom,
  which he confirms and sustains
By judgment and justice,
  both now and forever.
The zeal of the LORD of hosts will do this!
The word of the Lord.

———————

9   Is 61:0-11

A reading from the Book of the Prophet Isaiah

THUS says the LORD.
  Their descendants shall be renowned among the na-
    tions,
  and their offspring among the peoples;

All who see them shall acknowledge them
as a race the Lord has blessed.

I rejoice heartily in the Lord,
in my God is the joy of my soul;
For he has clothed me with a robe of salvation,
and wrapped me in a mantle of justice,
Like a bridegroom adorned with a diadem,
like a bride bedecked with her jewels.
As the earth brings forth its plants,
and a garden makes its growth spring up,
So will the Lord God make justice and praise
spring up before all the nations.
The word of the Lord.

---

10   Mi 5:1-4a

A reading from the Book of the Prophet Micah

THE Lord says:
You, Bethlehem-Ephrathah,
too small to be among the clans of Judah,
From you shall come forth for me
one who is to be ruler in Israel;
Whose origin is from of old,
from ancient times.
(Therefore the Lord will give them up, until the time
when she who is to give birth has borne,
And the rest of his brethren shall return
to the children of Israel.)
He shall stand firm and shepherd his flock
by the strength of the Lord,
in the majestic name of the Lord, his God;
And they shall remain, for now his greatness
shall reach to the ends of the earth;
he shall be peace.
The word of the Lord.

---

11   Zec 2:14-17

A reading from the Book of the Prophet Zechariah

SING and rejoice, O daughter Zion! See, I am coming to dwell among you, says the LORD. Many nations shall join themselves to the LORD on that day, and they shall be his people, and he will dwell among you, and you shall know that the LORD of hosts has sent me to you. The LORD will possess Judah as his portion in the holy land, and he will again choose Jerusalem. Silence, all mankind, in the presence of the LORD! for he stirs forth from his holy dwelling.—The word of the Lord.

READING I FROM THE NEW TESTAMENT DURING THE EASTER SEASON

1   Acts 1:12-14

A reading from the Acts of the Apostles

AFTER Jesus had been taken up to heaven, the Apostles returned to Jerusalem from the mount called Olivet, which is near Jerusalem, a sabbath day's journey away.

When they entered the city they went to the upper room where they were staying, Peter and John and James and Andrew, Philip and Thomas, Bartholomew and Matthew, James son of Alphaeus, Simon the Zealot, and Judas son of James. All these devoted themselves with one accord to prayer, together with some women, and Mary the mother of Jesus, and his brothers.—The word of the Lord.

---

2   Rv 11:19a; 12:1-6a, 10ab

A reading from the Book of Revelation

GOD'S temple in heaven was opened, and the ark of his covenant could be seen in the temple.

A great sign appeared in the sky, a woman clothed with the sun, with the moon under her feet, and on her head a crown of twelve stars. She was with child and wailed aloud in pain as she labored to give birth. Then another sign appeared in the sky; it was a huge red dragon, with seven heads and ten horns, and on its heads were seven diadems. Its tail swept away a third of the stars in the sky and hurled them down to the earth. Then the dragon stood before the woman about to give birth, to devour her child when she gave birth. She gave birth to a son, a male child, destined to rule all the nations with an iron rod. Her child was caught up to God and his throne. The woman herself fled into the desert where she had a place prepared by God.

Then I heard a loud voice in heaven say:

"Now have salvation and power come,
   and the Kingdom of our God
   and the authority of his Anointed."

The word of the Lord.

---

3   Rv 21:1-5a

A reading from the Book of Revelation

I, JOHN, saw a new heaven and a new earth. The former heaven and the former earth had passed away, and the sea was no more. I also saw the holy city, a new Jerusalem, coming down out of heaven from God, prepared as a bride adorned for her husband. I heard a loud voice from the throne saying, "Behold, God's dwelling is with the human race. He will dwell with them and they will be his people and God himself will always be with them as their God. He will wipe every tear from their eyes, and there shall be no more death or mourning, wailing or pain, for the old order has passed away."

The One who sat on the throne said, "Behold, I make all things new."—The word of the Lord.

RESPONSORIAL PSALM

1   1 Sm 2:1, 4-5, 6-7, 8abcd

℞. (see 1b) **My heart exults in the Lord, my Savior.**

"My heart exults in the LORD,
    my horn is exalted in my God.
I have swallowed up my enemies;
    I rejoice in my victory."—℞.

"The bows of the mighty are broken,
    while the tottering gird on strength.
The well-fed hire themselves out for bread,
    while the hungry batten on spoil.
The barren wife bears seven sons,
    while the mother of many languishes."—℞.

"The LORD puts to death and gives life;
    he casts down to the nether world;
    he raises up again.
The LORD makes poor and makes rich,
    he humbles, he also exalts."—℞.

"He raises the needy from the dust;
    from the dung heap he lifts up the poor,
To seat them with nobles
    and make a glorious throne their heritage."—℞.

2   Jdt 13:18bcde, 19

℞. (15:9d) **You are the highest honor of our race.**

"Blessed are you, daughter, by the Most High God,
    above all the women on earth;
    and blessed be the LORD God,
    the creator of heaven and earth."—℞.

"Your deed of hope will never be forgotten
    by those who tell of the might of God."—℞.

3
Ps 45:11-12, 14-15, 16-17

℟. (11) **Listen to me, daughter; see and bend your ear.**

Hear, O daughter, and see; turn your ear,
> forget your people and your father's house.
So shall the king desire your beauty;
> for he is your lord, and you must worship him.—℟.

All glorious is the king's daughter as she enters;
> her raiment is threaded with spun gold.
In embroidered apparel she is borne in to the king;
> behind her the virgins of her train are brought to
> you.—℟.

They are borne in with gladness and joy;
> they enter the palace of the king.
The place of your fathers your sons shall have;
> you shall make them princes through all the land.—℟.

4
Ps 113:1b-2, 3-4, 5-6, 7

℟. **Blessed be the name of the Lord for ever.**

℟. Or: **Alleluia.**

Praise, you servants of the LORD,
> praise the name of the LORD.
Blessed be the name of the LORD
> both now and forever.—℟.

From the rising to the setting of the sun
> is the name of the LORD to be praised.
High above all nations is the LORD;
> above the heavens is his glory.—℟.

Who is like the LORD, our God, who is enthroned on high
> and looks upon the heavens and the earth below?—℟.

He raises up the lowly from the dust;
> from the dunghill he lifts up the poor
To seat them with princes,
> with the princes of his own people.—℟.

5️⃣   Lk 1:46-47, 48-49, 50-51, 52-53, 54-55

℟. (49) **The Almighty has done great things for me, and holy is his Name.**

℟. Or: **O Blessed Virgin Mary, you carried the Son of the eternal Father.**

"My soul proclaims the greatness of the Lord,
    my spirit rejoices in God my Savior."—℟.

"For he has looked with favor on his lowly servant.
From this day all generations will call me blessed:
    the Almighty has done great things for me
    and holy is his Name."—℟.

"He has mercy on those who fear him
    in every generation.
He has shown the strength of his arm,
    he has scattered the proud in their conceit."—℟.

"He has cast down the mighty from their thrones,
    and has lifted up the lowly,
He has filled the hungry with good things,
    and the rich he has sent away empty."—℟.

"He has come to the help of his servant Israel
    for he has remembered his promise of mercy,
the promise he made to our fathers,
    to Abraham and his children for ever."—℟.

READING II FROM THE NEW TESTAMENT

1️⃣   Rom 5:12, 17-19

A reading from the Letter of Saint Paul to the Romans

BROTHERS and sisters: Through one man sin entered the world, and through sin, death, and thus death came to all men, inasmuch as all sinned.

For if, by the transgression of the one, death came to reign through that one, how much more will those who receive the abundance of grace and of the gift of justification come to reign in life through the one Jesus Christ. In conclusion, just as through one transgression condemnation came upon all, so, through one righteous act, acquittal and life came to all. For just as through the disobedience of the one man the many were made sinners, so, through the obedience of the one, the many will be made righteous.—The word of the Lord.

---

2   Rom 8:28-30

A reading from the Letter of Saint Paul to the Romans

BROTHERS and sisters: We know that all things work for good for those who love God, who are called according to his purpose. For those he foreknew he also predestined to be conformed to the image of his Son, so that he might be the firstborn among many brothers. And those he predestined he also called; and those he called he also justified; and those he justified he also glorified.—The word of the Lord.

---

3   Gal 4:4-7

A reading from the Letter of Saint Paul to the Galatians

BROTHERS and sisters: When the fullness of time had come, God sent his Son, born of a woman, born under the law, to ransom those under the law, so that we might receive adoption as sons. As proof that you are sons, God sent the spirit of his Son into our hearts, crying out, "Abba, Father!" So you are no longer a slave but a son, and if a son then also an heir, through God.—The word of the Lord.

---

4   Eph 1:3-6, 11-12

A reading from the Letter of Saint Paul to the Ephesians

BLESSED be the God and Father of our Lord Jesus Christ, who has blessed us in Christ with every spiritual blessing in the heavens, as he chose us in him, before the foundation of the world, to be holy and without blemish before him. In love he destined us for adoption to himself through Jesus Christ, in accord with the favor of his will, for the praise of the glory of his grace that he granted us in the beloved.

In him we were also chosen, destined in accord with the purpose of the One who accomplishes all things according to the intention of his will, so that we might exist for the praise of his glory, we who first hoped in Christ.—The word of the Lord.

ALLELUIA VERSE AND VERSE BEFORE THE GOSPEL

1   See Lk 1:28

Hail, Mary, full of grace, the Lord is with you;
blessed are you among women.

2   See Lk 1:45

Blessed are you, O Virgin Mary, who believed
that what was spoken to you by the Lord would be fulfilled.

3   See Lk 2:19

Blessed is the Virgin Mary who kept the word of God
and pondered it in her heart.

4   Lk 11:28

Blessed are those who hear the word of God
and observe it.

5

Blessed are you, holy Virgin Mary, deserving of all praise;
from you rose the sun of justice, Christ our God.

6

Blessed are you, O Virgin Mary;
without dying you won the martyr's crown
beneath the Cross of the Lord.

GOSPEL

1   Mt 1:1-16, 18-23 or 1:18-23

[If the "Short Form" is used, omit indented text in brackets.]

✝ A reading from the holy Gospel according to Matthew

THE book of the genealogy of Jesus Christ, the son of David, the son of Abraham.

Abraham became the father of Isaac, Isaac the father of Jacob, Jacob the father of Judah and his brothers. Judah became the father of Perez and Zerah, whose mother was Tamar. Perez became the father of Hezron, Hezron the father of Ram, Ram the father of Amminadab. Amminadab became the father of Nahshon, Nahshon the father of Salmon, Salmon the father of Boaz, whose mother was Rahab. Boaz became the father of Obed, whose mother was Ruth. Obed became the father of Jesse, Jesse the father of David the king.

David became the father of Solomon, whose mother had been the wife of Uriah. Solomon became the father of Rehoboam, Rehoboam the father of Abijah, Abijah the father of Asaph. Asaph became the father of Jehoshaphat, Jehoshaphat the father of Joram, Joram the father of Uzziah. Uzziah became the father of Jotham, Jotham the father of Ahaz, Ahaz the father of Hezekiah. Hezekiah became the father of Manasseh, Manasseh the father of Amos, Amos the father of Josiah. Josiah became the father of Jechoniah and his brothers at the time of the Babylonian exile.

After the Babylonian exile, Jechoniah became the father of Shealtiel, Shealtiel the father of Zerubbabel, Zerubbabel the father of Abiud. Abiud became the father of Eliakim, Eliakim the father of Azor, Azor the father of Zadok. Zadok became the father of Achim, Achim the father of Eliud, Eliud the father of Eleazar. Eleazar became the father of Matthan, Matthan the father of Jacob, Jacob the father of Joseph, the husband of Mary. Of her was born Jesus who is called the Christ.]

Now this is how the birth of Jesus Christ came about. When his mother Mary was betrothed to Joseph, but before they lived together, she was found with child through the Holy Spirit. Joseph her husband, since he was a righteous man, yet unwilling to expose her to shame, decided to divorce her quietly. Such was his intention when, behold, the angel of the Lord appeared to him in a dream and said, "Joseph, son of David, do not be afraid to take Mary your wife into your home. For it is through the Holy Spirit that this child has been conceived in her. She will bear a son and you are to name him Jesus, because he will save his people from their sins." All this took place to fulfill what the Lord had said through the prophet:

> *Behold, the virgin shall be with child and bear a son,*
>   *and they shall name him Emmanuel,*

which means "God is with us."—The Gospel of the Lord.

---

2   Mt 2:13-15, 19-23

✠ A reading from the holy Gospel according to Matthew

WHEN the magi had departed, behold, the angel of the Lord appeared to Joseph in a dream and said, "Rise, take the child and his mother, flee to Egypt, and stay there until I tell you. Herod is going to search for the child to destroy him." Joseph rose and took the child and his mother by night and departed for Egypt. He stayed there until the death of Herod, that what the Lord had said through the prophet might be fulfilled,

> *Out of Egypt I called my son.*

When Herod had died, behold, the angel of the Lord appeared in a dream to Joseph in Egypt and said, "Rise, take the child and his mother and go to the land of Israel, for those who sought the child's life are dead." He rose, took the child and his mother, and went to the land of Israel. But when he heard that Archelaus was ruling over Judea in place of his father Herod, he was afraid to go back there. And because he had been warned in a dream, he departed for the region of Galilee. He went and dwelt in a town called Nazareth, so that what had been spoken through the prophets might be fulfilled,

> *He shall be called a Nazorean.*

The Gospel of the Lord.

---

3   Mt 12:46-50

✣ A reading from the holy Gospel according to Matthew

WHILE Jesus was speaking to the crowds, his mother and his brothers appeared outside, wishing to speak with him. Someone told him, "Your mother and your brothers are standing outside, asking to speak with you." But he said in reply to the one who told him, "Who is my mother? Who are my brothers?" And stretching out his hand toward his disciples, he said, "Here are my mother and my brothers. For whoever does the will of my heavenly Father is my brother, and sister, and mother."—The Gospel of the Lord.

---

4   Lk 1:26-38

✣ A reading from the holy Gospel according to Luke

THE angel Gabriel was sent from God to a town of Galilee called Nazareth, to a virgin betrothed to a man named Joseph, of the house of David, and the virgin's name was Mary. And coming to her, he said, "Hail, full of grace! The Lord is with you." But she was greatly troubled at what was said and pondered what sort of greeting this might be. Then the angel said to her, "Do not be afraid, Mary, for you have found favor with God. Behold, you will conceive in your womb and bear a son, and you shall name him Jesus. He will be great and will be called Son of the Most High, and the Lord God will give him the throne of David his father, and he will rule over the house of Jacob forever, and of his Kingdom there will be no end." But Mary said to the angel, "How can this be, since I have no relations with a man?" And the angel said to her in reply, "The Holy Spirit will come upon you, and the power of the Most High will overshadow you. Therefore the child to be born will be called holy, the Son of God. And behold, Elizabeth, your relative, has also conceived a son in her old age, and this is the sixth month for her who was called barren; for nothing will be impossible for God." Mary said, "Behold, I am the handmaid of the Lord. May it be done to me according to your word." Then the angel departed from her.—The Gospel of the Lord.

5   Lk 1:39-47

✠ A reading from the holy Gospel according to Luke

MARY set out and traveled to the hill country in haste to a town of Judah, where she entered the house of Zechariah and greeted Elizabeth. When Elizabeth heard Mary's greeting, the infant leaped in her womb, and Elizabeth, filled with the Holy Spirit, cried out in a loud voice and said, "Most blessed are you among women, and blessed is the fruit of your womb. And how does this happen to me, that the mother of my Lord should come to me? For at the moment the sound of your greeting reached my ears, the infant in my womb leaped for joy. Blessed are you who believed that what was spoken to you by the Lord would be fulfilled."

And Mary said:

    "My soul proclaims the greatness of the Lord;
      my spirit rejoices in God my savior."

The Gospel of the Lord.

6   Lk 2:1-14

✠ A reading from the holy Gospel according to Luke

IN those days a decree went out from Caesar Augustus that the whole world should be enrolled. This was the first enrollment, when Quirinius was governor of Syria. So all went to be enrolled, each to his own town. And Joseph too went up from Galilee from the town of Nazareth to Judea, to the city of David that is called Bethlehem, because he was of the house and family of David, to be enrolled with Mary, his betrothed, who was with child. While they were there, the time came for her to have her child, and she gave birth to her firstborn son. She wrapped him in swaddling clothes and laid him in a manger, because there was no room for them in the inn.

Now there were shepherds in that region living in the fields and keeping the night watch over their flock. The angel of the Lord appeared to them and the glory of the Lord shone around them, and they were struck with great fear. The angel said to them, "Do not be afraid; for behold, I proclaim to you good news of great joy that will be for all the people. For today in the city of David a savior has been born for you who is Christ and Lord. And this will be a sign for you: you will find an infant wrapped in swaddling clothes and lying in a manger." And suddenly there was a multitude of the heavenly host with the angel, praising God and saying:

"Glory to God in the highest

and on earth peace to those on whom his favor rests."
The Gospel of the Lord.

----

7   Lk 2:15b-19

✠ A reading from the holy Gospel according to Luke

THE shepherds said to one another, "Let us go, then, to Bethlehem to see this thing that has taken place, which the Lord has made known to us." So they went in haste and found Mary and Joseph and the infant lying in the manger. When they saw this, they made known the message that had been told them about this child. All who heard it were amazed by what had been told them by the shepherds. And Mary kept all these things, reflecting on them in her heart.— The Gospel of the Lord.

----

8   Lk 2:27-35

✚ A reading from the holy Gospel according to Luke

S IMEON came in the Spirit into the temple; and when the
parents brought in the child Jesus to perform the custom of the law in regard to him, he took him into his arms
and blessed God, saying:

> "Lord, now let your servant go in peace;
>   your word has been fulfilled;
> my own eyes have seen the salvation
>   which you prepared in the sight of every people:
> a light to reveal you to the nations
>   and the glory of your people Israel."

The child's father and mother were amazed at what was
said about him; and Simeon blessed them and said to Mary
his mother, "Behold, this child is destined for the fall and rise
of many in Israel, and to be a sign that will be contradicted
and you yourself a sword will pierce so that the thoughts of
many hearts may be revealed."—The Gospel of the Lord.

9   Lk 2:41-52

✚ A reading from the holy Gospel according to Luke

E ACH year Jesus' parents went to Jerusalem for the feast
of Passover, and when he was twelve years old, they
went up according to festival custom. After they had completed its days, as they were returning, the boy Jesus
remained behind in Jerusalem, but his parents did not know
it. Thinking that he was in the caravan, they journeyed for a
day and looked for him among their relatives and acquaintances, but not finding him, they returned to Jerusalem to
look for him. After three days they found him in the temple,
sitting in the midst of the teachers, listening to them and
asking them questions, and all who heard him were
astounded at his understanding and his answers. When his
parents saw him, they were astonished, and his mother said
to him, "Son, why have you done this to us? Your father and

I have been looking for you with great anxiety." And he said to them, "Why were you looking for me? Did you not know that I must be in my Father's house?" But they did not understand what he said to them. He went down with them and came to Nazareth, and was obedient to them; and his mother kept all these things in her heart. And Jesus advanced in wisdom and age and favor before God and man.—The Gospel of the Lord.

10
Lk 11:27-28

✠ A reading from the holy Gospel according to Luke

WHILE Jesus was speaking, a woman from the crowd called out and said to him, "Blessed is the womb that carried you and the breasts at which you nursed." He replied, "Rather, blessed are those who hear the word of God and observe it."—The Gospel of the Lord.

11
Jn 2:1-11

✠ A reading from the holy Gospel according to John

THERE was a wedding in Cana at Galilee, and the mother of Jesus was there. Jesus and his disciples were also invited to the wedding. When the wine ran short, the mother of Jesus said to him, "They have no wine." And Jesus said to her, "Woman, how does your concern affect me? My hour has not yet come." His mother said to the servers, "Do whatever he tells you." Now there were six stone water jars there for Jewish ceremonial washings, each holding twenty to thirty gallons. Jesus told them, "Fill the jars with water." So they filled them to the brim. Then he told them, "Draw some out now and take it to the headwaiter." So they took it. And when the headwaiter tasted the water that had become wine, without knowing where it came from although the servers who had drawn the water knew, the headwaiter called the bridegroom and said to him, "Everyone serves good wine first, and then when people have drunk freely, an inferior one; but you have kept the good wine until now." Jesus did this as the beginning of his signs in Cana in Galilee and so revealed his glory, and his disciples began to believe in him.—The Gospel of the Lord.

---

12 Jn 19:25-27

✛ A reading from the holy Gospel according to John

STANDING by the cross of Jesus were his mother and his mother's sister, Mary the wife of Clopas, and Mary Magdalene. When Jesus saw his mother and the disciple there whom he loved, he said to his mother, "Woman, behold, your son." Then he said to the disciple, "Behold, your mother." And from that hour the disciple took her into his home.— The Gospel of the Lord.

READING I
FROM THE OLD TESTAMENT

1   2 Chr 24:18-22

A reading from the second Book of Chronicles

THE princes of Judah forsook the temple of the LORD, the God of their fathers, and began to serve the sacred poles and the idols; and because of this crime of theirs, wrath came upon Judah and Jerusalem. Although prophets were sent to them to convert them to the LORD, the people would not listen to their warnings. Then the spirit of God possessed Zechariah, son of Jehoiada the priest. He took his stand above the people and said to them: "God says, 'Why are you transgressing the LORD's commands, so that you cannot prosper? Because you have abandoned the LORD, he has abandoned you.'"

But the people conspired against him, and at the king's order they stoned him to death in the court of the LORD's temple. Thus King Joash was unmindful of the devotion shown him by Jehoiada, Zechariah's father, and slew his son. And as he was dying, he said, "May the LORD see and avenge."—The word of the Lord.

2   2 Mc 6:18, 21, 24-31

A reading from the second Book of Maccabees

ELEAZAR, one of the foremost scribes, a man of advanced age and noble appearance, was being forced to open his mouth to eat pork. Those in charge of that unlawful ritual meal took the man aside privately, because of their long acquaintance with him, and urged him to bring meat of his own providing, such as he could legitimately eat, and to pretend to be eating some of the meat of the sacrifice prescribed by the king.

He told them: "At our age it would be unbecoming to make such a pretense; many young men would think the ninety-year-old Eleazar had gone over to an alien religion. Should I thus pretend for the sake of a brief moment of life, they would be led astray by me, while I would bring shame and dishonor on my old age. Even if, for the time being, I avoid the punishment of men, I shall never, whether alive or dead, escape the hands of the Almighty. Therefore, by manfully giving up my life now, I will prove myself worthy of my old age, and I will leave to the young a noble example of how to die willingly and generously for the revered and holy laws."

He spoke thus, and went immediately to the instrument of torture. Those who shortly before had been kindly disposed now became hostile toward him because what he had said seemed to them utter madness. When he was about to die under the blows, he groaned and said: "The LORD in his holy knowledge knows full well that, although I could have escaped death, I am not only enduring terrible pain in my body from this scourging, but also suffering it with joy in my soul because of my devotion to him." This is how he died, leaving in his death a model of courage and an unforgettable example of virtue not only for the young but for the whole nation.—The word of the Lord.

---

3   2 Mc 7:1-2, 9-14

A reading from the second Book of Maccabees

IT happened that seven brothers with their mother were arrested and tortured with whips and scourges by the king, to force them to eat pork in violation of God's law. One of the brothers, speaking for the others, said: "What do you expect to achieve by questioning us? We are ready to die rather than transgress the laws of our ancestors."

At the point of death, the second brother said: "You accursed fiend, you are depriving us of this present life, but the King of the world will raise us up to live again forever. It is for his laws that we are dying."

After him the third suffered their cruel sport. He put out his tongue at once when told to do so, and bravely held out his hands, as he spoke these noble words: "It was from Heaven that I received these; for the sake of his laws I disdain them; from him I hope to receive them again." Even the king and his attendants marveled at the young man's courage, because he regarded his sufferings as nothing.

After he had died, they tortured and maltreated the fourth brother in the same way. When he was near death, he said, "It is my choice to die at the hands of men with the hope God gives of being raised up by him; but for you, there will be no resurrection to life."—The word of the Lord.

---

4   2 Mc 7:1, 20-23, 27b-29

A reading from the second Book of Maccabees

IT happened that seven brothers with their mother were arrested and tortured with whips and scourges by the king, to force them to eat pork in violation of God's law.

Most admirable and worthy of everlasting remembrance was the mother, who saw her seven sons perish in a single day, yet bore it courageously because of her hope in the LORD. Filled with a noble spirit that stirred her womanly heart with manly courage she exhorted each of them in the language of their forefathers with these words: "I do not know how you came into existence in my womb; it was not I who gave you the breath of life, nor was it I who set in order the elements of which each of you is composed. Therefore, since it is the Creator of the universe who shapes each man's beginning, as he brings about the origin of everything, he, in his mercy, will give you back both breath and life, because you now disregard yourselves for the sake of his law."

"Son, have pity on me, who carried you in my womb for nine months, nursed you for three years, brought you up, educated and supported you to your present age. I beg you, child, to look at the heavens and the earth and see all that is in them; then you will know that God did not make them out of existing things; and in the same way the human race came into existence. Do not be afraid of this executioner, but be worthy of your brothers and accept death, so that in the time of mercy I may receive you again with them."—The word of the Lord.

5   Wis 3:1-9

A reading from the Book of Wisdom

THE souls of the just are in the hand of God,
   and no torment shall touch them.
They seemed, in the view of the foolish, to be dead;
     and their passing away was thought an affliction
     and their going forth from us, utter destruction.
But they are in peace.
For if before men, indeed, they be punished,
     yet is their hope full of immortality;
Chastised a little, they shall be greatly blessed,
     because God tried them
     and found them worthy of himself.
As gold in the furnace, he proved them,
     and as sacrificial offerings he took them to himself.
In the time of their visitation they shall shine,
     and shall dart about as sparks through stubble;
They shall judge nations and rule over peoples,
     and the LORD shall be their King forever.
Those who trust in him shall understand truth,
     and the faithful shall abide with him in love:
Because grace and mercy are with his holy ones,
     and his care is with his elect.
The word of the Lord.

6   Sir 51:1-8

A reading from the Book of Sirach

I GIVE you thanks, O Lord and King;
I praise you, O God my savior!
I will make known your name,
   for you have been a helper and a protector to me.
You have kept back my body from the pit,
   and from the scourge of a slanderous tongue,
   from lips that went over to falsehood.
And in the sight of those who stood by,
   you have delivered me,
According to the multitude of the mercy of your name,
   and from them that did roar, prepared to devour me,
And from the power of those who sought my life;
   from many a danger you have saved me,
   from flames that hemmed me in on every side;
From the midst of unremitting fire when I was not burnt,
   from the deep belly of the nether world;
From deceiving lips and painters of lies,
   from the arrows of dishonest tongues.
My soul was at the point of death,
   my life was nearing the depths of the nether world;
They encompassed me on every side, but there was no
     one to help me,
   I looked for one to sustain me, but could find no one.
But then I remembered the mercies of the LORD,
   his kindness through ages past;
For he saves those who take refuge in him,
   and rescues them from every evil.
The word of the Lord.

READING I FROM THE NEW TESTAMENT
DURING THE EASTER SEASON

1️⃣   Acts 7:55-60

A reading from the Acts of the Apostles

STEPHEN, filled with the Holy Spirit, looked up intently to heaven and saw the glory of God and Jesus standing at the right hand of God, and he said,"Behold, I see the heavens opened and the Son of Man standing at the right hand of God."But they cried out in a loud voice, covered their ears, and rushed upon him together. They threw him out of the city, and began to stone him. The witnesses laid down their cloaks at the feet of a young man named Saul. As they were stoning Stephen, he called out,"Lord Jesus, receive my spirit."Then he fell to his knees and cried out in a loud voice, "Lord, do not hold this sin against them"; and when he said this, he fell asleep.—The word of the Lord.

2️⃣   Rv 7:9-17

A reading from the Book of Revelation

I, JOHN, had a vision of a great multitude, which no one could count, from every nation, race, people, and tongue. They stood before the throne and before the Lamb, wearing white robes and holding palm branches in their hands. They cried out in a loud voice:

"Salvation comes from our God, who is seated on the throne,
    and from the Lamb."

All the angels stood around the throne and around the elders and the four living creatures. They prostrated themselves before the throne, worshiped God, and exclaimed:

"Amen. Blessing and glory, wisdom and thanksgiving,
    honor, power, and might
    be to our God forever and ever. Amen."

Then one of the elders spoke up and said to me, "Who are these wearing white robes, and where did they come from?" I said to him, "My lord, you are the one who knows." He said to me, "These are the ones who have survived the time of great distress; they have washed their robes and made them white in the Blood of the Lamb.

"For this reason they stand before God's throne
> and worship him day and night in his temple.
The One who sits on the throne will shelter them.
They will not hunger or thirst anymore,
> nor will the sun or any heat strike them.
For the Lamb who is in the center of the throne will shepherd them
> and lead them to springs of life-giving water,
> and God will wipe away every tear from their eyes."

The word of the Lord.

---

3   Rv 12:10-12b

A reading from the Book of Revelation

I, JOHN, heard a loud voice in heaven say:
"Now have salvation and power come,
> and the Kingdom of our God
> and the authority of his Anointed.
For the accuser of our brothers is cast out,
> who accuses them before our God day and night.
They conquered him by the Blood of the Lamb
> and by the word of their testimony;
> love for life did not deter them from death.
Therefore, rejoice, you heavens,
> and you who dwell in them."

The word of the Lord.

---

4   Rv 21:5-7

A reading from the Book of Revelation

THE One who was seated on the throne said: "Behold, I make all things new." Then he said, "Write these words down, for they are trustworthy and true." He said to me, "They are accomplished. I am the Alpha and the Omega, the beginning and the end. To the thirsty I will give a gift from the spring of life-giving water. The victor will inherit these gifts, and I shall be his God, and he will be my son."—The word of the Lord.

RESPONSORIAL PSALM

1   Ps 31:3cd-4, 6 and 8ab, 16bc and 17

℟. (6) **Into your hands, O Lord, I commend my spirit.**

Be my rock of refuge,
a stronghold to give me safety.
You are my rock and my fortress;
for your name's sake you will lead and guide me.—℟.

Into your hands I commend my spirit;
you will redeem me, O LORD, O faithful God.
I will rejoice and be glad because of your mercy.—℟.

Rescue me from the clutches of my enemies and my persecutors,
Let your face shine upon your servant;
save me in your kindness.—℟.

---

2   Ps 34:2-3, 4-5, 6-7, 8-9

℟. (5) **The Lord delivered me from all my fears.**

I will bless the LORD at all times;
his praise shall be ever in my mouth.
Let my soul glory in the LORD;
the lowly will hear me and be glad.—℟.

Glorify the LORD with me,
let us together extol his name.
I sought the LORD, and he answered me
and delivered me from all my fears.—℟.

Look to him that you may be radiant with joy,
  and your faces may not blush with shame.
When the afflicted man called out, the LORD heard,
  and from all his distress he saved him.—R̝.

The angel of the LORD encamps
  around those who fear him, and delivers them.
Taste and see how good the LORD is;
  blessed the man who takes refuge in him.—R̝.

---

3   Ps 124:2-3, 4-5, 7cd-8

R̝. (7) **Our soul has been rescued like a bird from the fowler's snare.**

Had not the LORD been with us—
When men rose up against us,
  then would they have swallowed us alive
When their fury was inflamed against us.—R̝.

Then would the waters have overwhelmed us;
The torrent would have swept over us;
  over us then would have swept
  the raging waters.—R̝.

Broken was the snare,
  and we were freed.
Our help is in the name of the LORD,
  who made heaven and earth.—R̝.

---

4   Ps 126:1bc-2ab, 2cd-3, 4-5, 6

R̝. (5) **Those who sow in tears shall reap rejoicing.**

When the LORD brought back the captives of Zion,
  we were like men dreaming.
Then our mouth was filled with laughter,
  and our tongue with rejoicing.—R̝.

Then they said among the nations,
  "The LORD has done great things for them."
The LORD has done great things for us;
  we are glad indeed.—R̝.

Restore our fortunes, O LORD,
  like the torrents in the southern desert.
Those who sow in tears
  shall reap rejoicing.—℟.

Although they go forth weeping,
  carrying the seed to be sown,
They shall come back rejoicing,
  carrying their sheaves.—℟.

READING II FROM THE NEW TESTAMENT

1   Rom 5:1-5

A reading from the Letter of Saint Paul to the Romans

BROTHERS and sisters: Since we have been justified by
faith, we have peace with God through our Lord Jesus
Christ, through whom we have gained access by faith to this
grace in which we stand, and we boast in hope of the glory
of God. Not only that, but we even boast of our afflictions,
knowing that affliction produces endurance, and endurance,
proven character, and proven character, hope, and hope
does not disappoint, because the love of God has been
poured out into our hearts through the Holy Spirit that has
been given to us.—The word of the Lord.

---

2   Rom 8:31b-39

A reading from the Letter of Saint Paul to the Romans

BROTHERS and sisters: If God is for us, who can be
against us? He who did not spare his own Son but handed him over for us all, how will he not also give us everything else along with him? Who will bring a charge against
God's chosen ones? It is God who acquits us. Who will condemn? Christ Jesus it is who died—or, rather, was raised—
who also is at the right hand of God, who indeed intercedes

for us. What will separate us from the love of Christ? Will anguish, or distress, or persecution, or famine, or nakedness, or peril, or the sword? As it is written:

For your sake we are being slain all the day;
we are looked upon as sheep to be slaughtered.

No, in all these things we conquer overwhelmingly through him who loved us. For I am convinced that neither death, nor life, nor angels, nor principalities, nor present things, nor future things, nor powers, nor height, nor depth, nor any other creature will be able to separate us from the love of God in Christ Jesus our Lord.—The word of the Lord.

| 3 | 2 Cor 4:7-15

A reading from the second Letter of Saint Paul
to the Corinthians

BROTHERS and sisters: We hold this treasure in earthen vessels, that the surpassing power may be of God and not from us. We are afflicted in every way, but not constrained; perplexed, but not driven to despair; persecuted, but not abandoned; struck down, but not destroyed; always carrying about in the body the dying of Jesus, so that the life of Jesus may also be manifested in our body. For we who live are constantly being given up to death for the sake of Jesus, so that the life of Jesus may be manifested in our mortal flesh.

So death is at work in us, but life in you. Since, then, we have the same spirit of faith, according to what is written, *I believed, therefore I spoke,* we too believe and therefore speak, knowing that the one who raised the Lord Jesus will raise us also with Jesus and place us with you in his presence. Everything indeed is for you, so that the grace bestowed in abundance on more and more people may cause the thanksgiving to overflow for the glory of God.—The word of the Lord.

---

4   2 Cor 6:4-10

A reading from the second Letter of Saint Paul
to the Corinthians

BROTHERS and sisters: In everything we commend ourselves as ministers of God, through much endurance, in afflictions, hardships, constraints, beatings, imprisonments, riots, labors, vigils, fasts; by purity, knowledge, patience, kindness, in the Holy Spirit, in unfeigned love, in truthful speech, in the power of God; with weapons of righteousness at the right and at the left; through glory and dishonor, insult and praise. We are treated as deceivers and yet are truthful; as unrecognized and yet acknowledged; as dying and behold we live; as chastised and yet not put to death; as sorrowful yet always rejoicing; as poor yet enriching many; as having nothing and yet possessing all things.—The word of the Lord.

---

5   2 Tm 2:8-13; 3:10-12

A reading from the second Letter of Saint Paul to Timothy

BELOVED: Remember Jesus Christ, raised from the dead, a descendant of David: such is my Gospel, for which I am suffering, even to the point of chains, like a criminal. But the word of God is not chained. Therefore, I bear with everything for the sake of those who are chosen, so that they too may obtain the salvation that is in Christ Jesus, together with eternal glory. This saying is trustworthy:

If we have died with him
    we shall also live with him;
if we persevere
    we shall also reign with him.
But if we deny him
    he will deny us.
If we are unfaithful
    he remains faithful,
        for he cannot deny himself.

You have followed my teaching, way of life, purpose, faith, patience, love, endurance, persecutions, and sufferings, such as happened to me in Antioch, Iconium, and Lystra, persecutions that I endured. Yet from all these things the Lord delivered me. In fact, all who want to live religiously in Christ Jesus will be persecuted.—The word of the Lord.

---

6   Heb 10:32-36

A reading from the Letter to the Hebrews

BROTHERS and sisters: Remember the days past when, after you had been enlightened, you endured a great contest of suffering. At times you were publicly exposed to abuse and affliction; at other times you associated yourselves with those so treated. You even joined in the sufferings of those in prison and joyfully accepted the confiscation of your property, knowing that you had a better and lasting possession. Therefore, do not throw away your confidence; it will have great recompense. You need endurance to do the will of God and receive what he has promised.—The word of the Lord.

---

7   Jas 1:2-4, 12

A reading from the Letter of Saint James

CONSIDER it all joy, my brothers and sisters, when you encounter various trials, for you know that the testing of your faith produces perseverance. And let perseverance be perfect, so that you may be perfect and complete, lacking in nothing.

Blessed is the man who perseveres in temptation, for when he has been proved he will receive the crown of life that he promised to those who love him.—The word of the Lord.

8
1 Pt 3:14-17

A reading from the first Letter of Saint Peter

BELOVED: Even if you should suffer because of righteousness, blessed are you. Do not be afraid or terrified with fear of them, but sanctify Christ as Lord in your hearts. Always be ready to give an explanation to anyone who asks you for a reason for your hope, but do it with gentleness and reverence, keeping your conscience clear, so that, when you are maligned, those who defame your good conduct in Christ may themselves be put to shame. For it is better to suffer for doing good, if that be the will of God, than for doing evil.—The word of the Lord.

9
1 Pt 4:12-19

A reading from the first Letter of Saint Peter

BELOVED, do not be surprised that a trial by fire is occurring among you, as if something strange were happening to you. But rejoice to the extent that you share in the sufferings of Christ, so that when his glory is revealed you may also rejoice exultantly. If you are insulted for the name of Christ, blessed are you, for the Spirit of glory and of God rests upon you. But let no one among you be made to suffer as a murderer, a thief, an evildoer, or as an intriguer. But whoever is made to suffer as a Christian should not be ashamed but glorify God because of the name. For it is time for the judgment to begin with the household of God; if it begins with us, how will it end for those who fail to obey the Gospel of God?

And if the righteous one is barely saved,
where will the godless and the sinner appear?

As a result, those who suffer in accord with God's will hand their souls over to a faithful creator as they do good.—The word of the Lord.

10   1 Jn 5:1-5

A reading from the first Letter of Saint John

BELOVED: Everyone who believes that Jesus is the Christ is begotten by God, and everyone who loves the Father loves also the one begotten by him. In this way we know that we love the children of God when we love God and obey his commandments. For the love of God is this, that we keep his commandments. And his commandments are not burdensome, for whoever is begotten by God conquers the world. And the victory that conquers the world is our faith. Who indeed is the victor over the world but the one who believes that Jesus is the Son of God?—The word of the Lord.

ALLELUIA VERSE AND VERSE BEFORE THE GOSPEL

1   Mt 5:10

Blessed are they who are persecuted for the sake of righteousness,
for theirs is the Kingdom of heaven.

2   Jn 17:19

I consecrate myself for them,
so that they also may be consecrated in the truth.

3   2 Cor 1:3b-4a

Blessed be the Father of compassion and God of all encouragement,
who encourages us in our every affliction.

4   Jas 1:12

Blessed is the man who perseveres in temptation,
for when he has been proved he will receive the crown of life.

5

1 Pt 4:14

If you are insulted for the name of Christ, blessed are you, for the Spirit of God rests upon you.

6

See *Te Deum*

We praise you, O God,
we acclaim you as Lord;
the white-robed army of martyrs praise you.

GOSPEL

1

Mt 10:17-22

✠ A reading from the holy Gospel according to Matthew

JESUS said to his Apostles: "Beware of men, for they will hand you over to courts and scourge you in their synagogues, and you will be led before governors and kings for my sake as a witness before them and the pagans. When they hand you over, do not worry about how you are to speak or what you are to say. You will be given at that moment what you are to say. For it will not be you who speak but the Spirit of your Father speaking through you. Brother will hand over brother to death, and the father his child; children will rise up against parents and have them put to death. You will be hated by all because of my name, but whoever endures to the end will be saved."—The Gospel of the Lord.

2

Mt 10:28-33

✠ A reading from the holy Gospel according to Matthew

JESUS said to his Apostles: "Do not be afraid of those who kill the body but cannot kill the soul; rather, be afraid of the one who can destroy both soul and body in Gehenna. Are not two sparrows sold for a small coin? Yet not one of them falls to the ground without your Father's knowledge. Even all the hairs of your head are counted. So do not be afraid; you are worth more than many sparrows. Everyone who acknowledges me before others I will acknowledge before my heavenly Father. But whoever denies me before others, I will deny before my heavenly Father."—The Gospel of the Lord.

---

3   Mt 10:34-39

✛ A reading from the holy Gospel according to Matthew

JESUS said to his Apostles: "Do not think that I have come to bring peace upon the earth. I have come to bring not peace but the sword. For I have come to set

> a man 'against his father,
>   a daughter against her mother,
>   and a daughter-in-law against her mother-in-law;
>   and one's enemies will be those of one's house-
>   hold.'

"Whoever loves father or mother more than me is not worthy of me, and whoever loves son or daughter more than me is not worthy of me; and whoever does not take up his cross and follow after me is not worthy of me. Whoever finds his life will lose it, and whoever loses his life for my sake will find it."—The Gospel of the Lord.

---

4   Lk 9:23-26

✛ A reading from the holy Gospel according to Luke

JESUS said to all, "If anyone wishes to come after me, he must deny himself and take up his cross daily and follow me. For whoever wishes to save his life will lose it, but whoever loses his life for my sake will save it. What profit is there for one to gain the whole world yet lose or forfeit himself? Whoever is ashamed of me and of my words, the Son of Man will be ashamed of when he comes in his glory and in the glory of the Father and of the holy angels."—The Gospel of the Lord.

---

5   Jn 12:24-26

✠ A reading from the holy Gospel according to John

JESUS said to his disciples: "Amen, amen, I say to you, unless a grain of wheat falls to the ground and dies, it remains just a grain of wheat; but if it dies, it produces much fruit. Whoever loves his life loses it, and whoever hates his life in this world will preserve it for eternal life. Whoever serves me must follow me, and where I am, there also will my servant be. The Father will honor whoever serves me."—The Gospel of the Lord.

---

6   Jn 15:18-21

✠ A reading from the holy Gospel according to John

JESUS said to his disciples: "If the world hates you, realize that it hated me first. If you belonged to the world, the world would love its own; but because you do not belong to the world, and I have chosen you out of the world, the world hates you. Remember the word I spoke to you, 'No slave is greater than his master.' If they persecuted me, they will also persecute you. If they kept my word, they will also keep yours. And they will do all these things to you on account of my name, because they do not know the one who sent me."—The Gospel of the Lord.

---

7   Jn 17:11b-19

✠ A reading from the holy Gospel according to John

LIFTING his eyes to heaven, Jesus prayed, saying: "Holy Father, keep them in your name that you have given me, so that they may be one just as we are one. When I was with them I protected them in your name that you gave me, and I guarded them, and none of them was lost except the son of destruction, in order that the Scripture might be fulfilled. But now I am coming to you. I speak this in the world so that they may share my joy completely. I gave them your word, and the world hated them, because they do not belong to the world any more than I belong to the world. I do not ask that you take them out of the world but that you keep them from the Evil One. They do not belong to the world any more than I belong to the world. Consecrate them in the truth. Your word is truth. As you sent me into the world, so I sent them into the world. And I consecrate myself for them, so that they also may be consecrated in truth."—The Gospel of the Lord.

COMMON OF PASTORS

READING I FROM THE OLD TESTAMENT OUTSIDE THE EASTER SEASON

1   Ex 32:7-14

A reading from the Book of Exodus

THE LORD said to Moses, "Go down at once to your people, whom you brought out of the land of Egypt, for they have become depraved. They have soon turned aside from the way I pointed out to them, making for themselves a molten calf and worshiping it, sacrificing to it and crying out, 'This is your God, O Israel, who brought you out of the land of Egypt!' I see how stiff-necked this people is," continued the LORD to Moses. "Let me alone, then, that my wrath may blaze up against them to consume them. Then I will make of you a great nation."

But Moses implored the LORD, his God, saying, "Why, O LORD, should your wrath blaze up against your own people, whom you brought out of the land of Egypt with such great power and with so strong a hand? Why should the Egyptians say, 'With evil intent he brought them out, that he might kill them in the mountains and exterminate them from the face of the earth'? Let your blazing wrath die down; relent in punishing your people. Remember your servants Abraham, Isaac, and Israel, and how you swore to them by your own self, saying, 'I will make your descendants as numerous as the stars in the sky; and all this land that I promised, I will give your descendants as their perpetual heritage.'" So the LORD relented in the punishment he had threatened to inflict on his people.—The word of the Lord.

□2   Dt 10:8-9

A reading from the Book of Deuteronomy

MOSES summoned all of Israel and said to them: "At that time the LORD set apart the tribe of Levi to carry the ark of the covenant of the LORD, to be in attendance before the LORD and minister to him, and to give blessings in his name, as they have done to this day. For this reason, Levi has no share in the heritage with his brothers; the LORD himself is his heritage, as the LORD, your God, has told him."—The word of the Lord.

_____

□3   1 Sm 16:1b, 6-13a

A reading from the first Book of Samuel

THE LORD said to Samuel: "Fill your horn with oil, and be on your way. I am sending you to Jesse of Bethlehem, for I have chosen my king from among his sons."

As Jesse and his sons came to the sacrifice, Samuel looked at Eliab and thought, "Surely the LORD's anointed is here before him." But the LORD said to Samuel: "Do not judge from his appearance or from his lofty stature, because I have rejected him. Not as man sees does God see, because he sees the appearance but the LORD looks into the heart." Then Jesse called Abinadab and presented him before Samuel, who said, "The LORD has not chosen him." Next Jesse presented Shammah, but Samuel said, "The LORD has not chosen this one either." In the same way Jesse presented seven sons before Samuel, but Samuel said to Jesse, "The LORD has not chosen any one of these." Then Samuel asked Jesse, "Are these all the sons you have?" Jesse replied, "There is still the youngest, who is tending the sheep." Samuel said to Jesse, "Send for him; we will not begin the sacrificial banquet until he arrives here." Jesse sent and had the young man brought to them. He was ruddy, a youth handsome to behold and making a splendid appearance. The LORD said, "There—anoint him, for this is he!" Then Samuel, with the horn of oil in hand, anointed him in the midst of his brothers; and from that day on, the spirit of the LORD rushed upon David.—The word of the Lord.

4⃞   Is 6:1-8

A reading from the Book of the Prophet Isaiah

IN the year King Uzziah died, I saw the Lord seated on a high and lofty throne, with the train of his garment filling the temple. Seraphim were stationed above; each of them had six wings: with two they veiled their faces, with two they veiled their feet, and with two they hovered aloft.

"Holy, holy, holy is the LORD of hosts!" they cried, one to the other. "All the earth is filled with his glory!" At the sound of that cry, the frame of the door shook and the house was filled with smoke.

Then I said, "Woe is me, I am doomed! For I am a man of unclean lips, living among a people of unclean lips; yet my eyes have seen the King, the LORD of hosts!" Then one of the seraphim flew to me, holding an ember which he had taken with tongs from the altar.

He touched my mouth with it and said, "See, now that this has touched your lips, your wickedness is removed, your sin purged." Then I heard the voice of the Lord saying, "Whom shall I send? Who will go for us?" "Here I am," I said; "send me!"—The word of the Lord.

5⃞   Is 52:7-10

[For Missionaries]

A reading from the Book of the Prophet Isaiah

HOW beautiful upon the mountains
are the feet of him who brings glad tidings,
Announcing peace, bearing good news,
    announcing salvation, and saying to Zion,
    "Your God is King!"

Hark! Your sentinels raise a cry,
   together they shout for joy,
For they see directly, before their eyes,
   the LORD restoring Zion.
Break out together in song,
   O ruins of Jerusalem!
For the LORD comforts his people,
   he redeems Jerusalem.
The LORD has bared his holy arm
   in the sight of all the nations;
All the ends of the earth will behold
   the salvation of our God.
The word of the Lord.

---

6   Is 61:1-3d

A reading from the Book of the Prophet Isaiah

THE spirit of the Lord GOD is upon me,
   because the LORD has anointed me;
He has sent me to bring glad tidings to the lowly,
   to heal the brokenhearted,
To proclaim liberty to the captives
   and release to the prisoners,
To announce a year of favor from the LORD
   and a day of vindication by our God,
   to comfort all who mourn;
To place on those who mourn in Zion
   a diadem instead of ashes,
To give them oil of gladness in place of mourning,
   a glorious mantle instead of a listless spirit.
The word of the Lord.

---

7   Jer 1:4-9

A reading from the Book of the Prophet Jeremiah

THE word of the LORD came to me thus:
   Before I formed you in the womb I knew you,

before you were born I dedicated you,
a prophet to the nations I appointed you.

"Ah, Lord GOD!" I said,
"I know not how to speak; I am too young."

But the LORD answered me,

Say not, "I am too young."
To whomever I send you, you shall go;
whatever I command you, you shall speak.
Have no fear before them,
because I am with you to deliver you, says the LORD.

Then the LORD extended his hand and touched my mouth, saying,

See, I place my words in your mouth!
The word of the Lord.

---

8   Ez 3:17-21

A reading from the Book of the Prophet Ezekiel

THE word of the LORD came to me: Son of man, I have appointed you a watchman for the house of Israel. When you hear a word from my mouth, you shall warn them for me.

If I say to the wicked man, You shall surely die; and you do not warn him or speak out to dissuade him from his wicked conduct so that he may live: the wicked man shall die for his sin, but I will hold you responsible for his death. If, on the other hand, you have warned the wicked man, yet he has not turned away from his evil nor from his wicked conduct, then he shall die for his sin, but you shall save your life.

If a virtuous man turns away from virtue and does wrong when I place a stumbling block before him, he shall die. He shall die for his sin, and his virtuous deeds shall not be remembered; but I will hold you responsible for his death if you did not warn him. When, on the other hand, you have warned a virtuous man not to sin, and he has in fact not sinned, he shall surely live because of the warning, and you shall save your own life.—The word of the Lord.

---

9   Ez 34:11-16

A reading from the Book of the Prophet Ezekiel

THUS says the Lord GOD: I myself will look after and tend my sheep. As a shepherd tends his flock when he finds himself among his scattered sheep, so will I tend my sheep. I will rescue them from every place where they were scattered when it was cloudy and dark. I will lead them out from among the peoples and gather them from the foreign lands; I will bring them back to their own country and pasture them upon the mountains of Israel in the land's ravines and all its inhabited places. In good pastures will I pasture them, and on the mountain heights of Israel shall be their grazing ground. There they shall lie down on good grazing ground, and in rich pastures shall they be pastured on the mountains of Israel. I myself will pasture my sheep; I myself will give them rest, says the Lord GOD. The lost I will seek out, the strayed I will bring back, the injured I will bind up, the sick I will heal, but the sleek and the strong I will destroy, shepherding them rightly.—The word of the Lord.

READING I FROM THE NEW TESTAMENT DURING THE EASTER SEASON

1   Acts 13:46-49

[For Missionaries]

A reading from the Acts of the Apostles

PAUL and Barnabas spoke out boldly and said, "It was necessary that the word of God be spoken to you first, but since you reject it and condemn yourselves as unworthy of eternal life, we now turn to the Gentiles. For so the Lord has commanded us, *I have made you a light to the Gentiles, that you may be an instrument of salvation to the ends of the earth.*"

The Gentiles were delighted when they heard this and glorified the word of the Lord. All who were destined for eternal life came to believe, and the word of the Lord continued to spread through the whole region.—The word of the Lord.

---

2   Acts 20:17-18a, 28-32, 36

A reading from the Acts of the Apostles

FROM Miletus Paul had the presbyters of the Church at Ephesus summoned. When they came to him, he addressed them, "Keep watch over yourselves and over the whole flock of which the Holy Spirit has appointed you overseers, in which you tend the Church of God that he acquired with his own Blood. I know that after my departure savage wolves will come among you, and they will not spare the flock. And from your own group, men will come forward perverting the truth to draw the disciples away after them. So be vigilant and remember that for three years, night and day, I unceasingly admonished each of you with tears. And now I commend you to God and to that gracious word of his that can build you up and give you the inheritance among all who are consecrated."

When he had finished speaking he knelt down and prayed with them all.—The word of the Lord.

---

3   Acts 26:19-23

[For Missionaries]

A reading from the Acts of the Apostles

PAUL said: "King Agrippa, I was not disobedient to the heavenly vision. On the contrary, first to those in Damascus and in Jerusalem and throughout the whole country of Judea, and then to the Gentiles, I preached the need to repent and turn to God, and to do works giving evidence of repentance. That is why the Jews seized me when I was in the temple and tried to kill me. But I have enjoyed God's help to this very day, and so I stand here testifying to small and great alike, saying nothing different from what the prophets and Moses foretold, that the Christ must suffer and that, as the first to rise from the dead, he would proclaim light both to our people and to the Gentiles."—The word of the Lord.

RESPONSORIAL PSALM

1   Ps 16:1-2a and 5, 7-8, 11

℟. (see 5a) **You are my inheritance, O Lord.**

Keep me, O God, for in you I take refuge;
  I say to the LORD, "My Lord are you."
O LORD, my allotted portion and my cup,
  you it is who hold fast my lot.—℟.

I bless the LORD who counsels me;
  even in the night my heart exhorts me.
I set the LORD ever before me;
  with him at my right hand I shall not be disturbed.—℟.

You will show me the path to life,
  fullness of joys in your presence,
  the delights at your right hand forever.—℟.

2   Ps 23:1-3a, 4, 5, 6

℟. (1) **The Lord is my shepherd; there is nothing I shall want.**

The LORD is my shepherd; I shall not want.
  In verdant pastures he gives me repose;
Beside restful waters he leads me;
  he refreshes my soul.—℟.

Even though I walk in the dark valley
  I fear no evil; for you are at my side
With your rod and your staff
  that give me courage.—℟.

You spread the table before me
  in the sight of my foes;

You anoint my head with oil;
　　my cup overflows.—R̸.

Only goodness and kindness follow me
　　all the days of my life;
And I shall dwell in the house of the LORD
　　for years to come.—R̸.

―――――――――――

3　　　　　　　　　　　　Ps 40:2 and 4, 7-8a, 8b-9, 10

R̸. (8a and 9a) **Here I am, Lord; I come to do your will.**

I have waited, waited for the LORD,
　　and he stooped toward me and heard my cry.
And he put a new song into my mouth,
　　a hymn to our God.—R̸.

Sacrifice or offering you wished not,
　　but ears open to obedience you gave me.
Burnt offerings or sin-offerings you sought not;
　　then said I, "Behold I come."—R̸.

"In the written scroll it is prescribed for me,
To do your will, O my God, is my delight,
　　and your law is within my heart!"—R̸.

I announced your justice in the vast assembly;
　　I did not restrain my lips, as you, O LORD, know.—R̸.

―――――――――――

4　　　　　　　　　　　　Ps 89:2-3, 4-5, 21-22, 25 and 27

R̸. (2) **For ever I will sing the goodness of the Lord.**

The favors of the LORD I will sing forever;
　　through all generations my mouth shall proclaim your
　　　　faithfulness.
For you have said, "My kindness is established forever";
　　in heaven you have confirmed your faithfulness.—R̸.

"I have made a covenant with my chosen one,
　　I have sworn to David my servant:
Forever will I confirm your posterity
　　and establish your throne for all generations."—R̸.

"I have found David, my servant;
　　with my holy oil I have anointed him,
That my hand may be always with him,
　　and that my arm may make him strong."—℟.

"My faithfulness and my mercy shall be with him,
　　and through my name shall his horn be exalted.
He shall say of me, 'You are my father,
　　my God, the Rock, my savior.' "—℟.

5　　　　　　　　　　　　　　Ps 96:1-2a, 2b-3, 7-8a, 10

℟. (3) **Proclaim God's marvelous deeds to all the nations.**

Sing to the LORD a new song;
　　sing to the LORD, all you lands.
Sing to the LORD; bless his name.—℟.

Announce his salvation, day after day.
Tell his glory among the nations;
　　among all peoples, his wondrous deeds.—℟.

Give to the LORD, you families of nations,
　　give to the LORD glory and praise;
　　give to the LORD the glory due his name!—℟.

Say among the nations: The LORD is king.
He has made the world firm, not to be moved;
　　he governs the peoples with equity.—℟.

6　　　　　　　　　　　　　　　Ps 106:19-20, 21-22, 23

℟. (4a) **Remember us, O Lord, as you favor your people.**

Our fathers made a calf in Horeb
　　and adored a molten image;
They exchanged their glory
　　for the image of a grass-eating bullock.—℟.

They forgot the God who had saved them,
　　who had done great deeds in Egypt,
Wondrous deeds in the land of Ham,
　　terrible things at the Red Sea.—℟.

Then he spoke of exterminating them,
  but Moses, his chosen one,
Withstood him in the breach
  to turn back his destructive wrath.—℞.

---

7 Ps 110:1, 2, 3, 4

℞. (4b) **You are a priest for ever, in the line of Melchizedek.**

The LORD said to my Lord:"Sit at my right hand
  till I make your enemies your footstool."—℞.

The scepter of your power the LORD will stretch forth from
    Zion:
  "Rule in the midst of your enemies."—℞.

"Yours is princely power in the day of your birth, in holy
    splendor;
  before the daystar, like the dew, I have begotten you."—℞.

The Lord has sworn, and he will not repent:
  "You are a priest forever, according to the order of
    Melchizedek."—℞.

---

8 Ps 117:1bc, 2

℞. (Mk 16:15) **Go out to all the world and tell the Good
News.**

℞. Or: **Alleluia.**

Praise the LORD, all you nations;
  glorify him, all you peoples!—℞.

For steadfast is his kindness toward us,
  and the fidelity of the LORD endures forever.—℞.

READING II FROM THE NEW TESTAMENT

1 Rom 12:3-13

A reading from the Letter of Saint Paul to the Romans

BROTHERS and sisters: By the grace given to me I tell
everyone among you not to think of himself more high-

ly than one ought to think, but to think soberly, each according to the measure of faith that God has apportioned. For as
in one body we have many parts, and all the parts do not
have the same function, so we, though many, are one Body
in Christ and individually parts of one another. Since we
have gifts that differ according to the grace given to us, let
us exercise them: if prophecy, in proportion to the faith; if
ministry, in ministering; if one is a teacher, in teaching; if one
exhorts, in exhortation; if one contributes, in generosity; if
one is over others, with diligence; if one does acts of mercy,
with cheerfulness.

Let love be sincere; hate what is evil, hold on to what is
good; love one another with mutual affection; anticipate one
another in showing honor. Do not grow slack in zeal, be fervent in spirit, serve the Lord. Rejoice in hope, endure in
affliction, persevere in prayer. Contribute to the needs of the
holy ones, exercise hospitality.—The word of the Lord.

---

2   1 Cor 1:18-25

[For Missionaries]

A reading from the first Letter of Saint Paul to the
Corinthians

BROTHERS and sisters: The message of the cross is
foolishness to those who are perishing, but to us who are
being saved it is the power of God. For it is written:

I will destroy the wisdom of the wise,
and the learning of the learned I will set aside.

Where is the wise one? Where is the scribe? Where is the
debater of this age? Has not God made the wisdom of the
world foolish? For since in the wisdom of God the world did
not come to know God through wisdom, it was the will of
God through the foolishness of the proclamation to save
those who have faith. For Jews demand signs and Greeks
look for wisdom, but we proclaim Christ crucified, a stumbling block to Jews and foolishness to Gentiles, but to those

who are called, Jews and Greeks alike, Christ the power of God and the wisdom of God. For the foolishness of God is wiser than human wisdom, and the weakness of God is stronger than human strength.—The word of the Lord.

---

3   1 Cor 4:1-5

A reading from the first Letter of Saint Paul to the Corinthians

BROTHERS and sisters: Thus should one regard us: as servants of Christ and stewards of the mysteries of God. Now it is of course required of stewards that they be found trustworthy. It does not concern me in the least that I be judged by you or any human tribunal; I do not even pass judgment on myself; I am not conscious of anything against me, but I do not thereby stand acquitted; the one who judges me is the Lord. Therefore do not make any judgment before the appointed time, until the Lord comes, for he will bring to light what is hidden in darkness and will manifest the motives of our hearts, and then everyone will receive praise from God.—The word of the Lord.

---

4   1 Cor 9:16-19, 22-23

A reading from the first Letter of Saint Paul to the Corinthians

BROTHERS and sisters: If I preach the Gospel, this is no reason for me to boast, for an obligation has been imposed on me, and woe to me if I do not preach it! If I do so willingly, I have a recompense, but if unwillingly, then I have been entrusted with a stewardship. What then is my recompense? That, when I preach, I offer the Gospel free of charge so as not to make full use of my right in the Gospel.

Although I am free in regard to all, I have made myself a slave to all so as to win over as many as possible. To the weak I became weak, to win over the weak. I have become all things to all, to save at least some. All this I do for the sake of the Gospel, so that I too may have a share in it.—The word of the Lord.

---

5   2 Cor 3:1-6a

A reading from the second Letter of Saint Paul to the Corinthians

BROTHERS and sisters: Are we beginning to commend ourselves again? Do we need, as some do, letters of recommendation to you or from you? You are our letter, written on our hearts, known and read by all, shown to be a letter of Christ administered by us, written not in ink but by the Spirit of the living God, not on tablets of stone but on tablets that are hearts of flesh.

Such confidence we have through Christ toward God. Not that of ourselves we are qualified to take credit for anything as coming from us; rather, our qualification comes from God, who has indeed qualified us as ministers of a new covenant, not of letter but of spirit.—The word of the Lord.

---

6   2 Cor 4:1-2, 5-7

A reading from the second Letter of Saint Paul to the Corinthians

BROTHERS and sisters: Since we have this ministry through the mercy shown us, we are not discouraged. Rather, we have renounced shameful, hidden things; not acting deceitfully or falsifying the word of God, but by the open declaration of the truth we commend ourselves to everyone's conscience in the sight of God. For we do not preach ourselves but Jesus Christ as Lord, and ourselves as your slaves for the sake of Jesus. For God who said, *Let light shine out of darkness,* has shone in our hearts to bring to light the knowledge of the glory of God on the face of Jesus Christ.

But we hold this treasure in earthen vessels, that the surpassing power may be of God and not from us.—The word of the Lord.

7   2 Cor 5:14-20

A reading from the second Letter of Saint Paul to the
Corinthians

BROTHERS and sisters: The love of Christ impels us, once
we have come to the conviction that one died for all;
therefore, all have died. He indeed died for all, so that those
who live might no longer live for themselves but for him
who for their sake died and was raised.

Consequently, from now on we regard no one according
to the flesh; even if we once knew Christ according to the
flesh, yet now we know him so no longer. So whoever is in
Christ is a new creation: the old things have passed away;
behold, new things have come. And all this is from God, who
has reconciled us to himself through Christ and given us the
ministry of reconciliation, namely, God was reconciling the
world to himself in Christ, not counting their trespasses
against them and entrusting to us the message of reconciliation. So we are ambassadors for Christ, as if God were
appealing through us. We implore you on behalf of Christ, be
reconciled to God.—The word of the Lord.

---

8   Eph 4:1-7, 11-13

A reading from the Letter of Saint Paul to the Ephesians

BROTHERS and sisters, I, a prisoner for the Lord, urge
you to live in a manner worthy of the call you have
received, with all humility and gentleness, with patience,
bearing with one another through love, striving to preserve
the unity of the spirit through the bond of peace: one Body
and one Spirit, as you were also called to the one hope of
your call; one Lord, one faith, one baptism; one God and
Father of all, who is over all and through all and in all.

But grace was given to each of us according to the measure of Christ's gift.

And he gave some as Apostles, others as prophets, others
as evangelists, others as pastors and teachers, to equip the

holy ones for the work of ministry, for building up the Body of Christ, until we all attain to the unity of faith and knowledge of the Son of God, to mature manhood, to the extent of the full stature of Christ.—The word of the Lord.

---

9   Col 1:24-29

A reading from the Letter of Saint Paul to the Colossians

BROTHERS and sisters: I rejoice in my sufferings for your sake, and in my flesh I am filling up what is lacking in the afflictions of Christ on behalf of his Body, which is the Church, of which I am a minister in accordance with God's stewardship given to me to bring to completion for you the word of God, the mystery hidden from ages and from generations past. But now it has been manifested to his holy ones, to whom God chose to make known the riches of the glory of this mystery among the Gentiles; it is Christ in you, the hope for glory. It is he whom we proclaim, admonishing everyone and teaching everyone with all wisdom, that we may present everyone perfect in Christ. For this I labor and struggle, in accord with the exercise of his power working within me.—The word of the Lord.

---

10   1 Thes 2:2b-8

A reading from the first Letter of Saint Paul to the Thessalonians

BROTHERS and sisters: We drew courage through our God to speak to you the Gospel of God with much struggle. Our exhortation was not from delusion or impure motives, nor did it work through deception. But as we were judged worthy by God to be entrusted with the Gospel, that is how we speak, not as trying to please men, but rather God, who judges our hearts. Nor, indeed, did we ever appear with flattering speech, as you know, or with a pretext for greed— God is witness—nor did we seek praise from men, either from you or from others, although we were able to impose our weight as Apostles of Christ. Rather, we were gentle among you, as a nursing mother cares for her children. With such affection for you, we were determined to share with you not only the Gospel of God, but our very selves as well, so dearly beloved had you become to us.—The word of the Lord.

---

11   2 Tm 1:13-14; 2:1-3

A reading from the second Letter of Saint Paul to Timothy

BELOVED: Take as your norm the sound words that you heard from me, in the faith and love that are in Christ Jesus. Guard this rich trust with the help of the Holy Spirit who dwells within us. So you, my child, be strong in the grace that is in Christ Jesus. And what you heard from me through many witnesses entrust to faithful people who will have the ability to teach others as well. Bear your share of hardship along with me like a good soldier of Christ Jesus.—The word of the Lord.

---

12   2 Tm 4:1-5

A reading from the second Letter of Saint Paul to Timothy

BELOVED: I charge you in the presence of God and of Christ Jesus, who will judge the living and the dead, and by his appearing and his kingly power: proclaim the word; be persistent whether it is convenient or inconvenient; convince, reprimand, encourage through all patience and teaching. For the time will come when people will not tolerate sound doctrine but, following their own desires and insatiable curiosity, will accumulate teachers and will stop listening to the truth and will be diverted to myths. But you, be self-possessed in all circumstances; put up with hardship; perform the work of an evangelist; fulfill your ministry.—The word of the Lord.

13   1 Pt 5:1-4

A reading from the first Letter of Saint Peter

BELOVED: I exhort the presbyters among you, as a fellow presbyter and witness to the sufferings of Christ and one who has a share in the glory to be revealed. Tend the flock of God in your midst, overseeing it not by constraint but willingly, as God would have it, not for shameful profit but eagerly. Do not lord it over those assigned to you, but be examples to the flock. And when the chief Shepherd is revealed, you will receive the unfading crown of glory.—The word of the Lord.

ALLELUIA VERSE AND
VERSE BEFORE THE GOSPEL

1   Mt 23:9b, 10b

You have but one Father in heaven;
you have but one master, the Christ!

2   Mt 28:19a, 20bc

Go, and teach all nations, says the Lord;
I am with you always, until the end of the world.

3   Mk 1:17

Come after me, says the Lord,
and I will make you fishers of men.

4   Lk 4:18

The Lord sent me to bring glad tidings to the poor
and to proclaim liberty to captives.

5   Jn 10:14

I am the good shepherd, says the Lord;
I know my sheep, and mine know me.

6   Jn 15:5

I am the vine, you are the branches, says the Lord:
whoever remains in me and I in him will bear much fruit.

7   Jn 15:15b

I call you my friends, says the Lord,
for I have made known to you all that the Father has told me.

8   2 Cor 5:19

God was reconciling the world to himself in Christ,
and entrusting to us the message of reconciliation.

GOSPEL

1   Mt 9:35-38

✠ A reading from the holy Gospel according to Matthew

JESUS went around to all the towns and villages, teaching in their synagogues, proclaiming the Gospel of the Kingdom, and curing every disease and illness. At the sight of the crowds, his heart was moved with pity for them because they were troubled and abandoned, like sheep without a shepherd. Then he said to his disciples, "The harvest is abundant but the laborers are few; so ask the master of the harvest to send out laborers for his harvest."—The Gospel of the Lord.

---

2   Mt 16:13-19

[For a Pope]

✠ A reading from the holy Gospel according to Matthew

JESUS went into the region of Caesarea Philippi and he asked his disciples, "Who do people say that the Son of Man is?" They replied, "Some say John the Baptist, others Elijah, still others Jeremiah or one of the prophets." He said to them, "But who do you say that I am?" Simon Peter said in reply, "You are the Christ, the Son of the living God." Jesus said to him in reply, "Blessed are you, Simon son of Jonah. For flesh and blood has not revealed this to you, but my heavenly Father. And so I say to you, you are Peter, and upon this rock I will build my Church, and the gates of the netherworld shall not prevail against it. I will give you the keys to the Kingdom of heaven. Whatever you bind on earth shall be bound in heaven; and whatever you loose on earth shall be loosed in heaven."—The Gospel of the Lord.

---

3   Mt 23:8-12

✠ A reading from the holy Gospel according to Matthew

JESUS spoke to his disciples: "Do not be called 'Rabbi.' You have but one teacher, and you are all brothers. Call no one on earth your father; you have but one Father in heaven. Do not be called 'Master'; you have but one master, the Christ. The greatest among you must be your servant. Whoever exalts himself will be humbled; but whoever humbles himself will be exalted."—The Gospel of the Lord.

---

4   Mt 28:16-20

[For Missionaries]

✠ A reading from the holy Gospel according to Matthew

THE Eleven disciples went to Galilee, to the mountain to which Jesus had ordered them. When they saw him, they worshiped, but they doubted. Then Jesus approached and said to them, "All power in heaven and on earth has been given to me. Go, therefore, and make disciples of all nations, baptizing them in the name of the Father, and of the Son, and of the Holy Spirit, teaching them to observe all that I have commanded you. And behold, I am with you always, until the end of the age."—The Gospel of the Lord.

5   Mk 1:14-20

✛ A reading from the holy Gospel according to Mark

AFTER John had been arrested, Jesus came to Galilee proclaiming the Gospel of God:"This is the time of fulfillment. The Kingdom of God is at hand. Repent, and believe in the Gospel."

As he passed by the Sea of Galilee, he saw Simon and his brother Andrew casting their nets into the sea; they were fishermen. Jesus said to them, "Come after me, and I will make you fishers of men." Then they abandoned their nets and followed him. He walked along a little farther and saw James, the son of Zebedee, and his brother John. They too were in a boat mending their nets. Then he called them. So they left their father Zebedee in the boat along with the hired men and followed him.—The Gospel of the Lord.

6   Mk 16:15-20

[For Missionaries]

✛ A reading from the holy Gospel according to Mark

JESUS appeared to the Eleven and said to them: "Go into the whole world and proclaim the Gospel to every creature. Whoever believes and is baptized will be saved; whoever does not believe will be condemned. These signs will accompany those who believe: in my name they will drive out demons, they will speak new languages. They will pick up serpents with their hands, and if they drink any deadly thing, it will not harm them. They will lay hands on the sick, and they will recover." So then the Lord Jesus, after he spoke to them, was taken up into heaven and took his seat at the right hand of God. But they went forth and preached everywhere, while the Lord worked with them and confirmed the word through accompanying signs.—The Gospel of the Lord.

7   Lk 5:1-11

[For Missionaries]

✛ A reading from the holy Gospel according to Luke

WHILE the crowd was pressing in on Jesus and listening to the word of God, he was standing by the Lake of Gennesaret. He saw two boats there alongside the lake; the fishermen had disembarked and were washing their nets. Getting into one of them, the one belonging to Simon, he asked him to put out a short distance from the shore. Then he sat down and taught the crowds from the boat. After he had finished speaking, he said to Simon, "Put out into deep water and lower your nets for a catch." Simon said in reply, "Master, we have worked hard all night and have caught nothing, but at your command I will lower the nets." When they had done this, they caught a great number of fish and their nets were tearing. They signaled to their partners in the other boat to come to help them. They came and filled both boats so that the boats were in danger of sinking. When Simon Peter saw this, he fell at the knees of Jesus and said, "Depart from me, Lord, for I am a sinful man." For astonishment at the catch of fish they had made seized him and all those with him, and likewise James and John, the sons of Zebedee, who were partners of Simon. Jesus said to Simon, "Do not be afraid; from now on you will be catching men." When they brought their boats to the shore, they left everything and followed him.—The Gospel of the Lord.

———————

8   Lk 10:1-9

✛ A reading from the holy Gospel according to Luke

THE Lord Jesus appointed seventy-two disciples whom he sent ahead of him in pairs to every town and place he intended to visit. He said to them, "The harvest is abundant but the laborers are few; so ask the master of the harvest to send out laborers for his harvest. Go on your way; behold, I am sending you like lambs among wolves. Carry no money bag, no sack, no sandals; and greet no one along the way. Into whatever house you enter, first say, 'Peace to this household.' If a peaceful person lives there, your peace will rest on him; but if not, it will return to you. Stay in the same house and eat and drink what is offered to you, for the laborer deserves his payment. Do not move about from one house to another. Whatever town you enter and they welcome you, eat what is set before you, cure the sick in it and say to them, 'The Kingdom of God is at hand for you.'"—The Gospel of the Lord.

---

9 | Lk 22:24-30

✠ A reading from the holy Gospel according to Luke

AN argument broke out among the Apostles about which of them should be regarded as the greatest. Jesus said to them, "The kings of the Gentiles lord it over them and those in authority over them are addressed as 'Benefactors'; but among you it shall not be so. Rather, let the greatest among you be as the youngest, and the leader as the servant. For who is greater: the one seated at table or the one who serves? Is it not the one seated at table? I am among you as the one who serves. It is you who have stood by me in my trials; and I confer a kingdom on you, just as my Father has conferred one on me, that you may eat and drink at my table in my Kingdom; and you will sit on thrones judging the twelve tribes of Israel."—The Gospel of the Lord.

---

10 | Jn 10:11-16

✠ A reading from the holy Gospel according to John

JESUS said: "I am the good shepherd. A good shepherd lays down his life for the sheep. A hired man, who is not a shepherd and whose sheep are not his own, sees a wolf coming and leaves the sheep and runs away, and the wolf catches and scatters them. This is because he works for pay and has no concern for the sheep. I am the good shepherd, and I know mine and mine know me, just as the Father knows me and I know the Father; and I will lay down my life for the sheep. I have other sheep that do not belong to this fold. These also I must lead, and they will hear my voice, and there will be one flock, one shepherd."—The Gospel of the Lord.

11

Jn 15:9-17

✠ A reading from the holy Gospel according to John

JESUS said to his disciples: "As the Father loves me, so I also love you. Remain in my love. If you keep my commandments, you will remain in my love, just as I have kept my Father's commandments and remain in his love.

"I have told you this so that my joy might be in you and your joy might be complete. This is my commandment: love one another as I love you. No one has greater love than this, to lay down one's life for one's friends. You are my friends if you do what I command you. I no longer call you slaves, because a slave does not know what his master is doing. I have called you friends, because I have told you everything I have heard from my Father. It was not you who chose me, but I who chose you and appointed you to go and bear fruit that will remain, so that whatever you ask the Father in my name he may give you. This I command you: love one another."—The Gospel of the Lord.

12

Jn 21:15-17

[For a Pope]

✠ A reading from the holy Gospel according to John

AFTER Jesus had revealed himself to his disciples and eaten breakfast with them, he said to Simon Peter, "Simon, son of John, do you love me more than these?" Simon Peter answered him, "Yes, Lord, you know that I love you." Jesus said to him, "Feed my lambs." He then said to

Simon Peter a second time, "Simon, son of John, do you love me?" Simon Peter answered him, "Yes, Lord, you know that I love you." He said to him, "Tend my sheep." He said to him the third time, "Simon, son of John, do you love me?" Peter was distressed that he had said to him a third time, "Do you love me?" and he said to him, "Lord, you know everything; you know that I love you." Jesus said to him, "Feed my sheep."— The Gospel of the Lord.

COMMON OF DOCTORS
OF THE CHURCH

READING I FROM THE OLD TESTAMENT

1   1 Kgs 3:11-14

A reading from the first Book of Kings

THE LORD said to Solomon: "Because you have asked for this—not for a long life for yourself, nor for riches, nor for the life of your enemies, but for understanding so that you may know what is right—I do as you requested. I give you a heart so wise and understanding that there has never been anyone like you up to now, and after you there will come no one to equal you. In addition, I give you what you have not asked for, such riches and glory that among kings there is not your like. And if you follow me by keeping my statutes and commandments, as your father David did, I will give you a long life."—The word of the Lord.

---

2   Wis 7:7-10, 15-16

A reading from the Book of Wisdom

I PRAYED, and prudence was given me;
I pleaded, and the spirit of wisdom came to me.
I preferred her to scepter and throne,
And deemed riches nothing in comparison with her,
    nor did I liken any priceless gem to her;
Because all gold, in view of her, is a little sand,
    and before her, silver is to be accounted mire.
Beyond health and comeliness I loved her,
And I chose to have her rather than the light,
    because the splendor of her never yields to sleep.

Now God grant I speak suitably
    and value these endowments at their worth:

For he is the guide of Wisdom
    and the director of the wise.
For both we and our words are in his hand,
    as well as all prudence and knowledge of crafts.
The word of the Lord.

3   Sir 15:1-6

A reading from the Book of Sirach

HE who fears the LORD will do this;
    he who is practiced in the law will come to wisdom.
Motherlike she will meet him,
    like a young bride she will embrace him,
Nourish him with the bread of understanding,
    and give him the water of learning to drink.
He will lean upon her and not fall,
    he will trust in her and not be put to shame.
She will exalt him above his fellows;
    and in the midst of the assembly she will open his
        mouth
    and fill him with the spirit of wisdom and under-
        standing,
    and clothe him with the robe of glory.
Joy and gladness he will find,
    an everlasting name he will inherit.
The word of the Lord.

4   Sir 39:6e-10

A reading from the Book of Sirach

IF it pleases the LORD Almighty,
    he who studies the law of the Most High
    will be filled with the spirit of understanding;
He will pour forth his words of wisdom
    and in prayer give thanks to the LORD,
Who will direct his knowledge and his counsel,
    as he meditates upon his mysteries.
He will show the wisdom of what he has learned
    and glory in the law of the LORD's covenant.

Many will praise his understanding;
　　his fame can never be effaced;
Unfading will be his memory,
　　through all generations his name will live;
Peoples will speak of his wisdom,
　　and in assembly sing his praises.
The word of the Lord.

READING I FROM THE NEW TESTAMENT
DURING THE EASTER SEASON

1️⃣   Acts 2:14a, 22-24, 32-36

A reading from the Acts of the Apostles

ON the day of Pentecost, Peter stood up with the Eleven,
raised his voice, and proclaimed to them:
"You who are children of Israel, hear these words. Jesus
the Nazorean was a man commended to you by God with
mighty deeds, wonders, and signs, which God worked
through him in your midst, as you yourselves know. This
man, delivered up by the set plan and foreknowledge of
God, you killed, using lawless men to crucify him. But God
raised him up, releasing him from the throes of death,
because it was impossible for him to be held by it.

"God raised this Jesus; of this we are all witnesses.
Exalted at the right hand of God, he received the promise of
the Holy Spirit from the Father and poured it forth, as you
both see and hear. For David did not go up into heaven, but
he himself said:

The Lord said to my Lord,
'Sit at my right hand
　　until I make your enemies your footstool.'
Therefore let the whole house of Israel know for certain that
God has made him both Lord and Christ, this Jesus whom
you crucified."—The word of the Lord.

---

2   Acts 13:26-33

A reading from the Acts of the Apostles

WHEN Paul came to Antioch in Pisidia, he said in the synagogue: "My brothers, sons of the family of Abraham, and those others among you who are God-fearing, to us this word of salvation has been sent. The inhabitants of Jerusalem and their leaders failed to recognize him, and by condemning him they fulfilled the oracles of the prophets that are read sabbath after sabbath. For even though they found no grounds for a death sentence, they asked Pilate to have him put to death, and when they had accomplished all that was written about him, they took him down from the tree and placed him in a tomb. But God raised him from the dead, and for many days he appeared to those who had come up with him from Galilee to Jerusalem. These are now his witnesses before the people. We ourselves are proclaiming this good news to you that what God promised our fathers he has brought to fulfillment for us, their children, by raising up Jesus, as it is written in the second psalm, *You are my Son; this day I have begotten you.*"— The word of the Lord.

RESPONSORIAL PSALM

1   Ps 19:8, 9, 10, 11

℟. (10) **The judgments of the Lord are true, and all of them are just.**

℟. Or: (Jn 6.63) **Your words, Lord, are Spirit and life.**

The law of the LORD is perfect,
    refreshing the soul;
The decree of the LORD is trustworthy,
    giving wisdom to the simple.—℟.

The precepts of the LORD are right,
    rejoicing the heart;

The command of the LORD is clear,
enlightening the eye.—℟.

The fear of the LORD is pure,
enduring forever;
The ordinances of the LORD are true,
all of them just.—℟.

They are more precious than gold,
than a heap of purest gold;
Sweeter also than syrup
or honey from the comb.—℟.

---

2   Ps 37:3-4, 5-6, 30-31

℟. (30a) **The mouth of the just murmurs wisdom.**

Trust in the LORD and do good,
that you may dwell in the land and be fed in security.
Take delight in the LORD,
and he will grant you your heart's requests.—℟.

Commit to the LORD your way;
trust in him, and he will act.
He will make justice dawn for you like the light;
bright as the noonday shall be your vindication.—℟.

The mouth of the just tells of wisdom
and his tongue utters what is right.
The law of his God is in his heart,
and his steps do not falter.—℟.

---

3   Ps 119:9, 10, 11, 12, 13, 14

℟. (12b) **Lord, teach me your statutes.**

How can a young man be faultless in his way?
By keeping to your words.—℟.

With all my heart I seek you;
let me not stray from your commands.—℟.

Within my heart I treasure your promise,
  that I may not sin against you.—℟.

Blessed are you, O LORD;
  teach me your statutes.—℟.

With my lips I declare
  all the ordinances of your mouth.—℟.

In the way of your decrees
  I rejoice as much as in all riches.—℟.

READING II FROM THE NEW TESTAMENT

1   1 Cor 1:18-25

A reading from the first Letter of Saint Paul to the Corinthians

BROTHERS and sisters: The message of the cross is foolishness to those who are perishing, but to us who are being saved it is the power of God. For it is written:
  I will destroy the wisdom of the wise,
    and the learning of the learned I will set aside.
Where is the wise one? Where is the scribe? Where is the debater of this age? Has not God made the wisdom of the world foolish? For since in the wisdom of God the world did not come to know God through wisdom, it was the will of God through the foolishness of the proclamation to save those who have faith. For Jews demand signs and Greeks look for wisdom, but we proclaim Christ crucified, a stumbling block to Jews and foolishness to Gentiles, but to those who are called, Jews and Greeks alike, Christ the power of God and the wisdom of God. For the foolishness of God is wiser than human wisdom, and the weakness of God is stronger than human strength.—The word of the Lord.

---

2   1 Cor 2:1-10a

A reading from the first Letter of Saint Paul to the
Corinthians

WHEN I came to you, brothers and sisters, proclaiming
the mystery of God, I did not come with sublimity of
words or of wisdom. For I resolved to know nothing while I
was with you except Jesus Christ, and him crucified. I came
to you in weakness and fear and much trembling, and my
message and my proclamation were not with persuasive
words of wisdom, but with a demonstration of Spirit and
power, so that your faith might rest not on human wisdom
but on the power of God.

Yet we speak a wisdom to those who are mature, but not
a wisdom of this age, nor of the rulers of this age who are
passing away. Rather we speak God's wisdom, mysterious,
hidden, which God predetermined before the ages for our
glory, and which none of the rulers of this age knew; for, if
they had known it, they would not have crucified the Lord of
glory. But as it is written:

What eye has not seen, and ear has not heard,
   and what has not entered the human heart,
   what God has prepared for those who love him,
this God has revealed to us through the Spirit.—The word of
the Lord.

———————————

3   1 Cor 2:10b-16

A reading from the first Letter of Saint Paul to the
Corinthians

BROTHERS and sisters: The Spirit scrutinizes everything,
even the depths of God. Among men, who knows what
pertains to the man except his spirit that is within? Similarly,
no one knows what pertains to God except the Spirit of God.
We have not received the spirit of the world but the Spirit
who is from God, so that we may understand the things

freely given us by God. And we speak about them not with words taught by human wisdom, but with words taught by the Spirit, describing spiritual realities in spiritual terms.

Now the natural man does not accept what pertains to the Spirit of God, for to him it is foolishness, and he cannot understand it, because it is judged spiritually. The one who is spiritual, however, can judge everything but is not subject to judgment by anyone.

For *who has known the mind of the Lord, so as to counsel him?* But we have the mind of Christ.—The word of the Lord.

4

Eph 3:8-12

A reading from the Letter of Saint Paul to the Ephesians

BROTHERS and sisters: To me, the very least of all the holy ones, this grace was given, to preach to the Gentiles the inscrutable riches of Christ, and to bring to light for all what is the plan of the mystery hidden from ages past in God who created all things, so that the manifold wisdom of God might now be made known through the Church to the principalities and authorities in the heavens. This was according to the eternal purpose that he accomplished in Christ Jesus our Lord, in whom we have boldness of speech and confidence of access through faith in him.—The word of the Lord.

5

Eph 4:1-7, 11-13

A reading from the Letter of Saint Paul to the Ephesians

BROTHERS and sisters: I, a prisoner for the Lord, urge you to live in a manner worthy of the call you have received, with all humility and gentleness, with patience, bearing with one another through love, striving to preserve the unity of the Spirit through the bond of peace: one Body and one Spirit, as you were also called to the one hope of your call; one Lord, one faith, one baptism; one God and Father of all, who is over all and through all and in all.

But grace was given to each of us according to the measure of Christ's gift.

And he gave some as Apostles, others as prophets, others as evangelists, others as pastors and teachers, to equip the holy ones for the work of ministry, for building up the Body of Christ, until we all attain to the unity of faith and knowledge of the Son of God, to mature manhood, to the extent of the full stature of Christ.—The word of the Lord.

---

6   2 Tm 1:13-14; 2:1-3

A reading from the second Letter of Saint Paul to Timothy

BELOVED: Take as your norm the sound words that you heard from me, in the faith and love that are in Christ Jesus. Guard this rich trust with the help of the Holy Spirit that dwells within us.

My child, be strong in the grace that is in Christ Jesus. And what you heard from me through many witnesses entrust to faithful people who will have the ability to teach others as well. Bear your share of hardship along with me like a good soldier of Christ Jesus.—The word of the Lord.

---

7   2 Tm 4:1-5

A reading from the second Letter of Saint Paul to Timothy

BELOVED: I charge you in the presence of God and of Christ Jesus, who will judge the living and the dead, and by his appearing and his kingly power: proclaim the word; be persistent whether it is convenient or inconvenient; convince, reprimand, encourage through all patience and teaching. For the time will come when people will not tolerate sound doctrine but, following their own desires and insatiable curiosity, will accumulate teachers and will stop listening to the truth and will be diverted to myths. But you, be self-possessed in all circumstances; put up with hardship; perform the work of an evangelist; fulfill your ministry.—The word of the Lord.

ALLELUIA VERSE AND
VERSE BEFORE THE GOSPEL

1   Mt 5:16

Let your light shine before others,
that they may see your good deeds and glorify your heavenly Father.

2   Mt 23:9b, 10b

You have but one Father in heaven.
You have but one master, the Christ.

3   See Jn 6:63c, 68c

Your words, Lord, are Spirit and life;
you have the words of everlasting life.

4   Jn 15:5

I am the vine, you are the branches, says the Lord:
whoever remains in me and I in him will bear much fruit.

5   See Acts 16:14b

Open our hearts, O Lord,
to listen to the words of your Son.

6   1 Cor 1:18

The message about the cross is foolishness to those who are
perishing,
but to us who are being saved it is the power of God.

7   1 Cor 2:7

We speak God's wisdom, mysterious, hidden,
which God predetermined before the ages for our glory.

8

The seed is the word of God, Christ is the sower;
all who come to him will live for ever.

GOSPEL

1   Mt 5:13-19

✚ A reading from the holy Gospel according to Matthew

Jesus said to his disciples: "You are the salt of the earth. But if salt loses its taste, with what can it be seasoned? It is no longer good for anything but to be thrown out and trampled underfoot. You are the light of the world. A city set on a mountain cannot be hidden. Nor do they light a lamp and then put it under a bushel basket; it is set on a lampstand, where it gives light to all in the house. Just so, your light must shine before others, that they may see your good deeds and glorify your heavenly Father.

"Do not think that I have come to abolish the law or the prophets. I have come not to abolish but to fulfill. Amen, I say to you, until heaven and earth pass away, not the smallest letter or the smallest part of a letter will pass from the law, until all things have taken place. Therefore, whoever breaks one of the least of these commandments and teaches others to do so will be called least in the Kingdom of heaven. But whoever obeys and teaches these commandments will be called greatest in the Kingdom of heaven."— The Gospel of the Lord.

---

2   Mt 7:21-29

✚ A reading from the holy Gospel according to Matthew

JESUS said to his disciples: "Not everyone who says to me, 'Lord, Lord,' will enter the Kingdom of heaven, but only the one who does the will of my Father in heaven. Many will say to me on that day, 'Lord, Lord, did we not prophesy in your name? Did we not drive out demons in your name? Did we not do mighty deeds in your name?' Then I will declare to them solemnly, 'I never knew you. Depart from me, you evildoers.'

"Everyone who listens to these words of mine and acts on them will be like a wise man who built his house on rock. The rain fell, the floods came, and the winds blew and buffeted the house. But it did not collapse; it had been set solidly on rock. And everyone who listens to these words of mine but does not act on them will be like a fool who built his house on sand. The rain fell, the floods came, and the winds blew and buffeted the house. And it collapsed and was completely ruined."

When Jesus finished these words, the crowds were astonished at his teaching, for he taught them as one having authority, and not as their scribes.—The Gospel of the Lord.

---

3   Mt 13:47-52

✤ A reading from the holy Gospel according to Matthew

JESUS said to the crowds: "The Kingdom of heaven is like a net thrown into the sea, which collects fish of every kind. When it is full they haul it ashore and sit down to put what is good into buckets. What is bad they throw away. Thus it will be at the end of the age. The angels will go out and separate the wicked from the righteous and throw them into the fiery furnace, where there will be wailing and grinding of teeth.

"Do you understand all these things?" They answered, "Yes." And he replied, "Then every scribe who has been instructed in the Kingdom of heaven is like the head of a household who brings from his storeroom both the new and the old."—The Gospel of the Lord.

---

4   Mt 23:8-12

✝ A reading from the holy Gospel according to Matthew

JESUS said to his disciples: "Do not be called 'Rabbi.' You have but one teacher, and you are all brothers. Call no one on earth your father; you have but one Father in heaven. Do not be called 'Master'; you have but one master, the Christ. The greatest among you must be your servant. Whoever exalts himself will be humbled; whoever humbles himself will be exalted."—The Gospel of the Lord.

_____

5   Mk 4:1-10, 13-20 or 4:1-9

[If the "Short Form" is used, omit indented text in brackets.]

✝ A reading from the holy Gospel according to Mark

ON another occasion, Jesus began to teach by the sea. A very large crowd gathered around him so that he got into a boat on the sea and sat down. And the whole crowd was beside the sea on land. And he taught them at length in parables, and in the course of his instruction he said to them, "Hear this! A sower went out to sow. And as he sowed, some seed fell on the path, and the birds came and ate it up. Other seed fell on rocky ground where it had little soil. It sprang up at once because the soil was not deep. And when the sun rose, it was scorched and it withered for lack of roots. Some seed fell among thorns, and the thorns grew up and choked it and it produced no grain. And some seed fell on rich soil and produced fruit. It came up and grew and yielded thirty, sixty, and a hundredfold." He added, "Whoever has ears to hear ought to hear."

[And when he was alone, those present along with the Twelve questioned him about the parables. He said to them, "Do you not understand this parable? Then how will you understand any of the parables? The sower sows the word. These are the ones on the path where the word is sown. As soon as they hear, Satan comes at once and takes away the word sown in them. And these are the

ones sown on rocky ground who, when they hear the word, receive it at once with joy. But they have no roots; they last only for a time. Then when tribulation or persecution comes because of the word, they quickly fall away. Those sown among thorns are another sort. They are the people who hear the word, but worldly anxiety, the lure of riches, and the craving for other things intrude and choke the word, and it bears no fruit. But those sown on rich soil are the ones who hear the word and accept it and bear fruit thirty and sixty and a hundredfold."]
The Gospel of the Lord.

---

6   Lk 6:43-45

✠ A reading from the holy Gospel according to Luke

JESUS said to his disciples: "A good tree does not bear rotten fruit, nor does a rotten tree bear good fruit. For every tree is known by its own fruit. For people do not pick figs from thorn bushes, nor do they gather grapes from brambles. A good person out of the store of goodness in his heart produces good, but an evil person out of a store of evil produces evil; for from the fullness of the heart the mouth speaks."—The Gospel of the Lord.

READING I FROM THE OLD TESTAMENT

1   Sg 8:6-7

A reading from the Song of Songs

SET me as a seal on your heart,
  as a seal on your arm;
For stern as death is love,
    relentless as the nether world is devotion;
    its flames are a blazing fire.
Deep waters cannot quench love,
    nor floods sweep it away.
Were one to offer all he owns to purchase love,
    he would be roundly mocked.
The word of the Lord.

---

2   Hos 2:16bc, 17cd, 21-22

A reading from the Book of the Prophet Hosea

THUS says the LORD:
  I will lead her into the desert
and speak to her heart.
She shall respond there as in the days of her youth,
    when she came up from the land of Egypt.

I will espouse you to me forever:
I will espouse you in right and in justice,
    in love and in mercy;
I will espouse you in fidelity,
    and you shall know the LORD.
The word of the Lord.

READING I FROM THE NEW TESTAMENT
DURING THE EASTER SEASON

1   Rv 19:1, 5-9a

A reading from the Book of Revelation

I, JOHN, heard what sounded like the loud voice of a great multitude in heaven, saying:

"Alleluia!
Salvation, glory, and might belong to our God."

A voice coming from the throne said:

"Praise our God, all you his servants,
and you who revere him, small and great."

Then I heard something like the sound of a great multitude or the sound of rushing water or mighty peals of thunder, as they said.

"Alleluia!
The Lord has established his reign,
our God, the almighty.
Let us rejoice and be glad
and give him glory.
For the wedding day of the Lamb has come,
his bride has made herself ready.
She was allowed to wear
a bright, clean linen garment."

The linen represents the righteous deeds of the holy ones.

Then the angel said to me, "Write this: Blessed are those who have been called to the wedding feast of the Lamb."— The word of the Lord.

---

2   Rv 21:1-5a

A reading from the Book of Revelation

I, JOHN, saw a new heaven and a new earth. The former heaven and the former earth had passed away, and the sea was no more. I also saw the holy city, a new Jerusalem, coming down out of heaven from God, prepared as a bride adorned for her husband. I heard a loud voice from the throne saying, "Behold, God's dwelling is with the human race. He will dwell with them and they will be his people and God himself will always be with them as their God. He will wipe every tear from their eyes, and there shall be no more death or mourning, wailing or pain, for the old order has passed away."

The One who sat on the throne said, "Behold, I make all things new."—The word of the Lord.

RESPONSORIAL PSALM

1   Ps 45:11-12, 14-15, 16-17

℟. (11) **Listen to me, daughter; see and bend your ear.**

℟. Or: **The bridegroom is here; let us go out to meet Christ the Lord.**

Hear, O daughter, and see; turn your ear,
    forget your people and your father's house.
So shall the king desire your beauty;
    for he is your lord, and you must worship him.—℟.

All glorious is the king's daughter as she enters;
    her raiment is threaded with spun gold.
In embroidered apparel she is borne in to the king;
    behind her the virgins of her train are brought to
    you.—℟.

They are borne in with gladness and joy;
    they enter the palace of the king.
The place of your fathers your sons shall have;
    you shall make them princes through all the land.—℟.

___

2   Ps 148:1bc-2, 11-12, 13, 14

℟. (see 12a and 13a) **Young men and women, praise the name of the Lord.**

℟. Or: **Alleluia.**

Praise the LORD from the heavens;
>   praise him in the heights;
Praise him, all you his angels,
>   praise him, all you his hosts.—R̃.

Let the kings of the earth and all peoples,
>   the princes and all the judges of the earth,
Young men, too, and maidens,
>   old men and boys,
Praise the name of the LORD,
>   for his name alone is exalted.—R̃.

His majesty is above earth and heaven.
He has lifted up the horn of his people.
Be this his praise from all his faithful ones;
>   from the children of Israel, the people close to him.
>   Alleluia.—R̃.

READING II FROM THE NEW TESTAMENT

1   1 Cor 7:25-35

A reading from the first Letter of Saint Paul to the
Corinthians

BROTHERS and sisters: In regard to virgins, I have no
commandment from the Lord, but I give my opinion as
one who by the Lord's mercy is trustworthy. So this is what
I think best because of the present distress: that it is a good
thing for a person to remain as he is. Are you bound to a
wife? Do not seek a separation. Are you free of a wife? Then
do not look for a wife. If you marry, however, you do not sin,
nor does an unmarried woman sin if she marries, but such
people will experience affliction in their earthly life, and I
would like to spare you that.

I tell you, brothers, the time is running out. From now on,
let those having wives act as not having them, those weeping as not weeping, those rejoicing as not rejoicing, those
buying as not owning, those using the world as not using it
fully. For the world in its present form is passing away.

I should like you to be free of anxieties. An unmarried man is anxious about the things of the Lord, how he may please the Lord. But a married man is anxious about the things of the world, how he may please his wife, and he is divided. An unmarried woman or a virgin is anxious about the things of the Lord, so that she may be holy in both body and spirit. A married woman, on the other hand, is anxious about the things of the world, how she may please her husband. I am telling you this for your own benefit, not to impose a restraint upon you, but for the sake of propriety and adherence to the Lord without distraction.—The word of the Lord.

2️⃣   2 Cor 10:17—11:2

A reading from the second Letter of Saint Paul to the Corinthians

BROTHERS and sisters:"Whoever boasts, should boast in the Lord."For it is not the one who recommends himself who is approved, but the one whom the Lord recommends.

If only you would put up with a little foolishness from me! Please put up with me. For I am jealous of you with the jealousy of God, since I betrothed you to one husband to present you as a chaste virgin to Christ.—The word of the Lord.

ALLELUIA VERSE AND
VERSE BEFORE THE GOSPEL

1️⃣   Jn 14:23

Whoever loves me will keep my word
and my Father will love him,
and we will come to him.

2️⃣

This is the wise virgin, whom the Lord found waiting;
at his coming, she went in with him to the wedding feast.

3

Come, bride of Christ, and receive the crown,
which the Lord has prepared for you for ever.

GOSPEL

1   Mt 19:3-12

✠ A reading from the holy Gospel according to Matthew

S OME Pharisees approached Jesus, and tested him, saying, "Is it lawful for a man to divorce his wife for any
cause whatever?" He said in reply, "Have you not read that
from the beginning the Creator *made them male and female*
and said, *For this reason a man shall leave his father and
mother and be joined to his wife, and the two shall become
one flesh?* So they are no longer two, but one flesh. Therefore, what God has joined together, man must not separate."
They said to him, "Then why did Moses command that the
man give the woman a bill of divorce and dismiss her?" He
said to them, "Because of the hardness of your hearts Moses
allowed you to divorce your wives, but from the beginning it
was not so. I say to you, whoever divorces his wife (unless
the marriage is unlawful) and marries another commits
adultery." His disciples said to him, "If that is the case of a
man with his wife, it is better not to marry." He answered,
"Not all can accept this word, but only those to whom that is
granted. Some are incapable of marriage because they were
born so; some, because they were made so by others; some,
because they have renounced marriage for the sake of the
Kingdom of heaven. Whoever can accept this ought to
accept it."—The Gospel of the Lord.

✠ 2 ✠   Mt 25:1-13

✤ A reading from the holy Gospel according to Matthew

JESUS told his disciples this parable: "The Kingdom of heaven will be like ten virgins who took their lamps and went out to meet the bridegroom. Five of them were foolish and five were wise. The foolish ones, when taking their lamps, brought no oil with them, but the wise brought flasks of oil with their lamps. Since the bridegroom was long delayed, they all became drowsy and fell asleep. At midnight, there was a cry, 'Behold, the bridegroom! Come out to meet him!' Then all those virgins got up and trimmed their lamps. The foolish ones said to the wise, 'Give us some of your oil, for our lamps are going out.' But the wise ones replied, 'No, for there may not be enough for us and you. Go instead to the merchants and buy some for yourselves.' While they went off to buy it, the bridegroom came and those who were ready went into the wedding feast with him. Then the door was locked. Afterwards the other virgins came and said, 'Lord, Lord, open the door for us!' But he said in reply, 'Amen, I say to you, I do not know you.' Therefore, stay awake, for you know neither the day nor the hour."— The Gospel of the Lord.

3   Lk 10:38-42

✤ A reading from the holy Gospel according to Luke

JESUS entered a village where a woman whose name was Martha welcomed him. She had a sister named Mary who sat beside the Lord at his feet listening to him speak. Martha, burdened with much serving, came to him and said, "Lord, do you not care that my sister has left me by myself to do the serving? Tell her to help me." The Lord said to her in reply, "Martha, Martha, you are anxious and worried about many things. There is need of only one thing. Mary has chosen the better part and it will not be taken from her."—The Gospel of the Lord.

COMMON OF HOLY MEN AND WOMEN

READING I FROM THE OLD TESTAMENT

1
Gn 12:1-4a

A reading from the Book of Genesis

THE LORD said to Abram: "Go forth from the land of your kinsfolk and from your father's house to a land that I will show you.

"I will make of you a great nation,
and I will bless you;
I will make your name great,
so that you will be a blessing.
I will bless those who bless you
and curse those who curse you
All the communities of the earth
shall find blessing in you."

Abram went as the LORD directed him.—The word of the Lord.

2
Lv 19:1-2, 17-18

A reading from the Book of Leviticus

THE LORD said to Moses, "Speak to the whole assembly of the children of Israel and tell them: Be holy, for I, the LORD, your God, am holy.

"You shall not bear hatred for your brother in your heart. Though you may have to reprove your fellow citizen, do not incur sin because of him. Take no revenge and cherish no grudge against any of your people. You shall love your neighbor as yourself. I am the LORD."—The word of the Lord.

3
Dt 6:3-9

A reading from the Book of Deuteronomy

MOSES said to the people: "Hear, Israel, and be careful to observe these commandments, that you may grow and prosper the more, in keeping with the promise of the LORD, the God of your fathers, to give you a land flowing with milk and honey.

"Hear, O Israel! The LORD is our God, the LORD alone! Therefore, you shall love the LORD, your God, with all your heart, and with all your soul, and with all your strength. Take to heart these words which I enjoin on you today. Drill them into your children. Speak of them at home and abroad, whether you are busy or at rest. Bind them at your wrist as a sign and let them be as a pendant on your forehead. Write them on the doorposts of your houses and on your gates."— The word of the Lord.

---

4   Dt 10:8-9

A reading from the Book of Deuteronomy

MOSES summoned all of Israel and said to them: "At that time the LORD set apart the tribe of Levi to carry the ark of the covenant of the LORD, to be in attendance before the LORD and minister to him, and to give blessings in his name, as they have done to this day. For this reason, Levi has no share in the heritage with his brothers; the LORD himself is his heritage, as the LORD, your God, has told him."—The word of the Lord.

---

5   1 Kgs 19:4-9a, 11-15a

[For Religious]

A reading from the first Book of Kings

ELIJAH went a day's journey into the desert, until he came to a broom tree and sat beneath it. He prayed for death saying: "This is enough, O LORD! Take my life, for I am no better than my fathers." He lay down and fell asleep under the broom tree, but then an angel touched him and ordered him to get up and eat. He looked and there at his head was a hearth cake and a jug of water. After he ate and drank, he lay down again, but the angel of the LORD came back a second time, touched him, and ordered, "Get up and eat, else the journey will be too long for you!" He got up, ate, and drank; then strengthened by that food, he walked forty days and forty nights to the mountain of God, Horeb.

There he came to a cave, where he took shelter. Then the LORD said to him, "Go outside and stand on the mountain before the LORD; the LORD will be passing by." A strong and heavy wind was rending the mountains and crushing rocks before the LORD—but the LORD was not in the wind. After the wind there was an earthquake—but the LORD was not in the earthquake. After the earthquake there was fire—but the LORD was not in the fire. After the fire there was a tiny whispering sound. When he heard this, Elijah hid his face in his cloak and went and stood at the entrance of the cave. A voice said to him, "Elijah, why are you here?" He replied, "I have been most zealous for the LORD, the God of hosts. But the children of Israel have forsaken your covenant, torn down your altars, and put your prophets to the sword. I alone am left, and they seek to take my life." The LORD said to him, "Go, take the road back to the desert near Damascus."—The word of the Lord.

---

6 1 Kgs 19:16b, 19-21

[For Religious]

A reading from the first Book of Kings

THE LORD said to Elijah: "You shall anoint Elisha, son of Shaphat of Abel-meholah, as prophet to succeed you."

Elijah set out and came upon Elisha, son of Shaphat, as he was plowing with twelve yoke of oxen; he was following the twelfth. Elijah went over to him and threw his cloak over him. Elisha left the oxen, ran after Elijah, and said, "Please, let me kiss my father and mother goodbye, and I will follow you." Elijah answered, "Go back! Have I done anything to you?" Elisha left him and, taking the yoke of oxen, slaughtered them; he used the plowing equipment for fuel to boil their flesh, and gave it to his people to eat. Then he left and followed Elijah as his attendant.—The word of the Lord.

---

7   Tb 8:5-7

A reading from the Book of Tobit

ON their wedding night Tobiah arose from bed and said to his wife, "My love, get up. Let us pray and beg our Lord to have mercy on us and to grant us deliverance." She got up, and they started to pray and beg that deliverance might be theirs. He began with these words:

"Blessed are you, O God of our fathers;
    praised be your name forever and ever.
Let the heavens and all your creation
    praise you forever.
You made Adam and you gave him his wife Eve
    to be his help and support;
    and from these two the human race descended.
You said, 'It is not good for the man to be alone;
    let us make him a partner like himself.'
Now, Lord, you know that I take this wife of mine
    not because of lust,
    but for a noble purpose.
Call down your mercy on me and on her,
    and allow us to live together to a happy old age."

They said together, "Amen, amen."—The word of the Lord.

---

8   Tb 12:6-14a

[For Those Who Work for the Underprivileged]

A reading from the Book of Tobit

THE angel Raphael said to Tobit and his son: "Thank God! Give him the praise and the glory. Before all the living, acknowledge the many good things he has done for you, by blessing and extolling his name in song. Before all people, honor and proclaim God's deeds, and do not be slack in praising him. A king's secret it is prudent to keep, but the works of God are to be declared and made known. Praise them with due honor. Do good, and evil will not find its way to you. Prayer and fasting are good, but better than either is almsgiving accompanied by righteousness. A little with righteousness is better than abundance with wickedness. It is better to give alms than to store up gold; for almsgiving saves one from death and expiates every sin. Those who regularly give alms shall enjoy a full life; but those habitually guilty of sin are their own worst enemies.

"I will now tell you the whole truth; I will conceal nothing at all from you. I have already said to you, 'A king's secret it is prudent to keep, but the works of God are to be made known with due honor.' I can now tell you that when you, Tobit, and Sarah prayed, it was I who presented and read the record of your prayer before the Glory of the Lord; and I did the same thing when you used to bury the dead. When you did not hesitate to get up and leave your dinner in order to go and bury the dead, I was sent to put you to the test."—The word of the Lord.

---

9   Jdt 8:2-8

[For Widows]

A reading from the Book of Judith

JUDITH'S husband, Manasseh, of her own tribe and clan, had died at the time of the barley harvest. While he was in the field supervising those who bound the sheaves, he suffered sunstroke; and he died of this illness in Bethulia, his native city. Manasseh was buried with his fathers in the field between Dothan and Balamon. The widowed Judith remained three years and four months at home, where she set up a tent for herself on the roof of her house. She put sackcloth about her loins and wore widow's weeds. She fasted all the days of her widowhood, except sabbath eves and sabbaths, new moon eves and new moons, feastdays and holidays of the house of Israel. She was beautifully formed and lovely to behold.

Her husband, Manasseh, the son of Joseph, the son of Ahitub, the son of Melchis, the son of Eliab, the son of Nathanael, the son of Sarasadai, the son of Simeon, had left her gold and silver, servants and maids, livestock and fields, which she was maintaining. No one had a bad word to say about her, for she was a very God-fearing woman.—The word of the Lord.

---

10   Est C:1-7, 10

A reading from the Book of Esther

MORDECAI prayed: "O God of Abraham, God of Isaac, God of Jacob, blessed are you; O Lord God, almighty King, all things are in your power, and there is no one to oppose you in your will to save Israel. You made heaven and earth and every wonderful thing under the heavens. You are LORD of all, and there is no one who can resist you, LORD. You know all things. You know, O LORD, that gladly would I have kissed the soles of Haman's feet for the salvation of Israel. But I acted as I did so as not to place the honor of man above that of God. I will not bow down to anyone but you, my LORD and God. Hear my prayer; have pity on your inheritance and turn our sorrow into joy: thus we shall live to sing praise to your name, O LORD. Do not silence those who praise you."—The word of the Lord.

---

11   Prv 31:10-13, 19-20, 30-31

A reading from the Book of Proverbs

WHEN one finds a worthy wife,
    her value is far beyond pearls.
Her husband, entrusting his heart to her,
    has an unfailing prize.
She brings him good, and not evil,
    all the days of her life.
She obtains wool and flax
    and makes cloth with skillful hands.

She puts her hands to the distaff,
  and her fingers ply the spindle.
She reaches out her hands to the poor,
  and extends her arms to the needy.
Charm is deceptive and beauty fleeting;
  the woman who fears the LORD is to be praised.
Give her a reward of her labors,
  and let her works praise her at the city gates.
The word of the Lord.

---

12   Sir 2:7-13

A reading from the Book of Sirach

YOU who fear the LORD, wait for his mercy,
turn not away lest you fall.
You who fear the LORD, trust him,
  and your reward will not be lost.
You who fear the LORD, hope for good things,
  for lasting joy and mercy.
You who fear the LORD, love him
  and your hearts will be enlightened.
Study the generations long past and understand;
  has anyone hoped in the LORD and been disappoint-
    ed?
Has anyone persevered in his commandments and been
    forsaken?
  Has anyone called upon him and been rebuffed?
Compassionate and merciful is the LORD;
  he forgives sins, he saves in time of trouble
  and he is a protector to all who seek him in truth.
The word of the Lord.

---

13   Sir 3:17-24

A reading from the Book of Sirach

MY child, conduct your affairs with humility,
and you will be loved more than a giver of gifts.

Humble yourself the more, the greater you are,
  and you will find favor with God.
The greater you are,
  the more you must humble yourself in all things,
  and you will find grace before God.
For great is the power of God;
  by the humble he is glorified.
What is too sublime for you, seek not,
  into things beyond your strength search not.
What is committed to you, attend to;
  for it is not necessary for you to see with your eyes
  those things which are hidden.
With what is too much for you meddle not,
  when shown things beyond human understanding.
Their own opinion has misled many,
  and false reasoning unbalanced their judgment.
Where the pupil of the eye is missing, there is no light,
  and where there is no knowledge, there is no wisdom.
The word of the Lord.

14

Sir 26:1-4, 13-16

A reading from the Book of Sirach

BLESSED the husband of a good wife,
  twice-lengthened are his days;
A worthy wife brings joy to her husband,
  peaceful and full is his life.
A good wife is a generous gift
  bestowed upon him who fears the LORD;
Be he rich or poor, his heart is content,
  and a smile is ever on his face.

A gracious wife delights her husband,
  her thoughtfulness puts flesh on his bones;
A gift from the LORD is her governed speech,
  and her firm virtue is of surpassing worth.

Choicest of blessings is a modest wife,
>   priceless her chaste soul.
A holy and decent woman adds grace upon grace;
>   indeed, no price is worthy of her temperate soul.
Like the sun rising in the LORD's heavens,
>   the beauty of a virtuous wife is the radiance of her
>   home.

The word of the Lord.

15
                                                    Is 58:6-11

[For Those Who Work for the Underprivileged]

A reading from the Book of the Prophet Isaiah

THUS says the LORD:
This is the fasting that I wish:
>   releasing those bound unjustly,
>   untying the thongs of the yoke;
Setting free the oppressed,
>   breaking every yoke;
Sharing your bread with the hungry,
>   sheltering the oppressed and the homeless;
Clothing the naked when you see them,
>   and not turning your back on your own.
Then your light shall break forth like the dawn,
>   and your wound shall quickly be healed;
Your vindication shall go before you,
>   and the glory of the LORD shall be your rear guard.
Then you shall call, and the LORD will answer,
>   you shall cry for help, and he will say: Here I am!
If you remove from your midst oppression,
>   false accusation and malicious speech;
If you bestow your bread on the hungry
>   and satisfy the afflicted;
Then light shall rise for you in darkness,
>   and the gloom shall become for you like midday;
Then the LORD will guide you always
>   and give you plenty even on the parched land.

He will renew your strength,
> and you shall be like a watered garden,
> like a spring whose water never fails.

The word of the Lord.

---

16   Jer 20:7-9

A reading from the Book of the Prophet Jeremiah

YOU duped me, O LORD, and I let myself be duped;
you were too strong for me, and you triumphed.
All the day I am an object for laughter;
> everyone mocks me.
Whenever I speak, I must cry out,
> violence and outrage is my message;
The word of the LORD has brought me
> derision and reproach all the day.
I say to myself, I will not mention him,
> I will speak in his name no more.
But then it becomes like fire burning in my heart,
> imprisoned in my bones;
I grow weary holding it in,
> I cannot endure it.

The word of the Lord.

---

17   Mi 6:6-8

A reading from the Book of the Prophet Micah

WITH what shall I come before the LORD,
and bow before God most high?
Shall I come before him with burnt offerings,
> with calves a year old?
Will the LORD be pleased with thousands of rams,
> with myriad streams of oil?
Shall I give my first-born for my crime,
> the fruit of my body for the sin of my soul?
You have been told, O man, what is good,
> and what the LORD requires of you:

Only to do the right and to love goodness,
>   and to walk humbly with your God.
The word of the Lord.

---

18   Zep 2:3; 3:12-13

A reading from the Book of the Prophet Zephaniah

SEEK the LORD, all you humble of the earth,
>   who have observed his law;
Seek justice, seek humility;
>   perhaps you may be sheltered
>   on the day of the LORD's anger.

But I will leave as a remnant in your midst
>   a people humble and lowly,
Who shall take refuge in the name of the Lord:
>   the remnant of Israel.
They shall do no wrong
>   and speak no lies;
Nor shall there be found in their mouths
>   a deceitful tongue;
They shall pasture and couch their flocks
>   with none to disturb them.
The word of the Lord.

READING I FROM THE NEW TESTAMENT
DURING THE EASTER SEASON

1   Acts 4:32-35

[For Religious]

A reading from the Acts of the Apostles

THE community of believers was of one heart and mind,
and no one claimed that any of his possessions was his
own, but they had everything in common. With great power
the Apostles bore witness to the resurrection of the Lord
Jesus, and great favor was accorded them all. There was no

needy person among them, for those who owned property or houses would sell them, bring the proceeds of the sale, and put them at the feet of the Apostles, and they were distributed to each according to need.—The word of the Lord.

2

Rv 3:14b, 20-22

A reading from the Book of Revelation

" "The Amen, the faithful and true witness, the source of God's creation, says this:

" ' "Behold, I stand at the door and knock. If anyone hears my voice and opens the door, then I will enter his house and dine with him, and he with me. I will give the victor the right to sit with me on my throne, as I myself first won the victory and sit with my Father on his throne.

" ' "Whoever has ears ought to hear what the Spirit says to the churches." ' "—The word of the Lord.

3

Rv 19:1, 5-9a

A reading from the Book of Revelation

I, JOHN, heard what sounded like the loud voice of a great multitude in heaven, saying:

"Alleluia!
Salvation, glory, and might belong to our God."
A voice coming from the throne said:
"Praise our God, all you his servants,
and you who revere him, small and great."
Then I heard something like the sound of a great multitude or the sound of rushing water or mighty peals of thunder, as they said:
"Alleluia!
The Lord has established his reign,
our God, the almighty.
Let us rejoice and be glad
and give him glory.

For the wedding day of the Lamb has come,
  his bride has made herself ready.
She was allowed to wear
  a bright, clean linen garment."
(The linen represents the righteous deeds of the holy ones.)
  Then the angel said to me, "Write this: Blessed are those who have been called to the wedding feast of the Lamb."— The word of the Lord.

---

4   Rv 21:5-7

A reading from the Book of Revelation

THE One who was seated on the throne said: "Behold, I make all things new." Then he said, "Write these words down, for they are trustworthy and true." He said to me, "They are accomplished. I am the Alpha and the Omega, the beginning and the end. To the thirsty I will give a gift from the spring of life-giving water. The victor will inherit these gifts, and I shall be his God, and he will be my son."—The word of the Lord.

RESPONSORIAL PSALM

1   Ps 1:1-2, 3, 4 and 6

℟. (40:5a) **Blessed are they who hope in the Lord.**

℟. Or: (2a) **Blessed are they who delight in the law of the Lord.**

℟. Or: (Ps 92:13-14) **The just will flourish like the palm tree in the garden of the Lord.**

Blessed the man who follows not
  the counsel of the wicked
Nor walks in the way of sinners,
  nor sits in the company of the insolent,
But delights in the law of the LORD
  and meditates on his law day and night.—℟.

He is like a tree
  planted near running water,
That yields its fruit in due season,
  and whose leaves never fade.
    Whatever he does, prospers.—℞.

Not so, the wicked, not so;
  they are like chaff which the wind drives away.
For the LORD watches over the way of the just,
  but the way of the wicked vanishes.—℞.

---

2   Ps 15:2-3a, 3bc-4ab, 5

℞. (1) **The just one shall live on your holy mountain, O Lord.**

He who walks blamelessly and does justice;
  who thinks the truth in his heart
  and slanders not with his tongue.—℞.

Who harms not his fellow man,
  nor takes up a reproach against his neighbor;
By whom the reprobate is despised,
  while he honors those who fear the LORD.—℞.

Who lends not his money at usury
  and accepts no bribe against the innocent.
He who does these things
  shall never be disturbed.—℞.

---

3   Ps 16:1-2ab and 5, 7-8, 11

℞. (see 5a) **You are my inheritance, O Lord.**

Keep me, O God, for in you I take refuge;
  I say to the LORD, "My Lord are you."
O LORD, my allotted portion and my cup,
  you it is who hold fast my lot.—℞.

I bless the LORD who counsels me;
  even in the night my heart exhorts me.
I set the LORD ever before me;
  with him at my right hand I shall not be disturbed.—℞.

You will show me the path to life,
    fullness of joys in your presence,
    the delights at your right hand forever.—℟.

---

4   Ps 23:1-3, 4, 5, 6

℟. (1) **The Lord is my shepherd; there is nothing I shall want.**

The LORD is my shepherd; I shall not want.
    In verdant pastures he gives me repose;
Beside restful waters he leads me;
    he refreshes my soul.
He guides me on right paths
    for his name's sake.—℟.

Even though I walk in the dark valley
    I fear no evil; for you are at my side
With your rod and your staff
    that give me courage.—℟.

You spread the table before me
    in the sight of my foes;
You anoint my head with oil;
    my cup overflows.—℟.

Only goodness and kindness follow me
    all the days of my life;
And I shall dwell in the house of the LORD
    for years to come.—℟.

---

5   Ps 34:2-3, 4-5, 6-7, 8-9, 10-11

℟. **I will bless the Lord at all times.**

℟. Or: (9) **Taste and see the goodness of the Lord.**

I will bless the LORD at all times;
    his praise shall be ever in my mouth.
Let my soul glory in the LORD;
    the lowly will hear and be glad.—℟.

Glorify the LORD with me,
    let us together extol his name.

I sought the LORD, and he answered me
    and delivered me from all my fears.—R̲̂.

Look to him that you may be radiant with joy,
    and your faces may not blush with shame.
When the poor one called out, the LORD heard,
    and from all his distress he saved him.—R̲̂.

The angel of the LORD encamps
    around those who fear him, and delivers them.
Taste and see how good the LORD is;
    blessed the man who takes refuge in him.—R̲̂.

Fear the LORD, you his holy ones,
    for nought is lacking to those who fear him.
The great grow poor and hungry;
    but those who seek the LORD want for no good thing.—R̲̂.

---

6   Ps 103:1bc-2, 3-4, 8-9, 13-14, 17-18a

R̲̂. (1) **O bless the Lord, my soul!**

Bless the LORD, O my soul;
    and all my being, bless his holy name.
Bless the LORD, O my soul,
    and forget not all his benefits.—R̲̂.

He pardons all your iniquities,
    he heals all your ills,
He redeems your life from destruction,
    he crowns you with kindness and compassion.—R̲̂.

Merciful and gracious is the LORD,
    slow to anger and abounding in kindness.
He will not always chide,
    nor does he keep his wrath forever.—R̲̂.

As a father has compassion on his children,
    so the LORD has compassion on those who fear him,
For he knows how we are formed;
    he remembers that we are dust.—R̲̂.

But the kindness of the LORD is from eternity
    to eternity toward those who fear him,

And his justice toward his children's children
among those who keep his covenant.—℞.

---

7   Ps 112:1-2, 3-4, 5-7a, 7b-8, 9

℞. (1) **Blessed the man who fears the Lord.**

℞. Or: **Alleluia.**

Blessed the man who fears the LORD,
who greatly delights in his commands.
His posterity shall be mighty upon the earth;
the upright generation shall be blessed.—℞.

Wealth and riches shall be in his house;
his generosity shall endure forever.
Light shines through the darkness for the upright;
he is gracious and merciful and just.—℞.

Well for the man who is gracious and lends,
who conducts his affairs with justice;
He shall never be moved;
the just one shall be in everlasting remembrance.—℞.

An evil report he shall not fear;
his heart is firm, trusting in the LORD.
His heart is steadfast; he shall not fear
till he looks down upon his foes.—℞.

Lavishly he gives to the poor,
his generosity shall endure forever;
his horn shall be exalted in glory.—℞.

---

8   Ps 128:1-2, 3, 4-5

℞. **Blessed are those who fear the Lord.**

Blessed are you who fear the LORD,
who walk in his ways!
For you shall eat the fruit of your handiwork;
blessed shall you be, and favored.—℞.

Your wife shall be like a fruitful vine
in the recesses of your home;

Your children like olive plants
    around your table.—℟.

Behold, thus is the man blessed
    who fears the LORD.
The LORD bless you from Zion:
    may you see the prosperity of Jerusalem
    all the days of your life.—℟.

9

Ps 131:1bcde, 2, 3

℟. **In you, Lord, I have found my peace.**

O LORD, my heart is not proud,
    nor are my eyes haughty;
I busy not myself with great things,
    nor with things too sublime for me.—℟.

Nay rather, I have stilled and quieted
    my soul like a weaned child.
Like a weaned child on its mother's lap,
    so is my soul within me.—℟.

O Israel, hope in the LORD,
    both now and forever.—℟.

READING II FROM THE NEW TESTAMENT

1

Rom 8:26-30

A reading from the Letter of Saint Paul to the Romans

BROTHERS and sisters: The Spirit comes to the aid of our weakness; for we do not know how to pray as we ought, but the Spirit himself intercedes with inexpressible groanings. And the one who searches hearts knows what is the intention of the Spirit, because he intercedes for the holy ones according to God's will.

We know that all things work for good for those who love God, who are called according to his purpose. For those he foreknew he also predestined to be conformed to the image of his Son, so that he might be the firstborn among many brothers. And those he predestined he also called; and those he called he also justified; and those he justified he also glorified.—The word of the Lord.

2

1 Cor 1:26-31

A reading from the first Letter of Saint Paul to the Corinthians

CONSIDER your own calling, brothers and sisters. Not many of you were wise by human standards, not many were powerful, not many were of noble birth. Rather, God chose the foolish of the world to shame the wise, and God chose the weak of the world to shame the strong, and God chose the lowly and despised of the world, those who count for nothing, to reduce to nothing those who are something, so that no human being might boast before God. It is due to him that you are in Christ Jesus, who became for us wisdom from God, as well as righteousness, sanctification, and redemption, so that, as it is written, *Whoever boasts, should boast in the Lord.*—The word of the Lord.

3

1 Cor 12:31—13:13 or 13:4-13

[If the "Short Form" is used, omit indented text in brackets.]

A reading from the first Letter of Saint Paul to the Corinthians

BROTHERS and sisters:
[Strive eagerly for the greatest spiritual gifts. But I shall show you a still more excellent way.

If I speak in human and angelic tongues but do not have love, I am a resounding gong or a clashing cymbal. And if I have the gift of prophecy and comprehend all mysteries and all knowledge; if I have all faith so as to move mountains, but do not have love, I am nothing. If I give away everything I own, and if I hand my body over so that I may boast but do not have love, I gain nothing.]

Love is patient, love is kind. It is not jealous, love is not pompous, it is not inflated, it is not rude, it does not seek its own interests, it is not quick-tempered, it does not brood over injury, it does not rejoice over wrongdoing but rejoices with the truth. It bears all things, believes all things, hopes all things, endures all things.

Love never fails. If there are prophecies, they will be brought to nothing; if tongues, they will cease; if knowledge, it will be brought to nothing. For we know partially and we prophesy partially, but when the perfect comes, the partial will pass away. When I was a child, I used to talk as a child, think as a child, reason as a child; when I became a man, I put aside childish things. At present we see indistinctly, as in a mirror, but then face to face. At present I know partially; then I shall know fully, as I am fully known. So faith, hope, love remain, these three; but the greatest of these is love.— The word of the Lord.

---

4 2 Cor 10:17—11:2

A reading from the second Letter of Saint Paul to the Corinthians

B ROTHERS and sisters: *Whoever boasts, should boast in the Lord.* For it is not the one who recommends himself who is approved, but the one whom the Lord recommends.

If only you would put up with a little foolishness from me! Please put up with me. For I am jealous of you with the jealousy of God, since I betrothed you to one husband to present you as a chaste virgin to Christ.—The word of the Lord.

---

5 Gal 2:19-20

A reading from the Letter of Saint Paul to the Galatians

B ROTHERS and sisters: Through the law I died to the law, that I might live for God. I have been crucified with Christ; yet I live, no longer I, but Christ lives in me; insofar as I now live in the flesh, I live by faith in the Son of God

who has loved me and given himself up for me.—The word
of the Lord.

---

6   Gal 6:14-16

A reading from the Letter of Saint Paul to the Galatians

BROTHERS and sisters: May I never boast except in the
cross of our Lord Jesus Christ, through which the world
has been crucified to me, and I to the world. For neither does
circumcision mean anything, nor does uncircumcision, but
only a new creation. Peace and mercy be to all who follow
this rule and to the Israel of God.—The word of the Lord.

---

7   Eph 3:14-19

A reading from the Letter of Saint Paul to the Ephesians

BROTHERS and sisters: I kneel before the Father, from
whom every family in heaven and on earth is named,
that he may grant you in accord with the riches of his glory
to be strengthened with power through his Spirit in the
inner self, and that Christ may dwell in your hearts through
faith; that you, rooted and grounded in love, may have
strength to comprehend with all the holy ones what is the
breadth and length and height and depth, and to know the
love of Christ that surpasses knowledge, so that you may be
filled with all the fullness of God.—The word of the Lord.

---

8   Eph 6:10-13, 18

A reading from the Letter of Saint Paul to the Ephesians

BROTHERS and sisters: Draw your strength from the
Lord and from his mighty power. Put on the armor of
God so that you may be able to stand firm against the tactics
of the Devil. For our struggle is not with flesh and blood but
with the principalities, with the powers, with the world
rulers of this present darkness, with the evil spirits in the
heavens. Therefore, put on the armor of God, that you may

be able to resist on the evil day and, having done everything, to hold your ground.

With all prayer and supplication, pray at every opportunity in the Spirit. To that end, be watchful with all perseverance and supplication for all the holy ones.—The word of the Lord.

---

9   Phil 3:8-14

A reading from the Letter of Saint Paul to the Philippians

BROTHERS and sisters: I consider everything as a loss because of the supreme good of knowing Christ Jesus my Lord. For his sake I have accepted the loss of all things and I consider them so much rubbish, that I may gain Christ and be found in him, not having any righteousness of my own based on the law but that which comes through faith in Christ, the righteousness from God, depending on faith to know him and the power of his resurrection and the sharing of his sufferings by being conformed to his death, if somehow I may attain the resurrection from the dead.

It is not that I have already taken hold of it or have already attained perfect maturity, but I continue my pursuit in hope that I may possess it, since I have indeed been taken possession of by Christ Jesus. Brothers and sisters, I for my part do not consider myself to have taken possession. Just one thing: forgetting what lies behind but straining forward to what lies ahead, I continue my pursuit toward the goal, the prize of God's upward calling, in Christ Jesus.—The word of the Lord.

---

10   Phil 4:4-9

A reading from the Letter of Saint Paul to the Philippians

BROTHERS and sisters: Rejoice in the Lord always. I shall say it again: rejoice! Your kindness should be known to all. The Lord is near. Have no anxiety at all, but in everything, by prayer and petition, with thanksgiving, make your requests known to God. Then the peace of God that surpasses all understanding will guard your hearts and minds in Christ Jesus.

Finally, brothers and sisters, whatever is true, whatever is honorable, whatever is just, whatever is pure, whatever is lovely, whatever is gracious, if there is any excellence and if there is anything worthy of praise, think about these things. Keep on doing what you have learned and received and heard and seen in me. Then the God of peace will be with you.—The word of the Lord.

11

Col 3:12-17

A reading from the Letter of Saint Paul to the Colossians

BROTHERS and sisters: Put on, as God's chosen ones, holy and beloved, heartfelt compassion, kindness, humility, gentleness, and patience, bearing with one another and forgiving one another, if one has a grievance against another; as the Lord has forgiven you, so must you also do. And over all these put on love, that is, the bond of perfection. And let the peace of Christ control your hearts, the peace into which you were also called in one Body. And be thankful. Let the word of Christ dwell in you richly, as in all wisdom you teach and admonish one another, singing psalms, hymns, and spiritual songs with gratitude in your hearts to God. And whatever you do, in word or in deed, do everything in the name of the Lord Jesus, giving thanks to God the Father through him.—The word of the Lord.

12

1 Tm 5:3-10

[For Widows]

A reading from the first Letter of Saint Paul to Timothy

BELOVED: Honor widows who are truly widows. But if a widow has children or grandchildren, let these first learn to perform their religious duty to their own family and to make recompense to their parents, for this is pleasing to God. The real widow, who is all alone, has set her hope on God and continues in supplications and prayers night and day. But the one who is self-indulgent is dead while she lives. Command this, so that they may be irreproachable. And whoever does not provide for relatives and especially family members has denied the faith and is worse than an unbeliever.

Let a widow be enrolled if she is not less than sixty years old, married only once, with a reputation for good works, namely, that she has raised children, practiced hospitality, washed the feet of the holy ones, helped those in distress, involved herself in every good work.—The word of the Lord.

---

13   Jas 2:14-17

A reading from the Letter of Saint James

WHAT good is it, my brothers and sisters, if someone says he has faith but does not have works? Can that faith save him? If a brother or sister has nothing to wear and has no food for the day, and one of you says to them, "Go in peace, keep warm, and eat well," but you do not give them the necessities of the body, what good is it? So also faith of itself, if it does not have works, is dead.—The word of the Lord.

---

14   1 Pt 3:1-9

A reading from the first Letter of Saint Peter

YOU wives should be subordinate to your husbands so that, even if some disobey the word, they may be won over without a word by their wives' conduct when they observe your reverent and chaste behavior. Your adornment should not be an external one: braiding the hair, wearing gold jewelry, or dressing in fine clothes, but rather the hidden character of the heart, expressed in the imperishable beauty of a gentle and calm disposition, which is precious in the sight of God. For this is also how the holy women who hoped in God once used to adorn themselves and were subordinate to their husbands; thus Sarah obeyed Abraham, calling him "lord." You are her children when you do what is good and fear no intimidation.

Likewise, you husbands should live with your wives in understanding, showing honor to the weaker female sex, since we are joint heirs of the gift of life, so that your prayers may not be hindered.

Finally, all of you, be of one mind, sympathetic, loving toward one another, compassionate, humble. Do not return evil for evil, or insult for insult; but, on the contrary, a blessing, because to this you were called, that you might inherit a blessing.—The word of the Lord.

| **15** | 1 Pt 4:7b-11 |

A reading from the first Letter of Saint Peter

BELOVED: Be serious and sober-minded so that you will be able to pray. Above all, let your love for one another be intense, because love covers a multitude of sins. Be hospitable to one another without complaining. As each one has received a gift, use it to serve one another as good stewards of God's varied grace. Whoever preaches, let it be with the words of God; whoever serves, let it be with the strength that God supplies, so that in all things God may be glorified through Jesus Christ, to whom belong glory and dominion forever and ever. Amen.—The word of the Lord.

| **16** | 1 Jn 3:14-18 |

[For Those Who Work with the Underprivileged]

A reading from the first Letter of Saint John

BELOVED: We know that we have passed from death to life because we love our brothers. Whoever does not love remains in death. Everyone who hates his brother is a murderer, and you know that anyone who is a murderer does not have eternal life remaining in him. The way we came to know love was that he laid down his life for us; so we ought to lay down our lives for our brothers. If someone who has worldly means sees a brother in need and refuses him compassion, how can the love of God remain in him? Children, let us love not in word or speech but in deed and truth.—The word of the Lord.

---

17   1 Jn 4:7-16

A reading from the first Letter of Saint John

BELOVED, let us love one another, because love is of God; everyone who loves is begotten by God and knows God. Whoever is without love does not know God, for God is love. In this way the love of God was revealed to us: God sent his only-begotten Son into the world so that we might have life through him. In this is love: not that we have loved God, but that he loved us and sent his Son as expiation for our sins. Beloved, if God so loved us, we also must love one another. No one has ever seen God. Yet, if we love one another, God remains in us, and his love is brought to perfection in us.

This is how we know that we remain in him and he in us, that he has given us of his Spirit. Moreover, we have seen and testify that the Father sent his Son as savior of the world. Whoever acknowledges that Jesus is the Son of God, God remains in him and he in God. We have come to know and to believe in the love God has for us.

God is love, and whoever remains in love remains in God and God in him.—The word of the Lord.

---

18   1 Jn 5:1-5

A reading from the first Letter of Saint John

BELOVED: Everyone who believes that Jesus is the Christ is begotten by God, and everyone who loves the Father loves also the one begotten by him. In this way we know that we love the children of God when we love God and obey his commandments. For the love of God is this, that we keep his commandments. And his commandments are not burdensome, for whoever is begotten by God conquers the world. And the victory that conquers the world is our faith. Who indeed is the victor over the world but the one who believes that Jesus is the Son of God?—The word of the Lord.

ALLELUIA VERSE AND
VERSE BEFORE THE GOSPEL

1   Mt 5:3

Blessed are the poor in spirit;
for theirs is the Kingdom of heaven.

2   Mt 5:6

Blessed are those who hunger and thirst for righteousness,
for they will be satisfied.

3   Mt 5:8

Blessed are the clean of heart,
for they will see God.

4   See Mt 11:25

Blessed are you, Father, Lord of heaven and earth;
you have revealed to little ones the mysteries of the
    Kingdom.

5   Mt 11:28

Come to me, all you who labor and are burdened,
and I will give you rest, says the Lord.

6   Mt 23:11, 12b

The greatest among you must be your servant.
Whoever humbles himself will be exalted.

7

Lk 21:36

Be vigilant at all times
and pray that you may have the strength to stand before the
    Son of Man.

8

Jn 8:12

I am the light of the world, says the Lord;
whoever follows me will have the light of life.

9

Jn 8:31b-32

If you remain in my word, you will truly be my disciples,
and you will know the truth, says the Lord.

10

Jn 13:34

I give you a new commandment:
love one another as I have loved you.

11

Jn 14:23

Whoever loves me will keep my word
and my Father will love him
and we will come to him.

12

Jn 15:4a, 5b

Remain in me, as I remain in you, says the Lord;
whoever remains in me will bear much fruit.

13

Jn 15:9b, 5b

Remain in my love, says the Lord;
whoever remains in me and I in him will bear much fruit.

GOSPEL

1   Mt 5:1-12a

✝ A reading from the holy Gospel according to Matthew

WHEN Jesus saw the crowds, he went up the mountain, and after he had sat down, his disciples came to him. He began to teach them, saying:

"Blessed are the poor in spirit,
    for theirs is the Kingdom of heaven.
Blessed are they who mourn,
    for they will be comforted.
Blessed are the meek,
    for they will inherit the land.
Blessed are they who hunger and thirst for righteousness,
    for they will be satisfied.
Blessed are the merciful,
    for they will be shown mercy.
Blessed are the clean of heart,
    for they will see God.
Blessed are the peacemakers,
    for they will be called children of God.
Blessed are they who are persecuted for the sake of righ-
      teousness,
    for theirs is the Kingdom of heaven.

Blessed are you when they insult you and persecute you and utter every kind of evil against you falsely because of me. Rejoice and be glad, for your reward will be great in heaven."—The Gospel of the Lord.

---

2   Mt 5:13-16

✝ A reading from the holy Gospel according to Matthew

JESUS said to his disciples: "You are the salt of the earth. But if salt loses its taste, with what can it be seasoned? It is no longer good for anything but to be thrown out and trampled underfoot. You are the light of the world. A city set on a mountain cannot be hidden. Nor do they light a lamp and then put it under a bushel basket; it is set on a lampstand, where it gives light to all in the house. Just so, your light must shine before others, that they may see your good deeds and glorify your heavenly Father."—The Gospel of the Lord.

---

3   Mt 7:21-27

✤ A reading from the holy Gospel according to Matthew

JESUS said to his disciples:"Not everyone who says to me, 'Lord, Lord,' will enter the Kingdom of heaven, but only the one who does the will of my Father in heaven. Many will say to me on that day, 'Lord, Lord, did we not prophesy in your name? Did we not drive out demons in your name? Did we not do mighty deeds in your name?' Then I will declare to them solemnly, 'I never knew you. Depart from me, you evildoers.'

"Everyone who listens to these words of mine and acts on them will be like a wise man who built his house on rock. The rain fell, the floods came, and the winds blew and buffeted the house. But it did not collapse; it had been set solidly on rock. And everyone who listens to these words of mine but does not act on them will be like a fool who built his house on sand. The rain fell, the floods came, and the winds blew and buffeted the house. And it collapsed and was completely ruined."—The Gospel of the Lord.

---

4   Mt 11:25-30

✤ reading from the holy Gospel according to Matthew

AT that time Jesus exclaimed:"I give praise to you, Father, Lord of heaven and earth, for although you have hidden these things from the wise and the learned you have revealed them to the childlike. Yes, Father, such has been your gracious will. All things have been handed over to me by my Father. No one knows the Son except the Father, and no one knows the Father except the Son and anyone to whom the Son wishes to reveal him.

"Come to me, all you who labor and are burdened, and I will give you rest. Take my yoke upon you and learn from me, for I am meek and humble of heart; and you will find rest for yourselves. For my yoke is easy, and my burden light."—The Gospel of the Lord.

---

5   Mt 13:44-46

✢ A reading from the holy Gospel according to Matthew

JESUS said to the crowds:"The Kingdom of heaven is like a treasure buried in a field, which a person finds and hides again, and out of joy goes and sells all that he has and buys that field. Again, the Kingdom of heaven is like a merchant searching for fine pearls. When he finds a pearl of great price, he goes and sells all that he has and buys it."—The Gospel of the Lord.

---

6   Mt 16:24-27

✢ A reading from the holy Gospel according to Matthew

JESUS said to his disciples, "Whoever wishes to come after me must deny himself, take up his cross, and follow me. For whoever wishes to save his life will lose it, but whoever loses his life for my sake will find it. What profit would there be for one to gain the whole world and forfeit his life? Or what can one give in exchange for his life? For the Son of Man will come with his angels in his Father's glory, and then he will repay each one according to his conduct."—The Gospel of the Lord.

---

7   Mt 18:1-5

✢ A reading from the holy Gospel according to Matthew

THE disciples approached Jesus and said, "Who is the greatest in the Kingdom of heaven?" He called a child over, placed it in their midst, and said, "Amen, I say to you, unless you turn and become like children, you will not enter the Kingdom of heaven. Whoever humbles himself like this child is the greatest in the Kingdom of heaven. And whoever receives one child such as this in my name receives me."—The Gospel of the Lord.

---

8   Mt 19:3-12

[For Religious]

✠ A reading from the holy Gospel according to Matthew

SOME Pharisees approached Jesus and tested him, saying, "Is it lawful for a man to divorce his wife for any cause whatever?" He said in reply, "Have you not read that from the beginning the Creator *made them male and female* and said, *For this reason a man shall leave his father and mother and be joined to his wife, and the two shall become one flesh*? So they are no longer two, but one flesh. Therefore, what God has joined together, man must not separate." They said to him, "Then why did Moses command that the man give the woman a bill of divorce and dismiss her?" He said to them, "Because of the hardness of your hearts Moses allowed you to divorce your wives, but from the beginning it was not so. I say to you, whoever divorces his wife (unless the marriage is unlawful) and marries another commits adultery." His disciples said to him, "If that is the case of a man with his wife, it is better not to marry." He answered, "Not all can accept this word, but only those to whom that is granted. Some are incapable of marriage because they were born so; some, because they were made so by others; some, because they have renounced marriage for the sake of the Kingdom of heaven. Whoever can accept this ought to accept it."—The Gospel of the Lord.

9

Mt 19:27-29

✠ A reading from the holy Gospel according to Matthew

PETER said to Jesus, "We have given up everything and followed you. What will there be for us?" Jesus said to them, "Amen, I say to you that you who have followed me, in the new age, when the Son of Man is seated on his throne of glory, will yourselves sit on twelve thrones, judging the twelve tribes of Israel. And everyone who has given up houses or brothers or sisters or father or mother or children or lands for the sake of my name will receive a hundred times more, and will inherit eternal life."—The Gospel of the Lord.

10

Mt 22:34-40

✠ A reading from the holy Gospel according to Matthew

WHEN the Pharisees heard that Jesus had silenced the Sadducees, they gathered together, and one of them, a scholar of the law, tested him by asking, "Teacher, which commandment in the law is the greatest?" He said to him, "You shall love the Lord, your God, with all your heart, with all your soul, and with all your mind. This is the greatest and the first commandment. The second is like it: You shall love your neighbor as yourself. The whole law and the prophets depend on these two commandments." —The Gospel of the Lord.

11

Mt 25:1-13

✠ A reading from the holy Gospel according to Matthew

JESUS told his disciples this parable: "The Kingdom of heaven will be like ten virgins who took their lamps and went out to meet the bridegroom. Five of them were foolish and five were wise. The foolish ones, when taking their lamps, brought no oil with them, but the wise brought flasks of oil with their lamps. Since the bridegroom was long delayed, they all became drowsy and fell asleep. At midnight, there was a cry, 'Behold, the bridegroom! Come out to meet him!' Then all those virgins got up and trimmed their lamps. The foolish ones said to the wise, 'Give us some of your oil, for our lamps are going out.' But the wise ones replied, 'No, for there may not be enough for us and you. Go instead to the merchants and buy some for yourselves.' While they went off to buy it, the bridegroom came and those who were ready went into the wedding feast with him. Then the door was locked. Afterwards the other virgins came and said, 'Lord, Lord, open the door for us!' But he said in reply, 'Amen, I say to you, I do not know you.' Therefore, stay awake, for you know neither the day nor the hour."— The Gospel of the Lord.

---

12   Mt 25:14-30 or 25:14-23

[If the "Short Form" is used, omit indented text in brackets.]

✣ A reading from the holy Gospel according to Matthew

JESUS told his disciples this parable: "A man who was going on a journey called in his servants and entrusted his possessions to them. To one he gave five talents; to another, two; to a third, one—to each according to his ability. Then he went away. Immediately the one who received five talents went and traded with them, and made another five. Likewise, the one who received two made another two. But the man who received one went off and dug a hole in the ground and buried his master's money. After a long time the master of those servants came back and settled accounts with them. The one who had received five talents came forward bringing the additional five. He said, 'Master, you gave me five talents. See, I have made five more.' His master said to him, 'Well done, my good and faithful servant. Since you were faithful in small matters, I will give you great responsibilities. Come, share your master's joy.' Then the one who had received two talents also came forward and said, 'Master, you gave me two talents. See, I have made two more.' His master said to him, 'Well done, my good and faithful servant. Since you were faithful in small matters, I will give you great responsibilities. Come, share your master's joy.'

[Then the one who had received the one talent came forward and said, 'Master, I knew you were a demanding person, harvesting where you did not plant and gathering where you did not scatter; so out of fear I went off and buried your talent in the ground. Here it is back.' His master said to him in reply, 'You wicked, lazy servant! So you knew that I harvest where I did not plant and gather where I did not scatter? Should you not then have put my money in the bank so that I could have got it back with interest on my return? Now then! Take the talent from him and give it to the one with ten. For to everyone who has, more will be given and he will grow rich; but from the one who has not, even what he has will be taken away. And throw this useless servant into the darkness outside, where there will be wailing and grinding of teeth.' "]

The Gospel of the Lord.

---

13   Mt 25:31-46 or 25:31-40

[For Those Who Work for the Underprivileged]

[If the "Short Form" is used, omit indented text in brackets.]

✠ A reading from the holy Gospel according to Matthew

JESUS said to his disciples: "When the Son of Man comes in his glory, and all the angels with him, he will sit upon his glorious throne, and all the nations will be assembled before him. And he will separate them one from another, as a shepherd separates the sheep from the goats. He will place the sheep on his right and the goats on his left. Then the king will say to those on his right, 'Come, you who are blessed by my Father. Inherit the kingdom prepared for you from the foundation of the world. For I was hungry and you gave me food, I was thirsty and you gave me drink, a stranger and you welcomed me, naked and you clothed me, ill and you cared for me, in prison and you visited me.' Then the righteous will answer him and say, 'Lord, when did we see you hungry and feed you, or thirsty and give you drink? When did we see you a stranger and welcome you, or naked and clothe you? When did we see you ill or in prison, and visit you?' And the king will say to them in reply, 'Amen, I say to you, whatever you did for one of the least brothers of mine, you did for me.'

[Then he will say to those on his left, 'Depart from me, you accursed, into the eternal fire prepared for the Devil and his angels. For I was hungry and you gave me no food, I was thirsty and you gave me no drink, a stranger and you gave me no welcome, naked and you gave me no clothing, ill and in prison, and you did not care for me.' Then they will answer and say, 'Lord, when did we see you hungry or thirsty or a stranger or naked or ill or in prison, and not minister to your needs?' He will answer them, 'Amen, I say to you, what you did not do for one of these least ones, you did not do for me.' And these will go off to eternal punishment, but the righteous to eternal life."]

The Gospel of the Lord.

---

14   Mk 3:31-35

✠ A reading from the holy Gospel according to Mark

THE mother of Jesus and his brothers arrived. Standing outside they sent word to him and called him. A crowd seated around him told him, "Your mother and your brothers and your sisters are outside asking for you." But he said to them in reply, "Who are my mother and my brothers?" And looking around at those seated in the circle he said, "Here are my mother and my brothers. For whoever does the will of God is my brother and sister and mother."—The Gospel of the Lord.

---

15   Mk 9:34-37

[For Teachers]

✠ A reading from the holy Gospel according to Mark

JESUS' disciples had been discussing among themselves who was the greatest. Then he sat down, called the Twelve, and said to them, "If anyone wishes to be first, he shall be the last of all and the servant of all." Taking a child he placed it in their midst, and putting his arms around it he said to them, "Whoever receives one child such as this in my name, receives me; and whoever receives me, receives not me but the One who sent me."—The Gospel of the Lord.

---

16   Mk 10:13-16

✠ A reading from the holy Gospel according to Mark

PEOPLE were bringing children to Jesus that he might touch them, but the disciples rebuked them. When Jesus saw this he became indignant and said to them, "Let the children come to me; do not prevent them, for the Kingdom of God belongs to such as these. Amen, I say to you, whoever does not accept the Kingdom of God like a child will not enter it." Then he embraced them and blessed them, placing his hands on them.—The Gospel of the Lord.

---

17   Mk 10:17-30 or 10:17-27

[If the "Short Form" is used, omit indented text in brackets.]

[For Religious]

✠ A reading from the holy Gospel according to Mark

AS Jesus was setting out on a journey, a man ran up, knelt down before him, and asked him, "Good teacher, what must I do to inherit eternal life?" Jesus answered him, "Why do you call me good? No one is good but God alone. You know the commandments: *You shall not kill; you shall not commit adultery; you shall not steal; you shall not bear false witness; you shall not defraud; honor your father and your mother.*" He replied and said to him, "Teacher, all of these I have observed from my youth." Jesus, looking at him, loved him and said to him, "You are lacking in one thing. Go, sell what you have, and give to the poor and you will have treasure in heaven; then come, follow me." At that statement his face fell, and he went away sad, for he had many possessions.

Jesus looked around and said to his disciples, "How hard it is for those who have wealth to enter the Kingdom of God!" The disciples were amazed at his words. So Jesus again said to them in reply, "Children, how hard it is to enter the Kingdom of God! It is easier for a camel to pass through the eye of a needle than for one who is rich to enter the Kingdom of God." They were exceedingly astonished and said among themselves, "Then who can be saved?" Jesus looked at them and said, "For men it is impossible, but not for God. All things are possible for God."

[Peter began to say to him, "We have given up everything and followed you." Jesus said, "Amen, I say to you, there is no one who has given up house or brothers or sisters or mother or father or children or lands for my sake and for the sake of the Gospel who will not receive a hundred times more now in this present age: houses and brothers and sisters and mothers and children and lands, with persecutions, and eternal life in the age to come."]
The Gospel of the Lord.

18

Lk 6:27-38

✚ A reading from the holy Gospel according to Luke

JESUS said to his disciples: "To you who hear I say, love your enemies, do good to those who hate you, bless those who curse you, pray for those who mistreat you. To the person who strikes you on one cheek, offer the other one as well, and from the person who takes your cloak, do not withhold even your tunic. Give to everyone who asks of you, and from the one who takes what is yours do not demand it back. Do to others as you would have them do to you. For if you love those who love you, what credit is that to you? Even sinners love those who love them. And if you do good to those who do good to you, what credit is that to you? Even sinners do the same. If you lend money to those from whom you expect repayment, what credit is that to you? Even sinners lend to sinners, and get back the same amount. But rather, love your enemies and do good to them, and lend expecting nothing back; then your reward will be great and you will be children of the Most High, for he himself is kind to the ungrateful and the wicked. Be merciful, just as also your Father is merciful.

"Stop judging and you will not be judged. Stop condemning and you will not be condemned. Forgive and you will be forgiven. Give and gifts will be given to you; a good measure, packed together, shaken down, and overflowing, will be poured into your lap. For the measure with which you measure will in return be measured out to you."—The Gospel of the Lord.

 19

Lk 9:57-62

[For Religious]

✣ A reading from the holy Gospel according to Luke

AS Jesus and his disciples were proceeding on their journey, someone said to him, "I will follow you wherever you go." Jesus answered him, "Foxes have dens and birds of the sky have nests, but the Son of Man has nowhere to rest his head." And to another he said, "Follow me." But he replied, "Lord, let me go first and bury my father." But he answered him, "Let the dead bury their dead. But you, go and proclaim the Kingdom of God." And another said, "I will follow you, Lord, but first let me say farewell to my family at home." Jesus said to him, "No one who sets a hand to the plow and looks to what was left behind is fit for the Kingdom of God."—The Gospel of the Lord.

20

✛ A reading from the holy Gospel according to Luke

JESUS entered a village where a woman whose name was Martha welcomed him. She had a sister named Mary who sat beside the Lord at his feet listening to him speak. Martha, burdened with much serving, came to him and said, "Lord, do you not care that my sister has left me by myself to do the serving? Tell her to help me." The Lord said to her in reply, "Martha, Martha, you are anxious and worried about many things. There is need of only one thing. Mary has chosen the better part and it will not be taken from her."—The Gospel of the Lord.

21

[For Religious]

✛ A reading from the holy Gospel according to Luke

JESUS said to his disciples: "Do not be afraid any longer, little flock, for your Father is pleased to give you the Kingdom. Sell your belongings and give alms. Provide money bags for yourselves that do not wear out, an inexhaustible treasure in heaven that no thief can reach nor moth destroy. For where your treasure is, there also will your heart be."—The Gospel of the Lord.

22

✛ A reading from the holy Gospel according to Luke

JESUS said to his disciples: "Gird your loins and light your lamps and be like servants who await their master's return from a wedding, ready to open immediately when he comes and knocks. Blessed are those servants whom the master finds vigilant on his arrival. Amen, I say to you, he will gird himself, have them recline at table, and proceed to wait on them. And should he come in the second or third watch and find them prepared in this way, blessed are those servants. Be sure of this: if the master of the house had known the hour when the thief was coming, he would not have let his house be broken into. You also must be prepared, for at an hour you do not expect, the Son of Man will come."—The Gospel of the Lord.

23　　　　　　　　　　　　　　　　　　　　　　Lk 14:25-33

[For Religious]

✚ A reading from the holy Gospel according to Luke

GREAT crowds were traveling with Jesus, and he turned and addressed them, "If anyone comes to me without hating his father and mother, wife and children, brothers and sisters, and even his own life, he cannot be my disciple. Whoever does not carry his own cross and come after me cannot be my disciple. Which of you wishing to construct a tower does not first sit down and calculate the cost to see if there is enough for its completion? Otherwise, after laying the foundation and finding himself unable to finish the work the onlookers should laugh at him and say, 'This one began to build but did not have the resources to finish.' Or what king marching into battle would not first sit down and decide whether with ten thousand troops he can successfully oppose another king advancing upon him with twenty thousand troops? But if not, while he is still far away, he will send a delegation to ask for peace terms. In the same way, everyone of you who does not renounce all his possessions cannot be my disciple."—The Gospel of the Lord.

24　　　　　　　　　　　　　　　　　　　　　　Jn 15:1-8

✚ A reading from the holy Gospel according to John

JESUS said to his disciples: "I am the true vine, and my Father is the vine grower. He takes away every branch in me that does not bear fruit, and everyone that does he prunes so that it bears more fruit. You are already pruned because of the word that I spoke to you. Remain in me, as I remain in you. Just as a branch cannot bear fruit on its own unless it remains on the vine, so neither can you unless you remain in me. I am the vine, you are the branches. Whoever remains in me and I in him will bear much fruit, because without me you can do nothing. Anyone who does not remain in me will be thrown out like a branch and wither; people will gather them and throw them into a fire and they will be burned. If you remain in me and my words remain in you, ask for whatever you want and it will be done for you. By this is my Father glorified, that you bear much fruit and become my disciples."—The Gospel of the Lord.

<u>25</u>

Jn 15:9-17

✛ A reading from the holy Gospel according to John

JESUS said to his disciples: "As the Father loves me, so I also love you. Remain in my love. If you keep my commandments, you will remain in my love, just as I have kept my Father's commandments and remain in his love.

"I have told you this so that my joy might be in you and your joy might be complete. This is my commandment: love one another as I love you. No one has greater love than this, to lay down one's life for one's friends. You are my friends if you do what I command you. I no longer call you slaves, because a slave does not know what his master is doing. I have called you friends, because I have told you everything I have heard from my Father. It was not you who chose me, but I who chose you and appointed you to go and bear fruit that will remain, so that whatever you ask the Father in my name he may give you. This I command you: love one another."—The Gospel of the Lord.

---

26   Jn 17:20-26

✠ A reading from the holy Gospel according to John

JESUS raised his eyes to heaven and said: "Holy Father, I pray not only for these, but also for those who will believe in me through their word, so that they may all be one, as you, Father, are in me and I in you, that they also may be in us, that the world may believe that you sent me. And I have given them the glory you gave me, so that they may be one, as we are one, I in them and you in me, that they may be brought to perfection as one, that the world may know that you sent me, and that you loved them even as you loved me. Father, they are your gift to me. I wish that where I am they also may be with me, that they may see my glory that you gave me, because you loved me before the foundation of the world. Righteous Father, the world also does not know you, but I know you, and they know that you sent me. I made known to them your name and I will make it known, that the love with which you loved me may be in them and I in them."—The Gospel of the Lord.

APPENDIX I:
SELECTED MASSES AND PRAYERS

This section contains excerpts of selected Masses and Prayers that the celebrant may use on certain days of low rank. (See Tables of Choices of Masses and Texts, pp. [18]-[19].) For convenient reference the numbers attached to these Masses and Prayers in the *Sacramentary* have been retained. It is always preferable to use *Weekday* Readings, as indicated herein.

MASSES AND PRAYERS FOR VARIOUS NEEDS AND OCCASIONS

On Weekdays of Ordinary Time and certain other occasions, the complete Mass formulary found in the Sacramentary (processional chants and presidential prayers) or only the Opening Prayer may be taken from the following Masses and Prayers for Various Needs and Occasions. (See Introduction to Proper of Saints, pp. 433ff, and the Tables of Choices of Masses and Texts, pp. [18]-[19].)

1. FOR THE UNIVERSAL CHURCH

OPENING PRAYER

God our Father,
in your care and wisdom
you extend the kingdom of Christ to embrace the world
to give all men redemption.
May the Catholic Church be the sign of our salvation,
may it reveal for us the mystery of your love,
and may that love become effective in our lives.
Grant this . . . for ever and ever. R̹. **Amen.**

PRAYER OVER THE GIFTS

God of mercy,
look on our offering,
and by the power of this sacrament
help all who believe in you

to become the holy people you have called to be your own.
We ask this in the name of Jesus the Lord. ℟. **Amen.**

PRAYER AFTER COMMUNION

God our Father,
we are sustained by your sacraments;
we are renewed by this pledge of love at your altar.
May we live by the promises of your love which we receive,
and become a leaven in the world
to bring salvation to mankind.
Grant this through Christ our Lord. ℟. **Amen.**

---

2. FOR THE POPE

ENTRANCE ANT.
Mt 16:18-19

**You are Peter, the rock on which I will build my Church. The
gates of hell will not hold out against it. To you I will give
the keys of the kingdom of heaven.** → No. 2, p. 614

OPENING PRAYER

Father of providence,
look with love on N. our Pope,
your appointed successor to St. Peter
on whom you built your Church.
May he be the visible center and foundation
of our unity in faith and love.
Grant this . . . for ever and ever. ℟. **Amen.** ↓

READINGS AND INTERVENIENT CHANTS

*The current Weekday Readings and Intervenient Chants are
used.*

PRAYER OVER THE GIFTS

Lord,
be pleased with our gifts
and give guidance to your holy Church
together with N. our Pope,

to whom you have entrusted the care of your flock.
We ask this in the name of Jesus the Lord.
℟. **Amen.** → No. 21, p. 626

COMMUNION ANT. Jn 21:15, 17

Simon, son of John, do you love me more than these? Lord, you know all things; you know that I love you. ↓

PRAYER AFTER COMMUNION

God our Father,
we have eaten at your holy table.
By the power of this sacrament,
make your Church firm in unity and love,
and grant strength and salvation
to your servant N.,
together with the flock you have entrusted to his care.
Grant this through Christ our Lord.
℟. **Amen.** → No. 32, p. 660

---

3. FOR THE BISHOP

(Especially on the Anniversary of Ordination)

ENTRANCE ANT. Ez 34:11, 23-24

I will look after my sheep, says the Lord, and I will raise up one shepherd who will pasture them. I, the Lord, will be their God. → No. 2, p. 614

OPENING PRAYER

God, eternal shepherd,
you tend your Church in many ways,
and rule us with love.
Help your chosen servant N.
as pastor for Christ,
to watch over your flock.
Help him to be a faithful teacher,
a wise administrator, and a holy priest.
We ask this . . . for ever and ever. ℟. **Amen.** ↓

OR

God our Father, our shepherd and guide,
look with love on N. your servant,
your appointed pastor of the Church.
May his word and example inspire and guide the Church;
may he, and all those in his care,
come to the joy of everlasting life.
Grant this . . . for ever and ever. ℟. **Amen.** ↓

READINGS AND INTERVENIENT CHANTS

The current Weekday Readings and Intervenient Chants are used.

PRAYER OVER THE GIFTS

Lord,
accept these gifts which we offer for your servant N., your
    chosen priest.
Enrich him with the gifts and virtues of a true apostle
for the good of your people.
We ask this through Christ our Lord.
℟. **Amen.**   ➞ No. 21, p. 626

COMMUNION ANT.   Mt 20:28

**The Son of Man did not come to be served, but to serve, and
to give his life as a ransom for many.** ↓

PRAYER AFTER COMMUNION

Lord,
by the power of these holy mysteries
increase in our bishop N. your gifts of wisdom and love.
May he fulfill his pastoral ministry
and receive the eternal rewards
you promise to your faithful servants.
Grant this through Christ our Lord.
℟. **Amen.**   ➞ No. 32, p. 660

7. FOR THE PRIEST HIMSELF
ON THE ANNIVERSARY OF ORDINATION

OPENING PRAYER

Father,
unworthy as I am, you have chosen me
to share in the eternal priesthood of Christ
and the ministry of your Church.
May I be an ardent but gentle servant
of your gospel and your sacraments.
Grant this . . . for ever and ever. ℟. **Amen.**

PRAYER OVER THE GIFTS

Lord,
in your mercy, accept our offering
and help me to fulfill the ministry you have given me
in spite of my unworthiness.
Grant this through Christ our Lord. ℟. **Amen.**

PRAYER AFTER COMMUNION

Lord,
on this anniversary of my ordination
I have celebrated the mystery of faith
to the glory of your name.
May I always live in truth
the mysteries I handle at your altar.
Grant this in the name of Jesus the Lord. ℟. **Amen.**

---

9. FOR PRIESTLY VOCATIONS

ENTRANCE ANT.   Mt 9:38

Jesus says to his disciples: ask the Lord to send workers into his harvest.   ➙ No. 2, p. 614

OPENING PRAYER

Father,
in your plan for our salvation you provide shepherds for
your people.

Fill your Church with the spirit of courage and love.
Raise up worthy ministers for your altars
and ardent but gentle servants of the gospel.
Grant this . . . for ever and ever. ℟. **Amen.** ↓

READINGS AND INTERVENIENT CHANTS

The current Weekday Readings and Intervenient Chants are used.

PRAYER OVER THE GIFTS

Lord,
accept our prayers and gifts.
Give the Church more priests
and keep them faithful in their love and service.
Grant this in the name of Jesus the Lord.
℟. **Amen.** → No. 21, p. 626

COMMUNION ANT.   1 Jn 3:16

This is how we know what love is: Christ gave up his life for us; and we too must give up our lives for our brothers. ↓

PRAYER AFTER COMMUNION

Lord,
hear the prayers of those who are renewed
with the bread of life at your holy table.
By this sacrament of love
bring to maturity
the seeds you have sown
in the field of your Church;
may many of your people choose to serve you
by devoting themselves to the service of their brothers and
  sisters.
We ask this through Christ our Lord.
℟. **Amen.** → No. 32, p. 660

11. FOR RELIGIOUS VOCATIONS

ENTRANCE ANT. Mt 19:21

If you want to be perfect, go, sell what you own, give it all to the poor, then come, follow me. → No. 2, p. 614

OPENING PRAYER

Father,
you call all who believe in you to grow perfect in love
by following in the footsteps of Christ your Son.
May those whom you have chosen to serve you as religious
provide by their way of life
a convincing sign of your kingdom
for the Church and the whole world.
We ask this . . . for ever and ever. ℟. **Amen.** ↓

READINGS AND INTERVENIENT CHANTS

The current Weekday Readings and Intervenient Chants are used.

PRAYER OVER THE GIFTS

Father,
in your love accept the gifts we offer you,
and watch over those who wish to follow your Son more
    closely,
and to serve you joyfully in religious life.
Give them spiritual freedom
and love for their brothers and sisters.
We ask this through Christ our Lord.
℟. **Amen.** → No. 21, p. 626

COMMUNION ANT. See Mt 19:27-29

I solemnly tell you: those who have left everything and followed me will be repaid a hundredfold and will gain eternal life. ↓

PRAYER AFTER COMMUNION

Father, make your people grow strong
by sharing this spiritual food and drink.

Keep them faithful to the call of the gospel
that the world may see in them
the living image of your Son, Jesus Christ,
who is Lord for ever and ever.
℟. **Amen.**

→ No. 32, p. 660

12. FOR THE LAITY

OPENING PRAYER

God our Father,
you send the power of the gospel into the world
as a life-giving leaven.
Fill with the Spirit of Christ
those whom you call to live in the midst of the world
and its concerns;
help them by their work on earth
to build up your eternal kingdom.
We ask this . . . for ever and ever. ℟. **Amen.**

PRAYER OVER THE GIFTS

Father, you have given your Son
to save the whole world by his sacrifice.
By the power of this offering,
help all your people
to fill the world with the Spirit of Christ.
Grant this through Christ our Lord. ℟. **Amen.**

PRAYER AFTER COMMUNION

Lord,
you share with us the fullness of your love,
and give us new courage at this eucharistic feast.
May the people you call to work in the world
be effective witnesses to the truth of the gospel
and make your Church a living presence
in the midst of that world.
We ask this through Christ our Lord. ℟. **Amen.**

13. FOR UNITY OF CHRISTIANS

ENTRANCE ANT.
Jn 10:14-15

I am the Good Shepherd. I know my sheep, and mine know me, says the Lord, just as the Father knows me and I know the Father. I give my life for my sheep. → No. 2, p. 614

OPENING PRAYER

Almighty and eternal God,
keep together those you have united.
Look kindly on all who follow Jesus your Son.
We are all consecrated to you by our common baptism;
make us one in the fullness of faith
and keep us one in the fellowship of love.
We ask this . . . for ever and ever. ℟. **Amen.** ↓

OR

Lord,
lover of mankind,
fill us with the love your Spirit gives.
May we live in a manner worthy of our calling;
make us witnesses of your truth to all men
and help us work to bring all believers together
in the unity of faith and the fellowship of peace.
Grant this . . . for ever and ever. ℟. **Amen.** ↓

READINGS AND INTERVENIENT CHANTS
The current Weekday Readings and Intervenient Chants are used.

PRAYER OVER THE GIFTS

Lord,
by one perfect sacrifice
you gained us as your people.
Bless us and all your Church
with gifts of unity and peace.
We ask this in the name of Jesus the Lord.
℟. **Amen.**
→ No. 21, p. 626 (P 76)

COMMUNION ANT. See 1 Cor 10:17

Because there is one bread, we, though many, are one body, for we all share in the one loaf and in the one cup. ↓

PRAYER AFTER COMMUNION

Lord,
may this holy communion,
the sign and promise of our unity in you,
make that unity a reality in your Church.
We ask this through Christ our Lord.
℟. **Amen.**

→ No. 32, p. 660

14. FOR THE SPREAD OF THE GOSPEL

ENTRANCE ANT. Ps 67:2-3

May God bless us in his mercy; may he make his face shine on us, that we might know his ways on earth and his saving power among all the nations. → No. 2, p. 614

OPENING PRAYER

God our Father,
you will all men to be saved
and come to the knowledge of your truth.
Send workers into your great harvest
that the gospel may be preached to every creature
and your people, gathered together by the word of life
and strengthened by the power of the sacraments,
may advance in the way of salvation and love.
We ask this . . . for ever and ever. ℟. **Amen.** ↓

OR

God our Father,
you sent your Son into the world to be its true light.
Pour out the Spirit he promised us
to sow the truth in men's hearts
and awaken in them obedience to the faith.
May all men be born again to new life in baptism
and enter the fellowship of your one holy people.
Grant this . . . for ever and ever. ℟. **Amen.** ↓

READINGS AND INTERVENIENT CHANTS

The current Weekday Readings and Intervenient Chants are used.

PRAYER OVER THE GIFTS

Lord,
look upon the face of Christ your Son
who gave up his life to set all men free.
Through him may your name be praised
among all peoples from East to West,
and everywhere may one sacrifice be offered to give you
　　glory.
We ask this through Christ our Lord. R̶). **Amen.** ↓

PRAYER AFTER COMMUNION

Lord,
you renew our life with this gift of redemption.
Through this help to eternal salvation
may the true faith continue to grow throughout the world.
We ask this in the name of Jesus the Lord.
R̶). **Amen.**   → No. 32, p. 660

---

16. FOR PASTORAL OR SPIRITUAL MEETINGS

ENTRANCE ANT.   Mt 18:20

**Where two or three are gathered together in my name, says
the Lord, I am there among them.**

OR   Col 3:14-15

**To crown all things there must be love, to bind them togeth-
er and bring them to completion; and may the peace of
Christ rule in your hearts.**   → No. 2, p. 614

OPENING PRAYER

Lord,
pour out on us the spirit of understanding, truth, and peace.
Help us to strive with all our hearts
to know what is pleasing to you,

and when we know your will
make us determined to do it.
We ask this . . . for ever and ever. ℟. **Amen.** ↓

OR

God our Father,
your Son promised to be with all who gather in his name.
Make us aware of his presence among us
and fill us with his grace, mercy, and peace,
so that we may live in truth and love.
Grant this . . . for ever and ever. ℟. **Amen.** ↓

READINGS AND INTERVENIENT CHANTS

The current Weekday Readings and Intervenient Chants are used.

PRAYER OVER THE GIFTS

God our Father,
look with love on the gifts of your people.
Help us to understand what is right and good in your sight
and to proclaim it faithfully to our brothers and sisters.
We ask this through Christ our Lord.
℟. **Amen.**   → No. 21, p. 626

COMMUNION ANT.

**Where charity and love are found, God is there. The love of
Christ has gathered us together.** ↓

PRAYER AFTER COMMUNION

God of mercy,
may the holy gifts we receive
give us strength in doing your will,
and make us effective witnesses of your truth
to all whose lives we touch.
We ask this in the name of Jesus the Lord.
℟. **Amen.**   → No. 32, p. 660

17. FOR THE NATION, (STATE,) OR CITY

OPENING PRAYER

God our Father,
you guide everything in wisdom and love.
Accept the prayers we offer for our nation;
by the wisdom of our leaders and integrity of our citizens,
may harmony and justice be secured
and may there be lasting prosperity and peace.
We ask this . . . for ever and ever. R̸. **Amen.**

---

18. FOR THOSE WHO SERVE IN PUBLIC OFFICE

OPENING PRAYER

Almighty and eternal God,
you know the longings of men's hearts
and you protect their rights.
In your goodness,
watch over those in authority,
so that people everywhere may enjoy
freedom, security, and peace.
We ask this . . . for ever and ever. R̸. **Amen.**

---

19. FOR THE CONGRESS

OPENING PRAYER

Father,
you guide and govern everything with order and love.
Look upon the members of Congress
and fill them with the spirit of your wisdom.
May they always act in accordance with your will
and their decisions be for the peace and well-being of all.
We ask this . . . for ever and ever. R̸. **Amen.**

---

22. FOR PEACE AND JUSTICE

ENTRANCE ANT. See Sir 36:18-19

Give peace, Lord, to those who wait for you; listen to the prayers of your servants, and guide us in the way of justice.

➙ No. 2, p. 614

OPENING PRAYER

God our Father,
you revealed that those who work for peace
will be called your sons.
Help us to work without ceasing
for that justice
which brings true and lasting peace.
We ask this . . . for ever and ever. ℟. **Amen.** ↓

OR

Lord,
you guide all creation with fatherly care.
As you have given all men one common origin,
bring them together peacefully into one family
and keep them united in brotherly love.
We ask this . . . for ever and ever. ℟. **Amen.** ↓

READINGS AND INTERVENIENT CHANTS

The current Weekday Readings and Intervenient Chants are used.

PRAYER OVER THE GIFTS

Lord,
may the saving sacrifice of your Son, our King and peace-maker,
which we offer through these sacramental signs of unity and peace,
bring harmony and concord to all your children.
We ask this through Christ our Lord.
℟. **Amen.**

➙ No. 21, p. 626

COMMUNION ANT.   Mt 5:9

Happy the peacemakers; they shall be called sons of God. ↓

OR   Jn 14:27

Peace I leave with you, my own peace I give you, says the Lord. ↓

PRAYER AFTER COMMUNION

Lord, you give us the body and blood of your Son
and renew our strength.
Fill us with the spirit of love
that we may work effectively to establish among men
Christ's farewell gift of peace.
We ask this through Christ our Lord.
℟. **Amen.**   → No. 32, p. 660

---

25. FOR THE BLESSING OF HUMAN LABOR

ENTRANCE ANT.   Ps 90:17

May the goodness of the Lord be upon us, and give success to the work of our hands.   → No. 2, p. 614

OPENING PRAYER

God our Creator,
it is your will that man accept the duty of work.
In your kindness may the work we begin
bring us growth in this life
and help to extend the kingdom of Christ.
We ask this . . . for ever and ever. ℟. **Amen.** ↓

OR

God our Father,
by the labor of man you govern and guide to perfection
the work of creation.
Hear the prayers of your people
and give all men work that enhances their human dignity
and draws them closer to each other

in the service of their brothers.
We ask this . . . for ever and ever. R̞. **Amen.** ↓

READINGS AND INTERVENIENT CHANTS

The current Weekday Readings and Intervenient Chants are used.

PRAYER OVER THE GIFTS

God our Father,
you provide the human race with food for strength
and with the eucharist for its renewal;
may these gifts which we offer
always bring us health of mind and body.
Grant this through Christ our Lord.
R̞. **Amen.**   → No. 21, p. 626

COMMUNION ANT.   Col 3.17

**Let everything you do or say be in the name of the Lord
with thanksgiving to God.** ↓

PRAYER AFTER COMMUNION

Lord,
hear the prayers
of those who gather at your table of unity and love.
By doing the work you have entrusted to us
may we sustain our life on earth
and build up your kingdom in faith.
Grant this through Christ our Lord.
R̞. **Amen.**   → No. 32, p. 660

---

28. FOR THOSE WHO SUFFER FROM FAMINE

ENTRANCE ANT.   Ps 74:20, 19

**Lord, be true to your covenant, forget not the life of your
poor ones for ever.** ↓

OPENING PRAYER

All-powerful Father,
God of goodness,

you provide for all your creation.
Give us an effective love for our brothers and sisters
who suffer from lack of food.
Help us do all we can to relieve their hunger,
that they may serve you with carefree hearts.
We ask this . . . for ever and ever. ℟. **Amen.** ↓

READINGS AND INTERVENIENT CHANTS

The current Weekday Readings and Intervenient Chants are used.

PRAYER OVER THE GIFTS

Lord,
look upon this offering which we make to you
from the many good things you have given us.
This eucharist is the sign of your abundant life
and the unity of all men in your love.
May it keep us aware of our Christian duty.
We ask this through Christ our Lord.
℟. **Amen.** → No. 21, p. 626

COMMUNION ANT. Mt 11:28

Come to me, all you that labor and are burdened, and I will give you rest, says the Lord. ↓

PRAYER AFTER COMMUNION

God, all-powerful Father,
may the living bread from heaven
give us the courage and strength
to go to the aid of our hungry brothers and sisters.
We ask this through Christ our Lord.
℟. **Amen.** → No. 32, p. 660

---

32. FOR THE SICK

ENTRANCE ANT. Ps 6:3

Have mercy on me, God, for I am sick; heal me, Lord, my bones are racked with pain.

OR   See Is 53:4

The Lord has truly borne our sufferings; he has carried all our sorrows. → No. 2, p. 614

OPENING PRAYER

Father,
your Son accepted our sufferings
to teach us the virtue of patience in human illness.
Hear the prayers we offer for our sick brothers and sisters.
May all who suffer pain, illness or disease
realize that they are chosen to be saints,
and know that they are joined to Christ
in his suffering for the salvation of the world,
who lives and reigns with you and the Holy Spirit,
one God, for ever and ever. ℟. **Amen.** ↓

OR

All-powerful and ever-living God,
the lasting health of all who believe in you,
hear us as we ask your loving help for the sick;
restore their health,
that they may again offer joyful thanks in your Church.
Grant this . . . for ever and ever. ℟. **Amen.** ↓

READINGS AND INTERVENIENT CHANTS

The current Weekday Readings and Intervenient Chants are used.

PRAYER OVER THE GIFTS

God our Father,
your love guides every moment of our lives.
Accept the prayers and gifts we offer
for our sick brothers and sisters;
restore them to health
and turn our anxiety for them into joy.
We ask this in the name of Jesus the Lord.
℟. **Amen.**   → No. 21, p. 626

COMMUNION ANT. Col 1:24

I will make up in my own body what is lacking in the suffering of Christ, for the sake of his body, the Church. ↓

PRAYER AFTER COMMUNION

God our Father,
our help in human weakness,
show our sick brothers and sisters
the power of your loving care.
In your kindness make them well
and restore them to your Church.
We ask this through Christ our Lord.
℟. **Amen.** → No. 32, p. 660

33. FOR THE DYING

Mass for the Sick, p. 1256, *with the following prayers:*

OPENING PRAYER

God of power and mercy,
you have made death itself
the gateway to eternal life.
Look with love on our dying brother (sister)
and make him (her) one with your Son in his suffering and
    death,
that, sealed with the blood of Christ,
he (she) may come before you free from sin.
We ask this . . . for ever and ever. ℟. **Amen.**

PRAYER OVER THE GIFTS

Father, accept this sacrifice we offer
for our dying brother (sister),
and by it free him (her) from all his (her) sins.
As he (she) accepted the sufferings you asked him (her) to
    bear in this life,
may he (she) enjoy happiness and peace for ever in the life
    to come.
We ask this through Christ our Lord.
℟. **Amen.** → No. 21, p. 626

PRAYER AFTER COMMUNION

Lord,
by the power of this sacrament,
keep your servant safe in your love.
Do not let evil conquer him (her) at the hour of death,
but let him (her) go in the company of your angels
to the joy of eternal life.
We ask this through Christ our Lord.
℟. **Amen.**
→ No. 32, p. 660

---

34. IN TIME OF EARTHQUAKE

OPENING PRAYER

God our Father,
you set the earth on its foundation.
Keep us safe from the danger of earthquakes
and let us always feel the presence of your love.
May we be secure in your protection
and serve you with grateful hearts.
We ask this . . . for ever and ever. ℟. **Amen.**

---

35. FOR RAIN

OPENING PRAYER

Lord God,
in you we live and move and have our being.
Help us in our present time of trouble,
send us the rain we need,
and teach us to seek your lasting help
on the way to eternal life.
We ask this . . . for ever and ever. ℟. **Amen.**

---

36. FOR FINE WEATHER

OPENING PRAYER

All-powerful and ever-living God,
we find security in your forgiveness.

Give us the fine weather we pray for
so that we may rejoice in your gifts of kindness
and use them always for your glory and our good.
We ask this . . . for ever and ever. ℟. **Amen.**

---

38. FOR ANY NEED

ENTRANCE ANT.

I am the Savior of all people, says the Lord. Whatever their troubles, I will answer their cry, and I will always be their Lord.
→ No. 2, p. 614

OPENING PRAYER

God our Father,
our strength in adversity,
our health in weakness,
our comfort in sorrow,
be merciful to your people.
As you have given us the punishment we deserve,
give us also new life and hope as we rest in your kindness.
We ask this . . . for ever and ever. ℟. **Amen.** ↓

READINGS AND INTERVENIENT CHANTS

The current Weekday Readings and Intervenient Chants are used.

PRAYER OVER THE GIFTS

Lord,
receive the prayers and gifts we offer:
may your merciful love set us free from the punishment
we receive for our sins.
We ask this in the name of Jesus the Lord.
℟. **Amen.**
→ No. 21, p. 626

COMMUNION ANT.   Mt 11:28

Come to me, all you that labor and are burdened, and I will give you rest, says the Lord. ↓

PRAYER AFTER COMMUNION

Lord,
look kindly on us in our sufferings,
and by the death your Son endured for us
turn away from us your anger
and the punishment our sins deserve.
We ask this through Christ our Lord.
℟. **Amen.**   → No. 32, p. 660

---

39. IN THANKSGIVING

ENTRANCE ANT.   Eph 5:19-20

Sing and play music in your hearts to the Lord, always giving thanks for everything to God the Father in the name of our Lord Jesus Christ.   → No. 2, p. 614

OPENING PRAYER

Father of mercy,
you always answer your people in their sufferings.
We thank you for your kindness
and ask you to free us from all evil,
 that we may serve you in happiness all our days.
We ask this . . . for ever and ever. ℟. **Amen.** ↓

READINGS AND INTERVENIENT CHANTS

The current Weekday Readings and Intervenient Chants are used.

PRAYER OVER THE GIFTS

Lord,
you gave us your only Son
to free us from death and from every evil.
Mercifully accept this sacrifice
in gratitude for saving us from our distress.
We ask this through Christ our Lord.
℟. **Amen.**   → No. 21, p. 626 (P 40)

COMMUNION ANT. Ps 138:1

I will give thanks to you with all my heart, O Lord, for you have answered me. ↓

OR Ps 116:12-13

What return can I make to the Lord for all that he gives to me? I will take the cup of salvation, and call on the name of the Lord. ↓

PRAYER AFTER COMMUNION

All-powerful God,
by this bread of life
you free your people from the power of sin
and in your love renew their strength.
Help us grow constantly in the hope of eternal glory.
Grant this through Christ our Lord.
℟. **Amen.**

→ No. 32, p. 660

---

44. FOR RELATIVES AND FRIENDS

OPENING PRAYER

Father,
by the power of your Spirit
you have filled the hearts of your faithful people
with gifts of love for one another.
Hear the prayers we offer for our relatives and friends.
Give them health of mind and body
that they may do your will with perfect love.
We ask this . . . for ever and ever. ℟. **Amen.**

PRAYER OVER THE GIFTS

Lord,
have mercy on our relatives and friends
for whom we offer this sacrifice of praise.
May these holy gifts gain them the help of your blessing
and bring them to the joy of eternal glory.
We ask this through Christ our Lord. ℟. **Amen.**

PRAYER AFTER COMMUNION

Lord,
we who receive these holy mysteries
pray for the relatives and friends you have given us in love.
Pardon their sins.
Give them your constant encouragement
and guide them throughout their lives
until the day when we, with all who have served you,
will rejoice in your presence for ever.
Grant this through Christ our Lord.
℞. **Amen.** → No. 32, p. 660

VOTIVE MASSES

(For rules governing these Masses, see p. 1240)

2. HOLY CROSS

ENTRANCE ANT. See Gal 6:14

**We should glory in the cross of our Lord Jesus Christ, for he
is our salvation, our life and our resurrection; through him
we are saved and made free.** → No. 2, p. 614

OPENING PRAYER

God our Father,
in obedience to you
your only Son accepted death on the cross
for the salvation of mankind.
We acknowledge the mystery of the cross on earth.
May we receive the gift of redemption in heaven.
We ask this . . . for ever and ever. ℞. **Amen.** ↓

READINGS AND INTERVENIENT CHANTS

*The current Weekday Readings and Intervenient Chants are
used.*

PRAYER OVER THE GIFTS

Lord,
may this sacrifice once offered on the cross
to take away the sins of the world
now free us from our sins.

We ask this through Christ our Lord.
℟. **Amen.**   → No. 21, p. 626 (Pref. P 17)

COMMUNION ANT.   Jn 12:32

When I am lifted up from the earth, I will draw all men to myself, says the Lord. ↓

PRAYER AFTER COMMUNION

Lord Jesus Christ,
you are the holy bread of life.
Bring to the glory of the resurrection
the people you have redeemed by the wood of the cross.
We ask this through Christ our Lord.
℟. **Amen.**   → No. 32, p. 660

3. HOLY EUCHARIST
JESUS THE HIGH PRIEST

ENTRANCE ANT.   Ps 110:4

The Lord has sworn an oath and he will not retract: you are a priest for ever, in the line of Melchisedech. → No. 2, p. 614

OPENING PRAYER

Father,
for your glory and our salvation
you appointed Jesus Christ eternal High Priest.
May the people he gained for you by his blood
come to share in the power of his cross and resurrection
by celebrating his memorial in this eucharist,
for he lives and reigns with you and the Holy Spirit,
one God, for ever and ever. ℟. **Amen.** ↓

READINGS AND INTERVENIENT CHANTS

The current Weekday Readings and Intervenient Chants are used.

PRAYER OVER THE GIFTS

Lord,
may we offer these mysteries worthily and often,
for whenever this memorial sacrifice is celebrated

the work of our redemption is renewed.
We ask this through Christ our Lord.
℞. **Amen.** → No. 21, p. 626 (Pref. P 47-48)

COMMUNION ANT.
1 Cor 11:24-25

This body will be given for you. This is the cup of the new covenant in my blood; whenever you receive them, do so in remembrance of me. ↓

PRAYER AFTER COMMUNION

Lord,
by sharing in this sacrifice
which your Son commanded us to offer as his memorial,
may we become, with him, an everlasting gift to you.
We ask this through Christ our Lord.
℞. **Amen.** → No. 32, p. 660

5. PRECIOUS BLOOD

ENTRANCE ANT.
Rv 5:9-10

By your blood, O Lord, you have redeemed us from every tribe and tongue, from every nation and people: you have made us into the kingdom of God. → No. 2, p. 614

OPENING PRAYER

Father,
by the blood of your own Son
you have set all men free and saved us from death.
Continue your work of love within us,
that by constantly celebrating the mystery of our salvation
we may reach the eternal life it promises.
We ask this . . . for ever and ever. ℞. **Amen.** ↓

READINGS AND INTERVENIENT CHANTS

The current Weekday Readings and Intervenient Chants are used.

PRAYER OVER THE GIFTS

Lord,
by offering these gifts in this eucharist

may we come to Jesus, the mediator of the new covenant,
find salvation in the sprinkling of his blood
and draw closer to the kingdom
where he is Lord for ever and ever.
℟. **Amen.** → No. 21, p. 626 (Pref. P 17)

COMMUNION ANT. See 1 Cor 10:10

The cup that we bless is a communion with the blood of Christ; and the bread that we break is a communion with the body of the Lord. ↓

PRAYER AFTER COMMUNION

Lord,
you renew us with the food and drink of salvation.
May the blood of our Savior
be for us a fountain of water
springing up to eternal life.
We ask this through Christ our Lord.
℟. **Amen.** → No. 32, p. 660

6. THE SACRED HEART OF JESUS

ENTRANCE ANT. Ps 33:11, 19

The thoughts of his heart last through every generation, that he will rescue them from death and feed them in time of famine. → No. 2, p. 614

OPENING PRAYER

Lord God,
give us the strength and love of the heart of your Son
that, by becoming one with him,
we may have eternal salvation.
We ask this . . . for ever and ever. ℟. **Amen.** ↓

READINGS AND INTERVENIENT CHANTS

The current Weekday Readings and Intervenient Chants are used.

PRAYER OVER THE GIFTS

Father of mercy,
in your great love for us
you have given us your only Son.
May he take us up into his own perfect sacrifice,
that we may offer you fitting worship.
We ask this through Christ our Lord. ℟. **Amen.** ↓

PREFACE (P 45)

Father, all-powerful and ever-living God,
we do well always and everywhere to give you thanks
through Jesus Christ our Lord.

Lifted high on the cross,
Christ gave his life for us,
so much did he love us.
From his wounded side flowed blood and water,
the fountain of sacramental life in the Church.
To his open heart the Savior invites all men,
to draw water in joy from the springs of salvation.

Now, with all the saints and angels,
we praise you for ever: → No. 23, p. 627

COMMUNION ANT.   Jn 7:37-38

The Lord says: If anyone is thirsty, let him come to me; whoever believes in me, let him drink. Streams of living water shall flow out from within him. ↓

OR   Jn 19:34

One of the soldiers pierced Jesus' side with a lance, and at once there flowed out blood and water. ↓

PRAYER AFTER COMMUNION

Lord,
we have received your sacrament of love.
By becoming more like Christ on earth
may we share his glory in heaven,
where he lives and reigns for ever and ever.
℟. **Amen.** ————————————————— → No. 32, p. 660

7. HOLY SPIRIT

ENTRANCE ANT. Jn 16:13

When the Spirit of truth comes, says the Lord, he will lead you to the whole truth. → No. 2, p. 614

OPENING PRAYER

Lord,
may the Helper, the Spirit who comes from you,
fill our hearts with light
and lead us to all truth
as your Son promised,
for he lives and reigns with you and the Holy Spirit,
one God, for ever and ever. ℟. **Amen.** ↓

OR

God our Father,
no secret is hidden from you,
for every heart is open to you
and every wish is known.
Fill our hearts with the light of your Holy Spirit
to free our thoughts from sin,
that we may perfectly love you and fittingly praise you.
Grant this . . . for ever and ever. ℟. **Amen.** ↓

READINGS AND INTERVENIENT CHANTS

The current Weekday Readings and Intervenient Chants are used.

PRAYER OVER THE GIFTS

Father,
look with kindness
on the gifts we bring to your altar.
May we worship you in spirit and truth:
give us the humility and faith
to make our offering pleasing to you.
We ask this through Christ our Lord.
℟. **Amen.** → No. 21, p. 626 (Pref. P 55)

COMMUNION ANT. Jn 15:26; 16:14

The Lord says, the Spirit who comes from the Father will glorify me. ↓

PRAYER AFTER COMMUNION

Lord our God,
you renew us with food from heaven;
fill our hearts with the gentle love of your Spirit.
May the gifts we have received in this life
lead us to the gift of eternal joy.
We ask this through Christ our Lord.
℟. **Amen.** → No. 32, p. 660

8. BLESSED VIRGIN MARY

A Mass from the Common of the Blessed Virgin Mary, pp. 1032-1040, is used, in accord with the liturgical season.

THE IMMACULATE HEART OF MARY

See p. 1012.

MARY, MOTHER OF THE CHURCH

Common of the Blessed Virgin Mary, pp. 1032-1040.

OPENING PRAYER

God of mercies,
your only Son, while hanging on the cross,
appointed Mary, his mother,
to be our mother also.
Like her,
and under her loving care,
may your Church grow day by day,
rejoice in the holiness of its children,
and so attract to itself all the peoples of the earth.
We ask this . . . for ever and ever. ℟. **Amen.**

First Reading (Gn 3:9-15, 20), p. 1110, no. 1, or (Acts 1:12-14), p. 1117, no. 1.
Responsorial Psalm (Jdt 13), p. 1119, no. 2.
Alleluia, p. 1123, no. 5.
Gospel (Jn 19:25-27), p. 1131, no. 12.

PRAYER OVER THE GIFTS

Lord,
accept our gifts
and make them the sacrament of our salvation.
By its power
warm our hearts with the love of Mary,
Mother of the Church,
and join us more closely with her
in sharing the redeeming work of her Son.
We ask this through Christ our Lord. ℟. **Amen.** ↓

PREFACE (P 57-A)

℣. The Lord be with you. ℟. **And also with you.**
℣. Lift up your hearts. ℟. **We lift them up to the Lord.**
℣. Let us give thanks to the Lord our God. ℟. **It is right to give him thanks and praise.**

Father, all-powerful and ever-living God,
we do well always and everywhere to give you thanks;
we especially praise you and proclaim your glory
as we honor the Blessed Virgin Mary.

She received your Word in the purity of her heart,
and, conceiving in her virgin womb,
gave birth to our Savior
and so nurtured the Church at its very beginning.

She accepted God's parting gift of love
as she stood beneath the cross
and so became the mother of all those
who were brought to life
through the death of her only Son.

She joined her prayers with those of the apostles.
as together they awaited the coming of your Spirit,
and so became the perfect pattern of the Church at prayer.

Raised to the glory of heaven,
she cares for the pilgrim Church with a mother's love,
following its progress homeward
until the day of the Lord dawns in splendor.

Now with all the angels and saints,
we proclaim your glory
and join in their unending hymn of praise: ➙ No. 23, p. 627

PRAYER AFTER COMMUNION

Lord,
we have received the foretaste and promise
of the fullness of redemption.
We pray that your Church,
through the intercession of the Virgin Mother,
may proclaim the Gospel to all nations
and by the power of the Spirit
reach to the ends of the earth.
We ask this through Christ our Lord.
R̸. **Amen.** ➙ No. 32, p. 660

DAILY MASSES FOR THE DEAD

These Masses may be celebrated according to the rules given on p. 1240.

3C. FOR MORE THAN ONE PERSON OR FOR ALL THE DEAD

ENTRANCE ANT.

Give them eternal rest, O Lord, and let them share your glory. ➙ No. 2, p. 614

OPENING PRAYER

God, our creator and redeemer,
by your power Christ conquered death
and returned to you in glory.
May all your people who have gone before us in faith
share his victory
and enjoy the vision of your glory for ever,
where Christ lives and reigns with you and the Holy Spirit,
one God, for ever and ever. R̸. **Amen.** ↓

OR

God, our maker and redeemer,
in your mercy hear our prayer.
Grant forgiveness and peace
to our brothers (sisters) N. and N.
who longed for your mercy.
We ask this . . . for ever and ever. ℟. **Amen.** ↓

READINGS AND INTERVENIENT CHANTS

The current Weekday Readings and Intervenient Chants are used.

PRAYER OVER THE GIFTS

Lord,
receive this sacrifice
for our brothers and sisters.
On earth you gave them the privilege of believing in Christ:
grant them the eternal life promised by that faith.
We ask this through Christ our Lord.
℟. **Amen.**   → No. 21, p. 626 (Pref. P 77-81)

COMMUNION ANT.   1 Jn 4:9

**God sent his only Son into the world so that we could have
life through him.** ↓

PRAYER AFTER COMMUNION

Lord,
may our sacrifice bring peace and forgiveness
to our brothers and sisters who have died.
Bring the new life given to them in baptism
to the fullness of eternal joy.
We ask this through Christ our Lord. ℟. **Amen.**

OR

Lord of mercy,
may our prayer and sacrifice
free our brothers and sisters
and bring them to eternal salvation.

We ask this through Christ our Lord.
℞. **Amen.** _____ → No. 32, p. 660

VARIOUS PRAYERS FOR THE DEAD

1A. FOR A POPE

OPENING PRAYER

God our Father,
you reward all who believe in you.
May your servant, N. our Pope, vicar of Peter, and shepherd
    of your Church,
who faithfully administered the mysteries of your forgive-
    ness and love on earth,
rejoice with you for ever in heaven.
We ask this . . . for ever and ever. ℞. **Amen.**

PRAYER OVER THE GIFTS

Lord,
by this sacrifice which brings us peace,
give your servant, N. our Pope,
the reward of eternal happiness
and let your mercy win for us
the gift of your life and love.
We ask this through Christ our Lord. ℞. **Amen.**

PRAYER AFTER COMMUNION

Lord,
you renew us with the sacraments of your divine life.
Hear our prayers for your servant, N. our Pope.
You made him the center of the unity of your Church on
    earth,
count him now among the flock of the blessed in your king-
    dom.
Grant this through Christ our Lord. ℞. **Amen.**

_____

2A. FOR THE DIOCESAN BISHOP

OPENING PRAYER

All-powerful God,
you made N. your servant
the guide of your family.
May he enjoy the reward of all his work
and share the eternal joy of his Lord.
We ask this . . . for ever and ever. ℞. **Amen.**

PRAYER OVER THE GIFTS

Merciful God,
may this sacrifice,
which N. your servant offered during his life
for the salvation of the faithful,
help him now to find pardon and peace.
We ask this through Christ our Lord. ℞. **Amen.**

PRAYER AFTER COMMUNION

Lord,
give your mercy and love to N. your servant.
He hoped in Christ and preached Christ.
By this sacrifice may he share with Christ
the joy of eternal life.
We ask this through Christ our Lord. ℞. **Amen.**

3A. FOR A PRIEST

OPENING PRAYER

Lord,
you gave N. your servant and priest
the privilege of a holy ministry in this world.
May he rejoice for ever in the glory of your kingdom.
We ask this . . . for ever and ever. ℞. **Amen.**

PRAYER OVER THE GIFTS

All-powerful God,
by this eucharist may N. your servant and priest

rejoice for ever in the vision of the mysteries
which he faithfully ministered here on earth.
We ask this through Christ our Lord. R̠. **Amen.**

PRAYER AFTER COMMUNION

God of mercy,
we who receive the sacraments of salvation
pray for N. your servant and priest.
You made him a minister of your mysteries on earth.
May he rejoice in the full knowledge of your truth in heaven.
We ask this through Christ our Lord. R̠. **Amen.**

6A. FOR ONE PERSON

OPENING PRAYER

Lord,
those who die still live in your presence
and your saints rejoice in complete happiness.
Listen to our prayers for N. your son (daughter)
who has passed from the light of this world,
and bring him (her) to the joy of eternal radiance.
We ask this . . . for ever and ever. R̠. **Amen.**

PRAYER OVER THE GIFTS

Lord,
be pleased with this sacrifice we offer for N. your servant.
May he (she) find in your presence
the forgiveness he (she) always longed for
and come to praise your glory for ever
in the joyful fellowship of your saints.
We ask this through Christ our Lord. R̠. **Amen.**

PRAYER AFTER COMMUNION

Lord,
we thank you for the holy gifts we receive
and pray for N. our brother (sister).
By the suffering and death of your Son
free him (her) from the bonds of his (her) sins

and bring him (her) to endless joy in your presence.
We ask this through Christ our Lord. R̠. **Amen.**

11A. FOR SEVERAL PERSONS

OPENING PRAYER

Lord,
be merciful to your servants N. and N.
You cleansed them from sin in the fountain of new birth.
Bring them now to the happiness of life in your kingdom.
We ask this . . . for ever and ever. R̠. **Amen.**

PRAYER OVER THE GIFTS

Lord,
we offer you this sacrifice.
Hear our prayers for N. and N.,
and through this offering
grant our brothers (sisters) your everlasting forgiveness.
We ask this through Christ our Lord. R̠. **Amen.**

PRAYER AFTER COMMUNION

Lord,
we who receive your sacraments
ask your mercy and love.
By sharing in the power of this eucharist
may our brothers (sisters) win forgiveness of their sins,
enter your kingdom,
and praise you for all eternity.
We ask this through Christ our Lord. R̠. **Amen.**

---

13. FOR PARENTS

OPENING PRAYER

Almighty God,
you command us to honor father and mother.

In your mercy forgive the sins of my (our) parents
and let me (us) one day see them again
in the radiance of eternal joy.
We ask this . . . for ever and ever. ℟. **Amen.**

PRAYER OVER THE GIFTS

Lord,
receive the sacrifice we offer for my (our) parents.
Give them eternal joy in the land of the living,
and let me (us) join them one day in the happiness of the
  saints.
We ask this through Christ our Lord. ℟. **Amen.**

PRAYER AFTER COMMUNION

Lord,
may this sharing in the sacrament of heaven
win eternal rest and light for my (our) parents
and prepare me (us) to share eternal glory with them.
We ask this through Christ our Lord. ℟. **Amen.**

---

14. FOR RELATIVES, FRIENDS, AND BENEFACTORS

OPENING PRAYER

Father,
source of forgiveness and salvation for all mankind,
hear our prayer.
By the prayers of the ever-virgin Mary,
may our friends, relatives, and benefactors
who have gone from this world
come to share eternal happiness with all your saints.
We ask this . . . for ever and ever. ℟. **Amen.**

PRAYER OVER THE GIFTS

God of infinite mercy,
hear our prayers

and by this sacrament of our salvation
forgive all the sins of our relatives, friends, and benefactors.
We ask this through Christ our Lord. ℟. **Amen.**

PRAYER AFTER COMMUNION

Father all-powerful, God of mercy,
we have offered you this sacrifice of praise
for our relatives, friends, and benefactors.
By the power of this sacrament
free them from all their sins
and give them the joy of eternal light.
We ask this through Christ our Lord. ℟. **Amen.**

APPENDIX II

ALLELUIA VERSES
FOR WEEKDAYS OF THE YEAR

DECEMBER 1 TO DECEMBER 16

1 See Ps 80:4

Come and save us, LORD our
    God;
let your face shine upon us,
    that we may be saved.

2 Ps 85:8

Show us, LORD, your love,
and grant us your salvation.

3 Is 33:22

The LORD is our Judge, our
    Lawgiver, our King;
he it is who will save us.

4 Is 40:9-11

Raise your voice and tell the
    Good News:
Behold, the Lord GOD comes
    with power.

5 See Is 45:8

Let the clouds rain down the
    Just One,
and the earth bring forth a
    Savior.

6 Is 55:6

Seek the LORD while he may
    be found;
call him while he is near.

7 Lk 3:4, 6

Prepare the way of the Lord,
    make straight his paths:
All flesh shall see the salva-
    tion of God.

8

The Lord will come; go out to
    meet him!
He is the prince of peace

9

Behold, our Lord shall come
    with power;
he will enlighten the eyes of
    his servants.

10

Behold, the Lord comes to
    save his people;
blessed are those prepared to
    meet him.

11

Behold, the King will come,
    the Lord of earth:
and he will take away the
    yoke of our captivity.

12

The day of the Lord is near:
Behold, he comes to save us.

13

Come, O Lord, do not delay:
forgive the sins of your peo-
    ple.

14

Come, Lord, bring us your
    peace;
that we may rejoice before
    you with a perfect heart.

DECEMBER 17 TO DECEMBER 24

1

O Wisdom of our God Most High,
guiding creation with power and love:
come to teach us the path of knowledge!

2

O Leader of the House of Israel,
giver of the Law to Moses on Sinai:
come to rescue us with your mighty power!

3

O Root of Jesse's stem,
sign of God's love for all his people:
come to save us without delay!

4

O Key of David,
opening the gates of God's eternal Kingdom:
come and free the prisoners of darkness!

5

O Radiant Dawn,
splendor of eternal light, sun of justice:
come and shine on those who dwell in darkness and in the shadow of death!

6

O King of all nations and keystone of the Church:
come and save man, whom you formed from the dust!

7

O Emmanuel, our King, and Giver of Law:
come to save us, Lord our God!

BEFORE EPIPHANY

1   Jn 1:14a, 12a
The Word of God became flesh and dwelt among us.
To those who accepted him
he gave power to become the children of God.

2   Heb 1:1-2
In the past God spoke to our ancestors through the prophets:
in these last days, he has spoken to us through his Son.

3

A holy day has dawned upon us.
Come, you nations, and adore the Lord.
Today a great light has come upon the earth.

AFTER EPIPHANY

1   Mt 4:16
The people who sit in darkness have seen a great light;
on those dwelling in a land overshadowed by death,
light has arisen.

2   Mt 4:23
Jesus proclaimed the Gospel of the Kingdom
and cured every disease among the people.

3   Lk 4:18
The Lord sent me to bring glad tidings to the poor,
and to proclaim liberty to captives.

4   Lk 7:16
A great prophet has arisen in our midst
and God has visited his people.

5   See 1 Tm 3:16
Glory to you, O Christ, proclaimed to the Gentiles.
Glory to you, O Christ, believed in throughout the world.

VERSES BEFORE THE GOSPEL FOR THE WEEKDAYS OF LENT

*See p. 620 for the various responses
before and after each verse.*

See p. 620 for the various responses

1   Ps 51:12a, 14a
A clean heart create for me, O God;
give me back the joy of your salvation.

2   See Ps 95:8
If today you hear his voice, harden not your hearts.

3   Ps 130:5, 7bc
I hope in the LORD, I trust in his word;
with him there is kindness and plenteous redemption.

4   Ez 18:31
Cast away from you all the crimes you have committed, says the Lord,
and make for yourselves a new heart and a new spirit.

5   Ez 33:11
I take no pleasure in the death of the wicked man, says the Lord,
but rather in his conversion, that he may live.

6   JI 2:12-13
Even now, says the LORD,
return to me with your whole
    heart;
for I am gracious and merci-
    ful.

7   See Am 5:14
Seek good and not evil so that
    you may live,
and the LORD will be with you.

8   Mt 4:4b
One does not live on bread
    alone,
but on every word that comes
    forth from the mouth of
    God.

9   Mt 4:17
Repent, says the Lord;
the Kingdom of heaven is at
    hand.

10   See Lk 8:15
Blessed are they who have
    kept the word with a gen-
    erous heart
and yield a harvest through
    perseverance.

11   Lk 15:18
I will get up and go to my
    father and shall say to him:
Father, I have sinned against
    heaven and against you.

12   Jn 3:16
God so loved the world that he
    gave his only-begotten
    Son,
so that everyone who believes
    in him might have eternal
    life.

13   See Jn 6:63c, 68c
Your words, Lord, are Spirit
    and life;
you have the words of ever-
    lasting life.

14   Jn 8:12
I am the light of the world,
    says the Lord:
whoever follows me will have
    the light of life.

15   Jn 11:25a, 26
I am the resurrection and the
    life, said the Lord;
whoever believes in me will
    never die.

16   2 Cor 6:2b
Behold, now is a very accept-
    able time;
behold, now is the day of sal-
    vation

17
The seed is the word of God,
    Christ is the sower;
all who come to him will live
    for ever.

EASTER SEASON UP TO THE ASCENSION

1   Mt 4:4b
One does not live on bread
    alone,
but on every word that comes
    from the mouth of God.

2   See Lk 24:46, 26
Christ had to suffer and to rise
    from the dead,
and so enter into his glory.

3   Jn 3:14-15

The Son of Man must be lifted up,
so that everyone who believes in him
may have eternal life.

4   Jn 3:16

God so loved the world that he gave his only-begotten Son,
so that everyone who believes in him might have eternal life.

5   Jn 6:35ab

I am the bread of life, says the Lord;
whoever comes to me will never hunger.

6   See Jn 6:40

Everyone who believes in the Son has eternal life,
and I shall raise him on the last day, says the Lord.

7   Jn 6:51

I am the living bread that came down from heaven,
says the Lord;
whoever eats this bread will live forever.

8   Jn 6:56

Whoever eats my Flesh and drinks my Blood
remains in me and I in him, says the Lord.

9   See Jn 6:63c, 68c

Your words, Lord, are Spirit and life;
you have the words of everlasting life.

10   Jn 8:12

I am the light of the world, says the Lord;
whoever follows me will have the light of life.

11   Jn 8:31b-32

If you remain in my word, you will truly be my disciples,
and you will know the truth, says the Lord.

12   Jn 10:14

I am the good shepherd, says the Lord;
I know my sheep, and mine know me.

13   Jn 10:27

My sheep hear my voice, says the Lord;
I know them, and they follow me.

14   Jn 14:6

I am the way and the truth and the life, says the Lord;
no one comes to the Father except through me.

15   Jn 15:4a, 5b

Remain in me, as I remain in you, says the Lord;
whoever remains in me will bear much fruit.

16   Jn 15:15b

I call you my friends, says the Lord,
for I have made known to you all that the Father has told me.

17   Jn 20:29

You believe in me, Thomas,
    because you have seen
    me, says the Lord;
blessed are those who have
    not seen, but still believe!

18   Rom 6:9

Christ now raised from the
    dead, dies no more;
death no longer has power
    over him.

19   Col 3:1

If then you were raised with
    Christ,
seek what is above,
where Christ is seated at the
    right hand of God.

20   See Rv 1:5ab

Jesus Christ, you are the faith-
    ful witness,
the firstborn of the dead;
you have loved us and freed
    us from our sins by your
    Blood.

21

We know that Christ is truly
    risen from the dead;
victorious king, have mercy
    on us.

22

Nailed to the cross for our
    sake,
the Lord is now risen from the
    grave.

23

Christ is risen and shines
    upon us,
whom he has redeemed by his
    Blood.

24

Christ is risen, who made all
    things;
he has shown mercy on all
    people.

EASTER SEASON AFTER THE ASCENSION

1   Mt 28:19a, 20b

Go and teach all nations, says
    the Lord;
I am with you always, until
    the end of the world.

2   Jn 14:16

I will ask the Father,
and he will give another
    Advocate,
to be with you always.

3   See Jn 14:18

I will not leave you orphans,
    says the Lord;
I will come back to you, and
    your hearts will rejoice.

4   Jn 14:26

The Holy Spirit will teach you
    everything
and remind you of all I told
    you.

5   Jn 15:26b, 27a
The Spirit of truth will testify
    to me, says the Lord,
and you also will testify.

6   See Jn 16:7, 13
I will send to you the Spirit of
    truth, says the Lord;
he will guide you to all truth.

7   Jn 16:28
I came from the Father and
    have come into the world;
now I am leaving the world
    and going back to the
    Father.

8   See Jn 17:17b, 17a
Your word, O Lord, is truth;
consecrate us in the truth.

9   Jn 17:21
May they all be one as you,
    Father, are in me, and I in
    you,
that the world may believe
    that you sent me, says the
    Lord.

10   Col 3:1
If then you were raised with
    Christ,
seek what is above,
where Christ is seated at the
    right hand of God.

ORDINARY TIME

1   1 Sm 3:9; Jn 6:68c
Speak, O LORD, your servant
    is listening;
you have the words of ever-
    lasting life.

2   See Ps 19:9
Your words, O LORD, give joy
    to my heart,
your teaching is light to my
    eyes.

3   Ps 25:4b, 5a
Teach me your paths, my God,
and guide me in your truth.

4   See Ps 27:11
Teach me your way, O LORD,
    and lead me on a straight
    road.

5   Ps 95:8
If today you hear his voice,
harden not your hearts.

6   Ps 111:7b-8a
Your laws are all made firm, O
    LORD,
established for evermore.

7   Ps 119:18
Unveil my eyes, O Lord,
and I will see the marvels of
    your law.

8   Ps 119:27
Instruct me in the way of your
    rules,
and I will reflect on all your
    wonders.

9 Ps 119:34

Teach me the meaning of your law, O Lord,
and I will guard it with all my heart.

10 Ps 119:36a, 29b

Incline my heart, O God, to your decrees;
and favor me with your law.

11 Ps 119:88

In your mercy, give me life, O Lord,
and I will do your commands.

12 Ps 119:105

A lamp for my feet is your word,
and a light to my path.

13 Ps 119:135

Let your countenance shine upon your servant,
and teach me your statutes.

14 See Ps 130:5

I hope in the LORD,
my soul trusts in his word.

15 Ps 145:13cd

The LORD is faithful in all his words
and holy in all his deeds.

16 Ps 147:12a, 15a

Praise the LORD, Jerusalem;
God's word speeds forth to the earth.

17 Mt 4:4b

One does not live on bread alone,
but on every word that comes forth from the mouth of God.

18 See Mt 11:25

Blessed are you, Father, Lord of heaven and earth;
you have revealed to little ones the mysteries of the Kingdom.

19 See Lk 8:15

Blessed are they who have kept the word with a generous heart
and yield a harvest through perseverance.

20 See Jn 6:63c, 68c

Your words, Lord, are Spirit and life;
you have the words of everlasting life.

21 Jn 8:12

I am the light of the world, says the Lord;
whoever follows me will have the light of life.

22 Jn 10:27

My sheep hear my voice, says the Lord;
I know them, and they follow me.

23 Jn 14:6

I am the way and the truth and the life, says the Lord;
no one comes to the Father except through me.

24 Jn 14:23

Whoever loves me will keep
my word,
and my Father will love him,
and we will come to him.

25 Jn 15:15b

I call you my friends, says the
Lord,
for I have made known to you
all that Father has told me.

26 See Jn 17:17b, 17a

Your word, O Lord, is truth;
consecrate us in the truth.

27 See Acts 16:14b

Open our hearts, O Lord,
to listen to the words of your
Son.

28 2 Cor 5:19

God was reconciling the world
to himself in Christ
and entrusting to us the message of reconciliation.

29 See Eph 1:17-18

May the Father of our Lord
Jesus Christ
enlighten the eyes of our
hearts,
that we may know what is the
hope
that belongs to our call.

30 Phil 2:15d, 16a

Shine like lights in the world,
as you hold on to the word of
life.

31 See Col 3:16a, 17c

Let the word of Christ dwell in
you richly;
giving thanks to God the
Father through him.

32 See 1 Thes 2:13

Receive the word of God, not
as the words of men,
but as it truly is, the word of
God.

33 See 2 Thes 2:14

God has called us through the
Gospel,
to share in the glory of our
Lord Jesus Christ.

34 See 2 Tm 1:10

Our Savior Jesus Christ has
destroyed death
and brought life to light
through the Gospel.

35 Heb 4:12

The word of God is living and
effective,
able to discern reflections and
thoughts of the heart.

36 Jas 1:18

The Father willed to give us
birth by the word of truth,
that we may be a kind of firstfruits of his creatures.

37 Jas 1:21bc

Humbly welcome the word
that has been planted in
you
and is able to save your souls.

38	1 Pt 1:25

The word of the Lord remains
for ever;
this is the word that has been
proclaimed to you.

39	1 Jn 2:5

Whoever keeps the word of
Christ
the love of God is truly perfected in him.

For the Last Week

1	Mt 24:42a, 44

Stay awake!
For you do not know when the
Son of Man will come.

2	Lk 21:28

Stand erect and raise your
heads
because your redemption is at
hand.

3	Lk 21:36

Be vigilant at all times and
pray
that you may have the
strength to stand before
the Son of Man.

4	Rv 2:10c

Remain faithful until death,
and I will give you the crown
of life.

*The following texts for Sundays in Ordinary Time may also be
used in place of the texts proposed for each weekday.*

1	1 Sm 3:9; Jn 6:68c

Speak, O LORD, your servant
is listening;
you have the words of everlasting life.

2	See Mt 11:25

Blessed are you, Father, Lord
of heaven and earth;
you have revealed to little
ones the mysteries of the
Kingdom.

3	See Lk 19:38; 2:14

Blessed is the king who comes
in the name of the Lord.
Glory to God in the highest
and on earth peace to
those on whom his favor
rests.

4	Jn 1:14a, 12

The Word of God became
flesh and dwelt among us.
To those who accepted him
he gave power to become children of God.

5	See Jn 6:63c, 68c

Your words, Lord, are Spirit
and life;
you have the words of everlasting life.

6	Jn 8:12

I am the light of the world,
says the Lord:
whoever follows me will have
the light of life.

7   Jn 10:27

My sheep hear my voice, says
the Lord;
I know them, and they follow
me.

8   Jn 14:6

I am the way and the truth
and the life, says the Lord;
no one comes to the Father
except through me.

9   Jn 14:23

Whoever loves me will keep
my word,
and my Father will love him,
and we will come to him.

10   Jn 15:15b

I call you my friends, says the
Lord,
for I have made known to you
all that the Father has told
me.

11   See Jn 17:17b, 17a

Your word, O Lord, is truth;
consecrate us in the truth.

12   See Acts 16:14b

Open our hearts, O Lord,
to listen to the words of your
Son.

13   See Eph 1:17-18

May the Father of our Lord
Jesus Christ
enlighten the eyes of our
hearts,
that we may know what is the
hope
that belongs to our call.

Last Week in Ordinary Time

14   Mt 24:42a, 44

Stay awake!
For you do not know when the
Son of Man will come.

15   Lk 21:36

Be vigilant at all times and
pray
that you may have the
strength to stand before
the Son of Man.

16   Rv 2:10c

Remain faithful until death,
and I will give you the crown
of life.

TREASURY OF PRAYERS

MORNING PRAYER

MOST holy and adorable Trinity, one God in three Persons, I praise you and give you thanks for all the favors you have bestowed on me. Your goodness has preserved me until now. I offer you my whole being and in particular all my thoughts, words and deeds, together with all the trials I may undergo this day. Give them your blessing. May your Divine Love animate them and may they serve your greater glory.

I make this morning offering in union with the Divine intentions of Jesus Christ who offers himself daily in the holy Sacrifice of the Mass, and in union with Mary, his Virgin Mother and our Mother, who was always the faithful handmaid of the Lord.

Glory be to the Father, and to the Son, and to the Holy Spirit. Amen.

Prayer for Divine Guidance through the Day

Partial indulgence (No. 21)*

LORD, God Almighty, you have brought us safely to the beginning of this day. Defend us today by your mighty power, that we may not fall into any sin, but that all our words may so proceed and all our thoughts and actions be so directed, as to be always just in your sight. Through Christ our Lord. Amen.

---

*The indulgences quoted in this Missal are taken from *The Handbook of Indulgences* (published in 1991 by Catholic Book Publishing Co.).

Partial indulgence (No. 1)

Direct, we beg you, O Lord, our actions by your holy inspirations, and carry them on by your gracious assistance, that every prayer and work of ours may begin always with you, and through you be happily ended. Amen.

NIGHT PRAYERS

I ADORE you, my God, and thank you for having created me, for having made me a Christian and preserved me this day. I love you with all my heart and I am sorry for having sinned against you, because you are infinite Love and infinite Goodness. Protect me during my rest and may your love be always with me. Amen.

Eternal Father, I offer you the Precious Blood of Jesus Christ in atonement for my sins and for all the intentions of our Holy Church.

Holy Spirit, Love of the Father and the Son, purify my heart and fill it with the fire of your Love, so that I may be a chaste Temple of the Holy Trinity and be always pleasing to you in all things. Amen.

Plea for Divine Help

Partial indulgence (No. 24)

HEAR us, Lord, holy Father, almighty and eternal God, and graciously send your holy angel from heaven to watch over, to cherish, to protect, to abide with, and to defend all who dwell in this house. Through Christ our Lord. Amen.

COMMUNION PRAYERS

See pp. 609-612.

THE STATIONS OF THE CROSS

THE Stations of the Cross is a devotion in which we accompany, in spirit, our Blessed Lord in his sorrowful journey to Calvary, and devoutly meditate on his sufferings and death.

1. Jesus Is Condemned to Death
Dear Jesus, help me to sin no more and to be very obedient.

4. Jesus Meets His Mother
Dear Jesus, may your Mother console me and all who are sad.

2. Jesus Bears His Cross
Dear Jesus, let me suffer for sinners in union with you.

5. Jesus Is Helped by Simon
Dear Jesus, may I do all things to please you all day long.

3. Jesus Falls the First Time
Dear Jesus, help those who sin to rise and to be truly sorry.

6. Veronica Wipes His Face
Dear Jesus, give me courage and generosity to help others.

7. Jesus Falls a Second Time
Dear Jesus, teach us to be sorry for all our many sins.

11. Jesus Is Nailed to the Cross
Dear Jesus, keep me close to you from this moment until I die.

8. Jesus Speaks to the Women
Dear Jesus, comfort those who have no one to comfort them.

12. Jesus Dies on the Cross
Dear Jesus, be with me when I die and take me to heaven.

9 Jesus Falls a Third Time
Dear Jesus, show me how to be obedient and to be very kind.

13. He Is Taken from the Cross
Dear Jesus, teach me to place all my trust in your holy Love.

10. Stripped of His Garments
Dear Jesus, teach me to be pure in thought, word, and deed.

14. He Is Laid in the Tomb
Dear Jesus, help me to keep the commandments you have given.

THE HOLY ROSARY OF THE
BLESSED VIRGIN MARY

THE Rosary calls to mind the five Joyful, the five Sorrowful, and the five Glorious Mysteries in the life of Christ and His Blessed Mother. It is composed of fifteen decades, each decade consisting of one "Our Father," ten "Hail Marys," and one "Glory Be to the Father."

How to Say the Rosary

The Apostles' Creed *is said on the Crucifix; the* Our Father *is said on each of the Large Beads; the* Hail Mary *on each of the Small Beads; the* Glory Be to the Father *after the three Hail Marys at the beginning of the Rosary, and after each group of Small Beads.*

When the hands are occupied (driving a car, etc.) the indulgences for saying the Rosary may be gained as long as the beads are on one's person.

The Five Joyful Mysteries

1. The Annunciation
For love of humility.

2. The Visitation
For charity.

3. The Nativity
For poverty.

4. The Presentation
For obedience.

5. Finding in Temple
For piety.

The Five Sorrowful Mysteries

1. Agony in Garden
For true contrition.

2. Scourging at Pillar
For purity.

3. Crowned with Thorns.
For moral courage.

4. Carrying of Cross
For patience.

5. The Crucifixion
For final perseverance.

The Five Glorious Mysteries

1. The Resurrection
For faith.

2. The Ascension
For hope.

3. Descent of Holy Spirit
For love of God.

4. Assumption of B.V.M.
For devotion to Mary.

5. Crowning of B.V.M.
For eternal happiness.

GENERAL PRAYERS

Prayer to St. Joseph

O Blessed St. Joseph, loving father and faithful guardian of Jesus, and devoted spouse of the Mother of God, I beg you to offer God the Father his divine Son, bathed in blood on the Cross. Through the holy Name of Jesus obtain for us from the Father the favor we implore.

For the Sick

Father, your Son accepted our sufferings to teach us the virtue of patience in human illness. Hear the prayers we offer for our sick brothers and sisters. May all who suffer pain, illness or disease realize that they are chosen to be saints, and know that they are joined to Christ in his suffering for the salvation of the world, who lives and reigns with you and the Holy Spirit, one God, for ever and ever.

For Religious Vocations

Father, you call all who believe in you to grow perfect in love by following in the footsteps of Christ your Son. May those whom you have chosen to serve you as religious provide by their way of life a convincing sign of your kingdom for the Church and the whole world.

For the Assembly of National Leaders

Father, you guide and govern everything with order and love. Look upon the assembly of our national leaders and fill them with the spirit of your wisdom. May they always act in accordance with your will and their decisions be for the peace and well-being of all.

Prayer for Health

O Sacred Heart of Jesus, I come to ask of your infinite mercy the gift of health and strength that I may serve you more faithfully and love you more sincerely than in the past. I wish to be well and strong if this be your good pleasure and for your greater glory. Filled with high resolves and determined to perform my tasks most perfectly for love of you, I wish to be enabled to go back to my duties.

Prayer for Peace and Joy

Jesus, I want to rejoice in you always. You are near. Let me have no anxiety, but in every concern by prayer and supplication with thanksgiving I wish to let my petitions be made known in my communing with God.

    May the peace of God, which surpasses all understanding, guard my heart and my thoughts in you.

Prayer To Know God's Will

God the Father of our Lord Jesus Christ, the Author of glory, grant me spiritual wisdom and revelation. Enlighten the eyes of my mind with a deep knowledge of you and your holy will. May I understand of what nature is the hope to which you call me, what is the wealth of the splendor of your inheritance among the Saints, and what is the surpassing greatness of your power toward me.

Prayer for Civil Authorities

Almighty and everlasting God, you direct the powers and laws of all nations; mercifully regard those who rule over us, that, by your protecting right hand, the integrity of religion and the security of each country might prevail everywhere on earth. Through Christ our Lord. Amen.

Prayer for A Family

God of goodness and mercy, to your fatherly protection we commend our family, our household and all that belongs to us. We entrust all to your love and keeping. Fill our home with your blessings as you filled the holy house of Nazareth with your presence.

Above all else, keep far from us the stain of sin. We want you alone to rule over us. Help each one of us to obey the holy laws, to love you sincerely and to imitate the example of your holy guardian, Saint Joseph.

Lord, preserve us and our home from all evils and misfortunes. May we be ever resigned to your divine will even in the crosses and sorrows that you allow to come to us.

Finally, give all of us the grace to live in perfect harmony and love toward our neighbor. Grant that every one of us may deserve by a holy life the comfort of your holy sacraments at the hour of death.

Bless this house, God the Father, who created us, God the Son, who suffered for us upon the cross, and God the Holy Spirit, who sanctified us in baptism.

May the one God in three divine persons preserve our bodies, purify our minds, direct our hearts and bring us all to everlasting life.

Glory be to the Father, glory be to the Son, glory be to the Holy Spirit! Amen.

NEW RITE OF PENANCE
(Extracted from the Rite of Penance)

Texts for the Penitent

The penitent should prepare for the celebration of the sacrament by prayer, reading of Scripture, and silent reflection. The penitent should think over and should regret all sins since the last celebration of the sacrament.

RECEPTION OF THE PENITENT

The penitent enters the confessional or other place set aside for the celebration of the sacrament of penance. After the welcoming of the priest, the penitent makes the sign of the cross saying:

In the name of the Father, and of the Son, and of the Holy Spirit. Amen.

The penitent is invited to have trust in God and replies:

Amen.

READING THE WORD OF GOD

The penitent then listens to a text of Scripture which tells about God's mercy and calls man to conversion.

CONFESSION OF SINS AND ACCEPTANCE OF SATISFACTION

The penitent speaks to the priest in a normal, conversational fashion. The penitent tells when he or she last celebrated the sacrament and then confesses his or her sins. The penitent then listens to any advice the priest may give and accepts the satisfaction from the priest. The penitent should ask any appropriate questions.

PRAYER OF THE PENITENT AND ABSOLUTION
Prayer

Before the absolution is given, the penitent expresses sorrow for sins in these or similar words:

My God,
I am sorry for my sins with all my heart.
In choosing to do wrong
and failing to do good,

I have sinned against you
whom I should love above all things.
I firmly intend, with your help,
to do penance,
to sin no more,
and to avoid whatever leads me to sin.
Our Savior Jesus Christ
suffered and died for us.
In his name, my God, have mercy.

OR: Remember, Lord, your compassion and mercy
     which you showed long ago.
     Do not recall the sins and failings of my youth.
     In your mercy remember me, Lord, because of your
       goodness.

OR: Wash me from my guilt
     and cleanse me of my sin.
     I acknowledge my offense;
     my sin is before me always.

OR: Father, I have sinned against you
     and am not worthy to be called your son.
     Be merciful to me, a sinner.

OR: Father of mercy,
     like the prodigal son
     I return to you and say:
     "I have sinned against you
     and am no longer worthy to be called your son."
     Christ Jesus, Savior of the world,
     I pray with the repentant thief
     to whom you promised Paradise:
     "Lord, remember me in your kingdom."
     Holy Spirit, fountain of love,
     I call on you with trust:
     "Purify my heart,
     and help me to walk as a child of light."

OR: Lord Jesus,
     you opened the eyes of the blind,
     healed the sick,
     forgave the sinful woman,

and after Peter's denial confirmed him in your love.
Listen to my prayer,
forgive all my sins,
renew your love in my heart,
help me to live in perfect unity with my fellow
Christians
that I may proclaim your saving power to all the world.

OR: Lord Jesus;
     you choose to be called the friend of sinners.
     By your saving death and resurrection
     free me from my sins.
     May your peace take root in my heart
     and bring forth a harvest
     of love, holiness, and truth.

OR: Lord Jesus Christ,
     you are the Lamb of God;
     you take away the sins of the world.
     Through the grace of the Holy Spirit
     restore me to friendship with your Father,
     cleanse me from every stain of sin
     and raise me to new life
     for the glory of your name.

OR: Lord God,
     in your goodness have mercy on me:
     do not look on my sins,
     but take away all my guilt.
     Create in me a clean heart
     and renew within me an upright spirit.

OR: Lord Jesus, Son of God,
     have mercy on me, a sinner.

ABSOLUTION

If the penitent is not kneeling, he or she bows his or her head as the priest extends his hands (or at least extends his right hand).

God, the Father of mercies,
through the death and resurrection of his Son

has reconciled the world to himself
and sent the Holy Spirit among us
for the forgiveness of sins;
through the ministry of the Church
may God give you pardon and peace,
and I absolve you from your sins
in the name of the Father, and of the Son,
and of the Holy Spirit. Amen.

PROCLAMATION OF PRAISE OF GOD AND DISMISSAL

Penitent and priest give praise to God.

Priest: Give thanks to the Lord, for he is good.
Penitent: His mercy endures for ever.

Then the penitent is dismissed by the priest.

Form of Examination of Conscience

*This suggested form for an examination of conscience should
be completed and adapted to meet the needs of different individuals and to follow local usages.*

*In an examination of conscience, before the sacrament of
penance, each individual should ask himself these questions
in particular:*

1. What is my attitude to the sacrament of penance? Do I sincerely want to be set free from sin, to turn again to God, to
begin a new life, and to enter into a deeper friendship with God?
Or do I look on it as a burden, to be undertaken as seldom as
possible?

2. Did I forget to mention, or deliberately conceal, any grave
sins in past confessions?

3. Did I perform the penance I was given? Did I make repara-
tion for any injury to others? Have I tried to put into practice any
resolution to lead a better life in keeping with the Gospel?

*Each individual should examine his life in the light of God's
word.*

I. The Lord says: "You shall love the Lord your God with your whole heart."

1. Is my heart set on God, so that I really love him above all
things and am faithful to his commandments, as a son loves his

father? Or am I more concerned about the things of this world? Have I a right intention in what I do?

2. God spoke to us in his Son. Is my faith in God firm and secure? Am I wholehearted in accepting the Church's teaching? Have I been careful to grow in my understanding of the faith, to hear God's word, to listen to instructions on the faith, to avoid dangers to faith? Have I been always strong and fearless in professing my faith in God and the Church? Have I been willing to be known as a Christian in private and public life?

3. Have I prayed morning and evening? When I pray, do I really raise my mind and heart to God or is it a matter of words only? Do I offer my difficulties, my joys, and my sorrows? Do I turn to God in time of temptation?

4. Have I love and reverence for God's name? Have I offended him in blasphemy, swearing falsely, or taking his name in vain? Have I shown disrespect for the Blessed Virgin Mary and the saints?

5. Do I keep Sundays and feast days holy by taking a full part, with attention and devotion, in the liturgy, and especially in the Mass? Have I fulfilled the precept of annual confession and of communion during the Easter season?

6. Are there false gods that I worship by giving them greater attention and deeper trust than I give to God: money, superstition, spiritism, or other occult practices?

II. The Lord says: "Love one another as I have loved you."

1. Have I a genuine love for my neighbors? Or do I use them for my own ends, or do to them what I would not want done to myself? Have I given grave scandal by my words or actions?

2. In my family life, have I contributed to the well-being and happiness of the rest of the family by patience and genuine love? Have I been obedient to parents, showing them proper respect and giving them help in their spiritual and material needs? Have I been careful to give a Christian upbringing to my children, and to help them by good example and by exercising authority as a parent? Have I been faithful to my husband/wife in my heart and in my relations with others?

3. Do I share my possessions with the less fortunate? Do I do my best to help the victims of oppression, misfortune, and poverty? Or do I look down on my neighbor, especially the poor, the sick, the elderly, strangers, and people of other races?

4. Does my life reflect the mission I received in confirmation? Do I share in the apostolic and charitable works of the Church and in the life of my parish? Have I helped to meet the needs of the Church and of the world and prayed for them: for unity in the Church, for the spread of the Gospel among the nations, for peace and justice, etc.?

5. Am I concerned for the good and prosperity of the human community in which I live, or do I spend my life caring only for myself? Do I share to the best of my ability in the work of promoting justice, morality, harmony, and love in human relations? Have I done my duty as a citizen? Have I paid my taxes?

6. In my work or profession am I just, hard-working, honest, serving society out of love for others? Have I paid a fair wage to my employees? Have I been faithful to my promises and contracts?

7. Have I obeyed legitimate authority and given it due respect?

8. If I am in a position of responsibility or authority, do I use this for my own advantage or for the good of others, in a spirit of service?

9. Have I been truthful and fair, or have I injured others by deceit, calumny, detraction, rash judgment, or violation of a secret?

10. Have I done violence to others by damage to life or limb, reputation, honor, or material possessions? Have I involved them in loss? Have I been responsible for advising an abortion or procuring one? Have I kept up hatred for others? Am I estranged from others through quarrels, enmity, insults, anger? Have I been guilty of refusing to testify to the innocence of another because of selfishness?

11. Have I stolen the property of others? Have I desired it unjustly and inordinately? Have I damaged it? Have I made restitution of other people's property and made good their loss?

12. If I have been injured, have I been ready to make peace for the love of Christ and to forgive, or do I harbor hatred and the desire for revenge?

III. Christ our Lord says: "Be perfect as your Father is perfect."

1. Where is my life really leading me? Is the hope of eternal life my inspiration? Have I tried to grow in the life of the Spirit through prayer, reading the word of God and meditating on it, receiving the sacraments, self-denial? Have I been anxious to control my vices, my bad inclinations and passions, e.g., envy, love of food and drink? Have I been proud and boastful, thinking myself better in the sight of God and despising others as less important than myself? Have I imposed my own will on others, without respecting their freedom and rights?

2. What use have I made of time, of health and strength, of the gifts God has given to me to be used like the talents in the Gospel? Do I use them to become more perfect every day? Or have I been lazy and too much given to leisure?

3. Have I been patient in accepting the sorrows and disappointments of life? How have I performed mortification so as to "fill up what is wanting to the sufferings of Christ"? Have I kept the precept of fasting and abstinence?

4. Have I kept my senses and my whole body pure and chaste as a temple of the Holy Spirit consecrated for resurrection and glory, and as a sign of God's faithful love for men and women, a sign that is seen most perfectly in the sacrament of matrimony? Have I dishonored my body by fornication, impurity, unworthy conversation or thoughts, evil desires or actions? Have I given in to sensuality? Have I indulged in reading, conversation, shows, and entertainments that offend against Christian and human decency? Have I encouraged others to sin by my own failure to maintain these standards? Have I been faithful to the moral law in my married life?

5. Have I gone against my conscience out of fear or hypocrisy?

6. Have I always tried to act in the true freedom of the sons of God according to the law of the Spirit, or am I the slave of forces within me?

PRAYERS IN ACCORD WITH THE LITURGICAL YEAR

ADVENT SEASON

Prayer to Help Others Find Christ

O Lord Jesus, I thank you for the gift of faith and for the continual grace you give me to nourish and strengthen it. Enable me to cultivate the genuine desire for you that lies beneath the zealous search for justice, truth, love, and peace found in our contemporaries. Encourage these searchings, O Lord, and grant that all true seekers may look beyond the present moment and catch sight of your countenance in the world.

Prayer for Christ's Triple Coming

Lamb of God, you once came to rid the world of sin; cleanse me now of every stain of sin. Lord, you came to save what was lost; come once again with your salvific power so that those you redeemed will not be punished. I have come to know you in faith; may I have unending joy when you come again in glory.

Prayer for Christ's Coming in Grace

O Lord Jesus, during this Advent come to us in your grace. Come to prepare our hearts, minds, and bodies to welcome you on Christmas Day. Come to comfort us in sadness, to cheer us in loneliness, to refresh us in weariness, to strengthen us in temptations, to lead us in time of doubt, and to exult with us in joy.

CHRISTMAS SEASON

Prayer to Jesus, God's Greatest Gift

O Jesus, I believe that the greatest proof of God's love is his gift to us of you, his only Son. All love tends to become like that which it loves. You love human beings; therefore you became man. Infinite love and mercy caused you, the Second Person of the Blessed Trinity, to leave the Kingdom of eternal bliss, to descend from the throne of your majesty, and to become a helpless babe. Eventually you even suffered and died and rose that we might live.

You wished to enter the world as a child in order to show that you were true Man. But you become man also that we may become like God. In exchange for the humanity that you take from us you wish to make us share in your Divinity by sanctifying grace, so that you may take sole possession of us. Grant me the grace to love you in return with a deep, personal, and productive love.

Prayer for Christ's Rebirth in the Church

O Lord Jesus Christ, we ask you to incarnate in us your invisible Divinity. What you accomplished corporally in Mary accomplish now spiritually in your Church. May the Church's sure faith conceive you, its unstained intelligence give birth to you, and its soul united with the power of the Most High preserve you forever.

Prayer for Joy at the Birth of Jesus

Let the just rejoice, for their Justifier is born. Let the sick and infirm rejoice, for their Savior is born. Let captives rejoice, for their Redeemer is born. Let slaves rejoice, for their Master is born. Let free people rejoice, for their Liberator is born. Let all Christians rejoice, for Jesus Christ is born. *St. Augustine of Hippo*

Prayer To Know and Love Jesus

My Lord Jesus, I want to love you but you cannot trust me. If you do not help me, I will never do any good. I do not know you; I look for you but I do not find you. Come to me, O Lord. If I knew you, I would also know myself. If I have never loved you before, I want to love you truly now. I want to do your will alone; putting no trust in myself, I hope in you, O Lord. *St. Philip Neri*

Prayer That Christ May Be Known to All

O Lord, give us a new Epiphany when you will be manifested to the world: to those who do not know you, to those who deny you, and to all those who unconsciously long for you. Bring the day closer when all people will know and love you together with the Father and the Holy Spirit—and the Kingdom of God will have arrived.

SEASON OF LENT

Prayer To Be Freed of the Seven Deadly Sins

O meek Savior and Prince of Peace, implant in me the virtues of gentleness and patience. Let me curb the fury of anger and restrain all resentment and impatience so as to overcome evil with good, attain your peace, and rejoice in your love.

O Model of humility, divest me of all pride and arrogance. Let me acknowledge my weakness and sinfulness, so that I may bear mockery and contempt for your sake and esteem myself as lowly in your sight.

O Teacher of abstinence, help me to serve you rather than my appetites. Keep me from gluttony—the inordinate love of food and drink—and let me hunger and thirst for your justice.

O Lover of purity, remove all lust from my heart, so that I may serve you with a pure mind and a chaste body.

O Father of the poor, help me to avoid all covetousness for earthly goods and give me a love for heavenly things. Inspire me to give to the needy, just as you gave your life that I might inherit eternal treasures.

O Exemplar of love, keep me from all envy and ill-will. Let the grace of your love dwell in me that I may rejoice in the happiness of others and bewail their adversities.

O zealous Lover of souls, keep me from all sloth of mind or body. Inspire me with zeal for your glory, so that I may do all things for you and in you.

Prayer of Contrition

Merciful Father, I am guilty of sin. I confess my sins before you and I am sorry for them. Your promises are just; therefore I trust that you will forgive me my sins and cleanse me from every stain of sin. Jesus himself is the propitiation for my sins and those of the whole world. I put my hope in his atonement. May my sins be forgiven through his Name, and in his Blood may my soul be made clean.

Prayer To Know Jesus Christ

O Lord Jesus, like St. Paul, may I count everything as loss in comparison with the supreme advantage of knowing you. I want to know you and what your Passion and Resurrection can do. I also want to share in your sufferings in the hope that if I resemble you in death I may somehow attain to the resurrection from the dead.

Give me grace to make every effort to supplement faith with moral courage, moral courage with knowledge, knowledge with self-control, self-control with patience, patience with piety, piety with affection, and affection with love for all my brothers and sisters in Christ. May these virtues keep me both active and fruitful and bring me to the deep knowledge of you, Lord Jesus Christ.

Prayer To Appreciate the Mass

O Lord Jesus, in order that the merits of your sacrifice on the Cross might be applied to every soul of all time, you willed that it should be renewed upon the altar. At the Last Supper, you said: "Do this in remembrance of me." By these words you gave your Apostles and their successors the power to consecrate and the command to do what you yourself did.

I believe that the Mass is both a sacrifice and a memorial—reenacting your Passion, Death, and Resurrection. Help me to realize that the Mass is the greatest gift of God to us and our greatest gift to God.

EASTER SEASON

Prayer in Praise of Christ's Humanity

O risen Lord, your Body was part of your power, rather than you a part in its weakness. For this reason you could not but rise again, if you were to die—because your Body, once taken by you, never was or could be separated from you even in the grave.

I keep your most holy Body before me as the pledge of my own resurrection. Though I die, it only means I shall rise again.

Teach me to live as one who believes in the great dignity and sanctity of the material frame that you have given to me.

Prayer for the Fruits of Christ's Resurrection

God, the Father of lights, you have glorified the world by the light of the risen Christ. Brighten my heart today with the light of your faith. Through your risen Son you opened the gate of eternal life for all human beings. Grant to me as I work out my salvation daily the hope of eternal life.

You accepted the sacrifice of your Son and raised him from the dead. Accept the offering of my work, which I perform for your glory and the salvation of all people. Open my mind and heart to my brothers and sisters. Help us to love and serve one another.

Your Son rose to lift up the downtrodden, comfort the sorrowful, cure the sick, and bring joy to the world. Help all people to cast off sin and ignorance and enjoy Your Son's Paschal Victory.

Prayer to the Holy Spirit

Holy Spirit of light and love, you are the substantial Love of the Father and the Son; hear my prayer.

Bounteous bestower of most precious gifts, grant me a strong and living faith, which makes me accept all revealed truths and shape my conduct in accord with them. Give me a most confident hope in all Divine promises, which prompts me to abandon myself unreservedly to you and your guidance.

Infuse into me a love of perfect goodwill, that makes me accomplish God's will in all things and act according to God's least desires. Make me love not only my friends but my enemies as well in imitation of Jesus Christ who through you offered himself on the Cross for all people.

Holy Spirit, animate, inspire, and guide me, and help me to be always a true follower of Jesus.

Prayer to Christ Ascended into Heaven

O Lord Jesus, I adore you, Son of Mary, my Savior and my Brother, for you are God. I follow you in my thoughts, O firstfruits of our race, as I hope one day to follow you in my person into heavenly glory.

In the meantime, do not let me neglect the earthly task that you have given me. Let me labor diligently all my life with a greater appreciation for the present. Let me realize that only by accomplishing true human fulfillment can I attain Divine fulfillment and ascend to you at the completion of my work.

Prayer To Live a Full Life

O Lord, your Ascension into heaven marks the culmination of the Paschal Mystery, and it contains an important teaching for us. We may live life as an earthly reality and develop our human potential to its fullest. We may make use of the results of science to achieve a better life on this planet. But in our best moments we know that there must be more than all of this, a transcending Reality.

As Christians, we know that this Reality is your loving Father who awaits us with you and the Holy Spirit. Where you have gone, we ultimately will come—if we are faithful.

ORDINARY TIME

Prayer for a Productive Faith

O Lord, increase my faith and let it bear fruit in my life. Let it bind me fast to other Christians in the common certitude that our Master is the God-Man who gave his life for all. Let me listen in faith to the Divine word that challenges me.

Help me to strive wholeheartedly under the promptings of my faith in the building of a world ruled by love. Enable me to walk in faith toward the indescribable future that you have promised to all who possess a productive faith in you.

Prayer to Christ in the World

Lord Jesus, let us realize that every action of ours no matter how small or how secular enables us to be in touch with you. Let our interest lie in created things—but only in absolute dependence upon your presence in them. Let us pursue you and you alone through the reality of created things. Let this be our prayer—to become closer to you by becoming more human.

Let us become a true branch on the vine that is you, a branch that bears much fruit. Let us accept you in our lives in the way it pleases you to come into them: as Truth, to be spoken; as Life, to be lived; as Light, to be shared; as Love, to be followed; as Joy, to be given; as Peace, to be spread about; as Sacrifice, to be offered among our relatives and friends, among our neighbors and all people.

Prayer To Be Generous in Giving

Lord Jesus, you came to tell us that the meaning of life consists in giving. You told us that those who cling too tightly to what they have—without thought for others—

end up by losing everything. You gave us new values by which to measure the worth of a person's life.

Help me to realize it is not temporal success or riches or fame that necessarily gives life meaning. Rather it is the service rendered to others in your Name that brings fulfillment and makes my life worthwhile. May all my activity help build God's kingdom: my suffering bear genuine fruit, my obedience bring true freedom, and my death lead to eternal life.

Prayer To Discern God's Call

Heavenly Father, your call never comes to us in a vacuum; it comes to us in the circumstances of our ordinary lives.

Therefore, our response cannot be given only in the privacy of our own minds; it must overflow into our daily lives. You call us through our family, through our community or Church, and through the world.

Help me to see that when I say No to the legitimate requests of my family, my community, or my world, I say No to you. You have ordained that whatever advances the true progress of self, of the Church, and of the world is my way of saying Yes to your call. May I take advantage of the daily opportunities that you place at my disposal to answer your call affirmatively.

Prayer To Grow with the Church

O Lord Jesus, I know that all human relations take time if they are to grow and deepen. This is also true of my relations with You, the Father, and the Holy Spirit, which must grow over the course of my life.

But this growth is not automatic. Time means nothing unless I add my earnest efforts to it.

You have inspired Your Church to set aside special times when this growth can develop more intensely—the special Seasons of the Church year. If I fail to move toward you during these times, I waste precious opportunities and endanger my spiritual life.

Help me to take them seriously and make a real attempt to use them well, so that I may grow into the person you want me to be.

Prayer To Encounter God Frequently in Prayer

Heavenly Father, let me realize that, like all prayer, prayer of petition is primarily a means of encountering You and being sustained by you. You know what we need because you are a loving Father who watches over us. Yet you respect our freedom and wait for us to express our needs to you.

Let me have frequent recourse to you in prayer so that I will purify my intentions and bring my wishes into conformity with your own. Let me pray with fixed formulas as well as in my own words—whether they be long or short.

Above all, let me come before you with a heart moved by your Spirit and a will ready to conform to your holy Will.

INDICES

GENERAL INDEX

PROPER OF SEASONS

ORDER OF MASS

PROPER OF SEASONS (Cont'd)

TREASURY OF PRAYERS

INDICES

INDEX OF SAINTS

INDEX OF BIBLICAL READINGS

INDEX OF RESPONSORIAL PSALMS

INDEX OF PREFACES

WHY . . . Every Catholic should have a MISSAL . . . of his OWN!

AT MASS . . . for complete participation and understanding

- ✔ TO RECITE or SING . . . their parts with understanding and devotion.
- ✔ TO LISTEN . . . attentively to the Word of God.
- ✔ TO UNITE . . . with the Prayers of the Priest.
- ✔ TO HOLD . . . attention and increase their devotion.
- ✔ TO HELP . . . during short periods recommended for personal prayer.

AT HOME . . . to guide their Christian Life and personal spiritual reading

- ✔ TO PREPARE . . . themselves for Mass by reading over the texts and helpful commentary.
- ✔ TO SEE . . . the Liturgical Year as a whole.
- ✔ TO GUIDE . . . their lives in the spirit of the liturgy.
- ✔ TO MODEL . . . their prayers on liturgical sources.
- ✔ TO MEDITATE. . . often on the Word of God.

OTHER OUTSTANDING CATHOLIC BOOKS

HOLY BIBLE—Saint Joseph Edition of the completely modern translation called the New American Bible. In large type with Notes and Maps, Photographs, Family Record Pages and Bible Dictionary. **Ask for No. 611**

CATHOLIC PICTURE BIBLE—By Rev. L. Lovasik, S.V.D. Thrilling, inspiring and educational for all ages. Over 101 Bible stories retold in modern language, illustrated in glorious full color. **Ask for No. 435**

LIVES OF THE SAINTS—New Revised Edition. Short life of a Saint and prayer for every day of the year. Over 50 illustrations. Ideal for daily meditation and private study. **Ask for No. 870**

Wherever Catholic Books are Sold